The Physician's Guide to
Caring for Children
with Disabilities
and Chronic Conditions

The Physician's Guide to Caring for Children with Disabilities and Chronic Conditions

edited by

Robert E. Nickel, M.D.
Child Development and Rehabilitation Center, Eugene, Oregon
Oregon Health Sciences University, Portland

and

Larry W. Desch, M.D.
Hope Children's Hospital
Oak Lawn, Illinois

·P A U L·H·
BROOKES
PUBLISHING C?

Baltimore • London • Toronto • Sydney

Paul H. Brookes Publishing Co.
Post Office Box 10624
Baltimore, Maryland 21285-0624

www.brookespublishing.com

Typeset by Barton Matheson Willse & Worthington, Baltimore, Maryland.
Manufactured in the United States of America by
Sheridan Books, Ann Arbor, Michigan.

The information in this book evolved from a training program supported by a grant from the Maternal and Child Health Bureau, Health Resources and Services Administration, U.S. Department of Health and Human Services (Project MCJ-41R004).

The format of the Family and Physician Management Plan Summary forms located in the appendixes at the end of most chapters in this book were adapted from Cooley, W.C., Olson, A.L., & McAllister, J. (1994). *Care planning and next steps: Chronic condition management in the primary care setting: A provider's resource manual.* Lebanon: New Hampshire Partners in Health, Office Partners Project. The Guidelines for Care form located in the appendix at the end of Chapter 6 was adapted from Committee on Children with Disabilities. (1995). *Standards of care and outcome measures for children with cerebral palsy.* Columbus: Ohio Department of Health, Bureau for Children with Mental Handicaps. The Guidelines for Care form located in the appendix at the end of Chapter 13 was adapted from the Myelodysplasia Standards Committee. (1995). *Standards of care outcome measures for children with myelodysplasia (spina bifida).* Columbus: Ohio Department of Health, Bureau for Children with Mental Handicaps.

Library of Congress Cataloging-in-Publication Data

The physician's guide to caring for children with disabilities and
  chronic conditions/edited by Robert E. Nickel and Larry W. Desch.
     p.   cm.
  Includes bibliographical references and index.
  ISBN 1-55766-446-3
   1. Chronically ill children—Care.   2. Developmentally disabled
children—Care.   I. Nickel, Robert E.   II. Desch, Larry W.
  RJ380.P49   2000
  618.92—dc21

99-35344
CIP

British Library Cataloguing in Publication data are available from the British Library.

Contents

About the Editors

Robert E. Nickel, M.D., Clinical Director, Regional Services Center, Child Development and Rehabilitation Center, 901 East 18th Avenue, Eugene, Oregon, 97403; and Associate Professor, Department of Pediatrics, Oregon Health Sciences University, Portland, Oregon; rnickel@oregon.uoregon.edu

Dr. Nickel directs the Regional Services Center of the Child Development and Rehabilitation Center (CDRC), which is a major unit of Oregon Health Sciences University. The CDRC administers Title V services for children with special health care needs in Oregon, offers a variety of clinical services, and houses a research and training institute—the Oregon Institute on Disability and Development, which is a University Affiliated Program (UAP). The Eugene office of the CDRC is associated with the Center on Human Development, the UAP at the University of Oregon. Dr. Nickel completed fellowship training in developmental pediatrics at the University of Washington with Drs. Forrest C. Bennett and Jerry Sells. During this fellowship, he also worked regularly with Dr. David Shurtleff and the Birth Defects Clinic staff at Children's Hospital and Medical Center in Seattle.

Since completing his fellowship in 1980, Dr. Nickel has worked as a developmental pediatrician for the CDRC. In addition, he has directed the Eugene office since 1990. He represents the CDRC on the State Interagency Coordinating Council for Early Intervention/Early Childhood Special Education in Oregon and is a past chair of the Committee on Children with Disabilities of the Oregon Pediatric Society. He is a past president and a current curriculum committee member of the Northwest Society for Developmental and Behavioral Pediatrics. Dr. Nickel has written and lectured widely on the early identification of children with disabilities in the primary care office. He collaborated with Diane Bricker and Jane Squires in the development of *Ages & Stages Questionnaires: A Parent-Completed, Child-Monitoring System* (Paul H. Brookes Publishing Co., 1999) and developed the Infant Motor Screen. In addition, he has presented numerous workshops on caring for children with disabilities and chronic conditions in the primary care office and on improving the collaboration of health professionals with education staff and other community service providers.

Larry W. Desch, M.D., FAAP, Director of Developmental Pediatrics, Hope Children's Hospital, 4440 West 95th Street, Oak Lawn, Illinois, 60453; Department of Pediatrics, University of Illinois–Chicago; Larry.Desch@advocatehealth.com

Dr. Desch directs both the clinical and educational aspects of developmental pediatrics at Hope Children's Hospital, a major teaching affiliate of the University of Illinois College of Medicine, Department of Pediatrics. He completed his fellowship training in developmental disabilities at the University of Kansas Medical School and did postfellowship work for 3 years with Drs. Al Healy, Mark Wolraich, and James Blackman at the University of Iowa. Since then, Dr. Desch has served on the faculties of the University of Missouri and University of Wisconsin medical schools. He is a clinical associate professor at the University of Illinois–Chicago College of Medicine. Over the years, Dr. Desch has also assisted various state agencies that deal with children with a wide spectrum of disabilities and has served on a number of advisory boards and committees for children with disabilities of state chapters of the American Academy of Pediatrics (AAP) (including as a past chair of the committee in Missouri). He is also active in a number of national academic and professional organizations, including the AAP (the Section on Developmental and Behavioral Pediatrics and the Section on Children with Disabilities), the Society for Developmental Pediatrics, the Ambulatory Pediatrics Association, and the Midwest Society for Pediatric Research. Within the American Academy for Cerebral Palsy and Developmental Medicine, Dr. Desch serves as chair of the Continuing Education Committee. With the AAP, he is also involved in the development of the tertiary care component of the Medical Home for Children with Special Health Care Needs project. Dr. Desch has authored a considerable number of research papers and other scholarly publications, many of which deal with growth assessment of children with special needs and developmental neurophysiology. He has lectured widely to various groups about children with disabilities, particularly with regard to the early diagnosis and treatment of children with cerebral palsy.

Contributors

Janice L. Cockrell, M.D.
Clinical Associate Professor
Department of Pediatrics
Oregon Health Sciences University
Medical Director, Pediatric/Adolescent
  Rehabilitation
Legacy Emanuel Children's Hospital
2801 N. Gantenbein Avenue
Portland, Oregon 97227

Jay D. Eisenberg, M.D.
Pediatric Pulmonologist
Associate Professor
Department of Pediatrics
Oregon Health Sciences University
3181 S.W. Sam Jackson Park Road
UHN 56
Portland, Oregon 97201

Vivian Gedaly-Duff, D.N.Sc., R.N.
Associate Professor
Oregon Institute on Disabilities and Development
School of Nursing
Oregon Health Sciences University
3181 S.W. Sam Jackson Park Road
Mail Code: SN-5S
Portland, Oregon 97201

Christine Jepsen, R.N.
Nurse Consultant/Feeding Clinic Coordinator
Regional Services Center
Child Development and Rehabilitation Center
Oregon Health Sciences University
901 East 18th Avenue
Eugene, Oregon 97403

Lisa Letcher-Glembo, Ph.D.
Craniofacial Disorders Specialist
Legacy Emanuel Children's Hospital
2801 N. Gantenbein Avenue
Portland, Oregon 97227

Ronda M. Roberts, M.D.
Developmental and Behavioral Pediatrician
995 Willagillespie, Suite 100
Eugene, Oregon 97401

Kathleen Shelton, P.N.P., M.N., R.N.
Pediatric Nurse Practitioner and Doctoral
  Candidate
School of Nursing
Oregon Health Sciences University
3181 S.W. Sam Jackson Park Road
Portland, Oregon 97201

Jane Squires, Ph.D.
Associate Professor
Early Intervention/Special Education
Center on Human Development
Division of Special Education and Rehabilitation
College of Education
University of Oregon
Clinical Services Building
Eugene, Oregon 97403

Susan Stoeger, R.N.
Coordinator of Family Resource Center
Providence Child Center
830 N.E. 47th Avenue
Portland, Oregon 97213

Foreword

Children with neurodevelopmental and related disabilities and their families are increasingly relying on primary care providers. This phenomenon is likely to continue to escalate in the years ahead for two principal reasons. First, the prevalence of neurodevelopmental, neurobehavioral, and other chronic conditions and disabilities in the United States is increasing. This circumstance has been termed a *silent epidemic of neurodevelopmental dysfunction.* Contemporary biomedical technology has produced stunning increases in the survival of infants and children with potentially serious brain insults and other congenital defects and malformations. These "new survivors" are certainly at risk of experiencing the full range of long-term health and developmental morbidities. In addition, the persistent problems of prenatal drug exposure, environmental deprivation, and child abuse and neglect contribute immeasurably to the increasing number of children with developmental and behavioral dysfunction. The second reason for the continuing shift in the nature and focus of childhood primary health care is the dramatic reduction in serious infectious diseases witnessed during the last quarter of the 20th century. Accelerated vaccine development is certain to alter daily pediatric practice even further.

Because of these practice realities, pediatric primary health care providers must have the knowledge, skills, and attitudes necessary to serve this burgeoning group of health care consumers competently. The *medical home* concept is a community-based, family-centered model for providing ideal comprehensive care coordination for children with disabilities and their families. Unfortunately, many care providers today do not enter into medical practices with the desired chronic care interests and competencies and also do not enter practices that provide accessible, functional medical homes. The barriers to improved care for children with chronic conditions and their families are numerous: inadequate training at all levels of medical education, inadequate office management systems, inadequate reimbursement for the increased time required, productivity pressures of managed care, the inherent complexity and absence of immediate gratification in chronic care cases, and the historically low societal position and visibility of this population.

Thus, primary care physicians clearly must do better for these children and their families. Pediatric care providers should have a basic understanding of the major neurodevelopmental disabilities (i.e., developmental delay and mental retardation, cerebral palsy, autism, sensory impairments) in terms of their definitions, natural histories, etiologies, differential diagnoses, and interventions. They should appreciate the broad, overlapping spectrum of language and learning disorders. They must be aware of the common neurobehavioral co-morbidities, including attention-deficit/hyperactivity disorder (ADHD), oppositional defiant disorder (ODD), and anxiety and mood disorders. Parents should expect their child's primary care provider to be able to perform some type of developmental surveillance and screening, ensure appropriate developmental assessment, coordinate timely referrals to community agencies for optimal intervention services, and work with schools. Finally, pediatric care providers require competencies in caring for the broader population of children with special health care needs, including those with congenital defects and chronic illnesses as well as those who are at risk for developmental delays and disabilities.

This book is designed specifically with these needs in mind and to increase both the quantity and quality of community medical homes. It should be read and referenced by physicians, nurses, and others who care for or are in training to care for children with disabilities and chronic conditions and their families.

Forrest C. Bennett, M.D.
University of Washington
Seattle

Preface

This book evolved from a training program for primary care physicians and nurses entitled "Community Consultants in the Care of Children with Special Health Care Needs." The training program was developed with grant support from the Maternal and Child Health Bureau, Health Resources and Services Administration, U.S. Department of Health and Human Services (Project MCJ-41R004). The project was funded in the provider preparation category, and its goal was to enhance services for children with disabilities and chronic conditions through the primary health care office. The goal of the book is the same: to provide information and materials to support health professionals in providing a medical home for children with disabilities and chronic conditions.

This book is for primary care pediatricians, family practitioners, nurses, residents, nurses in training, and fellows in developmental pediatrics, as well as for physician's assistants and nurse practitioners, who are an essential part of the service system for children with disabilities and chronic conditions and their families in rural areas. The material in this book reflects the editors' and contributors' collective experiences in working with primary care physicians as developmental pediatricians and as members of specialty teams. It addresses numerous requests that we have received for specific, practical management information for the issues that these children face.

The original training program consisted of a written curriculum and four videotapes to complement the curriculum. This book contains the 17 chapters with appendixes that were included in the curriculum, as well as an additional chapter on children with sensory impairments. The topics for the curriculum were identified and prioritized by participants at an initial planning conference. Planning conference participants included primary care physicians, office nurses, community health nurses, care coordinators of managed care plans, and parents of children with disabilities. Each chapter addresses a specific topic and was developed to provide a comprehensive overview of its subject as well as practical management recommendations. The curriculum was reviewed by a variety of health care professionals and parents before final editing. The intent was to develop high-quality materials as expeditiously as possible.

This book would not have been possible without the dedicated efforts of all of the contributors, the many local and national reviewers of the curriculum, and the tireless staff at the Child Development and Rehabilitation Center (CDRC) of Oregon Health Sciences University. We specifically thank the following CDRC staff, who participated in grant activities:

Vivian Gedaly-Duff, D.N.Sc., R.N.,
    Project Co-coordinator
Marilyn S. Hartsell, M.Ed., Program Evaluation
Judith R. Hylton, M.S., Education Consultant
Christine Jepsen, R.N., Project Coordinator
Vanita Miller, Program Support
Murphy Novotny, Program Support

In addition, we thank Heather Shrestha, acquisitions editor at Paul H. Brookes Publishing Co., for her ongoing support and patience. Finally, we extend a very special thank you to Shirley May, who contributed innumerable extra hours and provided invaluable editorial assistance to ensure the timely completion and the quality of this book.

Acknowledgments

The time and expertise of the following individuals who reviewed the chapters of the curriculum were essential to the quality of the information and materials in this book:

Stephen Beals, M.D., Co-director, Southwest Craniofacial Center, Phoenix, Arizona; Professor of Plastic Surgery, Mayo Medical School, Rochester, Minnesota

Forrest C. Bennett, M.D., Professor, Department of Pediatrics, Center on Human Development and Disability, University of Washington, Seattle

Gail Bernstein, M.D., Associate Professor, Division of Child and Adolescent Psychiatry, University of Minnesota School of Medicine, Minneapolis

Cecile L. Betz, Ph.D., R.N., Associate Director, University of California at Los Angeles University Affiliated Program, Neuropsychiatric Institute

Robert Blakeley, Ph.D., former Director, Craniofacial Disorders Program, Child Development and Rehabilitation Center, Oregon Health Sciences University, Portland

Lauren Bridge, R.N., Parent, Family/Plan Coordinator, Families as Participants Project, Child Development and Rehabilitation Center, Oregon Health Sciences University, Portland

Janet Brockman, M.S., CCC-SLP, Program Director, Craniofacial Disorders Program, Child Development and Rehabilitation Center, Oregon Health Sciences University, Portland

J. Albert Browder, M.D., Associate Professor, Department of Pediatrics, Child Development and Rehabilitation Center, Oregon Health Sciences University, Portland

Sarojini Budden, M.D., Associate Professor, Department of Pediatrics, Child Development and Rehabilitation Center, Oregon Health Sciences University and Legacy Emanuel Children's Hospital, Portland

John Bussman, M.D., former Medical Director, Oregon Medical Assistance Program, Salem

Deanna Cheshire, R.N., Program Director, Spina Bifida Program, Regional Services Center, Child Development and Rehabilitation Center, Oregon Health Sciences University, Eugene

W. Carl Cooley, M.D., Developmental Pediatrician, Dartmouth-Hitchcock Medical Center, Lebanon, New Hampshire

Richard Coolman, M.D., Assistant Professor, Department of Pediatrics, Regional Services Center, Child Development and Rehabilitation Center, Oregon Health Sciences University, Eugene

Geraldine Dawson, Ph.D., Professor, Department of Psychology, University of Washington, Seattle

Suzanne Dixon, M.D., M.P.H., former Associate Professor, Department of Pediatrics, University of California at San Diego Medical Center; currently in private practice, Great Falls, Montana

Evelyn Eckberg, R.N., Graduate Student in Family Nursing, School of Nursing, Oregon Health Sciences University, Portland

Debra Eisert, Ph.D., Assistant Professor, Clinical Psychology, University of Oregon, and Regional Services Center, Child Development and Rehabilitation Center, Oregon Health Sciences University, Eugene

William R. Foran, Jr., Pediatric Physical Therapist, Child Development and Rehabilitation Center, Oregon Health Sciences University, Portland

Lisa Frenkel, M.D., Pediatrician, Infectious Disease Specialist, University of Washington School of Medicine and Children's Hospital and Medical Center, Seattle

Lydia Fusetti, M.D., Pediatrician, Corvallis Children's Clinic, Corvallis, Oregon

Jane Gilbert, parent of an adolescent with meningomyelocele, Eugene, Oregon

Steve Goins, M.D., Pediatric Neurologist, Eugene, Oregon

Ginger Gorham, M.S., Behavior Support Coordinator for Roseburg School District and Parent Co-chairperson for Oregon Interagency Coordinating Council for Early Intervention, Umpqua, Oregon

Marilyn Hartzell, parent of a child with cystic fibrosis and Program Evaluator, Child Development and Rehabilitation Center, Oregon Health Sciences University, Portland

Ross Hayes, M.D., Pediatric Physiatrist, Children's Hospital and Medical Center, Seattle, Washington

Susan Hayflick, M.D., Assistant Professor of Medical Genetics, Oregon Health Sciences University, Portland

David Hirsch, M.D., Pediatrician, Phoenix, Arizona

Kathi Hoffer, Ph.D., CCC-SLP, Professor, University of Oregon; Craniofacial Disorders Program

Coordinator, Regional Services Center, Child Development and Rehabilitation Center, Oregon Health Sciences University, Eugene

Leslie Houghton, M.S., R.D., Nutrition Consultant, Regional Services Center, Child Development and Rehabilitation Center, Oregon Health Sciences University, Eugene

Judith R. Hylton, M.S., Senior Instructor, University Affiliated Program, and Health Education Consultant, Special Projects Office for the Child Development and Rehabilitation Center, Oregon Health Sciences University, Portland

Christine Jepsen, R.N., Nurse Consultant, Feeding Clinic Coordinator, Regional Services Center, Child Development and Rehabilitation Center, Oregon Health Sciences University, Eugene

Jewel Johnson, parent of a child with a seizure disorder, Florence, Oregon

Doris Julian, Ed.D., R.N., Associate Professor Emeritus, School of Nursing; Past Training Coordinator of Nursing of University Affiliated Program, Child Development and Rehabilitation Center, Oregon Health Sciences University, Portland

Janet S. Lee, R.P.T., Pediatric Physical Therapist and Program Director, Neurodevelopmental Program, Regional Services Center, Child Development and Rehabilitation Center, Oregon Health Sciences University, Eugene

John Leidel, M.D., Developmental Pediatrician, Children's Program, Portland, Oregon

Gregory S. Liptak, M.D., Developmental Pediatrician, University of Rochester Medical Center, Rochester, New York

Dafne E. Mattiello, R.P.T., Pediatric Physical Therapist, Regional Services Center, Child Development and Rehabilitation Center, Oregon Health Sciences University, Eugene

Catherine M.V. McGovern-Zlotek, O.T.R., Pediatric Occupational Therapist, Regional Services Center, Child Development and Rehabilitation Center, Oregon Health Sciences University, Eugene

John F. McLaughlin, M.D., Professor, Department of Pediatrics, Center on Human Development and Disability, and Children's Hospital and Medical Center, University of Washington, Seattle

Eileen Miller, parent of a daughter with autism, Roseburg, Oregon

Michael Miller, M.D., Pediatrician, Infectious Disease Specialist, Oregon Health Sciences University, Portland

Kathleen Myers, M.D., M.P.H., Associate Professor, Department of Psychiatry, Oregon Health Sciences University, Portland

Maureen Oliverio, P.N.P., R.N., Pediatric Nurse Practitioner, Spina Bifida Clinic, Child Development and Rehabilitation Center, Oregon Health Sciences University, Portland

Joseph H. Piatt, M.D., Pediatric Neurosurgeon, Oregon Health Sciences University, Portland

Betty Presler, R.N., Ph.D., Program Co-coordinator, Shriner's Hospital, Lexington, Kentucky

Catherine Renken, R.N., Assistant Director, Services for Children with Special Health Needs, Child Development and Rehabilitation Center, Oregon Health Sciences University, Portland

Barry Russman, M.D., Pediatric Neurologist, Shriner's Hospital, Portland, Oregon

Clifford J. Sells, M.D., M.P.H., Director of Services for Children with Special Health Needs, Child Development and Rehabilitation Center; Professor of Pediatrics, Oregon Health Sciences University, Portland

Bryna Siegel, Ph.D., Developmental Psychologist, Langley Porter Neuropsychiatric Institute, University of California, San Francisco

Darryn Sikora, Ph.D., Clinical Psychologist, Assistant Professor, Department of Psychiatry and Child Development and Rehabilitation Center, Oregon Health Sciences University, Portland

Steven Skoog, M.D., Pediatric Urologist, Oregon Health Sciences University, Portland

Joyce Stratton, former Statewide Autism Specialist, Regional Program for Autism, Oregon Department of Education, Salem

Jane Thornton, R.N., Clinic Coordinator, Spina Bifida Clinic, Child Development and Rehabilitation Center, Oregon Health Sciences University, Portland

Bud Thoune, Executive Director, United Cerebral Palsy Association of Oregon and Southwest Washington, Portland, Oregon

Kent A. Vincent, M.D., Pediatric Orthopedist, Shriner's Hospital, Portland, Oregon, and Department of Orthopedics, Oregon Health Sciences University, Portland

Michael A. Wall, M.D., Pediatric Pulmonologist, Department of Pediatrics, Oregon Health Sciences University, Portland

David Willis, M.D., Pediatrician, Legacy Emanuel Hospital, Oregon Health Sciences University, Portland

Lynn S. Wolf, M.O.T., O.T.R., Pediatric Occupational Therapist, Children's Hospital and Medical Center, Seattle, Washington

Jonathon Zonana, M.D., Professor of Medical Genetics, Oregon Health Sciences University, Portland

Introduction

The American Academy of Pediatrics (AAP; 1992) has recommended that primary care pediatricians provide a medical home for children with disabilities and chronic conditions. The services provided by the child's medical home are preventive care, assurance of all necessary acute and chronic illness care, access to medical subspecialties and other specialized treatment services, and coordination of care with other community service providers and medical subspecialists. Care should be "accessible, family-centered, comprehensive, continuous, coordinated, compassionate and culturally competent" (AAP, Ad Hoc Task Force on Definition of the Medical Home, 1992, p. 774). The medical home can and should be provided by all interested pediatricians; however, in rural areas, the medical home may be provided by a family practitioner or, occasionally, by a nurse practitioner or physician's assistant who consults with a pediatrician.

Provision of a medical home to children with chronic conditions requires an enhanced level of knowledge and services from the primary care physician and the primary care office. The comprehensive management of children with chronic conditions in a medical home in collaboration with other community professionals and medical subspecialists is one example of secondary-level care. Another example of secondary-level care is a community-based, interdisciplinary clinic for children with disabilities staffed by a primary care pediatrician. This book reviews the information, materials, and services that primary care health professionals require to provide that level of care. Each chapter on a specific disability or condition identifies key competencies, discusses background information, provides specific information on diagnosis and management, and provides health education materials, including guidelines for care.

CONTENTS

This book contains 18 chapters, 14 of which describe specific conditions. The first 4 chapters provide general information that applies to all disabilities and chronic conditions. The 14 chapters on specific conditions focus on children with particular types of developmental disabilities. Also included are representative chapters on children with congenital defects (i.e., cleft lip and palate), acquired disabilities (i.e., brain injury, spinal cord injury), chronic illnesses (i.e., human immunodeficiency virus [HIV] infection, seizure disorders, chronic respiratory disorders), mental health disorders (e.g., anxiety disorders), and children who are at risk for developmental or behavior problems (i.e., children with prenatal drug exposure).

STRUCTURE OF THE CHAPTERS

Each chapter on a specific condition is organized according to the following outline:

- Key competencies
- Description of the condition
- Definition, classification, prevalence, and etiology
- Associated health and/or behavior problems
- Diagnosis and evaluation
- Early identification
- Components of the comprehensive evaluation
- Counseling the child and the family about the diagnosis
- Family strengths and support needs
- Management
- Periodic review and update of the management plan
- Education and behavior management
- Medical and surgical management
- Anticipatory guidance
- Important care coordination issues
- Appendix: Key components of care forms

KEY COMPETENCIES

Competencies may refer to an individual's skills and knowledge base as well as the individual's personal qualities (Wiggins, 1998). The key competencies identified in each chapter of this book focus on building the skills and knowledge bases of primary care physicians and nurses. Examples of skills include counseling the child and the family and performing a developmental screening test. Examples of a knowledge base include knowledge of community resources and of the medication management of a child with a particular type of disability, condition, or disorder. The areas of competence necessary to provide the enhanced level of services required of a medical home include

- Child Find (early identification)
- Diagnosis and evaluation of the chronic condition
- Knowledge of specific medical and surgical treatments and behavioral interventions
- Development and periodic update of a management plan
- Knowledge of education programs and other community services
- Child and family education, support, and counseling
- Care coordination

A primary care provider also must possess a number of personal capacities in order to provide a medical home. These capacities include the ability to be caring, committed, respectful, compassionate, flexible, adaptable, nonjudgmental, honest, open, and persistent. In a survey of parents of children with chronic conditions in five pediatric offices in Oregon, pediatricians were rated highest in providing supportive and respectful care and lowest in providing information to the family (Nickel, Jepsen, & Hartsell, 1998). The survey instrument was the Measure of Processes of Care (MPOC), which comprises five factors: enabling and partnership, providing general information, providing specific information about the child, providing coordinated and comprehensive care, and providing respectful and supportive care. These survey results attest to the supportive relationships that pediatricians establish with families but also underline the need for the primary care office to improve the provision of information about the child's health condition and community resources to families. Each chapter of this book provides materials for health professionals to use when counseling children and families about the child's condition and when providing them with anticipatory guidance.

DESCRIPTION OF THE CONDITION
This section reviews background information that forms the basis for diagnosis, evaluation, and treatment. Lists of diagnostic criteria are included as appropriate. A summary of this information may be useful when counseling the child and the family.

Diagnosis and Evaluation
One emphasis of the section on diagnosis and evaluation is the early identification and referral for diagnostic evaluation of children who are suspected of having the condition. The components of the com-

prehensive diagnostic evaluation also are described. A distinction is made between the tests and procedures used to diagnose the condition and the tests and procedures necessary to determine the cause or the etiology of the disorder. Conducting a family assessment to determine the family's strengths and support needs is another essential part of the comprehensive evaluation. This topic is discussed in detail in Chapters 1 and 3, and other discussion of family support services related to specific conditions are included in Chapters 5–18 on specific conditions.

Counseling the Child and the Family About the Diagnosis
Counseling the child and the family about the diagnosis of a disability or chronic condition is one of the greatest challenges for health professionals. This issue is discussed in detail in Chapter 3, which includes a section entitled "Techniques that Are Useful in Giving Bad News to the Family." Chapter 5 reviews the recommended steps to follow in discussing the diagnosis of a developmental disability with the child and the family. In addition, each chapter on a specific condition identifies special aspects of counseling the child and the family about that particular diagnosis (e.g., informing a child about the diagnosis of HIV infection).

MANAGEMENT
The section on management reviews in detail the educational, behavioral, medical, and surgical management strategies that are appropriate for children with that particular condition as well as certain associated health problems. The roles of the primary care office, specialists, and the specialty team are identified. Specific recommendations are made for monitoring the progress of children with each particular condition, when to consider referral to specialists or to the specialty team, the provision of anticipatory guidance, and coordination of care with other care providers.

As much as possible, specific treatment recommendations are supported by data from clinical research studies. Unfortunately, many of the data available on the efficacy of medications and other treatments are derived from small, open-label studies rather than from carefully designed, randomized, placebo-controlled, double-blind trials. An increasing recognition of the importance of evidence-based medical practice is developing. Evidence-based practice is a process that includes identification of clinical questions and relevant clinical research (best external evidence), a critical appraisal of that evidence for validity and usefulness (clinical applicability), integration of that analysis with one's own expertise and patient choice, and ongoing evaluation of one's own performance (Sackett, 1997). The "gold standard" or best external evidence is the large randomized trial or a systematic review of several randomized trials.

Care Coordination

Coordination of care among the primary care office, other community service providers, and medical subspecialists and specialty teams is a basic responsibility of the medical home. The components of care coordination as well as recommendations for specific procedures in the primary care office are discussed in Chapter 1. Each chapter also identifies important care coordination issues specific to that diagnosis (e.g., identification of the contact person for early intervention/early childhood special education for children with developmental delays). Additional materials on care coordination are available through the AAP's Medical Home Program (see the Appendix at the end of Chapter 1 for contact information).

Periodic Review and Update of the Management Plan

Another basic responsibility of the primary care office is to monitor the child's progress, including the child's response to services, the need for specialty consultation and reevaluation by the specialty team, and the family's need for support or enabling services. The management plan is the counterpart of the child's individualized education program, or IEP. It may contain recommendations from specialists or from the specialty team as well as from community service providers. It should be updated at least annually for most older children and more frequently for younger children.

KEY COMPONENTS OF CARE FORMS

The key components of care forms are located in the appendix of each chapter on a specific disability or chronic condition. They include

- Guidelines for care
- Management plan summary
- Resources

These forms were developed as abbreviated educational materials for primary care health professionals to use in providing anticipatory guidance or in counseling families about a diagnosis, as well as to assist care providers with a periodic review of the child's and family's service needs. The guidelines, management plans, and resource lists in this book

are designed to be photocopied and used in clinical practice. In addition, because the management plans are used for ongoing care coordination, they can be downloaded from the Brookes Publishing web site. Similarly, the resource lists can be downloaded to share with families. (Please see page iv, which outlines specific conditions for use of these forms.)

The guidelines for care are brief summaries of the material presented in each chapter. In general, they specify the role of the primary care office and the specialty team and recommend the frequency of reevaluation by the primary care physician and/or specialty team. They provide age-specific information about key clinical issues and concerns, related evaluations and key procedures, and involvement of specialists and community services. The guidelines provide a road-map of possible future clinical issues and service needs to use in providing anticipatory guidance to families.

The management plan summary is one of the key components of care forms included in the appendixes of most chapters. It provides a structured document to be used in the review of service needs and is provided in a checklist format to remind health care professionals of all possible clinical issues associated with each diagnosis. The child and the parents complete the first two pages, which review the child's current services and the child's and family's goals.

The "Resources" sections include information on national advocacy groups, and recommended brochures, newsletters, and books for professionals and families.

REFERENCES

American Academy of Pediatrics (AAP). (1992). *Managed care and children with special needs: The Medical Home Checklist.* Elk Grove Village, IL: Author.

American Academy of Pediatrics (AAP), Ad Hoc Task Force on Definition of the Medical Home. (1992). The medical home. *Pediatrics, 90*(5), 774.

Nickel, R.E., Jepsen, C., & Hartsell, M.S. (1998, September). *Parent ratings of the care of children with special health care needs (CSHCN) in pediatric offices.* Scientific poster presented at the annual meeting of the American Academy for Cerebral Palsy and Developmental Medicine, San Antonio, TX.

Sackett, D.L. (1997). Evidence-based medicine. *Seminars in Perinatology, 21*(1), 3–5.

Wiggins, N. (1998). Core roles and competencies of community health advisors. In E. Koch (Ed.), *A summary of the National Community Health Advisor Study: A policy research project of the University of Arizona* (pp. 11–17). Baltimore: The Annie E. Casey Foundation.

The Physician's Guide to
Caring for Children with Disabilities and Chronic Conditions

Children with Disabilities and Chronic Conditions and Their Service Needs

Robert E. Nickel

KEY COMPETENCIES

- Discuss secondary-level health services, and list the required areas of competency for primary care physicians and nurses
- Describe specific changes in office procedures that can facilitate improved care of children with disabilities and chronic conditions in the primary care office
- Identify the basic values that guide services to children with disabilities and chronic conditions and their families
- List the necessary qualifications of specialists who care for children with disabilities and chronic conditions
- Discuss instances when specialty team evaluations are necessary for appropriate diagnostic and management decisions

DESCRIPTION

Definition

Who are children with disabilities and chronic conditions? More than 200 disabilities and chronic conditions can affect children and adolescents, including asthma, diabetes, cerebral palsy, and spina bifida (Ireys, 1994). Most of these are rare, except for asthma. A variety of approaches have been used to describe this population, including the diagnosis of a chronic condition and the presence of functional limitations and increased service needs. In general, they are categorized within one of four groups:

1. Children with disabilities (e.g., cerebral palsy)
2. Children with chronic illnesses (e.g., diabetes, anxiety disorder)
3. Children with congenital defects (e.g., cleft lip and palate, congenital heart defect)
4. Children with health-related educational and behavior problems (e.g., learning disability, attention-deficit/hyperactivity disorder [ADHD])

State and federal Maternal and Child Health Bureau (MCH) programs adopted the phrase *children with special health care needs* to refer to this population. A group convened by the MCH developed the following definition of this term:

> Children with special health care needs are those who have or are at increased risk for a physical, developmental, behavioral, or emotional condition and who also require health and related services of a type or amount beyond that required by children generally. (McPherson, Arango, Fox, et al., 1998, p. 137)

Some investigators have included all children with a given diagnosis, regardless of whether the diagnosis is associated with functional limitations or increased service needs. In Oregon, however, the Medicaid program uses the eligibility criteria for Supplemental Security Income (SSI) to define children with special health care needs. This definition identifies a population with severe disabilities.

Prevalence

Of children younger than 18 years of age whose families participated in the 1994 National Interview Survey on Disability, 18% had a chronic physical, developmental, behavioral, or emotional condition and required more than the usual level of health and related services (Newacheck, Strickland, Shonkoff, et al., 1998). Approximately 11% of these children were uninsured, and 13% had one or more unmet health care needs in the year prior to the survey.

Service Needs

In general, the service needs of children with disabilities and chronic conditions are complex. They require services from a variety of sources, services continue over a long period of time, and the cost of care is high. Services may be provided by health, educational, and social services providers in local communities and at regional centers. Children with disabilities and chronic conditions require one-and-a-half times more visits to the primary care office, twice the time per visit, five to ten times more hospitalizations, and two to three times more physician time overall (DiVerde, 1995). These children manifest twice the number of behavior problems and miss at least twice the number of days of school compared with children without disabilities and chronic conditions (Perrin & MacLean, 1988).

Values that Guide Services   The care provided to children with disabilities and chronic conditions and their families should be community-based, family-centered, culturally competent, comprehensive, coordinated, and compassionate. Each child is unique, and family members are the experts in managing the care of their child. Families are partners with service providers; they are essential contributors to and participants in all treatment decisions. Services are provided in or near these children's home communities when possible, and the system of care honors and respects each family's cultural beliefs, values, and attitudes. Curriculum guidelines have been developed for culturally sensitive and competent health care for use in family practice and pediatric residency programs (Like, Steiner, & Rubel, 1996). Table 1.1 presents the key elements of family-centered care.

Primary, Secondary, and Tertiary Care Services   Health services for children with disabilities and chronic conditions can be categorized as primary care, secondary care, and tertiary care. A child with

Table 1.1.   Key elements of family-centered care

- Incorporating into policy and practice the recognition that the *family is the constant* in a child's life, while the service systems and support personnel within those systems fluctuate
- Facilitating *family–professional collaboration* at all levels of hospital, home, and community care:
  a.   Care of individual children
  b.   Program development, implementation, evaluation, and evolution
  c.   Policy formation
- Exchanging complete and unbiased information between families and professionals in a supportive manner at all times
- Incorporating into policy and practice the recognition and *honoring of cultural diversity*, strengths, and individuality within and across all families, including *ethnic, racial, spiritual, socioeconomic, educational, and geographic diversity*
- Recognizing and respecting *different methods of coping* and implementing comprehensive policies and programs that provide *developmental, educational, emotional, environmental, and financial supports* to meet the diverse needs of families
- Encouraging and facilitating *family-to-family support* and networking
- Ensuring that *hospital, home, and community service and support systems* for children needing specialized health and developmental care and their families are *flexible, accessible, and comprehensive* in responding to diverse family-identified needs
- *Appreciating families as families and children as children,* recognizing that they possess a wide range of strengths, concerns, emotions, and aspirations beyond their need for specialized health and developmental services and support

From Shelton, T.L., & Stepanek, J.S. (1994). *Family-centered care for children needing specialized health and developmental services* (3rd ed., p. vii). Alexandria, VA: Association for the Care of Children's Health; reproduced by permission from the Association for the Care of Children's Health.

a disability or chronic condition is first and foremost a child and has all the preventive health care needs of other children. Children with disabilities and chronic conditions must have access to *primary health care* through a medical home. The American Academy of Pediatrics' (AAP's) Ad Hoc Task Force on Definition of the Medical Home listed the following characteristics of a medical home:

- Provision of preventive care
- Assurance of ambulatory and inpatient care
- Provision of care over an extended period of time
- Identification of the need for subspecialty consultation and referrals
- Interaction with school and community agencies

- Maintenance of a central record and database containing all pertinent medical information (1992, p. 774)

The AAP, in collaboration with Family Voices, the federal Maternal and Child Health Bureau, the National Association of Children's Hospitals and Related Institutions, and Shriners Hospitals for Children, has developed a training program for health professionals to help ensure that all children have a medical home (see the "Resources" section in the Appendix at the end of this chapter).

Secondary-level health care refers to the comprehensive management of children with disabilities and chronic conditions by the primary care physician in a medical home in collaboration with parents and other community service providers and medical subspecialists as needed. It requires a commitment by the physician and the nurse to serve this population; an expanded knowledge of disabilities and chronic conditions; and changes in office procedures, including the provision of comprehensive care coordination. It can and should be provided by all interested primary care physicians. The following areas of competency are needed to provide secondary-level health services:

- Child Find (i.e., developmental screening and surveillance)
- Diagnosis of the disability or chronic condition (often in conjunction with specialists)
- Development and periodic updates of a management plan
- Knowledge of education programs and other community services
- Child and family education, support, and counseling, which should include the provision of written information regarding the condition and community services
- Care coordination

Tertiary care is provided by pediatric subspecialists. It requires a level of expertise and technology that may be found only at regional medical centers or in children's hospitals.

Basic Services Package   Children with disabilities and chronic conditions require a wide array of health and related services:

- Adequate primary and specialty medical and surgical care (inpatient and outpatient)
- Specialized nursing and support services
- Mental health services
- Assistive technologies
- Nutritional counseling and services
- Specialized dietary products

- Home health care
- Hospice care
- Care coordination
- Long-term physical and occupational therapy (habilitative and rehabilitative services)
- Long-term speech-language and hearing services
- Adaptive equipment and supplies
- Medications
- Specialized evaluations
- Enabling services (e.g., transportation to appointments with specialists, respite care)

Pediatricians should advocate for managed care contracts that provide a broad, comprehensive array of services for children with disabilities and chronic conditions (AAP, Committee on Children with Disabilities, 1998).

Referrals to Specialists Both primary care and specialty care providers require specialized knowledge and experience to serve children with disabilities and chronic conditions well. Specialists must have training and ongoing, regular experience specific to the diagnosis of, treatment of, and procedures for caring for children with disabilities and chronic conditions of a particular age group. Referral to an adult specialist who is untrained or inexperienced in treating children with a particular disability or chronic condition is not appropriate. In addition, there is a growing research base for clinical decision making in all disciplines with regard to providing care to children with disabilities and chronic conditions. Primary care physicians and specialists must participate in relevant continuing education activities to stay abreast of this information.

In general, it is not appropriate for specialists to provide primary care to children with disabilities and chronic conditions. In a few instances, the medical home may be provided by a medical subspecialist who offers specialty and all necessary primary care to the child and the family.

Specialty Team Evaluations For many children with disabilities and chronic conditions, evaluation by an experienced team of professionals is necessary for accurate diagnosis and optimal treatment planning. Evaluations by individual disciplines may result in incorrect diagnoses, inappropriate treatment recommendations, and increased cost of care. Parents are essential participants on the team with regard to both diagnostic and treatment decisions. Specialty teams include the child development, craniofacial, spina bifida, and neurodevelopmental teams. The following paragraphs highlight the importance of team evaluations for both diagnosis and management planning (see chapters on specific disabilities for more information).

1. *Diagnostic evaluations:* Children who are suspected of having autism, children with developmental delays and behavior problems, and children with severe behavior problems should be evaluated by an experienced child development team composed of a developmental pediatrician, a speech-language pathologist, and a psychologist. Other staff may be needed (e.g., an occupational therapist), depending on associated concerns. Care coordination should be provided by the medical social worker on the team or by the referral source if comprehensive care coordination is available. An accurate developmental diagnosis depends on the sharing of performance information across disciplines. The child's communication and cognitive abilities are critical components of an accurate diagnosis. Furthermore, care coordination in such cases involves medical, educational, and behavioral services. Decisions about the use of medication must be based on a thorough understanding of the functional intent of the problem behavior (see also Chapters 3 and 8).

2. *Management planning:* Children with certain known diagnoses (e.g., cleft lip and palate, spina bifida, cerebral palsy) require ongoing care by a team of experienced specialists who consult with the primary care physician and parents for the purposes of updating the management plan and handling specific management concerns. In these instances, the treatment recommendations of one professional directly affect those of another. Decisions about the timing of orthodontic care for children with cleft lip and palate may depend on the treatment recommendations of the pedodontist and the plastic surgeon and are assisted by information from the speech-language pathologist regarding voice quality and the need to address palatal insufficiency as part of the treatment plan. Recommendations for continence programs or therapy services for a child with spina bifida and a recent change in continence and gait depend on information from professionals in several disciplines. The child may have a symptomatic tethered cord and require surgical release before other treatment is begun. Similarly, treatment decisions with regard to children with cerebral palsy often require information from an orthopedist, a developmental pediatrician, and a physical therapist. Team evaluations promote appropriate care, long-term cost savings, and overall higher-quality care. Some children (e.g., children with human immunodeficiency virus [HIV] infection) may receive nearly all of their care related to their disability or chronic condition at a tertiary care medical center.

3. *Care coordination:* Liptak and Revell described the following components of care coordination, which mirror the competencies for providing secondary-level health services:

- Identify and assess the needs of children and their families (needs assessment)
- Plan and arrange for medical and nonmedical services (comprehensive care planning)
- Facilitate and coordinate services (including the training of community providers)
- Monitor services and patient progress (follow-up)
- Counsel, educate, train, and support patients and their families (empowerment) (1989, p. 465)

Regular exchange of information among the primary care and other service providers is critical for the effective coordination of services. A sample form (the Health Information Questionnaire for Children Receiving Early Intervention/Early Childhood Special Education [EI/ECSE] Services; Nickel, 1998) for the exchange of written information between the primary care office and early intervention (EI)/early childhood special education (ECSE) staff is provided in the Appendix at the end of this chapter. The Health Information Questionnaire was designed so that the health professional can provide important information to EI/ECSE staff with limited use of the health professional's time. The primary care provider should review the child's individualized family service plan (IFSP) or individualized education program (IEP) regularly and contribute health information to the development of the IFSP or IEP as needed. The IFSP and IEP are summaries of the child's educational and related services (see Chapter 5 for more details).

Care coordination may be available from exceptional needs care coordinators (ENCC) of managed care plans, nurses in state MCH programs (services for children with special health care needs), local EI and school staff, developmental disabilities care coordinators, and other agencies. It is important for the primary care physician and the nurse to be aware of local resources and to provide adequate time for care coordination in their office to collaborate fully with parents and community service providers.

4. *Enabling services:* Children with disabilities and chronic conditions and their families may require a variety of enabling or family support services. Without such supports, many families may be confused and overwhelmed by the complex and at times conflicting treatment recommendations of different service providers, miss appointments, and fail to follow up with needed services (Cooley, Olsen, & McAllister, 1994). For these families, enabling ser-

vices are necessary to ensure optimal medical outcomes. Enabling services include

- Respite care and child care
- Transportation to appointments
- Contact with other families who have children with similar disabilities or conditions (e.g., the Parent-to-Parent program of The Arc of the United States: A National Organization on Mental Retardation [more commonly called *The Arc*; formerly known as the Association for Retarded Citizens])
- Parent support groups (e.g., state and national chapters of the Spina Bifida Association of America, local autism parent groups)
- Advocacy and legal aid (e.g., state and national chapters of The Arc)
- Financial services (e.g., SSI)
- Counseling
- Assistance with care coordination

5. *Counseling the child and the family:* A particularly challenging role for the primary health care professional is counseling the parents of an infant or a child when the diagnosis of a developmental disability is first made. Health professionals must schedule adequate time, listen, be respectful and compassionate, provide information clearly and in understandable terms, and acknowledge the parents' reactions. Parents may be upset, confused, or angry. These reactions may be expressions of anxiety related to the start of the mourning process for the feelings of loss that they are experiencing (MacKeith, 1973; Nelson, 1989).

If possible, both parents should be present for the conference with the primary care physician regarding initial diagnosis, and other family members may be present also if the family so desires. Information should be shared completely yet in small amounts, with frequent checks to make sure that the parents understand it. The physician or nurse should also emphasize the child's positive aspects and strengths. The following list is a step-by-step guide for presenting the child's parents and other family members with information about the diagnosis:

- Begin with a review of the parents' concerns and observations.
- Review the results of the studies and evaluations that established the diagnosis.
- Ask the parents to compare these results with their observations.
- Discuss the natural history of the child's condition and associated problems as well as the prognosis, if appropriate.

- Recommend any further studies as needed to clarify the diagnosis or treatment recommendations.
- Review the child's IFSP or IEP with the family (AAP, Committee on Children with Disabilities, 1992), discuss medical treatment options, and make recommendations for the initial management plan. Clarify the responsibilities of the primary care office, the school, and other service providers.
- Discuss family support service needs and provide information about community services, including a parent-to-parent network.
- Review your office procedures for children with disabilities and chronic conditions. State clearly that the primary care physician and the parents are partners in the care of the child and that the parents will be involved in all treatment decisions.
- Provide written information about the condition and recommended treatments as well as resources for further information.

The following changes in office procedures (see, e.g., Cooley et al., 1994; Hirsch & Barela, 1995) are some of the necessary steps for providing secondary-level health services in the primary care office. These need to be complemented by an expanded knowledge base with regard to the management of specific problems.

1. *Identify children with disabilities and chronic conditions in your practice and code (i.e., flag) their charts as children with disabilities and chronic conditions:* Use a few criteria that are interpreted easily.

For example, use a brief questionnaire that parents can complete when checking in with the office receptionist (see Figure 1.1). Flag the chart of any child with one or more "yes" responses after clarification of any answers as needed with the family.

2. *Place the child's name on a priority list for office staff (e.g., at the receptionist's desk):* Note the optimal time of day for office appointments and any other special arrangements (e.g., limited tolerance for use of the waiting room, need for transportation). Children with disabilities and chronic conditions may best be scheduled as the first appointment in the morning or after lunch, and all appointments should be made for twice the amount of time usually allotted for children without disabilities (Cooley et al., 1994).

3. *Identify an office care coordinator for children with disabilities and chronic conditions:* Usually, an office nurse or nurse practitioner is responsible for establishing links with community agencies and ensuring timely and effective communication with representatives of these agencies as well as with families. This person supports and complements the care coordination activities of the physicians. When initiating a disability or chronic condition management plan (Cooley et al., 1994), it is important to discuss the special office procedures directly with the family and provide the name and telephone number of the primary care office care coordinator (if it is not the physician). The primary care office care coordinator should identify the appropriate contact person for the following agencies or services:

- Designated referral and evaluation agency for EI/ECSE services

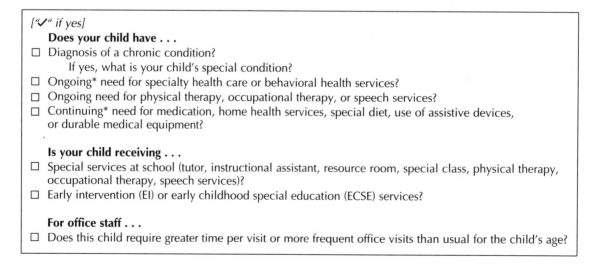

["✓" if yes]

Does your child have . . .

☐ Diagnosis of a chronic condition?
   If yes, what is your child's special condition?
☐ Ongoing* need for specialty health care or behavioral health services?
☐ Ongoing need for physical therapy, occupational therapy, or speech services?
☐ Continuing* need for medication, home health services, special diet, use of assistive devices, or durable medical equipment?

Is your child receiving . . .

☐ Special services at school (tutor, instructional assistant, resource room, special class, physical therapy, occupational therapy, speech services)?
☐ Early intervention (EI) or early childhood special education (ECSE) services?

For office staff . . .

☐ Does this child require greater time per visit or more frequent office visits than usual for the child's age?

Figure 1.1.   Checklist of questions a physician should ask parents to identify children with disabilities and chronic conditions in the primary care office. (*, *ongoing* or *continuing* means conditions have already lasted or are certain to last for at least 12 months.)

- Local interagency coordinating council (LICC) (i.e., the planning group for EI/ECSE)
- County health department and state MCH program (i.e., services for children with special health care needs)
- ENCCs of managed care plans
- Special education services in local school districts
- County and state developmental disabilities services organizations

4. *Identify an office staff member who will be responsible for authorizations and referral coordination:* This person primarily handles the logistical and financial aspects of authorization or reauthorization of services and supplies.

5. *Keep encounter data:* Data should include the number of outpatient visits and the length of each visit, the number of hospitalizations and the length of each stay, and other data as related to current contracts (e.g., laboratory, X rays, specialty referrals). Also estimate the amount of time per visit spent on telephone calls and other care coordination activities. Accurate data may be helpful to primary care physicians when negotiating with managed care plans for changes in the level of reimbursement for services.

6. *Provide information about the diagnosis and treatment options to the child and the family:* Families require information about their child's chronic condition, medical treatment, and community services. It is important to provide educational materials and discuss treatment options directly with older children and adolescents to facilitate these children's taking responsibility for appropriate aspects of their own care.

7. *Provide anticipatory guidance:* Anticipatory guidance for children with disabilities and chronic conditions builds on other programs such as Bright Futures and Guidelines for Adolescent Services (Elster & Kuznets, 1994; Green, 1994). In general, anticipatory guidance for children with disabilities and chronic conditions includes discussion of the following areas:

- Clinical information (e.g., symptoms of tethered cord for the child with spina bifida)
- Review of community resources
- School transition and transition from hospital to home (especially for children with complex medical needs)
- Promotion of social competence and self-esteem
- Promotion of self-care and independence

- Adolescent issues (e.g., diagnosis and treatment options, exercise and diet, sexuality; high-risk behaviors such as cigarette, drug, and alcohol use)
- Vocational planning
- Transition to adult services and independent living (see Schulzinger, 1998)

Transitions may be times of considerable stress for families (e.g., transitions from preschool to grade school, grade school to middle school, high school to adult services and independent living). Dependence and social isolation are problems for many adolescents and young adults with disabilities. Promotion of social competence, self-esteem, and individual responsibility for the individual's own care is a critical part of the management of children with disabilities and chronic conditions. Vocational planning, life skills (i.e., independent living skills), and social skills training programs are important services for many children with disabilities and chronic conditions.

8. *Review family strengths and support needs:* Maintain a family systems perspective and assist children and families in identifying goals and developing solutions. Brief, structured questionnaires such as the Family Needs Survey (Bailey & Simeonsson, 1988) may be useful as part of an open-ended interview (see Chapter 3 for further discussion of family assessment and support services).

9. *Identify the parent support groups and respite care resources in your community:* Provide families with information on local and national advocacy groups, including a contact person, address, telephone number, e-mail address, and web site address.

10. *Assist families in developing and maintaining a care notebook for their child:* Families should maintain an up-to-date file of their child's medical and educational records to facilitate the care of their child while they are on a family vacation or in the event that the family moves to a new community. The care notebook can also improve communication between health and educational service providers and communication between the primary care office and specialists.

Some families may also need a brief health data form to keep with them for use in the emergency room with physicians who may have no previous knowledge of their child's problems and limited time to read the child's medical record. The emergency data set developed by the American College of Emergency Physicians is one example (Carraccio, Dettmer, duPont, & Sacchetti, 1998). This form contains information about the child's physicians, diagnoses, current medications, baseline physical and laboratory data, common presenting problems, and recommended treatment.

11. *Periodically review the child's progress and update the office management plan:* The periodic review is best conducted at least annually for children who are stable and doing well and more often for younger children and in the first year or two of treatment. The following are the responsibilities of the primary care health professional:

- Monitor the child's response to services, including educational services
- Review the treatment of associated health problems and monitor for the development of new problems
- Determine the need for referral to specialists or to the specialty team
- Review ongoing needs for family support
- Provide anticipatory guidance, including written information, at appropriate times
- Assist the family with care coordination

Note that an important part of updating the management plan is a review of the child's educational progress, including a summary of the IEP for school-age children and of the IFSP for younger children receiving EI services. The Family and Physician Management Plan Summary for each disability or chronic condition reviewed in this book, located in the appendixes at the end of the chapter that covers the particular disability or chronic condition, was

developed to assist with the periodic review. It is presented in a checklist format as a reminder of most clinical issues associated with each condition.

12. *Review the need for structural changes in the office (e.g., wheelchair accessibility, number of parking spaces for people with disabilities):* In addition, consider 1) establishing a family advisory board for the primary care practice that includes parents of children with disabilities and chronic conditions or 2) evaluating consumer satisfaction regularly by another method (W.C. Cooley, personal communication, March 1996).

Cooley and co-workers (1994) developed a chronic condition management program to facilitate improvement in the care of children with disabilities and chronic conditions in the primary care office. This program identified specific changes in office procedures, such as creation of a priority list of children with disabilities and chronic conditions to assist with scheduling, use of guidelines for parents about care with regard to specific conditions, and the identification of office staff for care coordination responsibilities. Hirsch and Barela (1995) provided secondary-level health services successfully to more than 1,400 children with disabilities and chronic conditions in their pediatric practice in Phoenix. They noted the critical importance of keeping accurate patient encounter data. They have used this information to negotiate appropriate reimbursement with their state Medicaid agency and other payers.

REFERENCES

American Academy of Pediatrics (AAP), Ad Hoc Task Force on Definition of the Medical Home. (1992). The medical home. *Pediatrics, 90*(5), 774.

American Academy of Pediatrics (AAP), Committee on Children with Disabilities. (1992). Pediatrician's role in the development and implementation of an individualized education program (IEP) and/or an individualized family service plan (IFSP). *Pediatrics, 89*(2), 340–342.

American Academy of Pediatrics (AAP), Committee on Children with Disabilities. (1998). Managed care and children with special health care needs: A subject review. *Pediatrics, 102,* 657–660.

Bailey, D.B., Jr., & Simeonsson, R.J. (1988). Assessing needs of families with handicapped infants. *Journal of Special Education, 22*(1), 117–126.

Carraccio, C.L., Dettmer, K.S., duPont, M.L., & Sacchetti, A.D. (1998). Family member knowledge of children's medical problems: The need for universal application of an emergency data set. *Pediatrics, 102,* 367–370.

Cooley, W.C., Olson, A.L., & McAllister, J. (1994). *Chronic condition management in the primary care setting: A provider's resource manual.* Lebanon: New Hampshire Partners in Health, Office Partners Project.

DiVerde, M. (1995, January). Effective strategies for working with managed care programs: An Arizona practice shares its experiences. *Catch Quarterly, 3*(1), 4, 8.

Elster, A.B., & Kuznets, V.J. (Eds.). (1994). *American Medical Association guidelines for adolescent preventive services (GAPS): Recommendations and rationale.* Baltimore: Lippincott Williams & Wilkins.

Green, M. (Ed.). (1994). *Bright Futures: Guidelines for health supervision of infants, children, and adolescents.* Arlington, VA: National Center for Education in Maternal and Child Health.

Hirsch, D., & Barela, T. (1995, April). *Effective strategies for working with managed care programs.* Paper presented at the Families as Participants Conference, Washington, DC.

Ireys, H.T. (1994, November). *Children with special health care needs: Evaluating their needs and relevant service structures* (Background paper commissioned by the Institute of Medicine). Washington, DC: Institute of Medicine.

Like, R.C., Steiner, R.P., & Rubel, A.J. (1996). Recommended core curriculum guidelines on culturally sensitive and competent health care. *Family Medicine, 28*(4), 291–297.

Liptak, G.S., & Revell, G.M. (1989). Community physician's role in case management of children with chronic illnesses. *Pediatrics, 84*(3), 465–471.

MacKeith, R. (1973). The feelings and behavior of parents of handicapped children. *Developmental Medicine and Child Neurology, 15,* 524–527.

McPherson, M., Arango, P., Fox, H., et al. (1998). A new definition of children with special health care needs. *Pediatrics, 102,* 137–140.

Nelson, R.P. (1989). Community services for children with mental retardation. *Pediatric Annals, 18*(10), 615–621.

Newacheck, P.W., Strickland, B., Shonkoff, J.P., et al. (1998). An epidemiologic profile of children with special health care needs. *Pediatrics, 102*(1), 117–121.

Nickel, R.E. (1998). *Health Information Questionnaire for Children Receiving Early Intervention/Early Childhood Special Education (EI/ECSE) Services.* Portland: Oregon Health Sciences University.

Perrin, J.M., & MacLean, W.E. (1988). Children with chronic illness: The prevention of dysfunction. *Pediatric Clinics of North America, 35*(6), 1325–1337.

Schulzinger, R. (1998). *Key transition issues for youth with disabilities and chronic conditions: An occasional policy brief of the Institute of Child Health Policy.* Gainesville, FL: Institute of Child Health Policy.

Shelton, T.L., & Stepanek, J.S. (1994). *Family-centered care for children needing specialized health and developmental services* (3rd ed.). Alexandria, VA: Association for the Care of Children's Health.

1

Appendix

Health Information Questionnaire for Children Receiving
Early Intervention/Early Childhood Special Education (EI/ECSE) Services

Dear Health Care Provider: The information on this questionnaire will help us to learn whether health issues may affect this child's development and will help us to develop our plans for educational services. Thank you for your time and assistance. You do *not* need to copy your records for us. (Please provide details for any "Yes" answers.)

Child's name _____ Date of birth _____ County _____

Primary care provider _____ Person completing form _____

Address _____ Today's date _____

Telephone/fax_____

Best time to reach you in the office (if needed) _____

Yes No

1. ☐ ☐ Does this child have a neurologic problem (e.g., seizures/epilepsy, muscle weakness, hydrocephalus, cerebral palsy)? If yes, specify. _____

2. ☐ ☐ Does this child have an orthopedic problem (e.g., scoliosis, hand or foot deformity, hip dislocation)? If yes, specify. _____

3. ☐ ☐ Does this child have any birth defect or genetic problem (e.g., cleft palate, heart defect, Down syndrome)? If yes, specify. _____

4. ☐ ☐ Does this child have a chronic illness (e.g., diabetes, asthma, kidney problem)? If yes, specify. _____

5. ☐ ☐ Are there any concerns about this child's nutrition or growth? If yes, explain. _____

6. ☐ ☐ Is this child on a special diet? If yes, specify. _____

7. ☐ ☐ Does this child have difficulties with feeding (e.g., choking, gagging, coughing, vomiting, slow to complete a meal)? If yes, specify. _____

8. ☐ ☐ Does this child require special feeding techniques (e.g., adapted utensils, special positions)? If yes, specify. _____

9. ☐ ☐ Do you have any concerns about this child's hearing? If yes, specify. _____

10. ☐ ☐ Has this child's hearing been tested? If yes, please specify where, when, and what the results were. ____

11. ☐ ☐ Does this child have a history of chronic ear infections or tubes in ears? If yes, what is the child's current status? _____

12. ☐ ☐ Does this child have vision problems or wear eyeglasses? If yes, explain. _____

(continued)

The Physician's Guide to Caring for Children with Disabilities and Chronic Conditions, Nickel & Desch, copyright © 2000 by Paul H. Brookes Publishing Co.

Health Information Questionnaire for Children Receiving Early Intervention/Early Childhood Special Education (EI/ECSE) Services (continued)

Yes No

13. ☐ ☐ Does this child use assistive technology (e.g., wheelchair, prone stander, braces)? If yes, specify. _____
_____

14. ☐ ☐ Does this child need any health treatments daily (e.g., gastrostomy feedings, intermittent catheterization)? If yes, specify. _____
_____

15. ☐ ☐ Do any of these treatments need to be administered at school? If yes, specify. _____
_____

16. ☐ ☐ Does this child take medication every day? If yes, list the medication(s) and note any side effects of the medication of which school staff should be aware. _____
_____

17. ☐ ☐ Does this child need to receive the medication at school? If yes, what medication, at which dosage, and at what time? _____
_____

18. ☐ ☐ Does this child have any allergies to medications, food, or other substances? If yes, specify and describe the symptoms and any treatment that is needed if exposed to the allergen(s). _____
_____

19. ☐ ☐ Are any adaptations to the classroom schedule or to the environment required, or are special safety precautions necessary? If yes, describe. _____
_____

20. ☐ ☐ Are there any issues that you would like early intervention/early childhood special education staff to evaluate? to monitor? If yes, explain. _____
_____

21. ☐ ☐ Do you have any other concerns about this child's health of which school staff should be aware? If yes, please describe. _____
_____

22. ☐ ☐ Are immunizations up-to-date? *Please enclose a copy of the child's immunization record if available.*
_____
_____

☐ **Check here if parents would like the results of their child's early intervention/early childhood special education eligibility testing and a summary of the individualized family service plan (IFSP).**

Please return questionnaire to

Name _____

Program _____

Address _____

_____

Telephone/fax _____

The Physician's Guide to Caring for Children with Disabilities and Chronic Conditions, Nickel & Desch, copyright © 2000 by Paul H. Brookes Publishing Co.

RESOURCES ON CHILDREN WITH DISABILITIES AND CHRONIC CONDITIONS AND THEIR SERVICE NEEDS

Readings

Batshaw, M.L. (Ed.). (1997). *Children with disabilities* (4th ed.). Baltimore: Paul H. Brookes Publishing Co. (1-800-638-3775)

Capute, A.J., & Accardo, P.J. (Eds.). (1996). *Developmental disabilities in infancy and childhood* (2 vols.; 2nd ed.). Baltimore: Paul H. Brookes Publishing Co. (1-800-638-3775)

Porter, S., Haynie, M., Bierle, T., et al. (1997). *Children and youth assisted by medical technology in educational settings: Guidelines for care* (2nd ed.). Baltimore: Paul H. Brookes Publishing Co. (1-800-638-3775)

Singer, G.H.S., Powers, L.E., & Olson, A.L. (Eds.). (1996). *Redefining family support: Innovations in public–private partnerships.* Baltimore: Paul H. Brookes Publishing Co. (1-800-638-3775)

General Information

Centers for Disease Control and Prevention (CDC)
World Wide Web site: http://www.cdc.gov/

The CDC World Wide Web site provides access to publications such as *Morbidity and Mortality Weekly Report* (MMWR), prevention guidelines, and links to other departments and affiliates (e.g., the National Center for Health Statistics [NCHS]).

U.S. Food and Drug Administration (FDA)
World Wide Web site: http://www.fda.gov/

The FDA World Wide Web site publishes current notices on drug and device approvals, recalls, and so forth, as well as information about food-borne diseases.

healthfinder
World Wide Web site: http://www.healthfinder.gov/

This government-sponsored listing of health-related World Wide Web sites also has links to databases and on-line journals.

Internet Resources for Special Children (IRSC)
E-mail: julio_c@one.net
World Wide Web site: http://www.irsc.org/

IRSC provides excellent links to a variety of disability-specific World Wide Web sites (e.g., autism, cerebral palsy, hearing impairment).

Medscape
World Wide Web site: http://www.medscape.com/

Medscape offers access to literature searches through MEDLINE and provides medical information, graphics, and interactive quizzes.

National Library of Medicine
World Wide Web site: http://www.nlm.nih.gov/

The National Library of Medicine web site provides access to health databases, including MEDLINE and Pre-MEDLINE (PubMed at http://www.ncbi.nlm.nih.gov/PubMed/ or at http://www.ncbi.nlm.nih.gov/entrez/query.fcgi), as well as information on publications, research programs, and grants.

PEDINFO: An Index of the Pediatric Internet
World Wide Web site: http://www.pedinfo.org/

PEDINFO: An Index of the Pediatric Internet originated at the University of Alabama at Birmingham. It offers an online pediatric discussion group and provides condition-specific information and links to children's hospitals, professional organizations, and government agencies.

Professional Organizations

American Academy of Pediatrics (AAP)
141 Northwest Point Boulevard
Elk Grove Village, Illinois 60007-1098
Telephone: (800) 433-9016, (847) 228-5005
Fax: (847) 228-5097
E-mail: docp@aap.org
World Wide Web site: http://www.aap.org/

AAP encourages research, advocates for a variety of issues related to children and families, provides information and support to professionals, and publishes a journal, *Pediatrics,* and a newsletter, *Catch Quarterly.*

American Academy of Pediatrics
Medical Home Project Training Program
Training manager: Bob Moore, M.A.
Telephone: (800) 433-9016, ext. 4918
E-mail: bmoore@aap.org
World Wide Web site: http://www.aap.org/, then click on "Advocacy," then scroll down under the heading *Programs* and click on "National Center of Medical Home Initiatives for Children with Special Needs" (http://www.aap.org/advocacy/medhome.htm).

The AAP's medical home training program for health professionals includes guidelines for establishing contracts with health care plans, working with families, collaborating with health care professionals, and coordinating services.

2

Developmental Screening and Surveillance

Robert E. Nickel
Jane Squires

KEY COMPETENCIES 16
DESCRIPTION 16
  Definitions of Developmental Screening and Developmental Surveillance 16
  Rationale for the Use of a Developmental Monitoring Program in
    a Primary Care Office. 16
  Developmental Disabilities that Can Be Identified Through Developmental
    Monitoring Programs 17
  Advantages of Developmental Screening Tests as Part of a Monitoring Program 17
  Importance of Using Parent Report Measures 17
  Recommendations for a Developmental Monitoring Program. 17
CONCLUSIONS 25
REFERENCES 25
APPENDIX 28
  Resources on Developmental Screening and Surveillance 29

KEY COMPETENCIES

- Discuss the benefits of using parent report measures in developmental monitoring programs
- Become familiar with the administration and interpretation of at least one parent report measure; one general office screening tool; and targeted screening tools for cerebral palsy, language delay, and autism
- Construct a developmental monitoring program for your office that identifies risk factors in the newborn nursery and uses informal observations, parent report measures, and repeated measures at different ages

DESCRIPTION

Definitions of Developmental Screening and Developmental Surveillance

A *developmental screening* is a brief evaluation of developmental skills applied to a total population of children that is intended to identify those children with suspected disabilities who should be referred for a complete diagnostic assessment (Meisels, 1988). It does not provide a definitive diagnosis or a developmental quotient but rather raises red flags that indicate which children need further testing (Bennett, Nickel, Squires, & Woodward, 1997).

Developmental surveillance is part of the program of preventive health care recommended by the British Joint Working Party on Child Health Surveillance (Dworkin, 1989; Hutchison & Nicoll, 1988). In that program, the physician identifies parents' concerns and makes regular, skilled observations of a child's behavior in order to monitor the child's developmental progress. It is an informal, continuous process that may or may not involve the use of screening tests.

In this chapter, the terms *developmental monitoring* and *developmental surveillance* are used synonymously. The monitoring program that we recommend includes the identification of risk factors in the nursery and the use of formal screening tests with informal observations; repeated measures at different ages; and multiple sources of information, particularly parent report.

Rationale for the Use of a Developmental Monitoring Program in a Primary Care Office

Widespread support exists for the early identification of children with disabilities. Both the American Academy of Pediatrics (AAP; 1994) and the British Joint Working Party on Child Health Surveillance (Hutchison & Nicoll, 1988) have recommended routine monitoring of a child's developmental progress as part of preventive health care. In addition, at least 90% of pediatricians in two different surveys stated their support for the early identification of developmental problems and the provision of early intervention (EI) services for pre–school-age children with disabilities and their families (Scott, Lingaraju, Kilgo, et al., 1993; Wenger, McLaurin, Guild, et al., 1989).

In general, the benefits of EI services for children with a variety of disabilities have been well documented (Bricker, 1989; Guralnick, 1997, 1998; Shonkoff & Hauser-Cram, 1987), although additional research is needed to demonstrate the relative effectiveness of specific intervention strategies. Programs that are comprehensive in nature, are home based as well as center based, and include parents as well as their infants are the most effective. The Education of the Handicapped Act Amendments of 1986 (PL 99-457) and the Individuals with Disabilities Education Act (IDEA) Amendments of 1997 (PL 105-17) established requirements for early childhood special education (ECSE) and related services for children with disabilities ages 3–5 years and made recommendations for EI services for children from birth through 2 years of age. All states provide EI/ECSE services to eligible children through a combination of state and federal funds.

Primary care physicians and nurses are uniquely qualified to provide developmental monitoring programs and refer infants and children suspected of having disabilities for further evaluation and services. They have a knowledge of children's growth and development and have an ongoing relationship with the child and the child's family (Squires, Nickel, & Eisert, 1996). Furthermore, the AAP's Committee on Children with Disabilities made the following recommendations to primary care physicians:

1. Maintain and update knowledge about developmental issues, risk factors, screening techniques, and community resources for consultation and intervention.
2. Acquire skills in the administration and interpretation of a formal developmental screening technique.
3. Develop a strategy to provide periodic screening in the context of office-based primary care, including the following:
   - Developmental screening of all children in the practice
   - Recognizing abnormal appearance and functioning during health care maintenance examinations
   - Recognizing high-risk medical and environmental situations while taking routine medical and social histories

- Actively seeking observations and concerns from parents about their child's development
- Recognizing troubled parent–child interactions from history or observation
- Performing periodic rescreenings of practice populations to discover the possible emergence of new risk situations or the child's difficulty in meeting more advanced developmental expectations (1994, p. 864)

Developmental Disabilities that Can Be Identified Through Developmental Monitoring Programs

The term *developmental disabilities* refers to those conditions that originate in childhood, are likely to continue indefinitely, and are characterized by significant functional limitations in mental or physical abilities or both. These include developmental delay or mental retardation, cerebral palsy and related neuromuscular disorders, sensory impairments, autism, and learning and language disabilities.

The focus of this chapter is on the identification of pre–school-age children with developmental delay or mental retardation, cerebral palsy, language disorders, and autism. The identification of children with attention-deficit/hyperactivity disorder (ADHD), learning disabilities, and hearing and vision impairments is discussed in separate chapters. Attempts to identify children with learning disabilities prior to kindergarten have met with little success (Shapiro, Palmer, Antell, et al., 1990).

Advantages of Developmental Screening Tests as Part of a Monitoring Program

The routine use of screening tests improves the identification of children with mild developmental problems, helps the physician make appropriate referrals, and helps identify associated problems for children with more significant disabilities. These tests have known error rates and provide a structure within which professionals can make accurate observations. Studies have shown the Revised Denver Developmental Screening Test (R-DDST) to have low test sensitivity (i.e., misidentifies many children with disabilities as typically developing) and thus poor validity (Borowitz & Glascoe, 1986; Greer, Bauchner, & Zuckerman, 1989; Meisels & Margolis, 1988; Sciarillo, Brown, Robinson, et al., 1986). The Denver II test (Frankenburg, Dodds, Archer, et al., 1992a) has improved test sensitivity (i.e., improved identification of children with disabilities) but has a low specificity (i.e., it misidentifies many children who are developing typically as having disabilities) (Adesman, 1992; Frankenburg, Dodds, Archer, et al., 1992b; Glascoe, Ashford, & Chang, 1992; Glascoe,

Foster, & Wolraich, 1997). Other screening tests with established validity data, however, are available (see Tables 2.1–2.4). Physicians and nurses should be familiar with the error rates (i.e., validity), strengths, and limitations of the tests that they use.

The use of parent-completed questionnaires as screening tests can save time in the office and improve parent–physician communication. The questionnaire may identify issues that the family has failed to mention. Some parents fail to report their developmental concerns to the physician (Hickson, Altmemeier, & O'Connor, 1983). In one study, 70% of mothers had behavioral or developmental concerns regarding their children; however, only 28% had discussed those concerns with their pediatrician (Hickson et al., 1983).

Importance of Using Parent Report Measures

A principal concern about the use of developmental screening tests is that they require too much of professionals' time and thus are too costly (Glascoe et al., 1997). The use of parent-completed questionnaires requires little professional time and thus is a cost-effective way to identify parents' concerns, which is a central part of children's preventive health care. Parents witness a larger sample of their children's behavior and possess information that is unavailable to professionals (Squires, Nickel, & Bricker, 1990). Parents report their child's current developmental skills accurately (Lichtenstein & Ireton, 1984; Squires, Potter, Bricker, & Lamory, 1998). Use of a parent report measure gives the physician a relatively complete review of a child's current abilities and also focuses attention on areas of concern. In addition, Squires and Bricker (1991) showed that the use of these measures may increase parents' knowledge about child development and promote their involvement in developmental activities with their child.

Recommendations for a Developmental Monitoring Program

Types of Screening Tests Screening tests can be categorized as *general developmental screening tests* that cover all behavioral domains or as *targeted screens* that focus on one area of development. General screens and targeted screens can be *parent-completed measures* or *professionally administered* (i.e., in-office) *tests*. Tables 2.1–2.4 present information about a number of specific tests. The tools that the editors of this book recommend are marked with an asterisk. Figure 2.1 presents an algorithm for the use of a parent report measure, a general office screen, and targeted screens.

Table 2.1.   Parent-completed measures

Instrument	Age range	Description	Psychometrics/Utility
Denver Prescreening Developmental Questionnaire–Revised (Frankenburg, 1988; Frankenburg, Fandal, & Thornton, 1987)	Birth–6 years	Items taken from Denver Developmental Screening Test (DDST); parents answer questions until reaching ceiling of three consecutive "no" responses	Concurrent validity only with R-DDST; identified 84% of children rated abnormal on DDST; not recommended because of low sensitivity of R-DDST
Denver Prescreening Developmental Questionnaire–II (PDQ-II) (Frankenburg, 1998)	Birth–6 years	91 items taken from the Denver II; parents answer questions until reaching a ceiling of three consecutive "no" responses	No published data on PDQ-II are available; concurrent validity data for the PDQ–Revised (Frankenburg, Fandal, & Thornton, 1987) only with the Denver Developmental Screening Test–Revised (DDST–R) (Frankenburg, Dodds, Archer, et al., 1992b); not recommended
Ages & Stages Questionnaires* (Bricker, Squires, Mounts, et al., 1999)	4–60 months; questionnaires at 4, 6, 8, 10, 12, 14, 16, 18, 20, 22, 24, 27, 30, 33, 36, 42, 48, 54, and 60 months	30 items in areas of fine motor, gross motor, communication, adaptive, personal-social; completed by parents in 10–15 minutes (Spanish and French versions available)	Concurrent validity with standardized measures Sensitivity = .51–.90 Specificity = .81–.92 Reliability = .86–.91
Child Development Inventories* (Ireton, 1992)		Items taken from the Minnesota Child Development Inventory (Saylor & Brandt, 1986); 60–80 items on each inventory asking about child's development, possible problems, parent's concerns	Concurrent validity with standardized measures Sensitivity = .50–.76 Specificity = .76
Early Child Development Inventory* (Ireton, 1988)	1–3 years		
Infant Development Inventory* (Ireton, 1994)	Birth–15 months		
Preschool Developmental Inventory* (Ireton, 1984)	3–6 years		
Revised Parent Developmental Questionnaires (Knobloch, Stevens, Malone, et al., 1979)	Birth–36 months	Items from Gesell (Knobloch, Stevens, & Malone, 1980) in areas of gross motor, fine motor, adaptive, language, and personal-social	Concurrent validity with Gesell Underscreening 2.6%–10%; overscreening 6%; no other validity or reliability data available

*, Recommended tools.

Parent Report Measures In-depth, parent-completed questionnaires or interviews are recommended as the basic screens for all children. The use of parent report measures (see Table 2.1), however, may be inappropriate for certain families (e.g., parents with mental retardation, parents with a history of drug and alcohol abuse, families who speak a language other than English). A general office screening test should be used with these families.

The parent measure must be comprehensive as well as easy to complete and interpret. The challenge is to identify all or nearly all children with de-

Table 2.2. General office screening tests

Instrument	Age range	Description	Psychometrics/Utility
Battelle Developmental Inventory–Screening Test* (Newborg, Stock, & Wnek, 1984)	Birth–8 years	Items derived from Battelle Developmental Inventory. Two items per age level in personal-social, adaptive, gross motor, fine motor, receptive language, expressive language, and cognitive areas. Battelle has been adopted by several states under the Education of the Handicapped Act Amendments of 1986 (PL 99-457). Takes 30–35 minutes to administer.	Limited psychometric data on screening instrument. Preliminary validity data: Sensitivity = .80 Specificity = .74
Bayley Infant Neurodevelopmental Screener* (BINS) (Aylward, 1995)	3–24 months	Six-item sets grouped by age (3–4, 5–6, 7–10, 11–15, 16–20, and 21–24 months); items rated optimal or nonoptimal; cut scores identify low-, moderate-, and high-risk groups; takes 10 minutes to administer.	Good test–retest (.71–.84) and interrater reliability (.79–.96); 63%–80% agreement with full-length Bayley Scales of Infant Development (Bayley, 1969)
Brigance® screens (Brigance, 1977)	21–90 months	Seven forms, one for each 12-month age range. Measures speech-language, motor, readiness, and general knowledge at younger ages; takes 10–15 minutes to administer.	Normative data on 1,156 children. Cutoff scores for motor, language, readiness, and overall cutoff scores: Sensitivity = .72–.77 Specificity = .73–1.00
Denver II (Frankenburg et al., 1992a)	Birth–6 years	Revision of DDST. 150 items in personal-social, fine motor, adaptive, speech-language, and gross motor domains; language items added; some items deleted.	Renormed on 2,096 children from diverse backgrounds. High reliability. Preliminary validity data (Glascoe & Byrne, 1993): Sensitivity = .83 Specificity = .4
Developmental Indicators for the Assessment of Learning–3* (Mardell-Czudnowski & Goldenberg, 1998)	2.5–6 years	Designed to identify learning problems in domains of gross motor, fine motor, concepts, and communication. Designed for mass screenings; takes about 30 minutes to administer.	Strong psychometric data; norms revised in 1990.
Early Screening Inventory* (Meisels, Marsten, Wiske, & Henderson, 1997)	3–6 years	30 items in domains of visual-motor/adaptive; language and cognition; gross motor/body awareness; takes 15 minutes to administer.	Strong psychometric data. National standardization under way.
Miller Assessment for Preschoolers* (Miller, 1988)	2.0–5.8 years	27 items assess sensorimotor cognitive ability and combined abilities in five areas; takes 30 minutes to administer.	Validity: Identified 84% of preacademic problem children: Reliability = .81–.98
Revised Developmental Diagnosis Screening Inventory (Knobloch, Stevens, & Malone, 1980)	4 weeks–36 months	Selected items from full Gesell; domains of gross motor, fine motor, adaptive, language, personal-social; takes 15–20 minutes to administer.	Concurrent validity only with Gesell. Underscreening = 0% (sensitivity = 1.00); overscreening = 5.1% (specificity = .94). No reliability data available.

*, Recommended tools.

Table 2.3.   Language screening tests

Instrument	Age range	Description	Psychometrics/Utility
Bzoch-League Receptive Emergent Language Scale (Bzoch & League, 1978)	Birth–3 years	Three items testing receptive language and three items testing expressive language for each age interval	Limited psychometric data; administration time 15–30 minutes with interviewing skills necessary
Clinical Linguistic and Auditory Milestone Scale (Capute, Shapiro, Wachtel, et al., 1986)	Birth–3 years	Assesses language milestones through parent interview and child observation. Takes 3–5 minutes to administer.	Concurrent validity data with Bayley: Sensitivity = .66 Specificity = .74
Early Language Milestone Scale* (Coplan, 1993)	Birth–3 years	Domains of visual, auditory receptive, auditory expressive. Developed for use in medical offices. Takes 3 minutes to administer.	Validity data with several groups of children at high risk for being diagnosed with disabilities
Language Development Survey* (Rescorla, 1989)	24 months only	Vocabulary checklist completed by caregivers. Contains 300 words and general questions about word combinations.	High concurrent validity with Bayley (1969) and Reynell (Reynell & Gruber-Christian, 1990) scales; high reliability
MacArthur Communicative Development Inventories* (Fenson, Dale, Reznick, et al., 1993)	Infants: 8–16 months Toddlers: 16–30 months	Parent-completed checklists and questions covering expressive and receptive vocabulary, actions and gestures (infants), sentences and grammar (toddlers).	Excellent psychometric studies; inventories more in-depth than most first-level screening tools. Short forms for screening under development.

*, Recommended tools.

velopmental problems while identifying few false positives (i.e., misclassifying children who are developing typically as having disabilities) and using little of professionals' time. Ideally, the structure of the parent report measure should conform to the domains described in eligibility requirements for EI/ECSE services. Questions should cover cognitive development, physical development (gross and fine motor skills), communication, adaptive development (self-help), and socioemotional development.

Two examples of in-depth parent report measures are the *Ages & Stages Questionnaires (ASQ): A Parent-Completed, Child-Monitoring System, Second Edition* (Bricker, Squires, Mounts, et al., 1999), and the Child Development Inventories (CDI) (Ireton, 1992). The ASQ is a series of questionnaires for use with children from 4 to 60 months of age. Each questionnaire comprises 30 questions about specific skills or behaviors and 6 general questions that elicit parents' concerns. ASQ takes about 10–15 minutes for parents to complete. The CDI includes three separate questionnaires: the Infant Development Inventory (Ireton, 1994), the Early Child Development Inventory (Ireton, 1988), and the Preschool Developmental Inventory (Ireton, 1984). The Early Child Development and Preschool Development invento-

ries contain 60 questions about specific skills and a number of additional questions that elicit parents' concerns. Each inventory takes about 20–40 minutes for parents to complete. Children with suspect results on the parent report measure may have these results confirmed by testing with a general office screening test or may be referred directly for further evaluation (e.g., eligibility testing for EI/ECSE services).

An alternative method is to use a prescreening questionnaire, which requires little time for parents to complete or for professionals to interpret. These measures have been used to identify a subset of children who then require screening with a more thorough measure (Dworkin & Glascoe, 1997). Two examples are the Denver Prescreening Developmental Questionnaire (PDQ; Frankenburg et al., 1987) and the Parents' Evaluation of Developmental Status (PEDS; Glascoe, 1997b). The only validity data available for the PDQ are based on the R-DDST, and thus the PDQ is not a recommended test. The PEDS includes 10 questions that ask parents whether they have concerns about different aspects of their child's development and behavior. It is a systematic method by which to elicit parents' concerns. In one study involving children ages 4 years and older, the PEDS

Table 2.4. Neuromotor screening tests

Instrument	Age range	Description	Psychometrics/Utility
Alberta Infant Motor Scale (AIMS)* (Piper, Pinnell, Darrah, et al., 1994)	Birth– 18 months	Observational assessment; 54 items in prone, supine, sitting, and standing positions.	Normative data on 2,202 infants; concurrent validity data with Bayley (Bayley, 1969) and Peabody (Folio & DuBose, 1983) scales
Chandler Movement Assessment of Infants Screening Test (CMA-ST)* (Chandler, 1986)	2–12 months	37 items measure primitive reflexes, automatic reactions, and volitional movement; items scored on three-point scale.	Validity, reliability, and normative data pending
Infant Motor Screen* (Nickel, Renken, & Gallenstein, 1989)	4–16 months	25 items measure muscle tone, primitive reflexes, automatic reactions, and motor asymmetrics; items scored on three-point scale.	Predictive validity; at age 4 months: Sensitivity = 0.93 Specificity = 0.89 At age 8 months: Sensitivity = 1.00 Specificity = 0.96 Good interobserver reliability data; no normative data reported
Milani-Comparetti Motor Development Screening Test* (Ellison, Browning, Larson, & Denny, 1983; Milani-Comparetti & Gidoni, 1967; Tremblath, Kliewer, & Bruce, 1977)	Birth– 24 months	27 items measure volitional movement, automatic reactions, and primitive reflexes; original scoring system is descriptive.	Excellent normative and reliability data; two quantitative scoring systems have been used; limited predictive validity data
Harris Infant Neuromotor Test (HINT) (Harris, 1993)	3–12 months	22 items assess posture and movement, muscle tone, head circumference, eye muscle control, and behavior; includes four questions for parents.	Validity, reliability, and normative data pending
Primitive Reflex Profile (Capute, Accardo, Virong, et al., 1978)	Birth– 24 months	Nine items measure primitive reflexes; items are scored on a five-point scale.	Good normative data; limited predictive validity data; not recommended, because items measure primitive reflexes only

* Recommended tools.

had acceptable sensitivity for the identification of certain concerns (Glascoe, 1997a); however, no data are available on its use with children younger than age 4 years. The use of prescreening questionnaires is not recommended with children younger than age 4 years, because in-depth parent report measures such as the ASQ or the CDI provide much more information with little increase in the demand on professionals' time.

General Office Screens General developmental screens (see Table 2.2) administered by a physician, a nurse, or a nurse practitioner complement the results of the parent report measure. These tests are relatively brief (15–20 minutes to complete), yet the test items cover all appropriate developmental domains. These tools should be used to assess all children and families for whom the parent report measure is inappropriate and may be used to confirm suspect findings from the parent screen. General developmental screens help clarify the need for referral for EI/ECSE eligibility testing as well as other referrals. For example, the physician may refer a child who exhibits atypical behaviors and is delayed in all domains on the general screen for evaluation by an experienced child development team headed by a developmental pediatrician. Many primary care health professionals may choose to refer all children rated as suspect on the parent report measure for eligibility testing for EI/ECSE services rather than administer a general office screen.

Basic screen

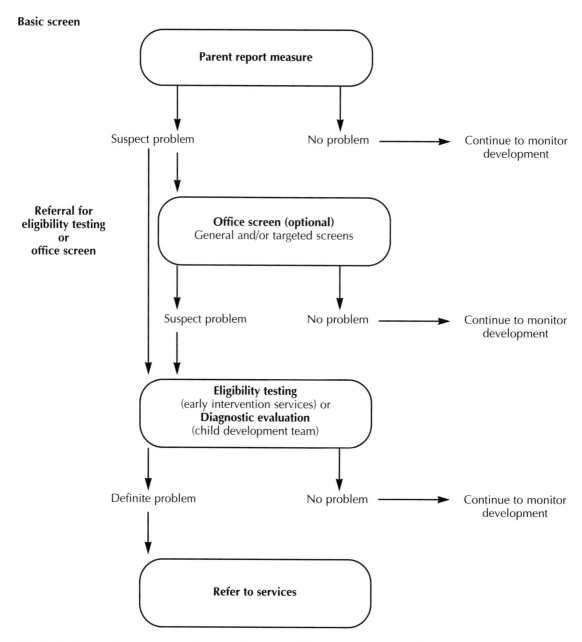

Figure 2.1.   A developmental screening procedure for a primary care office. (From Squires, J., Nickel, R.E., & Eisert, D. [1996]. Early detection of developmental problems: Strategies for monitoring young children in the practice setting. *Journal of Developmental and Behavioral Pediatrics, 17*[6], 422; adapted by permission.)

Targeted Screens   These tools include *neuromotor, language, autism,* and *behavioral screens.* Targeted screens have been developed to assist in the identification of specific conditions (e.g., cerebral palsy, language disorder). Targeted screens may be used primarily by health professionals who have a special interest in developmental disabilities.

The *language screen* should be used when parents express a concern about language development and for children who show delays in the lan-

guage or communication domains on general developmental screening tests. Language screens include both parent-completed and professionally administered measures. The instruments reviewed in Table 2.3 are for use with children from birth through 3 years of age. Targeted language screens for children older than age 3 years are available.

Neuromotor screens (see Table 2.4) are designed to assist in the identification of infants with cerebral palsy. These tests are discussed in greater detail in

Table 2.5.   Developmental monitoring protocol for infants and children who are at high risk for being diagnosed with disabilities

In addition to informal observations and review of parent concerns at each well-child visit, use the following:

- Determine the presence of biologic and environmental risk factors.
- Screen the development of children at 4, 8, 12, 18, 24, 36, and 48 months corrected age[a] and *when a parent expresses a specific concern.*[b]
- Use a professionally administered general developmental screening test and a neuromotor screen at 4 months corrected age.
- Use a parent report measure as the basic screen for all infants and children after the 4-month visit.
- Use a language screen for children from 18 months to 3 years of age who exhibit language delay on the general developmental screen and *when the parent expresses a concern about language delay.*

[a] The screening age should be the child's corrected age (i.e., the child's age as adjusted for the number of weeks of prematurity) up to 2 years of age.

[b] All infants who are identified by risk factors for hearing impairment should have a hearing screen prior to discharge from the neonatal intensive care unit (NICU) or audiologic testing with visually reinforced audiometry at or prior to 8 months of age (see Chapter 9).

Chapter 6. They should be used with infants up to 24 months of age when parents express concern about motor development or when the child is measured as having delays in motor skills on a general developmental screen. Targeted screening is particularly useful for clarifying the referral needs of children who have delayed motor skills. For example, the physician should refer a child who is suspected of having cerebral palsy to a developmental pediatrician or to a child neurologist and a physical therapist; however, the primary care physician may refer other children with motor delays for EI/ECSE eligibility testing.

Two targeted *screens for autism* are under development (Baron-Cohen, Allen, & Gillberg, 1992; Baron-Cohen, Cox, Baird, et al., 1996; Siegel, 1996). Both are available; however, limited reliability and validity data have been reported. Developmental screening for autism is discussed in Chapter 8. *Be-*

havioral questionnaires and *checklists* for identifying preschool and school-age children with behavior problems are reviewed in Chapter 6.

Ages at Which to Use Screening Tests   Developmental screening tests (in most cases, standardized parent report measures) should be used in addition to informal observations of behavior and unstructured parent interviews for all children at several ages (see Tables 2.5, 2.6). The use of repeated measures at different ages markedly improves the accuracy of a developmental monitoring program.

In addition, different developmental disabilities can be diagnosed at different ages. For example, cerebral palsy usually can be diagnosed by 12–18 months of age; however, a speech-language disorder is difficult to diagnose prior to 18 months of age. Thus, neuromotor screens are used up to 18–24 months of age, and use of language screens begins

Table 2.6.   Developmental monitoring protocol for infants and children who are at low risk for being diagnosed with disabilities

In addition to informal observations and review of parent concerns at each well-child visit, use the following:

- Determine the presence of biologic and environmental risk factors (if one or more are present, use the high-risk protocol).
- Screen the development of children at ages 6, 12, 18, 24, 36, and 48 months and *when a parent expresses a specific concern.*
- Use a parent report measure as the basic screen for all children at all screening ages.
- Use a neuromotor screen in addition to a general developmental screen for infants with delay in gross motor skills.
- Use a language screen for children from 18 months to 3 years of age with language delay on the general developmental screen *and when the parent expresses a concern about language delay.*

Table 2.7.   Ages for early diagnosis of developmental disabilities

Birth to 1 year	1–2 years	2–3 years	3–4 years
Mental retardation, moderate and severe	Mental retardation, moderate	Mental retardation, mild	Mental retardation, mild
Sensory impairments			
	Autism	Autism	
Cerebral palsy			
	Cerebral palsy	Language disorder	Language disorder

at 18 months of age and older. Table 2.7 presents the expected ages for early diagnosis of various developmental disorders.

Children Who Need to Be Monitored More Closely   A number of risk factors have been used to identify groups of children who are more likely to experience developmental problems (Kochanek & Buka, 1991). These factors include *biologic, environmental,* and *established* risk factors. Children with established risk factors (e.g., a child with Down syndrome) should be referred promptly to EI services by their physician and monitored for associated medical and developmental problems (e.g., autism). Biologic risk factors include premature birth, perinatal asphyxia, and neonatal seizures. Environmental risk factors include being born to a teenage mother,

maternal prenatal drug or alcohol use, and children of parents who themselves have developmental disabilities. Children with a combination of biologic and environmental factors are at greater risk for experiencing developmental problems than are children with either factor alone. Table 2.8 lists representative biologic and environmental risk factors.

Physicians and nurses should review each newborn and his or her family to determine whether biologic and environmental risk factors are present. If one or more risk factors are present, that infant and the infant's family should be followed according to the recommendations for the high-risk infant developmental monitoring protocol. Tables 2.5 and 2.6 present recommendations for the types of screening tests to use at specific ages for monitoring

Table 2.8.   Common biologic and environmental risk factors

Biologic factors	Environmental factors
Low birth weight (1,500 grams or less)	Maternal age less than 16 years
Small for gestational age (2 standard deviations or more below mean)	Parents with mental retardation or psychiatric disorder
Respiratory distress requiring mechanical ventilation	Parents' alcohol or substance abuse
Asphyxia (Apgar score of 4 or less at 5 minutes)	Lack of permanent housing
Neonatal seizures	Inadequate caregiving
Intracranial hemorrhage or periventricular leukomalacia	History of abuse and neglect in parent or sibling
Hyperbilirubinemia (levels exceeding need for exchange transfusion)	Extreme poverty
Major congenital anomalies	
Multiple minor physical anomalies	
Microcephaly and macrocephaly (more than 2 standard deviations below or above mean)	
Central nervous system infection	
Congenital infection (toxoplasmosis, other infections, rubella, cytomegalovirus, and herpes simplex virus [TORCH])	
Abnormal neonatal neurologic examination	
Maternal phenylketonuria (PKU) or human immunodeficiency virus (HIV) infection	
Prenatal teratogen exposure (e.g., Dilantin, valproic acid, alcohol or other substance abuse)	
Failure to thrive	

the development of children at high and low risk for being diagnosed with disabilities.

Children with biologic risk factors, particularly infants born prematurely, are at risk for cerebral palsy (Nelson & Ellenberg, 1979). Children with certain biologic or environmental risk factors (e.g., children exposed to drugs prenatally) have a higher rate of language disorders (Dixon, Breshnahan, & Zuckerman, 1990; Schneider, Griffith, & Chasnoff, 1989). Therefore, a developmental monitoring protocol that incorporates a neuromotor screen and a language screen in addition to other measures is recommended for infants and preschoolers when biologic and environmental risk factors are present. It is important for primary care physicians and nurses to coordinate their developmental monitoring activities with state programs that track infants who are at high risk for developmental delays (e.g., Babies First! of the Oregon State Health Division) and Child Find programs of local EI/ECSE staff or school districts.

How to Select a Screening Test Screening tests should meet certain standards or guidelines to ensure maximum efficiency and accuracy. Measures with established psychometric properties should be used. Tests should be valid (i.e., should have known accuracy in identifying the problem in question) as well as reliable (i.e., the test results should be reproducible). Acceptable validity and reliability is .70–.80 and greater (American Psychological Association, 1985). Other factors include the size of the normative sample, cultural sensitivity, comprehensiveness, utility in medical settings, and attractiveness to children.

CONCLUSIONS
The following statements review the major points of this chapter:

- Physicians and nurses are uniquely qualified to participate in Child Find activities (early identification of infants and young children with developmental disabilities).

- Physicians and nurses should use developmental screening tests along with informal observations to identify infants, toddlers, and preschool-age children with disabilities.

- Accurate developmental diagnosis depends on the use of parental information about their child's behavior in addition to observations by a professional and the use of repeated measures at different ages.

- A developmental monitoring program that uses a parent report measure as the basic screen is a cost-effective solution for a busy office practice.

- A separate developmental monitoring protocol should be used for children at high and low risk for being diagnosed with disabilities. Coordinate activities with state programs tracking infants who are deemed to be at high risk for having disabilities.

- Targeted neuromotor and language screens are useful additions whenever parents have expressed concerns about that aspect of their child's development and when children show delays in motor or language skills on the general developmental screen (see Chapters 6 and 8 for discussion of the use of behavioral and autism screens).

- Primary care physicians and nurses should become familiar with administration and scoring of at least one parent-completed measure, one general office screen, and targeted screens for cerebral palsy and language delay.

- Health care professionals should use screening tests with established psychometric properties that are culturally sensitive. Practitioners should also be familiar with the limitations of the screening tests that they use (e.g., the known error rates found in using the test).

REFERENCES

Adesman, A.R. (1992). Is the Denver II Developmental Test worthwhile? [Letter to the editor]. *Pediatrics, 90*(6), 1009–1011.

American Academy of Pediatrics (AAP), Committee on Children with Disabilities. (1994). Screening infants and young children for developmental disabilities. *Pediatrics, 93*(5), 863–865.

American Psychological Association (APA). (1985). *Standards for educational and psychological tests* (Rev. ed.). Washington, DC: Author.

Aylward, G.P. (1995). *Bayley Infant Neurodevelopmental Screener.* San Antonio, TX: The Psychological Corporation.

Baron-Cohen, S., Allen, J., & Gillberg, C. (1992). Can autism be detected at 18 months? *British Journal of Psychiatry, 161,* 839–843.

Baron-Cohen, S., Cox, A., Baird, G., et al. (1996). Psychological markers in the detection of autism in infancy in a large population. *British Journal of Psychiatry, 168*(2), 158–163.

Bayley, N. (1969). *Bayley Scales of Infant Development: Birth to two years.* New York: The Psychological Corporation.

Bennett, F.C., Nickel, R.E., Squires, J., & Woodward, B.J. (1997). Developmental screening/surveillance. In H.M. Wallace, J.C. MacQueen, R.F. Biehl, & J.A. Blackman

(Eds.), *Mosby's resource guide to children with disabilities and chronic illness* (pp. 236–247). St. Louis: C.V. Mosby.

Borowitz, K.C., & Glascoe, F.P. (1986). Sensitivity of the Denver Developmental Screening Test in Speech and Language Screening. *Pediatrics, 78*(6), 1075–1078.

Bricker, D.D. (1989). *Early intervention for at-risk and handicapped infants, toddlers, and preschool children* (2nd ed.). Palo Alto, CA: VORT Corp.

Bricker, D.D., Squires, J., Mounts, L., et al. (1999). *Ages & Stages Questionnaires (ASQ): A parent-completed, child-monitoring system* (2nd ed.). Baltimore: Paul H. Brookes Publishing Co.

Brigance, A. (1977). *Brigance® Inventory of Basic Skills.* North Billerica, MA: Curriculum Associates.

Bzoch, K.R., & League, R. (1978). *Assessing language skills in infancy: A handbook for the multidimensional analysis of emergent language.* Baltimore: University Park Press.

Capute, A.J., Accardo, P.F., Virong, E.P.G., et al. (1978). *Primitive reflex profile: Vol. 1. Monographs in developmental pediatrics.* Baltimore: University Park Press.

Capute, A.J., Shapiro, B.K., Wachtel, R.C., et al. (1986). The Clinical Linguistic and Auditory Milestone Scale (CLAMS). *American Journal of Diseases of Childhood, 140,* 694–698.

Chandler, L.S. (1986). Screening for movement dysfunction in infancy. *Physical and Occupational Therapy in Pediatrics, 6,* 171–190.

Coplan, J. (1993). *The Early Language Milestone Scale.* (2nd ed.). Austin, TX: PRO-ED.

Dixon, S.D., Breshnahan, K., & Zuckerman, B. (1990, June). Cocaine babies: Meeting the challenge of management. *Contemporary Pediatrics, 7*(6), 70–92.

Dworkin, P.H. (1989). British and American recommendations for developmental monitoring: The role of surveillance. *Pediatrics, 84*(6), 1000–1010.

Dworkin, P.H., & Glascoe, F.P. (1997). Early detection of developmental delays: How do you measure up? *Contemporary Pediatrics, 14*(4), 158–168.

Education of the Handicapped Act Amendments of 1986, PL 99-457, 20 U.S.C. §§ 1400 *et seq.*

Ellison, P.H., Browning, C.A., Larson, B., & Denny, J. (1983). Development of a scoring system for the Milani-Comparetti and Gidoni Method of assessing neurologic abnormality in infancy. *Physical Therapy, 63*(9), 1414–1423.

Fenson, L., Dale, P.S., Reznick, J.S., et al. (1993). *MacArthur Communicative Development Inventories (CDI).* San Diego: Singular Publishing Group.

Folio, M.R., & DuBose, R.F. (1983). *Peabody Developmental Motor Scales.* Hingham, MA: Teaching Resources.

Frankenburg, W.K. (1988). *Denver Prescreening Developmental Questionnaire–Revised (PDQ–R).* Denver: Denver Developmental Materials.

Frankenburg, W.K. (1998). *Denver Prescreening Developmental Questionnaire* (2nd ed.). Denver: Denver Developmental Materials.

Frankenburg, W.K., Dodds, J.B., Archer, P., et al. (1992a). *Denver II* (2nd ed.). Denver: Denver Developmental Materials.

Frankenburg, W.K., Dodds, J.B., Archer, P., et al. (1992b). The Denver II: A major revision and restandardization of the Denver Developmental Screening Test. *Pediatrics, 89*(1), 91–97.

Frankenburg, W.K., Fandal, A.W., & Thornton S.M. (1987). Revision of Denver Prescreening Developmental Questionnaire. *Journal of Pediatrics, 110*(4), 653–657.

Glascoe, F.P. (1997a). Parents' concerns about children's development: Prescreening technique or screening test? *Pediatrics, 99*(4), 522–528.

Glascoe, F.P. (1997b). *Parents' Evaluation of Developmental Status: Administration and scoring manual.* Nashville, TN: Ellsworth & Vandermeer Press.

Glascoe, F.P., Ashford, L.G., & Chang, B. (1992). The accuracy of the Denver II in developmental screening. *Pediatrics, 89,* 1221–1225.

Glascoe, F.P., & Byrne, K.E. (1993). The accuracy of three developmental screening tests. *Journal of Early Intervention, 17*(4), 368–379.

Glascoe, F.P., Foster, E.M., & Wolraich, M.L. (1997). An economic analysis of developmental detection methods. *Pediatrics, 99*(6), 830–837.

Greer, S., Bauchner, H., & Zuckerman, B. (1989). The Denver Developmental Screening Test: How good is its predictive validity? *Developmental Medicine and Child Neurology, 31,* 774–781.

Guralnick, M.J. (1998). Effectiveness of early intervention for vulnerable children: A developmental perspective. *American Journal on Mental Retardation, 102*(4), 319–345.

Guralnick, M.J. (Ed.). (1997). *The effectiveness of early intervention.* Baltimore: Paul H. Brookes Publishing Co.

Harris, S.R. (1993). *Harris Infant Neuromotor Test (HINT)* (Developmental ed. II). Vancouver, British Columbia, Canada: University of British Columbia.

Hickson, G.B., Altmemeier, W.A., & O'Connor, S. (1983, May). *Behavioral, developmental and parenting concerns of mothers seeking care in private offices: Opportunities for expansion of service.* Washington, DC: Ambulatory Pediatric Association.

Hutchison, T., & Nicoll, A. (1988, January). Developmental screening and surveillance. *British Journal of Hospital Medicine, 39*(1), 22–29.

Individuals with Disabilities Education Act (IDEA) Amendments of 1997, PL 105-17, 20 U.S.C. §§ 1400 *et seq.*

Ireton, H. (1984). *Preschool Developmental Inventory.* Minneapolis, MN: Behavior Science Systems.

Ireton, H. (1988). *Early Child Development Inventory.* Minneapolis, MN: Behavior Science Systems.

Ireton, H. (1992). *Child Development Inventories.* Minneapolis, MN: Behavior Science Systems.

Ireton, H. (1994). *Infant Development Inventory.* Minneapolis, MN: Behavior Science Systems.

Knobloch, H., Stevens, F., & Malone, A.F. (1980). *Manual of developmental diagnosis: The administration and interpretation of the Revised Gesell and Amatruda Developmental and Neurological Examination.* New York: HarperCollins.

Knobloch, H., Stevens, F., Malone, A.F., et al. (1979). The validity of parental reporting of infant development. *Pediatrics, 63*(6), 872–878.

Kochanek, T.T., & Buka, S.L. (1991, July). Using biologic and ecologic factors to identify vulnerable infants and toddlers. *Infants and Young Children,* 11–25.

Lichtenstein, R., & Ireton, H. (1984). *Preschool screening: Identifying young children with developmental and educational problems.* Orlando, FL: Grune & Stratton.

Mardell-Czudnowski, C., & Goldenberg, D. (1998). *Developmental Indicators for the Assessment of Learning–3*. Circle Pines, MN: American Guidance Service.

Meisels, S.J. (1988). Developmental screening in early childhood: The interaction of research and social policy. *Annual Review of Public Health, 9*, 527–550.

Meisels, S.J., & Margolis, L. (1988). Is the early and periodic screening, diagnosis, and treatment program effective with developmentally disabled children? *Pediatrics, 81*(2), 262–271.

Meisels, S.J., Marsten, D., Wiske, M., & Henderson, L. (1997). *Early Screening Inventory–Revised*. Ann Arbor, MI: Rebus.

Milani-Comparetti, A., & Gidoni, E.A. (1967). Routine developmental examination in normal and retarded children. *Developmental Medicine and Child Neurology, 9*(5), 631–638.

Miller, L.J. (1988). *Miller Assessment of Preschoolers*. San Antonio, TX: The Psychological Corporation.

Nelson, K.B., & Ellenberg, J.H. (1979). Neonatal signs as predictors of cerebral palsy. *Pediatrics, 64*, 225–232.

Newborg, J., Stock, J.R., & Wnek, L. (1984). *Battelle Developmental Inventory–Screening Test*. Hingham, MA: Teaching Resources.

Nickel, R.E., Renken, C.A., & Gallenstein, J.S. (1989). The Infant Motor Screen. *Developmental Medicine and Child Neurology, 31*, 35–42.

Piper, M.C., Pinnell, L.E., Darrah, J., et al. (1994). Construction and validation of the Alberta Infant Motor Scale (AIMS). *Canadian Journal of Public Health, 83* (Suppl. 2), S46–S50.

Rescorla, L. (1989). The Language Development Survey: A screening tool for delayed language in toddlers. *Journal of Speech and Hearing Disorders, 54*, 587–599.

Reynell, J.K., & Gruber-Christian, P. (1990). *Reynell Developmental Language Scales*. Los Angeles: Western Psychological Services.

Saylor, C.F., & Brandt, B.J. (1986). The Minnesota Child Development Inventory: A valid maternal report form for assessing development in infancy. *Journal of Developmental and Behavioral Pediatrics, 7*(5), 308–313.

Schneider, J.W., Griffith, D.R., & Chasnoff, I.J. (1989). Infants exposed to cocaine in utero: Implications for developmental assessment and intervention. *Infants and Young Children, 2*(1), 25–36.

Sciarillo, W.G., Brown, M.M., Robinson, N.M., et al. (1986). Effectiveness of the Denver Developmental Screening Test with biologically vulnerable infants. *Journal of Developmental and Behavioral Pediatrics, 7*(2), 77–83.

Scott, F.G., Lingaraju, S., Kilgo, J.L., et al. (1993). A survey of pediatricians on early identification and early intervention services. *Journal of Early Intervention, 17*, 129–138.

Shapiro, B.K., Palmer, F.B., Antell, S.E., et al. (1990). Detection of young children in need of reading help: Evaluation of specific reading disability formulas. *Clinical Pediatrics, 29*, 206–213.

Shonkoff, J.P., & Hauser-Cram, P. (1987). Early intervention for disabled infants and their families: A quantitative analysis. *Pediatrics, 80*(5), 650–658.

Siegel, B. (1996). *Pervasive Developmental Disorder Screening Test*. San Francisco: University of California, Langley-Porter Psychiatric Institute.

Squires, J., & Bricker, D.D. (1991). Impact of completing developmental questionnaires by at-risk mothers. *Journal of Early Intervention, 15*(2), 161–171.

Squires, J., Nickel, R.E., & Bricker, D.D. (1990). Use of parent-completed developmental questionnaires for Child-Find and screening. *Infants and Young Children, 3*(2), 46–57.

Squires, J., Nickel, R.E., & Eisert, D. (1996). Early detection of developmental problems: Strategies for monitoring young children in the practice setting. *Journal of Developmental and Behavioral Pediatrics, 17*(6), 420–427.

Squires, J., Potter, L., Bricker, D.D., & Lamory, S. (1998). Parent-completed developmental questionnaires: Effectiveness with low and middle income parents. *Early Childhood Research Quarterly, 13*(2), 347–356.

Tremblath, J.T., Kliewer, D., & Bruce, W. (1977). *The Milani-Comparetti Motor Developmental Screening Test*. Omaha: University of Nebraska Medical Center, C. Louis Meyer Children's Rehabilitation Institute, Media Resource Center.

Wenger, M., McLaurin, J., Guild, P., et al. (1989, November). *Physician involvement in planning for P.L. 99-457 Part H: Interagency coordinating council roles and system planning issues*. Chapel Hill, NC: Carolina Policy Studies Program.

2

Appendix

RESOURCES ON DEVELOPMENTAL SCREENING AND SURVEILLANCE

Bright Futures

World Wide Web site: http://www.brightfutures.org/index.html

A web site sponsored by the Maternal and Child Health Bureau, Health Resources and Services Administration, U.S. Department of Health and Human Services, and supported in part by Pfizer Pharmaceuticals Corp. that provides guidelines for health supervision for infants, children, and adolescents.

Pediatric Development and Behavior

All Children's Hospital
Department 7825
880 Sixth Street South
Saint Petersburg, Florida 33701
Telephone: (727) 502-8035
Fax: (727) 892-8244
E-mail: editor@dbpeds.org
World Wide Web site: http://www.dbpeds.org/

Information on a variety of topics in developmental and behavioral pediatrics, including information on developmental screening tests, linkages to professional groups, and condition-specific web sites.

Working with Families

Vivian Gedaly-Duff
Susan Stoeger
Kathleen Shelton

KEY COMPETENCIES

- Discuss the principles of a family perspective in caring for families of children with disabilities and chronic conditions
- Review the difficulties that families of children with disabilities and chronic conditions experience in their daily lives
- Describe the family interaction model and implications for families of children with disabilities and chronic conditions
- Discuss the effects of children with disabilities and chronic conditions on family members
- Discuss family support resources, including respite care and educational services
- Describe the assessment and techniques for giving bad news to the family

DESCRIPTION

Importance of a Family Perspective

Families are taught how to carry out the medical treatment and developmental care of their children but are not prepared for the daily and long-term effects that living with children with disabilities and chronic conditions may have on family members individually or on the family's life together. The purpose of this chapter is to discuss *family health*. Families are children's primary caregivers. They also comprise a special group of people who are growing and developing as individuals and as a group. The health and well-being of families and their children with disabilities and chronic conditions hang in a delicate balance like a mobile (Litman, 1974; May, 1992; Meister, 1991). If one part is moved, the entire mobile changes its shape. What happens to one family member affects all members. Family goals may be altered because resources go to the child with disabilities and chronic conditions. For example, mothers give up work to care for their children at home, and personal needs of other family members go unmet. Primary health care providers can support families by promoting the family's health, providing anticipatory guidance regarding potential problems, and referring the family to appropriate community resources to address specific concerns.

The assumption of this chapter is that optimal family health contributes to the health of children with disabilities and chronic conditions. The chronic nature of the conditions affecting such children and their families threatens families' health. In addition to meeting the needs of children with disabilities and chronic conditions, family members attempt to engage in the following basic family-related tasks that are essential to the survival and continuity of the family unit:

- To provide economic resources that secure shelter, food, and clothing
- To provide family resources that promote the emotional health of family members who can manage crises and experience nonmonetary achievement
- To ensure each individual's socialization as a member of society in school, at work, with regard to spirituality, and in community life
- To [allow family members eventually to] give birth, to adopt, or to contribute to the next generation
- To promote health and care for members during illness (Friedman, 1998c, p. 102)

No family is perfect in meeting all of the needs of its members. Family members have conflicting needs that are resolved at various times throughout the life span. Families that follow the recommendations of health professionals may be labeled *good families* (Satariano & Briggs, 1999). From a broader perspective, *good families* are those families that meet members' needs enough for the members to grow and develop (Hostler, 1991).

Prevalence of Families Living with Children with Disabilities and Chronic Conditions

Approximately 12.6 million families have a child younger than 18 years old with a chronic illness or disability (Newacheck, Strickland, Shonkoff, et al., 1998). Only 40,000 of these children are living in a long-term care institution (Newacheck, Hughes, McManus, et al., 1994). About 25,000 families have adopted children with chronic illnesses or disabilities (Leof, 1994). In 1996, the majority of all U.S. children younger than age 18 years lived in homes with two parents (68%); 32% lived in single-parent families (Federal Interagency Forum on Child and Family Statistics, 1997).

Noncategorical Approach

This chapter takes a noncategorical approach regarding disabling or chronic conditions. No distinction is made between mental, physical, or chronic disabilities or illnesses. The degree of burden that families experience seems to be related not to the diagnosis but to the intensity of caregiving and the visibility of the disability or condition (Pless & Nolan, 1991). Some researchers found that families of children with cognitive disabilities seemed to have more difficulties than families with children with physical disabilities or illnesses (Cole & Reiss, 1993). Other researchers, however, reported similar findings for both groups of families (Faux, 1993; Perrin, Newacheck, Pless, et al., 1993; Ray, 1995; Stoneman & Brody, 1993). Therefore, this chapter is based on literature about families of children with mental and physical disabilities and chronic illnesses. Families of such children are like other families. Primary care physicians' and families' knowing the factors that influence the care and rearing of a child with a disability or a chronic illness can improve the quality of family life.

Principles of Family-Centered Care

Family-centered care involves collaboration among families, health professionals, and others who deliver health care to children and families (Lash & Wertlieb, 1993). The principles of family-centered care include the following:

- Recognizing that families are the constant in these children's lives while the personnel in the health care system fluctuate
- Forming partnerships between families and health professionals in health care decisions
- Openly sharing information about all treatments, ethical concerns, and uncertainties with regard to health care
- Demonstrating cultural competence and sensitivity to the racial, ethnic, cultural, and socioeconomic diversity of families and their ways of coping
- Supporting and strengthening families' abilities to grow and develop

Families of children with disabilities and chronic conditions experience uncertainty related to their children's responses to treatment and developmental progress. Families learn that health professionals base decisions on theory, research, and clinical experience but cannot predict exactly how a specific child may respond until their interventions are completed (Paget, 1982). Families want to be informed partners of the health care team and need to know the different options for treating a particular problem. In a society that respects families' diversity, a health care team that includes the family is the appropriate model. This model is preferable to a hierarchical one with physicians at the top, nurses and other health professionals in between, and families at the bottom. The family perspective brings attention back to the fact that families ultimately care for themselves and their children (Gedaly-Duff & Heims, in press).

Difficulties that Families of Children with Disabilities and Chronic Conditions Experience

Parenting a child with disabilities and chronic conditions and coping with the associated stigma is a major challenge.

Parenting   *Parenting* refers to fostering the growth, development, and highest possible level of functioning of children. A major, twofold task of families of children with disabilities and chronic conditions is that of nurturing these children to become healthy, responsible, and creative adults while car-

ing for their disabilities and chronic illnesses. Yet, most parents have little formal education in parenting and caring for even healthy children (Grusec & Goodnow, 1994; Hoffman, 1994; Howard, 1991). They rely on their experience in their families of origin and "learn on the job" while raising their own children. Children with health care needs related to a disability or chronic condition increase the complexity of childrearing and family life.

After the initial shock of learning that they have a child with a disability or a chronic illness, the family grapples with first finding out about the treatment and management of the chronic illness or disability, and then with worrying about their family's and child's future. Parenting involves a comprehensive set of tasks that facilitate children's physical, mental, and social development. It encompasses teaching children how to take care of their physical health by carrying out daily routines of getting dressed, eating with the family, and sleeping at established bedtimes. Socially, it involves preparing children to relate to others by handling aggression, having friends, and participating in family and community activities. Ideally, families hope that their children will become self-supporting adults who contribute to society. Functional behaviors and developmental landmarks are the guidelines that parents use for evaluating their parenting efforts.

A number of factors can influence parenting, including marital satisfaction; parental conflict; the emotional climate of the home; the family's problem-solving style; the family structure; and the family's socioeconomic status, financial resources, and ethnicity (Stoneman & Brody, 1993). When parents are dissatisfied with their marriage and spousal conflict is high, inconsistent parenting and negative child outcomes may occur. For example, if a child with disabilities and chronic conditions presents with behavior problems, the health professional needs to determine whether both parents agree to a consistent method of handling the problem. If parents disagree and cannot resolve their different approaches, the issue may be more one of marital conflict than of the child's behavior.

Stigma and Normalization   Families of children with disabilities and chronic conditions may experience the stigma of being different. Goffman (1963/1986) defined *stigma* as the social intolerance of differences from norms. The emotions of disgrace and shame may be more significant than the physical evidence of differences. Families of children who display visible differences such as physical deformities, unusual behaviors, and special medical equipment may face anxiety and withdrawal of others who do not understand or accept the disability. People's apprehension may be associated with their own fears of vulnerability, and family friends may avoid families of children with disabilities and chronic conditions (Gallo, Breitmayer, Knafl, & Zoeller, 1991).

Families of children with disabilities and chronic conditions experience the contradiction of living with children who are atypical while trying to carry out their family lives. For example, one mother told the following story:

> One day, I was talking with a friend. I was telling her I was feeling really tired and wondering why I was feeling that way. My friend leaned over to me and said, "Having a son who has 50 seizures a day is not normal." She helped me realize I was so busy trying to be normal, I was overlooking that I was not living a normal life. (K. Shelton, personal communication, October 1996)

Many families strive for normalcy (Deatrick, Knafl, & Murphy-Moore, 1999; Deatrick, Knafl, & Walsh, 1988). Although families may find positive aspects and ways to achieve functional outcomes needed for activities such as daily living, going to school, and engaging in recreation, many barriers to achieving normalcy exist.

Family Interaction Model

The family interaction model involves the three concepts of family career; individual development; and patterns of health, disease, and illness (Gedaly-Duff & Heims, in press).

Family Career *Family career* refers to the experience of family life. It is like a motion picture showing the family's growth and development over time. It involves the reorganization of family roles and tasks as the family progresses through qualitatively different stages of development (Aldous, 1996; White, 1991). The concept of family career provides health care professionals with a dynamic view of family life. Family careers include *family developmental stages* and *transitions*.

Family Developmental Stages A family career consists of family life that changes predictably over time, moving through developmental stages such as establishing a family, childrearing and preparing children for the transition to adult life, and the eventual death of a parent or parent figure (Turk & Kerns, 1985). These changes many times do not occur in a linear fashion. For example, the birth of a child who has a chronic illness or disability may occur in the parents' early adulthood, middle adulthood, or late adulthood. Duvall's (Duvall & Miller, 1985) eight stages of family development describe expected changes that families who are rearing chil-

dren experience. The following are typical family developmental stages:

1. Family without children
2. Childbearing
3. Preschool
4. School age
5. Adolescence
6. Transition to adulthood
7. Middle adulthood
8. Retirement and old age

These family stages help health care professionals anticipate family reorganization that accommodates the growth and development of its members. For example, families expect their healthy school-age children to engage in certain personal hygiene tasks, self-care, and household chores. In contrast, families whose school-age children have disabilities may do most of these children's hygienic care for them.

Family Transitions *Family transitions* are developmental or situational events that signal a reorganization of family roles and tasks. Family developmental transitions occur at expected times congruent with the family's movement through the eight family stages described in the previous subsection. Situational events are unpredictable, temporary, and may occur at any time during a family career. Disease and illness are usually considered situational events, whereas disabilities or chronic illnesses last for the lifetimes of families and their children with disabilities and chronic conditions. The disability or illness, as a situational event, may delay families in reaching certain developmental milestones, and some families may never achieve particular milestones (Faber, 1975; Fewell, 1986). Families of children with disabilities and chronic conditions may experience renewed sadness, anxiety, and uncertainty as their children fail to make the developmental transition to an anticipated milestone. Transitions, both developmental and situational, are signals to health care professionals that families may be at risk for familial and health problems.

Seligman (1991) noted the following situational needs (see also Table 3.1) that may alter transitions at each developmental stage of families of children with disabilities and chronic conditions:

• *Childbearing:* Families may encounter their children's disability during prenatal testing for conditions such as Down syndrome and spina bifida. Other conditions, such as deafness, learning disabilities, and autism, may not be diagnosed until the children are older.

Table 3.1. Developmental stages and situational needs of families with children with disabilities and chronic conditions that may alter transitions at each stage

Stage	Developmental tasks	Situational needs that alter transitions
1. *Beginning family:* Married couple without children	a. Establish a mutually satisfying relationship b. Relate to kin network c. Family planning	a. Unprepared for the birth of children with disabilities; prenatal testing or visible anomalies at birth begin the coping process. b. In the United States, parents usually want to know their infants' diagnoses as early as possible.
2. *Early childbearing:* First birth up to developmental age 30 months	a. Integrate new baby into the family b. Reconcile conflicting needs of various family members c. Parental role development d. Accommodate to marital couple changes e. Expand relationships with extended family to adding grandparent and aunt and uncle roles	a. Learn the meaning of infants' behavior, symptoms, and treatments. b. Nurturing and parenting are hampered if children are not able to respond to parents' efforts to interact with them (e.g., not smiling or returning sounds in response to parental cooing). c. Search for adequate health care. d. Establish early intervention (EI) programs and other services (e.g., speech-language therapy, physical therapy).
3. *Family with pre–school-age children:* First child developmental ages 2½ years–5 years	a. Foster development of children b. Parents' privacy c. Increased competence of child d. Socializing of children e. Maintenance of the couple's relationship	a. Formal education of children with disabilities and chronic conditions may begin in infancy with EI programs; child and family transition to early childhood special education (ECSE) b. The child's failure to achieve developmental milestones (e.g., toilet training, self-feeding, language) may trigger the family's chronic sorrow. c. Families try to establish routines for themselves and their children.
4. *Family with school-age children:* Oldest child developmental ages 6–13 years	a. Letting children go b. Parents' needs balanced with children's needs c. Promoting school achievement d. Prepare for high-risk behavior related to drugs and sexual experimentation	a. The move of children from family care to community care requires creating new routines and relationships. b. Explain to school officials and others the needs of the child with disabilities and chronic conditions. c. Negotiate appropriate school services and curriculum. d. The child's behavior problems may isolate families.
5. *Family with adolescents:* Oldest child from developmental age 13 until the child leaves home	a. Loosening family ties b. Couple's relationship c. Parent–teen communication d. Maintenance of family's moral and ethical standards e. Promote safe sexual development	a. The child's continued dependency may lead to his or her never leaving home. b. The family examines how to continue family life with the child's increasing physical growth but ongoing dependence. c. High-risk behavior related to sexual activity and drugs may begin.
6. *Launching center family:* First through last child to leave home	a. Promote independence of children while maintaining their relationship with the family b. Couple's relationship: Build new life together c. Mid-life developmental crisis for adults	a. Financial costs do not decrease, because children with disabilities and chronic conditions may still require dependent-type care.

(continued)

Table 3.1.   *(continued)*

Stage	Developmental tasks	Situational needs that alter transitions
7. *Families in middle years:* Empty nest to retirement	a. Redefine activity and goals b. Provide healthy environment c. Meaningful relationships with aging parents d. Strengthen couple relationship	a. Redefine relationships with grown children and the child with disabilities and chronic conditions.
8. *Retirement to old age:* Retirement until death of parents	a. Cope with losses b. Living place c. Role changes d. Adjust to less income e. Chronic illness f. Mate loss g. Aware of death h. Life review	a. Make arrangements and/or "living trust" for child with disabilities and chronic conditions.

Adapted from Friedman (1998a) and Seligman and Darling (1997a).

- *Families with pre–school-age children:* Families watch for their children to achieve developmental milestones such as toilet training. Diapering a 3-year-old is not as easy as diapering a 1-year-old.
- *Families with school-age children:* Parents may experience a setback when they realize that their children do not fit into the traditional education system and need special education services and separate transportation systems. With their child's entry into school, families move beyond the boundaries of their family and thus need to explain their child's disability to others (e.g., schoolmates, teachers, other parents).
- *Families with adolescents and young adults:* As other children begin to separate from their families, the continued dependency of teenage children with disabilities and chronic conditions is a painful reminder of their inability to separate from the family. For parents of children with disabilities and chronic conditions, their child's 21st birthday can be stressful.
- *Transition to adulthood and the middle adulthood years:* Families expect to launch their children into adult life. With limited educational or work possibilities and inadequate community living arrangements, some families may have no options for securing independent living for their adult children (Wagner & Blackorby, 1996).
- *Retirement and old age:* Whereas most families anticipate rearing and caring for their children for approximately 20 years, families of children with disabilities and chronic conditions worry about who will care for their adult child with disabilities if they become unable to provide their child's care.

In addition to the ongoing situational needs related to their child's disability or chronic illness, families throughout their careers also may have problems with the following crises:

- *Personal relationships:* Personal relationships change when integrating a new baby or stepchild into the family or when a family member becomes a stepparent after divorce and remarriage.
- *Role and status:* Role and status change for an only child after the family has a new biological or adopted child.
- *Environment:* Familiar environments change when working parents move to a new job or a new house and the child must adapt to a new school, new friends, and a new community, or when families immigrate to a new country with a new language and a new culture and perhaps must work at lower-status jobs.
- *Physical and mental changes:* Physical and mental capabilities change when illness incapacitates other family members such as a working parent. Caregiving activities are shifted to other family members.
- *Loss of possessions:* Possessions may be lost during disasters such as fires, floods, and earthquakes. Family possessions and heirlooms are destroyed, and family structures and ways of interacting are altered (Rankin, 1989).

Individual Development   *Individual development* is the expected changes in humans associated with growth and development. In addition to the family's perspective, health professionals must also consider the needs of the individuals within the family (e.g., adults, siblings, children with disabilities and chronic conditions). Some family developmental stages are related to individual family members' growth and the differing needs associated with differently maturing family members. This subsection discusses research findings about the effect on mothers, fathers, siblings, and grandparents and other extended family members. It also includes two alternative family structures of divorced and single-parent families.

Mothers　Mothers of children with disabilities and chronic illness experience more depression, psychosocial problems, physical illness, and isolation than mothers of healthy children (Breslau, Salkever, & Staruch, 1982; Florian & Krulik, 1991; Jessop, Riessman, & Stein, 1988; Kazak & Marvin, 1984; Patterson, Leonard, & Titus, 1992; Shapiro & Tittle, 1986; Tavormina, Boll, Dunn, et al., 1981). Patterson and colleagues (1992) found that mothers had more physical illness symptoms than fathers and siblings did.

Mothers were tired and overwhelmed, and their physical health was often ignored by health professionals. Ray (1995) reported that fewer than 50% of the women had been getting 5 hours or more of sleep per night for months or years. A few mothers sought medical care for their fatigue. Even though they were told that their problem was stress, their doctors did not offer them any practical ways to reduce it.

Family income, social support, family environment, and marital satisfaction, as well as their children's disabilities and illness, affected mothers' physical and psychological health (Pelletier, Godin, LePage, & Dussault, 1994; Turner-Henson, Holaday, & Swan, 1992; Wallander, Varni, Babani, et al., 1989). For example, Fagan and Schor (1993) found that married or single mothers of children with spina bifida who had adult companionship had higher maternal satisfaction than did mothers without adult companionship. The support of a significant adult, either as a partner or as a spouse, was important to mothers' well-being.

Mothers usually handle the day-to-day care of their children. They master the technical and medical details of their children's care, but support for some of the daily care demands that they face has not been available (Ray & Ritchie, 1993; Stallard & Dickinson, 1994; Traustadottir, 1991). Health care professionals have focused on teaching the specific therapies that children with disabilities and chronic conditions need. Little attention has been given to how to handle these children's daily care along with family life. According to the mothers Trausta-

dottir (1991) studied, their responsibilities did not decrease over time but continued without relief as their families grew and changed.

Fathers　Only a few studies have compared fathers and mothers of children with disabilities and chronic conditions (Bailey & Simeonsson, 1988a; Cooper & Allred, 1992; King, King, & Rosenbaum, 1996). Prior to the mid-20th century, caregiving and childrearing were associated more with mothering than with fathering. Because fathers were perceived as less involved in the immediate care of their children, the ways in which they interacted and nurtured their children were ignored by researchers and clinicians (Lamb & Meyer, 1991; McKeever, 1981; Seligman & Darling, 1997a).

Bailey and Simeonsson (1988a) suggested that fathers have different needs than mothers do. McKeever (1981) found that fathers need more information about future expectations for their children. In comparison, mothers were focused on emotional support and worried about their ability to handle their children's everyday care. Lamb and Meyer (1991) suggested that fathers, because of their high expectations of their sons, were either intensely involved or totally withdrawn from their sons with disabilities and chronic conditions. Waisbren (1980) found that fathers were distressed about the impact of the children on their marriage. Gedaly-Duff (1990) found that fathers took responsibility for discussing their children's needs with their children's doctors. Stallard and Dickinson (1994) found that fathers felt marginalized and isolated from other parents and health care professionals. In addition, fathers were concerned about their children's education, the decision whether to have other children, and the widening gap in abilities between their own and other children.

King and colleagues (1996), however, found more similarities than differences between fathers and mothers. Both parents valued care that involved them as partners; helped them make decisions about their children's care; and aided them in coordinating the comprehensive care of their children's physical, socioemotional, and educational needs. Fathers felt rebuffed by health care professionals who assumed that they were not interested in their children's care. Clinic and office environments can facilitate more participation by fathers (King et al., 1996). Fathers may be involved with their children at home (e.g., doing physical treatments) and in the community (e.g., organizing softball games with volunteer firefighters to run or bat for the children) (Gedaly-Duff & Heims, in press).

Siblings The well-being of the sisters and brothers of children with disabilities and chronic conditions received increased attention by clinicians and researchers in the 1990s. Faux (1993) described negative effects, no differences, and positive effects on siblings of a brother or sister with disabilities and chronic conditions. Negative outcomes found included higher risk for depression, anxiety, withdrawal, and somatic complaints than siblings of children without disabilities (Cadman, Boyle, & Offord, 1988; Lavigne & Ryan, 1979; McHale & Gamble, 1989; Tritt & Esses, 1988). Also, increased aggression and conflict with peers and family members were documented among siblings of children with multiple chronic illnesses, developmental disabilities, and cystic fibrosis (Breslau, 1982; Breslau & Prabucki, 1987; Breslau, Weitzman, & Messenger, 1981; Gath, 1972; Labato, Barbour, Hall, & Miller, 1987; Tew & Laurence, 1973).

In contrast, other researchers found neither increased behavior problems (Vance, Fazan, Satterwhite, & Pless, 1980) nor significant differences between siblings of children with and without disabilities (Ferrari, 1984; Gallo et al., 1991). Some investigators described positive effects of being a sibling of a child with a disability or chronic condition. These included increased empathy and less self-centeredness (Harder & Bowditch, 1982), more helpfulness (Vance et al., 1980), and increased maturity and responsibility (Faux, 1991). In conclusion, being siblings of sisters and brothers with disabilities or chronic illness does not necessarily lead to a negative outcome. Rather, other factors such as the amount of time and attention parents spent on healthy siblings, consistent disciplinary practices, the degree of additional child care, and domestic chores assigned to siblings without disabilities may help to explain the mixed findings.

Siblings without disabilities often feel embarrassment, pride and protectiveness, stigmatization, and anger toward their sisters and brothers with disabilities or chronic illness:

- *Embarrassment,* when they had to bring their sibling with a disability to a school or play activity (It is important to remember that embarrassment and avoidance of siblings are common among healthy brothers and sisters.)
- *Pride,* when explaining the specialness of their sibling, and *protectiveness* when playmates tease their sibling
- *Stigmatization,* when they would not tell their peers about their sister or brother with a disability or chronic illness

- *Anger,* when they believed that their parents spent an unfair amount of time with their brother or sister with a disability or chronic condition or when they as children who were developing typically were disciplined when siblings with a disability were not. In the eyes of healthy siblings, this is unfair (Gallo et al., 1991; Ray, 1995).

Communication among siblings and other family members in families of children with disabilities or chronic illness may be a problem (Doherty & McCubbin, 1985; Faux, 1991, 1993; Patterson, 1995). Parents may want to protect their children from further hurt and avoid discussion about the disability. Healthy children who accompany their siblings and parents for visits with health professionals are rarely asked whether they have any questions. Yet, these children try to make sense of what is happening by interpreting what they have overheard. Lack of information and immaturity often lead to their misunderstanding the situation. For example, the healthy sibling may worry that they can "catch" the condition or that their wish to have a room for themselves caused a worsening of their sibling's condition. In turn, healthy siblings may try to protect their parents and not ask questions that could further upset their parents when they are already anxious (Chesler, Allswede, & Barbarin, 1991).

Being the sister or brother of a child with disabilities and chronic conditions may not be devastating, but neither is it easy. Health care professionals can educate siblings about the diagnosis, encourage them to talk about the hardships of being a sibling, acknowledge the sibling's feelings, and teach siblings how to answer the inevitable questions that they will encounter when playing or going to school.

Grandparents and Other Extended Family Members How grandparents, aunts, and uncles function as parts of families with or without children with disabilities is not fully recognized or researched (Kivett, 1991; Seligman & Darling, 1997a, 1997b). Yet, family well-being is affected indirectly and directly by grandparents and extended family members. Health professionals with a family perspective assume that families have intergenerational links.

Seligman and Darling (1997a) described possible responses of grandparents to the birth and rearing of their grandchildren with disabilities and chronic conditions. During the diagnosis stage, grandparents on both sides of the family may review the family's genealogy to prove that their side is not responsible for the child's disability or chronic condition. Grandparents may experience the dual hurt of the "loss" of the "perfect" grandchild and their offspring's ongoing burden of caring for the child whose disability or chronic condition will not go away or be treated easily. Because grandparents and parents who mourn the loss of their typical, healthy grandchild or child mourn simultaneously, they may be unable to support each other during this crisis stage of the child's disability or chronic illness.

Health care professionals may be able to anticipate the hurling back and forth of accusations between family members that intensifies the crisis (Seligman & Darling, 1997b). In-laws may accuse spouses of destroying their adult child's life. The accused spouse already feels guilty about the birth. The adult children in turn are caught between their parents and their spouses. Siblings who may sense the tension between their parents and grandparents may not know how to respond and experience increased confusion. If this hostility is not resolved, it may become a source of continuing intergenerational conflict.

Grandparenting also may have a direct influence on families with children with disabilities and chronic conditions. Grandparents may participate as daily or weekly child care service providers, mastering specific caregiving tasks such as suctioning, gavage feeding, and other specific treatments. Alternatively, they may contribute to other family life activities such as caring for the other children in the family, making meals, and doing other household chores. Visits to grandparents' homes may provide breaks from strict health care treatments and routines. If grandparents are part of the family's daily child care, however, they may need to provide care that is consistent with the parents' home routines. Parents and grandparents need to establish rules that fit the role of grandparenting and maintain necessary treatments or behavioral management (Landry-Meyer, 1999). During other transitions, such as divorce, grandparents may be separated from their grandchildren completely. Health care professionals may find themselves involved in the complex issues of grandparents' visitation rights (Purnell & Bagby, 1993).

Some grandparents are the primary caregivers of their grandchildren with disabilities and chronic conditions; for example, babies who are born with an addiction to drugs are often cared for by their grandparents because their parents continue to struggle with addiction and related difficulties (Jendrek, 1993;

Kelley, 1993; Landry-Meyer, 1999; Minkler & Roe, 1993). Grandparents who expected their parenting role to cease with the transition of their children to adulthood may find themselves resuming the role of parent. In these situations, health care professionals teach grandparents how to care for their grandchild and discuss the family support sources that can be useful to them (Kelley, 1993). Including grandparents and extended family members of children with disabilities and chronic conditions in family conferences and having workshops or evening clinics that provide information about therapies, education about specific disabilities, and discussion of appropriate expectations for growth and development are ways that primary care providers may facilitate extended family participation (Gable & Kotsch, 1981; Meyer & Vadasy, 1986).

Divorced and Single-Parent Families Research findings (e.g., Cooke, Bradshaw, Lawton, & Brewer, 1986; Hanson, in press; Hirsh, 1991) suggest that the birth of children with disabilities and chronic conditions does not lead to the situational crisis of marital difficulties and divorce. Statistically, families that have been reconstituted by divorce and remarriage and include a child with disabilities and chronic conditions are similar to the families of healthy children. For example, Cooke and colleagues (1986) found that families of 10-year-old children with disabilities and chronic conditions had experienced longer periods in single-parent households than healthy children but that overall they were no more likely than children in general to have only one parent. Cooke and colleagues used a representative nationwide sample of British families of children with disabilities ages 6–20 years and matched them on age and location with young people in the general British population. They found that families of children with and without disabilities were equally likely to live in two-parent households. Little evidence was found that the presence, type, and severity of the disability increased the likelihood of the parents' divorce or remarriage. Cooke and colleagues stated that the birth of a child with disabilities may increase the tension in an already fragile marriage, whereas in other marriages it may bring the parents closer together. Hirsh (1991) reported similar findings.

Divorced and single-parent families of children with disabilities and chronic conditions must find ways of working out new relationships among their extended families and friends (see Table 3.2). Because single-parent mothers, who usually earn less income than fathers, typically are awarded custody of children, they may have a greater need for family

Table 3.2. Divorce and family issues

Stages of divorce	Family issues
Predivorce	
1. Decision to divorce	Acceptance of one's own part in the failure of the marriage
2. Planning the breakup of the system	Working cooperatively on problems of custody, visitation, and finances
	Coping with extended family about the divorce
3. Separation	Mourning loss of intact family
	Restructuring marital and parent–child relationships and finances; adaptation to living apart
	Realignment of relationships with extended family; staying connected with spouse's extended family
Divorce	Mourning loss of intact family; giving up fantasies of reunion
	Retrieval of hopes, dreams, expectations from the marriage
	Staying connected with extended family
Postdivorce	
1. Single-parent (custodial household or primary residence)	Making flexible visitation arrangements with ex-spouse and his or her family
	Rebuilding own financial resources
	Rebuilding own social network
2. Single-parent (noncustodial)	Finding ways to continue effective parenting relationship with children
	Maintaining financial responsibilities to ex-spouse and children

Adapted from Carter and McGoldrick (1999).

support services (Hanson, in press). The issues of family divorce include the following:

- The decision to divorce and acceptance of one's own part in the failed marriage
- Planning the breakup of the system such as working out problems of custody, visitations, and finances, along with dealing with extended family about the divorce
- Separation and mourning the loss of the intact family, adapting to living apart, and realignment with the spouse's extended family
- The divorce and giving up the fantasy of reunion, and creating new hopes and dreams (Carter & McGoldrick, 1999, p. 375)

After the divorce, the custodial single parent has the continuing task of making flexible visitation arrangements with the ex-spouse and family and rebuilding his or her own financial resources and social network. Noncustodial single parents need to find ways to continue an effective parenting relationship with their children, maintain financial responsibilities, and rebuild their own social network (Carter & McGoldrick, 1999).

Patterns of Health, Disease, and Illness *Patterns of health, disease, and illness* refers to the behavior of family members to promote health and their responses to different characteristics and phases of the child's chronic condition.

Patterns of Health Families of children with disabilities and chronic conditions are challenged to

establish healthy patterns for themselves as couples and parents, for their children with and without disabilities, and for the family unit. *Health* refers to "a state of complete physical, mental, or social-emotional well-being, not merely to the absence of disease or infirmity" (Thomas & Craven, 1997, p. 845). Health promotion is achieved through family routines of eating, sleeping, recreation, school and/or work, and spiritual activities. Family resources such as strong ties of affection, a history of sharing in activities, flexible social roles, sharing responsibility for performing tasks, and open communication may have more effect on family well-being and functional outcomes than the medical diagnosis (Jessop et al., 1988; Patterson, 1991).

Patterns of Disease Chronic conditions may vary along several dimensions. These include the severity and type of impairment (physical or cognitive); the degree of visibility of the disability or disease; whether the trajectory of the condition is stable, relapsing, or progressive; the life expectancy of the child; the degree of pain or other symptoms the child experiences; and the level of dependency of the child or amount of caregiving the child requires (Rolland, 1999). These dimensions help determine the immediacy of the caregiving tasks and the impact of the child's disability or chronic condition on family life.

Patterns of Illness   Family responses vary with the phases of the chronic condition, which can be classified as *crisis, chronic,* or *terminal* (Rolland, 1999). Families reorganize their daily activities and use different approaches at each phase of the illness (Corbin & Strauss, 1988). Families in *crisis* at the onset of disability usually rally around their children and one another. Regular routines are suspended. For example, family members gather at the intensive care unit. Parents miss work, and siblings are cared for by their grandparents. Following the crisis phase is the *long-haul* or *chronic* phase. Families permanently reorganize their day-to-day lives to cope with the ongoing, incurable disease or disability. Family careers continue to unfold as the children grow and develop. For example, families experience siblings' jealousy of the attention that the child with a chronic illness receives. In addition, families later must cope with their adolescents with disabilities or chronic illness, who may ignore treatments, thereby aggravating their disease as they try to avoid appearing different from their peers.

Families again reorganize during the *terminal* phase of the chronic illness or disability. Not all conditions have a terminal phase, but those that do present families with the need to prepare for the death of and saying good-bye to the family member with a disability. Patterson (1995) wrote that families or family members may experience a child's death differently (e.g., a celebration of what that person's life meant for a family, relief and escape from the burden of care, a void in family life that was organized around the child's disability). Family rituals such as funerals help families to remember and to make the transition to ongoing life as they continue through their family careers. All family members are affected and need to be incorporated into the dying and mourning processes (McGoldrick & Walsh, 1999).

Families need different types of support and interventions at each illness phase (Rolland, 1999). During the crisis phase, clinicians begin to teach families the condition's signs and symptoms. During the chronic phase, clinicians continue to teach families; but in this phase, families teach clinicians about their child and family and how they as a family choose to cope with the illness or disability. The primary care provider's responsibility is to listen to and learn from the family. During the terminal phase, the health care provider must be mindful that few families have experienced the death of a child, so the uncertainty of how to behave and how to prepare may be frightening. Identifying which

illness phase families are experiencing guides the clinician's selection of the appropriate family intervention (Rolland, 1999).

Family Support Resources

Parent support programs, advocacy and educational services, and sibling programs are listed in the Appendix at the end of this chapter. *Respite care* is the temporary care of a child with a disability or chronic condition for the purpose of providing relief to family caregivers. Families need various types of respite care services, such as child care in case of emergencies and to allow for recreation and work (Diehl, Moffitt, & Wade, 1991; Horner, Rawlins, & Giles, 1987; O'Connor, Plaats, & Betz, 1992; Walker, Epstein, Taylor, et al., 1989). Families need respite care to promote overall family health (Folden & Coffman, 1993). The increased intensity of the care needed by children with disabilities and chronic conditions was found to influence all levels of family relationships and all family members (Diehl et al., 1991). Couples stated that they rarely did things together as husband and wife, that siblings took up most of their free time, and that their families could not function spontaneously.

Respite care services may be more difficult to locate for children with autism, severe behavior problems, or severe physical disabilities, especially epilepsy and cerebral palsy. Even when respite care is available, it may not fit families' needs. Many families fear leaving their children, especially children who use assistive technology (Diehl et al., 1991). Respite caregivers may lack appropriate education, and home routines are frequently disrupted. In addition, the difficulty of transporting their child to another location may prevent or shorten the parents' time alone.

Folden and Coffman (1993) reviewed the advantages of in-home and out-of-home respite services. *In-home services* include baby sitters, companions, home health aides, and nursing services; *out-of-home* services include residential facilities, private family homes, group homes, child care programs, and school programs. The following are the advantages of in-home services:

- Special equipment that the children use does not need to be moved.
- Children are in familiar surroundings.
- Transportation is not necessary to move children to an alternative setting.
- Special facilities are not needed, which may decrease the cost of providing services.

The following are the advantages of out-of-home services:

- Children with disabilities and chronic conditions receive additional stimulation.
- Family members can spend time together and concentrate on the other children in the family.
- Respite volunteers can care for several children who need services at one time, which may reduce the cost to families.
- Respite workers are more likely to be supervised.

Educational Services

Early Intervention and Early Childhood Special Education   Two programs that work with families to provide needed education services for young children with disabilities and chronic conditions are early intervention (EI) and early childhood special education (ECSE). The family participates in the development of the individualized family service plan (IFSP), which is a tool that specifically addresses the family's needs, strengths, and goals in addition to child-oriented services. EI and ECSE services and the development of the IFSP are described in detail in Chapter 5.

Transition to School-Age Services   The school attendance of the child with disabilities and chronic conditions is important in helping families to achieve their goal of socializing and preparing their child for the future. Integral to children's coping with their chronic illnesses and disabilities is relating to their peers, achieving academically, developing increased independence, and being a part of the school community. School attendance is as fundamental to children's development as the medical management of their disabilities and chronic conditions (Sexson & Madan-Swain, 1993). Since 1973, federal legislation has mandated that Head Start programs include children with disabilities and chronic conditions (American Academy of Pediatrics [AAP], 1973). The Individuals with Disabilities Education Act (IDEA) of 1990 (PL 101-476) and its amendments of 1991 (PL 102-119) and 1997 (PL 105-17) guarantee a free appropriate public education for all students with disabilities. The child's educational and related service needs are listed in the child's individualized education program (IEP; Vessey, Jackson, Rabin, & McFadden, 1996).

ECSE staff assist families in making the transition to school-age services. Inclusion of students with disabilities in a classroom environment that children who are developing typically would choose (e.g., a general education class in the neighborhood school) is a critical issue for many parents and educators. Some families, however, may feel that the physical and emotional effort required to place a child with disabilities and chronic conditions in a general school is excessive or may believe that their child is too vulnerable (e.g., at risk for contracting infectious diseases). Other parents may focus on the academic benefits rather than the social and developmental aspects of school and therefore choose home schooling.

Some schools may lack adequate resources to support school attendance and provide appropriate education services for children with disabilities and chronic conditions. Schools must have established emergency procedures, resources for medication administration, and the health procedures necessary to support the child's education program (e.g., intermittent catheterization). Schoolteachers may have little knowledge about particular disabling conditions, feel ambivalent about how to approach the child with a disability, be uncertain about how to handle the child's medical problems, lack the preparation to handle the reactions of other children to the child with a disability, and presume that the extra attention given to the child with disabilities may limit their ability to meet the needs of other children in the classroom (Sexon & Madan-Swain, 1993).

Finally, schoolchildren of all ages may need preparation for meeting their new classmate. They may have many questions about their classmate's condition, such as, "Is it contagious?" "Can we talk about it, or should we ignore it?" "Will _____ die of the condition?" "What will other kids think if I'm friends with _____?" "Will playing hard hurt _____?" From a family perspective, children with the disabilities and chronic conditions can be part of planning and can help determine what information is to be shared with their teachers and peers (Sexson & Madan-Swain, 1993).

Other Services   Families may require a variety of enabling or family support services in addition to respite and child care. For many families, enabling services are necessary to ensure optimal medical and educational outcomes for the child with a disability or chronic condition as well as the child's participation in community activities. These services are as follows:

- Respite care and child care
- Transportation to appointments
- Contact with other families who have children with similar conditions
- Parent support groups
- Advocacy

- Financial services (e.g., Supplemental Security Income [SSI])
- Training in behavior management
- Counseling
- Assistance with care coordination
- Adequate housing

For many families, meeting another family that has a child with a similar disability or chronic condition is an essential support service. It allows parents to see that families can reorganize, that the family career can move forward, and that the development of individual family members can be accommodated while the care needs of the child with disabilities and chronic conditions are met.

MANAGEMENT

Family Assessment

Ideally, the family assessment is a collaborative process between the health professional and the family. At its best, the family assessment is an ongoing process through which the physician or nurse teaches the family about the child's diagnosis, treatment options, and the natural history of the disability or condition, and the family informs the health professional about themselves, their values, their choices, and their concerns. The goal of the family assessment is to identify the family's strengths and resources as well as the difficulties a family may have in promoting health, preventing illness, and managing the child with disabilities and chronic conditions. A family assessment is needed for each family with a child with disabilities and chronic conditions.

Components of a Brief Family Assessment The family assessment forms the basis of recommendations for specific support services. It is best conducted in the format of an open-ended interview; however, a number of brief, structured questionnaires can be used to complement the information gathered in the interview (see Table 3.3). Use of a questionnaire clearly demonstrates the clinician's interest in addressing important family issues and provides a structure for gathering information and providing anticipatory guidance. Initial family assessments include the following components:

- Identification of the family's concerns and strengths
- Documentation of family structure, cultural and ethnic values, and preferred language

Table 3.3. Screening for family issues

Name	Author/year	Method	Comments
Family Needs Survey (FNS)	Bailey and Simeonsson (1988a, 1988b) Bailey and Blasco (1990)	Self-reporting instrument	35-item scale Six subscales: Information, Support, Explaining to Others, Community Services, Financial Needs, and Family Functioning Content and construct validity and internal consistency and test–retest reliability established 10 minutes to administer
Feetham Family Functioning Survey (FFFS)	Feetham and Humenick (1982) Roberts and Feetham (1982)	Self-reporting instrument	25 items Six areas of functioning measured: Household tasks, child care, sexual and moral relationships, interactions with family and friends, community involvement, and sources of support Content validity and reliability established 10 minutes to administer
Impact of Illness on the Family Scale	Stein and Riessman (1980)	Self-reporting instrument	33 items Areas of family functioning: Household tasks, child-rearing, financial concerns, interactions with family and friends, community involvement, sibling behavior Content validity and reliability established 15 minutes to administer
Parenting Stress Index–Short Form (PSI/SF)	Abidin (1995)	Self-reporting instrument	36 items Factor analysis validity, test–retest and internal consistency reliability established 10 minutes to administer

- Identification of members of the family or others who live in the household
- Identification of situational stressors (e.g., divorcing, moving, disease, illness) and family risk factors (e.g., drug and/or alcohol abuse)
- Recommendations for support services

Identification of the Family's Concerns and Strengths Begin the family assessment interview with a few general questions about other family members and the family's structure. Questions can include the following:

- How has the child's disability affected the family?
- What difficulties does the family experience?
- What has the family accomplished in the last year?
- What economic changes would the family like to make concerning the child's care?
- Looking ahead 10 years, what is the worst-case scenario the family foresees for itself?
- Looking ahead 10 years, what is the best-case scenario the family sees for itself? (J. Hale, personal communication, September 1997)

You may also use a structured questionnaire such as the Family Needs Survey (FNS) (Bailey & Blasco, 1990; Bailey & Simeonsson, 1988a, 1988b) or the Feetham Family Functioning Survey (FFFS) (Feetham & Humenick, 1982; Roberts & Feetham, 1982). These questionnaires screen areas of family life that may be affected by raising a child with disabilities or chronic conditions (e.g., economics, support, household tasks, marital relationships, community support).

Documentation of Family Structure, Cultural and Ethnic Values, and Preferred Language Understanding the context of the family structure and the family's religious or cultural values highlights nonmedical factors that may influence the family's care of their child with a disability or chronic condition. *Family structure* refers to who is living in the household (e.g., intact nuclear household, single-parent household, remarried family household, three-generation household, friends living in the household, boarders [i.e., non–nuclear family members]) and economic data (e.g., dual-earner household, migrant household, homeless, teen single-parent household).

The information on family structure enables the primary care provider to identify the family's past experiences with disabilities (if any) and the family's strengths, resources, and problems. Use the Family Members Short Form (see Figure 3.1) or the Family Genogram (see Figure 3.2) to obtain this information. The family genogram is a drawing of a family tree that records information about family members, relationships, resources, and communication patterns across three generations (McGoldrick, Gerson, & Shellenberger, 1999). It is recommended for families who are long-term clients of

Name (last, first)	Gender	Relationship	Date and place of birth	Occupation	Health status
1. [*Father's name*]					
2. [*Mother's name*]					
3. [*Child's name*]					
4.					
5.					
6.					
7.					
8.					

Figure 3.1. Family Members Short Form. List the family members and the roles of the family members who live in the household with the child with disabilities and chronic conditions as well as any extended family members who live in the household (e.g., grandparents, aunts, uncles). (Adapted from Friedman [1998b].)

FAMILY GENOGRAM

Essential genogram information for each generation is as follows:

- Child with a disability or chronic condition = Name, date of birth, education level attained, and salient diagnoses of the child with a disability or chronic condition (IP, index person)
- Parents = Names, dates of birth, occupations, education levels attained, and chronic illnesses or diseases of parents and other people living in the household
- Determine whether parents are partners or married. If married, give names of spouses and the name and sex of child with each spouse. Include dates of marriages, separations, and divorces.
- Paternal and maternal grandparents = Names, dates of birth, occupations, and chronic illnesses or diseases of grandparents or aunts and uncles as relevant. Include dates and causes of deaths.
- Of those family members listed, indicate those who were especially close, those who were cut off from each other, and those who were ovely dependent.

Adapted with permission from Like, R., Rogers, J., and McGoldrick, M. (1988). Genogram information categories for clinical practice. *Journal of Family Practice, 26*(4), 407–412.

A
Symbols to describe basic family membership and structure.

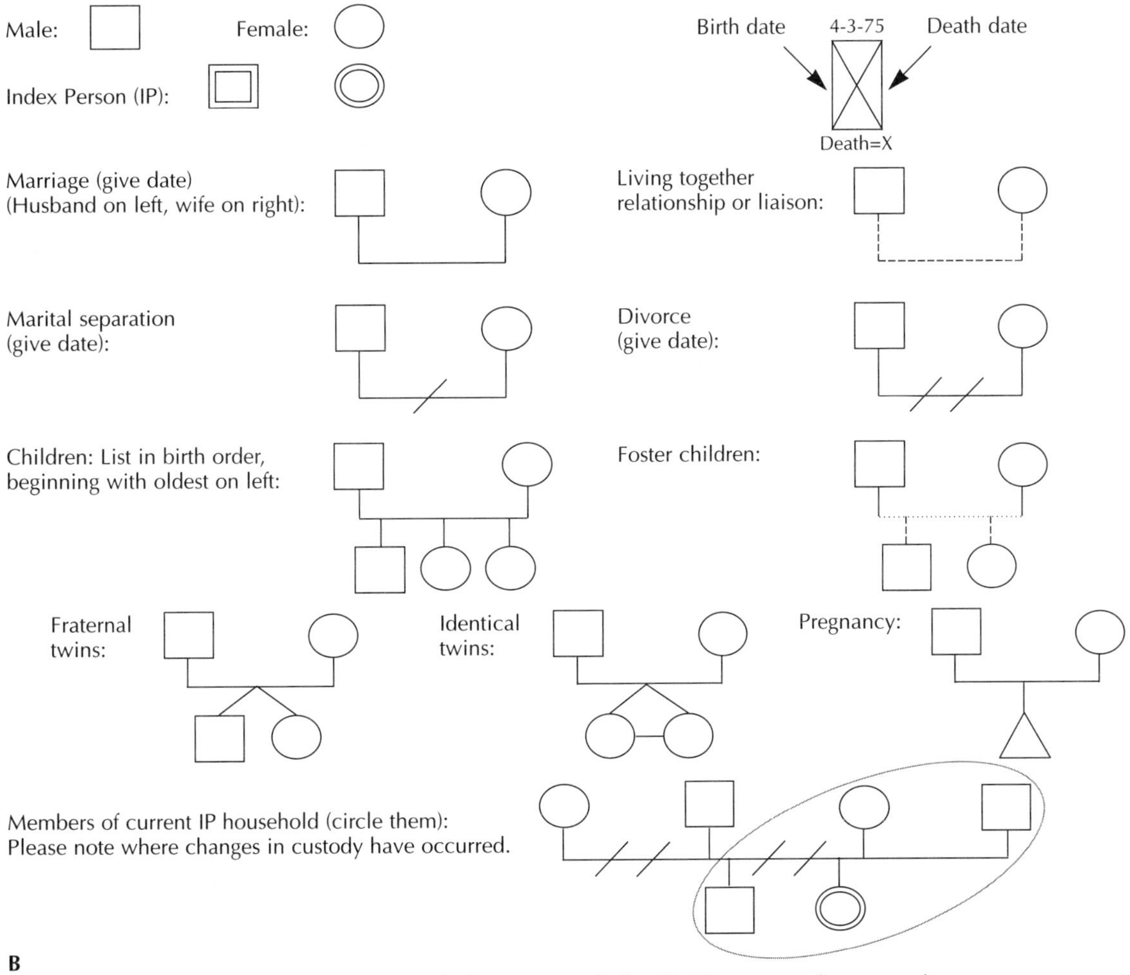

B
Family interaction patterns. The following symbols are optional. The clinician may prefer to note them on a separate sheet.

Figure 3.2. Family genogram. The symbols indicate the sex of family members, birth dates, dates of death, index person (IP) (i.e., family member of focus such as the child with a disability or chronic condition), marriages and dates thereof, marital separations and dates thereof, divorces and dates thereof, those who lived together or are living together, children and their ages, adopted or foster children, and members of the current IP's household, including other people who live with or care for family members. (From McGoldrick, M., Gerson, R., & Shellenberger, S. [1999]. *Genograms: Assessment and intervention* [2nd ed., p. 192]. New York: W.W. Norton; reprinted by permission.)

the practice, and information may be collected over the course of several sessions. When family information is gathered from only one family member, the clinician must take into account that this information is based on that particular family member's perspective. Figure 3.2 shows the symbols used in drawing a family genogram.

Identification of Situational Stressors and Family Risk Factors Families may experience situational stressors at any stage of family development or at any phase of the chronic condition. In addition, the presence of a child with disabilities and chronic conditions does not exempt families from the effects of other social problems, such as domestic violence; drug and alcohol abuse; criminal activity; physical, verbal, or sexual abuse; mental illness; significant death or other loss; and exposure to weapons. Each of these too-familiar conditions increases the family's stress and decreases the family's health. Any combination of these social problems and the presence of a child with disabilities and chronic conditions significantly increases the need for identification and problem solving to protect the family members and promote the health and safety of individual family members and the family as a unit. A primary health care provider is often a safe person with whom family members can discuss difficult problems. Simple, nonjudgmental questions asked periodically create opportunities to identify problems and help find solutions.

Comprehensive Assessment Some health professionals may choose to do an in-depth family assessment. This section describes one approach to conducting a comprehensive evaluation of family function based on the family interaction model. The objectives of the comprehensive family assessment are as follows:

- Identify family's concerns and strengths.
- Document the family's structure, cultural and ethnic values, and preferred language.
- Identify members of the family and others who live in the household.
- Review the adequacy of the family's housing, the family's current use of support services, the children's education, and the family's medical insurance coverage.
- Screen for situational stressors and familial risk factors.
- Identify the family's responses at different stages of the chronic condition.
- Identify the developmental stage of the family and screen for problems of daily life specific to that stage of caregiving.

- Evaluate the effect of the child with a disability or chronic condition on each family member.
- Screen for health promotion and prevention activities of the family and the child with a disability or chronic condition.
- Work out the logistics of receiving care and services.
- Determine the family's need for respite care.
- Make recommendations for additional support services.
- Identify the family's concerns and strengths (see previous discussion under the "Components of a Brief Family Assessment" heading).

Review the Adequacy of the Family's Housing, the Family's Current Use of Support Services, the Children's Education, and the Family's Medical Insurance Coverage Determine the family's type of housing (i.e., home or apartment) and which support services are being used by either individual family members or family groups. Learn which education services are being used by the child with a disability or chronic condition. Determine which related services are being used and which other professionals are involved (e.g., occupational therapy, physical therapy, speech-language therapy, social worker, visiting nurse). Include a list of the primary, secondary, and other medical insurance coverages that the family has (Adelmann, Bridge, & Krahn, 1997).

Identification of Situational Stressors Ask about job loss, family moves, and illnesses of other family members. Ask about family members' use of alcohol and drugs, the presence of weapons (e.g., guns, knives) in the home, incidents of violence (e.g., hitting, fighting), the use of harsh discipline at home, and family members' involvement with the police or the criminal justice system.

Identify Family Responses at Different Stages of the Disability or Chronic Condition Families behave differently in each stage of the child's disability or chronic condition. For example, during the initial crisis, when first learning that their child has a disability or chronic condition, families may trust that the condition can be corrected easily as if it were a broken leg that could be casted until its function was restored. Identify whether the family is experiencing the crisis phase or the "long-haul" phase of the child's illness. Brief questionnaires provided in the Appendix at the end of this chapter can be used to assess daily family life for each phase of the child's disability or chronic condition.

Identify the Developmental Stage of the Family and Screen for Problems of Daily Life Specific to that Stage of Caregiving A family's developmental stage is determined by the age of the oldest child in the family. The Primary Care Family Assessment forms (see the Appendix at the end of this chapter) include questions about the relevant tasks specific to each family developmental stage. These forms are useful to help structure the interview with families and to provide anticipatory guidance. Use the forms and questions that are specific to the developmental stage of each particular family.

Evaluate the Effect of the Child with Disabilities and Chronic Conditions on Each Family Member Mothers, fathers, siblings, and grandparents may be affected differently by the presence of a child with a disability or chronic condition in the family. For questions to ask family members to evaluate the effect on them of the birth of a child with disabilities and chronic conditions, please see the "Effect of Child's Disability on Family Members Interview" form in the Appendix at the end of this chapter.

Screen for Health Promotion and Prevention Activities Review the immunization record and dental practices of the child with a disability or chronic condition and the other children in the family. Determine the sleep and rest patterns of the family. What leisure or recreation activities does the family enjoy? Assess how the other children are doing with regard to school, making friends, and involvement in recreation activities. Ask whether the family has enrolled their child with a disability or chronic condition in camp and community recreation activities.

Logistics of Receiving Care and Services Determine how far away—in terms of both miles and time required for travel—health services are from the family's home, as well as the family's mode of transportation (Adelmann et al., 1997). What are the logistics of providing daily care? Ask the family to describe a typical day. In addition, sometimes problems can be detected by asking about the child's physical environment in the home (Ray, 1995). The following are some questions to ask the family:

- Are the stairs a problem?
- Are there enough electrical plugs in the home for the child to move from room to room with equipment?
- How many trips does it take to get all of the equipment and the child from the house to the car?
- Are the caregivers strong enough to lift the equipment?

- Where can the equipment be cleaned? Are the sinks in the home easily accessible?
- What community backup is available for medical emergencies?

Determine the Need for Respite Care Folden and Coffman (1993) suggested that clinicians use the following questions to evaluate the need for respite care:

- Do you sometimes feel that you are "going crazy" because you can never be alone?
- Do you have difficulty with finding temporary care for your child?
- Are you concerned that if a family emergency occurred, you would not have anyone with whom you could securely leave your child?
- Is it important that you and your spouse have some time alone together?
- Do you avoid going out because you feel that you are imposing on other people to help care for your child?
- Would you feel comfortable with leaving your child in the care of a well-trained respite care worker in your home or at another location?

Important Primary Care Family Interventions

Primary care family interventions may be needed during transitions through each family developmental stage; in each phase of the child's illness or disability; according to each family member's individual developmental needs; and in situational transitions related to the medical, educational, and social needs of the child with a disability or chronic condition.

Educate the Child and Family about the Child's Disability or Chronic Condition Explain to the child and the child's family the relationships between the signs and symptoms the child experiences and the child's disability or chronic condition. Include a description of how the tests help in interpreting the child's situation. Tell the family which signs and symptoms indicate that the condition is improving or worsening. The following are further protocols to follow in caring for families of children with disabilities and chronic conditions:

- Review the effects that the child with a disability or chronic condition may have on other family members (e.g., stress on parents, siblings, grandparents, friends).
- Discuss developmental issues related to the child's disability or chronic condition (e.g., mobility).
- Discuss the natural history of the disability or chronic condition and appropriate expectations of family members (e.g., how the disability or condition will eventually affect the child's self-care and independent living).

- Review the diagnosis and treatments with the child or with other appropriate family members (e.g., siblings).

Anticipatory Guidance

- Prepare family members for altered developmental transitions (e.g., transition from ECSE to kindergarten).
- Discuss chronic sorrow "flare-ups" during typically expected transition times (e.g., lack of expected school achievement).
- Discuss situational transitions as needed (e.g., change in jobs, moving, switching to new caregivers, divorce of parents).
- Discuss adolescence issues (e.g., sexuality, birth control, encouraging healthy behaviors).
- Encourage families to promote social competence, self-care, and individual responsibility in their child with a disability or chronic condition.
- Prepare for the transition of the child with a disability or chronic condition to independent living and adult services.
- Determine which supports and adult services will be needed for the child's transition to independent living.
- Discuss child's likely degree of dependency and begin guardianship discussions (e.g., with a lawyer) and financial planning for the future of the child with a disability or chronic condition.

Family Support and Advocacy
Explore the family's resources and connections with the community. Providing family support and advocacy can be accomplished in the following ways:

- Assist the family to meet another family with a child with a similar disability or chronic condition.
- Link the family with community resources (e.g., EI/ECSE services, respite care, advocacy groups, parent groups, sibling programs, recreation resources, organizations specific to their child's condition), and advocate for the family with those organizations and agencies.
- Be an empathetic listener, and allot sufficient time to meet with the family during office visits.

Referral to a Mental Health Professional
Consider referral of the family to a mental health professional when the following circumstances arise:

- The couple experiences marital conflict.
- Family problems develop that are based on strong emotional conflicts that cannot be resolved.
- Family members fixate on only one "right" way to manage a problem.
- Family members interact in a fixed, rigid pattern, particularly when two family members side against another family member (Heiney, 1999).

Fathers' Involvement in Clinic Visits
Linder and Chitwood (as cited in King et al., 1996) offered the following suggestions to increase the involvement of fathers in primary care office visits:

- Schedule appointments to fit fathers' schedules.
- Provide clinic services in the evenings and on weekends so that fathers can attend.
- Have father-and-mother conferences so that fathers do not have to rely solely on secondhand information via mothers for information from the clinic.

Techniques that Are Useful in Giving Bad News to the Family

Pediatricians and other primary care providers may face the difficult task of telling families that their children have a disability or a chronic illness. How families are informed influences their feelings of fear and hope for their future (Garwick, Patterson, Bennett, & Blum, 1995; Krahn, Hallum, & Kime, 1993). Garwick and colleagues (1995) found factors that influenced family reactions were previous knowledge and experience with chronic illness and disability, media exposure, and parents' suspicions that a problem existed before they received the diagnosis. Previous experience may have either positive or negative influences and thus may not always help families perceive an optimistic future. Watching movies and television programs about disabilities helped some families believe that they might be able to create a life with their child with a disability or chronic condition. Families that had no suspicion of a problem during the pregnancy or delivery experienced great shock. Krahn and colleagues (1993) listed the ways in which parents wanted to receive the news of their child's diagnosis:

- Inform family members together and in a private, quiet place, preferably with the baby present and held by the parents or by the professional. Parents wanted either their spouse or a friend with them. Being informed by telephone was particularly devastating.
- Be clear about the diagnosis, and also describe the positive characteristics of the child. Do not use offensive or insensitive terminology (e.g., *anomalies, abnormal*). Instead, identify the child's strengths, limitations, and the characteristics of the condition or disability. Families want to know what they as a family can do for the child.
- Give information at a pace that the family can follow. Ask questions and review aspects of the child's disability or chronic condition to allow families time to take in the information at a rate at which they can absorb and understand it.

- Provide accurate, up-to-date information on referrals and services.
- Parents prefer being informed in a compassionate and caring manner by an individual or a professional who knows them and their child.
- Most parents want to be told as soon as problems are suspected.

Potential Communication Problems of Families with Children with Disabilities and Chronic Conditions

Communication may be compromised among family members, between families and extended family members, and between families and health care providers (Anderson & Tomlinson, 1992; Butcher, 1994; Patterson, 1991; Thorne & Robinson, 1988). Patterson (1995) described various ways in which family members may react to living with a child with a chronic condition or a disability:

- Some family members avoid the emotional issues and focus instead on gathering information and learning new behaviors.
- Some family members have intense emotional reactions, and other family members may avoid them.
- Couples fear that talking about their situation with each other may upset the balance of their marital relationship (Doherty & McCubbin, 1985).
- Parents and siblings fear that talking about the situation may upset the balance of the parent–child relationship (Faux, 1991; Patterson, 1991, 1995; Stoneman & Brody, 1993).

Most of the time, families have strong-enough communication skills that they can discuss these issues once they are aware of them and have the opportunity to observe how the doctor or nurse models this type of communication. Referral is needed in the following circumstances:

- The doctor or nurse is uncomfortable with leading a discussion about emotional issues.
- Families become rigid and fixed in their daily routines.
- Families resist help from care providers.

Parents' Misperceptions of Vulnerability

Parents of children with chronic conditions or disabilities walk a tightrope of recognizing the vulnerability and limitations of their child while seeking to actively foster their child's growth, development, and highest level of functioning. Parents' misperceptions of their child's vulnerability frequently result in their overprotection or indulgence of their child. *Overprotection* is defined as an excess of parental control, expectation, or limit setting and is distinguished from *indulgence,* which is characterized by a lack of parental control, expectation, or limit setting. Thomasgard and Metz (1993) suggested that parents' misperceptions of their child's vulnerability can negatively affect the attachment between parent and child as well as the child's developmental outcome. Primary care providers are in an excellent position to offer parents a reality check for their perceptions of their child's vulnerability. Short scales or questionnaires (e.g., the Vulnerable Child/Overprotective Parent Scale; Wright, Mullen, West, & Wyatt, 1993) about parental overprotection can be used with parents when a service provider has concerns about overprotection or indulgence.

Families that Experience Chronic Sorrow

Families that see positive aspects of their situation and seem not to be overwhelmed have resiliency. In American society, upon learning of their child's diagnosis of a disability or chronic condition, families first experience grief, then they are supposed to reach a level of acceptance. In many families, acceptance does not develop. These families mourn the loss of their "perfect" child and experience chronic sorrow with grief flare-ups occurring during new crises or developmental transition periods.

For some families, the primary care provider's acknowledgment of grief and allowing them time to cope with their "loss" is sufficient support. Families that seem to be struggling, see their situation as tragic, and seem unable to manage it need a referral to a counselor to cope with their depression or continued grieving (Burke, Hainsworth, Eakes, & Lindgren, 1992).

Important Care Coordination Issues

The service needs of children with disabilities or chronic conditions and their families are often complex, and parents of these children often require assistance with care coordination. Care coordinators need to have a child-and-family focus, which means that care coordinators must have knowledge about families' experiences of chronic sorrow and grieving (Briskin & Liptak, 1995) and be sensitive to cultural differences such as specific familial and social interactions or dietary restrictions (Shah, 1997). The responsibilities of primary care providers for care coordination (see Chapter 1) include the following:

- Identify an office care coordinator who can be available to the child and family consistently.
- Create a resource file for family support services such as sibling groups, respite care, recreation services, and family counselors.

- Assist the family to develop a care notebook.
- Prioritize care for children with disabilities and chronic conditions in the office.
- Identify contacts for EI/ECSE services, county health departments, care coordinators of managed care plans, and county and state developmental disability services.

- Collaborate with other agencies that serve families of children with disabilities or chronic conditions and exchange information regularly with schools and other community service providers.
- Empower families of children with disabilities and chronic conditions to take an active role in planning and coordinating care.

REFERENCES

Abidin, R.R. (1995). *Parenting Stress Index–Short Form.* Odessa, FL: Psychological Assessment Resources.

Adelmann, B., Bridge, L., & Krahn, G. (1997). *PASSPORT: Managed care guide for children with special health care needs.* Unpublished manuscript. (Available from University Affiliated Program, Child Development and Rehabilitation Center, Oregon Health Sciences University, P.O. Box 574, Portland, OR 97207.)

Aldous, J. (1996). *Family careers: Rethinking the developmental perspective.* Thousand Oaks, CA: Sage Publications.

American Academy of Pediatrics (AAP). (1973). Committee on children with handicaps: Day care for handicapped children. *Pediatrics, 51,* 948.

Anderson, K., & Tomlinson, P. (1992). The family health system as an emerging paradigmatic view for nursing. *IMAGE: The Journal of Nursing Scholarship, 24*(1), 57–63.

Bailey, D.B., Jr., & Blasco, P.M. (1990). Parents' perspectives on a written survey of family needs. *Journal of Early Intervention, 14,* 196–203.

Bailey, D.B., Jr., & Simeonsson, R.J. (1988a). Assessing needs of families with handicapped infants. *Journal of Special Education, 22,* 117–127.

Bailey, D.B., Jr., & Simeonsson, R.J. (1988b). *Family assessment in early intervention.* Upper Saddle River, NJ: Merrill.

Breslau, N. (1982). Siblings of disabled children: Birth order and age-spacing effects. *Journal of Abnormal Child Psychology, 10,* 85–96.

Breslau, N., & Prabucki, K. (1987). Siblings of disabled children: Effects of chronic stress upon the family. *Archives of General Psychiatry, 44,* 1040–1046.

Breslau, N., Salkever, D., & Staruch, K.S. (1982). Women's labor force activity and responsibilities for disabled dependents: A study of families with disabled children. *Journal of Health and Social Behavior, 23,* 169–183.

Breslau, N., Weitzman, M., & Messenger, K. (1981). Psychologic functioning of siblings of disabled children. *Pediatrics, 67,* 344–353.

Briskin, H., & Liptak, G.S. (1995). Helping families with children with developmental disabilities. *Pediatric Annals, 24,* 262–266.

Burke, M.L., Hainsworth, M.A., Eakes, G.G., & Lindgren, C.L. (1992). Current knowledge and research on chronic sorrow: A foundation for inquiry. *Death Studies, 16,* 231–245.

Butcher, L. (1994). The family-focused perspective on chronic illness. *Rehabilitation Nursing, 19*(2), 70–74.

Cadman, D., Boyle, M., & Offord, D. (1988). The Ontario Child Health Study: Social adjustment and mental health of siblings of children with chronic health problems. *Developmental and Behavioral Pediatrics, 9,* 117–121.

Carter, B., & McGoldrick, M. (1999). The divorce cycle: A major variation in the American family life cycle. In B. Carter & M. McGoldrick (Eds.), *The expanded family life cycle: Individual, family and social perspectives* (3rd ed., pp. 373–398). Needham Heights, MA: Allyn & Bacon.

Chesler, M., Allswede, J., & Barbarin, O. (1991). Voices from the margin of the family: Siblings of children with cancer. *Journal of Psychosocial Oncology, 9*(4), 19–42.

Cole, R.E., & Reiss, D. (1993). *How do families cope with chronic illness?* Mahwah, NJ: Lawrence Erlbaum Associates.

Cooke, K., Bradshaw, J., Lawton, D., & Brewer, R. (1986). Child disablement, family dissolution and reconstitution. *Developmental Medicine and Child Neurology, 28,* 610–616.

Cooper, C.S., & Allred, K.W. (1992). A comparison of mothers' versus fathers' needs for support in caring for a young child with special needs. *Infant-Toddler Intervention, 2,* 205–221.

Corbin, J.M., & Strauss, A. (1988). Illness trajectories. In J.M. Corbin & A. Strauss, *Unending work and care: Managing chronic illness at home* (pp. 33–48). San Francisco: Jossey-Bass.

Deatrick, J.A., Knafl, K.A., & Murphy-Moore, C. (1999). Clarifying the concept of normalization. *IMAGE: The Journal of Nursing Scholarship, 3*(3), 209–214.

Deatrick, J.A., Knafl, K.A., & Walsh, M. (1988). The process of parenting a child with a disability: Normalization through accommodations. *Journal of Advanced Nursing, 13,* 15–21.

Diehl, S., Moffitt, K., & Wade, S. (1991). Focus group interview with parents of children with medically complex needs: An intimate look at their perceptions and feeling. *Children's Health Care, 20*(3), 170–178.

Doherty, W., & McCubbin, H. (1985). Families and health care: An emerging arena of theory, research, and clinical intervention. *Family Relations, 34,* 5–11.

Duvall, E.M., & Miller, B.C. (1985). Developmental tasks: Individual and family. In E.M. Duvall & B.C. Miller, *Marriage and family development* (6th ed., pp. 41–64). New York: HarperCollins.

Faber, B. (1975). Family adaptations to severely mentally retarded children. In M.J. Begab & S.A. Richardson (Eds.), *The mentally retarded and society: A social science perspective* (pp. 247–266). Baltimore: University Park Press.

Fagan, J., & Schor, D. (1993). Mothers of children with spina bifida: Factors related to maternal psychosocial functioning. *American Journal of Orthopsychiatry, 63,* 146–152.

Faux, S.A. (1991). Sibling relationships in families of congenitally impaired children. *Journal of Pediatric Nursing, 6*, 175–184.

Faux, S.A. (1993). Siblings of children with chronic physical and cognitive disabilities. *Journal of Pediatric Nursing, 8*(5), 305–317.

Federal Interagency Forum on Child and Family Statistics. (1997). *America's children: Key national indicators of well-being.* Washington, DC: National Maternal and Child Health Bureau Clearinghouse. (1-703-356-1964; http://www.cdc.gov/nchswww/data/amchild.pdf)

Feetham, S.L., & Humenick, S.S. (1982). The Feetham Family Functioning Survey. In S.S. Humenick, *Analysis of current assessment strategies in the health care of young children and childbearing families* (pp. 259–268). Stamford, CT: Appleton-Century-Crofts.

Ferrari, M. (1984). Chronic illness: Psychosocial effects on siblings: I. Chronically ill boys. *Journal of Child Psychology and Psychiatry, 25*(3), 459–476.

Fewell, R.R. (1986). A handicapped child in the family. In R.R. Fewell & P.F. Vadasy (Eds.), *Families of handicapped children: Needs and supports across the life span* (pp. 3–34). Austin, TX: PRO-ED.

Florian, V., & Krulik, T. (1991). Loneliness and social support of mothers of chronically ill children. *Social Science and Medicine, 32*, 1291–1296.

Folden, S., & Coffman, S. (1993). Respite care for families of children with disabilities. *Journal of Pediatric Health Care, 7*(3), 103–110.

Friedman, M.M. (1998a). Family developmental theory. In M.M. Friedman, *Family nursing: Research, theory, and practice* (4th ed., pp. 111–152). Stamford, CT: Appleton & Lange.

Friedman, M.M. (1998b). Family identifying data: Sociocultural assessment and intervention. In M.M. Friedman, *Family nursing: Research, theory, and practice* (4th ed., pp. 173–211). Stamford, CT: Appleton & Lange.

Friedman, M.M. (1998c). Structural-functional theory. In M.M. Friedman, *Family nursing: Research, theory, and practice* (4th ed., 99–110). Stamford, CT: Appleton & Lange.

Gable, H., & Kotsch, L.S. (1981). Extended families and young handicapped children. *Topics in Early Childhood Special Education, 1*, 29–35.

Gallo, A., Breitmayer, B., Knafl, K., & Zoeller, L. (1991). Stigma in childhood chronic illness: A well sibling perspective. *Pediatric Nursing, 17*(1), 21–25.

Garwick, A., Patterson, J., Bennett, F., & Blum, R. (1995). Breaking the news. How families first learn about their child's chronic condition. *Archives of Pediatric and Adolescent Medicine, 149*, 991–997.

Gath, A. (1972). The mental health of siblings of congenitally abnormal children. *Journal of Child Psychology and Psychiatry, 13*, 211–218.

Gedaly-Duff, V. (1990, March). *Family management of childhood pain. Phase 2: Parents' experiences in care of their children's repeated pain episodes associated with chronic illness such as juvenile rheumatoid arthritis.* Paper presented at the meeting of the Robert Wood Johnson Clinical Nurse Scholar program, University of Pennsylvania, Philadelphia.

Gedaly-Duff, V., & Heims, M. (in press). Family child health care. In S.M.H. Hanson (Ed.), *Family health care nursing: Theory, practice, and research* (2nd ed.). Philadelphia: F.A. Davis.

Goffman, E. (1986). *Stigma: Notes on the management of spoiled identity.* Upper Saddle River, NJ: Prentice-Hall. (Original work published 1963)

Grusec, J., & Goodnow, J. (1994). Impact of parental discipline methods on the child's internalization of values: A reconceptualization of current points of view. *Developmental Psychology, 30*(1), 4–19.

Hanson, S.M.H. (Ed.). (in press). Family nursing: An introduction. In S.M.H. Hanson (Ed.), *Family health care nursing: Theory, practice, and research* (2nd ed.). Philadelphia: F.A. Davis.

Harder, L., & Bowditch, B. (1982). Siblings of children with cystic fibrosis: Perceptions of the impact of the disease. *Children's Health Care, 10*, 116–120.

Heiney, S. (1999). Assessing and intervening with dysfunctional families. In G.D. Wegner & R.J. Alexander (Eds.), *Readings in family nursing* (2nd ed., pp. 392–402). Philadelphia: Lippincott Williams & Wilkins.

Hirsh, M. (1991). Dissolution and reconstitution of families with a disabled young person. *Developmental Medicine and Child Neurology, 33*, 1073–1079.

Hoffman, M. (1994). Discipline and internalization. *Developmental Psychology, 30*(1), 26–28.

Horner, M., Rawlins, P., & Giles, K. (1987). How parents of children with chronic conditions perceive their own needs. *American Journal of Maternal Child Nursing, 12*, 40–43.

Hostler, S. (1991). Family-centered care. *Development and Behavior: The Very Young Child, 38*(6), 1545–1560.

Howard, B. (1991). Discipline in early childhood. *Pediatric Clinics of North America, 38*(6), 1351–1369.

Individuals with Disabilities Education Act (IDEA) Amendments of 1991, PL 102-119, 20 U.S.C. §§ 1400 et seq.

Individuals with Disabilities Education Act (IDEA) Amendments of 1997, PL 105-17, 20 U.S.C. §§ 1400 et seq.

Individuals with Disabilities Education Act (IDEA) of 1990, PL 101-476, 20 U.S.C. §§ 1400 et seq.

Jendrek, M.P. (1993). Grandparents who parent their grandchildren: Effects on lifestyle. *Journal of Marriage and the Family, 55*, 609–621.

Jessop, D., Riessman, C., & Stein, R. (1988). Chronic childhood illness and maternal mental health. *Developmental and Behavioral Pediatrics, 9*(3), 147–156.

Kazak, A.D., & Marvin, R.S. (1984). Differences, difficulties, and adaptation: Stress and social networks in families with a handicapped child. *Family Relations, 33*, 67–77.

Kelley, S.J. (1993). Caregiver stress in grandparents raising grandchildren. *IMAGE: The Journal of Nursing Scholarship, 25*, 331–337.

King, G., King, S., & Rosenbaum, P. (1996). How mothers and fathers view professional caregiving for children with disabilities. *Developmental Medicine and Child Neurology, 38*, 397–407.

Kivett, V.R. (1991). The grandparent–grandchild connection. In S.K. Pfeifer & M.B. Sussman (Eds.), *Families: Intergenerational and generational connections* (pp. 267–290). Binghamton, NY: Haworth Press.

Krahn, G., Hallum, A., & Kime, C. (1993). Are there good ways to give "bad news"? *Pediatrics, 91*(3), 578–582.

Labato, D., Barbour, L., Hall, L., & Miller, C. (1987). Psychosocial characteristics of preschool siblings of handicapped and nonhandicapped children. *Journal of Abnormal Child Psychology, 15,* 329–338.

Lamb, M., & Meyer, D. (1991). Fathers of children with special needs. In M. Seligman (Ed.), *The family with a handicapped child* (2nd ed., 151–201). Needham Heights, MA: Allyn & Bacon.

Landry-Meyer, L. (1999). Research into action: Recommended intervention strategies for grandparent caregivers. *Family Relations, 48,* 381–389.

Lash, M., & Wertlieb, D. (1993). A model for family-centered service coordination for children who are disabled by traumatic injuries. *ACCH Advocate, 1*(1), 19–27, 39–41.

Lavigne, J., & Ryan, M. (1979). Psychologic adjustment of siblings with chronic illness. *Pediatrics, 63,* 616–627.

Leof, J. (1994). *Adopting children with developmental disabilities.* Rockville, MD: National Adoption Information Clearinghouse. (Available from National Adoption Information Clearinghouse, 5640 Nicholson Lane, Suite 300, Rockville, Maryland 20852; telephone: [301] 231-6512.)

Like, R., Rogers, J., & McGoldrick, M. (1988). Genogram information categories for clinical practice. *Journal of Family Practice, 26*(4), 407–412.

Litman, T. (1974). The family as a basic unit in health and medical care: A social-behavioral overview. *Social Science and Medicine, 8,* 495–519.

May, J. (1992). Rebalancing the mobile: The impact of chronic illness/disability on the family. *Journal of Rheumatology, 19*(Suppl. 33), 2–5.

McGoldrick, M., & Walsh, F. (1999). Death and the family life cycle. In B. Carter & M. McGoldrick (Eds.), *The expanded family life cycle: Individual, family, and social perspectives* (3rd ed., 185–201). Needham Heights, MA: Allyn & Bacon.

McGoldrick, M., Gerson, R., & Shellenberger, S. (1999). *Genograms: Assessment and intervention* (2nd ed.). New York: W.W. Norton.

McHale, S., & Gamble, W. (1989). Sibling relationships of children with disabled and nondisabled brothers and sisters. *Developmental Psychology, 25,* 421–429.

McKeever, P. (1981). Fathering the chronically ill child. *Maternal Child Nursing, 6,* 124–128.

Meister, S.B. (1991). Family well-being. In A.L. Whall & J. Fawcett (Eds.), *Family theory development in nursing: State of the science and art* (pp. 209–231). Philadelphia: F.A. Davis.

Meyer, D.J., & Vadasy, P.F. (1986). *Grandparent workshops: How to organize workshops for grandparents of children with handicaps.* Seattle: University of Washington Press.

Minkler, M., & Roe, K.M. (1993). *Family caregiver applications series: Vol. 2. Grandmothers as caregivers: Raising children of the crack cocaine epidemic.* Thousand Oaks, CA: Sage Publications.

Newacheck, P.W., Hughes, D.D., McManus, M.A., et al. (1994). *Meeting children's long term care needs under the Health Security Act's Home- and Community-Based Services Program.* San Francisco: University of California, San Francisco, Institute for Health Policy Studies.

Newacheck, P.W., Strickland, B., Shonkoff, J.P., et al. (1998). An epidemiologic profile of children with special health care needs. *Pediatrics, 102*(1), 117–121.

O'Connor, P., Plaats, S., & Betz, C. (1992). Respite care services to caretakers of chronically ill children in California. *Journal of Pediatric Nursing, 7*(4), 269–275.

Paget, M. (1982). Your son is cured now; you may take him home. *Culture, Medicine, and Psychiatry, 6,* 237–259.

Patterson, J. (1991). Family resilience to the challenge of a child's disability. *Pediatric Annals, 20*(9), 491–499.

Patterson, J. (1995). Disabilities. In D. Levinson (Ed.), *Encyclopedia of marriage and the family* (Vol. 1, pp. 160–172). New York: Macmillan Library Reference USA.

Patterson, J., Leonard, B.J., & Titus, J.C. (1992). Home care for medically fragile children: Impact on family health and well-being. *Journal of Developmental Behavior and Pediatrics, 13,* 248–255.

Pelletier, L., Godin, G., LePage, L., & Dussault, G. (1994). Social support received by mothers of chronically ill children. *Child: Care, Health, and Development, 20,* 115–131.

Perrin, E.C., Newacheck, P., Pless, I.B., et al. (1993). Issues involved in the definition and classification of chronic health conditions. *Pediatrics, 91*(4), 787–793.

Pless, B., & Nolan, T. (1991). Revision, replication and neglect: Research on maladjustment in chronic illness. *Journal of Child Psychology and Psychiatry, 32,* 347–365.

Purnell, M., & Bagby, B.H. (1993). Grandparents' rights: Implications for family specialists. *Family Relations, 42,* 173–178.

Rankin, S.H. (1989). Family transitions. In C.L. Gilliss, B.L. Highley, B.M. Robers, & I.M. Martinson (Eds.), *Toward a science of family nursing* (pp. 173–186). Menlo Park, CA: Addison Wesley Longman.

Ray, L. (1995). *Families and their children with special health care needs: An orientation for providers* (Contract No. 1600-02760). Seattle: Washington State Plan for Nurses, Department of Health, Department of Family and Community Health, Office of Children with Special Health Care Needs. (For copies of this manual, contact Dr. Kathryn E. Barnard, School of Nursing, University of Washington, Box 357920, Seattle, WA 98195; telephone [206] 543-9200.)

Ray, L., & Ritchie, J. (1993). Caring for chronically ill children at home: Factors that influence parents' coping. *Journal of Pediatric Nursing, 8*(4), 217–225.

Roberts, C.S., & Feetham, S.L. (1982). Assessing family functioning across three areas of relationships. *Nursing Research, 31,* 321–335.

Rolland, J.S. (1999). Chronic illness and the family life cycle. In B. Carter & M. McGoldrick (Eds.), *The expanded family life cycle: Individual, family, and social perspectives* (3rd ed., 492–511). Needham Heights, MA: Allyn & Bacon.

Satariano, H., & Briggs, N. (1999). The good family syndrome. In G.D. Wegner & R.J. Alexander (Eds.), *Readings in family nursing* (2nd ed., pp. 317–319). Philadelphia: Lippincott Williams & Wilkins.

Seligman, M. (Ed.). (1991). *The family with a handicapped child* (2nd ed.). Needham Heights, MA: Allyn & Bacon.

Seligman, M., & Darling, R.B. (1997a). Effects on fathers and grandparents. In M. Seligman & R.B. Darling, *Ordinary families, special children: A systems approach to childhood disability* (2nd ed., pp. 145–166). New York: Guilford Press.

Seligman, M., & Darling, R.B. (1997b). Introduction and conceptual framework: Social systems and family systems. In M. Seligman & R.B. Darling, *Ordinary families, special children: A systems approach to childhood disability* (2nd ed., pp. 1–35). New York: Guilford Press.

Sexson, S., & Madan-Swain, A. (1993). School reentry for the child with chronic illness. *Journal of Learning Disabilities, 26*(2), 115–125.

Shah, R. (1997). Improving services to Asian families and children with disabilities. *Child: Care, Health, and Development, 23,* 41–46.

Shapiro, J., & Tittle, K. (1986). Psychosocial adjustment of poor Mexican mothers of disabled and non-disabled children. *American Journal of Orthopsychiatry, 56,* 289–302.

Stallard, P., & Dickinson, F. (1994). Groups for parents of preschool children with severe disabilities. *Child: Care, Health, and Development, 20,* 197–207.

Stein, R.E.K., & Riessman, C.K. (1980). The development of an impact-on-family scale: Preliminary findings. *Medical Care, 18*(4), 465–472.

Stoneman, Z., & Brody, G.H. (1993). Sibling relations in the family context. In Z. Stoneman & P.W. Berman (Eds.), *The effects of mental retardation, disability, and illness on sibling relationships: Research issues and challenges* (pp. 3–30). Baltimore: Paul H. Brookes Publishing Co.

Tavormina, J.B., Boll, T.J., Dunn, N.J., et al. (1981). Psychosocial effects on parents of raising a physically handicapped child. *Journal of Abnormal Child Psychology, 9,* 121–131.

Tew, B., & Laurence, K. (1973). Mothers, brothers, and sisters of patients with spina bifida. *Developmental Medicine and Child Neurology, 15*(Suppl. 29), 269–276.

Thomas, C.L., & Craven, R.H., Jr. (Eds.). (1997). *Taber's cyclopedic medical dictionary: Thumb indexed* (18th ed.). Philadelphia: F.A. Davis Co.

Thomasgard, M., & Metz, W.P. (1993). Parental overprotection revisited. *Child Psychiatry and Human Development, 24*(2), 67–80.

Thorne, S., & Robinson, C. (1988). Health care relationships: The chronic illness perspective. *Research in Nursing and Health, 11,* 293–300.

Traustadottir, R. (1991). Mothers who care: Gender, disability, and family life. *Journal of Family Issues, 12*(2), 211–228.

Tritt, S., & Esses, L. (1988). Psychosocial adaptation of siblings with chronic medical illnesses. *American Journal of Orthopsychiatry, 58,* 211–220.

Turk, D.C., & Kerns, R.D. (1985). The family in health and illness. In D.C. Turk & R.D. Kerns (Eds.), *Health, illness, and families: A life-span perspective* (pp. 1–22). New York: John Wiley & Sons.

Turner-Henson, A., Holaday, B., & Swan, J.H. (1992). When parenting becomes caregiving: Caring for the chronically ill child. *Family and Community Health, 15*(2), 19–30.

Vance, J., Fazan, L., Satterwhite, B., & Pless, I. (1980). Effects of nephrotic syndrome on the family: A controlled study. *Pediatrics, 65,* 948–955.

Vessey, J.A., Jackson, P.L., Rabin, N., & McFadden, E. (1996). School and the child with a chronic condition. In P.L. Jackson & J.A. Vessey (Eds.), *Primary care of the child with a chronic condition* (pp. 72–85). St. Louis: C.V. Mosby.

Wagner, M., & Blackorby, J. (1996). Transition from high school to work or college: How special education students fare. *Future of Children, 6,* 103–120.

Waisbren, S.E. (1980). Parents' reaction after the birth of a developmentally disabled child. *American Journal of Mental Deficiency, 84,* 345–351.

Walker, D., Epstein, S., Taylor, A., et al. (1989). Perceived needs of families with children who have chronic health conditions. *Children's Health Care, 18*(4), 196–201.

Wallander, J.L., Varni, J.W., Babani, L., et al. (1989). The social environment and the adaptation of mothers of physically handicapped children. *Journal of Pediatric Psychology, 14*(3), 371–387.

White, J.M. (1991). *Dynamics of family development: A theoretical perspective.* New York: Guilford Press.

Wright, L., Mullen, T., West, K., & Wyatt, P. (1993). The VCOP Scale: A measure of overprotection in parents of physically vulnerable children. *Journal of Clinical Psychology, 49,* 790–798.

3

Appendix

Situational Stressors and Family Risks Assessment

Anticipatory Guidance for Families of Children with Disabilities and Chronic Conditions

Child's name _____ Person completing form _____ Today's date _____

Clinical issues and concerns	Situation and intervention
1. Right now, who is living at home with you and your child?	
2. Is everyone getting along well at home, or is there a lot of stress, arguing, or fighting?	
3. Has anybody ever been hit or hurt, pushed or shoved in a fight, or involved in arguments at your house?	
4. Is anybody in the family in trouble with the police or in jail?	
5. Is anybody worried that your children have been disciplined too harshly?	

The Physician's Guide to Caring for Children with Disabilities and Chronic Conditions, edited by Robert E. Nickel and Larry W. Desch, copyright © 2000 Paul H. Brookes Publishing Co.

Situational Stressors and Family Risks Assessment *(continued)*

Anticipatory Guidance for Families of Children with Disabilities and Chronic Conditions

Child's name _____ Person completing form _____ Today's date _____

Clinical issues and concerns	Situation and intervention
6. Is anybody worried that your children have been touched inappropriately or abused sexually?	
7. Is there anybody living with you or close to you who drinks a lot or uses illicit drugs?	
8. Are there guns, knives, or weapons at your house?	
9. Has anything major (e.g., death in the family, job loss, disasters, accidents) happened recently?	
10. What is the best part and the worst part of life for you right now?	

The Physician's Guide to Caring for Children with Disabilities and Chronic Conditions, edited by Robert E. Nickel and Larry W. Desch, copyright © 2000 Paul H. Brookes Publishing Co.

Brief Family Assessment During Initial Diagnosis or Crisis

Anticipatory Guidance for Families of Children with Disabilities and Chronic Conditions

Child's name _____   Person completing form _____   Today's date _____

Clinical issues and concerns	Situation and intervention
1. People behave differently in times of crisis. Some try to avoid talking about their problems, some overreact, others "keep a stiff upper lip." How does your family typically respond to crises?	
2. We need to establish a good relationship to work together to care for your child. In stressful times, do you want detailed information or more general information from me?	
3. What would be good times and places for us to meet and talk so that you don't feel rushed?	
4. Are there other family members whom you wish to participate in family meetings and to learn how to help care for your child?	
5. What kinds of support have been helpful to you in the past? How can we arrange to support you now?	
6. Parents going through a crisis with their child often feel out of control, fearful, angry, and misunderstood. How are you feeling right now?	

The Physician's Guide to Caring for Children with Disabilities and Chronic Conditions, edited by Robert E. Nickel and Larry W. Desch, copyright © 2000 Paul H. Brookes Publishing Co.

Brief Family Assessment Later in Crisis Phase

Anticipatory Guidance for Families of Children with Disabilities and Chronic Conditions

Child's name _____ Person completing form _____ Today's date _____

Clinical issues and concerns	Situation and intervention
1. Many parents are exhausted, feel depressed, or are worried by this time from the stress and disruption in their daily lives. What is it like for you right now?	
2. Are any parts of caring for your child particularly difficult for you to perform? What would be helpful?	
3. How are you managing to juggle your regular daily activities while caring for your child?	
4. Do you need more information now to help you understand your child's condition or how to explain it to others?	
[May use the Family Needs Survey (Bailey & Simeonsson, 1988a) at this time to guide discharge planning and a beginning family care plan for the "long haul."]	

The Physician's Guide to Caring for Children with Disabilities and Chronic Conditions, edited by Robert E. Nickel and Larry W. Desch, copyright © 2000 Paul H. Brookes Publishing Co.

Brief Family Assessment During "Long Haul" Phase of Chronic Conditions

Anticipatory Guidance for Families of Children with Disabilities and Chronic Conditions

Child's name _____   Person completing form _____   Today's date _____

Clinical issues and concerns	Situation and intervention
1. What effect does your child's condition have on each family member?	
2. Are there needs of other family members that are not being met because of the demands of caring for your child?	
3. How much burden exists in the family because of your child's condition? What would be helpful?	
4. How does your family cope with your child's condition? What do you tell others?	
5. Who is stressed in the family? Who is exhausted? Who is "going crazy"?	
6. What adaptations has the family had to make to accommodate your child's condition?	

The Physician's Guide to Caring for Children with Disabilities and Chronic Conditions, edited by Robert E. Nickel and Larry W. Desch, copyright © 2000 Paul H. Brookes Publishing Co.

Primary Care Family Assessment

Anticipatory Guidance for Families of Children with Disabilities and Chronic Conditions

Child's name _____   Person completing form _____   Today's date _____

Clinical issues and concerns	Currently a problem?	Questions to ask
Family developmental stage: Early childbearing (birth of first child–age 30 months)		
1. Integrate new baby into family		When you were expecting a baby, what did you think your baby might be like?
2. Reconcile competing needs of various family members		Are any family members feeling left out, or do they have unmet needs right now? Who?
3. Parental role development		What is it like for you being a parent of a child with special needs? (Assess for chronic sorrow.)
4. Accommodate to marital couple changes		How is your relationship with your partner right now? Do you need to talk about how parenting has affected your relationship?
Problems in daily life		
5. Concerns about diagnosis		What information and skills do you need right now to help you care for your child? What are your current perceptions of the severity and progression of your child's condition?

The Physician's Guide to Caring for Children with Disabilities and Chronic Conditions, edited by Robert E. Nickel and Larry W. Desch, copyright © 2000 Paul H. Brookes Publishing Co.

Primary Care Family Assessment *(continued)*

Anticipatory Guidance for Families of Children with Disabilities and Chronic Conditions

Child's name _____   Person completing form _____   Today's date _____

Clinical issues and concerns	Currently a problem?	Questions to ask
a. Activities of daily living b. Caregiving challenge		Who performs the special care tasks for your child? How do you divide the work? How has the diagnosis affected your family's activities of daily living? How are family routines reorganized to provide for your child's special needs?
c. Effect on mother and father d. Competing demands		Parents of children with disabilities and chronic conditions often withdraw or become overprotective. Which do you do? How do you manage the daily emotional demands and the daily care of your child?
6. Parenting concerns Child development Discipline methods		Do you have any current worries about your child? How do you think your child is developing? How is everyone adapting to the fact that your child isn't achieving or won't achieve a certain developmental milestone? What works in setting limits or coping with inappropriate behavior?
7. Need for respite Recreation and leisure Couple's time alone together		Caregiving is demanding. Are you fatigued? Exhausted or really stressed? On overload? What does your family do for fun right now? How often? Do you sometimes feel that you are "going crazy" because you can never be alone? How has having a child with a disability or chronic condition affected your relationship with your partner?

The Physician's Guide to Caring for Children with Disabilities and Chronic Conditions, edited by Robert E. Nickel and Larry W. Desch, copyright © 2000 Paul H. Brookes Publishing Co.

Primary Care Family Assessment *(continued)*

Anticipatory Guidance for Families of Children with Disabilities and Chronic Conditions

Child's name _____ Person completing form _____ Today's date _____

Clinical issues and concerns	Currently a problem?	Questions to ask
8. Child care entry		What are your thoughts about child care? How would you go about finding child care?
9. Normalization		What is "normal" family life for you right now? What is the hardest thing for the family now? Any difficulties explaining diagnosis to family, friends, or strangers? Any anger or embarrassment?
10. Family strengths and resources		What keeps you going right now? What help is most appreciated? What is the best thing about your family right now? What resources are available for fun and social support? Are these adequate for now?
Family developmental stage: Family of preschooler		
1. Meet needs for housing, nutrition, safety, and health of members		How well are your family members right now? What safety issues do you and your children face? Do you have enough beds and bedrooms for your family? What snacks do your children eat?
2. Integrate new children while meeting competing needs of family members		How do you manage the care of one more person in your family? What things have changed, and how do the other children behave when you care for the new baby?

The Physician's Guide to Caring for Children with Disabilities and Chronic Conditions, edited by Robert E. Nickel and Larry W. Desch, copyright © 2000 Paul H. Brookes Publishing Co.

Primary Care Family Assessment *(continued)*

Anticipatory Guidance for Families of Children with Disabilities and Chronic Conditions

Child's name _____ Person completing form _____ Today's date _____

Clinical issues and concerns	Currently a problem?	Questions to ask
3. Socialize children		Which "manners" are you teaching your preschooler right now?
4. Parental role development		Do you feel yourself starting to "let go" and let your child experience some consequences?
5. Accommodate to marital couple changes		How has the sexual curiosity of your child changed behaviors between you and your partner? How has a "high-maintenance" child changed the time you have with your partner?
Problems in daily life		
6. Activities of daily living Caregiving challenges Effect on mother and father Competing demands		How does the diagnosis affect your child's daily life right now? How are family routines reorganized to provide for your child's special needs? How does your preschooler act and react with mother and father? How do you manage all the demands on you right now?
7. Parenting concerns Child development Discipline methods		Do you have any current worries about your child? How do you think your child is developing right now? How are other children reacting to your child right now? What works in gaining cooperation in stopping inappropriate behavior?

The Physician's Guide to Caring for Children with Disabilities and Chronic Conditions, edited by Robert E. Nickel and Larry W. Desch, copyright © 2000 Paul H. Brookes Publishing Co.

Primary Care Family Assessment *(continued)*

Anticipatory Guidance for Families of Children with Disabilities and Chronic Conditions

Child's name _____ Person completing form _____ Today's date _____

Clinical issues and concerns	Currently a problem?	Questions to ask
8. Need for respite Recreation and leisure Couple time		Do you sometimes feel that you are "going crazy" because you can never be alone? What does your family do for fun right now? How often? Do you have time designated weekly for talking together about each other?
9. Child care entry		What arrangements do you have for child care? How is it working?
10. Normalization		What is "normal" family life like right now? What is the hardest thing right now?
11. Family strengths and resources		What keeps you going these days? What help is most appreciated now? Do you need more help?
Family developmental stage: Family of school-age children		
1. Balance parental needs with children's needs		Are there things you aren't doing at work or at home for yourself because of your children's needs?

The Physician's Guide to Caring for Children with Disabilities and Chronic Conditions, edited by Robert E. Nickel and Larry W. Desch, copyright © 2000 Paul H. Brookes Publishing Co.

Primary Care Family Assessment *(continued)*

Anticipatory Guidance for Families of Children with Disabilities and Chronic Conditions

Child's name _____   Person completing form _____   Today's date _____

Clinical issues and concerns	Currently a problem?	Questions to ask
2. Reconcile conflicting needs of family members		In which ways do you feel "overstretched" by family members' needs? How has the diagnosis affected the siblings?
3. Promote school achievement and friend relationships outside the family		Is school performance up to ability and grade level? Need an individualized education program or special accommodations? Tell me about your child's friends.
4. Parental role development		Do you have any worries that you are overprotecting or indulging your child because of his or her special needs?
5. Maintain couple, parent–child, extended family relationships		How are holidays celebrated at your house? Are extended family members as involved with your family as you would like?
Problems in daily life		
6. Concerns about diagnosis Activities of daily living Caregiving challenges Effect on mother and father Competing demands		What information about the diagnosis exists right now to help you through the school-age years? Who performs the special care your child needs? How do you divide the work? What routines have to be practiced to maintain school hours and the other demands of a day? What is it like for you to have a school-age child with special needs? How do you manage the daily emotional demands and daily care of a child with disabilities and chronic conditions?

The Physician's Guide to Caring for Children with Disabilities and Chronic Conditions, edited by Robert E. Nickel and Larry W. Desch, copyright © 2000 Paul H. Brookes Publishing Co.

Anticipatory Guidance for Families of Children with Disabilities and Chronic Conditions

Child's name _____   Person completing form _____   Today's date _____

Clinical issues and concerns	Currently a problem?	Questions to ask
7. Parenting concerns Child development Discipline methods		Do you have any worries about your child right now? How do you think your child is developing? What hobbies or interests does your school-age child enjoy? How do you encourage this? What works to encourage good behavior and discourage negative behavior?
8. Need for respite Recreation and leisure Couple time		Do you sometimes feel that you are "going crazy" because you can never be alone? What do you do for fun with school-age children? What is favorite "family fun"? When was the last time you were alone as a couple? Are there any signs of growing apart?
9. School experience		How is your child doing in school? What does your child do very well in school? Need any help getting special accommodations at school because of his or her diagnosis?
10. Normalization		What is "normal" for your family right now? How would you like to be more typical?
11. Family strengths and resources		What is the best thing about your family right now? What help is most important now? What resources are available for your family? Are these adequate?

The Physician's Guide to Caring for Children with Disabilities and Chronic Conditions, edited by Robert E. Nickel and Larry W. Desch, copyright © 2000 Paul H. Brookes Publishing Co.

Primary Care Family Assessment *(continued)*

Anticipatory Guidance for Families of Children with Disabilities and Chronic Conditions

Child's name _____   Person completing form _____   Today's date _____

Clinical issues and concerns	Currently a problem?	Questions to ask
Family developmental stage: Family with teens		
1. Loosen family ties as teens mature		How independent is your child now? How well does your teen care for his or her special needs?
2. Maintain communication with teen		What do you enjoy about teens today? What activities do you share with your teen?
3. Reconcile conflicting needs of various family members		Do any family members feel left out or resent that one person gets all the attention in the family? Is anybody upset, depressed, or worried a lot? Who is stressed? How do they show it?
4. Parental role development		What is it like being a parent of a teen with disabilities and chronic conditions? (Assess for chronic sorrow.)
5. Refocus on career and couple		What would you like to do to strengthen your relationship with your partner or spouse?

The Physician's Guide to Caring for Children with Disabilities and Chronic Conditions, edited by Robert E. Nickel and Larry W. Desch, copyright © 2000 Paul H. Brookes Publishing Co.

Primary Care Family Assessment *(continued)*

Anticipatory Guidance for Families of Children with Disabilities and Chronic Conditions

Child's name _____   Person completing form _____   Today's date _____

Clinical issues and concerns	Currently a problem?	Questions to ask
Problems in daily life		
6. Activities of daily living Caregiving challenges Effect on mother and father Competing demands		With children older, are family chores and self-care evenly shared among family members? How does the fact that your child is a teen affect how you manage the child's disability or chronic condition? How has "adolescent behavior" affected your role as a parent of a teen with a disability or chronic condition? How does the family manage all the demands of your family members now?
7. Parenting concerns Child development Discipline methods		What plans need to be in place for your child's future care as an adolescent and adult? Which adolescent milestones are most important to you? To your child? What would help to achieve these milestones? What works with setting limits for your teen? How does your teen strive for "more independence"?
8. Need for respite Recreation and leisure Couple time		What kind of break from the daily grind is refreshing for you? How can you take a break? What does your family do for fun right now? How often? Do you need more fun to relieve stress? Parents of teens often need to "rediscover" and reconnect with their partner after the years of parenting demands "wear you down." How can you take extra time together now?
9. School experience		What is school like for you and your child? What plans for future education, training, and life skills are needed?

The Physician's Guide to Caring for Children with Disabilities and Chronic Conditions, edited by Robert E. Nickel and Larry W. Desch, copyright © 2000 Paul H. Brookes Publishing Co.

Primary Care Family Assessment *(continued)*

Anticipatory Guidance for Families of Children with Disabilities and Chronic Conditions

Child's name _____   Person completing form _____   Today's date _____

Clinical issues and concerns	Currently a problem?	Questions to ask
10. Normalization		What is a "normal" day like at your house right now? What is the hardest part of having a teen with a disability or chronic condition in your family? Does your family look typical to others?
11. Family strengths and resources		What is the best thing about your family right now? What keeps you going? Who has been a support for you? What resources do you have or need to manage during the teen years?
Family developmental stage: Launching teens into adulthood		
1. Expand family circle via marriage and adult relationships		How does the diagnosis affect your teen's plans for adult relationships and having children? How will your family change as children leave home and start lives and families of their own?
2. Reconcile conflicts between various family members		How can your teen separate from your family to begin adult life and still be connected to you?
3. Parental role development		What do you have to "let go of" and what things do you need to "hang on to" as your teen approaches adulthood?

The Physician's Guide to Caring for Children with Disabilities and Chronic Conditions, edited by Robert E. Nickel and Larry W. Desch, copyright © 2000 Paul H. Brookes Publishing Co.

Primary Care Family Assessment *(continued)*

Anticipatory Guidance for Families of Children with Disabilities and Chronic Conditions

Child's name _____   Person completing form _____   Today's date _____

Clinical issues and concerns	Currently a problem?	Questions to ask
4. Build a new life together as teens leave		What kind of life do you imagine for yourself as your children leave home? What do you want to do with the rest of your life? What things have you put off doing?
5. Assist aging parents of married couple		How are your own parents managing? Will you be expected to care for them soon?
Problems in daily life		
6. Activities of daily living Caregiving challenges Effect on mother and father Competing demands		What changes in family mealtimes, activities, routines, and chores reflect having teens leaving home? What special needs still exist for your child because of the diagnosis? What does it mean to you that your teen is leaving home? How is it different from your partner's reactions? Are there more or fewer demands on you now than when your child was younger?
7. Parenting concerns Child development Discipline methods		What plans, worries, and hopes for the future do you have for your teen leaving home? What "leftover" developmental milestones have to be addressed so that your teen can be as independent as possible? What behavioral limits do you need to set now as your teen is leaving home?

The Physician's Guide to Caring for Children with Disabilities and Chronic Conditions, edited by Robert E. Nickel and Larry W. Desch, copyright © 2000 Paul H. Brookes Publishing Co.

Primary Care Family Assessment *(continued)*

Anticipatory Guidance for Families of Children with Disabilities and Chronic Conditions

Child's name _____   Today's date _____

Person completing form _____

Clinical issues and concerns	Currently a problem?	Questions to ask
8. Need for respite care Recreation and leisure Couple time		Has the need for respite increased or decreased as your teen has approached adulthood? What do you do for family fun now? Is there more or less time available and used for couple time?
9. Transition to work		What needs to happen so that your teen can make the transition to work?
10. Normalization		What is typical for your family right now? How does this match with what you had imagined typical family life would be at your house when teens left home?
11. Family strengths and resources		What are your hopes for the future? What resources are needed to make those hopes a reality?

The Physician's Guide to Caring for Children with Disabilities and Chronic Conditions, edited by Robert E. Nickel and Larry W. Desch, copyright © 2000 Paul H. Brookes Publishing Co.

Effect of Child's Disability on Family Members Interview

Child's name _____ Person completing form _____ Today's date _____

Mother

In which ways are you involved in the medical and educational care of your child? _____
_____

How do you take care of yourself (e.g., sleep, exercise, work, respite care, recreation time)? _____
_____

Who in the immediate and extended family, as well as close friends, is trained to care for the child (i.e., the alternate caregivers who can reduce the primary caregiver's burden)? _____
_____

What written information do you have on services in your clinic or in your community that are specific to your child and family? _____
_____

Who is coordinating services? _____
_____

How are services coordinated among all caregivers (e.g., school programs, therapists, family members) so that everyone is working toward the same goals? _____
_____

Have you met other families similar to yours? _____
_____

What worries you about how your child with a disability or chronic condition may be affecting your marriage? Do you worry about whether to have more children? _____
_____

What plans do you have for yourself, your child, and your family? _____
_____

Father

In which ways are you involved in the medical and educational care of your child? _____
_____

How do you take care of yourself (e.g., sleep, exercise, work, respite care, recreation time)? _____
_____

Who in the immediate and extended family, as well as close friends, is trained to care for the child (i.e., the alternate caregivers who can reduce the primary caregiver's burden)? _____
_____

What written information do you have on services in your clinic or in your community that are specific to your child and family? _____
_____

Who is coordinating services? _____
_____

How are services coordinated among all caregivers (e.g., school programs, therapists, family members) so that everyone is working toward the same goals? _____
_____

(continued)

The Physician's Guide to Caring for Children with Disabilities and Chronic Conditions, edited by Robert E. Nickel and Larry W. Desch, copyright © 2000 Paul H. Brookes Publishing Co.

Effect of Child's Disability on Family Members Interview (continued)

Have you met other families similar to yours? _____

_____

What worries you about how your child with a disability or chronic condition may be affecting your marriage? Do you worry about whether to have more children? _____

_____

What plans do you have for yourself, your child, and your family? _____

_____

Brothers and/or Sisters

What chores do you and your sister or brother with special needs do around the house?_____

_____

In which ways do you help out with your sister or brother?_____

_____

How are you doing in school? Are you doing as well as you would like to be doing?_____

_____

Who are your friends? What do you and your best friend like to do? _____

_____

I am going to start a sentence, and I want you to finish it:

"Sometimes I really need . . ."

_____

"The best thing about my family is . . ."

_____

"What I want my parents to know about being a sister or brother [*of a child with disabilities or chronic conditions*] is . . ."

_____

"I feel sad when . . ."

_____

Grandparents

Is there a family history of this disability or condition in your family? _____

_____

What do you worry about for your son or daughter (i.e., as the parent of a child with disabilities or chronic conditions)?_____

_____

What can you do for the family? _____

_____

What are you *unable* to do for the family?_____

_____

The Physician's Guide to Caring for Children with Disabilities and Chronic Conditions, edited by Robert E. Nickel and Larry W. Desch, copyright © 2000 Paul H. Brookes Publishing Co.

RESOURCES ON WORKING WITH FAMILIES

Readings

Featherstone, H. (1981). *A difference in the family: Living with a disabled child.* New York: Penguin USA. (1-800-253-6476)

Meyer, D.J. (Ed.). (1995). *Uncommon fathers: Reflections on raising a child with a disability.* Bethesda, MD: Woodbine House. (1-800-843-7323)

Meyer, D.J. (Ed.). (1997). *Views from our shoes: Growing up with a brother or sister with special needs.* Bethesda, MD: Woodbine House. (1-800-843-7323)

Meyer, D.J., & Vadasy, P. (1996). *Living with a brother or sister with special needs: A book for sibs* (2nd ed.). Seattle: University of Washington Press. (1-800-441-4115)

Powell, T.H., & Gallagher, P.A. (1993). *Brothers & sisters: A special part of exceptional families* (2nd ed.). Baltimore: Paul H. Brookes Publishing Co. (1-800-638-3775)

Pueschel, S.M., Scola, P.S., Weidenman, L.E., & Bernier, J.C. (1995). *The special child: A source book for parents of children with developmental disabilities* (2nd ed.). Baltimore: Paul H. Brookes Publishing Co. (1-800-638-3775)

Adolescents

KDWB Variety Family Center
University of Minnesota Gateway
200 Oak Street SE, Suite 160
Minneapolis, Minnesota 55455-2002
Telephone: (612) 626-2401
Fax: (612) 626-2134
World Wide Web sites: http://www.peds.umn.edu/peds-adol/, http://www.cyfc.umn.edu/NRL/

This center focuses on children and adolescents with disabilities and chronic illnesses and their families and includes clinical services, academic pediatrics, a family resource center, and a walk-in center where families can obtain materials related to their child's disability or chronic condition. Clinical services available at the center include the STAR Center, behavioral pediatrics, U Special Kids, pediatric psychology, and general pediatrics. The center also has a database and World Wide Web sites.

Information

The Family Village
The Waisman Center
University of Wisconsin–Madison
1500 Highland Avenue
Madison, Wisconsin 53705-2280
E-mail: familyvillage@waisman.wisc.edu
World Wide Web site: http://www.familyvillage.isc.edu/

Provides access to a great deal of information for parents and professionals; web site has linkages to a large number of other sites including alternative treatments, pharmaceuticals, and recreation and leisure activities.

**National Information Center for
Children and Youth with Disabilities (NICHCY)**
Post Office Box 1492
Washington, D.C. 20013
Voice/TDD: (800) 695-0285, (202) 884-8200
Fax: (202) 884-8441
E-mail: nichcy@aed.org
World Wide Web site: http://www.nichcy.org/

Provides wide variety of information to parents and professionals and referrals to other organizations.

National Organization for Rare Disorders, Inc. (NORD)
100 Route 37
Post Office Box 8923
New Fairfield, Connecticut 06812-8923
Telephone: (800) 999-NORD[6673], (203) 746-6518, (203) 746-6972 (TDD)
Fax: (203) 746-6481
E-mail: orphan@rarediseases.org
World Wide Web site: http://www.rarediseases.org/

Information center on rare disorders (e.g., inborn errors of metabolism); educates the public and professionals about these diseases.

**PACER (Parent Advocacy
Coalition for Educational Rights) Center**
4826 Chicago Avenue South
Minneapolis, Minnesota 55417-1098
Voice: (612) 827-2966, (800) 537-2237 (in Minnesota), (612) 827-7770 (TDD)
Fax: (612) 827-3065, (800) 848-4912
World Wide Web site: http://www.pacer.org/

Provides education and training to help parents understand the special education laws and to obtain appropriate school programs for their children; also provides information on child abuse prevention, newsletters, booklets, extensive written materials, videotapes.

Families

Beach Center on Families and Disability
University of Kansas
3111 Haworth Hall
Lawrence, Kansas 66045
Telephone: (913) 864-7600
E-mail: beach@dole.lsi.ukans.edu
World Wide Web site: http://www.lsi.ukans.edu/beach/beachhp.htm

Center that disseminates information about families with members who have disabilities; publishes newsletter and provides other information; also provides links to parent-to-parent support through state and local chapters.

Family Voices National Office
Post Office Box 769
Algodones, New Mexico 87001
Telephone: (888) 835-5669, (505) 867-2368
Fax: (505) 867-6517
E-mail: kidshealth@familyvoices.org
World Wide Web site: http://www.familyvoices.org/

Parent organization that provides advocacy and support, publishes a bimonthly newsletter, and has chapters in each state.

Federation for Children with Special Needs
1135 Tremont Street, Suite 420
Boston, Massachusetts 02120
Telephone: (617) 236-7210, (800) 331-0688 (toll-free in
    Massachusetts only)
Fax: (617) 572-2094
E-mail: fcsninfo@fcsn.org
World Wide Web site: http://www.fcsn.org/

Center for parents and parent groups, linkages to parent training centers in different states.

**National Parent to Parent Support
and Information System, Inc. (NPPSI)**
Post Office Box 907
Blue Ridge, Georgia 30513
Telephone: (800) 651-1151 (for parents), (706) 374-6250
    (Head Start) (TDD available)
Fax: (706) 374-3826
E-mail: nppsis@ellijay.com
World Wide Web site: http://www.nppsis.org/

Provides information and linkage to other families for support.

Fathers

The Fathers Network
ATTN: James May, Project Director
Kindering Center
16120 N.E. Eighth Street
Bellevue, Washington 98008-3937
Telephone: (206) 747-4004, extension 218,
    (206) 284-2859
Fax: (206) 747-1069, (206) 284-9664
E-mail: jmay@fathersnetwork.org
World Wide Web site: http://www.fathersnetwork.org/

Advocacy organization for fathers of children with disabilities, provides assistance with the development of fathers' groups, and publishes a quarterly newsletter.

Siblings

The Sibling Support Project
ATTN: Donald Meyer, Director
Children's Hospital and Regional Medical Center
Post Office Box 5371, CL-09
Seattle, Washington 98105-0371
Telephone: (206) 527-5712
Fax: (206) 527-5705
E-mail: dmeyer@chmc.org
World Wide Web site: http://www.chmc.org/departmt/
    sibsupp/

National program dedicated to the interests of brothers and sisters of people with special health and developmental needs; provides national directory of sibling workshops and publishes quarterly newsletter.

Transition to Work

**National Transition Alliance
for Youth with Disabilities (NTA)**
Transition Research Institute
University of Illinois
113 Children's Research Center
51 Gerty Drive
Champaign, Illinois 61820
Telephone: (217) 333-2325
E-mail: nta@aed.org
World Wide Web site: http://www.dssc.org/nta/

Provides information on transition from school to work, model programs, and information on technology.

Other Resources

Amazon.com (on-line bookseller)
World Wide Web site: http://www.amazon.com/

Search for books by topic (e.g., cerebral palsy), by title, or by author.

bn.com (on-line bookseller)
World Wide Web site: http://www.bn.com/

Provides "children with special needs" collection of books; search for books by topic, by title, or by author.

Exceptional Parent Magazine
555 Kinderkamack Road
Oradell, New Jersey 07649-1517
Telephone: (877) 372-7368, (201) 634-6550
Fax: (201) 634-6599
World Wide Web site: http://www.eparent.com/

Exceptional Parent Magazine provides practical information to parents and professionals involved in the care and education of children with disabilities and chronic conditions.

Nutrition and Growth

Christine Jepsen
Robert E. Nickel

KEY COMPETENCIES

- Take a feeding history and 24-hour history of dietary intake, and complete a standard observation of feeding
- Evaluate and diagnose failure to thrive (FTT) and gastroesophageal reflux (GER)
- List the indications for long-term enteral feedings and a Nissen fundoplication
- Describe the treatment of oral motor dysfunction and behavioral issues related to feeding
- List the indications for referral for a comprehensive evaluation by feeding specialists

DESCRIPTION

Children with disabilities and chronic conditions are at an increased risk of developing problems with nutrition and growth. They may be unable to ingest adequate calories because of oral motor dysfunction, may have gastroesophageal reflux (GER) with inadequate utilization of nutrients, or have high metabolic demands because of acute or chronic disorders. These problems can affect the course of a child's illness or disability significantly. Continued poor nutritional status can lead to failure to thrive (FTT), exacerbate other medical conditions (e.g., chronic lung disease), and interfere with developmental progress because of chronic fatigue and muscle weakness.

Nutrition and Growth Problems

Nutrition problems result from a decreased intake of adequate nutrients (e.g., oral motor dysfunction), the inability to utilize adequate calories (e.g., GER), increased utilization (e.g., hyperthyroidism), or loss of nutrients (e.g., malabsorption). Children with disabilities and chronic conditions may have nutritional needs comparable to those of other children, or their caloric needs may be greater or less than those of other children because of spasticity or differences in activity level and energy expenditure.

Growth problems include the failure to attain expected growth in weight, length, or head circumference based on established normative data. In general, a child's growth should fall between the 5th and the 95th percentiles on the National Center for Health Statistics (NCHS) growth curves, and a child's rate of growth should parallel the established growth curves. This chapter addresses the growth problems related to nutritional and feeding concerns, including a fall-off in the rate of linear growth, a fall-off in weight gain, and FTT.

Failure to Thrive The term *failure to thrive* refers specifically to children who present with either weight for length below the 5th percentile or a fall-off of growth velocity of at least two major percentile curves (e.g., a drop from the 25th to the 5th percentile).

FTT is the result of complex interactions among medical, nutritional, and psychosocial factors. It occurs predominantly in children younger than 18 months of age, with onset typically occurring between 3 months and 15 months. FTT often is classified as either organic or nonorganic, depending on whether a diagnosable condition that causes the growth delays is identified. Approximately 20% of FTT cases are attributed to known organic causes. Maternal deprivation, neglect, and environmental issues are contributing factors in FTT. A study of nonorganic FTT (Ramsey, Gisel, & Boutry, 1993) demonstrated that growth failure in children with this diagnosis often is secondary to a feeding-skills disorder and may, in fact, be neurophysiological rather than experiential or environmental in nature. Other studies have suggested that difficulties during the earlier stages of feeding development may interfere with the progression of more advanced feeding skills and may contribute to behavioral and interactional problems between mothers and infants. Excessive intake of juice leading to satiety but with a hypocaloric diet also has been suggested as a factor contributing to FTT.

Prevalence

One percent of all pediatric hospital admissions and five percent of admissions to teaching hospitals are due to nutritional or growth-related concerns (Kelsey, 1993). The majority of children with chronic illnesses or significant developmental delays have some level of compromise with regard to growth, nutrition, and/or feeding.

Etiology, Including Failure to Thrive

Nutrition problems with subsequent FTT result from decreased intake, inability to utilize nutrients fully, or increased utilization of nutrients.

Decreased Food Intake Decreased food intake results from oral motor dysfunction (e.g., cerebral palsy), mechanical impairment (e.g., cleft lip and/ or palate), and behavioral or psychosocial issues. The child must be able to take food into his or her mouth (e.g., suck, cleanse a spoon, bite off foods), form a bolus, and move the bolus to initiate a coordinated swallow.

Oral Motor Dysfunction A child with oral motor dysfunction may have difficulty with organizing and moving a bolus and may have an abnormal swallow. Also, an infant born prematurely with chronic lung disease often is unable to coordinate sucking, swallowing, and breathing.

Mechanical Impairment An infant with a cleft lip and/or palate often is unable to create adequate suction on a nipple to feed successfully unless adaptations are made to accommodate the structural defect. Other examples of mechanical impairment are tracheoesophageal fistula and pyloric stenosis.

Behavioral or Psychosocial Issues Feeding behavior is influenced by parenting skills, a child's temperament, a child's developmental skills, the family's eating patterns, and a child's chronic illness. In extreme cases, a caregiver may be withholding feedings from the child. Behavioral feeding problems can result secondarily from other feeding problems. For example, a family's overemphasis on feeding a child who is a picky eater can lead to increased struggles at meals. Feeding problems can be extremely stressful for families.

Inability to Utilize Nutrients Fully GER, malabsorption, chronic diarrhea, and other medical conditions may result in decreased utilization or increased loss of nutrients. *Gastroesophageal reflux* refers to the spontaneous return of gastric contents retrograde into the esophagus. Most babies spit up periodically, although only 1 in 500 has clinically significant GER (DiPalma, 1991). GER often is attributed to incompetence or relaxation of the lower esophageal sphincter, increased intraabdominal pressure, and alterations in gastric motility and emptying.

GER does improve with maturation: 60%–80% of infants are symptom-free by 18 months of age (DiPalma, 1991). The greatest improvements usually are seen when the child is between 8 and 10 months of age and begins to sit and when solids are introduced into the child's diet (Wolf & Glass, 1992). In those children with the most severe GER, the symptoms persist beyond age 18 months, and a small percentage of children with GER are still symptomatic at 4 years of age. The incidence of GER is higher in children with developmental delay or neurologic involvement. A study (Reyes, Cash, Green, & Booth, 1993) of GER in children with cerebral palsy reported significant reflux in 70%–75% of the children. Both nasogastric and gastrostomy feedings predispose an infant to GER. GER may manifest as emesis or may be "silent" and yet result in significant sequelae. GER can lead to esophagitis, FTT, stricture formation, reactive airway disease, aspiration, and/or apnea and bradycardia (Wolf & Glass, 1992).

Increased Utilization Children with chronic lung disease, congenital heart disease, hyperthyroidism, and other medical conditions may have increased caloric needs (see Chapter 18 for further discussion).

DIAGNOSIS AND EVALUATION

Measurements Used to Identify Disorders of Nutrition and Growth

Standard Anthropometric Measurements Length (i.e., height), weight, and head circumference should be obtained at each well-child visit. The weight-to-length ratio or body mass index (BMI) (i.e., weight-to-height or kilograms-per-meter ratio) also should be calculated. The most valuable information is the child's growth velocity, which is obtained by plotting a series of measurements over time. Often the length or weight of children with disabilities and chronic conditions is in less than the 5th percentile, but their growth rate parallels the normal curve. Accurate measurement is critical to the diagnosis of growth problems. The child's age corrected for prematurity should be used until the child is 2 years of age. In addition, accurate measurement of length or height may be impossible for children with cerebral palsy, who have contractures and do not stand. Alternative methods to measure linear growth include arm span, sitting height, crown–rump length, and segmental measurements of arms and legs (Stevenson, 1992).

Length The length of children younger than age 24 months and for children ages 24–36 months or older who are unable to stand independently should be measured in a recumbent position. These children's measurements should be noted as recumbent length on the growth curve. The most accurate length measurement can be obtained with a length-measuring device that has a headboard and movable footboard perpendicular to the surface on which the child is lying. The most accurate height measurement can be obtained with a measuring board and a right-angle headboard that can be attached to or separate from the measuring board.

Weight Infants and toddlers can be weighed on an infant scale. They should be weighed consistently in dry diapers or underpants only. A wheelchair scale is the most accurate means of measuring weight in a child with orthopedic impairments, although an alternative method is to measure the weight of an adult holding the child and then subtract the adult's weight from the first measurement. The use of weight for length or BMI also can indicate an adequate rate of weight gain for a small-stature child.

Alternative Methods of Measurement If an accurate length measurement cannot be obtained, measure the child's arm span. If neither an accurate length nor an adequate arm span can be measured, a sitting height or a crown–rump length or upper-arm length is recommended. Children with meningo-myelocele and other neuromotor or orthopedic impairments may require an arm span, sitting height, and crown–rump length measurement; alternatively, segmental measurements of the arm or leg may be required.

Arm Span   The arm span is the distance between the extended middle fingers of both hands when the child's arms are fully extended to the sides at right angles to the body and the back is straight. Arm span is a useful measurement for estimating the height of people with orthopedic and neuromotor problems affecting the legs (e.g., contractures, paralysis). It is more useful for children with meningomyelocele than for children with cerebral palsy. The arm span can be taken with the child standing with his or her back against a wall with arms outstretched. It is preferable to use an anthropometer (e.g., a sliding caliper), although a tape measure is often substituted. In children older than age 5 years who are developing typically, the ratio of arm span to height is 1:1. Arm span is not an accurate measurement for people with contractures of the upper extremities, nor is it accurate in children younger than age 5 or 6 years because of their changing proportions of limb length to body length.

Sitting Height   Sitting height can be obtained with the same equipment used to measure standing height. Sit the child on a box of known height, measure the child and the box, and subtract the measurement of the box. Ideally, the child's legs hang freely, the child's hands rest on his or her thighs, and his or her knees point straight ahead. This method is not accurate in measuring children with scoliosis or other spinal anomalies.

Crown–Rump Length   If a child has contractures or other impairments of the lower body, a crown–rump length measurement is more accurate than either a recumbent length or a sitting height measurement. A crown–rump length measurement is obtained as a recumbent length, except that the hips are bent to a 90° angle and the footboard is placed against the child's buttocks. The measurement should be noted as crown–rump length. This measurement method is not accurate for a child with scoliosis.

Segmental Measurements of Arms and Legs   A child with meningomyelocele or cerebral palsy with scoliosis and flexion contractures needs segmental measurement of upper-arm length, tibial length, or knee height (Stevenson, 1992). The tibial length is the easiest to obtain; however, children with meningomyelocele may experience undergrowth of the legs because of their neurologic impairment. The upper-arm length is the segmental measurement of choice for children with meningomyelocele when the arm span cannot be measured accurately. Use of an anthropometer is necessary to obtain upper-arm length.

Other Measures of Growth and Nutritional Status   A child who engages in minimal activity may appear underweight on the standard growth curves but may have adequate fat stores. Triceps skinfold and mid-upper-arm circumference measurements are used with children who appear underweight to determine whether further follow-up for FTT is indicated. The triceps skinfold thickness and the mid-upper-arm circumference together are used to calculate arm muscle circumference, arm muscle area, and arm fat area in children who have decreased muscle mass because of inactivity. These measurements provide good indicators of body fat and muscle stores. Weight alone is *not* an accurate indication of body fat, because of variations in body composition and possible decreased muscle mass. The best use of these measurements is to assess changes in growth percentiles over time.

Special Growth Charts   The NCHS growth charts are the most commonly used references in assessing children's growth. In addition to the charts for height, weight, and head circumference, specific growth charts are also available for sitting height and crown–rump lengths; preterm infants; height adjusted for parents' stature; and Down syndrome, Turner syndrome, and achondroplasia.

Office Procedures for the Assessment of Nutritional Status, Feeding Concerns, and Gastroesophageal Reflux

Further evaluation is indicated in cases of weight for height (or length) ratios below the 5th percentile, unexplained weight loss, a fall-off in linear growth, criteria for FTT being met, weight for height (or length) ratios above the 95th percentile, or an unexplained weight gain disproportionate to the height curve. In such cases, the physician should have the child's parents complete a 24-hour dietary recall, take a detailed feeding history, observe a feeding, and complete other aspects of the history and physical examination to help determine the need for laboratory tests, X rays, and referrals.

24-Hour Recall of Dietary Intake   Physicians or nurses should review dietary history briefly at all well-child visits. If a child presents with growth problems, then a detailed history should be taken. Ask the parents to complete the 24-hour recall of foods consumed (see the Appendix at the end of this chapter). It is important for parents to differen-

Table 4.1. General guidelines for caloric recommendations

Age	Caloric intake (in kilocalories per kilogram per day)
Infants born prematurely	80–120
Birth–2 months	110–120
3–6 months	100–110
6–12 months	100–110
1–3 years	80–100
3–5 years	60–80
5–10 years	55–75
10–15 years	40–55
15–22 years	40–45

tiate between foods their child has actually consumed and foods their child has been offered. They should list all foods and liquids and be as accurate as possible (e.g., tablespoons, bites, a quarter-sandwich). The child's dietary intake should be compared with the recommended dietary allowances (RDA) (promulgated by the Food and Nutrition Board of the National Academy of Sciences, National Research Council) for a child of that age. Caloric needs should be calculated based on the child's age, with adjustments made for catch-up growth as needed (see Table 4.1).

With regard to infants, rate the adequacy of dietary intake by calculating the known calories in the formula and milk (usually 20 calories per ounce) and baby foods ingested. Make a subjective judgment about the adequacy of the remainder of the diet for that day (e.g., soft table foods), then rate the 24-hour dietary recall as adequate or inadequate. An alternative is to refer the infant to a nutritionist or a dietician to complete the 24-hour calorie count. If the infant's 24-hour calorie intake is rated as inadequate, definitely consider referring the infant to a nutritionist and obtaining a formal 3-day diet history.

Feeding History If a child presents with growth problems or feeding concerns, then the physician or the nurse should take a detailed history of the parents' feeding procedures and the child's feeding behaviors. The feeding history should include the following:

- Schedule of meals
- Method of feeding
- Length of feedings
- Behavior during feeding
- Family's concerns about food intake or nutritional status
- A history of food allergies or milk intolerance

- Socioeconomic factors (e.g., family food resources, cultural influences on food choices)

Symptoms of Feeding Problems or Gastroesophageal Reflux Symptoms of feeding problems may include the following:

- History of poor appetite
- Poor sucking
- Feedings of abnormal duration (e.g., 45 minutes or longer)
- Abnormal feeding patterns (e.g., small, frequent feeds with intake less than 1 ounce)
- Crying during feeding
- Gagging easily
- Vomiting after feeding
- Difficulty with the transition to solid foods (Rokusek & Heinrichs, 1992)

Young infants with GER have been described as irritable, fussy, and jittery, and older infants with GER have been characterized as apathetic, withdrawn, and apprehensive with less vocalization (Ekvall, 1993). The GER may be "silent" and result in pneumonia (especially recurrent or chronic pneumonia). The possible symptoms of GER should be noted during the feeding history (see Table 4.2).

Indicators of Behavior-Based Feeding Problems Behavioral concerns should be addressed during the feeding history. Indicators of behavior-based feeding problems include the following:

- Meals that take longer than 20–30 minutes for no apparent reason (e.g., oral motor dysfunction)
- A limited range of foods accepted
- Use of multiple strategies to encourage food acceptance

Table 4.2. Gastroesophageal reflux symptoms

Recurrent vomiting or spitting up
Hematemesis
Arching (hyperextension) with feeding secondary to esophagitis
Respiratory symptoms
Torticollis secondary to esophagitis (Sandifer syndrome)
Choking
Frequent swallowing
Apnea
Anorexia
Refusal of feeding
Early satiety
Regurgitation (occasionally or frequently throughout the day, immediately after a feeding, several hours later, or during sleep)
Irritability

- Absence of set mealtimes and meal locations
- Noneating behaviors (e.g., refusing, gagging, vomiting, pica)

Observation of Feeding   A feeding should be observed in the office when there are concerns about the infant's growth or feeding. If these concerns are known in advance, request that the family bring the formula and solids as well as the utensils that are used at home. First observe solids, then formula or breast feeding. If possible, the caregiver should duplicate the home feeding method. The lungs should be auscultated before the feeding and after any coughing or choking and at the conclusion of the feeding. Determine whether the child's feeding skills are appropriate to the child's developmental level (see Table 4.3).

Positioning   Positioning during feeding should be assessed to ensure that poor positioning is not contributing to the child's feeding problems. The child's head, neck, and trunk should be aligned, and the child's hips should be flexed slightly (see Figures 4.1 and 4.2).

Bottle or Breast Feeding   Observe the child's oral reflexes, rooting, sucking, and suck-swallow-breathe pattern; and note any coughing or gagging. Observe the tongue for central grooving and normal position (i.e., bottom of the mouth with the tip touching the lower alveolar ridge). Note the strength of

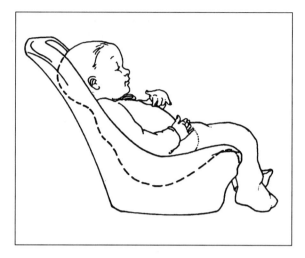

Figure 4.1.   Proper feeding position for the infant. (From Cloud, H. [1987]. *Team approach to pediatric feeding problems* [p. 206]. Chicago: American Dietetic Association; reprinted by permission.)

the suck. Observe jaw movement during feeding. The child's jaw should move with smooth, small, rhythmic excursions. Observe the swallow, and note any coughing or choking, the need for multiple swallows to clear the bolus, noisy breathing after feeding, and apnea during feeding.

Appropriate nipple selection for an infant with feeding problems can promote more typical feeding patterns. The rate of flow, shape, size, and consistency of the nipple should be considered (see Tables 4.4 and 4.5). A firm, narrow nipple provides greater proprioceptive input to the tongue and is helpful with a retracted tongue with poor central grooving. Flat, hypotonic tongues may respond to a round, firm nipple.

Spoon Feeding   Initially, the infant uses a sucking pattern to remove food from a spoon. Between ages 6 and 9 months, the infant with typical feeding skills stabilizes the jaw, cleanses food from the spoon with the upper lip, and begins to use the lower lip also. Observe the child's feeding pattern for lip closure, jaw stability, lateral movement of the tongue, chewing, and coordination of the swallow.

Signs of Oral Motor Dysfunction   Signs of oral motor dysfunction may include the following:

- Poor lip closure
- Excessive drooling
- Inability to handle secretions
- Inefficient or weak sucking
- Tonic biting
- Lack of age-appropriate chewing
- Tongue thrusting
- Sensory defensiveness

Table 4.3.   Typical feeding development

Age (in months)	Expected feeding behavior
Birth–3	Sucks to obtain all nutrients Head control developing rapidly
4–6	Trunk stability emerging Able to take food from a spoon
7–9	Munching Mouthing of toys Hand-to-mouth movement occurs Cup drinking begins
10–12	Pincer grasp acquired Cutting teeth Emerging independence Can hold cup or bottle
12–14	Brings filled spoon to mouth
15–18	Can scoop food and bring to mouth
20–24	Mature rotary chewing Food intake has decreased

From Cloud, H.H., & Bergman, J. (1991). Eating/feeding problems of children. *Nutrition Focus, 6*(6), 1. Used with permission. University of Washington, Center on Human Development and Disabilities.

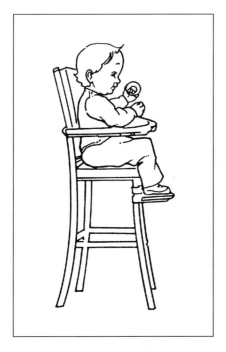

Figure 4.2. Good feeding position for a child ages 6–24 months, showing hip flexion and trunk and head in midline. Good foot support with a stool should continue throughout childhood. (From Cloud, H. [1987]. *Team approach to pediatric feeding problems* [p. 207]. Chicago: American Dietetic Association; reprinted by permission.)

- Cough or gag with feeding
- Inability to handle textured food at an appropriate age

Interventions Primary health care professionals may feel comfortable with recommendations to improve the position of the infant during feeding and a trial of different nipples. Other issues should be addressed by a feeding specialist. The following interventions can be useful, although consultation with a feeding specialist is often necessary to determine which interventions are appropriate and to instruct the family:

- Alter feeding position to provide alignment of head, neck, and trunk and 90° hip flexion.
- Provide cheek and jaw control with bottle or breast feeding.
- Evaluate nipples to ensure correct flow rate, firmness, and length for optimal feeds. Flow rate should be increased gradually. Nipple holes may be enlarged with a hot needle, boiling the nipple with a toothpick in the hole, or a single slit 1–3 millimeters long made with a scalpel.
- Use a flat, plastic spoon (e.g., small Equipment Shop Maroon Spoon), place downward pres-

Table 4.4. Situations in which modifying flow during sucking may be desirable

Infants who may require increased flow of liquid
The slow, poky feeder
The infant with poor endurance
An infant with a weak suck

Infants who may require slower flow of liquid
The infant with poor coordination of sucking, swallowing, and breathing
The very fast, eager feeder
An infant with a particularly strong suck

sure on the tongue, and bring the spoon straight out of the child's mouth rather than scraping the upper lip.
- Place foods in the child's mouth laterally.
- Try fork-mashed, soft, solid foods with children with a developmental age older than 6 months because it is more difficult for children with oral motor dysfunction to organize puréed foods into a bolus.

Medical Examination In addition to the measurement of growth parameters, the 24-hour dietary intake recall, feeding history, and observation of feeding, the physician should complete a medical and developmental history and perform a general physical and neuromotor examination of the child with disabilities and chronic conditions.

Prenatal and Perinatal History Determine whether the infant was small for gestational age (SGA) at birth or had intrauterine growth retardation (IUGR), and note the timing of onset of growth

Table 4.5. Comparison of nipples based on flow rate

High flow	SMA orthodontic
	Enfamil premature
	NUK
Medium flow	SMA standard
	Ross premature
	Enfamil Natural nipple
	SMA premature
Low flow	Enfamil standard
	Ross standard

problems (prenatally or postnatally). For infants with a birth history of SGA or IUGR, consider a teratogen (e.g., alcohol or substance abuse during pregnancy) or a genetic syndrome as the cause of their growth problems.

Developmental History and Testing   All children with problems of growth and nutrition should have a formal review of developmental progress with a parent-completed developmental questionnaire and/or a general office screen. Refer the child for eligibility testing for early intervention services or to an experienced child development team if the results of the screening tests are atypical.

Family History   The family history should include questions about growth and development problems among family members.

Medical History   The medical history should include questions about recurrent respiratory infections, bronchitis, asthma, pneumonia, and symptoms of GER (see Table 4.2).

Physical Examination   The physical examination should include an oral motor examination (to complement the observation of feeding), an evaluation of respiratory and cardiovascular status, a clinical assessment of nutritional status, a neuromotor examination, and evaluation for the presence of minor physical anomalies. Neuromotor screens are discussed in Chapters 2 and 6, and evaluation for minor anomalies is addressed in Chapter 5. If the oral motor examination of dentition, palate, gag reflex, tongue thrust, and oral motor sensitivity is suspicious, referral to a feeding specialist is indicated.

Infants who have unexplained respiratory disease that is unresponsive to pulmonary treatment may be experiencing GER. Reflux has been implicated as a causative factor of respiratory disease, specifically through aspiration of refluxed material; conversely, respiratory disease can cause reflux. Acid reflux in the esophagus has been suspected of increasing the amount of mucus secreted in the lungs and possibly changing the dynamics of the upper and lower airways (Wolf & Glass, 1992). Reflux is also suspected to cause bronchoconstriction, laryngospasm, and seizurelike episodes. Oximetry during feeding and/or a pneumogram may be useful in evaluating respiratory function with regard to feeding problems. Some medications used in the treatment of reactive airway disease may decrease lower esophageal tone or increase gastric acid secretion and potentially exacerbate GER (Wolf & Glass, 1992).

Further evaluation for possible cerebral palsy or a related neuromuscular disorder is indicated if the neuromotor examination is abnormal with evidence of hypertonia, hypotonia, abnormal reflexes, or delay in automatic reactions. Further evaluation is also indicated for children with multiple minor anomalies or a combination of minor and major anomalies. If a child has poor growth, developmental delay, and multiple minor anomalies, a high likelihood of a genetic syndrome exists. In that case, refer the child and family to a developmental pediatrician or a medical geneticist.

Comprehensive Evaluation of Infants with Failure to Thrive

Nutritional Evaluation   If the 24-hour recall of dietary intake is inadequate, refer the child and family to a registered dietitian for a 3-day food diary and analysis of protein, nutrient, and caloric intake. The 3-day food diary is usually analyzed by computer to determine whether RDA levels of proteins, nutrients, and calories are being met. Compare the child's fluid intake with the recommendations listed in Table 4.6. Calorie and vitamin requirements are based on underlying illnesses, medications, and activity levels. For example, children who are being administered anticonvulsants may need supplemental folic acid, calcium, and vitamins D and K.

Feeding Evaluation   An in-depth feeding evaluation for infants and children with apparent feeding disorders is recommended to determine the extent and character of the feeding problems and to make recommendations for improving the safety and success of oral feeding. Usually, a speech-language therapist and an occupational therapist, or at times a physical therapist, in conjunction with a registered dietician, perform the feeding evaluation. The occupational or physical therapist provides recommendations for positioning and the treatment of oral-tactile sensitivity, which is important for children with neuromotor disorders (e.g., cerebral palsy). Other professionals may participate on the team as needed (e.g., behavioral concerns, developmental

Table 4.6.   Fluid requirements for children

Child's weight (in kilograms)	Fluid intake requirements
1–10	100 milliliters per kilogram
10–20	1,000 milliliters plus 50 milliliters per kilogram for each kilogram over 10 kilograms
More than 20	1,500 milliliters plus 20 milliliters per kilogram for each kilogram over 20 kilograms

delay)—for example, a developmental pediatrician, a psychologist, a registered nurse, or a medical social worker.

The in-depth evaluation of feeding follows the same principles as are used in the office evaluation of feeding. Sensory processes in a child with neurologic impairment may be atypical and should also be evaluated. Characteristics of hypersensitivity include aversion to stimuli such as touching, textures, facial grimacing, eye blinking, gagging, and vomiting. Characteristics of hyposensitivity include impairment of taste or smell, decreased response to pressure, poor swallowing, and, at times, overstuffing.

If there are concerns about the safety of feeding (e.g., aspiration), arrange for an oral-pharyngeal motility study in conjunction with the feeding assessment. An *oral-pharyngeal motility study* (also referred to as a *modified barium swallow* or a *videofluoroscopic swallowing study*) is used to evaluate the swallow. The anatomy and physiology of the oral cavity and the pharynx can be viewed during swallowing. Difficulty with managing the bolus; risk of aspiration; and the oral, pharyngeal, and esophageal phases of swallowing can be observed clearly. The child is usually placed in the position that most closely approximates the feeding position used at home. A feeding specialist should participate in the examination. The feeding specialist either feeds the child or assists the caregiver with feeding to obtain appropriate information. A variety of barium-impregnated liquids and foods are given to the child. This study provides information about the safety of oral feeding as well as treatment recommendations to provide foods, feeding techniques, and positioning that are safest and decrease the risk of aspiration. An oral-pharyngeal motility study should be considered for the child with oral motor dysfunction with the following symptoms:

- Frequent coughing, gagging, or choking during meals
- Recurrent respiratory infections, especially right-upper-lobe pneumonia
- Wet, gurgly respirations or phonation with meals or just after meals
- Inadequate weight gain (after evaluation for and treatment of GER)
- Refusal of new textures
- Frequent irritability with feeding (after evaluation for and treatment of GER)
- Rigid feeding behaviors

If the child cannot be fed safely by mouth even with adaptations, then enteral feeding with a nasogastric or gastrostomy tube is recommended. It is important to determine whether GER is present in order to plan the type of feeding tube and necessity for antireflux measures.

Medical Evaluation The medical evaluation should include assessments to determine the cause of the FTT, including GER when indicated.

Evaluation for Failure to Thrive The laboratory evaluation rarely contributes to making the diagnosis; however, it may be helpful in planning treatment. Targeted workups may include a complete blood count (CBC); thyroid studies; measuring blood levels of albumin, iron, zinc, electrolytes, acid–base status, lead level, serum glucose, and blood urea nitrogen (BUN); liver function tests; and a urinalysis or a stool examination (including pH, stool-reducing substance, fat, parasites, eosinophils). A bone age study or a growth hormone evaluation may also be considered when the child's linear growth rate continues to be slower than what is expected for his or her age. A trial of non–cow's-milk formula may be initiated if the child's feeding history is suggestive of lactose intolerance or allergies.

Evaluation for Gastroesophageal Reflux If there are no identifiable causes of FTT or if the child's feeding history is suspicious for GER, then a basic workup for GER is indicated. A suspected diagnosis of GER can be confirmed by a barium swallow, a technetium scan, an esophageal pH study, or an endoscopy. Each of these procedures has strengths and limitations, which are described in the following list:

- *Barium swallow* (also known as an *esophagram*): The barium swallow is a procedure for evaluating the structure and function of the esophagus and stomach. Barium is given either orally or via nasogastric tube, and the esophagus and stomach are visualized while the infant is supine on a board. Swallowing may be seen initially during the study. Esophageal motility and mucosal signs of esophagitis can be observed, and reflux may be apparent either spontaneously or after abdominal pressure. As a sole test for GER, the barium swallow's value is limited because GER episodes may be missed and an evaluation of feeding and swallowing is incomplete.
- *Technetium scan* (also known as *gastroesophageal scintigraphy, milk scan*): Formula with a radioactive tracer is given to the infant, and gamma camera images are obtained every 5–30 seconds for 1–2 hours. The number of reflux episodes and the height of refluxed formula in the esophagus can be obtained. Gastric emptying can also be evaluated by assessing the quantity of food

remaining in the stomach after 1 hour. Both al-kaline and acidic reflux can be visualized. Lim-itations include oversensitivity because most infants have some reflux episodes, especially when feeding in a supine position. In addition, normative data are unavailable, and any GER episodes after the 1- to 2-hour test are not noted.

- *pH probe:* This 24-hour intraesophageal pH study has been useful in identifying GER and correlating GER episodes with feeding and ac-tivity. A pH probe connected to a portable, com-puterized recorder is inserted nasally and placed approximately 3 centimeters proximal to the lower esophageal sphincter. pH is continu-ously measured over a 24-hour period. Intra-esophageal pH is normally neutral to alkaline. All episodes of pH below 4 are defined as GER. The number and duration of episodes are recorded, and total reflux time is calculated. Episodes of less than 10 seconds' duration usu-ally are not recorded. Normative data are avail-able to confirm the presence of reflux. The diary of activities kept during the study can assist with correlating GER episodes with feeding, ac-tivity level, and sleep. Limitations include the inability to record alkaline reflux, which may be important for postfeeding reflux, especially in a child who tends to aspirate or have apneic events following feeding (Wolf & Glass, 1992); the unavailability of the height of reflux; and the cost of the procedure, which often requires a 24-hour hospitalization.
- *Endoscopy:* Esophagoscopy, esophageal manom-etry, laryngoscopy, and bronchoscopy may be useful in the evaluation of feeding and swallow-ing disorders. Esophagoscopy is used to view the esophagus and to obtain biopsy samples. It is used to visualize structural abnormalities and to diagnose esophagitis. Esophageal manometry measures the pressure in the upper and lower esophageal sphincters and often is used after a Nissen fundoplication to assess the competence of the sphincters. An incompetent lower eso-phageal sphincter has a pressure less than 5 mil-limeters mercury (HG) and a length less than 1.5 centimeters (Wolf & Glass, 1992). Laryngoscopy and bronchoscopy may reveal evidence of tra-cheal or bronchial damage resulting from GER.

MANAGEMENT OF ORAL MOTOR AND BEHAVIORAL FEEDING DISORDERS

Dietary Management

Dietary recommendations vary based on the under-lying cause of the child's undernutrition. Fre-quently, an increase in the total daily caloric intake is required. Determination of the number of calories needed is based on a formula for catch-up growth.

Catch-Up Growth Requirements Table 4.7 re-views the methods for calculating the calories and grams of protein required to support catch-up growth.

Increasing the Caloric Density of Solids and Formulas An increase in total daily caloric intake can be achieved by increasing the caloric density of the formula and other foods and/or by increasing the volume. Calories can be added to solids with the use of margarine, vegetable oil, 5% milk, half and half, and instant breakfast.

To maintain adequate protein content when in-creasing infant formula caloric density to 24 calories per ounce, it is best to increase the *concentration* of the formula rather than add Polycose (Ross Labora-tories; a glucose polymers formula made from corn-starch) or microlipids. An assessment of free water requirements is needed for a highly concentrated formula (e.g., 27 calories per ounce) or if renal in-sufficiency is present:

24-calorie formula

- *Liquid concentrate:* Mix one 13-ounce can of liq-uid concentrate with 9 ounces of water to make 22 ounces of 24-calories-per-ounce formula.
- *Powdered formula:* Mix three level scoops or tablespoons of powder with 5 ounces of water. For larger quantities, mix one-half cup plus one scoop (or 1 tablespoon) of powder with 15 ounces of water. Place the powdered formula in the bot-tle, and add water to the appropriate level (5 ounces or 15 ounces) for correct dilution.

Microlipids (safflower oil, 4.5 kilocalories per milliliter), medium-chain triglycerides (MCT) oil (Mead Johnson Nutritionals; 7.7 kilocalories per milliliter), or Polycose (liquid, 2 kilocalories per mil-liliter; powdered, 8 kilocalories per teaspoon) should be added to 24-calorie formula to increase the caloric density to more than 24 calories per ounce. Neither corn syrup nor honey should be used with children under 1 year of age, owing to the risk of infant botulism.

Specialized infant formulas are available for children older than 1 year of age. Pediasure (Ross Laboratories), Nutren Junior (Nestlé), Kindercal (Mead Johnson), and Peptamen Junior (Nestlé) all have 30 calories per ounce and are used for both oral and tube feedings for children between 1 and 10 years of age. Pediasure and Peptamen Junior are available with and without fiber. Ensure (Ross Lab-oratories), Ensure Plus (Ross Laboratories), and

Table 4.7.   Calculating catch-up growth requirements

1. Plot the child's height and weight on the National Center for Health Statistics (NCHS) growth charts.
2. Determine at which age the present weight would be at the 50th percentile (weight-age).
3. Determine the recommended calories per kilogram body weight for the child's weight-age (see Table 4.1).
4. Determine the child's ideal weight (the weight that is at the same percentile as the child's current length).
5. Multiply the recommended calories per kilogram of the child's body weight for weight-age by the child's ideal weight.
6. Divide the value in item 5 by the child's actual weight to obtain the catch-up growth requirement (kilocalories per kilogram per day).
7. Protein requirements for catch-up growth may be calculated in the same manner. Substitute the recommended dietary allowances (RDA) for protein per kilogram of body weight for the calories in item 3.

	Recommended grams of protein per kilogram		Recommended grams of protein per kilogram
Birth–6 months	2.2	(Males)	
6–12 months	1.6	11–14 years	1.0
1–3 years	1.2	15–18 years	.9
4–6 years	1.1	19–24 years	.8
7–10 years	1.0	(Females)	
		11–14 years	1.0
		15–18 years	.8
		19–24 years	.8

Adapted from Peterson, Washington, and Rathbun (1984).

Jevity (Ross Laboratories) are high-calorie formulas used in children older than 10 years of age. A variety of other specialty formulas also are available.

Dietary Management of Gastroesophageal Reflux   Thickened feedings can be used to lessen the number of reflux episodes because they increase the bulk of the formula and may be less likely to reflux into the esophagus. They also may increase the gastric emptying time. In addition, they increase the caloric density by 9 calories per tablespoon of cereal. One tablespoon of rice cereal per 1–2 ounces of formula is the recommended ratio to be given. Total daily intake of iron-fortified rice cereal should be monitored to prevent iron toxicity. Breast-fed infants do well with rice cereal mixed with breast milk or formula, given by spoon prior to nursing or when changing from one breast to the other. Solids by spoon may also be introduced at an earlier age. Smaller volume and more frequent feedings decrease the pressure on the lower esophageal sphincter. Carbonated beverages increase gastric distension with gas and should be avoided. A trial of predigested formula or hypoallergenic formula may be helpful because a small percentage of infants with GER do have fewer symptoms with these formulas (Borowitz & Borowitz, 1997). Ongoing dietary management includes taking the following steps:

- Regular assessment of caloric intake
- Provision of adequate nutrients for catch-up growth
- Careful instruction to the caregivers regarding type, quantities, and preparation of foods
- Long-term monitoring of growth

Feeding Management

Oral Motor Dysfunction   After the safety of oral feeding has been established for a child with significant oral motor dysfunction, a treatment plan is recommended to provide suitable textures, feeding techniques, and positioning. Specific techniques to facilitate optimal oral motor function should be taught to the child's caregivers. It is important that age-appropriate foods and feeding skills be integrated into a treatment program. Proper positioning during feeding provides stability and may be essential for the child who is having difficulty during feeding. Adaptations to feeding equipment (e.g., cut-out cups) and seating devices may also be recommended. Ongoing involvement of a feeding therapist is often needed to provide a progression of activities leading to feeding skill development.

Gastroesophageal Reflux   In severe cases of GER, a drip feeding of formula via nasogastric or gastrostomy tube decreases gastric volume. In some cases, a combination of smaller bolus feeds and a nighttime drip alleviates GER symptoms while allowing adequate caloric intake. Continuous drip feeds with the use of a pump should be considered for children with severe GER or children with intractable retching. Children with significant undernutrition often achieve rapid catch-up growth after placement of a gastrostomy tube. Weight should be monitored closely to avoid excessive weight gain, especially in the child with neurologic impairments.

To help decrease GER, use thickened feeds (as described in the "Dietary Management" section of this chapter); offer small, frequent feedings; position the child upright during and 20–30 minutes after meals; and minimize jostling after meals. Use of infant seats for feeding should be avoided because they may increase intraabdominal pressure and contribute to reflux. After feeding, also avoid positions that increase intraabdominal pressure, such as use of an infant swing, car seat, or feeder seat.

Medical Management

A team approach is often most effective in the management of undernutrition. Involvement of professionals specializing in the following disciplines may be indicated:

- Pediatrics
- Gastroenterology
- Nutrition
- Speech
- Therapy
- Nursing
- Social work
- Psychology

Methods of medical management may include hospitalization, medications, enteral feeding, and surgical interventions.

Hospitalization Hospitalization may be necessary to confirm the diagnosis, to determine whether adequate weight gain can be achieved with optimal nutritional intake, and to observe the infant–caregiver interaction. Hospitalization is recommended in the following situations:

(1) To protect the child from abuse when evidence of nonaccidental trauma is noted
(2) To protect a severely malnourished child from the sequelae of further starvation
(3) In extremely problematical parent–child interactions
(4) When practicality of distance and transportation preclude outpatient management (Sullivan, 1992)
(5) After failure of an adequate attempt at outpatient management (Levine, Carey, & Crocker, 1999, p. 403)

Medications Medications are indicated for children with moderate to severe symptoms of GER who do not respond to dietary and positional interventions (see Table 4.8). Medications are used to decrease acid production, neutralize gastric acid, and increase gastric motility. Children who receive medical therapy should be monitored at least monthly. It may take 6 weeks after initiation of therapy to determine the effi-

cacy of medical treatment. Treatment usually is not continued for longer than 6–12 months (Ekvall, 1993).

An initial medication regimen would include ranitidine (a histamine-2 blocker) and metoclopramide (a motility agent). Omeprazole has been effective for children with GER and esophagitis who are unresponsive to ranitidine or cimetidine and/or cisapride (Alliet, Raes, Bruneel, et al., 1998; Cucchiara, Minella, Campanozzi, et al., 1997). Cisapride was demonstrated (Khongphatthanayothin, Lane, Thomas, et al., 1998) to prolong the Q-T interval (electrocardiogram [EKG] interval that is a measure of ventricular repolarization) in some children and has been associated with serious cardiac arrhythmias in adults and children (Hill, Evangelista, Pizzi, et al., 1998). It should be used only if other medications are unsuccessful, and it is contraindicated in children with structural heart impairments and in children taking medications metabolized by the same enzymatic pathway in the liver (cytochrome P450 3A4 system, e.g., erythromycin). An EKG should be obtained before and a few days after initiating treatment to look for prolongation of the Q-T interval.

Enteral Feedings

Indications for Feeding Tubes Although it is preferable to feed children orally, enteral or tube feeding may be indicated if oral feeding is determined to be unsafe (e.g., because of aspiration) or if adequate nutrition cannot be supplied orally. Tube feeding may supplement oral feeding, or it may be used exclusively for nutrition. Following are the criteria for consideration of tube feeding:

- Inability to meet 80% of caloric needs by mouth
- No weight gain for 3 months
- Weight-to-height ratio at less than the 5th percentile
- Triceps skinfold measurement less than the 5th percentile
- Total feeding time greater than 4–6 hours per day
- Oral feeding deemed unsafe (Smith & Pederson, 1990, p. 1)

Options for nonoral feeding include nasogastric (NG) tubes, orogastric (OG) tubes, duodenal tubes, gastrostomies, and jejunostomies (see Table 4.9).

When nonoral feeding is indicated, planning should begin when the tube is placed for maintenance of oral motor integrity, prevention of oral hypersensitivity, and the transition back to oral feeding. Families should be counseled regarding feeding tube care, how long the tube is anticipated to be in place, and techniques to continue oral stimulation.

NG and OG tube feeding can be effective for short-term use in acute situations. If enteral feeding

Table 4.8.   Drugs used to treat gastroesophageal reflux in infants

Drug	Action	Dosage	Major side effects	Interaction with other drugs
Antacids (Gaviscon, Maalox, Mylanta)	Neutralizes gastric acid	Younger than age 12 months: ¼ to ½ teaspoon four times daily Older than age 12 months: 1 teaspoon four times daily (after feedings and before sleep at night)	Alterations in serum electrolyte and calcium levels in individuals with renal or metabolic disease	
Bethanechol (Duvoid, Urabeth, Urecholine)	Increases lower esophageal sphincter pressure Enhances motility in distal esophagus Stimulates parasympathetic system	.1–.2 milligrams per kilogram per dose three to four times daily (30–60 minutes before feedings and at bedtime)	Flushing skin (rare) Sweating (rare) Exacerbation of bronchospasm (contraindicated in asthma) Heart block (especially in patients prone to bradycardia)	Severe hypotension possible when given with ganglionic blocks
Cimetidine (Tagamet)	Histamine-2 blocker	20–40 milligrams per kilogram per day, divided in three doses (20 milligrams per kilogram per day in infants younger than age 4 months)	Drowsiness Decreased white blood cell count (rare) Increased liver enzyme activity (rare)	Inhibits cytochrome P-450 oxidase and increases levels of drugs metabolized by that system

Cisapride (Propulsid)	Increases lower esophageal sphincter pressure
	
	Accelerates gastric emptying
		.2 milligrams per kilogram four times daily (15 minutes before feedings and before sleep at night)	CAUTION: Cardiac arrhythmias, contraindicated in children with structural heart disease
			Central nervous system effects including:
			  Headache
			  Abdominal pain
			  Diarrhea
			  Nausea
			  Rhinitis
				Contraindicated with miconazole, fluconazole, erythromycin, clarithromycin, and troleandomycin (medications that inhibit cytochrome P-450 3A4)

Metoclopramide (Reglan)	Increases lower esophageal sphincter pressure
	
	Enhances gastric emptying
		.1 milligram per kilogram three to four times daily (20–30 minutes before feedings and at bedtime)	Central nervous system effects including:
			  Drowsiness
			  Irritability
			  Dystonic reactions	

Omeprazole (Prilosec)	Inhibits gastric acid pump	.5–3.3 milligrams-per-kilogram dose once daily before a meal (usual dose is a 1-milligram-per-kilogram dose)	Headache Diarrhea Nausea and vomiting	Increases half-life of diazepam, pheny-toin, and warfarin May increase absorp-tion of itraconazole, ketoconazole, iron salts, and ampicillin esters
Ranitidine HCL (Zantac)	Histamine-2 antagonist	4.0–5.0 milligrams per kilogram every 24 hours divided into two or three doses	Headache Gastrointestinal disturbance Insomnia Sedation Hepatotoxicity	Levels of theophylline, warfarin, may be increased

Table 4.9.   Strengths and limitations of various feeding tubes

Type of feeding tube	Insertion/destination	Strengths	Limitations
Nasogastric (NG) tube	Nose/stomach	No surgical placement required Oral feeding possible with tube in place	Insertion and presence in nose or throat is uncomfortable and may be aversive May trigger vagally mediated bradycardia May be cosmetically unacceptable for long-term use
Orogastric (OG) tube	Mouth/stomach	No surgical placement	Same as NG, plus difficult to feed orally with tube in place
Duodenal tube	Nose/duodenum	No surgical placement Bypasses stomach, so decreases risk of gastroesophageal reflux (GER)	Same as NG, though softer, so may have fewer hypersensitive responses Must use continuous-drip feeding Difficult to place and maintain in correct position
Gastrostomy tube (standard, percutaneous, button)	Surgically placed in stomach	No aversive oral-facial stimuli Despite surgical placement, can be removed easily when no longer needed Sits beneath clothing, cosmetically acceptable	Requires surgical placement Site needs daily care, requires trip to medical facility if tube falls out Potential risk for increased GER after tube placed
Jejunostomy tube	Surgically placed in jejunum, usually in association with gastrostomy	Same as gastrostomy Bypasses stomach, so reduces risk of GER	Requires surgical placement Site needs daily care, requires trip to hospital if tube falls out Requires continuous-drip feedings

is needed for longer than 6 weeks to 3 months, surgical placement of a gastrostomy tube should be considered. Long-term use of an NG or OG tube can interfere with swallowing and oral feeding and may cause erosion of the nasal and oral mucosa.

Types of Gastrostomy Tubes   Use of a gastrostomy tube has been associated with consistent weight gain. The Stamm gastrostomy tube, which requires a laparotomy, is commonly used. A silicone gastrostomy "button" is often inserted 4–6 weeks after insertion of the Stamm gastrostomy, although some surgeons place the button initially. The button is flush with the skin and has a one-way valve. The Bard Button (Bard Interventional Products Division), Ross Flexiflo (Ross Laboratories), and MicKey (Medical Innovations Corporation/Ballard Medical Products) are three commonly used models. Specialized tubing for bolus and drip feeding is available for all three button models.

The percutaneous endoscopic gastrostomy (PEG) tube is also used, particularly with children who are poor surgery candidates. The PEG tube is passed percutaneously under endoscopic guidance. The PEG tube has internal and external crossbars that stabilize the tube perpendicularly in a fistula between the gastric mucosa and the abdominal wall. Controversy surrounds the choice between the PEG and standard gastrostomies because the PEG tube is much easier to place, although antireflux measures may later be required. Children who have PEGs and develop significant GER may need to be fed via a jejunal feeding tube to decrease the risk of aspiration and esophagitis, or they may require a Stamm gastrostomy and antireflux surgery (e.g., Nissen fundoplication). Children with Stamm gastrostomies and Nissen fundoplications who continue to reflux may also require jejunal feeding.

Management of Gastrostomy Tubes The gastrostomy buttons need to be changed when the one-way valve malfunctions, when the MicKey balloon deteriorates, or when the child has grown significantly and use of a larger-size gastrostomy device is indicated. If the gastrostomy has been removed accidentally, the child may need to be seen by the physician immediately for a replacement. The Bard and Ross Flexiflo buttons, which can be painful to replace, are usually replaced by the gastroenterologist or the surgeon. The Bard and Ross Flexiflo buttons often last from 6 months to 1 year. The MicKey, which is inflated with water, can be replaced with minimal discomfort by caregivers who have been trained. The MicKey button usually lasts 3–6 months. The longevity of the MicKey button may be decreased by certain medications. Many caregivers like the locking feature of the tubing into the MicKey button. The locking mechanism decreases the likelihood of accidental disconnections with night drip feedings.

Regular site care is important because of possible leaking of gastric contents, formation of granulation tissue, and infection. Caregivers should be trained to detect the signs of infection, to cleanse the gastrostomy site with a mild soap and water, to rotate the button daily, to use liquid antacids topically, and to use silver nitrate sticks or Kenalog .5% twice daily to treat granulation tissue as needed.

Gastrostomy Tube Feeding Gastrostomy tube feeding is given by bolus, continuous drip, or a combination of both. When the gastrostomy tube is placed to augment caloric intake and oral feeding is safe, the timing and type of gastrostomy feeds are planned to promote oral feeding (e.g., a tube feeding might be given in the evening so that the child is hungry at mealtimes). Formula for gastrostomy feeds should be brought to room temperature for 15–20 minutes. Bolus feedings should be given for a minimum of 20 minutes, longer if the child is experiencing discomfort. The child should be seated with his or her head elevated or lying on his or her right side. For continuous feeding, the formula should be flushed through the tubing and then connected to the pump to prevent air from entering the stomach. Five to ten milliliters of water should be flushed through the gastrostomy tube after feeding. The gastrostomy tubing should be rinsed well after each feeding and after each time medication is given. The tubing may also be cleaned with white vinegar and rinsed well with water. Carbonated beverages may help to unclog blocked tubes. Cleaned tubes and syringes may be stored in the refrigerator in a clean container.

Many children with gastrostomies receive some feedings and related gastrostomy care at school. It is important that school personnel be adequately informed of a child's medical history (e.g., type of gastrostomy, fundoplication, feeding plan, previous complications) and medical needs. The child who has adequate developmental and cognitive skills should be an integral part of the planning for gastrostomy care and a feeding program.

Gastrostomy Tube Problems Children often achieve rapid catch-up growth when a gastrostomy tube is used for feeding. Growth parameters and caloric intake should be monitored every 2–3 months to make adjustments for inadequate or excessive weight gain.

Feeding via gastrostomy increases the likelihood of GER because of the increased pressure from the feeding (DiPalma, 1991). Rates for GER with gastrostomies vary from 14% to 44% in children without neurologic impairments and from 15% to 65% in children with neurologic impairments because of increased supine positioning, increased abdominal compression secondary to scoliosis, spasticity of the abdominal muscles, or other causes (Sullivan, 1992). The presence and severity of GER prior to gastrostomy placement should be evaluated carefully, with consideration given to the need for antireflux surgery at the time the type of gastrostomy is chosen.

Reintroduction of Oral Feeding Postgastrostomy If oral feeding is safe, initiation of an oral feeding program should begin shortly after surgery. The longer the interval with no oral stimulation or oral feeding, the more likely the child will be averse to oral feeding. For children who have not been fed orally, a long-term program of reintroduction of foods orally may be necessary. This reintroduction is often accomplished slowly in an outpatient setting. There are also a few inpatient programs that focus on an intensive treatment program.

Usually, if 1 ounce is consumed orally at each feeding, a program of tapering gastrostomy feeds and increasing table foods can be started. If the child is on a nighttime drip, begin by decreasing drip feeding in the early morning hours so that the child is hungry during the day. A bolus gastrostomy schedule is also gradually introduced to simulate a typical meal pattern. Two methods frequently used to increase oral feedings are 1) to decrease the gastrostomy feedings by 25% while offering foods orally at meals and snacks *or* 2) to have a period of 2 days every 3 weeks when only Pedialyte or water is given by gastrostomy and table foods are consumed orally. The quantity of oral foods consumed increases with each Pedialyte or water trial.

The process of making the transition to oral feeding can be difficult for families because it is more time-consuming than gastrostomy feeding and progress is often slow. A feeding specialist can help the family plan the transition and can address behavior issues related to feeding. Training in cardiopulmonary resuscitation and the Heimlich maneuver is recommended for all caregivers of children with oral motor dysfunction.

Fundoplication and Other Surgery   The Nissen fundoplication, an antireflux procedure involving a gastric fundal wrap around the esophagus to tighten the lower esophageal sphincter, is one treatment used to manage severe GER that has not responded to more conservative treatment. Table 4.10 reviews the management recommendations for mild, moderate, and severe GER. The Nissen is often used in conjunction with the Stamm gastrostomy.

Indications for Fundoplication   Antireflux surgery is recommended for infants with apnea who require gastrostomy feeding, children with repaired esophageal atresia (who are susceptible to reflux because of abnormal esophageal motility), children with peptic strictures or Barrett's esophagus, and some children with neurologic abnormalities (Orenstein, 1992). The evaluation for a fundoplication should include a barium esophagram to define the anatomy and a gastric emptying study to determine the need for pyloroplasty. Families should be counseled regarding the advantages and potential complications of a fundoplication.

Complications of Fundoplication   Complications of fundoplication are frequent and are due to the effectiveness of the wrap (e.g., gas bloat, retching), the failure of the wrap (e.g., herniation through the fundus), abnormalities of gastric emptying, and surgical complications (e.g., intraperitoneal leakage through a gastrostomy, small-bowel adhesions) (Orenstein, 1992). The child's retching may be decreased with smaller, more frequent feeds; use of continuous drip feedings; or medical management. As the fundoplication loosens, the retching usually improves and often disappears 6 months to 1 year postoperatively. Gas-bloat syndrome, the trapping of air in the stomach, is an uncomfortable side effect that may be relieved by venting the gastrostomy after feeds and other times as needed. When the fundal wrap herniates or breaks down, this can be documented with a barium esophagram. If breakdown occurs, the fundoplication may need to be revised.

Table 4.10.   Summary of gastroesophageal reflux management

Mild
Positioning (prone or upright; avoid infant seats)
Thickened feedings
Small, frequent feedings
Avoid carbonated beverages

Moderate
Positioning (prone or upright; avoid infant seats)
Thickened feedings
Earlier introduction of solids
Small, frequent feedings
Medications (see Table 4.8)

Severe
Positioning (prone or upright; avoid infant seats)
Thickened feedings
Earlier introduction of solids
Small, frequent feedings
Medications (see Table 4.8)
Enteral feedings, if oral feeding is unsafe or weight gain is inadequate
Surgical treatment (fundoplication)

Delayed gastric emptying is more common in children with neurologic impairments. When diagnosed preoperatively (e.g., barium esophagram, technetium scan), a pyloroplasty often is performed in conjunction with the Stamm gastrostomy and the Nissen fundoplication. Delayed gastric emptying can also occur postoperatively and may be related to vagal trauma or edema at the time of the fundoplication. It usually responds well to the use of a motility agent (see Table 4.8), and it resolves with time. It is important to note that children with esophageal dysmotility and swallowing dysfunction who are at risk for aspiration during feeding may be protected from reflux of gastric contents with a fundoplication but may continue to aspirate because of problems with handling their oral secretions.

Behavior Management
The management of behavior problems associated with feeding is interrelated to the dietary, feeding, and medical management of feeding issues. Children with certain feeding behavior problems may respond to basic interventions, and others may require a complex program that is best managed by a feeding team that includes a psychologist or a behavioral specialist.

Feeding Behavior Guidelines   Following are feeding guidelines for children with feeding behavior problems:

- Feeding should remain a pleasant experience for both the caregiver and the child, and forced feeding and punitive approaches should be avoided.
- Positive reinforcement and encouragement of self-feeding when appropriate are recommended.
- Although the parent determines what is presented to the child to eat as well as the manner in which food is presented, the child is responsible for whether and how much he or she eats.
- In general, children do best when meals are presented in a structured manner. That is, a scheduled mealtime (e.g., three meals and two to three snacks per day) and a planned meal place with minimal distractions are more conducive to appropriate behaviors at meals and adequate quantities of food consumed.

- Allow 1 hour before meals without food and beverages (except water) to stimulate hunger.
- Offer solids before liquids to avoid excessive consumption of liquids.
- Recognize the child's cues of hunger, satiety, and food preferences.
- Children do best with regard to feeding when mealtime is a time for social interaction, ideally with the family. Mealtimes are also an opportunity to model good eating behavior.
- Other factors to consider when planning behavioral modifications are the environment, the parent–child interaction, the particular behavior to be modified, optimization of the child's developmental and cognitive abilities, and parent teaching.

REFERENCES

Alliet, P., Raes, M., Bruneel, E., et al. (1998). Omeprazole in infants with cimetidine-resistant peptic esophagitis. *Journal of Pediatrics, 132*(2), 352–354.

Borowitz, S.M., & Borowitz, K.C. (1997). Gastroesophageal reflux in babies: Impact on growth and development. *Infants and Young Children, 10*(2), 14–26.

Cloud, H. (1987). *Team approach to pediatric feeding problems.* Chicago: American Dietetic Association.

Cloud, H.H., & Bergman, J. (1991). Eating/feeding problems of children. *Nutrition Focus, 6*(6), 1.

Cucchiara, S., Minella, R., Campanozzi, A., et al. (1997). Effects of omeprazole on mechanisms of gastroesophageal reflux in childhood. *Digestive Diseases and Sciences, 42*(2), 293–299.

DiPalma, J. (1991). Gastroesophageal reflux in infants. *American Family Practice, 43*(3), 857–864.

Ekvall, S.W. (Ed.). (1993). *Pediatric nutrition in chronic diseases and developmental disorders: Prevention, assessment, and treatment.* New York: Oxford University Press.

Gerber Products Co. (1997). *Nutrient values of Gerber baby foods.* Fremont, MI: Author.

Hill, S.L., Evangelista, J.K., Pizzi, A.M., et al. (1998). Proarrhythmia associated with cisapride in children. *Pediatrics, 101*(6), 1053–1056.

Kelsey, K. (1993). Failure to thrive. In S.W. Ekvall (Ed.), *Pediatric nutrition in chronic diseases and developmental disorders: Prevention, assessment, and treatment* (pp. 183–188, 203–217). New York: Oxford University Press.

Khongphatthanayothin, A., Lane, J., Thomas, D., et al. (1998). Effects of cisapride on QT interval in children. *Journal of Pediatrics, 133*(1), 51–56.

Levine, M.D., Carey, W.B., & Crocker, A.C. (Eds.). (1999). *Developmental-behavioral pediatrics* (3rd ed.). San Diego: Harcourt, Brace & Co.

Orenstein, S. (1992), Controversies in pediatric gastroesophageal reflux. *Journal of Pediatric Gastroenterology and Nutrition, 14,* 338–348.

Peterson, K., Washington, J.S., & Rathbun, J. (1984). Team management of failure to thrive. *Journal of the American Dietetic Association, 84,* 810–815.

Ramsey, M., Gisel, E.G., & Boutry, M. (1993). Nonorganic failure to thrive. *Developmental Medicine and Child Neurology, 35,* 285–297.

Reyes, A., Cash, A.J., Green, S.H., & Booth, I.W. (1993). Gastroesophageal reflux in children with cerebral palsy. *Child: Care, Health, and Development, 19,* 109–118.

Rokusek, C., & Heinrichs, E. (Eds.). (1992). *Nutrition and feeding for persons with special needs: A practical guide and resource manual* (2nd ed.). Vermillion: South Dakota Department of Education.

Smith, B., & Pederson, A. (1990). Tube feeding update. *Nutrition Focus, 5*(5), 1–6.

Stevenson, R.D. (1992). Measurement of growth in children with developmental disabilities. *Developmental Medicine and Child Neurology, 38,* 855–860.

Sullivan, P. (1992). Gastrostomy and the disabled child. *Developmental Medicine and Child Neurology, 34,* 547–555.

Wolf, L.S., & Glass, R.P. (1992). *Feeding and swallowing disorders in infancy: Assessment and management.* San Antonio, TX: Therapy Skill Builders.

4

Appendix

24-Hour Recall of Dietary Intake

Name _____   Date of dietary record _____

Date of birth _____   Height _____ centimeters _____ inches

Vitamin supplement? Yes ☐   No ☐   Weight _____ kilograms _____ pounds

Brand _____

Amount given _____ Per day ☐ Per week ☐   Weight-to-height ratio _____

Time	Food	Amount	FOR OFFICE USE ONLY

Daily intake rating: Adequate ☐   Inadequate ☐

The Physician's Guide to Caring for Children with Disabilities and Chronic Conditions, edited by Robert E. Nickel and Larry W. Desch, copyright © 2000 Paul H. Brookes Publishing Co.

CALORIC CONTENT OF GERBER BABY FOODS

	First foods		Second foods		Third foods	
Iron-fortified cereals	Cals./½ oz.		Cals./½ oz.			
	Barley	60	Mixed	60		
	Oatmeal	60	Oatmeal w/banana	60		
	Rice	60	Rice w/apple	60		
			Rice w/banana	60		
			Rice w/mixed fruit	60		
Vitamin C–fortified 100% juices	Cals./4 fl. oz.		Cals./4 fl. oz.		Cals./4 fl. oz.	
	Apple	60	Apple-banana	60	Apple-carrot	60
	Orange	60	Apple-cherry	60	Apple-sweet potato	70
	Pear	60	Apple-cranberry	60		
	White grape	60	Apple-grape	60		
	Mixed fruit	60				
	Apple-prune	70				
	Tropical blend	70				
Vitamin C–fortified fruits	Cals./2½ oz.		Cals./4 oz.		Cals./6 oz.	
	Peaches	30	Apple blueberry	60	Applesauce	90
	Applesauce	40	Applesauce	60	Apricots w/mixed fruit	100
	Pears	40	Applesauce apricot	60	Fruit salad	100
	Bananas	70	Pear pineapple	60	Banana pineapple	120
	Prunes (no vitamin C added)	70	Apricots w/mixed fruit	70	Peaches	110
			Peaches	70	Pears	120
			Pears	80	Plums w/apples	120
			Plums w/apples	80	Apple banana	130
			Prunes w/apples	90	Bananas w/apples and pears	140
			Bananas w/apples and pears	100	Banana strawberry	160
			Bananas	100		
Vegetables	Cals./2½ oz.		Cals./4 oz.		Cals./6 oz.	
	Carrots	25	Carrots	35	Broccoli carrots w/cheese	70
	Green beans	25	Green beans	35	Carrots	70
	Squash	25	Squash	35	Green beans w/rice	70
	Peas	35	Garden vegetables	45	Squash	70
	Sweet potatoes	45	Creamed spinach	50	Peas w/rice	90
	Potatoes	55	Mixed vegetables	50	Sweet potatoes	110
			Peas	50		
			Creamed corn	70		
			Sweet potatoes	70		
Meats and gravy			Cals./2½ oz.			
			Ham and ham gravy	70		
			Lamb and lamb gravy	70		
			Turkey and turkey gravy	70		
			Beef and beef gravy	80		
			Chicken and chicken gravy	80		
			Veal and veal gravy	100		
Dinners			Cals./4 oz.			
			Vegetable turkey	50		
			Turkey rice	60		
			Macaroni cheese	70		

CALORIC CONTENT OF GERBER BABY FOODS *(continued)*

	First foods	Second foods	Cals./4 oz.	Third foods	Cals./6 oz.
Dinners *(continued)*					
		Macaroni tomato beef	70	Chicken noodle	90
		Vegetable beef	70	Vegetable turkey	90
		Vegetable chicken	70	Bean and	
		Vegetable ham	70	egg noodle	100
		Chicken noodle	80	Lasagna	
		Vegetable bacon	90	w/meat sauce	100
		Broccoli and chicken	45	Turkey, rice, and	
		Apples and chicken	70	garden	
		Carrots and beef	70	vegetables	100
		Apples and ham	80	Vegetable chicken	100
		Pears and chicken	80	Vegetable pasta	100
		Sweet potatoes and		Vegetable beef	110
		turkey	80	Vegetable ham	110
				Spaghetti and	
				tomato sauce	
				with beef	130
Desserts			Cals./4 oz.		Cals./6 oz.
		Banana apple	80	Blueberry buckle	120
		Banana yogurt	80	Dutch apple	140
		Cherry vanilla pudding	80	Fruit medley	120
		Dutch apple	90	Apple banana	130
		Fruit medley	90	Peach cobbler	130
		Mixed fruit yogurt	90	Hawaiian delight	150
		Peach cobbler	90	Vanilla custard	
		Hawaiian delight	100	pudding	150
		Vanilla custard pudding	110		

Adapted from Gerber Products Co. (1997).

The Physician's Guide to Caring for Children with Disabilities and Chronic Conditions, edited by Robert E. Nickel and Larry W. Desch, copyright © 2000 Paul H. Brookes Publishing Co.

RESOURCES ON NUTRITION AND GROWTH

Readings

Kedesdy, J.H., & Budd, K.S. (1998). *Childhood feeding disorders: Biobehavioral assessment and intervention.* Baltimore: Paul H. Brookes Publishing Co. (1-800-638-3775)

Kessler, D.B., & Dawson, P. (Eds.). (1999). *Failure to thrive and pediatric undernutrition: A transdisciplinary approach.* Baltimore: Paul H. Brookes Publishing Co. (1-800-638-3775)

Macht, J. (1990). *Poor eaters: Helping children who refuse to eat.* New York: Plenum Publishing Corp. (781-871-6600)

Satter, E. (1987). *How to get your kid to eat . . . but not too much.* Palo Alto, CA: Bull Publishing Co. (1-800-676-2855)

Wolf, L.S., & Glass, R.P. (1992). *Feeding and swallowing disorders in infancy: Assessment and management.* San Antonio, TX: Therapy Skill Builders. (1-800-211-8378)

Discussion Groups

ChallengeNet
World Wide Web site: http://www.challengenet.com/

Information and support for parents of children with gastrostomy tubes and other types of tubes.

Pediatric/Adolescent Gastroesophageal Reflux Association (PAGER)
Post Office Box 1153
Germantown, Maryland 20875-1153
E-mail: gergroup@aol.com
World Wide Web site: http://www.reflux.org/

Nonprofit organization that provides information and support to families, teens, and professionals.

Children's Motility Disorder Foundation (CMDE)
Peachtree Center, South Tower
225 Peachtree Street, Suite 430
Atlanta, Georgia 30303
Telephone: (800) 809-9492, (404) 529-9200
Fax: (404) 529-9202
E-mail: emdf@motility.org
World Wide Web site: http://www.motility.org/index.htm

Organization dedicated to research and education related to gastrointestinal motility disorders including gastroesophageal reflux (GER) disease.

5

Developmental Delay and Mental Retardation

Robert E. Nickel

KEY COMPETENCIES

- Become familiar with the administration and interpretation of at least one parent report measure, one general office screen, and targeted screens for language and autism
- Evaluate a child with suspected developmental delay or mental retardation for the identification of minor physical anomalies
- List the eligibility requirements for early intervention and early childhood special education (EI/ECSE) services, and describe procedures for development of the individualized family service plan (IFSP)
- Describe the functional analysis of behavior, and review the medical component of the treatment of problem behaviors in children and adolescents with mental retardation
- Counsel families regarding alternative or controversial therapies
- Discuss the treatment options for menstrual care and contraception for women with mental retardation

DESCRIPTION

Definitions of Developmental Delay and Mental Retardation

Developmental delay is a descriptive term used to describe the skills of infants and young children. It refers to a general delay in skills across all or nearly all developmental domains (e.g., communication, motor, cognitive, adaptive, social, and emotional). Use of the term *developmental delay* prevents unjustified diagnostic conclusions and inappropriate predictions of future function because a single developmental assessment in early childhood may be poorly predictive of later function. Although it is possible to complete standardized intellectual assessments of children by the time they reach 3–4 years of age, accurate predictions of future intellectual function require repeated assessments and following the child's rate of developmental progress.

The American Association on Mental Retardation (AAMR) published (Luckasson, Coulter, Polloway, et al., 1992) an updated definition of *mental retardation* that is based on both intellectual and adaptive functioning as well as age of onset. The definition follows a three-step process in defining diagnosis, classification, and systems of support in four dimensions:

Step 1. Diagnosis of Mental Retardation (Dimension I: Intellectual Functioning and Adaptive Skills)

- The individual's intellectual functioning is approximately 70–75 (IQ score) or below.

- There are significant disabilities in two or more adaptive skill areas (e.g., communication, self-care, social skills).
- Age of onset is younger than 18 years.

Step 2. Classification and Description

- Describe the individual's strengths and weaknesses in reference to psychological/emotional considerations (Dimension II).
- Describe the individual's overall physical health and indicate the condition's etiology (Dimension III).
- Describe the individual's current environmental placement and the optimal environment that would facilitate his or her continued growth and development (Dimension IV).

Step 3. Profile and Intensities of Needed Supports

- Identify the kind and intensities of supports needed for each of the four dimensions.

This new definition broadens the concept of mental retardation and avoids sole reliance on the IQ score in determining the level of disability.

Classification of Mental Retardation

Mental retardation traditionally has been classified as mild, moderate, severe, or profound based on IQ score as follows:

1. Mild (educable mental retardation)
   (a) IQ score in the 55–70 range
   (b) 85% of individuals with mental retardation
2. Moderate (trainable mental retardation)
   (a) IQ score in 40–55 range
   (b) 10% of individuals with mental retardation
3. Severe
   (a) IQ score in 25–40 range
   (b) 3%–4% of individuals with mental retardation
4. Profound
   (a) IQ score of less than 25
   (b) 1%–2% of individuals with mental retardation (American Psychiatric Association, 1994, pp. 40, 41)

The descriptors *mild, moderate, severe,* and *profound* are not used in the AAMR definition in describing an individual's level of mental retardation. Instead, an individual's mental retardation is described with regard to the level of support he or she needs in activities of daily living (see Table 5.1). These descriptors are more functional and more directly related to the individual's need for services than the terms used previously.

Prevalence of Mental Retardation

The prevalence of mental retardation in childhood is generally agreed to be approximately 2%–3% in

Table 5.1. Examples of mental retardation intensities and supports

Intermittent: Supports are required on an "as-needed" basis. Person does not always need the support(s), or short-term supports are needed during life-span transitions (e.g., job loss, acute medical crisis).

Limited: Supports are time-limited but not of an intermittent nature and may require fewer staff members and less cost than more intense levels of support (e.g., time-limited employment training).

Extensive: Supports are characterized by regular involvement (e.g., daily) in at least some environments (e.g., work, home) that are not time-limited (e.g., long-term support).

Pervasive: Supports are characterized by consistent, high intensity and are required in all environments and are potentially life-sustaining in nature.

Adapted from Luckasson, Coulter, Polloway, et al. (1992).

the United States (McLaren & Bryson, 1987). About 85% of individuals affected have mild mental retardation (require intermittent supports and have mild adaptive disabilities) (Batshaw, 1993). Epidemiologic studies (Boyle, Yeargin-Allsopp, Doernberg, et al., 1991) reported a prevalence of mild mental retardation of 3.7–8.2 per 1,000 (well below the rate of 2 per 100 that McLaren and Bryson found) and a prevalence of .8–1.6 per 1,000 for severe mental retardation (requiring extensive supports). The reported prevalence for mild mental retardation may be low because of problems of ascertainment or concerns about labeling a child unnecessarily.

Etiology of Mental Retardation

Mental retardation can result from prenatal, perinatal, and postnatal factors. *Prenatal factors* include genetic disorders, birth defect syndromes, teratogens, chromosomal anomalies, isolated congenital central nervous system impairments, congenital infections, and intrauterine growth retardation. Genetic causes include disorders with autosomal dominant (e.g., tuberous sclerosis), autosomal recessive (e.g., phenylketonuria), and X-linked patterns of inheritance (e.g., Aicardi syndrome). Many newly described genetic mechanisms have been associated with mental retardation syndromes, including mitochondrial inheritance (e.g., amaurosis congenita of Leber), uniparental disomy (or both genes from the same parent) (e.g., maternal disomy with Prader-Willi syndrome), gene expansion disorders (e.g., fragile X syndrome), and microdeletion syndromes (e.g., velocardiofacial [VCF] syndrome).

Perinatal events that may lead to mental retardation include intraventricular hemorrhage with or without hydrocephalus, periventricular leukomala-

cia, perinatal asphyxia, and group B streptococcal meningitis. *Postnatal factors* include similar mechanisms of acute brain injury as well as environmental factors such as environmental neglect or deprivation and physical abuse (e.g., shaken baby syndrome). The effects of environmental neglect on development are usually subtle and additive to other factors.

Some children have a progressive or degenerative neurologic disorder. They usually show a period of apparently typical development followed by the onset of developmental regression and/or medical problems such as seizures (e.g., Rett syndrome, Cockayne syndrome). Please note, however, that in as many as 30%–40% of children, the specific cause of mental retardation cannot be established even after a comprehensive evaluation.

DIAGNOSIS AND EVALUATION

Procedures to Establish a Clinical Diagnosis of Mental Retardation

The pattern of development of children with mental retardation is dependent on the degree of their retardation. In general, the more severe the retardation, the earlier the onset and the more striking and generalized the individual's delays in development. Children with mild mental retardation (requiring intermittent support) often have language delays and demonstrate typical or near-typical gross motor and fine motor development. They may not receive a diagnosis of mental retardation until they reach 4–5 years of age, when they present with problems in preschool or their parents become more concerned about their slow progress in language development.

Children with moderate mental retardation (requiring limited support) show more generalized problems with development. They manifest significant delays in language abilities as well as gross motor and fine motor skills and self-help skills. They may have associated hyperactivity and a short attention span and can be identified as having mental retardation by 1–2 years of age.

In contrast to children with mild and moderate mental retardation, children with severe or profound mental retardation (requiring extensive or pervasive support) are likely to be diagnosed in the first months of life. Some may demonstrate hypotonia and feeding difficulties in the nursery. Others have an apparently normal neuromotor examination at nursery discharge but then show delayed development of visual interest in their environment and little or no early social engagement. These children frequently have associated birth defects and medical problems such as seizures.

Difficulties with the Early Diagnosis of Mental Retardation   Physicians often rely on motor milestones as an index of the rate of overall developmental progress. Yet children with mild mental retardation (requiring limited supports), who represent about 85% of all children with mental retardation, typically achieve motor milestones at expected ages in their first several years of life. Delay in language skills is a more reliable indicator of possible developmental problems (Shapiro, Palmer, & Capute, 1987).

Use of Developmental Screening Tests as Part of Developmental Surveillance   Before reading further in this section, please review the discussion in Chapter 2. Primary health care professionals should be familiar with administration and interpretation of a parent report screen, a general office screen, and targeted screens for language and autism. A parent-completed measure such as the *Ages & Stages Questionnaires: A Parent-Completed, Child-Monitoring System, Second Edition* (Bricker & Squires, 1999), is a recommended basic screen for all children in the primary care office.

The Battelle Developmental Inventory (BDI) Screening Test (Newborg, Stock, & Wnek, 1984) is a recommended general office screen. The Early Language Milestone Scale (Coplan, 1993) is a recommended targeted screen for the identification of toddlers and preschool-age children who have language disorders. A targeted screen for language helps to differentiate children with language delays from children with more global developmental problems. (Use of a targeted screen for autism is discussed in Chapter 8.) Consider use of an autism screen for children with atypical behaviors and children with delays in the language and social-emotional domains of a general screen.

Comprehensive Evaluation of a Child Suspected of Having Mental Retardation or Developmental Delays   Children who are highly suspected of having developmental delays on a clinical basis or who are experiencing delays in two or more skill areas on a screening test should be referred for comprehensive evaluation. The purposes of this evaluation are

- To confirm the presence of developmental delays
- To plan for early intervention (EI) and early childhood special education (ECSE) services
- To establish the cause of the child's developmental delays or mental retardation if possible
- To evaluate and treat associated medical problems

Referrals can be made directly for eligibility testing for EI/ECSE services to the contact person or agency in your locality. A multidisciplinary team evaluates the child to determine eligibility for education services. This is best done after a medical evaluation to determine an etiologic diagnosis.

Children who have complicated behavior problems, are suspected of having autism spectrum disorder (ASD), or have associated medical problems should be referred to an experienced child development team headed by a developmental pediatrician. In addition, referral to a developmental pediatrician or medical geneticist may be necessary to establish an etiologic diagnosis for those children referred directly for EI/ECSE eligibility testing.

The primary health care professional should have a good understanding of the types of comprehensive developmental evaluations that are appropriate at different ages.

General Developmental Evaluations for Use from Early Infancy to 3 Years of Age   The Revised Gesell Developmental Schedules (Knobloch, Stevens, & Malone, 1980) and the Bayley Scales of Infant Development: Birth to Two Years (Bayley, 1969) are two tests that commonly are used to evaluate children from early infancy to 3 years of age. The Revised Gesell Developmental Schedules have been restandardized for use with children from 4 weeks to 36 months of age. Test items are organized into five skill domains: adaptive (precursor of cognitive functioning for this test), gross motor, fine motor, communication, and personal-social. The percentage delay or a standard deviation score can be generated in each skill area. The Bayley Scales of Infant Development are useful through age 2.5 years and comprise mental, motor, and behavioral scales. The *Bayley Scales of Infant Development, Second Edition* (Bayley, 1993), include a wider age range (ages 2–42 months) and contain more test items than the 1969 version; however, the test administration time required by the 1993 version of the Bayley Scales is longer than the 1969 version.

Cognitive Assessments (3 Years of Age and Older)   The *Stanford-Binet Intelligence Scale, Fourth Edition* (Thorndike, Hagen, & Sattler, 1986), the Wechsler Preschool and Primary Scale of Intelligence–Revised (WPPSI–R; Wechsler, 1989), and the Wechsler Intelligence Scale for Children–Third Edition (WISC–III; Wechsler, 1991) are representative evaluations of intellectual skills or IQ score. The Stanford-Binet and the WPPSI–R are for use with older preschool-age children, and the WISC–III is for use with school-age children. The Stanford-Binet is for use with children older than 2 years of age. It is arranged into 15 tests in 4 categories, including verbal reasoning, quantitative reasoning, abstract visual reasoning, and short-term memory. The WPPSI–R is for use with children between the ages of 3 years and 7 years, 3 months. It has 11 subtests arranged into verbal and performance scales. Verbal, performance, and full-scale IQ scores are generated. The WISC–III is for use with children ages 6 years through 16 years, 11 months. It has 10 subtests and 3 supplemental subtests that are arranged into verbal and performance scales.

Children who have hearing impairments or who are experiencing significant delays in language skills development should be assessed with evaluations that do not depend on verbal instructions and contain few language items. The Hiskey-Nebraska Test of Learning Aptitude (Hiskey, 1966), which was developed specifically for use with deaf children, and the Leiter International Performance Scale–Revised (Roid & Miller, 1997) are two such assessments.

Evaluation of Adaptive Functioning Although a systematic assessment of intellectual skills is essential to the diagnosis of mental retardation, adaptive behavior also must be evaluated. The Vineland Adaptive Behavior Scales (Sparrow, Balla, & Cicchetti, 1984) and the Developmental Profile II (Alpern, Boll, & Shearer, 1980) are two such evaluations. The test items for the Vineland Adaptive Behavior Scales are arranged into four scales: motor, communication, daily living skills, and socialization. The age range is from younger than 1 year of age to 18 years of age and older. The Developmental Profile II is arranged into five scales: physical, self-help, social, academic, and communication. It is used with children within an age range from the first 6 months of life to 9 years of age. Both tests are completed by interviewing the child's parent(s). Other assessments are the Woodcock-Johnson Scales of Independent Behavior (Bruininks, Woodcock, Weatherman, & Hill, 1984), and the AAMR Adaptive Behavior Scale, Second Edition (Lambert, Nihira, & Leland, 1993).

Hearing and Vision Testing Every child who is suspected of experiencing developmental delays should receive formal audiologic testing with visually reinforced audiometry (VRA) as part of the comprehensive evaluation of developmental skills. If VRA cannot be completed because of the child's inability to follow test procedures, auditory brainstem-evoked potential (BAER or ABR) testing should be obtained. In addition, visual acuity screening should be conducted with all children who can cooperate with the usual test procedures (developmental age 3 years and older). A functional assessment of vision

should be performed during infancy by eliciting visual tracking of toys and observing for visual fixation, following, and the quality and persistence of the infant's visual interest (First & Palfrey, 1994). Formal evaluation by the ophthalmologist should be scheduled when there is concern about visual problems such as strabismus and as appropriate to assist with etiologic diagnosis. Chapter 9 provides further details about hearing and vision assessments.

Other Evaluations The assessment team at the child development center includes a developmental pediatrician, a psychologist, a speech-language pathologist, a special educator, an occupational therapist, a medical social worker, and a physical therapist. Some children require evaluation by service providers from only two disciplines (e.g., developmental pediatrics, psychology), whereas others require evaluations by professionals from additional disciplines. Children who are suspected of experiencing developmental delays or of having mental retardation often require evaluation of speech-language skills by a speech-language specialist and fine motor and visual perceptual skills by an occupational therapist. These evaluations are necessary to help identify associated problems and to clarify strengths and weaknesses in these skill areas to assist with treatment planning. For example, some children have associated motor planning problems or dyspraxia. In addition, a semistructured observation of play should be part of the comprehensive assessment of preschool-age children suspected of having autism. The evaluation of children with autism is discussed in Chapter 8.

Etiologic Evaluation

An accurate diagnosis of the cause of the developmental disorder:

- Identifies progressive or degenerative disorders (e.g., Rett syndrome, Cockayne syndrome)
- Identifies potentially treatable diseases (e.g., phenylketonuria, hypothyroidism)
- Provides information about the natural history of the child's disorder and associated medical problems (e.g., holoprosencephaly and limited survival to 1 year of age)
- May provide important genetic information (e.g., fragile X syndrome)

Laboratory Evaluation The laboratory evaluation of children with developmental delays may include the usual screening tests, such as the complete blood count and blood electrolytes; liver function tests; tests for thyroid function, lead level (especially if there is a history of pica), and creatine phosphokinase (e.g., to screen for Duchenne muscular dystrophy in boys with developmental delays and hypotonia); chromosomal and DNA (deoxyribonucleic acid) studies; urine and blood metabolic studies (e.g., urine amino acids, mucopolysaccharides); an electroencephalogram (EEG); and computed tomography (CT) or magnetic resonance imaging (MRI) brain scans. The following are the recommendations from a consensus conference of the American College of Medical Genetics for medical laboratory testing:

- Obtain blood chromosomal analysis (500-band level) on all individuals with unexplained developmental delay or mental retardation.
- Consider fragile X DNA testing in all individuals with unexplained developmental delay or mental retardation.
- Obtain metabolic testing *only* in the presence of suggestive clinical or physical findings.
- Obtain a cranial MRI brain scan (the imaging study of choice) for children without a known diagnosis, especially if the child has neurologic symptoms, abnormal head shape, microcephaly, or macrocephaly.
- Practice a stepwise approach to the diagnostic evaluation; a sequential evaluation, at times over the course of several years, may be necessary to determine the child's diagnosis. (Curry, Stevenson, Aughton, et al., 1997, p. 475)

In as many as 40% of children with mental retardation, no cause of mental retardation is found, even after a complete diagnostic evaluation. These children may have received all appropriate tests, including a CT or MRI brain scan; blood chromosomal analysis; and DNA studies, urine tests for metabolic studies, an ophthalmologic examination, X rays, and additional blood work. Yet other children may have a specific diagnosis established by a single test such as blood chromosomal analysis for a child with multiple birth defects suggestive of trisomy 13. The content of the workup should be based on each child's specific presentation. Clues from the *medical, developmental and behavioral*, and *family histories* as well as the *physical examination* assist in identifying the appropriate first tests.

Medical History   Take a complete pregnancy, perinatal, and postnatal medical history from the child's mother. The issues to address in the prenatal and perinatal history include

- Onset and quality of fetal motion
- Substance or alcohol use during the pregnancy
- Use of known teratogens (Dilantin, valproic acid)
- Breech presentation
- Presence of oligo- or polyhydramnios
- Labor or delivery complications
- Neonatal seizures
- Child's feeding behavior in the nursery

- Neurologic abnormalities in the nursery (e.g., persisting hypotonia, lethargy)

A definite history of inadequate fetal motion strongly suggests an early prenatal onset of a child's developmental delays. A mother's prenatal alcohol abuse should prompt a careful examination of her child for fetal alcohol syndrome. Many parents report minor labor and delivery problems; however, perinatal problems (e.g., perinatal asphyxia) are inadequate explanations for developmental delay or mental retardation unless there is a clear history of persistent hypotonia, neonatal seizures, or an abnormal neuromotor examination in the nursery.

Children with a history of episodic illness with vomiting and lethargy should be expeditiously evaluated for a metabolic disorder with appropriate urine, blood, and tissue studies. Children with a history of hearing loss, seizures, and developmental delay should be evaluated for peroxisomal disorders with blood tests for pipecolic, phytanic, and very long-chain fatty acids. The findings suggestive of a metabolic disorder in children with developmental delay include

- Episodic illness with vomiting and lethargy
- Failure to thrive
- Seizures (look first for a congenital defect of the brain)
- Hypotonia (particularly if combined with other findings on this list)
- Ataxia
- Hepatomegaly and hepatic dysfunction
- Cardiomyopathy
- Neurologic deterioration

Developmental and Behavioral History   Review the age of acquisition of major early motor and language milestones. As noted previously, delays in language milestones are a more reliable indicator of overall developmental problems than are delays in motor skills. Inquire about the child's social behaviors as well as a history of perseverative play and other atypical behaviors (see Chapter 8). In addition, ask the child's parents the following questions:

- When did you first become concerned about your child's development?
- Did your child experience a period of typical development?
- Has your child lost previously acquired skills?

Many disorders associated with mental retardation have a characteristic pattern of development. Girls with Rett syndrome usually present with a period of typical development followed by global regression of skills, including the loss of purposeful fine motor skills and the development of characteristic hand-wringing movements. Certain disorders are associated with a specific behavioral phenotype (e.g., extreme shyness, poor eye contact, and hyperactivity in boys with fragile X syndrome).

Family History A complete family history (going back at least three generations) should be taken from the parents of children being evaluated for developmental delays. Inquire about similar problems in parents (possible autosomal dominant disorder), siblings, and extended family members. Does the child physically resemble other family members? Are the child's parents related by blood (risk for autosomal recessive disorder)? Does the child's mother have a history of recurrent miscarriages or infertility (risk for parental balanced chromosome rearrangement)? Is there a family history of deaths in early infancy? Are there any individuals in the family with known genetic disorders or birth defects, developmental delays or mental retardation, seizure disorders or other neurologic problems, childhood-onset hearing loss, delayed speech or walking, school problems, attention-deficit/hyperactivity disorder (ADHD), or behavior or mental health disorders?

Children with fragile X syndrome often have a family history suggestive of an X-linked pattern of inheritance. The child's mother may have mild learning problems or mental retardation, and the child may have one or more maternal uncles with mental retardation. When a family history suggests X-linked inheritance for a girl or a boy with developmental delays, DNA testing for fragile X should be conducted.

Physical Examination

Growth The presence of intrauterine growth retardation likely documents a prenatal onset to that child's developmental problems. If it is associated with one or more major birth defects or multiple minor anomalies, blood chromosomal analysis and genetic consultation should be obtained. If the child has a postnatal onset of growth delays, the child's developmental problems may represent an acquired problem such as a metabolic or endocrine disorder (e.g., hypothyroidism) or a degenerative disorder (e.g., Rett syndrome, Cockayne syndrome).

Microcephaly and Macrocephaly Most children who are suspected of having mental retardation and have either microcephaly or macrocephaly should have a CT or MRI brain scan. The MRI is preferred to the CT in the workup of children with developmental delays because it is more sensitive to the detection of neuronal migration problems and other congenital defects of the central nervous system. The CT scan should be used if congenital cytomegalovirus (CMV) infection is suspected, because the CT scan is more sensitive than the MRI scan to the detection of intracranial calcifications.

Multiple Minor Anomalies The presence of a number (three or more) of minor physical anomalies strongly supports an early prenatal onset to that child's problems. Every primary care health professional should become comfortable with conducting a surface examination to identify minor anomalies such as single palmar creases, clinodactyly, hypertelorism, and midfacial hypoplasia (see, e.g., the representative examination in the Appendix at the end of this chapter).

Measurements should be taken whenever possible to confirm the clinical impression (e.g., inner canthal width for hypo- or hypertelorism) and should be compared with normative tables (see, e.g., Jones, 1997; see also Marden, Smith, & McDonald, 1964). Children with developmental delays and multiple minor anomalies should receive a blood chromosomal analysis and an evaluation by the medical geneticist.

Chromosomal Analysis and DNA Testing Most cytogenetics laboratories offer regular (metaphase) chromosomal analysis, high-resolution (prometaphase) analysis, fluorescent in situ hybridization (FISH), and a variety of special studies (e.g., uniparental disomy studies). In general, the indications for chromosomal analysis are

- Two or more major malformations
- Combination of major and minor anomalies
- Developmental delays and multiple minor anomalies (three or more)
- Developmental delays and short stature or failure to thrive
- Developmental delays and marked hypotonia (e.g., high-resolution chromosomal analysis and FISH or methylation study for Prader-Willi syndrome)
- Conotruncal congenital heart defect (e.g., high-resolution and FISH studies for chromosome 22q11 deletion)
- Ambiguous genitalia
- Mother with recurrent early pregnancy losses (three or more)

In addition, consider chromosomal analysis for all children with unexplained developmental delays or mental retardation.

The primary care physician initially should order a regular chromosome study for the child with developmental delays and multiple minor anomalies. The diagnosis of a microdeletion syndrome

Table 5.2.   DNA/RNA-based disease testing

The following are some of the disorders for which studies are available:

Trinucleotide repeat diseases
    Fragile X syndrome
    Huntington disease
    Kennedy disease
    Myotonic dystrophy
    Spinocerebellar ataxia type I

Duchenne/Becker muscular dystrophy (DMD/BMD)

Mitochondrial studies
    Syndrome of mitochondrial myopathy, encephalopathy, lactic acidosis, and strokelike episodes (MELAS)
    Syndrome of myoclonic epilepsy with ragged red fibers (MERRF)
    Southern analysis for deletion/duplication

Tay Sachs disease

Methylation studies
    Prader-Willi syndrome
    Angelman syndrome

such as Miller-Dieker syndrome (also called *lissencephaly syndrome*; cause is a visible deletion on chromosome #17) or VCF syndrome (associated with a deletion in the long arm of chromosome #22) requires a prometaphase study with FISH testing if the prometaphase study is normal. In most instances, these studies are best ordered by the developmental pediatrician or by the medical geneticist. It is important to diagnose microdeletion syndromes promptly because they can be inherited in families as apparent autosomal dominant traits with variable features. A parent of a child with VCF syndrome may have the deletion but manifest few of the clinical problems.

Finally, order DNA molecular testing from the DNA laboratory as the initial study if a disorder is suspected for which such definitive testing is available (e.g., fragile X syndrome) (see Table 5.2). Fragile X DNA testing should be considered strongly in all boys and girls with developmental delays when the etiology has not been established (Curry et al., 1997).

Genetic Consultation   Consider referring the child to the medical geneticist for the indications discussed in the previous section and in the following circumstances:

- Several family members are affected.
- The child has an episodic illness with vomiting and lethargy (also consider referral to the metabolic specialist).
- The child has a degenerative or progressive illness (also consider referral to the metabolic specialist).

- The child has ataxia (as many as 50% of children with ataxia and mental retardation have a genetic disorder).

The medical geneticist can help establish an etiologic diagnosis and provide critical information to families and physicians once the diagnosis is established. This information includes the natural history and treatment of the disorder, associated problems, and the availability of prenatal diagnosis. At times, other family members need to be tested (e.g., the parents of children with chromosomal syndromes that involve a translocation). One of the parents could be a translocation carrier, and thus the couple would have a much higher risk for recurrence. Consultation with the developmental pediatrician and genetic counselor instead of with the geneticist is appropriate for children with common chromosomal disorders.

Associated Medical and Behavior Problems
Children with developmental delays or mental retardation have a high incidence of associated problems. These problems include seizures, cerebral palsy, hearing and visual impairments, ASD, speech-language disorders, and behavior and mental health problems. Mental health problems include affective disorders (e.g., depression, mania), psychosis, ADHD, aggression, obsessive-compulsive disorder, stereotypies, and self-injurious behaviors (SIBs). In one study (Myers & Pueschel, 1991), the incidence of psychiatric disorders in 497 individuals with Down syndrome was 22.1%. Among individuals with mental retardation, 15%–20% experience seizures (Batshaw, 1993), and as many as 30% have problem behaviors or a mental health disorder (Lovell & Reiss, 1993).

The diagnostic evaluations for most of the associated problems are discussed in other chapters that cover these subjects specifically. The diagnostic evaluation for children with mental retardation and ADHD is similar to that for children without mental retardation and includes the use of parent and teacher behavioral questionnaires. Please note, however, that expectations for the child's attention span should be based on his or her developmental age rather than on his or her chronological age. The diagnosis of ADHD in children with severe or profound mental retardation (requiring extensive or pervasive support) is not appropriate.

The prevalence of affective disorders in individuals with mental retardation is 5%–15% (Lovell & Reiss, 1993). Assessment of affective symptoms in children with developmental disorders can be challenging, however. In general, the symptoms of depression in individuals with mild or moderate mental retardation (requiring intermittent or limited support) reflect standard diagnostic criteria (Marston, Perry, & Roy, 1997). Individuals with moderate and severe mental retardation (requiring intermittent and extensive support) show behavioral depressive equivalents such as increased irritability, aggression, tantrums, and SIBs; changes in social behavior (e.g., increased withdrawal); and changes in sleep patterns (Lovell & Reiss, 1993).

Family Strengths and Support Needs

Parents, siblings, grandparents, and other family members are the main source of support for individuals with disabilities. The great majority of individuals live in their family homes into adulthood. A broad array of community services support families in caring for children and adolescents with disabilities and chronic conditions. A careful assessment of the family and its social support network is a critical part of the diagnostic evaluation (please review Chapter 3).

Two types of formal assessment may be useful when used as part of an open-ended interview: a structured questionnaire on family needs (e.g., the Family Needs Survey; Bailey & Blasco, 1990; Bailey & Simeonsson, 1988a, 1988b) and a questionnaire on the impact of the child with disabilities and chronic conditions on the family (e.g., the Parenting Stress Index–Short Form; Abidin, 1995). The Family Needs Survey includes questions about the family's needs for

- Information
- Support
- Explaining the child's disability to others
- Community services
- Family functioning

Counseling Parents About the Diagnosis

Review the general recommendations for counseling parents about the diagnosis of a developmental disability in Chapters 1 and 3. *Developmental delay* is a provisional diagnosis. A diagnosis of mental retardation generally is not made until the child reaches 4–5 years of age, except for children with severe or profound developmental delays. Specific prognostic information can be provided if the etiology of the developmental delay has been established. Unfortunately, in as many as 40% of children, the cause of the developmental delay is unknown. Counseling in these situations is particularly challenging because the future is largely unknown. The health care professional should be cautious about providing any specific prognostic information for

preschool-age children, except for children who are clearly demonstrating severe or profound delay.

MANAGEMENT

Periodic Review and Update of the Management Plan

Once the etiologic diagnosis is established, most children with developmental delay or mental retardation can be managed by the primary care office in collaboration with educational and other community service providers. Reevaluate the child and the child's family, and update the management plan at least yearly (more frequently in the first year following the diagnosis and for young children). In general, the goals of the follow-up evaluation are to review the family's concerns; determine the child's rate of developmental or behavioral progress; review associated medical and behavior problems; and determine the need for additional services, including the need for referral to specialists or to a specialty team. It is also important to review information from educational service providers as well as families regularly (see Chapter 7 for discussion of the use of behavioral questionnaires).

Some children with developmental delay (e.g., children who experience difficult-to-control seizures) require ongoing management by a specialist (e.g., a pediatric neurologist). Other children need follow-up by the child development team. Consider referral for reevaluation by the child development team of children who

- Do not have an established etiologic diagnosis
- Have multiple and complicated associated medical problems
- Display difficult-to-manage behaviors
- Show regression in developmental skills
- Do not show expected progress after receiving services

Educational Services

Early Intervention and Early Childhood Special Education Services The principal treatment programs for children and adolescents with developmental delay or mental retardation are educational and behavioral in focus. Eligibility criteria for EI/ECSE services in the United States vary somewhat from state to state. For example, some states provide services for infants and toddlers who are at risk for developmental delays, but many other states do not. The following are representative criteria that a child from birth through 2 years of age must meet in order to receive EI services:

- The child has a diagnosed physical or mental condition that has a high probability of resulting in developmental delays as documented by a physician *or*
- The child experiences a developmental delay of 2 *SD* or more below the mean in *one or more* of the following developmental areas or 1.5 *SD* below the mean in *two or more* of the following developmental areas:
  a. Cognitive development
  b. Physical development
  c. Communication development
  d. Social or emotional development
  e. Adaptive development *and*
- The child's multidisciplinary team must determine that the child needs EI services as a result of the child's developmental delay

Similarly, from age 3 years through kindergarten, a child must meet the following criteria to receive ECSE services:

- The child meets the criteria for one of the disability categories for school-age children *or*
- The child experiences a developmental delay of 1.5 *SD* or more below the mean in *two or more* of the developmental areas listed for EI services *and*
- The multidisciplinary team must determine that the child needs special education services as a result of the disability

Individualized Family Service Plan   The individualized family service plan (IFSP) outlines the EI services that will be provided to the child and the family as determined by the multidisciplinary team, which includes the parents. Other community services, such as health care agencies, can also be part of the IFSP. The IFSP contains eight essential elements:

1. A statement of the child's current level of development
2. A statement of the family's resources and priorities (with the agreement of the family)
3. A statement of the major outcomes expected (major goals, procedures, and timelines)
4. A statement of the specific EI services to be provided
5. The projected dates for initiation of services and the duration of services
6. The name of the care coordinator
7. Steps to be taken to support the transition of the child to preschool (i.e., ECSE) services
8. Other needed health care and community services that are not required as part of EI

Children with disabilities and chronic conditions increasingly are receiving educational services at all levels. Physicians or nurses should participate in or contribute information to the IFSP conference. If the physician or nurse is unable to contribute directly to the IFSP conference, then he or she should review the plan with the parents to determine whether the health-related services are appropriate and contact educational staff as needed (American Academy of Pediatrics, [AAP], Committee on Children with Disabilities, 1992).

In general, EI services are provided in the home; for some children, they are also provided at a preschool or another developmental center. ECSE services are provided primarily in preschool classrooms, which may be in a center-based or community preschool. Services include parent support, care coordination, and structured developmental activities that may include physical, occupational, and speech-language therapy.

Special Education for Children and Adolescents from 6 to 21 Years of Age   The eligibility categories for children with disabilities ages 6 years and older include mental retardation, hearing impairments, visual impairments, multiple disabilities (e.g., deaf-blindness), speech-language impairments, serious emotional disturbance, orthopedic or other health impairments (including ADHD), autism, traumatic brain injury, and specific learning disabilities. In addition, children must also need special services in order to benefit from the education program because of their mental, physical, emotional, or learning problems.

Primary care physicians and nurses should be familiar with the contact person for EI/ECSE services in their community and a contact person for special education services in the local school district. The health professional should receive reports of all educational evaluations related to special services for children with developmental disabilities or mental retardation and also request yearly progress reports. Conversely, schools should be notified of any change in the child's medical management plan. Please review the American Academy of Pediatrics' position statements (AAP, 1990, 1993) on children with health impairments in schools and the provision of related services to children with disabilities.

Inclusion   Educational services must be provided to the extent appropriate in environments in which children without disabilities participate. Inclusion has replaced the concept of mainstreaming as the goal in education of children with disabilities. Inclusion is a broader concept that seeks ways to engage children with disabilities meaningfully in activities with their age peers without disabilities at school and in the community. The effects of including children with disabilities in general classrooms were studied extensively in the 1980s and 1990s (see, e.g., Close & Newman, 1990; Graves & Tracy, 1998). Results of studies have shown improved social interaction and peer relationships among students with disabilities in inclusive schools and classrooms, and a few studies have shown improved language development for the children with disabilities in inclusive environments (see Close & Newman, 1990). In addition, children with disabilities who participate in more inclusive educational environments participate in more inclusive recreation activities in the community (Modell, Rider, & Menchetti, 1997).

The success of inclusion depends on the information, training, and support available to teachers and parents. Not all children with disabilities are placed in an inclusive classroom appropriately with or without an instructional assistant. Some investigators (e.g., Mesibov & Shea, 1996) have questioned the benefits of inclusion, particularly for children with autism. Placement decisions can be controversial and at times confrontational issues for some parents and educators.

Medical Management of Mental Health and Problem Behaviors

A major treatment goal for individuals with developmental delay or mental retardation is the reduction of problem behaviors. The functional analysis of severe problem behaviors is a critical part of treatment planning for children with these problems, and quality-of-life and functional outcomes measures are important additions to more traditional measures to determine the benefit of specific interventions.

Functional Assessment of Behavior All behavior problems are shaped and modified by the environment. In general, misbehaviors serve a specific, often communicative, function in a given situation. For example, research studies (e.g., Day, Horner, & O'Neill, 1994) have shown that SIBs are maintained by different social functions such as escape from unpleasant demands or tasks and at other times to gain the attention of peers or adults. The functional assessment of specific behaviors includes analysis of the ABCs of behavioral analysis: assessment of *a*ntecedent events, the *b*ehavior displayed, and the *c*onsequences of the behavior. At times, simple environmental changes without the use of medications can eliminate a problem behavior such as aggression. The success of functional assessment depends on the experience of the behavioral consultant (see also Chapter 8).

Quality-of-Life and Functional Outcomes Measures Quality-of-life and functional outcomes measures are particularly important for documenting the progress of children with severe mental retardation (requiring extensive support). Traditional measures based on developmental milestones or a simple reduction in an undesirable target behavior in a restricted environment may have little relevance to treatment programs whose goal is to improve the child's function in his or her overall environment. The end result of behavioral support programs should be socially significant changes in the range of choices that children and families have in their lives—what people do, where they do it, and with which level of support (Newton, Horner, Ard, et al., 1994). Quality-of-life and functional outcomes measures incorporate and emphasize the importance of the family's goals in treatment planning.

A variety of quality-of-life scales and indicators as well as functional outcomes measures are used. Few have been developed specifically for children with mental retardation. The functional outcomes measures developed for use in adult and child rehabilitation programs are discussed in Chapter 6.

Use of Psychotropic Medications The management of mental health and behavior problems requires 1) a careful evaluation that includes functional analysis of the behaviors and 2) a comprehensive treatment program that includes behavior management alone or in combination with medication. The use of psychotropic medications for children and adults with mental retardation who live in institutions is high (30%–40%) (Gadow, 1997), the prevalence of medication use with individuals with mental retardation residing in the community has increased (Singh, Ellis, & Weschsler, 1997), and there is ongoing concern about the quality of treatment practices (Gadow, 1997; Singh et al., 1997). Information obtained from the child, the child's family, and school staff (the school's behavioral consultant, if available) is critical for the development of an appropriate management plan. Most children with mental retardation who are experiencing mental health and/or behavior problems require referral to an experienced child development team or to a child psychiatrist or other mental health professional.

Medications frequently have been used for the control of aggression in individuals with mental retardation. As a result, considerable skepticism exists with regard to the benefits of prescribing medication for this population, particularly the use of neuroleptics. In general, neuroleptics (e.g., haloperidol [Haldol]) can cause significant side effects, including cognitive slowing, tardive dyskinesia, neuroleptic malignant syndrome, and akathisia. The use of risperidone (Risperdal) instead of traditional neuroleptics, however, is associated with a decrease in the rate of these major side effects (Simon, Blubaugh, & Pippidis, 1996). In addition, other medications (e.g., selective serotonin reuptake inhibitors [SSRIs]) that do not have the major side effects of the neuroleptics are available and are effective for specific indications. Unfortunately, most of the information on medication use in children with mental retardation is from open label studies.

The benefits and the side effects of any medications should be discussed carefully with the child and the child's family prior to initiating treatment, as well as with educational staff if the family consents. In general, begin with the least toxic and safest medication that has demonstrated efficacy (Connor & Steingard, 1996; see Masi & Luccherino, 1997; Mercugliano, 1993). Dulcan (1992) developed sample handouts for families describing specific drugs.

For purposes of the present discussion, mental health and behavior problems are categorized as follows: affective or mood disorders (e.g., depression, mania), aggression, ADHD, obsessive-compulsive and anxiety disorders, psychotic disorders, sleep and eating disorders, and stereotypic behaviors and SIBs. Determine the child's principal problem behaviors to help decide which (if any) medication to recommend as part of the management of those behaviors. Some aggressive, stereotypic, and self-injurious behaviors may be related to anxiety and have a compulsive or perseverative component.

Affective or Mood Disorders The recognition and management of mood disorders in children with mental retardation are difficult. A child with mental retardation requiring extensive support and a sleep disturbance, irritability, and increased activity level, lability of mood, and SIBs may have a co-morbid mood disorder. Lithium remains the mainstay for the treatment of bipolar disorder. Side effects such as tremor and incontinence, however, may limit the use of lithium by individuals with mental retardation. Other treatment choices for bipolar disorder include valproic acid and carbamazepine. The use of valproic acid in young women has been associated with the development of polycystic ovaries (Vainionpaa, Rattya, Knip, et al., 1999). Tricyclic antidepressants (TCAs; e.g., imipramine, nortriptyline) are useful in the treatment of unipolar depression; however, induction of mania has been reported (Kastner, Friedman, Plummer, et al., 1990). Paroxetine (Paxil), an SSRI, was shown

(Masi, Marcheschi, & Pfanner, 1997) to be effective in an open label trial in adolescents with mental retardation and depression.

Aggression For most children, a careful functional analysis of the problem behaviors should be conducted prior to the use of medications. Many medications, including lithium, carbamazepine, beta blockers, valproic acid, and SSRIs, show modest benefits in the long-term treatment of aggression (Baumeister, Todd, & Sevin, 1993; Haspel, 1995; Kastner et al., 1990; Sovner, 1990). Aggression in some children improves with the treatment of target symptoms (e.g., impulsivity with stimulants, anxiety and obsessive-compulsive disorders with SSRIs) (Connor & Steingard, 1996). Neuroleptics (e.g., haloperidol, risperidone) may be required to treat acute episodes of aggression and agitation (Whitaker & Rao, 1992). Risperidone has fewer extrapyramidal side effects than neuroleptics; however, it is associated with increased appetite and weight gain.

Attention-Deficit/Hyperactivity Disorder The diagnosis of ADHD is based on expectations for the child's developmental age, and the diagnosis is determined by obtaining information from multiple sources by interview and the use of behavioral checklists. Stimulants are the medications of first choice for the treatment of motor overactivity and inattention in children with mental retardation. Studies have shown (e.g., Handen, Breaux, Gosling, et al., 1990) that these symptoms in children with mental retardation respond positively at rates similar to those found in children without mental retardation. Improvement in learning and social skills has not been documented, and many children with mental retardation continue to exhibit ongoing hyperactivity and related behavior problems (Aman, Pejeau, Osborne, et al., 1996; Handen, Janosky, & McAuliffe, 1997). (Please review Chapter 7 for a more complete discussion of medication management.)

Obsessive-Compulsive and Anxiety Disorders Children with mental retardation, particularly those who also have autism, may manifest perseverative and ritualistic behaviors that interfere with function significantly. A number of studies (Barak, Ring, Levy, et al., 1995; Bodfish & Madison, 1993; Brasic, Barnett, Kaplan, et al., 1994) have documented the benefits for these children of taking clomipramine, fluoxetine (Prozac), and other SSRIs. Some individuals with autism who have taken these medications also have shown modest improvement in their social behaviors. The use of clomipramine has been limited primarily by the anticholinergic side effects of urinary hesitancy and skin flushing. Induction of agitation also has been reported. An electrocardiogram needs to be obtained prior to the initiation of treatment and with dosage changes. Campbell, Schopler, Cueva, and Hallin (1996) recommended that clomipramine and TCAs be used cautiously with individuals with ASD. The side effects of SSRIs include tremor and difficulty with going to sleep as well as transient loss of appetite. Agitation has also been reported.

Psychotic Disorders Psychotic disorders are not discussed further here, because they are uncommon in childhood. Psychosis is a common reason for psychiatric inpatient treatment for individuals with intellectual disability (Raitasuo, Taiminen, & Salokangas, 1999). In addition, certain genetic disorders (e.g., VCF syndrome) are associated with a higher rate of schizophrenia in adults (Bassett, Hodgkinson, Chow, et al., 1998).

Sleep and Eating Disorders Sleep problems are common in children with mental retardation and autism, particularly in response to changes in the environment such as a family move. The most common sleep problems are difficulty with going to sleep and difficulty with returning to sleep after a nighttime awakening. The primary interventions are behavioral. Medications can be a short-term benefit to help reestablish a more typical sleep pattern. Clonidine can be used at bedtime because a principal side effect of clonidine is sedation. (Please review the discussion of clonidine in Chapter 7.)

In an open label study, melatonin was effective in improving the sleep patterns of 13 of 15 children with multiple disabilities (Jan, Espezel, & Appleton, 1994). Children responded at a dose of .5–5.0 milligrams. Previous studies (Alvarez, Dahlitz, Vignau, et al., 1992; Dahlitz, Alvarez, Vignau, et al., 1991) demonstrated that melatonin is beneficial in the treatment of adults who experience delayed sleep onset (i.e., patients went to sleep earlier but slept the same amount). Melatonin is not a pharmaceutical product, and thus the potency and purity of the tablets may vary. Jan, Freeman, and Fast (1999) reviewed a number of case reports, clinical trials, and a few controlled trials of the use of melatonin in children and adolescents with various disabilities and sleep disorders. Most of the studies they reviewed reported positive results (reduced sleep latency), including the two placebo-controlled trials (see Jan et al., 1999, for recommendations with regard to dose and administration).

Stereotypic and Self-Injurious Behaviors The efficacy of naltrexone, an opiate antagonist, in re-

ducing SIBs in individuals with mental retardation with or without autism has varied (Casner, Weinheimer, & Gualtieri, 1996; Willemsen-Swinkels, Buitelaar, Nijhof, & van England, 1995). SSRIs may reduce SIBs modestly (Hellings, Kelley, Gabrielli, et al., 1996), and risperidone was effective in reducing aggression and SIBs in an open label study of adults with mental retardation (Cohen, Ihrig, Lott, & Kerrick, 1998). The mainstay of the treatment of SIBs remains behavioral interventions based on a careful functional analysis.

Controversial Therapies

Many alternative or nonstandard therapies have been purported to benefit children with developmental delay or Down syndrome. These treatments include behavioral therapies as well as diets, vitamins, and medications. Table 5.3 lists the controversial therapies that have been used with children with Down syndrome.

Parents may seek information about controversial therapies for many reasons, including dissatisfaction with services or the unrealistic hope of a magic cure. The search for a magic cure is one stage in the adjustment of parents to the diagnosis of their child's developmental disability (Freeman, 1993). Parents may be particularly responsive to the claims of proponents of these therapies if their child has marked developmental delay and shows little progress or has marked behavior problems or an unknown etiologic diagnosis. The proponents of controversial therapies develop supportive relationships with families and provide parents with a great deal of anecdotal information about the effectiveness of that therapy. They may offer the possibility of a cure, state that all or nearly all children benefit, and indicate a need to begin intensive therapy right away because it will not be as effective

Table 5.3. Controversial therapies that have been used with children with Down syndrome or mental retardation

Megavitamins, trace minerals
U-series (Turkel)
Thyroid supplementation
Cell therapy
Dimethyl glycine (DMG)
Tryptophan
Piracetam (nootropics)
Growth hormone
Facial surgery
Craniosacral therapy
Patterning (Doman-Delacato)

later. These "red flags" are included on a list of questions for parents to review when considering a new treatment (Fields, 1994). Health care professionals may share the handout included as part of the Appendix at the end of Chapter 8 with parents to assist them in making the best decision about unsubstantiated treatments.

The responsibilities of health care professionals in counseling parents regarding controversial therapies are reviewed in detail in Chapter 8. If parents choose to pursue an unproved therapy, health care professionals should encourage them to use it in addition to, rather than in place of, established educational and medical treatments, and should assist families in monitoring for side effects. Structured assessments conducted before and after starting an unproved therapy may also help families in deciding whether there are true benefits.

Physicians and nurses also need to remain informed about controversial therapies through

- The Internet (e.g., the National Institutes of Health Office on Alternative Medicine [OAM]; see "Resources" listing in Chapter 8)
- Newsletters of advocacy groups
- Parent groups (local and national)
- Providers of alternative therapies (directly or through the Internet)
- Medical colleagues (e.g., developmental pediatricians)
- Educational service providers (e.g., the state department of education)
- Professional literature
- Medical meetings

Unfortunately, information available on the Internet is often from proponents of various therapies, and thus a balanced review of research data on effectiveness is not presented. National advocacy groups (e.g., the National Down Syndrome Society) provide useful information about unproved or nonstandard therapies on their web sites and in print. In addition, the OAM publishes a newsletter, and the web sites of both the OAM and the Rosenthal Center on Alternative Medicine at Columbia University offer the ability to search alternative medicine databases.

Ongoing Needs for Family Support

Primary care physicians and nurses can provide invaluable ongoing support to families by conducting a periodic review of the needs of individual family members: mothers, fathers, and siblings. Families experience many crises during the growth of their child with disabilities:

- When parents first learn about their child's diagnosis at the times of transition from EI to ECSE and from preschool to grade school services
- Introduction of new therapies (e.g., augmentative and alternative communication technology)
- Adolescence
- The transition to adult services (e.g., supported living, supported employment)
- The 21st birthday of the family member with disabilities and chronic conditions

Many communities have active fathers' networks as well as sibling workshops and support groups to address the needs of these two specific groups. A variety of books are available for siblings of children with disabilities (see the "Readings" and "Resources" sections in the Appendix at the end of this chapter).

Other important community services include state and county offices of the following: Developmental Disability Services, Department of Vocational Rehabilitation Services, The Arc of the United States: A National Organization on Mental Retardation (commonly referred to as "The Arc"; formerly called the Association for Retarded Citizens), and other advocacy groups that provide support to parents and educational staff. For example, many local chapters of The Arc provide parent-to-parent programs that put families of children with disabilities in contact with other families whose children have similar conditions. The Arc and other advocacy groups provide information on guardianship and the establishment of trusts to ensure continued support of the adult child with disabilities (see the "Resources" section in the Appendix at the end of this chapter).

Anticipatory Guidance

Certain issues are raised frequently by families, advocates, and professionals: transitions, social skills, vocational skills, self-care, independence, and sexuality and birth control (Patterson, Quint, Brown, et al., 1994). Health care professionals can help prepare families for transitions, promote social competence by encouraging inclusion in community activities with peers, and regularly promote self-care and independence during office visits. Social skills, vocational skills, and life skills training programs are critically important for some adolescents. Contact the local school district to determine the services that are available through the schools. In addition, review the "Resources" section in the Appendix at the end of this chapter for other appropriate agencies and organizations (e.g., The Arc).

Sexuality The American Academy of Pediatrics (1996) published the following recommendations for parents on sexuality education of children and adolescents with developmental disabilities. Adolescents and young adults with disabilities need detailed information about sexuality. The information provided must be appropriate for their intellectual level. Family life and social skills training programs are available and have been shown to be effective in 1) improving young people's understanding of the risks of sexual relationships and the need for responsible, caring behavior; and 2) changing behavior (e.g., training to decrease the risk of sexual abuse for men and women) (Carr & Purdue, 1988; Lindsay, Bellshaw, Culross, et al., 1992; McCabe, 1993). Of note, one third of the women with moderate mental retardation (requiring limited support) and one fourth of the women with mild mental retardation (requiring intermittent support) had been raped (Passer, Rauh, Chamberlain, et al., 1984). If men and women with disabilities are sexually active, they are also at risk for contracting sexually transmitted diseases, including hepatitis B and human immunodeficiency virus (HIV) infection.

Menstrual Hygiene and Birth Control Parents of young women with mental retardation are also concerned about the care of menstruation and the possibility of pregnancy. In one study, 50% of the women with moderate mental retardation (requiring limited support) had had sexual intercourse, as had 32% of those with mild mental retardation (requiring intermittent support) and 9% of those with severe mental retardation (requiring extensive support) (Passer et al., 1984). In general, menstrual hygiene proves to be less of a problem than parents anticipate prior to the onset of menses. Parents should wait until their daughters have experienced at least several periods prior to contemplating other treatment options. Programs that emphasize preparation, reassurance, and basic explanations have been successful in assisting women with intellectual disabilities to accept menstruation and to assist with their menstrual care (Taylor, Carlson, Gatlin, & Wilson, 1994).

The use of the injectable steroid medroxyprogesterone acetate (Depo-Provera Contraceptive Injection) and, to a lesser extent, combination birth control oral steroids (birth control pills) may improve menstrual hygiene by decreasing menstrual flow. Depo-Provera is given by intramuscular injection every 3 months. Most women experience a marked reduction in menstrual flow following the second injection as well as a reduction in menstrual cramps.

Contraception options for women include oral steroids, injectable steroids (medroxyprogesterone acetate), levonorgestrol (Norplant), intrauterine devices, barrier methods and spermicides, and sterilization (Haefner & Elkins, 1991; Wingfield, Healy, & Nicolson, 1994). The requirement for regular compliance limits the use of some methods, particularly barrier methods and spermicides. The use of intrauterine devices has been limited because of the side effects of cramping, irregular bleeding, and the potential for infection with continued sexual activity. Norplant is surgically implanted subcutaneously and changed every 5 years. Similar to Depo-Provera, its use requires no compliance by the woman. It may be associated with irregular bleeding, however, and can be difficult to remove. In women with mild or moderate mental retardation (requiring limited to intermittent support), use of combination birth control pills may be an appropriate first choice for contraception, unless reliability of pill taking cannot be guaranteed. In that case, use of medroxyprogesterone acetate (Depo-Provera) is an appropriate consideration. If the primary care physician or nurse is recommending the initiation of any method of contraception, referral should be made to a gynecologist who is experienced in the care of women with intellectual disabilities for a complete examination and appropriate counseling.

The use of condoms by men with cognitive disabilities is limited by the requirements for compliance and skilled knowledge of their use. Suppression of the pituitary hormones LH and FSH by testosterone alone or in combination with other agents has been a promising approach for male contraception (Behre, Baus, Kliesch, et al., 1995; Meriggiola, Bremner, Costantino, et al., 1998). Testosterone enanthate, however, must be given by weekly intramuscular injections and is associated with significant side effects and high cost (Comhaire, 1994). Testosterone buciclate can be given in monthly intramuscular injections, but few data are available on its efficacy. None of the hormonal methods have been studied adequately in men with cognitive disabilities. The most common method of male contraception is voluntary sterilization by vasectomy (Comhaire, 1994). The use of this method requires informed consent from the individual with mental retardation.

Surgical sterilization is still considered by some parents. In one study, 46% of parents of daughters with mental retardation attending an adolescent clinic had considered sterilization, and 26% were still seeking it (Passer et al., 1984). Sterilization can be accomplished by tubal ligation in women and by vasectomy in men. Most states have laws that provide clear protection of individuals with mental retardation against involuntary sterilization. People with mental retardation must consent to such procedures knowingly and voluntarily. The majority of women with mental retardation requiring limited support can understand the meaning of sterilization and its permanent implications (Leavesley & Porter, 1982). Further information is available through advocacy groups such as The Arc.

Important Care Coordination Issues

In addition to the general recommendations for care coordination discussed in Chapter 1, the following issues that are specific to children with developmental delay or mental retardation need to be addressed:

- Identify a local behavioral consultant who is experienced in the functional assessment of problem behaviors and a mental health professional who is experienced in working with children with developmental disabilities
- Develop a resource file on controversial therapies and know about the practitioners of such therapies in your area

Determine the most effective methods to exchange information with education agencies and other community service providers. Regular exchange of information is essential for effective coordination of services. Medical decisions about referrals to specialists, reevaluations by the child development team, or changes in medication management often depend on information provided by the school.

REFERENCES

Abidin, R.R. (1995). *Parenting Stress Index: Professional manual* (3rd ed.). Odessa, FL: Psychological Assessment Resources.

Alpern, G.D., Boll, T.J., & Shearer, M.S. (1980). *Developmental Profile II.* Aspen, CO: Psychological Development Publications.

Alvarez, B., Dahlitz, M.J., Vignau, J., et al. (1992). The delayed sleep phase syndrome: Clinical and investigative findings in 14 subjects. *Journal of Neurology, Neurosurgery, and Psychiatry, 55*(8), 665–670.

Aman, M.G., Pejeau, C., Osborne, P., et al. (1996). Four-year follow-up of children with low intelligence and ADHD. *Research in Developmental Disabilities, 17,* 417–432.

American Academy of Pediatrics (AAP). (1996). Sexuality education of children and adolescents with developmental disabilities. *Pediatrics, 97*(2), 275–278.

American Academy of Pediatrics (AAP), Committee on Children with Disabilities. (1992). Pediatrician's role in the development and implementation of an individual education plan (IEP) and/or an individual family service plan (IFSP). *Pediatrics, 89*(2), 340–342.

American Academy of Pediatrics (AAP), Committee on Children with Disabilities. (1993). Provision of related services for children with chronic disabilities. *Pediatrics, 92,* 879–881.

American Academy of Pediatrics (AAP), Committee on Children with Disabilities and Committee on School Health. (1990). Children with health impairments in schools. *Pediatrics, 86,* 636–637.

American Psychiatric Association (APA). (1994). *Diagnostic and statistical manual of mental disorders* (4th ed.). Washington, DC: American Psychiatric Press.

Bailey, D.B., & Blasco, P.M. (1990). Parents' perspectives on a written survey of family needs. *Journal of Early Intervention, 14,* 196–203.

Bailey, D.B., & Simeonsson, R.J. (1988a). Assessing needs of families with handicapped infants. *Journal of Special Education, 22,* 117–127.

Bailey, D.B., & Simeonsson, R.J. (1988b). *Family assessment in early intervention.* Upper Saddle River, NJ: Merrill.

Barak, Y., Ring, A., Levy, D., et al. (1995). Disabling compulsions in 11 mentally retarded adults: An open trial of clomipramine SR. *Journal of Clinical Psychiatry, 56,* 459–461.

Bassett, A.S., Hodgkinson, K., Chow, E.W., et al. (1998). 22q11 deletion syndrome in adults with schizophrenia. *American Journal of Medical Genetics, 81*(4), 328–337.

Batshaw, M.L. (1993). Mental retardation. *Pediatric Clinics of North America, 40*(3), 507–521.

Baumeister, A.A., Todd, M.E., & Sevin, J.A. (1993). Efficacy and specificity of pharmacological therapies for behavioral disorders in persons with mental retardation. *Clinical Neuropharmacology, 16*(4), 271–294.

Bayley, N. (1969). *Manual for the Bayley Scales of Infant Development.* San Antonio, TX: The Psychological Corporation.

Bayley, N. (1993). *Bayley Scales of Infant Development* (2nd ed.). San Antonio, TX: The Psychological Corporation.

Behre, H.M., Baus, S., Kliesch, S., et al. (1995). Potential of testosterone buciclate for male contraception: Endocrine differences between responders and nonresponders. *Journal of Clinical Endocrinology and Metabolism, 80*(8), 2394–2403.

Bodfish, J.W., & Madison, J.T. (1993). Diagnosis and fluoxetine treatment of compulsive behavior disorder of adults with mental retardation. *American Journal on Mental Retardation, 98*(3), 360–367.

Boyle, C.A., Yeargin-Allsopp, M., Doernberg, N.S., et al. (1991). Prevalence of selected developmental disabilities in children 3–10 years of age: The Metropolitan Atlanta Developmental Disabilities Surveillance Program. *Morbidity and Mortality Weekly Report, 45*(SS-2), 1–13.

Brasic, J.R., Barnett, J.Y., Kaplan, D., et al. (1994). Clomipramine ameliorates adventitious movements and compulsions in prepubertal boys with autistic disorder and severe mental retardation. *Neurology, 44*(7), 1309–1312.

Bricker, D.D., & Squires, J. (1999). *Ages & Stages Questionnaires (ASQ): A parent-completed, child-monitoring system* (2nd ed.). Baltimore: Paul H. Brookes Publishing Co.

Bruininks, R.H., Woodcock, R.W., Weatherman, R.F., & Hill, B.K. (1984). *Scales of Independent Behavior (SIB).* Itasca, IL: Riverside Publishing Co.

Campbell, M., Schopler, E., Cueva, J.E., & Hallin, A. (1996). Treatment of autistic disorder. *Journal of the American Academy of Child and Adolescent Psychiatry, 35*(2), 134–143.

Carr, J., & Purdue, D. (1988). Sexuality education for special needs adolescents. *Canadian Nurse, 84*(11), 26–29.

Casner, J.A., Weinheimer, B., & Gualtieri, C.T. (1996). Naltrexone and self-injurious behavior: A retrospective population study. *Journal of Clinical Psychopharmacology, 16,* 389–394.

Close, V.T., & Newman, J. (1990). *Mainstreaming: A guide for educators and parents* [Booklet]. Eugene: University of Oregon, Center on Human Development.

Cohen, S.A., Ihrig, K., Lott, R.S., & Kerrick, J.M. (1998). Risperidone for aggression and self-injurious behavior in adults with mental retardation. *Journal of Autism and Developmental Disorders, 28,* 229–233.

Comhaire, F.H. (1994). Male contraception: Hormonal, mechanical, and other. *Human Reproduction, 9*(Suppl. 2), 22–27.

Connor, D.F., & Steingard, R.J. (1996). A clinical approach to the pharmacotherapy of aggression in children and adolescents. *Annals of the New York Academy of Science, 794,* 290–307.

Coplan, J. (1993). *Early Language Milestone Scale* (2nd ed.). Austin, TX: PRO-ED.

Curry, C.J., Stevenson, R.E., Aughton, D., et al. (1997). Evaluation of mental retardation: Recommendations of a consensus conference. *American Journal of Medical Genetics, 72,* 468–477.

Dahlitz, M., Alvarez, B., Vignau, J., et al. (1991). Delayed sleep phase syndrome response to melatonin. *Lancet, 337*(8750), 1121–1124.

Day, H.M., Horner, R.H., & O'Neill, R.E. (1994). Multiple functions of problem behaviors: Assessment and intervention. *Journal of Applied Behavioral Analysis, 27,* 279–289.

Dulcan, M. (1992). Information for parents and youth on psychotropic medications. *Journal of Child and Adolescent Psychopharmacology, 2*(2), 81–101.

Fields, V. (1994). *Autism advocacy in Lane County: A handbook for parents and professionals.* Unpublished master's thesis, University of Oregon, Eugene.

First, L.R., & Palfrey, J.S. (1994). The infant or young child with developmental delay. *New England Journal of Medicine, 330*(7), 478–483.

Freeman, B.J. (1993). The syndrome of autism: Update and guidelines for diagnoses. *Infants and Young Children, 6*(2), 1–11.

Gadow, K.D. (1997). An overview of three decades of research in pediatric psychopharmacoepidemiology. *Journal of Child and Adolescent Psychopharmacology, 7,* 219–236.

Graves, P., & Tracy, J. (1998). Education for children with disabilities: The rationale for inclusion. *Journal of Paediatrics and Child Health, 34,* 220–225.

Haefner, H.K., & Elkins, T.E. (1991, December). Contraceptive management for female adolescents with mental retardation and handicapping disabilities. *Current Opinion in Obstetrics and Gynecology, 3*(6), 820–824.

Handen, B.L., Breaux, A.M., Gosling, A., et al. (1990). Efficacy of methylphenidate among mentally retarded children with attention-deficit/hyperactivity disorder. *Pediatrics, 86,* 6922–6930.

Handen, B.L., Janosky, J., & McAuliffe, S. (1997). Long-term follow-up of children with mental retardation/borderline intellectual functioning and ADHD. *Journal of Abnormal Child Psychology, 25,* 287–295.

Haspel, T. (1995). Beta-blockers and the treatment of aggression. *Harvard Review of Psychiatry, 2,* 274–281.

Hellings, J.A., Kelley, L.A., Gabrielli, W.F., et al. (1996). Sertraline response in adults with mental retardation and autistic disorder. *Journal of Clinical Psychiatry, 57,* 333–336.

Hiskey, M.S. (1966). *Hiskey-Nebraska Test of Learning Aptitude.* Lincoln, NE: Union College Press.

Jan, J.E., Espezel, H., & Appleton, R.E. (1994). The treatment of sleep disorders with melatonin. *Developmental Medicine and Child Neurology, 36,* 97–107.

Jan, J.E., Freeman, R.D., & Fast, D.K. (1999). Melatonin treatment of sleep–wake cycle disorders in children and adolescents. *Developmental Medicine and Child Neurology, 41,* 491–500.

Jones, K.L. (1997). *Smith's recognizable patterns of human malformation* (5th ed.). Philadelphia: W.B. Saunders Co.

Kastner, T., Friedman, D.L., Plummer, A.T., et al. (1990). Valproic acid for the treatment of children with mental retardation and mood symptomatology. *Pediatrics, 86*(3), 467–472.

Knobloch, H., Stevens, F., & Malone, A.F. (1980). *Manual of developmental diagnosis: The administration and interpretation of the revised Gesell and Armatruda Developmental and Neurological Examination.* New York: Harper-Collins.

Lambert, N., Nihira, K., & Leland, H. (1993). *AAMR Adaptive Behavior Scale–School (ABS–S:2)* (2nd ed.). Austin, TX: PRO-ED.

Leavesley, G., & Porter, J. (1982). Sexuality, fertility and contraception in disability. *Contraception, 26*(4), 417–441.

Lindsay, W.R., Bellshaw, E., Culross, G., et al. (1992). Increases in knowledge following a course of sex education for people with intellectual disabilities. *Journal of Intellectual Disability Research, 36*(6), 531–539.

Lovell, R.W., & Reiss, A.L. (1993). Dual diagnoses: Psychiatric disorders in developmental disabilities. *Pediatric Clinics of North America, 40*(3), 579–592.

Luckasson, R., Coulter, D.L., Polloway, E.A., et al. (1992). *Mental retardation: Definition, classification, and systems of supports* (Special 9th ed.). Washington, DC: American Association on Mental Retardation.

Marden, P.M., Smith, D.W., & McDonald, M.J. (1964). Congenital anomalies in the newborn infant, including minor variations. *Journal of Pediatrics, 6*(3), 357–371.

Marston, G.M., Perry, D.W., & Roy, A. (1997). Manifestations of depression in people with intellectual disability. *Journal of Intellectual Disability Research, 41,* 476–480.

Masi, G., & Luccherino, L. (1997). Psychiatric illness in mental retardation: An update on pharmacotherapy. *Panminerva Medica, 39,* 299–304.

Masi, G., Marcheschi, M., & Pfanner, P. (1997). Paroxetine in depressed adolescents with intellectual disability: An open label study. *Journal of Intellectual Disability Research, 41,* 268–272.

McCabe, M.P. (1993). Sex education programs for people with mental retardation. *Mental Retardation, 31*(6), 377–387.

McLaren, J., & Bryson, S.E. (1987). Review of recent epidemiological studies of mental retardation: Prevalence, associated disorders, and etiology. *American Journal on Mental Retardation, 92*(3), 243–254.

Mercugliano, M. (1993). Psychopharmacology in children with developmental disabilities. *Pediatric Clinics of North America, 40*(3), 593–615.

Meriggiola, M.C., Bremner, W.J., Costantino, A., et al. (1998). Low dose of cyproterone acetate and testosterone enanthate for contraception in men. *Human Reproduction, 13,* 1225–1229.

Mesibov, G.B., & Shea, V. (1996). Full inclusion and students with autism. *Journal of Autism and Developmental Disorders, 26,* 337–346.

Modell, S.J., Rider, R.A., & Menchetti, B.M. (1997). An exploration of the influence of educational placement on the community recreation and leisure patterns of children with developmental disabilities. *Perceptual Motor Skills, 85,* 695–704.

Myers, B.A., & Pueschel, S.M. (1991). Psychiatric disorders in persons with Down syndrome. *Journal of Nervous and Mental Disease, 179*(10), 609–613.

Newborg, J., Stock, J.R., & Wnek, L. (1984). *Battelle Developmental Inventory: Screening test.* Hingham, MA: Teaching Resources.

Newton, J.S., Horner, R.H., Ard, W.R., Jr., et al. (1994). A conceptual model for improving the social life of individuals with mental retardation. *Mental Retardation, 32,* 393–402.

Passer, A., Rauh, J., Chamberlain, A., et al. (1984). Issues in fertility control for mentally retarded female adolescents: II. Parental attitudes toward sterilization. *Pediatrics, 73*(4), 451–454.

Patterson, K.L., Quint, E., Brown, D., et al. (1994). Family views on sterilization for their mentally retarded children. *Journal of Reproductive Medicine, 39*(9), 701–706.

Raitasuo, S., Taiminen, T., & Salokangas, R.K. (1999). Characteristics of people with intellectual disability admitted for psychiatric inpatient treatment. *Journal of Intellectual Disability Research, 43*(pt. 2), 112–118.

Roid, G.H., & Miller, L.J. (1997). *Leiter International Performance Scale–Revised.* Wood Dale, IL: C.H. Stoelting Co.

Shapiro, B.K., Palmer, F.B., & Capute, A.J. (1987). The early detection of mental retardation. *Clinical Pediatrics, 26*(5), 215–220.

Simon, E.W., Blubaugh, K.M., & Pippidis, M. (1996). Substituting traditional antipsychotics with risperidone for individuals with mental retardation. *Mental Retardation, 34,* 359–366.

Singh, N.N., Ellis, C.R., & Weschsler, H. (1997). Psychopharmacoepidemiology of mental retardation: 1966 to 1995. *Journal of Child and Adolescent Psychopharmacology, 7,* 255–266.

Sovner, R. (1990). Drug profiles V: Beta blockers. *Habilitative Mental Healthcare Newsletter, 9*(9), 73–78.

Sparrow, S., Balla, D., & Cicchetti, D. (1984). *Vineland Adaptive Behavior Scales (VABS).* Circle Pines, MN: American Guidance Service.

Taylor, M., Carlson, B., Gatlin, J., & Wilson, J. (1994). Managing menstruation. *Medical Journal of Australia, 161,* 511–512.

Thorndike, R.L., Hagen, E.P., & Sattler, J.M. (1986). *Stanford-Binet Intelligence Scale: Guide for administering and scoring* (4th ed.). Itasca, IL: Riverside Publishing Co.

Vainionpaa, L.K., Rattya, J., Knip, M., et al. (1999). Valproate-induced hyperandrogenism during pubertal maturation in girls with epilepsy. *Annals of Neurology, 45*(4), 444–450.

Wechsler, D. (1989). *Wechsler Preschool and Primary Scale of Intelligence–Revised (WPPSI–R).* San Antonio, TX: The Psychological Corporation.

Wechsler, D. (1991). *Wechsler Intelligence Scale for Children (WISC)* (3rd ed.). San Antonio, TX: The Psychological Corporation.

Whitaker, A., & Rao, U. (1992). Neuroleptics in pediatric psychiatry. *Psychiatric Clinics of North America, 15*(1), 243–277.

Willemsen-Swinkels, S.H., Buitelaar, J.K., Nijhof, G.J., & van England, H. (1995). Failure of naltrexone hydrochloride to reduce self-injurious and autistic behavior in mentally retarded adults: Double-blind placebo-controlled studies. *Archives of General Psychiatry, 52,* 766–773.

Wingfield, M., Healy, D.L., & Nicolson, A. (1994). Gynaecological care for women with intellectual disability. *Medical Journal of Australia, 160*(9), 536–538.

5

Appendix

Guidelines for the Care of
Children and Adolescents with
Developmental Delay or Mental Retardation

Basic Team

The special care needs of children with developmental delay can be met by an experienced primary care physician working collaboratively with parents, early childhood educators, teachers, and other school staff. Some children and families require referral to an experienced child development team headed by a developmental pediatrician, and other children may need referral to a medical geneticist. Please note that the primary care physician continues to be responsible for coordinating the special services that these children require.

Regular members of the child development team include a developmental pediatrician, a psychologist, a speech-language pathologist, an occupational therapist, an audiologist, and a medical social worker. Many children do not require evaluation by all members of the team, and some children require additional evaluations (e.g., nutritionist, behavioral specialist).

Initial Evaluation

The objectives of the initial evaluation are to document the child's performance level in different developmental domains, make service recommendations, determine the cause of the disability, and identify associated medical problems. The responsibilities of the primary care physician and nurse are to complete family, developmental, and medical histories; perform a complete medical examination, including a surface evaluation for minor congenital anomalies; determine the needs for referral and for laboratory tests; and counsel the parents and the child about the diagnosis and recommended treatment.

Frequency of Visits

The child and the family are best followed monthly in the primary care office following the initial evaluation until associated medical problems are determined, the cause of the disability is identified and discussed, and the child is receiving general education services. Then reevaluate the child and the family in the office at least yearly to monitor his or her progress and to review the treatment of associated medical problems and more often for younger children and in the first year after the diagnosis. Some children may need to be seen more often by the primary care physician (e.g., children with seizures who are taking anticonvulsants). Some children require regular follow-up by the child neurologist, and other children may require reevaluation by the child development team. The management plan should be updated at each reevaluation and not less than yearly.

The Physician's Guide to Caring for Children with Disabilities and Chronic Conditions, edited by Robert E. Nickel and Larry W. Desch, copyright © 2000 Paul H. Brookes Publishing Co.

Guidelines for the Care of Children and Adolescents with Developmental Delay or Mental Retardation

The following elements are recommended by age group, and the listing is cumulative. Review all items indicated up through the actual age group of a child entering your practice for the first time as part of the initial evaluation.

AGE	KEY CLINICAL ISSUES/CONCERNS	EVALUATIONS/KEY PROCEDURES	SPECIALISTS
Birth–5 years (pre-school age)	*Growth/Nutrition* Failure to thrive Oral motor dysfunction Gastroesophageal reflux (GER) Microcephaly or macrocephaly	Growth parameters, diet record, nutrition and feeding assessment, workup for GER Special diet and feeding program, treatment for GER Cranial computed tomography (CT) or magnetic resonance imaging (MRI) scan as needed	Nutritionist, feeding specialist or team, pediatric gastroenterologist as needed
	Associated Medical Problems Hearing/vision Seizures Hypotonia Musculoskeletal: Hip dysplasia, scoliosis Sleep problems Constipation Toilet training Drooling **Note side effects of any medications.**	Hearing and vision testing Electroencephalogram Detailed neuromotor examination Hip ultrasound, X rays as needed Behavior management, occasional short-term medications Diet, medications (e.g., bulk agent), timed toilet training, adaptive seat as needed Behavioral therapy, occasional medication	Audiologist, ophthalmologist Child neurologist as needed Physical therapist, orthopedist as needed Developmental pediatrician (DPed), nurse specialist as needed Speech-language pathologist, rarely referral to otolaryngologist for older school-age children
	Cause of the Disability	Evaluation for minor anomalies Chromosomes, fragile X testing, cranial MRI scan, metabolic studies as needed	DPed or medical geneticist as needed
	Dental Care	Review oral hygiene	Dentist
	Associated Behavior/Mental Health Problems Autism spectrum disorder Aggression Hyperactivity/inattention Oppositional behavior Anxiety	Interview, behavior rating scales Functional analysis of behavior as needed Behavior management programs at home and school Medication as needed	Referral to child development team or psychologist, behavioral consultant, child psychiatrist as needed

The Physician's Guide to Caring for Children with Disabilities and Chronic Conditions, edited by Robert E. Nickel and Larry W. Desch, copyright © 2000 Paul H. Brookes Publishing Co.

Guidelines for the Care of Children and Adolescents with Developmental Delay or Mental Retardation (continued)

The following elements are recommended by age group, and the listing is cumulative. Review all items indicated up through the actual age group of a child entering your practice for the first time as part of the initial evaluation.

AGE	KEY CLINICAL ISSUES/CONCERNS	EVALUATIONS/KEY PROCEDURES	SPECIALISTS
Birth–5 years (pre-school age) (continued)	Developmental Progress, Early Intervention (EI)/Early Childhood Special Education (ECSE) Services Need for ancillary services: Physical therapy (PT), occupational therapy (OT), speech-language therapy Speech disorder Dyspraxic gait, ataxia, hypotonia, or cerebral palsy Fine motor and visual motor concerns	Request EI/ECSE report, review individualized family service plan (IFSP) with family Detailed musculoskeletal and neuromotor examinations	Referral for PT, OT, speech-language therapy as needed or for evaluation by child development team Collaborate with EI/ECSE staff
	Review of Diagnosis and Anticipatory Guidance Review IFSP or individualized education program (IEP) with family Transition from EI to ECSE and from ECSE to elementary school Sibling programs Discussion of alternative (controversial) therapies Promotion of self-care/independence Accident prevention	Family interview, educational materials, resource information, initiate care notebook Teacher interview, school conference as needed	DPed as needed Collaborate with EI/ECSE staff, child development team
	Family Support Services Respite care Parent groups Community health nurse Advocacy (e.g., The Arc) Financial services (e.g., Supplemental Security Income [SSI]) Other enabling services	Family interview, parent questionnaires (e.g., Family Needs Survey), provide resource information Care coordination	Medical social worker, referral to community health nurse, other community services as needed
	Collaboration with Community Services School Community health nurse Other service providers	Comprehensive care coordination with regular exchange of written information (at least yearly) with other service providers	Primary care office in collaboration with child development team

The Physician's Guide to Caring for Children with Disabilities and Chronic Conditions, edited by Robert E. Nickel and Larry W. Desch, copyright © 2000 Paul H. Brookes Publishing Co.

Guidelines for the Care of Children and Adolescents with Developmental Delay or Mental Retardation (continued)

The following elements are recommended by age group, and the listing is cumulative. Review all items indicated up through the actual age group of a child entering your practice for the first time as part of the initial evaluation.

AGE	KEY CLINICAL ISSUES/CONCERNS	EVALUATIONS/KEY PROCEDURES	SPECIALISTS
6–12 years (school-age)	*School Progress* Need for ancillary services: PT, OT, speech-language therapy	Behavior rating scales, school report, review IEP with family Detailed musculoskeletal and neuromotor examinations	Referral to child development team or individual evaluations by physical therapist, occupational therapist, speech-language therapist Collaborate with school staff
	Communication or Speech-Language Disorder	Evaluate need for augmentative and alternative communication (AAC) devices	Speech-language pathologist, AAC specialist as needed
	Associated Behavior/Mental Health Problems Autism Attention-deficit/hyperactivity disorder (ADHD) Oppositional behavior Anxiety Depression Aggression Obsessive-compulsive behavior Self-injurious behaviors (SIBs) and stereotypies	Behavior rating scales, functional analysis of behavior Behavior management programs at home and at school Medication management as needed Collaborate with school staff	Referral to child development team, behavioral consultant, or mental health professional as needed
	Social Skills Promote social competence Determine which supports are needed for involvement in peer group activities at school and in the community	Social skills program at school, encourage participation in community services	Psychologist, behavioral consultant, physical therapist, occupational therapist, adaptive physical education specialist as needed Collaborate with school staff
	Anticipatory Guidance Sports and leisure activities Transition to middle school	Provide resource information on community services Determine which supports are needed to encourage participation in community recreation and leisure activities	Primary care office in collaboration with child development team

The Physician's Guide to Caring for Children with Disabilities and Chronic Conditions, edited by Robert E. Nickel and Larry W. Desch, copyright © 2000 Paul H. Brookes Publishing Co.

Guidelines for the Care of Children and Adolescents with Developmental Delay or Mental Retardation *(continued)*

The following elements are recommended by age group, and the listing is cumulative. Review all items indicated up through the actual age group of a child entering your practice for the first time as part of the initial evaluation.

AGE	KEY CLINICAL ISSUES/CONCERNS	EVALUATIONS/KEY PROCEDURES	SPECIALISTS
13–21 years (adolescent and young adult)	*Self-Care/Independent Living* Determine which supports are needed to promote self-care and independent living skills	PT and OT services as needed Independent living skills program, social skills training as needed Service coordination	As needed, refer to physical therapist, occupational therapist, psychologist, medical social worker Collaborate with school, Developmental Disability Services
	Anticipatory Guidance Transitions to middle school and to high school	Adolescent, family, and teacher interviews; school conference as needed; review IEP with family	Primary care office in collaboration with child development team
	Sexuality and birth control, menstrual hygiene	Social skills training regarding sexuality, menstrual hygiene, birth control (e.g., Depo-Provera) as needed	Gynecologist as needed
	Vocational training Life skills programs (independent living) Encourage healthy behaviors (e.g., diet, exercise) Transition to adult services	Evaluation by vocational specialist, life skills training program as needed	Referrals to Developmental Disability Services, Department of Vocational Rehabilitation

The Physician's Guide to Caring for Children with Disabilities and Chronic Conditions, edited by Robert E. Nickel and Larry W. Desch, copyright © 2000 Paul H. Brookes Publishing Co.

Family and Physician Management Plan Summary for Children and Adolescents with Developmental Delay or Mental Retardation

This form will help you and your physician review current services and service needs. Please answer the questions about your current services on this page. Your physician will review your responses and complete the rest of the form.

Child's name _____ Today's date _____

Person completing the form _____

CURRENT SERVICES

1. Please list your/your child's current medications and any side effects.

2. What is your/your child's current school program?

   School name _____ Grade _____

   Teacher _____ Telephone _____

3. Do you/does your child receive any support services and other special programs at school (e.g., physical therapy, resource room)? Please list.

4. Who are your/your child's other medical and dental service providers?

   Dentist _____

   Neurologist _____

   Other _____

5. Who are your/your child's other community service providers?

   Speech-language pathologist _____

   Community health nurse _____

   Other _____

The Physician's Guide to Caring for Children with Disabilities and Chronic Conditions, edited by Robert E. Nickel and Larry W. Desch, copyright © 2000 Paul H. Brookes Publishing Co.

Family and Physician Management Plan Summary for Children and Adolescents with Developmental Delay or Mental Retardation *(continued)*

6. Do you/does your child also receive services from a child development team of specialists?

   Contact person _____

   Location _____

7. Have you/has your child had any blood tests, radiologic (i.e., X-ray) examinations, or other procedures since your/your child's last visit? If yes, please describe.

8. Have you/has your child been hospitalized or undergone surgery since your/your child's last visit? If yes, describe.

9. Please note your/your child's accomplishments since your last visit. Consider activities at home, in your neighborhood, or at school, as well as success with treatments.

10. What goals (i.e., skills) would you/your child like to accomplish in the next year? Consider activities at home, in your neighborhood, or at school as well as success with treatments.

11. What questions or concerns would you like addressed today?

Family and Physician Management Plan Summary for Children and Adolescents with Developmental Delay or Mental Retardation

The Management Plan Summary should be completed at each annual review and more often as needed. It is intended to be used with the Guidelines for Care, which provide a more complete listing of clinical issues at different ages and recommended evaluations and treatments.

Child's name _____   Person completing form _____   Today's date _____

Clinical issues	Currently a problem?	Evaluations needed	Treatment recommendations	Referrals made	Date for status check
Family's Questions					
Growth/Nutrition Feeding problems Slow weight gain Gastroesophageal reflux Obesity Short stature					
Associated Medical Problems Hearing loss Strabismus/vision problems Seizures Hypotonia Musculoskeletal issues (e.g., scoliosis, foot deformity) Drooling Sleep disorder Constipation Toilet training Sexuality, menstrual hygiene **Note any side effects of medications.**					
Cause of the Disability					

The Physician's Guide to Caring for Children with Disabilities and Chronic Conditions, edited by Robert E. Nickel and Larry W. Desch, copyright © 2000 Paul H. Brookes Publishing Co.

Family and Physician Management Plan Summary for
Children and Adolescents with Developmental Delay or Mental Retardation *(continued)*

Child's name _____   Person completing form _____   Today's date _____

Clinical issues	Currently a problem?	Evaluations needed	Treatment recommendations	Referrals made	Date for status check
Dental Care					
Associated Behavior/ Mental Health Problems Autism Aggression Inattention/hyperactivity Oppositional behavior Anxiety, depression Obsessive-compulsive behaviors Stereotypies Self-injurious behaviors (SIBs)					
Associated Developmental or Learning Issues Current school achievement Review early intervention (EI) or school services (individualized family service plan [IFSP] or individualized education program [IEP]) Speech-language disorder (need for augmentative and alternative communication devices)					
Need for Physical Therapy or Occupational Therapy Services Hypotonia Associated dyspraxia or cerebral palsy Fine motor/visual motor concerns					

The Physician's Guide to Caring for Children with Disabilities and Chronic Conditions, edited by Robert E. Nickel and Larry W. Desch, copyright © 2000 Paul H. Brookes Publishing Co.

Family and Physician Management Plan Summary for
Children and Adolescents with Developmental Delay or Mental Retardation *(continued)*

Child's name _____   Person completing form _____   Today's date _____

Clinical issues	Currently a problem?	Evaluations needed	Treatment recommendations	Referrals made	Date for status check
Behavior Management in the Home					
Behavior Management in the School					
Discussion of Alternative (Controversial) Therapies					
Social Skills Determine which supports are needed to promote involvement in peer group activities at school and in the community					
Self-Care/Independence					
Anticipatory Guidance List issues discussed and materials provided					
Family Support Services					

The Physician's Guide to Caring for Children with Disabilities and Chronic Conditions, edited by Robert E. Nickel and Larry W. Desch, copyright © 2000 Paul H. Brookes Publishing Co.
The Physician's Guide to Caring for Children with Disabilities and Chronic Conditions, edited by Robert E. Nickel and Larry W. Desch, copyright © 2000 Paul H. Brookes Publishing Co.

Family and Physician Management Plan Summary for
Children and Adolescents with Developmental Delay or Mental Retardation *(continued)*

Child's name _____ Person completing form _____ Today's date _____

Clinical issues	Currently a problem?	Evaluations needed	Treatment recommendations	Referrals made	Date for status check
Collaboration with Community Agencies School Developmental Disability Services Vocational Rehabilitation					
Comments					

Next update of the Management Plan Summary _____

Signature _____ Date _____
(Child and parent)

Signature _____ Date _____
(Health professional)

The Physician's Guide to Caring for Children with Disabilities and Chronic Conditions, edited by Robert E. Nickel and Larry W. Desch, copyright © 2000 Paul H. Brookes Publishing Co.

Family and Physician
Management Plan Summary for
Children and Adolescents with Down Syndrome

This form will help you and your physician review current services and service needs. Please answer the questions about your current services on this page. Your physician will review your responses and complete the rest of the form.

Child's name _____ Today's date _____

Person completing the form _____

CURRENT SERVICES

1. Please list your/your child's current medications and any side effects.

2. What is your/your child's current school program?

    School name _____ Grade _____

    Teacher _____ Telephone _____

3. Do you/does your child receive any support services and other special programs at school (e.g., physical therapy, resource room)? Please list.

4. Who are your/your child's other medical and dental service providers?

    Dentist _____

    Neurologist _____

    Geneticist _____

    Other _____

5. Who are your/your child's other community service providers?

    Physical therapist _____

    Community health nurse _____

    Other _____

The Physician's Guide to Caring for Children with Disabilities and Chronic Conditions, edited by Robert E. Nickel and Larry W. Desch, copyright © 2000 Paul H. Brookes Publishing Co.

Family and Physician Management Plan Summary
for Children and Adolescents with Down Syndrome *(continued)*

6. Do you/does your child also receive services from a child development team of specialists?

   Contact person _____

   Location _____

7. Have you/has your child had any blood tests, radiologic (i.e., X-ray) examinations, or other procedures since your last visit? If yes, please describe.

8. Have you/has your child been hospitalized or undergone surgery since your last visit? If yes, describe.

9. Please note your/your child's accomplishments since your last visit. Consider activities at home, in your neighborhood, or at school, as well as success with treatments.

10. What goals (i.e., skills) would you/your child like to accomplish in the next year? Consider activities at home, in your neighborhood, or at school, as well as success with treatments.

11. What questions or concerns would you like addressed today?

The Physician's Guide to Caring for Children with Disabilities and Chronic Conditions, edited by Robert E. Nickel and Larry W. Desch, copyright © 2000 Paul H. Brookes Publishing Co.

Family and Physician Management Plan Summary for Children and Adolescents with Down Syndrome

The Management Plan Summary should be completed at each annual review and more often as needed. It is intended to be used with the Guidelines for Care, which provide a more complete listing of clinical issues at different ages and recommended evaluations and treatments.

Child's name _____ Person completing form _____ Today's date _____

Clinical issues	Currently a problem?	Evaluations needed	Treatment recommendations	Referrals made	Date for status check
Family's Questions					
Growth/Nutrition Feeding problems Obesity					
Associated Medical Problems Congenital heart defect Visual concerns (e.g., strabismus, cataracts) Hearing concerns (e.g., recurrent acute otitis media, persistent serous otitis) Recurrent respiratory infections Hypothyroidism Musculoskeletal problems (e.g., hip dysplasia, atlantoaxial instability) Seizures Gastrointestinal problems (e.g., bowel atresia, Hirschsprung disease) Constipation Toilet training (determine need for adaptive seating) Sleep apnea Leukemia (rare) Sexuality, menstrual hygiene **Note any side effects of medications.**					
Dental Care Periodontitis					

The Physician's Guide to Caring for Children with Disabilities and Chronic Conditions, edited by Robert E. Nickel and Larry W. Desch, copyright © 2000 Paul H. Brookes Publishing Co.

Family and Physician Management Plan Summary for Children and Adolescents with Down Syndrome *(continued)*

Child's name _____ Person completing form _____ Today's date _____

Clinical issues	Currently a problem?	Evaluations needed	Treatment recommendations	Referrals made	Date for status check
Associated Behavior/ Mental Health Problems Autism Aggression Inattention/hyperactivity Oppositional behavior Anxiety, depression Obsessive-compulsive behavior Stereotypies Self-injurious behaviors (SIBs)					
Associated Developmental Problems Current school progress Review early intervention or school services (individualized family service plan [IFSP] or individualized education program [IEP]) Speech-language disorder (determine need for augmentative and alternative communication devices)					
Need for Physical or Occupational Therapy Services Hypotonia Associated dyspraxia or cerebral palsy Fine motor/visual motor concerns					

The Physician's Guide to Caring for Children with Disabilities and Chronic Conditions, edited by Robert E. Nickel and Larry W. Desch, copyright © 2000 Paul H. Brookes Publishing Co.

Family and Physician Management Plan Summary for Children and Adolescents with Down Syndrome *(continued)*

Child's name _____ Person completing form _____ Today's date _____

Clinical issues	Currently a problem?	Evaluations needed	Treatment recommendations	Referrals made	Date for status check
Behavior Management in the Home					
Behavior Management in the School					
Discussion of Alternative (Controversial) Therapies					
Social Skills Determine which supports are needed to promote involvement in peer group activities at school and in the community					
Anticipatory Guidance List issues discussed and materials provided					
Promote Self-Care/Independence					
Family Support Services					

The Physician's Guide to Caring for Children with Disabilities and Chronic Conditions, edited by Robert E. Nickel and Larry W. Desch, copyright © 2000 Paul H. Brookes Publishing Co.

Family and Physician Management Plan Summary for Children and Adolescents with Down Syndrome *(continued)*

Child's name _____ Person completing form _____ Today's date _____

Clinical issues	Currently a problem?	Evaluations needed	Treatment recommendations	Referrals made	Date for status check
Collaboration with Community Agencies Communication with schools Developmental Disability Services Vocational Rehabilitation					
Comments					

Next update of the Management Plan Summary _____

Signature _____ Date _____
        (Child and parent)

Signature _____ Date _____
        (Health professional)

The Physician's Guide to Caring for Children with Disabilities and Chronic Conditions, edited by Robert E. Nickel and Larry W. Desch, copyright © 2000 Paul H. Brookes Publishing Co.

Surface Evaluation for Minor Congenital Anomalies

The purpose of this examination is to provide a structure for making skilled observations to assist with the identification of children with birth defect syndromes and genetic problems. This examination is best integrated into the general physical examination. When first learning to evaluate a child thoroughly for minor anomalies, however, it is useful to conduct the examination from start to finish to become comfortable with every aspect of the examination.

Starting with the head and face, follow the sequence presented below. For each stage of the examination, a list of the most common anomalies is provided. Please remember to measure whatever can appropriately be measured (e.g., ear length, hand length, palpebral fissure length). Circle the anomalies that are present and describe or write in the measurements in the righthand column. Please also describe any anomalies next to the appropriate category that are not listed on the form.

Child's name _____ Date of birth _____ Today's date _____

Diagnosis or referral concerns _____

1. **Craniofacial**
   Flat or prominent nasal bridge
   Small mandible
   Flat or prominent occiput
   Metopic ridge
   Large posterior fontanelle
   Malar hypoplasia
   Anteverted nose
   Synophrys

2. **Ears**
   Preauricular tags or sinus
   Large or small ears
   Asymmetric size
   Low-set ears
   Posterior rotation (> 10%)
   Lack of usual fold of helix

3. **Eyes**
   Epicanthal folds
   Hypo- and hypertelorism
   Ptosis
   Short palpebral fissures
   Upward slant to palpebral fissures
   Downward slant to palpebral fissures

4. **Mouth**
   Bifid uvula
   High-arched palate
   Wide alveolar ridges
   Large tongue
   Thin upper lip
   Flat philtrum

5. **Skin/hair**
   Low hairline
   Frontal upsweep/aberrant hair whorl
   Alopecia of scalp
   Extra posterior cervical skin
   Large capillary hemangioma (other than on posterior neck)
   Café au lait spots
   Hypopigmented macules
   Deep sacral dimple
   Aplasia cutis congenita

(continued)

The Physician's Guide to Caring for Children with Disabilities and Chronic Conditions, edited by Robert E. Nickel and Larry W. Desch,
copyright © 2000 Paul H. Brookes Publishing Co.

Surface Evaluation for Minor Congenital Anomalies (continued)

6. **Chest**
   Short sternum
   Depressed sternum
   Wide-set or high-located nipples
   Shield chest

7. **Abdominal/perineal**
   Diastasis recti (> 3 centimeters)
   Umbilical hernia
   Inguinal hernia
   Small testes
   Hypospadias
   Small or hypoplastic genitals

8. **Hands**
   Single palmar crease
   Clinodactyly
   Other unusual crease pattern
   Camptodactyly
   Partial cutaneous syndactyly
   Proximally placed thumb
   Broad thumb
   Duplication of thumbnail
   Small or dysplastic nails
   Overlapping fingers
   Long fingers
   Small or large hands
   Short metacarpals

9. **Feet**
   Syndactyly of toes
   Overlapping toes
   Wide gap between toes
   Prominent heel
   Broad hallux
   Hallux valgus
   Hypoplastic nails
   Duplication of nail (rudimentary polydactyly)

Length _____ Weight _____ Head circumference _____

Comments _____

_____

_____

_____

_____

_____

_____

_____

(continued)

The Physician's Guide to Caring for Children with Disabilities and Chronic Conditions, edited by Robert E. Nickel and Larry W. Desch,
copyright © 2000 Paul H. Brookes Publishing Co.

Surface Evaluation for Minor Congenital Anomalies (continued)

Reference

Jones, K.L. (Ed.). (1997). *Smith's recognizable patterns of human malformation* (5th ed.). Philadelphia: W.B. Saunders Co.

Normal standards

Outer canthal distance (Jones, p. 764)
Inner canthal distance (Jones, p. 765)
Palpebral fissure length (Jones, p. 766)
Ear length (Jones, p. 768)
Total hand length (Jones, p. 760)
Palm length (Jones, p. 761)
Middle finger length (Jones, p. 761)
Foot length (Jones, p. 763)
Penile length (Jones, p. 769)

Notes (please review Jones, pp. 727–746)

1. Measure the outer and inner canthal distance with a plastic see-through ruler.
2. A flat nasal bridge and anteverted nose typically go together. Consider a nose anteverted if you can see straight into the nostrils when looking at the child from the front.
3. Ears are posteriorly rotated (slanted away from eye) if there is 15% slant away from the perpendicular (Jones, p. 730).
4. A sacral dimple is considered deep if the bottom cannot be seen without considerable stretching. It should be distinguished from a pilonidal sinus.
5. Measure penile length by resting one end of a ruler on the pubic bone and stretching the penis as much as possible. Measure to the tip of the glans.
6. Hypoplastic testes refers to small size and/or abnormal consistency. Hypoplasia of the labia majora may give the impression of a large clitoris (Jones, p. 734).
7. If the first metacarpal bone is short, the thumb will be proximally placed. If other metacarpals or metatarsals are short, the corresponding finger or toe will appear short. To check for a short metacarpal, have the child make a fist and check the knuckles. If a short metacarpal bone is present, the knuckle will be absent. A common example is relative shortness of the fourth or fifth metacarpal or metatarsal (Jones, p. 732).
8. Dysplastic nails are spoon-shaped, ridged, or otherwise malformed nails. The nails generally reflect the size and shape of the underlying distal phalanx (Jones, p. 731).
9. Partial syndactyly most commonly occurs between the third and fourth fingers and second and third toes. Less than 25% syndactyly between the second and third toes is considered normal.

RESOURCES ON DEVELOPMENTAL
DELAY AND MENTAL RETARDATION

Readings

American Academy of Pediatrics (AAP). (1997). *Genetic disorders and birth defects: A compendium of AAP guidelines and resources for the primary care practitioner.* Elk Grove Village, IL: Author. (Guidelines for the care of a number of genetic disorders and birth defects for the primary care practitioner and provides a number of condition-specific guidelines for care developed by AAP committees [e.g., Down syndrome, fragile X syndrome]; telephone: 1-800-433-9016; also available online: http://www.aap.org/search/search.htm)

American Academy of Pediatrics (AAP). (1997). *Health supervision re: Children with Down syndrome: Genetic disorders and birth defects: A compendium of AAP guidelines and resources for the primary care practitioner.* Elk Grove Village, IL: Author. (1-800-433-9016)

Binstock, C.L. (1997). *After your child's diagnosis: A practical guide for families raising children with disabilities.* Manassas, VA: E.M. Press. (1-800-727-4630)

Di Lima, S.N., Niemeyer, S., & Carson, J.R. (1997). *Caregiver education guide for children with developmental disabilities.* Gaithersburg, MD: Aspen Publishers. (1-800-638-8437)

Kroll, K., & Klein, E.L. (1995). *Enabling romance: A guide to love, sex and relationships for the disabled (and the people who care about them).* Bethesda, MD: Woodbine House. (1-800-843-7323)

Pueschel, S.M. (1990). *A parent's guide to Down syndrome: Toward a brighter future.* Baltimore: Paul H. Brookes Publishing Co. (1-800-638-3775)

Pueschel, S.M., & Pueschel, J.K. (1992). *Biomedical concerns in persons with Down syndrome.* Baltimore: Paul H. Brookes Publishing Co. (1-800-638-3775)

Schwartz, S., & Heller Miller, J.E. (1996). *The new language of toys: Teaching communication skills to children with special needs: A guide for parents and teachers* (Rev. ed.). Bethesda, MD: Woodbine House. (1-800-843-7323)

Siegel, B., & Silverstein, S.C. (1994). *What about me? Growing up with a developmentally disabled sibling.* New York: Insight Books.

Smith, R. (Ed.). (1993). *Children with mental retardation: A parent's guide* (The special needs collection). Bethesda, MD: Woodbine House. (1-800-843-7323)

Stray-Gundersen, K. (Ed.). (1995). *Babies with Down syndrome: A new parent's guide* (2nd ed.). Bethesda, MD: Woodbine House. (1-800-843-7323)

Thompson, M. (1992). *My brother, Matthew.* Bethesda, MD: Woodbine House. (1-800-843-7323)

Advocacy and Legal Assistance

Children's Defense Fund
25 E Street NW
Washington, D.C. 20001
Telephone: (800) 233-1200, (202) 628-8787
Fax: (202) 662-3550
E-mail: mlallen@childrensdefense.org
World Wide Web site: http://www.childrensdefense.org/

This organization provides information about legislation in health care, child welfare, and special education.

Disability Rights Education and Defense Fund (DREDF)
2212 Sixth Street
Berkeley, California 94710
Telephone/Voice/TTY: (510) 644-2555
Fax: (510) 841-8645
E-mail address: dlipton@dredf.org
World Wide Web site: http://www.dredf.org/

A law and policy center that provides information and referral regarding the rights of people with disabilities, including issues related to the Americans with Disabilities Act (ADA) of 1990 (PL 101-336).

Government Agency

**Office of Special Education
and Rehabilitative Services (OSERS)**
Communication and Media Support Services
U.S. Department of Education
330 C Street SW, Room 3132
Washington, D.C. 20202-2524
Telephone: (202) 205-8241
Fax: (202) 401-2608
World Wide Web site: http://www.ed.gov/offices/OSERS/

A government agency that provides a variety of services, including information in the areas of federal funding, legislation, and programs affecting individuals with disabilities.

National Organizations

**The Arc of the United States: A National
Organization on Mental Retardation**
(formerly the Association for Retarded Citizens)
National Headquarters Office
1010 Wayne Avenue, Suite 650
Silver Spring, Maryland 20910
Telephone: (301) 565-3842
Fax: (301) 565-5342
E-mail: info@thearc.org
World Wide Web site: http://thearc.org/

An organization dedicated to improving the lives of children and adults with mental retardation that provides a wide variety of information and publications as well as referrals to local chapters; its local programs include parent-to-parent and sibling programs and training of respite care providers.

National Down Syndrome Society (NDSS)

666 Broadway, Suite 800
New York, New York 10012-2317
Telephone: (212) 460-9330, (800) 221-4602
Fax: (212) 979-2873
E-mail address: info@ndss.org
World Wide Web site: http://www.ndss.org/

A national advocacy group that provides information, audiovisual aids, and summaries of research conferences, as well as publishing a newsletter.

National Down Syndrome Congress (NDSC)

7000 Peachtree-Dunwoody Road, NE
Lake Ridge 400 Office Park, Building 5, Suite 100
Atlanta, Georgia 30328
Telephone: (800) 232-NDSC (6372), (770) 604-9500
Fax: (770) 604-9898
E-mail address: NDSCcenter@aol.com
World Wide Web site: http://www.NDSCenter.org/

A referral and information center that publishes a regular newsletter.

National Fragile X Foundation

Post Office Box 190488
San Francisco, California 94119
Telephone: (800) 688-8765, (510) 763-6030
Fax: (510) 763-6223
E-mail address: natfragx@ix.netcom.com
World Wide Web site: http://www.fragilex.org/

This foundation provides information concerning diagnosis, treatment, and current research with regard to fragile X syndrome, as well as referrals to local resource centers. It also sponsors a biannual conference.

Professional Organization

American Association on Mental Retardation (AAMR)

444 North Capitol Street NW, Suite 846
Washington, D.C. 20001
Telephone: (202) 387-1968
Fax: (202) 387-2193
World Wide Web site: http://www.aamr.org/

A professional organization that encourages research and dissemination of information on community-based services for individuals with mental retardation and measures designated to reduce the incidence of mental retardation.

Recreation and Leisure Activities

Special Olympics International

1325 G Street NW, Suite 500
Washington, D.C. 20005-3104
Telephone: (202) 628-3630
Fax: (202) 824-0200
E-mail address: specialolympics@msn.com
World Wide Web site: http://www.specialolympics.org/

A national organization that sponsors local, state, and national athletic competitions for children and adults with mental retardation and is sanctioned by the U.S. Olympic Committee.

Other Resources

Ability Online Support Network

World Wide Web site: http://www.ablelink.org/

"Putting children and adolescents with disabilities in touch with the world," this e-mail system connects young people with disabilities or chronic conditions to peers and mentors with and without disabilities.

Cerebral Palsy

Robert E. Nickel

KEY COMPETENCIES

- Assess an infant with a neuromotor screen
- Plan the diagnostic workup for a child with cerebral palsy
- Counsel the parents of a child with the new diagnosis of cerebral palsy
- Conduct a musculoskeletal examination of a child with cerebral palsy, including observation of gait
- Describe the indications for physical therapy (PT) and occupational therapy (OT) services in children with cerebral palsy
- Discuss options for treating hypertonia and the musculoskeletal problems of children with cerebral palsy
- Construct a treatment plan for children with cerebral palsy and associated constipation, drooling, and urinary hesitancy

DESCRIPTION

Definition

Cerebral palsy is a group of disorders rather than a specific disease. It is characterized by a nonprogressive impairment of movement and posture resulting from brain injury or anomaly occurring early in development. The manifestations of the movement disorder may change with growth and maturation; however, the primary brain disorder is static.

Classification

Cerebral palsy is classified by the anatomical distribution of the dysfunction and the type of neurologic involvement. A child may manifest any of the following:

- *Hemiplegia* (one side of the body involved)
- *Diplegia* (both legs primarily involved or legs more involved than arms)
- *Quadriplegia* (total body involvement or arms more involved than legs)
- *Triplegia* (principal involvement of both legs and one arm)
- *Monoplegia* (single extremity involved)

The types of neurologic involvement are

- Spastic
- Dyskinetic (athetoid and dystonic)
- Ataxic
- Mixed (e.g., spastic-athetoid, spastic-ataxic)
- Atonic

Most commonly, children with hemiplegia or diplegia manifest spasticity; however, other types of neurologic involvement such as dystonia can also be seen (Scrutton, 1992). Further classification by the etiology, the severity (including functional skills), and the presence of associated problems can provide more specific information for families regarding their child's treatment needs and prognosis. Palisano, Kolobe, Haley, and colleagues (1995) published a standard system of classifying the gross motor function of children from 18 months to 6 years of age who have cerebral palsy. Children are categorized as being at one of five different levels of function based primarily on skills in sitting and walking as determined by the Gross Motor Function Measure (GMFM; Russell, Rosenbaum, Cadman, et al., 1989). Further development of this and similar systems of functional classification can assist in determining which services are needed and in comparing the results of different treatment.

Prevalence

The prevalence of moderate and severe cerebral palsy at school age is about 1.5–2.5 per 1,000 (Kuban & Leviton, 1994; Paneth, 1986a). These figures have remained relatively constant since the 1970s. An increase in the prevalence of cerebral palsy in certain populations (e.g., children born extremely prematurely) has been reported (Pharoah, Cooke, & Rosenbloom, 1989). The increased survival rate of small, premature infants is primarily responsible for the increased number of low birth weight infants with cerebral palsy (O'Shea, Preisser, Klinepeter, et al., 1998). The birthweight-specific rates of cerebral palsy among babies whose birthweight is 2,500 grams or more have remained stable (Munch, 1992).

Etiology

The brain insult or anomaly that results in cerebral palsy may occur prenatally, perinatally, or postnatally (in early childhood). *Prenatal* factors include chromosomal and genetic causes, isolated brain malformations or birth defect syndromes, neuronal migration disorders, congenital infections, and intrauterine ischemic events. Schizencephaly is an example of an intrauterine ischemic event that occurs at 10–12 weeks' gestation with secondary neuronal migration problems and resultant hemiplegic or quadriplegic pattern of cerebral palsy. Of interest, some cases of bilateral severe schizencephaly are familial and associated with mutations in the Homeobox gene *EMX2* (Granata, Farina, Faiella, et al., 1997).

Perinatal causes include premature birth with resultant periventricular leukomalacia (PVL) and/or intraventricular hemorrhage, perinatal asphyxia, perinatal infection, and metabolic disturbance (e.g., hyperbilirubinemia). *Postnatal* causes include infection (e.g., group B streptococcus meningitis) and acute brain injury secondary to child abuse (e.g., shaken-baby syndrome).

There is increasing recognition of the importance of the prenatal causes of cerebral palsy and a diminished emphasis on perinatal asphyxia and other perinatal factors. In one study (Truwit, Barkovitch, Kock, et al., 1992), more than half of the term infants who later developed cerebral palsy had evidence of prenatal brain injury on magnetic resonance imaging (MRI) scans, and half of those children demonstrated developmental anomalies of the brain.

Preterm infants with PVL represent about 35%–40% of the children with cerebral palsy; postnatal causes represent about 10% and genetic causes about 5% (Paneth, 1986b). Certain causes are associated with specific patterns of cerebral palsy. PVL results in spastic diplegia, a late-third-trimester ischemic event results in congenital spastic hemiplegia, and hyperbilirubinemia (i.e., kernicterus) may result in athetoid quadriplegia associated with sensorineural hearing loss.

DIAGNOSIS AND EVALUATION

Clinical Diagnosis

Signs of Cerebral Palsy in Infants Parents may express concern that their infant is persistently irritable, is difficult to feed, and feels stiff or floppy when they are caring for him or her. They may note that their infant is not developing motor skills as quickly as expected. In other situations, parents may comment on how early their infant can roll over or stand up. This may be due to spasticity or to atypical motor patterns (e.g., persistence of the neonatal positive support reflex with early standing). In this case, the infant is persistently on his or her toes with his or her legs touching or nearly touching each other.

Difficulties with Making the Diagnosis of Cerebral Palsy in Infants If the examiner relies solely on the evaluation of motor milestones, many infants with cerebral palsy will be missed or diagnosed much later than they otherwise might have been. A variety of studies (Check & Gallagher, 1985; Darrah, Piper, & Watt, 1998; Nelson, Bozynski, Genaze, et al., 1983; Nickel, Renken, & Gallenstein, 1989) showed that assessments based only on motor milestones are not reliable for the diagnosis of cerebral palsy in the baby's first year. Diagnostic accuracy can be improved by also evaluating the qualitative aspects of movement. This evaluation includes assessment of *primitive reflexes* (e.g., asymmetric tonic neck reflex,

tonic labyrinthine reflex-supine, neonatal positive support reflex), *automatic reactions* (e.g., parachute responses, truncal equilibrium responses), *motor asymmetries, muscle tone,* and *patterns of movement.*

Some infants continue to present diagnostic problems even with careful evaluation of motor milestones and qualitative aspects of movement. Certain infants born prematurely manifest a transient dystonia. They appear to have spasticity in the legs or an apparent spastic diplegia pattern of cerebral palsy when examined in their first year; however, these signs resolve after 1 year of age. In one study (Nelson & Ellenberg, 1982) of 229 one-year-old children who had been diagnosed with cerebral palsy, only 118 of the children still had the diagnosis of cerebral palsy at 7 years of age. Another problem with early diagnosis is that athetosis and ataxia may develop after 1 year of age. These infants typically manifest hypotonia, persistence of primitive reflexes, and delays in automatic reactions and motor milestones in the first year.

In summary, the diagnostic difficulties discussed in this section emphasize the importance of repeated examinations at different ages as well as evaluation of the qualitative aspects of movement in addition to motor milestones. Children with mild hemiplegia, diplegia, and extrapyramidal patterns of cerebral palsy may continue to be missed in diagnosis when evaluated early in their first year of life (Coolman, Bennett, Sells, et al., 1985); however, the diagnosis of cerebral palsy should not be missed beyond 18 months corrected age (i.e., age adjusted for weeks of prematurity).

Neuromotor Screening Tests Neuromotor screening tests can provide valuable assistance to heath care professionals in following infants and young children who have been diagnosed as being at risk for cerebral palsy. They provide a structure for making accurate observations, assist in referral decisions, and can be a mechanism for teaching parents and other professionals about infants' and young children's motor development (Chandler, 1986). A number of neuromotor screens are available, including the Infant Motor Screen (Nickel et al., 1989; see Table 6.1), the Primitive Reflex Profile (Capute, Palmer, Shapiro, et al., 1984), the Milani-Comparetti Motor Development Screening Test (Ellison, Browning, Larson, et al., 1983; Milani-Comparetti & Gidoni, 1967), and the Chandler Movement Assessment of Infants Screening Test (Chandler, 1986). All of these tests share a number of test items, and they generally are administered easily in a short amount of time (e.g., 10–15 minutes). Most of them offer lim-

Table 6.1.   Infant Motor Screen: Test items and examination sequence

1. *Sitting on caregiver's lap:*
   Asymmetric tonic neck reflex
   Tonic labyrinthine reflex—supine
   Muscle tone—arms/legs
   Passive trunk rotation (8) (part of test item Rolling)
   Palmar grasp
   Pull-to-sitting

2. *Sitting on examiner's lap:*
   Lateral head-righting
   Sitting tilting reaction (8)

3. *Vertical suspension:*
   Placing responses—hands/feet
   Vertical tilting reaction (12)
   Downward parachute

4. *Standing on firm surface:*
   Supporting reaction
   Standing tilting reaction (16)
   Lateral staggering reaction (16)

5. *Prone suspension:*
   Prone suspension
   Forward parachute (8)

6. *Sitting on firm surface:*
   Sideways parachute (8)
   Backward parachute (12)

7. *Supine on firm surface:*
   Tonic labyrinthine reflex—supine
   Asymmetric tonic neck reflex

8. *Observed responses during play on floor:*
   Rolling (8)
   Creeping (12)
   Standing up (12)

Note: Two asymmetry items are scored at 4 and 8 months and a third item is scored at 12 and 16 months. Numbers in parentheses indicate items added at 8, 12, and 16 months.

ited psychometric data. The Alberta Infant Motor Scale (AIMS) (Darrah et al., 1998; Piper, Pinnell, Darrah, et al., 1994) is a brief motor assessment that is based solely on the observation of posture and movement.

Observation of the amount and patterns of movement is a critical part of the evaluation of infants with suspect cerebral palsy (see Table 2.4, Chapter 2; become familiar with at least one of these tests for use in practice). A neuromotor screen should be part of the developmental monitoring program in the first year of life for all infants who are at high risk for cerebral palsy (identified by biologic risk factors) and may be used with full-term infants at low risk for cerebral palsy who present with delays in motor milestones. Prechtl, Einspieler, Cioni, and colleagues (1997) studied the usefulness of general (i.e., fidgety) movements in newborns and young infants in predicting later neurologic impairments. This method of detection was found to have greater specificity and sensitivity than cranial ultrasound. Determination of the role of this type of assessment in the early identification of infants with cerebral palsy requires additional research.

Comprehensive Neuromotor Assessment of an Infant Suspected of Having Cerebral Palsy   If an infant is suspected of having cerebral palsy based on concerns of the physician or the family or on the result of a screening test, the next step is to refer the infant for a comprehensive diagnostic evaluation. Referral is best made to an experienced neurodevelopmental team headed by a developmental pediatrician. Referral can also be made to a pediatric neurologist and a physical therapist. The basic team includes a developmental pediatrician, a physical therapist, an occupational therapist, an orthopedist (for older children), and a nurse. Not all members of the basic team may need to be involved in the initial evaluation. Other staff may be required, however, including a feeding specialist, a speech-language pathologist, a psychologist, a nutritionist, a social worker, an orthotist, a physiatrist, and a pediatric neurologist.

A comprehensive evaluation includes assessment of

- Growth, nutrition, and feeding
- The qualitative aspects of movement in addition to motor milestones
- Gross and fine motor skills
- Communication (i.e., speech-language development)
- Overall developmental progress
- Etiologic diagnosis
- Associated medical problems
- The family's strengths and need for support services

Two standardized instruments that evaluate the qualitative aspects of movement are the Movement Assessment of Infants (MAI) (Chandler, Andrews, & Swanson, 1980) and the Infant Neurological International Battery (INFANIB) (Ellison et al., 1983). Items from both of these tests evaluate the child's muscle tone, primitive reflexes, automatic reactions, and other movement patterns. These tests can be completed in 30–45 minutes by experienced examiners and are intended primarily for the use of physical and occupational therapists. Considerable data are available on the accuracy of the MAI for identifying infants with cerebral palsy at 4 and 8 months of age (Swanson, Bennett, Shy, et al., 1992).

Standardized assessments of general developmental progress are described in Chapter 5. The Bayley Scales of Infant Development (Bayley, 1969) and, more recently, the Bayley II (Bayley, 1993) are used frequently in the evaluation of infants who are suspected of having cerebral palsy. The Bayley Scales have mental, motor, and behavioral scales and thus provide an overview of the child's progress and associated developmental problems. The motor scale is based on the assessment of motor milestones.

Etiologic Diagnosis

Diagnostic Workup of the Child with Apparent Cerebral Palsy An accurate medical diagnosis identifies *progressive disorders* (e.g., ataxia telangiectasia) and *potentially treatable problems* (e.g., dopa-responsive dystonia) and provides *information about the natural history and associated problems* (e.g., schizencephaly, high risk for seizures); in addition, an accurate diagnosis may provide important *genetic information* (e.g., familial spastic paraplegia).

The content of the medical workup should be based on each child's specific presentation and may include a cranial MRI scan or computed tomography (CT) scan; metabolic testing with organic acids; blood tests, including chromosomal analysis; ophthalmologic exam; and audiologic testing. Clues from the history and physical examination as well as associated medical problems help determine the content of the etiologic workup. (Please review the discussion in Chapter 3.)

A child with a history of preterm birth and a typical spastic diplegia pattern of cerebral palsy may need no specific workup other than one to evaluate associated medical problems. A child born at term who presents with ataxia at 18 months of age, however, should have a full diagnostic workup to differentiate a possible progressive or degenerative disorder from cerebral palsy. Repeated examinations may be needed to demonstrate that the disorder is not progressive. As many as 50% of children with apparent ataxic cerebral palsy have a genetic basis for the disorder (Hughes & Newton, 1992). If one parent has spastic paraplegia, the child likely has familial spastic paraplegia, not cerebral palsy.

For an infant with spastic quadriplegia, marked developmental delay, and lissencephaly on a cranial MRI scan, a high-resolution chromosomal analysis should be done to look for deletion of chromosome 17p13, a condition which is associated with Miller-Dieker syndrome. Studies are available in research laboratories to identify the *LIS-1* gene, which is associated with Miller-Dieker syndrome and Type 1 lissencephaly (Isumi, Takashima, Kakita, et al., 1997), and the *XLIS* gene, which is associated with X-linked lissencephaly (Ross, Allen, Srivastava, et al., 1997).

The cranial MRI scan is much preferred to the CT scan for the etiologic workup of children with cerebral palsy because it is more sensitive to the detection of neuronal migration problems (e.g., schizencephaly) and other developmental anomalies (e.g., agenesis of the corpus callosum). The CT scan is still best for the detection of intracranial calcifications and should be used when detection of calcifications is critical for the diagnosis (e.g., in cases involving congenital cytomegalovirus [CMV] infection).

Diagnostic Evaluation of Associated Health and Developmental Problems Children with cerebral palsy may have additional developmental disabilities, including speech-language delays, learning disabilities, attention-deficit/hyperactivity disorder (ADHD), mental retardation, autism, and hearing and visual impairments (see Table 6.2). Associated medical problems include orthopedic issues (e.g., hip dislocation), seizures, strabismus, sensory disturbance, sleep apnea, dental caries and malocclusion, oral motor dysfunction, failure to thrive (FTT), precocious puberty, drooling, constipation, and urinary incontinence. Children with cerebral palsy may need assessment by a speech-language pathologist or a psychologist, audiologic testing, hip or spine X rays, and an electroencephalogram (EEG) as part of the initial diagnostic workup to evaluate associated problems.

The evaluation and treatment of some of these problems are discussed in detail in Chapters 4 and 17. Gastroesophageal reflux (GER), oral motor dysfunction, and related nutritional and growth problems are common in children with cerebral palsy. Accurate measurement of the rate of linear growth and weight gain may be difficult because of the presence of joint contractures, scoliosis, and difficulty in positioning the older child on the office scales. Additional measures for length (e.g., tibial length, upper-arm length) and nutritional status (e.g., skinfold thickness) should be used in some children (Stevenson, 1996). Nonnutritional factors also affect growth in children with cerebral palsy. Children with hemiplegia have undergrowth of the affected

Table 6.2.   Health and developmental problems associated with cerebral palsy

Growth/nutrition	Oral motor dysfunction Gastroesophageal reflux Poor weight gain, failure to thrive
Respiratory problems	Recurrent aspiration Chronic lung disease Recurrent apnea, sleep apnea
Hearing and vision	Sensorineural hearing loss Recurrent or persistent serous otitis Strabismus, visual impairment
Seizures	
Other medical concerns	Constipation Urinary urgency or incontinence Drooling Sleep disorder Precocious puberty
Dental	Malocclusion Caries
Problems with mobility and gait, seating and positioning, and upper-extremity function	
Musculoskeletal problems	Joint contractures Hip subluxation and dislocation Scoliosis Rotational abnormalities of legs Foot and ankle deformities Hand and arm deformities Osteopenia and fractures Joint and back pain
Associated communication problems	Speech-language disorder Language delay or disorder
Associated learning and behavioral problems	Developmental delay Mental retardation Specific learning disability Visual motor and visual perceptual dysfunction
Associated mental health and behavioral problems	Attention-deficit/hyperactivity disorder Low self-esteem Social isolation Depression

side proportionate to the severity of the neurologic impairment (Stevenson, Roberts, & Vogtle, 1995). In addition, some children with cerebral palsy have an apparent growth hormone deficiency (Coniglio, Stevenson, & Rogol, 1996).

Family Strengths and the Need for Support Services   Children with cerebral palsy and their families may require a number of enabling or family support services. Please review the discussion in Chapters 1 and 15.

Counseling the Parents About the Diagnosis

The most important and challenging role for the pediatrician in providing care to children with cere-

bral palsy is communicating with and supporting families (Wolraich, 1986). Families express a variety of reactions to the diagnosis of cerebral palsy, including shock, denial, sadness, anger, and guilt. The physician or nurse needs to identify these reactions in order to support parents in coping with the diagnosis. In most cases, the diagnosis of cerebral palsy should be a provisional diagnosis until 18–24 months of age. Please also review the discussion on counseling in Chapter 1.

Many parents want to know whether their child will be able to walk and talk and whether their child has mental retardation (Wolraich, 1986). In most cases, the answers to these questions are not available at the time of the diagnosis or perhaps even for months or years afterward. It is best to acknowledge the appropriateness of the questions and explain the difficulty of predicting the child's future level of function.

General information is available about the likelihood of the child's walking independently based on the child's development of specific early motor milestones. In one study, all of the children who had achieved head balance at 9 months of age walked independently or with support (da Paz, Burnett, & Braga, 1994). In contrast, those infants who had not achieved head balance by age 20 months did not walk. All children with spastic diplegia who were sitting independently by age 4 years walked; however, only 2 of 48 children with spastic quadriplegia who were not sitting at 4 years of age were able to walk. Previous studies reported similar data (Bleck, 1975; Molnar & Gordon, 1976).

MANAGEMENT

Periodic Review and Update of the Management Plan

Most children with cerebral palsy require ongoing management by the neurodevelopmental team. In general, older children are best evaluated at least yearly. Some children also require ongoing management by a specialist; for example, a child with difficult-to-control seizures needs to be seen regularly by a pediatric neurologist. A few children may require little or no consultation with specialists after the diagnosis is established and limited follow-up with the neurodevelopmental team (e.g., older children with mild diplegia or hemiplegia).

Reevaluate the child with cerebral palsy and the child's family in the primary care office, and update the child's management plan at least yearly, more frequently in the first year following the diagnosis and for young children. It is important to review information from families, the neurodevelopmental team, other specialists, and educational service providers regularly. Carefully review the child's growth and nutrition, and conduct a detailed musculoskeletal examination and observation of the child's gait as part of the periodic review. Consider prompt referral for reevaluation by the neurodevelopmental team for a child who shows any of the following symptoms:

- Regression in motor skills (e.g., deterioration in gait)
- Lack of expected developmental progress after receiving services

- Does not tolerate braces (e.g., ankle–foot orthoses [AFOs])
- Onset or worsening of joint contractures
- Onset or worsening of scoliosis or other orthopedic problems
- Multiple, complicated associated medical problems

Growth and Nutrition The management of GER, oral motor dysfunction, and related problems with nutrition and growth is discussed in detail in Chapter 4. The office assessment of growth and nutrition problems must include regular measurement of growth parameters and review of the signs and symptoms of oral motor dysfunction and GER and may include an observation of feeding for some infants and young children. Certain children require referral to a feeding specialist for evaluation and management. Other management options include special diets (e.g., high-calorie formulas), specialized feeding programs, medications for GER, enteral feedings, and fundoplication.

Musculoskeletal Examination and Observation of Gait The musculoskeletal examination is carried out in a systematic fashion to look for *structural changes*, to evaluate *muscle tone and strength*, and to assess *upper-extremity function* and *gait* (see Table 6.3). It is best integrated into the general physical and neurologic examination. This examination helps document changes in neuromotor status, determines the need for referral, and documents the benefit of interventions such as the use of braces. See the Appendix at the end of this chapter for a description of the methods and the scoring form for the Musculoskeletal Examination and Observation of Gait (Nickel, 1997).This examination is based in large part on Bleck (1979) and Dormans (1993).

Table 6.3. Clinical issues for the musculoskeletal examination

Structural changes
  Joint contractures
  Hip subluxation or dislocation
  Spine changes (scoliosis)
  Leg-length discrepancy
  Rotational abnormalities (pelvis, femur, tibia, and foot)
  Foot or ankle deformities
  Hand or arm deformities

Muscle tone and strength

Upper-extremity function (pinch, grasp, and release)

Clinical observation of gait

Adapted from Dormans (1993).

The gait cycle begins with the heel strike of the leading foot, followed sequentially by stance phase, toe-off, swing phase, and heel strike of the foot with which the cycle began. Of the entire gait cycle, 60% is in the stance phase and 40% is in the swing phase (Rose, Ounpuu, & DeLuca, 1991). The child should be observed when standing and when walking without braces, and again when wearing braces and using other assistive devices (e.g., AFOs, a posterior walker). Observe the position of the pelvis, and look for the presence of hip adduction, a crouch (hip and knee flexion), in- or outtoeing, and equinus or other foot-and-ankle deformities. Also note foot clearance, step length, gait stability, and velocity.

Evaluating the Progress
of Children with Cerebral Palsy

The comprehensive reevaluation by the neurodevelopmental team includes the following:

- Review of the family's questions and the child's medical history since the last evaluation
- Complete neurologic and musculoskeletal examinations of the child, including measurement of joint range of motion, muscle tone, and strength
- Review of feeding, nutrition, and growth
- Review of associated medical problems
- Assessment of gross and fine motor skills
- Assessment of functional skills
- Review of progress in communication skills, general development, and school
- Review of the family's support needs

Formal assessment by a speech-language pathologist and/or a psychologist may be required. Such evaluations should be coordinated with education staff to avoid duplication of services. Computerized gait analysis may be necessary based on the age of the child and the severity of the child's disabilities. Other evaluations that are of primary research interest at this time are the measurement of oxygen consumption and the efficiency of gait.

The National Center for Medical Rehabilitation Research (NCMRR) of the National Institutes of Health (NIH) developed a framework that describes the multiple dimensions of disability:

- Pathophysiology (e.g., periventricular leukomalacia)
- Impairment (e.g., spasticity, joint contractures)
- Functional limitations (e.g., difficulties with ambulation)
- Disability, or impairment in the child's ability to fulfill life functions (e.g., sports, a school play)
- Societal limitations (e.g., lack of wheelchair ramps, services not covered by insurance policies)

Use of the preceding model helps determine the benefit of interventions with regard to the different dimensions of the child's disability and focuses attention on the importance of functional measures and the child's and the family's goals. The benefits of treatment must be judged not only on changes in spasticity or joint contracture but also on change in function and the child's ability to participate in community activities.

Fine and Gross Motor Progress The Peabody Developmental Motor Scales (PDMS) (Folio & Fewell, 1983) are standardized, norm-referenced gross and fine motor scales that span from birth to 7 years of age. They are used widely by physical and occupational therapists to document motor progress in children with cerebral palsy. Test items assess typical motor milestones, including stacking blocks, cutting with scissors, jumping, and throwing a ball. Some investigators have reported, however, that the PDMS is not useful for detecting change over time in children with cerebral palsy (Palisano et al., 1995).

The GMFM (Russell et al., 1989) was developed as a standardized assessment to improve the detection of changes in gross motor skills development in children with cerebral palsy following specific interventions. GMFM consists of 85 items that measure the child's motor skills in different positions: lying and rolling, sitting, crawling, standing, kneeling and walking, and running and jumping. Items are scored on a four-point scale:

> 0 = Cannot initiate
> 1 = Initiates independently
> 2 = Partially completes
> 3 = Completes independently

The use of aids and orthoses is documented. The GMFM continues to focus primarily on changes in independent motor skills and may not be more sensitive than the PDMS in detecting changes in infants with cerebral palsy (Kolobe, Palisano, & Stratford, 1998).

Functional Skills Functional skill assessments evaluate the use of motor skills to accomplish day-to-day activities. Standardized assessments of functional skills are used concurrently with measures of motor skills such as the PDMS and the GMFM. The PDMS may not be helpful in measuring changes in children with severe cerebral palsy, owing to these children's slow rate of progress. Two assessment tools that measure the child's functional skills are the Pediatric Evaluation of Disability Inventory (PEDI) (Fedman, Haley, & Coryell, 1990; Haley, Coster, Ludlow, et al., 1992) and the Functional Independence Measure for Children (WeeFIM^SM) (State University of New York at Buffalo, 1993b; see also Hamilton & Granger, 1991; McCabe & Granger, 1990; Ottenbacher, Msall, Lyon, et al., 1997).

The PEDI and the WeeFIM are standardized assessments of children's functional abilities up to 7 years of age. They can also be used, however, to assess children of any age who have cerebral palsy and whose functional skills fall within the birth–7 years age range. The PEDI includes 42 items in three domains: self-care (e.g., grooming, hygiene), mobility (e.g., transfers, locomotion method, speed), and social function (e.g., functional communication, play, peer interaction). The items can be completed by the parent or by interview and observation by the professional. The need for caregiver assistance is also rated in all domains. The Tufts Assessment of Motor Performance (TAMP) is a similar functional assessment for use with older children and adults (Gans, Haley, Hallenborg, et al., 1988).

The WeeFIM includes 18 items in the following domains: self-care, sphincter control, transfers, locomotion, communication, and social cognition. The level of function is rated on a seven-point scale from a requirement of total assistance to complete independence. The WeeFIM is derived from previous work in adult rehabilitation with functional assessment. The WeeFIM can be completed by direct observation or by interview with a parent (Sperle, Ottenbacher, Braun, et al., 1997). The Functional Independence Measure (FIM^SM) (State University of New York at Buffalo, 1993a) can be used with older children and adults. The FIM has proved to be useful for evaluating people with cerebral palsy, people with spina bifida (Grimby, Andren, Holmgren, et al., 1996), and people with traumatic brain injury (Corrigan, Smith-Knapp, & Granger, 1997). The FIM can be completed in a telephone interview (FONE FIM^SM) as well as by direct observation (Chang, Chan, Slaughter, & Cartwright, 1997).

Computerized Gait Analysis Sophisticated objective analysis of gait in the laboratory is of both clinical and research importance. The value of quantitative gait analysis in clinical decision making was demonstrated in surgical decision making, choice of orthoses, and other aspects of treatment planning (Rose et al., 1991). Components of the gait analysis include the electromyogram (EMG) analysis with surface or fine-wire electrodes, videotaped motion analysis with three-dimensional kinematics, and kinetics and force plate analysis. *Kinematics* refers to joint angles and velocities, and *kinetics* refers to ground-reaction forces, joint movements, and pow-

ers. Measurements of kinematics and kinetics are taken in coronal, sagittal, and transverse planes with data generated on the hip, knee, and ankle. Standard gait parameters also include stride length, velocity, and cadence. Cadence is the number of steps taken per unit of time (measured in steps per minute).

Computerized gait analysis should be considered preoperatively in children who are candidates for orthopedic surgery if more than one procedure is contemplated. It is common practice to operate on all necessary joint levels (hip, knee, and ankle) at one time. Formal gait analysis is time- and labor-intensive and may not reflect the child's functional ambulation in the community (e.g., over uneven terrain). It should be complemented by the clinical analysis of gait.

Other Measures An additional measure in the gait laboratory is measurement of oxygen consumption by use of a lightweight, portable telemetry system (Bowen, Lennon, Castagno, et al., 1998; Corry, Duffy, Cosgrave, & Graham, 1996). Measurement of oxygen consumption provides additional objective data with which to assess the benefits of ambulatory aids as well as orthopedic surgical interventions. It was of particular research interest in the 1990s.

Quality-of-life measures or indicators such as participation in community activities, school attendance, and even the ability to sit at the dinner table provide more naturalistic measures of outcome success. They are particularly important for children with severe cerebral palsy and more accurately reflect the family's values and document the child's functional improvement relative to the family's goals.

Medical Management

Common Motor Patterns of Children with Hemiplegia, Diplegia, and Quadriplegia Almost all children with hemiplegia walk, usually by 18–24 months of age. The typical standing posture is equinus of the foot and ankle, knee and hip flexion, flexion of the elbow with forearm pronation, and flexion of the wrist and fingers with adduction of the thumb. Many children walk with knee hyperextension rather than flexion, with derotation of the affected side of the pelvis and decrease in step length. Children with hemiplegia also may have sensory problems in the affected hand and arm.

Most children with diplegia also walk, usually between 24 and 48 months of age. Standing posture is characterized by hip adduction and internal rotation, hip and knee flexion, equinus of the ankle, and valgus of the foot. Upper-limb involvement is usually minor. In addition, children with diplegia may have signifi-

cant truncal hypotonia and weakness. They walk
with decreased step length, adduction of the hips,
knee and hip flexion, intoeing, and equinus. Many
have impairments in standing equilibrium and
balancing responses and require assistive devices
(e.g., a posterior walker). Children with moderate
to severe diplegia, particularly children who are
nonambulatory, are at risk for hip subluxation or
dislocation.

Children with quadriplegia have total body involvement. Few walk, even with assistance. They
have truncal hypotonia and hypertonia of the extremities. The typical posture in the supine position
is flexion or extension of the arms with wrist and
finger flexion and adduction of the thumb, extension of the hips and knees, equinus posturing at foot
and ankle, and hip adduction and internal rotation.
Many children may also manifest hyperextension of
the head and neck as well as shoulder retraction.
They are at high risk for hip dislocation and scoliosis as well as for associated medical problems.

Treatment Goals   In general, the goal of treatment is to assist children with cerebral palsy to
develop to their full potential. Specific objectives
include

- Facilitating the child's motor progress during
  the developmental period
- Improving the quality or efficiency of the child's
  gait
- Improving the child's functional abilities
- Preventing secondary problems
- Facilitating the highest possible quality of life
  for the child (e.g., optimal nutrition and growth,
  social interaction, relief of pain)

The medical management program may include physical therapy (PT) and occupational therapy (OT); the use of braces and other assistive devices, positioning and seating equipment, and other
adaptive equipment; the use of various medical interventions, including medications; orthopedic and
neurosurgical interventions; and, perhaps most important, child and family support services. Treatment recommendations should be based on clearly
defined, realistic treatment objectives.

***Indications for Physical and Occupational
Therapy***   In general, indications for the provision
of PT and OT services include

- Regular therapy throughout the preschool years
- Rapid changes in motor skills
- Demonstration of emerging skills in standing
  and assisted walking
- High risk of developing progressive contractures

- Desire to maintain gains or improve function
  after surgical release of contractures
- Desire to improve endurance and speed through
  a cardiovascular and musculoskeletal conditioning program
- Other specific situations such as gait training
  with a new brace or other assistive device and
  the strengthening of specific muscles to improve
  the quality of gait

The effectiveness of any type of therapy services is
enhanced greatly by the active participation of parents in a home therapy program.

Previous studies (see Harris, 1987, 1997; Palmer, Shapiro, Wachtel, et al., 1988; Scherzer, Mike,
& Ilson, 1976) of the efficacy of PT for infants and
young children with cerebral palsy provided only
limited support for this treatment. Many of these
studies were compromised by limited outcome measures because they typically used only motor milestones, marked child-to-child variability, and lack of
a double-blind structure or a randomly assigned
control group. In addition, little or no research data
are available on the impact of PT on the family and
quality-of-life measures or on the efficacy of a given
frequency of therapy services (e.g., once per week
versus three times per week). Bower and McLellan
(1992) showed that there are significant positive
benefits for a short-term intensive PT program of
several hours per week that targets specific, realistic
goals. In addition, Damiano and colleagues (Damiano & Abel, 1998; Damiano, Kelly, & Vaughn, 1995)
demonstrated the benefits of muscle-strengthening
programs for some children with cerebral palsy. In
one study, strengthening of the knee extensor muscles resulted in increased force production with improved stride length and decreased crouch during
gait (Damiano et al., 1995).

Two critical issues related to the provision of
therapy services remain unresolved: What are medical versus educational therapy services? and, What
is the importance of maintenance versus rehabilitative therapy programs? Therapy services offered
in education environments focus on providing the
therapy support necessary so that a child may participate to the fullest possible extent in the education program. In certain instances, this approach
has neglected the medical need to monitor hip status, joint contractures, and scoliosis. Financial pressures have contributed to both the education and
health sectors' adopting narrower definitions of educational and medical necessities. Guidelines (Coolman, Foran, & Lee, 1997) for the provision of PT
and OT services developed by a multidisciplinary

group that included primary care physicians review the differences between medical and educational models and make recommendations for medically based therapy services in addition to services provided in the education environment.

In addition, regular therapy services are important for children with cerebral palsy who would show deterioration of function and development of secondary medical problems without these services (e.g., joint contracture). Even though children with cerebral palsy may not demonstrate improvement in motor skills in response to therapy, the success of the intervention is evident in these children's maintenance of function and improvement in their quality of life. Unfortunately, decisions about financial reimbursement for therapy services are based on an adult rehabilitation model and demonstrate little understanding of the different therapy requirements of children with cerebral palsy.

Braces, Assistive Devices, and Adaptive Equipment Physical and occupational therapists participate with other team members in recommending braces (i.e., orthoses), assistive devices, and adaptive equipment. Children with cerebral palsy should be provided with orthoses, assistive devices, and adaptive equipment as needed to allow them to have choices in posture, mobility, and self-care appropriate to their developmental age (e.g., independent sitting at age 6–9 months, standing at the end of the first year, active mobility in the second year).

In general, braces and hand splints are prescribed with the following treatment goals:

1. Prevent deformity
2. Support normal joint alignment
3. Facilitate function (Knutson & Clark, 1991)

Clinical experience and considerable research data (Abel, Juhl, Vaughan, & Damiano, 1998) demonstrate that lower-extremity orthotics (e.g., the ankle–foot orthosis [AFO]) increase gait velocity and step length and improve the stability of gait. Limited data are available on the efficacy of one type of brace versus another. For example, in one study (Carlson, Vaughan, Damiano, & Abel, 1997), the solid AFO was superior to the supramalleolar orthosis in children with spastic diplegia.

Appropriate seating and positioning for children with quadriplegia or moderate to severe diplegia are critical for the treatment of secondary orthopedic deformities as well as improvement in these children's function and quality of life (see Table 6.4). The goals for adaptive seating are to

1. Improve function, including independent mobility

2. Prevent the progression of deformity
3. Improve comfort and alleviate pain
4. Facilitate transportation
5. Improve quality of life (Piggott, 1987)

Children who have complicated seating needs (i.e., most children with quadriplegia) should be evaluated by an experienced neurodevelopmental team, which optimally includes a pediatric physiatrist. The neurodevelopmental team's recommendations for manual or power-driven wheelchairs are much more likely to result in an appropriate device and the realization of long-term cost savings.

Types of Assistive Technology and Their Use by Children with Cerebral Palsy The importance of AT in enabling children with cerebral palsy to participate to their maximum potential in the school and home environments is uniformly accepted (Todis, 1993). Positioning devices make it possible for students with cerebral palsy to join their classmates in a variety of activities at tables, on the floor, and in standing positions. Power-driven wheelchairs provide children with severe cerebral palsy the independent mobility that they need to choose their own workstation and activities and to join in their friends' activities.

Studies have documented the benefits of powered mobility for children as young as 2 years of age who have no other options for independent mobility (Butler, 1988). Similarly, computer technology has enabled children with limited fine motor skills and handwriting ability to keep up with homework and express their thoughts and feelings in writing (Desch, 1986; Todis, 1993). Preschool-age children

Table 6.4. General principles for adaptive seating

Provide a stable base of support
Always begin positioning strategies at the pelvis for seating
Equalize weight bearing
To avoid specific points of pressure
Through all weight-bearing surfaces
To provide symmetrical base of support
Work proximal to distal when making postural modifications
Correct a flexible deformity
Support a fixed deformity
Provide sufficient support without restricting function
Use commercially available equipment rather than custom-made equipment whenever possible
Consider the use of multiple devices
Consider each patient's individuality

Adapted from Piggott (1987).

with cerebral palsy should be evaluated for their capacity to use computers prior to when computer use will be required in order for them to complete their schoolwork.

Finally, augmentative and alternative communication (AAC) devices allow children with severe motor speech disorders the ability to express their needs, make choices, and interact with their friends and family in a more natural way than they would be able to otherwise (Todis, 1993). AAC programs should be initiated in the child's second year of life. AAC devices range from picture communication symbol boards to small computers with voice output.

Evaluation of children with regard to recommending assistive devices, including powered mobility, computer use, and AAC, requires a highly knowledgeable team of professionals with combined expertise in seating and positioning; switch access; computer hardware and software; and gross and fine motor, cognitive, and speech-language development. Early and consistent use of appropriate assistive devices may facilitate a higher degree of independence, job success, and social function as an adult (Desch, 1986).

Definitions of Spasticity, Dystonia, and Muscle Tone *Spasticity* refers to the increase in velocity-dependent resistance to muscle stretch that is manifested by exaggerated deep-tendon reflexes as a result of hyperexcitability of the spinal stretch reflex (Katz & Rymer, 1989). *Muscle tone* is the sensation of resistance to passive range of motion at a joint. The mechanical properties of the muscle and connective tissue, spasticity, and dystonia (i.e., rigidity) all may contribute to muscle tone.

The term *hypertonia* is not synonymous with *spasticity*. Spasticity is related to dysfunction of the pyramidal system, and dystonia is related to dysfunction of the extrapyramidal system. *Dystonia* refers to involuntary, sustained muscle contractions that often result in twisting, abnormal postures (Greene, 1992). It is characterized by consistent resistance to passive movement of the extremity and the absence of hyperactive deep-tendon reflexes. Differentiation of spasticity and dystonia is critical because some interventions for spasticity do not benefit dystonia (e.g., selective dorsal rhizotomy). Table 6.5 presents one measure of muscle tone, the Ashworth Scale (Ashworth, 1964, p. 541).

Hypertonia is only one of several neuromotor impairments that contribute to the functional problems of children with cerebral palsy. These problems include

- Hypertonia (spasticity and dystonia)
- Muscle weakness and easy fatigability

- Loss of dexterity or selective motor control
- Involuntary movement
- Impaired balance and ataxia

The management plan must consider all neuromotor impairments. The presence of muscle weakness affects recommendations for the treatment of spasticity. For example, selective dorsal rhizotomy is contraindicated in children who have spasticity and proximal muscle weakness. In such instances, marked reduction in spasticity may result in loss of function.

Decisions about the management of hypertonicity must be based on a careful neuromotor assessment; musculoskeletal examination; and, for some children, gait analysis. The decision must involve the therapists, the orthopedist, the developmental pediatrician or physiatrist, a neurosurgeon, and the child and family. Treatment goals must be realistic and must target functional change or important quality-of-life goals.

Use of Oral Medications to Treat Spasticity Oral medications have limited usefulness in the treatment of children with cerebral palsy. Antispasticity drugs include baclofen, diazepam and other benzodiazepines, and dantrolene (Gracies, Elovic, McGuire, et al., 1997; Gracies, Nance, Elovic, et al., 1997; Milia & Jackson, 1977; Young & Delwaide, 1981). Baclofen is a gamma-aminobutyric acid (GABA) agonist that acts principally on the spinal cord. Diazepam and benzodiazepines facilitate the action of GABA and act both centrally and at the spinal cord level. Dantrolene inhibits the release of calcium from the sarcoplasmic reticulum of the muscle, thereby decreasing the force of muscle contraction and producing muscle weakness.

The usefulness of these medications is limited by their frequent side effects, particularly sedation and weakness, as well as by their modest positive effects. Children who have oral motor dysfunction may show deterioration in feeding skills while tak-

Table 6.5. Measurement of muscle tone: The Ashworth Scale

0 = No increase in tone

1 = Slight increase in tone, giving a "catch" when affected part(s) moved in flexion or extension

2 = More marked increase in tone but affected part(s) easily flexed

3 = Considerable increase in tone; passive movement difficult

4 = Affected part(s) rigid in flexion or extension

From Ashworth, B. (1964). Preliminary trial of carisoprodol in multiple sclerosis. *Practitioner, 192,* 541; reprinted by permission.

ing these medications. Oral dantrolene appears to be more effective with spasticity of cerebral origin, and baclofen appears to be more effective with spasticity of spinal cord origin (Gracies, Elovic, et al., 1997). Tizanidine, an antispasticity agent that is used in adults with multiple sclerosis and spinal cord injury, may prove useful in treating spasticity in children (Smith, Birnbaum, Carter, et al., 1994; Young, 1994). It is an alpha-2-adrenergic agonist that increases presynaptic inhibition of motor neurons. It should not be used with another alpha-2-adrenergic agonist (e.g., clonidine). In addition, the use of tizanidine can be associated with an increase in liver enzymes, and three deaths from liver failure in people who took tizanidine were reported ("Tizanidine for Spasticity," 1997). Liver function tests must be monitored carefully when dantrium or tizanidine is prescribed.

A trial of oral medications in a child with severe spasticity may be indicated, particularly with the goal of improving ease of care. Diazepam may be useful in the treatment of frequent startle episodes that interfere with function and the treatment of persistent or recurrent muscle cramps at night.

Electrical Stimulation and Electromyogram Biofeedback
Research studies (see Colborne, 1994; Lee & Inman, 1990) on the use of functional electrical stimulation (FES) and EMG biofeedback to improve the gait of individuals with cerebral palsy have documented improvement on laboratory measures but limited functional change in gait. For example, in one study (Colborne, 1994), children with a hemiplegia pattern of cerebral palsy were treated with FES to the anterior tibialis to improve active dorsiflexion during the swing phase of gait. Stimulation intensity was set to effect active dorsiflexion of the foot to just less than the full passive range of motion. The children who received FES showed improvement in passive range of motion as compared with matched controls but showed no difference from matched controls in the knee and ankle motion on gait analysis (Colborne, 1994).

Pape, Kirsch, Galil, and colleagues (1993) reported decreased spasticity and improved motor skills in five children with cerebral palsy who received 6 months of therapeutic electrical stimulation (TES). TES provides low-intensity stimulation and does not cause active muscle contraction, so it can be used continuously. A number of children have been treated with TES at several centers; however, the benefits have not been confirmed in placebo-controlled, blind trials. In addition, the mechanism by which TES may result in functional benefits is not known. A randomized controlled trial of TES in chil-

dren after selective dorsal rhizotomy did show statistically significant functional change as measured by the GMFM (Steinbok, Reiner, & Kestle, 1997).

Phenol Neurolysis and Use of Botulinum Toxin
Phenol intramuscular neurolysis has been used for the treatment of spasticity in children with cerebral palsy since the 1970s (Gracies, Elovic, et al., 1997). Indications have been to improve function, improve ease of hygiene, and treat pain secondary to spasticity. The motor point of the nerve is located by the use of electrical stimulation with a fine wire electrode, and phenol is injected at this site. The effects of a phenol block last 9–12 months, and the injection can be repeated. The major limitations are the pain and discomfort associated with the procedure.

Botulinum toxin was used initially to treat strabismus as well as focal dystonias. Since the 1990s, it has been used to treat spasticity in children with cerebral palsy (Cosgrove, Corry, & Graham, 1994; Chutorian & Root, 1994; Koman, Mooney, Smith, et al., 1993; Russman, Tilton, & Gormley, 1997). Improvements have been demonstrated in the upper and lower extremities, muscle tone, range of motion, gait pattern, positioning, and other measures (Corry, Cosgrove, Duffy, et al., 1998; Corry, Cosgrove, Walsh, et al., 1997; Simpson, 1997).

Botulinum toxin interferes with the release of acetylcholine at the neuromuscular junction. The effects of one injection last approximately 3 months. Repeated injections may last 4–6 months. The major advantages of botulinum toxin for intramuscular neurolysis are the ease of the procedure, the decrease in the pain associated with the injection, and the comparative absence of side effects from the injection. A few children may develop minor pain at the site of the injection or a mild flulike illness that lasts for a few days. Treatment indications include

- Prevent progression of muscle contractures (to allow normal muscle growth and postpone surgery)
- Dynamic spasticity interfering with use of braces or causing functional impairment in gait (e.g., child with dynamic spasticity in gastrocnemius and poor tolerance of AFOs)
- Presurgical assessment if the functional benefit of muscle release is unclear (e.g., adolescent with dystonic varus deformity of the foot)
- Alleviation of pain because of spasticity or dystonia if other treatments are unsuccessful (e.g., child with idiopathic dystonia and shoulder pain)

There is general agreement that EMG localization of muscle motor points is not necessary. Botulinum toxin diffuses readily in the muscle; however, large muscles do require several injection sites (e.g., three in the medial hamstring). For this reason, botulinum toxin is usually used in children with conscious sedation with a medication such as oral or intranasal Versed. Only two or three muscles can be treated with botulinum toxin at one time because of the limitations of a total body dose. The major disadvantage of botulinum toxin is its high cost.

Surgical Management

Management of Orthopedic Problems in the Lower Extremity and Back The orthopedic problems of children with cerebral palsy include

- Joint contractures
- Hip subluxation and dislocation
- Scoliosis, lordosis, and kyphosis
- Rotational deformities
- Foot and ankle deformities
- Arm and hand deformities
- Joint pain
- Osteopenia and fractures

The surgical management of lower-extremity problems and scoliosis is discussed in the subsection that follows. Please note that many orthopedic surgeries treat the consequences of spasticity. Ideal management of the child with cerebral palsy includes control of abnormal tone to prevent the need for muscle or tendon releases to treat joint contractures.

Lower Extremity Two basic types of orthopedic surgeries are performed: 1) soft tissue surgery that includes tendon or muscle releases and length-

ening to correct imbalance between agonist and antagonist muscles and 2) bone surgery to correct fixed structural deformities. The goals of orthopedic surgery are 1) to prevent or to control the progression of structural deformity that would compromise maximal independence as an adult and 2) to improve function, including the quality and efficiency of gait.

Orthopedic surgery is best avoided in the child's preschool years, unless there is a structural deformity (e.g., hip subluxation or flexion contractures of the legs that prevent standing). The best results of orthopedic surgery are achieved when children are between 5 and 8 years of age. It is common practice to analyze all aspects of deformity in the legs and operate at all necessary joints (hips, knees, and ankles) at one time (Nene, Evans, & Patrick, 1993). It is important to note that orthopedic surgery reduces not the spasticity itself but the consequences of the spasticity. Joint contractures can recur. Review the orthopedic surgeries of the lower extremity listed in Table 6.6.

Hip Problems Common hip problems include flexion contracture, adduction contracture, internal rotation, and subluxation or dislocation. Hip subluxation and dislocation are usually problems in nonambulators (Scrutton, 1989). Plain hip radiographs remain the mainstay for diagnosis. Recommendations for the ages of children at which to obtain hip X rays to document their hip status are presented in the Guidelines for Care in the Appen-

Table 6.6. Orthopedic surgeries of the lower extremity

Clinical problem	Representative surgery
Hip flexion contracture	Lengthening of psoas tendon
Adduction contracture	Adductor tenotomy
Subluxation and dislocation	Adductor release with or without iliopsoas tenotomy
	Varus osteotomy of proximal femur
	Acetabular augmentation
Internal rotation	Derotational osteotomy
Knee flexion contracture (crouched knee)	Lengthening of hamstrings
Stiff knee	Rectus femoris release or transfer
Tibial torsion	Derotational osteotomy
Ankle equinus	Lengthening of Achilles tendon or aponeurosis
Spastic pes varus	Split transfer of posterior tibialis tendon
	Anterior transfer of posterior tibialis tendon
Spastic pes planus	Modified extraarticular subtalar arthrodesis

Adapted from Park and Owen (1992).

dix at the end of this chapter. Please note that the clinical examination does not predict hip subluxation, and even the clinical signs of dislocation can be subtle. The migration percentage (i.e., the percentage by which the femoral head is uncovered by the acetabulum) and the acetabular index are two X-ray measures of hip stability (Cornell, 1995). The value of hip abduction orthoses to prevent hip dislocation remains controversial. Surgical treatment may include adductor tenotomy, iliopsoas lengthening, varus derotation osteotomy of the proximal femur, and acetabular augmentation.

Knee Problems Knee problems include the crouched knee (i.e., flexion contracture due to hamstring spasticity), stiff knee due to rectus femoris spasticity, and recurvatum at the knee (Sutherland & Davids, 1993). Treatment of the knee flexion contracture may be ineffective unless it is combined with treatment of co-existing flexion contractures at the hip and ankle. In addition, lengthening of the hamstrings to treat flexion contracture of the knee occasionally may result in a stiff-kneed gait because of the associated spasticity of the rectus femoris. Treatment of the spastic rectus femoris is by surgical release or transfer.

Foot and Ankle Problems Common foot and ankle problems include equinus and spastic pes planus, which are common in the child with spastic diplegia (Bleck, 1990). The use of braces (i.e., solid AFOs) and physical therapy are the principal means by which to prevent fixed equinus contractures. The two surgical treatments of a fixed heel cord contracture are lengthening of the Achilles tendon or the aponeurosis. If surgery is required in a child prior to 5 years of age, there is a high risk of recurrent contracture, especially in a child with hemiplegia. The major risk of Achilles tendon or aponeurosis lengthening in ambulatory children with cerebral palsy, however, is overcorrection and subsequent crouched gait. The risk for overcorrection is significantly less if surgery is performed after a child reaches 8 years of age (Borton, Walker, Nattrass, & Graham, 1998).

Subtalar extraarticular arthrodesis (also called *the Grice procedure*) may be indicated for treatment of spastic pas planus or valgus foot deformity. Surgical treatment should be postponed until the child is 8 years of age or older for the best surgical result. Surgery may be less successful in children with more serious involvement (e.g., children with quadriplegia) (Alman, Craig, & Zimbler, 1993).

Scoliosis Spinal deformity in children with cerebral palsy includes scoliosis, kyphosis, and lordosis. Scoliosis tends to be the most severe in children with spastic quadriplegia. The presence of hip subluxation or dislocation and an asymmetric sitting posture with pelvic obliquity may contribute to the progression of scoliosis. Scoliosis may progress regardless of treatment during the adolescent growth spurt. Contracture of the hamstrings may contribute to kyphosis, and iliopsoas contracture may contribute to lordosis, because of anterior pelvic tilt. Common interventions for scoliosis include proper positioning or seating in a wheelchair, the use of bracing or body jackets, and the use of specially designed total-contact seating systems.

Once the scoliotic curve has progressed beyond 40%, it is likely to progress and require surgical stabilization (Rinsky, 1990; Saito, Ebara, Ohotsuka, et al., 1998). Segmental instrumentation is usually combined with arthrodesis (i.e., fusion) of the spine to the pelvis. Anterior surgery combined with posterior instrumentation and fusion may be necessary to improve the correction of the spines of children with severe scoliotic curves. Optimal preoperative nutritional status does improve the child's postoperative outcome (Jevsevar & Karlin, 1993). The benefits of surgical stabilization of scoliosis in children with severe or profound neurodevelopmental disabilities remain controversial (Cassidy, Craig, Perry, et al., 1994; Comstock, Leach, & Wenger, 1998; Majd, Muldowny, & Holt, 1997). In one study (Cassidy et al., 1994), no clinical differences were noted between a group of 17 people with severe cerebral palsy who were living in institutions and had had scoliosis surgeries and a similar group of 20 people who had not had surgery. Health care workers, however, believed that the individuals who had had the fusion surgery were more comfortable. Treatment recommendations for surgical stabilization of the spine must be individualized and based on realistic goals of improving the individual's function, ease of care, and quality of life.

Osteopenia and Fractures Some children with quadriplegia or severe diplegia have decreased bone mineral density (i.e., osteopenia) and recurrent fractures. One time of high risk for fractures is following removal of a hip spica cast (Henderson, 1997). Children with cerebral palsy and seizures who are taking anticonvulsants are at increased risk for osteopenia (Jones & Sambrook, 1994; Sheth, Wesolowski, Jacob, et al., 1995). In one study (Baer, Kozlowski, Byler, et al., 1997), ambulatory status and the use of anticonvulsants by children who were not ambulatory were the strongest predictors of osteopenia. In addition, 50% of the study group received less than the recommended daily intake of calcium, and 70% received less than the recommended intake of vitamin D.

Blood calcium, phosphate, and alkaline phosphatase levels are not accurate indicators of low bone mineral density (Henderson, Lin, & Greene, 1995). The bone density of children with cerebral palsy who are not ambulatory should be monitored as needed with energy X-ray absorptiometry (Lin & Henderson, 1996). Review these children's calcium and vitamin D intake, and consider prescribing vitamin D supplementation. Studies report conflicting results regarding the benefits of standing on increasing bone mineral density (e.g., use of a standing frame by a child who is not ambulatory). Treatment with biphosphonates to inhibit osteoclastic bone resorption has been successful in adults with postmenopausal osteoporosis; however, their use in children with cerebral palsy who experience recurrent fractures is controversial because of concern about the inhibition of bone mineralization (Shaw, White, Fraser, & Rosenbloom, 1994).

Upper Extremity   Only a small number of children with cerebral palsy (e.g., children with hemiplegia) have indications for surgical treatment of dynamic or fixed structural deformities of the upper extremity. Surgical decisions must be based on the extent of the fixed and dynamic deformity, sensation in the hand, and the intelligence and motivation level of the child (see Koman, Gelberman, Toby, et al., 1990; Waters & Van Heest, 1998).

Neurosurgical Treatments for Spasticity

Selective Dorsal Rhizotomy   Selective dorsal rhizotomy (SDR) is a neurosurgical procedure intended to reduce spasticity by severing selected dorsal rootlets of the spinal cord from spinal levels L2 to S1 or S2 (Cahan, 1988; McLaughlin, Bjornson, Astley, et al., 1994; Peacock & Arens, 1982). The fibers to be cut are identified by their abnormal responses to direct electrical stimulation. A definite reduction in spasticity is noted postoperatively, and many children demonstrate improvement in ambulatory status. Considerable variability between children in outcomes occurs, however (McLaughlin et al., 1994). The ideal candidate appears to be the child with spastic diplegia who was born prematurely, has some functional ambulation with or without assistive devices, and has good trunk control. Relative contraindications to SDR include prior orthopedic surgery, fixed joint contractures, the presence of dystonia or athetosis, and significant truncal or proximal muscle weakness.

The maximum benefit of the procedure is generally not noted until 6–12 months postoperatively. Most children demonstrate significant weakness in the initial weeks postsurgery and require frequent therapy services for 6–12 months. These therapy services are generally provided on a schedule of 2 hours per day prior to hospital discharge, three times weekly for 6 months, and then twice weekly for another 6 months.

SDR does not prevent progression of hip subluxation or dislocation, rotational deformities, or valgus foot deformities. Sensory loss and neurogenic bladder dysfunction have been rare problems postoperatively. SDR may prevent joint contractures resulting from spasticity if performed before the child reaches 4 years of age. In one study, children who received SDR before 4 years of age required fewer Achilles tendon and hamstring lengthenings than children who received SDR after age 4 (Chicoine, Park, & Kaufman, 1997).

The role of SDR versus intrathecal baclofen or optimal traditional management with therapy, bracing, and orthopedic surgery remains controversial. Results from three double-blind randomized trials of SDR versus similar level of therapy services without SDR for children with spastic diplegia were reported (McLaughlin, Bjornson, Astley, et al., 1998; Steinbock, Reiner, Beauchamp, et al., 1997; Wright, Sheil, Drake, et al., 1998). All three of the centers where the trials were conducted (Vancouver, Toronto, and Seattle) reported significant reductions in spasticity; however, only two reported significant functional gains as measured by the GMFM. In addition, some investigators (see Hays, McLaughlin, Bjornson, et al., 1998; Steinbok, Reiner, Beauchamp, et al., 1997) have questioned the electrophysiologic methods for determining which rootlets are to be cut.

Intrathecal Baclofen   Baclofen is a GABA-agonist and acts at the spinal cord level. Although it has been only modestly effective in controlling the spasticity associated with cerebral palsy when given orally, baclofen has been shown to be effective when given intrathecally. Small amounts can be given intrathecally, avoiding the central side effects of baclofen. The effect of a single intrathecal dose lasts only for a few hours; therefore, baclofen is given intrathecally by a continuous infusion pump that is surgically placed subcutaneously (Albright, Barron, Fasick, et al., 1993; Albright, Cervi, Singletary, et al., 1991). Two groups of children with cerebral palsy are potential candidates for intrathecal baclofen (ITB): individuals with severe hypertonicity (where the treatment goal is to facilitate care) and individuals who have mild to moderate hypertonicity (where the treatment goal is to improve function).

Nonrandomized clinical research studies (Albright, 1996; Albright, Barry, Painter, & Schultz, 1998; Gerszten, Albright, & Barry, 1997) showed that ITB does reduce spasticity and dystonia significantly and improve ambulation and quality of life. Doses can be titrated to avoid loss of function due to weakness. ITB also may decrease the need for subsequent orthopedic surgery (Gerszten, Albright, & Johnstone, 1998). Significant side effects have been reported, including dizziness, sedation, respiratory depression, and hypotension. In addition, ITB may result in mechanical complications and postoperative infections (Armstrong, Steinbok, Cochrane, et al., 1997). ITB may be the treatment of choice for individuals with ambulatory potential who have proximal weakness and spasticity or dystonia that interferes with function. Ongoing research is required to clarify specific treatment indications, long-term benefits, and the relative benefits of ITB versus traditional management with orthopedic surgery.

Management of Drooling, Constipation, and Urinary Hesitancy or Incontinence

Drooling Drooling is a typical phenomenon of infancy and usually subsides by 15–18 months of age (Blasco & Allaire, 1992). Children with cerebral palsy, especially those with quadriplegia or right hemiplegia, may continue to drool beyond school age. Persistent drooling can cause significant social problems, interfere with day-to-day activities, and cause minor skin irritation. Excess secretions may also precipitate recurrent gagging, coughing, and vomiting that can be confused with GER. The goal of treatment is to improve these children's overall quality of life and social functioning. The treatment options include various behavioral therapies, medications, and surgeries. In general, medications are considered for treating school-age and, in rare cases, preschool-age children (see Table 6.7). Surgical intervention may be considered in an older school-age child or adolescent, particularly if the use of medications was unsuccessful. Research data with regard to any of these treatment methods are limited (Blasco & Allaire, 1992).

Adults with cerebral palsy and parents of children with cerebral palsy report frustration with behavioral methods (Blasco & Allaire, 1992). The drooling is reduced only as long as the person maintains concentration on the behavioral intervention and returns when the person's focus is on another task. Verbal cuing is one method that directs the child's awareness to the drooling and encourages regular swallowing.

The anticholinergic drugs atropine, scopolamine, benztropine (Cogentin), benzhexol (Artane), and glycopyrrolate (Robinul) have been used to decrease drooling in children with cerebral palsy (Blasco & Allaire, 1992; Camp-Bruno, Winsberg,

Table 6.7. Medications for the management of drooling

Representative drug	Initial treatment dosage
Atropine sulfate	.1–.4 milligrams one to three times daily
Benztropine	Start .5–2 milligrams once daily
Glycopyrrolate	1–2 milligrams one to three times daily
Benzhexol	1 milligram twice daily
Transdermal scopolamine	One patch changed twice weekly in older children and adolescents

Green-Parsons, et al., 1989; Lewis, Fontana, Mehallick, et al., 1994; Reddihough, Johnson, Staples, et al., 1990). All are used primarily for other medical purposes; for example, Cogentin and Artane are used as adjuncts to the treatment of movement disorders. Studies (Bachrach, Walter, & Trzcinski, 1998; Blasco & Stansbury, 1996; Camp-Bruno et al., 1989) have provided cause for some optimism regarding the effectiveness of some of these medications for drooling. In one study (Camp-Bruno et al., 1989), as many as two thirds of the children in the sample did show significant reductions in the amount of drooling, although drooling was not eliminated in any of the children. The side effects of the medications for drooling include sedation, irritability, blurred vision, constipation, lowering of seizure threshold, and urinary retention. Make sure that constipation is adequately treated and that seizures, if present, are well controlled before starting a child on any of these medications.

Glycopyrrolate (i.e., Robinul) does not appear to have the central side effects of the other medications and thus may be the appropriate first choice for a medication trial. Several studies (Bachrach et al., 1998; Blasco & Stansbury, 1996; Stern, 1997) reported clinically significant reductions in drooling in most children; however, many reported that children experienced side effects, including dry mouth, thick secretions, flushing, and urinary retention.

In general, three surgical approaches alone or in combination have been used to reduce drooling: The salivary glands have been removed, the secretory ducts have been ligated or relocated, and the secretory motor nerves to the glands have been severed or crushed (Burton, 1991; O'Dwyer & Conlon, 1997; Webb, Reddihough, Johnson, et al., 1995). Laser photocoagulation is a reported alternative to ligation of the parotid duct (Wong, Chang, Chen, & Chen, 1997). Representative surgical procedures for drooling are as follows:

- Removal of submandibular glands and repositioning of parotid ducts (i.e., the Wilke procedure)

- Relocation of submandibular ducts with or without removal of sublingual glands
- Ligation of parotid ducts with or without submandibular gland excision

Different physicians favor various procedures. No consensus exists with regard to the most effective approach. Postoperative complications include infection, dry mouth with thick mucoid saliva, worsening of dental problems, and increased difficulty with chewing and swallowing (Hallet, Lucas, Johnston, et al., 1995). Surgical treatment of drooling has resulted in the loss of oral feeding skills and the requirement for gastrostomy placement (Stevenson, Allaire, & Blasco, 1994). Transtympanic sectioning of the chorda tympani and tympanic nerve has largely been abandoned by most surgeons because of reports of the return of drooling after a few months and loss of taste (Blasco & Allaire, 1992). A few otolaryngologists continue to advocate this procedure (Burton, 1991).

The Teacher Drool Scale (TDS; see Table 6.8) (Camp-Bruno et al., 1989) is one qualitative method for following the effectiveness of any of the interventions described in this subsection. It can be completed by both teachers and parents on a daily basis during a medication trial. Another method is to count the number of bib or towel changes during the day.

Constipation Constipation and impaction with secondary stool incontinence are common problems for children with cerebral palsy. A number of factors predispose these children to constipation: decreased mobility, decreased fluid and fiber intake in the diet, difficulty with positioning the child securely on the toilet, and side effects of med-

Table 6.8.   Teacher Drool Scale (TDS)

1. No drooling
2. Infrequent drooling, small amount
3. Occasional drooling, on and off all day
4. Frequent drooling, but not profusely
5. Constant drooling, always wet

Adapted from Camp-Bruno et al. (1989).

ications. Anorectal manometry has demonstrated some incoordination of the sphincter and pelvic floor musculature but typical rectal functioning (Agnarsson, McCarthy, Clayder, et al., 1993).

Questions about constipation and incontinence should be part of each update of a child's management plan. If present, constipation and associated impaction should be treated vigorously. Treatment failures result from too little treatment for too short a period of time. Children should be monitored closely for at least 6 months after the initiation of treatment. The treatment program (see Table 6.9) includes review of positioning and seating alternatives, behavioral management programs, dietary alterations, a cleanout program to treat the impaction, a maintenance program to ensure continued appropriate stool consistency, and occasionally an emptying program to train regular emptying.

Adequate oral fluid intake and increase in dietary fiber are the mainstays of treatment. Fiber products or bulk agents include wheat bran (i.e., cellulose); Fruiteze (i.e., soluble fiber from puréed dates, prunes, and raisins; for more information, contact Fruit-Eze, Inc., 1075 N.W. Murray Road, Suite 276, Portland, OR 97229-5892, 800-743-1941); and a

Table 6.9.   Management of constipation in children with cerebral palsy

Treatment issues	Treatment recommendations
Review of positioning and seating	Obtain an adaptive toilet seat with adequate support as needed
Address behavioral issues	Implement behavior management program as needed
Dietary alterations	Increase fluid and fiber in the diet and decrease dairy products (watch calcium and vitamin D intake)
	If on enteral feeding, use formula with fiber
	Refer to a nutritionist as needed
Cleanout program	Minimum of one enema on 2 consecutive days, followed by oral bisacodyl tablets or magnesium citrate on the third day (oil-retention enemas should be used if standard enemas are not effective prior to oral medications)
Maintenance program	Initially use a bulk agent with a lubricant (mineral oil) if the child has an impaction or a history of chronic constipation
Emptying program	Use oral senna, enema, or suppository as needed to ensure at least every other day regular emptying

variety of products that contain psyllium, methylcellulose, or polycarbophil. Lactulose also has been effective in the treatment of constipation. In addition, stimulant laxatives (e.g., oral bisacodyl) may be helpful after the use of enemas to clean out an impaction and occasionally for training regular bowel habits (e.g., use of bisacodyl suppositories or oral senna).

Urinary Hesitancy or Incontinence As many as 30% of children with cerebral palsy express complaints related to the lower urinary tract (Mayo, 1992). The principal problems in children with cerebral palsy who have been referred for urologic evaluation are daytime urgency incontinence and difficulty with initiating a urinary stream (Mayo, 1992; McNeal, Hawtrey, Wolraich, et al., 1983; Reid & Borzyskowski, 1993). Urologic evaluation should include voiding cystourethrogram and urodynamics. Hyperreflexia of the bladder and urgency with bladder fullness is commonly found in urodynamic studies. Evidence of upper-tract damage is rarely found if renal ultrasound is performed.

The treatment program is individualized based on the results of the urologic evaluation and includes use of anticholinergic medication (e.g., oxybutynin, hyoscyanine), and occasionally antibiotics and clean intermittent catheterization. Rarely, surgical intervention is indicated. Almost all children improve with treatment, although difficulty with voiding has proved more difficult to manage, especially if it is associated with urgency with bladder fullness (Mayo, 1992). Please note that concomitant treatment of constipation may result in improved bladder emptying.

Anticipatory Guidance

Adolescence is generally a time for the exploration of new social roles and increasing independence (Wadsworth & Harper, 1993). Social skills such as interpersonal problem solving and making friends develop from observation of and interaction with other adolescents. Unfortunately, adolescents with cerebral palsy and other physical disabilities often have limited interaction with peers and inconsistent or negative social feedback from them (Blum, Resnick, Nelson, et al., 1991). Research (see Wadsworth & Harper, 1993) showed that adolescents with physical disabilities view having friends as being very important, but they have limited contact with friends outside school and show negligible participation in organized social activities. Adolescent girls with cerebral palsy rate themselves as being less competent in social and athletic skills and as having less romantic appeal (King, Shultz, Steel, et al., 1993). Boys rate themselves as being less competent in academic and athletic skills and as having

less romantic appeal. In a more encouraging study (Magill-Evans & Restall, 1991), adolescent girls reported lower self-esteem in adolescence but were similar to controls in adulthood. In the same study, boys were found to be similar to controls as adolescents and as adults.

Parents and health professionals need to be aware of the importance of social competence for adolescents with cerebral palsy, to recognize that lack of social skills is among the primary factors leading to job failure and adjustment problems as adults, and to understand that specific social skills training programs can be effective (Wadsworth & Harper, 1993). Interventions with adolescents with cerebral palsy generally focus on building self-care and independent living and job skills. Little attention may have been paid to social isolation or a need for the adolescent to develop new social roles. Health professionals need to work with other community professionals to support families in providing typical social experiences for children with cerebral palsy at *all* ages. Children and adolescents need to practice social skills on a daily basis and thus need encouragement to participate regularly in recreational, social, and educational groups and to develop and maintain close friendships.

Important Care Coordination Issues

Education staff are responsible for implementing the health procedures needed to support the child's full participation in education programs. These procedures may include specialized oral feeding programs, gastrostomy feeding, tracheostomy care, or the administration of oxygen for some children while they are at school. In addition, some children with cerebral palsy need special emergency management plans. School staff need information about and at times training in specific procedures from health professionals. Collaboration among the primary care office, schools, and the neurodevelopmental team is essential for the optimal management of children with cerebral palsy and their families.

Home health nursing services also provide invaluable support to some families for gastrostomy feeding and other specialized services. In addition to the general recommendations for care coordination provided in Chapter 1, the primary care office also should identify

- The contact people for EI/ECSE services and in the school district who supervise health procedures in education environments and facilitate exchange of information
- The contact person for home health nursing services in the community

REFERENCES

Abel, M.F., Juhl, G.A., Vaughan, C.L., & Damiano, D.L. (1998). Gait assessment of fixed ankle–foot orthoses in children with spastic diplegia. *Archives of Physical Medicine and Rehabilitation, 79*(2), 126–133.

Agnarsson, U., McCarthy, G., Clayder, G.S., et al. (1993). Anorectal function of children with neurological problems: II. Cerebral palsy. *Developmental Medicine and Child Neurology, 35,* 903–908.

Albright, A.L. (1996). Intrathecal baclofen in cerebral palsy movement disorders. *Journal of Child Neurology, 11*(Suppl. 1), S29–S35.

Albright, A.L., Barron, W.B., Fasick, M.P., et al. (1993). Continuous intrathecal baclofen infusion for spasticity of cerebral origin. *JAMA: Journal of the American Medical Association, 270*(20), 2475–2477.

Albright, A.L., Barry, M.J., Painter, M.J., & Shultz, B. (1998). Infusion of intrathecal baclofen for generalized dystonia in cerebral palsy. *Journal of Neurosurgery, 88*(1), 73–76.

Albright, A.L., Cervi, A., Singletary, J., et al. (1991). Intrathecal baclofen for spasticity in cerebral palsy. *JAMA: Journal of the American Medical Association, 265*(11), 1418–1422.

Alman, B.A., Craig, C.L., & Zimbler, S. (1993). Subtalar arthrodesis for stabilization of valgus hindfoot in patients with cerebral palsy. *Journal of Pediatric Orthopaedics, 13*(5), 634–641.

American Academy of Orthopaedic Surgeons. (1965). *Joint motion: Method of measuring and recording.* Rosemont, IL: Author.

Armstrong, R.W., Steinbok, P., Cochrane, D.D., et al. (1997). Intrathecally administered baclofen for treatment of children with spasticity of cerebral palsy. *Journal of Neurosurgery, 87*(3), 409–414.

Ashworth, B. (1964). Preliminary trial of carisoprodol in multiple sclerosis. *Practitioner, 192,* 540–542.

Bachrach, S.J., Walter, R.S., & Trzcinski, K. (1998). Use of glycopyrrodate and other anticholinergic medications for sialorrhea in children with cerebral palsy. *Clinical Pediatrics (Philadelphia), 37*(8), 485–490.

Baer, M.T., Kozlowksi, B.W., Byler, E.M., et al. (1997). Vitamin D, calcium, and bone status in children with developmental delay in relation to anticonvulsant use and ambulatory status. *American Journal of Clinical Nutrition, 65*(4), 1042–1051.

Bayley, N. (1969). *Manual for the Bayley Scales of Infant Development.* San Antonio, TX: The Psychological Corp.

Bayley, N. (1993). *Bayley Scales of Infant Development* (2nd ed.). San Antonio, TX: The Psychological Corp.

Blasco, P.A., & Allaire, J.H. (1992). Drooling in the developmentally disabled: Management practices and recommendations. *Developmental Medicine and Child Neurology, 34,* 849–862.

Blasco, P.A., & Stansbury, J.C. (1996). Glycopyrrolate treatment of chronic drooling. *Archives of Pediatrics and Adolescent Medicine, 150*(9), 932–935.

Bleck, E.E. (1975). Locomotor prognosis in cerebral palsy. *Developmental Medicine and Child Neurology, 17,* 18–25.

Bleck, E.E. (1979). Musculoskeletal examination of the child with cerebral palsy. *Pediatric Annals, 8*(10), 606–613.

Bleck, E.E. (1990). Current concepts review: Management of the lower extremities in children who have cerebral palsy. *Journal of Bone and Joint Surgery, 72A*(1), 140–144.

Blum, R.W., Resnick, M.D., Nelson, R., et al. (1991). Family and peer issues among adolescents with spina bifida and cerebral palsy. *Pediatrics, 88*(2), 280–285.

Borton, D., Walker, K., Nattrass, G., & Graham, H.K. (1998). *Calf lengthening in cerebral palsy: Risk factor outcome analysis.* Paper presented at the annual meeting of the American Academy for Cerebral Palsy and Developmental Medicine, San Antonio, TX.

Bowen, T.R., Lennon, N., Castagno, P., et al. (1998). Variability of energy-consumption measures in children with cerebral palsy. *Journal of Pediatric Orthopaedics, 18*(6), 738–742.

Bower, E., & McLellan, D.L. (1992). Effect of increased exposure to physiotherapy on skill acquisition of children with cerebral palsy. *Developmental Medicine and Child Neurology, 34,* 25–39.

Burton, M.J. (1991), Annotation: The surgical management of drooling. *Developmental Medicine and Child Neurology, 33,* 1110–1116.

Butler, C. (1988, Summer). Powered tots: Augmentative mobility for locomotor disabled youngsters. *Tot Line, 4*(9), 18–19. (*Note: Tot Line* is the publication of the Section of Pediatrics, American Physical Therapy Association.)

Cahan, L.D. (1988). Selective dorsal rhizotomy for children with cerebral palsy. In G.T. Tindall (Ed.), *Contemporary neurosurgery* (pp. 1–6). Philadelphia: Lippincott Williams & Wilkins.

Camp-Bruno, J.A., Winsberg, B.G., Green-Parsons, A.R., et al. (1989). Efficacy of benztropine therapy for drooling. *Developmental Medicine and Child Neurology, 31,* 309–319.

Capute, A.J., Palmer, F.B., Shapiro, B.K., et al. (1984). Primitive reflex profile: A quantitation of primitive reflexes in infancy. *Developmental Medicine and Child Neurology, 26,* 375–383.

Carlson, W.E., Vaughan, C.L., Damiano, D.L., & Abel, M.F. (1997). Orthotic management of gait in spastic diplegia. *American Journal of Physical Medicine and Rehabilitation, 76*(3), 219–225.

Cassidy, C., Craig, C.L., Perry, A., et al. (1994). A reassessment of spinal stabilization in severe cerebral palsy. *Journal of Pediatric Orthopedics, 14*(6), 731–739.

Chandler, L.S. (1986). Screening for movement dysfunction in infancy. *Physical and Occupational Therapy in Pediatrics, 6,* 171–190.

Chandler, L.S., Andrews, M., & Swanson, M. (1980). *Movement Assessment of Infants (MAI).* Rolling Bay, WA: A.H. Larson.

Chang, W.C., Chan, C., Slaughter, S.E., & Cartwright, D. (1997). Evaluating the FONE FIM: Part II. Concurrent validity and influencing factors. *Journal of Outcome Measures, 1,* 259–285.

Check, D., & Gallagher, R.J. (1985). *Infant motor assessment: Bayley Scales of Infant Development compared with the Chicago Infant Neuromotor Assessment.* Paper presented to the annual meeting of the American Academy for Cerebral Palsy and Developmental Medicine, Seattle, WA.

Chicoine, M.R., Park, T.S., & Kaufman, B.A. (1997). Selective dorsal rhizotomy and rates of orthopedic surgery in children with spastic cerebral palsy. *Journal of Neurosurgery, 86,* 34–39.

Chutorian, A.M., & Root, L. (1994), Management of spasticity in children with botulinum A toxin. *International Pediatrics, 9*(Suppl. 1), 35–43.

Colborne, R.G. (1994). Feedback of triceps surae EMG in gait of children with cerebral palsy: A controlled study. *Archives of Physical Medicine and Rehabilitation, 75,* 40–44.

Comstock, C.P., Leach, J., & Wenger, O.R. (1998). Scoliosis in total-body-involvement cerebral palsy: Analysis of surgical treatment and patient and caregiver satisfaction. *Spine, 23*(12), 1412–1424.

Coniglio, S.J., Stevenson, R.D., & Rogol, A.D. (1996). Apparent growth hormone deficiency in children with cerebral palsy. *Developmental Medicine and Child Neurology, 38,* 797–804.

Coolman, R., Foran, W., & Lee, J. (1997). *Oregon guidelines for medically based outpatient physical therapy and occupational therapy for children with special health needs in the managed care environment.* Portland: Oregon Health Sciences University.

Coolman, R.B., Bennett, F.C., Sells, C.J., et al. (1985). Neuromotor development of graduates of the neonatal intensive care unit: Patterns encountered in the first two years of life. *Developmental and Behavioral Pediatrics, 6*(6), 327–333.

Cornell, M.S. (1995). Review article: The hip in cerebral palsy. *Developmental Medicine and Child Neurology, 37,* 3–18.

Corrigan, J.D., Smith-Knapp, K., & Granger, C.V. (1997). Validity of the functional independence measure for persons with traumatic brain injury. *Archives of Physical Medicine and Rehabilitation, 78,* 828–834.

Corry, I.S., Cosgrove, A.P., Duffy, C.M., et al. (1998). Botulinum toxin A compared with stretching casts in the treatment of spastic equinus: A randomised prospective trial. *Journal of Pediatric Orthopedics, 18*(3), 304–311.

Corry, I.S., Cosgrove, A.P., Walsh, E.G., et al. (1997). Botulinum toxin A in the hemiplegic upper limb: A double-blind trial. *Developmental Medicine and Child Neurology, 39*(3), 185–193.

Corry, I.S., Duffy, C.M., Cosgrave, A.P., & Graham, H.K. (1996). Measurement of oxygen consumption in disabled children by the Cosmed K2 portable telemetry system. *Developmental Medicine and Child Neurology, 38*(7), 585–593.

Cosgrove, A.P., Corry, I.S., & Graham, H.K. (1994). Botulinum toxin in the management of the lower limb in cerebral palsy. *Developmental Medicine and Child Neurology, 36,* 386–396.

da Paz, A.C., Burnett, S.M., & Braga, L.W. (1994). Walking prognosis in cerebral palsy: A 22-year retrospective analysis. *Developmental Medicine and Child Neurology, 36*(2), 130–134.

Damiano, D.L., & Abel, M.F. (1998). Functional outcomes of strength training in spastic cerebral palsy. *Archives of Physical Medicine and Rehabilitation, 79*(2), 119–125.

Damiano, D.L., Kelly, I.E., & Vaughn, C.L. (1995). Effects of quadriceps femoris muscle strengthening on crouch gait in children with spastic diplegia. *Physical Therapy, 75,* 658–671.

Darrah, J., Piper, M., & Watt, M.J. (1998). Assessment of gross motor skills of at-risk infants: Predictive validity of the Alberta Infant Motor Scale. *Developmental Medicine and Child Neurology, 40*(7), 485–491.

Desch, L.W. (1986). High technology for handicapped children: A pediatrician's viewpoint. *Pediatrics, 77,* 71–87.

Dormans, J.P. (1993). Orthopedic management of children with cerebral palsy. *Pediatric Clinics of North America, 40*(3), 645–657.

Ellison, P.H., Browning, C.A., Larson, B., et al. (1983). Development of a scoring system for the Milani-Comparetti and Gidoni method of assessing neurologic abnormality in infancy. *Physical Therapy, 63,* 1414–1423.

Fedman, A.B., Haley, S.M., & Coryell, J. (1990). Concurrent and constructive validity of the pediatric evaluation of disability inventory. *Physical Therapy, 70*(10), 602–610.

Folio, M.R., & Fewell, R.R. (1983). *Peabody Developmental Motor Scales and Activity Cards (PDMS).* Itasca, IL: Riverside Publishing Co.

Gans, B.M., Haley, S.M., Hallenborg, S.C., et al. (1988). Description and interobserver reliability of the Tufts Assessment of Motor Performance. *American Journal of Physical Medicine and Rehabilitation, 67*(5), 202–210.

Gerszten, P.C., Albright, A.L., & Johnstone, G.F. (1998). Intrathecal baclofen infusion and subsequent orthopedic surgery in patients with spastic cerebral palsy. *Journal of Neurosurgery, 88*(6), 1009–1013.

Gerszten, P.C., Albright, A.L., & Barry, M.J. (1997). Effect on ambulation of continuous intrathecal baclofen infusion. *Pediatric Neurosurgery, 27*(1), 40–44.

Gracies, J.-M., Elovic, E., McGuire, J., et al. (1997). Traditional pharmacological treatments for spasticity: Part I. Local treatments. *Muscle and Nerve Supplement, 6,* S61–S91.

Gracies, J.M., Nance, P., Elovic, E., et al. (1997). Traditional pharmacological treatments for spasticity: Part II. General and regional treatments. *Muscle and Nerve Supplement, 6,* S92–S120.

Granata, T., Farina, L., Faiella, A., et al. (1997). Familial schizencephaly associated with EMX2 mutation. *Neurology, 48,* 1403–1406.

Greene, P. (1992). Baclofen in the treatment of dystonia. *Clinical Neuropharmacology, 15,* 276–288.

Grimby, G., Andren, E., Holmgren, E., et al. (1996). Structure of a combination of Functional Independence Measure and Instrumental Activity Measure items in community-living persons: A study of individuals with cerebral palsy and spina bifida. *Archives of Physical Medicine and Rehabilitation, 77,* 1109–1114.

Haley, S.M., Coster, W.J., Ludlow, L.H., et al. (1992). *Pediatric Evaluation of Disability Inventory (PEDI) version 1.0: Developmental, standardization, and administration manual.* Boston: New England Medical Center Hospitals.

Hall, J.G., Froster-Iskenius, U.G., & Allanson, J.E. (1989). *Handbook of normal physical measurements.* New York: Oxford University Press.

Hallett, K.B., Lucas, J.O., Johnston, T., et al. (1995). Dental health of children with cerebral palsy following sialodochoplasty. *Special Care in Dentistry, 15*(6), 234–238.

Hamilton, B.B., & Granger, C.V. (1991). *WeeFIM.* Buffalo: Research Foundation of the State University of New York.

Harris, S.R. (1987). Early intervention for children with motor handicaps. In M.J. Guralnick & F.C. Bennett (Eds.), *The effectiveness of early intervention for at-risk and handicapped children* (pp. 175–212). San Diego: Academic Press.

Harris, S.R. (1997). The effectiveness of early intervention for children with cerebral palsy and related motor disabilities. In M.J. Guralnick (Ed.), *The effectiveness of early intervention* (pp. 327–347). Baltimore: Paul H. Brookes Publishing Co.

Hays, R.M., McLaughlin, J.F., Bjornson, K.F., et al. (1998). Electrophysiological monitoring during selective dorsal rhizotomy, and spasticity and GMFM performance. *Developmental Medicine and Child Neurology, 40,* 233–238.

Henderson, R.C. (1997). Bone density and other possible predictors of fracture risk in children and adolescents with spastic quadriplegia. *Developmental Medicine and Child Neurology, 39,* 224–227.

Henderson, R.C., Lin, P.P., & Greene, W.B. (1995). Bone-mineral density in children and adolescents who have spastic cerebral palsy. *Journal of Bone and Joint Surgery American, 77*(11), 1671–1681.

Hughes, I., & Newton, R. (1992). Annotation: Genetic aspects of cerebral palsy. *Developmental Medicine and Child Neurology, 34,* 80–86.

Isumi, H., Takashima, S., Kakita, A., et al. (1997). Expression of the LIS-1 gene product in brain anomalies with a migration disorder. *Pediatric Neurology, 16*(1), 42–44.

Jevsevar, D.S., & Karlin, L.I. (1993). The relationship between preoperative nutritional status and complications after an operation for scoliosis in patients who have cerebral palsy. *Journal of Bone and Joint Surgery, 75A*(6), 880–884.

Jones, G., & Sambrook, P.N. (1994). Drug-induced disorders of bone metabolism: Incidence, management, and avoidance. *Drug Safety, 10*(6), 480–490.

Katz, R.T., & Rymer, W.Z. (1989). Review article: Spastic hypertonia: Mechanics and measurement. *Archives of Physical Medicine and Rehabilitation, 70,* 144–154.

King, G.A., Shultz, I.Z., Steel, K., et al. (1993). Self-evaluation and self-concept of adolescents with physical disabilities. *American Journal of Occupational Therapy, 47*(2), 132–140.

Knutson, L.M., & Clark, D.E. (1991). Orthotic devices for ambulation in children with cerebral palsy and myelomeningocele. *Physical Therapy, 71*(12), 947–959.

Kolobe, T.H., Palisano, R.J., & Stratford, P.W. (1998). Comparison of two outcome measures for infants with cerebral palsy and infants with motor delays. *Physical Therapy, 78,* 1062–1072.

Koman, L.A., Gelberman, R.H., Toby, E.B., et al. (1990). Cerebral palsy: Management of the upper extremity. *Clinical Orthopedics and Related Research, 253,* 62–74.

Koman, L.A., Mooney, J.F., III, Smith, B., et al. (1993). Management of cerebral palsy with botulinum-A toxin: Preliminary investigation. *Journal of Pediatric Orthopedics, 13,* 489–495.

Kuban, K.C.K., & Leviton, A. (1994). Review article: Cerebral palsy. *New England Journal of Medicine, 330*(3), 188–195.

Lee, J.S., & Inman, D. (1990). *Use of surface electromyography to teach children with cerebral palsy to improve motor control.* Scientific poster presented to the annual meeting of the American Academy for Cerebral Palsy and Developmental Medicine, Orlando, FL.

Lewis, D.W., Fontana, C., Mehallick, L.K., et al. (1994). Transdermal scopolamine for reduction of drooling in developmentally delayed children. *Developmental Medicine and Child Neurology, 36*(6), 484–486.

Lin, P.P., & Henderson, R.C. (1996). Bone mineralization in the affected extremities of children with spastic hemiplegia. *Developmental Medicine and Child Neurology, 38*(9), 782–786.

Magill-Evans, J.E., & Restall, G. (1991). Self-esteem of persons with cerebral palsy: From adolescence to adulthood. *American Journal of Occupational Therapy, 45*(9), 819–825.

Majd, M.E., Muldowny, D.S., & Holt, R.T. (1997). Natural history of scoliosis in the institutionalized adult cerebral palsy population. *Spine, 22*(13), 1461–1466.

Mayo, M.E. (1992). Lower urinary tract dysfunction in cerebral palsy. *Journal of Urology, 147,* 419–420.

McCabe, M.A., & Granger, V. (1990). Content validity of a pediatric functional independence measure. *Applied Nursing Research, 3,* 120–122.

McCormick, M.C., Charney, E.B., & Stemmler, M.M. (1986). Assessing the impact of a child with spina bifida on the family. *Developmental Medicine and Child Neurology, 28,* 53–56.

McLaughlin, J.F., Bjornson, K.F., Astley, S.J., et al. (1994). The role of selective dorsal rhizotomy in cerebral palsy: Critical evaluation of a prospective clinical series. *Developmental Medicine and Child Neurology, 36,* 755–769.

McLaughlin, J.F., Bjornson, K.F., Astley, S.J., et al. (1998). Selective dorsal rhizotomy: Efficacy and safety in an investigator-masked randomized clinical trial. *Developmental Medicine and Child Neurology, 40*(4), 220–232.

McNeal, D.M., Hawtrey, C.E., Wolraich, M.L., et al. (1983). Symptomatic neurogenic bladder in a cerebral-palsied population. *Developmental Medicine and Child Neurology, 25,* 612–616.

Milani-Comparetti, A., & Gidoni, E. (1967). Routine developmental examination in normal and retarded children. *Developmental Medicine and Child Neurology, 9,* 631–638.

Milla, P.G., & Jackson, A.D.M. (1977). A controlled trial of baclofen in children with cerebral palsy. *Journal of International Medical Research, 5,* 398–404.

Molnar, G.E., & Gordon, S.U. (1976). Cerebral palsy: Predictive value of selected clinical signs for early prognostication of motor function. *Archives of Physical Medicine and Rehabilitation, 57,* 153–158.

Munch, L. (1992). Annotations: Cerebral palsy epidemiology: Where are we now and where are we going? *Developmental Medicine and Child Neurology, 34,* 547–555.

Nelson, K.B., & Ellenberg, J.H. (1982). Children who "outgrew" cerebral palsy. *Pediatrics, 69*(5), 529–536.

Nelson, M.N., Bozynski, M.E.A., Genaze, D., et al. (1983, October). *Comparative evaluation of motor development of ≤ 1200 gram infants during the first postnatal year using the Bayley Scales versus the Milani-Comparetti.* Paper presented to the annual meeting of the American Academy for Cerebral Palsy and Developmental Medicine, Chicago.

Nene, A.V., Evans, G.A., & Patrick, J.H. (1993). Simultaneous multiple operations for spastic diplegia. *Journal of Bone and Joint Surgery, 75B*(3), 488–494.

Nickel, R.E. (1997). *The musculoskeletal exam and clinical observation of gait.* Portland: Oregon Health Sciences University.

Nickel, R.E., Renken, C.A., & Gallenstein, J.A. (1989). The Infant Motor Screen. *Developmental Medicine and Child Neurology, 31,* 35–42.

O'Dwyer, T.P., & Conlon, B.J. (1997). The surgical management of drooling: A 15-year follow-up. *Clinical Otolaryngology, 22,* 284–287.

Okamoto, G.A., McEwen, I., Marlowe, K., et al. (1983). Prescriptions for physical and occupational therapy in school. *Archives of Physical Medicine and Rehabilitation, 64,* 429–431.

O'Shea, T.M., Preisser, J.S., Klinepeter, K.L., et al. (1998). Trends in mortality and cerebral palsy in a geographically based cohort of very low birth weight neonates born between 1982 and 1994. *Pediatrics, 101*(4), 642–647.

Ottenbacher, K.J., Msall, M.E., Lyon, N.R., et al. (1997). Interrater agreement and stability of the Functional Independence Measure for Children (WeeFIM[SM]): Use in children with developmental disabilities. *Archives of Physical Medicine and Rehabilitation, 78,* 1309–1315.

Palisano, R., Rosenbaum, P., Walter, S., et al. (1997). Development and reliability of a system to classify gross motor function in children with cerebral palsy. *Developmental Medicine and Child Neurology, 39,* 214–223.

Palisano, R.J., Kolobe, T.H., Haley, S.M., et al. (1995). Validity of the Peabody Developmental Gross Motor Scale as an evaluative measure of infants receiving physical therapy. *Physical Therapy, 11,* 939–951.

Palmer, F.B., Shapiro, B.K., Wachtel, R.C., et al. (1988). The effects of physical therapy on cerebral palsy: A controlled trial in infants with spastic diplegia. *New England Journal of Medicine, 318*(3), 803–808.

Paneth, N. (1986a). Birth and the origins of cerebral palsy. *New England Journal of Medicine, 315*(2), 124–126.

Paneth, N. (1986b). Etiologic factors in cerebral palsy. *Pediatric Annals, 15*(3), 193–201.

Pape, K.E., Kirsch, S.E., Galil, A., et al. (1993). Neuromuscular approach to the motor deficits of cerebral palsy: A pilot study. *Journal of Pediatric Orthopaedics, 13*(5), 628–633.

Park, T.S., & Owen, J.H. (1992). Review article: Surgical management of spastic diplegia in cerebral palsy. *New England Journal of Medicine, 326*(11), 745–749.

Peacock, W.J., & Arens, L.J. (1982). Selective posterior rhizotomy for the relief of spasticity in cerebral palsy. *South African Medical Journal, 62,* 119–124.

Pharoah, P.O.D., Cooke, T., & Rosenbloom, L. (1989). Acquired cerebral palsy. *Archives of Disease in Childhood, 64,* 1013–1016.

Piggott, K.P. (1987). *Adapted seating and mobility for the disabled child: Clinical assessment and problem-solving.* Instructional course presented at the annual meeting of the American Academy for Cerebral Palsy and Developmental Medicine, Boston.

Piper, M.C., Pinnell, L.E., Darrah, J., et al. (1994). Construction and validation of the Alberta Infant Motor Scale (AIMS). *Canadian Journal of Public Health, 83*(Suppl. 2), S46–S50.

Prechtl, H.F.R., Einspieler, C., Cioni, G., et al. (1997). An early marker for neurological deficits after perinatal brain lesions. *Lancet, 349*(9062), 1361–1363.

Reddihough, D., Johnson, H., Staples, M., et al. (1990). Use of benzhexol hydrochloride to control drooling of children with cerebral palsy. *Developmental Medicine and Child Neurology, 32,* 985–989.

Reid, C.J., & Borzyskowski, M. (1993). Lower urinary tract dysfunction in cerebral palsy. *Archives of Disease in Childhood, 68*(6), 739–742.

Rinsky, L.A. (1990). Surgery of spinal deformity in cerebral palsy: Twelve years in the evolution of scoliosis management. *Scoliosis Management in Cerebral Palsy, 253,* 100–109.

Rose, S.A., Ounpuu, S.A., & DeLuca, P.A. (1991). Strategies for the assessment of pediatric gait in the clinical setting. *Physical Therapy, 71*(12), 961–980.

Ross, M.E., Allen, K.M., Srivastava, A.K., et al. (1997). Linkage and physical mapping of X-linked lissencephaly/SBH (*XLIS*): A gene causing neuronal migration defects in human brain. *Human Molecular Genetics, 6*(4), 555–562.

Russell, D.J., Rosenbaum, P.L., Cadman, D.T., et al. (1989). The Gross Motor Function Measure: A means to evaluate the effects of physical therapy. *Developmental Medicine and Child Neurology, 31,* 341–352.

Russman, B.S., Tilton, A., & Gormley, M.E., Jr. (1997). Cerebral palsy: A rational approach to a treatment protocol, and the role of botulinum toxin in treatment. *Muscle and Nerve Supplement, 6,* S181–S193.

Saito, N., Ebara, S., Ohotsuka, K., et al. (1998). Natural history of scoliosis in spastic cerebral palsy. *Lancet, 351*(9117), 1687–1692.

Scherzer, A.L., Mike, V., & Ilson, J. (1976). Physical therapy as a determinant of change in the cerebral palsied infant. *Pediatrics, 58*(1), 47–52.

Scrutton, D. (1989). Review article: The early management of hips in cerebral palsy. *Developmental Medicine and Child Neurology, 31,* 108–116.

Scrutton, D. (1992). The classification of the cerebral palsies [Letter to the editor]. *Developmental Medicine and Child Neurology, 34,* 833–837.

Shaw, N.J., White, C.P., Fraser, W.D., & Rosenbloom, L. (1994). Osteopenia in cerebral palsy. *Archives of Disease in Childhood, 71,* 235–238.

Sheth, R.D., Wesolowski, C.A., Jacob, J.C., et al. (1995). Effect of carbamazepine and valproate on bone mineral density. *Journal of Pediatrics, 127*(2), 256–262.

Simpson, D.M. (1997). Clinical trials of botulinum toxin in the treatment of spasticity. *Muscle and Nerve Supplement, 6,* S169–S175.

Smith, C., Birnbaum, G., Carter, J.L., et al. (1994). Tizanidine treatment of spasticity caused by multiple sclerosis: Results of a double-blind, placebo-controlled trial. *Neurology, 44*(11)(Suppl. 9), S34–S42.

Sperle, P.A., Ottenbacher, K.J., Braun, S.L., et al. (1997). Equivalence reliability of the Functional Independence Measure for Children (WeeFIM) administration methods. *American Journal of Occupational Therapy, 51*(1), 35–41.

State University of New York at Buffalo. (1993a). *Guide for the Uniform Data Set for Medical Rehabilitation (FIM), version 4.0.* Buffalo, NY: Author.

State University of New York at Buffalo. (1993b). *Guide for the Uniform Data Set for Medical Rehabilitation for Children (WeeFIM), version 4.0.* Buffalo, NY: Author.

Steinbok, P., Reiner, A.M., Beauchamp, R., et al. (1997). A randomized clinical trial to compare selective posterior rhizotomy plus physiotherapy with physiotherapy alone in children with spastic diplegic cerebral palsy. *Developmental Medicine and Child Neurology, 39,* 178–184.

Steinbok, P., Reiner, A.M., & Kestle, J.R.W. (1997). Therapeutic electrical stimulation following selective posterior rhizotomy in children with spastic diplegic cerebral palsy: A randomized clinical trial. *Developmental Medicine and Child Neurology, 39,* 515–520.

Stern, L.M. (1997). Preliminary study of glycopyrrolate in the management of drooling. *Journal of Pediatrics and Child Health, 33*(1), 52–54.

Stevenson, R.D. (1996). Measurement of growth in children with developmental disabilities. *Developmental Medicine and Child Neurology, 38,* 855–860.

Stevenson, R.D., Allaire, J.H., & Blasco, P.A. (1994). Deterioration of feeding behavior following surgical treatment of drooling. *Dysphagia, 9*(1), 22–25.

Stevenson, R.D., Roberts, C.D., & Vogtle, L. (1995). The effects of non-nutritional factors on growth in cerebral palsy. *Developmental Medicine and Child Neurology, 37,* 124–130.

Sutherland, D.H., & Davids, J.R. (1993). Common gait abnormalities of the knee in cerebral palsy. *Clinical Orthopaedics and Related Research, 288,* 139–147.

Swanson, M.W., Bennett, F.C., Shy, K.K., et al. (1992). Identification of neurodevelopmental abnormality at four and eight months by the movement assessment of infants. *Developmental Medicine and Child Neurology, 34,* 321–337.

Tizanidine for spasticity. (1997). *Medical Letter, 39*(1004), 62–63.

Todis, B. (1993). The impact of technology on academic and social integration. *Oregon Conference Monograph, 5,* 1–8.

Truwit, C.L., Barkovitch, A.J., Kock, T.K., et al. (1992). Cerebral palsy: MR findings in 40 patients. *American Journal of Neuroradiology, 13,* 67–78.

Wadsworth, J.S., & Harper, D.C. (1993). The social needs of adolescents with cerebral palsy. *Developmental Medicine and Child Neurology, 35,* 1015–1024.

Waters, P.M., & Van Heest, A. (1998). Spastic hemiplegia of the upper extremity in children. *Hand Clinics, 14*(1), 119–134.

Webb, K., Reddihough, D.S., Johnson, H., et al. (1995). Long-term outcome of saliva-control surgery. *Developmental and Child Neurology, 37,* 755–762.

Wolraich, M.L. (1986). Counseling families of children with cerebral palsy. *Pediatric Annals, 15*(3), 239–244.

Wong, A.M., Chang, C.J., Chen, L.R., & Chen, M.M. (1997). Laser intraductal photocoagulation of bilateral parotid ducts for reducing drooling of cerebral palsied children: A preliminary report. *Journal of Clinical Laser Medicine and Surgery, 15*(2), 65–69.

Wright, F.V., Sheil, E.M.H., Drake, J.M., et al. (1998). Evaluation of selective dorsal rhizotomy for the reduction of spasticity in cerebral palsy: A randomized controlled trial. *Developmental Medicine and Child Neurology, 40,* 239–247.

Young, R.R. (1994). Spasticity: A review. *Neurology, 44*(11, Suppl. 9), S12–S20.

Young, R.R., & Delwaide, P.J. (1981). Drug therapy: Spasticity (2 parts). *New England Journal of Medicine, 304*(1), 28–33 (part 1), 96–99 (part 2).

6

Appendix

Guidelines for the Care of Children and Adolescents with Cerebral Palsy

Basic Team

The special care needs of children with cerebral palsy are best met by an experienced, coordinated team of pediatric specialists working collaboratively with parents, the primary care physician, and other service providers. Not all members of the basic team may be needed at each visit, and other professionals may be required. These include but are not limited to a child neurologist, a neurosurgeon, an ophthalmologist, a nutritionist, a feeding specialist, and a psychologist. Parents of children with cerebral palsy or people with cerebral palsy should be encouraged to participate actively as part of the team. Please note that though a coordinated team is needed to manage the range of specialty services required, all children require a medical home. The primary care physician is responsible for preventive and acute illness care and for coordinating special services.

Regular members of the child development team include a developmental pediatrician or physiatrist, a medical social worker, a nurse, an orthopedist, an orthotist, physical and occupational therapists, and a speech-language pathologist.

Initial Evaluation

The initial evaluation should be performed as soon as a diagnosis of cerebral palsy is suspected. The following components are recommended: family, medical, and developmental histories; developmental and behavioral assessments; a physical examination, including neuromotor and musculoskeletal assessments; and other tests as indicated. Other tests may include X rays and laboratory tests, a hearing and vision evaluation, an educational evaluation, an assessment of the child's communication skills and needs, and a nutrition and feeding evaluation. An initial management plan that is inclusive of all needed services should be developed.

Frequency of Visits

As the child with cerebral palsy grows and develops, additional needs may become evident that require further evaluation or treatment. In general, the primary care physician should review the child's progress and update the office management plan at least yearly and more often for young children and in the first 2 years of treatment. Children with cerebral palsy also require regular follow-up by the team of specialists. Clear and regular communication among service providers is critical. The child should be reevaluated by the neurodevelopmental team several times per year in the first 2–3 years, twice annually until the child reaches 5 years of age, and at least annually thereafter.

The Physician's Guide to Caring for Children with Disabilities and Chronic Conditions, edited by Robert E. Nickel and Larry W. Desch, copyright © 2000 Paul H. Brookes Publishing Co.

Guidelines for the Care of Children and Adolescents with Cerebral Palsy

The following elements are recommended by age group, and the listing is cumulative. Review all items indicated up through the actual age group of a child entering your practice for the first time as part of the initial evaluation.

AGE	KEY CLINICAL ISSUES/CONCERNS	EVALUATIONS/KEY PROCEDURES	SPECIALISTS
Birth–3 years (infants and toddlers)	*Growth/Nutrition/Feeding* Slow weight gain or linear growth Failure to thrive Oral motor dysfunction Gastroesophageal reflux (GER) Gastrostomy care	Growth parameters, diet record, nutrition and feeding assessment, evaluation of GER (pH study), modified barium swallow as needed Special diet or feeding program, medication (acid blocker and/or motility agent) or fundoplication for GER Gastrostomy as needed	Nutritionist, feeding specialist or team, pediatric gastroenterologist as needed
	Associated Medical Problems Hearing and vision Seizures Chronic respiratory problems/aspiration	Hearing and vision testing Electroencephalogram Chest X ray, workup for GER and swallowing dysfunction	Audiologist, ophthalmologist Child neurologist as needed Pediatric gastroenterologist as needed
	Constipation	Diet, cleanout for impaction, medication (bulk agents)	Developmental pediatrician (DPed), nurse specialist as needed
	Muscle cramps	Regular stretching, warm bath and massage, ibuprofen, diazepam (rarely)	
	Sleep problems	Behavioral management, occasionally short-term medications	
	Drooling	Behavioral therapy, occasionally medications	Speech-language pathologist as needed
	Note side effects of any medications.		
	Cause of the Disability	Evaluation for minor anomalies Cranial magnetic resonance imaging (MRI) or computed tomography (CT) scan, other testing as needed	DPed, medical geneticist as needed
	Dental Care Caries Malocclusion	Review oral hygiene	Dentist
	Ambulation and Mobility Need for physical therapy (PT) services Need for bracing and adaptive equipment	Detailed neuromotor and musculoskeletal examinations	Physical therapist, DPed, orthopedist, orthotist as needed
	Seating and Positioning Need for specialized seating device	Detailed neuromotor and musculoskeletal examinations	Physical therapist, occupational therapist, physiatrist, equipment vendor as needed

The Physician's Guide to Caring for Children with Disabilities and Chronic Conditions, edited by Robert E. Nickel and Larry W. Desch, copyright © 2000 Paul H. Brookes Publishing Co.

Guidelines for the Care of Children and Adolescents with Cerebral Palsy *(continued)*

The following elements are recommended by age group, and the listing is cumulative. Review all items indicated up through the actual age group of a child entering your practice for the first time as part of the initial evaluation.

AGE	KEY CLINICAL ISSUES/CONCERNS	EVALUATIONS/KEY PROCEDURES	SPECIALISTS
Birth–3 years (infants and toddlers) *(continued)*	*Upper-Extremity Function and Visual Motor Skills* Need for occupational therapy services Fine motor/visual motor skills	Detailed musculoskeletal examination, assessment of fine motor and visual motor skills	Occupational therapist, DPed, orthopedist as needed
	Musculoskeletal Problems Joint contractures Hip subluxation or dislocation Scoliosis Foot and ankle deformities Arm and hand deformities Rotational deformities of the legs Osteopenia and fractures	Detailed musculoskeletal examination, hip X rays at age 2 years or before, back and other X rays as needed	Physical therapist, occupational therapist, DPed; orthopedist as needed and at least yearly after 3 years of age
	Communication, Developmental Progress, Early Intervention (EI) Services Need for EI services Language delay or speech disorder Developmental delay	Developmental surveillance Referral for eligibility testing for EI services as needed	Referral to child development team, speech-language pathologist, or psychologist as needed
	Review of Diagnosis and Anticipatory Guidance Information on diagnosis and management Review the individualized family service plan (IFSP) with family as needed Transition from EI to early childhood special education (ECSE) or to community preschool participation Promote self-care and independence	Family interview, provide educational materials and resource information, initiate care notebook Teacher interview, school conference as needed	Primary care office in collaboration with the neurodevelopmental team
	Family Support Services Respite Parent groups Community health nurse Advocacy (e.g., United Cerebral Palsy Association) Financial services (Supplemental Security Income [SSI]) Other enabling services	Family interview, parent questionnaires (e.g., Family Needs Survey), provide resource information Service coordination, referral to community services as needed	Medical social worker, referral to community health nurse as needed

The Physician's Guide to Caring for Children with Disabilities and Chronic Conditions, edited by Robert E. Nickel and Larry W. Desch, copyright © 2000 Paul H. Brookes Publishing Co.

Guidelines for the Care of Children and Adolescents with Cerebral Palsy *(continued)*

The following elements are recommended by age group, and the listing is cumulative. Review all items indicated up through the actual age group of a child entering your practice for the first time as part of the initial evaluation.

AGE	KEY CLINICAL ISSUES/CONCERNS	EVALUATIONS/KEY PROCEDURES	SPECIALISTS
Birth–3 years (infants and toddlers) *(continued)*	*Collaboration with Community Services* Early intervention Community health nurse Other community providers	Comprehensive service coordination with regular exchange of written information (at least yearly) with other service providers, care conference as needed	Primary care office in collaboration with neuro-developmental team
3–5 years (pre-school age)	*Review of Medical or Surgical Treatment Approaches for Hypertonicity*	Detailed musculoskeletal and neuromotor examinations, gait analysis as needed	DPed, orthopedist, physical therapist, occupational therapist, neurosurgeon as needed
	Need for Special Technology Power-drive wheelchair Augmentative and alternative communication (AAC) Computer use for written work	Assessment of language and cognitive skills, evaluation of fine motor dexterity and speed AAC clinic, power-drive wheelchair assessment Assessment of visual acuity as needed	Physical therapist, occupational therapist, speech-language, pathologist, psychologist, ophthalmologist as needed
	Developmental Progress, Early Childhood Special Education (ECSE) Services	Developmental surveillance, referral for eligibility testing for ECSE as needed Intellectual or educational evaluation, assessment of visual perceptual and visual motor skills as needed and prior to kindergarten entry	Psychologist, speech-language pathologist, or referral to child development team as needed Collaborate with preschool or grade school staff
	Self-Care/Independence	Evaluation of functional skills (PEDI or WeeFIM)	Physical therapist and occupational therapist (family and all professionals)
	Toilet Training/Constipation/Urinary Incontinence	Treat constipation first; use adaptive seating as needed and refer for voiding cystourethrogram (VCUG) and urodynamics as needed	DPed, nurse specialist, urologist as needed
	Drooling	Oral motor therapy (birth–3 years), other behavioral therapies, medication, and (rarely) surgery (older school-age child)	DPed, nurse specialist, speech-language pathologist as needed, rarely otolaryngologist (ENT)
	Anticipatory Guidance Treatment of hypertonicity Transition to grade school Review IFSP or individualized education program (IEP) with the family	Family and teacher interviews, school conference as needed	Primary care office in collaboration with neuro-developmental team

The Physician's Guide to Caring for Children with Disabilities and Chronic Conditions, edited by Robert E. Nickel and Larry W. Desch, copyright © 2000 Paul H. Brookes Publishing Co.

Guidelines for the Care of Children and Adolescents with Cerebral Palsy *(continued)*

The following elements are recommended by age group, and the listing is cumulative. Review all items indicated up through the actual age group of a child entering your practice for the first time as part of the initial evaluation.

AGE	KEY CLINICAL ISSUES/CONCERNS	EVALUATIONS/KEY PROCEDURES	SPECIALISTS
6–12 years (school-age)	*Associated Learning/Behavior Problems* Learning disability Mental retardation Attention-deficit/hyperactivity disorder (ADHD)	Behavior checklists, school progress report, review IEP Intellectual and achievement testing as needed	DPed, psychologist, speech-language pathologist or referral to child development team as needed Collaborate with school staff
	Reassess Need for Physical and Occupational Therapy Services	Assessment of fine and gross motor and functional skills	Physical therapist, occupational therapist, DPed, orthopedist as needed
	Patient Education Regarding Diagnosis and Treatment	Patient educational materials	DPed, nurse specialist, physical therapist, and occupational therapist
	Social Skills Promote social competence Involvement in peer group activities at school and in the community (determine which supports are needed)	Social skills program at school as needed Service coordination, referral to community resources, mentor program	Physical therapist, occupational therapist, psychologist, adaptive physical education specialist as needed Collaborate with school staff
	Anticipatory Guidance Discuss diagnosis and management with child Promote self-care and independence Recreation and leisure activities Review IEP with family Transition to middle school	Referral to community services; provide educational materials; conduct family and teacher interviews, school conference as needed	Primary care office in collaboration with neurodevelopmental team Referral to physical therapist, occupational therapist, adaptive physical education specialist as needed
13–21 years (adolescent and young adult)	*Community Mobility and Driver Training*	Driver training assessment; assessment of cognitive skills, visual acuity, and visual fields as needed	Physical therapist, occupational therapist, physiatrist, psychologist, ophthalmologist as needed
	Self-Care/Independent Living Determine which supports are needed	Outpatient physical therapy (PT) and occupational therapy (OT) services as needed; consider inpatient rehabilitation evaluation Independent living skills program, social skills training as needed	Physical therapist, occupational therapist, psychologist, medical social worker, vocational specialist as needed

The Physician's Guide to Caring for Children with Disabilities and Chronic Conditions, edited by Robert E. Nickel and Larry W. Desch, copyright © 2000 Paul H. Brookes Publishing Co.

Guidelines for the Care of Children and Adolescents with Cerebral Palsy *(continued)*

The following elements are recommended by age group, and the listing is cumulative. Review all items indicated up through the actual age group of a child entering your practice for the first time as part of the initial evaluation.

AGE	KEY CLINICAL ISSUES/CONCERNS	EVALUATIONS/KEY PROCEDURES	SPECIALISTS
13–21 years (adolescent and young adult) *(continued)*	*Anticipatory Guidance* Promote healthy behaviors (exercise program, weight control, muscle-stretching program) Sexuality and birth control High-risk behavior Career planning and higher education Social isolation Transition to adult medical services	Patient educational materials Gynecologic examination for sexually active women Adolescent, family, and teacher interviews; school conference as needed Career counseling, evaluation by vocational specialist as needed Encourage involvement in after-school and community activities, mentor programs	Primary care office in collaboration with neuro-developmental team Referral to gynecologist as needed Referral to Department of Vocational Rehabilitation, mental health professional as needed

The Physician's Guide to Caring for Children with Disabilities and Chronic Conditions, edited by Robert E. Nickel and Larry W. Desch, copyright © 2000 Paul H. Brookes Publishing Co.

Family and Physician Management Plan Summary for Children and Adolescents with Cerebral Palsy

This form will help you and your physician review current services and service needs. Please answer the questions about your current services on this page. Your physician will review your responses and complete the rest of the form.

Child's name _____ Today's date _____

Person completing the form _____

CURRENT SERVICES

1. Please list your/your child's current medications and any side effects.

2. What braces and special equipment do you/does your child use now?

3. What is your/your child's current school program?
   School name _____ Grade _____
   Teacher _____ Telephone _____

4. Do you/does your child receive any support services and other special programs at school (e.g., physical therapy, resource room)? Please list.

5. Who are your/your child's other medical and dental service providers?
   Dentist _____
   Neurologist _____
   Orthopedist _____
   Other _____

The Physician's Guide to Caring for Children with Disabilities and Chronic Conditions, edited by Robert E. Nickel and Larry W. Desch, copyright © 2000 Paul H. Brookes Publishing Co.

Family and Physician Management Plan Summary
for Children and Adolescents with Cerebral Palsy *(continued)*

6. Who are your/your child's other community service providers?

    Physical therapist _____

    Community health nurse _____

    Other _____

7. Do you/does your child also receive services from a neurodevelopmental team of specialists?

    Contact person _____

    Location _____

8. Have you/has your child had any blood tests, radiologic (X-ray) examinations, or other procedures since your last visit? If yes, please describe.

9. Have you/has your child been hospitalized or undergone surgery since your last visit? If yes, describe.

10. Please note your/your child's accomplishments since your last visit. Consider activities at home, in your neighborhood, or at school, as well as success with treatments.

11. What goals (i.e., skills) would you/your child like to accomplish in the next year? Consider activities at home, in your neighborhood, or at school, as well as success with treatments.

12. What questions or concerns would you like addressed today?

The Physician's Guide to Caring for Children with Disabilities and Chronic Conditions, edited by Robert E. Nickel and Larry W. Desch,
copyright © 2000 Paul H. Brookes Publishing Co.

Family and Physician Management Plan Summary for Children and Adolescents with Cerebral Palsy

The Management Plan Summary should be completed at each annual review and more often as needed. It is intended to be used with the Guidelines for Care, which provide a more complete listing of clinical issues at different ages and recommended evaluations and treatments.

Child's name _____   Person completing form _____   Today's date _____

Clinical issues	Currently a problem?	Evaluations needed	Treatment recommendations	Referrals made	Date for status check
Family's Questions					
Growth/Nutrition/Feeding Feeding problems Slow weight gain, linear growth Questions about specialized feeding, gastrostomy care					
Associated Medical Problems Recurrent respiratory problems or aspiration Gastroesophageal reflux (GER) Seizures Toilet training (assess need for adaptive seating) Constipation, urinary incontinence Drooling Muscle cramps Hearing loss Strabismus/visual problems Sleep disorder, sleep apnea **Note any side effects of medications.**					
Cause of the Disability					

The Physician's Guide to Caring for Children with Disabilities and Chronic Conditions, edited by Robert E. Nickel and Larry W. Desch, copyright © 2000 Paul H. Brookes Publishing Co.

Family and Physician Management Plan Summary for Children and Adolescents with Cerebral Palsy *(continued)*

Child's name _____ Person completing form _____ Today's date _____

Clinical issues	Currently a problem?	Evaluations needed	Treatment recommendations	Referrals made	Date for status check
Dental Care					
Ambulation and Mobility Describe current ambulatory status Questions about physical therapy, braces, adaptive equipment Need for power-drive wheelchair					
Seating and Positioning					
Upper-Extremity Function and Visual Motor Skills					
Musculoskeletal Problems Recent change in contractures, gait, scoliosis					
Associated Developmental or Learning Issues Current school achievement Review early intervention (EI) or school services (individualized family service plan [IFSP] or individualized education program [IEP]) Developmental delay or mental retardation Learning disabilities					

The Physician's Guide to Caring for Children with Disabilities and Chronic Conditions, edited by Robert E. Nickel and Larry W. Desch, copyright © 2000 Paul H. Brookes Publishing Co.

Family and Physician Management Plan Summary for Children and Adolescents with Cerebral Palsy *(continued)*

Child's name _____ Person completing form _____ Today's date _____

Clinical issues	Currently a problem?	Evaluations needed	Treatment recommendations	Referrals made	Date for status check
Associated Behavior/Mental Health Problems					
Social Skills Involvement in peer group activities in school and community (determine which supports are needed)					
Self-Care/Independence					
Family Support Services					
Treatment of Hypertonicity					
Communication/Speech Questions about speech services Need for augmentative and alternative communication (AAC) device(s) or a computer for written communication					

The Physician's Guide to Caring for Children with Disabilities and Chronic Conditions, edited by Robert E. Nickel and Larry W. Desch, copyright © 2000 Paul H. Brookes Publishing Co.

Family and Physician Management Plan Summary for Children and Adolescents with Cerebral Palsy *(continued)*

Child's name _____   Person completing form _____   Today's date _____

Clinical issues	Currently a problem?	Evaluations needed	Treatment recommendations	Referrals made	Date for status check
Anticipatory Guidance List issues discussed and materials provided					
Collaboration with Community Agencies School					
Comments					

Next update of the Management Plan Summary _____

Signature _____ Date _____
          (Child and parent)

Signature _____ Date _____
          (Health professional)

The Physician's Guide to Caring for Children with Disabilities and Chronic Conditions, edited by Robert E. Nickel and Larry W. Desch, copyright © 2000 Paul H. Brookes Publishing Co.

Musculoskeletal Examination Scoring Form

Child's name _____ Date of birth _____ Today's date _____

Diagnosis _____

Equipment/braces _____

Surgeries _____

Examiner _____

A. Structural changes

1. Joint contractures: Rate 0 (none), 1(present), 2 (severe)[a]

Hip	R _____	L _____	Elbow	R _____	L _____
Knee	R _____	L _____	Forearm	R _____	L _____
Ankle	R _____	L _____	Wrist	R _____	L _____
Toes	R _____	L _____	Thumb	R _____	L _____
Shoulder	R _____	L _____	Fingers	R _____	L _____

   Please describe type of contracture (e.g., hip flexion contracture) _____
   _____
   _____

2. Straight-leg raising (popliteal angle): Rate 0 (full), 1 (limited), 2 (severely limited)
   R _____   L _____

3. Hip subluxation or dislocation: Rate 0 (not present), 1 (suspect), 2 (definite)
   R _____   L _____

4. Spine changes: Rate 0 (not present), 1 (present), 2 (severe)
   Scoliosis _____ Lordosis _____ Kyphosis _____

5. Leg-length discrepancy in supine (in centimeters): R _____ L _____
   Clinical difference in stance (in centimeters): _____

6. Foot and ankle deformities: Rate 0 (not present), 1 (present), 2 (severe)
   R _____   L _____
   Describe type _____
   _____

7. Rotational abnormalities of legs: Rate 0 (none), 1 (present), 2 (severe)
   Femoral anteversion   R _____   L _____
   Internal or external tibial torsion   R _____   L _____

8. Arm and/or hand deformities: Rate 0 (not present), 1 (present), 2 (severe)
   R _____   L _____
   Describe type _____
   _____

[a] The normal range of motion for different joints is given in Section E at the end of this form. In general, a rating of *severe* or *severely limited* for any of the test items reflects a problem that has a marked impact on function. For example, a hip flexion contracture of greater than 30° usually makes independent standing and walking very difficult.

_____

(continued)

The Physician's Guide to Caring for Children with Disabilities and Chronic Conditions, edited by Robert E. Nickel and Larry W. Desch, copyright © 2000 Paul H. Brookes Publishing Co.

Musculoskeletal Examination Scoring Form (continued)

9. Congenital defects   Rate 0 (not present), 1 (present), 2 (severe)

   R_____   L_____

   Please describe_____

   _____

   _____

B. **Muscle tone and strength**

1. Trunk in sitting: Rate 0 (sits with trunk erect), 1 (trunk rounded, occasional use of hands for support), 2 (requires hands for support in sitting), or 9 (not able to sit) _____

Tone	*Strength*
Rate 0 (normal),	Rate 0 (normal),
1 (definite hypertonicity),	1 (definite weakness),
2 (severe hypertonicity), or	2 (severe weakness), or
9 (hypotonicity)	9 (cannot evaluate)

2. Upper extremity

   Hand grip   R_____   L_____

   Shoulder extensors   R_____   L_____

   Biceps/brachioradialis R_____   L_____

   Pronator teres   R_____   L_____

3. Lower extremity

   Hip adductors   R_____   L_____

   Rectus femoris   R_____   L_____

   Hamstrings   R_____   L_____

   Gastrocnemius/soleus R_____   L_____

   Clonus present?   R_____   L_____

   Ankle dorsiflexion   R_____   L_____

   Coming to stand
   (or coming to tall kneel) R_____   L_____

   One-leg standing
   (hip abductors)   R_____   L_____

   Walking on heels   R_____   L_____

   Walking on toes   R_____   L_____

4. Other activities

   Wheelbarrow walk
   (or crawling)   R_____   L_____

   Push-up   R_____   L_____

   Sit-up   R_____   L_____

C. **Upper-extremity function**

1. Involuntary movement, dysmetria, or dystonia _____

   Please describe and note impact on function_____

   _____

2. Active range of motion: Rate 0 (full), 1 (limited), 2 (severely limited)

   Elbow extension   R_____   L_____

   Supination   R_____   L_____

   Wrist extension   R_____   L_____

   Thumb abduction   R_____   L_____

   Thumb extension   R_____   L_____

   Finger extension   R_____   L_____

(continued)

The Physician's Guide to Caring for Children with Disabilities and Chronic Conditions, edited by Robert E. Nickel and Larry W. Desch, copyright © 2000 Paul H. Brookes Publishing Co.

Musculoskeletal Examination Scoring Form (continued)

                             Rate 0 (adequate), 1 (inadequate), 2 (severely impaired)

3.   Grasp/release of block R _____   L _____
      Pincer grasp   R _____   L _____

D. Observation of gait

1.   Standing
     Rate 0 (not present), 1 (definite),   Rate 0 (adequate), 1 (inadequate),
     2 (severe)   2 (severely impaired)

Pelvic obliquity, retraction, or anterior tilt	R _____	L _____	Standing balance _____
Hip adduction	R _____	L _____	
Crouch (hip and knee flexion)	R _____	L _____	Base of support (centimeters) _____
In or out toeing	R _____	L _____	
Equinus	R _____	L _____	
Other foot and/or ankle deformities	R _____	L _____	

Comments _____
_____
_____

2.   Walking without braces
     Rate 0 (not present), 1 (definite),   Rate 0 (adequate), 1 (inadequate),
     2 (severe)   2 (severely impaired)

Exaggerated truncal sway with pelvic drop	R _____	L _____	Clearance of foot	R ___	L ___
Pelvic obliquity, retraction, or anterior tilt	R _____	L _____	Step length	R ___	L ___
Stability	R _____	L _____	Velocity	R ___	L ___
Hip adduction	R _____	L _____	Arm swing/posture	R ___	L ___
Crouch (hip and knee flexion)	R _____	L _____			
In or out toeing	R _____	L _____			
Equinus	R _____	L _____			
Other foot and/or ankle deformities	R _____	L _____			

Comments _____
_____
_____

3.   Walking with braces
     Rate 0 (not present), 1 (definite),   Rate 0 (adequate), 1 (inadequate),
     2 (severe)   2 (severely impaired)

Exaggerated truncal sway with pelvic drop	R _____	L _____	Clearance of foot	R ___	L ___
Pelvic obliquity or anterior tilt	R _____	L _____	Step length	R ___	L ___
Hip adduction	R _____	L _____	Stability	R ___	L ___

_____

(continued)

The Physician's Guide to Caring for Children with Disabilities and Chronic Conditions, edited by Robert E. Nickel and Larry W. Desch, copyright © 2000 Paul H. Brookes Publishing Co.

Crouch (hip and knee flexion)   R _____   L _____   Velocity   R _____ L _____

In or out toeing   R _____   L _____   Arm swing/posture   R _____ L _____

Equinus   R _____   L _____

Other foot and/or
ankle deformities   R _____   L _____

Comments (Note the presence of ataxia, involuntary movement, or dystonia. List current braces and assistive devices, and note any differences when wearing braces.) _____

_____

_____

4. Ambulatory status (*please circle*)

Community ambulator

- Walks without braces or aids *or*
- Walks with braces or other aids, no wheelchair *or*
- Walks with braces or other aids, uses wheelchair for long distances

Household ambulator

- Walks with braces or other aids in home or school (classroom) only *and*
- Uses wheelchair for long distances

Nonfunctional ambulator

- Walks with braces or other aids only in therapy *and*
- Scoots or crawls and uses wheelchair for mobility

Nonambulator

- Rolls, scoots, or crawls and uses wheelchair for mobility
- Nonindependent mobility

E. **Range of motion**[b]

Hip   130° flexion to 0°–10° extension
             20°–30° adduction to 60° abduction (with hips flexed)[c]
             40°–50° internal to 30°–45° external rotation

Knee   120°–150° flexion to 5°–10° extension

Ankle   20°–30° dorsiflexion to 40°–50° plantarflexion

Shoulder   150°–170° forward flexion to 40° extension
             95° internal to 40°–60° extension

Elbow   150° flexion to 0°–10° extension

Forearm   80°–90° pronation to 80°–90° supination

Wrist   50°–60° flexion to 35°–60° extension

[b] Data from Hall, Froster-Iskenius, and Allanson (1989, pp. 281–285).
[c] Data from Joint Motion Method of Measuring and Recording, American Academy of Orthopedic Surgeons (1965, pp. 84–85).

RESOURCES ON CEREBRAL PALSY

Readings

Dormans, J.P., & Pellegrino, L. (Eds.). (1998). *Caring for children with cerebral palsy: A team approach.* Baltimore: Paul H. Brookes Publishing Co. (1-800-638-3775)

Finnie, N.R., Bavin, J., Bax, M., et al. (1997). *Handling the young child with cerebral palsy at home* (3rd ed.). Portsmouth, NH: Butterworth-Heinemann Medical. (1-800-366-2665)

Geralis, E. (1998). *Children with cerebral palsy: A parents' guide* (2nd ed.). Bethesda, MD: Woodbine House. (1-800-843-7323)

Kriegsman, K.H., Zaslow, E.L., & D'Zmura-Rechsteiner, J. (1992). *Taking charge: Teenagers talk about life and physical disabilities.* Bethesda, MD: Woodbine House. (1-800-843-7323)

McAnaney, K.D. (1992). *I wish . . .: Dreams and realities of parenting a special needs child.* Sacramento: United Cerebral Palsy Association of California.

Miller, F., & Bachrach, S.J. (1998). *Cerebral palsy: A complete guide for caregiving.* Baltimore: Johns Hopkins University Press. (1-800-537-5487)

Moran, G. (1995). *Imagine me on a sit-ski!* Morton Grove, IL: A. Whitman. (1-800-255-7675)

Schleichkorn, J. (1993). *Coping with cerebral palsy: Answers to questions parents often ask* (2nd ed.). Austin, TX: PRO-ED. (1-800-897-3202; 512-451-3246)

National Organizations

National Easter Seal Society
230 West Monroe Street, Suite 1800
Chicago, Illinois 60606
Telephone: (312) 726-6200, TDD: (312) 726-4258; (800) 221-6827
Fax: (312) 726-1494
World Wide Web site: http://www.hqeaster-seals.org/

The Easter Seal Society is a national organization with 170 local affiliates dedicated to increasing the independence of people with disabilities and offering a range of services and programs.

United Cerebral Palsy Associations (UCPA)
1660 L Street, NW, Suite 700
Washington, D.C. 20036
Telephone: (800) 872-5827, Voice: (202) 776-0406, TDD: (202) 973-7197
Fax: (202) 776-0414
E-mail: ucpnatl@ucpa.org
World Wide Web site: http://www.ucpa.org/

UCPA is a national organization with 160 local affiliates. It provides a number of direct services to children and adults with cerebral palsy and funds training programs for professionals and research.

Professional Organization

American Academy for Cerebral Palsy and Developmental Medicine (AACPDM)
6300 North River Road, Suite 727
Rosemont, Illinois 60018-4226
Telephone: (847) 698-1635
Fax: (847) 823-0536
E-mail: woppenhe@ucla.edu
World Wide Web site: http://www.aacpdm.org/

A multidisciplinary scientific society that fosters professional education and research on problems associated with cerebral palsy and related disabilities.

Recreation and Leisure Activities

Mobility International USA (MIUSA)
Post Office Box 10767
Eugene, Oregon 97440
Telephone (voice/TTY): (541) 343-1284
Fax: (541) 343-6812

A national organization dedicated to promoting and facilitating travel and educational exchange programs for people with disabilities; MIUSA also publishes resource books and a quarterly newsletter.

Disabled Sports USA (DS/USA)
Kirk M. Bauer, Executive Director
451 Hungerford Drive, Suite 100
Rockville, Maryland 20850
Telephone: (301) 217-0960, TDD: (301) 217-0693
Fax: (301) 217-9840
E-mail: dsusa@dsusa.org
World Wide Web site: http://www.dsusa.org/

A national network of local chapters offering year-round sports and recreation opportunities for people with physical, neuromuscular, and visual impairments.

Wheelchair Sports, USA
3595 East Fountain Boulevard, Suite L1
Colorado Springs, Colorado 80910-1740
Telephone: (719) 574-1150
Fax: (719) 574-9840
E-mail: wsusa@aol.com
World Wide Web site: http://www.wsusa.org/

This is the governing body of various wheelchair sports, including swimming, archery, weightlifting, track and field, table tennis, and air weapons; it also publishes a newsletter.

Technology

ABLEDATA
8455 Colesville Road, Suite 935
Silver Spring, Maryland 20910
Telephone: (800) 227-0216, (301) 588-9285
E-mail: kabelknap@aol.com
World Wide Web site: http://www.abledata.com/

ABLEDATA is a national database on assistive technology and rehabilitation equipment.

Center for Accessible Technology
2547 8th Street, Suite 12-A
Berkeley, California 94710
Telephone (voice/TTY): (510) 841-3224
E-mail: info@cforat.org
World Wide Web site: http://www.el.net/CAT

A resource and demonstration center on adaptive technology that sponsors seminars for parents and professionals, provides assessment services; a small membership fee is required.

Closing the Gap, Inc.
526 Main Street
Henderson, Minnesota 56004
Telephone: (507) 248-3294
Fax: (507) 248-3810
E-mail: info@closingthegap.com
World Wide Web site: http://www.closingthegap.com/

An organization that publishes a newspaper on computers and children with disabilities.

Trace Research and Development Center
University of Wisconsin–Madison
5901 Research Park Boulevard
Madison, Wisconsin 53719-1252
Telephone: (608) 262-6966, TTY: (608) 263-5408
Fax: (608) 262-8848
E-mail: web@trace.wisc.edu
World Wide Web site: http://www.trace.wisc.edu/

A research and development center for communication devices.

Transition and Employment

DO-IT
University of Washington
E-mail: doit@u.washington.edu
World Wide Web site: http://www.washington.edu/doit/

Programs to support high school students with disabilities who have an interest in science, engineering, and math; includes a 2-week summer program at the University of Washington, equipment loans for DO-IT scholars, on-line support, and an e-mail discussion group (doitsem@u.washington.edu).

HEATH Resource Center
One Dupont Circle, Suite 800
Washington, D.C. 20036-1193
Telephone (voice/TTY): (202) 939-9320, TTY: 800-544-3284
Fax: (202) 833-4760

A clearinghouse on information related to educating or training people with disabilities after high school; the center also publishes a newsletter and resource papers.

Attention-Deficit/Hyperactivity Disorder and Related Disorders

Robert E. Nickel

KEY COMPETENCIES

- Discuss the problems in diagnosing attention-deficit/hyperactivity disorder (ADHD) in preschool-age children
- Use behavior rating questionnaires as part of the diagnostic evaluation and to follow treatment effects
- Describe the objectives of the comprehensive diagnostic evaluation
- Construct a management plan for the child with ADHD that incorporates recommendations for behavior management in the home and school
- Discuss the medications used to treat ADHD, including alternatives to stimulants and recommendations for the treatment of ADHD with co-morbid conditions (e.g., ADHD and anxiety disorder)

DESCRIPTION

Definition

ADHD is a neurobehavioral syndrome characterized by persistent inattention, distractibility, overarousal, and impulsivity and is associated with low self-esteem and impaired academic achievement. It is a developmental disability that has a pervasive impact on many, if not all, aspects of daily life for the child and his or her family. Previous diagnostic terms for this disorder have included *minimal brain dysfunction (MBD), hyperkinesis, hyperactivity,* and *attention deficit disorder.*

Attention problems can be *primary,* as in ADHD; *secondary;* or *situational* (Levine, 1990a). Children with secondary attention deficits have inattention as a result of a learning disability, anxiety, depression, medication use (e.g., phenobarbital), substance abuse, environmental neglect or abuse, or physical problems (e.g., anemia). Situational inattention occurs only in specific circumstances and often results from a mismatch of a child and a given set of expectations. This distinction is important when considering the diagnosis and treatment of ADHD. For example, secondary attention problems caused by a learning disability or substance abuse are treated by appropriate educational strategies or by stopping the substance abuse. Situational attention problems are treated by improving the match between a child and his or her specific environmental circumstances.

Classification

Research studies have clearly demonstrated two major behavioral factors in ADHD: inattention and hyperactivity-impulsivity (McBurnett, Pfiffner, Willcutt, et al., 1999). The *Diagnostic and Statistical Manual of Mental Disorders, Fourth Edition* (DSM-IV; American Psychiatric Association [APA], 1994) defines three subtypes of ADHD:

- ADHD, Predominantly Inattentive Type (ADHD-I)
- ADHD, Predominantly Hyperactive-Impulsive Type (ADHD-HI)
- ADHD, Combined Type (ADHD-C; criteria for both Hyperactive/Impulsive and Inattentive types are met)

The two subtypes defined by high levels of inattention (ADHD-I and ADHD-HI) are associated with academic impairment, and the two subtypes defined by high levels of hyperactivity and impulsivity (ADHD-HI and ADHD-C) are associated with social skills impairment and externalizing behavior problems (McBurnett et al., 1999). ADHD-HI is a clinically significant subtype in some studies (Neuman, Todd, Heath, et al., 1999) but not in others (McBurnett et al., 1999).

The diagnostic criteria for ADHD are presented in Table 7.1. Symptoms must be present before age 7 years, must persist for at least 6 months, and must result in significant dysfunction in day-to-day activities in two or more settings (e.g., at school and at home). In addition, clear evidence of clinically significant impairment in social, academic, or occupational functioning must exist, and symptoms must not be better explained by a diagnosis of autism or another mental disorder (APA, 1994).

Prevalence

In general, ADHD occurs in 3%–5% of children (Barkley, 1998). The prevalence varies from .09% to 14.3% in different studies (Szatmari, Offord, & Boyle, 1989). Two epidemiologic studies (Baumgaertel, Wolraich, & Dietrich, 1995; Wolraich, Hannah, Pinnock, et al., 1996) reported somewhat higher prevalence rates for ADHD when DSM-IV rather than DSM-III-R criteria were used. In one study, the prevalence of ADHD as diagnosed by using DSM-IV criteria was 11.4% as compared with 7.4% as diagnosed with DSM-III–R criteria (Wolraich et al., 1996). The higher prevalence rates in both studies were due to new cases of the predominantly inattentive type of ADHD.

ADHD occurs more frequently in boys. The male-to-female ratio with regard to ADHD diagnoses is close to 3:1 in classroom samples; however, clinic-based samples often show a disproportionately high male-to-female ratio (6:1–8:1) because of the bias toward referring children (usually boys) who exhibit aggressive behaviors (Szatmari et al., 1989). In addition, there is a somewhat greater prevalence of ADHD in families in lower socioeconomic groups.

Table 7.1. Diagnostic criteria for attention-deficit/hyperactivity disorder

1. **Inattention** (six or more of the following symptoms)
    a. Often fails to give close attention to details or makes careless mistakes in schoolwork, work, or other activities
    b. Often has difficulty sustaining attention in tasks or play activities
    c. Often does not seem to listen when spoken to directly
    d. Often does not follow through on instructions and fails to finish schoolwork, chores, or duties in the workplace (not because of oppositional behavior or failure to understand instructions)
    e. Often has difficulty organizing tasks and activities
    f. Often avoids, dislikes, or is reluctant to engage in tasks that require sustained mental effort (e.g., schoolwork, homework)
    g. Often loses things necessary for tasks or activities (e.g., toys, school assignments, pencils, books, tools)
    h. Is often easily distracted by extraneous stimuli
    i. Is often forgetful in daily activities

2. **Hyperactivity** (six or more of the following symptoms of hyperactivity-impulsivity)
    a. Often fidgets with hands or feet or squirms in seat
    b. Often leaves seat in classroom or in other situations in which remaining seated is expected
    c. Often runs about or climbs excessively in situations in which doing so is inappropriate
    d. Often has difficulty playing or engaging in leisure activities quietly
    e. Is often "on the go" or often acts as if "driven by a motor"
    f. Often talks excessively

    Impulsivity
    g. Often blurts out answers before questions have been completed
    h. Often has difficulty awaiting turn
    i. Often interrupts or intrudes on others (e.g., butts into conversations or games)

Adapted with permission from *Diagnostic and Statistical Manual of Mental Disorders, Fourth Edition.* Copyright © 1994 American Psychiatric Association.

Etiology

In General The interaction of genetic, biologic, and environmental factors results in the behavioral complex of ADHD. Biologic influences include a variety of mechanisms of brain injury that may occur prenatally, perinatally, or postnatally. Prenatal factors include maternal drug or alcohol abuse (fetal alcohol syndrome and fetal alcohol effects). Perinatal factors include prematurity and group B

streptococcal neonatal meningitis. Postnatal mechanisms of brain injury include meningitis, metabolic encephalopathy (Reye syndrome), traumatic brain injury, and lead exposure. The degree of lead exposure or blood lead level that may result in attention and learning problems remains controversial.

Family dysfunction, poor child management techniques, and parental psychopathology are more common in families of children with ADHD than in controls (Whalen, Henker, & Hinshaw, 1985). Although these factors may correlate with poor behavioral outcome, family dysfunction alone does not cause ADHD. Allergies, food additives (e.g., food dyes, aspartame), and dietary sugar have all been suggested as causes of ADHD. A great deal of research interest has been shown for these proposed etiologies, but with largely negative results. For example, no evidence exists that sugar ingestion alone can change a child with typical attention and activity levels into a child with ADHD (Kinsbourne, 1994).

The principal importance of genetic factors as causes of ADHD are increasingly being recognized, and the emphasis on brain injury as a cause of ADHD is diminishing (Barkley, 1993). Monozygotic (i.e., identical) twin studies have shown a high concordance for ADHD. Family studies have shown that relatives of children with ADHD have a much higher risk for ADHD as well as antisocial personality disorder, alcohol abuse, and depression (Biederman, Faraone, Keenan, et al., 1990; Cantwell, 1972). Molecular genetic studies have focused on three candidate genes: the *D4* dopamine receptor gene, the dopamine transporter gene (*DAT1*), and the *D2* dopamine receptor gene (Faraone & Biederman, 1998). The *DAT1* gene appears to be more strongly linked to the combined subtype of ADHD, and the strength of the linkage increases with symptom severity (Waldman, Rowe, Abramowitz, et al., 1998).

Physiologic Basis It is generally accepted that the brain has both anterior and posterior attentional systems. The anterior system is responsible for executive functions and working memory, and the posterior system is responsible for disengaging from current stimuli and engaging new stimuli (Pliszka, McCracken, & Maas, 1996). Executive functions include the ability to inhibit responses, to initiate, to sustain or shift attention, to plan, and to organize. *Working memory* refers to gaining access to information and internal manipulation of that information to solve a problem (Pliszka et al., 1996). Children with ADHD manifest a variety of impairments in executive functions and a poor working memory. This pattern of impairments is similar to that seen in adults with frontal lobe dysfunction (Faraone & Biederman, 1998).

The anterior attentional system is composed of the prefrontal cortex and basal ganglia (the cortical-striatal-thalamic system) (Castellanos, 1997). Dopamine is the primary neurotransmitter in the prefrontal cortex and basal ganglia, although norepinephrine is an important neurotransmitter in certain regions (e.g., the locus ceruleus), and the posterior attentional system is primarily noradrenergic (Pliszka et al., 1996). The positive response of the majority of children with ADHD to stimulant medications that act as dopaminergic and noradrenergic neurotransmitter agonists has focused attention on the role of catecholamines in ADHD. Other evidence supports the interaction of dopaminergic, noradrenergic, and serotonergic neurotransmitter systems (Hunt, 1993).

Evidence from studies using magnetic resonance imaging (MRI), positron emission tomography (PET), and single photon emission tomography (SPECT) scans supports the involvement of the prefrontal cortex and basal ganglia in ADHD. In one study, anatomic MRI scan measurements of the prefrontal cortex and caudate correlated with task performance on response inhibition tasks (Casey, Castellanos, Giedd, et al., 1997). Functional MRI has demonstrated differences in frontal and striatal activation in children with ADHD and modulation by methylphenidate (Ritalin) (Vaidya, Austin, Kirkorian, et al., 1998). In addition, high-resolution SPECT imaging has revealed decreased perfusion of the prefrontal cortex in children and adolescents with ADHD (Amen & Carmichael, 1997). In another study, PET scans demonstrated a global decrease in brain glucose metabolism in adults with ADHD, with the greatest decrease occurring in the premotor cortex and superior prefrontal cortex (Zametkin, Nordahl, Gross, et al., 1990).

Learning Disabilities and Behavior Problems
ADHD is associated with learning disabilities (20%–25%), oppositional defiant disorder (60%), conduct disorder (45%), anxiety disorders (20%), and depression and mood disorders (20%), and it can co-occur with mental retardation (Barkley, 1998; Hechtman, 1993; Pliszka, 1998). Fifty percent of children with ADHD have no associated conditions; however, 20% of children with ADHD have two or more co-morbid conditions (Hechtman, 1993).

Learning Disabilities Children with learning disabilities form a large heterogeneous group that in-

cludes approximately 5% of school-age children (Shapiro & Gallico, 1993). About the same number of boys and girls have learning disabilities (Shaywitz, Shaywitz, Fletcher, & Escobar, 1990). The learning disorders described in DSM-IV include *reading disorder* (dyslexia), *mathematics disorder* (dyscalculia), and *disorder of written expression* (written language disorder) (see Table 7.2). Nonverbal learning disabilities have been described as an additional type of learning disability. Children with nonverbal learning disabilities have poor social skills, visual-perceptual problems, and difficulty with mathematics and reading comprehension. Nonverbal learning disabilities are discussed in Chapter 13. Children with mathematics disorder usually also experience short-term memory problems, visuospatial problems, and difficulty with written work (Siegel, 1992).

Twenty-five percent of children with learning disabilities also have ADHD. Conversely, 20%–25%

Table 7.2. Diagnostic criteria for learning disabilities

Reading disorder
- Reading achievement is substantially below that expected, given the person's chronological age, measured intelligence, and age-appropriate education.
- The reading difficulties significantly interfere with academic achievement or activities of daily living that require reading skills.
- If a sensory deficit is present, the reading difficulties are in excess of those usually associated with it.

Mathematics disorder
- Mathematical ability is substantially below that expected, given the person's chronological age, measured intelligence, and age-appropriate education.
- The difficulties with mathematics significantly interfere with academic achievement or activities of daily living that require mathematical ability.
- If a sensory deficit is present, the difficulties with mathematics are in excess of those usually associated with it.

Disorder of written expression
- Writing skills are substantially below those expected, given the person's chronological age, measured intelligence, and age-appropriate education.
- The difficulties with writing skills significantly interfere with academic achievement or activities of daily living that require the composition of written texts.
- If a sensory deficit is present, the difficulties with writing skills are in excess of those usually associated with it.

Adapted with permission from *Diagnostic and Statistical Manual of Mental Disorders, Fourth Edition.* Copyright © 1994 American Psychiatric Association.

of children with ADHD have learning disabilities (Pliszka, 1998). The reading problems of children with ADHD and learning disabilities are usually more severe and more resistant to intervention (Lyon, 1996). In another study, children with ADHD and co-morbid learning disabilities had poorer school and intellectual functioning and higher rates of depression than children with ADHD who had no learning disabilities (Faraone, Biederman, Mennin, et al., 1997).

Dyslexia, or specific developmental reading disorder, is the most common learning disability. The educational diagnosis of learning disabilities in school-age children is based on the discrepancy between intellectual potential and academic achievement. Controversy about the use of a discrepancy definition of reading disability is ongoing (Beitchman & Young, 1997; Lyon, 1996). The basic impairment in reading skills is independent of the discrepancy between achievement and intellectual potential. Most children with dyslexia have a primary problem with phonological awareness (e.g., difficulty with recognizing words, reading nonwords [i.e., decoding], associating sounds with letters) (Lyon, 1996; Shaywitz, 1998). Phonological awareness impairments can be identified in kindergarten and are predictive of word identification and spelling skills as many as 11 years later (MacDonald & Cornwall, 1995).

Oppositional Defiant Disorder and Conduct Disorder   The association of ADHD with aggressive behaviors and the diagnosis of oppositional defiant disorder (ODD) or conduct disorder is an important clinical and public health problem. Children with ADHD and aggression account for the preponderance of children with poor outcomes as adolescents and adults. ADHD, ODD, and conduct disorder are characterized in DSM-IV as disruptive behavior disorders. Approximately 2%–16% of children in the general population are diagnosed with ODD (APA, 1994); however, as many as 60% of children with ADHD meet the diagnostic criteria for this diagnosis. ODD and conduct disorder are more prevalent in children who have had a succession of different caregivers and in families that use harsh, inconsistent, and neglectful parenting practices (APA, 1994). Children and adolescents with ODD and conduct disorder are also at increased risk for anxiety and mood disorders.

ODD is characterized by recurrent negative, defiant, disobedient, and hostile behaviors toward parents and other authority figures. Table 7.3 presents the diagnostic criteria for ODD. These behaviors

Table 7.3. Diagnostic criteria for oppositional defiant disorder

A pattern of negativistic, hostile, and defiant behavior lasting at least 6 months (four or more of the following symptoms must be present):

1. Often loses temper
2. Often argues with adults
3. Often actively defies or refuses to comply with adults' requests or rules
4. Often deliberately annoys people
5. Often blames others for his or her mistakes or misbehavior
6. Is often touchy or easily annoyed by others
7. Is often angry and resentful
8. Is often spiteful or vindictive

Adapted with permission from *Diagnostic and Statistical Manual of Mental Disorders, Fourth Edition.* Copyright © 1994 American Psychiatric Association.

must result in a clinically significant impairment in social, academic, or occupational functioning and must not be better explained by another mental health disorder.

Conduct disorder is characterized by recurrent and persistent violation of age-appropriate societal rules. Specific behaviors include theft, lying, running away, arson, truancy, damage to property, cruelty to animals, and fighting. Approximately 6%–16% of boys and 2%–9% of girls in the general population (APA, 1994) and 45% of children with ADHD develop conduct disorder. Conduct disorder is more common in boys and can be diagnosed as early as 5–6 years of age. Children with ODD may progress to demonstrate behaviors consistent with the diagnosis of conduct disorder. The earlier the diagnosis of conduct disorder, the worse the prognosis for persisting problems and the development of adult antisocial personality disorder. Table 7.4 presents the diagnostic criteria for conduct disorder. Conduct disorder is classified as either childhood-onset (one criterion present before 10 years of age) or adolescent-onset, and the severity of the disorder is rated as mild, moderate, or severe.

Anxiety Disorders   Twenty percent of children and adolescents with ADHD also manifest an anxiety disorder (Hechtman, 1993). Anxiety disorders are common in childhood and can be protracted and associated with significant functional impairment. Anxiety disorders are discussed in detail in Chapter 10. Epidemiologic studies indicate that the overlap between ADHD and anxiety disorders oc-

Table 7.4.   Diagnostic criteria for conduct disorder

A repetitive and persistent pattern of behavior in which the basic rights of others or major age-appropriate societal norms or rules are violated (three or more of the following criteria must have been present in the past 12 months, with at least one present in the past 6 months):

Aggression toward people and animals

1. Often bullies, threatens, or intimidates others
2. Often initiates physical fights
3. Has used a weapon that can cause serious physical harm to others (e.g., bat, broken bottle, knife, gun)
4. Has been physically cruel to people
5. Has been physically cruel to animals
6. Has stolen while confronting a victim (e.g., mugging, purse snatching, armed robbery)
7. Has forced someone into sexual activity

Destruction of property

8. Has deliberately engaged in fire setting with the intention of causing serious damage
9. Has deliberately destroyed others' property (other than by fire setting)

Deceitfulness or theft

10. Has broken into someone else's house, building, or car
11. Often lies to obtain goods or favors or to avoid obligations (i.e., "cons" others)
12. Has stolen items of nontrivial value without confronting a victim (e.g., shoplifting without breaking and entering; forgery)

Serious violations of rules

13. Often stays out at night despite parental prohibitions, beginning before age 13 years
14. Has run away from home overnight at least twice while living in parental or parental surrogate home (or once without returning for a lengthy period)
15. Is often truant from school, beginning before age 13 years

Adapted with permission from *Diagnostic and Statistical Manual of Mental Disorders, Fourth Edition.* Copyright © 1994 American Psychiatric Association.

curs at levels that far exceed chance rates (Tannock, 1993). When ADHD and anxiety disorders occur together, they both should be seen as primary and co-morbid disorders. Children with anxiety disorders may be restless, fidgety, and unable to concentrate, but they *do not* show the persistent and pervasive pattern of behavioral disinhibition, hyperactivity, and poor sustained attention beginning in early childhood that is typical of ADHD (Barkley, 1993). The principal reason for the diagnosis of co-morbid anxiety disorder is the greater risk for children with ADHD and anxiety disorders to have adverse reactions to stimulant medications.

Children with the inattentive subtype of ADHD have fewer serious problems with aggres-

sion and conduct; are less impulsive; and are more likely to be characterized as shy, unhappy, anxious, and socially withdrawn. Approximately 43% of children with the inattentive subtype of ADHD have a concomitant diagnosis of anxiety disorder or depression; by contrast, 10% of children with the hyperactive-impulsive subtype of ADHD receive these co-morbid diagnoses (Lahey & Carlson, 1991).

Depression and Mood Disorders   Up to 30% of children and adolescents with ADHD may also manifest major depression or other mood disorders (Barkley, 1998; Hechtman, 1993). Major depression is seen more commonly with the inattentive subtype of ADHD. Families of children with ADHD have a high rate of mood disorders. Conversely, children of parents with major depressive disorders show elevated rates of major depressive disorder, ADHD, and major depressive disorder with ADHD (Wilens, 1993). Children with major depressive disorder manifest pervasive irritability, dysphoria, social withdrawal, and at times suicidal ideation. Prepubertal children with bipolar disorder may show a chronic, nonepisodic, rapid-cycling, mixed manic state and may present with features of ADHD and/or conduct disorder (Geller & Luby, 1997); however, the diagnosis of bipolar disorder in these children is controversial if the children do not have a relapsing or remitting clinical picture (Biederman, Klein, Pine, et al., 1998; Hechtman, 1999).

Tourette Syndrome   Tourette syndrome is a familial disorder characterized by the presence of chronic motor and vocal tics. In a study of 42 children with Tourette syndrome, the mean age of tic onset was 5.6 years; tics worsened until 10.0 years of age and then declined steadily (Leckman, Zhang, Vitale, et al., 1998). By 18 years of age, nearly half of the group was tic-free. About 50% of children and adolescents with Tourette syndrome also have ADHD (Cohen, Riddle, & Leckman, 1992). In most children with Tourette syndrome and ADHD, the behavioral symptoms of inattention and poor impulse control with or without hyperactivity precede the development of tics by 2–3 years of age (Singer, Brown, Quaskey, et al., 1995).

The diagnosis of Tourette syndrome and ADHD has important management implications. Stimulant medications may exacerbate motor and vocal symptoms in as many as 50% of children with established tics (Singer et al., 1995) and may provoke the appearance of tics in children prior to the diagnosis of Tourette syndrome. Children with Tourette syndrome and ADHD, however, experience a significant dose-related improvement in ADHD-related behavior with methylphenidate (Ritalin) (Castellanos, Giedd, Elia, et al., 1997). In a double-blind, placebo-controlled study of children with Tourette syndrome and ADHD, the use of methylphenidate was associated with significant improvement in ADHD-related behaviors without worsening of tic severity (Gadow, Sverd, Nolan, & Sprafkin, 1995). In addition, in another study, children with ADHD who received methylphenidate exhibited a similar appearance of new tics and similar rates of worsening or improvement of existing tics after 1 year as children with ADHD who received placebo (Law & Schachar, 1997).

Other Disorders Children with developmental delays or mental retardation often manifest some of the behavioral features of ADHD because of their delays (Barkley, 1998). The additional diagnosis of ADHD is appropriate only if these children exceed attentional expectations for their developmental or mental age. Many children with autism spectrum disorder (ASD) manifest multiple behaviors consistent with inattention and hyperactivity-impulsivity. Because of the pervasive nature of the impairments of children with ASD, the additional diagnosis of ADHD is not warranted (Barkley, 1998). Similarly, an additional diagnosis of ADHD for a child with severe mental retardation (requiring extensive or pervasive support) is not recommended.

DIAGNOSIS AND EVALUATION

Behavior Profile of Infants and Preschool-Age Children with Attention-Deficit/Hyperactivity Disorder

In infancy, children with ADHD may have a difficult temperament with low adaptability, low persistence, low threshold, and high intensity of response. Children with ADHD may experience irregular sleep patterns, may be picky eaters, and may have a generally negative relationship with their parents. The quality of the mother–infant relationship may have a profound influence on the infant's subsequent behavior (Campbell, Breaux, Ewing, et al., 1986; Tynan & Nearing, 1994).

As preschoolers, children with ADHD exhibit a high degree of "nuisance" behaviors. They are aggressive, impulsive, noncompliant, and fearless. Their behavior is erratic, they show poor judgment, and their social skills are poorly developed. Preschool children with ADHD may be unpopular with their peers and have difficulty adapting to child care and preschool because of problems with turn taking and following rules.

Difficulties with Diagnosing Attention-Deficit/Hyperactivity Disorder in Preschool-Age Children

Symptoms of ADHD in preschool-age children can resemble typical toddler behavior or the "terrible twos." In free-play situations, the behavior of preschoolers with ADHD may be like that of preschool-age children without ADHD; however, in structured situations, preschoolers with ADHD may be more aggressive and oppositional. Nearly 50% of children diagnosed as having ADHD at 3 years of age still have that diagnosis in later childhood (Tynan & Nearing, 1994). Three-year-old children with hyperactivity and aggression, noncompliance, and a negative mother–child relationship are more likely to show persisting problems (Campbell et al., 1986). Whether use of DSM-IV criteria for ADHD improves the accuracy of the diagnosis in this age group is uncertain.

Difficulties with Diagnosing Learning Disabilities in Preschool-Age Children

The identification of learning disabilities in preschool-age children remains difficult (Shapiro & Gallico, 1993). Preschool-age children who experience developmental delay, language disorder, or behavior disturbance or who have a family history of learning disabilities are at an increased risk for developing specific learning disabilities (Shapiro & Gallico, 1993). School readiness tests are generally poor predictors of which children will later show learning disabilities; however, as commented previously, tests of phonemic awareness and letter–sound association at school entry can predict which children will subsequently have reading problems. Risk factors for reading problems in preschool-age children include a history of language delay, trouble playing rhyming games, and confusing words that sound alike (Shaywitz, 1998).

Use of Behavior Rating Questionnaires in the Primary Care Office

Approximately 38% of pediatricians are already using questionnaires for some purpose in their practice, and another 36% express interest in using questionnaires (Sturner, 1991). Pediatricians use them because they are efficient, provide more complete information, help parents organize their thoughts, and enhance parents' sense of participation in the appointment (Sturner, Eisert, Mabe, & Thomas, 1985).

The use of behavior rating questionnaires can improve the identification and treatment of children with psychosocial or learning problems. These children are being underidentified by primary care physicians (Little, Murphy, Jellinek, et al., 1994). Behavior rating questionnaires are useful for three purposes: *to screen for problems, to provide a comprehensive overview of behaviors to assist in diagnosis,* and *to follow the treatment of specific problems* such as ADHD. Primary care physicians and nurses should become familiar with the use of at least one behavior rating scale for each of these purposes. As discussed in Chapter 2, standardized questionnaires should be used because they have known psychometric properties and known error rates. Questionnaires should be used as part of the comprehensive evaluation of the child with possible ADHD and related behavior problems and to follow treatment effects. Table 7.5 presents representative questionnaires in the categories of screening, diagnostic evaluation, and treatment follow-up.

Behavior Questionnaires for Screening The primary goal of screening for behavior problems is to clarify the need for further evaluation or for referral (Sturner, 1991). The questionnaire should be brief yet comprehensive, with clearly identified cutoff scores. The Pediatric Symptom Checklist (Little et al., 1994) is an example of a general behavioral screen for use with children 4–10 years of age.

Comprehensive Behavior Questionnaires Use a comprehensive behavior questionnaire with parents who feel that their child has behavior problems. Behavior rating scales are available for completion by parents, teachers, and older children and adolescents. The Child Behavior Checklist (CBCL) Parent (Achenbach, 1991a), Teacher (Achenbach, 1991b), and Youth Self-Report (Achenbach, 1991c) forms are recommended as comprehensive diagnostic questionnaires. The CBCL should be used as part of the diagnostic process and not to make a final diagnosis. Unlike other questionnaires, it asks some open-ended questions and provides areas to record school testing results.

The Conners' Parent and Teacher Rating Scales–Revised (CPRS–R; CTRS–R) (Conners, 1997) are based on extensive normative data. These questionnaires have been used widely as part of a comprehensive evaluation of children suspected of having ADHD and for follow-up with regard to medication effects. The CPRS–R: Long Form (Conners, 1997), the CTRS–R: Long Form (Conners, 1997), and the Conners'-Wells' Adolescent Self-Report Scale: Long Form (CASS:L) (Conners, 1997) can be used in place of the CBCL as part of the diagnostic evaluation. The CPRS-R:L and CTRS-R:L include an ADHD Index and a DSM-IV Checklist.

Questionnaires to Monitor the Results of Treatment The Home and School Situations Questionnaires–Revised (HSQ–R and SSQ–R, respectively) (Barkley & Murphy, 1998) are useful ad-

juncts to other questionnaires as part of the diagnostic evaluation and to follow treatment effects. The HSQ–R and SSQ–R evaluate the situation and the degree to which the child is manifesting attentional problems. Other types of Conners' questionnaires (Short Form and Conners' Global Index–Teacher [Conners, 1997]) also are available and are most appropriate to use in following treatment effects.

Comprehensive Evaluation

The primary care physician is the appropriate professional to coordinate the evaluation of a child for ADHD and related behavior problems. ADHD has a biologic basis, it can affect most aspects of the child's and the family's functioning, and children with ADHD frequently experience associated mental health and developmental problems. After establishing the diagnosis of ADHD, the use of medication is an important part of the comprehensive management program. The primary objectives of the diagnostic evaluation are as follows:

- Document the child's behavior in different environments
- Identify associated developmental or learning problems
- Determine the etiology of the child's ADHD if possible
- Identify and evaluate associated medical problems
- Determine the presence of associated mental health disorders
- Review the family's strengths, resources, and support needs
- Review the school's current resources and previous experiences with children with ADHD
- Counsel the parent and the child about the diagnosis

Document the Child's Behavior in Different Environments Obtaining information about the child's behavior from parents (home), teachers (school), the child, and through direct observations (office) is critical. DSM-IV criteria require evidence of clinically significant impairment of function in two or more environments. Obtain information by using behavior rating questionnaires; conducting parent, child, and teacher interviews; and making direct observations in the office. Do not rely on behavioral observations made in the office to confirm or to refute a diagnosis of ADHD, because the child may not manifest behaviors usually seen in other environments in the relatively brief and structured office visit.

The use of objective assessment techniques to diagnose attentional problems remains controversial. Tests of the various aspects of executive func-

Table 7.5. Behavior rating scales

	Age range	Focus	Number of items	Psychometric data
A. Screening				
Pediatric Symptom Checklist* (Little, Murphy, Jellinek, et al., 1994)	4–16 years	General behavior	35 items	Concurrent validity with Child Behavior Checklist for 4- and 5-year-olds
Behavior Checklist (Rickham & Graham, 1971)	Preschool- and school-age	General behavior	21 items	No normative validity data reported
Behavior Questionnaire (Willoughby & Haggerty, 1964)	18 months to 6 years	Behavior development	28 items	No normative or reliability data
B. Diagnostic evaluation				
Child Behavior Checklist: Parent, Teacher, and Youth Self-Report forms* (Achenbach, 1991a, 1991b, 1991c)	4–18 years	Withdrawn Somatic complaints Anxious/depressed Thought problems Attention problems Delinquent Aggressive	100 items	Extensive normative, reliability, and validity data
Conners' Parent Rating Scales–Revised–Long Form* (CPRS–R:L)	3–17 years	14 subscales	80 items	Recently revised, large normative sample, and good reliability and limited validity data
Conners' Teacher Rating Scales–Revised–Long Form* (CTRS-R:L)	3–17 years	13 subscales	59 items	
Conners'-Wells' Adolescent Self-Report Scale–Long Form* (CASS:L) (Conners, 1997)	12–17 years	10 subscales	87 items	
ANSER Questionnaires for Parents (P), School (S) (Aggregate Neurobehavioral Student Health and Education Review), and Student (Levine, 1980)	3–12 years Student (9+ years)	Development (S) Behavior Health (P) Development Attention Behavior	Very long	No normative or validity data available
ADDH Comprehensive Teacher Rating Scale* (ACTeRS) (Ullman, Sleator, & Sprague, 1991)	5–12 years	Attention Hyperactivity Social skills Oppositional behavior	24 items	Good normative and reliability data, limited validity data
Preschool Behavior Questionnaire (Behar & Stringfield, 1974) (teachers only)	3–6 years	Hostile-aggressive Anxious-fearful Hyperactive-distractible	30 items	Good normative and reliability data

* Recommended scales.

(continued)

Table 7.5.   *(continued)*

	Age range	Focus	Number of items	Psychometric data
C. Treatment follow-up				
Conners' Parent Rating Scales–Revised–Short Form* (CPRS–R:S)	3–17 years	Oppositional Cognitive problems Hyperactivity ADHD Index	27 items (CPRS–R:S)	Recently revised, large normative sample, good reliability data and limited validity data
Conners' Teacher Rating Scales–Revised–Short Form* (CTRS–R:S)	3–17 years	Same as above	28 items (CTRS–R:S)	
Conners'-Wells' Adolescent Self-Report Scales–Short Form* (CASS:S) (Conners, 1997)	12–17 years	Same as above	27 items (CASS:S)	
Conners' Global Index–Parent* (CGI–P) (Conners, 1997)	3–17 years	Emotional lability Reckless-Impulsive	10 items	
Conners' Global Index–Teacher* (CBI–T) (Conners, 1997)	3–17 years	Same as above	10 items	
Home Situations Questionnaire* (Barkley, 1997)	6–12 years	Inattention severity Problem settings Compliance situations Leisure situations	16 items	HSQ-R and SSQ-R are useful for following treatment of ADHD
School Situations Questionnaire* (Barkley, 1997)	6–12 years	Inattention severity Problem settings	12 items	Normative, reliability, and validity data available

* Recommended scales.

tioning include the Gordon Diagnostic System (Gordon, 1983), and the Conners' Continuous Performance Test (Conners, 1995), the Test of Variables of Attention (TOVA) (Greenberg, 1990) (sustained attention test), Matching Familiar Figures (Kagan, Rosman, Day, et al., 1964) and Go–No Go (Drewe, 1975) tests (response inhibition), and the Wisconsin Card Sorting Test (Grant & Berg, 1993) (concept function and flexibility). These tests are of continuing research interest and utility; however, they may have significant false negative rates (e.g., Gordon Diagnostic System; Gordon [1983]), and they are unreliable for diagnostic purposes (Barkley, 1993; Koelega, 1995). These tests do offer the clinician the opportunity to observe the child's behavior under conditions requiring attention and self-control and may prove to be useful in the diagnosis of the inattentive subtype of ADHD or, in certain instances, monitoring treatment effects. In one study, clinicians who used the TOVA correctly identified 80% of children with ADHD and 72% of controls (Forbes, 1998). Children who were misclassified by

the TOVA, however, were identified correctly by teacher ratings, and vice versa.

Parent Interview   The ADHD Clinic Parent Interview (see Barkley, 1998) is one example of a comprehensive interview. Important features in conducting the parent interview are as follows:

• Review parents' current concerns
• Obtain prenatal and perinatal data about the child
• Obtain the child's developmental history and temperament and behavioral history
• Review the child's school history
• Review the child's previous diagnoses, treatments, and associated medical problems
• Obtain the child's social and family history
• Identify the child's strengths, and identify the family's strengths and need for support services
• Review the results from behavior rating scales used with the child
• Complete checklists of the DSM-IV diagnostic criteria for ADHD, conduct disorder, and ODD as needed

The parent interview builds rapport between the physician and the parents, clarifies the parents' current concerns, provides a broad range of information, determines the need for family support services, and helps determine the diagnostic and treatment plan for the child. Information obtained from the child's parents has been shown to have a low level of agreement with that obtained from teachers (Newcorn, Halperin, Schwartz, et al., 1994). The reliability of parent information is improved, however, if questions are asked about the child's current behavior and questions are specific to information related to ADHD (Barkley, 1998).

Ask the parents to describe their current concerns about their child. Start by asking them their principal concerns or the behaviors of their child that they would like to see changed or improved. Clarify the situations in which these behaviors occur, the frequency of these behaviors, and the interventions that have been used previously. Any parental disagreement regarding these concerns should be identified clearly. Ask about the child's strengths or what the parents like about their child. The review of medical problems should include any known illness or event that may have resulted in the child's current learning or behavior problems. Ask about the child's functioning prior to this illness or injury as well as any specific diagnoses and ongoing treatments. The child's social history should include discussion of the child's peer relationships, participation in after-school activities such as clubs and sports, and a description of the child's sibling relationships.

Finally, complete a review of the DSM-IV diagnostic criteria for ADHD. Ask parents to complete a standardized checklist such as the ADHD Rating Scale–IV (DuPaul, Power, Anastopoulos, & Reid, 1998) or review these criteria in an interview. When interviewing parents, ask them to answer "yes" only if they think the given behavior (e.g., "often fidgets with his hands or feet or squirms in seat") occurs much more frequently than usual in children of the same age (Barkley, 1998).

Child Interview For older children and adolescents, the child interview can be complemented by the completion of a behavior rating questionnaire such as the CBCL Youth Self-Report (Achenbach, 1991c) form or the Self-Administered Student Profile of the ANSER system (Levine, 1980). The child interview is also an opportunity to make further behavioral observations. Ask the child why he or she is visiting the clinic, then provide a full explanation as needed. Ask the child specifically the child's own view of his or her learning or behavior problems or conflicts at school and at home. Review

the child's school history, also emphasizing the activities that the child enjoys and the child's own perceived strengths. Finally, ask the child what he or she would like to see changed or improved at home and at school related to these learning problems. If a child has difficulty responding, ask the child what he or she would wish to be changed if given three wishes. Please note that children and adolescents with ADHD typically underreport behavior difficulties (Barkley, 1998). Table 7.6 lists additional questions that can be used in the child interview (Levine, 1990b).

Teacher Interview Optimally, the physician completes a telephone interview with the child's teacher in addition to administering a teacher behavior rating scale. The teacher interview should include a review of the child's current school program, academic progress, behavior in the classroom and in other school situations, and peer relationships. Ask the teacher about his or her previous communications with the child's parents and whether he or she and the child's parents have a cooperative relationship. Determine which adaptations have been made in the classroom; the types of support services, if any, that are being provided; and whether the child has an individualized education program (IEP) or Section 504 plan. The child's ADHD (or other disabling condition) must substantially limit his or her ability to benefit from the education program to be eligible for educational support services through Section 504 of the Rehabilitation Act of 1973 (PL 93-112). Also request the results of any previous intellectual or achievement evaluations completed by school staff.

Associated Developmental or Learning Problems
The evaluation of the child with ADHD should be

Table 7.6.   Questions for the child interview

What's it like on your bus, in the cafeteria, or at recess (or physical education) at your school?

Are there some groups of kids at school whom you don't like much? Which are the good and bad groups?

Do you think there are any groups of kids who don't like you much?

Are you pretty popular with other kids?

Are there any kids you can really talk to and trust?

A lot of kids call each other names. Do kids call each other names in your school? What are some of the names? Do you ever get called names? Which ones?

Are there things that other kids do that make you mad?

If there were a kid you liked and wanted to be friends with, how would you try to make friends with that kid?

Do you worry about what other kids think about you? What sorts of things worry you most often?

Adapted from Levine (1990b).

done in close collaboration with educational personnel. School staff may have completed intellectual and achievement testing of the child or have experienced staff available to do so. Similarly, early childhood special education staff can provide an appropriate evaluation for preschool-age children with ADHD. Many children with ADHD require evaluation by a speech-language pathologist for language disorders and by an occupational therapist for fine motor problems such as dyspraxia, as well as by a psychologist and/or a special educator. Testing should include at least intellectual and academic achievement or general developmental testing (for preschool-age children). Please also review the discussion of the diagnostic evaluation in Chapter 5.

Some children are best referred to an experienced child development team headed by a developmental pediatrician for some or all of these assessments. Consider referral for children who

- Have associated chronic medical problems (e.g., seizure disorder on anticonvulsant medication)
- Have significant anxiety or suspected depression, ODD, or conduct disorder
- Possibly have autism spectrum disorder (ASD)
- When school resources for evaluation are insufficient or exhausted
- If school staff have declined to evaluate the child even though both parents and physician agree that evaluation is appropriate

Identify Associated Medical Problems and Etiology of the Child's Attention-Deficit/Hyperactivity Disorder   The results of the routine physical and neurologic examination are often normal in children with ADHD. Children with ADHD may manifest an increased number of so-called soft neurologic signs or neuromotor immaturities. For example, the child with ADHD may show poor right–left discrimination, inconsistent hand preference, or synkinesis with the contralateral hand during fine motor activities. These findings are not diagnostic; they are also found in children with learning disabilities, ASD, and mental retardation and in many children who are otherwise developing typically. Furthermore, the absence of "soft" signs does not rule out the diagnosis of ADHD. A careful evaluation of fine motor skills including bilateral coordination skills may help the primary care physician decide whether to refer the child to an occupational therapist. The physician may decide to perform a comprehensive neurodevelopmental examination that includes a detailed evaluation of minor neurologic signs and motor skills such as the Pediatric Early Elementary Examination (PEEX) (Levine, 1983) for

children 4–6 years of age. This examination is quite lengthy, however, and thus is of limited utility in a primary care office.

A child with ADHD may also have an increased number (three or more) of minor physical anomalies (e.g., bilateral hair whorls, single palmar crease, epicanthal folds) (Waldrop & Goering, 1971). These anomalies are not specific to children with ADHD and also are found in children with learning disabilities as well as in children with genetic syndromes. The presence of an increased number of minor physical anomalies should prompt further consideration of a genetic disorder or syndrome. A number of genetic disorders or syndromes are associated with learning disabilities or mental retardation and ADHD. These include neurofibromatosis (autosomal dominant genetic disorder), velocardiofacial syndrome (microdeletion of chromosome 22q11), Turner syndrome (chromosomal disorder), fragile X syndrome (gene expansion disorder), and fetal alcohol syndrome (teratogen). Please see Chapter 5 for a review of the evaluation of minor anomalies. Referral to a developmental pediatrician or to a medical geneticist should be considered for children with three or more minor physical anomalies as well as learning and behavior problems.

Children with ADHD do not need routine laboratory studies as part of the diagnostic workup. Further evaluation is indicated to identify the cause of possible secondary inattention, to identify and evaluate associated medical problems, and to identify possible genetic syndromes. Recommendations for lab work (e.g., complete blood count [CBC], lead level, thyroid studies, blood chromosomal analysis, electroencephalogram, computed tomography or magnetic resonance imaging scan) should be based on the results of the medical and developmental history or the physical examination. ADHD has been associated with generalized resistance to thyroid hormone, a rare genetic disorder (Hauser, Zametkin, Martinez, et al., 1993); however, routine thyroid studies are not indicated in children with ADHD (Toren, Karasik, Eldar, et al., 1997).

Associated Mental Health Disorders   The parent, child, and teacher interviews, as well as behavior rating questionnaires, help determine the presence of associated mental health problems and the need for further evaluation of the child with ADHD. Some children with ADHD (e.g., children suspected of having depression or an anxiety or thought disorder) require referral to a child psychiatrist or other mental health professional.

Family Strengths, Resources, and Support Needs
An important part of the evaluation of children with ADHD is the assessment of family strengths, resources, and support needs. In general, families of children with ADHD have more problems than families of children who do not have ADHD (Hechtman, 1997). The physician must determine the capabilities of parents to understand the diagnosis and treatment recommendations and to follow through with the management plan. Behavior management in the home is a critical component of the management of children with ADHD, and training the parents in behavior management may be a necessary support service. Some families may have a high level of distress and may require referral for individual, couples, or family counseling.

To assist with the evaluation of child and family functioning, physicians may ask parents to complete questionnaires such as the Family Needs Survey (Bailey & Simeonsson, 1988), the Parenting Stress Index Short Form (Abidin, 1995), or the Parenting Practices Scale (Strayhorn & Weidman, 1988). The Parenting Practices Scale provides information on the parents' use of specific behavior management techniques in the home. Information derived from the questionnaires may assist families to identify appropriate goals and needed supports. (Please also review Chapter 3.)

School Resources and Experience with Children with Attention-Deficit/Hyperactivity Disorder As part of the teacher interview, it is important to determine the school's and teacher's previous experience with children with ADHD, the need to provide educational materials to school staff on ADHD or associated health problems, and the availability of staff to monitor the child's school performance in conjunction with medical management. Is there an experienced staff member (e.g., behavioral consultant, special educator) available to support the teacher in the implementation of a behavior management program?

Counseling the Parents and the Child About the Diagnosis General recommendations for counseling families about the new diagnosis of a developmental disability are reviewed in Chapter 1. In addition, explain the following three basic principles to the family:

1. ADHD is a disability.
2. ADHD may be a lifelong disability. (As many as 50% of adolescents with ADHD show persistent problems with ADHD into adulthood.)
3. Medication is the only specific treatment for inattention and impulsivity; however, restruc-

turing the child's environment at home and at school, implementing a behavior management program, and addressing the child's learning problems can improve the child's behavior and self-esteem and his or her success at school (Barkley, 1998).

A considerable amount of information about the diagnosis and treatment of ADHD is available for parents and for children with ADHD (see the Appendix at the end of this chapter). Provide written information to families on clinical issues as well as parent support groups and other community resources (e.g., the family's local chapter of Children and Adults with Attention Deficit Disorders [CHADD]).

MANAGEMENT

Periodic Review and Update of the Management Plan
In general, a multimodal treatment program that incorporates parent education about the diagnosis, parent training in behavior management, behavior management programs at home and in school, medication management, appropriate educational services, and needed family support services is recommended (Dulcan, 1997). Individual counseling for children with ADHD is primarily indicated for the treatment of associated mental health problems. Cognitive behavior therapy is probably the most widely used individual therapy other than pharmacotherapy. The results of cognitive behavior therapy alone for ADHD have been disappointing; however, studies (e.g., Shaywitz, Fletcher, & Shaywitz, 1997) have reported benefits of cognitive behavior therapy in addition to medication management. An important focus of the management of children and adolescents with ADHD is identifying and promoting areas of competence (child strengths) and building the child's social skills and self-esteem.

Reevaluate the child and family in the primary care office and update the management plan at least twice yearly and more often in the first year of treatment and for younger children. Some children need ongoing management by specialists (e.g., a pediatric neurologist for a child with Tourette syndrome, a child psychiatrist for a child with a co-morbid affective disorder). Other children may need referral to a developmental pediatrician and child development team. Consider referral to specialists or to a child development team for children who

- Display ongoing or worsening behavior problems
- Do not make expected progress in school

- Either fail to respond to stimulants or experience significant side effects with stimulants
- Experience onset or worsening of tics or some symptoms of anxiety or depression
- Exhibit skill regression
- Experience developmental delay or are suspected of having ASD

Behavior Management

Optimally, parents should participate in a structured parent training or counseling program designed specifically for the behavior management of children with ADHD. Unfortunately, such programs may be unavailable in the family's community. Contact ADHD or child development centers or the local or statewide chapter of CHADD for information on parent training resources. For families with a high level of stress and parental discord, marital counseling for the parents may be the appropriate first intervention.

Table 7.7 lists the core principles and strategies for managing children with ADHD in the home. This checklist is provided to health professionals and parents as a guide to understanding the basics of a behavior management program. It is not a substitute for the parent training program, which typically involves several weeks' commitment, structured teaching, role playing, and practice in individual problem-solving strategies.

Educational Management

The collaboration of teachers and other school personnel, parents, and health professionals is essential to the successful treatment of children and adolescents with ADHD. School staff help determine whether a child has either ADHD or academic skills difficulties, termed *specific learning disabilities*, or both, and they determine a child's eligibility for special education services under the Individuals with Disabilities Education Act (IDEA) Amendments of 1997 (PL 105-17) and Section 504 of the Rehabilitation Act of 1973 (PL 93-112). In addition, school staff provide a comprehensive education and behavior management program and assist in evaluating the effects of other treatments (e.g., stimulant medication).

Regular and clear communication between the teacher and the child's parents and between the teacher and health professionals is critical. Teacher–parent communication may include daily or weekly report cards or notes. DuPaul and Stoner listed the following components of effective home–school communication:

- Agree on daily and/or weekly goals that are stated in a *positive* manner—the child's parents' agreement must be obtained prior to implementation.
- Obtain the child's input with regard to goals and contingencies.
- Include both academic and behavioral goals.
- Target a small number of goals at a time.
- Provide quantitative feedback about the child's school performance (the teacher's responsibility).
- Provide feedback by subject or by class as needed (the teacher's responsibility).
- Communicate regularly (either daily or weekly).
- Tie home-based contingencies to the child's school performance, and use both short- and long-term consequences (the parents' responsibility).
- Modify goals and procedures as necessary. (1994, p. 116)

Regular completion of behavior rating scales and maintaining other specific data records, as well as conducting telephone interviews, are the basis for effective teacher–health professional communication. Contacts should be more frequent during medication trials, when medication dosage is changed, or when there is a focus on a specific problem behavior. Data records that identify a *few target behav-*

Table 7.7. Home strategies for managing a child with attention-deficit/hyperactivity disorder

1. Remember that attention-deficit/hyperactivity disorders (ADHD) is a disability. Distinguish between noncompliance (*won't*) and inability (*can't*).
2. Keep the home organized, and establish regular daily routines.
3. Create a quiet, nondistracting area for homework. Avoid overstimulating situations when possible.
4. Post rules, chores, and responsibilities.
5. Make directions short, clear, and simple.
6. Give immediate, frequent feedback.
7. Reinforce positive behavior; tell the child what is the expected behavior, then agree on a reward.
8. Use extrinsic rewards (toys, tokens, or privileges), and make frequent changes in rewards.
9. Plan ahead to anticipate potential problem situations. Review two or three rules with the child specific to a problem situation, then have the child repeat the rules to you.
   a. Set up a small, immediate reward that the child can earn if the rules are followed. Review the rules and reward with the child.
   b. Set up a small, immediate consequence for breaking the rules. Review this consequence with the child.
   When you enter the situation, deliver the reward or consequence immediately after the occurrence of the positive or negative behavior.
10. Maintain consistency among parents and caregivers.
11. Maintain a sense of priorities, and "choose your battles."
12. Schedule regular free time or outlets for your child, and engage in pleasurable activities with your child regularly.
13. Take a break periodically.

Adapted from Barkley (1993) and Berman (1995).

iors in *specific situations* and are *completed daily* can be effective adjuncts to behavior rating scales. The short Conners' questionnaires or similar forms can be used to gather this information.

Teachers implement both positive and negative consequences in response to a child's behavior in the classroom. Studies of children with ADHD show that a combination of positive consequences (e.g., token reinforcement) and negative consequences (e.g., response cost) is the most effective in increasing on-task behavior, seatwork productivity, and academic accuracy (DuPaul & Stoner, 1994). Positive consequences include positive teacher attention, token reinforcement (i.e., the use of tokens to reward positive behavior that can be exchanged later for privileges), and contingency contracts between the teacher and the student ("If I do this, I will get that"). Negative consequences include ignoring, reprimands, response cost (i.e., losing tokens or privileges), and time-out. Table 7.8 lists basic classroom strategies for managing children with ADHD.

Medication Management

For in-depth discussion of medication management of ADHD, please see Dulcan, Bregman, Weller, and Weller (1998). Stimulant medications and behavior modification strategies in the home and in school are the two most common interventions for ADHD. Pharmacotherapy is best used in combination with behavioral and educational approaches (Barkley, 1998; Dulcan, 1997). The appropriate use of medication may make these other approaches more effective. In one study (Wolraich, Lindgren, Stromquist, et al., 1990), however, 88% of children with ADHD were treated with stimulants by a pediatrician or a family practitioner, and only 22% were treated with behavior modification.

The National Institute of Mental Health (NIMH) and the U.S. Department of Education have co-sponsored a study at six centers comparing multimodal treatment and medication management with minimal support (Arnold, Abikoff, Cantwell, et al., 1997; Greenhill, Abikoff, Arnold, et al., 1996; MTA Cooperative Group, 1999). The study had four treatment groups: medication only, intensive behavioral treatment only, combined treatment, and a control group of children treated by community professionals. The results of medication treatment only and combined treatment were superior to behavioral treatment alone and community treatment (MTA Cooperative Group, 1999). Behavioral treatment offered no additional benefit to children who were also receiving pharmacotherapy but may have provided modest advantages for children with co-morbid conditions (oppositional, aggressive, and internalizing

Table 7.8. Classroom strategies for managing a child with attention-deficit/hyperactivity disorder

1. Place the child with attention-deficit/hyperactivity disorder (ADHD) in a class with a low student–teacher ratio.
2. Provide structure (i.e., routines) and consistency in class.
3. Post class rules and students' responsibilities.
4. Seat the child with ADHD near the teacher.
5. When possible, limit distracting stimuli.
6. Surround the child with ADHD with good role models.
7. Divide work into small, manageable amounts.
8. Schedule more difficult subjects in the morning, and intersperse with high- and low-interest tasks.
9. Simplify and repeat directions both verbally and visually (e.g., by writing on the chalkboard). Establish eye contact with the child with ADHD during instructions. Provide frequent, direct feedback from teacher to the child with ADHD.
10. Distinguish between noncompliance and inability.
11. Provide frequent, positive feedback, and avoid negativism in comments and directions to the child with ADHD.
12. Use extrinsic rewards (e.g., tokens, privileges).
13. Develop a hierarchy of classroom consequences (e.g., head down at desk; fine in token system; time-out in a corner [not in a hallway], then time-out in the principal's office).
14. Anticipate potential problem situations (e.g., assemblies, field trips).
15. Prepare the child with ADHD in advance for transitions or changes in classroom routines.
16. Talk briefly and privately with the child with ADHD during class as needed.
17. Avoid embarrassing the child with ADHD in front of peers, and avoid giving a child with ADHD public reminders to take medication.
18. Teach a child with ADHD how to organize materials in order to complete and hand in schoolwork and homework.
19. Encourage the child with ADHD to ask for help, and teach the child how to ask for help.
20. Teach self-monitoring (e.g., teach the child with ADHD to record his or her own work productivity and behavior) by use of a daily report card.
21. Allow frequent breaks.
22. Involve the child with ADHD in prosocial physical activities.
23. Enhance the child's self-esteem by focusing on the child's strengths.

Adapted from Barkley (1993) and Berman (1995).

symptoms) and certain outcomes (teacher-rated social skills and parent–child relationships). Rigorous medication management was important. Two thirds of the children in the community control group were treated with medication; however, these children fared less well than children who received medication management as part of the study.

A number of factors should be considered before initiating a trial of medication:

- *Severity of the ADHD symptoms and problem behaviors:* Some data suggest that the more severe the child's ADHD behaviors, the greater the probability that the child will show a positive response to stimulants.
- *Prior use of other treatments:* Implement home and classroom behavior management strategies before the use of medications if ADHD symptoms are mild. Use behavioral strategies first with preschool-age children because children at that age respond less well to stimulants and in general experience more side effects (Barkley, 1988). Severe symptoms and a high level of family stress, however, may indicate the need for a medication trial before other treatments to improve the treatments' effectiveness.
- *Presence of an anxiety disorder:* Children with ADHD and a co-morbid anxiety disorder are less likely to respond positively to stimulant medications.
- *Parents' attitudes toward the use of medications:* Provide parents with adequate information and time to understand the rationale for prescribing medications and other therapies. Parents should not be hurried into agreeing to the initiation of a medication trial. Consider the use of a placebo-controlled trial if either the child's parents or the child's teacher feels strongly that medications should or should not be used.
- *Adequacy of parent and teacher supervision:* Before medication treatment is initiated, parents and teachers must be in agreement about committing the necessary time and providing the necessary data to determine the short- and long-term success of the medication trial.
- *The child's attitude toward medication:* The rationale for the use of medication should be explained fully to the child. If the child is not in at least tacit agreement with medication use, he or she may sabotage the trial. (DuPaul & Stoner, 1994, pp. 153–154)

Some children with ADHD should be referred to a developmental pediatrician, a child psychiatrist, or a neurologist for consultation specifically regarding medication management. Consider referral for children who

- Respond inadequately to stimulants
- Have autism or mental retardation
- Have associated anxiety or depression
- Are suspected of having ODD or conduct disorder

Children who are receiving pharmacotherapy for ADHD should be followed closely for side effects (see Table 7.9). The Side Effects Rating Scale (Barkley & Murphy, 1998) is available to monitor the response of children to prescribed stimulants. Please also review the discussion of medication management in Chapter 10. Many of the medications used for the treatment of ADHD have not been approved by the Food and Drug Administration (FDA) for use

Table 7.9. Side effects of stimulants

Mild increase in heart rate/increase in blood pressure
Headache
Difficulty falling asleep
Dizziness/dry mouth
Decrease in appetite
Stomach discomfort
Constipation
Irritability/moodiness
Excessive crying
Rebound overactivity
Decrease in rate of growth (does not lead to permanent growth impairment)
Onset or exacerbation of tic disorder
Nervous habits (e.g., picking at skin) and stereotypic movements
Elevated liver enzymes (a side effect of taking pemoline [Cylert])

Adapted from Dulcan, Bregman, Weller, and Weller (1998).

by children. Methylphenidate (Ritalin) and dextroamphetamine (Dexedrine) are the exceptions. An FDA rule ("Regulations Requiring Manufacturers to Assess the Safety and Effectiveness of New Drugs," 1998) that became effective April 1, 1999, requires manufacturers of new drugs that may be beneficial to children to provide information on the safety and efficacy of that drug in pediatric patients at the time it is approved for adult indications.

Stimulant Medications For in-depth discussion of stimulant medications, please review Greenhill, Halperin, and Abikoff (1999), as well as Tables 7.10 and 7.11. Methylphenidate (Ritalin) is the drug of first choice for medication management of children with ADHD because 70%–80% of children respond positively while taking it: They tend to display improved attention, better behavior control, improvement in some measures of academic success (e.g., individually assigned written work), and gains in certain social skills (e.g., compliance) (Barkley, 1977; Barkley, DuPaul, & McMurray, 1991; DuPaul, Barkley, & McMurray, 1994). When implementing a trial of methylphenidate (see Dulcan et al., 1998),

- Identify target behaviors for improvement and obtain baseline data, including growth, heart rate, blood pressure, and behavior rating questionnaires.
- Use a 0.3-milligrams-per-kilogram dose as a guide for the initiation of treatment with methylphenidate (Ritalin). Begin with one morning dose for the first few days to observe for side effects, then prescribe two daily doses—one in the

Table 7.10. Stimulant medications

Drug name	Dosage sizes	Half-life	Usual single-dose range	Dosage frequency	Maximum daily dose
Methylphenidate (Ritalin)	5, 10, 20 milligrams 20 milligrams slow release	3–4 hours	2.5–20 milligrams (.3–.7 milligrams per kilogram)	Two to four times daily	60 milligrams
Dextroamphetamine (Dexedrine)	5 milligrams/ 5 milliliters elixir 5-milligram tablet; 5-, 10-, 15-milligram spansules	4–6 hours	2.5–20 milligrams (generally half the dose of Ritalin; .15–.5 milligrams per kilogram)	Two to three times daily	40 milligrams
Adderall (dextroam-phetamine saccha-rate and sulfate and amphetamine aspartate and sulphate)	5-, 10-, 20-, 30-milligram tablets	6–8 hours	2.5–20 milligrams	Two to three times daily	40 milligrams
Pemoline (Cylert) (not recommended as first-line drug for the treatment of attention-deficit/ hyperactivity dis-order because of rare assocation with liver failure)	18.75-, 37.5-, 75-milligram tablets	7–8 hours	18.75–112.5 (.5–2.5 mil-ligrams per kilogram per day)	Once or twice daily	112.5 milligrams

From Dulcan, M.K., Bregman, J., Weller, E.B., & Weller, R. (1998). Treatment of childhood and adolescent disorders. In A.F. Schatzberg & C.B. Nemeroff (Eds.), *The American Psychiatric Press textbook of psychopharmacology* (2nd ed., p. 811). Washington, DC: American Psychiatric Press; adapted by permission.

early morning and another at noon. The interval between the doses as well as the dosage itself should be individualized for each child. The child's body weight may not be a good predictor of dose response to methylphenidate. The recommended maximum daily dose is 0.8–1.0 milligram per kilogram (Dulcan, 1994).

- Add a third daily dose if needed in the late afternoon, usually at a lower amount than morning doses (e.g., half). In a study of 25 boys with ADHD, three equal doses per day were found to be superior to two daily doses on a parent-completed rating scale (Stein, Blondis, Schnitzler, et al., 1996). The children who received three

Table 7.11. Interactions of stimulants with commonly used psychotropics

Medication	Effects of interactions
Sympathomimetics (e.g., ephedrine, pseudoephedrine)	Increase the effects of both medications
Antihistamines	May diminish effectiveness of stimulants
Monoamine oxidase inhibitors (MAOIs)	Decrease stimulant metabolism, increase level of both medications; potential for serious side effects
Tricyclic antidepressants (TCAs)	May alter TCA levels, increase in effect of both medications; with imipramine (Tofranil) may cause confusion, lability, aggressiveness
Anticonvulsants	May increase or decrease anticonvulsant levels

From Wilens, T.E., & Biederman, J. (1992). The stimulants. *Psychiatric Clinics of North America (Pediatric Pharmacology), 15*(1), 195; reprinted by permission of W.B. Saunders Co.

daily doses experienced some decrease in appetite and no change in sleep duration.

- Consider recommending that the child stay off medication on weekends and for summer holidays, particularly if the child experiences significant side effects from taking the medication (e.g., decreased appetite, concerns about growth). If the child has a summer holiday from medication, it should be restarted at least 1 week before school starts in the fall.
- The child's response to the long-acting version of methylphenidate (Ritalin SR) is unpredictable. It may be useful in children who experience a short duration of action (2–3 hours) with standard methylphenidate, in children who experience a severe rebound effect in the afternoon, and in cases in which the medication cannot be given at school.
- Try a different stimulant if the child does not respond positively to methylphenidate. As many as 20% of children respond positively to a different stimulant (Barkley, 1998).
- Dextroamphetamine (Dexedrine) may have longer duration of action (1–2 hours or longer) than methylphenidate, and the dose is approximately half that of methylphenidate.
- Dextroamphetamine may cause more side effects for some children (e.g., appetite suppression, growth concerns) and has a higher abuse potential.
- The long-acting form of dextroamphetamine (Dexedrine Spansule) offers more dose flexibility and is more predictable in its action than Ritalin SR.
- Adderall is an alternative to Dexedrine. It has been effective in clinical trials and has a duration of action similar to that of dextroamphetamine (Dexedrine) (Warneke, 1990).
- Monitor the child's liver function tests closely when treating the child with pemoline (Cylert), which has been shown to be a cause of liver failure in rare cases. It is no longer considered a first-line drug for the treatment of ADHD.
- Use stimulants cautiously if the child has tics, a family history of Tourette syndrome, or seizures.
- Substance abuse, agitated behavior, cardiac disorders, glaucoma, thought disorder, and marked anxiety are relative contraindications to the use of stimulants.

A number of other medications have been used to treat children with ADHD. Methylphenidate prescribed with three-times-daily dosing was the initial medication used with children in the National Institute of Mental Health (NIMH) Collaborative Multisite Multimodal Treatment Study (Greenhill et al., 1996). If methylphenidate was unsuccessful, the child was switched to dextroamphetamine and then, if necessary, to pemoline (the protocol was altered after the drug alert concerning pemoline and liver failure) and finally to imipramine. If none of these was satisfactory, other medications were tried, including clonidine, nortriptyline, and bupropion.

Tricyclic Antidepressants For more in-depth discussion of tricyclic antidepressants (TCAs), please review Geller, Reising, Leonard, and colleagues (1999), as well as Tables 7.12 and 7.13. The TCAs imipramine (Tofranil), desipramine (Norpramine), amitryptyline (Elavil), and nortriptyline (Pamelor) have both anticholinergic and noradrenergic effects. Use of a TCA is indicated for children and adolescents with ADHD when stimulants are ineffective or contraindicated if stimulants are partially effective, if stimulants produce unacceptable side effects, or if the child has co-morbid anxiety or mild depression. In general, stimulants are still the first choice for children with ADHD and co-morbid anxiety disorders (Hechtman, 1993). TCAs have modest positive effects on inattention and impulsivity, improve mood, and decrease irritability and aggressiveness. The advantage of TCAs is their long duration of action and once-or-twice-daily dosing schedule. The disadvantages include the potential for cardiac arrhythmias and for lethal overdose. For this reason, TCAs should be dispensed in limited amounts to safeguard against overdoses, either purposeful or accidental. Consider consultation with a developmental pediatrician, a child neurologist, or a psychiatrist before using these medications.

Imipramine is the TCA of first choice. It is the least expensive medication among TCAs but has more anticholinergic side effects than the others. Desipramine has the best efficacy data, but several cases of sudden death in children with ADHD taking desipramine have been reported. Because exer-

Table 7.12.   Side effects of tricyclic antidepressants

Dry mouth
Constipation
Blurred vision
Delayed urination (uncommon)
Cardiac conduction slowing (risk for arrhythmias)
Tachycardia
Agitation or confusion
Decrease in seizure threshold
High blood pressure and skin rash

Table 7.13. Interactions of tricyclic antidepressants with other medications

Tricyclic antidepressants (TCAs) increase the effects of stimulants, antidepressants, anticholinergics, thyroid medications, and Dilantin.

TCAs decrease the antihypertensive effects of clonidine and quanethidine.

Methylphenidate may increase the plasma level of TCAs.

Severe toxic reaction is possible when TCAs are used with monoamine oxidase inhibitors (MAOIs).

Adapted from Chappell (1994).

cise was temporally related to the collapse of three of the children who died suddenly, Waslick, Walsh, Greenhill, and colleagues (1999) examined the effects of desipramine on exercise in 22 children and adults. Desipramine had minor effects on these individuals' cardiovascular response to exercise; however, their serum norepinephrine levels were elevated, and one adult did have a brief run of ventricular tachycardia during exercise (Waslick et al., 1999). Further research is needed to clarify the cardiovascular risks associated with the use of desipramine, particularly during exercise. Some investigators recommend that desipramine not be used, because safer TCAs are available (Popper, 1997).

Nortriptyline may be as effective as desipramine, although experience in its use with children is minimal. Clomipramine has been shown to be effective for obsessive-compulsive disorder and may be useful in treating children with ADHD who also exhibit significant obsessive-compulsive behaviors. The principal problem with clomipramine is its anticholinergic side effects.

When implementing a trial with imipramine (see Dulcan et al., 1998, pp. 808, 818–820), use the following procedure:

- Obtain a baseline electrocardiogram (EKG), heart rate, and blood pressure; conduct a physical examination; and obtain a family history for the child. In obtaining the family's medical history, ask specifically about any family history of sudden death, cardiac arrhythmias, or heart disease. Do not start the TCA or decrease and stop the TCA if the EKG shows prolonged PR, QRS, or QT interval (Chappell, 1994).
- Prescribe imipramine in twice-a-day dosing for older children and adults, and three times per day for prepubertal children.
- Start with a prescription of 10–25 milligrams per day (0.5–1.0 milligrams per kilogram per day) and increase the dose every 1–2 weeks.

- Use a maintenance dose of 2–3 milligrams per kilogram daily, and a maximum dose of 5 milligrams per kilogram daily.
- Repeat the EKG at the maintenance dose or at 3 milligrams per kilogram per day and for each 1 milligram per kilogram per day above that level. Plasma drug levels may be helpful (e.g., to identify children who are slow metabolizers of TCAs); however, no clear relationship to drug effect exists. When discontinued, TCAs should be tapered over a 2- to 3-week period to avoid a flulike anticholinergic withdrawal syndrome.

Few data exist to support the combination of a TCA with a stimulant, and no data are available that compare the effect of Ritalin with a TCA as opposed to Ritalin with a selective serotonin reuptake inhibitor (SSRI). Ritalin may increase TCA blood levels and increase the possibility of side effects. However, some practitioners use Ritalin with low dosages of a TCA with good effects (Dulcan, 1994).

Clonidine (Catapres) Please review Dulcan and colleagues (1998), as well as Tables 7.14 and 7.15. Clonidine is an alpha-2-noradrenergic agonist. It is marketed primarily as a treatment for high blood pressure. It may be used *instead of stimulants* if tics are present or develop while the child is taking stimulants and for children and adolescents with ADHD who exhibit high degrees of arousal and explosive or aggressive behaviors. It may be used *in combination with stimulants* for the child with ADHD and tics, when there is a partial stimulant response, or if the stimulant dose is limited by side effects. Fifty to seventy percent of children respond positively, with more improvement in problem behaviors than in inattention being recorded (Barkley, 1998). Clonidine can also be used as a *single bedtime dose* for the treatment of insomnia in children who are taking stimulants. In a study of 62 children with ADHD, the sleep disturbances of 85% of the chil-

Table 7.14. Side effects of clonidine

Sedation
Dry mouth
Constipation
Skin rash (to the clonidine patch)
Headache
Dizziness
Stomachache/nausea
Depression
Orthostatic hypotension
Risk for cardiac arrhythmias

Table 7.15. Clonidine and guanfacine

Drug name	Dosage sizes	Half-life	Dose range	Dosage frequency	Maximum daily dose
Clonidine (Catapres)	.1-, .2-, .3-milligram tablets (skin patches also available)	8 hours Peak effect: 1–2 hours	.025–.1 milligrams	Three to four times per day	.4 milligrams per day
Guanfacine (Tenex)	1.0, 2.0 milligrams	17 hours Peak effect: 1–4 hours	.5–1.5 milligrams	Twice per day	3.0 milligrams per day

Adapted from Chappell (1994).

dren improved with this treatment (Prince, Wilens, Biederman, et al., 1996).

There have been four case reports (three deaths and one episode of hypotension) of serious side effects in children taking clonidine and methylphenidate (Popper, 1995). The role of clonidine in these cases is not clear; however, this combination should be used cautiously (Wilens & Spencer, 1999). Obtain a baseline EKG before starting a child on clonidine, and follow the child's blood pressure and EKG carefully. If clonidine is discontinued, taper the dosage slowly to avoid rebound hypertension. The side effects of clonidine are reviewed in Table 7.14. Concomitant use of central nervous system depressants and anticholinergic agents increases the potential for side effects (Chappell, 1994). Consider consultation with a developmental pediatrician, a child neurologist, or a psychiatrist before using clonidine or guanfacine. When implementing a trial with clonidine (see Chappell, 1994; Dulcan et al., 1998),

- Start with a single dose of .025–.05 milligrams at bedtime or in the morning if the child is exhibiting highly aroused behaviors. To minimize sedation, increase the dose by only .025–.05 milligrams per day every 3 days until the child is receiving three or four daily doses (unless clonidine is being used only for the treatment of insomnia).
- Use a maintenance dose of 3–6 micrograms per kilogram per day or .15–.4 milligrams per day.
- Consider use of transdermal clonidine (a skin patch). Three dosage sizes are available that are equivalent to a .1-, .2-, or .3-milligram daily dose. Change the patch every 5 days.
- Expect to see a therapeutic response within 2–4 weeks; however, the maximum effect may not be seen for 2 or more months.
- Do not stop clonidine suddenly, because there is a possibility of the child's experiencing rebound hypertension and tachycardia.

Guanfacine (Tenex) Guanfacine is a long-acting alpha-2-adrenergic agonist similar to clonidine. Research studies (Cohn & Caliendo, 1997; Hunt, Arnsten, & Asbell, 1995) have documented positive effects with a decrease in hyperactivity, aggression, and oppositionality, as well as a modest effect on inattention. It can be taken two or three times per day. Begin treatment with .5 milligrams once daily, then increase the dosage by .5 milligrams every 3 days. The side effects are similar to those of clonidine.

Other Medications Please review Emslie, Walkup, Pliszka, and Ernst (1999). A variety of other medications have been used to treat ADHD, including fluoxetine (Prozac) and other SSRIs, bupropion (Wellbutrin), and carbamazepine (Tegretol), buspirone (Buspar), and venlafaxine (Effexor). Fluoxetine, other SSRIs, and venlafaxine may aggravate ADHD symptoms (Olvera, Pliszka, Luh, & Tatum, 1996; Popper, 1997). SSRIs may be useful for the child with ADHD and co-morbid anxiety, depression, or obsessive-compulsive symptomatology; however, little information is available on the use of SSRIs in combination with stimulants. Methylphenidate does increase the blood levels of fluoxetine. In a study of seven children and adults with ADHD and major depression, improvement in ADHD symptoms required the addition of methylphenidate to fluoxetine or sertraline treatment. The combination of these drugs was found to be tolerated well (Findling, 1996).

Bupropion is an antidepressant that has an affinity for serotonin receptors, enhances norepinephrine availability, and is a weak dopamine agonist (Riggs, Leon, Mikulich, & Pottle, 1998). It may be most useful in children with ADHD and anxiety or depressive symptoms, children with ADHD who have done poorly with other medications, and adolescents with ADHD and a history of substance abuse. A number of studies (see Barrickman, Perry, Allen, et al., 1995; Conners, Casat, Gualtieri, et al.,

1996; Malhotra & Santosh, 1998) have demonstrated the effectiveness of bupropion in treating children and adolescents with ADHD, and bupropion has been found to be tolerated well. In a double-blind crossover study of 15 children with ADHD, bupropion was found to be as effective as methylphenidate (Barrickman et al., 1995). In addition, bupropion has a low abuse potential, and an open label study (Riggs et al., 1998) demonstrated its effectiveness in adolescents with ADHD, conduct disorder, and a history of substance abuse.

Unproved or Controversial Treatments
Barkley (1993) listed the following unproved or disproved therapies for ADHD:

- Dietary management
- Megavitamin or orthomolecular therapies
- Sensory integration therapy
- Chiropractic manipulations
- Ocular motor exercises or optometrics
- Traditional play therapy
- Relaxation training or electromyogram (EMG) biofeedback
- EEG biofeedback

The results of self-control and social skills training provided in a clinical environment may not generalize to the school or the community; however, some practitioners disagree and have found these programs to be effective (J. Liedel, personal communication, November 1995). Social skills training offered in the school environment can be effective, especially for children diagnosed as having the inattentive subtype of ADHD (i.e., children who are shy and anxious yet not aggressive or acting out). Play therapy may be useful for younger children with co-morbid conditions such as anxiety or mood disorders. (For a review of controversial therapies, see Goldstein & Ingersoll, 1992; Silver, 1987; please also review the discussion of controversial therapies in Chapters 5 and 8.)

Anticipatory Guidance
As adolescents, 15%–20% of children with ADHD have minimal or no problems; 60%–70% continue to show symptoms of ADHD; and 25% exhibit significant antisocial behaviors (Hechtman, 1993). As adults, 30%–40% have minimal or no problems; 40%–50% experience modest problems; and 10% have severe problems, including antisocial behavior, psychiatric illness, and an increase in suicide risk. Factors that may predict poor outcome in adolescence and adulthood include male gender; hyperactive-impulsive subtype of ADHD; ADHD with co-morbid aggression, ODD, or conduct dis-

order; decreased intellectual potential; parental pathology; and low socioeconomic status of the child's family. In addition, ADHD is strongly associated with psychoactive substance abuse in adolescents and adults (Mannuzza, Klein, Bessler, et al., 1993; Wilens, Biederman, & Mick, 1997). Adolescents with ADHD begin drug use at an earlier age, and their substance abuse problems are more severe than those of adolescents without ADHD (Horner & Scheibe, 1997).

Vocational education programs can be helpful for adolescents with ADHD and learning disabilities (Evers, 1996). The skills necessary for success in the workplace are similar to the skills necessary for success in school: organization, planning, attention, completion of tasks, and meeting deadlines. An important part of vocational counseling is matching the person's interests and areas of competence with specific job requirements. (For a review of adolescent and adult outcomes studies, see Barkley, 1998, and Dulcan, 1997.)

Hechtman (1985) and Thorley (1988) suggested that stimulant treatment does not seem to have a significant effect on outcomes in adolescence. Some data do suggest, however, that multimodal (comprehensive) treatment and longer treatment result in better academic and social outcomes (Satterfield, Satterfield, & Cantwell, 1981). Few research studies have addressed the effects of multimodal treatment programs. Preliminary results from the NIMH multi-center, multimodal treatment study showed that medication management is superior to behavioral treatment and that intensive behavioral treatment offers limited additional benefit to children who receive rigorous medication management (MTA Cooperative Group, 1999). The results of this 14-month trial did not address the long-term effects of medication or multimodal treatment, however.

Important Care Coordination Issues
In addition to the general recommendations for care coordination discussed in Chapter 1, the primary care office should

- Identify a local resource for parent training related to the behavior management of children with ADHD
- Identify the contact person for early childhood special education, special education services, and behavioral support in the local school district(s)
- Exchange information with schools and other community service providers regularly
- Identify the contact person for the local chapter of CHADD

REFERENCES

Abidin, R.R. (1995). *Parenting Stress Index Short Form.* Odessa, FL: Psychological Assessment Resources.

Achenbach, T.M. (1991a). *Manual for the Child Behavior Checklist and Revised Child Behavior Profile.* Burlington: University of Vermont.

Achenbach, T.M. (1991b). *Manual for the Child Behavior Checklist and Youth Self-Report.* Burlington: University of Vermont.

Achenbach, T.M. (1991c). *Manual for the Teacher Report Form and the Child Behavior Profile.* Burlington: University of Vermont.

Amen, D.G., & Carmichael, B.D. (1997). High-resolution brain SPECT imaging in ADHD. *Annals of Clinical Psychiatry, 9,* 81–86.

American Psychiatric Association (APA). (1994). *Diagnostic and statistical manual of mental disorders* (4th ed.). Washington, DC: Author.

Arnold, L.E., Abikoff, H.B., Cantwell, D.P., et al. (1997). National Institute of Mental Health Collaborative Multimodal Treatment Study of Children with ADHD (MTA): Design challenges and choices. *Archives of General Psychiatry, 54,* 865–870.

Bailey, D.B., Jr., & Simeonsson, R.J. (1988). Assessing needs of families with handicapped infants. *Journal of Special Education, 22*(1), 117–126.

Barkley, R.A. (1977). The effects of methylphenidate on various measures of activity level and attention in hyperkinetic children. *Journal of Abnormal Child Psychology, 5,* 351–369.

Barkley, R.A. (1988). The effects of methylphenidate on the interactions of preschool ADHD children with their mothers. *Journal of the American Academy of Child and Adolescent Psychiatry, 27,* 336–341.

Barkley, R.A. (1993, April). Attention-deficit hyperactivity disorder workshop, Portland, OR.

Barkley, R.A. (1997). *Defiant children: A clinician's manual for assessment and parent training* (2nd ed.). New York: Guilford Press.

Barkley, R.A. (1998). *Attention-deficit disorder: A handbook for diagnosis and treatment* (2nd ed.). New York: Guilford Press.

Barkley, R.A., DuPaul, G.J., & McMurray, M.B. (1991). Attention deficit disorder with and without hyperactivity: Clinical response to three dose levels of methylphenidate. *Pediatrics, 87,* 519–531.

Barkley, R.A., & Murphy, K.R. (1998). *Attention-deficit disorder: A clinical workbook* (2nd ed.). New York: Guilford Press.

Barrickman, L.L., Perry, P.J., Allen, A.J., et al. (1995). Bupropion versus methylphenidate in the treatment of attention-deficit hyperactivity disorder. *Journal of the American Academy of Child and Adolescent Psychiatry, 34,* 649–657.

Baumgaertel, A., Wolraich, M.L., & Dietrich, M. (1995). Comparison of diagnostic criteria for attention deficit disorders in a German elementary school sample. *Journal of the American Academy of Child and Adolescent Psychiatry, 34,* 629–638.

Behar, L., & Stringfield, S. (1974). Behavior Rating Scale for the Pre-school Child. *Developmental Psychology, 10,* 601–610.

Beitchman, J.H., & Young, A.R. (1997). Learning disorders with a special emphasis on reading disorders: A review of the past 10 years. *Journal of the American Academy of Child and Adolescent Psychiatry, 36,* 1020–1032.

Berman, B. (1995, April). *Attention deficit disorder: Early indicators and diagnostic issues.* Paper presented at the Conference on Children with Special Needs, Contemporary Forums, San Francisco.

Biederman, J., Faraone, S.V., Keenan, K., et al. (1990). Family-genetic and psychosocial risk factors in DSM-III attention deficit disorder. *Journal of the American Academy of Child and Adolescent Psychiatry, 29,* 526–533.

Biederman, J., Klein, R.G., Pine, D.S., et al. (1998). Resolved: Mania is mistaken for ADHD in prepubertal children. *Journal of the American Academy of Child and Adolescent Psychiatry, 37,* 1091–1099.

Campbell, S.B., Breaux, A.M., Ewing, L.J., & Szumowski, E.K. (1986). Correlates and predictors of hyperactivity and aggression: A longitudinal study of parent-referred problem preschoolers. *Journal of Abnormal Child Psychology, 14*(2), 217–234.

Cantwell, D.P. (1972). Psychiatric illness in the parents of hyperactive children. *Archives of General Psychiatry, 27,* 414–427.

Casey, B.J., Castellanos, F.X., Giedd, J.N., et al. (1997). Implication of right frontostriatal circuitry in response inhibition and attention-deficit/hyperactivity disorder. *Journal of the American Academy of Child and Adolescent Psychiatry, 36,* 374–383.

Castellanos, F.X. (1997). Toward a pathophysiology of attention-deficit/hyperactivity disorder. *Clinical Pediatrics, 36,* 281–393.

Castellanos, F.X., Giedd, J.N., Elia, J., et al. (1997). Controlled stimulant treatment of ADHD and comorbid Tourette's syndrome: Effects of stimulant and dose. *Journal of the American Academy of Child and Adolescent Psychiatry, 36,* 589–596.

Chappell, P.B. (1994, October). *ADHD: Nonstimulants.* Paper presented at the annual meeting of the American Academy of Child and Adolescent Psychiatry, New York City.

Cohen, D.J., Riddle, M.A., & Leckman, J.F. (1992). Pharmacotherapy of Tourette's syndrome and associated disorders. *Psychiatric Clinics of North America, 15*(1), 109–129.

Cohn, L.M., & Caliendo, G.C. (1997). Guanfacine use in children with attention deficit hyperactivity disorder. *Annals of Pharmacotherapy, 31,* 918–919.

Conners, C.K. (1995). *Conners' Continuous Performance Test* [Software]. North Tonawanda, NY: Multi-Health Systems, Inc.

Conners, C.K. (1997). *Conners' Rating Scales–Revised technical manual.* North Tonawanda, NY: Multi-Health Systems, Inc.

Conners, C.K., Casat, C.D., Gualtieri, C.T., et al. (1996). Bupropion hydrochloride in attention deficit disorder with hyperactivity. *Journal of the American Academy of Child and Adolescent Psychiatry, 35,* 1314–1321.

Drewe, E.A. (1975). Go–no go learning after frontal lobe lesions in humans. *Cortex, 11,* 8–16.

Dulcan, M.K. (1994, October). *The treatment of ADHD with psychostimulants.* Paper presented at the annual meeting of the American Academy of Child and Adolescent Psychiatry, Psychopharmacology Institute, New York City.

Dulcan, M.K. (1997). Practice parameters for the assessment and treatment of children, adolescents, and adults with attention-deficit/hyperactivity disorder. *Journal of the American Academy of Child and Adolescent Psychiatry, 36*(10 Suppl.), S85–S121.

Dulcan, M.K., Bregman, J., Weller, E.B., & Weller, R. (1998). Treatment of childhood and adolescent disorders. In A.F. Schatzberg & C.B. Nemeroff (Eds.), *The American Psychiatric Press textbook of psychopharmacology* (2nd ed., pp. 803–850). Washington, DC: American Psychiatric Press.

DuPaul, G.J., Barkley, R.A., & McMurray, M.G. (1994). Response of children with ADHD to methylphenidate: Interaction with internalizing symptoms. *Journal of the American Academy of Child and Adolescent Psychiatry, 33*(6), 844–903.

DuPaul, G.J., Power, T.J., Anastopoulos, A.D., & Reid, R. (1998). *ADHD Rating Scale–IV: Checklists, norms, and clinical interpretation.* New York: Guilford Press.

DuPaul, G.J., & Stoner, G. (1994). *ADHD in the schools: Assessment and intervention strategies.* New York: Guilford Press.

Emslie, G.J., Walkup, J.T., Pliszka, S.R., & Ernst, M. (1999). Nontricyclic antidepressants: Current trends in children and adolescents. *Journal of the American Academy of Child and Adolescent Psychiatry, 38*(5), 517–528.

Evers, R.B. (1996). The positive force of vocational education: Transition outcomes for youth with learning disabilities. *Journal of Learning Disabilities, 29*(1), 69–78.

Faraone, S.V., & Biederman, J. (1998). Neurobiology of attention-deficit hyperactivity disorder. *Biological Psychiatry, 15*, 951–958.

Faraone, S.V., Biederman, J., Mennin, D., et al. (1997, October). *ADHD and learning disability: A prospective four-year follow-up study.* Abstract presented at the annual meeting of the American Academy of Child and Adolescent Psychiatry, Toronto.

Findling, R.L. (1996). Open-label treatment of comorbid depression and attentional disorders with co-administration of serotonin reuptake inhibitors and psychostimulants in children, adolescents, and adults: A case series. *Journal of Child and Adolescent Psychopharmacology, 6*, 165–175.

Forbes, G.B. (1998). Clinical utility of the Test of Variables of Attention (TOVA) in the diagnosis of attention-deficit/hyperactivity disorder. *Journal of Clinical Psychology, 54*, 461–476.

Gadow, K.D., Sverd, J., Nolan, E.E., & Sprafkin, J. (1995). Efficacy of methylphenidate for ADHD in children with tic disorder. *Archives of General Psychiatry, 52*, 444–455.

Geller, B., & Luby, J. (1997). Child and adolescent bipolar disorder: A review of the past 10 years. *Journal of the American Academy of Child and Adolescent Psychiatry, 36*(9), 1168–1176.

Geller, B., Reising, D., Leonard, H.L., et al. (1999). Clinical review of tricyclic antidepressant use in children and adolescents. *Journal of the American Academy of Child and Adolescent Psychiatry, 38*(5), 513–516.

Goldstein, S., & Ingersoll, B. (1992, Fall/Winter). Controversial treatments for children with attention deficit hyperactivity disorder. *Chadder: Newsletter of Children and Adults with Attention Deficit Disorders (CHADD)*, 1–4.

Gordon, M. (1983). *The Gordon Diagnostic System.* Dewitt, NY: Gordon Systems.

Grant, D., & Berg, F. (1993). *Wisconsin Card Sorting Test.* Odessa, FL: Psychological Assessment Resources.

Greenberg, L. (1990). *Test of Variables of Attention (TOVA).* Minneapolis, MN: Attention Technology Systems.

Greenhill, L.L., Abikoff, H.B., Arnold, E., et al. (1996). Medication treatment strategies in the MTA study: Relevance to clinicians and researchers. *Journal of the American Academy of Child and Adolescent Psychiatry, 34*, 1304–1313.

Greenhill, L.L., Halperin, J.M., & Abikoff, H. (1999). Stimulant medications. *Journal of the American Academy of Child and Adolescent Psychiatry, 38*(5), 503–512.

Hauser, P., Zametkin, A.J., Martinez, P., et al. (1993). Attention-deficit hyperactivity disorder in people with generalized resistance to thyroid hormone. *New England Journal of Medicine, 328*(14), 997–1001.

Hechtman, L. (1985). Adolescent outcome of hyperactive children treated with stimulants in childhood: A review. *Psychopharmacological Bulletin, 21*, 178–191.

Hechtman, L. (1993, October). *Various types of adolescent and adult outcome.* Paper presented at the 40th annual meeting of the American Academy of Child and Adolescent Psychiatry, San Antonio, TX.

Hechtman, L. (1997). Families of children with attention deficit hyperactivity disorder: A review. *Canadian Journal of Psychiatry, 42*(2), 211.

Hechtman, L. (1999). ADHD and bipolar disorder. *ADHD Report, 7*(2), 1–4.

Horner, B.R., & Scheibe, K.E. (1997). Prevalence and implications of attention-deficit hyperactivity disorder among adolescents in treatment for substance abuse. *Journal of the American Academy of Child and Adolescent Psychiatry, 36*(1), 30–36.

Hunt, R.D. (1993, October). *Neurobiological subtypes of ADHD.* Paper presented at the 40th annual meeting of the American Academy of Child and Adolescent Psychiatry, San Antonio, TX.

Hunt, R.D., Arnsten, A.F., & Asbell, M.D. (1995). An open trial of guanfacine in the treatment of attention-deficit hyperactivity disorder. *Journal of the American Academy of Child and Adolescent Psychiatry, 34*, 50–54.

Individuals with Disabilities Education Act (IDEA) Amendments of 1997, PL 105-17, 20 U.S.C. §§ 1400 *et seq.*

Kagan, J., Rosman, B.L., Day, L., et al. (1964). Information processing in the child: Significance of analytic and reflective attitudes. *Psychological Monographs, 78*(578).

Kinsbourne, M. (1994). Sugar and the hyperactive child. *New England Journal of Medicine, 330*(5), 355–356.

Koelega, H.S. (1995). Is the Continuous Performance Task useful in research with ADHD children? Comments on a review. *Journal of Child Psychology and Psychiatry, 36*, 1477–1493.

Lahey, B.B., & Carlson, C.L. (1991). Validity of the diagnostic category of attention deficit disorder without hyperactivity: A review of the literature. *Journal of Learning Disabilities, 24*(2), 110–120.

Law, S., & Schachar, R. (1997, October). *Does methylphenidate cause tics?* Abstract presented at the annual meeting of the American Academy of Child and Adolescent Psychiatry, Toronto.

Leckman, J.F., Zhang, H., Vitale, A., et al. (1998). Course of the tic severity in Tourette syndrome: The first two decades. *Pediatrics, 102,* 14–19.

Levine, M.D. (1980). *The ANSER System: Self-administered student profile for developmental, behavioral, and health assessment.* Boston: Educators Publishing Service.

Levine, M.D. (1983). *Pediatric Early Elementary Examination (PEEX): Response booklet.* Cambridge, MA: Educators Publishing Service.

Levine, M.D. (1990a). *Patterns of attentional dysfunction: Their clinical significance in childhood.* Paper presented to the annual meeting of the Oregon Pediatric Society, Eugene, OR.

Levine, M.D. (1990b). *Social ability, sociability, social inability, and social liability.* Paper presented to the annual meeting of the Oregon Pediatric Society, Eugene, OR.

Little, M., Murphy, J.M., Jellinek, M.S., et al. (1994). Screening 4- and 5-year-old children for psychosocial dysfunction: A preliminary study with the Pediatric Symptom Checklist. *Journal of Developmental and Behavioral Pediatrics, 15*(3), 191–197.

Lyon, G.R. (1996, Spring). Learning disabilities. *Future of Children, 6*(1), 54–76.

MacDonald, G.W., & Cornwall, A. (1995). The relationship between phonological awareness and reading and spelling achievement eleven years later. *Journal of Learning Disabilities, 28*(8), 523–527.

Malhotra, S., & Santosh, P.J. (1998). An open clinical trial of buspirone in children with attention-deficit/hyperactivity disorder. *Journal of the American Academy of Child and Adolescent Psychiatry, 37,* 364–365.

Mannuzza, S., Klein, R.G., Bessler, A., et al. (1993). Adult outcome of hyperactive boys: Educational achievement, occupational rank, and psychiatric status. *Archives of General Psychiatry, 50*(7), 565–576.

McBurnett, K., Pfiffner, L.J., Willcutt, E., et al. (1999). Experimental cross-validation of DSM-IV types of attention-deficit/hyperactivity disorder. *Journal of the American Academy of Child and Adolescent Psychiatry, 38,* 17–24.

MTA Cooperative Group. (1999). A 14-month randomized clinical trial of treatment strategies for attention-deficit/hyperactivity disorder: Multimodal Treatment Study of Children with ADHD. *Archives of General Psychiatry, 56*(12), 1073–1086.

Neuman, R.J., Todd, R.D., Heath, A.C., et al. (1999). Evaluation of ADHD typology in three contrasting samples: A latent class approach. *Journal of the American Academy of Child and Adolescent Psychiatry, 38,* 25–33.

Newcorn, J.H., Halperin, J.M., Schwartz, S., et al. (1994). Parent and teacher ratings of attention-deficit hyperactivity disorder symptoms: Implications for case identification. *Journal of Developmental and Behavioral Pediatrics, 15*(2), 86–91.

Olvera, R.L., Pliszka, S.R., Luh, J., & Tatum, R. (1996). An open trial of venlafaxine in the treatment of attention-deficit/hyperactivity disorder in children and adolescents. *Journal of Child and Adolescent Psychopharmacology, 6*(4), 241–250.

Pliszka, S.R. (1998). Comorbidity of attention-deficit/hyperactivity disorder with psychiatric disorder: An overview. *Journal of Clinical Psychiatry, 59*(Suppl. 7), 50–58.

Pliszka, S.R., McCracken, J.T., & Maas, J.W. (1996). Catecholamines in attention-deficit hyperactivity disorder: Current perspectives. *Journal of the American Academy of Child and Adolescent Psychiatry, 35,* 264–271.

Popper, C.W. (1995). Combining methylphenidate and clonidine: Pharmacologic questions and news reports about sudden death. *Journal of Child and Adolescent Psychopharmacology, 5*(3), 157–166.

Popper, C.W. (1997). Antidepressants in the treatment of attention-deficit/hyperactivity disorder. *Journal of Clinical Psychiatry, 58,* 14–31.

Prince, J.B., Wilens, T.E., Biederman, J., et al. (1996). Clonidine for sleep disturbances associated with attention-deficit hyperactivity disorder: A systematic chart review of 62 cases. *Journal of the American Academy of Child and Adolescent Psychiatry, 35,* 599–605.

Regulations requiring manufacturers to assess the safety and effectiveness of new drugs and biological products. (1998). 63(231) Fed. Reg. 66,631–66,672.

Rehabilitation Act of 1973, PL 93-112, 29 U.S.C. §§ 701 *et seq.*

Rickham, N., & Graham, P.J. (1971). A behavioral screening questionnaire for use with three-year-old children: Preliminary findings. *Journal of Child Psychology and Psychiatry, 12,* 5–33.

Riggs, P.D., Leon, S.L., Mikulich, S.K., & Pottle, L.C. (1998). An open trial of bupropion for ADHD in adolescents with substance use disorders and conduct disorder. *Journal of the American Academy of Child and Adolescent Psychiatry, 37,* 1271–1278.

Satterfield, J., Satterfield, B., & Cantwell, D. (1981). Three-year multimodality treatment study of 100 hyperactive boys. *Journal of Pediatrics, 98,* 680–688.

Shapiro, B.K., & Gallico, R.P. (1993). Learning disabilities. *Child with Developmental Disabilities, 40*(3), 491–505.

Shaywitz, B.A., Fletcher, J.M., & Shaywitz, S.E. (1997). Attention-deficit/hyperactivity disorder. *Advances in Pediatrics, 44,* 331–367.

Shaywitz, S.E. (1998). Dyslexia. *Current Concepts, 338,* 307–312.

Shaywitz, S.E., Shaywitz, B.A., Fletcher, J.M., & Escobar, M.D. (1990). Prevalence of reading disability in boys and girls: Results of the Connecticut Longitudinal Study. *JAMA: Journal of the American Medical Association, 264*(8), 998–1002.

Siegel, L.S. (1992, March). *Is IQ justified in the diagnosis of LD?* Paper presented at the Developmental Disabilities Colloquium, Johns Hopkins Medical Institution, Baltimore.

Silver, L.B. (1987). The "magic cure": A review of the current controversial approaches for treating learning disabilities. *Journal of Learning Disabilities, 20*(8), 498–512.

Singer, H.S., Brown, J., Quaskey, S., et al. (1995). The treatment of attention-deficit hyperactivity disorder in Tourette's syndrome: A double-blind placebo-controlled study with clonidine and desipramine. *Pediatrics, 956*(1), 74–81.

Stein, M.A., Blondis, T.A., Schnitzler, E.R., et al. (1996). Methylphenidate dosing: Twice daily versus three times daily. *Pediatrics, 98,* 748–756.

Strayhorn, J.M., & Weidman, C.S. (1988). A parent practices scale and its relation to parent and child mental health. *Journal of the American Academy of Child and Adolescent Psychiatry, 27*(5), 613–618.

Sturner, R.A. (1991). Parent questionnaires: Basic office equipment? *Journal of Developmental and Behavioral Pediatrics, 12*(1), 51–54.

Sturner, R.A., Eisert, D.C., Mabe, A., & Thomas, P. (1985). Questionnaire use in pediatric practice: Survey of practice. *Clinical Pediatrics, 24*(11), 638–641.

Szatmari, P., Offord, D.R., & Boyle, M.H. (1989). Ontario Child Health Study: Prevalence of attention deficit disorder with hyperactivity. *Journal of Child Psychology and Psychiatry and Allied Disciplines, 30*(2), 219–230.

Tannock, R. (1993, October). *Attention deficit hyperactivity disorders with anxiety disorders.* Paper presented at the 40th annual meeting of the American Academy of Child and Adolescent Psychiatry, San Antonio, TX.

Thorley, G. (1988). Adolescent outcome for hyperactive children. *Archives of the Diseases of Childhood, 63,* 1181–1183.

Toren, P., Karasik, A., Eldar, S., et al. (1997). Thyroid function in attention deficit and hyperactivity disorder. *Journal of Psychiatric Research, 31,* 359–363.

Tynan, W.D., & Nearing, J. (1994). The diagnosis of attention deficit hyperactivity disorder in young children. *Infants and Young Children, 6*(4), 13–20.

Ullmann, R.K., Sleator, E.K., & Sprague, R.L. (1991). *ADHD Comprehensive Teacher's Rating Scale (ACTeRS).* Champaign, IL: MetriTech.

Vaidya, C.J., Austin, G., Kirkorian, G., et al. (1998). Selective effects of methylphenidate in attention deficit hyperactivity disorder: A functional magnetic resonance study. *Proceedings of the National Academy of Science USA, 24,* 14,494–14,499.

Waldman, I.D., Rowe, D.C., Abramowitz, A., et al. (1998). Association and linkage of the dopamine transporter gene and attention-deficit hyperactivity disorder in children: Heterogeneity owing to diagnostic subtype and severity. *American Journal of Human Genetics, 63,* 1767–1776.

Waldrop, M.F., & Goering, J.D. (1971). Hyperactivity and minor physical anomalies in elementary school children. *American Journal of Orthopsychiatry, 41*(4), 602–607.

Warneke, L. (1990). Psychostimulants in psychiatry. *Canadian Journal of Psychiatry, 35*(1), 3–10.

Waslick, B.D., Walsh, B.T., Greenhill, L.L., et al. (1999). Cardiovascular effects of desipramine in children and adults during exercise testing. *Journal of the American Academy of Child and Adolescent Psychiatry, 38*(2), 179–186.

Whalen, C.K., Henker, B., & Hinshaw, S.P. (1985). Cognitive behavioral therapies for hyperactive children: Premises, problems, and prospects. *Journal of Abnormal Child Psychology, 13,* 391–410.

Wilens, T.E. (1993, October). *Comorbidity of ADHD with mood or substance use disorders.* Paper presented at the 40th annual meeting of the American Academy of Child and Adolescent Psychiatry, San Antonio, TX.

Wilens, T.E., & Biederman, J. (1992). The stimulants. *Psychiatric Clinics of North America, 15*(1), 191–222.

Wilens, T.E., Biederman, J., & Mick, E. (1997). Attention deficit hyperactivity disorder (ADHD) is associated with early onset substance use disorders. *Journal of Nervous and Mental Disease, 185*(8), 475–482.

Wilens, T.E., & Spencer, T.J. (1999). Combining methylphenidate and clonidine: A clinically sound medication option. *Journal of the American Academy of Child and Adolescent Psychiatry, 38*(5), 614–622.

Willoughby, J.A., & Haggerty, R.J. (1964). A simple behavior questionnaire for preschool children. *Pediatrics, 36,* 798–806.

Wolraich, M.L., Hannah, J.N., Pinnock, T.Y., et al. (1996). Comparison of diagnostic criteria for attention-deficit hyperactivity disorder in a county-wide sample. *Journal of the American Academy of Child and Adolescent Psychiatry, 35,* 319–324.

Wolraich, M.L., Lindgren, S., Stromquist, A., et al. (1990). Stimulant medication use by primary care physicians in the treatment of attention deficit hyperactivity disorder. *Pediatrics, 86*(1), 95–101.

Zametkin, A.J., Nordahl, T.E., Gross, M., et al. (1990). Cerebral glucose metabolism in adults with hyperactivity of childhood onset. *New England Journal of Medicine, 323,* 1361–1366.

7

Appendix

Guidelines for the Care of Children and Adolescents with Attention-Deficit/Hyperactivity Disorder

Basic Team

The special care needs of children with attention-deficit/hyperactivity disorder (ADHD) can be met by an experienced primary care physician who works collaboratively with parents, teachers, and other school staff. Some children with ADHD and their families require referral to an experienced child development team headed by a developmental pediatrician, and others may need referral to a child neurologist or a mental health professional. Please note that the primary care physician continues to be responsible for coordinating the special services that children with ADHD require.

Regular members of the child development team include a developmental pediatrician, a psychologist, a speech-language pathologist, an occupational therapist, an audiologist, and a medical social worker. Some children with ADHD require evaluation by only a developmental pediatrician and a psychologist.

Initial Evaluation

The objectives of the initial evaluation are to document the child's behavior in different environments, identify associated developmental problems, clarify the cause of the child's ADHD if possible, and identify associated medical and mental health problems. The responsibilities of the primary care physician and nurse are to conduct parent, child, and teacher interviews; perform a complete medical examination; review behavior rating scales; and counsel the parents and the child about the diagnosis and recommended treatment.

Frequency of Visits

The child and the family should be followed monthly by the primary care office following the initiation of the treatment program. This is particularly important for children who are starting on a medication trial. Reevaluate the child and family in the office twice yearly if the child is stable and doing well with the treatment program and more frequently for younger children and in the first year of treatment. In addition, the physician and office staff should conduct telephone interviews with the child's parents and teachers and obtain behavior rating scales and other specific follow-up data as needed (e.g., during medication trials, with change in medication dosage, to update the Management Plan). The Management Plan should be updated as needed at each reevaluation and not less than yearly.

The Physician's Guide to Caring for Children with Disabilities and Chronic Conditions, edited by Robert E. Nickel and Larry W. Desch, copyright © 2000 Paul H. Brookes Publishing Co.

Guidelines for the Care of Children and Adolescents with Attention-Deficit/Hyperactivity Disorder

The following elements are recommended by age group, and the listing is cumulative. Review all items indicated through the actual age group of a child entering your practice for the first time as part of the initial evaluation.

AGE	KEY CLINICAL ISSUES/CONCERNS	EVALUATIONS/KEY PROCEDURES	SPECIALISTS
Birth–5 years (pre-school age)	*Growth/Nutrition*	Growth parameters, diet history	Nutritionist as needed
	Associated Medical Problems Hearing or vision	Hearing and vision testing as needed	Audiologist, ophthalmologist as needed Nutritionist as needed
	Motor and vocal tics		Child neurologist as needed
	Seizures	Electroencephalogram (EEG)	Pediatric gastroenterologist, urologist as needed
	Constipation	Diet, medication (e.g., bulk agent), GI referral as needed	
	Encopresis	Biofeedback treatment, counseling as needed	
	Enuresis	UA/culture as needed, behavioral or other management	
	Sleep disorder	Behavior management or, occasionally, medication	
	Note any side effects of medications.		
	Dental Care	Review oral hygiene	Dentist
	Associated Behavior and Mental Health Problems Aggression Oppositional behaviors Anxiety Obsessive-compulsive behaviors	Family and teacher interviews, behavior rating scales and preschool information at least twice yearly, more frequently if on medication	Child development team or individual appointments with psychologist, child psychiatrist as needed
	Associated Developmental or Learning Problems Need for early intervention/early childhood special education (EI/ECSE) Language delay or speech-language disorder Developmental delay	Developmental screening and surveillance Referral for eligibility testing for EI/ECSE services as needed	Evaluation by child development team or speech-language pathologist as needed
	Behavior Management in the Home Consistency and anticipation Structure and predictability Positives before negatives Immediate and frequent feedback Identify problem situations (e.g., trip to store)	Family interview, educational materials Refer parents to community services (behavior management programs specifically for children with attention-deficit/hyperactivity disorder [ADHD]) as needed	

The Physician's Guide to Caring for Children with Disabilities and Chronic Conditions, edited by Robert E. Nickel and Larry W. Desch, copyright © 2000 Paul H. Brookes Publishing Co.

Guidelines for the Care of Children and Adolescents with Attention-Deficit/Hyperactivity Disorder *(continued)*

The following elements are recommended by age group, and the listing is cumulative. Review all items indicated through the actual age group of a child entering your practice for the first time as part of the initial evaluation.

AGE	KEY CLINICAL ISSUES/CONCERNS	EVALUATIONS/KEY PROCEDURES	SPECIALISTS
Birth–5 years (pre-school age) *(continued)*	*Behavior Management*	Teacher interview, behavior rating scales, and other data collection as needed	
	Family Support Services Respite care Parent group (e.g., Children and Adults with Attention-Deficit Disorders [CHADD]) Community health nurse Advocacy Financial (e.g., Supplemental Security Income [SSI] for children with severe or multiple problems)	Family interview, use parent questionnaire (family assessment), and provide resource information to the parents	Community health nurse, mental health professional as needed Collaborate with community services
	Review of Diagnosis and Anticipatory Guidance Need for parent training in behavior management Review individualized family service plan (IFSP) with family Accident prevention Discussion of alternative (controversial) therapies Transition to grade school	Child and family interviews, educational materials Teacher interview, school conference as needed	Primary care physician; collaborate with child development team as needed
6–12 years (school-age child)	*Follow-Up of Medication Treatment*	Behavior rating scales and teacher report at least twice yearly Check growth, blood pressure, heart rate, tics, side effects at least twice yearly if child is stable and doing well Electrocardiogram (EKG), lab work as needed for specific medications	Collaborate with developmental pediatrician (DPed) or child psychiatrist as needed
	Associated Learning Disabilities	Intellectual and achievement testing as needed	Referral to child development team as needed, collaborate with school staff

The Physician's Guide to Caring for Children with Disabilities and Chronic Conditions, edited by Robert E. Nickel and Larry W. Desch, copyright © 2000 Paul H. Brookes Publishing Co.

Guidelines for the Care of Children and Adolescents with Attention-Deficit/Hyperactivity Disorder *(continued)*

The following elements are recommended by age group, and the listing is cumulative. Review all items indicated through the actual age group of a child entering your practice for the first time as part of the initial evaluation.

AGE	KEY CLINICAL ISSUES/CONCERNS	EVALUATIONS/KEY PROCEDURES	SPECIALISTS
6–12 years (school-age *(continued)*	*Associated Behavior or Mental Health Problems* Oppositional defiant disorder (ODD) Conduct disorder Tourette syndrome Anxiety disorders Depression, bipolar disorder	Child, parent, and teacher interviews; behavior rating scales as noted previously Review medication management	Referral to child deveopment team or mental health professional as needed, collaborate with school staff
	Social Skills Promote social competence Involvement in peer group activities at school and in community (determine which supports are needed)	School-based social skills program or referral to community services as needed	Collaborate with school staff
	Anticipatory Guidance Sports and leisure activities (highly structured small-group activities, noncompetitive, and with adult supervision) Promote self-care and independence	Referral to community services as indicated	
13–21 years (adolescent–young adult)	*Anticipatory Guidance* Transition to middle school and high school Encourage healthy behaviors (diet, exercise) High-risk behavior (substance use and abuse, promiscuity) Career planning Transitions to adult services and independent living	Adolescent, parent, and teacher interviews, school conference as needed Referrals to career counseling, vocational specialist as needed	Primary care office, collaborate with mental health professional as needed

The Physician's Guide to Caring for Children with Disabilities and Chronic Conditions, edited by Robert E. Nickel and Larry W. Desch, copyright © 2000 Paul H. Brookes Publishing Co.

Family and Physician Management Plan Summary for Children and Adolescents with Attention-Deficit/Hyperactivity Disorder

This form will help you and your physician review current services and service needs. Please answer the questions about your current services on this page. Your physician will review your responses and complete the rest of the form.

Child's name _____ Today's date _____

Person completing the form _____

CURRENT SERVICES

1. Please list your/your child's current medications and any side effects.

2. What is your/your child's current school program?

   School name _____ Grade _____

   Teacher _____ Telephone _____

3. Do you/does your child receive any support services and other special programs at school (e.g., physical therapy, resource room)? Please list.

4. Who are your/your child's other medical and dental service providers?

   Dentist _____

   Neurologist _____

   Other _____

5. Who are your/your child's other community service providers?

   Behavioral or mental health specialist _____

   _____

   Other _____

Family and Physician Management Plan Summary for Children and Adolescents with Attention-Deficit/Hyperactivity Disorder *(continued)*

6. Do you/does your child also receive services from a child development team of specialists?

   Contact person _____

   Location _____

7. Have you/has your child had any blood tests, radiologic (X-ray) examinations, or other procedures since your last visit? If yes, please describe.

8. Have you/has your child been hospitalized or received surgery since your last visit? If yes, describe.

9. Please note your/your child's accomplishments since your last visit. Consider activities at home, in your neighborhood, or at school, as well as success with treatments.

10. What goals (e.g., skills) would you/your child like to accomplish in the next year? Consider activities at home, in your neighborhood, or at school, as well as success with treatments.

11. What questions or concerns would you like addressed today?

The Physician's Guide to Caring for Children with Disabilities and Chronic Conditions, edited by Robert E. Nickel and Larry W. Desch, copyright © 2000 Paul H. Brookes Publishing Co.

Family and Physician Management Plan Summary for Children and Adolescents with Attention-Deficit/Hyperactivity Disorder

The Management Plan Summary should be completed at each annual review and more often as needed. It is intended to be used with the Guidelines for Care, which provide a more complete listing of clinical issues at different ages as well as recommended evaluations and treatments.

Child's name _____   Person completing form _____   Today's date _____

Clinical issues	Currently a problem?	Evaluations needed	Treatment recommendations	Referrals made	Date for status check
Family's Questions					
Growth/Nutrition					
Dental Care					
Associated Medical Problems Hearing and vision concerns Seizures Tics or Tourette syndrome Constipation, enuresis Sleep disorder **Note any side effects of medications.**					

The Physician's Guide to Caring for Children with Disabilities and Chronic Conditions, edited by Robert E. Nickel and Larry W. Desch, copyright © 2000 Paul H. Brookes Publishing Co.

Family and Physician Management Plan Summary for Children and Adolescents with Attention-Deficit/Hyperactivity Disorder *(continued)*

Child's name _____ Person completing form _____ Today's date _____

Clinical issues	Currently a problem?	Evaluations needed	Treatment recommendations	Referrals made	Date for status check
Associated Developmental or Learning Problems Describe current school achievement Review school services (individualized family service plan [IFSP] or individualized education program [IEP]) Learning disability Speech-language disorder					
Review of Behavioral Questionnaires					
Behavior Management in the Home					
Behavior Management in the School					
Family Support Services					

The Physician's Guide to Caring for Children with Disabilities and Chronic Conditions, edited by Robert E. Nickel and Larry W. Desch, copyright © 2000 Paul H. Brookes Publishing Co.

Family and Physician Management Plan Summary for
Children and Adolescents with Attention-Deficit/Hyperactivity Disorder *(continued)*

Child's name _____ Person completing form _____ Today's date _____

Clinical issues	Currently a problem?	Evaluations needed	Treatment recommendations	Referrals made	Date for status check
Associated Behavior or Mental Health Issues Aggression Oppositional behavior, oppositional defiant disorder Conduct disorder Anxiety, depression Obsessive-compulsive behaviors High-risk behaviors					
Discussion of Alternative (Controversial) Therapies					
Social Skills Involvement in peer group activities at school, and in the community (determine which supports are needed)					
Self-Care/Independence					
Anticipatory Guidance List issues discussed and materials provided					

Family and Physician Management Plan Summary for
Children and Adolescents with Attention-Deficit/Hyperactivity Disorder *(continued)*

Child's name _____ Person completing form _____ Today's date _____

Clinical issues	Currently a problem?	Evaluations needed	Treatment recommendations	Referrals made	Date for status check
Collaboration with Community Agencies Schools					
Comments:					

Next update of the Management Plan Summary _____

Signature _____ Date _____
 (Child and parent)

Signature _____ Date _____
 (Health professional)

The Physician's Guide to Caring for Children with Disabilities and Chronic Conditions, edited by Robert E. Nickel and Larry W. Desch, copyright © 2000 Paul H. Brookes Publishing Co.

RESOURCES ON ATTENTION-DEFICIT/
HYPERACTIVITY DISORDER AND RELATED DISORDERS

Readings

Alexander-Roberts, C. (1995). *ADHD and teens: A parent's guide to making it through the tough years.* Dallas, TX: Taylor Publishing Co. (contains a foreword by P.T. Elliott) (1-800-677-2800)

Barkley, R.A. (1995). *Taking charge of ADHD: The complete, authoritative guide for parents.* New York: Guilford Press. (1-800-365-7006)

Fowler, M.C. (1999). *Maybe you know my kid? A parent's guide to identifying, understanding, and helping your child with attention deficit hyperactivity disorder* (3rd ed.). Secaucus, NJ: Carol Publishing Group. (1-800-447-2665)

Goldstein, S., & Goldstein, M. (1992). *Hyperactivity: Why won't my child pay attention? A complete guide to ADD for parents, teachers, and community agencies.* New York: John Wiley & Sons. (1-800-225-2945)

Kennedy, P., Terdal, L., & Fusetti, L. (1993). *The hyperactive child book: A pediatrician, a child psychologist, and a mother team up to offer the most practical, up-to-date guide to treating, educating, and living with your ADHD child.* New York: St. Martin's Press. (1-800-221-7945)

Kilcarr, P.J., & Quinn, P.O. (1997). *Voices from fatherhood: Fathers, sons, and ADHD.* Philadelphia: Brunner/Mazel. (1-800-821-8312)

Latham, P.S., & Latham, P.H. (1997). *Attention deficit disorder and the law: A guide for advocates* (2nd ed.). Washington, DC: JKL Communications. (202-223-5097)

Levine, M.D. (1990). *Keeping a head in school: A student's book about learning abilities and learning disorders.* Cambridge, MA: Educators Publishing Service. (1-800-435-7728)

Moss, D.M. (1989). *Shelley, the hyperactive turtle* (The special needs collection). Bethesda, MD: Woodbine House. (1-800-843-7352)

Osman, B.B. (1997). *Learning disabilities and ADHD: A family guide to living and learning together.* New York: John Wiley & Sons. (1-800-225-2945)

Shapiro, L.E., & Shore, H.M. (Eds.). (1993). *Sometimes I drive my mom crazy, but I know she's crazy about me: A self-esteem book for ADHD children.* King of Prussia, PA: Center for Applied Psychology.

Silver, L.B. (1999). *Dr. Larry Silver's advice to parents on attention-deficit hyperactivity disorder* (2nd ed.). New York: Times Books. (1-800-733-3000)

National Organizations

Children and Adults with Attention-Deficit/Hyperactivity Disorder (CHADD)
8181 Professional Place, Suite 201
Landover, Maryland 20785
Telephone: (800) 233-4050, (301) 306-7070
Fax: (301) 306-7090
E-mail: national@chadd.org
World Wide Web site: http://www.chadd.org/

A national parent organization with more than 400 local chapters that provides information and support, publishes a magazine, *CHADDER,* and a newsletter, *Chadderbox,* and supports a national call-in center: (800) 233-4050 (8:00 A.M.–5:30 P.M. Eastern Time).

Learning Disabilities Association (LDA) of America
4156 Library Road
Pittsburgh, Pennsylvania 15234-1349
Telephone: (412) 341-1515
Fax: (412) 344-0224
E-mail: ldanatl@usaor.net
World Wide Web site: http://www.ldanatl.org/

A national information and referral service (formerly Association for Children and Adults with Learning Disabilities) with 700 local chapters, LDA publishes a quarterly newsletter, *Newsbriefs,* and journal, *Learning Disabilities Multidisciplinary Journal,* sponsors professional conferences, and requires an annual membership fee.

**International Dyslexia Association
(formerly the Orton Dyslexia Society)**
The Chester Building, Suite 382
8600 LaSalle Road

Baltimore, Maryland 21286-2044
Telephone: (410) 296-0232, (800) 222-3123
Fax: (410) 321-5069
World Wide Web site: http://www.interdys.org/

An international organization with 43 branches that supports research, disseminates research information through conferences and publications, and sponsors support groups for college students with dyslexia as well as a web site designed for teenagers with dyslexia (http://www.ldteens.org/).

National Attention Deficit Disorder Association (ADDA)
1788 Second Street, Suite 200
Highland Park, Illinois 60035
Telephone: (847) 432-ADDA (2332)
Fax: (847) 432-5874
E-mail: mail@add.org
World Wide Web site: http://www.add.org/

A national organization that provides information and referral services to families and professionals.

Further Information

LD Online
World Wide Web site: http://www.ldonline.org/

A service of the Learning Project at public broadcasting station WETA in Washington, D.C., that provides information on learning disabilities and attention-deficit/hyperactivity disorder; a resource list; a calendar of events; an electronic newsletter; bulletin boards, chat rooms for parents, students, and teachers; and a special "Ask the Expert" bulletin board.

Autism and Pervasive Developmental Disorders

Robert E. Nickel

KEY COMPETENCIES

- Discuss the classification of pervasive developmental disorders (PDDs)
- Describe the characteristic behaviors of infants and toddlers with autism and the characteristics of children with high-functioning autism (HFA)
- Discuss the difficulties with making an early diagnosis of autism
- Use developmental screening tests to identify toddlers and preschool-age children who are suspected of having autism
- Review the basic components of educational and behavioral services for children with autism
- Describe the medical management of challenging behavior
- Counsel families about alternative and/or controversial therapies

DESCRIPTION

Definition of Autism

Autism is a behavioral syndrome that begins before age 3 years and is characterized by impairments in social interaction, verbal and nonverbal communication, and play. Although some early investigators speculated that autism was caused by abnormal parenting, autism clearly is a developmental disorder that has an organic basis.

In 1943, Kanner first used the term *early infantile autism* to describe a group of 11 children who exhibited extreme aloofness; were unable to develop relationships with people; and had delayed speech and repetitive, simple play patterns. In 1978, Rutter proposed four essential characteristics of infantile autism:

- A lack of social interest and responsiveness
- Impairments in language ability, including the failure to develop speech or the development of peculiar speech patterns
- Bizarre motor behavior, including limited play patterns and ritualistic and compulsive behaviors (e.g., hand flapping, toe walking)
- Onset before 30 months of age (1978, p. 19)

Classification of Autism and Pervasive Developmental Disorders

Autistic disorder is one subtype of the pervasive developmental disorders (PDDs). The subtypes of PDD and the criteria used to diagnose autistic disorder have changed significantly from the *Diagnostic and Statistical Manual of Mental Disorders, Third Edition* (DSM-III; American Psychiatric Association, 1977), to DSM-III-R (American Psychiatric Association, 1987) and DSM-IV (American Psychiatric Association, 1994). Table 8.1 compares the PDD

Table 8.1. Subtypes of pervasive developmental disorders

Diagnostic and Statistical Manual of Mental Disorders, Third Edition (DSM-III)

Infantile autism

Infantile autism, residual state

Childhood-onset pervasive developmental disorder (PDD)

Childhood-onset PDD, residual state

Atypical PDD

DSM-III-R

Autistic disorder

PDD not otherwise specified (PDD-NOS)

DSM-IV

Autistic disorder

Rett syndrome

Childhood disintegrative disorder

Asperger syndrome

PDD-NOS (includes atypical autism)

Adapted with permission from the *Diagnostic and Statistical Manual of Mental Disorders.* Copyright © 1980, 1987, 1994 American Psychiatric Association.

subtypes described in DSM-III, DSM-III-R, and DSM-IV.

The changes in the diagnostic criteria for autism in DSM-IV were made to improve diagnostic accuracy, to shorten the list of criteria, and to improve compatibility with the *International Classification of Diseases, Tenth Edition* (ICD-10; Lord, 1993). The use of DSM-III-R criteria seems to have overdiagnosed autism in children with severe or profound mental retardation (those requiring extensive or pervasive support) and to have underdiagnosed autism in children without mental retardation (Lord, 1993). Table 8.2 reviews the DSM-IV diagnostic criteria for autistic disorder. To arrive at a diagnosis of autistic disorder under DSM-IV criteria, the child's symptoms must have been present prior to 3 years of age and, as with the other PDD subtypes, must not be better explained by another PDD or a mental health disorder.

The term *pervasive developmental disorder* can be confusing to some families, particularly if educational staff have used the term *autism*. Use of the term *autistic spectrum disorder* in addition to *pervasive developmental disorder* may enhance the family's understanding and acceptance of the diagnosis and treatment recommendations.

Diagnostic Criteria for Other Pervasive Developmental Disorders

Asperger Syndrome   Asperger syndrome (AS) was first described in 1944 by Hans Asperger, who regarded the syndrome as a personality disorder. The children he described began speaking at a typi-

Table 8.2.　Diagnostic criteria for autistic disorder

A child must meet six or more of the following criteria with at least two from (1), and one each from (2) and (3).

(1)　Qualitative impairment in social interaction
- Marked impairment in the use of multiple nonverbal behaviors such as eye-to-eye gaze, facial expression, body postures, and gestures to regulate social interaction
- Failure to develop peer relationships appropriate to developmental level
- A lack of spontaneous seeking to share enjoyment, interests, or achievements with other people (e.g., by a lack of showing, bringing, or pointing out objects of interest)
- Lack of social or emotional reciprocity

(2)　Qualitative impairments in communication
- Delay in, or total lack of, the development of spoken language (not accompanied by an attempt to compensate through alternative modes of communication such as gesture or mime)
- In individuals with adequate speech, marked impairment in the ability to initiate or sustain a conversation with others
- Stereotyped and repetitive use of language or idiosyncratic language
- Lack of varied, spontaneous make-believe play or social imitative play appropriate to developmental level

(3)　Restricted repetitive and stereotyped patterns of behavior, interests, and activities
- Encompassing preoccupation with one or more stereotyped and restricted patterns of interest that is abnormal either in intensity or focus
- Apparently inflexible adherence to specific, nonfunctional routines or rituals
- Stereotyped and repetitive motor mannerisms (e.g., hand or finger flapping or twisting, complex whole-body movements)
- Persistent preoccupation with parts of objects

Adapted with permission from the *Diagnostic and Statistical Manual of Mental Disorders, Fourth Edition.* Copyright © 1994 American Psychiatric Association.

cal age, but the content and quality of their speech and language was atypical. He also noted impairments in these children's social skills, repetitive and stereotypic play, and isolated areas of interest; but they had no impairment in abstract thinking ability (Tsai, 1997). In 1981, Wing recommended that AS be considered part of the autism spectrum. She noted that some children with AS are slow to talk and some have cognitive delays. She also noted that children with AS are clumsy, have pedantic (i.e., monotonous) speech, and all-absorbing interests.

The controversy about whether AS is a valid subtype and which factors differentiate AS from high-functioning autism (HFA) or pervasive developmental disorder not otherwise specified (PDD-NOS) has not been resolved (Ghaziuddin, Tsai, & Ghaziuddin, 1992; Szatmari, 1991; Volkmar, Klin, & Pauls, 1998). Research studies that have compared children with AS with children with HFA primarily have noted differences with regard to language and social skills (Szatmari, Archer, Fisman, et al., 1995; Volkmar, Klin, & Pauls, 1998). One study (Ozonoff, Rogers, & Pennington, 1991) noted significant differences between the two groups in neuropsychological assessments (e.g., theory of mind tests). Other authors (Ghaziuddin, Butler, Tsai, et al., 1994; Gha-

ziuddin & Gerstein, 1996) suggested that clumsiness and pedantic speech (common in AS) may help differentiate AS from HFA. The critical difference may be that children with AS achieve higher full-scale and verbal IQ scores compared to children with HFA (Ramberg, Ehlers, Nyden, et al., 1996).

Table 8.3 presents representative behaviors for children with AS, and Table 8.4 reviews the DSM-IV diagnostic criteria for AS. DSM-IV criteria for AS specify that the child must not have significant cognitive or language delays and that symptoms must result in clinically significant impairment in social, occupational, or other important areas of functioning.

Rett Syndrome　Rett syndrome (RS) is a rare neurodevelopmental disorder with unknown etiology that affects girls exclusively. Genetic studies (see, e.g., Ellaway & Christodoulou, 1999) strongly suggest that RS involves a gene located on the X chromosome. The onset of RS symptoms occurs after a period of typical development of at least several months, although researchers (Kerr, 1995; Leonard & Bower, 1998) have reported differences in the development of girls with RS beginning at birth. The period of developmental regression usually begins in the first 2 years of life. Affected individuals develop a number of characteristic features, including a fall-

226 Nickel

Table 8.3. Representative behaviors of children with Asperger syndrome

Communication
- No general delay in language; grammar and vocabulary are usually good
- Speech is sometimes stilted and repetitive
- Voice tends to be flat, emotionless, and pedantic
- One-sided conversations that revolve around special interests

Cognition
- Obsessed with specific topics (e.g., weather patterns, music)
- No general delay in cognitive skills
- May have nonverbal learning disabilities
- Lack common sense

Social interaction
- Often described as eccentric
- Insensitive to others' feelings or intentions
- Inappropriate approach to initiate social interaction
- Lack of friends

Adapted from Center for the Study of Autism (1990).

Table 8.4. Diagnostic criteria for Asperger syndrome

A child must meet two or more of the criteria from (1) and at least one from (2).

(1) Qualitative impairment in social interaction
- Marked impairment in the use of multiple nonverbal behaviors such as eye-to-eye gaze, facial expression, body postures, and gestures to regulate social interaction
- Failure to develop peer relationships appropriate to developmental level
- A lack of spontaneous seeking to share enjoyment, interests, or achievements with other people (e.g., by a lack of showing, bringing, or pointing out objects of interest to other people)
- Lack of social or emotional reciprocity

(2) Restricted repetitive and stereotyped patterns of behavior, interests, and activities
- Encompassing preoccupation with one or more stereotyped and restricted patterns of interest that is abnormal either in intensity or focus
- Apparently inflexible adherence to specific, nonfunctional routines or rituals
- Stereotyped and repetitive motor mannerisms (e.g., hand or finger flapping or twisting, complex whole-body movements)
- Persistent preoccupation with parts of objects

Adapted with permission from the *Diagnostic and Statistical Manual of Mental Disorders, Fourth Edition.* Copyright © 1994 American Psychiatric Association.

off in the rate of head growth, loss of purposeful hand skills, development of stereotypic hand movements (e.g., hand wringing, hand washing), dyspraxic or shuffling gait, little interest in the social environment, and severe impairments in speech-language and cognitive skills. Children with RS also may experience episodes of hyperventilation, breath-holding spells, seizures, scoliosis, and poor growth. Hagberg and Witt-Engerstrom (1986) suggested a four-stage model of the progression of symptoms in RS:

1. Early-onset stagnation stage (6 months to 1½ years of age)
2. Rapid developmental regression (1–2 years of age)
3. Pseudostagnation stage (3–4 years of age or longer)
4. Late motor deterioration (late school age or early adolescence)

More recent data have shown that girls with RS remain stable after the period of regression and may show limited improvement (Budden, 1997). For all children suspected of having RS, conduct a complete medical or laboratory evaluation to determine the cause of their neurologic deterioration. Table 8.5 reviews the DSM-IV diagnostic criteria for RS.

Childhood Disintegrative Disorder (Heller Syndrome) The hallmark of childhood disintegrative disorder (CDD), also referred to as *Heller syndrome*, is marked regression in multiple areas following

typical development through 2 years of age or older. No specific factor has been associated with the onset of the child's developmental regression in CDD. Children with CDD demonstrate striking and severe impairments in communication, social skills, and self-care and experience a limited recovery (Volkmar, 1992). In one study (Volkmar, 1992), 42% of children recovered no speech and 35% only recovered the use of single words. The etiology of CDD is unknown. Clearly, all children with CDD should receive a vigorous evaluation to identify any known metabolic or neurodegenerative disorder and any possibility of medical treatment. Table 8.6 presents the DSM-IV diagnostic criteria for CDD.

Pervasive Developmental Disorder Not Otherwise Specified The diagnostic category *pervasive developmental disorder not otherwise specified* (PDD-NOS) is for children who demonstrate significant and persistent impairments in reciprocal social interaction, verbal and nonverbal communication, stereotypic behaviors, and restricted activities or interests but who do *not* meet the diagnostic criteria for autistic disorder. DSM-IV does not list specific diagnostic criteria for PDD-NOS.

Table 8.5. Diagnostic criteria for Rett syndrome

Apparently normal prenatal and perinatal development

Apparently normal psychomotor development through the first 5 months after birth

Normal head circumference at birth

Deceleration of head growth between ages 5 and 48 months

Loss of previously acquired purposeful hand skills between ages 5 and 30 months with the subsequent development of stereotyped hand movements (e.g., hand wringing, hand washing)

Loss of social engagement early in the course (although often social interaction develops later)

Appearance of poorly coordinated gait or trunk movements

Severely impaired expressive and receptive language development with severe psychomotor retardation

Adapted with permission from the *Diagnostic and Statistical Manual of Mental Disorders, Fourth Edition.* Copyright © 1994 American Psychiatric Association.

Prevalence

Epidemiologic studies (Tsai & Ghaziuddin, 1997) have reported the prevalence of autism to be between 2 and 3 per 10,000 children. Use of the DSM-III-R criteria suggests a prevalence of autism of approximately 4–5 per 10,000 children; for PDD-NOS, the prevalence rate is 10–15 children per 10,000. A French epidemiologic study (Fombonne, Du Mazaubrun, Cans, & Grandjean, 1997) noted a prevalence rate of autism of 5.35 per 10,000 children and a prevalence rate of all PDDs of 16.3 per 10,000 children. A review (Fombonne, 1999) of 23 epidemiologic surveys of autism published between 1966 and 1998 noted that prevalence rates significantly increased with the year of publication of the study. The median rate for the prevalence of autism for 11 surveys conducted since 1989 was 7.2 per 10,000. The increase in the prevalence of autism is due in large part to improvements in diagnosis and to a lesser extent to changes in the diagnostic criteria. Studies (see Tsai, 1997) have shown no consistent difference in prevalence rates between rural and urban areas, and individuals with autism are found in all socioeconomic groups. Three boys for every girl are diagnosed with autism; however, girls with autism usually have more severe impairments (Tsai & Ghaziuddin, 1997).

Etiology

Autism is a behavioral syndrome with multiple known causes that represent different genetic mechanisms and types of brain injury. Autism has been reported in association with tuberous sclerosis and

Table 8.6. Diagnostic criteria for childhood disintegrative disorder

(1) Normal development for at least the first 2 years after birth including appropriate verbal and non-verbal communication, social relationships, play, and adaptive behavior

(2) Loss of previously acquired skills (before age 10 years) in two or more of the following areas:
  • Expressive or receptive language
  • Social skills or adaptive behavior
  • Bowel or bladder control
  • Play
  • Motor skills

(3) Abnormal function in one or more of the following areas:
  • Qualitative impairment in social interaction (criteria similar to child with autism)
  • Qualitative impairment in communication
  • Restricted, repetitive, and stereotyped patterns of behavior, interests, and activities

Adapted with permission from the *Diagnostic and Statistical Manual of Mental Disorders, Fourth Edition.* Copyright © 1994 American Psychiatric Association.

neurofibromatosis (autosomal dominant), phenylketonuria (autosomal recessive), fragile X syndrome (gene expansion disorder), Down syndrome (chromosome disorder), congenital cytomegalovirus, rubella infections, neonatal intracranial hemorrhage, perinatal asphyxia, lead encephalopathy, and viral encephalitis (Folstein & Piven 1991; Tsai & Ghaziuddin, 1997).

Most individuals with autism, however, have no identifiable cause for their developmental disabilities and chronic conditions (Barton & Volkmar, 1998; Gillberg & Coleman, 1996). In one study, only 30% of individuals with classic autism had a specific medical etiology identified (Gillberg & Coleman, 1996). Children with autism have an increased number of prenatal and perinatal complications; but these findings are not consistent for all children with autism, are not specific to autism, and are not useful predictors of autism (Nelson, 1991).

Twin and Family Studies The prevalence of autism in the siblings of children with autism has been estimated to be 2%–3% (Folstein & Piven, 1991); however, Ritvo, Jorde, Mason-Brothers, and co-workers (1989) reported a sibling recurrence risk of 8.6% from an epidemiologic study of 207 families in Utah, basing their estimate on stoppage rules. The stoppage rules assume that families who have a child with a severe disability may stop having children, and thus the prevalence of that disorder in siblings is reduced artificially.

The reported (Folstein & Piven, 1991) concordance rate has varied from 36% to 96% for monozygotic twins and from 0% to 24% for dizygotic twins. Family studies (e.g., Bolton, Pickles, Murphy, & Rutter, 1998; DeLong & Nohria, 1994; Spiker, Lotspeich, Kraemer, et al., 1994) have shown an increased incidence of cognitive disorders, language disorders, social skills impairments, obsessive-compulsive disorder, and major affective disorders in siblings and first-degree relatives. In one study (Gillberg, Gillberg, & Steffenburg, 1992), Asperger syndrome was found to be more common in siblings and parents of children with autism than in first-degree relatives of children who were developing typically.

Thus, considerable evidence points to a higher genetic liability for autism in siblings of children with autism and to a higher liability for both social and cognitive impairments in siblings and other first-degree relatives (Folstein & Piven, 1991). The exact genetic mechanisms are as yet unknown. Interstitial duplications of chromosome region 15q11–15q13 have been associated with autism in a number of children (Repetto, White, Bader, et al., 1998; Schroer, Phelan, Michaelis, et al., 1998). A candidate gene in this region is the gamma-aminobutyric acid A receptor subunit gene (Cook, Courchesne, Cox, et al., 1998). In addition, studies have reported conflicting results with regard to the association of autism with the serotonin transporter gene (Cook, Courchesne, Lord, et al., 1997; Klauck, Poustka, Benner, et al., 1997).

Neuroanatomic and Neuropathologic Studies
No consensus exists with regard to the area or areas of the brain that are damaged or disordered in autism. Computed tomography (CT) scans and anatomic magnetic resonance imaging (MRI) studies have shown no consistent changes in supratentorial structures for individuals with autism (Courchesne, 1991). The findings that have been reported (Courchesne, 1991; Piven, Berthier, Starkstein, et al., 1990) in some patients include focal neuronal migration abnormalities (involving frontal, parietal, and occipital regions), cortical volume loss, ventricular enlargement, and right–left asymmetries.

Anatomic MRI studies have reported conflicting results with regard to the presence of cerebellar hypoplasia. Courchesne and co-workers (Courchesne, 1991; Courchesne, Yeung-Courchesne, Press, et al., 1988; Murakami et al., 1989) reported a decrease in the size of the cerebellar vermis as well as the cerebellar hemispheres on MRI scans in the majority of individuals with autism. They (Courchesne, Saitoh, Yeung-Courchesne et al., 1994) subsequently expanded and reanalyzed their data and reported two subgroups of individuals with autism: one with cere-

bellar vermian hypoplasia and the other with vermian hyperplasia. These findings were not replicated in other studies (Piven, Saliba, Bailey, & Arndt, 1997; Ritvo & Garber, 1988), and cerebellar hypoplasia also was noted in children with fragile X syndrome (Reiss, 1988). Yet to be demonstrated is how these cerebellar abnormalities relate to the complex cognitive and behavior problems that individuals with autism exhibit.

Neuropathologic studies on a limited number of individuals have shown abnormalities in specific areas of the limbic system, including the hippocampus and amygdala (increase in cell number and decrease in cell size) and in the cerebellum (loss of Purkinje cells and, to a lesser extent, loss of granular cells) (Bauman, 1991; Kemper & Bauman, 1993). A variety of evidence has strengthened interest in impairments in the medial temporal lobe (the hippocampus and the amygdala) and the limbic system in the etiology of autism. Bachevalier (1994) reported an animal model for autism that resulted from damage to the medial temporal lobe. Four infants with autism were noted to have bilateral hippocampal sclerosis on MRI scans (DeLong & Heinz, 1997), and Hoon and Reiss (1992) reported on a child with PDD and left temporal oligodendroglioma. In addition, functional MRI scans have shown that parts of the temporal lobe have a specific role in the recognition of facial expressions (Schultz, 1997), and individuals with autism have impairments in the recognition of facial expressions and emotions.

Immunologic Studies
A number of research studies (Cook, Perry, Dawson, et al., 1993; Plioplys, Greaves, Kazemi, & Silverman, 1994; Singh, Warren, Odell, & Cole, 1991; Stubbs, 1990; Stubbs, Crawford, Burger, et al., 1977; Warren, Cole, Odell, et al., 1990) have explored possible immunologic causes of autism. These studies noted differences in cell-mediated immunity, immune response to vaccination, and natural killer cell activity. Differences have been inconsistent and have varied across studies. A few researchers (see Gupta, Aggarwall, & Heads, 1996) speculated that autism has an autoimmune basis, and, in fact, monthly intravenous immunoglobulin (IVIG) has been used to treat a few children with autism. In an open label study (Plioplys, 1998), only 1 in 10 children showed a positive response to monthly IVIG treatment, and thus it should be considered a nonstandard treatment. As of 2000, no animal or clinical research data exist to support the theory that immune complexes cause autism.

A preliminary report in *Lancet* noted an association between mumps, measles, and rubella vaccination; inflammatory bowel disease; and autism

(Wakefield, Murch, Anthony, et al., 1998). Subsequent review by other investigators provided no support for this finding, however (Fombonne, 1998; Peltola, Patja, Leinikki, et al., 1998).

Biochemical Models Two biochemical models resulted in rapid, enthusiastic introduction of drug treatments for autism: the use of fenfluramine to reduce blood serotonin levels and the use of opiate antagonists. Serotonin is a neurotransmitter in the brain and the peripheral nervous system. Several studies (see, e.g., Ho, Lockitch, Eaves, et al., 1986) demonstrated that as many as one third of individuals with autism have high blood serotonin levels. Fenfluramine, a sympathomimetic amine that has been used for appetite suppression, has been demonstrated to lower blood serotonin levels (Geller, Ritvo, Freeman, et al., 1982; Ho et al., 1986). The initial report (Geller et al., 1982) of fenfluramine treatment of three boys with autism (one of whom had demonstrated a dramatic IQ score increase) in the *New England Journal of Medicine* was followed by enthusiastic publicity; however, a subsequent controlled study (Ho et al., 1986) found no consistent behavioral or developmental effects. Fenfluramine may have improved some children's attention; however, the children's blood serotonin levels were unrelated to apparent drug effect (Ho et al., 1986). In addition, in a 1997 study, the use of fenfluramine combined with phentermine for appetite suppression in adult women was associated with the development of valvular heart disease (Connolly, Crary, McGoon, et al., 1997).

A great deal of research (Chamberlain & Herman, 1990; Herman, 1991) has explored the relationship of opiate peptides to autism and self-injurious behaviors (SIBs). Chamberlain and Herman (1990) speculated that a subgroup of individuals with autism and SIBs have hypersecretion of beta-endorphin and related brain opioids. A few studies (e.g., Herman, 1991) reported elevated cerebrospinal fluid (CSF) opioid peptide concentration in children with autism and lower plasma levels in children with autism and SIBs. Based on these research data, naltrexone, an opiate antagonist, has been used to treat children with autism with and without SIBs. Modest dose-related improvements in SIBs and other behaviors (primarily hyperactivity) have been reported (Herman, 1991; Kolmen, Feldman, Handen, et al., 1995; Panksepp & Lensing, 1991). In one study (Kolmen et al., 1995), 8 of 13 of the children with autism did show a positive response, primarily a decrease in hyperactivity. In a follow-up study (Kolmen, Feldman, Handen, et al., 1997), however, only 3 of 11 children improved in two or more settings,

and overall only 11 of 24 children improved while taking naltrexone. Naltrexone did not result in improvement in communication skills, a basic impairment in children with autism (Feldman, Kolmen, & Gonzaga, 1999).

Of interest, data also exist to support involvement of the dopamine and norepinephrine neurotransmitter systems in autism. For example, children with severe autism may have high CSF homovanillic acid (HVA) levels, and neuroleptics (e.g., haloperidol) that are dopamine receptor blocking agents may be modestly effective in the treatment of autism (Herman, 1991). In addition, dopamine agonists such as stimulants may cause the worsening of certain behaviors in children with autism (Tsai & Ghaziuddin, 1997).

Psychological Theories Psychological theories that emerged in the 1980s and 1990s focused on impairment of social interaction as the primary feature of autism. One theory stipulates that children with autism lack a theory of mind (Baron-Cohen, 1989, 1991). This theory states that children with autism are not able to attribute mental states to others. Children who are developing typically have a theory of mind at about 4 years of age. They understand that people have beliefs and desires about the world and that these determine a person's behavior. If children with autism lack a theory of mind, they cannot attribute beliefs or wants to others to help explain a person's particular behavior (Happé, 1994). Such an impairment could account for impairments in social skills, communication, and imagination. Other researchers (see Klin, Volkmar, & Sparrow, 1992), however, have argued that social impairments in infancy (e.g., lack of shared affect, lack of imitation of facial expressions, lack of anticipation of being picked up) cannot be explained by a lack of the theory of mind (Klin et al., 1992). Some individuals with autism do pass first-order and even second-order theory of mind tests (Baron-Cohen, 1989, 1991; Happé, 1994; Ozonoff, Rogers, & Pennington, 1991).

Frith (see Happé, 1994) proposed that individuals with autism lack the ability to draw different pieces of information together in context to construct higher levels of meaning, which represents an impairment in central coherence. One example of central coherence is the ability to recognize the meaning of ambiguous words by context, such as *son* and *sun*, *meet* and *meat*, and *pair* and *pear*. Another example is the ability to pronounce two homographs correctly based on context, such as "He made a deep bow" versus "He had a pink bow" (Happé, 1994). Children with autism give the most frequent pronunciation of the word regardless of sentence context

(Happé, 1994). Adults with autism have more difficulty with achieving central coherence than adults with AS (Jolliffe & Baron-Cohen, 1999).

Another theory maintains that children with autism have an impairment in their ability to perceive and respond to the affective expressions of others and that their difficulties in social interaction and communication are secondary (Hobson, 1989). Further research will help to clarify the relationship of these different theories to the other cognitive impairments and behavior problems reported in individuals with autism (e.g., impairment in executive functions, verbal IQ score).

DIAGNOSIS AND EVALUATION

Issues in Early Identification

In 1988, Siegel, Pliner, Eschler, and Elliott surveyed 75 families of children with autism. Parents, on average, first raised concerns about their children's development when their children were 1½ years of age. Yet, on average, initial diagnoses were not made until the children reached 2½ years of age, and definitive diagnoses were not established, on average, until the children reached 4½ years of age. Ninety-two percent of parents first discussed their concerns with their children's primary care physician. Siegel and colleagues identified the following factors to explain the delay in diagnosis:

- Autism may have different manifestations at different ages (i.e., infants and toddlers may not show the full-blown syndrome).
- Physicians need to use developmental screening tests
- Screening tests for autism need to be developed
- Referral to an experienced child development team is important in making a prompt and correct diagnosis

Characteristic Behaviors of Infants and Toddlers with Austim   An infant with autism may appear to be a perfect baby. The child may never complain, rarely cry, and be indifferent to being held. The infant with autism also may be persistently irritable, difficult to console, and rigid when held, however. Smiling, cooing, and anticipation of feeding may be absent or slow to develop in the infant. Older infants and toddlers with autism are delayed in play with toys. They show little or no imitative play, comfort seeking, or empathetic response to another's emotion (Dawson, 1992). They may have a qualitative, not necessarily quantitative, difference in eye contact. Their gaze may be directed to a spot on the parent's forehead or may not be combined with facial expressions and vocalizations (Dawson, 1992).

Children with autism at 2–3 years old may show little interest in shared activities or pretend play. They do not use joint attention behaviors such as pointing to indicate interests or showing objects to parents. Their language is delayed, and they make little use of gestures or facial expressions to indicate their wants. Table 8.7 lists the characteristic behaviors of children with autism in infancy and in their second and third years. Some infants and toddlers with autism appear to develop typically until 18–24 months of age, when they experience regression in skills. It is important that these children be evaluated carefully in an attempt to identify the cause of their regression.

Characteristics of Children with High-Functioning Autism   Most investigators define HFA as autism without mental retardation (i.e., nonverbal IQ score greater than 70). Children with HFA have delayed speech and unusual speech patterns. They demonstrate persistent though less severe symptoms than children who have autism and mental retardation. They may appear to make social attachments but lack an understanding of or an interest in other people's thoughts or feelings. Few if any children with HFA make friends, and they tend to function poorly in group play situations. Their speech is monotonous; they may speak perseveratively about an overriding interest without noticing that the listener is uninterested (Stine, 1986; Tsai & Scott-Miller, 1988).

Difficulties with Making an Early Diagnosis of Autism   A number of characteristics of children with autism can make the diagnosis of autism difficult in preschool-age children:

- Typical appearance and typical motor development
- Apparent difficult temperament with hyperactivity
- Isolated areas of typical or above-average skills
- Typical early development with regression suggesting autism

Many children with autism do have a typical physical appearance and typical motor development. Children with HFA may appear to have only a difficult temperament. They may be hyperactive, have a low threshold of response, and respond negatively when approached. These children may not comply with parents' requests or a professional's attempts to complete developmental testing. Adults may assume that the child *will not* do something rather than that the child *cannot* do it. In addition, some children with autism have isolated areas of above-average skills (e.g., mathematics ability,

Table 8.7. Characteristic behaviors of children with autism

INFANCY

Motor
- Inactive, hypotonic, and rarely cries
  or
- Irritable, inconsolable, and/or rigid when held; may arch away from close physical contact

Sensory
- May appear unresponsive to voice, but jolts or panics at environmental sounds
- Refuses food with rough texture
- Adverse reaction to wool fabrics; prefers smooth surfaces
- May panic at change in lighting
- Preoccupied with observing own hand and finger movements

Social
- No or delayed social smile
- Avoidance of eye contact when held
- Fleeting eye contact at a distance
- Lack of anticipatory response to being picked up
- Seems content to be left alone
- Fails to follow visually the coming and going of primary caregiver
- Little imitative play (e.g., Peek-a-boo, Pat-a-cake, wave bye-bye)
- Fails to show normal 8-month-old's stranger anxiety

Some infants may show social attachment to familiar adults.

Language
- Delayed or absent coo and/or expressive vocalization
- Failure to imitate words and sounds
- Little communicative use of gesture
- Delayed speech

SECOND AND THIRD YEARS

Motor
Some children may show . . .
- Toe walking
- Rocking
- Head banging
- Whirling and other perseverative movements

Perceptual
- Withdraws from environmental stimulation
- Engages in self-stimulation
- Preoccupied with spinning objects

Social
- No shared affect
- No empathy for another's distress
- Little interest in shared activities
- No "joint attention" behavior such as pointing or showing
- Moves adult's hand as if it were a tool
- Insists on sameness and ritualizes routines

Language
- Little use of gestures or facial expression to compensate for speech delay
- Echolalia, and delayed echolalia unrelated to social context
- Pronoun reversals
- Voice atonal, hollow, arrhythmic (pedantic)

Play
- No pretend or imaginative play
- Little appropriate use of toys
- Preoccupied with impersonal, "narrow" subjects (e.g., television commercials)

Adapted from Dawson (1992); Kalmanson and Pekarsky (1987).

visuospatial skills). If assessment is based primarily on these skill areas, these children may appear to be functioning typically. As many as 30% of children with autism appear to develop typically until regression in communication, play, and social behaviors occurs at 18–24 months of age (Rapin, 1997). These children subsequently show developmental progress but demonstrate poorer cognitive function than children with autism who did not have a period of regression (Tuchman & Rapin, 1997).

The difficulties with the diagnosis of autism in preschool-age children underline the importance of a careful assessment to establish the diagnosis of autism. Evaluation by an experienced child development team is the most expedient way to an accurate diagnosis and referral to appropriate services.

Use of Developmental Screening Tests Physicians and nurses should use a parent report measure as the basic developmental screening test for autism in the primary care office (see Chapter 2). Pay particular attention to the language and personal-social domains of the test. In Siegel's study (Siegel et al., 1988), 94% of parents of children with autism were first concerned about language development, 84% were first concerned with social development, and only 34% were first concerned with motor development. Consider use of one of the targeted screens for autism to complement information obtained from the parent report measure or general office screen. Please review the discussion on developmental screening and surveillance in Chapter 2.

Two targeted screens for autism are under development: the Childhood Autism Test (CHAT) (Baron-Cohen, Allen, & Gillberg, 1992; Baron-Cohen, Cox, Baird, et al., 1996) and the Pervasive Developmental Disorder Screening Test (PDDST) (Siegel, 1996). The PDDST is a parent-completed questionnaire.[1] Reliability and validity data for both tests are limited. In addition, supplement developmental information with observations of play between the parent and the child. Observe for imitative and pretend play, shared affect, "joint attention" behaviors such as pointing and showing, and how the child requests "help." A scoring form for a brief, semistructured observation of play for use in the primary care office is provided in the Appendix at the end of this chapter (Nickel, 1996).

Comprehensive Diagnostic Evaluation

The responsibilities of the primary care office are to

- Identify and refer children suspected of having autism and their families for a comprehensive evaluation
- Complete medical or laboratory testing to determine the etiology of the disability if possible and to evaluate for associated problems
- Counsel families about the diagnosis and treatment recommendations
- Review families' strengths and their need for support services

Refer children who are suspected of having autism to an experienced child development team headed by a developmental pediatrician or a child psychiatrist. Children who are suspected of having autism include children who have

- Delays in language and personal-social domains on a general developmental screen
- A suspect rating on a targeted screen for autism
- A typical developmental screen but atypical communication and social behavior

Table 8.8 lists the components of the comprehensive evaluation of a child with suspected autism and his or her family. Please also review the discussion in Chapter 5 of the comprehensive evaluation of the child who is suspected of having developmental delays. The choice of cognitive and communication evaluations is based on the child's apparent developmental age. In addition, the cognitive evaluation should not be highly dependent on verbal abilities. The Hiskey-Nebraska Test of Learning

Aptitude (Hiskey, 1966), the Leiter International Performance Scale–Revised (Roid & Miller, 1997), and the Test of Nonverbal Intelligence, Second Edition (TONI-2; Brown, Sherbenou, & Johnsen, 1990) are examples of nonverbal intelligence tests. The Leiter was revised and standardized in the late 1990s on the basis of evaluations of 1,719 children who were developing typically and 692 children with atypical development (Roid & Miller, 1997). The TONI-2 is a relatively brief, language-free measure of abstract or figural problem solving for use with children from 5 years of age to 8 years, 11 months of age (Brown et al., 1990).

Every child who is suspected of having autism also should receive formal audiologic testing with visually reinforced audiometry or, if the child is uncooperative, auditory brainstem-evoked response testing (see Chapter 9). Once the comprehensive diagnostic evaluation has been completed, the child with autism and the child's family should be referred for early intervention/early childhood special education (EI/ECSE) services.

Developmental History Review the developmental history described in Chapter 5. The questions about environmental interactions, early social interest, and early communicative behaviors are important in the evaluation of children suspected of having autism. Was your baby "easy"? Was he or she hard to feed? Did he or she like being held, and did she actively cuddle? When did he or she start to babble and play gestural games such as Pat-a-cake? When did your baby begin to look at you when you called his name? When did your baby begin to use gestures to indicate wants, such as by pointing with the index finger? Does your child look at you during feeding and during joint play?

Ask parents to bring videotapes of their child, if available, from home to an appointment. In a study of home videotapes of first birthday parties of children with autism, observation for the behaviors *pointing*, *showing objects*, *looking at others*, and *orienting to name* correctly identified 10 of 11 children with autism and 10 of 11 controls (Osterling & Dawson, 1994).

Observation of Play All diagnostic evaluations for autism should include careful observation of interactive play between the child and the child's parent or caregiver. A variety of toys should be provided, including toys with which the child is familiar. The examiner observes for *imitative play* (e.g., Pat-a-cake, simple gestures), *pretend play*, or *imaginative play* (e.g., a toy telephone, a doll, dress-up clothes), *reciprocal play* (e.g., a shared activity such as playing ball), *interest in books*, and *requests for* "*more*" *or* "*help*." Does the child point to indicate

---

[1]The PDDST is available from Bryna S. Siegel, Ph.D., Department of Psychiatry, Langley Porter Neuropsychiatric Institute, University of California, Campus Box 0984, San Francisco, CA 94143-0984.

Table 8.8.   Components of the comprehensive diagnostic evaluation and representative assessments

Initial assessments

History and physical examination, including developmental history

Observation of interactive play between child and caregiver

Audiologic assessment

General developmental evaluation

Gesell and Amatruda's Developmental Diagnosis (Knobloch, 1980; Knobloch & Pasamanick, 1974)

Bayley Scales of Infant Development (Bayley, 1993)

Cognitive assessment

Kaufman Assessment Battery for Children (Kaufman & Kaufman, 1983)

Stanford-Binet Intelligence Test, Fourth Edition (Thorndike, Hagen, & Sattler, 1986)

Wechsler Intelligence Scale of Children–III (Wechsler, 1991)

Wechsler Intelligence Scale of Children–Revised (Wechsler, 1989)

Hiskey-Nebraska Test of Learning Aptitude (Hiskey, 1966)

Leiter International Performance Scale–Revised (Roid & Miller, 1997)

Merrill-Palmer Scale of Mental Tests (Stutsman, 1948)

Test of Nonverbal Intelligence, Second Edition (TONI–2) (Brown, Sherbenou, & Johnsen, 1990)

Assessment of adaptive functioning

Vineland Adaptive Behavior Scales (Sparrow, Balla, & Cicchetti, 1984)

Woodcock-Johnson Scale of Independent Behavior (Bruininks, Woodcock, Weatherman, & Hill, 1984)

Communication assessment

Preschool Language Scale–3 (Zimmerman, Steiner, & Pond, 1991)

Test of Auditory Comprehension of Language–Revised (Carrow-Woolfolk, 1985)

Test of Language Development–Primary (Newcomer & Hammill, 1996)

Test of Language Competence–Expanded Edition (Wiig & Secord, 1988)

Motor development (as needed)

Beery Buktenica VMI: Developmental Test of Visual-Motor Integration (Beery, 1997)

Peabody Developmental Motor Scales (Folio & Fewell, 1983)

Bruininks-Oseretsky Test of Motor Proficiency (Bruininks, 1978)

Autism scales

Childhood Autism Rating Scale (Schopler, Reichler, & Renner, 1988)

Behavioral Observation Scale for Autism (Freeman, Schroth, Ritvo, et al., 1980)

Autism Behavior Checklist of the Autism Screening Instrument for Educational Planning (Krug, Aric, & Almond, 1993)

Family needs

Family Needs Survey (Bailey & Simeonsson, 1988)

Parenting Stress Index (Abidin, 1995)

Medical and laboratory evaluation (see pages 235–236)

Note: In general, only one assessment is needed in each domain.

wants, show objects to the parent, look at the parent's face, and respond to his or her own name (the four behaviors from the study of first-birthday videotapes)? How does the child attempt to get help? Is looking at the parent associated with smiling and vocalization? Is showing an object associated with looking at the parent's face? Does the child demonstrate shared affect while playing?

Autism Scales   A number of behavioral scales or checklists have been developed to assist in the identification of children with autism (Morgan, 1988). Some are based on an interview (e.g., Autism Diagnostic Interview–Revised; Lord, Rutter, & Le Couteur, 1994), and some are based on direct observation, such as the Behavioral Observation Scale for Autism (Freeman, Schroth, Ritvo, et al., 1980) and the Childhood Autism Rating Scale (CARS; Schopler, Reichler, & Renner, 1988). CARS is a 15-item scale developed for use with preschool-age children, although it has proved to be useful for adolescents and young adults also (Garfin, McCallon, & Cox, 1988). With CARS, the behavioral reactions of the child are observed during a structured evaluation procedure. CARS is one of the most widely used scales in clinical practice. It has adequate interrater reliability and internal consistency. The diagnostic criteria are close in content to those of DSM-III-R (Van Bourgondien, Marcus, & Schopler, 1992). Each item is rated on a four-point scale:

- No evidence of impairment
- Mild impairment
- Moderate impairment
- Severe impairment

Items included in CARS are relationships with people, affect, adaptation to environmental change, anxiety, and verbal and nonverbal communication. Some investigators are concerned that CARS over-identifies autism in children who in actuality have severe mental retardation (requiring extensive support).

The Autism Diagnostic Interview–R (ADI–R), the Autism Diagnostic Observation Schedule (ADOS; Lord, Rutter, Goode, et al., 1989), and the Pre-Linguistic Autism Diagnostic Observation Schedule (PL-ADOS; DiLavore, Lord, & Rutter, 1995) reflect more closely the diagnostic criteria for autism in DSM-IV. The ADOS and the PL-ADOS are based on standard play observations. These evaluations initially were developed for use in clinical research but also may be used in clinical settings. Participation in a training workshop and demonstration of adequate interrater reliability are required to use these instruments in clinical research.

Family Assessment   Careful clinical assessment of the family and its social support network is also an important part of the diagnostic evaluation (Freeman, 1993). Families may experience the following sequence of adaptations when advised they have a child with a developmental disability:

1. Denial (It is not true.)
2. Distortion (My child is just slow.)
3. Projection (It is the doctor's [e.g., obstetrician's] fault.)
4. Search for a magical cure (Parents experiment with the use of alternative therapies.)
5. Exclusion (Parents consider institutionalization of their child as opposed to reordering family life completely to adapt to their child's disability.)
6. Adjustment and acceptance (Freeman, 1993, p. 8)

Studies (see Harris, 1994) have documented that parents of children with autism experience significant stress. For example, mothers of preschool-age children with autism report greater stress than mothers of children with mental retardation or mothers of children who are developing typically.

Ask parents to complete questionnaires such as the Parenting Stress Index–Short Form (PSI–SF;

Abidin, 1995) and the Family Needs Survey (Bailey & Simeonsson, 1988). The PSI–SF contains 36 questions and Total Stress, Parenting Distress, Parent–Child Dysfunctional Interaction, and Difficult Child subscales. Use these measures in an open-ended format to allow families to raise additional needs or concerns (Bailey, 1988). In addition, ask specifically about the parents' need for support in the management of their child's problem behaviors (e.g., aggressive or destructive behavior, tantrums, SIBs). The problem behaviors of children with autism can be stressful and may need *immediate* attention. The following services may be useful to some or all families of children with autism:

- Appropriate education programs for the child
- Parent training to manage the child's problem behaviors
- Respite care
- Support groups, including those geared for parents, fathers, or siblings
- Other support services
  a. Individual or couples counseling for parents
  b. Counseling for siblings
  c. Financial and legal advice and assistance
  d. Other enabling services (e.g., transportation)

Medical or Laboratory Evaluation

A specific etiology is identified in only a minority of children with autism, even after thorough testing. An accurate diagnosis of the cause of the child's autism, however, accomplishes the following:

- Identifies progressive or degenerative disorders (e.g., Batten's disease)
- Identifies potentially treatable diseases (e.g., Landau-Kleffner syndrome)
- Provides information about the natural history of the child's autism and associated medical problems (e.g., tuberous sclerosis, seizures)
- Provides genetic information (e.g., fragile X syndrome)

Differential Diagnosis   Autism is a behavioral syndrome. It is highly associated with mental retardation, and, for some children, it is associated with an identifiable medical condition. It is important to differentiate autism from other PDDs as well as from disorders that present in a similar manner. The differential diagnosis of a child with autism should include

- Fragile X syndrome
- Asperger syndrome
- Rett syndrome
- CDD
- Landau-Kleffner syndrome (LKS), often with an electroencephalogram (EEG) pattern of contin-

uous spike-and-wave discharges during slow-wave sleep (CSWS)

- Progressive or degenerative disorders (e.g., late infantile neuronal ceroid lipofuscinosis, Batten's disease, metachromatic leukodystrophy)
- Sensory impairments
- Developmental language disorders
- Attention-deficit/hyperactivity disorder (ADHD)
- Reactive attachment disorder
- Other psychiatric disorders, including manic depressive disorder, schizophrenia, elective mutism, and obsessive-compulsive disorder

Landau-Kleffner Syndrome LKS is an acquired epileptic aphasia in a child who has previously shown typical development. It is a rare disorder characterized by the gradual or abrupt loss of language, inattentiveness to nonspeech sounds, and other behavior problems (e.g., hyperactivity) in association with seizures and multifocal spike and spike-and-wave discharges on the EEG (Echenne, Cheminal, Rivier, et al., 1992; Lerman, Lerman-Sagie & Kivity, 1991; Paquier, Van Dongen, & Loonen, 1992; Tharpe & Olson, 1994). It appears most commonly between 2 and 5 years of age (Morrell, Whisler, & Smith, 1995). The sleep EEG may show CSWS. This EEG pattern also has been associated with language loss and behavioral symptoms (Soprano, Garcia, Caraballo, et al., 1994).

Seizures in LKS may become apparent before, concurrently with, or after the loss of language. In fact, 20%–30% of children do not show overt behavioral seizures (Paquier et al., 1992). The results of treatment of LKS with anticonvulsants alone have been disappointing. Many children, however, respond dramatically to adrenocorticotropic hormone (ACTH) or corticosteroid therapy. Some children who have failed to respond adequately to other treatments have been treated with multiple subpial transection, a technique that eliminates the capacity of cortical tissue to generate seizures while preserving normal physiologic function (Buelow, Aydelott, Pierz, & Heck, 1996; Gordon, 1997; Morrell et al., 1995). In one study (Morrell et al., 1995), 7 of 14 children recovered age-appropriate language following surgery. LKS also has been described in association with an astrocytoma of the left temporal lobe (Solomon, Carson, Pavlakis, et al., 1993). Therefore, all children who are suspected of having LKS should be evaluated carefully for a focal lesion.

Autistic Regression As commented previously, as many as 30% of children with autism experience a period of regression. In one study, the mean age of regression was 21 months (Tuchman & Rapin, 1997). Tuchman and Rapin (1997) suggested that autistic regression may result from subclinical seizures similar to LKS. In their study, epileptiform EEGs were demonstrated in 14% of children with a history of regression and in only 6% of children with autism but without a history of regression. Other investigators (Nass, Gross, & Devinsky, 1998) noted that the EEG findings seen in autistic regression overlap with those seen in LKS. Tuchman and Rapin (1997) recommended that all children with autistic regression who have characteristic EEG findings be considered for treatment with anticonvulsants and steroids.

Other Disorders A careful clinical evaluation differentiates children with autism from children with ADHD, developmental language disorders, attachment disorders, and other psychiatric disorders. Children with ADHD may show language problems and some atypical behaviors (e.g., overreaction to some stimuli). Children with ADHD attempt to communicate, however, and also readily join in social activities and exhibit imaginative play. Children with developmental language disorders may show some atypical behaviors; however, they do not manifest sensory disturbances (e.g., over- or underreactivity), do attempt to communicate with gestures and facial expressions, and demonstrate imaginative play (Tsai & Ghaziuddin, 1997). Children with attachment disorders have experienced marked psychosocial deprivation and generally improve rapidly when placed in an appropriately responsive psychosocial environment (Richters & Volkmar, 1994). Children with autism rarely if ever develop thought disorders with delusions and hallucinations. The age of onset of symptoms for autism is less than 3 years of age, and the onset of childhood schizophrenia is most often in the preadolescent and adolescent years. Formal hearing and vision testing identifies children with sensory impairments. Please note, however, that autism can occur in association with hearing and vision impairments.

Medical and Laboratory Tests Careful medical, developmental, and family histories as well as the physical examination determine which tests to perform to evaluate the etiology of the child's developmental disability. The recommendations in the subsections that follow are provided as guidelines only.

Children with High-Functioning Autism Medical and laboratory tests are used primarily to identify associated medical problems (e.g., seizures). Unless the child's history or physical examination points to a specific diagnosis, routine tests (e.g., urine for metabolic screen, blood chromosomal analysis) are unlikely to provide useful information. The cranial MRI scan is primarily of research interest. If the child has macrocephaly or microcephaly, however, an MRI scan may provide useful diagnostic and perhaps treatment information (e.g., for a child with hydrocephalus).

Similarly, if a child has a positive family history for autism or mental retardation, a fragile X deoxyribonucleic acid (DNA) test should be obtained. In general, all children suspected of having autism should receive a fragile X study. The characteristic physical features of fragile X syndrome are not routinely present in prepubertal boys. In addition, young girls with fragile X syndrome may not show striking physical features (Gillberg, 1991) but do show autistic behaviors (Mazzocco, Kates, Baumgardner, et al., 1997). Representative tests include the following:

- Audiologic testing
- Fragile X DNA test
- EEG scan (if possible seizures) and cranial MRI scan (if macro- or microcephaly)
- Blood lead level (if there is a history of pica)

Children with Autism and Developmental Delay or Mental Retardation   Children who have been diagnosed with autism as well as developmental delay or mental retardation should be evaluated as per the recommendations in Chapter 5 for children with developmental delay or mental retardation. In general, all children with autism and mental retardation should receive fragile X DNA testing. The combination of the early onset of seizures, autism, and mental retardation requiring extensive support suggests tuberous sclerosis (Gillberg, 1991; Smalley, 1998). A careful past medical history, family history, and dermatologic examination using a Wood's lamp will help identify the 1%–4% of individuals with autism who have tuberous sclerosis. In addition, the primary health care professional should be familiar with an evaluation for minor physical anomalies to assist in the identification of a child with a genetic disorder or a birth defect syndrome. Consider referral to a medical geneticist or a developmental pediatrician for assistance in establishing an etiologic diagnosis. Representative tests include the following:

- Audiologic testing
- Fragile X DNA test, blood chromosomal analysis
- EEG scan (if possible seizures) and cranial MRI scan (if macro- or microcephaly)
- Ophthalmologic examination
- Blood lead level (if there is a history of pica)

In addition, consider obtaining urine for a metabolic screen if suggestive symptoms are present.

Children with Autistic Behaviors and Regression in Skills After a Period of Typical Development   Children who show regression in developmental skills or who have abnormal neurologic signs should have a thorough and prompt diagnostic evaluation. The diagnostic possibilities include potentially treatable conditions such as LKS and conditions that show a static course after the initial regression (Heller syndrome), and relentlessly progressive illnesses (e.g., Batten's disease, metachromatic leukodystrophy). These children may require a wide variety of tests as well as referrals to a pediatric neurologist, a medical geneticist, and a metabolic disease specialist. In addition to the tests recommended for children with autism and developmental delay, consider doing the following tests:

- Electroretinogram
- Conjunctival or skin biopsy
- Blood lysosomal enzymes and other specialized metabolic studies
- EEG with a prolonged sleep record in children with autistic regression and children suspected of having LKS to detect EEG abnormalities during slow wave sleep
- Cranial MRI scan and other studies as indicated

Associated Medical, Developmental, and Behavior Problems

Children with autism may demonstrate a variety of other problems, including mental retardation, seizures, cerebral palsy, and vision and hearing impairments. Approximately 25%–33% of individuals with autism have seizures (Tsai & Ghaziuddin, 1997). Onset is commonly in adolescence. In addition, the EEG is abnormal in one third or more of individuals with autism. The most common findings are diffuse or focal spike or slow wave and paroxysmal spike-and-wave discharges. In one study (Tuchman & Rapin, 1997), 11% of children with autism had clinical seizures; however, 21% had epileptiform EEGs.

Among individuals with autism, 70%–75% have mental retardation (Tsai & Ghaziuddin, 1997). Behavior problems can include hyperactivity, inattention, aggression, tantrums, noncompliance, SIBs, stereotypies, obsessive-compulsive behaviors, sleep disorders, and affective disorders. The identification of a co-morbid affective disorder in children with developmental disabilities can be particularly difficult. The symptoms of affective disorders in a child with developmental disabilities are reviewed in Chapter 3. The diagnosis of ADHD is not appropriate in a child with autism; however, hyperactivity and inattention are significant problems for many children with autism. These behaviors should be identified as principal problem behaviors so that specific behavior management strategies can be devised. The identification and management of associated behavior and psychiatric problems may require referral to a child psychiatrist or another mental health professional who is experienced in the care of individuals with autism.

Counseling the Parents of a Child with Autism

General recommendations for counseling the parents of a child with a disability are presented in Chapter 3. In most cases, the initial counseling of parents regarding the diagnosis of autism is done by members of the child development team. It is important, however, for the primary health care professional to schedule a conference with the family, keeping in mind the following goals:

- Review diagnostic information and treatment recommendations
- Assist the family with service coordination
- Provide the family with support and advocacy as needed

The health care professional should be cautious about providing any specific prognostic information for families of preschool-age children, except for families of children who clearly demonstrate severe or profound delays. The outcome of individuals with autism relates to three principal factors: IQ score, the presence or absence of speech, and the severity of the disorder (Tsai & Ghaziuddin, 1997). In general, cognitive test scores, especially those determined at school age, are predictive of later outcome (Freeman, 1993; Nordin & Gillberg, 1998). Children with seizures, mental retardation, and other disabilities in addition to autism have the greatest impairment. Children with autism who receive intensive early intervention services, especially children with HFA, have improved outcomes, which may include participation in general classes by the time they reach school age.

A subgroup of individuals with autism and typical IQ scores are able to live and work independently, but these individuals rarely marry. Such individuals do continue to demonstrate definite personality, social, and cognitive impairments (Freeman, 1993). The overwhelming majority of individuals with autism require some degree of continued supervision in social situations and support in employment. Many individuals with autism show an increase in their symptoms in adolescence (Gillberg, 1991). These symptoms include hyperactivity, aggressiveness, destructiveness (usually against themselves), insistence on sameness, and unpredictability.

Some show an apparent permanent deterioration in functional skills.

MANAGEMENT

The management of children with autism is primarily educational and behavioral. Medical management can be helpful in conjunction with educational and behavioral services for specific mental health or behavior problems and for associated medical problems. Individualized, psychoanalytically oriented play therapy is not an effective treatment. Counseling may be helpful for adolescents with HFA who exhibit obsessive-compulsive behaviors, anxiety, or depression (Campbell, Schopler, Cueva, & Hallin, 1996). Pharmacotherapy may be useful for the treatment of the associated medical, mental health, and behavior problems of children with autism.

Some children with autism require ongoing management by a specialist (e.g., a pediatric neurologist for the child with difficult-to-control seizures). Other children may require little or no specialty consultation after the diagnosis is established and require limited follow-up with the child development team. Consider referral for reevaluation by the child development team in the following situations:

- Disagreement about the diagnosis of autism
- Multiple and complicated associated medical problems
- Difficult-to-manage behaviors
- Regression in developmental skills
- Lack of expected progress in services
- Making a transition between programs
- Questions about nonstandard or alternative treatments

Periodic Review and Update of the Management Plan

Reevaluate the child and family in the primary care office and update the management plan at least yearly, and more frequently in the first year following the diagnosis and with young children. The objectives of the periodic review are to discuss the family's current concerns; to determine the child's rate of developmental or behavioral progress; to review associated medical and behavioral problems; and to determine the need for additional services, including the need for referral to specialists or to a specialty team.

It is important to review information from educational service providers as well as from families regularly. Request a school progress report, including a summary of the most recent individualized family service plan (IFSP) or individualized education program (IEP), prior to meeting with the family. Please also review the discussion on the use of behavioral questionnaires in Chapter 6.

Educational and
Behavioral Treatment Approaches

Young children with autism are eligible for EI/ECSE services. The eligibility criteria for obtaining EI/ECSE services and the process for developing the IFSP are reviewed in Chapter 5. EI/ECSE programs offer a combination of educational and behavioral interventions as well as family support services.

In general, the education and behavioral programs that are the most successful begin early, are intensive and highly structured, address the child's communication and social skills impairments, and are oriented to the individual child's needs. They involve parents and include various professionals, including special educators, speech-language pathologists, autism specialists, and occupational therapists. The speech-language pathologist is a critical part of the program for children with speech-language delays. Few empirical data, however, are available to assist parents and professionals in deciding what level of intensity of services and which types of programs are best for different child characteristics (e.g., HFA versus severe autism).

Dawson and Osterling (1997) reviewed eight model preschool programs for children with autism and other PDDs. All programs reported success in fostering integration in general school programs and/or significant developmental progress for a substantial number of students. All programs provided at least 15 hours of school-based services per week, and the average number of hours of such services was 27. Some of the programs were based on the principles of applied behavior analysis; others emphasized developmental principles and focused on language and social development through incidental teaching, an integrated preschool using peer models, and a highly structured teaching environment. Although the programs' philosophies varied, the programs had the following common features:

- Curriculum emphasizing the ability to attend, to imitate, to comprehend and use language, to play appropriately with toys, and to interact socially
- Highly supportive teaching environment (initial 1:1 to 1:2 staff-to-student ratio)
- A highly structured environment (predictability and routine)
- Functional approaches to problem behaviors
- Facilitation of the transitions from preschool to kindergarten or first grade
- Involvement of parents in the education process

Structured teaching using the Treatment and Education of Autistic and Communications Handicapped Children (TEACCH) program (Schopler, 1994) and a program of early, intensive behavior modification developed by Lovaas (1987) are two different intervention programs for children with autism. Both programs were represented in the eight model preschools reviewed by Dawson and Osterling (1997).

TEACCH Program and Structured Teaching

The TEACCH program was developed in response to the nondirective and psychodynamic treatment programs of the 1950s and 1960s. The TEACCH program emphasizes structuring the environment to promote skill acquisition and facilitating independence (Dawson & Osterling, 1997; Schopler, Mesibov, & Hearsey, 1995). Structured teaching, a component of the TEACCH program, builds on the relative strengths of individuals with autism (e.g., processing of visual information and rote memory for routines or lists) and accommodates their weaknesses (e.g., difficulty with adapting to change and to transitions) (Schopler, 1994; Schopler et al., 1995). It is a system for organizing the physical space of the school by provision of a transition area, visually clear schedules of the day's activities, and start-and-finish boxes at individual work-study stations. Structured teaching can be implemented in the classroom, at home, and in the workplace. The TEACCH program was developed in North Carolina and has been implemented throughout the United States.

Lovaas Method of Early, Intensive Behavior Modification

A variety of interventions using behavioral techniques have been used for children with autism. In 1987, Lovaas reported the results of early, intensive behavior modification in 19 individuals who were 7 years of age. A follow-up study (McEachin, Smith, & Lovaas, 1993) was reported in 1993, when the original participants' mean age was 11.5 years. In the initial report, 47% of the experimental group achieved a normal IQ score, compared with 2% of the control group. In general, these results were maintained at follow-up. The Lovaas method is based on discrete trial training. It involves presentation of a stimulus (a command or a request), the response, then reinforcement (reward or correction) (Buckmann, 1995). This home-based treatment program involves 30–40 hours per week of one-to-one therapy, building from simple behaviors to more complex behaviors.

A number of investigators (Foxx, 1993; Greenspan, 1992; Kazdin, 1993; Mesibov, 1993) criticized the results of the research studies by Lovaas and

McEachin and co-workers. They noted the lack of random assignment to experimental and control groups, the small sample size, the high initial IQ scores in the treatment group, and the unexplained underrepresentation of children with HFA in the control group. Greenspan (1992) criticized the directive, repetitive, and rigid character of the therapy as well as the focus on isolated skills. Additional controversy has been generated by the claim that a cure or recovery from autism is possible for the majority of children if this therapy is started early.

Sheinkopf and Siegel (1998) completed a study of 11 children with autism or PDD who received intensive behavior modification therapy matched with 11 children who received conventional EI services. Children who received at least 15 hours per week of services showed significant gains in their IQ scores whether they received behavior modification therapy or conventional EI services. (The group that received an average of 21.2 hours of behavior modification therapy per week made greater gains than the group that received 15.8 hours of EI services per week; however, the differences were not statistically significant.) Thus, a critical issue may be the number of hours of intervention. Both the review by Dawson and Osterling (1997) and the study by Sheinkopf and Siegel (1998) suggested that at least 15 hours and as many as 25 hours per week are needed to support significant developmental gains. Of note, however, is that parents were taught to use behavioral interventions in the home in all of the programs that Dawson and Osterling reviewed. Thus, the actual hours of intervention were probably greater than 15 in these programs.

Functional Assessment of Problem Behavior

All behavior problems are shaped and modified by the child's environment. In general, misbehaviors serve specific, often communicative, functions in given situations. A child's SIBs may be maintained by different social functions, such as escape from unpleasant demands or tasks and to gain the attention of peers or adults. Aggressive behaviors or tantrums may be a child's way of communicating that the situation is aversive (Day, Horner, & O'Neill, 1994). A successful behavioral intervention is to change the environment to make the task less aversive or to teach the child a different way to communicate the need (e.g., using manual signs or pictures).

The functional assessment of specific behaviors includes review of the "ABCs" of behavioral analysis: *a*ntecedent events, *b*ehavior displayed, and *c*onsequences of the behaviors (Foster-Johnson & Dunlap, 1993; Frea, Koegel, & Koegel, 1994). Com-

pletion of a functional assessment prior to starting a behavioral intervention is standard practice. In fact, in most cases, a behavioral intervention program should be implemented before the use of medications. The objective of functional assessment is to understand the structure and function of the child's problem behaviors in order to teach and develop effective alternatives (Foster-Johnson & Dunlap, 1993). Functional assessment involves description of the problem behavior, prediction of the times when and situations in which it will occur, definition of the function that that behavior fulfills for the individual, and systematic manipulation of specific variables that may or may not result in the problem behavior. The successful completion of the functional assessment and implementation of a behavioral management plan may require a coordinated school-based team with support as needed from an experienced behavioral consultant.

Medical Management of Associated Behavior Problems

Aman, Van Bourgondien, Wolford, and Sarphare (1995) surveyed 853 caregivers regarding the use of psychotropic medications, anticonvulsants, and vitamins by individuals with autism. Among the individuals they studied, 22.1% were taking at least one psychotropic medication, and 6.4% were taking two. The medications prescribed most frequently were neuroleptics (12.2%), stimulants (6.6%), anxiolytics and hypnotics (6.3%), and antidepressants (6.1%). Caregivers were most satisfied with the individuals' reactions to anticonvulsants, antidepressants, and stimulants. They were least satisfied with individuals' reactions to mood stabilizers, neuroleptics, antihypertensives (i.e., clonidine), and sedative/hypnotics (Aman et al., 1995).

In general, no medication has been effective in treating the core symptoms of autism. A number of medications may be effective in treating some of the problem behaviors associated with autism. Unfortunately, few placebo-controlled, double-blind trials have been undertaken with children. Much of the data on the use of medications is from single case reports or open label studies. Table 8.9 lists the medications shown to benefit specific problem behaviors of children with autism. (Please also review the discussion on the use of psychotropic medications in Chapter 5.)

Children with autism are prone to experiencing side effects from medications; therefore, medications should be started at low doses, then the dosage level should be increased slowly (Rapin, 1991). Care should be taken in using multiple drugs because

Table 8.9.   Medications used in the treatment of children with autism and pervasive
developmental disorders

Problem behaviors	Medications	
Inattention/hyperactivity	Stimulants	Naltrexone
	Buspirone	Clonidine
Obsessive-compulsive behaviors	Fluoxetine	Fluvoxamine
	Clomipramine	Other selective serotonin reuptake inhibitors (SSRIs)
Stereotypies and self-injurious behaviors	Naltrexone	Other SSRIs
	Fluoxetine	Risperidone
	Haloperidol	
Aggression (disruptive behaviors)	Propranolol	Carbamazepine
	Valproic acid	Risperidone
	Haloperidol	
Sleep disorder	*Long-term*	*Short-term*
	Melatonin (limited data)	Diphenhydramine
		Diazepam
		Trazodone
Anxiety	Fluoxetine	Buspirone
	Other SSRIs	
Affective or mood disorders, manic depressive illness	Fluoxetine	Lithium
	Other SSRIs	Valproic acid
		Carbamazepine

a number of psychotropic and nonpsychotropic medications are metabolized by the hepatic cytochrome P450 system. Baker, Urichuk, and Coutts (1998) reviewed drug metabolism and drug–drug interactions in detail.

Haloperidol and Other Neuroleptics Haloperidol (Haldol) is the best studied of neuroleptic medications. Campbell, Anderson, Deutsch, and Green (1984) reported modest improvements in attention, cognitive performance, and social interactions, along with a decrease in aggression and hyperactivity, with the use of low-dose haloperidol in some children with autism. Unfortunately, the risk of side effects with the use of neuroleptics is significant, including tardive and withdrawal dyskinesias and acute dystonic reactions. Approximately 29%–33% of children with autism develop drug-related dyskinesias, primarily withdrawal dyskinesias (Campbell & Cueva, 1995). In a long-term prospective study of 118 children with autism who were treated with haloperidol, 40 children (33.9%) developed dyskinesias, 5 with TD and 35 with WD (Campbell, Armenteros, Malone, et al., 1997). In general, use haloperidol and related neuroleptics only for specific behaviors that are unresponsive to other interventions (e.g., acute aggression).

Risperidone (Risperdal) is a neuroleptic with fewer extrapyramidal side effects. It has been shown to be effective in several open label studies in children and a double-blind, placebo-controlled study in adults with autism (McDougle, Holmes, Carlson, et al., 1998; Nicolson, Awad, & Sloman, 1998). It may be particularly useful for individuals with explosive aggression and SIBs (Horrigan & Barnhill, 1997). Its principal side effects are weight gain and sedation.

Methylphenidate and Other Stimulants Stimulant medications should be used cautiously in children with autism and hyperactivity and/or inattention. Although they may be helpful with some children, they may worsen (e.g., increase the frequency of stereotypies and SIBs) behavior in other children (Rapin, 1991). Stimulants may be more effective in children with HFA and inattention and/or hyperactivity (Gilman & Tuchman, 1995).

Clomipramine, Fluoxetine, and Other Selective Serotonin Reuptake Inhibitors A number of studies (Brasic, Barnett, & Kaplan, 1994; Bodfish & Madison, 1993; DeLong, Teague, & Kamran, 1998; McDougle, Naylor, Cohen, et al., 1996) have demonstrated the effectiveness of clomipramine, fluoxetine (Prozac), and other selective serotonin reuptake inhibitors (SSRIs) in the treatment of children with autism with or without obsessive-compulsive behaviors. The response of children with autism to fluoxetine in one study (DeLong et al., 1998) was strongly associated with a family history of major depressive disorder. Both clomipramine and fluoxetine also have been reported to be useful for treating specific stereotypies (e.g., trichotillomania [excessive hair pulling]) in individuals with autism. In one case report (Holttum, Lubetsky, & Eastman, 1994), the use of clomipramine and behavioral treatment was more effective than either treatment alone. Fluvoxamine (Luvox) is an SSRI that is chemically unrelated to clomipramine and fluoxetine. Preliminary studies (DeWulf, Hendricks, & Lesaffre, 1995; Freeman, Trimble, Deakin, et al., 1994) have shown it to be effective for control of obsessive-compulsive behaviors.

The effectiveness of these medications has been limited primarily by their side effects, such as anticholinergic side effects with clomipramine. Campbell and co-workers (1996) recommended that clomipramine and tricyclic antidepressants (TCAs) be used judiciously in children with PDDs. An EEG needs to be obtained prior to initiation of treatment with clomipramine and with each dosage change. A toxic serotonin syndrome (TSS) can result from high doses of serotonergic agents or interaction between these drugs and monoamine oxidase inhibitors (MAOIs) and other drugs such as 5-hydroxytryptophan (Sokolenko & Kutcher, 1998). Symptoms may vary from mild to severe and typically include elevated mood, tremor, myoclonus, and shivering. A combination of any of the following agents may be associated with TSS: buspirone, carbamazepine, dextromethorphan, lithium, L-tryptophan, MAOIs, marijuana, meperidine, methylene dioxymethamphetamine (MDMA; street name: *ecstasy*), SSRIs, TCAs, and trazodone.

Naltrexone and Fenfluramine Please review the previous discussion of fenfluramine and naltrexone in this chapter. The use of fenfluramine with children with autism has been discontinued because of lack of efficacy and the risk of cardiac side effects. The use of naltrexone has resulted in modest improvement in behavior in less than 50% of children in one double-blind trial (Kolmen et al., 1997) and no change in communication skills (Feldman et al., 1999). Naltrexone has a long half-life and may be given daily or every other day. It has few side effects; however, liver function tests must be monitored (Gilman & Tuchman, 1995). Naltrexone has a bitter taste, and its use has been limited in part by difficulties in administration. Rarely, some individuals have a paradoxical increase in SIBs when treated with naltrexone because of the extinction burst phenomenon (Benjamin, Seek, Tresise, et al., 1995). Campbell and Harris (1996) reviewed the pros and cons of using naltrexone with children with autism.

Use of Alternative Therapies

A variety of alternative therapies have been purported to benefit children with autism. A number of other terms have been used to refer to these therapies, including *unproved, nontraditional, nonstandard,* and *controversial.* The following operational definition of *alternative treatments* is based on the characteristics of those therapies and the claims of their proponents:

- Based on overly simplified scientific theories
- Purported to be effective for a variety of conditions
- Claims that most children respond dramatically and that some may be cured
- Supported by anecdotal reports only
- Initiated with little attention to specific treatment objectives
- Claim to have no remarkable side effects and that thus research studies are not needed (Nickel, 1996, p. 30)

Table 8.10 lists the alternative behavioral therapies, vitamin supplements, and dietary and medication treatments that have been used with children with autism. References specific to many of these treatments and to several 1990s review articles on controversial therapies are provided in the Appendix at the end of this chapter.

The responsibilities of primary health care professionals in counseling families about alternative therapies are as follows:

- Ensure that families have access to standard services and are involved actively in all treatment decisions.
- Attempt to determine an etiologic diagnosis.
- Discuss alternative therapies as part of the initial management plan and whenever asked about them.
- Be knowledgeable about standard and nonstandard treatments or refer the family for consultation.
- Schedule ample time for discussion. Make sure your comments are not taken as an endorsement of a particular alternative therapy. Discuss the placebo effect and the importance of controlled research.
- Support the parents' desire to do everything possible to help their child.
- Provide information about the specific treatment, discuss decision making, and emphasize the "red flags" (e.g., a claim of a cure or that every child benefits from the treatment).
- Identify any confounding factors (e.g., opinions of relatives, more than one treatment started).
- Be willing to support a trial of alternative therapy in selected situations. Require clear treatment objectives and pre- and posttesting.
- If parents decide to use an alternative treatment, encourage them to use it in addition to standard or tried-and-true treatments.
- Remain actively involved even if you do not agree with the parents' decision. (Nickel, 1996, p. 37)

Alternative and unproved treatments should be discussed openly with parents. The information that they receive from proponents of therapies or from other parents is likely to be biased and limited. The

242 Nickel

Table 8.10. Alternative treatments for children with autism and pervasive developmental disorders

Medications, vitamins, and diets	Behavioral treatments
Feingold diet	Facilitated communication
Hypoallergenic diet for cerebral allergies	Auditory integration training
Megavitamins and minerals	Craniosacral therapy
Vitamin B_6 and magnesium	Patterning (Doman-Delacato method)
Dimethyl glycine (DMG)	Music therapy
Antifungal therapy (diet and medication)	Holding therapy
Intravenous immunoglobulin (IVIG)	Rhythmic entrainment
Adrenocorticotropic hormone (ACTH)	Brushing/massage
Secretin	Squeeze therapy

Adapted from Nickel (1996).

list of questions developed by Fields (1994), "Questions for Parents to Ask Themselves Regarding Specific Treatments" (see the Appendix at the end of this chapter), is a useful handout to provide to families when counseling them about alternative therapies.

Health care professionals also must remain informed about alternative and unproved therapies. For example, secretin is an unproved therapy for autism that has received widespread attention in the media, through parent groups, and on the Internet based initially on a report on three children with autism (Horvath, Stefanatos, Sokolski, et al., 1998). The three children described in the report received secretin to stimulate pancreatobiliary secretion as part of upper-gastrointestinal endoscopy for evaluation of their gastrointestinal problems. All three showed improvements in gastrointestinal symptoms and in their behavior within 5 weeks of the secretin infusion. Useful resources for information on alternative therapies are discussed in Chapter 5 and are listed in the Appendix at the end of this chapter.

Family Support Services and Anticipatory Guidance

Health professionals should review the need for family support services as part of the periodic review and update of the management plan. The presence of a developmental disability in a child magnifies the degree of stress that the child's family may experience. Parents, especially mothers, may become depressed by the sense of failure in meeting their child's needs (Harris, 1994). In general, emotional support from a spouse and adequate social support improve a family's adaptation to their child's disability. A child with difficult-to-manage behaviors, however, may significantly increase marital discord. In this instance, respite care and parent training to manage the problem behaviors rather

than marital counseling may be the best solution. Services must be individualized for each family. Studies (e.g., Harris, 1994) have shown clearly that raising a child with a severe developmental disability may have a negative impact on some families and yet strengthen others.

The nurse or the physician should provide anticipatory guidance to families regarding the im-pact of the child's disability on the child's siblings as well as times of potential increase in stress (e.g., transitions between school programs and to adult services). Most siblings of children with autism are resilient to their brother's or sister's special needs (Harris, 1994). The children who develop a positive relationship with their sibling with autism usually have a good factual understanding of the disability and view both their parents and their peers as responding positively to the disability (Harris, 1994). Health professionals may need to schedule individual appointments with siblings to discuss the disability and their interactions with their sibling with autism.

Important Care Coordination Issues

In addition to the general recommendations for care coordination discussed in Chapter 1, the primary care office should

- Identify the contact person for a child development team experienced in the evaluation and management of children with autism
- Identify the contact person for EI/ECSE and special education services
- Have updated lists of other community service providers, including a behavioral consultant who is experienced in functional assessment of problem behaviors of individuals with autism
- Develop a resource file on alternative therapies and know the practitioners of nonstandard therapies in the local area or region

REFERENCES

Abidin, R.R. (1995). *Parenting Stress Index Manual* (3rd ed.). Odessa, FL: Psychological Assessment Resources.

Aman, M.G., Van Bourgondien, M.E., Wolford, P.L., & Sarphare, G. (1995). Psychotropic and anticonvulsant drugs in subjects with autism: Prevalence and patterns of use. *Journal of the American Academy of Child and Adolescent Psychiatry, 34,* 1672–1681.

American Psychiatric Association (APA). (1977). *Diagnostic and statistical manual of mental disorders* (3rd ed.). Washington, DC: Author.

American Psychiatric Association (APA). (1987). *Diagnostic and statistical manual of mental disorders* (3rd ed. rev.). Washington, DC: Author.

American Psychiatric Association (APA). (1994). *Diagnostic and statistical manual of mental disorders* (4th ed.). Washington, DC: Author.

Bachevalier, J. (1994). Review: Medial temporal lobe structures and autism: A review of clinical and experimental findings. *Neuropsycholgia, 32*(6), 627–648.

Bailey, D.B., Jr. (1988). Assessing family stress and needs. In D.B. Bailey, Jr., & R.J. Simeonsson, *Family assessment in early intervention.* Upper Saddle River, NJ: Merrill.

Bailey, D.B., Jr., & Simeonsson, R.J. (1988). Assessing needs of families with handicapped infants. *Journal of Special Education, 22*(1), 117–126.

Baker, G.B., Urichuk, L.J., & Coutts, R.T. (1998). Drug metabolism and metabolic drug–drug interactions in psychiatry. *Child and Adolescent Psychopharmacology News, 3,* S1–S8.

Baron-Cohen, S. (1989). The autistic child's theory of mind: A case of specific developmental delay. *Journal of Child Psychology and Psychiatry, 30*(2), 285–297.

Baron-Cohen, S. (1991). The development of a theory of mind in autism: Deviance and delay? *Psychiatric Clinics of North America, 14*(1), 33–51.

Baron-Cohen, S., Allen, J., & Gillberg, C. (1992). Can autism be detected at 18 months? The needle, the haystack, and the CHAT. *British Journal of Psychiatry, 161,* 839–843.

Baron-Cohen, S., Cox, A., Baird, G., et al. (1996). Psychological markers in the detection of autism in infancy in a large population. *British Journal of Psychiatry, 168*(2), 158–163.

Barton, M., & Volkmar, F.R. (1998). How commonly are known medical conditions associated with autism? *Journal of Autism and Developmental Disorders, 28,* 273–278.

Bauman, M.L. (1991). Microscopic neuroanatomic abnormalities in autism. *Pediatrics, 87*(5, Suppl. pt. 2), 791–796.

Bayley, N. (1993). *Bayley Scales of Infant Development: Second Edition Manual.* San Antonio, TX: The Psychological Corporation.

Beery, K.E. (1997). *The Beery Buktenica VMI: Developmental Test of Visual-Motor Integration with supplemental developmental tests of visual perception and motor coordination: Administration, scoring, and teaching manual* (4th ed. rev.). Parsippany, NJ: Modern Curriculum Press.

Benjamin, B., Seek, A., Tresise, L., et al. (1995). Case study: Paradoxical response to naltrexone treatment of self-injurious behavior. *Journal of the American Academy of Child and Adolescent Psychiatry, 34*(2), 238–242.

Bodfish, J.W., & Madison, J.T. (1993). Diagnosis and fluoxetine treatment of compulsive behavior disorder of adults with mental retardation. *American Journal on Mental Retardation, 98*(3), 360–367.

Bolton, P.F., Pickles, A., Murphy, M., & Rutter, M. (1998). Autism, affective and other psychiatric disorders: Patterns of familial aggregation. *Psychological Medicine, 28,* 385–395.

Brasic, J.R., Barnett, J.Y., & Kaplan, D. (1994). Clomipramine ameliorates adventitious movements and compulsions in prepubertal boys with autistic disorder and severe mental retardation. *Neurology, 44*(7), 309–312.

Brown, L., Sherbenou, R.J., & Johnsen, S.K. (1990). *Test of Nonverbal Intelligence (TONI–2): A language-free measure of cognitive ability* (2nd ed.). Austin, TX: PRO-ED.

Bruininks, R.H. (1978). *Bruininks-Oseretsky Test of Motor Proficiency: Examiner's manual.* Circle Pines, MN: American Guidance Service.

Bruininks, R.H., Woodcock, R.W., Weatherman, R.F., & Hill, B.K. (1984). *Scales of Independent Behavior (SIB).* Itasca, IL: Riverside Publishing Co.

Buckmann, S. (1995). Lovaas revisited: Should we have ever left? *Indiana Resource Center for Autism Newsletter, 8*(3), 1–7.

Budden, S.S. (1997). Rett syndrome: Habilitation and management reviewed. *European Child and Adolescent Psychiatry, 6,* 103–107.

Buelow, J.M., Aydelott, P., Pierz, D.M., & Heck, B. (1996). Multiple subpial transection for Landau-Kleffner syndrome. *AORN Journal, 63,* 727–744.

Campbell, M., Anderson, L.T., Deutsch, S.I., & Green, W.H. (1984). Psychopharmacological treatment of children with the syndrome of autism. *Pediatric Annals, 13*(4), 309–316.

Campbell, M., Armenteros, J.L., Malone, R.P., et al. (1997). Neuroleptic-related dyskinesias in autistic children: A prospective, longitudinal study. *Journal of the American Academy of Child and Adolescent Psychiatry, 36,* 835–843.

Campbell, M., & Cueva, J.E. (1995). Psychopharmacology in child and adolescent psychiatry: A review of the past seven years: Part I. *Journal of the American Academy of Child and Adolescent Psychiatry, 34*(9), 1124–1132.

Campbell, M., & Harris, J.C. (1996). Resolved: Autistic children should have a trial of naltrexone. *Journal of the American Academy of Child and Adolescent Psychiatry, 35*(2), 246–251.

Campbell, M., Schopler, E., Cueva, J.E., & Hallin, A. (1996). Treatment of autistic disorder. *Journal of the American Academy of Child and Adolescent Psychiatry, 35*(2), 134–143.

Carrow-Woolfolk, E. (1985). *Test for Auditory Comprehension of Language–Revised (TACL–R).* Itasca, IL: Riverside Publishing Co.

Center for the Study of Autism. (1990). *Asperger's syndrome: Information for families and professionals* [Handout]. Newberg, OR: Author.

Chamberlain, R.S., & Herman, B.H. (1990). A novel biochemical model linking dysfunctions in brain melatonin, proopiomelanocortin peptides, and serotonin in autism. *Biological Psychiatry, 28,* 773–793.

Connolly, H.M., Crary, J.L., McGoon, M.D., et al. (1997). Valvular heart disease associated with fenfluramine-phentermine. *New England Journal of Medicine, 337,* 581–588.

Cook, E.H., Courchesne, R.Y., Cox, N.J., et al. (1998). Linkage-disequilibrium mapping of autistic disorder, with 15q11–15q13 markers. *American Journal of Human Genetics, 62,* 1077–1083.

Cook, E.H., Courchesne, R.Y., Lord, C., et al. (1997). Evidence of linkage between the serotonin transporter and autistic disorder. *Molecular Psychiatry, 2,* 247–250.

Cook, E.H., Perry, B.D., Dawson, G., et al. (1993). Receptor inhibition by immunoglobulins: Specific inhibition by autistic children, their relatives, and control subjects. *Journal of Autism and Developmental Disorders, 23*(1), 67–78.

Courchesne, E. (1991). Neuroanatomic imaging in autism. *Pediatrics, 87*(5, Suppl. pt. 2), 781–790.

Courchesne, E., Saitoh, O., Townsend, J.P., et al. (1994). Cerebellar hypoplasia and hyperplasia in infantile autism. *Lancet, 343*, 63–64.

Courchesne, E., Saitoh, O., Yeung-Courchesne, R., et al. (1994). Abnormality of cerebellar vermian lobules VI and VII in patients with infantile autism: Identification of hypoplastic and hyperplastic subgroups with MR imaging. *American Journal of Radiology, 162*, 123–130.

Courchesne, E., Yeung-Courchesne, R., Press, G.A., et al. (1988). Hypoplasia of cerebellar vermal lobules VI and VII in autism. *New England Journal of Medicine, 318*(21), 1349–1354.

Dawson, G. (1992, April). *Educational planning for children with pervasive developmental disorders.* Paper presented at the meeting of the Northwest Society for Developmental and Behavioral Pediatrics, Portland, OR.

Dawson, G., & Osterling, J. (1997). Early intervention in autism. In M.J. Guralnick (Ed.), *The effectiveness of early intervention* (pp. 307–326). Baltimore: Paul H. Brookes Publishing Co.

Day, H.M., Horner, R.H., & O'Neill, R.E. (1994). Multiple functions of problem behaviors: Assessment and intervention. *Journal of Applied Behavior Analysis, 27*(2), 279–289.

DeLong, G.R., & Heinz, E.R. (1997). The clinical syndrome of early-life bilateral hippocampal sclerosis. *Annals of Neurology, 42*(1), 11–17.

DeLong, G.R., Teague, L.A., & Kamran, M.M. (1998). Effects of fluoxetine treatment in young children with idiopathic autism. *Developmental Medicine and Child Neurology, 40*, 551–562.

DeLong, R. (1994). Children with autistic spectrum disorder and a family history of affective disorder. *Developmental Medicine and Child Neurology, 36*, 674–688.

DeLong, R., & Nohria, C. (1994). Psychiatric family history and neurological disease in autistic spectrum disorders. *Developmental Medicine and Child Neurology, 36*, 441–448.

DeWulf, M., Hendricks, B., & Lesaffre, E. (1995). Epidemiological data of patients treated with fluvoxamine: Results from a 12-week non-comparative multicentre study. *International Clinical Psychopharmacology, 9*(Suppl. 4), 67–72.

DiLavore, P.C., Lord, C., & Rutter, M. (1995). The Prelinguistic Autism Diagnostic Observation Schedule. *Journal of Autism and Developmental Disorders, 25*, 355–379.

Echenne, B., Cheminal, R., Rivier, F., et al. (1992). Epileptic electro-encephalographic abnormalities and developmental dysphasias: A study of 32 patients. *Brain and Development, 14*(4), 216–225.

Ellaway, C., & Christodoulou, J. (1999). Rett syndrome: Clinical update and review of recent genetic advances. *Journal of Pediatrics and Child Health, 35*(5), 419–426.

Famularo, R., & Kinscherff, R. (1992). Pediatric psychopharmacology. In M.D. Levine, W.B. Carey, & A.C. Crocker (Eds.), *Developmental-behavioral pediatrics* (2nd ed., pp. 740–753). Philadelphia: W.B. Saunders Co.

Farber, J.M. (1996). Autism and other communication disorders. In A.J. Capute & P.J. Accardo (Eds.), *Developmental disabilities in infancy and childhood: Vol. II. The spectrum of developmental disabilities* (2nd ed., pp. 347–364). Baltimore: Paul H. Brookes Publishing Co.

Feldman, H.M., Kolmen, B.K., & Gonzaga, A.M. (1999). Naltrexone and communication skills in young children with autism. *Journal of the American Academy of Child and Adolescent Psychiatry, 38*(5), 587–593.

Fields, V. (1994). *Autism advocacy in Lane County: A handbook for parents and professionals.* Unpublished master's thesis, University of Oregon, Eugene.

Folio, M.R., & Fewell, R.R. (1983). *Peabody Developmental Motor Scales and Activity Cards (PDMS): Manual.* Itasca, IL: Riverside Publishing Co.

Folstein, S.E., & Piven, J. (1991). Etiology of autism: Genetic influences. *Pediatrics, 87*(5, Suppl. pt. 2), 767–773.

Fombonne, E. (1998). Inflammatory bowel disease and autism. *Lancet, 351*, 955.

Fombonne, E. (1999). The epidemiology of autism: A review. *Psychological Medicine, 29*(4), 769–786.

Fombonne, E., Du Mazaubrun, C., Cans, C., & Grandjean, H. (1997). Autism and associated medical disorders in a French epidemiological survey. *Journal of the American Academy of Child and Adolescent Psychiatry, 36*, 1561–1569.

Foster-Johnson, L., & Dunlap, G. (1993). Using functional assessment to develop effective, individualized interventions for challenging behaviors. *Teaching Exceptional Children, 25*, 44–57.

Foxx, R.M. (1993). Sapid effects awaiting independent replication. *American Journal on Mental Retardation, 97*(4), 375–376.

Frea, W.D., Koegel, L.K., & Koegel, R.L. (1994). *Understanding why problem behaviors occur: A guide for assisting parents in assessing causes of behavior and designing treatment plans.* Santa Barbara: University of California, Santa Barbara.

Freeman, B.J. (1993). The syndrome of autism: Update and guidelines for diagnosis. *Infants and Young Children, 6*(2), 1–11.

Freeman, B.J., Schroth, P., Ritvo, E., et al. (1980). The Behavior Observation Scale for Autism (BOS): Initial results of factor analyses. *Journal of Autism and Developmental Disorders, 10*(3), 343–346.

Freeman, C.P., Trimble, M.R., Deakin, J.F., et al. (1994). Fluvoxamine versus clomipramine in the treatment of obsessive compulsive disorder: A multicenter randomized, double-blind, parallel group comparison. *Journal of Clinical Psychiatry, 55*(7), 301–305.

Garfin, D.G., McCallon, D., & Cox, R. (1988). Validity and reliability of the Childhood Autism Rating Scale with autistic adolescents. *Journal of Autism and Developmental Disorders, 18*(3), 367–377.

Geller, E., Ritvo, E.R., Freeman, B.J., & Yuwiler, A. (1982). Preliminary observations on the effect of fenfluramine on blood serotonin and symptoms in three autistic boys. *New England Journal of Medicine, 307*(3), 165–169.

Ghaziuddin, M., Butler, E., Tsai, L., & Ghaziuddin, N. (1994). Is clumsiness a marker for Asperger syndrome? *Journal of Intellectual Disability Research, 38*, 519–527.

Ghaziuddin, M., & Gerstein, L. (1996). Pedantic speaking style differentiates Asperger syndrome from high-functioning autism. *Journal of Autism and Developmental Disorders, 26*, 585–595.

Ghaziuddin, M., Tsai, L.Y., & Ghaziuddin, N. (1992). Brief report: A comparison of the diagnostic criteria for Asperger syndrome. *Journal of Autism and Developmental Disorders, 22*(4), 643–648.

Gillberg, C. (1991). Outcome in autism and autistic-like conditions. *Journal of the American Academy of Child and Adolescent Psychiatry, 30*(3), 375–382.

Gillberg, C., & Coleman, M. (1996). Autism and medical disorders: A review of the literature. *Developmental Medicine and Child Neurology, 38*(3), 191–202.

Gillberg, C., Gillberg, I.C., & Steffenburg, S. (1992). Siblings and parents of children with autism: A controlled population-based study. *Developmental Medicine and Child Neurology, 34*(5), 389–398.

Gilman, J.T., & Tuchman, R.F. (1995). Autism and associated behavioral disorders: Pharmacotherapeutic intervention. *Annals of Pharmacotherapy, 29*, 47–56.

Gordon, N. (1997). The Landau-Kleffner syndrome: Increased understanding. *Brain and Development, 19*, 311–316.

Greenspan, S.I. (1992). Reconsidering the diagnosis and treatment of very young children with autistic spectrum or pervasive developmental disorder. *Zero to Three, 13*(2), 1–9.

Gupta, S., Aggarwall, S., & Heads, C. (1996). Brief report: Dysregulated immune system in children with autism: Beneficial effects of intravenous immune globulin on autistic characteristics. *Journal of Autism and Developmental Disorders, 26*(4), 439–452.

Hagberg, B., & Witt-Engerstrom, I. (1986). Rett syndrome: A suggested staging system for describing impairment profile with increasing age toward adolescence. *American Journal of Medical Genetics, 1*(Suppl.), 47–59.

Happé, F.G.E. (1994). An advanced test of theory of mind: Understanding of story characters' thoughts and feelings by able autistic, mentally handicapped, and normal children and adults. *Journal of Autism and Developmental Disorders, 24*(2), 129–154.

Harris, S.L. (1994). Treatment of family problems in autism. In E. Schopler & G.B. Mesibov (Eds.), *Behavioral issues in autism* (pp. 161–175). New York: Plenum Publishing Corp.

Herman, B.H. (1991). Effects of opioid receptor antagonists in the treatment of autism and self-injurious behavior. In J.J. Ratey (Ed.), *Progress in psychiatry series: Vol. 32. Mental retardation: Developing pharmacotherapies* (pp. 107–137). Washington, DC: American Psychiatric Press.

Hiskey, M.A. (1966). *Hiskey-Nebraska Test of Learning Aptitude*. Lincoln, NE: College-View Printers.

Ho, H.H., Lockitch, G., Eaves, L., & Jacobson, B. (1986). Blood serotonin concentrations and fenfluramine therapy in autistic children. *Journal of Pediatrics, 108*(3), 465–469.

Hobson, R.P. (1989). Beyond cognition: A theory of autism. In G. Dawson (Ed.), *Autism: Nature, diagnosis, and treatment* (pp. 22–45). New York: Guilford Press.

Holttum, J.R., Lubetsky, M.J., & Eastman, L.E. (1994). Comprehensive management of trichotillomania in a young autistic girl. *Journal of the American Academy of Child and Adolescent Psychiatry, 33*(4), 577–581.

Hoon, A.H. Jr., & Reiss, A.L. (1992). The mesial-temporal lobe and autism: Case report and review. *Developmental Medicine and Child Neurology, 34*(3), 252–259.

Horrigan, J.P., & Barnhill, L.J. (1997). Risperidone and explosive aggressive autism. *Journal of Autism and Developmental Disorders, 27*, 313–323.

Horvath, K., Stefanatos, G., Sokolski, K.N., et al. (1998). Improved social and language skills after secretin administration in patients with autistic spectrum disorders. *Journal of the Association for Academic Minority Physicians, 9*(1), 9–15.

Jolliffe, T., & Baron-Cohen, S. (1999). A test of central coherence theory: Linguistic processing in high-functioning adults with autism or Asperger syndrome: Is local coherence impaired? *Cognition, 71*(2), 149–185.

Kalmanson, B., & Pekarsky, J.H. (1987). Infant–parent psychotherapy with an autistic toddler. *Zero to Three, 7*(3), 1–6.

Kanner, L. (1943). Autistic disturbances of affective contact. *Nervous Child, 2*, 217–250.

Kaufman, A.S., & Kaufman, N.L. (1983). *Administration and scoring manual for the Kaufman Assessment Battery for Children (K-ABC)*. Circle Pines, MN: American Guidance Service.

Kazdin, A.E. (1993). Replication and extension of behavioral treatment of autistic disorder. *American Journal on Mental Retardation, 97*(4), 377–379.

Kemper, T.L., & Bauman, M.L. (1993). The contribution of neuropathologic studies to the understanding of autism. *Neurologic Clinics, 11*, 175–187.

Kerr, A.M. (1995). Early clinical signs in the Rett disorder. *Neuropediatrics, 26*, 67–71.

Klauck, S.M., Poustka, F., Benner, A., et al. (1997). Serotonin transporter (5-HTT) gene variants associated with autism? *Human Molecular Genetics, 6*, 2233–2238.

Klin, A., Volkmar, F.R., & Sparrow, S.S. (1992). Autistic social dysfunction: Some limitations of the theory of mind hypothesis. *Journal of Child Psychology and Psychiatry, 33*(5), 861–876.

Knobloch, H. (1980). *Manual of developmental diagnosis: The administration and interpretation of the revised Gesell and Amatruda developmental and neurologic examination*. New York: HarperCollins.

Knobloch, H., & Pasamanick, B. (Ed.). (1974). *Gesell and Amatruda's developmental diagnosis: The evaluation and management of normal and abnormal neuropsychologic development in infancy and early childhood* (3rd ed.). New York: HarperCollins.

Kolmen, B.K., Feldman, H.M., Handen, B.L., & Janosky, J.E. (1995). Naltrexone in young autistic children: A double-blind, placebo-controlled crossover study. *Journal of the American Academy of Child and Adolescent Psychiatry, 34*(2), 223–231.

Kolmen, B.K., Feldman, H.M., Handen, B.L., & Janosky, J.E. (1997). Naltrexone in young autistic children: Replication study and learning measures. *Journal of the American Academy of Child and Adolescent Psychiatry, 36*, 1570–1578.

Krug, D.A., Arick, J.R., & Almond, P.A. (1993). *Autism Screening Instrument for Educational Planning (ASIEP-2)*. Austin, TX: PRO-ED.

Leonard, H., & Bower, C. (1998). Is the girl with Rett syndrome normal at birth? *Developmental Medicine and Child Neurology, 40*, 115–121.

Lerman, P., Lerman-Sagie, T., & Kivity, S. (1991). Effect of early corticosteroid therapy for Landau-Kleffner syndrome. *Developmental Medicine and Child Neurology, 33*(3), 257–260.

Lord, C. (1993, October). *Diagnosis and assessment of autism and pervasive developmental disorders*. Symposium presented at the 40th annual meeting of the American Academy of Child and Adolescent Psychiatry, San Antonio, TX.

Lord, C., Rutter, M., Goode, S., et al. (1989). Autism Diagnostic Observation Schedule: A standardized observation of communicative and social behavior. *Journal of Autism and Developmental Disorders, 19*(2), 185–212.

Lord, C., Rutter, M., & Le Couteur, A. (1994). Autism Diagnostic Interview–Revised: A revised version of a diagnostic interview for caregivers of individuals with possible pervasive developmental disorders. *Journal of Autism and Developmental Disorders, 24*(5), 659–685.

Lovaas, O.I. (1987). Behavioral treatment and normal educational and intellectual functioning in young autistic children. *Journal of Consulting and Clinical Psychology, 55*(1), 3–9.

Mazzocco, M.M., Kates, W.R., Baumgardner, T.L., et al. (1997). Autistic behaviors among girls with fragile X syndrome. *Journal of Autism and Developmental Disorders, 27*, 415–435.

McDougle, C.J., Holmes, J.P., Carlson, D.C., et al. (1998). A double-blind, placebo-controlled study of risperidone in adults with autistic disorder and other pervasive developmental disorders. *Archives of General Psychiatry, 55*, 633–641.

McDougle, C.J., Naylor, S.T., Cohen, D.J., et al. (1996). A double-blind, placebo-controlled study of fluvoxamine in adults with autistic disorder. *Archives of General Psychiatry, 53*, 1001–1008.

McEachin, J.J., Smith, T., & Lovaas, O.I. (1993). Long-term outcome for children with autism who received early intensive behavioral treatment. *American Journal on Mental Retardation, 97*(4), 359–372.

Mesibov, G.B. (1993). Treatment outcome is encouraging. *American Journal on Mental Retardation, 97*(4), 379–380.

Morgan, S. (1988). Diagnostic assessment of autism: A review of objective scales. *Journal of Psychoeducational Assessment, 6*, 139–151.

Morrell, F., Whisler, W.W., & Smith, M.C. (1995). Landau-Kleffner syndrome: Treatment with subpial intracortical transection. *Brain, 118*, 1529–1546.

Murakami, J.W., Courchesne, E., Press, G., et al. (1989). Reduced cerebellar hemisphere size and its relationship to verbal hypoplasia in autism. *Archives of Neurology, 46*, 689–694.

Nass, R., Gross, A., & Devinsky, O. (1998). Autism and autistic epileptiform regression with occipital spikes. *Developmental Medicine and Child Neurology, 40*, 543–458.

Nelson, K.B. (1991). Prenatal and perinatal factors in the etiology of autism. *Pediatrics, 87*(5, Suppl. pt. 2), 761–766.

Newcomer, P., & Hammill, D. (1996). *Test of Language Development–Primary (TOLD–P:3).* Austin, TX: PRO-ED.

Nickel, R.E. (1996). Controversial therapies for young children with developmental disabilities. *Infants and Young Children, 8*(4), 29–40.

Nicolson, R., Awad, G., & Sloman, L. (1998). An open trial of risperidone in young autistic children. *Journal of the American Academy of Child and Adolescent Psychiatry, 37*, 372–376.

Nordin, V., & Gillberg, C. (1998). The long-term course of autistic disorders: Update on follow-up studies. *Acta Psychiatrica Scandinavica, 97*, 99–108.

Osterling, J., & Dawson, G. (1994). Early recognition of children with autism: A study of first birthday home videotapes. *Journal of Autism and Developmental Disorders, 24*(3), 247–257.

Ozonoff, S., Rogers, S.J., & Pennington, B.F. (1991). Asperger's syndrome: Evidence of an empirical distinction from high-functioning autism. *Journal of Child Psychology and Psychiatry, 32*(7), 1107–1122.

Panksepp, J., & Lensing, P. (1991). Brief report: A synopsis of an open-trial of naltrexone treatment of autism with four children. *Journal of Autism and Developmental Disorders, 21*(2), 243–249.

Paquier, P.F., Van Dongen, H.R., & Loonen, C.B. (1992). The Landau-Kleffner syndrome or "acquired aphasia with convulsive disorder": Long-term follow-up of six children and a review of the recent literature. *Archives of Neurology, 49*, 354–359.

Peltola, H., Patja, A.N., Leinikki, P., et al. (1998). No evidence for measles, mumps, and rubella vaccine-associated inflammatory bowel disease or autism in a 14-year prospective study. *Lancet, 351*, 1327–1328.

Piven, J., Berthier, M.L., Starkstein, S.E., et al. (1990). Magnetic resonance imaging evidence for a defect of cerebral cortical development in autism. *American Journal of Psychiatry, 147*(6), 734–739.

Piven, J., Saliba, K., Bailey, J., & Arndt, S. (1997). An MRI study of autism: The cerebellum revisited. *Neurology, 49*, 546–551.

Plioplys, A.V. (1998). Intravenous immunoglobulin treatment of children with autism. *Journal of Child Neurology, 13*, 79–82.

Plioplys, A.V., Greaves, A., Kazemi, K., & Silverman, E. (1994). Lymphocyte function in autism and Rett syndrome. *Neuropsychobiology, 29*(1), 12–16.

Ramberg, C., Ehlers, S., Nyden, A., et al. (1996). Language and pragmatic functions in school-age children on the autism spectrum. *European Journal of Disorders of Communication, 31*, 387–413.

Rapin, I. (1991). Autistic children: Diagnosis and clinical features. *Pediatrics, 87*(5, Suppl. pt. 2), 751–760.

Rapin, I. (1997). Autism. *Current Concepts, 337*, 97–104.

Reiss, A.L. (1988). Cerebellar hypoplasia and autism [Letter to the editor]. *New England Journal of Medicine, 319*(17), 1152–1153.

Repetto, G.M., White, L.M., Bader, P.J., et al. (1998). Interstitial duplications of chromosome region 15q11–15q13: Clinical and molecular characterization. *American Journal of Medical Genetics, 79*, 82–89.

Richters, M.M., & Volkmar, F.R. (1994). Reactive attachment disorder of infancy or early childhood. *Journal of the American Academy of Child and Adolescent Psychiatry, 33*(3), 328–332.

Ritvo, E., & Garber, H.J. (1988). Cerebellar hypoplasia and autism [Letter to the editor]. *New England Journal of Medicine, 319*(17), 1152.

Ritvo, E.R., Jorde, L.B., Mason-Brothers, A., et al. (1989) The UCLA–University of Utah epidemiologic survey of autism: Recurrence risk estimates and genetic counseling. *American Journal of Psychiatry, 146*(8), 1032–1036.

Roid, G.H., & Miller, L.J. (1997). *Leiter International Performance Scale–Revised.* Wood Dale, IL: C.H. Stoelting Co.

Rutter, M. (1978). Diagnosis and definition. In M. Rutter & E. Schopler (Eds.), *Autism: A reappraisal of concepts and treatment* (pp. 1–25). New York: Plenum Publishing Corp.

Schopler, E. (1994). A statewide program for the treatment and education of autistic and related communication handicapped children (TEACCH). *Child and Adolescent Psychiatric Clinics of North America, 3*(1), 91–103.

Schopler, E., Mesibov, G.B., & Hearsey, K. (1995). Structured teaching in the TEACCH system. In E. Schopler

& G.B. Mesibov (Eds.), *Learning and cognition in autism* (pp. 243–268). New York: Plenum Publishing Corp.

Schopler, E., Reichler, R.J., & Renner, B.R. (1988). *The Childhood Autism Rating Scale (CARS)*. Los Angeles: Western Psychological Services.

Schroer, R.J., Phelan, M.C., Michaelis, R.C., et al. (1998). Autism and maternally derived aberrations of chromosome 15q. *American Journal of Medical Genetics, 76,* 327–336.

Schultz, R.T. (1997, October). *Asperger's syndrome: Neuropsychology and neuroimaging.* Paper presented to the annual meeting of the American Academy of Child and Adolescent Psychiatry, Toronto.

Sheinkopf, S.J., & Siegel, B. (1998). Home based behavioral treatment of young children with autism. *Journal of Autism and Developmental Disorders, 28*(1), 15–23.

Siegel, B. (1996). *Pervasive Developmental Disorder Screening Test.* San Francisco: University of California, Langley Porter Psychiatric Institute.

Siegel, B., Pliner, C., Eschler, J., & Elliott, G.R. (1988). How children with autism are diagnosed: Difficulties in identification of children with multiple developmental delays. *Developmental and Behavioral Pediatrics, 9*(4), 199–204.

Singh, V.K., Warren, R.P., Odell, J.D., & Cole, P. (1991). Changes of soluble interleukin-2, interleukin-2 receptor, T8 antigen, and interleukin-1 in the serum of autistic children. *Clinical Immunology and Immunopathology, 61,* 448–455.

Smalley, S.L. (1998). Autism and tuberous sclerosis. *Journal of Autism and Developmental Disorders, 28,* 407–414.

Sokolenko, M., & Kutcher, S. (1998). Mini-review: Paroxetine. *Child and Adolescent Psychopharmacology News, 3*(3), 1–5, 8.

Solomon, G.E., Carson, D., Pavlakis, S., et al. (1993). Intracranial EEG monitoring in Landau-Kleffner syndrome associated with left temporal lobe astrocytoma. *Epilepsia, 34*(3), 557–560.

Soprano, A.M., Garcia, E.F., Caraballo, R., & Fejerman, N. (1994). Acquired epileptic aphasia: Neuropsychologic follow-up of 12 patients. *Pediatric Neurology, 11*(3), 230–235.

Sparrow, S., Balla, D., & Cicchetti, D. (1984). *Vineland Adaptive Behavior Scales (VABS)*. Circle Pines, MN: American Guidance Service.

Spiker, D., Lotspeich, L., Kraemer, H.C., et al. (1994). Genetics of autism: Characteristics of affected and unaffected children from 37 multiplex families. *American Journal of Medical Genetics (Neuropsychiatric Genetics), 54*(27), 27–35.

Stine, L. (1986). *Identifying high functioning children with autism.* Bloomington: Indiana Resource Center for Autism, Institute for the Study of Developmental Disabilities.

Stubbs, E. (1990, Spring). Update on autism. *CDRC News, VI*(1), 1–4.

Stubbs, E.G., Crawford, M.I., Burger, D.R., & Vanderbark, A.A. (1977). Depressed lymphocyte responsiveness in autistic children. *Journal of Autism and Childhood Schizophrenia, 7,* 49–55.

Stutsman, R. (1948). *Merrill-Palmer Scale of Mental Tests.* Wood Dale, IL: C.H. Stoelting Co.

Szatmari, P. (1991). Asperger's syndrome: Diagnosis, treatment, and outcome. *Psychiatric Clinics of North America, 14*(1), 81–93.

Szatmari, P., Archer, L., Fisman, S., et al. (1995). Asperger's syndrome and autism: Differences in behavior, cognition, and adaptive functioning. *Journal of the American Academy of Child and Adolescent Psychiatry, 34*(12), 1662–1671.

Tharpe, A.M., & Olson, B.J. (1994). Landau-Kleffner syndrome: Acquired epileptic aphasia in children. *Journal of the American Academy of Audiology, 5*(2), 146–150.

Thorndike, R.L., Hagen, E.P., & Sattler, J.M. (1986). *Stanford-Binet Intelligence Scale* (4th ed.). Itasca, IL: Riverside Publishing Co.

Tsai, L.Y. (1997). Other pervasive developmental disorders. In J.M. Weiner (Ed.), *Textbook of child and adolescent psychiatry* (2nd ed., pp. 255–280). Washington, DC: American Psychiatric Press, American Academy of Child and Adolescent Psychiatry.

Tsai, L.Y., & Ghaziuddin, M. (1997). Autistic disorder. In J.M. Weiner (Ed.), *Textbook of child and adolescent psychiatry* (2nd ed., pp. 219–254). Washington, DC: American Psychiatry Press, American Academy of Child and Adolescent Psychiatry.

Tsai, L.Y., & Scott-Miller, D. (1988). Higher functioning autistic disorder. *Focus on Autistic Behavior, 2*(6), 1–8.

Tuchman, R.F., & Rapin, I. (1997). Regression in pervasive developmental disorders: Seizures and epileptiform electroencephalogram correlates. *Pediatrics, 99*(4), 560–566.

Van Bourgondien, M.E., Marcus, L.M., & Schopler, E. (1992). Comparison of DSM-III-R and Childhood Autism Rating Scale diagnoses of autism. *Journal of Autism and Developmental Disorders, 22*(4), 493–505.

Volkmar, F.R. (1992). Childhood disintegrative disorder: issues for DSM-IV. *Journal of Autism and Developmental Disorders, 22*(4), 625–641.

Volkmar, F.R., Klin, A., & Pauls, D. (1998). Nosological and genetic aspects of Asperger syndrome. *Journal of Autism and Developmental Disorders, 28,* 457–463.

Wakefield, A.J., Murch, S.H., Anthony, A., et al. (1998). Ileal-lymphoid-nodular hyperplasia, non-specific colitis, and pervasive developmental disorder in children. *Lancet, 351,* 637–641.

Warren, R.P., Cole, P., Odell, D., et al. (1990). Detection of maternal antibodies in infantile autism. *Journal of the American Academy of Child and Adolescent Psychiatry, 6,* 873–877.

Wechsler, D. (1989). *Wechsler Preschool and Primary Scale of Intelligence–Revised.* San Antonio, TX: The Psychological Corp.

Wechsler, D. (1991). *Wechsler Intelligence Scale for Children* (3rd ed.). San Antonio, TX: The Psychological Corp.

Weizman, A., Weizman, R., Szekely, G.A., et al. (1982). Abnormal immune response to brain tissue antigen in the syndrome of autism. *American Journal of Psychiatry, 7,* 1462–1465.

Whitaker, A.M., & Rao, U. (1992). Neuroleptics in pediatric psychiatry. *Psychiatric Clinics of North America, 15*(1), 243–277.

Wiig, E.H., & Secord, W. (1988). *Test of Language Competence–Expanded Edition.* San Antonio, TX: The Psychological Corp.

Wing, L. (1981). Asperger's syndrome: A clinical account. *Psychological Medicine, 11,* 115–129.

Zimmerman, I.L., Steiner, V.G., & Pond, R.E. (1991). *Preschool Language Scale (PLS–3)*. San Antonio, TX: The Psychological Corp.

8

Appendix

Guidelines for the Care of Children and Adolescents with Autism and Pervasive Developmental Disorders

Basic Team

The special care needs of children with autism can be met by the primary care physician working collaboratively with parents, an experienced child development team, early childhood educators, teachers, and other school staff. Some children and families require referral to a child neurologist or child psychiatrist, and other children may need referral to a behavioral consultant. Please note that the primary care physician continues to be responsible for coordinating the special services that these children require.

Regular members of the child development team include a developmental pediatrician, a psychologist, a speech-language pathologist, an occupational therapist, an audiologist, and a medical social worker. Many children do not see all members of the team, and some children require additional evaluations (e.g., nutritionist, behavioral specialist).

Initial Evaluation

The objectives of the initial evaluation by the child development team are to confirm the diagnosis of autism, to determine the presence of other developmental and behavior problems, to establish the cause of the child's developmental problems if possible, and to review the support needs of the child's family. The responsibilities of the primary care physician and the nurse are to identify and refer children who are suspected of having autism; to perform a complete medical examination of such children including evaluation for minor anomalies; to evaluate and treat associated medical problems; and to counsel the parents and children about the diagnosis and recommended treatment.

Frequency of Visits

The child and family are best followed monthly in the primary care office following the initial evaluation until associated medical problems are evaluated, family support needs have been addressed and discussed, and the child is receiving needed educational services. Reevaluate the child and family in the office at least yearly to monitor his or her progress and review the treatment of associated behavior and medical problems, and more frequently for younger children and children in the first year after beginning treatment. Some children may need to be seen more often by the primary care physician (e.g., children with seizures who are taking anticonvulsants). Many children benefit from reevaluation by the child development team. Some children require regular follow-up by a child neurologist or a child psychiatrist. The management plan should be updated as needed at each reevaluation and not less than yearly.

Guidelines for the Care of Children and Adolescents with Autism and Pervasive Developmental Disorders

The following elements are recommended by age group, and the listing is cumulative. Review all items indicated up through the actual age group of a child entering your practice for the first time as part of the initial evaluation.

AGE	KEY CLINICAL ISSUES/CONCERNS	EVALUATIONS/KEY PROCEDURES	SPECIALISTS
Birth–5 years (pre-school age)	*Growth/Nutrition*	Growth parameters, diet record	Nutritionist, feeding specialist as needed
	Associated Medical Problems		
	Hearing/vision	Audiologic testing, vision testing, referral to ophthalmologist as needed	Audiologist, opthalmologist as needed
	Gastroesophageal reflux (GER)	Workup for GER, trial of medication, positioning, and diet change	Pediatric gastroenterologist as needed
	Seizures	Electroencephalogram (EEG), referral to child neurologist as needed	Child neurologist as needed
	Neuromotor concerns (e.g., hypotonia, dyspraxia, toe walking)	Detailed neuromotor evaluation as needed	Physical/occupational therapist as needed
	Sleep problems	Behavioral management, occasional short-term medications	Developmental pediatrician (DPed), nurse specialist as needed
	Constipation	Diet, medication (e.g., bulk agent)	
	Toilet training		
	Drooling	Behavioral management, occasional medications	Speech-language pathologist, DPed as needed
	Note any side effects of medications.		
	Dental Care	Review oral hygiene	Dentist
	Cause of the Developmental Disability Consider pervasive developmental disorder (PDD), fragile X syndrome, or Landau-Kleffner syndrome	Evaluation for minor anomalies Fragile X study, chromosomes, magnetic resonance imaging (MRI) scan, and so forth as needed Obtain EEG with prolonged sleep record if regression in skills occurs	DPed, medical geneticist as needed
	Associated Behavior or Mental Health Problems Aggression Hyperactivity or inattention Oppositional behavior Avoidant behavior Anxiety Perseverative behaviors Self-injurious behaviors (SIBs) or stereotypies	Family and teacher interviews, behavior rating scales, functional analysis of behavior Parent training in behavior management	DPed, child psychiatrist, or other mental health professional as needed Referral to child development team, behavioral consultant as needed

The Physician's Guide to Caring for Children with Disabilities and Chronic Conditions, edited by Robert E. Nickel and Larry W. Desch, copyright © 2000 Paul H. Brookes Publishing Co.

Guidelines for the Care of Children and Adolescents with Autism and Pervasive Developmental Disorders *(continued)*

The following elements are recommended by age group, and the listing is cumulative. Review all items indicated up through the actual age group of a child entering your practice for the first time as part of the initial evaluation.

AGE	KEY CLINICAL ISSUES/CONCERNS	EVALUATIONS/KEY PROCEDURES	SPECIALISTS
Birth–5 years (pre-school age) *(continued)*	*Developmental Progress, Early Intervention/ Early Childhood Special Education (EI/ECSE) Services* Need for physical therapy, occupational therapy, speech-language therapy, behavioral support Developmental delay or mental retardation Speech-language disorder Dyspraxia	Developmental surveillance Request EI/ECSE report, review individualized family service plan (IFSP) with family	Referral to child development team as needed Speech-language pathologist, physical and occupational therapists as needed
	Review of Diagnosis and Anticipatory Guidance Review IFSP with family Need for parent training in behavior management Discuss alternative therapies Transition from EI to ECSE and from ECSE to grade school Sibling programs	Family interview, educational materials (e.g., handouts on alternative therapies), initiate care notebook Teacher interview, school conference	Primary care office; collaborate with child development team and EI/ECSE staff as needed
	Family Support Services Respite care Parent group Community health nurse Advocacy (e.g., Autism Society of America) Financial services (Supplemental Security Income [SSI]) Other enabling services	Family interview, use parent questionnaire (e.g., Family Needs Survey) as needed; provide resource information Care coordination; collaboration with school, Developmental Disability (DD) services, and other agencies	Medical social worker, community health nurse, and other community services as needed

The Physician's Guide to Caring for Children with Disabilities and Chronic Conditions, edited by Robert E. Nickel and Larry W. Desch, copyright © 2000 Paul H. Brookes Publishing Co.

Guidelines for the Care of Children and Adolescents with Autism and Pervasive Developmental Disorders (continued)

The following elements are recommended by age group, and the listing is cumulative. Review all items indicated up through the actual age group of a child entering your practice for the first time as part of the initial evaluation.

AGE	KEY CLINICAL ISSUES/CONCERNS	EVALUATIONS/KEY PROCEDURES	SPECIALISTS
6–12 years (school-age)	*School Progress* Need for ancillary services Physical therapy, occupational therapy, speech-language therapy	Family and teacher interviews, behavior rating scales, school report as needed; review individualized education program (IEP) with family	Evaluation by child development team as needed; collaborate with school staff
	Associated Behavior or Mental Health Problems Sleep disorder Hyperactivity or inattention Oppositional behaviors Anxiety Depression Aggression Obsessive-compulsive behaviors SIBs or stereotypies	Interviews, behavior rating scales, functional analysis of behavior Medication management as needed	Referral to child development team or individual appointments with DPed, psychologist, behavioral consultant, and child psychiatrist as needed
	Social Skills, Recreation and Leisure Activities Involvement in peer group activities at school and in the community (determine which supports are needed)	School-based program and referral to community services as needed	Physical therapist, occupational therapist, adaptive PE specialist, psychologist, and behavioral consultant as needed; collaborate with school staff
13–21 years (adolescent–young adult)	*Self-Care/Independent Living* Determine which supports are needed	Outpatient occupational therapy and physical therapy services as needed Independent living skills program, social skills training as needed	Medical social worker, physical therapist, occupational theapist, psychologist as needed
	Anticipatory Guidance Transitions to middle school and high school Sexuality, menstrual hygiene, and birth control Vocational training Life skills programs Encourage healthy behaviors (e.g., diet, exercise) Transition to adult services	Adolescent, family and teacher interviews, school conference as needed; review IEP with family Social skills training regarding sexuality, menstrual hygiene; birth control as needed (e.g., Depo-Provera) Career counseling, evaluation by vocational specialist as needed Care coordination; collaboration with school staff, DD services, other agencies	Primary care office in collaboration with child development team and school staff Referral to gynecologist as needed Referral to Department of Vocational Rehabilitation

The Physician's Guide to Caring for Children with Disabilities and Chronic Conditions, edited by Robert E. Nickel and Larry W. Desch, copyright © 2000 Paul H. Brookes Publishing Co.

Family and Physician Management Plan Summary for Children and Adolescents with Autism and Pervasive Developmental Disorders

This form will help you and your physician review current services and service needs. Please answer the questions about your current services on this page. Your physician will review your responses and complete the rest of the form.

Child's name _____ Today's date _____

Person completing the form _____

CURRENT SERVICES

1. Please list your/your child's current medications and any side effects.

2. What is your/your child's current school program?

    School name _____ Grade _____

    Teacher _____ Telephone _____

3. Do you/does your child receive any support services and other special programs at school (e.g., physical therapy, resource room)? Please list.

4. Who are your/your child's other medical and dental service providers?

    Dentist _____

    Neurologist _____

    Other _____

5. Who are your/your child's other community service providers?

    Speech-language pathologist _____

    Community health nurse _____

    Other _____

The Physician's Guide to Caring for Children with Disabilities and Chronic Conditions, edited by Robert E. Nickel and Larry W. Desch, copyright © 2000 Paul H. Brookes Publishing Co.

Family and Physician Management Plan Summary for Children and Adolescents with Autism and Pervasive Developmental Disorders *(continued)*

6. Do you also receive services from a child development team of specialists?

   Contact person _____

   Location _____

7. Have you/has your child had any blood tests, radiologic (X-ray) examinations, or other procedures since your last visit? If yes, please describe.

8. Have you/has your child been hospitalized or received surgery since your last visit? If yes, describe.

9. Please note your child's accomplishments since your last visit. Consider activities at home, in your neighborhood, or at school, as well as success with treatments.

10. What goals (skills) would you/your child like to accomplish in the next year? Consider activities at home, in your neighborhood, or at school, as well as success with a treatment.

11. What questions or concerns would you like to address today?

Family and Physician Management Plan Summary for Children and Adolescents with Autism and Pervasive Developmental Disorders

The Management Plan Summary should be completed at each annual review and more often as needed. It is intended to be used with the Guidelines for Care, which provide a more complete listing of clinical issues at different ages and recommended evaluations and treatments.

Child's name _____ Person completing form _____ Today's date _____

Clinical issues	Currently a problem?	Evaluations needed	Treatment recommendations	Referrals made	Date for status check
Family's Questions					
Cause of the Developmental Disability Fragile X DNA testing results					
Growth/Nutrition					
Dental Care					
Other Medical Issues Hearing or vision concerns Seizures Neuromotor concerns (e.g., hypotonia, toe walking) Drooling Sleep disorder Constipation or diarrhea Toilet training Sexuality, menstrual hygiene **Note any side effects of medications.**					

The Physician's Guide to Caring for Children with Disabilities and Chronic Conditions, edited by Robert E. Nickel and Larry W. Desch, copyright © 2000 Paul H. Brookes Publishing Co.

Family and Physician Management Plan Summary for
Children and Adolescents with Autism and Pervasive Developmental Disorders *(continued)*

Child's name _____ Person completing form _____ Today's date _____

Clinical issues	Currently a problem?	Evaluations needed	Treatment recommendations	Referrals made	Date for status check
Associated Developmental or Learning Issues Current school progress Review early intervention (EI) or school services (individualized family service plan [IFSP] or individualized education program [IEP]) Developmental delay or mental retardation Speech-language disorder; assess need for augmentative communication					
Need for Physical and Occupational Therapy Services Hypotonia or toe walking Associated dyspraxia or cerebral palsy Fine motor or visual motor concerns					
Associated Behavior or Mental Health Issues Aggression Inattention or hyperactivity Oppositional behavior Anxiety, depression Obsessive-compulsive behaviors Stereotypies Self-injurious behaviors (SIBs)					

The Physician's Guide to Caring for Children with Disabilities and Chronic Conditions, edited by Robert E. Nickel and Larry W. Desch, copyright © 2000 Paul H. Brookes Publishing Co.

Family and Physician Management Plan Summary for Children and Adolescents with Autism and Pervasive Developmental Disorders *(continued)*

Child's name _____ Person completing form _____ Today's date _____

Clinical issues	Currently a problem?	Evaluations needed	Treatment recommendations	Referrals made	Date for status check
Behavior Management in the Home					
Behavior Management in the School					
Discussion of Alternative Therapies					
Social Skills Involvement in group activities at school, in community (determine which supports are needed)					
Promote Self-Care/Independence					
Family Support Services					
Anticipatory Guidance List issues discussed and materials provided					

The Physician's Guide to Caring for Children with Disabilities and Chronic Conditions, edited by Robert E. Nickel and Larry W. Desch, copyright © 2000 Paul H. Brookes Publishing Co.

Family and Physician Management Plan Summary for Children and Adolescents with Autism and Pervasive Developmental Disorders *(continued)*

Child's name _____   Person completing form _____   Today's date _____

Clinical issues	Currently a problem?	Evaluations needed	Treatment recommendations	Referrals made	Date for status check
Collaboration with Community Agencies					
Schools					
Comments					

Next update of the Management Plan Summary _____

Signature _____ Date _____
            (Child and parent)

Signature _____ Date _____
            (Health professional)

The Physician's Guide to Caring for Children with Disabilities and Chronic Conditions, edited by Robert E. Nickel and Larry W. Desch, copyright © 2000 Paul H. Brookes Publishing Co.

Questions for Parents to Ask Themselves Regarding Specific Treatments

Child's name _____ Date of birth _____ Person completing form _____

1. What characteristic behaviors of autism am I trying to target? Does the treatment that I am considering target these characteristic behaviors?

2. Are there any harmful side effects associated with this treatment?

3. What positive effects of treatment would I hope to see?

4. What short-term and long-term effects might I see with this treatment?

5. Can this treatment be integrated into my child's current program?

6. What is the cost of the treatment?

7. Will my insurance company pay for the treatment?

8. How much time does the treatment take? Can I realistically devote the time required to the treatment?

9. Has this treatment been validated scientifically?

10. Have I researched the treatment?

11. Was I able to interview other parents and professionals about the treatment? If so, list stated pros, cons, and other areas of interest.

12. Do proponents of the treatment claim that this procedure can help nearly everyone? Do proponents offer the possibility of a "cure," state that treatment must be done early or else is not effective, claim that treatment benefits a variety of conditions? If so, these should be seen as "red flags" to be more careful in considering this technique.

13. What do my pediatrician and other professionals involved with my child think about the treatment's appropriateness?

From Fields, V. (1994). *Autism advocacy in Lane County: A handbook for parents and professionals.* Unpublished master's thesis, University of Oregon, Eugene; reprinted by permission.

Observation of Play

The purpose of the play observation is to improve the quality of behavioral observations in the primary care office. It is not a screening test. It provides a structure to look for specific social, communicative, and play behaviors to assist in the identification of children through 3 years of age who are suspected of having autism or other pervasive developmental disorders (PDDs).

The play observation is best incorporated at the end of the physician's interview with the parents and prior to the physical examination. Look for the target behaviors while the child is playing during the interview, then allow 10–15 minutes for the structured observation of play.

TOYS: Have books and a number of toys available, including toys that can be used for pretend or make-believe play and reciprocal play, and "cause-and-effect" toys such as a Jack-in-the-Box or a See 'n Say toy (a pull-string toy). Your toy box can include a toy telephone with push buttons or a dial that spins, a doll with removable clothes, two plastic bowls or cups and two spoons, a 6-inch-diameter ball, a toy car, a pull toy (e.g., a train), a tower and plastic rings, blocks, a shape sorter, and books.

METHODS

1. Begin by telling the parents that you want to watch them play with their child to learn more about their child's behavior. Ask the parents if they have brought any of the child's toys from home. Then encourage the parents to play as if they were at home and use the child's own toys as well as those in the toy box.

   Wait and observe (several minutes).

   [*Skip Item #2 if the parents and the child are already playing actively on the floor near the toy box.*]

2. Next, ask the parents to sit down next to the box of toys. If the child is not engaged actively in playing near the toy box, ask one of the parents to pick up a toy to show the child and to call the child by name. If the child does not come in response to being called, ask one of the parents to place the child next to the toys.

   Wait and observe.

3. Now instruct one of the parents to show the child the toy telephone (or a bowl and a spoon). If the child does not begin to play with the toy telephone (or the bowl and the spoon), instruct one of the parents to model dialing, pretend to talk on the telephone (or pretend to eat from the bowl with the spoon), and then offer the telephone receiver (or the pretend spoonful) to the child.

   Wait and observe.

   If the child begins to play with the toy telephone, ask one of the parents to imitate the child (do whatever the child does right after the child does it) and/or to elaborate slightly on the child's play.

4. Next, ask one of the parents to show the child a book. If the child does not begin to look at the book, instruct the parent to begin talking about a picture in the book and to show that picture to the child while pointing at it. If the child begins to look at the book, ask the parent to follow the child's lead and imitate and/or elaborate slightly on what the child is doing.

   Wait and observe.

5. Next, ask one of the parents to call the child's name, point to an easily observed toy or object in the room, and say, "Look at the [name of toy]!" Does the child look where his or her parent is pointing, not just at the parent's hand? If the child does not look at the parent when the child's name is called, ask the parent to touch the child on the shoulder and again call the child's name, point at an object, and say, "Look at the [name of toy]!"

6. At some point during the child's play, pretend that you (the examiner) hurt your finger and feign crying loudly. Does the child notice? Look concerned? Try to comfort?

7. Demonstrate blowing bubbles, then close the jar of bubbles and hold the jar in front of you. Wait and observe how the child responds. Does the child request more? If so, how? Next, make sure the lid is tightly closed and hand the jar to the child. Does the child request help? If so, how? Alternatively, show the child an attractive toy or food item, then place it into a clear plastic jar and screw the lid on tightly so that the child cannot open it. Hand the jar to the child, and observe how the child responds. Does the child request help? If so, how?

Observation of Play

Name _____ Date of birth _____ Today's date _____

Examiner _____

Family's concerns _____

Scoring (check [✓] each time behavior occurs)	Description (circle and add description as needed)
1. Communication	
❑ Uses gestures (please list)	In imitation To request
❑ Uses words (please list)	In imitation To request
❑ Makes requests (e.g., "help" or "more")	Looks at examiner's or With vocalization parent's face
2. Social	
❑ Seeks contact with parent	Then looks at parent's face With vocalization
❑ Looks at parent's face	And smiles with parent
❑ Looks at examiner's face	And smiles with examiner
❑ Responds to name	

(continued)

Observation of Play (continued)

Scoring (check [✓] each time behavior occurs)	Description (circle and add description as needed)
❑ Shows (i.e., brings) toy to parent	Then looks at parent's face With vocalization
❑ Points to toy or book	Then looks at parent's face With vocalization
❑ Looks where parent has pointed	
❑ Notices the examiner crying (typical by 1 year of age)	Looks concerned (typical by 2 years of age) Tries to comfort (typical by 2–4 years of age)

3. Play
    ❑ Imitates
 	
    ❑ Pretends	

(continued)

Observation of Play (continued)

General observations (e.g., very active, tantrums, passive or stares into space, flat affect, perseverative play such as spinning toys, stereotypic behavior such as hand flapping):

Impression (*please circle*):   Autism is present   Suspected   Not present

Action taken:

REFERENCES

Baron-Cohen, S., Allen, J., & Gillberg, C. (1992). Can autism be detected at 18 months? The needle, the haystack, and the CHAT. *British Journal of Psychiatry, 161,* 839–843.

Osterling, J., & Dawson, G. (1994). Early recognition of children with autism: A study of first birthday home videotapes. *Journal of Autism and Developmental Disabilities, 24*(3), 247–257.

Siegel, B. (1996). *The world of the autistic child: Understanding and treating autistic spectrum disorders* (pp. 94–95). New York Oxford University Press.

RESOURCES ON AUTISM AND
PERVASIVE DEVELOPMENTAL DISORDERS

Readings

Cohen, D.J., Donnellan, A.M., & Paul, R. (Eds.). (1988). *Handbook of autism and pervasive developmental disorders.* New York: John Wiley & Sons. (1-800-225-5945)

Dawson, G. (1989). *Autism: Nature, diagnosis, and treatment.* New York: Guilford Press. (1-800-365-7006)

Gerlach, E.K. (1993). *Autism treatment guide.* Eugene, OR: Four Leaf Press.

Grandin, T., & Scariano, M.M. (1996). *Emergence: Labeled autistic.* New York: Warner Books. (212-522-7200)

Harris, S.L. (1994). *Siblings of children with autism: A guide for families* (Topics in autism series). Bethesda, MD: Woodbine House. (1-800-843-7323)

Hart, C.A. (1993). *A parent's guide to autism: Answers to the most common questions.* New York: Pocket Books. (1-800-223-2336)

Koegel, R.L., & Koegel, L.K. (Eds.). (1995). *Teaching children with autism: Strategies for initiating positive inter-actions and improving learning opportunities.* Baltimore: Paul H. Brookes Publishing Co. (1-800-638-3775)

Myles, B., & Simpson, R.L. (1998). *Asperger's syndrome: A guide for educators and parents.* Austin, TX: PRO-ED. (1-800-897-3202)

Powers, M.D. (Ed.). (1989). *Children with autism: A parent's guide.* Bethesda, MD: Woodbine House. (1-800-843-7323)

Schopler, E., Mesibov, G.B., & Kunce, L.J. (1998). *Asperger syndrome or high-functioning autism?* New York: Plenum Publishing Corp. (781-871-6600)

Siegel, B. (1996). *The world of the autistic child: Understanding and treating autistic spectrum disorders.* New York: Oxford University Press. (1-800-451-7556)

Volkmar, F.R. (Ed.). (1998). *Autism and pervasive developmental disorders.* New York: Cambridge University Press. (1-800-221-4512)

Williams, D. (1992). *Nobody nowhere: The extraordinary autobiography of an autistic.* New York: Times Books. (1-800-733-3000)

National Organizations

Aspen of America, Inc.
Post Office Box 2577
Jacksonville, Florida 32203-2577
Telephone: (904) 745-6741
E-mail: aspen@cybermax.net
World Wide Web site: http://www.asperger.org/

National clearinghouse of information on Asperger syndrome, high-functioning autism, nonverbal learning disabilities, hyperlexia, and pervasive developmental disorder not otherwise specified.

Autism Research Institute
4182 Adams Avenue
San Diego, California 92116
Fax: (619) 563-6840
World Wide Web site: http://www.autism.com/ari/

Information and referral center for parents and professionals; publishes quarterly newsletter, *Autism Research Review International.*

Autism Society of America (ASA)
7910 Woodmont Avenue, Suite 300
Bethesda, Maryland 20814-3015
Telephone: (800) 3-AUTISM, (301) 657-0881
Fax: (301) 657-0869
World Wide Web site: http://www.autism-society.org/

National organization with local chapters, provides advocacy and information about diagnosis and treament of autism for parents, family members, and professionals.

Autism Services Center
605 9th Street, Prichard Building
Post Office Box 507
Huntington, West Virginia 25710-0507
Telephone: (304) 525-8014
Fax: (304) 525-8026

Provides information and advocacy, training and consultation, and direct-care services locally (e.g., behavioral support in group homes).

Online Asperger Syndrome Information and Support (OASIS)
E-mail: bkirby@udel.edu
World Wide Web site: http://www.udel.edu/bkirby/asperger/

Information; referral; and support for individuals with Asperger syndrome, their families, and professionals.

Resources on Alternative Medicine

National Center for Complementary and Alternative Medicine, National Institutes of Health
NCCAM Clearinghouse
Post Office Box 8218
Silver Spring, Maryland 20907-8218
Telephone: (888) 644-6226, (888) 644-6226 (TDY/TTY)
Fax: (301) 495-4957
E-mail: nccam-info@nccam.nih.gov
World Wide Web site: http://nccam.nih.gov/

Provides information on research grants and programs and a search of alternative medicine databases and publishes quarterly newsletter, *Complementary and Alternative Medicine.*

The Richard and Hinda Rosenthal Center for Complementary and Alternative Medicine
College of Physicians and Surgeons
Columbia University
630 West 168th Street, Box 75
New York, New York 10032
Telephone: (212) 543-9550
Fax: (212) 543-2845
World Wide Web site: http://cpmcnet.columbia.edu/dept/rosenthal/

Provides a variety of information including legal and regulatory issues, courses at medical schools, research centers; provides linkages to other sites and professional associations, and directory of databases.

9

Visual and Hearing Impairments

Larry W. Desch

KEY COMPETENCIES

- Discuss the major genetic and nongenetic etiologies for visual and hearing impairments
- List the various conditions that can be associated with visual and hearing impairments, including disorders such as cerebral palsy
- List the various risk factors for the development of visual and hearing impairments, including premature birth
- Discuss the findings and implications of cortical blindness (i.e., central visual inattention) and delayed visual maturation, especially with regard to their possible relationship with other neurodevelopmental problems
- Describe the methods used to screen for visual and hearing impairments, and specify the various age groups and problems for which each of these methods is appropriate
- Describe the various medical and educational treatments for visual impairments and the role of the primary care physician in ensuring children's access to the appropriate specialists so that these treatments or therapies can be provided
- Describe the various medical treatment options for hearing impairments and the role of the primary care physician in ensuring children's access to appropriate specialists for evaluation and management
- Provide resource information and support to assist families in learning about and deciding on options for educational and related services for children with severe to profound hearing impairment

SECTION I: VISUAL IMPAIRMENTS

Definition of Visual Impairment

Visual impairment refers to decreased visual function that is due to disease, disorder, or loss of any of the structures of the visual system. Problems can exist with the outer layers of the eye itself (e.g., opacity of the cornea), the anterior chamber (e.g., glaucoma), the lens (e.g., congenital cataracts), the retina, the optic nerve, or optic radiations within the brain or with movement of the extraocular muscles. In addition, the cerebral visual cortex may be diseased or damaged, which interferes with the decoding and processing of the information received through the rest of the visual pathways.

Vision is important to the overall development of a child. Motor ability, coordination, learning ability, and behavior are closely linked to the quality of a child's vision. The impairment of vision, therefore,

is a disability that should be recognized as early as possible in order to facilitate learning and to lessen the impact of visual disability on the child's emotional and personal development. Many of the problems that cause visual impairment can be treated and/or remediated, and thus such secondary impairments and disabilities can be prevented.

Classification of Visual Impairments

Buncic (1987) described the following two categories of the lesser degrees of visual impairment, also known as being *partially sighted:* 1) individuals with *impaired vision* have impaired vision in either one or both eyes, even when wearing eyeglasses, and 2) individuals with *low vision* are not able to read ordinary newspaper print using eyeglasses with both eyes or have "no useful vision" in either eye. People who are partially sighted have visual acuity that is better than 20/200 without correction but worse than 20/70 with correction.

The term *blindness* refers to complete impairment or the most severe degree of impairment of vision (Bishop, 1991). The legal definition of *blindness* (e.g., for purposes of qualifying for federal programs such as Supplemental Security Income [SSI]) is determined by a visual acuity for distance vision of 20/200 or less in the best eye with the best correction *or* the widest diameter of a visual field in either eye being at an angle of less than 20°. This narrowed visual field is known as *tunnel vision.*

Prevalence of Visual Impairments

Visual impairments are not uncommon. It is estimated that 38 million people worldwide are blind and that another 110 million people have visual impairments, many of whom are at risk for blindness (Thylefors, Negrel, Pararajasegaram, & Dadzie, 1995). Most of these people are adults, and many have adult-onset diseases such as macular degeneration or cataracts. About 1 in 3,000 children have blindness, which is congenital in about half of the children, and another 30%–40% have loss of vision before age 1 year (Foster, 1988). Blindness is more common in select groups such as infants who are born extremely prematurely. In one study (Lorenz, Wooliever, Jetton, & Paneth, 1998), the incidence of blindness among infants born extremely prematurely was found to be 8%.

Although the overall prevalence of visual impairments is low, the presence of visual impairments in infants and children is frequently associated with multiple developmental disabilities (Menacker, 1993). Visual abnormalities occur in about 40% of children with multiple disabilities whose primary diagnosis is not related to vision (Warburg, Frederiksen, & Ratt-

Table 9.1. Etiology of visual impairments based on onset

Prenatal onset
- Developmental brain abnormalities
- Chorioretinitis from infections (viral infections or toxoplasmosis)
- Genetic syndromes (e.g., CHARGE association: congenital malformations of coloboma [absence of part of the eye or retina], heart disease, choanal atresia [nasal blockage], retarded growth, mild to profound mental retardation, genital anomalies, and ear anomalies and deafness; trisomy 13)

Perinatal onset
- Retinopathy of prematurity
- Infections (e.g., gonorrhea, herpes)
- Hypoxic ischemic encephalopathy
- Metabolic disorders

Postnatal onset
- Genetic syndromes (e.g., tuberous sclerosis)
- Trauma
- Infections (e.g., orbital cellulitis)
- Strabismus (not always associated with vision loss)
- Amblyopia

leff, 1979). In many children with neurologic impairments, such as children with cerebral palsy, the primary visual problem is strabismus that is due to the imbalance of extraocular muscles. Schenk-Rootlieb, van Nieuwenhuizen, van der Graaf, and colleagues (1992) demonstrated that more than 70% of children with cerebral palsy had significant visual acuity problems, some of which were detected by previous eye examinations.

Etiology of Visual Impairments

The causes of visual impairments, like those of many other disabilities, are related to prenatal, perinatal, or postnatal events or a combination of these (see Tables 9.1 and 9.2). The various etiologies can be subdivided further into genetic or environmental causation.

Prenatal and Perinatal Causes of Visual Impairment

Genetic Causes Nearly half of the congenital or progressive visual disorders in children are due to inherited disorders. These fall into three main categories: autosomal dominant, autosomal recessive, and sex-linked genetic disorders (McKusick, 1998). Some relatively common eye disorders such as colobomas, isolated congenital cataracts, or aniridia are inherited as autosomal dominant disorders. Congenital retinal aplasia (i.e., congenital amaurosis of Leber), which accounts for 10%–20% of the causes of blindness among children who are congenitally blind, and oculocutaneous albinism

are examples of autosomal recessive disorders. Sex-linked disorders that mainly cause visual problems are rare but include disorders such as certain types of Ehlers-Danlos syndrome, ocular albinism, and some forms of congenital cataracts. *The Causes of Blindness in Childhood: A Study of 776 Children with Severe Visual Handicaps,* the classic book on vision impairments by Fraser and Friedmann, noted that "preliminary estimates suggest that no less than 19 autosomal dominant, 30 autosomal recessive, and 10 sex-linked genetic entities played a part in causation of childhood blindness" (1967, p. 47). (For further information about these conditions, see the "Resources" section located in the Appendix at the end of this chapter.)

Chromosomal disorders can also include ocular defects as part of the presentation. Defects of the visual system are commonly seen with various trisomies and deletions. Children with Down syndrome (trisomy 21), for example, commonly develop cataracts (Roizen, Mets, & Blondis, 1994). Table 9.3 lists representative genetic conditions that may be associated with visual problems.

Infectious Causes for Visual Impairments Infectious agents are important causes of congenital visual impairment. The most common infectious etiologies are the toxoplasmosis, rubella, cytomegalovirus, and herpes simplex (TORCH) group of infectious agents (Bale, 1992). Until the early 1980s, rubella was the

Table 9.2. Etiology of visual impairments based on location

Peripheral eye
- Corneal clouding from infection or metabolic disorders
- Trauma
- Strabismus (not always associated with vision loss)

Anterior eye
- Cataracts of the lens from metabolic disorders
- Glaucoma
- Iris abnormalities (e.g., coloboma of the iris in CHARGE association: congenital malformations of coloboma [absence of part of the eye or retina], heart disease, choanal atresia [nasal blockage], retarded growth, mild to profound mental retardation, genital anomalies, and ear anomalies and deafness)

Posterior eye
- Retinopathy of prematurity
- Chorioretinitis (e.g., toxoplasmosis)
- Optic nerve (e.g., neuritis)

Brain (e.g., "cortical blindness")
- Trauma
- Hypoxic ischemic encephalopathy
- Developmental brain abnormalities (e.g., schizencephaly)
- Amblyopia

Table 9.3.   Selected genetic conditions that have associated eye problems

Eye abnormality	Genetic conditions	Associated findings
Cataracts	Osteogenesis imperfecta	Bone disease, blue sclera
	Galactosemia	Hypoglycemia, developmental delays, vomiting, diarrhea
	Lowe syndrome	Mental retardation, hypotonia, metabolic acidosis, rickets
	Pseudo and pseudo-pseudo hypoparathyroidism	Mental retardation, short stature, muscle weakness, convulsions
Dislocated lens	Homocystinuria	Tall stature, mental retardation, seizures, kyphoscoliosis
	Marfan syndrome	Tall stature, lax joints, cardiac disease
Iris changes	Trisomy 13, trisomy 18	Corneal changes, coloboma
	CHARGE association: Congenital malformations of coloboma, (absence of part of the eye or retina), heart disease, choanal atresia (nasal blockage), retarded growth, mild to profound mental retardation, genital anomalies, and ear anomalies and deafness	
Retinal changes	Albinism syndromes	Skin hypopigmentation, mental retardation (occasionally) and neurologic dysfunction
	Tuberous sclerosis	Seizures, mental retardation, depigmented iris
	Neuronal ceroid lipofuscinosis (Batten disease)	Progressive central nervous system (CNS) deterioration, blindness
Macular changes	Gangliosidosis (Tay-Sachs syndrome, Sandhoff syndrome)	Cherry-red macula, deafness, seizures, CNS deterioration
	Niemann-Pick syndrome (sphingomyelin lipidosis)	Cherry-red macula, hepatosplenomegaly, CNS deterioration
	Metachromatic leukodystrophy (sulfatide lipidosis)	Progressive motor disability, seizures, loss of deep tendon reflexes (DTRs)
Optic atrophy	Krabbe disease (globoid cell leukodystrophy)	Excessive irritability, progressive muscular rigidity, seizures

most common of all of the causes of visual impairment. This was due to the high incidence of chorioretinitis. Chorioretinitis is a severe destructive process of the retina that usually leads to blindness. During the most recent rubella epidemic (1964–1965), about 15% of children who were infected by intrauterine rubella developed significant visual impairments (Newcomb, 1977). Most of these children also had other significant disorders, such as hearing loss, which occurred in 90% of them (Fraser, 1976). Fortunately, large-scale vaccination programs reduced the significance of rubella as a cause of visual impairment in the last 2 decades of the 20th century. In some populations, however, such as individuals who have immigrated recently to the United States, vaccination coverage may be inadequate. Therefore, for these infants and children who are at risk for inadequate vaccination coverage, laboratory investigations to determine the etiology of a visual impairment should also include tests for rubella.

Chorioretinitis is also a frequent occurrence following congenital toxoplasmosis or cytomegalovirus (CMV) infections (Bale, 1992); congenital syphilis is less common than those two infections but can also cause eye problems such as keratitis of the cornea. All three of these diseases are rare, and there have been no successful vaccination programs developed as yet for any of these three infections. Toxoplasmosis, however, is treatable with antibiotics, which can be given both to the mother during her pregnancy and postnatally to the newborn. In some cases, spiramycin has been given to the mother during the pregnancy to prevent congenital infection. Treatment of the infant with congenital toxoplasmosis with pyrimethamine and sulfadiazine (given with folinic acid to prevent hematological problems) has been shown to be somewhat effective, especially in preventing or reducing the severity of the chorioretinitis (Guerina, Hsu, Meissner, et al., 1994).

Retinopathy of Prematurity A frequent perinatal cause of visual impairment related to perinatal events is *retinopathy of prematurity* (ROP). This disorder was previously called *retrolental fibroplasia* (RLF) and initially was thought to be caused exclusively by excessive oxygen administration. In the 1990s, however, a better understanding of the primary role that prematurity has in causation emerged. Oxygen administration does play a role in ROP, and careful monitoring of oxygen delivered to babies born prematurely decreased the incidence of ROP in the 1980s and 1990s. Oxygen excess and prematurity are not the only factors correlated with the development of ROP, though. Several studies (see, e.g., Flynn, 1992) have proved that term infants, without being given oxygen, can develop classic ROP on rare occasions. ROP is far more common, however, in infants who are born prematurely or are small for gestational age, especially those who require a high concentration of oxygen during the first few days of life. ROP occurs in almost 5% of babies who weigh less than 1,500 grams at birth. The incidence of ROP is higher (about 15%) for those infants who are extremely low birth weight (500–1,000 grams) (Keith & Doyle, 1995). Although the incidence of visual impairments that are due to ROP continues to be high, the incidence of blindness that is due to ROP is low, and only about 500 infants per year are blind as the direct result of ROP (Phelps, 1993).

Cortical Blindness (Central Visual Inattention) and Visual Maturational Delay On rare occasions, infectious diseases such as meningitis as well as hypoxic events or trauma may cause damage to the visual cortex and lead to cortical blindness. Damage to the visual cortex is usually associated with widespread cortical damage; thus, cortical blindness is usually associated with a number of other disabilities, including cerebral palsy and mental retardation (Williamson, Desmond, Andrew, & Hicks, 1987). Complete cortical blindness is unusual, and many infants and younger children show some limited visual recovery. For these reasons, careful assessment of these children's vision is required (Dutton, Ballantyne, Boyd, et al., 1996; Roland, Jan, Hill, & Wong, 1986).

On occasion, an infant may present with obvious visual impairments but experience improvements in visual function with time. This improvement can be due to what has been called *visual maturational delay*, a diagnosis that should be considered for any infant who is older than 2–3 months of age and has normal pupillary and oculomotor movements. There have been children who have had this disorder at an early age and subsequently experienced typical vision development without any evidence of long-term visual or developmental problems (Mellor & Fielder, 1980). Most of the time, however, visual maturational delay is but one feature of a significant neurodevelopmental disorder (Tresidder, Fielder, & Nicholson, 1990). The overall developmental prognosis for children who have cortical blindness or visual maturational delays is dependent in large part on the presence of other disabilities, the severity of the other disabilities, and the responsiveness of these children's disabilities to therapy.

Postnatal Causes of Visual Impairment Postnatal causes of visual impairment include strabismus and amblyopia, traumatic injury to the eyes or the brain, and a relatively few infectious diseases. Complications of infections such as orbital cellulitis or meningitis or Toxocara canis (visceral larva migrans) also can lead to blindness in rare cases. Connective tissue diseases such as Marfan syndrome can cause blindness secondary to the generalized problem of improper development of connective tissue. Postnatal causes of visual impairment are relatively uncommon; in Fraser and Friedmann's (1967) classic study, they accounted for only 11% of the total number of cases of blindness surveyed.

Strabismus and Amblyopia Probably the most important postnatal cause of visual impairment is imbalance of the extraocular muscles or problems with innervation of these muscles. Imbalance of the extraocular muscle movements then results in a condition called *strabismus*. Strabismus or misalignment of the eyes is common in children who have some type of central nervous system (CNS) disease; however, a significant number of children with strabismus have no other CNS disorder. Strabismus can also result from defects in the eye itself, such as cataracts or damaged retina; from poor visual acuity in one eye; or from actual problems of the extraocular muscles, such as congenital shortening. With strabismus, one eye may consistently turn inward (i.e., esotropia) or outward (i.e., exotropia), or both eyes may alternate in the direction in which they deviate (e.g., alternating esotropia). A tendency for an eye to turn inward or outward but not consistently is known as *esophoria* or *exophoria*, respectively.

Most untreated cases of strabismus result in *amblyopia*, which is defined as a progressive visual loss in an eye without any evidence of intraocular disease. Amblyopia is caused by a child's not using an eye because the eye cannot get a clear image on the retina and therefore cannot develop an adequate fixation reflex. If a child does not develop a fixation reflex by having normal bilateral vision by age 6–7 years, amblyopia is likely to occur and to be permanent, even though proper therapy may be initiated eventually. Amblyopia may be secondary to any event preventing the development of the visual fixation reflex, such as congenital cataract; strabismus; or any marked visual acuity discrepancy between the eyes, a disorder known as *anisometropia.* Amblyopia therefore can occur only in an immature CNS. In an older child who develops strabismus (i.e., extraocular muscle imbalance), strabismus would likely lead to double vision but without permanent CNS changes. The phenomenon of amblyopia represents one of several examples of serious developmental disorders that can result from problems occurring during what are known as *critical periods* (Daw, 1998). Chapter 2 addresses other areas of development that need to be assessed during these critical periods.

Strabismus causes amblyopia that is due to the loss of fusion or binocular vision. The loss of fusion or binocular vision usually results in one eye being used to a much lesser extent, and thus the visual pathways for that eye actually deteriorate. Strabismus does not always lead to loss in visual acuity in one eye, however. For example, vision loss does not usually occur with lateral deviation of one eye (i.e., exotropia) or with alternating strabismus in which each eye alternates with fixation. Visual acuity in these cases often is normal in each eye when the eyes are tested separately. Even though normal bilateral acuity may exist, the development of normal *stereoscopic* vision requires normal function and alignment of both eyes. In either of these two situations, strabismus results in the impairment of depth perception, which can lead to secondary problems such as motor incoordination.

Diagnosis and Evaluation

The proper assessment of visual disorders necessitates making a correct etiologic diagnosis of the visual impairment as well as determining whether the child has any associated conditions or problems secondary to the visual impairment. In the large majority of children with severe visual impairments, these requirements call for an interdisciplinary team approach to properly evaluate the child along with his or her parents. The team approach is often required because of the complicated nature of the child's delays and behaviors, which may include autistic-like behaviors or delay in motor skills (Jan, Groenveld, Sykanda, & Hoyt, 1987). For lesser degrees of visual impairment, the input of only one or a few profes-

Table 9.4.   Vision screening and referral for infants and toddlers

Complete medical and family history (i.e., risk factors)

A newborn examination, including
  General inspection of the eyes
  Visualization of the red reflex (reflection off the vascular retina)
  Evaluation of ocular motility

An evaluation, by age 3–4 months, of
  Eye fixation and following responses
  Muscle imbalance (Bruekner test, cover–uncover test)
  Pupillary responses and red reflex
  Corneal light reflex (Hirschberg)

A second examination with visual acuity testing by age 3 or 4 years (see criteria below)

Criteria for referral to pediatric ophthalmologist
Inability to fixate and/or follow by 4–6 months

A comparative difference in any way in the appearance of one eye from the other

Suspected strabismus (e.g., abnormal Hirschberg, Bruekner, or cover–uncover test)

An abnormal pupillary or red reflex

Adapted from American Academy of Pediatrics (AAP), Committee on Practice and Ambulatory Medicine (1986).

sionals may be required. Therefore, it is important for the primary care physician to do routine developmental surveillance and screening in order to make appropriate referrals based on the specific developmental or physical problems uncovered by these processes (see Chapter 2). Tables 9.4 and 9.5 outline the steps in vision screening and the criteria for referral to a pediatric ophthalmologist.

Although the exact risks for certain groups are somewhat uncertain and no agreed-upon risk criteria exist, some groups of infants and young children warrant careful follow-up by a primary care physician and early referral for suspected developmental problems. These infants and young children include infants who were born prematurely, infants and children with developmental delays or hearing impairments, those with neurologic problems such as seizures, and those who have a positive family history for vision problems.

General Inspection, Red Reflexes, and Ocular Motility

Cloudy Cornea   Glaucoma is a rare disorder in infants and children. Increased irritability, cloudy cornea, excessive tearing, and photophobia are common symptoms of glaucoma in infants and children. The cornea itself is usually large in childhood

Table 9.5.   Vision screening guidelines for children of preschool age and older

Ages and tested function	Recommended tests	Referral criteria
Ages 3–5 years		
Distance visual acuity	Snellen letters Snellen numbers Tumbling E's HOTV Picture tests Allen test LH test	Less than four of six correct on 20-feet line with either eye tested monocularly (i.e., less than 10/20 or 20/40) *or* Two-line difference between range (i.e., 10/12.5 and 10/20 [10-feet testing] or 20/25 and 20/40 [20-feet testing])
Ocular alignment	Unilateral cover test at 10 feet or 3 meters Random-dot-E stereoscope at 40 centimeters (630 seconds of arc)	Any eye movement *or* Less than four of six correct
Ages 6 years and older		
Distance visual acuity	Snellen letters Snellen numbers Tumbling E's HOTV Picture tests Allen test	Less than four of six correct on 15-feet line with either eye tested at 10 feet monocularly (i.e., less than 10/15 or 20/30) *or* Two-line difference between eyes, even within the passing range (i.e., 10/10 and 10/15 [10-feet testing] or 20/20 and 20/30 [20-feet testing])
Ocular alignment	Unilateral cover test at 10 feet or 3 meters Random-dot-E stereo test at 40 centimeters (630 seconds of arc)	Any eye movement *or* Less than four of six correct

Adapted from guidelines developed by the American Academy of Pediatrics (AAP) Section on Ophthalmology Executive Committee, 1991–1992 (Wasserman, Croft, & Brotherton, 1992).

Tests are listed in order of decreasing cognitive difficulty. The highest test that the child is capable of performing should be used. In general, the Tumbling E's test or the HOTV test should be used with children ages 3–5 years, and Snellen letters or numbers should be used with children 6 years and older.

Testing distance of 10 feet is recommended for all visual acuity tests (20 feet is better but is often impractical).

A line of figures is preferred to single figures (e.g., Snellen letters versus HOTV).

The nontested eye should be covered by an occluder held by the examiner or by an adhesive occlusive patch applied to the child's eye; the examiner must ensure that it is not possible for the child to look around the edges of the occluder with the nontested eye.

glaucoma, with the diameter of the cornea being greater than 12 millimeters. Glaucoma is often associated with other disorders such as neurofibromatosis, hydrocephalus, or the rubella syndrome.

"White Pupil"   "White pupil" (i.e., leukocoria) is an abnormal red reflex. Disorders causing this presentation include cataracts, colobomas, chorioretinitis, ROP, detached retina, and persistent primary vitreous. Occasionally, optic atrophy appears as white or pale optic discs and is associated with CNS disorders.

Nystagmus   Nystagmus is commonly caused by disorders of the eye itself, of the visual system, or of the CNS. The presence of nystagmus often indicates a serious pathology such as CNS disorders, bilateral cataracts, or severe chorioretinitis. A form of congenital inherited nystagmus exists in which vi-

sion is normal and no other neurologic abnormalities are present (Burde, Savino, & Trobe, 1992).

Fixation and Following   Observe whether the infant's eyes stare (i.e., fixate) at a stationary target (e.g., face, toy, light) and pursue (i.e., follow) a moving target at arm's length. If possible, test each eye separately with one eye occluded at a time.

Eye Alignment   As previously mentioned, strabismus is common in children with disabling conditions, and therefore careful examination for strabismus during the physical examination of an infant or a child with disabilities is indicated. The first step in screening for strabismus is a careful eye examination while observing for associated problems such as head tilt. If problems exist with the muscles of one eye, a child may have to hold his head at an angle in order to avoid double vision.

Screens for Ocular Misalignment (Strabismus)

1. *Corneal light reflex test (the Hirschberg test):* The Hirschberg test compares the position of corneal light reflection in both eyes. If the child's eyes are aligned, the light reflection appears symmetrically in both eyes; if the child's eyes are not aligned, one reflection is displaced. Sometimes having the infant or child fixate on a small toy held adjacent to the penlight is useful. Shine the penlight onto both corneas. Determine the child's eye alignment as follows:

Corneal light reflex test (the Hirschberg test)

Position of reflection	Ocular alignment
Symmetric (both central or nasal)	Normal
Outwardly displaced	Convergent misalignment (esotropia)
Inwardly displaced	Divergent misalignment (exotropia)
Downwardly displaced	Vertical misalignment (hypertropia)

2. *Cover–uncover test:* Have the child fixate on an eye chart or an object that is at least 5–10 feet away. For younger children, use an attention-getting device such as a toy, and, if necessary, have the parent talk to the child. Cover the child's right eye quickly with a whole hand or an occluder, and observe the child's left eye for a fixational movement. Uncover both of the child's eyes. Cover the child's left eye, and observe the child's right eye for a fixational movement. Sometimes children demonstrate their strabismus only while looking at objects in directions other than straight ahead; therefore, the target for the child's eyes' should be moved both horizontally and vertically during the cover–uncover test. Determine the child's eye alignment as follows:

Cover–uncover test

Eye movement	Ocular alignment
None	Normal
Outward	Esotropia
Inward	Exotropia
Downward or upward	Hypertropia

3. *Bruekner test:* The Bruekner test, which is done similarly to the Hirschberg test, is also helpful in detecting even small degrees of strabismus. In this test, the examiner looks through an ophthalmoscope at *both* of an infant's or young child's eyes simultaneously. By darkening the room and being at least 4–6 feet away, the examiner can look at the corneal light reflexes and the red reflexes (retinal reflections) of both eyes at the same time. Even small differences detected between the eyes during the Bruekner test warrant enough concern for a referral.

If strabismus is demonstrated, it is usually one of three types. The first type is *esotropia* or *esophoria* (the *-phoria* suffix indicates a latent tendency toward misalignment). Esophoria involves a convergent deviation or a turning in of the eyes. The second type, exotropia or exophoria, is a divergent deviation or turning outward of the eyes (commonly referred to as *walleye*). A third condition, called *alternating strabismus,* exists in which either eye is used for fixation and seeing while the other eye deviates. Amblyopia in this condition is rare because the eye that is being primarily used for vision alternates.

Assessment of Visual Acuity of Infants and Young Children Until the 1990s, it was believed that routine testing for visual acuity was not possible in children younger than age 3 years or in those with significant mental retardation secondary to their inability to cooperate. Several methodologies can be implemented to assess visual acuity in infants more completely. These methods include optokinetic nystagmus (OKN), preferential looking tests, and photo screening.

Optokinetic Nystagmus and Other Reflexes OKN can often be elicited easily, even in infants, by the use of a rotating drum with alternating light and dark stripes (Friendly, 1993; Lewis, Maurer, & Brent, 1989). OKN, however, obtains a high false positive rate because many infants and children do not focus long enough on the stripes for the nystagmus to be elicited. Other visual reflexes such as closure of the eyelids to a bright light should be present at birth. Later-appearing reflexes such as horizontal or vertical following or blinking to a visual threat (both occurring normally at about 3 months of age) should be done over time as the child's developmental progress is followed in the primary care office.

Preferential Looking Tests Preferential looking tests are an important advancement in the methodology of visual acuity testing of infants or other individuals who are nonverbal and minimally cooperative (e.g., those with mental retardation requiring extensive support). With most preferential looking tests, the child is shown a card with stripes or one that is blank. Studies (e.g., Shenk-Rootlieb et al., 1992; Teller, McDonald, Preston, et al., 1986) have demonstrated that infants and others who are nonverbal fixate preferentially on a striped pattern rather than on a less novel stimulus. Although other systems are available (e.g., Mackie, McCulloch, Sauners, et al., 1995), the most common preferential looking system is the Teller Acuity Card test (Teller et al., 1986). While performing the Teller Acuity Card test, the examiner uses cards with thinner and thinner stripe widths until the child's fixation response disappears. The use of preferential looking testing can therefore be used to estimate visual acuity, and an approximate Snellen notation value can be given. Although relatively easy to administer, a preferential looking test can overestimate a child's visual acuity in cases of amblyopia and sometimes can underestimate it in situations in which abnormal eye movements are present (e.g., with nystagmus) (Friendly, 1993). Considerable patience and skill are required, but preferential looking testing can also be quite useful in assessing the vision of children and adults who have severe cognitive or motor impairments (Hertz & Rosenberg, 1992).

Photo Screening   A technology emerged in the 1990s that improved on the usual methods of assessing infants' and children's eye alignment and to a lesser degree the estimation of their visual acuity. This procedure is called *photorefraction testing* and makes use of instant photography (i.e., by using a Polaroid camera). Photorefraction technology uses a camera and flash to photograph the red reflex in order to better evaluate the potential for an abnormality in the child's eyes. If a refractive error is found, then the equipment can also provide a close estimate of the degree of vision correction needed (i.e., using eyeglasses).

Photo screening methods can have a high degree of sensitivity and specificity for both strabismus and refractive errors. In one study, Ottar, Scott, and Holgado (1995) found a sensitivity of 82% for strabismus and 91% for refractive errors by using a photo screening method. The accuracy of the photo screening results varies widely, however, depending on who is doing the testing. In another study (Tong, Enke-Miyazaki, Bassin, et al., 1998), sensitivities were found in the range of 37%–88%, and the range of specificities was 40%–88%. Tong and colleagues stated that the differences noted "were not positively correlated with the ophthalmological knowledge" (1998, p. 861) of the examiners. Therefore, photo screening seems to be a promising method, but further refinement of photo screening methodology may be needed before it becomes accepted more widely as a way to perform universal visual screening of infants. Photo screening can be useful in screening infants, young children, or other children without verbal ability who may have risk factors for visual problems, such as premature birth (Gallo & Lennerstrand, 1991). Three commercial systems for photo screening are available in the United States: the MTI Photo Screener, the Welch-Allyn SureSight, and VisiScreen OSS-C (for the addresses of the companies that manufacture these

screening systems, see the "Resources" section of the Appendix at the end of this chapter). Similar systems are available in other countries (Cooper, Bowling, Hall, et al., 1996; Schworm, Kau, Reindl, et al., 1997).

Assessment of Visual Acuity for Preschool-Age and Older Children   For older children, especially those who are developing typically, more useful and specific tests of visual acuity are available (see Table 9.5). It is usually helpful to have parents practice these tests with their children at home before the tests are conducted in the office (Wasserman et al., 1992). With school-age children, the primary care physician may need only ensure that accurate and appropriate screenings are taking place in the school system.

HOTV and Allen Tests   Charts such as the HOTV letter-matching test (Jenkins, Prager, Mazow, et al., 1983) or the Allen Picture Test of Visual Acuity (Allen, 1957) can readily be used with most preschool children. The HOTV test uses a chart on the wall and a small card both with the letters *H, O, T,* and *V* on them. Because the wall chart letters get progressively smaller and the child points to matching letters on his or her card, eventually a level of acuity can be estimated. Testing by using the Allen Picture Cards is conducted as follows: The child is asked to identify standard pictures (e.g., house, telephone) of a standardized size verbally while standing at a distance of 10 or—ideally—20 feet. Measurement is identical to that used in Snellen testing (see the subsection that immediately follows).

Snellen Illiterate E Test (Tumbling E's)   The Snellen Illiterate E ("Tumbling E's") chart can also be used successfully with children, especially those with no physical disabilities, beginning at about age 3 years; but it may require some training of the child with regard to how to respond during the test. The procedure for Tumbling E's is as follows: The child is asked to identify (by hand gestures or, preferably, by using gestures with both arms) the orientation of E's of diminishing size and at various orientations. The acuity estimation is carried out in the same manner as that used with Snellen testing.

Some children, even at age 5 or 6 years, may have difficulty with the Tumbling E's test, especially with the E's that face left and right. This difficulty is similar to the problems that young children have at this age with backward writing of letters and numbers. Using both arms to indicate the direction of the E's seems to lead to more accurate results, especially when the test is practiced at home. Prevent Blindness America makes available home testing kits for parents to use (see the Appendix at the end of this chapter for contact information for this organization). By the time children are in the second grade, most can respond accurately when using a Snellen letter or number chart (see the subsection immediately following).

Snellen Test at a Distance   Testing with a Snellen chart (numbers or letters) at a distance of 20 feet is the "gold standard" and arguably the most accurate method of vision testing of school-age children. Acuity is expressed by a numerator and a denominator, with the numerator being the testing distance (20 feet, or 6 meters) and the denominator being the smallest line of print the child can read at that testing distance. A person with a 20/60 visual acuity can see at a distance of 20 feet what a person with normal acuity can see from a distance of 60 feet.

The child should stand at a designated distance (again, ideally 20 feet) from a well-illuminated Snellen chart. Each eye should be tested separately with the child wearing his or her eyeglasses or contact lenses when applicable. For each eye, record the smallest line of Snellen print that the child can read. If most letters or numbers on a line are identified correctly, give the child credit for reading that line.

If the child's visual acuity is poorer than seeing the largest Snellen letter (either 20/200 or 20/400), the child should continually be moved closer to the Snellen chart as needed until he or she is able to read the largest symbol on the chart correctly. If the viewing distance is 5 feet, the child's visual acuity is recorded as 5/200 or 5/400, depending on the size of the largest symbol. If the child still cannot see the largest letter on the chart at a viewing distance of 3 feet, a descriptive estimation of the visual impairment can be made by one of the following methods, listed in order of decreasing visual function: *counting fingers,* meaning that the child can count fingers at a specified distance that is generally measured between 1 and 5 feet; *hand movements,* meaning that the child can distinguish horizontal from vertical hand motions at a distance of 1 foot; and *light perception,* meaning that the child can see a bright light shined directly into the eye.

In addition to the routine vision screening tests for children, several additional tests can be done with only a minimal increase in time and expense. Tests for color vision can be done in older preschool children. Tests for stereoscopic vision using random dot stereograms or specialized eyeglasses with holographic prints that can be used with older children are available as well (Simons, 1996).

If the vision assessment finds evidence of visual acuity problems, the National Society for the Prevention of Blindness (1973) has recommended that a referral to an ophthalmologist be made in the following situations:

- Vision poorer than 20/50 in children younger than 3 years old
- Vision poorer than 20/40 in children older than 4 years of age
- Any difference in visual acuity between the two eyes if this finding is confirmed twice, even if the scores for the individual eyes are within the passing range (This finding might indicate a condition of amblyopia.)

Children with any abnormal physical findings such as white pupil (i.e., leukocoria) or strabismus should also be referred to an ophthalmologist immediately.

Diagnostic Testing   Beyond routine assessment, ophthalmologists commonly employ two additional techniques to evaluate the visual system: visual evoked potentials (VEPs) and electroretinograms (ERGs). VEPs are often used in assessing infants who have congenital cataracts, are suspected of blindness, or have severe strabismus. ERGs are used when a child is suspected of having a visual impairment in which a retinal disorder is suspected or when there is a family history of retinal dystrophy. Using both of these techniques can determine whether the problem is in the eye itself, in the optic nerve, or in the brain. VEPs are also used to assess the presence of increased intracranial pressure (Desch, 1998; York, 1986).

Associated Medical and Behavior Problems

For children who have been diagnosed with visual impairments, the child's physician can play an important role by assessing the child for any of the disabilities that may be associated with visual impairments, including hearing impairments (see Section II of this chapter). The primary care physician needs to evaluate growth and development carefully (see Chapters 2 and 4) and assess for minor dysmorphic features (see Chapter 5). For example, infants who are born prematurely who develop ROP may also have neuromotor problems such as cerebral palsy; with these infants, careful evaluation for any abnormal motor findings is indicated. If cerebral palsy is diagnosed, usually it is the spastic diplegic type because both this type of cerebral palsy and ROP are related to having been born prematurely. Often, brain imaging studies (e.g., a magnetic resonance imaging [MRI] scan) are indicated to evaluate for CNS damage or disorders such as septo-optic dysplasia.

The opposite also holds true. When examining infants who are demonstrating neuromotor delays or problems, the physician should be aware that these infants are at a significant risk for having visual impairments. Optic atrophy or optic nerve hypoplasia is commonly seen in children with the spastic quadriplegic type of cerebral palsy, presumably because of the severe CNS damage that these children have sustained (Menaker, 1993). In addition, some infants who have primary or secondary developmental disorders of the brain can exhibit a visual maturational delay. This condition should be diagnosed as early as possible because starting early intervention (EI) services for these infants and young children may help to alleviate potential further problems that might occur if visual maturational delay went undetected.

Children who are known to have severely impaired vision often exhibit unusual stereotypic behaviors called *blindisms*. These behaviors, such as waving of the hands, rocking, and other mannerisms, are believed to be a type of self-stimulatory activity (Dekker & Koole, 1992). Similar types of behavior are sometimes also seen in individuals with autism or in children with mental retardation requiring extensive support, and the behaviors are not usually the result of any visual impairment. Certain mannerisms, however, such as eye pressing and prolonged light gazing, seem more common in children with visual impairments.

Jan, Friedman, McCormick, and colleagues (1983) demonstrated that children with bilateral optic nerve disorders do not demonstrate eye-pressing behavior, whereas those with retinal disorders tend to exhibit frequent eye-pressing stimulatory behavior. They hypothesized that self-stimulation occurs when the "demand of the brain for meaningful information is not adequately met" (1983, p. 762). During the examination of a child with visual impairment, assessment of these behaviors should detail the frequency and ease of elimination of these behaviors by substituting other developmentally appropriate activities. These observations can be helpful when designing therapeutic or EI programs.

Because adequate vision is so important to a child's ideal developmental progress, assessment of intelligence and learning abilities of children with visual impairments should be done only when properly validated instruments can be used. Investigators have demonstrated that the average IQ scores of children with visual impairments are slightly lower than those of children without disabilities (Warburg, 1983; Warburg, Fredericksen, & Rattleff, 1979). These findings are controversial, however, because they generally used testing instruments that are based on the performance of children who have

normal vision. Educators of children with visual impairments are an important resource for determining whether a given education or intellectual assessment tool can or should be used in intelligence testing of children with visual impairments. The etiology for the child's visual impairment is also important to consider when evaluating the child's intellectual capability (see the Appendix at the end of this chapter for a list of representative tests that have been used with children who have visual impairments). Wodrich (1997) described several psychological tests that are appropriate to use in testing children with visual problems.

Medical and Surgical Management
When a visual disorder is suspected, the primary responsibility of the primary care office is prompt referral to a pediatric ophthalmologist. If the diagnosis of a visual disorder is made early, then medical treatment can often preserve the best possible vision in one or both of the child's eyes. Early treatment of strabismus, for example, can prevent amblyopia (Smith, Thompson, Woodruff, & Hiscox, 1995). Initial treatment for strabismus frequently consists of patching the stronger eye to force the muscles of the weaker eye into proper alignment. The eye patch is usually taped over the eye but can be attached to the child's eyeglasses. A possible alternative is for the child to wear eyeglasses on which one lens is blocked somewhat (e.g., by using translucent but not transparent tape). This method is less effective, because in many cases the child can peer around the edges of the eyeglasses. Botulinum toxins have occasionally been used to help treat strabismus by paralyzing extraocular mucles (Rayner, Hollick, & Lee, 1999). Also, the use of atropine drops in the better eye to help strengthen the weaker eye has been successful in improving some strabismus (Foley-Nolan, McCann, & O'Keefe, 1997).

Sometimes surgical treatment for strabismus is necessary. This treatment involves surgically altering the length of some of the extraocular muscles. The specific goals for surgical treatment of strabismus are to allow the development of good binocular vision, fusion, and stereoscopic depth perception. Occasionally, however, strabismus can occur as a result of a nonremedial defect such as an optic nerve lesion. Surgery for strabismus can be done in those situations, but it is done essentially for cosmetic reasons only.

Medical management of visual impairments should be pursued in all children, despite the presence of other disabilities such as severe mental retardation (requiring extensive support) (Woodruff, Hiscox, Thompson, et al., 1994). Vision is such an important factor in learning that serious secondary problems result if vision impairments are not treated or are remediated simply because of the presence of other developmental disabilities such as cerebral palsy or severe mental retardation (requiring extensive support). In these situations, the child's degree of mental retardation likely could worsen secondary to the inappropriate management of a visual impairment.

In addition to active treatment of vision impairment, prevention of further vision loss is also important. If the vision in one eye is significantly worse than in the opposite eye, an important preventive measure is to ensure the protection of the less involved or more normal eye. Children with this diagnosis should be followed closely by a pediatric ophthalmologist and, more important, should wear a protective lens over the better eye even if that lens has no corrective ability. The main purpose of the lens in such cases is to protect the good eye from possible trauma.

Educational and Therapeutic Management

In caring for children with significant visual impairments, it is important to address three limitations that result from the visual impairment and then to develop therapeutic and educational interventions to alleviate these three limitations:

1. The child will have limited visual experiences because the visual sense is impaired.
2. The child will experience limitations in the ability to move about unassisted.
3. The child will experience limitations in his or her ability to control and interact with his or her environment.

As soon as a child's visual impairment is diagnosed, which optimally occurs within the first year of life, remediation should be instituted as soon as possible to work on the three areas just listed. Research has shown that intellectual impairment, motor or coordination disability, psychopathology, and abnormal behavior are not necessarily features associated with all children with visual impairments (Moller, 1993; Simeonsson, Chen, & Hu, 1995). These secondary problems may occur but are often preventable or ameliorable if adequate interventions are instituted early.

Research has shown, for example, that some delays in the motor development of children with visual impairments are possible but that these delays can be minimized with proper therapy (Moller,

1993). Walking and crawling are often delayed because of the child's deficiencies in early visual-motor coordination and by some degree of fear that may be present (Cass, Sonkesen, & McConachie, 1994). The early mobility of children with visual impairments is therefore decreased, thereby causing further and longer-lasting delays in motor development. Cass and colleagues' research and other studies, however, have shown that children with visual impairments are capable of learning and developing spatial orientation and spatial perception. These children can be assisted to learn ways of using other feedback modalities such as cutaneous, thermal, time sense, and muscular memory to help them with their independent mobility. Early intervention with physical therapy, therefore, is indicated to assist with these children's transitions and overall gross motor development.

Language development, especially that which occurs beyond 2 years of age, also can be delayed because of the child's lack of association between certain words and what is *not* seen in the environment because of the vision loss. Language delays can be associated with later problems in learning. Lowenfeld (1980) reported that a slower rate of learning school-related knowledge appears to exist in this population. In general, blind children are linguistically about 2 years behind children without visual impairments. Part of this delay may be due to the fact that it takes three to four times longer to learn by reading braille than by reading printed material.

Important changes have occurred in the education of children with visual impairments during the 1990s. Previously, these children were served in institutional facilities for the blind. Self-contained classrooms for children with even severe visual impairments have been developed for general public schools, with as much inclusion with students without disabilities as feasible occurring in some parts of the United States. Although full inclusion has not yet been realized, this phenomenon is becoming increasingly more common and has achieved some degree of success thus far. Physicians who are able to remain informed about such school inclusion programs in their communities can often be quite assistive to parents in obtaining adequate education programs for children with visual impairments.

In the 1990s, considerable innovations and improvements in technology occurred, such that many children with low vision and children who are blind are able to participate in many if not most general classroom activities alongside their peers without disabilities. In particular, the many improvements in computers, such as text-to-speech conversion capabilities and low-vision optical and video aids, have enabled children with low vision and children who are blind to expand their learning beyond the traditional braille books and audiotapes. Most children with visual impairments need considerable assistance in learning to use these forms of equipment and classroom modifications to make the devices and aids as functional as possible for these children in a general classroom setting. (For a listing of resources that can be useful in making modifications to a general classroom curriculum or to assist in the development of an appropriate individualized education program [IEP], please see the "Readings" heading in the "Resources" section of the Appendix at the end of this chapter.)

As noted previously, it is important that diagnosis and remediation be carried out as soon as possible upon suspicion that an infant or child has a visual impairment. The first 2–3 years of life is a critical period for helping the child with visual impairment to achieve his or her maximum potential. Parents should be assisted by appropriate professionals' working with their child. Counseling should be provided when the parents are having difficulty coping with their child's problems. Specialists in EI programs for infants and children with visual impairments are becoming more available and can offer parents considerable help by beginning the remediation process for these infants and later with helping them make the transition to school. Organizations that work with individuals who are blind and state departments of education are the best resources to contact for information about infant stimulation programs (see the Appendix at the end of this chapter). Many of these organizations and programs have also expanded to address the special needs of children who have both visual impairment and multiple disabilities.

SECTION II: HEARING IMPAIRMENTS

Definition of Hearing Impairment

Hearing impairment is a general term that includes many different disorders and degrees of hearing loss. The hearing impairment may result from *conductive* hearing loss, *sensorineural* hearing loss, or a combination of both. A conductive hearing loss usually involves the lower sound frequencies and is due to problems related to the middle ear. This type of hearing loss could be the result of fluid in the middle ear, tympanic membrane (TM) dysfunction, or problems related to the ossicles. Some forms of conductive hearing loss are permanent (e.g., absence of middle-ear structures), but most are temporary (e.g., middle-ear effusion). Sensorineural hearing loss

usually involves a higher-frequency hearing loss, is usually permanent, and is sometimes progressive, both in degree and in extent. This kind of hearing loss is due to problems with the cochlea; the eighth cranial nerve; or, rarely, the auditory portions of the brain. Conditions may also exist in which both conductive and sensorineural hearing loss are present. This general description of hearing impairment is incomplete because the degree of hearing loss is often what is most important. As with other medical terms that are subjective, professionals disagree with regard to the classification of the degree of hearing impairment.

Classification of Hearing Impairments

The U.S. Health, Education, and Welfare Advisory Committee on the Education of the Deaf listed three degrees of hearing impairment (Berg & Fletcher, 1970). The following are functional definitions that are based on the degree of an individual's ability to hear and understand ordinary speech:

- *Hard of hearing:* People who are classified as hard of hearing usually have a moderate hearing loss (40- to 70-decibel loss) and usually require hearing aids or other amplification to understand speech. As children, they are able to attend school with children without hearing impairments but frequently require support services.

- *Partially hearing:* People who are classified as partially hearing have a severe hearing loss (70- to 90-decibel loss) such that as children they usually require special education with prolonged auditory training, along with specialized speech-language and communication skills training. These individuals also benefit from hearing aids and other amplification methods.

- *Deaf:* The deaf classification usually refers to people who have profound bilateral hearing loss (greater than 90-decibel loss) and depend totally on their vision or other senses for learning language and communication. Usually, as children, deaf people have such severe degrees of hearing loss that amplification, even though often useful for other purposes (e.g., some awareness of sounds), may be of little use in helping them understand or develop spoken language.

Another method of classifying hearing impairments in children is to determine the age of onset of the hearing loss (Schein & Delk, 1974). Three categories are used in this method of classifying hearing loss:

- *Prelingual:* Prelingual hearing loss occurs prior to the development of speech-language ability.

- *Prevocational:* Prevocational hearing loss starts after age 2–3 years and before the onset of the individual's work experience (usually prior to 18 or 19 years of age).
- *Late-onset:* A late-onset hearing impairment occurs in older adolescents or adults.

The latter classification system is useful in helping to address the individual's ultimate prognosis. If a child has an early-onset (i.e., prelingual) hearing loss of severe degree, the child is likely to have problems with speech-language development and to need an educational placement in a specialized classroom or a school for the deaf. In addition, these children, as adults, often have difficulty in competing successfully in many vocational environments. With this categorization as well as with the others, it is important to recognize that the individual's hearing loss may not be unchanging. It is extremely important, though not easy, to recognize progressive hearing loss (Levi, Tell, & Feinwesser, 1993).

Prevalence of Hearing Impairments

The incidence and prevalence rates of hearing impairments among the general population, as one might imagine, vary depending on the classification system and definitions that are used (Herrgard, Karjalainen, Martikainen, & Heinonen, 1995). One study (Kvaerner & Arnesen, 1994) in Norway, a country with an excellent medical tracking system, found that approximately 1 in 1,000 infants had a congenital severe to profound hearing loss (mostly sensorineural loss) and that this prevalence is doubled by childhood age, primarily because of an increase in conductive hearing loss. A study (Holt & Hotton, 1994) done in the United States reported that approximately 1.8% of children younger than 18 years of age have a hearing impairment, a figure that combined both sensorineural and conductive loss. This latter incidence rate may be somewhat low because it may not include those children who have a unilateral but clinically significant hearing loss (Brookhouser, Worthington, & Kelly, 1991).

Etiology of Hearing Impairments

A review of the etiology of hearing impairments in children can be done best by discussing the causes that occur during prenatal, perinatal, or postnatal development. Sensorineural hearing loss, for example, can be divided into prenatal, perinatal, or postnatal onset and into genetic and nongenetic causes (Chan, 1994), as follows:

Prenatal causes
- Inherited conditions (most common)
- Viral infections (e.g., CMV, rubella)

Perinatal causes
- Hypoxic ischemic encephalopathy (HIE)
- Hyperbilirubinemia
- Infections (primarily meningitis)
- Ototoxic drugs (e.g., furosemide, aminoglycosides)

Postnatal causes
- Infections (primarily meningitis)
- Recurrent, prolonged otitis media with effusion
- Ototoxic drugs
- Inherited conditions (i.e., progressive disorders)

Prenatal Causes Fraser (1976) found that among children living in schools for the deaf, approximately 40%–60% had deafness that had a genetic etiology. Of these inherited conditions, about 50% were autosomal recessive, 25% were autosomal dominant, and 2% were X-linked. The remainder had one of a variety of syndromic genetic conditions associated with other birth defects. Researchers in the United States (e.g., Schein & Delk, 1974) have also demonstrated inherited factors to be important and have noted that the risk of deafness for offspring when both parents are congenitally deaf is four times greater than when only one parent is congenitally deaf.

Although the continuing improvements in genetic evaluation methods make it difficult to assign a definite number, approximately 80% of children who inherit sensorineural hearing impairment do so as an autosomal recessive disorder (McKusick, 1998). In general, autosomal recessive hearing loss is nonsyndromic and therefore is not associated with any other birth defects. Approximately 50% of nonsyndromic childhood recessive hearing loss is caused by various mutations in a gene on chromosome 13, the connexin 26 (Cx26) gene (*GJB2*), with a carrier rate for these mutations being nearly 3% (Kelley, Harris, Comer, et al., 1998). Although these mutations usually lead to severe or profound sensorineural hearing loss, there is a wide variation in the degree of loss from mild/moderate to profound, even within a single family, which suggests that other factors, including environmental ones, may serve to modify the effects of the mutations. Despite this variability in presentation, it has been recommended that all newborns who have hearing loss have testing done for the Cx26 mutations (Cohn, Kelley, Fowler, et al., 1999). If the testing finds mutations present, a high risk for severe to profound hearing impairments is indicated. Aggressive therapies such as cochlear implants may therefore be considered (see discussion under the "Medical Management of Sensorineural Hearing Loss" heading in this chapter). Table 9.6 describes some of the more common genetic conditions related to hearing impairment.

The prenatal environmental causes of congenital deafness are nearly as important as the genetic causes. Several environmental toxins, such as mercury compounds, are known to cause hearing loss in infants if the mother is exposed to them during her pregnancy; however, prenatal infections are the principal etiologic factors. Until 1980, congenital rubella infection was the most common acquired cause of severe sensorineural hearing loss. The last true rubella epidemic in the United States occurred in 1964–1965 and accounted for nearly half of the total number of cases of hearing impairment in children born during those years (Bale, 1992). Since the advent of routine rubella vaccination of children, the cycles of rubella epidemics have been eliminated; therefore, rubella is much less a threat to the developing fetus in most countries.

Since 1990, there has been increasing recognition that another viral agent, CMV, can also damage the infant's developing auditory system. In its most well-recognized form, cytomegalic inclusion disease, CMV infection of the fetus causes widespread neurologic and hematologic problems as well as sensorineural hearing loss. Those infants who survive usually have severe hearing impairments (Hanshaw, 1994). Probably more important, however, are those cases of "asymptomatic" CMV infection, in which the newborn does not display the classic picture of cytomegalic inclusion disease but in whom neurologic problems such as sensorineural hearing loss may develop months and sometimes 1 year or more after birth (Schildroth, 1994). Limited research data indicate that sensorineural hearing loss occurs in about 10% of these infants who are asymptomatic and that their hearing loss may be progressive (Williamson, Demmer, & Percy, 1992). Asymptomatic CMV infections appear to occur 10 times more often than the severe forms of CMV infection (Hanshaw, 1994).

Perinatal Causes With improvements in newborn intensive care and increasing survival of low birth weight infants, the relative importance of perinatal factors as causes of hearing impairment has

Table 9.6. Selected genetic disorders associated with hearing impairment

Examples of syndromes	Inheritance pattern	Type of hearing loss	Other findings
Down syndrome	Chromosomal	Conductive, occasionally sensorineural	Small auricles, narrow ear canals, high incidence of middle-ear infections
Trisomy 13, trisomy 18	Chromosomal	Sensorineural, (assumed) stable	Severe central nervous system (CNS) malformations
Treacher-Collins syndrome	Autosomal dominant	Conductive or mixed	Micrognathia, deformed auricles, defects of ear canal and middle ear
Waardenburg syndrome	Autosomal dominant	Sensorineural, stable	Unusual facial appearance, irises of different colors, white forelock, absent organ of Corti
Laurence-Moon-Biedle syndrome	Autosomal recessive	Sensorineural, progressive	Retinitis pigmentosa, mental retardation, obesity, extra fingers or toes
Usher syndrome	Autosomal recessive	Sensorineural, progressive in Usher type III	Retinitis pigmentosa; CNS effects, including vertigo, loss of smell, mental retardation, epilepsy; half have psychosis
CHARGE association: Congenital malformations of coloboma (absence of part of the eye or retina), heart disease, choanal atresia (nasal blockage), retarded growth, mild to profound mental retardation, genital anomalies, and ear anomalies and deafness	Assumed multifactorial	Mixed, progressive	Eye, gastrointestinal, and other malformations

been increasing. Adverse perinatal events are estimated to be responsible for about 10%–20% of cases of hearing loss in children (Fraser, 1976). Profound congenital deafness occurs in about .1% of low-risk pregnancies and in about 1.7% (approximately 20 times as commonly) of high-risk pregnancies (Simmons, 1980). Significant hypoxic events, sepsis, neonatal meningitis, or the toxic effects of furosemide or aminoglycoside antibiotics can result in significant sensorineural hearing impairment (Chan, 1994). Perinatal anoxic events such as those seen with premature babies also are potential causes of CNS damage, including damage to the auditory system. Children with hearing loss that is due to hypoxic damage are likely to have other evidence of CNS damage, such as seizure disorders or cerebral palsy.

Another well-known cause of hearing loss is hyperbilirubinemia, which at very high levels causes damage to the brain known as *kernicterus.* Although it is well accepted that high bilirubin levels, especially in babies born prematurely, can lead to auditory damage, whether any threshold values exist in which damage is certain to occur is unclear. Some changes in the evoked response audiometric measures (e.g., brainstem auditory evoked response audiometry [BAER]) have been found beginning at serum bilirubin levels of 20–22 milligrams per deciliter. These effects were reversible with a decrease in serum levels, such as with the use of exchange transfusions (Nwaesei, 1984). The changes in BAER that are due to hyperbilirubinemia are mainly transient; however, one study (Funato, Teraoka, Tamai, & Shimida, 1996) suggested that a delay in the improvement of the abnormalities seen might prove useful in predicting a chronic neurologic problem. More studies of this type clearly are needed to better assess the risk to the developing auditory system of high bilirubin levels. What has become better recognized is that frequently certain events or problems need to occur together in order for hyperbilirubinemia to lead to CNS damage. These issues include situations such as acidosis, certain medications that displace bilirubin, and extremes of gestational age.

Postnatal Causes

Conductive Hearing Loss Hearing impairments that are due to conductive losses are most likely to occur in the postnatal and early childhood period. Middle-ear effusions are the major cause of conductive hearing losses in this period and are most common during the first 2 years of life (Shapiro & Bluestone, 1995). Studies (see, e.g., Eimas & Kavanagh, 1986) have suggested that chronic conductive hearing loss that is due to middle-ear disease is related to language impairment, auditory processing problems, and learning disabilities. Methodologic problems in many of these studies make their interpretation difficult, however. Paradise (1981) published an extensive review on this subject that has stood the test of time. Certain groups of children have an increased risk for conductive hearing loss. For example, children who have Down syndrome are particularly susceptible to experiencing conductive hearing loss, possibly because of their skull shape and secondary eustachian tube dysfunction. A study (Roizen, Wolters, Nicol, & Blondis, 1993) of adults who have Down syndrome found that between 50% and 75% of the individuals studied had some degree of hearing impairment. Children who have cleft palates also have a higher incidence of conductive hearing loss (Muntz, 1993).

Sensorineural Hearing Loss Sensorineural hearing loss can occur as a result of factors arising in the postnatal or childhood period. The principal factors causing sensorineural hearing loss are infectious etiologies such as meningitis or encephalitis; but some of the medications used in treating such infections, such as aminoglycosides, are also ototoxic. The addition of steroids to the usual treatment for meningitis (especially that due to Hemophilus influenza), if given very early in the course of the illness, has decreased the incidence of later hearing loss significantly. Despite this potential treatment, Fortnum and Davis (1993) demonstrated in a long-term follow-up study that up to 10% of children who had a previously diagnosed bacterial meningitis develop a significant sensorineural hearing loss that is due to damage to the cochlea. For children with many of the inherited conditions that cause deafness, hearing impairment begins later in childhood or in young adulthood. Careful review of the child's family history, coupled with proper evaluation and follow-up, is therefore necessary to identify individuals with inherited hearing impairments.

Diagnosis and Evaluation

Early identification of the presence and etiology of a hearing impairment is important, for the following reasons:

- Proper diagnosis leads to more timely and more useful genetic counseling.
- The exact diagnosis can lead to early identification of problems associated with the condition.
- A specific diagnosis should lead to earlier and more appropriate treatment and services.

In a study by Yoshinaga-Itano, Sedey, Coulter, and Mehl (1998), children whose hearing loss was identified before 6 months of age demonstrated significantly better language scores than children whose hearing loss was identified after 6 months of age. The infants' language differences were independent of test age, communication mode, degree of hearing loss, or the family's socioeconomic status. The study's authors concluded that early identification and early intervention must be considered the potential explanation for the language advantage in the group identified prior to 6 months of age. In addition, it is essential that *any* hearing loss, even mild conductive hearing loss, be detected early in children who have other disabling conditions. An undiagnosed hearing loss unnecessarily compounds the developmental and behavioral difficulties of a child with mental retardation or other disabilities.

Early Identification   The primary purpose of routine early assessments of hearing is to detect the infant's hearing impairment at the earliest possible age. Early assessment and diagnosis are the first crucial steps that should lead to early treatment or remediation of the child's hearing impairment. Adequate hearing is directly related to the child's development of language. A child's language skills are likely to be impaired permanently if the child does not have adequate hearing during the first 2 years of life (a "critical period"), even if the child's hearing impairment is remedied completely later. The following are methods for early identification of infants' hearing loss:

- Use of risk factors ("at-risk criteria")
- Electrophysiologic testing (screening or diagnostic) of those infants with an identified risk factor
- Universal newborn hearing screening, followed by diagnostic testing of those with positive screenings

Use of Risk Factors   The most common assessment method begins with a determination of the presence or absence of a number of risk factors for developing hearing loss, called a *prescreening technique,* which is a process that should occur shortly after birth for every newborn and in some cases prior to the mother's pregnancy. The Joint Committee on Infant Hearing of the American Academy of Pediatrics (AAP; 1995) published a list of risk criteria and made recommendations with regard to assessment of newborns' hearing (see Table 9.7).

Direct referral to an experienced pediatric audiologist or possibly to a neonatal intensive care follow-up program should be made if an infant

meets one or more of the AAP criteria. The diagnostic evaluation can be accomplished in children older than 6 months of age by assessing their behavioral responses to sounds (i.e., behavioral observation audiometry) or in younger infants or those with developmental delays by determination of electrophysiologic responses (i.e., evoked potential audiometry). These diagnostic methods are discussed later in this chapter under the "Hearing Screening of Older Infants and Children" heading. Use of risk criteria is a good prescreening tool because many infants who meet one or more of these criteria actually are diagnosed after further assessments as having significant hearing impairment. Only about 50% of children found to have a hearing loss at age 2–3 years, however, have one of these risk criteria present (Brookhouser, 1996).

Electrophysiologic Testing of Infants Identified by Risk Factors   Electrophysiologic testing is the methodology that is used most widely; however, great variations in the procedures used for audiologic testing exist. An infant may be referred for a diagnostic test (e.g., BAER with sedation), or an electrophysiologic screening test such as an automated BAER (e.g., ALGO), or EOAE testing. In addition, many neonatal intensive care units (NICUs) have expanded the list of risk factors to include any infant who spends 2 or more days in the NICU. If an NICU uses an expanded list of risk criteria, the audiologic evaluation is likely to be an electrophysiologic screening test.

Universal Newborn Hearing Screening   Universal newborn hearing screening of infants in the first 1–2 days of life, performed while the newborn is still in the birth hospital, was recommended in 1993 by a panel of experts at a consensus conference convened by the National Institutes of Health (NIH) (AAP, Joint Committee on Infant Hearing, 1995). The AAP Task Force on Newborn and Infant Hearing (1999) endorsed universal screening and defined the important components and parameters of a screening system. Despite these recommendations, controversy about universal newborn hearing screening remains, especially regarding what constitutes the best practice in implementation of a complete screening and follow-up program. The number of states that have started or are planning such programs has been increasing steadily. The following screening methods have been employed in various states:

1. *Transient Evoked Otoacoustic Emissions (TEOAE or TOAE) testing*
   - Broadband (click) stimulus
   - Tests only cochlear response

Table 9.7.   Factors that may be associated with sensorineural and/or conductive hearing loss

Neonates (birth through 28 days)

Family history of hereditary childhood sensorineural hearing loss

In utero infections, such as cytomegalovirus (CMV), rubella, syphilis, herpes, and toxoplasmosis

Craniofacial anomalies, including those with morphologic abnormalities of the pinna and ear canals

Birth weight of less than 1,500 grams (3.3 pounds)

Hyperbilirubinemia at a serum level requiring exchange transfusion

Ototoxic medications, including but not limited to the aminoglycosides, used in multiple courses or in combination with loop diuretics

Bacterial meningitis

Apgar scores of 0–4 at 1 minute or 0–6 at 5 minutes

Mechanical ventilation lasting 5 days or longer

Stigmata or other findings associated with a syndrome known to include a sensorineural and/or conductive hearing loss

Infants and toddlers (29 days through 2 years) (especially when certain health conditions have developed)

Parent and caregiver concerns regarding hearing, speech-language, and/or developmental delay

Bacterial meningitis and other infections associated with sensorineural hearing loss

Head trauma associated with loss of consciousness or with skull fracture

Stigmata or other findings associated with a syndrome known to include a sensorineural and/or conductive hearing loss

Ototoxic medications, including but not limited to chemotherapeutic agents or aminoglycosides, used in multiple courses or in combination with loop diuretics

Recurrent or persistent otitis media with effusion for at least 3 months

Infants and young children (29 days through 6 years) (those who have conditions that require periodic monitoring of hearing)

Some newborns and infants may pass their initial hearing screenings but require periodic monitoring of their hearing to detect delayed-onset sensorineural and/or conductive hearing loss (e.g., after asymptomatic CMV infection). Infants with these indicators require a hearing evaluation at least every 6 months until age 3 years and at appropriate intervals thereafter.

Factors that may be associated with delayed-onset sensorineural hearing loss include:

Family history of hereditary childhood hearing loss

In utero infection such as CMV, rubella, syphilis, herpes, or toxoplasmosis

Neurofibromatosis type II and neurodegenerative disorders

Factors that may be associated with later-onset conductive hearing loss include:

Recurrent or persistent otitis media with effusion

Anatomic deformities and other disorders that affect eustachian tube function

Neurodegenerative disorders

From American Academy of Pediatrics, Joint Commission on Infant Hearing (1995).

2. *Distortion Product Otoacoustic Emission (DPOAE) testing*
   - Frequency-specific stimuli
   - Tests only cochlear responses

3. *Automated Auditory Brainstem Responses*
   - Objective measure
   - Tests cochlea, peripheral nerve, and brainstem functions

Of the three methods just listed, TEOAE testing is the least costly and thus appears to be the most feasible for universal infant hearing screening. Three states have developed universal hearing screening programs, and others are developing them as well, that primarily make use of EOAE testing as the screening paradigm. Of these states, Rhode Island has been doing universal newborn hearing screening since 1989. Since 1993, when the NIH-sponsored consensus conference endorsed TEOAE as the method of choice to screen for hearing loss in infants, TEOAE has gained acceptance in other countries (AAP, Joint Committee on Infant Hearing, 1995; Meredith, Stephens, Hogan, et al., 1994). TEOAE makes use of a phenomenon in which the cochlea, in addition to responding to sound, actually produces a tiny, transient sound wave in response to the sound stimulus (Champlin, 1996). The apparatus for TEOAE is similar to that of an immittance audiometer (i.e., tympanometer) in that a probe with a microphone and speaker is inserted into the ear canal to do the testing.

No response is found when the infant's hearing loss is greater than approximately 30 decibels.

The acceptance of TEOAE and related testing systems (e.g., distortion product otoacoustic emissions) as methods by which to do universal hearing screening has been delayed because of the problems of a somewhat high false positive rate, especially for newborns, of up to 10%–15% (Bantock & Croxson, 1998; Doyle, Burggraf, Fujikawa, & Kim, 1997; Huynh, Pollack, & Cunningham, 1996). Researchers (Vohr, Cary, Moore, & Letourneau, 1998) in Rhode Island, using careful standardized techniques, decreased the first stage fail rate to about 8%; however, this fail rate is still unacceptably high to some professionals and administrators. Much of this high false positive rate in newborns' hearing assessments is undoubtedly due to debris in the ear canals of many newborns or to transient fluid in their middle ears (Brass & Kemp, 1994). BAER tests have been used routinely since 1990 to test neonates at high risk for hearing loss (e.g., those in the NICU). BAER testing is expensive and limited to facilities with the technical skills and equipment, however. An automated screening system based on auditory evoked potentials is a cost-effective alternative. Two of these devices, called the *ALGO-1* and *ALGO-2*, are used quite frequently in NICUs throughout the United States and in other countries (Doyle et al., 1997; Stewart, Bibb, & Pearlman, 1993). The ALGO devices compare the evoked responses of the infant being tested to a computerized model of the normal waves. The ALGO devices can be used quite successfully by people with no audiologic training, because they essentially report only *Pass, Fail,* or *Could not test* as the results of the screening. These automated BAER systems have also been used quite successfully as part of statewide universal newborn hearing screening programs in Hawaii and Colorado (Downs, 1995; Johnson, Kuntz, Sia, et al., 1997).

The methods used to identify hearing impairment in newborns (i.e., TEOAE, DPOAE, automated ABR) are accepted nearly universally as valid and reliable measurement tools. These methods can be expected to identify at least 85%–90% of cases of congenital hearing impairments. The false positive rate, though initially relatively high at about 10%, should be expected to fall to about 3%–5% with improvements in equipment and as personnel become more experienced in a particular screening method.

Hearing screening of well newborns before discharge from the hospital is more effective and less expensive than diagnostic testing with BAER or vi-

sual reinforcement audiometry (VRA), which cannot be performed reliably with most infants until they reach 6 months of age and older. If newborn hearing screening is done only on babies who are identified by risk factors (see Table 9.7), the costs will be lower but only about 45%–50% of cases will be identified. Hearing screening of newborns who are at risk for hearing loss, in conjunction with later visual reinforcement audiometry, is likely to be more expensive and less effective than universal newborn hearing screening. An essential feature of any newborn hearing screening program is a system to ensure quality control. Quality control must include the proper training of personnel and ongoing evaluations of their performance.

Newborn hearing screening (especially if universal) must be considered as only the first step in a system which will 1) provide for further assessment, 2) determine the etiologic diagnosis, and 3) provide equipment (e.g., hearing aids) and habilitation for the children who are diagnosed with hearing impairments. It is this *system* that has been absent in most, if not all, universal screening programs set up in the United States thus far. Many potential problems are associated with newborn hearing screening programs, which may be especially troublesome if the system is universal. These include parents' anxiety about any false positive results and possibly delayed diagnoses due to false negative results. These risks seem manageable, however, especially when compared with the importance of the expected benefits.

Any newborn hearing screening program, even if it is universal, cannot identify any of the acquired or progressive hearing losses that occur later in childhood. Behavioral screening methods and surveillance methods (e.g., parent questionnaires about their child's hearing and language) are needed to identify these cases, which may account for as many as 20% of all permanent childhood hearing problems. The presence of inherited hearing disorders, many of which are progressive, necessitates yearly evaluations (Levi et al., 1993).

If the results of an initial hearing screening by electrophysiologic responses are equivocal, then the infant should be seen for a full diagnostic evaluation by an audiologist. The diagnostic test for young infants is BAER with sedation (see Table 9.8). Frequency-specific BAER testing is available at some centers and has the advantage of giving information about the infant's hearing ability for specific frequencies (Frattali, Sataloff, Hirshout, et al., 1995; Stapells & Oates, 1997). DPOAE testing also gives information about infants' hearing levels at specific

Table 9.8. Brainstem auditory evoked responses

Sound-activated electrical potentials
*   From auditory nerve and brainstem
*   With latencies up to about 20 milliseconds

Potentials are measured from scalp electrodes using many signal presentations and time-locked computer averaging of responses

Patient must be very quiet and not be moving or asleep

frequencies (Kimberley, 1995). For some disorders, such as those associated with external ear deformities, DPOAE testing needs to be done in conjunction with an otolaryngologist (ENT). In addition to referral, the physician should also examine the child carefully for other major and minor congenital anomalies that might be associated with the hearing disorder. These include cardiac defects, dysmorphic features (see Chapter 5), abnormal development, or neurologic findings (see Chapter 6).

Hearing Screening of Older Infants and Children   For older infants and children, as with younger infants, the use of risk criteria is important (see Table 9.7). With a child's increasing age, however, the comparative incidence of conductive hearing loss increases; therefore, problems such as recurrent otitis media and chronic middle-ear effusion are the principal factors to be considered. By older infancy and early childhood, parents or other caregivers can be asked to state any concerns that they may have about their child's hearing or with speech-language development (which can be related to the child's hearing status). This process can be incorporated into routine developmental surveillance easily, especially with regard to assessing a child's speech-language development (see Chapter 2). The following questions can be added to the routine office procedures easily as a way to gather additional information and can be considered a type of prescreening test for children's hearing and speech-language problems:

*   Is the child responding to sounds around him or her (e.g., doors shutting, telephone ringing)?
*   Is the child turning his or her head to the sound of a voice or to other sounds?
*   Is the child imitating words or sounds that are made to him or her?
*   Does the child try to locate or find interesting sounds that he or she hears, such as from a toy?
*   Does the child's speech seem to be like that of other children of his or her age?
*   Is the child always trying to turn up the television to a high volume?

*   Is the child continuing to gain more understanding of words and increasing his or her vocabulary as he or she is getting older?

If parents express any concerns in answering these questions or if there is a strong suspicion of a hearing impairment because of speech-language delays or a family history of hearing problems, referral to an audiologist or an otolaryngologist is warranted. For preschool-age children, particularly for those children with disabilities, a formal audiologic evaluation should be considered carefully every 1–2 years.

Hearing assessment is appreciably easier when a child reaches a developmental age of 2–3 years. Hearing screening with older children using standard audiometric equipment can be performed easily and with a high degree of accuracy. Table 9.9 describes the basic screening audiometry technique to be used with older children. Tympanometry or similar impedance techniques are also helpful in determining the presence of middle-ear disease, which can lead to a conductive hearing loss.

Impedance Audiometry   After the age of 9 months, impedance audiometry (tympanometry or reflectance) can be helpful and can be done routinely (see Table 9.10; see also Page, Kramer, Novak, et al., 1995). By this age, conductive hearing loss, which usually is due to middle-ear effusion, is the predominant cause of hearing impairment. An abnormal finding on tympanometry, especially if it is a condition lasting for more than 2 months, is often indicative of a conductive hearing loss and should lead to referral of the child for further audiologic assessment or possibly to an otolaryngologist. Abnormal findings on tympanograms and their probable causes include

*   *Peak at negative pressure:* Partial vacuum in the middle ear ("sluggish middle ear")
*   *Rounded peak, shallow tympanogram:* Possible effusion or thickened tympanic membrane
*   *Flat tympanogram with a normal ear canal volume:* Probable effusion or impacted cerumen
*   *Flat tympanogram with a large ear canal volume:* Probable tympanic membrane (TM) perforation or patent pressure-equalizing (PE) tube
*   *Machine will not start:* TM perforation; volume too large to obtain a pressure seal
*   *Very high peak:* Floppy eardrum, ossicular discontinuity

Interpretation of acoustic reflex responses is as follows:

*   *When responses occur at 80- to 90-decibel hearing level (HL):* Hearing threshold no worse than about 60-decibel HL

Table 9.9. Pure-tone screening audiometry using earphones, for children older than 3 years of age

Determination of the ability to hear at specific frequencies that are important for communication, development, and education. Use of earphones is required.

Procedure can be done in an office setting in a quiet location. Audiometer must be calibrated behaviorally every month and electroacoustically every year.

Screening failure = Failure to hear any tone in either ear

Test level (in decibels of hearing loss)	Test frequency (in Hertz)			
	500	1,000	2,000	4,000
	20[a]	20	20	20

[a]Not needed if acoustic reflex test was normal

- *When responses occur at 100- to 110-decibel HL:* Hearing threshold no worse than about 80-decibel HL
- *No responses:* No information about hearing (i.e., could be normal)

On rare occasions, chronic middle-ear effusions lead to permanent hearing loss. A conservative approach in such cases is to follow all children with middle-ear effusions until the effusion has cleared spontaneously or until the effusion has lasted for a prolonged period (more than 3–4 months) (see discussion under the "Management of Conductive Hearing Loss" heading in this chapter). The following conditions warrant a referral to an audiologist and possibly to an otolaryngologist:

- Persistent (i.e., longer than 3–4 months) bilateral middle-ear fluid

Table 9.10. Acoustic impedance procedures

Tympanometry

Measurement of sound reflected from the ear canal, eardrum, and middle ear as pressure is varied in the ear canal

Assessment of function of the conducting mechanism (especially eustachian tube dysfunction and eardrum mobility)

Acoustic reflex tests

Measurement of a change in eardrum tension caused by acoustic activation of the middle-ear muscles (requires pressure change as with tympanometry)

Assessment of the integrity of the entire acoustic reflex; typically used to assess sensory and neural function

Reflectance audiometry (spectral gradient acoustic reflectometry)

Measures sound reflectance off the tympanic membrane

If fluid is present, most of sound is reflected back

Less informative than tympanometry

Much less costly than tympanometry; a home version is available

- Family concern about the child's hearing status
- Associated speech-language delays
- Risk factors present (e.g., family history, passive smoking)
- Disorders that are associated with conductive hearing loss (e.g., Down syndrome, cleft palate, craniofacial abnormalities)
- Concern about hearing in a child who has developmental delays or sensory impairments (e.g., mental retardation, visual impairment, sensorineural hearing loss)

Children with Down syndrome, as a group, are at higher risk for conductive hearing loss. These children should be followed carefully and frequently to detect the presence of any hearing loss. Likewise, children with other craniofacial abnormalities, such as cleft palate deformities, should also be evaluated frequently during early childhood because this population is also at high risk for conductive hearing loss. Because of the high risks for chronic middle-ear effusion, some children who have either Down syndrome or a cleft palate have tympanostomy tubes inserted surgically early in life as a prophylactic measure in an attempt to prevent conductive hearing loss.

Audiologic Assessment of Toddlers and Young Children Children as young as 6 months of age may be able to be tested successfully to determine frequency-specific information by VRA and older children by a similar method known as *conditioned play orienting response (COR) testing* (Gravel & Traquina, 1992). The components of VRA are as follows:

- Soundproof booth (most common)
- Ideally, two loudspeakers placed to either side are used, above which are darkened enclosures holding a large, animated toy.
- Child in parent's lap (with parent being instructed not to help child)

- Reinforcement established by presenting a sound while animating the toy with a light on in the enclosure
- Once the young child is conditioned, the enclosure is not lighted until *after* the child responds to the sound
- Different frequencies of sound are presented to establish a profile of the infant's hearing ability

The components of COR testing are as follows:

- Similar to VRA with a soundproof booth
- Two speakers placed at 45° angles to the child (seated on parent's lap or in a small chair)
- Child needs to be conditioned to *localize* the sound source (e.g., drops a block in a bucket in response to hearing a tone).
- Can be used with earphones to establish ear-specific profiles

On occasion, BAER testing is needed for children who are difficult to test or for children with developmental disabilities. BAER testing with sedation can be used quite successfully with children with mental retardation requiring extensive support who cannot respond to routine methods of audiometric testing (Gans & Gans, 1993; Stein, Kraus, McGee, et al., 1995). Assessment of these children's hearing is difficult because their behavioral responses to sounds are not always reliable.

Management of Hearing Impairments

As with other developmental disabilities in infancy and childhood, the treatment of hearing impairment should start with trying to *prevent* further hearing loss and by preventing those disabilities that are secondary to the primary condition. This goal can be accomplished through the use of three levels of prevention activities. Both primary care physicians and specialists have an important role in all three levels of prevention. At the primary level of prevention, physicians can

- Ensure that genetic counseling is done with parents who are at risk of having future babies with sensorineural hearing impairments because of proved or suspected genetic hearing loss
- Help to ensure that all women have rubella vaccinations before pregnancies, and determine women's immune status for rubella
- Maintain caution (e.g., doing drug-level testing) when prescribing ototoxic drugs such as furosemide or aminoglycoside antibiotics to the mother
- Give guidance to pregnant women to avoid situations of exposure to infectious agents such as toxoplasmosis and CMV

- Monitor closely and prevent problems due to blood incompatibility (e.g., Rh or ABO blood groups)

Secondary prevention activities to be done during the perinatal period include the prevention of hypoxia, hyperbilirubinemia, and acidosis in premature infants as well as minimizing the exposure of the newborn to any ototoxic drugs. Tertiary prevention activities involve early diagnosis and treatment of hearing loss to prevent or to ameliorate the subsequent development of secondary behavioral and developmental disabilities. The rest of this chapter addresses tertiary level prevention and management, especially with regard to sensorineural hearing impairments.

Medical Management of Sensorineural Hearing Loss For infants with hearing impairments who are less than 6 months of age, therapy consists of

- Initial and periodic audiologic reevaluation
- Otolaryngologic treatment as needed
- Referral for genetic counseling and evaluation when indicated

Because some genetic conditions (e.g., Alport syndrome) are associated with renal disease, a screening urinalysis and possibly a renal ultrasound test should also be obtained. Some hearing loss is also associated with visual problems, which warrant a referral to a pediatric ophthalmologist.

The audiologist often has a crucial role at this stage of a child's development because of the responsibility for selecting appropriate hearing aids and counseling the family about ways to cope with their child's hearing impairment. The most appropriate audiologic approach is to attempt to use whatever degree of residual hearing is left to its best advantage (including amplification) and to structure the child's environment so that the child can use auditory clues to facilitate learning. This technique is known as *auditory training* or *aural rehabilitation,* which is discussed later in this chapter.

Hearing Aids Infants usually adapt well to wearing hearing aids. It is usually the older child, at 2–3 years of age, who has more difficulty when first beginning to use a hearing aid. Some parents may develop a certain amount of resistance during the institution of the use of hearing aids or other therapies, and their resistance needs to be addressed. Support and encouragement from the primary care physicians and the specialists can be helpful in alleviating their resistance.

In the first few years of their infant's life, the parents of a child with hearing impairment are extremely important components of any program that is being implemented to help stimulate the child's speech-language development and the child's functional use of residual hearing. Speech-language pathologists and audiologists are necessary to design these specific programs to help parents maximize their child's abilities. The child needs to use nonauditory cues in the environment and use amplification successfully when indicated to provide some degree of auditory input to help in the child's learning and language development.

Cochlear Implants   One promising technological device with the potential for widespread use but also possible misuse among children and adults with hearing impairments is the cochlear implant (Balkany, Hodges, & Goodman, 1996; Cohen, 1995). A cochlear implant is an electronic device in which electrodes are placed in the cochlea surgically in order to stimulate the child's auditory nerve directly. An external microphone, amplifier, signal processors, and related electronics transmit sound-generated signals through the skin to the receiver, which is placed subcutaneously behind the ear. This device converts sound waves picked up by the external microphone into electrical impulses that are then sent to the auditory nerve by the implanted electrodes. Both children and adults who have undergone this implant procedure have developed some awareness of sounds and can discriminate between certain sounds.

The main candidates for cochlear implants are young children, adolescents, and adults who developed some language prior to the development of a profound hearing loss (i.e., postlingual deafness) (Langman, Quigley, & Souliere, 1996). These people are likely to develop improved speech recognition as well as better speech intelligibility, although considerably less than that expected for people of their age. Cochlear implants should also be considered for those young children who are prelingually deaf. Even with extensive speech-language therapy, however, the chances that these children will be able to use spoken language for their entire communication needs are low. Studies (e.g., Miyamoto, Kirk, Todd, et al., 1995) have indicated that using cochlear implants leads to somewhat better speech production and understanding than that which would be expected from the use of hearing aids by young children with profound hearing loss.

A Consensus Development Panel of the NIH and the U.S. Food and Drug Administration (FDA) approved cochlear implants for use in children as young as 2 years of age (Anonymous, 1995). At age 2 years, however, a child may well be past the neu-

rodevelopmental peak for acquiring language abilities. A few centers are doing studies (see Anonymous, 1995) in younger children to determine whether early implantation leads to better language abilities. It may also be found that there is an ideal age at which time this surgery should be done to have the most successful outcomes with the least complications. In addition, the technology of cochlear implants continues to improve; a device that is current in 2000 will not be state-of-the-art in the near future.

The surgery required for cochlear implantation usually further damages the cochlea as well as any residual hearing that these children might have had (Miyamoto, 1995). This damage is a significant concern because most children with hearing impairments are not totally deaf at birth, and many have a progressive hearing loss but with an unknown time line of progressivity. Therefore, cochlear implantation is being done primarily with children and adults who have profound hearing loss in both ears. In many children less than 2 years of age, however, testing them accurately for the extent of their hearing loss is extremely difficult.

A second concern about cochlear implants regards their use in older children who have prelingual deafness. For these children and for some adults, the use of cochlear implants has not resulted in any useful speech or any understanding of spoken language; they have developed only some improvement in their awareness of ambient sounds. A survey (Rose, Vernon, & Pool, 1996) of a large number of schools for the deaf demonstrated that about half of the children who received cochlear implants stopped using them and expressed disappointment in the results of the implant.

Educational and Therapeutic Management of Sensorineural Hearing Loss   Early intervention services and aural rehabilitation should be initiated shortly after the diagnosis of hearing impairment is made. It is important that services begin as soon as possible to help ensure that the child achieves optimum development of intellectual, speech-language, and emotional functioning (Afzali-Nomani, 1995). The audiologist determines the most appropriate type of hearing aid and fits the aid to the child. The speech-language therapist works closely with the audiologist to help the child improve sound recognition and responsiveness and to work on vocal imitation, speech development, or American Sign Language (ASL) if indicated.

At about 3 years of age, a child with significant hearing impairment is enrolled in a special education classroom either with other children with hearing impairments or in inclusive programs in which they receive specialized supports but learn alongside children without disabilities. The intellectual abilities of the child, the presence of other impairments, the degree of the child's hearing impairment, and the availability of services in the community determine which education environment is appropriate for each child. Usually, a child who has a moderately severe hearing loss (greater than a 60- to 70-decibel hearing loss with hearing aids) requires placement in classes tailored specifically for deaf children.

Education Programs: Approaches and Methods
For many years, continuing controversy has existed about which educational methods are best for school-age children who have severe to profound hearing impairments. Basically, four major viewpoints about methodology can be considered. The first method emphasizes the traditional aural/oral method, which relies on speechreading (i.e., watching the lips and face of the speaker), written language, and auditory training. The second method emphasizes the manual method, using English-oriented sign language (possibly incorporating ASL), fingerspelling, and other systems to help facilitate English sentence structure and language learning. Total communication, the third and most common system, uses elements of both the aural/oral and the sign language methods. The total communication approach concentrates on those communication methods that seem to be the most successful with the child. Total communication tries to use whichever of the child's senses are available—for example, visual, auditory, or tactile—in order to maximize learning communication and overall skills (Dolman, 1992). In a survey (Jordan, Gustason, & Rosen, 1976) of programs for children with hearing impairments done in the mid-1970s, approximately 95% of the 795 programs had changed to a total communication approach. A fourth system that is gaining much favor rapidly is essentially an outgrowth of total communication and is called the *bilingual* or *bicultural approach* (Wood, 1992). In this system, children are initially taught ASL at a level that is quite functional for them. Following this step, the child is taught English essentially as a second language by using whichever methods are appropriate, including aural/oral, ASL or other sign language, or cued speech (i.e., using speech coupled with specific signs to help improve receptive accuracy).

Prior to the 1970s, children with hearing impairments were placed either in special schools for the deaf or in general classrooms for children without disabilities with minimal or no additional modifications to their education programs. Neither of these alternatives is ideal for all families. The enactment of the Education for All Handicapped Children Act of 1975 (PL 94-142), which was reauthorized in 1990 and renamed the Individuals with Disabilities Education Act (IDEA; PL 101-476), as well as the requirement that all children with disabilities receive an individualized education program (IEP), has resulted in improvements in individual instruction and classroom modifications for children with disabilities. Well-constructed and well-implemented IEPs have allowed children with hearing impairments to be placed in general classrooms with children without disabilities, but with extensive speech-language and auditory assistance (Afzali-Nomani, 1995).

Newer electronic devices, developed in part because of changes in the computer and electronics industry, are becoming more available for use by children and adults with hearing impairments. Devices such as visual alerting devices for an alarm clock or a telephone are inexpensive but effective aids. Closed captioning on television and with videotapes for people with hearing impairments is also becoming more popular and allows for more learning and socialization experiences. Many theaters and concert halls are offering amplification devices or sign language interpreters for audience members with hearing impairments. These new devices are being used more often with children, and therefore such systems will be highly functional for them when they reach adulthood.

Associated Medical and Developmental Problems Many children who have hearing impairments have other disabilities as well. A survey (Schein & Delk, 1974) of children with hearing impairments that was conducted in the early 1970s found that about 40% of children who were in schools for the deaf had a second disability, and about 7% had two other disabilities. Behavior problems, mental retardation, severe visual problems, and cerebral palsy are among the most common additional impairments found in this population. The detrimental effects of these other disabilities are often more than additive to the developmental risks associated with the hearing impairment and often result in severe problems with language, learning, and other areas of development.

Children with known hearing loss require other evaluations in addition to medical and audiologic testing. In school-age children with significant hearing impairments (i.e., hard-of-hearing, deaf), it is important to assess their general cognitive functioning periodically with tests that have been designed for and validated on populations with hearing impairments. For example, tests such as the Hiskey-Nebraska or the Leiter International Performance Scale (Roid & Miller, 1997) have been validated using children with hearing impairments (Wodrich, 1997). These tests require much less verbal language ability, which is an ability that is impaired when there is significant hearing loss. In the past, some children with hearing impairments have received a label of mental retardation inappropriately, only to have that label changed when they were retested with appropriate tests. Gallaudet College, located in Washington, D.C., is the U.S. college for the deaf and people with hearing impairments. It has available lists of psychological, educational, and vocational tests that are appropriate for use with people with hearing impairments (Zieziula, 1982).

Using an interdisciplinary approach when multiple impairments are present, such as a child who is deafblind or a child with cerebral palsy and hearing impairment, is important so that management is comprehensive and follow-up care is coordinated properly. This approach may require referral to a multidisciplinary developmental center. In locations where such centers are not readily available, the primary care physician can coordinate the assessment and treatment services in cooperation with school personnel and other professionals.

Role of the Primary Care Physician   The primary care physician can help in the education and support of the parents and assist them in becoming knowledgeable advocates for their children. This physician is the person who is primarily responsible for assuring that a child's conductive hearing loss does not complicate his or her sensorineural hearing loss. Middle-ear effusion with conductive hearing loss can be an added complication in children with sensorineural hearing loss, and therefore regularly scheduled examinations in the primary care office are necessary for appropriate follow-up of these children.

Some parents may mistakenly think that ASL will prevent their child's future development of good speech-language skills. These parents need to be counseled that this is not true and that sign language may actually aid in their child's speech-language development. The primary care physician can assist in this counseling in conjunction with school personnel and other professionals. The parents of a child with severe or profound hearing impairment can have great difficulties in coping with

the demands of the habilitation program and with their emotional acceptance of the child. These parents are suddenly placed into a situation in which they have to teach language to their child in an unfamiliar way and also have the responsibilities of taking care of a child with a disability. Physicians, audiologists, and educational specialists can be helpful to such parents by directing them to appropriate resources and professionals. A listing of schools and classes for the deaf across the United States is published annually in the April edition of the *American Annals of the Deaf*. The April 1998 issue ("Educational Programs for Deaf Students," 1998) devoted 91 pages to listing education programs for deaf students.

Common Misconceptions About Hearing Impairments and Their Treatment   Following are some common misconceptions about hearing impairments and their treatment:

- *A child's use of ASL will prevent his or her learning of oral speech:* On the contrary, a number of studies (e.g., Geers & Schick, 1988; Mallery-Ruganis & Fischer, 1991) have shown that learning signs may actually improve a child's other language and speech acquisition.
- *Learning ASL impairs a child's reading skills:* Although it is true that children with profound hearing impairments, on average, have lower reading ability compared with their peers without disabilities, this discrepancy is present even among people who were taught only by an aural/oral approach.
- *Hearing aids are unnecessary for people who use ASL:* Many people who primarily use ASL use hearing aids as a safety measure to help them perceive some environmental sounds.
- *Use of ASL isolates a person:* Although it is true that most people who primarily use ASL to communicate prefer to be part of a community of other people who use ASL, people with hearing impairments who do not use ASL and do not have good aural/oral skills can actually become more isolated.

Management of Conductive Hearing Loss   The previous discussion in this chapter centers mainly on the management of children with a severe to profound sensorineural hearing loss. Wide variations of opinion exist with regard to the significance of conductive hearing loss, especially that which is due to middle-ear effusion. In order to diagnose a conductive hearing loss properly, formal audiologic testing is necessary to determine the differences between air and bone conduction of sound (the "air–bone gap") to ensure that no underlying sensorineural hearing loss exists as well.

Numerous studies (see, e.g., Eimas & Kavanagh, 1986; Gordon, 1986; Peters, Grievink, van Bon, et al., 1997) have demonstrated that language and learning problems are likely as a result of chronic conductive hearing loss of even a moderate degree (30- to 40-decibel hearing loss). Paradise (1981), in a critical review of the literature, found that conductive hearing loss, language delays, and intellectual impairments can occur with chronic middle-ear disease; however, these impairments seem to dissipate over time once the individual's hearing loss has been resolved. No studies in the 1990s presented conflicting data; however, one study noted that the presence of chronic middle-ear disease, when coupled with other risk factors such as low birth weight or premature birth, does increase the risk for later language and education problems significantly (Peters, Grievink, van Bon, et al., 1997).

Therefore, treatment for middle-ear effusion should be done if the effusion is longstanding or if significant hearing loss or other risk factors (e.g., premature birth) are present. Studies have reported conflicting results regarding the effectiveness of antibiotics, antihistamines, and/or decongestants in treating persistent serous otitis media. Good evidence exists, however, that surgical treatment such as ear tube placement can indeed improve hearing in most cases immediately following surgery. Occasionally, hearing loss does not improve despite the ear tube placement, and rarely such a procedure might worsen hearing acutely (Desch & Laskowski, 1982). Table 9.11 reviews the AAP's (1994) guidelines on the treatment of otitis media with effusion in children. The AAP guidelines have been updated to reflect technical improvements and additional information was reported after their initial 1994 publication.

A technological development has also led to another option for dealing with middle-ear effusion, which may also be useful in situations where surgery for PE tube placement is not applicable. A company has developed and received FDA approval for a laser device that can quickly make a small hole in the TM. Laser-assisted tympanostomy using this laser device, known as the *OtoLAM*, has so far been done in an office setting with several hundred children, with no reports of any serious side effects (based on information from the company web site, www.earinfections.com). In one study, approximately 80% of the children who had the procedure were free of effusion after a minimum follow-up period of 3 months (Silverstein, Kuhn, Choo, et al., 1996).

Table 9.11.   Managing otitis media with effusion in young children

Diagnostic and evaluative

Otitis media with effusion is common in young children.

Visualization of the tympanic membranes is necessary.

Pneumatic otoscopy can be used to assess middle-ear effusion. This is difficult because of the problems in ensuring an adequate seal of the ear canal.

Tympanometry *or* spectral gradient acoustic reflectometry can be performed to confirm the presence of effusion (but its use does not negate the need to visualize tympanic membranes).

A child who has fluid in both middle ears for a total of 3 months should undergo a hearing test. (Before 3 months of effusion have occurred, a hearing test is optional but might be indicated for an infant or child with developmental problems.)

Therapeutic

Observation *or* antibiotic therapy is a treatment option for children with effusion that has been present for less than 4–6 months and at any time for children *without* a 20-decibel hearing loss or worse loss in the better-hearing ear.

For the child who has had bilateral effusion for a total of 3 months and who has a *bilateral* hearing deficiency (as above), bilateral myringotomy with tube insertion becomes an additional treatment option. Placement of tubes is recommended after a total of 4–6 months of bilateral effusion *with* a bilateral hearing impairment.

For a child who is at risk for chronic middle-ear effusion, such as children who have a cleft palate, craniofacial disorders, or Down syndrome, tympanostomy tube insertion should be considered strongly as a prophylactic measure, especially if the tube can be inserted when anesthesia is being done for other reasons (e.g., for cleft repairs).

Adapted from American Academy of Pediatrics, Otitis Media Guideline Panel (1994).

A conservative treatment approach is to follow the child with middle-ear disease with monthly tympanometric examinations to assess the child's middle-ear function. Hearing screening should be done when there is tympanometric evidence of conductive hearing loss (e.g., a flat tympanogram). If the child has effusions that persists for longer than 3–4 months, referral to both an audiologist and an otolaryngologist is required. Another option is to manage the hearing loss caused by middle-ear effusion by using a "loaner" hearing aid, which will acutely improve a child's hearing (Desch & Laskowski, 1982; Jardine, Griffiths, & Midgley, 1999). This option is often followed when removal of middle-ear fluid is not possible (e.g., ear canals are extremely small, high risk from sedation or anesthesia making surgery inadvisable). This method requires close monitoring by an audiologist because of the variations in the degree of hearing loss that can occur over time and is appropriate only for children who are likely to have persistent conductive hearing loss.

CONCLUSION

Anticipatory Guidance and Family Support Services

The physician can play an important role in the emotional development and education of children with visual or hearing impairments by assisting parents in exploring all educational and therapeutic options and by helping to eliminate some of the common misconceptions about these impairments. About 90% of children who are deaf have parents without hearing impairments; therefore, it is important that the parents and siblings participate by acquiring some ASL or other communication skills that may be needed (Kluwin & Gaustad, 1991). More than 90% of children with visual impairments have parents with no significant vision problems. These families, therefore, may need guidance in how to modify their homes or make other changes to accommodate the needs of their child with a visual impairment. For children with visual and/or hearing impairments, major changes in family activities are often required, and thus these families sometimes may need extended social, psychological, and financial support.

As mentioned in Chapter 3, many families experience crises during the life of their child with disabilities. This is certainly true for most families of children with severe visual or hearing problems. The Appendix at the end of this chapter lists many national organizations (most of which have local or state chapters) that can be assistive to families in coping with important issues. Important sources for assistance and information are the state offices for Vocational Rehabilitation and Developmental Disability services as well as services provided for children with special health care needs (Title V).

Important Care Coordination Issues

Chapter 1 lists general recommendations for care coordination to assist primary care health professionals in supporting children with developmental disabilities and chronic conditions and their families. For infants and children with visual and/or hearing impairments to receive optimal and timely diagnoses and care, access to experienced audiologists, ophthalmologists, otolaryngologists, educators, speech-language therapists, social workers, and nurses, as well as developmental pediatricians is necessary. To provide adequate care coordination, the primary care physician should develop and update periodically a resource file on state organizations and services, national and local parent support groups, appropriate specialists, educational personnel, and other community service providers.

REFERENCES

Afzali-Nomani, E. (1995). Educational conditions related to successful full inclusion programs involving deaf and hard of hearing children. *American Annals of the Deaf, 140*, 396–401.

Allen, H.F. (1957). A new picture series for preschool vision testing. *American Journal of Ophthalmology, 44,* 38.

American Academy of Pediatrics (AAP), Committee on Practice and Ambulatory Medicine. (1986). Vision screening and eye examination in children. *Pediatrics, 77,* 918–919.

American Academy of Pediatrics (AAP), Joint Committee on Infant Hearing. (1995). Joint Committee on Infant Hearing 1994 position statement. *Pediatrics, 95*(1), 152–156.

American Academy of Pediatrics (AAP), Otitis Media Guideline Panel. (1994). Managing otitis media with effusion in young children. *Pediatrics, 94*(5), 766–773.

American Academy of Pediatrics (AAP), Task Force on Newborn and Infant Hearing. (1999). Newborn and infant hearing loss: Detection and intervention. *Pediatrics, 103*(2), 527–530.

Anonymous. (1995). NIH Consensus Conference: Cochlear implants in adults and children. *JAMA: Journal of the American Medical Association, 274*(24), 1955–1961.

Bale, J.F., Jr. (1992). Congenital infections and the nervous system. *Pediatric Clinics of North America, 39,* 669–690.

Balkany, T., Hodges, A.V., & Goodman, K.W. (1996). Ethics of cochlear implantation in young children. *Otolaryngology: Head and Neck Surgery, 114,* 748–755.

Bantock, H.M., & Croxson, S. (1998). Universal hearing screening using transient otoacoustic emissions in a community health clinic. *Archives of Diseases in Childhood, 78*(3), 249–252.

Berg, F.S., & Fletcher, S.G. (Eds.). (1970). *The hard of hearing child: Clinical and educational management.* Orlando, FL: Grune & Stratton.

Bishop, V.E. (1991). Preschool visually impaired children: A demographic study. *Journal of Visual Impairment and Blindness, 85,* 69–74.

Brass, D., & Kemp, D.T. (1994). The objective assessment of transient evoked otoacoustic emission in neonates. *Ear and Hearing, 15,* 371–377.

Brookhouser, P.E. (1996). Sensorineural hearing loss in children. *Pediatric Clinics of North America, 43,* 1195–1216.

Brookhouser, P.E., Worthington, D.W., & Kelly, W.J. (1991). Unilateral hearing loss in children. *Laryngoscope, 101,* 1264–1274.

Buncic, J.R. (1987). The blind child. *Pediatric Clinics of North America, 34,* 1403–1414.

Burde, R.M., Savino, P.J., & Trobe, J.D. (1992). Nystagmus and other periodic eye disorders. In R.M. Burde, P.J. Savino, & J.D. Trobe, *Clinical decisions in neuro-ophthalmology* (2nd ed., pp. 157–202). St. Louis: Mosby–Year Book.

Cass, H.D., Sonkesen, P.M., & McConachie, H.R. (1994). Developmental setback in severe visual impairment. *Archives of Diseases of Childhood, 70,* 192–196.

Champlin, C.A. (1996). Physiologic measures of auditory and vestibular function. In F.N. Martin & J.G. Clark (Eds.), *Hearing care for children* (pp. 94–127). Needham Heights, MA: Allyn & Bacon.

Chan, K.H. (1994). Sensorineural hearing loss in children: Classification and evaluation. *Otolaryngological Clinics of North America, 27,* 473–486.

Cohen, N.L. (1995). The ethics of cochlear implants in young children. *Advances in Oto-Rhino-Laryngology, 50,* 1–3.

Cohn, E.S., Kelley, P.M., Fowler, T.W., et al. (1999). Clinical studies of families with hearing loss attributable to mutations in the connexin 26 gene (GJB2/DFNB1). *Pediatrics, 103*(3), 546–550.

Cooper, C.D., Bowling, F.G., Hall, J.E., et al. (1996). Evaluation of photoscreener instruments in a childhood population: Otago photoscreener and Dortmans video-photorefractor. *Australian and New Zealand Journal of Ophthalmology, 24,* 347–355.

Daw, N.W. (1998). Critical periods and amblyopia. *Archives of Ophthalmology, 116,* 502–505.

Dekker, R., & Koole, F.D. (1992). Visually impaired children's visual characteristics and intelligence. *Developmental Medicine and Child Neurology, 34,* 123–133.

Desch, L.W. (1998). Longitudinal stability of visual evoked responses in children with hydrocephalus. *Developmental Medicine and Child Neurology, 40*(Suppl.), 36.

Desch, L.W., & Laskowski, R.P. (1982). Testing and stuffing cotton balls in your ears. *Pediatrics, 69,* 829–830.

Dolman, D. (1992). Some concerns about using whole language approaches with deaf children. *American Annals of the Deaf, 137,* 278–282.

Downs, M.P. (1995). Universal hearing screening: The Colorado story. *International Journal of Pediatric Otorhinolaryngology, 39,* 257–259.

Doyle, K.J., Burggraf, B., Fujikawa, S., & Kim, J. (1997). Newborn hearing screening by otoacoustic emissions and automated auditory brainstem response. *International Journal of Pediatric Otorhinolaryngology, 41*(2), 111–119.

Dutton, G., Ballantyne, J., Boyd, G., et al. (1996). Cortical visual dysfunction in children: A clinical study. *Eye, 10,* 302–309.

Education for All Handicapped Children Act of 1975, PL 94-142, 20 U.S.C. §§ 1400 *et seq.*

Educational programs for deaf students. (1998). *American Annals of the Deaf, 143,* 71–162.

Eimas, P.D., & Kavanagh, J.F. (1986). Otitis media, hearing loss, and child development: A NICHD conference summary. *Public Health Reports, 101*(3), 289–293.

Flynn, J.T. (1992). The premature retina: A model for the in vivo study of molecular genetics? *Eye, 6,* 161–162.

Foley-Nolan, A., McCann, A., & O'Keefe, M. (1997). Atropine penalisation versus occlusion as the primary treatment for amblyopia. *British Journal of Ophthalmology, 81*(1), 54–57.

Fortnum, H., & Davis, A. (1993). Hearing impairment in children after bacterial meningitis: Incidence and resource implications. *British Journal of Audiology, 27,* 43–52.

Foster, A. (1988). Childhood blindness. *Eye, 2*(Suppl.), S27–S36.

Fraser, G.R. (1976). *The causes of profound deafness in childhood: A study of 3,535 individuals with severe hearing loss present at birth or of childhood onset.* Baltimore: The John Hopkins University Press.

Fraser, G.R., & Friedmann, A.I. (1967). *The causes of blindness in childhood: A study of 776 children with severe visual handicaps.* Baltimore: The John Hopkins University Press.

Frattali, M.A., Sataloff, R.T., Hirshout, D., et al. (1995). Audiogram construction using frequency-specific auditory brainstem response (ABR) thresholds. *Ear, Nose, and Throat Journal, 74*(10), 691–698.

Friendly, D.S. (1993). Development of vision in infants and young children. *Pediatric Clinics of North America, 40,* 693–703.

Funato, M., Teraoka, S., Tamai, H., & Shimida, S. (1996). Follow-up study of auditory brainstem responses in hyperbilirubinemic newborns treated with exchange transfusion. *Acta Paediatrica Japonica, 38,* 17–21.

Gallo, J.E., & Lennerstrand, G. (1991). A population study of ocular abnormalities in premature children aged 5 to 10 years. *American Journal of Ophthalmology, 111,* 539–547.

Gans, D., & Gans, K.D. (1993). Development of a hearing test protocol for profoundly involved multi-handicapped children. *Ear and Hearing, 14,* 128–140.

Geers, A.E., & Schick, B. (1988). Acquisition of spoken and signed English by hearing impaired children of hearing-impaired or hearing parents. *Journal of Speech and Hearing, 53,* 136–143.

Gordon, N. (1986). Intermittent deafness and learning. *Developmental Medicine and Child Neurology, 28*(3), 364–369.

Gravel, J.S., & Traquina, D.N. (1992). Experience with the audiologic assessment of infants and toddlers. *International Journal of Pediatric Otolaryngology, 23,* 59–71.

Guerina, N.G., Hsu, H.W., Meissner, H.C., et al. (1994). Neonatal serologic screening and early treatment for congenital toxoplasm gondii infection. *New England Journal of Medicine, 330*(26), 1858–1863.

Hanshaw, J.B. (1994). Congenital cytomegalovirus infection. *Pediatric Annals, 23,* 124–128.

Herrgard, E., Karjalainen, S., Martikainen, A., & Heinonen, K. (1995). Hearing loss at the age of 5 years of children born preterm: A matter of definition. *Acta Paediatrica, 84,* 1160–1164.

Hertz, B.G., & Rosenberg, J. (1992). Effect of mental retardation and motor disability on testing with visual acuity cards. *Developmental Medicine and Child Neurology, 34,* 115–122.

Holt, J., & Hotton, S. (1994). *Demographic aspects of hearing impairment: Questions and answers* (3rd ed.). Washington, DC: Gallaudet University, Center for Assessment and Demographic Studies.

Huynh, M.T., Pollack, R.A., & Cunningham, R.A. (1996). Universal newborn hearing screening: Feasibility in a community hospital. *Journal of Family Practice, 42*(5), 487–490.

Individuals with Disabilities Education Act (IDEA) of 1990, PL 101-476, 20 U.S.C. §§ 1400 *et seq.*

Jan, J.E., Friedman, R.D., McCormick, A.Q., et al. (1983). Eye pressing by visually-impaired children. *Developmental Medicine and Child Neurology, 25*(6), 755–762.

Jan, J.E., Groenveld, M., Sykanda, A.M., & Hoyt, C.S. (1987). Behavioral characteristics of children with permanent cortical visual impairment. *Developmental Medicine and Child Neurology, 29*(5), 571–576.

Jardine, A.H., Griffiths, M.V., & Midgley, E. (1999). The acceptance of hearing aids for children with otitis media with effusion. *Journal of Laryngology and Otology 113*(4), 314–317.

Jenkins, P.F., Prager, P.C., Mazow, M.L., et al. (1983). Preliterate vision screening: A comparative study. *American Orthoptic Journal, 33,* 91–97.

Johnson, J.L., Kuntz, N.L., Sia, C.C., et al. (1997). Newborn hearing screening in Hawaii. *Hawaii Medical Journal, 56,* 352–355.

Jordan, I., Gustason, G., & Rosen, R. (1976). Current communication trends at programs for the deaf. *American Annals of the Deaf, 121,* 527–532.

Keith, C.G., & Doyle, L.W. (1995). Retinopathy of prematurity in extremely low birth weight infants. *Pediatrics, 95,* 42–45.

Kelley, P.M., Harris, D.J., Comer, B.C., et al. (1998). Novel mutations in the connexin 26 gene (GJB2) that cause autosomal recessive (DFNB1) hearing loss. *American Journal of Human Genetics, 62*(4), 792–799.

Kimberley, B.P. (1995). Distortion product emission features and the prediction of pure tone thresholds. *Laryngoscope, 105*(4 pt. 1), 349–353.

Kluwin, T.N., & Gaustad, M.G. (1991). Predicting family communication choices. *American Annals of the Deaf, 136*(1), 28–34.

Kvaerner, K.J., & Arnesen, A.R. (1994). Hearing impairment in Oslo born children 1989–1991: Incidence, etiology, and diagnostic delay. *Scandinavian Audiology, 23,* 233–239.

Langman, A.W., Quigley, S.M., & Souliere, C.R., Jr. (1996). Cochlear implants in children. *Pediatric Clinics of North America, 43,* 1217–1231.

Levi, H., Tell, L., & Feinwesser, M. (1993). Progressive hearing loss in hard-of-hearing children. *Audiology, 32,* 132–136.

Lewis, T.L., Maurer, D., & Brent, H.P. (1989). Optokinetic nystagmus in normal and visually deprived children: Implications for cortical development. *Canadian Journal of Psychology, 43,* 121–140.

Lorenz, J.M., Wooliever, D.E., Jetton, J.R., & Paneth, N. (1998). A quantitative review of mortality and developmental disability in extremely premature newborns. *Archives of Pediatrics and Adolescent Medicine, 152,* 425–435.

Lowenfeld, B. (1980). Psychological problems of children with impaired vision. In W.M. Cruickshank (Ed.), *Psychology of exceptional children and youth* (4th ed.). Upper Saddle River, NJ: Prentice-Hall.

Mackie, R.T., McCulloch, D.L., Sauners, K.J., et al. (1995). Comparison of visual assessment tests in multiply handicapped children. *Eye, 9,* 136–141.

Mallery-Ruganis, D., & Fischer, S. (1991). Characteristics that contribute to effective simultaneous communication. *American Annals of the Deaf, 136*(5), 401–408.

McKusick, V.A. (1998). *Mendelian inheritance in man: A catalog of human genes and genetic disorders* (12th ed.). Baltimore: The Johns Hopkins University Press.

Mellor, D.H., & Fielder, A.R. (1980). Dissociated visual development: Electrodiagnostic studies in infants who are "slow to see." *Developmental Medicine and Child Neurology, 22*(3), 327–335.

Menacker, S.J. (1993). Visual function in children with developmental disabilities. *Pediatric Clinics of North America, 40,* 659–674.

Meredith, R., Stephens, D., Hogan, S., et al. (1994). Screening for hearing loss in an at-risk neonatal population using evoked otoacoustic emissions. *Scandinavian Audiology, 23,* 187–193.

Miyamoto, R.T. (1995). Cochlear implants. *Otolaryngologic Clinics of North America, 28,* 287–294.

Miyamoto, R.T., Kirk, K.I., Todd, S.L., et al. (1995). Speech perception skills of children with multichannel cochlear implants or hearing aids. *Annals of Otology, Rhinology, and Laryngology, 166* (Suppl.), 334–337.

Moller, M.A. (1993). Working with visually impaired children and their families. *Pediatric Clinics of North America, 40*(4), 881–890.

Muntz, H.R. (1993). An overview of middle ear disease in cleft palate children. *Facial Plastic Surgery, 9,* 177–180.

National Society for the Prevention of Blindness. (1973). *A guide for eye inspection and testing visual acuity of pre-school age children: A screening process.* New York: Author.

Newcomb, R.P. (1977). The causes of blindness in children: A review of the literature. *Journal of the American Optometric Association, 48,* 499–503.

Nwaesei, C.G. (1984). Changes in auditory brainstem responses in hyperbilirubinemic infants before and after exchange transfusion. *Pediatrics, 74*(5), 800–803.

Ottar, W.L., Scott, W.E., & Holgado, S.I. (1995). Photoscreening for amblyogenic factors. *Journal of Pediatric Ophthalmology and Strabismus, 32,* 289–295.

Page, A., Kramer, S., Novak, J., et al. (1995). Tympanometric screening in elementary school children. *Audiology, 34,* 6–12.

Paradise, J.L. (1981). Otitis media during early life: How hazardous to development? A critical review of the evidence. *Pediatrics, 68*(6), 869–873.

Peters, S.A., Grievink, E.H., van Bon, W.H., et al. (1997). The contribution of risk factors to the effect of early otitis media with effusion on later language, reading, and spelling. *Developmental Medicine and Child Neurology, 39,* 31–39.

Phelps, D.L. (1993). Retinopathy of prematurity. *Pediatric Clinics of North America, 40,* 705–714.

Rayner, S.A., Hollick, E.J., & Lee, J.P. (1999). Botulinum toxin in childhood strabismus. *Strabismus, 7*(2), 103–111.

Roid, G.H., & Miller, L.J. (1997). *Leiter International Performance Scale-Revised.* Wood Dale, IL: C.H. Stoelting Co.

Roizen, N.J., Mets, M.B., & Blondis, T.A. (1994). Ophthalmic disorders in children with Down syndrome. *Developmental Medicine and Child Neurology, 36,* 594–600.

Roizen, N.J., Wolters, C., Nicol, T., & Blondis, T.A. (1993). Hearing loss in children with Down syndrome. *Journal of Pediatrics, 123,* S9–S12.

Roland, E.H., Jan, J.E., Hill, A., & Wong, P.K. (1986). Cortical visual impairment following birth asphyxia. *Pediatric Neurology, 2,* 133–137.

Rose, D.E., Vernon, M., & Pool, A.F. (1996). Cochlear implants in prelingually deaf children. *American Annals of the Deaf, 141,* 258–262.

Schein, J.D., & Delk, M.T. (1974). *The Deaf population of the United States.* Silver Spring, MD: National Association of the Deaf.

Schenk-Rootlieb, A.J., van Nieuwenhuizen, O., van der Graaf, Y., et al. (1992). The prevalence of cerebral visual disturbance in children with cerebral palsy. *Developmental Medicine and Child Neurology, 34,* 473–480.

Schildroth, A. (1994). Congenital cytomegalovirus and deafness. *American Journal of Audiology, 3,* 27–38.

Schworm, H.D., Kau, C., Reindl, B., et al. (1997). Photoscreening for early detection of amblyopic eye changes. *Klinische Monatsblatter fur Augenheilkunde [Clinical Monthly Letter for Eye Diseases], 210,* 158–164.

Shapiro, A.M., & Bluestone, C.D. (1995). Otitis media reassessed: Up-to-date answers to some basic questions. *Postgraduate Medicine, 97,* 73–76.

Silverstein, H., Kuhn, J., Choo, D., et al. (1996). Laser-assisted tympanostomy. *Laryngoscope, 106*(9 pt. 1), 1067–1074.

Simeonsson, R.J., Chen, J., & Hu, Y. (1995). Functional assessment of Chinese children with the ABILITIES index. *Disability and Rehabilitation, 17*(1), 400–410.

Simmons, F.B. (1980). Patterns of deafness in newborns. *Laryngoscope, 90,* 448–453.

Simons, K. (Ed.). (1996). *Early visual development: Normal and abnormal.* New York: Oxford University Press.

Smith, L.K., Thompson, J.R., Woodruff, G., & Hiscox, F. (1995). Factors affecting treatment compliance in amblyopia. *Journal of Pediatric Ophthalmology and Strabismus, 32,* 98–101.

Stapells, D.R., & Oates, P. (1997). Estimation of the pure-tone audiogram by the auditory brainstem response: A review. *Audiology and Neuro-otology, 2*(5), 257–280.

Stein, L., Kraus, N., McGee, T., et al. (1995). New developments in the clinical application of auditory evoked potentials with children with multiple handicaps. *Scandinavian Audiology, 40*(Suppl.), 18–30.

Stewart, D.L., Bibb, K.W., & Pearlman, A. (1993). Automated newborn hearing testing with the ALGO-1 Screener. *Clinical Pediatrics, 32,* 308–311.

Teller, D.Y., McDonald, M.A., Preston, K., et al. (1986). Assessment of visual acuity in infants and children: The acuity card procedure. *Developmental Medicine and Child Neurology, 28*(6), 779–789.

Thylefors, B., Negrel, A.D., Pararajasegaram, R., & Dadzie, K.Y. (1995). Global data on blindness. *Bulletin of the World Health Organization, 73,* 115–121.

Tong, P.Y., Enke-Miyazaki, E., Bassin, R.E., et al. (1998). Screening for amblyopia in preverbal children with photoscreening photographs: National Children's Study Group. *Opthalmology, 105,* 856–863.

Tresidder, J., Fielder, A.R., & Nicholson, J. (1990). Delayed visual maturation: Ophthalmic and neurodevelopmental aspects. *Developmental Medicine and Child Neurology 33*(10), 872–881.

Vohr, B.R., Cary, L.M., Moore, P.E., & Letourneau, K. (1998). The Rhode Island Hearing Assessment Program: Experience with statewide hearing screening (1993–1998). *Journal of Pediatrics, 133,* 353–357.

Warburg, M. (1983). Why are the blind and severely visually impaired children with mental retardation much more retarded than the sighted children? *Acta Ophthalmologica, 157*(Suppl.), 72–81.

Warburg, M., Frederiksen, P., & Rattleff, J. (1979). Results of a screening of blindness among 7,720 mentally retarded children in Denmark. *Clinics in Developmental Medicine, 73,* 56–67.

Wasserman, R.C., Croft, C.A., & Brotherton, S.E. (1992). Preschool vision screening in pediatric practice: A study from the Pediatric Research in Office Settings. *Pediatrics, 89,* 834–838.

Williamson, W.D., Demmer, G.J., & Percy, A.K. (1992). Progressive hearing loss in infants with asymptomatic congenital cytomegalovirus infection. *Pediatrics, 89,* 862–866.

Williamson, W.D., Desmond, M.M., Andrew, L.P., & Hicks, R.N.(1987). Visually impaired infants in the 1980's: Survey of etiological factors and additional handicapping conditions in a school population. *Clinical Pediatrics, 26,* 241–244.

Wodrich, D.L. (1997). *Children's psychological testing: A guide for nonpsychologists* (3rd ed.). Baltimore: Paul H. Brookes Publishing Co.

Wood, D. (1992). Total communication in the education of deaf children. *Developmental Medicine and Child Neurology, 34,* 266–269.

Woodruff, G., Hiscox, F., Thompson, J.R., et al. (1994). Factors effecting the outcome of children treated for amblyopia. *Eye, 8,* 627–631.

York, D.H. (1986). Non-invasive monitoring of intracranial pressure with visual evoked potentials. *Clinical Neuroscience, 2,* 3–7.

Yoshinaga-Itano, C., Sedey, A.L., Coulter, D.K., & Mehl, A.L. (1998). Language of early- and later-identified children with hearing loss. *Pediatrics, 102,* 1161–1171.

Zieziula, F.R. (Ed.). (1982). *Assessment of hearing impaired persons.* Washington, DC: Gallaudet College Press.

9

Appendix

Guidelines for the Care of
Children and Adolescents with Visual Impairments

Basic Team

The special care needs of infants and children who have visual impairments, especially those with severe degrees of impairment, are best met by an experienced, coordinated, interdisciplinary team of specialists who will work collaboratively with parents, the primary care physician, and other service providers. Not all members of the team are needed at every visit, and other professionals may be required at certain times; for example, a medical geneticist may be needed as part of the diagnostic evaluation. The parents of children with visual impairments and people who themselves have visual impairments should be actively encouraged to participate as part of the team. All of these children require a medical home to provide routine medical care and to assist with the coordination of services. The primary care physician is responsible for providing the medical home.

Regular members of the basic team are a developmental pediatrician, a low vision specialist, a medical social worker, a nurse or nurse practitioner, an occupational therapist, a pediatric ophthalmologist, a psychologist, a special education teacher, a teacher of students with visual impairments, and a vision resources therapist or teacher.

Initial Evaluation

The objectives of the initial evaluation are to clarify the extent of the visual impairment and to identify the cause of the disability and associated medical and developmental problems. The initial diagnostic workup will be coordinated by the primary care physician in conjunction with the specialists. The number and type of laboratory tests and procedures will vary depending on the type and number of associated medical problems and disabilities. All infants and children who have a serious visual impairment should have an evaluation to determine an etiologic diagnosis. An initial plan for educational and other services should be developed as quickly after the initial diagnosis as possible.

Frequency of Visits

The infant or child with a visual impairment should be reevaluated by the specialty team several times per year in the first 2 to 3 years after the diagnosis is established, twice a year until school age, and then once a year. If the vision loss is progressive, more frequent visits may be required. Children with multiple disabilities may require follow-up by other specialists (e.g., the pediatric neurologist and neurodevelopmental team for a child with visual impairment, seizures, mental retardation, and cerebral palsy). The responsibilities of the primary care physician are: 1) to evaluate and treat acute medical conditions; 2) to monitor the child's development and progress in services, and to update an office management plan at least yearly; 3) to obtain family, medical, and developmental histories and share pertinent information with specialists; 4) to assist the family and specialty team in communication with school staff and other providers; and 5) to provide ongoing support to the child and family.

The Physician's Guide to Caring for Children with Disabilities and Chronic Conditions, edited by Robert E. Nickel and Larry W. Desch,
copyright © 2000 Paul H. Brookes Publishing Co.

Guidelines for the Care of Children and Adolescents with Visual Impairments

The following elements are recommended by age group, and the listing is cumulative. Review all items indicated up through the actual age group of a child entering your practice for the first time as part of the initial evaluation.

AGE	KEY CLINICAL ISSUES/CONCERNS	EVALUATIONS/KEY PROCEDURES	SPECIALISTS
Birth–5 years (pre-school age)	*Growth/Nutrition* Failure to thrive Oral motor dysfunction Short stature Microcephaly or macrocephaly	Growth parameters, diet record, nutrition, and feeding assessment Special diet and feeding program as needed Cranial computed tomography or magnetic resonance imaging (MRI) scan as needed	Nutritionist, feeding specialist or team, endocrinologist as needed
	Associated Medical Problems Hearing loss Seizures Neuromotor problems (e.g., hypotonia, cerebral palsy) Sleep problems Constipation	Hearing testing in all children Electroencephalogram Detailed neuromotor exam Behavioral management, occasional short-term medications Diet, medications (e.g., bulk agent), timed toilet training, adaptive seat as needed	Audiologist Child neurologist as needed Physical therapist (PT), developmental pediatrician (DPed), nurse specialist as needed
	Note side effects of any medications.		
	Dental Care	Review oral hygiene	Dentist
	Cause of the Visual Impairment	Evaluation for minor anomalies Chromosomes, cranial MRI scan, metabolic studies as needed	DPed or medical geneticist as needed
	Management of the Visual Disorder and Associated Visual Problems Retinopathy of prematurity (ROP) Strabismus/amblyopia Glaucoma Microophthalmia (e.g., clinical anophthalmia and need for ocular prosthesis)	Detailed ophthalmologic and visual motor exam Glasses, patching, surgical correction as needed	Pediatric ophthalmologist, vision specialist
	Associated Behavior and Mental Health Problems Autistic-like behaviors Aggression Hyperactivity/inattention Oppositional behavior Anxiety	Interview, behavior rating scales Functional analysis of behavior as needed Behavior management programs at home and school Medication as needed	Referral to child development team or psychologist, behavioral consultant, child psychiatrist as needed

The Physician's Guide to Caring for Children with Disabilities and Chronic Conditions, edited by Robert E. Nickel and Larry W. Desch, copyright © 2000 Paul H. Brookes Publishing Co.

Guidelines for the Care of Children and Adolescents with Visual Impairments (continued)

The following elements are recommended by age group, and the listing is cumulative. Review all items indicated up through the actual age group of a child entering your practice for the first time as part of the initial evaluation.

AGE	KEY CLINICAL ISSUES/CONCERNS	EVALUATIONS/KEY PROCEDURES	SPECIALISTS
Birth–5 years (pre-school age) (continued)	*Developmental Progress, Early Intervention/ Early Childhood Special Education (EI/ECSE) Services* Need for ancillary services: Physical therapy (PT), occupational therapy (OT), speech-language therapy Delayed gross motor milestones Fine motor concerns Delayed speech-language skills	Developmental surveillance Referral for EI/ECSE services, review individualized family service plan (IFSP) with family Detailed musculoskeletal and neuromotor examination, evaluation of speech-language and motor skills	Referral to physical therapist, occupational therapist, speech-language pathologist as needed or for evaluation by child development team Collaborate with EI/ECSE staff
	Review of Diagnosis and Anticipatory Guidance Review IFSP or individualized education program (IEP) with family Transition from EI to ECSE and from ECSE to elementary school Sibling programs Promotion of self-care/independence Accident prevention	Family interview, educational materials, resource information, initiate care notebook Teacher interview, school conference as needed	Primary care office in collaboration with specialty team
	Family Support Services Respite care Parent group Community health nurse Advocacy Financial services (Supplemental Security Income [SSI]) Other enabling services (e.g., Lions Club Eye Services)	Family interview, parent questionnaires (e.g., Family Needs Survey), provide resource information Referral to community services	Medical social worker, community health nurse as needed
	Collaboration with Community Services School Community health nurse Other providers	Comprehensive care coordination with regular exchange of written information (at least yearly) with other providers	Primary care office in collaboration with specialty team

The Physician's Guide to Caring for Children with Disabilities and Chronic Conditions, edited by Robert E. Nickel and Larry W. Desch, copyright © 2000 Paul H. Brookes Publishing Co.

Guidelines for the Care of Children and Adolescents with Visual Impairments *(continued)*

The following elements are recommended by age group, and the listing is cumulative. Review all items indicated up through the actual age group of a child entering your practice for the first time as part of the initial evaluation.

AGE	KEY CLINICAL ISSUES/CONCERNS	EVALUATIONS/KEY PROCEDURES	SPECIALISTS
6–12 years (school-age)	*School Progress* Need for teacher for the visually impaired, School for the Blind Need for adaptive materials/low vision aides (e.g., Kurzweil Reader)	Behavioral rating scales, school report, review IEP with family Referral to School for the Blind as needed Evaluation of functional vision	Ophthalmologist, low vision specialist Referral to child development team as needed Collaborate with school staff
	Need for PT and OT services Mobility Self-care/independence	Detailed neuromotor examination, review of activities of daily living and necessary supports	Physical therapist, occupational therapist, low vision specialist
	Associated Behavior or Mental Health Problems Autistic-like behaviors Attention-deficit/hyperactivity disorder (ADHD) Oppositional behavior Anxiety, depression Aggression Self-injurious behaviors (SIBs) and stereotypies	Behavioral rating scales, functional analysis of behavior Behavior management programs at home and at school Medication management as needed Collaborate with school staff	Referral to child development team, behavioral consultant, or mental health professional as needed
	Social Skills Promote social competence Involvement in peer group activities at school and in the community (determine which supports are needed)	Social skills program at school, encourage participation in community services	Psychologist, behavioral consultant, physical therapist, occupational therapist, adaptive physical education specialist as needed Collaborate with school staff
	Anticipatory Guidance Sports and leisure activities Transition to middle school Link with other children/adults with visual impairment	Provide resource information on community services Encourage participation in community recreational and leisure activities Refer to advocacy groups, School for the Blind	Primary care office in collaboration with specialty team

The Physician's Guide to Caring for Children with Disabilities and Chronic Conditions, edited by Robert E. Nickel and Larry W. Desch, copyright © 2000 Paul H. Brookes Publishing Co.

Guidelines for the Care of Children and Adolescents with Visual Impairments *(continued)*

The following elements are recommended by age group, and the listing is cumulative. Review all items indicated up through the actual age group of a child entering your practice for the first time as part of the initial evaluation.

AGE	KEY CLINICAL ISSUES/CONCERNS	EVALUATIONS/KEY PROCEDURES	SPECIALISTS
13–21 years (adolescents, young adults)	*Self-Care/Independent Living* Determine which supports are needed to promote self-care and independent living skills	Evaluation of equipment and support needs, OT services as needed Independent living skills program, social skills training as needed	Low vision specialist, occupational therapist, psychologist, medical social worker as needed Collaborate with school staff
	Anticipatory Guidance Transition to middle school and high school Encourage healthy behaviors (diet, exercise) Sexuality and birth control, high risk behaviors Vocational training/career planning/higher education Life skills programs (independent living) Transition to adult services	Adolescent, family, and teacher interviews; school conference as needed; review IEP with family Evaluation by vocational specialist, life skills training program as needed	Primary care office in collaboration with specialty team Gynecologist as needed Referral to state services for the visually impaired, developmental disability services, department of vocational rehabilitation as needed

The Physician's Guide to Caring for Children with Disabilities and Chronic Conditions, edited by Robert E. Nickel and Larry W. Desch, copyright © 2000 Paul H. Brookes Publishing Co.

Family and Physician Management Plan Summary for Children and Adolescents with Visual Impairments

This form will help you and your physician review current services and service needs. Please answer the questions about your current services on this page. Your physician will review your responses and complete the rest of the form.

Child's name _____ Today's date _____

Person completing the form _____

CURRENT SERVICES

1. Please list your/your child's current medications and any side effects.

2. What is your/your child's current school program?

   School name _____ Grade _____

   Teacher _____ Telephone _____

3. Does your child receive any support services at school (e.g., occupational therapy, low-vision specialist)? Please list.

4. Who are your/your child's other medical and dental service providers?

   Ophthalmologist _____

   Neurologist _____

   Dentist _____

   Other _____

5. Who are your/your child's other community service providers?

   Teacher of visually impaired _____

   Low-vision specialist _____

   Other _____

Family and Physician Management Plan Summary for Children and Adolescents with Visual Impairments *(continued)*

6. Do you also receive services from a specialist team?

   Contact person _____

   Location _____

7. Have you/has your child had visual acuity testing, blood tests, radiologic (i.e., X-ray) examinations, or other procedures since your last visit? If yes, please describe.

8. Have you/has your child been hospitalized or undergone surgery since your last visit? If yes, describe.

9. Please note your/your child's accomplishments since your/your child's last visit. Consider activities at home, in your neighborhood, or at school, as well as success with treatments.

10. What goals (i.e., skills) would you/your child like to accomplish in the next year? Consider activities at home, in your neighborhood, or at school, as well as success with a treatment.

11. What questions or concerns would you like addressed today?

The Physician's Guide to Caring for Children with Disabilities and Chronic Conditions, edited by Robert E. Nickel and Larry W. Desch, copyright © 2000 Paul H. Brookes Publishing Co.

Family and Physician Management Plan Summary for Children and Adolescents with Visual Impairments

The Family and Physician Management Plan Summary should be completed at each annual review and more often as needed. It is intended to be used with the Guidelines for Care, which provide a more complete listing of clinical issues at different ages and recommended evaluations and treatments.

Child's name _____ Person completing form _____ Today's date _____

Clinical issues	Currently a problem?	Evaluations needed	Treatment recommendations	Referrals made	Date for status check
Family's Questions					
Cause of the Visual Impairment					
Growth/Nutrition/Feeding Feeding problems Inadequate weight gain or obesity Short stature Microcephaly or macrocephaly					
Dental Care					
Management of the Visual Disorder and Associated Visual Problems Retinopathy of prematurity (ROP) Strabismus/amblyopia Glaucoma Microophthalmia (e.g., clinical anophthalmia and need for ocular prosthesis)					

The Physician's Guide to Caring for Children with Disabilities and Chronic Conditions, edited by Robert E. Nickel and Larry W. Desch, copyright © 2000 Paul H. Brookes Publishing Co.

Family and Physician Management Plan Summary for Children and Adolescents with Visual Impairments *(continued)*

Child's name _____ Person completing form _____ Today's date _____

Clinical issues	Currently a problem?	Evaluations needed	Treatment recommendations	Referrals made	Date for status check
Associated Medical Issues Hearing concerns Seizures Neuromotor problems (e.g., hypotonia, cerebral palsy) Sleep disorder					
Developmental and School Progress Current school achievement Review individualized family service plan (IFSP) or individualized education program (IEP) with family Teacher for the visually impaired Need for adaptive materials/low vision aides (e.g., Kurzweil Reader)					
Need for Physical or Occupational Therapy Services Mobility Associated hypotonia, dyspraxia, ataxia, or cerebral palsy Fine motor concerns					
Social Skills Involvement in peer group activities at school and in community (determine which supports are needed) Involvement with other children and adults with visual impairments					

The Physician's Guide to Caring for Children with Disabilities and Chronic Conditions, edited by Robert E. Nickel and Larry W. Desch, copyright © 2000 Paul H. Brookes Publishing Co.

Family and Physician Management Plan Summary for Children and Adolescents with Visual Impairments *(continued)*

Child's name _____   Person completing form _____   Today's date _____

Clinical issues	Currently a problem?	Evaluations needed	Treatment recommendations	Referrals made	Date for status check
Self-Care/Independence					
Family Support Services					
Anticipatory Guidance List issues discussed and materials provided					
Collaboration with Community Agencies School Low-vision specialist, state school for students with visual impairment					
Comments					

Next update of the Management Plan Summary _____

Signature _____ Date _____

(Child and parent)

Signature _____ Date _____

(Health professional)

The Physician's Guide to Caring for Children with Disabilities and Chronic Conditions, edited by Robert E. Nickel and Larry W. Desch, copyright © 2000 Paul H. Brookes Publishing Co.

Guidelines for the Care of
Children and Adolescents with Hearing Impairments

Basic Team

The special care needs of infants and children who have hearing impairments, especially those with severe degrees of impairment, are best met by an experienced, coordinated, interdisciplinary team of specialists who will work collaboratively with parents, the primary care physician, and other service providers. Not all members of the team are needed at every visit, and other professionals may be required at certain times; for example, a medical geneticist may be needed as part of the diagnostic evaluation. The parents of children with hearing impairments and people who themselves have hearing impairments should be actively encouraged to participate as part of the team. All of these children require a medical home to provide routine medical care and to assist with the coordination of services. The primary care physician is responsible for providing the medical home.

Regular members of the basic team are a developmental pediatrician, an audiologist, a medical social worker, a nurse or nurse practitioner, an occupational therapist, an otolaryngologist (ENT), a psychologist, a special education teacher, and a teacher of students with hearing impairments.

Initial Evaluation

The objectives of the initial evaluation are to clarify the extent of the hearing impairment and to identify the cause of the disability and associated medical and developmental problems. The initial diagnostic workup will be coordinated by the primary care physician in conjunction with the specialists. The number and type of laboratory tests and procedures will vary depending on the type and number of associated medical problems and disabilities. All infants and children who have a hearing impairment should have an evaluation to determine an etiologic diagnosis. An initial plan for educational and other services should be developed as quickly after the initial diagnosis as possible.

Frequency of Visits

The infant or child with a hearing impairment should be reevaluated by the specialty team several times per year in the first 2 to 3 years after the diagnosis is established, twice a year until school age, and then once a year. If the hearing loss is progressive, more frequent visits may be required. Children with multiple disabilities may require follow-up by other specialists (e.g., the pediatric neurologist and neurodevelopmental team for a child with hearing impairment, seizures, mental retardation, and cerebral palsy). The responsibilities of the primary care physician are: 1) to evaluate and treat acute medical conditions; 2) to monitor the child's development and progress in services, and to update an office management plan at least yearly; 3) to obtain family, medical, and developmental histories and share pertinent information with specialists; 4) to assist the family and specialty team in communication with school staff and other providers; and 5) to provide ongoing support to the child and family.

The Physician's Guide to Caring for Children with Disabilities and Chronic Conditions, edited by Robert E. Nickel and Larry W. Desch,
copyright © 2000 Paul H. Brookes Publishing Co.

Guidelines for the Care of Children and Adolescents with Hearing Impairments

The following elements are recommended by age group and the listing is cumulative. Review all items indicated up through the actual age group of a child entering your practice for the first time as part of the initial evaluation.

AGE	KEY CLINICAL ISSUES/CONCERNS	EVALUATIONS/KEY PROCEDURES	SPECIALISTS
Birth–5 years (pre-school age)	*Growth/Nutrition*	Growth parameters, diet record	Nutritionist as needed
	Associated Medical Problems		
	Recurrent otitis media or persistent serous otitis media	Monitor middle-ear function	Audiologist, otolaryngologist (ENT) as needed
	Strabismus/visual problems	Vision testing	Ophthalmologist
	Seizures	Electroencephalogram (EEG)	Child neurologist as needed
	Neuromotor concerns (e.g., hypotonia, ataxia)	Detailed neuromotor examination	Physical therapist, developmental pediatrician (DPed) as needed
	Sleep problems	Behavior management, occasional short-term medications	
	Renal disease	Urinalysis, consider renal ultrasound	Urologist, nephrologist as needed
	Note side effects of any medications.		
	Dental Care	Review oral hygiene	Dentist
	Cause of the Hearing Impairment	Evaluation for minor anomalies	DPed or medical geneticist as needed
		Chromosomes, cranial magnetic resonance imaging (MRI) scan, metabolic studies as needed	
	Management of the Hearing Loss (Aural Habilitation)	Audiologic testing including tympanometry at least annually and as needed	Audiologist, speech-language pathologist (SLP), ENT
	Hearing aids and other adaptive equipment (e.g., FM transmitter system)	Family interview, educational materials, behavioral management as needed	Referral to behavioral specialist as needed
	Monitor middle-ear function		
	Monitor for progressive hearing loss		
	Review indications for cochlear implant		
	Compliance with hearing aides/treatment program		
	Communication/Language Progress	Monitor communication (speech and ASL) and language skills	SLP, specialty team
	Speech-language delay	Referral to community services	
	Sign language classes for family	Family interview, educational materials	
	Review educational choices (e.g., aural/oral, American Sign Language (ASL), total communication, bilingual/bicultural)		

The Physician's Guide to Caring for Children with Disabilities and Chronic Conditions, edited by Robert E. Nickel and Larry W. Desch, copyright © 2000 Paul H. Brookes Publishing Co.

Guidelines for the Care of Children and Adolescents with Hearing Impairments *(continued)*

The following elements are recommended by age group and the listing is cumulative. Review all items indicated up through the actual age group of a child entering your practice for the first time as part of the initial evaluation.

AGE	KEY CLINICAL ISSUES/CONCERNS	EVALUATIONS/KEY PROCEDURES	SPECIALISTS
Birth–5 years (pre-school age) *(continued)*	*Associated Behavior Problems* Autistic-like behaviors Hyperactivity/inattention Noncompliance/oppositional behavior	Interview, behavioral rating scales Behavior management programs at home and school as needed	Referral to child development team or psychologist, behavioral consultant as needed
	Developmental Progress, Early Intervention (EI)/Early Childhood Special Education (ECSE) services Need for ancillary services; PT, OT (e.g., neuromotor or fine motor/visual motor concerns)	Developmental surveillance Request EI/ECSE report, review individualized family service plan (IFSP) with family Detailed neuromotor exam, assessment of visual motor skills	Referral to physical therapist, occupational therapist, psychologist as needed, or for evaluation by child development team Collaborate with EI/ECSE staff
	Review of Diagnosis and Anticipatory Guidance Training for family in sign language Discuss educational choices, transition to School for the Deaf Review IFSP or individualized education program (IEP) with family Transition from EI to ECSE and ECSE to grade school Sibling programs Discussion of alternative (controversial) therapies Promotion of self-care/independence	Family interview, educational materials, resource information, initiate care notebook Referral to community services for course in sign language Teacher interview, school conference as needed	Speech-language pathologist (SLP), specialty team in collaboration with EI/ECSE staff
	Family Support Services Respite care Parent group Advocacy Financial services (Supplemental Security Income [SSI]) Other enabling services	Family interview, parent questionnaires (e.g., Family Needs Survey), provide resource information	Medical social worker, referral to community services as needed
	Collaboration with Community Services Educational services Other providers	Comprehensive care coordination with regular exchange of written information (at least yearly) with other providers	Primary care office in collaboration with specialty team

The Physician's Guide to Caring for Children with Disabilities and Chronic Conditions, edited by Robert E. Nickel and Larry W. Desch, copyright © 2000 Paul H. Brookes Publishing Co.

Guidelines for the Care of Children and Adolescents with Hearing Impairments *(continued)*

The following elements are recommended by age group and the listing is cumulative. Review all items indicated up through the actual age group of a child entering your practice for the first time as part of the initial evaluation.

AGE	KEY CLINICAL ISSUES/CONCERNS	EVALUATIONS/KEY PROCEDURES	SPECIALISTS
6–12 years (school-age)	*School Progress—Need for Special Education, PT, OT*	School report, review IEP with family as needed Detailed neuromotor examination	Referral to child development team or individual evaluations by physical therapist, occupational therapist, psychologist Collaborate with school staff
	Communication/Language Progress Review requirements for speech-language support, need for FM transmitter system in classroom	Monitor communication/language progress	SLP, audiologist as needed Collaborate with school staff
	Social Skills Promote social competence Involvement in peer group activities at school and in the community (what supports are needed?)	Social skills program at school as needed, encourage participation in community services	SLP, psychologist, occupational therapist as needed Collaborate with school staff
	Anticipatory Guidance Discussion of diagnosis and management with child Sports and leisure activities Transition to middle school Link with other children/adults with hearing impairment, users of ASL (as indicated)	Provide resource information on community services Encourage participation in community recreational and leisure activities (determine which supports are needed) Referral to advocacy groups, School for the Deaf	Specialty team in collaboration with primary care office
13–21 years (adolescents, young adults)	*Self-Care/Independent Living* Determine which supports are needed	OT services as needed Independent living skills program, social skills training as needed	SLP, audiologist, occupational therapist, psychologist as needed Collaborate with school staff
	Anticipatory Guidance Transition to middle school and high school Encourage healthy behaviors (e.g., diet, exercise) Sexuality and birth control, high-risk behaviors Career planning, higher education (e.g., Gallaudet College) Transition to adult services	Adolescent, family and teacher interviews, school conference as needed, review IEP with family Evaluation by vocational specialist as needed	Primary care office in collaboration with specialty team Gynecologist as needed

The Physician's Guide to Caring for Children with Disabilities and Chronic Conditions, edited by Robert E. Nickel and Larry W. Desch, copyright © 2000 Paul H. Brookes Publishing Co.

Family and Physician Management Plan Summary for Children and Adolescents with Hearing Impairments

This form will help you and your physician review current services and service needs. Please answer the questions about your current services on this page. Your physician will review your responses and complete the rest of the form.

Child's name _____ Today's date _____

Person completing the form _____

CURRENT SERVICES

1. Please list your/your child's current medications and any side effects.

2. What is your/your child's current school program?

    School name _____ Grade _____

    Teacher _____ Telephone _____

3. Do you/does your child receive any support services and other special programs at school (e.g., speech therapy)? Please list.

4. Who are your/your child's other medical and dental service providers?

    Audiologist _____

    Otolaryngologist _____

    Dentist _____

    Other _____

5. Who are your/your child's other community service providers?

    Speech-language pathologist _____

    Community health nurse _____

    Other _____

The Physician's Guide to Caring for Children with Disabilities and Chronic Conditions, edited by Robert E. Nickel and Larry W. Desch, copyright © 2000 Paul H. Brookes Publishing Co.

Family and Physician Management Plan Summary for
Children and Adolescents with Hearing Impairments *(continued)*

6. Do you/does your child also receive services from a child development team of specialists?

    Contact person _____

    Location _____

7. Have you/has your child had hearing testing or other procedures since your last visit? If yes, please describe.

8. Have you/has your child been hospitalized or received surgery since your last visit? If yes, describe.

9. Please note your/your child's accomplishments since your/your child's last visit. Consider activities at home, in your neighborhood, or at school, as well as success with treatments.

10. What goals (i.e., skills) would you/your child like to accomplish in the next year? Consider activities at home, in your neighborhood, or at school, as well as success with a treatment.

11. What questions or concerns would you like addressed today?

The Physician's Guide to Caring for Children with Disabilities and Chronic Conditions, edited by Robert E. Nickel and Larry W. Desch, copyright © 2000 Paul H. Brookes Publishing Co.

Family and Physician Management Plan Summary for Children and Adolescents with Hearing Impairments

The Family and Physician Management Plan Summary should be completed at each annual review and more often as needed. It is intended to be used with the Guidelines for Care, which provide a more complete listing of clinical issues at different ages and recommended evaluations and treatments.

Child's name _____ Person completing form _____ Today's date _____

Clinical issues	Currently a problem?	Evaluations needed	Treatment recommendations	Referrals made	Date for status check
Family's Questions					
Cause of the Hearing Impairment					
Growth/Nutrition/Feeding					
Dental Care					
Management of the Hearing Loss Current hearing level with/without aids Use of aides/other adaptive equipment Monitor middle-ear function Monitor for progressive loss Review use of cochlear implants Compliance					

The Physician's Guide to Caring for Children with Disabilities and Chronic Conditions, edited by Robert E. Nickel and Larry W. Desch, copyright © 2000 Paul H. Brookes Publishing Co.

Family and Physician Management Plan Summary for Children and Adolescents with Hearing Impairments *(continued)*

Child's name _____ Person completing form _____ Today's date _____

Clinical issues	Currently a problem?	Evaluations needed	Treatment recommendations	Referrals made	Date for status check
Communication/Language Progress Speech-language delay Review educational choices Sign language classes for the family					
Associated Medical Problems Visual problems Seizures Neuromotor concerns (e.g., hypotonia, ataxia) Renal disease Sleep disorder **Note side effects of any medications.**					
Developmental/School Progress Developmental surveillance Current school achievement Review individualized family service plan or individualized education program with family					
Associated Behavior Problems Inattention/hyperactivity Oppositional behavior Anxiety, depression Aggression					

The Physician's Guide to Caring for Children with Disabilities and Chronic Conditions, edited by Robert E. Nickel and Larry W. Desch, copyright © 2000 Paul H. Brookes Publishing Co.

Family and Physician Management Plan Summary for Children and Adolescents with Hearing Impairments *(continued)*

Child's name _____ Person completing form _____ Today's date _____

Clinical issues	Currently a problem?	Evaluations needed	Treatment recommendations	Referrals made	Date for status check
Need for Physical or Occupational Therapy Services Associated dyspraxia, ataxia, or cerebral palsy (physical therapy [PT] evaluation) Fine motor/visual motor concerns (occupational therapy [OT] evaluation)					
Social Skills Involvement in peer group activities at school, in community Involvement with children and adults with hearing impairment					
Promote Self-Care/Independence					
Family Support Services					
Anticipatory Guidance List issues discussed and materials provided					

The Physician's Guide to Caring for Children with Disabilities and Chronic Conditions, edited by Robert E. Nickel and Larry W. Desch, copyright © 2000 Paul H. Brookes Publishing Co.

Family and Physician Management Plan Summary for Children and Adolescents with Hearing Impairments *(continued)*

Child's name _____ Person completing form _____ Today's date _____

Clinical issues	Currently a problem?	Evaluations needed	Treatment recommendations	Referrals made	Date for status check
Collaboration with Community Agencies School					
Comments					

Next update of the Management Plan Summary _____

Signature _____ Date _____
(Child and parent)

Signature _____ Date _____
(Health professional)

The Physician's Guide to Caring for Children with Disabilities and Chronic Conditions, edited by Robert E. Nickel and Larry W. Desch, copyright © 2000 Paul H. Brookes Publishing Co.

RESOURCES ON VISUAL IMPAIRMENTS

Readings

American Foundation for the Blind. (1993). *AFB directory of services for blind and visually impaired persons in the United States* (24th ed.). New York: Author. (212-502-7600)

Blakely, K., Lang, M.A., Kushner, B., & Iltus, S. (1995). *Toys and play: A guide to fun and development for children with impaired vision.* Long Island City, NY: Lighthouse Industries. (1-800-829-0500)

Brown, L.B., Simmons, C., & Methwin, E. (1994). *Oregon Project Curriculum for Visually Impaired and Blind Preschool Children (OPC).* Medford, OR: Jackson County Education Service District.

Curran, E.P. (1988). *Just enough to know better (a braille primer).* Boston: National Braille Press. (1-800-548-7323)

Ferrell, K.A. (1996). *Reach out and teach: Materials for parents of visually handicapped and multihandicapped young children.* New York: American Foundation for the Blind. (212-502-7600)

Harrison, F. (1993). *Living and learning with blind children: A guide for parents and teachers of visually impaired children.* Toronto: University of Toronto Press. (1-800-565-9523)

Hazekamp, J., & Huebner, K.M. (1989). *Program planning and evaluation for blind and visually impaired students: National guidelines for educational excellence.* New York: American Foundation for the Blind. (212-502-7600)

Holbrook, M.C. (Ed.). (1996). *Children with visual impairments: A parents' guide.* Bethesda, MD: Woodbine House. [Available from Woodbine House, 6510 Bells Mill Road, Bethesda, MD 20817; telephone: 1-800-843-7323 (outside the Washington, D.C., calling area); (301) 897-3570 (within the Washington, D.C., calling area).]

Pogrund, R.L., Fazzi, D.L., & Lampert, J.S. (Eds.). (1992). *Early focus: Working with young blind and visually impaired children and their families.* New York: American Foundation for the Blind. (212-502-7600)

Scott, E., Jan, J., & Freeman, R. (1995). *Can't your child see?* (2nd ed.). Austin, TX: PRO-ED. (PRO-ED, 8700 Shoal Creek Boulevard, Austin, TX 78757-6897; Telephone: 1-800-897-3202.)

Warren, D.H. (1994). *Blindness and children: An individual differences approach.* New York: Cambridge University Press. (1-800-221-4512)

National Organizations and Product Information

American Council of the Blind (ACB)
1155 15th Street NW, Suite 1004
Washington, D.C. 20005
Telephone: (800) 424-8666, (202) 467-5081
Fax: (202) 467-5085
E-mail: ncrabb@acces.diges.net
World Wide Web site: http://acb.org/

An advocacy and public policy group for parents that provides information and referrals regarding educational rights and with regard to other topics.

American Foundation for the Blind (AFB)
11 Penn Plaza, Suite 300
New York, New York 10001
Telephone: (212) 502-7600
Fax: (212) 501-7774
E-mail: afbinfo@afb.net
World Wide Web site: http://www.afb.org/

A national organization with six regional offices, AFB works with schools and other organizations to provide information and referrals, public education, and consultation to individuals with visual impairments; produces talking books and other materials; and publishes a journal, *Journal of Visual Impairment and Blindness,* and a directory, *Directory of Services for Blind and Visually Impaired Persons in the U.S.*

The American Printing House for the Blind (APH)
1839 Frankfort Avenue
Post Office Box 6085
Louisville, Kentucky 40206-0085
Telephone: (502) 895-2405, (800) 223-1839
Fax: (502) 899-2274
World Wide Web site: http://www.aph.org/

A nonprofit publishing house for people with visual impairments, including books in braille and large-type formats,

recordings, and computer disks; a variety of educational materials are also available.

Lighthouse International
111 East 59th Street
New York, New York 10022-1202
Telephone: (800) 829-0500, (212) 821-9200,
(212) 821-9713 (TTY)
Fax: (212) 821-9705
E-mail: info@lighthouse.org
World Wide Web site: http://www.lighthouse.org/

The Lighthouse provides pamphlets about infants and young children with visual impairments and information about different testing methods for detecting visual impairments; a newsletter as well as materials in Spanish are also available.

Medical Technology Innovations, Inc. (MTI)
615 Centerville Road
Lancaster, Pennsylvania 17601
Telephone: (800) 277-1710 (U.S. and Canada only),
(717) 892-6770
Fax: (717) 892-6788
World Wide Web site:
http://www.photoscreener.com/home.html

MTI develops and sells vision-screening equipment (e.g., MTI PhotoScreener) and other medical devices.

National Association for
Parents of the Visually Impaired (NAPVI)
Post Office Box 317
Watertown, Massachusetts 02272
Telephone: (617) 972-7441, (800) 562-6265
Fax: (617) 972-7444
World Wide Web site: http://www.spedex.com/napvi/

A national organization of, by, and for parents of children who have visual impairments, this group has local support groups and provides information and referrals, including materials on special education services and materials in Spanish.

National Library Services for the Blind and Physically Handicapped

1291 Taylor Street NW
Washington, D.C. 20542
Telephone: (202) 707-5100 (Voice), (202) 707-0744 (TDD)
Fax: (202) 707-0712
E-mail: nls@loc.gov
World Wide Web site: http://www.loc.gov/nls

A national library service that provides braille and recorded books and magazines by loan to individuals who cannot read standard print because of their visual or physical disabilities.

National Organization of Parents of Blind Children (NOPBC)

1800 Johnson Street
Baltimore, Maryland 21230
Telephone: (410) 659-9314
E-mail: nfb@access.digex.net
World Wide Web site: http://www.nfb.org/brochure.htm

The NOPBC is a consumer group within the National Federation of the Blind (NFB) that responds to questions about blindness, refers people to appropriate resources, and offers a publications list. *Postsecondary Education and Career Development: A Resource Guide* can be ordered directly by mail from the organization's headquarters address. The NFB has a number of scholarships available for postsecondary education for students who are blind. *The Braille Monitor* is a monthly publication available without cost to members. The NFB also sponsors JOB, a job listing and referral service.

Prevent Blindness America (formerly the National Society to Prevent Blindness)

500 East Remington Road
Schaumburg, Illinois 60173
Telephone: (708) 843-2020, (800) 331-2020
E-mail: info@preventblindness.org
World Wide Web site: http://www.prevent-blindness.org/

An organization that provides information and referrals, including a "home-practice test" for children to learn to respond to a Snellen "Tumbling E" test and materials in Spanish.

Vision Research Corp.

211 Summit Parkway, Suite 105
Birmingham, Alabama 35209
Telephone: (205) 942-8011
Fax: (205) 942-0701
E-mail: info@vision-research.com
World Wide Web site: http://www.vision-research.com/index.html

Vision Research Corp. developed and sells the VisiScreen OSS-C, a vision-screening device, and also contracts for vision screening of large groups (e.g., schools).

Welch Allyn Medical Products

4341 State Street Road
Post Office Box 220
Skaneateles Falls, New York 13153
Telephone: (800) 535-6663, (315) 685-4100
Fax: (315) 685-3361
World Wide Web site: http://www.welchallyn.com/medical/

Welch Allyn produces the SureSight and other medical diagnostic equipment for vision and hearing assessment.

RESOURCES ON HEARING IMPAIRMENTS

Readings

Adams, J.W. (1988). *You and your hearing-impaired child: A self-instructional guide for parents.* Washington, DC: Gallaudet University. (Available at the Gallaudet University Bookstore, 800 Florida Avenue NE, Washington, DC 20002; Telephone: 1-800-451-1073.)

Alpiner, J.G., & McCarthy, P.A. (1993). *Rehabilitative audiology: Children and adults.* Philadelphia: Lippincott Williams & Wilkins. (1-800-638-3030)

Densham, J. (1995). *Deafness, children and the family: A guide to professional practice.* Brookfield, VT: Ashgate Publishing Co. (1-800-535-9544)

Gorlin, R.L., Tortello, H.V., & Cohen, M.M. Jr. (1995). *Hereditary hearing loss and its syndromes.* New York: Oxford University Press. (1-800-451-7556)

Gregory, S. (1995). *Deaf children and their families.* New York: Cambridge University Press. (1-800-221-4512)

Luterman, D.M. (1991). *When your child is deaf: A guide for parents.* Timonium, MD: York Press. (Available at York Press, P.O. Box 504, Timonium, MD 21094; Telephone: 1-800-962-2763.)

Medwid, D.K., & Westom, D.C. (1995). *Kid-friendly parenting with deaf and hard of hearing children.* Washington, DC: Clerk Books.

Ross, M. (Ed.). (1990). *Hearing-impaired children in the mainstream.* Timonium, MD: York Press. (Available at York Press, P.O. Box 504, Timonium, MD 21094; Telephone: 1-800-962-2763.)

Rushmer, N. (1994). Supporting families of hearing impaired infants and toddlers. *Seminars in Hearing, 15,* 160–172. (American Speech-Language-Hearing Association, 1-800-498-2071)

Schwartz, S. (Ed.). (1996). *Choices in deafness: A parents guide to communication options.* Bethesda, MD: Woodbine House. [Available from Woodbine House, 6510 Bells Mill Road, Bethesda, MD 20817; Telephone: 1-800-843-7323 (outside the Washington, D.C., calling area); (301) 897-3570 (within the Washington, D.C., calling area).

National Organizations and Further Information

Alexander Graham Bell Association for the Deaf and Hard of Hearing
3417 Volta Place NW
Washington, D.C. 20007-2778
Telephone: 202-337-5220 (Voice/TTY)
Fax: (202) 337-8314
World Wide Web site: http://www.agbell.org/

This group, the umbrella organization for International Organization for the Education of the Hearing Impaired (IOEHI), Parents' Section (PS), and Oral Hearing Impaired Section, provides general information and information on resources and encourages improved communication, better public understanding, and detection of early hearing loss, as well as provides scholarships and training for teachers.

American Society for Deaf Children
Post Office Box 3355
Gettysburg, Pennsylvania 17325
Telephone (voice; TTY): (800) 942-2732, (717) 334-7922
Fax: (717) 334-8808
E-mail: asdc1@aol.com
World Wide Web site: http://deafchildren.org/

An organization for parents that provides a variety of materials, facilitates family networking, and organizes conferences.

John Tracy Clinic
806 West Adams Boulevard
Los Angeles, California 90007
Telephone: (800) 522-4582, (213) 748-5481,
   TTY: (213) 747-2924
Fax: (213) 749-1651
World Wide Web site: http://www.johntracyclinic.org/

An excellent resource for families of young children through age 5 years who have a hearing impairment, this organization offers a free correspondence course and many information packets and also has Spanish materials available.

National Association of the Deaf (NAD)
814 Thayer Avenue
Silver Spring, Maryland 20910-4500
Telephone: (301) 587-1788 (Voice), (301) 587-1789 (TTY)
Fax: (301) 587-1791
E-mail: NADinfo@nad.org
World Wide Web site: http://www.nad.org/

A consumer advocacy organization with 51 state associations and affiliates. Its programs include legislative advocacy; community leadership and empowerment; educational choices and alternatives; public awareness and information dissemination; interpreter assessment and certification; communication, media, and technology accessibility; and youth programs. An annual membership fee covers subscriptions to two publications: *NAD Broadcaster* and *The Deaf American Monograph.*

National Cued Speech Association (NCSA)
Grafe Media
1715 Eighth Street East
Menomonie, Wisconsin 54751
Telephone: (715) 232-9467
E-mail: info@cuedspeech.com
World Wide Web site: http://www.cuedspeech.com/

An advocacy organization that provides information and referral as well as networking with local parent groups.

Helen Keller National Center for Deaf-Blind Youths and Adults
111 Middle Neck Road
Sands Point, New York 11050
Telephone: (516) 944-8900 (voice), (516) 944-8637 (TTY)
Fax: (516) 944-7302
World Wide Web site: http://www.helenkeller.org/

An organization that provides advocacy and referral information for agencies and parent groups, including information about educational resources.

National Deaf Education Network and Clearinghouse
(formerly National Information Center on Deafness [NICD])
Gallaudet University
800 Florida Avenue NE
Washington, D.C. 20002-3695
Telephone: (202) 651-5051 (Voice), (202) 651-5052 (TTY)
Fax: (202) 651-5054
E-mail: clearinghouse.infotogo@gallaudet.edu
World Wide Web site: http://www.gallaudet.edu/~nicd

This national information and referral service related to deafness has a multitude of resources available for individuals with hearing impairment, their families, and professionals.

OtoLAM (ESC Sharplan Medical Systems)
E-mail: info@escmed.com
World Wide Web sites: http://www.earinfections.com/,
http://www.escmed.com/

ESC Sharplan Medical Systems developed and distributes the OtoLAM laser-assisted tympanostomy device for treatment of otitis media.

Self Help for Hard of Hearing People (SHHH)
7910 Woodmont Avenue, Suite 1200
Bethesda, Maryland 20814
Telephone: (301) 657-2248 (Voice), (301) 657-2249 (TTY)
Fax: (301) 913-9413
World Wide Web site: http://www.shhh.org/

An advocacy group mainly for adults that focuses on milder forms of hearing impairment and provides information on products such as FM transmitters as well as referrals to agencies and local groups.

Anxiety Disorders

Robert E. Nickel

KEY COMPETENCIES 322

DESCRIPTION 322
    Definition 322
    Classification 322
    Prevalence. 330
    Co-morbidity 330
    Etiology 331

DIAGNOSIS AND EVALUATION 331
    Identification 331
    Comprehensive Evaluation 332
    Counseling the Parents and the Child About the Diagnosis 335
    Counseling Families About School Refusal, Persistent Fears,
        and Behavioral Inhibition 335

MANAGEMENT 336
    Periodic Review and Update of the Management Plan. 336
    Cognitive-Behavioral and Psychodynamic Therapies 337
    Medication Management (Pharmacotherapy) 338
    Family Support Services 339
    Important Care Coordination Issues 339

REFERENCES 340

APPENDIX 345
    Guidelines for the Care of Children and Adolescents with Anxiety Disorders 346
    Family and Physician Management Plan Summary for Children
        and Adolescents with Anxiety Disorders 350
    Resources on Anxiety Disorders 355

KEY COMPETENCIES

- Discuss the classification of anxiety disorders
- Describe common childhood fears and behavioral inhibition in children
- Discuss the use of temperament and behavioral rating questionnaires
- List factors that help determine when to refer the child to mental heath professionals
- Review the basic components of cognitive-behavioral therapies and medication management of children with anxiety disorders
- Describe the important care coordination issues in the management of children and adolescents with anxiety disorders

DESCRIPTION

Definition

Anxiety disorders are a group of closely related disorders that are characterized by persistent and excessive anxiety about objects, strangers, specific situations, or being separated from parents or other family members that result in significant disruption in daily function at home, at school, or in the community.

Classification

Table 10.1 presents the classification of anxiety disorders from the *Diagnostic and Statistical Manual of Mental Disorders, Fourth Edition* (DSM-IV; American Psychiatric Association [APA], 1994). The anxiety disorders of children and adolescents are included in two categories: anxiety disorders and other disorders of infancy, childhood, and adolescence. Little research delineating specific and distinct parameters for anxiety disorders has been conducted (Beidel, 1991). Unlike autism and attention-deficit/hyperactivity disorder (ADHD), the changes in DSM-IV from previous editions of the manual regarding anxiety disorders were not based on large field trials (Werry, 1994). Whether these disorders are distinct clinical entities with overlapping symptoms or different manifestations of the same underlying process is unresolved (Biederman, Rosenbaum, Chaloff, & Kagan, 1995). In one study, 50%–85% of individuals with the diagnosis of social phobia also met the criteria for avoidant disorder (Liebowitz et al., 1991). The DSM-III-R (APA, 1987) diagnosis of avoidant disorder is conceptualized as social phobia in DSM-IV. In another study (Beidel, 1991), the diagnostic validity of social phobia was supported; however, the validity of overanxious disorder (OAD) was not. The DSM-III-R diagnosis of OAD is included in the diagnosis of generalized anxiety disorder (GAD) in DSM-IV.

Table 10.1. Classification of anxiety disorders

Anxiety Disorders	ICD-9 Codes
Panic disorder without agoraphobia	.300.01
Panic disorder with agoraphobia	.300.21
Agoraphobia without history of panic disorder	.300.22
Specific phobia	.300.29
Social phobia	.300.23
Obsessive-compulsive disorder	.300.3
Posttraumatic stress disorder	.309.81
Acute stress disorder	.308.3
Generalized anxiety disorder	.300.02
Anxiety disorder due to a general medical condition	.293.89
Other Disorders of Infancy, Childhood, or Adolescence	
Separation anxiety disorder	.313.21
Selective mutism	.313.23
Reactive attachment disorder of infancy or early childhood	.313.89

Adapted with permission from *Diagnostic and Statistical Manual of Mental Disorders, Fourth Edition.* Copyright © 1994 American Psychiatric Association.

ICD-9, *International Classification of Diseases, Ninth Revision* (World Health Organization, 1980).

Furthermore, some investigators (see Greenspan, 1991) have questioned the usefulness of DSM-IV for infants and toddlers. *The Diagnostic Classification of Mental Health and Developmental Disorders of Infancy and Early Childhood* (ZERO TO THREE/National Center for Clinical Infant Programs, 1994) was developed in part to describe the earliest manifestations of behavior problems that have been categorized in diagnostic systems developed for older children and adults. It is intended to complement other approaches and includes the categories of traumatic stress disorders and anxiety disorders of infancy and early childhood.

In addition, *The Classification of Child and Adolescent Diagnosis in Primary Care: Diagnostic and Statistical Manual for Primary Care* (DSM-PC) (Wolraich, Felice, & Drotar, 1996) was developed to help primary health care professionals identify psychosocial factors in their patients and determine appropriate interventions. DSM-PC describes developmental variations, problems, and disorders. Some disorders that are included are those defined in DSM-IV. It remains to be seen how useful DSM-PC will be in differentiating children with developmental variations or situational problems from children with disorders who need referral to mental health professionals.

Separation anxiety disorder (SAD), GAD, specific phobias, social phobia, panic disorder, obsessive-compulsive disorder (OCD), posttraumatic stress disorder (PTSD), and reactive attachment disorder of infancy or early childhood (RAD) are the anxiety disorders discussed in this chapter.

Separation Anxiety Disorder Children with SAD experience excessive anxiety about being separated from home, their parents, or another person to whom they are attached emotionally (APA, 1994). The problem must last for at least 4 weeks and result in significant impairment in function at school, with friends, or with the family. The core feature is intense anxiety at the time of separation or when apart from the parent and fear that the parent may be hurt or die (Jellinek & Kearns, 1995). The child may be reluctant or refuse to attend school or camp or to sleep at a friend's house. These children may not be able to stay in a room by themselves. They may try to stay close to the parent throughout the day. They may also have difficulty at bedtime and insist that someone stay with them until they fall asleep (APA, 1994).

The symptoms of SAD vary with age. Young children (ages 5–8 years) are the most likely to worry about harm to a parent and exhibit school refusal; children ages 9–12 years report excessive distress at the time of separation; and adolescents (ages 13–16 years) report somatic complaints (e.g., headache, stomachache, nausea, dizziness) and may display school refusal (Francis, Last, & Strauss, 1987). SAD occurs more often in prepubertal girls than in other age groups. The average age at the time of referral for evaluation is 9.1 years (Last, Hersen, Kazdin, et al., 1987a).

The most common presentation of SAD is school refusal (Jellinek & Kearns, 1995), and the most common cause of school refusal in preadolescents is SAD (Last & Strauss, 1990). Of note, some children and adolescents refuse to go to school because of excessive fear about some specific aspect of school (e.g., a bully, specific activity), which represents specific or social phobia. These children are generally older and exhibit more severe school refusal (Last & Strauss, 1990). School refusal can also result from depression or conduct disorder (CD) (Leonard & Rapoport, 1991). In one study of school refusers, 18 of 26 adolescents (69%) met the diagnostic criteria for depression, 16 (62%) met the criteria for an anxiety disorder, and 13 (50%) met the criteria for both (Bernstein & Garfinkel, 1986). Bernstein and Garfinkel emphasized the difficulty in differentiating severe anxiety from depression in this population. Table 10.2 lists the DSM-IV diagnostic

criteria for SAD. SAD may be a risk factor for the development of panic disorder in adults, although this relationship remains controversial (please see the discussion under the "Panic Disorder" subheading later in this section).

Generalized Anxiety Disorder In DSM-IV, the category OAD was included in the previous adult category of GAD. The predominate feature of GAD continues to be excessive worry that is not focused on a particular event or object and is accompanied by somatic complaints such as fatigue, irritability, headache, and stomachache or by trouble concentrating or falling asleep (Silverman & Ginsberg, 1995). GAD is a common problem in childhood. In one study (Last, Hersen, Kazdin, et al., 1987a), 52% of referrals to an outpatient psychiatric clinic had the diagnosis of OAD. OAD has a high co-morbidity with other anxiety disorders (Strauss, 1994). Adolescents have co-morbid depression or specific phobia, and younger children have co-morbid SAD or ADHD. Children with GAD worry about past and future events, social acceptability, and meeting others' expectations. They are perfectionistic and may request nearly constant reassurance. *Clinically significant worrying is more than 3 days per week (more days than not) for 6 months.* Children with severe GAD are noted to worry constantly. GAD can seriously inter-

Table 10.2. Diagnostic criteria for separation anxiety disorder

Three or more of the following criteria must be present:

- Recurrent and excessive distress when separation from home or from major attachment figures is anticipated or occurs
- Persistent and excessive worry about losing, or possible injury/illness of, major attachment figures
- Persistent and excessive worry that an untoward event will result in separation from major attachment figures (e.g., getting lost, being kidnapped)
- Persistent reluctance or refusal to go to school or elsewhere because of fear of separation
- Persistent and excessive fear or reluctance to be alone without major attachment figures at home or without significant adults in other settings
- Persistent reluctance or refusal to go to sleep without being near a major attachment figure or to sleep away from home
- Repeated nightmares involving the theme of separation
- Repeated complaints of physical symptoms (e.g., headaches, stomachaches) when separation from major attachment figures is anticipated or occurs

Adapted with permission from the *Diagnostic and Statistical Manual of Mental Disorders, Fourth Edition.* Copyright © 1994 American Psychiatric Association.

Table 10.3. Diagnostic criteria for generalized anxiety disorder

Excessive anxiety and worry about a number of events or activities that occur more days than not for at least 6 months

The person finds it difficult to control the worry and anxiety, which causes clinically significant distress or impairment in social, occupational, or other important areas of functioning.

The anxiety and worry are associated with three or more of the following six symptoms (only one symptom is required in children):

1) Restlessness or feeling keyed up or on edge
2) Being easily fatigued
3) Difficulty concentrating or mind going blank
4) Irritability
5) Muscle tension
6) Sleep disturbance (difficulty falling or staying asleep or restless, unsatisfying sleep)

The disturbance is not better explained by another mental health disorder or by the effects of medication or substance abuse.

Adapted with permission from the *Diagnostic and Statistical Manual of Mental Disorders, Fourth Edition.* Copyright © 1994 American Psychiatric Association.

fere with 1) academic performance because of the child's inability to complete assignments and because of poor test performance (both due to fear of failure) and 2) social relationships. OAD has been associated with school refusal (Strauss, 1994).

GAD is best characterized by what it is not. It is not worry about having a panic attack (panic disorder), being embarrassed in public (social phobia), being contaminated (OCD), or being separated from home or from a parent (SAD), and it is not worry as part of PTSD, a direct effect of taking medication or using illicit drugs, or an association with a medical illness (e.g., hyperthyroidism). Table 10.3 lists the DSM-IV criteria for GAD.

Specific Phobia (Formerly Simple Phobia) A *phobia* is a marked and persistent fear of a specific object or situation that the person attempts to avoid or endures with intense anxiety (APA, 1994). Anticipation of exposure to the stimulus may be associated with intense anxiety. For example, a child who is afraid of dogs may refuse to walk down a certain street due to the fear of a dog appearing. The more severe the phobia, the more extreme the avoidance behavior and the greater the impairment in function (Silverman & Rabian, 1994). Parents typically seek treatment when their child's behavior becomes disruptive to both the child's and the family's daily activities. Table 10.4 lists the criteria for specific phobias. Symptoms must have been present for at least

6 months, and the symptoms must not be accounted for better by another mental disorder.

Common phobias include animals, loud noises, the dentist, darkness, thunder and lightning (younger children); and bodily injury, school performance, and social fears (adolescents) (Silverman & Rabian, 1994). DSM-IV lists the following subcategories of phobias:

- Animal type (e.g., dogs)
- Natural environment type (e.g., storms)
- Blood-injection-injury type (e.g., seeing blood)
- Situational type (e.g., flying)
- Other type (e.g., loud noises)

The onset of specific phobias is in childhood. In one study, the mean age of onset for animal phobias was 6.9 years; for blood phobia, it was 8.8 years (Ost, 1987).

Social Phobia The core feature of *social phobia* is marked and persistent fear of social and performance situations that may result in embarrassment (APA, 1994). Situations that are commonly associated with social phobia are eating, drinking, speaking, and writing in public; going to parties or other social events; talking to authority figures; and using public rest rooms (Beidel & Randall, 1994). Table 10.5 lists the diagnostic criteria for social phobia. In order to meet DSM-IV criteria, symptoms must have lasted for at least 6 months and are not described better by another mental disorder or the effects of medication or substance abuse.

Children previously diagnosed with avoidant disorders in accordance with DSM-III–R criteria would most likely be diagnosed with social phobia under DSM-IV criteria. Children with *avoidant disorder* avoid interaction with strangers. They want to make friends but believe that others would not like

Table 10.4. Diagnostic criteria for specific phobia

Marked and persistent fear that is excessive or unreasonable, cued by the presence or anticipation of a specific object or situation.

Exposure to the phobic stimulus results in an immediate anxiety response, which may take the form of a panic attack. The anxiety may be expressed by crying, tantrums, freezing, or clinging in children.

The person recognizes that the fear is excessive or unreasonable (not required in children).

The phobic situation(s) is avoided or endured with intense anxiety or distress.

Symptoms significantly interfere with the person's normal routine, occupational or school functioning, social activities or relationships, or there is marked distress about having the phobia.

Adapted with permission from the *Diagnostic and Statistical Manual of Mental Disorders, Fourth Edition.* Copyright © 1994 American Psychiatric Association.

Table 10.5. Diagnostic criteria for social phobia

Marked and persistent fear of social or performance situations in which the person fears that he or she will act in a way that will be humiliating or embarrassing (in peer settings as well as in interactions with adults)

Exposure to the feared social situation results in anxiety, which may take the form of a panic attack. The anxiety may be expressed in children by crying, tantrums, freezing, or shrinking from social situations with unfamiliar people.

The person recognizes that the fear is excessive or unreasonable (not required in children).

The feared social or performance situations are avoided or endured with intense anxiety or distress.

Symptoms significantly interfere with the person's normal routine, occupational or school functioning, or social activities or relationships, or there is marked distress about having the phobia.

Adapted with permission from the *Diagnostic and Statistical Manual of Mental Disorders, Fourth Edition.* Copyright © 1994 American Psychiatric Association.

to be friends with them or fear being teased and called "stupid" (Francis & D'Elia, 1994). If children's social anxiety becomes overwhelming, they may become inarticulate or mute. Approximately 4% of young children with speech-language disorders have the diagnosis of avoidant disorder (Beidel & Randall, 1994). In a comparison of children with social phobia, social phobia and avoidant disorder, and avoidant disorder alone, the only significant difference among the groups was the children's age at referral: The children with avoidant disorder were younger (Francis, Last, & Strauss, 1992). This difference reflected trends seen in children who are developing typically (e.g., fear of strangers occurs before fear of social situations). Based on these findings, Francis and colleagues questioned whether avoidant disorder and social phobia are distinct disorders.

Of note, some researchers in the 1990s (Black & Uhde, 1994; Dow, Sonies, Scheib, et al., 1995; Dummit, Klein, Tancer, et al., 1997; Leonard & Dow, 1995) suggested that *selective mutism* is best characterized as an anxiety disorder. In one study (Black & Uhde, 1994), 97% of children with selective mutism were diagnosed with social phobia or avoidant disorder or both, and 30% were diagnosed with simple phobia. Children with selective mutism may have shy, inhibited temperaments; a family history of anxiety disorders; and speech-language delay or developmental delay (Dow et al., 1995). Occasionally, selective mutism follows a long hospitalization or a traumatic event (reactive mutism) (Hayden, 1980). The essential feature of selective mutism is persistent failure to speak in social situations (e.g., school) in spite of

speaking with some family members or friends (APA, 1994). These children need a comprehensive evaluation that includes intellectual and achievement testing. Most children outgrow selective mutism; however, it occasionally persists for several years during elementary school (Leonard & Dow, 1995). Leonard and Dow (1995) recommend a referral for evaluation and for treatment if symptoms persist for more than 6 months.

Panic Disorder   A *panic attack* is a discrete episode of rapid onset characterized by intense fear and discomfort (APA, 1994). It may last for minutes or for hours. Four or more of the symptoms delineated in DSM-IV (see Table 10.6) must be present for an episode to be characterized as a panic attack. An episode with fewer than four symptoms is referred to as a *limited-systems attack* (Dummit & Klein, 1994). Of note, panic attacks can occur occasionally among people without a diagnosis of panic disorder and in association with other anxiety disorders. The diagnosis of panic disorder depends on the individual's experiencing spontaneous (i.e., uncued) panic attacks. These episodes occur unexpectedly, "out of the blue," and are not triggered by an anxiety-provoking situation (i.e., cued panic attack).

The peak age of diagnosis of panic disorder was 15–19 years in one study (Von Korff, Eaton, & Keyl, 1985). In another study (Thyer, Parrish, Curtis, et al., 1985), 13% of adults reported the onset of symptoms prior to 10 years of age. The occurrence

Table 10.6. Diagnostic criteria for panic attack

A discrete period of intense fear or discomfort

Four or more of the following symptoms develop abruptly and reach a peak within 10 minutes:

1) Palpitations, pounding heart, or accelerated heart rate
2) Sweating
3) Trembling or shaking
4) Sensations of shortness of breath or smothering
5) Feeling of choking
6) Chest pain or discomfort
7) Nausea or abdominal distress
8) Feeling dizzy, unsteady, lightheaded, or faint
9) Derealization (feelings of unreality) or depersonalization (being detached from oneself)
10) Fear of losing control or going crazy
11) Fear of dying
12) Paresthesias (tingling, prickling, or burning skin sensation)
13) Chills or hot flushes

Adapted with permission from the *Diagnostic and Statistical Manual of Mental Disorders, Fourth Edition.* Copyright © 1994 American Psychiatric Association.

Table 10.7. Diagnostic criteria for panic disorder with agoraphobia

All three of the following criteria must be met:

1) Recurrent, unexpected panic attacks
2) One or more of the attacks has been followed by at least one of the following symptoms that has lasted one month or more:
    • Persistent concern about having additional attacks
    • Worry about the implications of the attack or its consequences (e.g., losing control, having a heart attack, going crazy)
    • A significant change in behavior related to the attacks
3) The presence of agoraphobia

Adapted with permission from the *Diagnostic and Statistical Manual of Mental Disorders, Fourth Edition.* Copyright © 1994 American Psychiatric Association.

of spontaneous panic attacks before puberty is the source of ongoing controversy (Dummit & Klein, 1994; Vitiello, Behar, Wolfson, & McLeer, 1990). Most studies (see Dummit & Klein, 1994) of anxiety disorders in children report few or no spontaneous attacks in preadolescents.

Most individuals with panic disorder develop some degree of *agoraphobia* (Black, 1995). *Agoraphobia* is the fear and avoidance of places or situations in which the person fears a panic attack may occur, in which he or she would have no help if a panic attack were to occur, or from which escape would be difficult or embarrassing (Black, 1995). A person with mild agoraphobia might avoid crowded public places; however, a person with severe symptoms might refuse to leave home. Table 10.7 lists the diagnostic criteria for panic disorder with agoraphobia (PDAG). The person's panic attacks must not be explained better by another mental disorder or be effects of medication or substance abuse.

Up to half of the adults with PDAG report a history of SAD (Black, 1995). Conversely, children with SAD are at increased risk of developing PDAG as adults (Black, 1995), and they might even develop PDAG during childhood (Biederman, Rosenbaum, Bolduc-Murphy, et al., 1993). In addition, the risk that children of a parent with panic disorder will develop SAD is three times higher than that of children of parents without panic disorder (Weissman, Leckman, Merikangas, et al., 1984). Several authors (e.g., Black, 1995; Klein, 1981) suggested that panic disorder and SAD may be different manifestations of the *same* disorder, although this theory remains controversial (Moreau & Follett, 1993).

Finally, a careful search should be made for medical disorders in people who experience panic attacks, including *problems that may have precipitated* the panic attacks (e.g., hyperthyroidism and substance abuse), *disorders that mimic* panic attacks (e.g., seizures), and *co-occurring problems* (e.g., mitral valve prolapse). Mitral valve prolapse has been reported (Dummit & Klein, 1994) in association with panic disorder in adults and children; however, the prevalence and significance of this co-morbidity are not clear.

Obsessive-Compulsive Disorder *Obsessive-compulsive disorder* is characterized by recurrent obsessions and compulsions that cause marked distress and are severe enough to be time consuming and/or to interfere with functioning significantly (APA, 1994). Obsessions are persistent thoughts that the individual perceives as senseless and intrusive; yet, they are a product of his or her own mind. The person attempts to ignore or suppress these thoughts. Compulsions are repetitive, purposeful behaviors performed in response to an obsession according to specific rules or in a stereotypic fashion (Leonard & Rapoport, 1991). They serve to alleviate anxiety, and, in general, the person recognizes the behavior as excessive and unreasonable.

The mean age of onset of symptoms was 10 years in a study (Swedo, Rapoport, Leonard, et al., 1989) of 70 children and adolescents with OCD at the National Institute of Mental Health (NIMH). Boys had an earlier age of onset than girls did. The clinical presentation of children with OCD is similar to that of adults with OCD (Leonard, 1997). The most common ritual in the NIMH study was cleaning (hand washing, bathing, and tooth brushing) (55% of subjects). *Repeating rituals,* such as going up and down stairs, were common (51%), as were *checking behaviors,* such as making sure appliances were turned off (45%). Other common rituals were *counting* (18%) and *ordering or arranging* (17%). The most common obsession was with dirt, germs, and contamination (40%). The children whom Swedo and colleagues studied reported an inner sense that "it didn't feel right" until the obsessive thinking or compulsive action was completed. Table 10.8 reviews the diagnostic criteria for OCD. The obsessions or compulsions must be time consuming and result in significant disruption of the person's home, school, work, or social life.

Almost all children with OCD have a combination of obsessions and compulsions (Swedo et al., 1989). Individuals with an early onset (less than 6 years of age) were more likely to have compulsions (i.e., rituals; Rettew, Swedo, Leonard, et al.,

1992). Individual symptoms vary over time, and children may be good at hiding their symptoms. The following are symptoms that suggest an OCD diagnosis:

- Spending long, unproductive hours on homework
- Erasing test papers and homework excessively
- Retracing letters or words or rereading paragraphs
- Dramatic increase in laundering clothes
- Insistence on wearing clothes or using towels only once
- Stopping up toilets from too much paper (due to an obsession about germs)
- Long, rigid bedtime or hygiene rituals
- Exaggerated need for reassurance
- Requests for family members to repeat phrases
- Preoccupying fear of harm being done to oneself or to others
- Persistent fear that one has an illness
- Hoarding useless objects (Leonard & Rapoport, 1991)

Children with Tourette syndrome (TS) were excluded from the NIMH study (Swedo et al.,

Table 10.8. Diagnostic criteria for obsessive-compulsive disorder

Obsessions
1) Recurrent and persistent thoughts, impulses, or images that are experienced as intrusive and inappropriate and that cause marked anxiety or distress
2) The thoughts, impulses, or images are not simply excessive worries about real-life problems.
3) The person attempts to ignore or suppress such thoughts, impulses, or images or to neutralize them with some other thought or action.
4) The person recognizes that the obsessive thoughts, impulses, or images are a product of his or her own mind (not imposed from without as in a thought disorder).

Compulsions
1) Repetitive behaviors (e.g., hand washing, ordering, checking) or mental acts (e.g., counting, repeating words silently) that the person feels driven to perform according to strict rules
2) The behaviors or mental acts are attempts to reduce distress or prevent some dreaded event or situation; however, these behaviors or mental acts either are not connected in a realistic way to the situation or are clearly excessive.

The person recognizes that the obsession or compulsion is excessive or unreasonable (not required in children).

Adapted with permission from the *Diagnostic and Statistical Manual of Mental Disorders, Fourth Edition.* Copyright © 1994 American Psychiatric Association.

1989); however, TS is closely associated with OCD. Obsessive-compulsive symptoms may be present in children with TS and usually are present in adults with TS. In addition, first-degree relatives of children with TS have an increased risk for OCD (March, Leonard, & Swedo, 1995). Some cases of OCD and tic disorders appear to be triggered by streptococcal infections in a manner similar to that seen in Sydenham's chorea (Allen, Leonard, & Swedo, 1995a; Kiessling, Marcotte, & Culpepper, 1993; Swedo & Leonard, 1994). *Sydenham's chorea* is an involuntary movement disorder that develops after infection with group A beta-hemolytic streptococcal bacteria. It is an autoimmune disorder of the basal ganglia associated with antineuronal antibodies. OCD occurs at a higher rate in children who have Sydenham's chorea than in children who have rheumatic fever and no chorea. In children with Syndenham's chorea and OCD, obsessive-compulsive behaviors improve with treatment with penicillin or plasmapheresis to eliminate antineuronal antibodies (Allen et al., 1995a). Improved identification of children with the proposed pediatric autoimmune neuropsychiatric disorders associated with streptococcal infections (PANDAS) allows the evaluation of new treatment and prevention strategies (Swedo, Leonard, Garvey, et al., 1998).

Posttraumatic Stress Disorder Major stress reactions to traumatic events have been recognized for several centuries. The description of PTSD and its three major groups of symptoms resulted from a study of the persisting problems of Vietnam War veterans (Yule, 1994). DSM-III–R was the first edition of DSM to make reference to PTSD in children. Since the mid-1980s, considerable research has been done on PTSD and children exposed to natural disasters, kidnapping, and violence. Children are as susceptible to PTSD as adults are. According to DSM-IV, PTSD is characterized by

- Exposure to a traumatic event that involves feelings of intense fear, helplessness, or horror
- Persistent reexperiencing of the traumatic event
- Avoidance of stimuli associated with the trauma or a general numbing of emotional responsiveness
- Persistently increased arousal (APA, 1994)

A traumatic event may be experienced or witnessed and may include severe accidents or injuries (e.g., burns, animal bites), kidnapping or hostage situations, sexual and physical abuse, major disasters (e.g., hurricanes), and life-threatening illnesses. American societal conditions sometimes place children at risk of witnessing the rape, murder, or suicide of family members (Pynoos, Nader, & March, 1991). The likelihood of an individual's developing PTSD is directly proportional to the magnitude and type of stress that the individual experienced because of the traumatic event (Pynoos et al., 1991). Traumatic events are differentiated into two types: type 1, a sudden, unexpected single incident, and type 2, chronic, expected, repeated incidents (Terr, 1991). Type 2 traumatic events usually involve childhood physical and/or sexual abuse. When the episode of abuse is perpetrated by a trusted authority figure, the impact on the child may be more severe and long-lasting. In one study (McLeer, Deblinger, Atkins, et al., 1988), at least 75% of children who had been sexually abused by their natural fathers, as compared with 25% who had been sexually abused by another trusted adult, developed PTSD. No children who had been abused by an older child met the full criteria for PTSD.

Traumatic events may be reexperienced by children with PTSD as intrusive images, such as the moment of extreme fear or helplessness. Children may reexperience their trauma through *traumatic dreams, traumatic play,* and other *reenactment behaviors.* Reenactment can be understood as action memories. For example, a child who was trapped in a well may squeeze into small spaces (Pynoos et al., 1991). Children may modify the action to minimize their distress (e.g., a child may repetitively catch the bullet before it strikes him or her) (Pynoos et al., 1991). Reenactment behavior can also be risky and dangerous. Finally, sexualized play, self-mutilation, or suicidal behaviors may represent reenactment by child victims of physical or sexual abuse and should always prompt a search for the possible source of abuse (Amaya-Jackson & March, 1995).

Certain objects, places, activities, conditions (e.g., a storm), and feelings of helplessness may become *traumatic reminders* to children of the source of their fear or distress. Children may avoid specific locations or objects and may discontinue engaging in pleasurable activities. Adolescents may report feeling numb, but younger children may report only not knowing how they feel or trying to keep an emotion from emerging (Pynoos et al., 1991). Young children may become withdrawn and display limited affect and play (Scheeringa, Zeanah, Drell, & Larrieu, 1995).

The fourth criterion for PTSD is an increased state of arousal (APA, 1994). Children may manifest a sleep disorder, difficulty with concentrating, irritability and aggression, or hypervigilance and exaggerated startle in certain situations (e.g., at bedtime for a child who has been sexually abused). Sleep disturbances are especially common in children with PTSD (Scheeringa et al., 1995).

Little research has been done regarding PTSD in preschool-age children (see Scheeringa et al., 1995; Terr, 1988). The diagnosis may be difficult in children with limited expressive language abilities. Scheeringa and co-workers (1995) reviewed the case reports of 20 infants and preschoolers who had been traumatized severely between the ages of 3 months and 47 months. They found that these children did show many persistent symptoms of impairment similar to those of older children and adults. Symptoms included aggressive play; distress at toileting, bathing, or bedtime; and sleep disturbance. They also concluded that the DSM-IV criteria were not sufficiently sensitive to diagnose PTSD in preschool-age children and proposed an alternative set of criteria for this population. These criteria were objective and based on observable behaviors (see Table 10.9).

Anxiety and depression are common accompaniments of PTSD in adults and children. PTSD can also exaggerate or mimic externalizing behavior disorders. Before diagnosing ADHD, oppositional defiant disorder (ODD), or CD, it is important to rule out PTSD as the reason for a child's deteriorating school performance, poor attention, or aggression (Amaya-Jackson & March, 1995; Pynoos et al., 1991). Preexisting learning disabilities (LD) can also be exacerbated by PTSD.

Reactive Attachment Disorder of Infancy and Early Childhood   RAD is included in this discussion of anxiety disorders because many children with RAD have additional DSM-IV diagnoses, including PTSD. RAD is characterized by markedly disturbed social relatedness secondary to grossly inadequate or pathological care. Considerable improvement generally results when the infant or young child is placed in a nurturing caregiving environment. There are two types of RAD: 1) inhibited (in which an infant or young child fails to initiate or respond and is inactive and apathetic) and 2) disinhibited (in which an older infant or young child forms indiscriminate attachments). The onset of RAD occurs in the first year or two of life and by definition before 5 years of age (APA, 1994). The child's symptoms must not be explained better by developmental delay, mental retardation, or PDD.

A number of terms have been applied to children with RAD, including anaclitic depression, nonorganic failure to thrive (NOFTT), and psychosocial dwarfism. Children with RAD have a constellation of symptoms and may demonstrate abnormalities of growth, development, and behavior.

Table 10.9.   Proposed diagnostic criteria for posttraumatic stress disorder in preschool-age children

A.   Exposure to a traumatic event
1)   The child experienced, witnessed, or was confronted with an event or events that involved actual or threatened death or serious injury to him- or herself or to others.

B.   Reexperiencing (one item needed)
1)   Posttraumatic play: Compulsively repetitive, represents part of the trauma, fails to relieve anxiety, and is less elaborate and imaginative than usual play
2)   Play reenactment: Represents part of the trauma but lacks the monotonous repetition and other characteristics of posttraumatic play
3)   Recurrent recollections of the traumatic event other than what is revealed in play, and which are not necessarily distressing
4)   Nightmares: May have obvious links to the trauma or be of increased frequency with unknown content
5)   Episodes with objective features of a flashback or dissociation
6)   Distress at exposure to reminders of the event

C.   Numbing of responsiveness (one item needed)
1)   Constriction of play: Child may have constriction of play and still have posttraumatic play or play reenactment.
2)   Socially more withdrawn
3)   Restricted range of affect
4)   Loss of acquired developmental skills, especially language regression and toilet training

D.   Increased arousal (one item needed)
1)   Night terrors
2)   Difficulty going to sleep that is not related to being afraid of having nightmares or fear of the dark
3)   Night-waking not related to nightmares or night terrors
4)   Decreased concentration: Marked decrease in concentration or attention span compared to before the trauma
5)   Hypervigilance
6)   Exaggerated startle response

E.   New fears and aggression (one item needed)
1)   New aggression
2)   New separation anxiety
3)   Fear of toileting alone
4)   Fear of the dark
5)   Any other new fears of things or situations not obviously related to the trauma

F.   Duration of disturbance greater than 1 month

Adapted from Scheeringa et al. (1995).

They may experience chronic malnourishment and dehydration with evident growth delay and show signs of nonaccidental injuries (e.g., physical or sexual abuse). They may also present with a feeding disorder, pica, or rumination. These infants and children may have a number of additional mental health and developmental problems, including developmental delay, expressive and receptive language disorder, ADHD, ODD, and PTSD. RAD cannot be diagnosed if the child meets the criteria for PDD. The estimated prevalence of RAD is 1% (Richters & Volkmar, 1994). RAD has been diagnosed in premature infants who have received prolonged care in the neonatal intensive care unit (NICU) (Goodfriend, 1993). Such cases emphasize the importance of the focus since the 1990s on the developmental care of infants in the NICU.

The appropriateness of RAD as a diagnostic label and the diagnostic criteria for RAD continue to be controversial. Zeanah, Mammen, and Lieberman (1993) argued that the principle feature of RAD is a profound disturbance in the infant's attachment to the primary caregiver and proposed criteria that focus on attachment and differ from the DSM-IV criteria. Richters and Volkmar (1994) supported the concept of RAD as a disorder of social relatedness and atypical development, not as one of attachment. They recommended that the diagnosis of RAD be maintained, that the requirement of pathological parenting be dropped (the history may be unclear), and that criteria detailing the other possible developmental problems of these children be added.

The impairments in social relatedness demonstrated by infants and young children with RAD are responsive to treatment. In fact, RAD is wholly preventable. The basis of treatment is placement of the child in a consistent, nurturing caregiving environment. Early intervention/early childhood special education (EI/ECSE) services are appropriate for associated developmental problems; behavioral or therapy services and medication are appropriate for associated sleep disorder, ADHD, ODD, and PTSD. Unfortunately, some of these children (e.g., those with oppositional behaviors) may live in a succession of foster homes.

Prevalence

All children occasionally feel anxious, sad, or fearful. Girls report more fears than boys do (Bernstein & Borchardt, 1991). In addition, a substantial number of school-age children and adults label themselves as shy. Shyness is the tendency to feel awkward or anxious during social interactions especially with unfamiliar people. A developmental peak in shyness occurs in adolescence; however, fewer than 50% of children who were shy as early adolescents still consider themselves shy at age 21 (Cheek, Parker, & Zuckerman, 1995).

Stranger anxiety and separation anxiety are expected developmental phenomena in older infants and toddlers, and performance anxiety is seen in older school-age children and adolescents. Fears are common in children 3–5 years of age and throughout adolescence. Ritualistic behavior is seen in many children as part of typical development. Young children may insist on things being done "just so" and have elaborate bedtime rituals (Leonard, Goldberger, Rapoport, et al., 1990). These typical developmental rituals are usually gone by 8–9 years of age and are different in content than the rituals of OCD, which usually begin later (Leonard et al., 1990).

The distinction between "normal" fears or shyness and a disorder is based on the number, severity, and duration of symptoms and on the child's age and culture. For example, age-equivalent sim-

ple fear responds to reassurance and does not significantly interfere with the child's daily activities. A phobia does *not* respond to reassurance and *does* result in significant functional impairment.

In general, child and parent reports about anxiety symptoms often do not agree. In studies that use both child and parent reports, the prevalence rates for anxiety disorders are higher because children report more symptoms than their parents do (Bernstein & Borchardt, 1991). In addition, some studies have not used functional impairment criteria. The use of functional criteria results in a significant decrease in the prevalence of the anxiety disorders (Bernstein & Borchardt, 1991). Table 10.10 presents the prevalence data for each subcategory of the anxiety disorders.

Co-morbidity

In general, a high level of co-morbidity exists among anxiety disorders; however, there appears to be little or no association between phobia disorders and the other anxiety and panic disorders (Costello & Angold, 1995). As stated previously, this co-morbidity may reflect overlapping symptoms of distinct disorders, or each disorder may be a different manifestation of the same problem. In clinic populations, as many as 33% of children and adolescents with SAD and 15% of children and adolescents with OAD have a second anxiety disorder diagnosis (Last, Strauss, & Francis, 1987). In the general population, 36%–39% of children with one anxiety disorder have a second (Anderson, Williams, McGee, et al., 1987).

Children and adolescents with anxiety disorders are also more likely to have co-morbid depression, ADHD, and other externalizing behavior disor-

Table 10.10.   Prevalence of anxiety disorders in childhood and adolescence

Name of disorder	Children (%)	Adolescents (%)	Lifetime prevalence (%)
Separation anxiety disorder	2.0–5.4	.7	
Overanxious disorder	2.6–5.9	7.3	3.7 (GAD)
Simple phobia	2.3–9.0	4.7	3.6
Social phobia	1.0		
Panic disorder/agoraphobia			.6–1.0
Obsessive-compulsive disorder		.3–.4(3.0[a])	1.9
Posttraumatic stress disorder			.3–1.4 (9.0[b])

Adapted from Anderson (1994), Bernstein and Borchardt (1991).

[a] The 3% prevalence figure is from an epidemiologic study of adolescents in the southeastern United States (Valleni-Basile, Garrison, Jackson, et al., 1994).

[b] The prevalence of posttraumatic stress disorder in young urban adults may be as high as 9% (Robins, Helzer, Croughan, et al., 1981).

GAD, generalized anxiety disorder.

ders. In one study, 17% of the children with anxiety disorders also had depression (Anderson et al., 1987); in another study, 12% of adolescents with an anxiety disorder also had a depressive disorder (McGee, Feehan, Williams, et al., 1990). In addition, children with depression are three to four times more likely than children without depression to have an anxiety disorder (Costello & Angold, 1995). Children with ODD or CD are two to three times more likely than children without these disruptive behavior disorders to have an anxiety disorder. Approximately 20% of children and adolescents with ADHD also manifest an anxiety disorder (Barkley, 1998a), including 43% of children with the inattentive subtype and 10% of children with the impulsive-hyperactive subtype of ADHD (Lahey & Carlson, 1991).

In the NIMH study (Swedo et al., 1989) of OCD, only 26% (18 individuals) had OCD as their only diagnosis. Depression was present in 35% of the group, and anxiety disorders were present in 40%. Thirty-three percent of the sample manifested a disruptive behavior disorder or substance abuse.

Etiology

Anxiety disorders are most likely due to the interaction of biologic (i.e., temperamental) and genetic factors with environmental events, including the developmental experiences of care and attachment (Tonge, 1994). For example, a traumatic event is necessary for the diagnosis of PTSD, and the majority of adults with social phobia report the onset of their disorder after a traumatic event (Beidel & Randall, 1994).

Family Studies The causes of most childhood anxiety disorders are poorly understood. A number of studies (see Last, Hersen, Kazdin, et al., 1987b; Last, Hersen, Kazdin, et al., 1991) have documented an increased risk for anxiety disorders in first-degree relatives of children with anxiety disorders. Conversely, other studies (see Turner, Biedel, & Costello, 1987; Weissman et al., 1984) have noted an increased incidence of anxiety disorders in children of parents who have a diagnosed anxiety disorder. In a study of children with anxiety disorders (Last, Hersen, Kazdin, et al., 1991), 34.6% of their first-degree relatives also had an anxiety disorder, including 50% of the first-degree relatives of children with OAD. In another study (Riddle, Scahill, King, et al., 1992), 15 of 21 children and adolescents with OCD had a parent with OCD (19%) or a parent with obsessive-compulsive symptoms (52%). As commented earlier, the children of parents who have PDAG have three times the risk of developing SAD (Weissman et al., 1984).

Biochemical Studies and Brain Imaging The major neurotransmitter systems involved in anxiety disorders include noradrenergic and serotonergic systems. Evidence also implicates neuropeptide Y (NPY) and cholecystokinin (CCK) as modulators of anxious behaviors (Sallee & Greenawald, 1995). The locus ceruleus (one of the basal ganglia) is a major noradrenergic nucleus and is proposed as a common pathway for the production of fear and acute panic attack (Sallee & Greenawald, 1995). Both animal and clinical studies have demonstrated that serotonin plays a major role in mediating fear and anxiety. Finally, the hypothalamic-pituitary-adrenal (HPA) axis has been implicated in stress and anxiety. A variety of stressful events are associated with an increase in blood cortisol levels. Of interest, patients with anxiety disorders have a hyperactive HPA as measured by stimulation of the HPA with cortisol-releasing factor (CRF).

Brain imaging studies of children and adults with OCD have reported conflicting results. In one study (Luxenberg, Swedo, Flament, et al., 1988), computed tomography (CT) scans demonstrated bilaterally small caudate nuclei in 10 young adults with OCD; however, studies utilizing magnetic resonance imaging (MRI) scans have not confirmed these findings (Sallee & Greenawald, 1995). Functional neuroimaging studies of individuals with OCD (e.g., studies using positron emission tomography [PET]) have demonstrated hypermetabolism of the orbital frontal cortex, the caudate, and the anterior cingulate gyrus (Rauch, Savage, Alpert, et al., 1997; Saxena, Brody, Schwartz, & Baxter, 1998).

Psychodynamic Theory Traditionally, psychodynamic theories have explained anxiety as resulting from unresolved childhood conflicts and have emphasized the individuals' difficulties with mastery of the developmental issues of separation and autonomy. Some of the family studies can be interpreted to support a psychodynamic model in that parents' psychopathology may make anxiety disorders more likely in their children. Torgersen (1983) demonstrated, however, a higher concordance rate for anxiety disorders in monozygotic twins than in dizygotic twins, thus supporting a strong role for genetics.

DIAGNOSIS AND EVALUATION

Identification

Behavioral Inhibition Infants who appear shy and who respond to novelty (e.g., to a new situation or to an unfamiliar person) by withdrawing have been referred to as being *behaviorally inhibited.*

Kagan, Reznick, Clarke, and co-workers (1984) reported that 15%–20% of European American children fit that profile and are shy and fearful as toddlers and cautious, quiet, and introverted when they reach school age. Of note, other studies have shown that behavioral inhibition in children is associated with PDAG with or without depressive illness in parents and that behavioral inhibition is a significant risk factor for the later development of an anxiety disorder (Biederman et al., 1993).

It is useful to identify children who are behaviorally inhibited so that parents can be given appropriate guidance. These children are similar to the "slow-to-warm-up" children whom Chess and Thomas (1986) described. Use of a temperament questionnaire, such as the Early Infancy Temperament Questionnaire (EITQ) or the Toddler EITQ (Medoff-Cooper, Carey, & McDevitt, 1993), helps to supplement direct observations of the child. These questionnaires assist in the identification of temperamental style but do not measure behavioral inhibition.

If you do not use structured questionnaires, ask questions about the child's personality or temperament. Important temperamental traits are *intensity* and *threshold of response, adaptability, response to novelty*, and *persistence versus distractibility*. Such information is also useful in identifying other children who may be difficult to parent, such as "the difficult child" (Chess & Thomas, 1986) who exhibits high-intensity response, low persistence, and high distractibility. In a study (Little, 1983) concerning the use of temperament questionnaires in pediatric practice, 90% of parents reported a better understanding of their child, 87% thought completing the questionnaire was worthwhile, and 57% reported that it changed their approach to parenting.

Behavioral Rating Questionnaires Pediatricians identify only about one in five children who have behavior or emotional problems (Jellinek, Little, Murphy, & Pagano, 1995). The use of behavioral rating questionnaires can improve the identification of these children, including children with anxiety disorders. Questionnaires are also efficient, provide more complete information than behavioral rating scales, help parents organize their thoughts, and enhance a parent's sense of participation in the appointment (Sturner, Eisert, Mabe, & Thomas, 1985).

These questionnaires can be used for three purposes: 1) *screen for problems,* 2) to provide a comprehensive overview of behaviors to *assist in diagnosis,* and 3) to *follow treatment* of specific problems (Eisert, Sturner, & Mabe, 1991). The Pediatric Symptom Checklist (Little, Murphy, Jellinek, et al., 1994) is a general behavior screen for use with children

4–10 years of age. Please also review the discussion of behavioral rating scales in Chapter 7.

Supplemental Questions Ask both parents and children the appropriate questions; interview older children separately. The child's problems with anxiety may be underestimated if only the parent is asked. If a behavioral screen is not used, supplement the usual history during well-child visits with the following questions in order to identify the child's risk for an anxiety disorder (see Cheek, et al., 1995, p. 286; Jellinek & Kearns, 1995, p. 58):

- Is there a family history of anxiety disorder, panic attacks, or depression?
- Is either parent anxious or depressed?
- Is your child shy in new situations or when meeting new people?
- Are you worried that your child is too shy to make friends or do well in school?
- Does your child have any difficulty with staying with babysitters, sleeping overnight at a friend's house, or going to school?
- How many days of school has your child missed during this school year? The previous school year?
- Does your child worry a lot? What does he or she worry about?
- Does your child's worry or fear keep him or her from engaging in usual activities?
- Have you noticed a change in your child's behavior? More distractibility, school grades dropping, sleep problems?

Comprehensive Evaluation

A critical issue for the primary care health professional is to differentiate between acute situational anxiety symptoms and a chronic anxiety disorder. Children with situational anxiety symptoms can often be managed by practical advice, reassurance, and monitoring (Mattison, 1989). Children with a chronic anxiety disorder, however, require a comprehensive evaluation in collaboration with a mental health professional (see Table 10.11). The objectives of the diagnostic evaluation of the child with a suspected anxiety disorder are to

- Document the child's behavior in different environments
- Confirm the diagnosis of an anxiety disorder
- Identify associated mental health and learning problems
- Determine the presence of associated medical problems
- Determine the need for family support services

The responsibilities of the primary care physician and nurse are to obtain parent, child, and school

Table 10.11. Components of the comprehensive evaluation for the child or adolescent suspected of having an anxiety disorder

- Parent, child, and teacher interviews
- Behavior questionnaires–parent, youth, and teacher forms (e.g., Achenbach Child Behavior Checklist [CBCL] [Achenbach, 1991a])
- School information
- Intellectual and achievement testing (as needed)
- Medical examination
- Assessment of family strengths and support needs
- Semistructured diagnostic interviews (mental health professional)

    Schedule for Affective Disorders and Schizophrenia for School-Age Children: Epidemiologic Version–5 (K-SADS-E–5) (Orvaschel, 1995)

    Anxiety Disorders Interview Schedule for DSM-IV: Child Version (ADIS for DSM-IV:C) (Silverman & Albano, 1996)

- Self-report measures (mental health professional)

    State-Trait Anxiety Inventory for Children (STAIC) (Spielberger, Edwards, & Lushene, 1973)

    Revised Children's Manifest Anxiety Scale (RCMAS) (Reynolds & Richmond, 1985)

    Revised Fear Survey Schedule for Children (Ollendick, 1983)

information; review the results of behavior rating scales; conduct the medical examination; make a referral to the mental health professional; and review the results of the evaluation and recommendations for treatment with the child and family.

Parent, Child, and Teacher Interviews Please review the discussion on parent, child, and teacher interviews in Chapter 7. An accurate diagnosis of an anxiety disorder depends on obtaining information from multiple sources: the parent, the child, child care, and the school. Information must include both the type of the problem and how it affects the child's functioning in different situations.

Children underreport disruptive behavior (Barkley, 1998a); however, they are better reporters of the symptoms of anxiety (Schwab-Stone, Fallon, Briggs, & Crowther, 1994). Ideally, the physician completes a telephone interview with the teacher in addition to using a teacher behavior rating scale (e.g., Teacher Report Form; Achenbach, 1991b). This interview should include a review of the child's academic progress, the child's behavior in the classroom as well as in other situations, the child's relationship with the teacher, and the child's peer relationships. Additional questions for the parent and child include the following:

- What is the nature of the child's worries or fears? (For example, if the child is refusing to go

to school, is the child's refusal caused by fear of separation or fear of someone or something at school?)
- Does the child's fear or worry significantly interfere with his or her activities in the home, at school, or in the community?
- Do the parents and child remember a specific trigger of the worry or fear?
- How do the parents respond to their child's anxiety?
- What do the parents think is causing their child's anxiety?
- What treatments have been tried in the past?
- Are there any important situational factors (e.g., new school or teacher, move to new home, divorce)? (adapted from Jellinek & Kearns, 1995, p. 58)

Behavioral Questionnaires Use comprehensive behavioral questionnaires to obtain information from parents, the child, and the school. The Child Behavior Checklist (CBCL) has Parent (Achenbach, 1991a), Teacher (Achenbach, 1991b), and Youth Self-Report (Achenbach, 1991c) forms. The CBCL can identify children who are having significant behavior problems, but it should not be used for making a final diagnosis. The CBCL has both internalizing and externalizing dimensions; however, it does not discriminate well between anxiety and depression (Werry, 1994). Better agreement exists between the Teacher and Parent forms for externalizing problems than for internalizing (Strauss, 1994).

The Conners' Parent and Teacher Rating Scales were revised and renormed in the late 1990s (Conners, 1997). The Conners'-Wells' Adolescent Self-Report Scale is available for use with adolescents 12–17 years of age (Conners, 1997). The Preschool Behavior Questionnaire (Behar, 1977; Behar & Stringfield, 1974) is a teacher questionnaire for use with 3- to 6-year-olds. It has hostile-aggressive, anxious-fearful, and hyperactivity-distractibility scales. Please also review Table 7.5 in Chapter 7.

Intellectual and Achievement Testing and Other School Information Many children suspected of having an anxiety disorder need intellectual and achievement testing to identify a possible associated learning disability or to clarify the diagnosis. An anxiety disorder can cause secondary problems with inattention, distractibility, and poor school performance. Conversely, a child with LD may manifest symptoms of anxiety that are directly related to the difficult academic subjects. Some children may also require a speech-language evaluation. Children with speech-language impairments are more likely to have anxiety disorders. In one study, SAD and avoidant disorder were more prevalent in kindergarten-age children with speech-language problems than in controls (Beitchman, Nair, Clegg, et al., 1986). If the school has not completed intellectual and achievement testing, a referral can be made to the clinical psychologist or the child development team to complete this testing.

Medical Examination   The principal goals of the medical examination are to look for a possible medical cause for the child's anxiety disorder and to identify any medical problems associated with the disorder. Identifying a medical cause and associated medical problems related to anxiety disorders is particularly important in children with school refusal. The parents and the child must be reassured that the child is healthy and that the somatic complaints are signs of stress or symptoms of anxiety. Somatic complaints are a common manifestation of anxiety and depression in adolescents with school refusal (Bernstein, Massie, Thuras, et al., 1997).

The differential diagnosis of anxiety disorders includes other anxiety, affective, and disruptive behavior disorders (see Table 10.12). It also includes anxiety as a manifestation of ongoing abuse, anxiety as a symptom of a medical illness (e.g., hyperthyroidism), and medical problems misdiagnosed as an anxiety disorder. For example, partial complex seizures have been misdiagnosed as panic attacks, and other medical disorders can cause symptoms similar to panic attacks (Dummit & Klein, 1994). Finally, anxiety may be a response to a serious medical condition such as cancer.

The medical examination should be meticulous, and the results are usually normal. Observe for vocal and motor tics that would support the diagnosis of TS (observation of tics in the physician's office is not necessary for the diagnosis), and any physical evidence of nonaccidental injuries. Of interest, children with anxiety disorders may show an increase in the number of "soft" neurologic signs or neuromotor immaturities (Hooper & March, 1995). Their presence is not critical to the diagnosis. Panic disorder can be associated with mitral valve prolapse. The frequency of this association in children is not known; however, this condition is generally believed to be benign (Dummit & Klein, 1994).

Family Assessment   Careful assessment of the family and the social support network can be an important part of the diagnostic evaluation. Use a family systems perspective, and assist the family in identifying strengths as well as areas of concern. Optimally, the family assessment leads to the identification of family goals and potential solutions. Please review Chapter 3 and Coleman's (1997) article. Asking parents to complete a questionnaire such as the Parenting Stress Index–Short Form (Abidin, 1995) or the Family Needs Survey (Bailey & Simeonsson, 1988) can be helpful if it is used as part of an open-ended interview.

Referral to a Mental Health Professional or a Child Development Team   Many children do require referral to a child psychiatrist or psychologist or to a child development team headed by a developmental pediatrician to confirm the diagnosis. Consider referral in the following circumstances:

- The child has persisting symptoms (longer than 3–6 months).
- Symptoms significantly interfere with the child's or family's daily activities.
- Anxiety symptoms are associated with a chronic medical condition or learning disability.
- Parents have limited abilities to assist the child with treatment (e.g., a parent with an anxiety disorder or depression).

If the principal issues are establishing a diagnosis and initiating treatment including medication, it may be most appropriate to refer to a child psychiatrist. If the focus is primarily for diagnosis and behavioral interventions, consider referral to the clinical psychologist (Jellinek & Kearns, 1995). If the

---

Table 10.12.   Differential diagnosis of anxiety disorders in children and adolescents

Separation anxiety disorder
Social phobia
Panic disorder
Generalized anxiety disorder
Specific phobia
Obsessive-compulsive disorder
Tourette syndrome
Posttraumatic stress disorder
Depression
Attention-deficit/hyperactivity disorder
Oppositional defiant disorder/conduct disorder
Seizure disorder
Physical abuse
Excessive coffee drinking
Effect of medication
Drug or alcohol abuse
Hyperthyroidism
Cardiac arrhythmia
Hypoglycemia and related metabolic disorders
Pheochromocytoma (catecholamine-releasing tumor)
Systemic lupus erythematosus

Adapted with permission from the *Diagnostic and Statistical Manual of Mental Disorders, Fourth Edition.* Copyright © 1994 American Psychiatric Association.

child has significant learning or medical problems in addition to the suspected anxiety disorder, however, refer the child and family to a child development team (with a clinical psychologist) headed by a developmental pediatrician.

Semistructured Diagnostic Interviews and Self-Report Measures   A semistructured diagnostic interview, a self-report measure, and behavioral observations are parts of the evaluation by the mental health professional. Examples of semistructured diagnostic interviews are the Schedule for Affective Disorders and Schizophrenia for School-Age Children (K-SADS) (Kaufman, Birmaher, Brent, et al., 1997; Orvaschel, 1995) and the Anxiety Disorders Interview Schedule for DSM-IV: Child Version (ADIS for DSM-IV:C) (Silverman & Albano, 1996). The ADIS for DSM-IV:C is a specially designed instrument for the assessment of anxiety disorders. It provides data about symptoms, etiology, course, and functional impact. Self-report measures include the State-Trait Anxiety Inventory for Children (STAIC) (Spielberger, Edwards, & Lushene, 1973), the Revised Children's Manifest Anxiety Scale (RCMAS) (Reynolds & Richmond, 1985), and the Revised Fear Survey Schedule for Children (FSSC–R) (Ollendick, 1983). The FSSC-R measures five factors: fear of failure and criticism, the unknown, injury and small animals, danger and death, and medical fears. It may be used with children and adolescents 7–18 years of age. Physiologic measures (e.g., heart rate, surface electromyogram [EMG], skin conductance) may also be used at times (e.g., in the evaluation of specific phobias).

Counseling the Parents and the Child About the Diagnosis

In General   In most cases, the initial counseling of the parents and the child is done by the mental health professional or the child development team. It is important, however, for the primary care physician to schedule a family conference with the following goals:

- Review of diagnostic information and treatment recommendations
- Assistance with service coordination
- Provision of support and advocacy to families as needed
- Clarification of the responsibilities of the primary care office and the mental health professional for ongoing management

Schedule ample time for the appointment, and be sure that the appropriate reports are available: school information, behavioral questionnaire results, and reports from the mental health evalua-

tion. Please also review the general list of recommendations for counseling in Chapter 1.

Stability of the Diagnosis and Prognosis   Children with symptoms of anxiety who do not have an anxiety disorder and have no family history of anxiety or affective disorder generally do well. Their risk for an anxiety disorder or for other mental health problems is similar to that of the general population (Bell-Dolan, Last, & Strauss, 1990). The outcomes for children with a diagnosed anxiety disorder depend on the specific disorder. A substantial number of individuals continue to have mental health problems as adults. As noted previously, children with SAD are at risk for PDAG as adults. Leonard, Swedo, Lenane, and colleagues (1993) reported on a 2- to 7-year follow-up of 54 children treated for OCD. Only 11% were asymptomatic, and 43% continued to meet DSM-III–R diagnostic criteria for OCD. In general, children with OCD continue to experience significant problems as adults. The prognosis for children with PTSD depends on the character of the traumatic event. Children who experience repeated traumatic episodes (type 2; Terr, 1991) from a trusted adult are at high risk for experiencing a variety of mental health problems, including depression and borderline personality disorder.

Counseling Families about School Refusal, Persistent Fears, and Behavioral Inhibition

School Refusal   School refusal should be managed as a psychosocial "emergency." The principal treatment strategy for the children with mild to moderate problems is to return the child to regular school attendance as soon as possible. The child can return to school even while a medical evaluation for somatic complaints is in progress. In fact, a return to school may be diagnostic (Schmitt, 1995). The following list of measures (adapted from Schmitt, 1995, and Jellinek & Kearns, 1995) should be taken to help parents cope with a child who refuses to go to school:

- Talk with the parents, the child, and school staff.
- Discuss your assessment of the basis for the child's school refusal (e.g., separation anxiety versus phobia versus CD).
- Emphasize that, after a thorough evaluation and appropriate testing, the child is found to be healthy. (Avoid unnecessary tests.)
- Agree on a time line (1–2 weeks) and procedures for returning to school (e.g., one of the parents will drive the child to and from school, the parent may walk the child to the classroom initially).
- Make necessary changes at school (e.g., if the child is fearful of specific situations). In general, changing teachers and schools is of no benefit.

- Agree on the procedures to follow when the child "feels" sick before school (e.g., parent takes the child's temperature and calls the physician for an elevated temperature) and during school (e.g., visit to the office for a temperature check and possible call to the physician). If the child's temperature is not elevated and there is no other clear sign of medical illness, the child should go to school or return to the classroom.
- Be available and supportive to the child and family. Meet with them as frequently as needed. Some families may require twice-weekly visits until the situation stabilizes.
- Discuss the criteria for referral to a mental health professional (e.g., if school refusal persists for 2 weeks or more).

Persistent Fears The important distinction is between a "normal" fear that does respond to reassurance and a phobia that significantly interferes with activities at home, in school, or in the community and responds poorly to reassurance (Augustyn, 1995). Common fears in early childhood include separation, falling, animals or insects, bedtime, monsters or ghosts, divorce or loss of a parent, and getting lost. Common fears in older childhood and adolescence include social rejection, new situations, dating, and sexual relations. Take the following steps to help the child and parents cope with persistent fears of the child:

- Discuss the fear with the child and parents to correct any misunderstandings.
- Respect the child's tendency initially to withdraw from the source of the fear.
- Agree on a plan to gradually introduce the stimulus of the fear with appropriate support.
- Parents may have to take concrete action with young children (e.g., looking into a closet or under the bed) but should minimize it. Provide rational explanations (e.g., say, "The sound is from the heating system") because certain actions (e.g., "monster proofing" a bedroom) may reinforce a child's fear that monsters are real. (Adapted from Augustyn, 1995, p. 142)

Consider referral to a mental health professional if using the measures just described is unsuccessful. Parents and professionals should avoid using fears as threats, exaggerating or ignoring fears, having unrealistic expectations of the child's ability to cope with fearful situations, or overprotecting the child. Overprotection may reinforce the child's fear of the object or situation (Augustyn, 1995).

Behavioral Inhibition Fifteen to twenty percent of children fit the description of the *behaviorally inhibited* or *slow-to-warm-up child* (Kagan et al., 1984).

These children are likely to respond to a new situation by withdrawing. Use the following measures to diagnose and treat the child who displays behavioral inhibition:

- Determine if there is a family history of anxiety or affective disorder (if yes, the child's risk for developing an anxiety disorder is increased).
- Talk to the parent and the child, and also talk to the child's teachers as needed (if the child agrees).
- Acknowledge and respect the child's shy temperament (i.e., emphasis on everyone being different in size, appearance, and personality).
- Discuss preparing the child for new experiences (e.g., visiting a new school before classes start, rehearsing a book report), and avoid overpreparation because the child may become more anxious.
- Review how to arrange successful social experiences for the child (e.g., initially invite one friend to the child's home to play for several hours, arrange a structured after-school activity with another child and an adult available for supervision).
- Parents need to be supportive, consistent, and persistent in exposing the child to new experiences. Avoid overprotection or pressure.
- Discuss ways to cope with embarrassment and teasing. Shy children may be embarrassed easily (adapted from Cheek et al., 1995, pp. 286–287).

MANAGEMENT

Periodic Review and Update of the Management Plan

In general, a multimodal treatment program that incorporates psychotherapy and pharmacotherapy is recommended for children and adolescents with anxiety disorders (American Academy of Child and Adolescent Psychiatry [AACAP], 1997, 1998a, 1998b; Dow et al., 1995). In most instances, children and adolescents with anxiety disorders are best co-managed by the primary health care professional and the mental health professional. The following are the responsibilities of the primary care health professional:

- Monitor the child's progress in services, including educational services.
- Determine the need for referral to the mental health professional or to other specialists.
- Review the child's response to medications and any side effects the child experiences.
- Provide advocacy and determine the need for additional family support services.
- Assist the family with care coordination.

Reevaluate the child and family in the primary care office, and update the management plan at least annually and more often for younger children and in

Cognitive-Behavioral and Psychodynamic Therapies

Cognitive-Behavioral Therapy The basis of cognitive-behavioral therapy (CBT) is therapist-controlled exposure to the stimulus. Exposure-based strategies include *gradual exposure* and *flooding*. In gradual exposure, the child makes a list of the least feared to the most feared situations, and treatment starts with the least feared situations to facilitate success. In flooding, the exposure begins with the most anxiety-provoking stimulus and is usually paired with *response prevention* (E/RP) (i.e., preventing the child from avoiding the stimulus or performing a ritual). In flooding, exposure is repeated and prolonged until the child experiences a marked decrease in anxiety (Francis & Beidel, 1995).

Various *anxiety management strategies* also are employed (e.g., *relaxation training* with progressive muscle relaxation and breathing training). *Contingency management* (e.g., use of positive and negative reinforcement, shaping of behaviors), *modeling*, and *cognitive strategies* (e.g., self-talk, problem solving, self-instruction) are other techniques used in CBT. *Systemic desensitization* is a three-step CBT program that incorporates 1) relaxation training, 2) construction of an anxiety hierarchy, and 3) gradual exposure paired with relaxation training (Francis & Beidel, 1995).

CBT for children and adolescents with OCD also involves three steps: 1) information gathering, 2) therapist-assisted E/RP, and 3) homework (March et al., 1995; March, Mulle, & Herbel, 1994). Practice or homework and parents' involvement are important parts of all CBT programs. Various programs for treating OCD use gradual exposure or flooding as well as relaxation training and cognitive strategies. CBT is effective in decreasing the symptoms of OCD. CBT in combination with pharmacotherapy results in a greater reduction of symptoms and decreases in relapse rates (March et al., 1994).

Behavioral therapies are the treatment of choice for specific phobias (Allen et al., 1995b). Gradual exposure with relaxation training, contingency management, and modeling and cognitive strategies has been effective in treating specific phobias and GAD (Francis & Beidel, 1995). In a controlled study, 47 children and adolescents with OAD, SAD, or avoidant disorder were treated for 16 weeks with a combination of gradual exposure, relaxation training, contingency management, and self-control techniques (Kendall, 1994). The control group spent 8 weeks on a waiting list. The individuals receiving the CBT treatment program showed a significant reduction in anxiety in comparison to the control group posttreatment and at a 1-year follow-up.

CBT for children with social phobia also emphasizes modification of maladaptive self-statements such as "What if I do something wrong?" (a cognitive strategy) (Beidel & Morris, 1995). In addition, those children with social phobia who have social skills impairments need modeling and social skills training (Beidel & Morris, 1995). The mainstays of therapy for PTSD are a mixture of CBT, support, and psychodynamic psychotherapy (Amaya-Jackson & March, 1995). A central element of PTSD therapies is the controlled exposure to traumatic cues to facilitate mastery.

Psychodynamic Psychotherapy Psychodynamic psychotherapy has been described as a derivative of child psychoanalysis (Keith, 1995). It encourages greater participation of parents in treatment; the therapist provides more active support and practical guidance. Appointments are less frequent than with classic child psychoanalysis (AACAP, 1997). The following are the basic principles of psychodynamic psychotherapy:

1. The child produces "material" through play and verbalization, and thus therapy proceeds at the child's pace.
2. The therapist listens or interprets the material based on the child's defenses (e.g., avoidance, repression), wishes and impulses, and transference (e.g., a child with SAD becomes distressed at the therapist's absences or vacations) (Keith, 1995).

Psychodynamic therapy may be frequent (one or more times per week) and at times is long term. It has not been shown to be effective for children and adolescents with OCD (March, 1995), and only limited research data are available on its efficacy with other anxiety disorders. It is widely practiced, and case reports have demonstrated its effectiveness (AACAP, 1997). Individual sessions can be helpful to provide support, to educate the child about the disorder, to address maladaptive behaviors, and to help the child to master separation, enhance self-esteem, and develop age-appropriate behaviors.

Other psychotherapy options include group therapy and family therapy (see Wells, 1995). These may be appropriate for certain children and families (e.g., group therapy for the older child and adolescent with PTSD). CBT in a group setting has been effective in treating panic disorder in adults (Martinsen, Olsen, Tonset, et al., 1998). Individual therapy for parents may be necessary for those parents who are anxious or depressed (Popper, 1993).

the first year of treatment. Request a current progress report from the mental health professional and from the child's education program.

Medical Management (Pharmacotherapy)

Pharmacotherapy is an important part of the medical management of many children and adolescents with anxiety disorders. Research studies (see AACAP, 1997; Bernstein, Borchardt, & Perwien, 1996) have demonstrated the effectiveness of many medications. Unfortunately, most of the research studies have "open label" methodology and are not "blinded" with an appropriate control group. In addition, few such studies have involved young children.

Most medications that have been used to treat anxiety are approved for marketing by the U.S. Food and Drug Administration (FDA), but not for use with children. Methylphenidate and dextroamphetamine are exceptions. A federal regulation promulgated by the FDA ("Regulations Requiring Manufacturers to Assess the Safety and Effectiveness of New Drugs," 1998) that took effect April 1, 1999, requires manufacturers of new drugs to provide information on how to use the medication safely and effectively with pediatric patients. At present, it is appropriate for physicians to prescribe commercially available medications for children and adolescents based on their best medical judgment (Popper, 1993). The specific use of these medications, however, should be supported by published research studies. (For a resource for general information sheets on a number of antianxiety medications to provide to parents and children, see Dulcan, 1992; for a review of the pharmacotherapy of anxiety disorders, see Allen, Leonard, & Swedo, 1995b; Bernstein et al., 1996; Birmaher, Yelovich, & Renaud, 1998; Popper, 1993; and Riddle, Bernstein, Cook, et al., 1999. Also review the detailed discussion of medication management in Chapter 7.)

When prescribing psychotropic medications to children and adolescents, review all treatment options in detail with the family and explain the benefits as well as potential side effects of the medication carefully. Make sure that families understand that some medications may not take effect for several weeks, and psychotropic medications may need several dosage adjustments. In addition specifically discuss possible interaction of prescription medications, alcohol, and recreational drugs with adolescents.

A number of scales for measuring the benefits of psychotropic medications with reasonable reliability and validity are available. These include the Yale-Brown Obsessive Compulsive Scale (YBOCS; Goodman, Price, Rasmussen, et al., 1989), the Yale Global Tic Severity Scale (Leckman, Riddle, Hardin, et al., 1989), and the Anxiety Rating for Children–Revised (Bernstein et al., 1996). Structured checklists are also available to assist in following side ef-

fects. Three examples are the Side Effects Rating Scale for children with ADHD (Barkley, 1998b), the side effects profile checklist for buspirone (Kutcher, Reiter, Gardner, et al., 1992), and the SSRI Anti-Depressant Monitoring for Side Effects (Kutcher, Reiter, & Gardner, 1995).

Commonly used medications for the treatment of anxiety disorders include selective serotonin reuptake inhibitors (SSRIs), benzodiazepines, and tricyclic antidepressants (TCAs). Other medications include buspirone, beta-adrenergic blocking agents, and monoamine oxidase inhibitors (MAOIs). Research (see Labellarte, Walkup, & Riddle, 1998) regarding the role of SSRIs in the treatment of anxiety disorders in children is encouraging. Antihistamines (diphenhydramine and hydroxyzine) that were used widely in the 1970s and 1980s appear to be of limited value (Popper, 1993). Children who are prescribed TCAs should be monitored closely (e.g., pulse, blood pressure, cardiac rhythms) because of their risk of developing potentially serious cardiac arrhythmias (AACAP, 1997). Stimulant medications should be used with care in children with ADHD and a co-morbid anxiety disorder because of the potential of exacerbating anxiety symptomatology (Popper, 1993).

Separation Anxiety Disorder and School Refusal

Four placebo-controlled trials with TCAs with a total of 140 children (three with imipramine and one with clomipramine; Berney, Kolvin, Bhate, et al., 1981; Bernstein, Garfinkel, & Borchardt, 1990; Gittleman-Klein & Klein, 1971, 1973; Klein, Koplewicz, & Kanner, 1992) reported conflicting results. Allen and coworkers (1995b) concluded that imipramine may be helpful in some children, but the proof is lacking. A number of case reports (see Popper, 1993) noted improvement with clonazepam (a benzodiazepine); however, a controlled trial of clonazepam in 12 children (11 of whom had SAD) showed no significant increase in benefit from medicine over placebo (Graae, Milner, Rizzotto, & Klein, 1994). In two open label studies (Birmaher, Waterman, Ryan, et al., 1994; Fairbanks, Pine, Tancer, et al., 1997) of children with mixed anxiety disorders, most children and adolescents with SAD or social phobia showed moderate to marked improvement with fluoxetine with few side effects.

Overanxious Disorder

Open label studies and/or case reports (see Popper, 1993) have noted benefits derived from using benzodiazepines (e.g., clonazepam, alprazolam) and buspirone. A controlled trial (Simeon, Ferguson, Knott, et al., 1992) of alprazolam with 30 children and adolescents with OAD and avoidant disorder, however, showed no significant benefit. As noted previously, fluoxetine resulted in moderate to marked improvement in 17 of 21 children and adolescents with OAD, SAD, or social phobia (Birmaher et al., 1994).

Panic Disorder Controlled trials (Moroz & Rosenbaum, 1999; Nair, Bakish, Saxena, et al., 1996; Pohl, Wolkow, & Clary, 1998) in adults have documented the efficacy of several medications, including clonazepam, sertraline (an SSRI), and imipramine; however, few placebo-controlled studies are available for children and adolescents. In a long-term placebo-controlled study (Kutcher & Mackenzie, 1988), nine of 12 adolescents with panic disorder improved with clonazepam. A number of case reports also have noted clinical improvement with clonazepam and imipramine (Popper, 1993). In addition, in an open label study (Renaud, Birmaher, Wassick, & Bridge, 1999), nine of 12 children and adolescents with panic disorder were much to very much improved on SSRIs without significant side effects.

Social Phobia The benefit of SSRIs for social phobia in children and adolescents has not been demonstrated clearly. In an open label study (Fairbanks et al., 1997) of children with mixed anxiety disorders, 8 of 10 children with social phobia improved on fluoxetine. In another open label study (Dummitt, Klein, Tancer, et al., 1996), 15 of 21 children with selective mutism improved on fluoxetine; however, few differences were noted in a placebo-controlled study (Black & Uhde, 1994) of fluoxetine in 15 children and adolescents with selective mutism, social phobia, or avoidant disorder. Liebowitz and co-workers (1991) reported significant improvement in adults with social phobia when treated with the MAOI phenelzine (80 individuals, 64% positive response), buspirone (nine individuals, 60% positive response), and fluoxetine (12 individuals, 58% positive response).

Obsessive-Compulsive Disorder OCD is perhaps the most thoroughly studied of the anxiety disorders. Clomipramine, fluoxetine, and other SSRIs appear to be beneficial for children and adolescents with OCD; however, controlled trials are few (Grados, Scahill, & Riddle, 1999; Leonard, 1997; March & Leonard, 1996; Riddle et al., 1992). In a placebo-controlled, cross-over trial (Leonard & Rapoport, 1989) of clomipramine and desipramine, clomipramine was found to be superior to placebo. The response to desipramine was similar to placebo, and many children relapsed when switched from clomipramine to desipramine. In another study (Riddle et al., 1992), 44% of subjects who received fluoxetine responded positively compared to 27% of the control group. Finally, fluvoxamine, paroxetine, and sertra-

line were found to be beneficial in open trials (Alderman, Wolkow, Chung, & Johnston, 1998; Apter, Ratzoni, King, et al., 1994; Rosenberg, Stewart, Fitzgerald, et al., 1999) with children and adolescents with OCD.

Posttraumatic Stress Disorder A variety of medications have been used to treat the anxiety, depression, and other problems associated with PTSD; however, few research studies with children have been reported (Donnelly, Amaya-Jackson, & March, 1999; Perry & Azad, 1999). These medications include SSRIs, benzodiazepines, clonidine, propranolol, buspirone, TCAs, and phenelzine (an MAOI). Clonidine has been effective as a single bedtime dose in treating children who have sleep disorders associated with PTSD (Harmon & Riggs, 1996; Pynoos & Nader, 1993). Propranolol reduced aggressivity and symptoms of anxiety in an open label study of 11 children with acute PTSD (Famularo, Kinscherff, & Fenton, 1988).

Family Support Services
A critical part of each reevaluation is a review of the family's goals and the family's need for support services. As commented previously, parents who are anxious or depressed also may need to be referred for individual psychotherapy services. A variety of services may be required to support families in the care of their child with an anxiety disorder:

- Appropriate behavior and psychotherapy treatments for the child
- Parent training in specific behavioral management strategies
- Support groups for parents, fathers, and siblings
- Other support services
  a. Individual counseling for parents
  b. Couples counseling for parents
  c. Counseling for siblings
  d. Financial or legal advice or assistance
  e. Other enabling services (e.g., respite care, transportation)

Important Care Coordination Issues
General recommendations for changes in office procedures to facilitate the care of children with disabilities and chronic conditions are discussed in detail in Chapter 1. In addition to those general recommendations, the primary care office should

- Identify the contact person for ECSE, special education services, and school nursing services in the local school district
- Have an updated list of the local mental health service providers with expertise in the treatment of anxiety disorders in children (medication management and CBT)

- Clearly identify who is responsible for medication management (the primary care physician, the child psychiatrist, or the developmental pediatrician)
- Regularly exchange information with schools and mental health service providers, and iden-

tify a specific time when you or the office care coordinator can be contacted
- Provide resource information to families on parent support and advocacy groups (e.g., the Tourette Syndrome Association) (please see the Appendix at the end of this chapter)

REFERENCES

Abidin, R.R. (1995). *Parenting Stress Index Manual* (3rd ed.). Lutz, FL: Psychological Assessment Resources.

Achenbach, T.M. (1991a). *Manual for Child Behavior Checklist/4-18 and 1991 Profile.* Burlington: University of Vermont, Department of Psychiatry.

Achenbach, T.M. (1991b). *Manual for the Teacher's Report Form and 1991 Profile.* Burlington: University of Vermont, Department of Psychiatry.

Achenbach, T.M. (1991c). *Manual for the Youth Self-Report and 1991 Profile.* Burlington: University of Vermont, Department of Psychiatry.

Alderman, J., Wolkow, R., Chung, M., & Johnston, H.F. (1998). Sertraline treatment of children and adolescents with obsessive-compulsive disorder or depression: Pharmacokinetics, tolerability, and efficacy. *Journal of the American Academy of Child and Adolescent Psychiatry, 37,* 386–394.

Allen, A.J., Leonard, H.L., & Swedo, S.E. (1995a). Case study: A new infection-triggered, autoimmune subtype of pediatric OCD and Tourette's syndrome. *Journal of the American Academy of Child and Adolescent Psychiatry, 34*(3), 307–311.

Allen, A.J., Leonard, H.L., & Swedo, S.E. (1995b). Current knowledge of medications for the treatment of childhood anxiety disorders. *Journal of the American Academy of Child and Adolescent Psychiatry, 34*(8), 976–986.

Amaya-Jackson, L., & March, J.S. (1995). Posttraumatic stress disorder. In J. March (Ed.), *Anxiety disorders in children and adolescents* (pp. 276–300). New York: Guilford Press.

American Academy of Child and Adolescent Psychiatry. (1997). Practice parameters for the assessment and treatment of children and adolescents with anxiety disorders. *Journal of the American Academy of Child and Adolescent Psychiatry, 36*(10, Suppl.), S69–S84.

American Academy of Child and Adolescent Psychiatry. (1998a). Practice parameters for the assessment and treatment of children and adolescents with obsessive-compulsive disorder. *Journal of the American Academy of Child and Adolescent Psychiatry, 37*(10, Suppl.), S27–S45.

American Academy of Child and Adolescent Psychiatry. (1998b). Summary of the practice parameters for the assessment and treatment of children and adolescents with posttraumatic stress disorder. *Journal of the American Academy of Child and Adolescent Psychiatry, 37*(9), 997–1001.

American Psychiatric Association (APA). (1987). *Diagnostic and statistical manual of mental disorders* (3rd ed. rev.). Washington, DC: Author.

American Psychiatric Association (APA). (1994). *Diagnostic and statistical manual of mental disorders* (4th ed.). Washington, DC: Author.

Anderson, J.C. (1994). Epidemiological issues. In T.H. Ollendick, N.J. King, & W. Yule (Eds.), *International handbook of phobic and anxiety disorders in children and adolescents* (pp. 43–66). New York: Plenum Press.

Anderson, J.C., Williams, S., McGee, R., et al. (1987). DSM-III disorders in preadolescent children. *Archives of General Psychiatry, 44,* 69–76.

Apter, A., Ratzoni, G., King, R.A., et al. (1994). Fluvoxamine open-label treatment of adolescent inpatients with obsessive-compulsive disorder or depression. *Journal of the American Academy of Child and Adolescent Psychiatry, 33*(3), 342–348.

Augustyn, M. (1995). Fears. In S. Parker & B. Zuckerman (Eds.), *Behavior and developmental pediatrics: A handbook for primary care* (pp. 140–142). Boston: Little, Brown & Co.

Bailey, D.B., Jr., & Simeonsson, R.J. (1988). Assessing needs of families with handicapped infants. *Journal of Special Education, 22*(1), 117–126.

Barkley, R.A. (1998a). *Attention deficit hyperactivity disorder: A handbook for diagnosis and treatment* (2nd ed.). New York: Guilford Press.

Barkley, R.A. (1998b). Side Effects Rating Scale. In R.A. Barkley & K.R. Murphy, *Attention-deficit disorder: A clinical workbook* (2nd ed., p. 132). New York: Guilford Press.

Behar, L.B. (1977). The Preschool Behavior Questionnaire. *Journal of Abnormal Child Psychology, 5*(3), 265–275.

Behar, L.B., & Stringfield, S. (1974). A behavior rating scale for the preschool child. *Developmental Psychology, 10,* 601–610.

Beidel, D.C. (1991). Social phobia and overanxious disorder in school-age children. *Journal of the American Academy of Child and Adolescent Psychiatry, 30*(4), 545–552.

Beidel, D.C., & Morris, T.L. (1995). Social phobia. In J. March (Ed.), *Anxiety disorders in children and adolescents* (pp. 181–211). New York: Guilford Press.

Beidel, D.C., & Randall, J. (1994). Social phobia. In T.H. Ollendick, N.J. King, & W. Yule (Eds.), *International handbook of phobic and anxiety disorders in children and adolescents* (pp. 111–130). New York: Plenum Publishing Corp.

Beitchman, J.H., Nair, R., Clegg, M.A., et al. (1986). Prevalence of psychiatric disorders in children with speech and language disorders. *Journal of the American Academy of Child and Adolescent Psychiatry, 25,* 528–535.

Bell-Dolan, D.J., Last, C.G., & Strauss, C.C. (1990). Symptoms of anxiety disorders in normal children. *Journal of the American Academy of Child and Adolescent Psychiatry, 29,* 759–765.

Berney, T., Kolvin, I., Bhate, S.R., et al. (1981). School phobia: A therapeutic trial with clomipramine and short-term outcome. *British Journal of Psychiatry, 138,* 110–118.

Bernstein, G.A., & Borchardt, C.M. (1991). Anxiety disorders of childhood and adolescence: A critical review.

Journal of the American Academy of Child and Adolescent Psychiatry, 30(4), 519–532.

Bernstein, G.A., Borchardt, C.M., & Perwien, A.R. (1996). Anxiety disorders in children and adolescents: A review of the past 10 years. *Journal of the American Academy of Child and Adolescent Psychiatry, 35*(9), 1110–1119.

Bernstein, G.A., & Garfinkel, B.D. (1986). School phobia: The overlap of affective and anxiety disorders. *Journal of the American Academy of Child Psychiatry, 25*(2), 235–241.

Bernstein, G.A., Garfinkel, D.D., & Borchardt, C.M. (1990). Comparative studies of pharmacotherapy for school refusal. *Journal of the American Academy of Child and Adolescent Psychiatry, 29,* 773–781.

Bernstein, G.A., Massie, E.D., Thuras, P.D., et al. (1997). Somatic symptoms in anxious-depressed school refusers. *Journal of the American Academy of Child and Adolescent Psychiatry, 36*(5), 661–668.

Biederman, J., Rosenbaum, J.F., Bolduc-Murphy, E.A., et al. (1993). Behavioral inhibition as a temperamental risk factor for anxiety disorders. *Child and Adolescent Psychiatric Clinics of North America, 2,* 667–684.

Biederman, J., Rosenbaum, J.F., Chaloff, J., & Kagan, J. (1995). Behavioral inhibition as a risk factor. In J.S. March (Ed.), *Anxiety disorders in children and adolescents* (pp. 61–81). New York: Guilford Press.

Birmaher, B., Waterman, G.S., Ryan, N., et al. (1994). Fluoxetine for childhood anxiety disorders. *Journal of the American Academy of Child and Adolescent Psychiatry, 33*(7), 993–999.

Birmaher, B., Yelovich, A.K., & Renaud, J. (1998). Pharmacologic treatment for children and adolescents with anxiety disorders. *Pediatric Clinics of North America, 45*(5), 1187–1204.

Black, B. (1995). Separation anxiety disorder and panic disorder. In J.S. March (Ed.), *Anxiety disorders in children and adolescents* (pp. 212–234). New York: Guilford Press.

Black, B., & Uhde, T.W. (1994). Treatment of elective mutism with fluoxetine: A double-blind, placebo-controlled study. *Journal of the American Academy of Child and Adolescent Psychiatry, 33,* 1000–1006.

Cheek, J.M., Parker, S., & Zuckerman, B. (Eds.). (1995). *Behavior and developmental pediatrics: A handbook for primary care.* Boston: Little, Brown & Co.

Chess, S., & Thomas, A. (1986). *Temperament in clinical practice.* New York: Guilford Press.

Coleman, W.L. (1997). Family-focused pediatrics: Solution-oriented techniques for behavioral problems. *Contemporary Pediatrics, 14*(7), 121–134.

Conners, C.K. (1997). *Conners' Rating Scales–Revised technical manual.* North Tonawanda, NY: Multi-Health Systems.

Costello, E.J., & Angold, A. (1995). Epidemiology. In J.S. March (Ed.), *Anxiety disorders in children and adolescents* (pp. 109–124). New York: Guilford Press.

Donnelly, C.L., Amaya-Jackson, L., & March, J.S. (1999). Psychopharmacology of pediatric posttraumatic stress disorder. *Journal of Child and Adolescent Psychopharmacology, 9*(3), 203–220.

Dow, S.P., Sonies, D.B., Scheib, D., et al. (1995). Practical guidelines for the assessment and treatment of selective mutism. *Journal of the American Academy of Child and Adolescent Psychiatry, 34*(7), 836–846.

Dulcan, M.K. (1992). Information for parents and youth on psychotropic medications. *Journal of Child and Adolescent Psychopharmacology, 2*(2), 81–101.

Dummit, E.S., & Klein, R.G. (1994). Panic disorder. In T.H. Ollendick, N.J. King, & W. Yule (Eds.), *International handbook of phobic and anxiety disorders in children and adolescents* (pp. 241–266). New York: Plenum Publishing Corp.

Dummit, E.S., Klein, R.G., Tancer, N.K., et al. (1996). Fluoxetine treatment of children with selective mutism: An open trial. *Journal of the American Academy of Child and Adolescent Psychiatry, 35*(5), 615–621.

Dummit, E.S., Klein, R.G., Tancer, N.K., et al. (1997). Systematic assessment of 50 children with selective mutism. *Journal of the American Academy of Child and Adolescent Psychiatry, 36*(5), 653–660.

Eisert, D.C., Sturner, R.A., & Mabe, P.A. (1991). Questionnaires in behavioral pediatrics: Guidelines for selection and use. *Developmental and Behavioral Pediatrics, 12*(1), 42–54.

Fairbanks, J.M., Pine, D.S., Tancer, N.K., et al. (1997). Open fluoxetine treatment of mixed anxiety disorders in children and adolescents. *Journal of Child and Adolescent Psychopharmacology, 7*(1), 17–29.

Famularo, R., Kinscherff, R., & Fenton, T. (1988). Propranolol treatment for childhood posttraumatic stress disorder, acute type. A pilot study. *American Journal of Diseases of Children, 142*(11), 1244–1247.

Francis, G., & Beidel, D. (1995). Cognitive-behavioral psychotherapy. In J. March (Ed.), *Anxiety disorders in children and adolescents* (pp. 321–340). New York: Guilford Press.

Francis, G., & D'Elia, F.A. (1994). Avoidant disorder. In T.H. Ollendick, N.J. King, & W. Yule (Eds.), *International handbook of phobic and anxiety disorders in children and adolescents* (pp. 131–144). New York: Plenum Publishing Corp.

Francis, G., Last, C.G., & Strauss, C.C. (1987). Expression of separation anxiety disorder: The roles of age and gender. *Child Psychiatry and Human Development, 18*(2), 82–89.

Francis, G., Last, C.G., & Strauss, C.C. (1992). Avoidant disorder and social phobia in children and adolescents. *Journal of the American Academy of Child and Adolescent Psychiatry, 31*(6), 1086–1089.

Gittelman-Klein, R., & Klein, D.F. (1971). Controlled imipramine treatment of school phobia. *Archives of General Psychiatry, 25,* 204–207.

Gittelman-Klein, R., & Klein, D.F. (1973). School phobia: Diagnostic considerations in the light of imipramine effects. *Journal of Nervous and Mental Disease, 156,* 199–215.

Goodfriend, M.S. (1993). Treatment of attachment disorder of infancy in a neonatal intensive care unit. *Pediatrics, 91*(1), 139–142.

Goodman, W.K., Price, L.H., Rasmussen, S.T., et al. (1989). The Yale-Brown Obsessive Compulsive Scale. *Archives of General Psychiatry, 46,* 1006–1016.

Graae, F., Milner, J., Rizzotto, L., & Klein, R.G. (1994). Clonazapam in childhood anxiety disorders. *Journal of the American Academy of Child and Adolescent Psychiatry, 33,* 372–376.

Grados, M., Scahill, L., & Riddle, M.A. (1999). Pharmacotherapy in children and adolescents with obsessive-compulsive disorder. *Child and Adolescent Psychiatric Clinics of North America, 8*(3), 617–634.

Greenspan, S.I. (1991). Clinical assessment of emotional milestones in infancy and early childhood. *Pediatric Clinical of North America, 38*(6), 1371–1385.

Harmon, R.J., & Riggs, P.D. (1996). Clonidine for posttraumatic stress disorder in preschool children. *Journal of the American Academy of Child and Adolescent Psychiatry, 35*(9), 1247–1249.

Hayden, T.L. (1980). Classification of elective mutism. *Journal of the American Academy of Child Psychiatry, 19*(1), 118–133.

Hooper, S.R., & March, J.S. (1995). Neuropsychology. In J. March (Ed.), *Anxiety disorders in children and adolescents* (pp. 35–60). New York: Guilford Press.

Jellinek, M.S., & Kearns, M.E. (1995). Separation anxiety. *Pediatrics in Review, 16*(2), 57–61.

Jellinek, M.S., Little, M., Murphy, M., & Pagano, M. (1995). The Pediatric Symptom Checklist: Support for a role in a managed care environment. *Archives of Pediatric Adolescent Medicine, 149*, 740–744.

Kagan, J., Reznick, J.S., Clarke, C., et al. (1984). Behavioral inhibition to the unfamiliar. *Child Development, 55*, 2212–2225.

Kaufman, J., Birmaher, B., Brent, D., et al. (1997). Schedule for Affective Disorders and Schizophrenia for School-Age Children–Present and Lifetime Version (K-SADS-PL): Initial reliability and validity data. *Journal of the American Academy of Child and Adolescent Psychiatry, 36*, 980–988.

Keith, C. (1995). Psychodynamic psychotherapy. In J. March (Ed.), *Anxiety disorders in children and adolescents* (pp. 386–400). New York: Guilford Press.

Kendall, P.C. (1994). Treating anxiety disorders in youth: Results of a randomized clinical trial. *Journal of Consulting and Clinical Psychology, 62*, 100–110.

Kiessling, L.S., Marcotte, A.C., & Culpepper, L. (1993). Antineuronal antibodies in movement disorders. *Pediatrics, 92*, 39–43.

Klein, D.F. (1981). Anxiety reconceptualized. In D.F. Klein & J. Rabkin (Eds.), *Anxiety: New research and changing concepts* (pp. 235–263). Philadelphia: Lippincott-Raven.

Klein, R.G., Koplewicz, H.S., & Kanner, A. (1992). Imipramine treatment of children with separation anxiety disorder. *Journal of the American Academy of Child and Adolescent Psychiatry, 31*, 21–28.

Kutcher, S., Reiter, S., & Gardner, D. (1995). Pharmacotherapy: Approaches and applications. In J. March (Ed.), *Anxiety disorders in children and adolescents* (pp. 341–385). New York: Guilford Press.

Kutcher, S.P., & Mackenzie, S. (1988). Successful clonazapam treatment of adolescents with panic disorder. *Journal of Clinical Psychopharmacology, 8*, 229–300.

Kutcher, S.P., Reiter, S., Gardner, D.M., et al. (1992). The pharmacotherapy of anxiety disorders in children and adolescents. *Psychiatric Clinics of North America, 15*, 41–68.

Labellarte, M.J., Walkup, J.T., & Riddle, M.A. (1998). The new antidepressants: Selective serotonin reuptake inhibitors. *Pediatric Clinics of North America, 45*(5), 1137–1155.

Lahey, B.B., & Carlson, C.L. (1991). Validity of the diagnostic category of attention deficit disorder without hyperactivity: A review of the literature. *Journal of Learning Disabilities, 24*(2), 110–120.

Last, C.G., Hersen, M., Kazdin, A.E., et al. (1987a). Comparison of DSM-III separation anxiety and overanxious disorders: Demographic characteristics and patterns of comorbidity. *Journal of the American Academy of Child and Adolescent Psychiatry, 26*(4), 527–531.

Last, C.G., Hersen, M., Kazdin, A.E., et al. (1987b). Psychiatric illness in the mothers of anxious children. *American Journal of Psychiatry, 144*(12), 1580–1583.

Last, C.G., Hersen, M., Kazdin, A.E., et al. (1991). Anxiety disorders in children and their families. *Archives of General Psychiatry, 48*(10), 928–934.

Last, C.G., & Strauss, C.C. (1990). School refusal in anxiety-disordered children and adolescents. *Journal of the American Academy of Child and Adolescent Psychiatry, 29*, 31–35.

Last, C.G., Strauss, C.C., & Francis, G. (1987). Comorbidity among childhood anxiety disorders. *Journal of Nervous and Mental Disease, 175*(12), 726–730.

Leckman, J.F., Riddle, M.A., Hardin, M.T., et al. (1989). The Yale Global Tic Severity Scale: Initial testing of a clinician-rated scale of tic severity. *Journal of the American Academy of Child and Adolescent Psychiatry, 28*(4), 566–573.

Leonard, H., & Dow, S. (1995). Selective mutism. In J. March (Ed.), *Anxiety disorders in children and adolescents* (pp. 235–250). New York: Guilford Press.

Leonard, H.L. (1997). New developments in the treatment of obsessive-compulsive disorder. *Journal of Clinical Psychiatry, 58*(Suppl. 14), 39–47.

Leonard, H.L., & Rapoport, J.L. (1989). Pharmacotherapy of childhood obsessive-compulsive disorder. *Psychiatric Clinics of North America, 12*(4), 963–970.

Leonard, H.L., & Rapoport, J.L. (1991). Obsessive-compulsive disorder. In J.M. Werner (Ed.), *Textbook of child and adolescent psychiatry* (pp. 323–329). Washington, DC: American Psychiatric Press.

Leonard, H.L., Goldberger, E.L., Rapoport, J.L., et al. (1990). Childhood rituals: Normal development or obsessive compulsive symptoms. *Journal of the American Academy of Child and Adolescent Psychiatry, 29*, 17–23.

Leonard, H.L., Swedo, S.E., Lenane, M.C., et al. (1993). A 2- to 7-year follow-up study of 54 obsessive-compulsive children and adolescents. *Archives of General Psychiatry, 50*(6), 429–439.

Liebowitz, M.R., Schneier, F.R., Hollander, E., et al. (1991). Treatment of social phobia with drugs other than benzodiazepines. *Journal of Clinical Psychiatry, 52*(11), 10–15.

Little, D.L. (1983). Parent acceptance of routine use of the Carey and McDevitt Infant Temperament Questionnaire. *Pediatrics, 71*(1), 104–106.

Little, M., Murphy, J.M., Jellinek, M.S., et al. (1994). Screening 4- and 5-year-old children for psychosocial dysfunction: A preliminary study with the Pediatric Symptom Checklist. *Journal of Developmental and Behavioral Pediatrics, 15*(3), 191–197.

Luxenberg, J.S., Swedo, S.E., Flament, S.E., et al. (1988). Neuroanatomic abnormalities in obsessive-compulsive disorder detected with quantitative X-ray computed tomography. *American Journal of Psychiatry, 145*, 1089–1093.

March, J.S., Mulle, K., & Herbel, B. (1994). Behavioral psychotherapy for children and adolescents with obsessive-compulsive disorder: An open trial of a new protocol-driven treatment package. *Journal of the American*

Academy of Child and Adolescent Psychiatry, 33(3), 333–341.

March, J.S. (1995). Cognitive-behavioral psychotherapy for children and adolescents with OCD: A review and recommendations for treatment. *Journal of American Academy of Child and Adolescent Psychiatry, 34*(1), 7–18.

March, J.S., & Leonard, H.L. (1996). Obsessive-compulsive disorder in children and adolescents: A review of the past 10 years. *Journal of the American Academy of Child and Adolescent Psychiatry, 35,* 1265–1273.

March, J.S., Leonard, H.L., & Swedo, S. (1995). Obsessive-compulsive disorder. In J.S. March (Ed.), *Anxiety disorders in children and adolescents* (pp. 251–275). New York: Guilford Press.

Martinsen, E.W., Olsen, T., Tonset, E., et al. (1998). Cognitive-behavioral group therapy for panic disorder in the general clinical setting: A naturalistic study with 1-year follow-up. *Journal of Clinical Psychiatry, 59,* 437–442.

Mattison, R.E. (1989). Pediatrics management of anxiety disorders. *Pediatric Annals, 18*(2), 114–118.

McGee, R., Feehan, M., Williams, S., et al. (1990). DSM-III disorders in a large sample of adolescents. *Journal of the American Academy of Child and Adolescent Psychiatry, 29*(4), 611–619.

McLeer, S.V., Deblinger, E., Atkins, M.S., et al. (1988). Post-traumatic stress disorder in sexually abused children. *Journal of the American Academy of Child and Adolescent Psychiatry, 27*(5), 650–654.

Medoff-Cooper, B., Carey, W.B., & McDevitt, S.C. (1993). The Early Infancy Temperament Questionnaire. *Developmental and Behavioral Pediatrics, 14*(4), 230–235.

Moreau, D., & Follett, C. (1993). Panic disorder in children and adolescents. *Child and Adolescent Psychiatry Clinics of North America, 2,* 581–602.

Moroz, G., & Rosenbaum, J.F. (1999). Efficacy, safety, and gradual discontinuation of clonazepam in panic disorder: A placebo-controlled, multicenter study using optimized dosages. *Journal of Clinical Psychiatry, 60*(9), 604–612.

Nair, N.P., Bakish, D., Saxena, B., et al. (1996). Comparison of fluvoxamine, imipramine, and placebo in the treatment of outpatients with panic disorder. *Anxiety, 2*(4), 192–198.

Ollendick, T.H. (1983). Reliability and validity of the Revised Fear Survey Schedule for Children (FSSC–R). *Behaviour Research and Therapy, 21*(6), 685–692.

Orvaschel, H. (1995). *Schedule for Affective Disorders and Schizophrenia for School-Age Children: Epidemiologic Version–5 (K-SADS-E–5).* Fort Lauderdale, FL: Nova Southeastern University.

Ost, L. (1987). Age of onset in different phobias. *Journal of Abnormal Psychology, 96,* 123–145.

Perry, B.D., & Azad, I. (1999). Posttraumatic stress disorders in children and adolescents. *Current Opinion in Pediatrics, 11*(4), 310–316.

Pohl, R.B., Wolkow, R.M., & Clary, C.M. (1998). Sertraline in the treatment of panic disorder: A double-blind multicenter trial. *American Journal of Psychiatry, 155,* 1189–1195.

Popper, C.W. (1993). Psychopharmacologic treatment of anxiety disorders in adolescents and children. *Journal of Clinical Psychiatry, 54*(5), 52–63.

Pynoos, R.S., & Nader, K. (1993). Issues in the treatment of posttraumatic stress in children and adolescents. In J.P. Wilson & B. Raphael (Eds.), *International handbook of traumatic stress syndromes* (pp. 535–549). New York: Plenum Publishing Corp.

Pynoos, R.S., Nader, K., & March, J.S. (1991). Posttraumatic stress disorder. In J.M. Werner (Ed.), *Textbook of child and adolescent psychiatry* (pp. 339–348). Washington, DC: American Psychiatric Press.

Rauch, S.L., Savage, C.R., Alpert, N.M., et al. (1997). Probing striatal function in obsessive-compulsive disorder: A PET study of implicit sequence learning. *Journal of Neuropsychiatry and Clinical Neuroscience, 9,* 568–573.

Regulations requiring manufacturers to assess the safety and effectiveness of new drugs and biological products. (1998). 63(231) Fed. Reg. 66,631–66,672.

Renaud, J., Birmaher, B., Wassick, S.C., & Bridge, J. (1999). Use of selective serotonin reuptake inhibitors for the treatment of childhood panic disorder: A pilot study. *Journal of Child and Adolescent Psychopharmacology, 9*(2), 73–83.

Rettew, D.C., Swedo, S.E., Leonard, H.L., et al. (1992). Obsessions and compulsions across time in 79 children and adolescents with obsessive-compulsive disorder. *Journal of the American Academy of Child and Adolescent Psychiatry, 31*(6), 1050–1056.

Reynolds, C.R., & Richmond, B.O. (1985). *Revised Children's Manifest Anxiety Scale (RCMAS) manual.* Los Angeles: Western Psychological Services.

Richters, M.M., & Volkmar, F.R. (1994). Reactive attachment disorder of infancy or early childhood. *Journal of the American Academy of Child and Adolescent Psychiatry, 33*(3), 328–332.

Riddle, M.A., Bernstein, G.A., Cook, E.H., et al. (1999). Anxiolytics, adrenergic agents, and naltrexone. *Journal of the American Academy of Child and Adolescent Psychiatry, 38*(5), 546–556.

Riddle, M.A., Scahill, L., King, R.A., et al. (1992). Double-blind crossover trial of fluoxetine and placebo in children and adolescents with obsessive-compulsive disorder. *Journal of the American Academy of Child and Adolescent Psychiatry, 31,* 1062–1069.

Robins, L.N., Helzer, J.E., Croughan, J., et al. (1981). The National Institute of Mental Health Diagnostic Interview Schedule: Its history, characteristics, and validity. *Archives of General Psychiatry, 149,* 475–481.

Rosenberg, D.R., Stewart, C.M., Fitzgerald, K.D., et al. (1999). Paroxetine open-label treatment of pediatric outpatients with obsessive-compulsive disorder. *Journal of the American Academy of Child and Adolescent Psychiatry, 38*(9), 1180–1185.

Sallee, R., & Greenawald, J. (1995). Neurobiology. In J. March (Ed.), *Anxiety disorders in children and adolescents* (pp. 3–34). New York: Guilford Press.

Saxena, S., Brody, A.L., Schwartz, J.M., & Baxter, L.R. (1998). Neuroimaging and frontal-subcortical circuitry in obsessive-compulsive disorder. *British Journal of Psychiatry Supplement, 35,* 26–37.

Scheeringa, M.S., Zeanah, C.H., Drell, M.J., & Larrieu, J.A. (1995). Two approaches to the diagnosis of posttraumatic stress disorder in infancy and early childhood. *Journal of the American Academy of Child and Adolescent Psychiatry, 34*(2), 191–200.

Schmitt, B.D. (1995). In S. Parker & B. Zuckerman (Eds.), *Behavior and developmental pediatrics: A handbook for primary care* (pp. 251–255). Boston: Little, Brown & Co.

Schwab-Stone, M., Fallon, F., Briggs, M., & Crowther, B. (1994). Reliability of diagnostic reporting for children aged 6–11 years: A test–retest study of the Diagnostic Interview Schedule for Children–Revised. *American Journal of Psychiatry, 151*(7), 1048–1054.

Silverman, W.K., & Albano, A.M. (1996). *Anxiety disorders interview schedule for DSM-IV: Child Version–Child Interview Schedule.* San Antonio, TX: The Psychological Corporation.

Silverman, W.K., & Ginsberg, G. (1995). Specific phobias and generalized anxiety disorder. In J. March (Ed.), *Anxiety disorders in children and adolescents* (pp. 151–180). New York: Guilford Press.

Silverman, W.K., & Rabian, B. (1994). Specific phobias. In T.H. Ollendick, N.J. King, & W. Yule (Eds.), *International handbook of phobic and anxiety disorders in children and adolescents* (pp. 87–110). New York: Plenum Publishing Corp.

Simeon, J.G., Ferguson, H.B., Knott, V., et al. (1992). Clinical, cognitive, and neurophysiological effects of alprazolam in children and adolescents with overanxious and avoidant disorders. *Journal of the American Academy of Child and Adolescent Psychiatry, 31*, 29–33.

Spielberger, C.D., Edwards, C.D., & Lushene, R.E. (1973). *State-Trait Anxiety Inventory for Children.* Palo Alto, CA: Consulting Psychologists Press.

Strauss, C.C. (1994). Overanxious disorder. In T.H. Ollendick, N.J. King, & W. Yule (Eds.), *International handbook of phobic and anxiety disorders in children and adolescents* (pp. 187–206). New York: Plenum Publishing Corp.

Sturner, R.A., Eisert, D.C., Mabe, A., & Thomas, P. (1985). Questionnaire use in pediatric practice: Survey of practice. *Clinical Pediatrics, 24*(11), 638–641.

Swedo, S.E., & Leonard, H.L. (1994). Childhood movement disorders and obsessive compulsive disorder. *Journal of Clinical Psychiatry, 55*(Suppl.), 32–37.

Swedo, S.E., Leonard, H.L., Garvey, M., et al. (1998). Pediatric autoimmune neuropsychiatric disorders associated with streptococcal infections: Clinical description of the first 50 cases. *American Journal of Psychiatry, 155*, 264–271.

Swedo, S.E., Rapoport, J.L., Leonard, H., et al. (1989). Obsessive-compulsive disorder in children and adolescents. *Archives of General Psychiatry, 46*, 335–341.

Terr, L. (1988). Case study: What happens to early memories of trauma? A study of twenty children under age five at the time of documented traumatic events. *Journal of the American Academy of Child and Adolescent Psychiatry, 27*(1), 96–104.

Terr, L.C. (1991). Childhood traumas: An outline and overview. *American Journal of Psychiatry, 148*, 10–19.

Thyer, B.A., Parrish, R.T., Curtis, G.C., et al. (1985). Age of onset of DSM-III anxiety disorders. *Comprehensive Psychiatry, 26*, 113–122.

Tonge, B. (1994). Separation anxiety disorder. In T.H. Ollendick, N.J. King, & W. Yule (Eds.), *International handbook of phobic and anxiety disorders in children and adolescents* (pp. 145–168). New York: Plenum Publishing Corp.

Torgersen, S. (1983). Genetic factors in anxiety disorders. *Archives of General Psychiatry, 40*, 1085–1089.

Turner, S.M., Biedel, D.C., & Costello, A. (1987). Psychopathology in the offspring of anxiety disordered patients. *Journal of Consulting and Clinical Psychology, 55*, 229–235.

Valleni-Basile, L.A., Garrison, C.Z., Jackson, K.L., et al. (1994). Frequency of obsessive-compulsive disorder in a community sample of young adolescents. *Journal of the American Academy of Child and Adolescent Psychiatry, 33*(6), 782–791.

Vitiello, B., Behar, D., Wolfson, D., & McLeer, S.V. (1990). Diagnosis of panic disorder in prepubertal children. *Journal of the American Academy of Child and Adolescent Psychiatry, 29*, 782–784.

Von Korff, M.R., Eaton, W.W., & Keyl, P.M. (1985). The epidemiology of panic attacks and panic disorder: Results of three community surveys. *American Journal of Epidemiology, 122*(6), 970–981.

Weissman, M.M., Leckman, J.F., Merikangas, K.R., et al. (1984). Depression and anxiety disorders in parents and children: Results from the Yale Family Study. *Archives of General Psychiatry, 41*, 845–852.

Wells, K.C. (1995). Family therapy. In J. March (Ed.), *Anxiety disorders in children and adolescents* (pp. 401–419). New York: Guilford Press.

Werry, J.S. (1994). Diagnostic and classification issues. In T.H. Ollendick, N.J. King, & W. Yule (Eds.), *International handbook of phobic and anxiety disorders in children and adolescents* (pp. 21–42). New York: Plenum Publishing Corp.

Wolraich, M.L., Felice, M.E., & Drotar, D. (Eds.). (1996). *The classification of child and adolescent mental diagnoses in primary care: Diagnostic and Statistical Manual for Primary Care (DSM-PC): Child and Adolescent Version.* Elk Grove Village, IL: American Academy of Pediatrics.

World Health Organization (WHO). (1980). *International classification of diseases* (9th rev.). Geneva: Author.

Yule, W. (1994). Posttraumatic stress disorder. In T.H. Ollendick, N.J. King, & W. Yule (Eds.), *International handbook of phobic and anxiety disorders in children and adolescents* (pp. 223–240). New York: Plenum Publishing Corp.

Zeanah, D.H., Mammen, O.K., & Lieberman, A.F. (1993). Disorders of attachment. In C.H. Zeanah (Ed.), *Handbook of infant mental health* (pp. 332–349). New York: Guilford Press.

ZERO TO THREE/National Center for Clinical Infant Programs. (1994). *Diagnostic Classification: 0–3. Diagnostic classification of mental health and developmental disorders of infancy and early childhood.* Arlington, VA: Author.

Appendix

Guidelines for the Care of Children and Adolescents with Anxiety Disorders

Basic Team

The special care needs of children with anxiety disorders can be met by the primary care physician working collaboratively with parents, mental health professionals (e.g., child psychiatrists, psychologists, social workers), and school staff. Some children and families require referral to an experienced child development team headed by a developmental pediatrician, and other children may need referral to a child neurologist. Please note that the primary care physician continues to be responsible for coordinating the special services that these children require.

Regular members of the child development team include the developmental pediatrician, psychologist, speech-language pathologist, occupational therapist, audiologist, and medical social worker. Most children do not require evaluation by all team members.

Initial Evaluation

The objectives of the initial evaluation are to document the child's behavior in different environments, to identify associated developmental problems, and to identify associated medical and mental health problems. The responsibilities of the primary care physician and nurse are to complete parent, child, and teacher interviews; perform a complete medical examination; review behavior rating scales; determine the need for referral to a mental health professional or a child development team; and counsel the parents and child about the diagnosis and recommended treatment.

Frequency of Visits

Follow-up of the child with an anxiety disorder is dependent on the specific disorder and the severity of the symptoms. Almost all children are co-managed with a mental health professional. In general, the child and family are best followed monthly in the primary care office following the initiation of the treatment program. This is particularly important for children starting on a medication trial. Then reevaluate the child and family twice yearly to monitor progress and side effects of medication if the child is stable and doing well with the treatment program, more often for young children and in the first year of treatment. In addition, the physician and office staff should have frequent telephone contact with parents and teachers and regularly obtain behavior rating scales and other specific follow-up data (weekly at first and then with any medication dosage change). The management plan should be updated as needed at each reevaluation and not less than yearly.

The Physician's Guide to Caring for Children with Disabilities and Chronic Conditions, edited by Robert E. Nickel and Larry W. Desch, copyright © 2000 Paul H. Brookes Publishing Co.

Guidelines for the Care of Children and Adolescents with Anxiety Disorders

The following elements are recommended by age group, and the listing is cumulative. Review all items indicated up through the actual age group of a child entering your practice for the first time as part of the initial evaluation.

AGE	KEY CLINICAL ISSUES/CONCERNS	EVALUATIONS/KEY PROCEDURES	SPECIALISTS
Birth–5 years (infant, toddler, and preschool age)	*Growth/Nutrition*	Growth parameters, diet history	Nutritionist as needed
	Associated Medical Problems Hearing/vision Motor and vocal tics	Hearing and vision testing as needed	Audiologist, ophthalmologist as needed
	Seizures	Electroencephalogram (EEG), referral to child neurologist as needed	Child neurologist
	Constipation Encopresis Enuresis	Diet, medication (e.g., bulk agent) Biofeedback treatment, counseling as needed, urinalysis/culture as needed, behavior or other management	Pediatric gastroenterologist, urologist as needed
	Sleep disorder	Behavior management, occasionally short-term medications	
	Note any side effects of medications.		
	Dental Care	Review oral hygiene	Dentist
	Associated Behavior/ Mental Health Problems Hyperactivity/inattention Aggression Oppositional behaviors Other anxiety disorders Eating disorder	Family and teacher interviews, behavioral rating scales, and preschool information at least twice yearly, more frequently if on medication	Child development team or individual appointments with psychologist, child psychiatrist as needed Referral to nutritionist, feeding specialist as needed
	Developmental Progress, Early Intervention (EI)/Early Childhood Special Education (ECSE) Services Language delay/speech disorder Developmental delay	Developmental screening and surveillance Referral for eligibility testing for EI/ECSE as needed	Evaluation by child development team or speech-language pathologist as needed
	Behavior Management in the Home	Family interview, educational materials Parent training in behavior management, referral to community services as needed	Referral to mental health professional as needed Collaboration with school staff

The Physician's Guide to Caring for Children with Disabilities and Chronic Conditions, edited by Robert E. Nickel and Larry W. Desch, copyright © 2000 Paul H. Brookes Publishing Co.

Guidelines for the Care of Children and Adolescents with Anxiety Disorders (continued)

The following elements are recommended by age group, and the listing is cumulative. Review all items indicated up through the actual age group of a child entering your practice for the first time as part of the initial evaluation.

AGE	KEY CLINICAL ISSUES/CONCERNS	EVALUATIONS/KEY PROCEDURES	SPECIALISTS
Birth–5 years (infant, toddler, and preschool age) (continued)	Behavior Management in the Preschool	Teacher interview, behavioral rating scales, or other data collection	Collaboration with school staff, mental health professional
	Family Support Services Respite care Parent group Counseling Advocacy (e.g., Obsessive-Compulsive Foundation) Financial (e.g., Supplemental Security Income [SSI] for children with severe or multiple problems)	Family interview, use parent questionnaire (e.g., Family Needs Survey), provide resource information Care coordination, collaboration with school and community agencies	Medical social worker, referral to community services as needed
	Review of Diagnosis and Anticipatory Guidance Common childhood fears Behavioral inhibition School refusal, problem situations (e.g., fear of dogs) Transition to grade school Review individualized family service plan (IFSP) or individualized education program (IEP) with family as needed	Family interview, educational materials Teacher interview, school report, conference as needed	Primary care office in collaboration with mental health professional as needed
6–12 years (school-age)	Follow-up of Medication Treatment	Child, parent, and teacher interviews; behavioral rating scales and school report at least twice yearly Check growth, blood pressure and heart rate, tics, side effects at least twice yearly Electrocardiogram (EKG), lab work as needed for specific medications	Referral to child psychiatrist as needed
	Associated Learning Disabilities	Intellectual and achievement testing as needed	Referral to child development team as needed, collaborate with school staff

The Physician's Guide to Caring for Children with Disabilities and Chronic Conditions, edited by Robert E. Nickel and Larry W. Desch, copyright © 2000 Paul H. Brookes Publishing Co.

Guidelines for the Care of Children and Adolescents with Anxiety Disorders *(continued)*

The following elements are recommended by age group, and the listing is cumulative. Review all items indicated up through the actual age group of a child entering your practice for the first time as part of the initial evaluation.

AGE	KEY CLINICAL ISSUES/CONCERNS	EVALUATIONS/KEY PROCEDURES	SPECIALISTS
6–12 years (school-age) *(continued)*	*Associated Behavior/ Mental Health Problems* Attention-deficit/hyperactivity disorder (ADHD) Oppositional defiant disorder (ODD) Conduct disorder (CD) Other anxiety disorders Depression, bipolar disorder	Child, parent, and teacher interviews; behavioral rating scales and school report at least twice yearly Review medication management	Referral to mental health professional or child development team as needed, collaborate with school staff
	Social Skills Involvement in peer-group activities at school and in the community (determine which supports are needed) Promote social competence	School-based program and referral to community services as needed	Collaborate with school staff
	Anticipatory Guidance Sports and leisure activities (structured small-group activities, noncompetitive, adult supervision) Promote self-care and independence	Referral to community services as indicated	Primary care office Referral to physical or occupational therapists, adaptive physical education specialist as needed
13–21 years (adolescents– young adults)	*Anticipatory Guidance* Transition to middle school and high school Encourage healthy behaviors (diet, exercise) High-risk behaviors (substance use or abuse, promiscuity) Career planning Transition to adult services and/or independent living	Adolescent, parent, and teacher interviews; school report; conference as needed Referral to career counseling, vocational specialist as needed	Primary care office in collaboration with mental health professional and school staff as needed
	Collaboration with Community Agencies School Mental health professional	Regular exchange of information (at least yearly), care conference as needed	Primary care office

The Physician's Guide to Caring for Children with Disabilities and Chronic Conditions, edited by Robert E. Nickel and Larry W. Desch, copyright © 2000 Paul H. Brookes Publishing Co.

Family and Physician Management Plan Summary for Children and Adolescents with Anxiety Disorders

This form will help you and your physician review current services and service needs. Please answer the questions about your current services on this page. Your physician will review your responses and complete the rest of the form.

Child's name _____   Today's date _____

Person completing the form _____

CURRENT SERVICES

1. Please list your/your child's current medications and any side effects.

2. What is your/your child's current school program?

    School name _____   Grade _____

    Teacher _____   Telephone _____

3. Do you/does your child receive any support services or other special programs at school (e.g., physical therapy, resource room)? Please list.

4. Who are your/your child's other medical and dental service providers?

    Dentist _____

    Child psychiatrist _____

    Other _____

5. Who are your/your child's other community service providers?

    Behavioral or mental health specialist _____

    Other _____

The Physician's Guide to Caring for Children with Disabilities and Chronic Conditions, edited by Robert E. Nickel and Larry W. Desch, copyright © 2000 Paul H. Brookes Publishing Co.

Family and Physician Management Plan Summary for Children and Adolescents with Anxiety Disorders *(continued)*

6. Have you/has your child had any blood tests, radiologic (X-ray) examinations, or other procedures since your last visit? If yes, please describe.

7. Have you/has your child been hospitalized or received surgery since your last visit? If yes, please describe.

8. Please note your/your child's accomplishments since your/your child's last visit. Consider activities at home, in your neighborhood, or at school, as well as success with treatments.

9. What goals (i.e., skills) would you/your child like to accomplish in the next year? Consider activities at home, in your neighborhood, or at school, as well as success with a treatment.

10. What questions or concerns would you like addressed today?

Family and Physician Management Plan Summary for Children and Adolescents with Anxiety Disorders

The Management Plan Summary should be completed at each annual review and more often as needed. It is intended to be used with the Guidelines for Care, which provide a more complete listing of clinical issues at different ages and recommended evaluations and treatments.

Child's name _____ Person completing form _____ Today's date _____

Clinical issues	Currently a problem?	Evaluations needed	Treatment recommendations	Referrals made	Date for status check
Family's Questions					
Growth/Nutrition					
Associated Medical Problems Hearing/vision concerns Seizures Tics or Tourette syndrome Constipation Encopresis Enuresis Sleep disorder **Note any side effects of medications.**					
Dental Care					
Associated Behavior/ Mental Health Problems Inattention, hyperactivity Aggression Oppositional behaviors Other anxiety disorders Depression Eating disorder High-risk behaviors					

Family and Physician Management Plan Summary for Children and Adolescents with Anxiety Disorders *(continued)*

Child's name _____ Person completing form _____ Today's date _____

Clinical issues	Currently a problem?	Evaluations needed	Treatment recommendations	Referrals made	Date for status check
Review of Behavioral Questionnaires					
Behavior Management in the Home					
Behavior Management in the School					
Associated Developmental or Learning Problems Current school achievement Review school services (individu-alized education program [IEP]) Learning disability Speech-language disorder					
Social Skills Involvement in group activities at school, in community					
Self-Care and Independence					
Family Support Services					

The Physician's Guide to Caring for Children with Disabilities and Chronic Conditions, edited by Robert E. Nickel and Larry W. Desch, copyright © 2000 Paul H. Brookes Publishing Co.

Family and Physician Management Plan Summary for Children and Adolescents with Anxiety Disorders *(continued)*

Child's name _____ Person completing form _____ Today's date _____

Clinical issues	Currently a problem?	Evaluations needed	Treatment recommendations	Referrals made	Date for status check
Anticipatory Guidance List issues discussed and materials provided					
Collaboration with Community Agencies School Mental health agency					
Comments					

Next update of the Management Plan Summary _____

Signature _____ Date _____
(Child and parent)

Signature _____ Date _____
(Health professional)

The Physician's Guide to Caring for Children with Disabilities and Chronic Conditions, edited by Robert E. Nickel and Larry W. Desch, copyright © 2000 Paul H. Brookes Publishing Co.

RESOURCES ON ANXIETY DISORDERS

Readings

Brown, J.L., & Davis, J. (1995). *No more monsters in the closet: Teaching your children to overcome everyday fears and phobias.* New York: Prince Paperbacks.

Foa, E., & Wilson, R. (1991). *Stop obsessing: How to overcome your obsessions and compulsions.* New York: Bantam Books. (1-800-223-6834)

Foster, C.H. (1994). *Polly's magic games: A child's view of obsessive-compulsive disorder.* Ellsworth, ME: Dilligaff.

Haerle, T. (1992). *Children with Tourette syndrome: A parents' guide.* Bethesda, MD: Woodbine House. (1-800-843-7323)

Hughes, S. (1990). *Ryan: A mother's story of her hyperactive/Tourette syndrome child.* Duarte, CA: Hope Press. (626-303-0644)

March, J.S. (1995). *Anxiety disorders in children and adolescents.* New York: Guilford Press. (1-800-365-7006)

March, J.S., & Mulle, K. (1998). *OCD in children and adolescents: A cognitive-behavioral treatment manual.* New York: Guilford Press. (1-800-365-7006)

Ollendick, T.H., King, N.J., & Yule, W. (Eds.). (1994). *International handbook of phobic and anxiety disorders in children and adolescents.* New York: Plenum Publishing Corp. (781-871-6600)

Rapoport, J.L. (1988). *The boy who couldn't stop washing.* New York: E.P. Dutton. (212-366-2000)

Information

Anxiety Disorders Education Program
(National Institute of Mental Health)
World Wide Web site: http://www.nimh.nih.gov/anxiety/

A program dedicated to increasing awareness about anxiety disorders among the public and professionals; it also provides lists of publications and conferences.

Obsessive-Compulsive Foundation (OCF)
337 Notch Hill Road
North Branford, Connecticut 06471
Telephone: (203) 315-2190
Fax: (203) 315-2196
E-mail: info@ocfoundation.org
World Wide Web site: http://www.ocfoundaton.org/

A national organization with local affiliates for people with obsessive-compulsive disorder (OCD), their families, and professionals; this group also provides information on OCD and its treatment, as well as on support groups, and publishes a newsletter.

National Organizations

Anxiety Busters
Post Office Box 11402
Philadelphia, Pennsylvania 19111
Telephone: (215) 635-3337
Fax: (215) 635-3972
Free anxiety helpline: (215) 635-4700 (10:00 A.M.–
   10:00 P.M. Eastern time, 7 days per week)
World Wide Web site: http://www.anxietybusters.com/

An advocacy and support group that makes self-help tapes available as well as its telephone helpline; it also publishes a quarterly newsletter.

Anxiety Disorders Association of America (ADAA)
11900 Parklawn Drive, Suite 100
Rockville, Maryland 20852
Telephone: (301) 231-9350
Fax: (301) 231-7392
E-mail: anxdis@adaa.org
World Wide Web site: http://www.adaa.org/

A national organization that provides information and support, and its World Wide Web site offers links to a variety of related World Wide Web sites.

Tourette Syndrome Association
42-40 Bell Boulevard
Bayside, New York 11361
Telephone: (718) 224-2999
Fax: (718) 279-9596
E-mail: tourette@ix.netcom.com
World Wide Web site: http://tsa.mgh.harvard.edu/

An association that provides advocacy, information, and referral and publishes a quarterly newsletter.

Professional Organization

American Academy of
Child and Adolescent Psychiatry (AACAP)
3615 Wisconsin Avenue, NW
Washington, D.C. 20016
Telephone: (202) 966-7300
Fax: (202) 966-2891
World Wide Web site: http://www.aacap.org/

A professional organization that promotes research and education on mental disorders that children and adolescents experience.

11

Prenatal Drug Exposure

Robert E. Nickel

KEY COMPETENCIES

- Review the effects of alcohol and other drugs on the pregnancy, the fetus, the newborn, and the child's long-term growth and development
- Demonstrate knowledge of drug use patterns and basic pharmacology
- Describe the characteristics of fetal alcohol syndrome (FAS), and complete an examination for minor physical anomalies
- List the associated social, mental health, and medical problems of pregnant women who abuse alcohol and other drugs
- Discuss the signs of the neonatal abstinence syndrome (NAS) in narcotic withdrawal and the neurobehavioral abnormalities associated with the mother's prenatal cocaine use, and conduct a neonatal neurobehavioral examination
- Discuss the identification and treatment of infectious diseases that may be transmitted from mother to child, such as human immunodeficiency virus (HIV), hepatitis B and C, and sexually transmitted diseases (STDs)
- Develop a comprehensive management plan for the infant who has been exposed to drugs prenatally and the family

DESCRIPTION

Problem of Prenatal Drug Exposure

The prevalence of legal and illegal drug use by pregnant women varies considerably from area to area and from hospital to hospital. Research studies (Chasnoff, Landress, & Barrett, 1990; Vega, Kolody, Hwang, et al., 1993) have reported that approximately 5%–15% of all newborns (approximately 375,000 births per year) are exposed prenatally to illegal drugs (see Table 11.1). Prenatal alcohol and other drug use by expectant mothers continues to be a significant public health problem in the United States. Expectant mothers' use of these drugs may alter the course of the pregnancy, affect the developing fetus, and have a long-term impact on their children's development. Expectant parents' use of alcohol and other drugs also may interfere with their ability to parent and their infant's ability to elicit and respond to caregiving activities.

In the 1960s and early 1970s, marijuana, sedatives, hallucinogens, and amphetamines were the illicit drugs abused most commonly. Cocaine use became more prevalent in the 1980s first because it decreased in cost and then as the result of the development in 1985 of a smokeable cocaine (i.e., "crack"). This chapter discusses the most com-

monly abused drugs: cigarettes (i.e., nicotine), alcohol, marijuana, cocaine and methamphetamines (i.e., stimulants), and heroin and methadone (i.e., opiates). The following questions are raised and discussed with regard to each category of drugs: What is the effect of their use on the course of the pregnancy, the fetus, and the newborn? What are the long-term consequences of prenatal use? Finally, the management of these women and their infants is discussed.

Methodologic Problems in Research Studies

The actual prevalence of prenatal drug abuse is unknown. Many problems interfere with the collection of accurate data. In general, prenatal drug use is identified by

- Clinical judgment
- Self-report measures (e.g., structured interview, questionnaire)
- Urine testing
- Newborn hair sample analysis
- Meconium analysis

Numerous studies have noted the inaccuracy of *clinical judgment*. The likelihood of a physician referral is determined in part by the physician's beliefs about which women abuse drugs and which drugs are important. In a study in Florida (Chasnoff et al., 1990), physicians significantly underreported pregnant women who were abusing drugs; however, underreporting was greater for white women than for nonwhite women, and use of cocaine was reported much more often than use of marijuana.

Self-report measures also significantly underestimate the prevalence of drug use when compared to urine testing. In one study (Hingson, Zuckerman, Amaro, et al., 1986), pregnant women were more likely to report drug use if they were told their urine would be tested for drugs (63%) than if they were not told (41%). Urine testing identified an additional five women who were abusing drugs and did not self-reveal. A core characteristic of addictive disease is denial of the drug use to oneself as well as to others.

Urine tests are accurate only for drug use that has occurred in the previous 2–3 days (the previous 1 week for marijuana) and may not reflect the actual prevalence of drug use during the pregnancy. Urine toxicology is not often obtained early in the pregnancy. In one study (Ryan, Wagner, Schultz, et al., 1994), approximately one third of mothers who were abusing cocaine had received no prenatal care. Two newer methods, *newborn hair* and *meconium analysis*, improve the identification of maternal substance use during the pregnancy. Infant hair samples can detect mothers' drug use in the last trimester (Forman, Klein, Barks, et al., 1994; Kline, Ng, Schittini, et al., 1997), and meconium samples can identify maternal drug use in the second and third trimesters (Behnke & Eyler, 1993). In one study (Ursitti, Klein, & Koren, 1997), neonatal hair testing confirmed prenatal cocaine use at a rate 5.5 times greater than a previous population-based study in those nurseries. These methods still do not offer information with regard to the pattern of maternal drug use—amount, purity (i.e., strength), frequency, or timing of the mother's drug use during the pregnancy—and they do not indicate which drugs were used together. Urine and meconium testing are the best options (Kwong & Ryan, 1997). Meconium testing requires increased time, and testing of neonatal hair is technically demanding.

Outcome studies are confounded by additional methodologic problems. Many studies routinely follow pregnant women of low socioeconomic status who are in drug treatment programs. These studies miss the group with potentially the best outcomes (women from the middle and upper socioeconomic strata) as well as the group with potentially the worst outcomes (women of low socioeconomic status who continue to abuse drugs and avoid prenatal care) (Myers, Olson, & Kaltenbach, 1992). In addition, women who abuse one drug are likely to smoke, drink alcohol, and abuse other drugs.

A number of psychosocial factors may also add to the infant's risk for subsequent developmental and behavior problems. Pregnant women who abuse drugs are more likely to be single, poor, urban, and undernourished, and they may have been victims of physical and/or sexual abuse. Approximately 25% of these women have other psychiatric diagnoses (Grella, 1997), and as a group, they are more likely than other women to maltreat their children (Williams-Peterson, Myers, Degen, et al., 1994). Finally, studies with unfavorable outcomes are more likely to be published regardless of their degree of scientific rigor (Koren, Shear, Graham, et al., 1989).

Prevalence of Prenatal Maternal Drug Use

Both indirect and direct methods have been used to determine the prevalence of prenatal maternal drug use. An *indirect* method is to measure the prevalence of drug use in women of child-bearing age. Among women 15–44 years of age, 18% reported using marijuana and 5% reported using cocaine in the previous month; only 6% of married women 22–44 years of age reported using marijuana, and only 2% reported using cocaine in the previous month (National Institute on Drug Abuse [NIDA],

Table 11.1. Prevalence of prenatal maternal use of cigarettes, alcohol, and illegal drugs

Drugs	Prevalence (%)
Cigarettes	13.6
Alcohol	35–40 (any alcohol use)
	5 (six or more drinks per week in first 6–8 weeks[a] of pregnancy)
Marijuana	10–12
Cocaine	3–12
Heroin/methadone	1–2
Total illegal drug use	5–15

Adapted from Guyer, MacDorman, and Martin (1998).
[a] Floyd, Decoufle, and Hungerford (1999).

1990). Several studies (Day, Wagener, & Taylor, 1985; Fried, 1993; Tennes, Avitable, Blackard, et al., 1985) have noted that women may stop or decrease their level of drug use when they realize that they are pregnant.

Direct methods by which to determine the prevalence of prenatal exposure include routinely testing the following individuals: pregnant women who are in prenatal care, new mothers after delivery in the hospital, or newborns in the hospital just after birth (Robins, Mills, Krulewitch, et al., 1993). It is estimated that 99% of all babies in the United States are born in a hospital. Testing women who deliver in a hospital or their newborns avoids the potential bias of testing pregnant women in prenatal care, because many women who are using drugs receive inadequate or no prenatal care. Table 11.1 presents prevalence figures for prenatal maternal smoking as well as alcohol and illegal drug use. These data were compiled from a number of studies (see Guyer, MacDorman, & Martin, 1998) that used direct methods.

Studies of the prevalence of prenatal drug use have found conflicting results with regard to the importance of age, race, and urban versus suburban residence. In a general population study (Johnson, McCarter, & Ferencz, 1987), overall drug use was greater among white women than among Black women, and their patterns of drug use were different. White women tended to abuse marijuana, methamphetamines, and psychedelics; Black women were more likely to abuse cocaine and multiple drugs. Other studies (Forman, 1994; Vega et al., 1993) noted higher rates of prenatal drug use among young Black women in urban populations. In contrast, Chasnoff and co-workers (1990) found similar rates of drug use in white and nonwhite pregnant women in Pinellas County, Florida, when tested at the first prenatal visit in public and private clinic populations. In Toronto, 12.5% of pregnant women from a downtown urban hospital versus 3% of women at a suburban hospital were positive by urine screen for one or more illicit drugs (Forman, 1994). Kokotailo and co-workers (1992) studied drug use in pregnant adolescents 13–18 years of age. They found that 17% were abusing alcohol or other drugs by self-report, urine test, or provider report, and 22% smoked cigarettes; marijuana was the most common illicit drug abused.

Illicit drug use is strongly associated with cigarette smoking, heavy drinking, and polydrug abuse (Johnson et al., 1987). In a study in Dallas, 75% of pregnant women who were using cocaine were also using methamphetamines, heroin, and/or sedatives, including alcohol. In Oregon, the prevalence of illegal drug use by pregnant women was 5.2%. Women who were abusing illegal drugs were five times more likely to smoke cigarettes and 2.5 times more likely to drink alcohol (Oregon Health Division, 1990). All drug use must be considered polydrug use. Separation of the specific contribution of individual drugs as well as medical and social conditions to adverse outcomes is difficult.

Effects of the Most Commonly Abused Legal and Illegal Drugs

Cigarette Smoking (Nicotine)

Effect on the Pregnancy, the Fetus, and the Newborn Maternal smoking has been associated with a number of adverse outcomes, including an increased rate of spontaneous abortions, stillbirths, perinatal mortality, and prematurity (Finnegan, 1994; Fried, 1993). Cigarette smoking is the largest single risk factor for low birth weight (Chomitz, Cheung, & Lieberman, 1995; Jacobson et al., 1994). In one study (Jacobson et al., 1994), alcohol and smoking had more effect on the birth weight of infants of women who abused drugs than cocaine and opiates did. Infants of average smokers weigh approximately 150–250 grams less at birth than other infants (Fried, 1993). The incidence of the births of low birth weight infants could be reduced by 20% if women did not smoke during pregnancy (Chomitz et al., 1995; Oregon Health Division, 1992). A possible physiologic mechanism may be fetal hypoxia secondary to decreased uteroplacental blood flow. The placental vascular resistance is increased in maternal smokers, and placentas may be smaller and show signs of chronic ischemia (Fried, 1993).

Women who smoke are likely to drink alcohol and caffeine. In one study (Peacock, Bland, & Anderson, 1991), pregnant women who smoked and drank alcohol (one or more drinks per day) and coffee (five or more cups per day) had a significantly increased risk for giving birth to an infant with intrauterine growth retardation (IUGR), although other studies (e.g., Day, Richardson, Geva, & Robles, 1994) have not confirmed this finding.

Long-Term Consequences Evidence links maternal cigarette smoking with an increased risk for infants' experiencing sudden infant death syndrome (SIDS), although the relative contributions of smoking during pregnancy and infants' postnatal exposure to secondhand cigarette smoke are not clear (Behnke & Eyler, 1993; Kandall & Gaines, 1991). In two large studies (Haglund & Cnattingius, 1990; Malloy, Kleinman, Land, et al., 1988), cigarette smoking doubled the risk for SIDS. In another study (MacDorman, Cnattingius, Hoffman, et al., 1997), infants born to women who smoked 10 or more cigarettes per day had two to nearly four times greater risk of SIDS than infants of women who were nonsmokers. In addition, infants' postnatal growth (i.e., length) is reduced when prenatally exposed to cigarette smoking, and this effect continues into adolescence (Behnke & Eyler, 1993).

No consistent effect of cigarette smoking on infants' cognitive development has been noted. In a study (Fried & Watkinson, 1988) of 217 one-year-old children, the average Mental Developmental Index (MDI) of the Bayley Scales of Infant Intelligence (Bayley, 1993) for infants of nonsmokers was 109.5; however, the MDI for 1-year-olds of women who smoked heavily during pregnancy was 96.5. This difference was not seen at follow-up at 2 years of age; however, in a subsequent study by the same investigators, infants' prenatal exposure to cigarette smoking was associated with poorer language development and lower cognitive scores at ages 36 and 48 months (Fried & Watkinson, 1990). Two studies (Denson, Nanson, & McWatters, 1975; Nichols & Chen, 1981) also have linked maternal smoking with hyperactivity in young children.

Alcohol Alcohol is the most widely used drug in the United States among all age groups and at all socioeconomic levels (NIDA, 1990).

Effect on the Pregnancy, the Fetus, and the Newborn A number of adverse pregnancy outcomes have been reported, including an increase in perinatal mortality, stillbirths, abruptio placenta, and prematurity (Behnke & Eyler, 1993); however, studies have reported conflicting results. Consistent evidence exists that high levels of alcohol exposure (more than two drinks per day) are associated with poor fetal growth; however, studies (Behnke & Eyler, 1993; Mills, Graubard, Harley, et al., 1984) have reported inconsistent or no effect for low (less than one drink per day) or moderate alcohol intake (one to two drinks per day). Jacobson and co-workers (1994) studied 470 newborns of women who abused alcohol or cocaine or both during pregnancy. Many of these women also smoked cigarettes and abused opiates. When other factors were controlled, alcohol was strongly correlated with decreased birth length, and smoking and alcohol were correlated with decreased birth weight.

A safe amount of alcohol consumption for pregnant women has not been determined. Even when the mother stops drinking during the second trimester of pregnancy, the infant may be at risk for developmental and behavior problems. Coles and colleagues (1987) conducted a study of three groups of pregnant women—those who never drank, those who stopped during the second trimester, and those who drank throughout the pregnancy. They found differences in these women's infants' motor performance, autonomic regulation, and reflexive behavior 1 month after birth. The third group of infants demonstrated the greatest impairments. Only the babies whose mothers never drank achieved expected performance on the Neonatal Behavioral Assessment Scale (NBAS) (Brazelton, 1984).

Prenatal maternal alcohol abuse is strongly associated with birth defects. Reports consistent with the association of alcohol and birth defects were present in Greek and Roman mythology (Jones, 1986). *Fetal alcohol syndrome* (FAS) was first described by Jones and co-workers in 1973. FAS is characterized by low birth weight, microcephaly, heart defects, facial dysmorphic features, poor growth, developmental delay, fine motor impairment, and inattention and hyperactivity (see Table 11.2). A few children with FAS have a cleft lip and palate, and occasionally children with FAS have meningomyelocele. Jones and colleagues' original reports emphasize three principal criteria for the diagnosis of FAS: pre- and/or postnatal growth retardation, abnormal brain function reflected in developmental disabilities, and characteristic facial features (Clarren & Smith, 1978). Approximately 30% of the infants of women who were *heavy* drinkers during pregnancy have FAS (Streissguth, Landesman-Dwyer, Martin, et al., 1980). Abel and Sokol (1991) estimated the prevalence of FAS at less than one per 1,000 live births. Other authors (Sampson, Streissguth, Bookstein, et al., 1997) have suggested that the prevalence of FAS and alcohol-related neurodevelopmental problems may be as high as 9.1 per 1,000.

Newborns with FAS have been found to be slow to habituate to stimuli and to have poor ratings on the NBAS, as evidenced by poor state regulation and more abnormal reflexes than infants who are developing typically (Coles et al., 1985). Approximately three fourths of infants with FAS are irritable and display tremulousness and jitteriness (Olson, 1994). Similar neurobehavioral irregularities can be seen in other infants with IUGR.

Table 11.2. Features observed in children with fetal alcohol syndrome

Growth and development	Skeletal	Craniofacial	Other
Prenatal and postnatal growth deficiency	Tapering terminal phalanges	Microcephaly	Ventricular septal defects
Developmental delay	Camptodactyly	Short palpebral fissures	Atrial septal defects
Fine motor dysfunction	Flexion contractures at elbows	Ptosis	Tetralogy of Fallot, great vessel anomalies
Mental retardation	Radioulnar synostosis	Epicanthal folds	Cleft lip and/or cleft palate
Hyperactivity and poor attention span	Hypoplastic finger- and toenails	Micrognathia	Myopia, strabismus
Speech problems	Altered palm or crease patterns	Maxillary hypoplasia	Small teeth with faulty enamel
Poor coordination, hypotonia		Hypoplastic long or smooth philtrum	Dental malocclusion
Social skills impairments		Thin vermillion of upper lip	Hearing loss
		Short, upturned nose	Microphthalmia, blepharophimosis
			Hypospadias; small, rotated kidneys; hydronephrosis
			Meningomyelocele

Adapted from American Academy of Pediatrics (1993).

The label *fetal alcohol effects* (FAE) has been applied to children who have some but not all of the characteristics of FAS when there is a maternal history of moderate to heavy alcohol use. FAE, however, is not a specific diagnosis and may not be recognized easily (Olson, 1994). Some clinicians and investigators have used the label indiscriminately (Aase et al., 1995). Diagnosing a child with FAE can provide access to services for some children; however, it can also prevent further evaluation for other potential causes of the child's problems. Aase, Jones, and Clarren (1995) recommended abandoning the use of the FAE label in the clinical setting and simply recording the known findings. These infants and children should be monitored regularly for developmental progress and behavioral issues. Astley and Clarren (1995, 1996) developed a quantitative, multivariate case definition of FAS based on facial photographs to improve the identification of children with significant neurodevelopmental problems related to prenatal alcohol.

Long-Term Consequences   Approximately 75% of individuals with FAS have mild to moderate developmental delay or mental retardation. Children with FAS may have poor coordination, hyperactivity, impulsivity or distractibility, language problems, and social skills impairments (Olson, 1994). These difficulties tend to persist into adulthood. Studies of adults with FAS (Streissguth, Aase, Clarren, et al., 1991) have noted potentially debilitating functional problems with cognitive skills, behavior, effective communication, and socialization. Prenatal exposure to alcohol also has been associated with reduced postnatal growth in children who do not have FAS. In one study (Day et al., 1994), children who were prenatally exposed to alcohol had smaller height, weight, and head circumference at 6 years of age than children without prenatal alcohol exposure.

Marijuana   Most women who are regular users of marijuana continue to use marijuana during pregnancy. In one study, 75% of 18- to 25-year-old women who were heavy marijuana users were still using at the end of the third month of the pregnancy, and 63% were still using at the end of the pregnancy (Richardson et al., 1993).

Effect on the Pregnancy, the Fetus, and the Newborn   No consistent effects have been found for prenatal marijuana use on birthweight or length of gestation (Behnke & Eyler, 1993; Fried, 1993; Richardson, Day, & McGauhey, 1993). Only 4 of more than 12 studies of maternal marijuana use and infant birthweight have reported a significant relationship between these factors (Fried, 1993). In one study, heavy maternal marijuana use that was identified by positive urine tests was associated with a significant reduction in infants' birthweight and birth length (Zuckerman, Frank, Hingson, et al., 1989). One study (Gibson, Baghurst, & Colley, 1983) noted an increased rate of prematurity; however, a more recent study (Shiono, Klebanoff, Nugent, et al., 1995) did not.

The adverse effects of marijuana may be potentiated by other factors. In an animal study (Charlebois & Fried, 1980), marijuana exposure and a low-protein diet resulted in an increased number of stillbirths compared to rats that received a regular or high-protein diet. A significant proportion of all adolescent women have inadequate nutritional status based on weight-for-height ratio (Sargent, Schulken, Kemper, et al., 1994), which may compound the effects of marijuana use in adolescents who are pregnant. In addition, marijuana use may be a marker for other drug use or adverse social factors. It may best be considered a "red flag" rather than a direct cause of adverse outcomes.

No consistent effects have been noted for prenatal maternal marijuana use and major or minor congenital anomalies (Day et al., 1994; Fried, 1993). One study (Hingson et al., 1982) of women who were regular marijuana users during their pregnancies (who compose 2% of mothers of all newborns who have been exposed to marijuana) did report a fivefold increase of the probability of newborns' having facial features of FAS. Some studies of newborns who have been exposed to marijuana have noted poor visual habituation, high-pitched cry, tremors, exaggerated startles, and disturbed sleep patterns in some infants (Fried & Makin, 1987); however, other studies have not confirmed these findings (Fried, 1993).

Long-Term Consequences   In general, long-term follow-up studies (Fried, 1993; Richardson et al., 1993) have demonstrated that infants born to mothers who use marijuana experience normal growth and development through 5–6 years of age. In the Ottawa Prenatal Prospective Study (Fried & Watkinson, 1990), the children of heavy users of marijuana scored lower in memory and verbal abilities at 48 months of age. In a subsequent study (Fried, Watkinson, & Siegel, 1997), however, prenatal marijuana exposure was not related to later reading and language test performance at 9–12 years of age. Dahl and co-workers (1995) reported an increased rate of disruptions within sleep (i.e., increased number of arousals) and decreased sleep efficiency during electroencephalogram (EEG) sleep studies in children who were exposed to marijuana prenatally versus children who were not.

Cocaine Marijuana and cocaine are the illegal drugs abused most frequently during pregnancy in most areas of the United States. Cocaine (benzoylmethylecgonine) is a powerful central nervous system (CNS) stimulant and local anesthetic derived from the leaves of the cocoa plant (*Erythroxylon coca*). When used to induce a "high," it is taken intranasally (i.e., by snorting), smoked (i.e., "crack" cocaine), or injected intravenously alone or in combination with other drugs (Chasnoff, 1992). Cocaine can cause vasoconstriction, uterine irritability, and fetal hypoxia. It also has a direct effect on brain adrenergic neurotransmitter systems with resultant CNS irritability (Chasnoff, 1992).

Effect on the Pregnancy, the Fetus, and the Newborn Prenatal maternal cocaine use has been associated with an increased rate of spontaneous abortions, precipitous labor, abruptio placenta, and stillbirths (Behnke & Eyler, 1993; Chasnoff, 1992; MacGregor, Keith, Chasnoff, et al., 1987; Singer, Arendt, Song, et al., 1994). Hypertension, strokes, cardiac arrhythmias, and ischemic events have been reported in pregnant women who use cocaine and other adult cocaine users. Prenatal maternal cocaine use also is definitely associated with low birth weight, decreased birth length, and decreased head circumference (Chasnoff, 1992; Chiriboga, Brust, Bateman, & Hauser, 1999; Oro & Dixon, 1987; Zuckerman & Frank, 1994). Disagreement exists, however, with regard to whether infants who have been exposed to cocaine prenatally have lower birth weight predominately because of prematurity or IUGR, as well as with regard to the importance of associated risk factors such as maternal nutrition or smoking (Jacobson et al., 1994; King, Perlman, Laptook, et al., 1995; Kliegman, Madura, Kiwi, et al., 1994; Miller, Boudreaux & Regan, 1995; Zuckerman & Frank, 1994). In a study of women abusing alcohol or cocaine or both during pregnancy, Jacobson and co-workers (1994) concluded that the effect of cocaine on birth weight was an indirect consequence of shorter gestation and poorer maternal nutrition. Other studies (see Eyler, Behnke, Conlon, et al., 1998) have noted smaller head and chest circumferences in infants born to women who used cocaine and smoked during pregnancy, and infants with reduced birth weight of women who used cocaine while pregnant had received inadequate prenatal care and had smoked during pregnancy (Miller et al., 1995).

Women who use cocaine only during the first trimester have improved pregnancy outcomes compared to women who continue their cocaine use throughout their pregnancies (Chasnoff, Griffith, MacGregor, et al., 1989; Graham, Dimitrakoudis, Pellegrini, et al., 1989). For example, Chasnoff and co-workers (1989) studied women who used cocaine during the first trimester only, women who used cocaine throughout the pregnancy, and pregnant women who were nonusers of cocaine. The outcomes of the pregnancies of first-trimester cocaine users were no different from those of nonusers with regard to the rates of prematurity and low birth weight.

Infants who were exposed to cocaine prenatally do not appear to experience an increased number of minor anomalies as compared to infants who were not exposed to cocaine prenatally or who had a birth defects syndrome. Studies have reported conflicting results with regard to the rate of major birth defects (Behnke & Eyler, 1993). Doering and co-workers (1989) concluded that the great majority of newborns who were exposed to cocaine in the womb do not have congenital birth defects. However, prenatal maternal cocaine use occasionally has been associated with urogenital anomalies, necrotizing enterocolitis and intestinal atresia, congenital heart defects, limb reduction defects, limb–body wall deficits, cerebral hypoxic-ischemic injury, intraventricular hemorrhage, and infarctions (Chasnoff, 1992; Dixon & Bejar, 1989; Viscarello, Ferguson, Nores, et al., 1992). These anomalies appear to be due to the vasoconstrictive properties of cocaine (Hoyme, Jones, Dixon, et al., 1990).

Two studies (King et al., 1995; Singer, Yamashita, Hawkins, et al., 1994) reported conflicting data with regard to the incidence of intraventricular hemorrhage (IVH) in preterm infants who were exposed to cocaine prenatally. Although King and co-workers did not identify an increase in CNS ultrasonographic abnormalities (e.g., IVH), the infants whom they studied did show evidence of altered behavior consistent with drug effect and had changes in Doppler flow velocity of the anterior cerebral arteries consistent with the vasoconstrictive effects of cocaine.

Infants who are exposed to cocaine in utero may experience increased tremulousness and startles, a low threshold for overstimulation, decreased interactive behaviors, and increased state lability (Chasnoff, 1992; Frank, Bresnaham, & Zuckerman, 1993). These findings are more apparent in newborns who were exposed prenatally to cocaine recently (i.e., those who are acutely intoxicated). Dixon and Bejar (1989) identified a variety of minor

CNS abnormalities in one third of neonates exposed to cocaine prenatally, a sixfold increase over the matched group who had not been exposed to cocaine.

Long-Term Consequences Early studies (see Howard, Beckwith, Rodning, et al., 1989) of infants who had been exposed to cocaine in utero reported an increased risk for developmental delay, physical problems, lack of representational play, and deviant attachment patterns. Studies published in the 1990s presented a somewhat more optimistic picture.

In general, children who were exposed to cocaine prenatally perform similarly to children who were not on measures of cognitive development and intellectual potential through 6–9 years of age (Chasnoff, Anson, Hatcher, et al., 1998; Hurt, Malmud, Betancourt, et al., 1997; Myers, Olson, & Kaltenbach, 1992; Wasserman, Kline, Bateman, et al., 1998). In a longitudinal study, Chasnoff and co-workers (1992) found that infants and toddlers who had been exposed prenatally to cocaine and/or multiple drugs were not significantly different from controls at 12, 18, and 24 months of age when tested with the Bayley Scales of Infant Intelligence (Bayley, 1993). Significantly more children who were exposed to cocaine in utero, however, scored greater than one standard deviation (*SD*) below the mean on both the MDI and the Performance Development Index (PDI). When tested with the Stanford-Binet Intelligence Scale (Thorndike, Hagen, & Sattler, 1986) at 3 years of age, the IQ scores of children who had been exposed to cocaine prenatally were not significantly different from those of children who had not, except on the verbal reasoning subscale (see Table 11.3) (Griffith, Azuma, & Chasnoff, 1994). About one third of the children who had been exposed prenatally to multiple drugs did have delays in language development or were rated as more de-

structive and more aggressive on the Child Behavior Checklist (Achenbach, 1991). Other studies have noted language delays (Nulman, Rovet, Altmann, et al., 1994), significantly more behavior problems in the first grade (Delaney-Black, Covington, Templin, et al., 1998), and impairments in sustained attention on a computerized vigilance task (Richardson, Conroy, & Day, 1996).

Chasnoff and co-workers (1992) reported that the mean head circumference for infants exposed to cocaine or multiple drugs prenatally remained significantly smaller than infants who did not experience prenatal drug exposure, and these differences persisted to age 3 years (Griffith et al., 1994). Other studies, however, did not note this association when other factors were controlled (Jacobson, Jacobson, Sokol, et al., 1994).

These data indicate that there is a vulnerable subset of this population, although most children who have experienced prenatal cocaine exposure have a typical developmental course. Additional research is needed to determine the prevalence of self-regulatory problems among these children and the impact of such problems on these children's school achievement, as well as their difficulties with affect or attachment in their social and emotional development. The effects of prenatal cocaine exposure also may be compounded by mothers' prenatal polydrug use and an inadequate caregiving environment (Koren, Nulman, Rovet, et al., 1998). For example, the passive exposure of infants to crack cocaine is a significant problem that contributes to an increase in upper- and lower-respiratory illness in certain inner-city populations (Lustbader, Mayes, McGee, et al., 1998).

Initial reports noted a high rate of SIDS in infants who had been exposed prenatally to cocaine (Chasnoff, Burns, & Burns, 1987). Subsequent stud-

Table 11.3.   Mean 3-year Stanford-Binet standard age IQ scores by group

	Cocaine with polydrug use (N = 92)		Polydrug use without cocaine (N = 23)		Controls (N = 25)	
	M	*SD*	*M*	*SD*	*M*	*SD*
Overall test	94.4	9.4	93.2	9.3	98.5	12.8
Verbal reasoning	89.3	8.2	90.3	10.9	95.2	11.8
Abstract/visual reasoning	93.5	11.9	90.1	9.6	98.2	13.9
Quantitative reasoning	99.9	10.1	98.9	10.5	102.4	10.9
Short-term memory	99.3	8.5	99.9	9.4	101.7	12.9

Adapted from Griffith et al. (1994).

SD, standard deviation; *M*, mean.

ies have not confirmed this finding. The risk for SIDS appears to be only slightly higher (8.5 per 1,000) than the risk reported for children living in poverty in general (4–5 per 1,000) and lower than the risk for infants who are exposed to heroin or methadone prenatally (15–20 per 1,000) (Frank et al., 1993; Ostrea, Ostrea, & Simpson, 1997).

Methamphetamine Methamphetamine is another powerful stimulant with effects similar to those of cocaine. The state of Oregon is ranked third in the United States by the Food and Drug Administration in the illegal production of marijuana and methamphetamines. Areas of California and Native American reservations are also significantly affected by the abuse of this drug. Methamphetamine may be snorted, ingested, smoked (in a crystalline form called *ice*), or injected intravenously. Methamphetamine has a much longer duration of action than cocaine and produces an agitated high with a rapid rise in blood pressure. Adult morbidities are essentially the same as those for cocaine.

The illegal production of methamphetamine is associated with many potentially toxic chemicals, including lead acetate (Burton, 1990). In fact, lead poisoning has been reported in one user (Oregon Health Division, 1992). The effects of methamphetamines on the pregnancy, the fetus, and the newborn and older children have received limited research attention save in northern Europe, where amphetamines were the drug of choice in the 1970s and 1980s.

Infants who were carried to term but were exposed to methamphetamine or cocaine in the womb have shown a similar incidence and pattern of abnormalities on cranial ultrasonography as well as growth and behavioral irregularities (Dixon & Bejar, 1989). The abnormalities seen in both groups of infants include IVH, small areas of echodensity, and ventricular enlargement. In another study (Billing, Eriksson, Steneroth, et al., 1985), 4-year-old children who had been exposed to amphetamines in utero had lower IQ scores than those who had not been exposed, and more children who had been exposed to amphetamines prenatally were rated as "problem" children. Data from European studies do suggest ongoing behavior and school problems in this population.

Heroin and Methadone (Opiates)

Effect on the Pregnancy, the Fetus, and the Newborn In general, studies have shown that infants who were exposed to opiates prenatally have lower birth weights and are born prematurely (see Behnke

& Eyler, 1993; van Baar, Soepatmi, Gunning, et al., 1994). In one study (Kandall, Albin, Gartner, et al., 1977), infants born to women who had been maintained on methadone had higher birth weights than women who were dependent on heroin but were not in treatment; however, this finding has not been confirmed by other studies (Lifschitz & Wilson, 1991; Zuckerman & Bresnahan, 1991). Many methadone users "chip" (i.e., use heroin) in the seventh month of pregnancy and later because of the failure of clinics to increase or maintain their dose of methadone during that time. Please note that methadone maintenance remains an essential part of a comprehensive service program for women who are addicted to opiates during pregnancy to improve the health of the women and the outcomes of their pregnancies (Kandall, Doberczak, Jantunen, & Stein, 1999).

Infants who have been exposed prenatally to opiates may have smaller head circumference and birth length in addition to low birth weight (Jacobson et al., 1994; Soepatmi, 1994; van Baar et al., 1994). The decrease in infants' birth weight and length may be related to other factors (e.g., maternal cigarette smoking, maternal alcohol use, poor maternal nutrition, inadequate prenatal maternal care). Maternal opiate use during pregnancy has not been associated with an increased risk for major congenital anomalies.

The newborn drug withdrawal syndrome known as neonatal abstinence syndrome (NAS) is a well-known, predictable consequence of opiate dependency in pregnant women. NAS is characterized by hyperirritability, tremors, hypertonicity, high-pitched cry, sleep disturbance, nasal stuffiness, poor feeding, fever, and diarrhea (Kaltenbach & Finnegan, 1986). These symptoms can be reversed by the administration of an opiate. Please note that infants who were exposed in utero to opiates and cocaine experience a higher rate of NAS than infants exposed prenatally to heroin alone (Fulroth, Phillips, & Durand, 1989). In addition, infants of mothers maintained on methadone may have more prolonged withdrawal symptoms lasting up to 1 month (Rajegowda, Glass, Evans, et al., 1972; Wilson, 1989). The onset of infants' withdrawal from heroin is during the first day; however, infants' methadone withdrawal may not begin until 3–5 days of age, depending on the amount and timing of the mother's last dose.

Long-Term Consequences In general, most studies (e.g., Behnke & Eyler, 1993; Kaltenbach, 1994) have reported that infants and children who were exposed to opiates prenatally are developing

Table 11.4.   Cognitive functioning in infants and children with and without prenatal narcotic exposure

Authors	Age (in years)	Methadone/heroin MDI	(SD)	Controls MDI	(SD)
Strauss et al. (1976)	1.00	113.4	(10.2)	114.8	(11.3)
Chasnoff et al. (1986)	2.00	98.7	(16.0)	96.2	(15.9)
Hans (1989)	2.00	92.0	(13.1)	95.8	(12.4)
Lifschitz et al. (1985)	3–5	85.3	(15.7)	89.4	(10.8)
Wilson (1989)	3–5	90.4	(13.0)	89.4	(13)
Kaltenbach and Finnegan (1989)	4.5	106.51	(12.96)	106.05	(13.1)
Strauss et al. (1979)	5	86.8	(13.3)	86.2	(16.3)

From Brown, E.R., & Zuckerman, B. (1991). The infant of the drug-abusing mother. *Pediatric Annals, 20*(10), 558; reprinted with permission from Slack, Inc.

MDI, Bayley Scales of Infant Development, Mental Development Index (Bayley, 1993); *SD*, standard deviation.

typically (see Table 11.4). In one study (Wilson, Desmond, & Wait, 1981), infants who had been exposed to heroin and methadone in utero were developing within the normal range at 1 year of age save for minor motor problems and poor attention spans. Another study (Bunikowski, Grimmer, Heiser, et al., 1998) reported mild psychomotor delay at 1 year of age.

Wilson (1989) also reported that the cognitive performance of a group of children who had been exposed to heroin in utero varied widely over time, suggesting that these changes reflected at least in part changes in the children's home environment. Children with smaller head circumferences at birth were more likely to exhibit behavior problems and attain lower cognitive scores. Van Baar and co-workers (1994) followed a group of children who had been exposed prenatally to heroin and methadone to 5.5 years of age. The group who had been exposed to these drugs had lower cognitive scores and showed more behavior problems than children who had not. No group differences were noted for motor development; however, the group of children who had been exposed to heroin and methadone before birth remained smaller in head circumference, weight, and length than children who had not. Rosen and Johnson (1982) reported follow-up data for 18-month-old children who had been exposed to methadone prenatally. The children who had been exposed to methadone before birth had lower Bayley MDI and PDI scores than children who had not, but both groups of children were developing within the normal range. Prenatal opiate exposure has been associated with SIDS in several studies with an approximate incidence of 15–20 per 1,000 live births (Finnegan, 1979; Frank et al., 1993; Householder, Hatcher, Burns, et al., 1982; Kandall, Gaines, Habel, et al., 1993).

Associated Social, Mental Health, and Medical Problems of Pregnant Women Who Abuse Drugs

Obstetrical Complications   The most common obstetrical complication in women who abuse drugs and have no prenatal care is preterm birth. The incidence of low birth weight is approximately 50% in infants born to these mothers. Other obstetrical complications include fetal loss, abruptio placenta, amnionitis, preeclampsia, premature rupture of fetal membranes, postpartum hemorrhage, and septic thrombophlebitis (Roberts & Pinkerton, 1989).

Social Problems   Many of the pregnant women who abuse illegal drugs are single, poorly educated, and urban and have a poor social support network. They may have a personal history of physical or sexual abuse and may be victims of domestic violence. In addition, they may live with partners who abuse drugs. They are likely to be unemployed and may be homeless or live in substandard housing. Most of these women began their drug use in adolescence, and their perspectives and approaches to problem solving may be similar to that seen in the adolescent stage of psychosocial development. These women are also more likely than other women to have been raised by parents who were substance abusers.

Mental Health Problems   Pregnant women who abuse drugs have low self-esteem. They may feel powerless and often feel guilty and ashamed of their continued drug use. Many are clinically depressed or have other psychiatric diagnoses (e.g., posttraumatic stress disorder [PTSD], borderline personality disorder) (Grella, 1997). Some of these women have an associated developmental disability and an organic brain syndrome with clinical depression that follows cocaine or amphetamine cessation. As a group, they are at a high risk for abusing their children. In one study (Williams-Petersen, Myers, Degen, et al., 1994), more than one half of the group of pregnant women who were abusing drugs scored in the extreme risk range on a measure of child abuse potential. In another study (Wasserman & Leventhal, 1993), 47 infants who had been exposed to cocaine before birth were followed to 2 years of age. By 2 years of age, 23% of children who had been exposed to cocaine prenatally had been maltreated, versus 4% of children who had not been exposed to cocaine in the womb. Physical abuse of 11% of children who had been exposed to cocaine before birth, versus 2% of children who had not, had occurred.

Other Medical Problems The potential medical problems of pregnant women who abuse drugs are numerous and vary from inconsequential to life threatening (see Table 11.5). Women who abuse drugs intravenously are at high risk for contracting human immunodeficiency virus (HIV) infection and hepatitis B and C, as well as other complications related to sharing and reusing needles (e.g., abscesses, cellulitis, septicemia). They may have one or more sexually transmitted diseases (STDs), including syphilis, gonorrhea, herpes simplex, and chlamydia; in addition, they may be carriers of group B streptococcal infection. They may have poor nutrition and receive inadequate prenatal care.

MANAGEMENT

Identification

Drug-Use History to Be Administered by Health Professionals Before reading this section, please review Werner, Joffe, and Graham (1999). Family practitioners, pediatricians, and nurses should take a detailed drug history as part of counseling women of child-bearing age about the risks of use of alcohol and other drugs prior to and during pregnancy. This history should include legal drugs (prescription drugs, cigarettes, and alcohol) and illegal drugs. If the woman is using one or more drugs, ask her about

- Duration of use and age when use started
- Frequency of use and amount of drugs used
- Route of administration
- Social context of use (when and where she uses)
- Previous treatment for drug abuse and support group involvement
- Family history of alcohol or drug abuse
- Interest in treatment (Kandall, 1993)

Obstetricians, family practitioners, and midwives should also take a detailed drug use history from pregnant women during their first prenatal visit as part of counseling them about the risk of al-

Table 11.5. Medical complications in pregnant women who abuse drugs

Anemia (iron and folic acid deficiencies)
Human immunodeficiency virus infection
Other infections
  Abscesses
  Cellulitis
  Septicemia
  Urinary tract infections
  Tuberculosis
  Tetanus
Poor nutrition
Sexually transmitted diseases
  Syphilis
  Gonorrhea
  Herpes simplex
  Chlamydia
Hepatitis B and C
Group B streptococcus carrier
Consequences of physical violence: Suicidal and risk-taking behaviors

cohol and other drug use during pregnancy. Self-reported tobacco use of pregnant adolescents should serve as a "red flag" to ask in detail about their use of alcohol and illicit drugs (Archie, Anderson, & Gruber, 1997). Women who acknowledge drug use should be referred for appropriate treatment services and followed closely during the pregnancy. Indirect indicators such as multiple job or address changes, prolonged unemployment, previous incarceration, or involvement with Child Protective Services also should prompt more detailed and repeated questions about pregnant women's drug and alcohol use.

Risk Factors for Prenatal Maternal Drug Use The health professional cannot rely on the drug history or the self-report of the pregnant woman to identify all infants who could be exposed to alcohol or other drugs during pregnancy. Certain factors have been associated with an increased risk of drug use in pregnant women. These include preterm delivery, abruptio placenta, inadequate prenatal care, STDs, and low socioeconomic status of the mother (Ryan et al., 1994), as well as contextual factors such as availability of substances and neighborhood poverty and disorganization (Wallace, 1999). Some investigators (e.g., Neuspiel, 1995) have raised the concern that certain factors (e.g., low socioeconomic status, lack of prenatal care) are strongly biased by social class and lack of access to care. Other factors may be protective, such as strong ethnic identification and family-held traditional values and beliefs (Wallace, 1999). Table 11.6 provides a comprehensive list of risk factors for prenatal substance abuse. Some are more meaningful than others. For example, Ryan and co-workers (1994) studied 1,201 mother–infant pairs. They found that 28% of the women who had received inadequate prenatal care were using cocaine, compared with 8% of the total study population.

Some hospitals do have formal guidelines that indicate when to test mothers and their newborns for substance abuse. The use of guidelines may increase the identification of infants with drug ex-

Table 11.6. Risk factors associated with prenatal maternal substance abuse

Medical

Inadequate prenatal care
Premature delivery
Sexually transmitted diseases
Human immunodeficiency virus infection
Hepatitis
Abruptio placenta
Meconium staining
Intrauterine growth retardation
Microcephaly

Social

Previous drug use
Prostitution
Frequent changes of residence or employment
History of abuse or neglect of another child
History of serious mental illness
Repeated foster home placement in either parent
History of abuse when parent was a child
History of violent behavior or jail sentence in either parent
Relinquishment of child for adoption is sought, then reversed

Other

Mother's negative comments about the baby
Mother's behaviors indicating lack of maternal attachment and bonding
    Does not want to hold, feed, or name the baby
    Avoids eye contact and touching the baby
    No signs of cuddling or talking to the baby
    Disparaging remarks about the baby
    Feeds baby in a mechanical or other inappropriate way
    Spanks the newborn or directs overt anger toward the baby
Inadequate visiting or telephone patterns if mother is discharged before baby
Reluctance to come in for the baby when his or her discharge is approved

From Roberts, D., & Pinkerton, R.D. (1989). *Women, drugs, and babies: Guidelines for medical and protective services response to infants endangered by drug abuse during pregnancy.* Salem, OR: Department of Human Resources, Children's Services Division; adapted by permission.

posure and eliminate the biases of individual physicians or nurses but may formalize systematic prejudice. Which mothers or infants should be tested? The best answer to this question is determined by local professional groups. In general, screening of the newborn's urine should be done for the purposes of medical evaluation and treatment.

Should the infant be tested without parents' permission? This is another controversial issue. In general, the mother should be asked for permission prior to testing her infant. If the infant shows signs and symptoms of possible prenatal substance exposure, testing can be done without parental permission as part of an evaluation for possible child abuse. If the physician decides to test the infant, the infant's parents should be notified and the reasons for the testing should be discussed with them directly. Practitioners need to remain knowledgeable about current legal standards with regard to these issues.

Testing Methods for Illegal Drugs   Most hospitals continue to rely on urine testing; however, a number of studies have reported that testing of meconium is more sensitive and easier to obtain than urine testing (Lewis, Moore, Leikin, et al., 1995; Ryan et al., 1994). In one study (Ryan et al., 1994), urine testing missed 25% of the meconium samples that were positive for cocaine and metabolites, and meconium sampling identified all the positive urine samples. Meconium testing can be done by most hospital laboratories with current technology for urine testing (Ryan et al., 1994). Rapid immunoassays of urine specimens are sensitive; but in the case of amphetamines and opiates, they are not specific. Amphetamines may cross-react with over-the-counter cold medicines. Other testing methods may be used that increase specificity, but they require larger volumes of urine that may decrease drug concentrations below detectable levels.

As commented previously, the use of meconium can detect drug use during the last several months of the pregnancy. Cocaine and its metabolites (ecgonine and benzolyecgonine) and amphetamines are present in the urine for only a few days, and marijuana is present in the urine for up to 1 week. Alcohol is present in the urine for only a few hours.

Signs of the Neonatal Abstinence Syndrome and Neurobehavioral Abnormalities Reflecting Drug Exposure   Babies who were exposed to drugs prenatally are most often identified when their mothers come to the hospital in labor or when the newborn has problems in the nursery (Dixon, Bresnahan, & Zuckerman, 1990). Infants who have unexplained lethargy, poor feeding, altered sleep, respiratory

Table 11.7. Signs of the neonatal abstinence syndrome

Irritability
High-pitched cry
Wakefulness
Tremulousness
Excoriations due to constant movement
Hypertonia
Seizures
Sweating
Tachypnea
Fever
Frequent yawning
Nasal stuffiness and/or sneezing
Poor feeding
Excessive sucking
Regurgitation and vomiting
Loose or watery stool

Adapted from Finnegan (1981).

problems, or signs of NAS should be screened for prenatal drug or alcohol exposure. Table 11.7 lists the signs of NAS. Although not related to drug withdrawal per se, most of these signs have been seen as part of the drug effects of stimulants and the gradual CNS recovery from exposure to these agents.

Physical Examination for Minor and Major Anomalies It is important to conduct a careful physical examination for minor and major birth defects of newborns who were exposed to drugs during pregnancy to identify

- Infants with FAS
- Infants with isolated birth defects that are associated with maternal alcohol or other drug exposure
- Infants with an apparent birth defect syndrome that may be unrelated to alcohol or drug exposure

Please review the discussion of the examination for minor physical anomalies in Chapter 5. The physical examination should include careful measurement and recording of the infant's birth weight, length, and head circumference. Referral to a developmental pediatrician or a medical geneticist may be helpful to confirm a diagnosis of FAS and to help to determine the diagnosis in infants with multiple anomalies (i.e., three or more minor anomalies), especially when the anomalies are associated with IUGR.

Management of the Infant or Child

Newborns The highest priorities of the health professional for an infant with documented prena-

tal drug exposure are to identify and treat the NAS and to evaluate for possible mother–infant transmission of a number of potentially serious infectious diseases, including the following:

- Syphilis
- Hepatitis B and C
- HIV
- Other STDs
- Group B streptococcus
- Cytomegalovirus (CMV)

Treatment of Neurobehavioral Abnormalities, Including Neonatal Abstinence Syndrome Treatment of the neonate should primarily be supportive and includes swaddling; use of low lighting and sound levels; and frequent, small feedings. With the proper supportive care, the majority of infants with NAS do not require pharmacological treatment. Table 11.8 reviews the medical treatment of opiate withdrawal symptoms. The infant should be monitored with an abstinence scoring method such as the Neonatal Abstinence Scoring System (Finnegan, 1981) (see Figure 11.1); consider prescribing pharmacologic treatment for infants with a score of 8 or more on this measure (Finnegan, Mitros, & Hopkins, 1979). Limited research data are available to support any specific pharmacologic treatment of NAS. In a review of 14 studies, Theis and co-workers (1997) noted that none of the studies were double-blind and most had other methodologic problems. They questioned the use of paregoric because it contains the central stimulant camphor and a large amount of alcohol.

Evaluate the Mother and Child for Transmission of Infectious Diseases All pregnant women should be tested for hepatitis B surface antigen (HB$_s$Ag), and all neonates should receive hepatitis B vaccine (HBV). Infants who are delivered to women with chronic hepatitis B infection should also receive hepatitis B immunoglobin (HBIG) immediately after birth (CDC, 1994). Women who have not been tested previously must receive HB$_s$Ag testing promptly to ensure HBIG treatment of the infant during the first 12 hours after birth if the infant is positive for HB$_s$Ag. If testing cannot be completed within this time frame, consider giving the infant HBIG and HBV as soon after delivery as possible. Please review Chapter 11 for recommendations regarding the antenatal treatment of mothers with HIV and treatment of their infants.

Women and men who are involved in intravenous drug use, who received blood or blood products before 1992, or who have secured hemodialysis should be screened for hepatitis C virus (HCV)

Table 11.8.   Pharmacologic treatment of opiate withdrawal

Drug	Dose	Considerations
Paregoric (.4 milligrams MS/cc)	.2 milliliters every 3 hours (by mouth) up to maximum of .4 milliliters every 3 hours After stabilization for 5 days, taper the dose cautiously. Gradually decrease the dose every other day by .05 milliliter dose as tolerated.	Add phenobarbital if abstinence syndrome remains uncontrolled. Observe infant for 1–2 days after discontinuing drugs.
Phenobarbital	Initial dose of 5 milligrams-per-kilogram (intramuscular or intravenous) then maintenance dose of 3–5 milligrams-per-kilogram per day (by mouth, intramuscular, or intravenous) given every 8 hours Increase as needed by 1 milligram-per-kilogram to a maximum of 10 milligrams-per-kilogram per day.	Monitor for constipation. Serum phenobarbital should be monitored when clinically indicated. Excessive phenobarbital dose may cause poor feeding and lethargy.
	After stabilization for 3–5 days, taper the dose cautiously. Reduce by 25% every other day or as clinically indicated.	Some infants may require small doses for months.

Adapted from Kandall (1993).

(CDC, 1998). The AAP (1998) recommends screening for HCV in all infants born to mothers who are infected with HCV. The vertical transmission of HCV is low, except for women who are also infected with HIV and women who are positive for hepatitis C ribonucleic acid (RNA) (Resti, Azzari, Mannelli, et al., 1998).

Evaluate the Infant or Child for Other Medical Problems   Infants with prenatal cocaine exposure also may have transient increases in blood pressure that do not require treatment and electrocardiogram (EKG) changes indicating minor ischemia (Dixon et al., 1990). Blood pressure should be followed until it is normal, usually for 1–3 days. Prenatal maternal cocaine use has also been reported in association with infants' necrotizing enterocolitis and intestinal atresia. Infants with persistent vomiting and abdominal distention must be evaluated for these problems. Children with marked neurobehavioral abnormalities (e.g., hyporesponsiveness) should receive a cranial ultrasound and other assessments as needed.

Document the Infant's Neurobehavioral Status   Many infants who were exposed to drugs before birth show few or no signs of neurobehavioral dysfunction, and other such infants may have severe NAS (e.g., infants who were exposed to opiates). Document the infant's neurobehavioral status initially and again prior to discharge. Use an examination such as the Neurological Assessment of the Pre-Term and Full-Term Newborn (Dubowitz,

Dubowitz, & Mercuri, 1999). The neonatal neurologic examination includes neurobehavioral items as well as items that assess the infant's movement, tone, and reflexes. Look for the signs of the "classic" infant with prenatal drug exposure: lethargy, poor responsiveness, hypertonicity, tremulousness, and irritability when alert. These infants may be overstimulated easily and exhibit poor eye contact when feeding. They also may have poor coordination of suck and swallow as well as oral hypersensitivity.

Examine the baby with the mother or primary caregiver present so that she can see the baby's abilities and appropriate management techniques can be demonstrated (see Table 11.9). Focus on the positive findings regarding the infant's status as well as the infant's problems. Infants with persistent feeding dysfunction may need a referral to the feeding specialist prior to discharge. Breast feeding is generally not recommended for infants of women who abuse drugs because of the potential for further exposing the infant to drugs through the breast milk. In some instances, breast feeding may be appropriate (e.g., with regard to women who have been in treatment programs consistently during their pregnancy and have abstained from drugs for some months, women who are taking low doses of methadone and tapering their dose postpartum). The infant may be discharged from the hospital when

- All assessments have been completed (including notification of Child Protective Services if needed)

- The infant is feeding well orally and gaining weight
- The infant has shown sufficient recovery from NAS
- Management techniques (e.g., feeding, positioning) have been demonstrated to the mother or primary caregiver

Signs and symptoms	Scoring
Central nervous system disturbances	
High-pitched cry *or*	2
Continuous high-pitched cry	3
Sleeps < 1 hour after feeding *or*	3
Sleeps < 2 hours after feeding *or*	2
Sleeps < 3 hours after feeding	1
Hyperactive Moro reflex *or*	2
Markedly hyperactive Moro reflex	3
Mild tremors disturbed *or*	1
Moderate to severe tremors disturbed	2
Mild tremors undisturbed *or*	3
Moderate to severe tremors undisturbed	4
Increased muscle tone	2
Excoriation (specify area)	1
Myoclonic jerks	3
Generalized convulsions	5
Metabolic/vasomotor/respiratory disturbances	
Sweating	1
Fever < 101° F (99° F–100.8° F) *or*	1
Fever > 101° F	2
Frequent yawning (more than three or four times per minute)	1
Mottling	1
Nasal stuffiness	1
Sneezing (more than three or four times per minute)	1
Nasal flaring	2
Respiratory rate > 60 breaths per minute *or*	1
Respiratory rate > 60 breaths per minute with retractions	2
Gastrointestinal disturbances	
Excessive sucking	1
Poor feeding	2
Regurgitation *or*	2
Projectile vomiting	3
Loose stools *or*	2
Watery stools	3
Total score	____

Figure 11.1. Neonatal Abstinence Scoring System. (Adapted from Finnegan [1981].)

- The mother or primary caregiver and the health professional agree on a follow-up plan (e.g., weekly appointment in the primary care office) (adapted from Dixon, Bresnahan, & Zuckerman, 1990)

Infants and Older Children

Monitor Growth and Development A review of the mother's (or the primary caregiver's) comfort and skill with feeding and positioning the infant at each follow-up appointment is particularly important. Monitor the weight, length, and head circumference of the infant carefully. Infants with prenatal drug exposure are at risk for either organic or nonorganic failure to thrive. Infants with prenatal drug exposure who are small for their gestational age may not show catch-up growth but should maintain the expected growth velocity for children their age (i.e., growth pattern parallel to the normal growth curve).

The development of all infants who were exposed to drugs before birth should be monitored carefully. Most infants with prenatal drug exposure experience a typical developmental course, but this depends on their postnatal environment. Refer the following infants with prenatal drug exposure to local early intervention (EI) services:

- Diagnosis of FAS
- Marked neurobehavioral difficulties
- Condition likely to result in developmental delay
- Microcephaly (head circumference smaller than 2 *SD* from the mean)
- Persistent ventriculomegaly
- Posthemorrhagic hydrocephalus
- Large areas of periventricular leukomalacia

In many states, funds are not available to provide EI services to infants and their families identified solely by biologic and social risk factors. These women and their infants may be eligible for other

Table 11.9. Management techniques for newborns and young infants with prenatal drug exposure

- Keep lights dim and noise levels low.
- Follow consistent, predictable routines.
- Use a pacifier.
- Move the baby slowly; use a calm, soothing voice.
- Give gentle massage (avoid bouncing and patting; avoid massage if irritability results).
- Use swaddling and gentle rocking as needed.
- Use a front pack to carry the baby.
- Follow the baby's cues especially when he or she is overstimulated. (The infant may show gaze or head aversion, frowning, and grimacing.)

Adapted from Dixon, Bresnahan, and Zuckerman (1990).

support services. Contact the county health department or EI providers to determine which services are available in your area.

For infants at high risk for developmental problems and any infant and toddler with language delay, obtain formal audiologic testing for hearing loss. Also carefully monitor the child's neuromotor status. Infants with prenatal drug exposure may show a period of hypertonicity or stiffness associated with tremulousness in the first year. In general, this circumstance does not require specific referral or treatment. The findings of a consistent pattern of motor asymmetries (e.g., right-sided hypertonicity or stiffness), however, may indicate a hemiplegia and require a referral for further evaluation and possible treatment. Language delay and behavior problems may be signs of underlying, often complex cognitive difficulties. Consider referral of children who are experiencing these difficulties to a child development team.

Anticipatory Guidance   Review the problems that infants with prenatal drug exposure may exhibit with the parents or other primary caregivers (e.g., hypertonicity, sleep disturbance, tremulousness), as well as their natural history and management suggestions. Typically, these problems improve slowly and have resolved by the end of the first year. Review expected developmental milestones with parents, particularly the child's understanding of discipline. Women who use drugs may have little knowledge of typical child development and may have a directive and coercive parenting style. They may never have experienced good parenting practices themselves when they were growing up. Teach parents to play with their infants by first simply imitating what their infant does.

Toddlers who are active, distractible, and impulsive are difficult to manage. Their parents require regular support and instruction in behavior management techniques. Consider a referral to birth-to-three parenting groups, an early referral to preschool and Head Start programs, and/or a referral to EI/early childhood special education (ECSE) services. Guidelines for the care of young children with self-regulatory problems at home and in preschool are included in the publication *Improving Treatment for Drug-Exposed Infants* (Kandall, 1993). Modeling of appropriate management techniques by primary care office staff at *all* office visits is often more helpful than providing parents with instruction and reading materials. Table 11.10 presents recommendations for the management of children with prenatal cocaine exposure to 5 years of age.

Table 11.10.   The first 5 years: Guidelines for the management of infants and young children with prenatal cocaine exposure

First 2 months
Establish weekly or biweekly visits.
Monitor neurologic and behavioral status.
Look for irritability, sleeping and eating disturbances, slightly elevated temperature, excessive weight gain or poor weight gain, diarrhea, and vomiting.
Advise soothing; swaddling; quiet rocking; decreased stimulation; and quiet, calm handling.
Prescribe mild sedation if needed (rarely): Phenobarbital 5 milligrams-per-kilogram per day divided into two or three doses; avoid if possible, and wean early.
Check infectious disease issues as needed; receive second hepatitis B vaccine.
Refer children who have tested positive for human immunodeficiency virus (HIV) to pediatric acquired immunodeficiency syndrome (AIDS) center.
Support baby's caregivers, and know your community's resources.

2–6 months
Establish monthly visits.
Monitor neurologic abnormalities.
Repeat ultrasounds of previously identified abnormalities.
Repeat VDRL (Venereal Disease Research Laboratories), third hepatitis B vaccine; monitor for cytomegalovirus in urine and for infections previously identified.
Refer HIV-positive children to a pediatric AIDS center.
Assess health and welfare of siblings.
Support parents' drug treatment involvement.
Be alert to any evidence of postnatal drug exposure.
Advocate for stable home placement as needed.
Monitor child's development and behavior at each visit.

8–18 months
Conduct formal, standardized assessments of motor function, speech-language development, and behavior.
Be alert to language delays and behavior problems.
Refer for further psychological testing as needed.

Yearly from ages 2–5 years
Repeat standardized developmental assessments.
Provide general good health care.

From Dixon, S.D., Bresnahan, K., & Zuckerman, B. (1990). Cocaine babies: Meeting the challenge of management. *Contemporary Pediatrics, 7*(6), 83; reprinted by permission from Medical Economics Co.

The most important part of the treatment of infants with prenatal drug exposure is a consistent, nurturing caregiving environment.

Management of the Mother and the Family
The mothers of infants who were exposed to drugs before birth may display a wide variety of needs and problems that require an array of services. The best treatment for the infant is to assist the mother and father to recover from addiction (Kandall, 1993), and the best time to provide treatment

is early in the pregnancy. As commented, the outcome for infants is improved if women stop using drugs after the first trimester and if they are provided with comprehensive services. The goals of treatment are to ensure a safe, nurturing caregiving environment and to keep families intact if possible. Identify mutual goals with parents, and engage their positive motivation in specific good parenting activities and practices. It is important to identify the factors that place these infants at risk, as well as the positive factors in these infants' and families' lives.

Completion of a formal management plan for infants with prenatal drug exposure and their families is useful because many have ongoing service needs from a number of different community providers. Update the management plan at each reevaluation as needed. The management of these children and families requires the collaboration of a number of community service providers. Substance abuse is a chronic, relapsing disorder. The health care professional must be aware of this problem and maintain regular communication with other agencies serving the family to ensure the safety of the infant and young child. Missed appointments and erratic behavior in the primary care office or over the telephone may be signs that the mother's or parents' addiction has recurred.

"One-stop shopping" with the provision of multiple services at one site and a multilevel model of treatment that includes short- and long-term residential and intensive outpatient treatment may be critical to serving this population (Kaltenbach & Finnegan, 1998). Comprehensive treatment has been shown to increase the likelihood of term birth, decrease the number of perinatal complications, and decrease the number of repeat pregnancies involving prenatal drug exposure (Burkett, Gomez-Marin, Yasin, & Martinez, 1998). A comprehensive treatment program includes the following:

- Legal advocacy
- Child Protective Services
- Prenatal medical care for women
- Treatment of other maternal health problems
- Pediatric care
- HIV testing and counseling
- Preconception education and family planning services
- Women's chemical dependency treatment (e.g., residential treatment, drug-free housing)
- Education and job training
- Coordination of social services with outreach services available

- Developmental assessment of children and referral to EI services
- Child care, therapeutic child care, and children's mental health services
- Care coordination using professionals trained in substance abuse counseling
- Parenting education
- Mental health services
- Support groups
- Transportation
- Housing
- Domestic violence counseling
- Respite care
- Training in life management skills (e.g., money management) (Kandall, 1993)

Some children cannot be maintained safely with the biologic family. The recommendations regarding management of infants and children in foster care are similar to the recommendations discussed previously. The focus must be on supporting the foster family to ensure a consistent nurturing environment instead of sequential placements in different foster homes. Foster parents require anticipatory guidance and education regarding infants with prenatal drug exposure and may also require ongoing support services (e.g., parents' support groups, respite care).

Important Care Coordination Issues
Manage infants with prenatal drug exposure similarly to other children with disabilities and chronic conditions. Follow the general recommendations for changes in office procedures discussed in Chapter 1 (e.g., identify an office care coordinator, use the key components of care forms). The following are specific care coordination responsibilities of the primary health care professional for the management of these families:

- Identify an office staff member to be a support or contact person for the family.
- Identify the contact people with Child Protective Services, EI/ECSE services, and the county health department.
- Maintain an up-to-date list of other community service providers, including support groups for parents with children from birth to 3 years of age, Head Start, and other preschool programs.
- Be aware of the drug treatment programs in the community and in the state.
- Regularly exchange information with other service providers, especially with regard to children and families continuing in Child Protective Services and children in foster care.

REFERENCES

Aase, J.M., Jones, K.L., & Clarren, S.K. (1995). Do we need the term "FAE"? *Pediatrics, 95*(3), 428–430.

Abel, E.L., & Sokol, R.L. (1991). A revised conservative estimate of the incidence of FAS and its economic impact. *Alcoholism: Clinical and Experimental Research, 15*, 514–524.

Achenbach, T.M. (1991). *Manual for the Child Behavior Checklist/4–18 and 1991 profile.* Burlington: University of Vermont, Department of Psychiatry.

American Academy of Pediatrics (AAP), Committee on Infectious Diseases. (1998). Hepatitis C virus infection. *Pediatrics, 101*(3 pt. 1), 481–485.

American Academy of Pediatrics (AAP), Committee on Substance Abuse and Committee on Children with Disabilities. (1993). Fetal alcohol syndrome and fetal alcohol effects. *Pediatrics, 91*(5), 1004–1006.

Archie, C.L., Anderson, M.M., & Gruber, E.L. (1997). Positive smoking history as a preliminary screening device for substance use in pregnant adolescents. *Journal of Pediatric and Adolescent Gynecology, 10*, 13–17.

Astley, S.J., & Clarren, S.K. (1995). A fetal alcohol syndrome screening tool. *Alcoholism: Clinical and Experimental Research, 19*(6), 1565–1571.

Astley, S.J., & Clarren, S.K. (1996). A case definition and photographic screening tool for the facial phenotype of fetal alcohol syndrome. *Journal of Pediatrics, 129*(1), 33–41.

Bayley, N. (1993). *Bayley Scales of Infant Development: Birth to two years* (2nd ed.). San Antonio, TX: The Psychological Corporation.

Behnke, M., & Eyler, F.D. (1993). The consequences of prenatal substance use for the developing fetus, newborn, and young child. *International Journal of the Addictions, 28*(13), 1341–1391.

Billing, L., Eriksson, M., Steneroth, G., et al. (1985). Preschool children of amphetamine-addicted mothers: I. Somatic and psychomotor development. *Acta Paediatrica Scandinavia, 74*, 179–184.

Brazelton, T.B. (1984). *The Neonatal Behavioral Assessment Scale: Vol. 88. Clinics in developmental medicine.* Philadelphia: J.B. Lippincott Co.

Brown, E.R., & Zuckerman, B. (1991). The infant of the drug-abusing mother. *Pediatric Annals, 20*(10), 555–563.

Bunikowski, R., Grimmer, I., Heiser, A., et al. (1998). Neurodevelopmental outcome after prenatal exposure to opiates. *European Journal of Pediatrics, 157*, 724–730.

Burkett, G., Gomez-Marin, O., Yasin, S.Y., & Martinez, M. (1998). Prenatal care in cocaine-exposed pregnancies. *Obstetrics and Gynecology, 92*(2), 193–200.

Burton, B.T. (1990). Methamphetamine. *Oregon Poison Center: Poison Press, 1*(3), 1–4.

Centers for Disease Control and Prevention (CDC). (1994). Recommendations of the U.S. Public Health Service Task Force on the use of Zidovudine to reduce perinatal transmission of human immunodeficiency virus. *Morbidity and Mortality Weekly Report, 43*(11) [entire issue].

Centers for Disease Control and Prevention (CDC). (1998). Recommendations for the prevention and control of hepatitis C virus (HCV) infection and HCV-related chronic disease. *Morbidity and Mortality Weekly Report, 47*(RR-19), 23–24.

Charlebois, A.T., & Fried, P.A. (1980). Interactive effects of nutrition and cannabis upon rat perinatal development. *Developmental Psychobiology, 13*(6), 591–605.

Chasnoff, I.J. (1992, August). Cocaine, pregnancy, and the growing child. *Current Problems in Pediatrics, 22*(7), 302–321.

Chasnoff, I.J., Anson, A., Hatcher, R., et al. (1998). Prenatal exposure to cocaine and other drugs: Outcome at four to six years. *Annals of the New York Academy of Science, 846*, 314–328.

Chasnoff, I.J., Burns, K.A., & Burns, W.J. (1987). Cocaine use in pregnancy: Perinatal morbidity and mortality. *Neurotoxicology and Teratology, 9*(4), 291–293.

Chasnoff, I.J., Burns, K.A., Burns, W.J., & Schnoll, S.H. (1986). Prenatal drug exposure: Effects on neonatal and infant growth and development. *Neurobehavioral Toxicology and Teratology, 8*(4), 357–362.

Chasnoff, I.J., Griffith, D.R., Frerer, C., et al. (1992). Cocaine/polydrug use in pregnancy: Two-year follow-up. *Pediatrics, 89*(2), 284–289.

Chasnoff, I.J., Griffith, D.R., MacGregor, S., et al. (1989). Temporal patterns of cocaine use in pregnancy. *JAMA: Journal of the American Medical Association, 261*(12), 1741–1744.

Chasnoff, I.J., Landress, H.J., & Barrett, M.E. (1990). The prevalence of illicit-drug or alcohol use during pregnancy and discrepancies in mandatory reporting in Pinellas County, Florida. *New England Journal of Medicine, 322*(17), 1202–1206.

Chiriboga, C.A., Brust, J.C.M., Bateman, D., & Hauser, W.A. (1999). Dose-response effect of fetal cocaine exposure on newborn neurologic function. *Pediatrics, 103* 79–85.

Chomitz, V.R., Cheung, L.W., & Lieberman, E. (1995). The role of lifestyle in preventing low birth weight. *Future of Children, 5*(1), 121–138.

Clarren, S.K., & Smith, D.W. (1978). The fetal alcohol syndrome. *New England Journal of Medicine, 298*, 1063–1067.

Coles, C.D., Smith, I., Femhoff, P.M., et al. (1985). Neonatal neurobehavioral characteristics as correlates of maternal alcohol use during gestation. *Alcoholism, 9*, 454–459.

Coles, C.D., Smith, I.E., & Falek, A. (1987). Prenatal alcohol exposure and infant behavior: Immediate effects and implications for later development. *Advances in Alcohol and Substance Abuse, 6*(4), 87–104.

Dahl, R.E., Scher, M.S., Williamson, D.E., et al. (1995). A longitudinal study of prenatal marijuana use: Effects on sleep and arousal at age 3 years. *Archives of Pediatric and Adolescent Medicine, 149*, 145–150.

Day, N.L., Richardson, G.A., Geva, D., & Robles, N. (1994). Alcohol, marijuana, and tobacco: Effects of prenatal exposure on offspring growth and morphology at age six. *Alcohol Clinical and Experimental Research, 18*, 786–794.

Day, N.L., Wagener, D.K., & Taylor, P.M. (1985). Measurement of substance use during pregnancy: Methodologic issues. In *National Institute on Drug Abuse (NIDA) Research Monograph, 56*, 36–47.

Delaney-Black, V., Covington, C., Templin, T., et al. (1998). Prenatal cocaine exposure and child behavior. *Pediatrics, 102*, 945–950.

Denson, R., Nanson, J.L., & McWatters, M.A. (1975). Hyperkinesis and maternal smoking. *Canadian Psychiatric Association Journal, 20*(3), 183–187.

Dixon, S.D., & Bejar, R. (1989). Echoencephalographic findings in neonates associated with maternal cocaine and methamphetamine use: Incidence and clinical correlates. *Journal of Pediatrics, 115,* 770–778.

Dixon, S.D., Bresnahan, K., & Zuckerman, B. (1990, June). Cocaine babies: Meeting the challenge of management. *Contemporary Pediatrics, 7*(6), 70–92.

Doering, P.L., Davidson, C.L., LaFrance, L., et al. (1989). Effects of cocaine on the human fetus: A review of clinical studies. *DICP, 23,* 639–645.

Dubowitz, L.M.S., Dubowitz, V., & Mercuri, E. (1999). *Neurological assessment of the pre-term and full-term newborn infant* (2nd ed.). New York: Cambridge University Press.

Eyler, F.D., Behnke, M., Conlon, M., et al. (1998). Birth outcome from a prospective, matched study of prenatal crack/cocaine use: I. Interactive and dose effects on health and growth. *Pediatrics, 101*(2), 229–237.

Finnegan, L.P. (1979). In utero opiate dependence and sudden infant death syndrome. *Clinical Perinatology, 6*(1), 163–180.

Finnegan, L.P. (1981). Neonatal Abstinence Scoring System. In *Drug dependence in pregnancy: Clinical management of mother and child* (pp. 83–91). Washington, DC: U.S. Department of Health and Human Services, National Institute on Drug Abuse.

Finnegan, L.P. (1994). Perinatal morbidity and mortality in substance using families: Effects and intervention strategies. *Bulletin on Narcotics, 45*(1), 19–43.

Finnegan, L.P., Mitros, T.F., & Hopkins, L.E. (1979). Management of neonatal narcotic abstinence utilizing a phenobarbital loading dose method. In *National Institute on Drug Abuse (NIDA) Research Monograph, 27,* 247–253.

Floyd, R.L., Decoufle, P., & Hungerford, D.W. (1999). Alcohol use prior to pregnancy recognition. *American Journal of Preventive Medicine, 17*(2), 101–107.

Forman, R., Klein, J., Barks, J., et al. (1994). Prevalence of fetal exposure to cocaine in Toronto, 1990–1991. *Clinical and Investigative Medicine, 17*(3), 206–211.

Frank, D.A., Bresnaham, K., & Zuckerman, B.S. (1993). Maternal cocaine use: Impact on child health and development. *Advances in Pediatrics, 40,* 65–99.

Fried, P.A. (1993). Prenatal exposure to tobacco and marijuana: Effects during pregnancy, infancy, and early childhood. *Clinical Obstetrics and Gynecology, 36*(2), 319–337.

Fried, P.A., & Makin, J.E. (1987). Neonatal behavioural correlates of prenatal exposure to marijuana, cigarettes and alcohol in a low risk population. *Neurotoxicology and Teratology, 9*(1), 1–7.

Fried, P.A., & Watkinson, B. (1988). 12- and 24-month neurobehavioral follow-up of children prenatally exposed to marijuana, cigarettes, and alcohol. *Neurotoxicology and Teratology, 10*(4), 305–313.

Fried, P.A., & Watkinson, B. (1990). 36- and 48-month neurobehavioral follow-up of children prenatally exposed to marijuana, cigarettes, and alcohol. *Journal of Developmental and Behavioral Pediatrics, 11,* 49–58.

Fried, P.A., Watkinson, B., & Siegel, L.S. (1997). Reading and language in 9- to 12-year-olds prenatally exposed to cigarettes and marijuana. *Neurotoxicology and Teratology, 19,* 171–183.

Fulroth, R., Phillips, B., & Durand, D.J. (1989). Perinatal outcome of infants exposed to cocaine and/or heroin in utero. *American Journal of Diseases of Children, 143,* 905–910.

Gibson, G.T., Baghurst, P.A., & Colley, D.P. (1983). Maternal alcohol, tobacco and cannabis consumption and the outcome of pregnancy. *Australian and New Zealand Journal of Obstetrics and Gynaecology, 23*(1), 15–19.

Graham, K., Dimitrakoudis, D., Pellegrini, E., et al. (1989). Pregnancy outcome following first trimester exposure to cocaine in social users in Toronto, Canada. *Veterinary and Human Toxicology, 31,* 143–148.

Grella, C.E. (1997). Services for perinatal women with substance abuse and mental health disorders: The unmet need. *Journal of Psychoactive Drugs, 29,* 67–78.

Griffith, D.R., Azuma, S.D., & Chasnoff, I.J. (1994). Three-year outcome of children exposed prenatally to drugs. *Journal of the American Academy of Child and Adolescent Psychiatry, 33*(1), 20–27.

Guyer, B., MacDorman, M.F., & Martin, J.A. (1998). Annual summary of vital statistics: 1997. *Pediatrics, 102*(6), 1333–1349.

Haglund, B., & Cnattingius, S. (1990). Cigarette smoking as a risk factor for sudden infant death syndrome: A population-based study. *American Journal of Public Health, 80*(1), 29–32.

Hans, S.L. (1989). Developmental consequences of prenatal exposure to methadone. *Annals of the New York Academy of Science, 562,* 195–207.

Hingson, R., Alpert, J.J., Day, N., et al. (1982). Effects of maternal drinking and marijuana use on fetal growth and development. *Pediatrics, 70*(4), 539–546.

Hingson, R., Zuckerman, B., Amaro, H., et al. (1986). Maternal marijuana use and neonatal outcome: Uncertainty posed by self-reports. *American Journal of Public Health, 76*(6), 667–670.

Householder, J., Hatcher, R., Burns, W., et al. (1982). Infants born to narcotic-addicted mother. *Psychological Bulletin, 92,* 453–468.

Howard, J., Beckwith, L., Rodning, C., et al. (1989). The development of young children of substance-abusing parents: Insights from seven years of intervention and research. *Zero to Three, 9,* 8–12.

Hoyme, H.E., Jones, K.L., Dixon, S.D., et al. (1990). Prenatal cocaine exposure and fetal vascular disruption. *Pediatrics, 85,* 743–747.

Hurt, H., Malmud, E., Betancourt, L., et al. (1997). Children with in utero cocaine exposure do not differ from control subjects on intelligence testing. *Archives of Pediatric and Adolescent Medicine, 151,* 1237–1241.

Jacobson, J.L., Jacobson, S.W., Sokol, R.J., et al. (1994). Effects of alcohol use, smoking, and illicit drug use on fetal growth in black infants. *Journal of Pediatrics, 124*(5 pt. 1), 757–764.

Johnson, S.F., McCarter, R.J., & Ferencz, C. (1987). Changes in alcohol, cigarette, and recreational drug use during pregnancy: Implications for interventions. *American Journal of Epidemiology, 126,* 695–702.

Jones, K.L. (1986). Fetal alcohol syndrome. *Pediatric Review, 8,* 122–126.

Jones, K.L., Smith, D.W., Ulleland, C.M., & Streissguth, A.P. (1973). Pattern of malformation in offspring of chronic alcoholic mothers. *Lancet, 1*(815), 1267–1271.

Kaltenbach, K.A., & Finnegan, L.P. (1989). Prenatal narcotic exposure: Perinatal and developmental effects. *Neurotoxicology, 10*(3), 597–604.

Kaltenbach, K., & Finnegan, L. (1998). Prevention and treatment issues for pregnant cocaine-dependent women and their infants. *Annals of the New York Academy of Science, 846,* 329–334.

Kaltenbach, K., & Finnegan, L.P. (1986). Neonatal abstinence syndrome, pharmacotherapy and developmental outcome. *Neurobehavioral Toxicology and Teratology, 8*(4), 353–355.

Kaltenbach, K.A. (1994). Effects of in-utero opiate exposure: New paradigms for old questions. *Drug and Alcohol Dependence, 36,* 83–87.

Kandall, S.R. (1993). *Improving treatment for drug-exposed infants: Treatment improvement protocol (TIP) series.* Washington, DC: U.S. Department of Health and Human Services.

Kandall, S.R., Albin, S., Gartner, L.M., et al. (1977). The narcotic-dependent mother: Fetal and neonatal consequences. *Early Human Development, 1*(2), 159–169.

Kandall, S.R., Doberczak, T.M., Jantunen, M., & Stein, J. (1999). The methadone-maintained pregnancy. *Clinical Perinatology, 26*(1), 173–183.

Kandall, S.R., & Gaines, J. (1991). Maternal substance use and subsequent sudden infant death syndrome (SIDS) in offspring. *Neurotoxicology and Teratology, 13*(2), 235–240.

Kandall, S.R., Gaines, J., Habel, L., et al. (1993). Relationship of maternal substance abuse to subsequent sudden infant death syndrome in offspring. *Journal of Pediatrics, 123*(1), 120–126.

King, T.A., Perlman, J.M., Laptook, A.R., et al. (1995). Neurologic manifestations of in utero cocaine exposure in near-term infants. *Pediatrics, 96*(2 pt. 1), 259–264.

Kliegman, R.M., Madura, D., Kiwi, R., et al. (1994). Relation of maternal cocaine use to the risks of prematurity and low birth weight. *Journal of Pediatrics, 124*(5 pt. 1), 751–756.

Kline, J., Ng, S.K., Schittini, M., et al. (1997). Cocaine use during pregnancy: Sensitive detection by hair assay. *American Journal of Public Health, 87,* 352–358.

Kokotailo, P.K., Adger, H., Jr., Duggan, A.K., et al. (1992). Cigarette, alcohol, and other drug use by school-age pregnant adolescents: Prevalence, detection, and associated risk factors. *Pediatrics, 90*(3), 328–334.

Koren, G., Nulman, I., Rovet, J., et al. (1998). Long-term neurodevelopmental risks in children exposed in utero to cocaine: The Toronto Adoption Study. *Annals of the New York Academy of Science, 846,* 306–313.

Koren, G., Shear, H., Graham, K., et al. (1989). Bias against the null hypothesis: The reproductive hazards of cocaine. *Lancet, 2,* 1440–1442.

Kwong, T.C., & Ryan, R.M. (1997). Detection of intrauterine illicit drug exposure by newborn drug testing: National Academy of Clinical Biochemistry. *Clinical Chemistry, 43*(1), 235–242.

Lewis, D.E., Moore, C.M., Leikin, J.B., & Koller, A. (1995). Meconium analysis for cocaine: A validation study and comparison with paired urine analysis. *Journal of Analytical Toxicology, 19*(3), 148–150.

Lifschitz, M.H., & Wilson, G.S. (1991). Patterns of growth and development in narcotic-exposed children. In M.M. Kilbey & K. Asghar (Eds.), *National Institute on Drug Abuse research monographs: Methodological issues in controlled studies on effects of prenatal exposure to drug abuse, 114,* 323–339.

Lifschitz, M.H., Wilson, G.S., Smith, E.O., & Desmond, M.M. (1985). Factors affecting head growth and intellectual function in children of drug addicts. *Pediatrics, 75*(2), 269–274.

Lustbader, A.S., Mayes, L.C., McGee, B.A., et al. (1998). Incidence of passive exposure to crack/cocaine and clinical findings in infants seen in an outpatient service. *Pediatrics, 102,* e5.

MacDorman, M.F., Cnattingius, S., Hoffman, H.J., et al. (1997). Sudden infant death syndrome and smoking in the United States and Sweden. *American Journal of Epidemiology, 146*(3), 249–257.

MacGregor, S.N., Keith, L.G., Chasnoff, I.J., et al. (1987). Cocaine use during pregnancy: Adverse perinatal outcome. *American Journal of Obstetrics and Gynecology, 157*(3), 686–690.

Malloy, M.H., Kleinman, J.C., Land, G.H., et al. (1988). The association of maternal smoking with age and cause of infant death. *American Journal of Epidemiology, 128*(1), 46–55.

Maternal drug abuse and drug exposed children: Understanding the problem. (1992). Washington, DC: U.S. Department of Health and Human Services.

Miller, J.M., Jr., Boudreaux, M.C., & Regan, F.A. (1995). A case-control study of cocaine use in pregnancy. *American Journal of Obstetrics and Gynecology, 172*(1 pt. 1), 180–185.

Mills, J.L., Graubard, B.I., Harley, E.E., et al. (1984). Maternal alcohol consumption and birth weight: How much drinking in pregnancy is safe? *JAMA: Journal of the American Medical Association, 252,* 1875–1879.

Myers, B.J., Olson, H.C., & Kaltenbach, K. (1992). Cocaine-exposed infants: Myths and misunderstandings. *Zero to Three: National Center for Clinical Infant Programs, 13*(1), 1–5.

National Institute on Drug Abuse (NIDA). (1990). *National Household Survey on Drug Abuse: Population estimates, 1990* (National Institute on Drug Abuse Pub. No. [ADM] 91-1732). Rockville, MD: U.S. Department of Health and Human Services, National Institute on Drug Abuse.

Neuspiel, D.R. (1995). Screening neonates for intrauterine cocaine exposure. *Journal of Pediatrics, 126*(2), 323–324.

Nichols, P.L., & Chen, T.C. (1981). *Minimal brain dysfunction: A prospective study.* Mahwah, NJ: Lawrence Erlbaum Associates.

Nulman, I., Rovet, J., Altmann, D., et al. (1994). Neurodevelopment of adopted children exposed in utero to cocaine. *Canadian Medical Association Journal, 151*(11), 1591–1597.

Olson, H.C. (1994, January). The effects of prenatal alcohol exposure on child development. *Infants and Young Children, 6*(3), 10–25.

Oregon Health Division. (1990). Perinatal substance abuse in Oregon. *Communicable Disease Summary, 39*(21), 1–2.

Oregon Health Division. (1992). Lead poisoning in a methamphetamine user. *Communicable Disease Sumary, 41*(16), 1.

Oro, A.S., & Dixon S.D. (1987, October). Perinatal cocaine and methamphetamine exposure: Maternal and neonatal correlates. *Journal of Pediatrics, 111*(4), 571–578.

Ostrea, E.M., Jr., Ostrea, A.R., & Simpson, P.M. (1997). Mortality within the first 2 years in infants exposed to cocaine, opiate, or cannabinoid during gestation. *Pediatrics, 100,* 79–83.

Peacock, J.L., Bland, J.M., & Anderson, H.R. (1991). Effects on birthweight of alcohol and caffeine consumption in smoking women. *Journal of Epidemiology and Community Health, 45,* 159–163.

Rajegowda, B.K., Glass, L., Evans, H.E., et al. (1972). Methadone withdrawal in newborn infants. *Journal of Pediatrics, 81*(3), 532–534.

Resti, M., Azzari, C., Mannelli, F., et al. (1998). Mother to child transmission of hepatitis C virus: Prospective study of risk factors and timing of infection in children born to workmen seronegative for HIV-1: Tuscany Study Group on Hepatitis C Virus Infection. *British Medical Journal, 317,* 437–441.

Richardson, G.A., Conroy, M.L., & Day, N.L. (1996). Prenatal cocaine exposure: Effects on the development of school-age children. *Neurotoxicology and Teratology, 18,* 627–634.

Richardson, G.A., Day, N.L., & McGauhey, P.J. (1993). The impact of prenatal marijuana and cocaine use on the infant and child. *Clinical Obstetrics and Gynecology, 36*(2), 302–318.

Roberts, D., & Pinkerton, R.M. (Eds.). (1989). *Women, drugs and babies: Guidelines for medical and protective services response to infants endangered by drug use during pregnancy.* Department of Human Resources, Children's Services Division, Salem, OR.

Robins, L.N., Mills, J.L., Krulewitch, C., et al. (1993). Effects of in utero exposure to street drugs. (1993). *American Journal of Public Health, 83*(Suppl.), 9–32.

Rosen, T.S., & Johnson, H.L. (1982). Children of methadone-maintained mothers: Follow-up to 18 months of age. *Journal of Pediatrics, 101*(2), 192–196.

Ryan, R.M., Wagner, C.L., Schultz, J.M., et al. (1994). Meconium analysis for improved identification of infants exposed to cocaine in utero. *Journal of Pediatrics, 125,* 435–440.

Sampson, P.D., Streissguth, A.P., Bookstein, F.L., et al. (1997). Incidence of fetal alcohol syndrome and prevalence of alcohol-related neurodevelopmental disorder. *Teratology, 56*(5), 317–326.

Sargent, R.G., Schulken, E.D., Kemper, K.A., et al. (1994). Black and white adolescent females' pre-pregnancy nutrition status. *Adolescence, 29*(116), 845–858.

Shiono, P.H., Klebanoff, M.A., Nugent, R.P., et al. (1995). The impact of cocaine and marijuana use on low birth weight and preterm birth: A multicenter study. *American Journal of Obstetrics and Gynecology, 172*(1 pt. 1), 19–27.

Singer, L., Arendt, R., Song, L.Y., et al. (1994). Direct and indirect interactions of cocaine with childbirth outcomes. *Archives of Pediatrics and Adolescent Medicine, 148*(9), 959–964.

Singer, L.T., Yamashita, T.S., Hawkins, S., et al. (1994). Increased incidence of intraventricular hemorrhage and developmental delay in cocaine-exposed, very low birth weight infants. *Journal of Pediatrics, 124,* 765–771.

Soepatmi, S. (1994). Developmental outcomes of children of mothers dependent on heroin or heroin/methadone during pregnancy. *Acta Paediatrica, 404,* 36–39.

Strauss, M.E., Lessen-Firestone, J.K., Chavez, C.J., & Stryker, J.C. (1979). Children of methadone-treated women at five years of age. *Pharmacology, Biochemistry, and Behavior, 11*(Suppl.), S3–S6.

Strauss, M.E., Starr, R.H., Ostrea, E.M., et al. (1976). Behavioral concomitants of prenatal addiction to narcotics. *Journal of Pediatrics, 89*(5), 842–846.

Streissguth, A.P., Aase, J.M., Clarren, S.K., et al. (1991). Fetal alcohol syndrome in adolescents and adults. *JAMA: Journal of the American Medical Association, 265*(15), 1961–1967.

Streissguth, A.P., Landesman-Dwyer, S., Martin, J.C., et al. (1980). Teratogenic effects of alcohol in humans and laboratory animals. *Science, 209,* 353–361.

Tennes, K., Avitable, N., Blackard, C., et al. (1985). Marijuana: Prenatal and postnatal exposure in the human. In *National Institute on Drug Abuse (NIDA) Research Monographs, 59,* 48–60.

Theis, J.G., Selby, P., Ikizler, Y., & Koren, G. (1997). Current management of the neonatal abstinence syndrome: A critical analysis of the evidence. *Biology of the Neonate, 71*(6), 345–356.

Thorndike, R.L., Hagen, E.P., & Sattler, J.M. (1986). *Stanford-Binet Intelligence Scale* (4th ed.). Itasca, IL: Riverside Publishing Co.

Ursitti, F., Klein, J., & Koren, G. (1997). Clinical utilization of the neonatal hair test for cocaine: A four-year experience in Toronto. *Biology of the Neonate, 72*(6), 345–351.

van Baar, A., & Graaff, B.M.T. (1994). Cognitive development at preschool-age of infants of drug-dependent mothers. *Developmental Medicine and Child Neurology, 36,* 1063–1075.

van Baar, A.L., Soepatmi, S., Gunning, W.B., et al. (1994). Development after prenatal exposure to cocaine, heroin and methadone. *Acta Paediatrica, 404,* 40–46.

Vega, W.A., Kolody, B., Hwang, J., et al. (1993). Prevalence and magnitude of perinatal substance exposures in California. *New England Journal of Medicine, 329*(12), 850–854.

Viscarello, R.R., Ferguson, D.D., Nores, J., et al. (1992). Limb–body wall complex associated with cocaine abuse: Further evidence of cocaine's teratogenicity. *Obstetrics and Gynecology, 80*(3 pt. 2), 523–526.

Wallace, J.M., Jr. (1999). The social ecology of addiction: Race, risk, and resilience. *Pediatrics, 103*(5 pt. 2), 1122–1127.

Wasserman, D.R., & Leventhal, J.M. (1993). Maltreatment of children born to cocaine-dependent mothers. *American Journal of the Diseases of Children, 147,* 1324–1328.

Wasserman, G.A., Kline, J.K., Bateman, D.A., et al. (1998). Prenatal cocaine exposure and school-age intelligence. *Drug and Alcohol Dependence, 50,* 203–210.

Werner, M.J., Joffe, A., & Graham, A.V. (1999). Screening, early identification, and office-based intervention with children and youth living in substance-abusing families. *Pediatrics, 103,* 1099–1112.

Williams-Petersen, M.G., Myers, B.J., Degen, H.M., et al. (1994). Drug-using and nonusing women: Potential for child abuse, child-rearing attitudes, social support, and affection for expected baby. *International Journal of the Addictions, 29*(12), 1631–1643.

Wilson, G.S. (1989). Clinical studies of infants and children exposed prenatally to heroin. *Annals of the New York Academy of Sciences, 562,* 183–194.

Wilson, G.S., Desmond, M.M., & Wait, R.B. (1981). Follow-up of methadone-treated and untreated narcotic-dependent women and their infants: Health, development, and social implications. *Journal of Pediatrics, 98*(5), 716–722.

Zuckerman, B., & Bresnahan, K. (1991). Developmental and behavioral consequences of prenatal drug and alcohol exposure. *Pediatric Clinics of North America, 38,* 1387–1406.

Zuckerman, B., & Frank, D.A. (1994). Prenatal cocaine exposure: Nine years later. *Journal of Pediatrics, 124,* 731–733.

Zuckerman, B., Frank, D.A., Hingson, R., et al. (1989). Effects of maternal marijuana and cocaine use on fetal growth. *New England Journal of Medicine, 320*(12), 762–768.

Appendix

Guidelines for the Care of Children and Adolescents with Prenatal Drug Exposure

Basic Team

The special care needs of children with prenatal drug exposure can be met by the primary care physician working collaboratively with parents, community health service providers, drug treatment programs, Child Protective Services, early intervention/early childhood special education (EI/ECSE) staff, and community services. Some children and families require referral to an experienced child development team headed by a developmental pediatrician, and other children may need referral to a child neurologist. Please note that the primary care physician continues to be responsible for coordinating the special services that these children may require. Most of these children follow a typical developmental course, and primary health care is their most common unmet need.

Regular members of the child development team include a developmental pediatrician, a psychologist, a speech-language pathologist, an occupational therapist, an audiologist, and a medical social worker. Many children do not require evaluation by all team members.

Initial Evaluation

The objectives of the initial evaluation of the newborn with prenatal drug exposure are to determine the presence of neurobehavioral abnormalities and the neonatal abstinence syndrome, to look for minor physical anomalies suggesting fetal alcohol syndrome, and to identify associated medical problems such as hepatitis B infection or human immunodeficiency virus infection. A primary responsibility of the primary care physician is to determine the need for involvement of Child Protective Services and to assist the family in identifying needed support services, including drug treatment for the mother.

Frequency of Visits

The infant and parent are best followed regularly in the primary care office in the first months following nursery discharge to monitor growth, feeding, sleep organization, and neurobehavioral status and to review the family's support needs. Then, follow the child and family per routine well-child visits. The child's neurobehavioral and developmental status and family stress and coping should be checked at each visit. In addition, the physician and office staff should have regular contact with other caregivers. The management plan should be updated as needed at each reevaluation.

Guidelines for the Care of Children and Adolescents with Prenatal Drug Exposure

The following elements are recommended by age group, and the listing is cumulative. Review all items indicated up through the actual age group of a child entering your practice for the first time as part of the initial evaluation.

AGE	KEY CLINICAL ISSUES/CONCERNS	EVALUATIONS/KEY PROCEDURES	SPECIALISTS
Birth–5 years (pre-school age)	*Growth/Nutrition* Microcephaly Intrauterine growth retardation (IUGR) Failure to thrive (FTT) Oral motor dysfunction	Obtain cranial ultrasound or computed tomography (CT) scan, evaluate for congenital infection as needed Growth parameters, diet history, feeding evaluation as needed	Nutritionist, feeding specialist as needed
	Associated Medical Problems Hearing/vision Neonatal abstinence syndrome (NAS) and neurobehavioral abnormalities Seizures Neuromotor problems (e.g., stiffness, tremulousness)	Hearing and vision testing, as needed Environmental/behavior management, occasionally short-term medications Electroencephalogram (EEG) Detailed neuromotor examination	Audiologist, ophthalmologist as needed Child neurologist as needed Physical therapist as needed
	Maternally transmitted infections (e.g., human immunodeficiency virus [HIV], hepatitis B and C, sexually transmitted diseases [STDs])	Perinatal HIV and hepatitis B core antigen (Hb_sAg) testing if not done prenatally, hepatitis B immunoglobulin (HBIG) and hepatitis B vaccine (HBV) to infant if mother is positive for Hb_sAg, test infant for other STDs as needed	Referral to HIV/infectious disease specialist as needed
	Sleep disorder	Behavior management, occasional short-term medications	
	Dental Care	Review oral hygiene	Dentist
	Associated Behavior/ Mental Health Problems Lethargy/poor quality of alertness (infant) Irritability (infant) Hyperactivity/inattention Aggression Oppositional behavior Attachment disorder Eating disorder	Family and teacher interviews, behavioral rating scales, and preschool information as needed Therapeutic child care as needed Parent training in behavior management	Referral to child development team, psychologist, child psychiatrist as needed
	Developmental Progress, Early Intervention/ Early Childhood Special Education (EI/ECSE) Services Language delay/speech-language disorder Developmental delay Evaluate for fetal alcohol syndrome (FAS)	Developmental screening and surveillance Evaluation for minor anomalies Early referral to community preschool or Head Start Referral for eligibility testing for EI/ECSE services as needed	Evaluation by child development team or individual evaluations by psychologist, speech-language pathologist as needed Referral to developmental pediatrician or medical geneticist as needed

The Physician's Guide to Caring for Children with Disabilities and Chronic Conditions, edited by Robert E. Nickel and Larry W. Desch, copyright © 2000 Paul H. Brookes Publishing Co.

Guidelines for the Care of Children and Adolescents with Prenatal Drug Exposure *(continued)*

The following elements are recommended by age group, and the listing is cumulative. Review all items indicated up through the actual age group of a child entering your practice for the first time as part of the initial evaluation.

AGE	KEY CLINICAL ISSUES/CONCERNS	EVALUATIONS/KEY PROCEDURES	SPECIALISTS
Birth–5 years (pre-school age) *continued*	*Behavior Management in the Home*	Family and teacher interviews, school report Referral to a birth-to-3 parent group Referral for parent training in behavior management as needed	Referral to mental health professional, child development team as needed Collaboration with preschool staff
	Behavior Management in the Preschool	Teacher interview, behavior rating scales or other method of data collection	Referral to mental health professional as needed Collaboration with preschool staff
	Family Support Services (*needs may be complex*) Respite care Community health nurse Drug treatment for parents Counseling, job training Advocacy Other enabling services	Family interview; use parent questionnaire (e.g., Family Needs Survey), provide resource information	Medical social worker, community health nurse, mental health specialist as needed
	Review of Diagnosis and Anticipatory Guidance Irritability/stiffness/tremulousness Need for positive discipline and consistency Accident prevention Transition to grade school	Family interview; provide educational materials Teacher interview, school report, review individualized family service plan (IFSP) with family as needed	Primary care office
	Collaboration with Community Agencies Child Protective Services Drug treatment programs (parent) EI/ECSE services County health department	Care coordination, regular information exchange with other caregivers	Primary care office
	Associated Learning Disabilities	Intellectual and achievement testing as needed	Referral to child development team as needed, collaborate with school staff

The Physician's Guide to Caring for Children with Disabilities and Chronic Conditions, edited by Robert E. Nickel and Larry W. Desch, copyright © 2000 Paul H. Brookes Publishing Co.

Guidelines for the Care of Children and Adolescents with Prenatal Drug Exposure *(continued)*

The following elements are recommended by age group, and the listing is cumulative. Review all items indicated up through the actual age group of a child entering your practice for the first time as part of the initial evaluation.

AGE	KEY CLINICAL ISSUES/CONCERNS	EVALUATIONS/KEY PROCEDURES	SPECIALISTS
6–12 years (school-age)	*Associated Behavior and Mental Health Problems* Attention-deficit/hyperactivity disorder (ADHD) Oppositional defiant disorder (ODD) Conduct disorder (CD) Anxiety Depression	Child, parent, and teacher interviews; behavioral rating scales; school report as noted previously Review medication management	Referral to mental health professional, child development team as needed
	Social Skills Involvement in peer-group activities at school and in community (determine which supports are needed) Promote social competence	School-based social skills program and referral to community services as needed	
	Anticipatory Guidance Sports and leisure activities (highly structured small-group activities, noncompetitive, adult supervision) Promote self-care and independence	Provide resource information and refer to community services as indicated	Primary care office Referral to physical or occupational therapists, adaptive physical education specialist as needed
13–21 years (adolescents–young adults)	*Anticipatory Guidance* Transition to middle school and high school Encourage healthy behaviors (e.g., diet, exercise) High-risk behaviors (e.g., substance use and abuse, sexuality) Career planning Transition to adult services and independent living	Adolescent, parent, and teacher interviews; school report and conference as needed Referral to career counseling, vocational specialist as needed	Primary care office in collaboration with school and mental health professional as needed Referral to gynecologist as needed
	Collaboration with Community Services School Mental health professional Child Protective Services	Regular exchange of information (at least yearly), care conference as needed	Primary care physician

The Physician's Guide to Caring for Children with Disabilities and Chronic Conditions, edited by Robert E. Nickel and Larry W. Desch, copyright © 2000 Paul H. Brookes Publishing Co.

Family and Physician Management Plan Summary for Children and Adolescents with Prenatal Drug Exposure and Their Families

This form will help you and your physician review current services and service needs. Please answer the questions about your current services on this page. Your physician will review your responses and complete the rest of the form.

Child's name _____ Today's date _____

Person completing the form _____

CURRENT SERVICES

1. Please list your/your child's current medications and any side effects.

2. What is your/your child's current school program?

   School name _____ Grade _____

   Teacher _____ Telephone _____

3. Do you/does your child receive any support services and other special programs at school (e.g., physical therapy, resource room)? Please list.

4. Who are your/your child's other medical and dental service providers?

   Dentist _____

   Neurologist _____

   Other _____

5. Who are your/your child's other community service providers?

   Behavior or mental health specialist _____

   _____

   Other _____

Family and Physician Management Plan Summary for Children and Adolescents with Prenatal Drug Exposure and Their Families *(continued)*

6. Do you also receive services from a child development team of specialists?

   Contact person _____

   Location _____

7. Have you/has your child had any blood tests, radiologic (X-ray) examinations, or other procedures since your last visit? If yes, please describe.

8. Have you/has your child been hospitalized or received surgery since your last visit? If yes, describe.

9. Please note accomplishments since your last visit. Consider activities at home, in your neighborhood, or at school, as well as success with treatments.

10. What goals (i.e., skills) would you/your child like to accomplish in the next year? Consider activities at home, in your neighborhood, or at school, as well as success with a treatment.

11. What questions or concerns would you like addressed today?

Family and Physician Management Plan Summary for Children and Adolescents with Prenatal Drug Exposure and Their Families

The Management Plan Summary should be completed at each annual review and more often as needed. It is intended to be used with the Guidelines for Care, which provide a more complete listing of clinical issues at different ages, as well as recommended evaluations and treatments.

Child's name _____ Person completing form _____ Today's date _____

Clinical issues	Currently a problem?	Evaluations needed	Treatment recommendations	Referrals made	Date for status check
Family's Questions					
Growth/Nutrition Intrauterine growth retardation (IUGR) Slow weight gain, failure to thrive (FTT)					
Associated Medical Problems Microcephaly Hearing loss Strabismus or vision problems Neurodevelopmental concerns (e.g., neonatal abstinence syndrome [NAS], difficult temperament) Seizures Maternally transmitted infections (e.g., human immunodeficiency virus [HIV], hepatitis B) Sleep disorder					
Dental Care					

The Physician's Guide to Caring for Children with Disabilities and Chronic Conditions, edited by Robert E. Nickel and Larry W. Desch, copyright © 2000 Paul H. Brookes Publishing Co.

Family and Physician Management Plan Summary for
Children and Adolescents with Prenatal Drug Exposure and Their Families *(continued)*

Child's name _____ Person completing form _____ Today's date _____

Clinical issues	Currently a problem?	Evaluations needed	Treatment recommendations	Referrals made	Date for status check
Associated Behavior/Mental Health Problems Inattention/hyperactivity Aggression Oppositional behaviors Anxiety, depression Attachment disorder High-risk behavior					
Associated Developmental/ Learning Problems Developmental surveillance Describe current school achievement Review early intervention (EI) or other school services (individualized family service plan [IFSP] or individualized education program [IEP]) Learning disability Speech-language disorder					
Physical Therapy (PT) or Occupational Therapy (OT) Services Hypertonicity in infancy Associated dyspraxia or cerebral palsy Questions about fine motor or visual motor skills					

The Physician's Guide to Caring for Children with Disabilities and Chronic Conditions, edited by Robert E. Nickel and Larry W. Desch, copyright © 2000 Paul H. Brookes Publishing Co.

Family and Physician Management Plan Summary for Children and Adolescents with Prenatal Drug Exposure and Their Families *(continued)*

Child's name _____ Person completing form _____ Today's date _____

Clinical issues	Currently a problem?	Evaluations needed	Treatment recommendations	Referrals made	Date for status check
Review of Behavior Questionnaires					
Behavior Management in the Home					
Behavior Management in the School					
Social Skills Involvement in group activities at school and in the community (determine which supports are needed)					
Self-Care and Independence					
Family Support Services					
Anticipatory Guidance List issues discussed and materials provided					

The Physician's Guide to Caring for Children with Disabilities and Chronic Conditions, edited by Robert E. Nickel and Larry W. Desch, copyright © 2000 Paul H. Brookes Publishing Co.

Family and Physician Management Plan Summary for
Children and Adolescents with Prenatal Drug Exposure and Their Families *(continued)*

Child's name _____   Person completing form _____   Today's date _____

Clinical Issues	Currently a problem?	Evaluations needed	Treatment recommendations	Referrals made	Date for status check
Collaboration with Community Agencies School Child Protective Services Drug treatment program (parent)					
Comments					

Next update of the Management Plan Summary _____

Signature _____ Date _____
　　　　　(Child and parent)

Signature _____ Date _____
　　　　　(Health professional)

The Physician's Guide to Caring for Children with Disabilities and Chronic Conditions, edited by Robert E. Nickel and Larry W. Desch, copyright © 2000 Paul H. Brookes Publishing Co.

RESOURCES ON PRENATAL DRUG EXPOSURE

Readings

Child Welfare League of America (CWLA). (1991). *Homeworks: At home training resources for foster and adoptive parents.* Edison, NJ: Author. (This is a series of three "self-instruction workshops" that can be used individually or in collaboration with a social worker. CWLA Publishing House: CWLA, c/o CSSC, P.O. Box 78161, Raritan Center Parkway, Edison, NJ 08818-7816; 908-225-1900. The titles of the workbooks include "Helping Children and Youth Manage Separation and Loss"; "Helping Children and Youth Develop Positive Attachments"; "Helping Children and Youth and Families Manage the Impact of Placement")

Cook, P.S., Petersen, R.C., & Moore, D.T. (1990). *Alcohol, tobacco, and other drugs may harm the unborn.* Washington, DC: U.S. Department of Health and Human Services, U.S. Public Health Service, Substance Abuse, Alcohol, Drug Abuse, and Mental Health Services Administration (SAMHSA), Center for Substance Abuse Prevention. (1-800-354-8824)

Dorris, M. (1989). *The broken cord: A family's ongoing struggle with fetal alcohol syndrome.* New York: Harper-Collins. (1-800-242-7737)

Edelstein, S.B., & Howard, J. (1995). *Children with prenatal, alcohol and or other drug exposure: Weighing the risks of adoption.* Washington, DC: Child Welfare League of America Press. (908-225-1900)

Fomufod, A.K. (Ed). (1992). *Substance use in pregnancy: Helping the mother.* Washington, DC: Howard University Hospital, Department of Pediatrics and Child Health.

(204 Georgia Avenue, N.W., Washington, DC 20060; telephone: 202-865-4564; attn: Davine White)

Kandall, S.R. (1993). *Improving treatment for drug-exposed infants: Treatment Improvement Protocol (TIP) series.* Rockville, MD: U.S. Department of Health and Human Services, U.S. Public Health Service, Substance Abuse and Mental Health Services Administration (SAMHSA), Center for Substance Abuse Treatment. (5600 Fishers Lane, Rockville, MD 20857; telephone: 301-443-3820)

National Institute on Drug Abuse (NIDA). *NIDA Notes.* Washington, DC: U.S. Department of Health and Human Services, Public Health Service, National Institutes of Health. (1-888-644-6432)

Soby, J.M. (1994). *Prenatal exposure to drugs–alcohol: Characteristics and educational implications of fetal alcohol syndrome and cocaine: Polydrug effects.* Springfield, IL: Charles C Thomas Publishing Co. (1-800-258-8980)

Streissguth, A.P. (1997). *Fetal alcohol syndrome: A guide for families and communities.* Baltimore: Paul H. Brookes Publishing Co. (1-800-638-3775)

U.S. Department of Health and Human Services. (1993). *Pregnancy and exposure to alcohol and other drug use.* Washington, DC: U.S. Department of Health and Human Services, U.S. Public Health Service, Substance Abuse and Mental Health Services Administration, Center for Substance Abuse and Mental Health Services Administration, Center for Substance Abuse Prevention. (1-800-354-8824)

National Organizations

Center for Substance Abuse Prevention (CSAP), Substance Abuse and Mental Health Services Administration (SAMHSA)
5600 Fishers Lane, Rockwall II
Rockville, Maryland 20857
Telephone: (301) 443-0365
E-mail: nnadal@samhsa.gov
World Wide Web site: http://www.samhsa.gov/csap/index.htm

CSAP provides information and referrals, as well as links to other agencies; its services include the National Clearinghouse for Alcohol and Drug Information (NCCD) (http://www.health.org).

Center for Substance Abuse Treatment (CSAT), Substance Abuse and Mental Health Services Administration (SAMHSA)
5600 Fishers Lane, Rockwall II
Rockville, Maryland 20857
Telephone: (301) 443-3820
E-mail: lyoung@samhsa.gov
World Wide Web site: http://www.samhsa.gov/csat/csat.htm

CSAT provides information and referrals as well as links to other agencies; it provides a national drug and alcohol treatment routing service (1-800-622-HELP).

The National Center on Addiction and Substance Abuse (CASA) at Columbia University
Columbia University
152 West 57th Street, 12th floor
New York, New York 10019-3310
Telephone: (212) 841-5200
Fax: (212) 956-8020
World Wide Web site: http://www.casacolumbia.org/

CASA provides information and referrals, as well as links to other organizations.

National Organization on Fetal Alcohol Syndrome
418 C Street NE
Washington, D.C. 20002
Telephone: (202) 785-4585
Fax: (202) 466-6456
E-mail: nofas@erols.com
World Wide Web site: http://www.nofas.org/

This national information and advocacy group is dedicated to eliminating birth defects caused by maternal alcohol consumption during pregnancy and to improving the quality of life of those families and individuals who are affected by fetal alcohol syndrome.

12

Human Immunodeficiency Virus Infection

Robert E. Nickel

KEY COMPETENCIES

- Discuss the classification of human immunodeficiency virus (HIV) infection in children and adolescents
- Describe the modes of transmission of the HIV virus and factors that may increase the likelihood of maternal-to-infant transmission
- Describe the clinical problems of children and adolescents with acquired immunodeficiency syndrome (AIDS)
- Review the developmental and learning problems of children with HIV infection
- Counsel the family of child with HIV infection about HIV infection and AIDS
- List the advantages of a prompt diagnosis of HIV infection in pregnant women and infants
- Review the zidovudine (ZDV) treatment protocol to decrease mother–infant HIV transmission
- Review the general treatment recommendations for children and adolescents with HIV infection, including prophylaxis against *pneumocystis carinii* pneumonia (PCP)
- Discuss the comprehensive service needs of these children and families

DESCRIPTION

Definitions

Acquired immunodeficiency syndrome (AIDS) is the symptomatic clinical manifestation of impaired cellular immunity due to infection with the human immunodeficiency virus type 1 (HIV-1). The first cases of AIDS in adults were reported in 1981 and in children 1 year later (Conlon, 1992). The virus responsible for AIDS was first termed the *lymphadenopathy associated virus* (LAV) by French scientists and *human T-lymphotropic virus-III* (HTLV-III) by U.S. investigators (Parks, 1987). Subsequently, the name *human immunodeficiency virus* (HIV) became generally accepted.

AIDS in children and adolescents is still a uniformly fatal illness that is characterized by multi-system involvement including lymphadenopathy, recurrent infections, malignancies, and a progressive encephalopathy. The time from age of diagnosis of the HIV infection to the onset of symptoms and the diagnosis of AIDS varies considerably from child to child. In one study (Pliner, Weedon, Thomas, et al., 1998), the mean age of onset of AIDS was 4.1 years. Forty-eight percent of children infected with HIV perinatally had developed AIDS by 3 years of age; however, it was estimated that 33% would remain AIDS-free to 13 years of age. The use of newer, more potent antiretroviral drugs provides hope that the progression of the disease can be slowed, and prospective identification and treatment of pregnant women with HIV infection will reduce the incidence of perinatal transmission (Melvin & Frenkel, 1997–1998).

Classification

Infants and Children   A revised classification system for HIV infection in children (younger than 13 years of age) was published by the U.S. Public Health Service in 1994 (Centers for Disease Control and Prevention [CDC], 1994b). In this system, children are classified into different categories based on infection status, clinical status, and immunologic status. Table 12.1 presents the overall classification of pediatric HIV infections in children. Tables 12.2, 12.3, and 12.4 present the infection, clinical, and immunologic categories necessary for classification. Children are placed in one of four clinical categories: N (asymptomatic), A (mildly symptomatic), B (moderately symptomatic), and C (severely symptomatic). The letter classification is followed by a number that indicates the immunologic status of the child (e.g., N1 for asymptomatic and no evidence of suppression). Children who are exposed to HIV perinatally (HIV infection status not determined) are identified by placing an E in front of the letter and number (e.g., EN1).

Adolescents   HIV infection and AIDS are classified in the same way with regard to adolescents (i.e., individuals 13–19 years of age) as they are in

Table 12.1.   Pediatric human immunodeficiency virus (HIV) classification

	Clinical categories			
Immunologic categories	N: No signs/ symptoms	A: Mild signs/ symptoms	B: Moderate signs/symptoms	C: Severe signs/symptoms
1: No evidence of suppression	N1	A1	B1	C1
2: Evidence of moderate suppression	N2	A2	B2	C2
3: Severe suppression	N3	A3	B3	C3

From Centers for Disease Control and Prevention (CDC). (1994b). Revised classification system for human immunodeficiency virus infection in children less than 13 years of age. *Morbidity and Mortality Weekly Report, 43*(RR-12), 2.

Children whose HIV infection status is not confirmed are classified by using this grid with a letter E (for perinatally exposed) placed before the appropriate classification code (e.g., EN2).

Table 12.2. Infection status

HIV-Infected

1. A child < 18 months of age who is known to be HIV seropositive or born to an HIV-infected mother or whose mode of transmission is unknown

   - Has positive results on two separate determinations (excluding cord blood) using one or more of the following HIV detection tests:
     HIV virus culture
     HIV polymerase chain reaction (PCR)
     HIV antigen (p24) (not recommended as the only test) OR
   - Meets diagnosis of AIDS based on the 1987 AIDS case definition

2. A child ≥ 18 months of age born to an HIV-infected mother or a child infected by blood, blood products, or other known mode of transmission such as sexual contact who

   - Is HIV antibody positive by repeated reactive enzyme immunoassay (EIA) and confirmatory test (e.g., Western blot, immunofluorescence assay [IFA]) OR
   - Meets any of the criteria in (1) above

Perinatally Exposed (Prefix E)

A child who does not meet the criteria above who

- Is HIV seropositive by EIA and confirmatory test (e.g., Western blot, IFA) and < 18 months old at the time of test OR
- Has unknown antibody status but was born to a mother known or assumed to be HIV-infected

Seroreverter (SR)

Age equivalent child born to an HIV-infected mother who

- Has been documented to be HIV antibody negative (two or more negative EIA tests after 6 months of age) AND
- Has no other laboratory evidence of infection (has not had two positive viral detection tests if performed) AND
- Has not had an AIDS-defining condition

From Centers for Disease Control and Prevention (CDC). (1994b). Revised classification system for human immunodeficiency virus infection in children less than 13 years of age. *Morbidity and Mortality Weekly Report, 43*(RR-12), 3.

adults. Adolescents acquire HIV infection primarily by engaging in high-risk behaviors, including intravenous drug use (IVDU) and unprotected sex with an infected partner. HIV infection in women in the northwestern and southern United States is often *not* associated with drug use. Table 12.5 lists the indicator diseases in the 1987 surveillance case definition for AIDS in adolescents and adults. This list has been expanded to also include all HIV-infected people who have

- Less than 200 CD_4+ (T-helper lymphocytes) count or T lymphocyte (thymus-derived lymphocytes) percentage of total lymphocytes less than 14%
- Pulmonary tuberculosis

Table 12.3. Clinical status

Category N: Not Symptomatic

Children who have no signs or symptoms considered to be the result of HIV infection or who have only 1 of the conditions listed in Category A

Category A: Mildly Symptomatic

Children who have two or more of the conditions listed below but none of the conditions listed in Categories B and C

- Lymphadenopathy (≥ 0.5 cm at ≥ 2 sites; bilateral = 1 site)
- Hepatomegaly
- Splenomegaly
- Dermatitis
- Parotitis
- Recurrent or persistent upper respiratory infection, sinusitis, or otitis media

Category B: Moderately Symptomatic

Children who have symptomatic conditions attributed to HIV infection other than those listed in Category A or C. Examples of conditions in clinical Category B include *but are not limited to*

- Anemia (< 8 gm/dl), neutropenia (< 1,000/mm), or thrombocytopenia (< 100,000/mm) persisting ≥ 30 days
- Bacterial meningitis, pneumonia, or sepsis (single episode)
- Candidiasis, oropharyngeal (thrush), persisting (> 2 months) in child > 6 months of age
- Cardiomyopathy
- Cytomegalovirus infection, with onset before 1 month of age
- Diarrhea, recurrent or chronic
- Hepatitis
- Herpes simplex stomatitis, recurrent (≥ 2 episodes within 1 year)
- Herpes simplex virus (HSV), bronchitis, pneumonitis, or esophagitis with onset before 1 month of age
- Herpes zoster (shingles) involving at least two distinct episodes or more than one dermatome
- Leiomyosarcoma
- Lymphoid interstitial pneumonia or pulmonary lymphoid hyperplasia complex (LIP/PLH)
- Nephropathy
- Nocardiosis
- Persistent fever > 1 month
- Toxoplasmosis, onset before 1 month of age
- Varicella, disseminated (complicated chickenpox)

Category C: Severely Symptomatic

Children who have any condition listed in the 1987 surveillance case definition for AIDS, with the exception of LIP

From Centers for Disease Control and Prevention (CDC). (1994b). Revised classification system for human immunodeficiency virus infection in children less than 13 years of age. *Morbidity and Mortality Weekly Report, 43*(RR-12), 6.

- Recurrent bacterial pneumonia
- Invasive cervical cancer (CDC, 1993)

Prevalence

Children younger than 13 years of age represent approximately .4% and adolescents (13–19 years of

Table 12.4.   Immunologic status

Immunologic category	Age of child		
	0–11 months	1–5 years	6–12 years
1. No evidence of suppression	≥ 1,500 (≥ 25%)	≥ 1,000 (≥ 25%)	≥ 500 (≥ 25%)
2. Evidence of moderate suppression	75–1,499 (15%–24%)	500–999 (15%–24%)	200–499 (15%–24%)
3. Severe suppression	< 750 (< 15%)	< 500 (< 15%)	< 200 (< 15%)

From Centers for Disease Control and Prevention (CDC). (1994b). Revised classification system for human immunodeficiency virus infection in children less than 13 years of age. *Morbidity and Mortality Weekly Report, 43*(RR-12), 6.

age) represent .5% of all cases of AIDS reported in the United States for the period October 1992–September 1993 (CDC, 1994c). AIDS was the seventh leading cause of death for children 1–4 years of age in 1992 (National Center for Health Statistics, 1993) and the sixth leading cause of death for children 5–14 years of age in the United States in 1997 (CDC, 1998a). For every child diagnosed with AIDS, however, it is estimated that there are 10 children with HIV infection (Gwynn, Pappaioanou, George, et al., 1991).

In the United States, the HIV seroprevalence among women giving birth remained stable from 1989 to 1994 at 1.5–1.7 per 1,000 women (Davis, Rosen, Steinberg, et al., 1998). Because almost all children with HIV are infected by perinatal transmission, the incidence of new HIV infection in children can be estimated from the number of births to women with HIV infection. For example, approximately 6,600 infants were born to mothers with HIV infection in 1993 (Bertolli, Caldwell, Lindgren, et al., 1995). The rate of transmission is estimated at 15%–25%; therefore, 900–1,650 infants were born infected with HIV in 1993 (Bertolli, Caldwell, Lindgren, et al., 1995). The rate of transmission is potentially lower (8%) with antenatal treatment of the mother with zidovudine (ZDV) and postnatal treatment of the infant (see subsequent discussion under the "Use of Zidovudine" heading in this chapter).

Black children account for approximately 50% and Hispanic children 25% of all pediatric AIDS cases (Bertolli et al., 1995). The majority of all cases (54% in 1993) reported were in four states (New York, New Jersey, Florida, and California), and five cities (Miami; Newark, N.J.; New York; Philadelphia; and Washington, D.C.) accounted for 40% of prenatally acquired AIDS cases in 1993. Thus, HIV infection in children is strongly linked to large, urban minority populations. HIV infection, however, is becoming more widespread. The HIV sero-

prevalence in childbearing women increased in the South through 1991 and then stabilized through 1994, and the seroprevalence in the Northeast declined from 1989 through 1994 (Davis et al., 1998). The revision of the surveillance case definition of AIDS in 1993 resulted in a significant increase (111%) in the prevalence of AIDS for that year compared with 1992 (CDC, 1994c). The new definition included more women and more intravenous drug users (Chaisson, Stanton, Gallant, et al., 1993).

Etiology

Virus   HIV is a retrovirus. This family of viruses is characterized by diploid linear single-stranded ribonucleic acid (RNA) that is surrounded by a protein capsid and a glycoprotein coat (Parks, 1987). The glycoprotein coat or envelope contains a region for attachment to the host cell and a region to which neutralizing antibodies can bind. Both are important to the virus' infectivity. Parts of the envelope are highly variable from virus to virus, and this characteristic appears to be important in allowing "escape" from immunologic control. Figure 12.1 depicts the life cycle of the virus CD_4+ or helper T_4 lymphocyte. HIV infection results in immunosuppression by causing both T-cell abnormalities (e.g., decrease in CD_4+ cells and cell-mediated immunity) and B-cell (bone marrow–derived lymphocytes) abnormalities (e.g., failure to produce antibody after immunization and hypergammaglobulinemia) (Amman, 1987).

Transmission

Infants and Children   Before 1985, the majority of cases of AIDS in children 1–12 years of age were caused by contaminated blood products or clotting factors (Conlon, 1992). With the universal screening of blood donors and the heat treatment of clotting products, however, estimates in the mid-1990s of the risk of HIV transmission from transfusion were 1 per 500,000 (Lackritz, Satten, Aberle-Grasse, et al.,

Table 12.5. Revision of case definition for acquired immunodeficiency syndrome (AIDS) for surveillance purposes: Indicator diseases

- Candidiasis of the esophagus, trachea, bronchi, or lungs
- Cryptococcosis, extrapulmonary
- Cryptosporidiosis with diarrhea persisting > 1 month
- Cytomegalovirus disease of an organ other than liver, spleen, or lymph nodes in a patient > 1 month of age
- Herpes simplex virus infection causing a mucocutaneous ulcer that persists longer than 1 month; or bronchitis, pneumonitis, or esophagitis for any duration affecting a patient > 1 month of age
- Kaposi's sarcoma
- Lymphoma of the brain (primary)
- Lymphoid interstitial pneumonia and/or pulmonary lymphoid hyperplasias (LIP/PLH complex) affecting a child < 13 years of age
- *Mycobacterium avium* complex or *M. Kansasii* disease, disseminated (at a site other than or in addition to lungs, skin, or cervical or hilar lymph nodes)
- *Pneumocystis carinii* pneumonia
- Progressive multifocal leukoencephalopathy
- Toxoplasmosis of the brain affecting a patient 1 month of age
- Bacterial infections, multiple or recurrent (any combination of at least two within a 2-year period), of the following types affecting a child < 13 years of age: Septicemia, pneumonia, meningitis, bone or joint infection, or abscess of an internal organ or body cavity (excluding otitis media or superficial skin or mucosal abscesses) caused by *Haemophilus*, *Streptococcus* (including pneumococcus) or other pyogenic bacteria
- Coccidioidomycosis, disseminated (at a site other than or in addition to lungs or cervical or hilar lymph nodes)
- HIV encephalopathy (also called "HIV dementia," "AIDS dementia," or "subacute encephalitis due to HIV")
- Histoplasmosis, disseminated (at a site other than or in addition to lungs or cervical or hilar lymph nodes)
- Isosporiasis with diarrhea persisting > 1 month
- Other non-Hodgkin's lymphoma of B-cell or unknown immunologic phenotype and the following histologic types:
  a. Small noncleaved lymphoma (either Burkitt or non-Burkitt type)
  b. Immunoblastic sarcoma (equivalent to any of the following, although not necessarily all in combination: immunoblastic lymphoma, large-cell lymphoma, diffuse histiocytic lymphoma, diffuse undifferentiated lymphoma, or high-grade lymphoma)
  Note: Lymphomas are not included here if they are of T-cell immunologic phenotype or if their histologic type is not described or is described as "lymphocytic," "lymphoblastic," "small cleaved," or "plasmacytoid lymphocytic."
- Any mycobacterial disease caused by mycobacteria other than *M. Tuberculosis*, disseminated (at a site other than or in addition to lungs, skin, or cervical or hilar lymph nodes)
- Disease caused by *M. tuberculosis*, extrapulmonary (involving at least one site outside the lungs, regardless of whether there is concurrent pulmonary involvement)
- Salmonella (nontyphoid) septicemia, recurrent
- HIV wasting syndrome (emaciation, "slim disease")

From Centers for Disease Control and Prevention (CDC). (1994b). Revised classification system for human immunodeficiency virus infection in children less than 13 years of age. *Morbidity and Mortality Weekly Report, 43*(RR-12), 4S–5S.

1995). During the 1990s, almost all new cases of HIV infection in children resulted from perinatal transmission (Bertolli et al., 1995; CDC 1997). In one study (Bertolli et al., 1995), only 5% of cases in children were the result of blood transfusion or a use of clotting factors, 1.5% had no risk factor identified, and two cases were from HIV-seronegative blood donors who later seroconverted. As of June 1994, a total of seven cases of AIDS infection in children involved sexual contact with an adult as a possible mode of transmission (Bertolli et al., 1995).

In the early 1990s, the rate of mother–infant transmission in the United States was 15%–25% (Working Group on Mother-to-Child Transmission of HIV, 1995). Transmission of HIV can be *in utero*, *during labor and delivery*, and *through breast feeding*. In utero transmission has been documented (Peckham

& Gibb, 1995) by the identification of HIV in aborted fetal tissue (Phuapradit, Panburana, Jaovisidha, et al., 1999) and is supported by the observation that about 30%–50% of infants with HIV infection have HIV in their blood in the first week of life (Peckham & Gibb, 1995). HIV has been cultured from breast milk, and late postpartum transmission has been documented (Leroy, Newell, Dabis, et al., 1998) in developing countries where breast feeding is the norm. Breast feeding is contraindicated for HIV-infected mothers in developed (i.e., industrialized) countries.

The factors that increase the likelihood of mother-to-infant transmission include

- High viral load (maternal HIV-1 ribonucleic acid [RNA] levels) with low CD_4+ count and advanced clinical disease in the mother

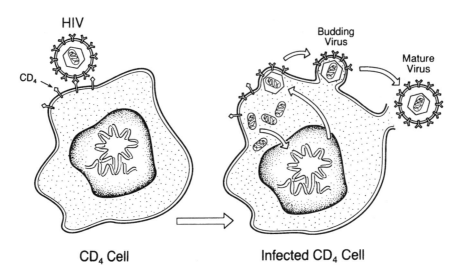

Figure 12.1.   Destruction of T$_4$(CD$_4$) cells by HIV. The CD$_4$ lymphocyte is critical to immune defense and its destruction is the major cause of the progressive immunodeficiency disorder that is the hallmark of HIV infection. One mechanism of destruction involves HIV entering and replicating in the CD$_4$ cell and then budding from the damaging cell membrane. (From Conlon, C.J. [1993]. New threats to development in children with disabilities. In M.L. Batshaw & Y.M. Perret [Eds.], *Children with disabilities: A medical primer* [3rd ed., p. 123]. Baltimore: Paul H. Brookes Publishing Co.; reprinted by permission.)

- Chorioamnionitis
- Sexually transmitted diseases (STDs)
- Vaginal delivery
- Other possible factors
  a. Prematurity
  b. Use of forceps and/or scalp electrodes
  c. Episiotomy, vaginal lacerations, and/or traumatic delivery
  d. Prolonged rupture of fetal membranes (European Collaborative Study, 1999; Mofenson, Lambert, Stiehm, et al., 1999; Peckham & Gibb, 1995)

The maternal HIV-1 RNA level is an important determinant of the risk of transmission (European Collaborative Study, 1999; Mofenson et al., 1999). In a study (Mofenson et al., 1999) of 480 women taking zidovudine and their infants, transmission did not occur if the maternal HIV-1 RNA levels were less than 500 copies per milliliter. A metaanalysis (International Perinatal HIV Group, 1999) of data from 15 studies reported a reduction of transmission by approximately 50% for infants delivered by elective cesarean section. In a study (Towers, Deveikis, Asrat, et al., 1998), that involved 108 individuals, the rate of mother–infant transmission of HIV infection was 5.7% for infants delivered by "bloodless" cesarean section and 20% in the control group. Another study (European Collaborative Study, 1999) reported significant reduction in transmission for pregnant women with HIV infection who had had elective cesarean sections independent of the maternal HIV-1 RNA levels.

Clinical Problems

Identification and treatment of pregnant women with HIV infection, treatment of infants with HIV exposure, and the use of prophylaxis for *pneumocystis carinii* pneumonia (PCP) can delay the onset of symptoms markedly in infants who are HIV-infected (Maldonado, Araneta, & Hersh, 1998). Lymphadenopathy (69.5%), splenomegaly (62.4%), and hepatomegaly (58.4%) were the most common signs of HIV infection in the first year (Galli, de Martino, Toro, et al., 1995). Early onset of clinical signs, early positive viral culture (indicating in utero transmission), high viral load, and thymic dysfunction (CD4 and CD8 counts less than 5% of expected) predict those infants who will experience rapid progression of HIV infection (Diaz, Hanson, Cooper, et al., 1998; Dickover, Dillon, Leung, et al., 1998; Nahmais, Clark, Kourtis, et al., 1998; Shearer, Quinn, LaRussa, et al., 1997).

Acquired Immunodeficiency Syndrome Indicator Diagnoses   Table 12.6 lists the most common AIDS indicator diagnoses. The peak age of onset for PCP is 3–6 months. It has a high mortality rate and is generally a poor prognostic sign (Peckham & Gibb, 1995). HIV encephalopathy is common in infants with rapid clinical progression. Opportunistic infections include PCP; cytomegalovirus (CMV); and Epstein-Barr virus (EBV), which also may be involved in the pathogenesis of lymphocytic interstitial pneumonia (LIP) (Peckham & Gibb, 1995). In a cohort of children receiving antiretroviral treatment

Table 12.6. Most common acquired immunodeficiency syndrome (AIDS) indicator diseases among 5,734 pediatric AIDS cases reported in the United States through June 1994

Indicator disease	Number of cases	Percentage
Pneumocystis carinii pneumonia	2,041	36
Lymphoid interstitial pneumonia	1,385	24
Recurrent serious bacterial infections	1,138	20
Candida esophagitis	884	15
Wasting syndrome	820	14
Human immunodeficiency virus (HIV) encephalopathy	781	14
Cytomegalovirus disease	457	8
Mycobacterium avium complex	357	6
Candidiasis of lung	229	4
Chronic herpes simplex	226	4

From Bertolli et al. (1995). Epidemiology of HIV disease in children. *Immunology and Allergy Clinics of North America, 15*(2), 200; reprinted with permission from W.B. Saunders Co.

Note: Some children have more than one diagnosis.

and PCP prophylaxis, the most common AIDS indicator diagnoses were LIP (54%), wasting syndrome (29%), esophagitis (21%), and encephalopathy (17%) (Oleske, 1994).

Children with Rapid Progression or Slow Progression Almost all newborns who are infected with HIV are asymptomatic. Studies have confirmed that there is a group of children with rapid progression of symptoms (about 15%–25%) and a group of children whose progression is much slower (Peckham & Gibb, 1995). Many of the individuals in the group with rapid progression have an AIDS diagnosis prior to 1 year of age, whereas the other group has a median age of 6 years for the diagnosis of AIDS (Bertolli et al., 1995). Persaud and co-workers (1992) reported on 32 children whose HIV infection was first diagnosed at 4 years of age or older. The median age of diagnosis was 6.1 years. Eight individuals (25%) were asymptomatic at their initial visit; however, six of the eight had lymphadenopathy but no hepatosplenomegaly, and one had lymphadenopathy and hepatosplenomegaly. Ten of the twenty-four symptomatic children (42%) had recurrent bacterial infections. A small but increasing subgroup of children who do not develop AIDS until they are older than 10 years of age has been identified. With current management, as many as 33% of children with HIV infection are expected to survive into adolescence without developing AIDS (Pliner et al., 1998).

Human Immunodeficiency Virus Encephalopathy Progressive neurologic problems have been reported in 9%–19% of infants and children with HIV infection in Europe (CDC, 1994b). Studies (Cooper, Hanson, Diaz, et al., 1998; Lobato, Caldwell, Ng, et al., 1995; Roy, Geoffroy, Lapointe, et al., 1992) in the United States have reported progressive encephalopathy in 20%–30% of children with HIV infection. Cooper and co-workers (1998) found that progressive encephalopathy was diagnosed in 21% of children with HIV infection. It was the first AIDS-defining condition in 67% of these children and was associated with high viral load, immunodeficiency, and shortened survival.

Common presentations include developmental regression, loss of motor milestones, and spasticity. In fact, an infant with HIV encephalopathy can present similarly to an infant with the spastic diplegia form of cerebral palsy. Neurologic signs may also include ataxia, tremors, bradykinesia, and dysphagia (Zuckerman, Sanchez, & Conway, 1998). Most children with HIV encephalopathy show cerebral atrophy on a computed tomography (CT) or magnetic resonance imaging (MRI) scan. Approximately 30% show calcification of the basal ganglia (Kauffman, Sivit, Fitz, et al., 1992; Roy et al., 1992). Children with basal ganglia calcification on the CT scan and those with decreasing or low CD_4+ counts may be particularly at risk for progressive encephalopathy (Fowler, 1994). Pathological studies (see, e.g., Wiestler, Leib, Brustle, et al., 1992) have shown a leukoencephalopathy (loss of myelin and absence of inflammation) as well as encephalitis (inflammatory reaction with multinucleated giant cells). Opportunistic infections, tumors, and/or hemorrhage can also cause focal or diffuse central nervous system (CNS) pathology in the child with AIDS.

Developmental, Learning, Emotional, and Behavior Problems Developmental problems have been reported in 75%–90% of children with HIV infection (CDC, 1994b). In the older child, these include inattention, memory problems, depression, learning disabilities, visual-perceptual problems, and speech-language disorder. Papola and co-workers (1994) studied the learning problems of 86 school-age children, 44% of whom were functioning in the low average to average range of intelligence and 56% of whom were functioning in the borderline range or lower. Of the children studied, 50% had language impairments and 42% had emotional or behavioral disorders. In the younger child, developmental problems include developmental delay, language delay, and gross motor delay. Children may show a loss of skills or developmental regression, or they may exhibit a plateau in skill acquisition. In a study by Coplan and co-workers (1998), language delay was the first sign of developmental regression in young children with HIV infection.

Clinical Problems of Older Children Some children who do not show symptoms until 6–7 years of age develop chronic pulmonary problems related to LIP and recurrent bacterial infections. In one study (Oleske, 1994), respiratory problems occurred in 79 of 93 school-age children with HIV infection. LIP is a chronic, progressive lung disease characterized by diffuse interstitial thickening of the lungs, with occasional nodules (Pitt, 1991). On microscopic examination, diffuse infiltration with lymphocytes and plasma cells is apparent. Pitt (1991) found that LIP occurred in 30%–50% of children with perinatally acquired HIV and was associated with hypoxia and oxygen dependence (Pitt, 1991). In the Pacific Northwest region of the United States, LIP is encountered rarely with current management (L. Frenkel, personal communication, March 1996).

Older children and adolescents with HIV infection may have multisystem involvement with a number of associated disorders in the heart (cardiomyopathy), gastrointestinal (GI) tract (e.g., chronic diarrhea, malabsorption, esophagitis), liver (e.g., hepatitis), kidneys (e.g., nephrotic syndrome, renal failure [rarely]), pancreas (e.g., pancreatitis), and skin disorders. Malignancies include non-Hodgkin's lymphomas and leiomyosarcoma (Oleske, 1994). One of the more debilitating problems for older children with HIV infection is chronic wasting as a result of multiple oral and GI complications.

Grubman and co-workers (1995) reported on 42 children older than 9 years of age at the time of the study who were infected with HIV perinatally.

Among this group, 36 (85.7%) had experienced the onset of symptoms after age 48 months. The median age at follow-up was 12 years, 10 months. Of the total sample studied, 23.8% remained asymptomatic. Table 12.7 lists the AIDS-defining illnesses noted in the symptomatic children whom Grubman and colleagues studied. Seventy-six percent of the children were orphaned because of their mothers' deaths. In addition, 76% were in general classes (one third were behind in academic areas), and 23.8% were in special education classes.

Differences Between Pediatric and Adult Cases of Acquired Immunodeficiency Syndrome The major differences between AIDS in children and AIDS in adolescents and adults include

- Children have a more rapid onset of clinical symptoms and more rapid progression to death.
- Serious bacterial sepsis is a major problem in children.
- Acute mononucleosis-like presentation is rare in children.
- Progressive neurologic disease due to primary HIV infection is more pronounced in children.
- LIP is more common in children.
- Kaposi's sarcoma is rare in children.
- Hypergammaglobulinemia may be pronounced in children (Barrett, 1988).

Factors that May Contribute to Developmental and Behavior Problems

HIV infection in women is associated with IVDU, particularly in the northeastern United States. In fact, investigators have referred to the *dual epidemics* of HIV and drug abuse. Women who abuse drugs are more likely to be single, poor, and urban and to smoke cigarettes and drink alcohol (please review Chapter 11). Maternal HIV infection is independently associated with infants' low birth weight and prematurity (Abrams, Matheson, Thomas, et al.,

Table 12.7. AIDS-defining conditions in children older than 7 years of age who were infected perinatally

Lymphocytic interstitial pneumonia (LIP)	31.0%
Wasting syndrome	16.7
Candida esophagitis	11.9
Progressive encephalitis	11.9
Pneumocystis carinii pneumonia (PCP)	4.8
Mycobacterium avium complex	4.8
Herpes simplex—persistent/extensive	2.4
Pulmonary tuberculosis	4.8
CD$_4$+ count less than 200 and child older than 13 years of age	16.7

Adapted from Grubman et al. (1995).

1995; Temmerman, Chomba, Ndinya-Achda, et al., 1994). Prenatal maternal alcohol and drug abuse compound these problems (Mauri, 1995). Prenatal maternal alcohol and other drug abuse are also associated with long-term developmental and behavioral consequences for children, including developmental delay, inattention, and hyperactivity. This situation may be further complicated by the death of a parent, an inadequate caregiving environment in the biological home, care in a sequence of foster homes, or prolonged hospitalizations. In addition, limited data are available on the potential deleterious effects of antiretroviral drugs on the developing fetus.

DIAGNOSIS AND EVALUATION

Advantages of a Prompt Diagnosis of Human Immunodeficiency Virus in Pregnant Women

A prompt diagnosis of HIV infection in pregnant women is critical to

- Allow antenatal treatment of the mother and postnatal treatment of the infant with HIV exposure with ZDV to decrease the risk of mother–infant transmission
- Provide prophylaxis against PCP to all infants who have been exposed to HIV
- Instruct the mother with HIV to avoid breast feeding her infant
- Allow early identification and treatment of the infant with HIV infection
- Modify the immunization schedule for the infant with HIV infection
- Provide careful follow-up and prompt treatment of infections in the infant with HIV infection

Who Should Be Tested for Human Immunodeficiency Virus Infection?

The following individuals should be tested for HIV infection:

- Individuals with high-risk behaviors
- All pregnant women
- Mothers with risk factors who were not tested during their pregnancies
- Infants and children with atypical or unusual illnesses suggestive of HIV

Individuals with High-Risk Behaviors High-risk behaviors include IVDU, history of STDs, and high-risk sexual practices (e.g., failure to use condoms, multiple sexual partners). Physicians and nurses must include detailed drug and sexual histories (and related counseling) as part of routine adolescent health care. Studies have shown that the

great majority of adolescents want information about HIV, STDs, and safe sex. They prefer, however, that the health care professional initiate the discussion (Rawitscher, Saitz, & Friedman, 1995). In addition, a significant percentage of adolescents with high-risk behaviors obtain HIV testing if it is offered confidentially. In one study (Goodman, Tipton, Hecht, et al., 1994), 41% of adolescent females with high-risk behaviors obtained testing the same day as their scheduled appointment in a general pediatrics clinic.

All Pregnant Women The CDC (1995b) and the American College of Obstetricians and Gynecologists and the American Academy of Pediatrics (1995) jointly recommended that all pregnant women should receive HIV education and counseling, as well as HIV testing with their consent. Maldonado and co-workers (1995) showed that a significant percentage (24%) of women with HIV infection report no risk factor, a significant percentage of infants with HIV infection are asymptomatic, and a comprehensive prenatal HIV screening program is strongly correlated with an early age at diagnosis of HIV infection in these infants. The failure of some women with HIV infection to receive prenatal care has been a critical obstacle to implementing these recommendations fully. From 1993 to 1996, the percentage of pregnant women who were offered prenatal treatment with ZDV and in whom HIV infection was diagnosed prior to delivery increased from 68% to 81% in Louisiana, Michigan, New Jersey, and South Carolina (CDC, 1998e).

Mothers with Risk Factors Who Were Not Tested During their Pregnancies Mothers with risk factors who were not tested during pregnancy should be tested for HIV as well as for hepatitis B (hepatitis B surface antigen [HB$_s$Ag] testing). Women who use intravenous drugs or who do not practice safe sex are at high risk for chronic hepatitis B infection as well as for HIV infection. If the mother is HB$_s$Ag-positive, the infant should receive passive immunization (hepatitis B immunoglobulin [HBIG]) promptly after birth, as well as active immunization.

Infants and Children with Atypical or Unusual Illnesses Suggestive of Human Immunodeficiency Virus The illnesses suggestive of HIV infection include AIDS-indicator diseases and the following:

- Diffuse lymphadenopathy with or without hepatosplenomegaly
- Persistent or recurrent infections that are not responsive to the usual treatments

- Children with developmental delay or apparent motor delay and spasticity, especially if they have experienced a loss of skills
- Children with failure to thrive (FTT) or chronic diarrhea
- Malignancies that are highly associated with HIV infection (e.g., leiomyosarcoma)

Human Immunodeficiency
Virus Testing Methodology

The diagnosis of HIV infections in infants born to mothers with HIV infection can be made by growing the virus in culture, detection of the viral genome by polymerase chain reaction (PCR), viral antigen (p24) testing, or detection of the HIV antibody after the age of 18 months (Peckham & Gibb, 1995). The sensitivity of viral culture or PCR is only approximately 40% in the first week of life but 90% (or higher for PCR) after 1 month of age. A definite diagnosis in an infant requires a positive result by HIV culture, PCR, or antigen testing on *two* separate occasions. Viral culture and PCR are the preferred tests to establish the diagnosis of HIV infection in infants. PCR for viral RNA may be more sensitive than PCR for viral deoxyribonucleic acid (DNA); however, data on these tests are limited (CDC, 1998a). Identifying the HIV antibody is not a reliable test in infants because of their transplacental acquisition of maternal antibody. The median time to disappearance of the antibody is 10 months (CDC, 1994a). Repeatedly positive HIV antibody tests after 18 months of age, however, do confirm the diagnosis. HIV antibody is tested initially by reactive enzyme immunoassay (EIA) and confirmed by western blot or immunofluorescent assay.

The recommendations for testing HIV-exposed infants are as follows:

- Obtain viral culture or PCR on *all* infants of mothers with HIV infection at 48 hours of age (do p24 antigen testing only if viral culture and PCR are not available)
- If test results in the first bulleted item are negative, repeat culture or PCR at 1 month and between 3 and 6 months of age
- If test results obtained in the second bulleted item are negative again, do HIV antibody testing when the infant reaches 15 and 18 months of age
- If the viral culture or PCR is positive, confirm the result with a second culture or PCR at the time the positive result is obtained (CDC, 1998a)

Children who have negative viral cultures or PCR tests, do not have an AIDS-defining illness, and have two or more negative antibody (i.e., EIA) tests after 6 months of age *are not* infected with HIV (i.e., "seroreverter") (CDC, 1998a).

Evaluation for Associated Problems

Infants and Children Newborns who have been exposed to HIV are at risk for a number of problems associated with maternal high-risk behaviors:

- Other infections
  a. Hepatitis B and C
  b. Syphilis
  c. Herpes simplex
  d. Chlamydia
  e. Other STDs
- Low birth weight and small for gestational age
- Fetal alcohol syndrome (FAS)
- Isolated birth defects associated with maternal alcohol or other drug use

All pregnant women with HIV infection should be tested for hepatitis B and C, and all neonates should receive a hepatitis B vaccine (HBV). Infants delivered to women with chronic hepatitis B infection should also receive HBIG immediately after birth (CDC, 1994a). Women who have not been tested previously must receive HB$_s$Ag testing promptly to ensure HBIG treatment of the infant during the first 12 hours after birth if the mothers are HB$_s$Ag-positive. If testing cannot be completed within this time frame, consider giving the infant HBIG and HBV as soon after delivery as possible. The vertical transmission of hepatitis C virus (HCV) is generally low; however, the risk of transmission is increased by maternal co-infection with HIV (Granovsky, Minkoff, Tess, et al., 1998). The AAP (1998) has recommended screening infants if the mother is positive for HCV. The infant should be tested by PCR for HCV RNA at 1–2 months of age or for anti-HCV antibodies after 12 months of age (CDC, 1998c).

Perform a careful physical examination of the infant for minor or major anomalies (see the Appendix at the end of Chapter 5) and a neurobehavioral examination as part of the evaluation of an infant with prenatal drug exposure (Chapter 10). A few infants with HIV infection may have FAS, and some manifest neonatal abstinence syndrome (NAS).

Adolescents The adolescent with HIV may experience a variety of associated social (e.g., homeless), mental health (e.g., depression), and medical problems (e.g., hepatitis) similar to those discussed with regard to women who abuse alcohol and/or other drugs during pregnancy (see Chapter 10). This is particularly true for gay and bisexual adolescents. Depression and suicide attempts are common among these adolescents (Sells & Remafedi, 1995). In addition, many live in dysfunctional homes or are homeless. Adolescents with hemophilia who were infected by contaminated clotting factors are a special group (see Brown, Schultz, & Gragg, 1995).

Mothers and Families The care of most families with members who have HIV is complicated by the difficulties inherent in delivering services to the most disenfranchised population in the United States (Myers & Weitzman, 1991). Mothers with HIV infection usually have a number of social, mental health, and medical problems similar to those of women who abuse alcohol and/or other drugs during their pregnancy. They require a comprehensive array of services. Please review the discussion in Chapter 10. The social and mental health problems of these women are compounded by the social stigma of the AIDS diagnosis as well as their guilt concerning their infant with HIV and concerns about the future.

Counseling the Child and the
Family About the Diagnosis and Prognosis

Counseling the child and family about HIV infection is complicated by uncertainty about the diagnosis (confirmation of the diagnosis in infants who have been exposed to HIV may take several months) and the rate at which the infant's and mother's HIV will progress, maternal guilt and isolation, and the mother's concerns about her own death and the subsequent care of her children (Cooper, Pelton, & LeMay, 1988). For the adolescent male, it may involve disclosure of his homosexuality to the family. Please review the general comments on counseling in other chapters. In addition, address each of the following issues that are specific to HIV infection:

- Discuss the differences between HIV infection and AIDS.
- Emphasize HIV infection as a chronic illness.
- Emphasize the positive aspects of care that can improve quality of life (e.g., PCP prophylaxis).
- Discuss the risk of HIV transmission and prevention thereof
  a. In subsequent pregnancies
  b. Among household members
  c. In the school or in the community
- Discuss the importance of prompt evaluation of intercurrent illnesses.
- Help the parents and the child identify social supports (i.e., individuals with whom they can share the diagnosis).
- Emphasize the confidentiality of the individuals' medical records (i.e., that it will be the parents' choice with whom to share medical information).

- Clarify the responsibilities of the primary care office and the responsibilities of the AIDS specialist.
- Discuss with the parents when and how to disclose the diagnosis to the child and whether to notify school authorities.
- Specifically, review the transmission of HIV infection and the importance of contraception with adolescents who have HIV infection.

One of the most challenging issues with regard to HIV is discussion of the diagnosis with the child or adolescent. A critical question is when to disclose the diagnosis and the terminal nature of the illness to the child because of the high level of public misunderstanding and fear regarding AIDS (Spiegel & Mayers, 1991). In the study by Grubman and co-workers (1995), disclosure of the HIV diagnosis had been made to 57% of children with HIV and 33.3% of these children's schools. Discussion of the diagnosis with the child is best conceptualized as a process rather than a single event (Spiegel & Mayers, 1991). The Committee on Pediatric AIDS of the AAP (1999) strongly endorses disclosure that is individualized to the child's developmental level, clinical status, and social circumstances.

The explanation of the illness must be appropriate for the level of understanding of the individual child. In general, school-age children are capable of understanding how the body works and can accept that they have a serious illness even though they are asymptomatic (Spiegel & Mayers, 1991). Older children and adolescents must be informed fully about their HIV diagnosis, and they should participate in all decisions about their care. Anxiety concerning the terminal nature of the illness may not be manifested directly. Studies (e.g., Spiegel & Mayers, 1991) have shown that children have a greater awareness of their illness than suspected; however, expressions of their anxiety are rare.

MANAGEMENT AND PREVENTION

Periodic Review and
Update of the Management Plan

The management of the child and adolescent with HIV infection is rapidly evolving and increasingly complex (Melvin & Frenkel, 1997–1998). These children and their families require ongoing management by the HIV specialist and other professionals at the HIV treatment center. The primary care physician co-manages the child with HIV infection with the HIV specialist. These children may need frequent visits to the primary care office, depending on the presence of associated health problems.

Regularly review information from families, the HIV specialist, schools, and other community providers. Update an office management plan as needed and at least yearly for older children who are doing well. The management responsibilities of the primary care health professional are to

- Evaluate and manage newborns with HIV exposure
- Initiate prophylaxis for pneumocystis in all infants with HIV exposure
- Collaborate with the HIV specialist in treatment regimens for the child with HIV infection
- Modify the immunization schedule for infants and children with HIV infection
- Regularly review the response to services, including educational services
- Review ongoing needs for family support
- Assist the family with care coordination

Service Needs of Families with Children and Adolescents with Human Immunodeficiency Virus Infection   The service needs of mothers and families of children and adolescents with HIV infection are great (Levine, 1995). Ideally, services are comprehensive and intensive, with "one-stop" shopping or multiple services available at one center (Levine & Allen, 1995). Women with HIV infection are coping with their own chronic illness and may experience further social isolation because of the social stigma of the AIDS diagnosis. At times, the psychosocial needs of these families can appear to be overwhelming. A comprehensive treatment program may include the following services:

- Legal advocacy
- Child Protective Services
- Prenatal care for pregnant women with HIV
- HIV testing and counseling
- Treatment for HIV-related conditions
- Treatment of other maternal health problems
- Pediatric care of the infant with HIV
- Hospice care
- Preconceptional education about family planning services
- Women's chemical dependency treatment
- Education and job training
- Coordination of social services
- Developmental assessment of children
- Child care
- Care coordination
- Parenting education
- Mental health services
- Support groups
- Transportation
- Home health nurses or aides

- Housing
- Domestic violence counseling
- Respite care
- Training in life management skills (Kandall, 1993)

Treatments to Decrease Perinatal Transmission

Use of Zidovudine   The results of the AIDS Clinical Trials Group (ACTG) Protocol 076 clearly demonstrated reduction in mother-to-infant transmission with the use of ZDV (CDC, 1994a; Conner & Mofenson, 1995). The trial included women who had CD_4+ counts greater than 200, no prior antiretroviral therapy, and started prenatal care before 34 weeks of gestation. The treatment protocol comprised three components—antenatal, intrapartum, and neonatal—as follows:

- Women with HIV infection were treated with 100 milligrams of ZDV taken orally five times daily starting anywhere from the 14th to the 34th week of gestation and continuing throughout the pregnancy.
- During labor, these women also received a 2-milligrams-per-kilogram ZDV intravenously (IV) in the first hour and then 1 milligram per kilogram per hour until delivery.
- Their newborns were treated with a 2-milligrams-per-kilogram dose of ZDV every 6 hours for the first 6 weeks after birth (CDC, 1994a).

The HIV transmission rate was 25.5% in the placebo group (184 children) and 8.3% in the ZDV group (180 children) (Conner & Mofenson, 1995). In addition, other studies (CDC, 1998b; Matheson, Abrams, Thomas, et al., 1995) have reported a decrease in maternal transmission among women with advanced HIV, variable CD_4+ counts, and prior ZDV therapy when all three components of the ZDV treatment protocol were followed.

In 1998, the CDC Working Group on Antiretroviral Therapy recommended offering standard antiretroviral treatment (combination drug therapy) to pregnant women with HIV infection, incorporating the ZDV treatment protocol into the combination therapy, and counseling women about the unknown effects of antiretroviral drugs on the fetus. Their recommendations for the use of ZDV chemoprophylaxis (CDC, 1998b) included four scenarios:

1. Use the full ZDV protocol with women with HIV infection who have had no prior antiretroviral therapy.
2. Add ZDV or substitute ZDV for another nucleoside analogue after 12 weeks' gestation, and

use the intrapartum and neonatal components of the ZDV chemoprophylaxis protocol with women with HIV infection who are receiving antiretroviral therapy.

3. Use the intrapartum and neonatal components of ZDV chemoprophylaxis with women with HIV infection who are in labor and have had no prior antiretroviral therapy.

4. Offer the neonatal component of the ZDV protocol for infants born to women with HIV infection who received no antiretroviral therapy during the pregnancy.

ZDV is the only drug that has been demonstrated to reduce the rate of mother–infant transmission. Therefore, ZDV should be included as one component if combination antiretroviral therapy is initiated in pregnant women with HIV (CDC, 1998b). In addition, pregnant women in their first trimester should be counseled to consider delaying initiation of antiretroviral therapy until after 12 weeks of gestation because of the unknown effects of antiretroviral drugs on the developing fetus.

Other Treatment Methods   Table 12.8 lists a number of other treatment methods to decrease mothers' transmission of HIV infection to their infants. These include avoidance of breast feeding, cesarean section delivery, and the use of antiretroviral drugs other than ZDV. As commented previously, a metaanalysis of data from 15 studies showed a 50% reduction of transmission associated with elective cesarean section and approximately an 87% reduction with cesarean section combined with ZDV prophylaxis (International Perinatal HIV Group, 1999). No consistent research data exist on the efficacy of the other methods noted. Cleansing of the birth canal and passive immunization were still being

Table 12.8.   Approaches to reducing the transmission of human immunodeficiency virus (HIV) from mother to child

Avoidance of breast feeding
Antiretroviral therapy (antenatal, intrapartum, and
   neonatal)
   Zidovudine (ZDV)
   Other antiretroviral agents (ZDV is the only anti-
   retroviral with demonstrated efficacy.)
Reduction in peripartum exposure
   Cesarean section
   Avoidance of intrapartum invasive procedures (e.g., use
   of forceps)
   Vaginal disinfection
   Treatment of sexually transmitted diseases (STDs)
Passive immunotherapy for the mother or infant (or both)
Active immunization

Adapted from Peckham and Gibb (1995).

studied in the late 1990s, and efforts to develop an effective vaccine continue (Peckham & Gibb, 1995).

Prophylaxis Against
***Pneumocystis Carinii* Pneumonia**

Infants and Children   In adolescents and adults with HIV, a CD_4+ count less than 200 is a useful indicator to start prophylaxis against PCP. In infants, however, the CD_4+ count is higher than it is in older children and adults, and it may fall rapidly (Peckham & Gibb, 1995). Because of this factor, the CDC (1995a) recommended that all infants who have been exposed to HIV receive prophylaxis against PCP in the following manner:

• Initiate PCP prophylaxis in all infants with HIV exposure at 4–6 weeks of age after completion of ZDV chemoprophylaxis.

• Continue PCP prophylaxis until 12 months of age for all infants with HIV infection and infants whose infection status has not yet been determined.

• PCP prophylaxis should be discontinued among infants in whom HIV infection has been reasonably excluded on the basis of two or more viral diagnostic tests (i.e., HIV culture, PCR).

Start prophylaxis with trimethoprim-sulfamethoxazole (TMP-SMX) after ZDV chemoprophylaxis is discontinued (see Table 12.9). Dapsone and pentamidine can be used in infants who cannot tolerate TMP-SMX; however, these drugs may not be as effective as TMP-SMX (Peckham & Gibb, 1995).

Adolescents and Adults   The CDC (1992) recommended prophylaxis against PCP in adolescents and adults who have a CD_4+ count less than 200. Individuals with constitutional symptoms such as thrush or unexplained fever greater than 100° F for greater than or equal to 2 weeks should also receive prophylaxis, even if their CD_4+ counts are greater than 200. Start treatment with TMP-SMX at a dose of one double-strength tablet every day, 7 days a week. Leucovorin does *not* need to be given with this regimen (CDC, 1992). A substantial percentage of individuals cannot tolerate TMP-SMX secondary to pruritus, rash, leukopenia, or increase of transaminases. Dapsone or desensitization to TMP-SMX is usually tried then (Mirochnick, Cooper, McIntosh, et al., 1999). Aerosolized pentamidine is an alternative treatment. Prophylaxis is continued for life.

Antiretroviral Therapy

Indications for Antiretroviral Treatment   Antiretroviral treatment is indicated in all children with symptoms of HIV infection (clinical category A, B, or C) and with children in whom there is evidence

Table 12.9. Drug regimens for PCP prophylaxis for children 4 weeks of age or older

Recommended regimen

- Trimethoprim-sulfamethoxazole (TMP-SMX) 150 milligrams TMP per square meter per day with 750 milligrams SMX per square meter per day administered orally in divided doses twice a day (b.i.d.) three times per week on consecutive days (e.g., Monday, Tuesday, Wednesday).

Acceptable alternative TMP-SMX dosage schedules

- 150 milligrams TMP per square meter per day with 750 milligrams SMX per square meter per day administered orally *as a single dose* three times per week on consecutive days (e.g., Monday, Tuesday, Wednesday)
- 150 milligrams TMP per square meter per day with 750 milligrams SMX per square meter per day orally divided twice per day and *administered 7 days per week*
- 150 milligrams TMP per square meter per day with 750 SMX per square meter per day administered orally divided twice per day and administered three times per week on *alternate days* (e.g., Monday, Wednesday, Friday)

Alternative regimens if TMP-SMX is not tolerated

- **Dapsone**[a]
  2 milligrams per kilogram (not to exceed 100 milligrams) administered orally once daily
- **Aerosolized pentamidine**[a] (children 5 years of age or older)
  300 milligrams administered via Respirgard II inhaler monthly

From Centers for Disease Control and Prevention (CDC). (1995b). 1995 revised guidelines for prophylaxis against pneumocystis carinii pneumonia for children infected with or perinatally exposed to human immunodeficiency virus. *Morbidity and Mortality Weekly Report, 44*(RR-4), 9.

[a]If neither dapsone nor aerosolized pentamidine is tolerated, some clinicians use intravenous pentamidine (4 milligrams per kilogram) administered every 2–4 weeks.

of immune suppression (immune categories 2 or 3) (CDC, 1998a). Therapy is also recommended for all infants with HIV infection who are less than 12 months of age, owing to the high risk of disease progression and the lower predictive value of immunologic and viral tests. The National Pediatric Research Center Working Group on Antiretroviral Treatment (1998) recommended two general approaches for children 12 months of age or older: 1) Treat all HIV-infected children regardless of age or clinical status, *or* 2) defer treatment in children with normal immunologic status and low viral load. If treatment is deferred, indicators for subsequent initiation of treatment are high or increasing viral load, declining CD_4+ counts, and the development of clinical symptoms. The indicators for the treatment of adolescents with HIV who were infected sexually or through intravenous drug use in adolescence are the same as those for adults (CDC, 1998d). The

dosage of medication for HIV infection or opportunistic infections is determined by the adolescent's pubertal status. Adolescents who are in early puberty should be treated based on pediatric dosing schedules (CDC, 1998d).

Antiretroviral Agents There are three types of antiretroviral agents: nucleoside reverse transcriptase inhibitors (NRTI), non-nucleoside reverse transcriptase inhibitors, and protease inhibitors. ZDV, didanosine (DDI), zalcitabine (DDC), stavudine (D4T), and lamivudine (3TC) are nucleoside reverse transcriptase inhibitors. Non-nucleoside reverse transcriptase inhibitors include nevirapine, delavirdine, and lovridine. Protease inhibitors include saquinavir, indinavir, ritonavir, and nelfinavir.

Combination therapy is recommended for infants, children, and adolescents (CDC, 1998a). It is the best approach to reducing viral load, maintaining health, and delaying progression of the disease (Barrett & Sleasman, 1997). Monotherapy is not recommended, except for the use of ZDV to prevent mother–infant transmission. The combination of a protease inhibitor with two NRTIs (i.e., a three-drug combination) is recommended by the Working Group on Antiretroviral Treatment as the preferred initial treatment regimen. This combination has been effective in adults and in a limited number of trials with children (Melvin, Mohan, Arcuino, et al., 1997; Rutstein, Feingold, Meislich, et al., 1997; Wintergerst, Hoffmann, Solder, et al., 1998). One study (Chougnet, Fowke, Mueller, et al., 1998) reported significantly reduced viral loads and increased CD_4+ counts but a lack of improvement in other immune parameters with triple-drug treatment.

A variety of side effects have been reported, including nausea, diarrhea, abdominal pain, elevated liver function tests, and hematuria (protease inhibitors); anemia and neutropenia (ZDV); and pancreatitis, peripheral retinal depigmentation, and peripheral neuropathy (DDI). Antiretroviral therapy and the medical management of pediatric HIV infection was reviewed in detail in the October 1998 Supplement to *Pediatrics*.

Other Components of the Management Plan
Other components of medical management of children with HIV infection and their families are as follows (AAP, 1997; Hoernle & Reid, 1995):

- Obtain a complete blood count (CBC) and differential before ZDV chemoprophylaxis in the newborn with HIV, and repeat monthly during treatment.
- Follow CD_4+ counts and viral load every 3 months in children with HIV. (Viral load and CD_4+ counts are independent predictors of

disease status and the risk of progression; Palumbo, Raskino, Fiscus, et al., 1998.)

- Treat infections early and aggressively.
- Modify the schedule for routine active immunizations:
  a. No varicella vaccine
  b. Use an inactivated polio virus (IPV) vaccine (siblings should also receive IPV vaccine)
  c. Add a pneumococcal vaccine at age 2 years for children who are symptomatic for HIV infection
  d. Administer a measles, mumps, and rubella (MMR) vaccine unless the child is severely immunodepressed (immune category 3)
- Use passive immunization for significant exposure to measles, varicella, hepatitis B, and tetanus.
- Use tetanus immune globulin for tetanus-prone wounds regardless of the child's immunization status.
- Do annual tuberculosis (TB) skin testing, and determine the TB status of the mother and other household members.
- Use monthly intravenous immunoglobulin (IVIG) for children with recurrent bacterial infections, hypogammaglobulinemia, or poor response to routine immunizations (Hoernle & Reid, 1995).
- Monitor growth and development carefully (every 3–6 months in infants and young children):
  a. Provide nutritional support services as needed
  b. Refer children with developmental problems for early intervention/early childhood special education (EI/ECSE) services
- Monitor the child's neuromotor status regularly (every 3–6 months in infants and young children):
  a. Refer the child with apparent progressive encephalopathy for appropriate support services (e.g., physical therapy)
- Provide comprehensive psychosocial services, including hospice care.
- Provide ongoing advocacy, support, and counseling to the child and family.
- Obtain an ophthalmologic examination every 3–6 months to monitor for cytomegalovirus (CMV) retinitis in children who are immunocompromised and have a history of CMV infection.
- Consider prophylaxis for mycobacterium avium complex (MAC) in children who are severely immunocompromised.

Important Care Coordination Issues

Comprehensive educational and rehabilitative services are important components of the treatment of children with HIV infection. In addition to the general recommendations for care coordination discussed in Chapter 1, the responsibilities of the primary care office are to

- Identify the contact person for EI/ECSE services and the county health department, as well as school nurses in the community
- Be aware of drug treatment programs in your community and state
- Maintain an up-to-date list of other community services, including support groups for families with children with HIV; support groups for gay, lesbian, and bisexual youth; and support groups for foster parents
- Exchange information with other service providers regularly, and attend school conferences as needed

Prevention

Initiatives to prevent the spread of HIV infection have focused on

- Public education about HIV and AIDS
- Preventing high-risk behaviors among students
- Targeted education or intervention programs for specific groups (e.g., IVDUs, people who attend clinics for STDs, gay males)

Public Information Programs Public information programs sponsored by the CDC (1993) have included the following high-priority messages:

- How HIV is and is not transmitted
- How to avoid becoming infected
- What to do if infection is suspected
- The benefits of knowing one's serologic status, including the benefits of early diagnosis and treatment for HIV

One approach has been to encourage people in all high-risk groups to obtain HIV testing so that they know their HIV status. Table 12.10 provides a partial list of individuals who are at risk for contracting HIV. As many as 50% of women with HIV in Seattle, however, have no identified risk factor for HIV (L. Frenkel, personal communication, March 1996). This potentiality emphasizes the importance of public education about HIV and AIDS, education programs for students, and individual counseling of women of childbearing age by health professionals. The Committee on Pediatric AIDS of the AAP (1998) recommended that HIV and AIDS education be incorporated into health education programs for students in grades K–12.

Preventing High-Risk Behavior Among Students A great deal of research has focused on educational programs for HIV testing of adolescents who engage in high-risk behaviors (secondary prevention) and education of adolescents in general (primary pre-

Table 12.10. Individuals who are at risk for human immunodeficiency virus (HIV) infection

- Men who have had sex with other men
- People who are substance abusers, including intravenous drug users (IVDUs), especially those who share needles and other drug paraphernalia
- People who exchange sex for drugs, money, housing, or food
- People with sexually transmitted diseases (STDs), especially those with a history of repeatedly contracting STDs
- Youth in high-risk situations, including runaways, youth who have had STDs, youth who are homosexual or bisexual, juvenile offenders, young IVDUs, and young people who barter or sell sex
- Women in high-risk situations, including those whose partners have HIV infections or who engage in high-risk behavior
- People in the correctional and criminal justice systems
- Homeless people in high-risk situations
- People who are or have partners with one of the previously listed risk factors

Adapted from Centers for Disease Control and Prevention (CDC) (1993).

vention). Another strategy has been the provision of free condoms in school-based clinics or in medical offices. The percentage of students who have received HIV education at school has increased from 50% in 1989 to 83% in 1991 (Holtzman, Mathis, Kann, et al., 1995). In addition, educational efforts to encourage young people to delay the onset of first sexual intercourse and to decrease the number of young people who become sexually active have been modestly effective. Data from the Youth Risk Behavior Survey for 1991, 1993, 1995, and 1997 demonstrated the percentage of U.S. high school students who had ever had sexual intercourse decreased modestly from 54.2% in 1991 to 48.4% in 1997, and that their use of condoms increased (CDC, 1998f). Only 58.6% of students who were sexually active, however, reported that either they or their partner used a condom during their last sexual intercourse. A randomized trial of Safer Choices (Coyle, Basen-Engquist, Kirby, et al., 1999), a multicomponent HIV, STD, and pregnancy prevention program for high school youth in California and Texas, resulted in a reduced frequency of intercourse without a condom and increased use of a condom during last intercourse.

Studies have demonstrated (Stevenson, Gay, & Josar, et al., 1995; Sunwood et al., 1995) that educational programs at schools that include the use of videotapes about and presentations by people with AIDS are effective at increasing students' knowledge about HIV. These programs have inconsistent effects on changing behaviors, however (e.g., obtaining HIV testing following HIV counseling). In addition, studies (Rickert, Gottlieb, Jay, et al., 1992; Sunwood et al., 1995) have reported inconsistent results in changing high-risk behaviors of adolescents. The effects of educational programs have been greater for adolescents in high-risk groups (e.g., individuals at an STD clinic).

High-Risk Groups (Secondary Prevention) Another strategy has been to target interventions at high-risk groups, including individuals at STD clinics; IVDUs; and youth who are gay, lesbian, or bisexual. Prevention programs for IVDUs have focused on decreasing drug use as well as increasing the use of safe needles and safe sex practices, as well as making available STD and HIV treatment and counseling services. As part of a comprehensive approach to the treatment and prevention of illicit drug use, the American Academy of Pediatrics (1994) recommended

- Targeted risk reduction education to IVDUs
- Bleach decontamination of used equipment
- Reconsideration of drug paraphernalia laws that prevent the purchase of sterile needles
- Consideration of needle exchange programs

Interventions with individuals at STD clinics and with youth who are gay, lesbian, or bisexual generally have focused on changing high-risk behavior and providing HIV testing. Studies have documented modest changes in high-risk behaviors with targeted education programs. For example, two studies (Remafedi, 1994; Rotheram-Borus, Reid, & Rosario, 1994) of adolescents who are gay or bisexual documented increased condom use and a decreased number of sexual partners, and in another study (Rotheram-Borus et al., 1994), the intervention effects were maintained for 12 months.

REFERENCES

Abrams, E.J., Matheson, P.B., Thomas, P.A., et al. (1995). Neonatal predictors of infection monitored prospectively from birth: New York City Perinatal HIV Transmission Collaborative Study Group. *Pediatrics, 96*(3), 451–458.

American Academy of Pediatrics (AAP) and the American College of Obstetricians and Gynecologists. (1995, August). *Joint statement on human immunodeficiency virus screening by the American Academy of Pediatrics and the American College of Obstetricians and Gynecologists.* Elk Grove Village, IL, and Washington, DC: Authors.

American Academy of Pediatrics (AAP), Committee on Pediatric AIDS. (1997). Evaluation and medical treatment of the HIV-exposed infant. *Pediatrics, 99,* 909–917.

American Academy of Pediatrics (AAP), Committee on Pediatric AIDS. (1998). Human immunodeficiency virus/acquired immunodeficiency syndrome education in schools. *Pediatrics, 101*, 933–935.

American Academy of Pediatrics (AAP), Committee on Pediatric AIDS. (1999). Disclosure of illness status to children and adolescents with HIV infection. *Pediatrics, 103*, 164–166.

American Academy of Pediatrics (AAP), Provisional Committee on Pediatric AIDS. (1994). Reducing the risk of human immunodeficiency virus infection associated with illicit drug use. *Pediatrics, 94*(6), 945–947.

American Academy of Pediatrics, Committee on Infectious Diseases. (1998). Hepatitis C virus infection. *Pediatrics, 101*(3 pt. 1), 481–485.

Amman, A. (1987). The immunology of pediatric AIDS. In *Report of The Surgeon General's Workshop on Children with HIV Infection and their Families* (pp. 13–17) (DHHS Publication No. HRS-D-MC 87-1). Washington, DC: U.S. Department of Health and Human Services.

Barrett, D.J. (1988). The clinicians guide to pediatric AIDS. *Contemporary Pediatrics, 5*, 24–47.

Barrett, D.J., & Sleasman, J.W. (1997). Pediatric AIDS: So now what do we do? *Contemporary Pediatrics, 14*(6), 111–124.

Bertolli, J., Caldwell, B., Lindgren, M.L., et al. (1995). Epidemiology of HIV disease in children. *Immunology and Allergy Clinics of North America, 15*(2), 193–204.

Brown, L.K., Schultz, J.R., & Gragg, R.A. (1995). HIV-infected adolescents with hemophilia: Adaptation and coping: The Hemophilia Behavioral Intervention Evaluation Project. *Pediatrics, 96*(3), 459–463.

Centers for Disease Control and Prevention (CDC). (1992). Recommendations for prophylaxis against pneumocystis carinii pneumonia for adults and adolescents infected with human immunodeficiency virus. *Morbidity and Mortality Weekly Report, 41*(4), 1–11.

Centers for Disease Control and Prevention (CDC). (1993). *Annual report: Division of STD/HIV Prevention, 1993* (pp. 65–118). Washington, DC: U.S. Department of Health and Human Services.

Centers for Disease Control and Prevention (CDC). (1994a). Recommendations of the U.S. Public Health Service Task Force on the Use of Zidovudine to Reduce Perinatal Transmission of Human Immunodeficiency Virus. *Morbidity and Mortality Weekly Report, 43*(11) [Entire issue].

Centers for Disease Control and Prevention (CDC). (1994b). Revised classification system for human immunodeficiency virus infection in children less than 13 years of age. *Morbidity and Mortality Weekly Report, 43*(RR-12), 1–9.

Centers for Disease Control and Prevention (CDC). (1994c). Update: Impact of the expanded AIDS surveillance case definition for adolescents and adults on case reporting: United States, 1993. *Morbidity and Mortality Weekly Report, 43*(9), 160–161, 167–170.

Centers for Disease Control and Prevention (CDC). (1995a). 1995 revised guidelines for prophylaxis against pneumocystis carinii pneumonia for children infected with or perinatally exposed to human immunodeficiency virus. *Morbidity and Mortality Weekly Report, 44*(RR-4), 1–11.

Centers for Disease Control and Prevention (CDC). (1995b). U.S. Public Health Service recommendations for human immunodeficiency virus counseling and voluntary testing for pregnant women. *Morbidity and Mortality Weekly Report, 44*(RR-7), 1–15.

Centers for Disease Control and Prevention (CDC). (1997). Update: Perinatally acquired HIV/AIDS—United States, 1997. *Morbidity and Mortality Weekly Report, 46*(46), 1086–1092.

Centers for Disease Control and Prevention (CDC). (1998a). Guidelines for the use of antiretroviral agents in pediatric HIV infection. *Morbidity and Mortality Weekly Report, 47*(RR-4), 1–43 [see also errata *MMWR, 47*, 315].

Centers for Disease Control and Prevention (CDC). (1998b). Public Health Service task force recommendations for the use of antiretroviral drugs in pregnant women infected with HIV-1 for maternal health and for reducing perinatal HIV-1 transmission in the United States. *Morbidity and Mortality Weekly Report, 47*(RR-2), 1–30 [see also errata *MMWR 47*, 287; *MMWR, 47*, 315].

Centers for Disease Control and Prevention (CDC). (1998c). Recommendations for the prevention and control of hepatitis C virus (HCV) infection and HCV-related chronic disease. *Morbidity and Mortality Weekly Report, 47*(RR-19), 23–24.

Centers for Disease Control and Prevention (CDC). (1998d). Report of the NIH panel to define principles of therapy of HIV infection and guidelines for the use of antiretroviral agents in HIV-infected adults and adolescents. *Morbidity and Mortality Weekly Report, 47*(RR-5), 43–82.

Centers for Disease Control and Prevention (CDC). (1998e). Success in implementing Public Health Service guidelines to reduce perinatal transmission of HIV: Louisiana, Michigan, New Jersey, and South Carolina, 1993, 1995, and 1996. *Morbidity and Mortality Weekly Report, 47*(33), 688–691 [see also erratum *MMWR, 47*, 718].

Centers for Disease Control and Prevention (CDC). (1998f). Trends in sexual risk behaviors among high school students: United States, 1991–1997. *Morbidity and Mortality Weekly Report, 47*(36), 749–752.

Chaisson, R.E., Stanton, D.L., Gallant, J.E., et al. (1993). Impact of the 1993 revision of the AIDS case definition on the prevalence of AIDS in a clinical setting. *AIDS, 7*(6), 857–862.

Chougnet, C., Fowke, D.R., Mueller, B.U., et al. (1998). Protease inhibitor and triple-drug therapy: Cellular immune parameters are not restored in pediatric AIDS patients after 6 months of treatment. *AIDS, 12*(18), 2397–2406

Conlon, C.J. (1992). New threats to development. In M.L. Batshaw & Y.M. Perret (Eds.), *Children with disabilities: A medical primer* (3rd ed., pp. 111–136). Baltimore: Paul H. Brookes Publishing Co.

Conner, E.M., & Mofenson, L.M. (1995). Zidovudine for the reduction of perinatal human immunodeficiency virus transmission: Pediatric AIDS clinical trials group Protocol 076: Results and treatment recommendations. *Pediatric Infectious Diseases Journal, 14*, 536–541.

Cooper, E.R., Hanson, C., Diaz, C., et al. (1998). Encephalopathy and progression of human immunodeficiency virus disease in a cohort of children with perinatally acquired human immunodeficiency virus infection: Women and Infants Transmission Study Group. *Journal of Pediatrics, 132*, 808–812.

Cooper, E.R., Pelton, S.I., & LeMay, M. (1988). Acquired immunodeficiency syndrome: A new population of children at risk. *Pediatric Clinics of North America, 35*(6), 1365–1387.

Coplan, J., Contello, K.A., Cummingham, C.K., et al. (1998). Early language development in children exposed to or infected with human immunodeficiency virus. *Pediatrics, 102,* e8.

Coyle, K., Basen-Engquist, K., Kirby, D., et al. (1999). Short-term impact of safer choices: A multicomponent, school-based HIV, other STD, and pregnancy prevention program. *Journal of School Health, 69*(5), 181–188.

Davis, S.F., Rosen, D.H., Steinberg, S., et al. (1998). Trends in HIV prevalence among childbearing women in the United States, 1989–1994. *Journal of Acquired Immune Deficiency Syndromes and Human Retrovirology, 19,* 158–164.

Diaz, C., Hanson, C., Cooper, E.R., et al. (1998). Disease progression in a cohort of infants with vertically acquired HIV infection observed from birth: The Women and Infants Transmission Study (WITS). *Journal of Acquired Immune Deficiency Syndromes and Human Retrovirology, 18,* 221–228.

Dickover, R.E., Dillon, M., Leung, K.M., et al. (1998). Early prognostic indicators in primary perinatal human immunodeficiency virus type 1 infection: Importance of viral RNA and the timing of transmission on long-term outcome. *Journal of Infectious Disease, 178,* 375–387.

European Collaborative Study. (1999). Maternal viral load and vertical transmission of HIV-1: An important factor but not the only one. *AIDS, 13*(11), 1377–1385.

Fowler, M.G. (1994). Pediatric HIV infection: Neurologic and neuropsychologic findings. *Acta Paediatrica Supplement, 400,* 59–62.

Galli, L., de Martino, M., Toro, P.A., et al. (1995). Onset of clinical signs in children with HIV-1 perinatal infection: Italian register for HIV infection in children. *AIDS, 9*(5), 455–461.

Goodman, E., Tipton, A.C., Hecht, L., et al. (1994). Perseverance pays off: Health care providers' impact on HIV testing decisions by adolescent females. *Pediatrics, 94*(6), 878–882.

Granovsky, M.O., Minkoff, H.L., Tess, B.H., et al. (1998). Hepatitis C virus infection in the Mothers and Infants Cohort Study. *Pediatrics, 102*(2 pt. 1), 355–359.

Grubman, S., Gross, E., Lerner-Weiss, N., et al. (1995). Older children and adolescents living with perinatally acquired human immunodeficiency virus infection. *Pediatrics, 95*(5), 657–663.

Gwynn, M., Pappaioanou, M., George, J.R., et al. (1991). Prevalence of HIV infection in childbearing women in the United States: Surveillance using newborn blood samples. *JAMA: Journal of the American Medical Association, 265,* 1704–1708.

Hoernle, E.H., & Reid, T.E. (1995). Human immunodeficiency infection in children. *American Journal of Health-System Pharmacy, 52,* 961–979.

Holtzman, D., Mathis, M.P., Kann, L., et al. (1995). Trends in risk behaviors for HIV infection among U.S. high school students. *AIDS Education and Prevention, 7*(3), 265–277.

International Perinatal HIV Group. (1999). The mode of delivery and the risk of vertical transmission of human immunodeficiency virus type 1: A meta-analysis of 15 prospective cohort studies. *New England Journal of Medicine, 340*(13), 977–987.

Kandall, S.R. (1993). *Improving treatment for drug-exposed infants: Treatment improvement protocol (TIP) series.* Washington, DC: U.S. Department of Health and Human Services.

Kauffman, W.M., Sivit, C.J., Fitz, C.R., et al. (1992). CT and MR evaluation of intracranial involvement in pediatric HIV infection: A clinical-imaging correlation. *American Journal of Neuroradiology, 13*(3), 949–957.

Lackritz, E.M., Satten, G.A., Aberle-Grasse, J., et al. (1995). Estimated risk of transmission of the human immunodeficiency virus by screened blood in the United States. *New England Journal of Medicine, 333*(26), 1721–1725.

Leroy, V., Newell, M.L., Dabis, F., et al. (1998). International multicentre pooled analysis of late postnatal mother-to-child transmission of HIV-1 infection: Ghent International Working Group on Mother-to-Child Transmission of HIV. *Lancet, 352,* 597–600.

Levine, C. (1995). Orphans of the HIV epidemic: Unmet needs in six U.S. cities. *AIDS Care, 7*(1), 57–62.

Levine, C., & Allen, M.H. (1995). Social interventions in the care of human immunodeficiency virus (HIV)–infected pregnant women. *Seminars in Perinatology, 19*(4), 323–329.

Lobato, M.N., Caldwell, M.B., Ng, P., et al. (1995). Encephalopathy in children with perinatally acquired human immunodeficiency virus infection. *Journal of Pediatrics, 126*(5), 710–715.

Maldonado, Y.A., Araneta, R.G., & Hersh, A.L. (1998). Pneumocystic carinii pneumonia prophylaxis and early clinical manifestations of severe perinatal human immunodeficiency virus type 1 infection: Northern California Pediatric HIV Consortium. *Pediatric Infectious Disease Journal, 17,* 398–402.

Maldonado, Y.A., Wang, N.E., & Caldwell, B. (1995). Factors associated with early clinical recognition of children with perinatal human immunodeficiency virus infection: Northern California Pediatric HIV Consortium. *Journal of Infectious Diseases, 171,* 689–692.

Matheson, P.B., Abrams, E.J., Thomas, P.A., et al. (1995). Efficacy of antenatal zidovudine in reducing perinatal transmission of human immunodeficiency virus type 1. *Journal of Infectious Diseases, 172,* 353–358.

Mauri, A., Piccione, E., Deiana, P., et al. (1995). Obstetric and perinatal outcome in human immunodeficiency virus–infected pregnant women with and without opiate addiction. *European Journal of Obstetrics, Gynecology, and Reproductive Biology, 58*(2), 135–140.

Melvin, A.J., & Frenkel, L.M. (1997–1998). Pediatric HIV disease: New developments in treatment and prevention. *AIDS Clinical Review,* 109–127.

Melvin, A.J., Mohan, K.M., Arcuino, L.A., et al. (1997). Clinical, virologic and immunologic responses of children with advanced human immunodeficiency virus type 1 disease treated with protease inhibitors. *Pediatric Infectious Disease Journal, 16,* 968–974.

Mirochnick, M., Cooper, E., McIntosh, K., et al. (1999). Pharmacokinetics of dapsone administered daily and weekly in human immunodeficiency virus–infected children. *Antimicrobial Agents and Chemotherapy, 43*(11), 2586–2591.

Mofenson, L.M., Lambert, J.S., Stiehm, E.R., et al. (1999). Risk factors for perinatal transmission of human immunodeficiency virus type 1 in women treated with zidovudine: Pediatric AIDS Clinical Trials Group Study 185 Team. *New England Journal of Medicine, 341*(6), 385–393.

Myers, A., & Weitzman, M. (1991). Pediatric HIV disease: The newest chronic illness of childhood. *Pediatrics Clinics of North America, 38*(1), 169–194.

Nahmais, A.J., Clark, W.S., Kourtis, A.P., et al. (1998). Thymic dysfunction and time of infection predict mortality in human immunodeficiency virus-infected infants: CDC Perinatal AIDS Collaborative Transmission Study Group. *Journal of Infectious Disease, 178*, 680–685.

National Center for Health Statistics. (1993). *Annual summary of births, marriages, divorces and deaths: United States (1992) monthly vital statistics report.* Hyattsville, MD: U.S. Public Health Service.

Oleske, J. (1987). Natural history of HIV infection: II. In *Report of The Surgeon General's Workshop on children with HIV infection and their families* (DHHS Publication No. HRS-D-MC 87-1, pp. 24–26. Washington, DC: U.S. Department of Health and Human Services.

Oleske, J.M. (1994). The many needs of the HIV-infected child. *Hospital Practice, 29*(9), 63–69.

Palumbo, P.E., Raskino, C., Fiscus, S., et al. (1998). Predictive value of quantitative plasma HIV RNA and CD4+ lymphocyte count in HIV-infected infants and children. *JAMA: Journal of the American Medical Association, 279*, 756–761.

Papola, P., Alvarez, M., & Cohen, H.J. (1994). Developmental and service needs of school-age children with human immunodeficiency virus infection: A descriptive study. *Pediatrics, 94*(6), 914–918.

Parks, W. (1987). The human immunodeficiency virus. In *Report of the Surgeon General's Workshop on children with HIV infection and their families* (DHHS Publication No. HRS-D-MC 87-1, pp. 11–13). Washington, DC: U.S. Department of Health and Human Services.

Peckham, C., & Gibb, D. (1995). Mother-to-child transmission of the human immunodeficiency virus. *New England Journal of Medicine, 333*(5), 299–302.

Persaud, D., Chandwani, S., Rigaud, M., et al. (1992). Delayed recognition of human immunodeficiency virus infection in preadolescent children. *Pediatrics, 90*(5), 688–691.

Phuapradit, W., Panburana, P., & Jaovisidha, A. (1999). Maternal viral load and vertical transmission of HIV-1 in mid-trimester gestation. *AIDS, 13*(14), 1927–1931.

Pitt, J. (1991). Lymphocytic interstitial pneumonia. In P.J. Edelson (Ed.), *The pediatric clinics of North America: Childhood AIDS* (pp. 89–96). Philadelphia: W.B. Saunders Co.

Pliner, V., Weedon, J., Thomas, P.A., et al. (1998). Incubation period of HIV-1 in perinatally infected children: New York City Perinatal HIV Transmission Collaborative Study Group. *AIDS, 12*, 759–766.

Rawitscher, A., Saitz, R., & Friedman, L.S. (1995). Adolescents' preferences regarding human immunodeficiency virus (HIV)–related physician counseling and HIV testing. *Pediatrics, 96*(1), 52–58.

Remafedi, G. (1994). Cognitive and behavioral adaptations to HIV/AIDS among gay and bisexual adolescents. *Journal of Adolescent Health, 15*(2), 142–148.

Rickert, V.I., Gottlieb, A.A., Jay, M.S., et al. (1992). Is AIDS education related to condom acquisition? *Clinical Pediatrics, 31*(4), 205–210.

Rotheram-Borus, M.J., Reid, H., & Rosario, M. (1994). Factors mediating changes in sexual HIV risk behaviors among gay and bisexual male adolescents. *American Journal of Public Health, 83*(12), 1938–1946.

Roy, S., Geoffroy, G., Lapointe, N., et al. (1992). Neurological findings in HIV-infected children: A review of 49 cases. *Canadian Journal of Neurological Sciences, 19*(4), 453–457.

Rutstein, R.M., Feingold, A., Meislich, D., et al. (1997). Protease inhibitor therapy in children with perinatally acquired HIV infection. *AIDS, 11*, F107–F111.

Sells, C.W., & Remafedi, G. (1995). Gay, lesbian, and bisexual youth. In S. Parker & B. Zuckerman (Eds.), *Behavioral and developmental pediatrics: A handbook for primary care* (pp. 157–160). Boston: Little, Brown & Co.

Shearer, W.T., Quinn, T.C., & LaRussa, P. (1997). Viral load and disease progression in infants infected with human immunodeficiency virus type 1: Women and Infants Transmission Study Group. *New England Journal of Medicine, 336*(19), 1337–1342.

Spiegel, L., & Mayers, A. (1991). Psychosocial aspects of AIDS in children and adolescents. *Pediatric Clinics of North America, 38*(1), 153–167.

Stevenson, H.C., Gay, K.M., & Josar, L. (1995). Culturally sensitive AIDS education and perceived AIDS risk knowledge: Reaching the "know-it-all" teenager. *AIDS Education and Prevention, 7*(2), 134–144.

Sunwood, J., Brenman, A., Escobedo, J., et al. (1995). School-based AIDS education for adolescents. *Journal of Adolescent Health, 16*(4), 309–315.

Temmerman, M., Chomba, E.N., Ndinya-Achda, J., et al. (1994). Maternal human immunodeficiency virus-1 infection and pregnancy outcome. *Obstetrics and Gynecology, 83*(4), 495–501.

Towers, C.V., Deveikis, A., Asrat, T., et al. (1998). A "bloodless cesarean section" and perinatal transmission of the human immunodeficiency virus. *American Journal of Gynecology, 179*, 708–714.

Wiestler, O.D., Leib, S.L., Brustle, O., et al. (1992). Neuropathology and pathogenesis of HIV encephalopathies. *Acta Histochemica Supplement, 42*, 107–114.

Wintergerst, U., Hoffmann, F., Solder, B., et al. (1998). Comparison of two antiretroviral triple combinations including the protease inhibitor indinavir in children infected with human immunodeficiency virus. *Pediatric Infectious Disease Journal, 17*, 495–499.

Working Group on Antiretroviral Therapy and Medical Management of Infants, Children, and Adolescents with HIV Infection. (1998). Antiretroviral therapy and medical management of pediatric HIV infection and 1997 USPHS/IDSA report on the prevention of opportunistic infections in people infected with human immunodeficiency virus. *Pediatrics, 102*(4 Suppl.), 1005–1085.

Working Group on Mother-To Child Transmission of HIV. (1995). Rates of mother-to-child transmission of HIV-1 in Africa, America, and Europe: Results from 13 perinatal studies. *Journal of Acquired Immune Deficiency Syndromes and Human Retrovirology, 8*(5), 506–510.

Zuckerman, G.B., Sanchez, J.L., & Conway, E.E., Jr. (1998). Neurologic complications of HIV infections in children. *Pediatric Annals, 27*, 635–639.

Appendix

Guidelines for the Care of Children and Adolescents with Human Immunodeficiency Virus Infection

Basic Team

The special care needs of children with human immunodeficiency virus (HIV) infection can be met by the primary care physician working collaboratively with parents, the HIV center, early childhood educators, teachers, and other community service providers. Children with HIV and their families may require a wide variety of psychosocial, educational, and medical services. Please note that an important responsibility of the primary care physician is to work with other service providers to coordinate the special services that these children require.

Initial Evaluation

The objectives of the initial evaluation of the newborn of a mother with HIV infection are to determine the presence of neurobehavioral abnormalities (if prenatal drug exposure is also present) and to identify associated medical problems such as hepatitis B and C exposure. In addition, the responsibilities of the primary care physician are to contact the HIV center and initiate zidovudine (ZDV) prophylaxis with the infant, to obtain HIV testing of the infant, to initiate pneumocystis prophylaxis after completion of the ZDV, to determine the need for involvement of Child Protective Services (if prenatal drug exposure is also present), and to assist the family in identifying needed support services, including drug treatment for the mother.

Frequency of Visits

The infant with exposure to HIV and the child's family should be seen regularly in the primary care office in the first months following nursery discharge to monitor growth, antiretroviral treatment to prevent HIV transmission, *pneumocystis carinii* prophylaxis (PCP), and neurodevelopmental status; to clarify infection status; and to review family support needs.

The primary care office should continue to follow children with HIV infection regularly in conjunction with the HIV center. In general, reevaluate children with HIV infection in the office every 3 months in the first 2 years after birth to monitor growth, neurologic status, developmental progress, antiretroviral treatment, and family support needs. Then reevaluate these children in the office every 6 months if they are stable and doing well with the treatment program. Update the office management plan at each reevaluation as needed and at least yearly.

Infants with HIV exposure who are *not* infected (i.e., seroreverters) should be followed as per recommendations in the protocol for children with prenatal drug exposure, if appropriate.

The Physician's Guide to Caring for Children with Disabilities and Chronic Conditions, edited by Robert E. Nickel and Larry W. Desch, copyright © 2000 Paul H. Brookes Publishing Co.

Guidelines for the Care of Children and Adolescents with Human Immunodeficiency Virus Infection

The following elements are recommended by age group, and the listing is cumulative. Review all items indicated up through the actual age group of a child entering your practice for the first time as part of the initial evaluation.

AGE	KEY CLINICAL ISSUES/CONCERNS	EVALUATIONS/KEY PROCEDURES	SPECIALISTS
Birth–5 years (pre–school age)	*Diagnosis and Follow-Up Testing* HIV testing Treatment of infants with HIV exposure *Pneumocystis carinii* prophylaxis (PCP) exposure Antiretroviral treatment of HIV-infected infants	Obtain initial HIV testing (culture, PCP) Begin antiretroviral protocol for newborns with exposure to HIV in conjunction with HIV specialist Begin PCP with all infants with exposure to HIV at 4–6 weeks of age Consider antiretroviral treatment of all infants with HIV exposure, follow CD_4+ counts and viral load every 3 months	HIV specialist or center
	Growth/Nutrition Microcephaly Intrauterine growth retardation (IUGR) Failure to thrive (FTT) Oral motor dysfunction	Obtain cranial ultrasound or computed tomography (CT) scan as needed for newborns Growth parameters, diet history, feeding evaluation as needed	Nutritionist, feeding specialist as needed
	Associated Medical Problems (especially when child has had prenatal drug exposure) Hearing/vision Neurobehavioral abnormalities (e.g., neonatal abstinence syndrome [NAS]) Seizures Neuromotor problems (e.g., spasticity) Fetal alcohol syndrome (FAS) or multiple minor anomalies Maternally transmitted infections (e.g., hepatitis B and C, sexually transmitted diseases [STDs])	Hearing and vision testing as needed Environmental/behavioral arrangement, occasional short-term medications Electroencephalogram (EEG) Detailed neuromotor examination Evaluation for minor anomalies Maternal hepatitis B surface antigen (Hb_sAg) testing if not done previously, hepatitis B immunoglobulin (HBIG) and hepatitis B virus (HBV) to infant if mother is Hb_sAg-positive; screen infant if mother is HIV-positive Infant testing for other STDs as needed	Audiologist, ophthalmologist as needed Child neurologist, developmental pediatrician (DPed), physical therapist (PT) as needed HIV/infectious disease specialist in collaboration with primary care
	Sleep disorder	Behavior management; occasionally, short-term medications for sleep disorder	
	Pain management	Comprehensive pain management as needed	

The Physician's Guide to Caring for Children with Disabilities and Chronic Conditions, edited by Robert E. Nickel and Larry W. Desch, copyright © 2000 Paul H. Brookes Publishing Co.

Guidelines for the Care of Children and Adolescents with Human Immunodeficiency Virus Infection *(continued)*

The following elements are recommended by age group, and the listing is cumulative. Review all items indicated up through the actual age group of a child entering your practice for the first time as part of the initial evaluation.

AGE	KEY CLINICAL ISSUES/CONCERNS	EVALUATIONS/KEY PROCEDURES	SPECIALISTS
Birth–5 years (pre-school age) *(continued)*	*HIV-Related Complications* PCP Other opportunistic infections Lymphocytic interstitial pneumonia (LIP) Encephalopathy Wasting syndrome Esophagitis Recurrent bacterial infections	Use monthly intravenous immunoglobulin if recurrent bacterial infections, hypergammaglobulinemia, or poor response to immunizations Repeat CT scan as needed, neurologic examinations every 3 months for early identification and prompt referral to services Comprehensive nutritional support as needed Treat infections early and aggressively	HIV specialist/center, nutritionist
	Immunizations Modified schedule	No varicella vaccine; use inactivated polio vaccine (and with siblings), add pneumococcal vaccine at age 2 years; use passive immunization for exposure to measles, chickenpox, hepatitis B, and tetanus	Primary care office
	Dental Care	Review oral hygiene	Dentist
	Associated Behavior Problems/Mental Health Issues (especially when child also has had prenatal drug exposure) Inattention, hyperactivity Aggression Oppositionality Anxiety	Child and family interviews, behavioral rating scales, and preschool information	Referral to child development team, mental health professional as needed
	Developmental Progress, Early Intervention (EI)/Early Childhood Special Education (ECSE) Services Developmental delay Language delay/speech disorder Gross motor delay Regression	Developmental screening and surveillance every 3–6 months Detailed musculoskeletal and neuromotor examinations Referral for eligibility testing for EI/ECSE services as needed	Evaluation by child development team, or individual evaluations by psychologist, speech-language pathologist, physical therapist as needed

The Physician's Guide to Caring for Children with Disabilities and Chronic Conditions, edited by Robert E. Nickel and Larry W. Desch, copyright © 2000 Paul H. Brookes Publishing Co.

Guidelines for the Care of Children and Adolescents with Human Immunodeficiency Virus Infection *(continued)*

The following elements are recommended by age group, and the listing is cumulative. Review all items indicated up through the actual age group of a child entering your practice for the first time as part of the initial evaluation.

AGE	KEY CLINICAL ISSUES/CONCERNS	EVALUATIONS/KEY PROCEDURES	SPECIALISTS
Birth–5 years (pre–school age) *(continued)*	*Review of Diagnosis and Anticipatory Guidance* Immunizations Prevention of transmission Prophylaxis of PCP Counseling the child Transitions from EI to ECSE and from ECSE to grade school Informing the school Health of parent	Child and family interviews, provide educational materials, initiate care notebook Review individualized family service plan (IFSP) with family, conduct teacher interview, have school conference as needed	Primary care office in collaboration with HIV specialist/center
	Family Support Services (needs may be complex) Respite care Parent group Community health services Drug treatment for parents Counseling, job training Financial services (Supplemental Security Income [SSI])	Family interview; use parent questionnaire (e.g., Family Needs Survey); provide resource information Care coordination	Medical social worker, referral to community services as needed
	Collaboration with Community Agencies (especially in cases involving history of maternal drug use) HIV center Drug treatment program (parent) EI/ESCE services County Health Department Child Protective Services	Comprehensive care coordination with regular exchange of written information with other providers (at least yearly); care conference as needed	Primary care office
6–12 years (school-age)	*HIV-Related Complications* Wasting syndrome Mycobacterium avium complex (MAC) Pancreatitis Nephrotic syndrome Tuberculosis Malignancies Cytomegalovirus (CMV) retinitis	Consider prophylactic treatment for MAC in severely immunocompromised children Regular ophthalmologic examinations in severely immunocompromised individuals with history of CMV	HIV specialist or center

The Physician's Guide to Caring for Children with Disabilities and Chronic Conditions, edited by Robert E. Nickel and Larry W. Desch, copyright © 2000 Paul H. Brookes Publishing Co.

Guidelines for the Care of Children and Adolescents with Human Immunodeficiency Virus Infection *(continued)*

The following elements are recommended by age group, and the listing is cumulative. Review all items indicated up through the actual age group of a child entering your practice for the first time as part of the initial evaluation.

AGE	KEY CLINICAL ISSUES/CONCERNS	EVALUATIONS/KEY PROCEDURES	SPECIALISTS
6–12 years (school-age) *(continued)*	*Associated Developmental/Learning Disabilities/Need for Ancillary Services* Physical therapy, occupational therapy, speech-language therapy	Intellectual and achievement testing as needed Detailed musculoskeletal and neuromotor exam	Referral to child development team as needed, collaborate with school staff
	Associated Behavior/ Mental Health Problems Attention-deficit/hyperactivity disorder (ADHD) Oppositional defiant disorder (ODD)/ conduct disorder (CD) Anxiety Depression	Child, family, and teacher interviews; behavioral rating scales; and school report as indicated previously	Referral to mental health professional or child development team as needed, collaborate with school staff
	Social Skills/Recreation and Leisure Activities Involvement in peer group activities at school and in community (determine which supports are needed)	Social skills program at school, encourage participation in after-school and community activities Referral to community services as needed	Mental health professional, physical therapist, occupational therapist, adaptive physical education specialist as needed Collaborate with school staff
	Anticipatory Guidance Ongoing counseling of child and family Review of diagnosis with child Promote self-care/independence	Referral to community services as indicated	Primary care office in collaboration with HIV center
13–21 years (adolescents– young adults)	*Anticipatory Guidance* Transition to middle school and high school Career planning, higher education Encourage healthy behaviors (e.g., exercise, diet) High-risk behaviors (substance use or abuse, sexuality) Prevention of HIV transmission Progression of the illness Transition to adult medical services	Adolescent and family interviews; provide educational materials Teacher interview, school conference as needed	Primary care office in collaboration with HIV center Referral to gynecologist as needed

The Physician's Guide to Caring for Children with Disabilities and Chronic Conditions, edited by Robert E. Nickel and Larry W. Desch, copyright © 2000 Paul H. Brookes Publishing Co.

Family and Physician Management Plan Summary for Children and Adolescents with Human Immunodeficiency Virus Infection

This form will help you and your physician review current services and service needs. Please answer the questions about your current services on this page. Your physician will review your responses and complete the rest of the form.

Child's name _____ Today's date _____

Person completing the form _____

CURRENT SERVICES

1. Please list your/your child's current medications and any side effects.

2. What is your/your child's current school program?

   School name _____ Grade _____

   Teacher _____ Telephone _____

3. Do you/does your child receive any support services and other special programs at school (e.g., physical therapy, resource room)? Please list.

4. Who are your/your child's other medical and dental service providers?

   HIV treatment center _____

   Dentist _____

   Other _____

5. Who are your/your child's other community service providers?

   Physical therapist _____

   Community health nurse _____

   Other _____

The Physician's Guide to Caring for Children with Disabilities and Chronic Conditions, edited by Robert E. Nickel and Larry W. Desch, copyright © 2000 Paul H. Brookes Publishing Co.

Family and Physician Management Plan Summary for Children and Adolescents with Human Immunodeficiency Virus Infection *(continued)*

6. Have you/has your child had any blood tests, radiologic (X-ray) examinations, or other procedures since your last visit? If yes, please describe.

7. Have you/has your child been hospitalized or received surgery since your last visit? If yes, describe.

8. Please note your/your child's accomplishments since your last visit. Consider activities at home, in your neighborhood, or at school, as well as success with treatments.

9. What goals (i.e., skills) would you/your child like to accomplish in the next year? Consider activities at home, in your neighborhood, or at school, as well as success with a treatment.

10. What questions or concerns would you like addressed today?

Family and Physician Management Plan Summary for Children and Adolescents with Human Immunodeficiency Virus Infection

The *Family and Physician Management Plan Summary* should be completed at each annual review and more often as needed. It is intended to be used with the *Guidelines for Care*, which provide a more complete listing of clinical issues at different ages as well as recommended evaluations and treatments.

Child's name _____ Person completing form _____ Today's date _____

Clinical issues	Currently a problem?	Evaluations needed	Treatment recommendations	Referrals made	Date for status check
Family's Questions					
HIV Diagnosis and Follow-Up Testing CD$_4$+ count and viral load Treatment of infants with HIV exposure *Pneumocystis carinii* prophylaxis (PCP) Antiretroviral treatment of infants with HIV infection Adjust immunization protocol					
Growth/Nutrition					

The Physician's Guide to Caring for Children with Disabilities and Chronic Conditions, edited by Robert E. Nickel and Larry W. Desch, copyright © 2000 Paul H. Brookes Publishing Co.

Family and Physician Management Plan Summary for
Children and Adolescents with Human Immunodeficiency Virus Infection *(continued)*

Child's name _____   Person completing form _____   Today's date _____

Clinical issues	Currently a problem?	Evaluations needed	Treatment recommendations	Referrals made	Date for status check
Associated Medical Problems Prenatal alcohol or other drug exposure Hearing loss Strabismus/vision problems Neurobehavioral concerns (e.g., neonatal abstinence syndrome [NAS], difficult temperament) Seizures Maternally transmitted infections (e.g., hepatitis B, hepatitis C) Sleep disorder Pain management **Note any side effects of medications.**					
HIV-Related Complications PCP Other opportunistic infections Lymphocytic interstitial pneumonia (LIP) Encephalopathy Wasting syndrome Esophagitis Recurrent bacterial infections					
Dental Care					

Family and Physician Management Plan Summary for
Children and Adolescents with Human Immunodeficiency Virus Infection *(continued)*

Child's name _____ Person completing form _____ Today's date _____

Clinical issues	Currently a problem?	Evaluations needed	Treatment recommendations	Referrals made	Date for status check
Need for PT or OT Services HIV encephalopathy Hypertonicity, regression in skills Need for bracing or adaptive equipment					
Associated Behavior/ Mental Health Problems Inattention or hyperactivity Aggression Oppositional behaviors Anxiety, depression Attachment disorder High-risk behavior					
Associated Developmental/ Learning Disabilities Current school achievement level Review early intervention or other school services (individualized family service plan [IFSP] or individualized education program [IEP]) Developmental delay Speech-language disorder Learning disabilities					
Social Skills Involvement in peer-group activities at school and in the community (determine which supports are needed)					

The Physician's Guide to Caring for Children with Disabilities and Chronic Conditions, edited by Robert E. Nickel and Larry W. Desch, copyright © 2000 Paul H. Brookes Publishing Co.

Family and Physician Management Plan Summary for Children and Adolescents with Human Immunodeficiency Virus Infection *(continued)*

Child's name _____ Person completing form _____ Today's date _____

Clinical issues	Currently a problem?	Evaluations needed	Treatment recommendations	Referrals made	Date for status check
Self-Care and Independence					
Family Support Services					
Anticipatory Guidance List issues discussed and materials provided					
Collaboration with Community Agencies School					
Comments					

Next update of the Management Plan Summary _____

Signature _____ Date _____
(Child and parent)

Signature _____ Date _____
(Health professional)

The Physician's Guide to Caring for Children with Disabilities and Chronic Conditions, edited by Robert E. Nickel and Larry W. Desch, copyright © 2000 Paul H. Brookes Publishing Co.

RESOURCES ON HUMAN IMMUNODEFICIENCY VIRUS INFECTION

Readings

Association for the Care of Children's Health (ACCH). (1990). *Family-centered care for children with HIV infection: Checklists.* Bethesda, MD: Author. (Association for the Care of Children's Health, 7910 Woodmont Avenue, Suite 300, Bethesda, MD 20814; 301-654-6549; four checklists to help hospitals, communities, early intervention programs, and early childhood programs provide family-centered services)

Best, A., & Wiener, L.S. (Eds.), & Pizzo, P.A., & Wiener, L.S. (Compilers). (1996). *Be a friend: Children who live with HIV speak.* Morton Grove, IL: A. Whitman. (1-800-255-7675)

Crocker, A.C., Cohen, H.J., & Kastner, T.A. (1992). *HIV infection and developmental disabilities: A resource for service providers.* Baltimore: Paul H. Brookes Publishing Co. (1-800-638-3775)

Draimin, B.H. (1993). *Coping when a parent has AIDS.* New York: Rosen Publishing Group. (1-800-237-9932)

National Pediatric HIV Resource Center. (1988). *Jimmy and the eggs virus.* Newark, NJ: Author. (National Pediatric HIV Resource Center, 15 South 9th Street, Newark, NJ 07107; 201-268-8251, 1-800-362-0071; a child's viewpoint of what it is like to receive the diagnosis of HIV infection; requires supervised use)

National Pediatric HIV Resource Center. (1992). *Legal issues in pediatric HIV practice: A handbook for health care providers.* Newark, NJ: Author. (National Pediatric HIV Resource Center, 15 South 9th Street, Newark, NJ 07107; 201-268-8251, 1-800-362-0071)

National Pediatric HIV Resource Center. (1993, February). *Serving young people at risk for HIV infection: Case studies of adolescent-focused HIV prevention and services delivery programs.* Newark, NJ: Author. (National Pediatric HIV Resource Center, 15 South 9th Street, Newark, NJ 07107; 201-268-8251, 1-800-362-0071)

National Pediatric HIV Resource Center. (n.d.). *Parent information booklet series* (10 vols.). Newark, NJ: Author. (National Pediatric HIV Resource Center, 15 South 9th Street, Newark, NJ 07107; 201-268-8251, 1-800-362-0071; 10 individual booklets address diagnosis, treatment, and management of HIV in children as well as issues of parents' feelings, telling the child, and the services that families need; available in English and Spanish)

Pizzo, P.A., & Wilfert, C.M. (1994). *Pediatrics AIDS: The challenges of HIV infection in infants, children, and adolescents.* Philadelphia: Lippincott Williams & Wilkins. (1-800-638-3030)

Quackenbush, M., & Villarreal, S. (1992). *Does AIDS hurt? Educating young children about AIDS: Suggestions for parents, teachers, and other care providers of children to age 10.* Santa Cruz, CA: ETR Associates. (1-800-321-4407)

Tasker, M. (1992). *How can I tell you?* Bethesda, MD: Association for the Care of Children's Health (ACCH).

Walter, V.A., & Gross, M. (1996). *HIV/AIDS information for children: A guide to issues and resources.* Bronx, NY: H.W. Wilson Co. (1-800-367-6770)

Information

AIDS Clinical Trials Information Service (ACTIS)
Post Office Box 6421
Rockville, Maryland 20849-6421
Telephone: (800) TRIALS-A (874-2572), (888) 480-3739 (TTY), (301) 519-0459 (International)
Fax: (301) 519-6616
E-mail: ACTIS@actis.org
World Wide Web site: http://www.actis.org/

A service that provides information about AIDS/HIV clinical trials conducted by the National Institutes of Health and the Food and Drug Administration.

National Prevention Information Network (NPIN)
Centers for Disease Control and Prevention (CDC)
Post Office Box 6003
Rockville, Maryland 20849-6003
Telephone: 800-458-5231, 800-243-7012 (TTY)
Fax: (888) 282-7681
E-mail: info@cdcnpin.org
World Wide Web site: http://cdcnpin.org/

A national reference, referral, and publications distribution service for HIV and AIDS information.

National AIDS Hotline, Centers for Disease Control and Prevention (CDC)
Telephone: (800) 342-AIDS (2437) (English),
(800) 344-SIDA (7432) (Spanish); 800-243-7889 (TTY/TDD)

This hotline provides confidential information on transmission and prevention, testing, local referrals, and educational materials weekdays 9:00 A.M.–7:00 P.M. Eastern time.

HIV/AIDS Treatment Information Service (ATIS)
Post Office Box 6303
Rockville, Maryland 20849-6303
Telephone: (800) HIV (448)-0440, (888) 480-3739 (TTY)
Fax: (301) 519-6616
E-mail: atis@hivatis.org
World Wide Web site: http://www.hivatis.org/

National Pediatric and Family HIV Resource Center (NPHRC)
University of Medicine and Dentistry of New Jersey
30 Bergen Street–ADMC #4
Newark, New Jersey 07103
Telephone: (973) 972-0410, (800) 362-0071
Fax: (973) 972-0399
World Wide Web site: http://www.pedhivaids.org/

This center provides information and referrals, as well as a book list and links to other organizations.

National Organizations

National Association of People with AIDS
1413 K Street, NW, 7th Floor
Washington, D.C. 20005
Telephone: (202) 898-0414
Fax: (202) 898-0435
E-mail address: bfranklin@napwa.org
World Wide Web site: http://www.napwa.org/

National Hemophilia Foundation
116 West 32nd Street, 11th floor
New York, New York 10001
Telephone: (212) 219-8180
Fax: (212) 328-3777
World Wide Web site: http://www.hemophilia.org/

This foundation publishes a quarterly newsletter, *HIV Treatment Information Exchange.*

Further Information

American Foundation for AIDS Research: (800) 392-6327
AIDS Treatment Data Network: (800) 734-7104
AIDS Treatment News: (800) TREAT1-2 (873-2812)
Teens Teaching AIDS Prevention Program (TTAPP)
    National Hotline: (800) 234-TEEN (8336)

Meningomyelocele and Related Neural Tube Defects

Robert E. Nickel

KEY COMPETENCIES

- Discuss the causes of neural tube defects (NTDs)
- Review the use of folic acid for the primary prevention of NTDs
- Describe the methods used for the prenatal diagnosis of NTDs and issues in prenatal counseling about NTDs and associated problems
- Use a neonatal neurologic examination and evaluation for minor anomalies to evaluate a newborn with meningomyelocele
- Discuss the counseling of the parents of a newborn with meningomyelocele
- Describe the signs, symptoms, and treatment of common neurosurgical problems in children with meningomyelocele
- Discuss the signs and symptoms and treatment of common urologic problems in children with meningomyelocele
- Describe the treatment alternatives for urinary and bowel incontinence
- Describe the treatment of constipation and impaction and the prevention of decubiti
- Discuss the treatment of common orthopedic problems of children with meningomyelocele
- Use a musculoskeletal examination and observation of gait to evaluate a child with meningomyelocele
- Discuss issues that are important for adolescents and young adults with meningomyelocele

DESCRIPTION

Definition of Meningomyelocele

Meningomyelocele is a birth defect of the spine. It is an "open" neural tube defect (NTD) that results from a primary defect in neural tube closure and can occur at any level of the spine: cervical, thoracic, lumbar, and sacral. Meningomyelocele can cause variable paralysis of the muscles in the legs and sensory loss, and it is often associated with a number of potentially serious medical problems, including hydrocephalus, Chiari type II malformation, tethered cord, scoliosis, ankle–foot deformities, and bowel and bladder incontinence.

Embryology of Neural Tube Defects

The neural tube consists of the brain and the spinal cord. It is formed by two processes: *primary* and *secondary neurulation.* The brain and the spinal cord to the second sacral vertebral segment develop by *primary neurulation.* The neural plate forms neural folds that fuse to form the neural tube within the first 4 weeks of embryonic development. The distal spinal cord develops by *secondary neurulation.* Neural crest cells form a mass of cells in the midline. These cells then form canals and finally one tubular structure that joins with the spinal cord that has developed by primary neurulation. This process occurs from the fourth to the eighth weeks of embryonic development (Shurtleff & Lemire, 1995).

Research (Chatkupt, Hol, Shugart, et al., 1995; Keynes & Krumlauf, 1994; Lopez, David, & Crockard, 1997) has focused on the role of homeobox genes (e.g., *PAX, HOX*) in the development of the neural tube and the axial skeleton. Homeobox genes control the segmental development of the embryo. Mutation in the *PAX-3* gene is present in most cases of Waardenburg syndrome, type 1 (Pandya, Xia, Landa, et al., 1996; Tassabehji, Read, Newton, et al., 1992). The principal manifestations of this autosomal dominant disorder are hearing impairment, white forelock, lateral displacement of medial canthi, and occasionally NTDs. However, mutations in *PAX-3* genes have not been demonstrated in families that have two or more members with NTDs (Chatkupt et al., 1995).

Classification of Neural Tube Defects

NTDs can result from problems with primary neurulation (meningomyelocele) or secondary neurulation (lipomeningomyelocele). They can affect the brain (anencephaly), the spinal cord (meningomyelocele), or both (craniorachischisis), and they can be "open" (meningomyelocele) or "closed" (lipomeningomyelocele or meningocele). *Spinal dysraphism* and *spina bifida* are general terms that refer to NTDs that affect the spine. Table 13.1 reviews the classification of NTDs.

Causes

NTDs can be caused by teratogens (e.g., valproic acid, alcohol), chromosomal disorders (usually tri-

Table 13.1.   Classification of neural tube defects

Defects of the brain

- *Anencephaly:* Severe open neural tube defect (NTD) not compatible with life
- *Encephalocele:* Open or closed NTD, protrusion of brain and meninges through a defect in the skull
- *Craniomeningocele:* Closed NTD, a protrusion of meninges only through a skull defect

Defects of the spinal cord

- *Meningomyelocele:* Open NTD; other terms include *spina bifida aperta, myelocele,* and *myelodysplasia*
- *Meningocele:* Closed NTD, protrusion of meninges through a spinal defect
- *Myelocystocele:* Closed NTD, multicystic lesion that is continuous with the central canal of the spinal cord, associated with extrophy of the cloaca
- *Lipomeningomyelocele, lipomeningocele, and lipomyelocystocele:* Closed NTDs associated with fatty tumors
- *Diastematomyelia:* Fibrous bands or bone and cartilaginous spur in the spinal canal often associated with a split spinal cord

Defects of both brain and spinal cord

- *Craniorrhachischisis:* Open NTD involving entire spine not compatible with life

Adapted from Shurtleff, Lemire, and Warkany (1986).

Table 13.2.   Causes of neural tube defects

Teratogens

- Valproic acid (Depakene and Depakote) and other anticonvulsants
- Isotretinoin (Accutane) for the treatment of acne and etretinate (Tegison) for the treatment of psoriasis
- Methotrexate and aminopterin for the treatment of cancer and certain other diseases (e.g., psoriasis)
- Alcohol (meningomyelocele is an occasional finding in fetal alcohol syndrome [FAS])
- Thalidomide

Chromosomal disorders

- Trisomy 18 or trisomy 13
- Microdeletion of chromosome 22q11

Autosomal dominant and recessive disorders

- Autosomal dominant
    Waardenburg syndrome, type 1 (meningomyelocele)
    Anterior meningocele and sacral agenesis
    Neurofibromatosis type 1 (anterior thoracic and lumbar meningoceles)
- Autosomal recessive
    Meckel syndrome (encephalocele)

Sporadic disorders (e.g., amniotic band sequence)
Maternal insulin-dependent diabetes mellitus

Sources: Dodson (1989), Nickel and Magenis (1996), Rose and Mennuti (1993), Shurtleff et al. (1986).

somy 18 or trisomy 13), microdeletion of chromosome 22 (22q11), maternal insulin-dependent diabetes mellitus, rare autosomal dominant and recessive disorders, and some sporadic disorders. Table 13.2 lists some of the known causes of NTDs. Most NTDs do not have an identifiable cause and are due to the interaction of genetic predisposition and maternal environmental factors. Certain factors are known to predispose individuals to the development of NTDs, including folate deficiency and high vitamin A intake. Table 13.3 reviews these factors. Studies (Greenland & Ackerman, 1995; McMichael, Dreosti, Ryan, & Robertson, 1994; Shurtleff & Lemire, 1995) have reported conflicting results on the risk associated with zinc deficiency and the use of clomiphene for the treatment of infertility.

Prevalence

In the United States, the incidence of all NTDs is 1–2 per 1,000 births (Rose & Mennuti, 1993), and the birth incidence of spina bifida (meningomyelocele) declined from a peak of .59 per 1,000 in 1984 to .32 per 1,000 in 1990 (Lary & Edmonds, 1996). The birth incidence of spina bifida has declined in other areas of the world also. In the United Kingdom, for example, the birth incidence was 1.5–4.5 per 1,000 before 1980 and .74–2.5 per 1,000 after 1980 (Shurtleff & Lemire, 1995). The prevalence of NTDs is higher in families of Celtic extraction (Irish, Welsh, and Scotch), fami-

lies of German ancestry, families of Hispanic origin, and families of low socioeconomic status (Chatkupt, Skurnick, Jaggi, et al., 1994; Lary & Edmonds, 1996; Shurtleff, Lemire, & Warkany, 1986). The prevalence of NTDs is lower in Asian American and African American families (Lary & Edmonds, 1996).

Primary Prevention

Folic Acid Supplementation   All women of child-bearing age should take .4 milligrams of folic acid daily (Centers for Disease Control and Preven-

Table 13.3.   Factors that predispose infants to neural tube defects

Folate deficiency

- Studies, MRC Vitamin Study Research Group (1991) and Czeizel and Dudas (1992), suggest that as many as 50% of neural tube defects (NTDs) can be prevented by intake of folic acid

High vitamin A intake

- Intake over 10,000 units per day

Heat exposure

- Use of hot tubs or saunas
- Maternal fever

Maternal obesity

- Risk is unrelated to folic acid

Sources: Milunsky et al. (1992), Rothman et al. (1995), Werler et al. (1996).

tion [CDC], 1992; Crandall, Corson, Evans, et al., 1998). Studies (Czeizel & Dudas, 1992; MRC Vitamin Study Research Group, 1991) have shown that folic acid supplementation reduces the risk of recurrence and first occurrence of NTDs by more than 50%. The recommendation for supplemental folic acid is in addition to the daily intake of foods containing natural folate or foods fortified with folic acid. Women who are at increased risk for having a baby with an NTD should consider taking 4 milligrams of folic acid daily at least 1 month (preferably 3 months) before conception and for the first trimester of the pregnancy. This recommendation includes women who

• Have had a previous baby with an NTD or whose spouses have had a previous baby with an NTD
• Themselves (or whose spouses) have an NTD
• Have diabetes
• Are taking valproic acid or other anticonvulsants (Pacific Northwest Regional Genetics Group [PacNoRGG], 1999)

Women with the characteristics just listed should take the increased dose of folate under the supervision of a physician. Large doses of folate can mask the signs of vitamin B_{12} deficiency. In addition, these women should not take their 4 milligrams of folic acid by increasing the dose of multivitamins, because this can result in their taking harmful levels of other vitamins (PacNoRGG, 1999).

Other Methods Avoid prescribing isotretinoin (Accutane) and etretinate (Tegison) for women of childbearing age. Review anticonvulsant management prior to the pregnancy of women who are taking anticonvulsants, and counsel women to avoid the use of alcohol during pregnancy. In addition, counsel women about other factors that predispose their babies to NTDs, such as high vitamin A intake and the use of hot tubs.

Prenatal Diagnosis

Maternal Serum Alpha-Fetoprotein Measurement of maternal serum alpha-fetoprotein (MSAFP) is used to screen for open NTDs. MSAFP testing should be offered to all pregnant women at 15–20 weeks' gestation. It is often done in combination with measurement of human chorionic gonadotropin and unconjugated estriol (triple marker screen), which also screens for trisomies 21, 18, and 13. An elevated MSAFP (2.0–2.5 times the median value) identifies 80% of fetuses with open meningomyelocele and 90% of fetuses with anencephaly (Rose & Mennuti, 1993). An elevated MSAFP can also be explained by other factors such as incorrect gestational dates (the norms for MSAFP are strongly dependent on gestational age).

Amniocentesis and High-Resolution Ultrasound Pregnant women with elevated MSAFP and women at high risk for having a baby with an NTD should be offered testing with high-resolution ultrasound and amniocentesis. In a study (Omtzigt, Los, Hagenaars, et al., 1992) of pregnant women taking valproic acid, MSAFP identified only two of five fetuses with NTDs. The combination of MSAFP and ultrasound identifies about 90% of fetuses with meningomyelocele (Platt, Feuchtbaum, Filly, et al., 1992) and nearly all fetuses with anencephaly (Rose & Mennuti, 1993). The accuracy of ultrasound, however, may be limited by the amount of experience the examiner has had with prenatal ultrasound.

Amniocentesis confirms the presence of an open NTD. Amniotic alpha-fetoprotein (AFP) and acetylcholinesterase levels are high with open NTDs. Acetylcholinesterase is specific to open NTDs. If the AFP is high and the acetylcholinesterase is not detectable, the fetus likely has another open defect (e.g., gastroschisis). Normal amniocentesis and ultrasound following an elevated MSAFP exclude an open NTD with a high degree of confidence (Rose & Mennuti, 1993). Chromosomal analysis of amniotic fluid identifies fetuses with chromosomal disorders. In one study (Babcook, Goldstein, & Filly, 1995), 9 of 52 (17%) fetuses with open NTDs had abnormal karyotypes, and 2 of the 9 (21%) had no other anomalies identified by ultrasound. The presence of a chromosomal disorder is critical information for prenatal counseling.

High-resolution ultrasonography (US) also can provide limited prognostic information about the open NTD. US may identify other anomalies and can identify the level of the defect with reasonable accuracy. A study of 28 newborns (Babcook, 1995) found 78% agreement within one spinal level between the prenatal US and the clinical examination of the newborn. The ultrasound is not helpful in predicting postnatal hydronephrosis or bladder function, and lower-extremity motion on prenatal US is not predictive of later motor function.

Prenatal Counseling

Optimally, prenatal counseling is provided by members of the spina bifida team and the perinatologist. Schedule ample time for an appointment that both parents and other support people can attend. Make sure that the results of all prenatal tests, including chromosomal analysis, are available. If the fetus has a congenital heart defect and/or cleft palate, request fluorescent in situ hybridization

(FISH) testing for the 22q11 microdeletion in addition to chromosomal analysis. If the fetus has one or more anomalies in addition to the NTDs or abnormal chromosomal analysis or FISH testing, consider referral to the medical geneticist prior to prenatal counseling. The goals of prenatal counseling are to answer the parents' questions, to provide general information about the birth defect, and to review functional outcomes and the treatment services available. Specific questions that may be asked include the following:

- Will my child walk?
- Will he or she have mental retardation?
- Will she or he be able to attend our neighborhood school?
- Will he or she be able to have a family?

In general, avoid specific predictions, and provide a range of outcomes. Most children with spina bifida, even those with higher levels of paralysis, can walk with appropriate bracing (Charney, Melchionni, & Smith, 1991). Approximately 50% of children with spina bifida and high levels of paralysis (thoracic level) have mental retardation. In addition, about 85% of children with spina bifida require a ventriculoperitoneal shunt for the treatment of hydrocephalus, and nearly all experience bowel and bladder incontinence (McLaughlin & Shurtleff, 1979).

The prenatal ultrasound may provide limited prognostic information. If the fetus has microcephaly or another brain malformation (e.g., agenesis of the corpus callosum), the risk for mental retardation is increased. The fetus with a large thoracic NTD on ultrasound is likely to have a high motor functional level and is at an increased risk for having mental retardation and learning problems. Specific prognostic information is available for the fetus with spina bifida and trisomy 18 or another chromosomal syndrome. Only 5%–10% of infants with trisomy 18 survive the first year, and all have severe mental retardation (i.e., require extensive support) (Jones, 1997).

Finally, review information about labor and delivery management, including the recommendation that the birth take place at a regional center with the support of an experienced spina bifida team and discussion of the possible benefits of cesarean section delivery. Families may need assistance from the health professional in identifying social supports within their extended family and community. Some families may require more than one counseling session as they experience grief at the "loss" of a child who is expected not to have congenital impairments or disabilities.

Evaluation and Management of the Fetus with Meningomyelocele in the Third Trimester

Premature Delivery Ventricular size of fetuses with meningomyelocele should be followed in the third trimester by sequential ultrasonography every 1–2 weeks (Rekate, 1991b). Ninety-four percent of fetuses with meningomyelocele have ventriculomegaly after 24 weeks of gestation (Babcook, 1995). Occasionally, the fetus demonstrates progressive or marked ventriculomegaly and may benefit from premature delivery in order to treat the hydrocephalus. Delivery after the demonstration of fetal lung maturity minimizes the risks to the baby (Rekate, 1991a).

Fetal Surgery The benefit of fetal surgery for hydrocephalus (ventriculoamniotic shunt) has not been demonstrated (Rekate, 1991b). Research (Adzick, Sutton, Crombleholme, & Flake, 1998; Bruner, Tulipan, & Richards, 1996; Meuli-Simmen, Meuli, Hutchins, et al., 1995) has suggested that fetal surgery to close the exposed neural plate late in the second trimester may preserve neurologic function; however, the data supporting this procedure are extremely limited. Amniotic fluid has been demonstrated to be toxic to the exposed neural plate in fetal sheep, and neurologic damage can be prevented by fetal surgery (Meuli, Meuli-Simmen, Yingling, et al., 1996).

Cesarean Section Delivery Studies (Hill & Beattie, 1994; Cochrane, Aronyk, Sawatzky, et al., 1991; Luthy, Wardinsky, Shurtleff, et al., 1991; Shurtleff, Luthy, Nyberg, et al., 1994) have provided conflicting data on the benefit of cesarean section prior to labor in preserving neurologic function (improving motor outcomes). Luthy and co-workers (1991) compared the outcomes of 47 infants delivered by cesarean section prior to the onset of labor with 37 infants delivered by cesarean section after the onset of labor and 78 infants delivered vaginally. At age 2 years, the level of paralysis in the children studied was three segments below the anatomic level of the defect for infants delivered by cesarean section prior to labor but only one level below for infants delivered vaginally or by cesarean section after labor. At 4 years of age, those in the group delivered by cesarean section prior to labor were experiencing more late complications; however, similar differences in neurologic outcomes persisted (Shurtleff et al., 1994). The presence of intact amniotic membranes appeared to be a critical factor. Infants born by cesarean section before or after labor were similar if their amniotic membranes were intact. Other authors (Cochrane et al., 1991; Hill & Beattie, 1994) have not noted differences in motor outcome, and the results of Luthy and colleagues may have been affected by the selection bias of women having cesarean section deliveries after receiving prenatal diagnoses. Luthy and colleagues recommended several contraindications to cesarean section prior to labor. These include fetuses with trisomy 18, trisomy 13, or another lethal disorder and fetuses that have not demonstrated knee and ankle motion (Shurtleff & Lemire, 1995).

Associated Medical and Developmental Problems

Table 13.4 lists the medical and developmental problems that may be experienced by children and adolescents with meningomyelocele. Each will be discussed in greater detail in the following section.

EVALUATION AND MANAGEMENT OF NEWBORNS WITH MENINGOMYELOCELE

Optimally, the mother is transported for delivery to a regional center with a team of professionals who are experienced in the care of newborns and children with meningomyelocele. If the baby is not born in a hospital or other location where consultation with an experienced team can be obtained, the infant should be transported to the regional center when stable.

An experienced treatment team includes a developmental pediatrician, a nurse, a neurosurgeon, an orthopedist, a urologist, physical and occupational therapists, and a medical social worker. These clinicians work collaboratively with the primary care physician, the neonatologist, and the family. Depending on the problems of each newborn, some of these professionals may have limited contact with the infant and family. Other members of the treatment team become involved during outpatient follow-up and may include a physiatrist, a nutritionist, a psychologist, a speech-language pathologist, and a special educator. Finally, the child with meningomyelocele may require consultation by other medical professionals, including a pediatric neurologist, a medical geneticist, or an ophthalmologist.

The responsibilities of the primary care physician or the neonatologist are to

- Take a complete family, pregnancy, and perinatal history
- Perform a physical examination to identify
  a. Physiologic stability
  b. Additional major and minor anomalies
  c. Musculoskeletal deformities
  d. Apparent motor function level
- Request initial laboratory and radiologic tests

- Arrange for consultation or transport for evaluation by an experienced treatment team
- Participate in treatment planning with parents and team members
- Most important, provide emotional support to parents, assist them in identifying social supports within their extended family and the community, and advocate for sufficient time for parents to make treatment decisions

Evaluation Prior to Back Closure

Initial Care of the Exposed Neural Plaque   The neural plaque of infants with meningomyelocele is usually exposed at the center of the defect. The first priority is to protect the wound from infection. Follow these steps in the acute care of the exposed neural plaque:

- Handle the infant with sterile gloves.
- Use sterile linen, drapes, and clothing.
- Cover first with moist, sterile dressing and then plastic wrap.
- Keep moist with Ringer's lactate or sterile saline (some researchers [e.g., G.S. Liptak, personal communication, February 1997] recommend avoiding moist dressings because of the risk of drying and adhering to the wound during transport).
- Avoid trauma; keep the infant in a prone or a side-lying position.
- Obtain a cerebrospinal fluid (CSF) culture from the subarachnoid space ventral to the NTD and start the infant on antibiotics as if treating neonatal meningitis (unless the NTD is skin-covered) (Shurtleff & Stuntz, 1986).

Physical Examination   The first objective of the physical examination is to assess physiologic stability and treat related problems as needed. Other objectives of the physical examination are to identify

- Additional major and minor anomalies
- Musculoskeletal deformities
- The apparent level of neuromotor impairment
- Any other factor that may influence functional outcomes

Any newborn with two or more major defects (including the NTD) or three or more minor anomalies may have a chromosomal disorder or birth defect syndrome. If unfamiliar with a structured examination for minor anomalies, please review the Surface Evaluation for Minor Congenital Anomalies form located in the Appendix at the end of Chapter 5.

Conduct a neonatal neurologic and musculoskeletal examination, paying specific attention to motor and/or sensory function. If unfamiliar with a structured neonatal neurologic examination (e.g., Dubowitz), please review the section "Neonatal

Table 13.4.   Medical and developmental problems associated with meningomyelocele

Problems with ambulation (described in motor functional levels)
- Thoracic; high, mid, and low lumbar; and sacral

Musculoskeletal problems
- Foot–ankle deformities (present in most children with spina bifida)
- Hip problems (e.g., dislocation or subluxation)
- Knee deformities (e.g., flexion and extension contractures)
- Rotational deformities of legs (e.g., internal tibial torsion)
- Scoliosis, kyphosis, lordosis
- Osteopenia/fractures of the legs

Upper-extremity problems
- Weakness/hypotonia or spasticity
- Incoordination

Hydrocephalus
- About 85% of infants with meningomyelocele have hydrocephalus and require a cerebrospinal fluid (CSF) shunt for treatment

Chiari type II malformation
- Present in almost all infants and severe symptoms in about 20% of infants

Other brain malformations (e.g., agenesis of the corpus callosum)

Hydromyelia or syringomyelia
- Present on magnetic resonance imaging (MRI) in 20%–40%

Tethered cord (nearly all children with meningomyelocele are at risk)

Other spinal anomalies
- Hypoplastic spinal cord
- Spinal arachnoid cysts
- Diastematomyelia and diplomyelia

Other congenital defects (if present, evaluate for a chromosomal disorder or birth defect syndrome)
- About 3% of children with meningomyelocele have a cleft lip or palate or a congenital heart defect
- Orthopedic defects (e.g., radial hypoplasia)
- Renal anomalies

Seizures (occur in 15% of children and adults with meningomyelocele)

Decubiti (i.e., pressure ulcers), **burns, and abrasions** (all children with meningomyelocele are at risk)

Growth and nutrition
- In some infants, oral motor dysfunction and failure to thrive (FTT) caused by symptomatic Chiari type II malformation
- Obesity (most children with high lumbar or thoracic motor levels)
- Apparent growth hormone deficiency in a few children
- Precocious puberty in a few children

Urologic problems (present in nearly all children and adults with meningomyelocele)
- Incontinence
- Hydronephrosis
- Vesicourethral reflux
- Recurrent urinary tract infections
- Stones (calculi)
- Renal damage/dysfunction

Bowel problems (present in nearly all children and adults with meningomyelocele)
- Incontinence
- Constipation or impaction
- Rectal prolapse

Eye problems
- In one study, only 27% of children with meningomyelocele definitely had normal visual function (Gaston, 1991)

Nonverbal learning disabilities (NVLD)

Visual motor dysfunction

Mental retardation
- 50% of children with high lumbar or thoracic levels
- About 15% of children with low lumbar or sacral levels

Psychosocial problems
- Low self-esteem, depression, social isolation, and unemployment as young adults

Sexual dysfunction and infertility as adults
- In females, vaginal lubrication problems; fertility is normal
- In males, lack of psychogenic erections and failure or retrograde ejaculation (especially if level above mid-lumbar); most males are infertile

Latex allergy
- Present in as many as 50% of older children with meningomyelocele

Autonomic dysreflexia
- Significant risk if spinal level above midthoracic (T4–T6)

Adapted from McLaughlin and Shurtleff (1979).

Neurologic Examination" in Chapter 11. Carefully assess the newborn's
- Alertness
- Cranial nerve function including visual and auditory orienting, strength and/or pattern of sucking
- Position at rest

- Passive range of motion
- Spine and hips
- Muscle consistency and resistance to passive stretch
- Muscle bulk and presence of palpable tendons (e.g., medial hamstring tendons)

- Extremity size or length and symmetry
- Volitional movement
- Sensory level
- Leakage of urine or meconium with crying
- Resting anal sphincter tone

Use a pinprick to supplement the neonatal neurologic examination (e.g., Dubowitz) and to assist in determining approximate sensory and motor levels. Start distally and work proximally, first with the upper extremities and then with the lower extremities. Make the distinction between the motion of the legs to stimulation of the foot (possibly because of a spinal reflex) and movement of the legs in response to stimulation of the trunk or the upper extremities (likely volitional motion). Watch for leakage of urine or meconium during crying, and note resting anal sphincter tone. The presence of an anal wink reflex is not helpful in determining the degree of neurogenic bowel dysfunction. Similarly, a tight sphincter is not indicative of normal function. Note the presence of orthopedic problems, particularly scoliosis or kyphosis, hip dislocation or subluxation, club feet or other foot deformities, and flexion contractures of the hips and knees.

Prenatal, Perinatal, and Family Histories Maternal illness (e.g., diabetes), use of medication (e.g. valproic acid), and potential teratogens (e.g., alcohol) are important pieces of information to help determine the cause of the NTD. Perinatal complications (e.g., asphyxia) may affect an infant's developmental prognosis. In addition, a family history in a first-degree relative of NTD, congenital heart defect, or cleft palate suggests a specific genetic cause (e.g., the 22q11 deletion). If the infant's parents have experienced two or more miscarriages prior to the current pregnancy, either the mother or the father may be a translocation carrier of a chromosomal abnormality. Please review the discussion of family history in Chapter 5.

Radiologic and Laboratory Evaluation The radiologic and laboratory evaluation of the newborn with meningomyelocele includes

- Cranial ultrasound
- Renal and bladder ultrasound
- Serum creatinine and blood urea nitrogen (BUN)
- Urinalysis and urine culture
- Measurement of postvoid residual urine volume
- Chromosomal analysis and FISH testing for the 22q11 deletion as needed

The objectives of the cranial US are to determine ventricular size and cortical mantel thickness and to identify other central nervous system (CNS) malfor-

mations. If the newborn has markedly asymmetric neurologic function, also request a spinal magnetic resonance imaging (MRI) scan to identify a hemimyelocele (Byrd & Radkowski, 1991). The objectives of the renal or bladder US are to clarify anatomy and determine the presence of hydronephrosis.

Also obtain serum creatinine (Cr), BUN, urinalysis, and urine culture as part of the initial laboratory evaluation. If the Cr is obtained in the first 24–48 hours after birth, the value reflects maternal levels and, if elevated, must be repeated later in the first week after birth. Request bladder catheterization to measure the postvoid residual urine volume. Optimally, this measurement is obtained immediately following spontaneous voiding. This information helps determine the need for treatment of inadequate bladder emptying or increased bladder outlet resistance.

If amniotic fluid chromosomal analysis has not been obtained, request blood chromosomal analysis as needed. All babies with two or more major anomalies or three or more minor anomalies should be considered for chromosomal analysis, even when a clear history of exposure to a teratogen or maternal diabetes has been determined. Babies with congenital heart defects, especially those with conotruncal defects, and babies with cleft palate and additional features of velocardiofacial (VCF) syndrome (e.g., dysmorphic facial features, long fingers) or DiGeorge sequence (e.g., hypocalcemia, thymic aplasia) should be tested for the 22q11 deletion (Nickel, Pillers, Merkens, et al., 1994). Approximately 3% of children with meningomyelocele have the 22q11 microdeletion (Nickel & Magenis, 1996). If the results of these studies are normal, evaluation by the medical geneticist will assist in the diagnosis of a specific birth defect syndrome (e.g., fetal alcohol syndrome [FAS]).

Counseling the Family
About the Initial Treatment Plan

The initial counseling session should be timely and led by a member of the spina bifida team. The purpose of this meeting is to discuss the initial treatment of the infant with the infant's parents. Parents should receive general information about NTDs and associated medical and developmental conditions; participate in a discussion of the cause of the NTD in their baby; be given a description of the problems that have been identified, additional evaluations needed, and probable functional outcomes; and receive suggestions for recommended treatments. For most babies, initial treatment includes surgical closure of the NTD and possible treatment of hydrocephalus if marked ventriculomegaly is present on the US. No active treatment is appropriate for newborns with severe or profound disability and little likelihood of survival (e.g., trisomy 18, trisomy 13). In these cases, active treatment would serve only to prolong the infant's pain and discomfort.

Prenatal diagnosis and counseling of the family facilitates the discussion of the initial treatment of the newborn markedly. Unfortunately, if the infant has been transported for care, discussion of treatment must be conducted by telephone with one or both of the parents. Transport of the mother prior to delivery can prevent this circumstance from arising. It is critical that parents are actively involved in all treatment decisions. They need adequate information, counseling, and emotional support, as well as ample time to make treatment decisions.

Surgical Closure of the Neural Tube Defect

Surgical closure of the NTD is usually done by 24–48 hours of age to prevent infection and further loss of neurologic function (Noetzel, 1989). Approximately 75% of defects can be closed primarily without special techniques, and roughly 25% are large and difficult to close (Ramasastry & Cohen, 1995). A variety of approaches have been developed to close large back defects. One widely used method is the creation of bipedicle skin flaps by bilateral relaxing incisions. The use of latissimus dorsi gluteus maximus musculocutaneous flaps is a more technically difficult operation; however, it eliminates the need for relaxing incisions, preserves muscle function, and maintains a good vascular supply (Ramasastry & Cohen, 1995). The use of split-thickness skin grafts to the open NTD is not an appropriate long-term treatment because of the potential for trauma and scarring to the neural plaque.

Several factors may delay the timing of back closure, including CSF infection, other illness (e.g., respiratory distress syndrome), evaluation for a possible chromosomal disorder or a birth defect syndrome, and delay in the parents' decision making. Some authors have stated that back closure can be delayed for several days if necessary for treatment planning without increasing the risk of infection or worsening the motor prognosis (Charney, Weller, Sutton, et al., 1985). In one study (Charney et al., 1985), no difference was noted in the rate of ventriculitis, developmental delay, or worsening of paralysis among 52 infants who received "early" surgery (by 48 hours after birth): 32 infants had "delayed" back closure (3–7 days after birth), and 12 infants had "late" surgery (1 week–10 months of age).

Evaluation and Management Subsequent to Back Closure

Neurosurgical Problems The principal neurosurgical problems in the neonatal period other than closure of the NTD are ventriculomegaly and hydrocephalus and symptomatic Chiari type II malformation.

Ventriculomegaly and Hydrocephalus Hydrocephalus that requires placement of a CSF shunt is present in about 85% of children with meningomyelocele. These children's hydrocephalus is usually due to the Chiari type II malformation, which causes obstruction of the flow of CSF from the fourth ventricle or posterior fossa (Dias & McLone, 1993). In addition, many children who have not been shunted show some degree of ventricular enlargement.

Most infants are not born with overt hydrocephalus (Pang, 1995). CSF leaks from the open NTD prior to closure and thus decompresses the ventricular system. After back closure, all infants should be monitored for progressive ventriculomegaly with serial cranial ultrasound examinations. Most infants have a CSF shunt placed by 2–3 weeks of age (Noetzel, 1989). Ventriculoperitoneal shunts are the treatment of choice because they have certain advantages over ventriculoatrial shunts: The abdomen has a vast absorptive capacity, the abdomen can accept sufficient catheter length for many years of growth, and insertion or revision is technically less complex (Kanev & Park, 1993). The indications for shunt placement in the young infant are

- Marked ventriculomegaly
- Progressive ventriculomegaly
- Poor back healing
- Ventriculomegaly with symptomatic Chiari type II malformation (Rekate, 1991b)

Infants who are born with marked ventriculomegaly that is not due to brain atrophy can be treated by ventriculoperitoneal shunt placement at the time of back closure, placement of ventriculostomy (external ventricular drainage), or delayed placement of a shunt when the CSF has been documented to be sterile. Placement of the shunt at the time of back closure avoids a second surgery (Dias & McLone, 1993), and two studies (Miller, Pollack, Pang, & Albright, 1996; Parent & McMillan, 1995) reported no increase in shunt infection or dysfunction with simultaneous placement of the shunt and back closure. The use of external drainage is rarely necessary, because a shunt usually can be placed by 3–7 days of age (Rekate, 1991b). Some infants de-

434   Nickel

velop a CSF accumulation or leak that complicates healing of the closure site yet continues to decompress the ventricular system. External ventricular drainage and revision of the back closure may be required to treat this complication (Pang, 1995).

Transcranial Doppler ultrasound is a method developed for detecting or monitoring increased intracranial pressure (i.e., hydrocephalus). It measures intracranial blood flow and generates a resistance index (RI) and a pulsatility index (PI). An increasing PI or RI can indicate worsening hydrocephalus; however, both indexes have a broad range of normal and are affected by the infant's heart rate (Hanlo, Gooskens, Nijhuis, et al., 1995). They may be useful in monitoring an individual child (Goh & Minns, 1995).

Symptomatic Chiari Type II Malformation   Almost all children with meningomyelocele have the Chiari type II malformation. Clinically significant problems develop in up to 20% of infants and young children and can be life threatening (Shurtleff, 1986). The MRI scan is the evaluation of choice to document the child's anatomy. The MRI findings, however, do not correlate with the severity of symptoms. The Chiari II is characterized by

- Small posterior fossa with obliteration of the cisterna magna
- Caudal displacement of the medulla, lower pons, and cerebellar vermis and an elongated fourth ventricle through the foramen magnum
- Caudal displacement of the cervical spinal cord and kinking of the medulla

Almost all newborns have no symptoms related to the Chiari type II malformation. Symptoms may develop in the first 2–3 months and are reviewed in Table 13.5. Brainstem auditory evoked potentials (BAEPs) have not been shown to be a useful screening test for identifying infants who will develop brainstem dysfunction. In one study (Worley, Erwin, Schuster, et al., 1994), 10 of 11 infants with brainstem dysfunction had abnormal BAEPs; however, 10 of 25 infants without symptoms also had abnormal BAEPs. In another study (Barnet, Weiss, & Shaer, 1993) of 16 infants, BAEPs did not differentiate those with or without symptoms. The evaluation and treatment of the symptomatic Chiari II malformation are discussed in the next section.

Urologic Problems   Nearly all infants and children with meningomyelocele have some degree of neurogenic bladder dysfunction. Clinical problems in the newborn include urinary tract infections (UTIs), hydronephrosis, vesicoureteral reflux (VUR), the "high-risk" bladder, and poor bladder emptying (high bladder outlet resistance). The high pressure or

"high-risk" bladder is strongly correlated with VUR, hydronephrosis, and renal damage. In one study, 68% of 22 individuals with high bladder pressure had VUR, and 82% had hydronephrosis; however, none of the 20 individuals with low bladder pressures had VUR, and only two had hydronephrosis (McGuire, Woodside, Bordeu, & Weiss, 1981). The high-risk bladder is characterized by

- Filling pressure or leak point pressure 40 centimeters of water or more
- Bladder detrusor muscle *dyssynergia* (muscle contracts without relaxation of the external sphincter)
- Decreased bladder compliance
- Detrusor hypertonia or detrusor hyperreflexia
- Fibrotic detrusor (Fernandes, Reinberg, Vernier, & Gonzalez, 1994)

The principal objective of urologic management is the prevention of UTIs and renal damage by the early identification and treatment of the high-risk bladder, VUR, hydronephrosis, and poor bladder emptying (high bladder outlet resistance).

Table 13.5. Symptoms of Chiari type II malformation in infants and children with meningomyelocele

Infants (signs and symptoms of brainstem dysfunction)
- Feeding problems
    Choking
    Nasal regurgitation
    Poor suck
    Prolonged feeding time
    Aspiration
    Failure to thrive (FTT)
    Depressed gag
    Tongue fasciculations
    Paralysis of soft palate
- Apnea
- Weak cry
- Bradycardia
- Laryngeal stridor due to abductor paralysis of vocal cords
- Cyanotic breath-holding spells in the older infant and young child
- Upper-extremity weakness or hypotonia
- Stiff hands (will not open to hold bottle)
- Arching of neck (opisthotonus)

Older children (principally symptoms of cervical cord and cerebellar dysfunction)
- Stiff arms and hands
- Unsteady gait with frequent falls
- Poorly coordinated arm movements
- Upper-extremity spasticity or weakness
- Sensory loss in arms (pain and temperature sensation)
- Neck pain
- Facial numbness
- Respiratory compromise

Source: Rauzzino and Oakes (1995).

In addition to the studies performed on the newborn, obtain a voiding cystourethrogram (VCUG) and urodynamics when the infant is approximately 8 weeks of age. The renal US is an excellent screen for hydronephrosis (Bailey, 1991); however, 15% of the infants with normal upper tracts have VUR (Bailey, 1991). Urodynamic studies identify infants with high-risk bladders, and the postvoid residual can be measured as part of this evaluation. Some authors obtain VCUG and urodynamics only as needed based on clinical findings. In addition, urodynamics are not available at many centers. If urodynamics are not available for young infants, repeat the renal and bladder US at 3 months of age.

Clean intermittent catheterization (CIC) with anticholinergic medication (e.g., oxybutynin) is the mainstay of treatment for the high-risk bladder with or without VUR or hydronephrosis. In general, CIC must be performed at least four times daily to be effective. In one study, 24 of 26 (92%) infants with high-risk bladders and VUR and/or hydronephrosis who were managed with CIC and anticholinergics maintained normal upper urinary tracts; 27 of 56 (48%) infants who were managed without CIC, however, showed deterioration (Kasabian, Bauer, Dyro, et al., 1992). In another study, 22 of 31 (71%) children showed decreases in bladder pressure to less than 40 centimeters of water with CIC and anticholinergics. VUR resolved in 7 of 10 and hydronephrosis resolved in 3 of 4 infants (Hernandez, Hurwitz, Foote, et al., 1994). If CIC and oxybutinin fail or the family is unable to perform CIC, vesicostomy is indicated. In one study (Krahn & Johnson, 1993), 90% of infants had stabilization of the upper urinary tracts following vesicostomy. Vesicostomy is a temporary measure best suited for children younger than 2 years of age (Bauer & Joseph, 1990).

VUR associated with a low-risk bladder can be treated by prophylactic antibiotics alone. The use of antibiotics results in a significant reduction in the incidence of pyelonephritis. Phenoxybenzamine or other alpha-adrenergic blocking agents (e.g., prazosin) can be used to treat poor bladder emptying associated with low bladder pressure; however, the response is modest. In one study, 21 of 37 (57%) infants responded to 1–3 milligrams of phenoxybenzamine per day by decreasing residual urine volumes from more than 30 milliliters to less than 15 milliliters (Kimura, Mayo, & Shurtleff, 1986). Most were later treated with CIC. Sphincterotomy and urethral dilation are effective at lowering outlet resistance; however, they are contraindicated because of the high rate of subsequent incontinence (Bauer & Joseph, 1990).

Orthopedic Problems   The principal problems of the newborn are hip subluxation or dislocation, equinovarus foot deformities (clubfeet), hip and knee flexion contractures, and congenital kyphosis. There is no agreement in the literature concerning the treatment of hip subluxation or dislocation in the newborn. Treatment recommendations include passive range-of-motion exercises with or without abduction splinting of the hip (Mayfield, 1991) and casting followed by splinting (Tachdjian, 1990). The use of abduction splints (e.g., Pavlic harness) may contribute to the development of an abduction and external rotation contracture (Carroll, 1987). Little or no research data are available to support any of these recommendations. The primary treatment objective is to maintain range of motion.

Equinovarus foot deformities are treated by serial casting or strapping followed by bracing. Most investigators agree that only modest correction is accomplished by either treatment unlike the response of idiopathic clubfeet (Tachdjian, 1990). Some authors (e.g., Schafer & Dias, 1983b) have stated that partial correction by these methods decreases the risk for skin breakdown at surgery. Surgical correction is generally done at 8–12 months of age.

Hip and knee flexion contractures, as well as ankle dorsi- and plantarflexion contractures, in the newborn are treated by passive range-of-motion exercises monitored by the physical therapist. Scoliosis is generally not a problem for the newborn, unless there are vertebral anomalies causing a congenital scoliosis (e.g., hemivertebrae). However, infants born with a large NTD may have a significant congenital kyphosis that can increase the difficulty of back closure and complicate positioning. In general, congenital kyphosis requires no specific treatment in the newborn. Some orthopedists perform apical kyphectomy with wire fixation in conjunction with back closure (Pang, 1995). Infants must then wear a thoracolumbar spinal orthosis (TLSO) until they are at least 2 years of age. The role of apical kyphectomy with wire fixation or short-segment fusion in the infant or young child is controversial.

Neuromotor Functional Levels   An accurate assessment of neuromotor function is difficult in the newborn. Spinal reflexive movement can be misinterpreted as volitional movement and result in an overly optimistic judgment about motor function; conversely, transient weakness or paralysis from spinal cord shock can result in an overly pessimistic assessment (McLaughlin & Shurtleff, 1979). A careful neuromotor examination that starts in the upper extremities and trunk and moves distally to proximally minimizes the error of interpreting spinal reflexive movement as volitional movement. In addition, if a neonate has good muscle bulk and palpable tendons, spinal cord shock may account for the lack of active function in those muscles. These difficulties underline the importance of serial examinations to determine accurate motor and sensory levels. Motor level is the best predictor of functional status.

The physical therapist completes a detailed neuromotor assessment of the infant and provides the family with instructions for passive range-of-motion exercises, positioning and handling techniques, and appropriate developmental activities (Ryan, Ploski, & Emans, 1991). Positioning alternatives may be limited in the young infant by delayed healing of the back closure and treatment of hydrocephalus.

Other Problems Nearly all infants and children have some degree of neurogenic bowel dysfunction. In infancy, the treatment priority is prevention of constipation. Please review the discussion on management of the neurogenic bowel in the following section. Some infants develop significant feeding dysfunction related to the Chiari type II malformation and require evaluation by a feeding specialist as well as implementation of a specialized oral feeding program. Other infants with obvious visual problems (e.g., marked strabismus, visual inattention) require consultation by the ophthalmologist.

Counseling Families Prior to the Infant's Discharge from the Neonatal Intensive Care Unit Discharge planning should begin early in the infant's hospitalization. The plan is reviewed in detail during the discharge conference. Schedule ample time so that all of the family's questions can be discussed. This conference should provide a summary of the child's treatment in the hospital and treatment recommendations from all of the professionals involved in the child's care. The following issues are addressed:

- Review of general information on NTDs and the problems associated with meningomyelocele
- Discussion of the child's condition, treatment in the hospital, and ongoing treatment recommendations (e.g., home exercise, positioning and handling recommendations)
- Review of discharge medications, scheduled appointments, and referrals to community services (e.g., early intervention [EI] services)
- Presentation of individual educational materials on spina bifida and initiation of a care notebook
- Anticipatory guidance in the form of handouts on prevention, symptoms of shunt obstruction and infection, symptoms of Chiari II malforma-

tion, and symptoms of UTIs (available from the Spina Bifida Association of America [SBAA] and from most spina bifida teams)
- Review of family support and resource needs (e.g., community health nurse referral)
- Assistance for families in establishing contact with another family with a child with meningomyelocele (e.g., through a local Parent-to-Parent program or in a clinic) when appropriate

Important Care Coordination Issues Clear and regular communication among service providers is highly important. The infant and family require services from a variety of health, education, and social service providers. All infants with meningomyelocele require primary care in a medical home in their local community, as well as regular follow-up by the team of specialists to provide needed services and to assist with care coordination. The components of comprehensive care coordination for children with disabilities and chronic conditions are reviewed in Chapter 1. In addition to the general recommendations discussed in Chapter 1, the responsibilities of primary health care professionals in coordinating the care of children with meningomyelocele and their families are as follows:

- Identify the contact people for the team of spina bifida specialists, EI services, and the county health department in the family's community.
- Clarify with the family the responsibilities of different service providers (e.g., who the family should call first with specific questions—almost always the primary care physician).
- Review with the child and family educational materials provided to the family by the team of specialists, and clarify any misunderstandings.

EVALUATION AND MANAGEMENT OF INFANTS AND CHILDREN WITH MENINGOMYELOCELE

In general, infants are evaluated by the spina bifida team at least every 3–6 months, preschool-age children are evaluated every 6–12 months, and children ages 1 year and older are evaluated yearly. Some children also require individual appointments with specialists to address specific issues (e.g., the pediatric neurosurgeon and the child with possible symptoms of shunt dysfunction). Because of the changing nature of the clinical problems of children with meningomyelocele, regular examination and accurate data collection (for comparison from one visit to the next) and collaboration among all service providers are critical to successful management. For example, teachers or school therapists may be the first to notice changes indicative of serious medical problems.

The primary care office and the spina bifida team work collaboratively with children with spina bifida and their families. The responsibilities of the primary care health professional are to

- Evaluate interval problems and provide necessary acute care
- Review the treatment of associated health problems periodically, and monitor for the development of new problems
- Monitor the child's response to services, including educational services
- Review ongoing needs for family support (review Chapters 1 and 3)
- Provide anticipatory guidance in conjunction with the spina bifida team
- Assist the family with care coordination

Periodic Review and Update of the Management Plan

Review the child's progress periodically, and update the office management plan at least yearly for older children and more frequently for young children. It is important to review regularly information from families, the spina bifida team, educational staff, and other community service providers. Review growth and nutrition carefully, and conduct a detailed musculoskeletal examination and observation of gait (see the Appendix at the end of Chapter 6) as part of the periodic review. Measure the child's head circumference at each well-child visit and obtain a urine specimen to screen for urinary tract infections. Many signs or symptoms should serve as "red flags" that signify the need for *prompt* reevaluation by the spina bifida team or the appropriate specialist. These red flags include

- Rapid head growth
- Oral motor dysfunction, apnea, or stridor
- Onset or worsening of joint contractures
- Onset or worsening of scoliosis
- Deterioration in gait
- Change in the success of continence programs
- Weakness or spasticity in upper extremities
- Poor tolerance of braces
- Recurrent urinary tract infections
- Deterioration of school performance

Neurosurgical Problems

Before reading the subsections that follow, please review Table 13.6.

Ventriculomegaly and Hydrocephalus Children who have not had a CSF shunt placed as a

neonate require close follow-up for signs and symptoms of hydrocephalus (see Table 13.7). The child's head circumference (occipitofrontal circumference [OFC]) should be measured at all medical appointments. An increased velocity of head growth may be the only sign of increased intracranial pressure and progressive ventriculomegaly. Obtain cranial US at regular intervals—for example, weekly in the first weeks after birth and then at 6, 12, and 18 weeks and again at 6 months of age (Rekate, 1991b). The computed tomography (CT) scan can be used in place of the US and must be used when the infant's anterior fontanelle has closed. Children who have stable and normal ventricular size after 6 months of age do not need routine imaging studies (Rekate, 1991b). The recommendations for placement of a CSF shunt are

- Progressive ventriculomegaly
- Ventriculomegaly and symptoms of brainstem dysfunction (Chiari type II malformation)
- Ventriculomegaly and hydromyelia or syringomyelia
- Ventriculomegaly and developmental delay
- Infants who do not establish an adequate cortical mantel (smaller than 3 centimeters) by 5–6 months of age (Rekate, 1991b)
- Children younger than 3 years of age who have stable, moderate, or severe ventriculomegaly (McLone & Partington, 1993)

Continue to monitor the status of children with stable and mild ventriculomegaly with head growth and cranial US or CT scans. Research data are not available to assess the costs of not shunting (loss of intellectual potential) versus the complications of CSF shunts (e.g., infection, obstruction).

Endoscopic third ventriculostomy (ETV) has been used to treat noncommunicating hydrocephalus; however, limited research data exist with regard to its use with children with meningomyelocele (Jones, Kowk, Stening, & Vonau, 1996; Teo & Jones, 1996). ETV does offer the possibility of long-term control of increased intracranial pressure without the use of a shunt. In one study (Teo & Jones, 1996), ETV was performed in 69 individuals with hydrocephalus and spina bifida, with a success rate of 72%. The success rate was 80% when ETV was performed after 6 months of age in individuals who had been shunted previously. In addition, isosorbide and acetazolamide with furosemide have been studied as treatment alternatives to CSF shunts. Benefit has not been demonstrated for either regimen (Liptak, Gellerstedt, & Klionsky, 1992; Shinnar, Gammon, Bergman, et al., 1985). In addition, the use of acetazolamide and furosemide is associated with hypercalciuria and a

Table 13.6.   Neurosurgical problems of children with meningomyelocele

Condition	Age	Evaluations (in addition to the history and physical)	Treatment
Hydrocephalus/ ventriculomegaly	All	Cranial ultrasonography (US) or computed tomography (CT) scan	Ventriculoperitoneal shunt Alternative: Ventriculoatrial shunt
Shunt obstruction/ shunt infection	All	Cranial US or CT scan Shunt tap Radionuclide shunt study Cerebrospinal fluid (CSF) pressure monitoring	Shunt revision Antibiotics Shunt removal and antibiotics External drainage
Symptomatic Chiari type II malformation	All, most common in the first 2 months after birth (brainstem dysfunction)	Cranial magnetic resonance imaging (MRI) scan Pneumocardiogram Direct laryngoscopy Feeding assessment	Ventriculoperitoneal shunt or shunt revision Posterior fossa decompression Supportive care (including tracheostomy and gastrostomy)
Hydromyelia or syringomyelia	Infant and older child	Cranial, spinal MRI scan Somatosensory evoked potentials Electromyogram (EMG)	Ventriculoperitoneal shunt or revision Craniocervical (posterior fossa) decompression Alternative: Syringopleural or syringoperitoneal shunt
Symptomatic tethered cord (diastematomyelia and spinal arachnoid cysts can present in a similar manner)	Preschool-age child or older	Spinal MRI scan Urodynamics Somatosensory evoked potentials EMG	Surgical untethering

high risk for renal calculi (Stafstrom, Gilmore, & Kurtin, 1992).

Shunt Obstruction and Infection   The principal complications of shunts are obstruction and infection. Fifty percent of children require at least one shunt revision, and twenty percent require multiple revisions (Dias & McLone, 1993). The incidence of shunt infection per procedure varies among centers from 2% to 13% (Rekate, 1991c). Infection is the major cause of morbidity and mortality with CSF shunts. In general, there are three degrees of severity of shunt infection: infection of the distal shunt without ventriculitis, infection of the shunt with low-grade ventriculitis associated with recurrent shunt obstruction, and infection of the shunt with ventriculomeningitis (Shurtleff et al., 1986). The latter is associated with the highest risk for brain damage. Shunt infection is often associated with obstruction. The signs and symptoms of shunt infection and obstruction are listed in Tables 13.8 and 13.9.

The use of the mechanical properties of the shunt valve to diagnose shunt malfunction is unreliable (Rekate, 1991c). Radiologic assessment usually leads to the diagnosis; however, the CT scan

may show no change in children who have had persistently large ventricles (Desch, in press). Radiographs of the head, chest, and abdomen may detect disconnection or kinking of the shunt. At times, a shunt tap, radionuclide shunt study, or prolonged pressure monitoring may be necessary to diagnose shunt infection and obstruction (Rekate, 1991c).

Antibiotic Prophylaxis with Dental Procedures   Children with ventriculoatrial (VA) or ventriculoperitoneal (VP) shunts are at increased risk for shunt infections after dental procedures and should receive antibiotic prophylaxis as per the recommendations of the American Heart Association to prevent bacterial endocarditis. The need for prophylactic antibiotics for children with VP shunts is controversial (Acs & Cozzi, 1992; Helpin, Rosenberg, Sayany, & Sanford, 1998).

Symptomatic Chiari Type II Malformation   Symptomatic Chiari type II malformation is a major cause of morbidity and mortality in infants with meningomyelocele, and the results of treatment continue to be disappointing. A severe Chiari II on an MRI scan, however, does not predict severe symptoms. The cranial MRI scan documents the infant's anatomy. Infants with symptoms of Chiari

Table 13.7. Signs and symptoms of increased intracranial pressure and progressive hydrocephalus

Infants
- Large head circumference
- Rapid head growth
- Full fontanelle
- Split cranial sutures
- Dilated scalp veins
- Sunset sign
- Limitation of upward gaze
- Irritability
- Lethargy
- Apnea

Children and adolescents
- Signs and symptoms as listed for cerebrospinal fluid (CSF) shunt obstruction (see Table 13.9)
- Bradycardia
- Stridor
- Papilledema (may occur late)
- Onset or worsening of strabismus
- Onset or worsening of seizures
- Vomiting
- Opisthotonos (hyperrextension of head and neck)
- Other signs of symptomatic Chiari type II malformation

Sources: Dias and McLone (1993); Shurtleff, Stuntz, and Hayden (1986).

type II malformation may require a pneumocardiogram and direct laryngoscopy to assist with treatment planning and to monitor the brainstem dysfunction. Placement of a CSF shunt or revision of an existing shunt to control hydrocephalus is the first treatment option. If symptoms persist, the next treatment option is posterior fossa decompression and laminectomy. The benefit of this surgery to infants with significant brainstem dysfunction has not been established (Rauzzino & Oakes, 1995).

The age at presentation and severity of symptoms may be the principal factors that determine outcome. In one study (Rauzzino & Oakes, 1995), 23% of 13 infants who presented with severe symptoms at younger than 3 months of age died, 16% had poor outcomes, and 62% had good outcomes. Fifty percent of infants with vocal cord paralysis died. In contrast, none of 12 infants who presented after 3 months of age died or had a poor outcome. Some authors claim that if surgery is performed be-

Table 13.8. Signs and symptoms of cerebrospinal fluid shunt infection

Swelling, redness, and tenderness along shunt tubing
Fever
Irritability
Lethargy
Signs of shunt obstruction

Table 13.9. Signs and symptoms of cerebrospinal fluid shunt obstruction

Infants
Signs and symptoms as listed for increased intracranial pressure (see Table 13.7)

Toddler and preschool-age children
Rapid head growth
Full fontanelle (if still open)
Irritability
Decrease in activity level
Behavior change
Changes in speech
Loss of previously learned skills
Lethargy
Papilledema (may occur late)
Onset or increase in strabismus
Recurring headaches (not helped by lying down)
Onset or increase in seizures

Older children and adolescents
Poor school performance (one of the most frequent signs)
Staring spells that mimic absence seizures
Personality change
Decreased activity
Lethargy
Increase in eating and weight gain or decrease in eating and weight loss
Papilledema (may be the only sign in some individuals)
Decreased visual acuity
Onset or increase in strabismus
Recurring headaches that do not improve with lying down
Onset or worsening of seizures
Signs and symptoms of symptomatic hydromyelia or syringomyelia
Signs and symptoms of symptomatic tethered cord

Progression of symptoms
(may be rapid in older child and adolescent)
Persistent frontal headache (behind the eyes)
Recurrent vomiting
Somnolence
Pain of headache down to neck
Refusal to eat
Opisthotonos
Coma
A change in vital signs (progressing to cardiorespiratory arrest)
Presence of Chiari type II malformation predisposes older children and adolescents to sudden cardiorespiratory arrest

Sources: Dias and McLone (1993) and Shurtleff, Stuntz, and Hayden (1986).

fore severe symptoms develop, outcomes improve. In one study (Rauzzino & Oakes, 1995), four of four infants operated on within 4 days of presentation recovered fully, two of thirteen operated on after 4 days died, and six required tracheostomy and gastrostomy. If symptoms do not improve following treatment of hydrocephalus, consider posterior fossa decompression in infants and older children with Chiari II and the following symptoms:

In the infant

- Stridor at rest or stridor that is progressive
- Aspiration pneumonia due to palatal dysfunction or gastroesophageal reflux (GER)
- Central apnea with or without cyanosis
- Recurrent cyanotic breath-holding spells
- Opisthotonus

In the older child

- Upper-extremity spasticity if functionally significant or progressive
- Progressive ataxia if functionally significant

Symptomatic Hydromyelia and Syringomyelia

Hydromyelia is the distention of the central canal of the spinal cord with communication to the fourth ventricle, and *syringomyelia* is distention of the central canal with obstruction. These terms are used interchangeably for purposes of this discussion. Both relate to disturbance of normal CSF flow at the craniocervical junction because of the infant's Chiari II. Distention of the central canal is present in 20%–40% of MRI scans in children with meningomyelocele (Rauzzino & Oakes, 1995). The distention may be local, or it may involve the entire spinal cord. Table 13.10 lists the signs and symptoms of hydromyelia and syringomyelia.

Treatment is based on the presence of clinical symptoms, not on the MRI findings. Some authors recommend a baseline MRI of the spine; others do not. The MRI study clarifies the extent of the hydromyelia or syringomyelia and the severity of the Chiari II; documents the low-lying cord (i.e., "tethered" spinal cord); and detects spinal arachnoid cyst,

Table 13.10. Signs and symptoms of hydromyelia and syringomyelia in children with meningomyelocele

- Neck and occipital pain
- Weakness of the upper extremities
- Sensory loss in the arms (may be asymmetric)
- Atrophy of hand muscles
- Headache
- Hyperextension of head and neck (retrocollis)
- Fasciculations of tongue
- Loss of deep tendon reflexes (DTRs) in arms
- Increase in DTRs in legs
- Onset or worsening of spasticity of legs
- Onset or worsening of hip and knee flexion contractures
- Onset or worsening of scoliosis
- Cranial nerve and brainstem dysfunction (onset can be rapid)
- Horner's syndrome (complete or partial)

Source: Nohria and Oakes (1994).

hypoplastic cord, or diastematomyelia if present. If clinical symptoms develop, repeat the spinal MRI scan to look for anatomic change in the syrinx. The use of somatosensory evoked potentials (SSEPs) of the median nerve for the diagnosis of symptomatic hydromyelia and syringomyelia is primarily of research interest at this time (Krieger & Sclabassi, 1995). The electromyogram (EMG) can also be used; however, a baseline study is necessary, and it is a painful procedure that young children tolerate poorly.

The first treatment consideration is control of hydrocephalus. Placement or revision of a ventriculoperitoneal shunt may result in improvement in some infants (Milhorat, Miller, Johnson, et al., 1993). After treatment of hydrocephalus, most investigators agree that the principal treatment objective is decompression of the craniocervical junction (i.e., posterior fossa decompression) to correct the physiologic defect in CSF fluid dynamics (Nohria & Oakes, 1994). In general, most children stabilize, and some improve. In one study (Nohria & Oakes, 1994), there was improvement in pain, stabilization, and modest improvement in scoliosis; however, little or no return of sensory or motor function occurred. Some authors (Rauzzino & Oakes, 1995) have recommended follow-up MRI and clinical assessment 3–6 months after decompression. If a large syrinx and clinical symptoms persist, they recommend placing a syringoperitoneal or syringopleural shunt. Others (e.g., Rekate, 1991a) have recommended the syringopleural or syringoperitoneal shunt as a primary treatment.

Symptomatic Tethered Cord

Almost all children with meningomyelocele are found to have a low-lying cord on their spinal MRI scan (i.e., the conus terminates below the second lumbar vertebral body). The diagnosis of tethered cord is based on clinical symptoms. Symptoms may appear at any age; however, tethered cord often presents at 5–8 years of age. The diagnosis and management decisions may be complicated by the presence of hydromyelia or syringomyelia, diastematomyelia, or arachnoid cyst. Table 13.11 reviews the signs and symptoms of tethered cord.

The spinal MRI scan documents the infant's anatomy and detects associated neurosurgical problems. Urodynamics are useful to document changes in bladder function to help confirm the diagnosis of symptomatic tethering. SSEPs are also useful in following individuals at risk for tethering (Krieger & Sclabassi, 1995). In one study (Boor, Schwarz, Reitter, & Voth, 1993), SSEPs identified 14 of 15 individuals with symptomatic tethering, and these symptoms improved in 8 of 10 after surgery. Motor-evoked po-

Table 13.11.   Signs and symptoms of tethered cord in
children with meningomyelocele

Back and leg pain (may be radicular)
Change in bladder or bowel incontinence
Onset or worsening of spasticity in legs
Weakness of legs
Change in sensory level in legs
Dysesthesias of feet
Gait deterioration
Onset or worsening of flexion contractures of hip
    and knee
Onset or worsening of foot deformity
Progression of hip subluxation or dislocation
Onset or worsening of scoliosis

Sources: Herman et al. (1993) and Rekate (1991a).

tentials, phase MRI scans to measure longitudinal
motion of the cord, and US scans to assess cord motion are primarily of research use at this time.

The treatment of symptomatic tethered cord is
surgical release of the "tethered" cord. Most individuals stabilize or improve. Back pain improves in as
many as 90% of these individuals; sensory and motor
deficits may improve modestly (Herman et al., 1993).
Scoliosis stabilizes for smaller curves (Hartford,
Banta, & Smith, 1995) and in children with low lumbar and sacral motor levels; however, in children
with high lumbar and thoracic motor levels, scoliosis
may progress (Reigel, Tchernoukha, Bazmi, et al.,
1994) and bladder function is unlikely to improve
(Boemers, van Gool, & de Jong, 1995). Please note
that the scientific rigor of the existing research studies on tethered cord is limited (Liptak, 1995).

Urologic Problems

Infants and young children with meningomyelocele
are at high risk for change in urologic status. Without regular follow-up and treatment, as many as
50% show evidence of upper-tract deterioration by 5
years of age (Bauer & Joseph, 1990). In one study, 8
of 26 infants with low-risk bladders as newborns
showed deterioration in the first 6 months of life
(Roach, Switters, & Stone, 1993). Please review Table
13.12 for general recommendations on the evaluation and treatment of each urologic problem. Table
13.13 lists medications that are useful in the management of these issues. Most of these evaluations
should be repeated at regular intervals. Repeat the
renal and bladder US at 6 and 12 months of age and
yearly thereafter (Fernandes et al., 1994). Repeat urodynamics at 6–12 months of age and then as needed
(Stone, 1995). Other authors (e.g., Fernandes et al.,
1994) have recommended repeating urodynamics
for children with high-risk bladders yearly until they

reach 2 years of age. If urodynamics are not available
in young infants, repeat the renal and bladder US at
3 months of age. If a VCUG is not obtained from a
newborn, the VCUG should be performed at 6–12
months of age (Fernandes et al., 1994). Repeat the
VCUG as needed for children with low-risk bladders
and no VUR; however, repeat the VCUG yearly until
3 years of age for children with high-risk bladders
or until reflux disappears. Request a renal scan as
needed for further evaluation of renal damage. The
dimercaptosuccinic acid (DMSA) renal scan with
single photon emission tomography (SPECT) scan is
the most sensitive in detecting renal scars.

Urinary Tract Infections   Perform urine dipstick tests on the urine of all children at all regular
clinic visits. Obtain a urine culture when a UTI is
suspected and when *either* the leukocyte esterase
or nitrate test strip is positive (Liptak, Campbell,
Stewart, et al., 1993). In a study (Hoberman & Wald,
1997) of children without spina bifida, the sensitivity of either a positive leukocyte esterase or nitrate
for UTI was 78.7%, and specificity was 98.3%. An alternative to screening with a urine dipstick test is to
obtain a urine culture if there is pyuria on the microscopic examination of unspun urine.

Bacteriuria is common in children on CIC. In
one study (Rudy & Woodside, 1991), more than 60%
had bacteriuria but only 3% had febrile infections.
Do not treat a child with bacteriuria who does not
have symptoms of a UTI or leukocytes on urinalysis,
unless the child has VUR (Kimura et al., 1986).
Asymptomatic bacteriuria with VUR has been associated with renal damage (Fernandes et al., 1994).
Table 13.14 lists the symptoms of UTIs in children
with meningomyelocele. Please note that children
who have had bladder augmentation have mucous,
leukocytes, and bacteria in the urinary sediment.
Obtain a urine culture if children with bladder augmentation have an apparent febrile UTI or experience a change in continence associated with other
signs of infection.

Urinary Incontinence   Continence programs
are generally initiated at 3–4 years of age after the
child and family are comfortable with a bowel continence program. In general, CIC with oxybutinin is
the initial program for most children with meningomyelocele. Nonlatex catheters are used, and CIC is
performed about every 4 hours. A frequency of less
than 3 hours tends to be disruptive to both school and
home routines. In general, most children with meningomyelocele can begin to learn self-catheterization by
5–6 years of age. Table 13.15 lists the four types of
neurogenic bladder dysfunction that are based on the

Table 13.12.   Urologic problems of children with meningomyelocele

Condition	Age	Evaluation	Treatment
Hydronephrosis	All	Renal ultrasound	Clean intermittent catheterization (CIC) and anticholinergics
Vesicoureteral reflux	All	Voiding cystourethrogram	Prophylactic antibiotics CIC and anticholinergics Surgical reimplantation
High outlet resistance (large postvoid residual)	All	Postvoid residual	CIC Alternative: Alpha-adrenergic blocking agent

High-risk bladder	All	Urodynamics	CIC and anticholinergics
			Alternatives:
			  Vesicostomy
			  Bladder augmentation

Recurrent urinary tract infections (UTIs)	All	Screen with nitrite and leukocyte esterase test strips or urine culture (if reflux, hydronephrosis, or infection is suspected)	Prophylactic antibiotics (one-fourth to one-third treatment dose) Acidification of the urine with juices such as cranberry or grape or supplemental vitamin C Complete bladder emptying (use CIC or alpha-adrenergic blocking agent) Intravesical gentamycin or neomycin (limited data)
Renal damage	All	Renal scan as needed	Prevention
Renal stones (calculi)	Older children and adolescents	IVP, renal scan	High risk with ileal loop or Mitrofanoff procedure or after bladder augmentation Treatment similar to patients without meningomyelocele

Source: Bauer and Joseph (1990).

presence or absence of the high-risk bladder and the adequacy of outlet resistance (i.e., external sphincter tone). Identification of the type of bladder dysfunction is helpful in planning a continence program. In general, children with low-risk bladders and adequate outlet resistance do well on CIC and anticholinergic medication.

Bladder Augmentation   If the high-risk bladder is unresponsive to anticholinergic medication and CIC, consider *bladder augmentation* surgery. Bladder augmentation increases bladder capacity, decreases bladder pressure, and stabilizes the upper urinary tracts (Bailey, 1991). The rate of continence varies from 63% to 100% in different studies. Most children need to continue on CIC to ensure complete bladder emptying, and some children also need to continue on anticholinergics because of the presence of uninhibited contractions (Rudy & Woodside, 1991). Two types of augmentation are in general use: the *enterocystoplasty* (uses a segment of

bowel) and the *gastrocystoplasty* (uses part of the stomach). Both have noteworthy side effects (see Table 13.16). The enterocystoplasty is the most common because of the risk for peptic ulceration with gastrocystoplasty. Autoaugmentation of the bladder (removal of the detrusor muscle from the dome of the bladder) and use of a deepithelialized segment of sigmoid are being studied as alternatives; however, research data are as yet limited. Children who have had enterocystoplasty need regular bladder irrigations to remove mucous and decrease the risk for UTIs and bladder stones.

Transurethral Bladder Stimulation   Transurethral bladder stimulation has been used to increase bladder capacity and to improve continence. It is time-consuming. Twenty 90-minute sessions are required in one treatment series (Boone, Roehrborn, & Hurt, 1992). Initial studies were encouraging, especially the reported increase in bladder capacity (Kaplan, Richards, & Richards, 1989).

Table 13.13.   Medications used in the management of urologic problems

Medication	Oral dosage
Anticholinergic	
Oxybutynin chloride (Ditropan)[a]	.2 milligrams per kilogram two to four times a day, extended-release tablet available for adults and children ages 12 years and older
Propantheline	.5 milligrams per kilogram two to four times a day
Hyoscyamine sulfate (Levsin)	1/2 to 1 tablet or 1/2 to 1 teaspoon two to four times a day (children 2–12 years of age), extended-release tablet available for adults and children ages 12 years and older
Tolterodine tartrate (Detrol)	1–2 milligrams twice a day (adults and children ages 12 years and older)
Alpha-adrenergic blocking agents	
Phenoxybenzamine	.5 milligrams per kilogram two to three times a day or 1–3 milligrams per day for an infant
Prazosin	.1–.3 milligrams per kilogram two to three times a day
Sympathomimetic	
Ephedrine	.5 milligrams per kilogram two times a day to 1.0 milligram per kilogram three times a day
Pseudoephedrine	.4 milligrams per kilogram two times a day to .9 milligrams per kilogram three times a day

Adapted from Bauer and Joseph (1990).

[a]May use intravesical oxybutynin if oral meds not tolerated due to side effects.

Unfortunately, later studies (Boone et al., 1992; Decter, Snyder, & Laudermilch, 1994) from other centers have failed to confirm those results. Continuous low-intensity electrical stimulation through skin electrodes has been used to improve bladder capacity and continence (Balcom, Wiatrak, Biefeld, et al., 1997). Further research is required to clarify the possible benefits of this procedure.

Ileal Loop Diversion and Undiversion The ileal loop and nonrefluxing colon loop diversions are contraindicated because of the high rate of side effects, including recurrent infection, stones, and deterioration of the upper tracts (Bailey, 1991; Koch, McDougal, Hall, et al., 1992). In fact, *undiversion* (undoing of the ileal loop) is an appropriate treatment consideration in adolescents and young adults who have had this surgery in the past. Indications include renal deterioration and stomal problems as

Table 13.14.   Symptoms of urinary tract infections in children with meningomyelocele

Strong urine odor
Cloudy urine
Sandy particles in urine
Increase in urine mucous
Increase in wetness (incontinence)
Onset of perineal rash (due to increased wetness)
Bloody urine
Lethargy
Fever

Source: Kimura et al. (1986).

well as the desire for an improved quality of life (Herschorn, Rangaswamy, & Radomski, 1994). In one study (Herschorn et al., 1994), 18 of 20 young adults required bladder augmentation as part of undiversion, 17 of the 20 were continent after surgery, and all had stable upper tracts.

Mitrofanoff Procedure In older children and adolescents who have difficulty with CIC, the Mitrofanoff procedure (i.e., appendicovesicostomy) improves the ease of CIC and improves continence. The stoma of the appendix is placed in an easy-to-reach position on the abdomen (e.g., the umbilicus), and children perform CIC through the "continent" conduit of the appendix. Complications include stomal problems and stones (Duckett & Lotfi, 1993). The Mitrofanoff procedure also may be indicated if outlet procedures have failed.

Outlet Procedures Inadequate outlet resistance can be treated by the *artificial urinary sphincter* and several different *outlet procedures*. The artificial sphincter provides satisfactory continence in most children and is the procedure of choice in boys, according to some authors (Fernandes et al., 1994). In one study (Gonzalez, Merino, & Vaughn, 1995), 85% of 46 children had satisfactory continence and 87% of these children's sphincters were working well after 25 months. The rate of reoperation was only 7 per 1,000 child months. Other authors have experienced higher rates of complications and are less enthusiastic about the use of the artificial sphincter (Rudy & Woodside, 1991; Stone, 1995). Some children have deterioration

Table 13.15.   Treatment of urinary incontinence

Condition	Treatment
Low-risk bladder and high or adequate outlet resistance	Clean intermittent catheterization (CIC),[a] anticholinergic as needed
Low-risk bladder and low outlet resistance	CIC, anticholinergic, and sympatheminetic as needed Alternative: Outlet procedure
High-risk bladder and high or adequate outlet resistance	CIC and anticholinergic Alternative: Bladder augmentation
High-risk bladder and low outlet resistance	CIC and anticholinergic, sympatheminetic as needed Alternative: Bladder augmentation, outlet procedure as needed

[a]If the child has difficulty performing CIC, consider using the Mitrofanoff procedure.

of the upper tracts after placement of the artificial sphincter or other outlet procedures. This factor underlines the importance of adequate evaluation of the bladder, including urodynamics, before implementing a procedure to increase outlet resistance.

No agreement exists with regard to the outlet procedure of choice. Surgeries that increase outlet resistance include the pubovaginal sling (may be the procedure of choice in girls [Rudy & Woodside, 1991]), bladder neck reconstruction (Young-Dees-Leadbetter procedure or modification), and urethral lengthening (Kropp procedure or modification). In general, these procedures improve continence by creation of a one-way flap valve. Studies report satisfactory rates of continence following all of these procedures. Some children have difficulty with catheterizing after the Kropp procedure, and all children must do regular CIC postoperatively (Kropp & Angwao, 1986). It is contraindicated if compliance is an issue. In addition, injections of

Table 13.16.   Side effects of bladder augmentation surgery

Enterocystoplasty (cecum, sigmoid, small bowel)
- Mucous production increases risk of infection and stones and can block catheters
    Regular bladder irrigation required
- Nearly all have compensated hyperchloremic acidosis
- Osteopenia in long-term follow-up
- Risk of adenocarcinoma at anastomosis (about 30 cases reported worldwide)
- Bladder perforation
- Do not use ileocecal segment, because of resultant diarrhea and increase in fecal incontinence

Gastrocystoplasty (stomach)
- Metabolic alkalosis and hypokalemia
- Hematuria, dysuria and risk for peptic ulcer
    Children must take histamine-2 blockers
- Increased risk for stones

Sources: Fernandes et al. (1994) and Rudy and Woodside (1991).

glutaraldehyde cross-linked collagen have been used to treat inadequate outlet resistance. Research data are limited, and the injections appear to be less useful in children with spina bifida who require regular CIC than in other groups (Bomalaski, Bloom, McGuire, & Panzl, 1996).

External Collection Devices   Finally, *external collection devices* (penile collector or condom catheter) can effectively treat incontinence in males if other measures are unsuccessful or are contraindicated. Good skin care and hygiene are important. Some males are difficult to fit, and a method more compatible with sexual function needs to be found by adolescence (Kimura et al., 1986).

Neuromotor Dysfunction

The overall goal of treatment is to maximize the child's function, independence, and self-esteem and to facilitate the highest possible quality of life (Ryan et al., 1991). Treatment modalities include physical therapy (PT) and occupational therapy (OT), braces (i.e., orthoses), wheelchairs, other assistive devices and adaptive equipment, medical interventions, and surgeries.

Physical and Occupational Therapy Services   PT and OT services include assessment, stretching (passive range of motion), activities to facilitate movement and posture, gait training, muscle-strengthening exercises, recommendations for braces and assistive devices, and parent training. Formal assessments include passive range of motion, muscle strength, tests of fine and gross motor development (e.g., Peabody Developmental Motor Scales; Folio & Fewell, 1983), functional assessments (e.g., the Pediatric Evaluation of Disability Inventory [PEDI]; Haley, Coster, Ludlow, et al., 1992), and quality-of-life measures. Please review the discussion of assessment in Chapter 6. The indications for PT services are as follows:

- Regular therapy for the infant and young child to facilitate motor progress, except for infants with sacral motor function
- Infant or young child with motor delays greater than expected for motor level
- Regular therapy in preschool years for children with significant spasticity
- Gait training when the child receives a new brace or assistive device
- Children who are at high risk for progressive contractures
- Postoperatively to maintain gains or to improve function after release of a contracture
- Cardiovascular and musculoskeletal conditioning programs to improve strength, endurance, and speed

Orthotic Management Physical and occupational therapists participate with other team members to recommend braces and assistive devices. In general, children with meningomyelocele are provided with braces and related equipment as needed to allow them choices in posture, mobility, and self-care appropriate to the child's developmental age. For example, a standing frame or parapodium may be prescribed at 1 year of age to facilitate indepen-

dent standing in the child with a thoracic motor level. The child may be transitioned to a swivel walker and then the reciprocating gait orthosis (RGO) to facilitate independent ambulation. In one study (Charney et al., 1991), 52% of 87 children with high motor levels achieved independent ambulation by age 5 years with appropriate bracing.

Table 13.17 reviews general recommendations for orthotic management specific to different motor function levels. In general, the treatment goals are to 1) prevent progression of deformity, 2) support normal joint alignment, and 3) facilitate function (Knutson & Clark, 1991). Clinical experience and research data demonstrate that lower-extremity orthotics increase gait velocity and step length, improve stability of gait, and decrease energy consumption. Some braces may interfere with active mobility. Children with midlumbar motor levels and above also require a wheelchair to improve mobility and access to the environment. Introduce the wheelchair when it is apparent that it will enhance the child's mobility and independence. This should occur as early as 18 months for some children (Ryan et al., 1991). Early wheelchair use does not result in cessation of ambulation; rather, it results in an increase in activity level

Table 13.17. Motor function levels and orthotic management of children with meningomyelocele

Motor level	Muscle function	Orthosis	Age
Thoracic (T12 and above) and high lumbar (L1 and L2)	Abdominals, hip flexors (high lumbar)	Initial: Standing frame or parapodium	1 year
		HKAFO or RGO	2–3 years
		Parawalker (HGO) (use wheelchair for community mobility)	Older children and adolescents
Midlumbar (L3)	Above muscles, hip adductors, knee extensors	Initial: Standing frame or parapodium	1 year
		HKAFO or RGO	2–3 years
		HKAFO or KAFO (if strong quadriceps, AFO) (most use wheelchair for community mobility)	Preschool-age and older children
Lowlumbar (L4 and L5)	Above muscles, knee flexors (medial hamstrings), ankle plantar flexors, hip extensors, toe flexors, and foot intrinsic muscles	KAFO or AFO (most are community ambulators with braces; may use wheelchair for sports)	1 year and older
Sacral	Above muscles, knee flexors (lateral hamstrings), ankle plantar flexors, hip extensors, toe flexors, and foot intrinsic muscles	AFO, UCBL, or no braces (all walk with or without braces)	1 year and older

Adapted from Ryan et al. (1991).

HKAFO, hip–knee–ankle–foot orthosis; RGO, reciprocating gait orthosis; HGO, hip guidance orthosis; KAFO, knee-ankle-foot orthosis; AFO, ankle-foot orthosis; UCBL, University of California, Berkeley Laboratory orthosis.

Table 13.18. Classification of ambulatory status

Community ambulator
Walks without braces or aids or
Walks with braces or aids, no wheelchair or
Walks with braces or aids, uses wheelchair for long
  distances

Household ambulator
Walks with braces or aids in home or school
  (classroom) only and
Uses wheelchair for long distances

Nonfunctional ambulator
Walks with braces or aids only in therapy and
Scoots or crawls and uses wheelchair for mobility

Nonambulator
Scoots or crawls and uses wheelchair for mobility

Source: Ryan et al. (1991).

and mobility. Table 13.18 reviews a classification of ambulatory status that incorporates use of braces, aids, and wheelchairs.

Orthopedic Problems
Please review Table 13.19 before reading the following subsections.

Hip Subluxation or Dislocation Most investigators agree that reduction of the dislocated hip is not indicated in children who do not have the potential for community ambulation (high-lumbar and thoracic motor levels). These children are treated with anterior release of hip flexion contractures as needed to allow bracing for standing and limited ambulation. Continuing controversy exists, however, with regard to the treatment of children with mid- and low-lumbar motor levels. These children are at relatively high risk for subluxation, and most of them have the potential for community ambulation (because of their strong quadriceps). Several studies have demonstrated that dislocation does not affect walking ability or increase the risk of a painful hip (Crandall, Birkebak, & Winter, 1989; Sherk, Melchionne, & Smith, 1987). A 1992 study (Keggi, Banta, & Walton, 1992) found no causal relationship between unilateral dislocation and scoliosis. In addition, surgery can cause postoperative hip stiffness, fractures, and heterotopic calcification (21% of 24 children in one study; Bouchard & D'Astous, 1991), with resultant loss of function (Sherk et al., 1987). Proponents of surgical reduction argue that hip reduction improves the range of motion and quality of gait and may decrease the need for bracing (Fraser et al., 1995). They recommend that surgery be delayed until after age 2 years to assess ambulatory potential and do all needed surgeries at one time to decrease the risk of stiffness (Lindseth, Dias, & Drennan, 1991).

Flexion Contractures Flexion contractures of the hip and knee and plantarflexion contractures of the ankle can be treated by passive range-of-motion exercises (i.e., stretching), bracing (i.e., ankle–foot orthoses [AFOs]), and surgery. In general, a hip flexion contracture of 30° or more, a knee flexion contracture of 20° or more, and a plantarflexion contracture of 10° or more require surgical release (see Schafer & Dias, 1983a, 1983c). All have a significant risk for recurrence.

Foot Deformities The goal of the treatment of foot deformities is a supple, plantigrade foot (see Schafer & Dias, 1983b). Some authors recommend against arthrodesis because of the risk of skin problems in a rigid nonplantigrade foot (Karol, 1995).

Scoliosis and Kyphosis Surgical treatment of scoliosis and kyphosis is delayed as long as possible to allow for truncal growth. The use of a brace (e.g., the thoracolumbosacral orthosis [TLSO]) delays the age for surgery if the scoliotic curve is less than 40° (Muller & Nordwall, 1994). The combination of anterior and posterior fusion with Luque instrumentation appears to be superior to anterior or posterior fusion alone (Banta, 1990; Karol, 1995). The risks of spinal surgery include wound infection, pseudoarthrosis, and loss of ambulatory and self-care skills (if fusion includes the pelvis). In one study (Muller & Nordwall, 1994), 4 of 14 children lost the ability to come to a sitting position. In another study (Boemers, Soorani-Lunsing, de Jong, & Pruijs, 1996), 3 of 16 children were unable to do self-catheterization postoperatively. One author (Karol, 1995) recommended against fusion to the pelvis to prevent the loss of ambulatory skills. Other authors (Banta, Romness, Thomson, et al., 1999) consider fusion to the pelvis essential to control spinal rotation and pelvic obliquity. The role of early apical kyphectomy with wire fixation or limited fusion to treat congenital kyphosis is undefined (Mayfield, 1991).

Bowel Problems
The primary problems are constipation with or without impaction and incontinence. The principal treatment goal in the first year is prevention of constipation. Rectal prolapse is an uncommon complication in infants or young children with chronic constipation.

Rectal Prolapse Most infants can be treated by gentle reduction of the prolapse with a gloved hand and lubricant, followed by treatment of the constipation. If children have recurrent prolapse in spite of adequate treatment of chronic constipation, surgical treatment can provide excellent results (e.g., posterior repair and suspension of the rectum; Ashcraft, Garred, Holder, et al., 1990).

Table 13.19.   Representative orthopedic problems in children with meningomyelocele

Condition	Evaluation	Treatment
Scoliosis, developmental	X rays: Sitting anterior/posterior and lateral of spine	Bracing if spinal curve is greater than 20°
		Consider surgery if spinal curve is greater than 40°
		Anterior or posterior fusion with Luque instrumentation
Kyphosis, congenital	X rays: Anterior/posterior and lateral of spine	Bracing thoracolumbosacral orthosis (TLSO)
		Anterior or posterior fusion with Luque instrumentation if recurrent decubiti, loss of sitting balance, severe or progressive deformity
		Apical kyphectomy in infant or young child is controversial
Hip subluxation or dislocation	Hip ultrasound, X rays: Anterior/posterior and lateral of pelvis	Passive range of motion for flexion contracture
		If community ambulator, surgical treatment is controversial
		If not a community ambulator, use anterior release of hip flexion contracture to allow bracing
Clubfeet	X rays: Anterior/posterior and lateral of feet	Serial casts or strapping and bracing (newborn)
		Posterior medial foot release (8–12 months of age)
		Talectomy (for recurrence)
		Triple arthrodesis as needed (adolescent)
Hip flexion contracture	Range of motion	Passive range of motion
		Anterior release for contracture greater than 30°
Knee flexion contracture	Range of motion	Posterior release of knee if contracture is greater than 20°
Equinus	Range of motion	Passive range of motion, bracing (ankle–foot orthosis [AFO])
		If contracture is greater than 10°, release of Achilles tendon (posterior capsulotomy if severe contracture)
Calcaneus foot	Range of motion	Passive range of motion (infant)
		Bracing (AFO)
		Anterior tibialis transfer or anterior release (ages 5 years and older)
Fractures	Clinical examination and X ray	Soft cast with rapid return to weight bearing (usual bracing for fractures of epiphysis)

Constipation Please also review the discussion on the treatment of constipation in children with cerebral palsy in Chapter 6. Constipation in children with meningomyelocele is caused by

- Relative obstruction due to high external sphincter tone or decrease in the intrinsic innervation of the colon (Liptak et al., 1992)
- Decreased fluid intake
- Increased fluid loss
- Low bulk (soluble and insoluble fiber) content of the diet
- Diet high in constipating foods (e.g., milk products)
- Decreased activity level
- Medications (e.g., anticholinergic medications) (Wicks & Shurtleff, 1986)

The primary treatment of constipation is dietary management with supplemental bulk agents and adequate nondairy oral fluids. The greatest difficulty with the use of dietary programs and bulk agents is compliance. Children may be picky eaters with a low fluid intake. Studies of older adults have shown that psyllium is more effective than placebo (Cheskin, Kamal, Crowell, et al., 1995), that methyl cellulose is also effective and may result in improved compliance (Swartz, 1989), and that psyllium with senna (a mild stimulant) is more effective than psyllium alone (Marlett, Li, Patrow, & Bass, 1987) or lactulose (Passmore, Davies, Flanagan, et al., 1993). Bulk agents must be taken with sufficient fluid. Fruiteze® (puréed dates, raisins, and prunes; for more information, contact Fruit-Eze, Inc., 1075 N.W. Murray Road, Suite 276,

Table 13.20. Management of bowel incontinence in children with meningomyelocele

Bowel management program	Representative products
Timed with or without digital stimulation	Glycerin suppositories
Timed with glycerin suppository	Per Diem (psyllium with senna)
Timed with bulk agent with or without senna	Senekot tablets and Metamucil or Citrucel or Fiberall wafers
Timed with bisacodyl suppositories	Dulcolax suppositories, Magic Bullet suppositories
Timed with Theravac minienemas	Theravac minienemas
Timed with expansion enema	Two 8-ounce saline enemas given rapidly in sequence
Enema continence catheter	20 milliliters per kilogram high-volume saline enema every 2–3 days
Biofeedback training	Anal plug electrode
Appendicocecal enterostomy and cecostomy with antegrade enema	Saline and phosphate[a] enemas (volume as needed) daily to every other day or 30–60 milliliters of saline and glycerol daily

[a]Regular use of phosphate enemas may result in hyperphosphatemia.

Portland, OR 97229-5892, 800-743-1941) and various recipes for high-fiber cookies or muffins are good sources of soluble fiber.

Stool Impaction Intermittent impaction is a common accompaniment of chronic constipation. A plain radiograph of the abdomen (kidneys, ureters, bladder [KUB]) can help determine the degree of impaction or colon dilation. A variety of techniques have been used for disimpaction of the colon. Most involve the use of saline and oil enemas and then oral cathartics after elimination of the distal impaction. Oil enemas are necessary if saline enemas are not successful. Oral cathartics such as oral bisacodyl, magnesium citrate, or polyethylene glycol (GoLYTELY®) can be used to ensure complete emptying of the bowel once the distal impaction has been eliminated by enemas. The most common mistake with disimpaction is not treating it vigorously enough. One regimen follows:

- Use saline or mineral oil enemas daily to twice a day until hard stool is removed.
- Then use oral bisacodyl daily to twice daily for 2 days. (GoLYTELY is given once by mouth or by nasogastric tube.)
- Then return to the regular bowel program with bulk agent and oral mineral oil for a variable period of time (months).

Bowel Incontinence A bowel continence program is initiated at 2–3 years of age. The first program is a timed program (regular toileting at the same time each day) with or without digital stimulation. The basic goal of most programs is daily, complete rectal emptying. Success requires consistency and patience. Constipation and impaction must be treated before initiating or changing a bowel program. The overall effectiveness of bowel programs

is 75%–85%, and the rate of success increases with age (Shurtleff, 1986). Table 13.20 lists representative bowel continence programs.

Senna has a predictable 8- to 10-hour onset of action, so it can be given the night before a morning timed program. High-volume saline enemas have been associated with electrolyte disturbances, can cause mucosal irritation (Liptak & Revell, 1992), and may increase the risk for irritable bowel syndrome (Shurtleff, 1986). Biofeedback training with the anal plug electrode has been used to treat bowel incontinence. In one study (Whitehead, Parker, Bosmajian, et al., 1986), biofeedback training was found to be no more effective than behavior modification alone. A subgroup of individuals with sacral motor level and two or more bowel movements per day did have specific benefit.

Surgical approaches include the appendicocecal enterostomy and the cecostomy (Biggar, Morrison, Chait, et al., 1999; DePeppo, Iacobelli, DeGennaro, et al., 1999; Graf, Strear, Bratton, et al., 1998; Malone, Curry, & Osborne, 1998). Both provide "continent" conduits for the use of antegrade continence enemas. The appendicocecal enterostomy operates by the same principle as the Mitrofanoff procedure. Enema solutions have included saline, phosphate, tap water, polyethylene glycol-electrolyte solution, phosphosoda, Fleets, and glycerol (Graf et al., 1998). The enema volume has varied from 80 milliliters to 1 liter in studies, and enema frequency is generally daily to every other day (Graf et al., 1998). The use of daily enemas of 30–60 milliliters of saline and glycerol has been effective (L. Covert, personal communication, October 1999). The use of these procedures can significantly improve bowel continence for a child who has continuing stool accidents as well as the child's ability to perform a bowel program independently.

Table 13.21. Classification of pressure ulcers

Stage I
- Redness of intact skin that persists for more than 30 minutes with elimination of pressure

Stage II
- Partial thickness skin loss (appears as an abrasion, blister, or shallow crater)

Stage III
- Full thickness skin loss involving damage to subcutaneous tissue (may extend to, but not through, fascia; may or may not undermine adjacent tissue)

Stage IV
- Full thickness skin loss with damage to muscle, bone, or connective tissue

Adapted from Yarkony (1994).

Table 13.22. Steps in the prevention of pressure ulcers

Good nutrition
- Maintain adequate protein, calorie, vitamin, mineral, and fluid intake

Good perineal hygiene and skin care
- Moisture and poor hygiene significantly increase risk for ulcers

Daily skin checks
- Areas of redness that persist for more than 30 minutes raise a risk of ulcer formation

Regular (every 15–20 minutes) pressure relief (wheelchair pushups)
- Use of specialized wheelchair cushion does not eliminate the need to do regular pressure relief

Wheelchair cushions
- Use gel cushions (they reduce pressure and shear but not friction and moisture)
- Foam cushions reduce pressure somewhat but not shear, friction, or moisture
- Sheepskin pads do not relieve pressure

Improve sitting posture and balance
- Consider contoured foam cushion or custom sitting orthosis for patient with significant pelvic obliquity (reduces pressure and improves posture and balance better than standard foam, gel, or multiple-cell air-filled cushions)

Sources: Quigley and Curley (1996); Yarkony (1994).

Pressure Ulcers or Decubiti

Decubiti and other types of skin breakdown (e.g., burns, abrasions) are common in children with meningomyelocele. Pressure ulcers are more frequent in children with high motor levels; however, skin breakdown over the legs is equally common in children with any motor functional level (Shurtleff, 1986). Risk factors include inactivity, poor nutrition, poor hygiene, and ill-fitting casts and braces. Table 13.21 presents one classification system of pressure ulcers, and Table 13.22 lists important steps for the prevention of decubiti. The basic principles for the topical treatment of pressure ulcers are as follows:

- Remove the source of pressure or irritation.
- Cleanse and debride the wound.
- Treat associated infection if present.
- Protect healthy tissue and keep the wound hydrated.

Wound healing is improved in a moist environment (Yarkony, 1994). Hydrocolloid dressings (e.g., Duoderm) are excellent for partial thickness (stage II) and full thickness (stage III) ulcers with minimal exudate. In an animal model, they are superior to polyurethane film, wet-to-dry dressings, and air exposure (Yarkony, 1994). Hydrocolloids are not appropriate for infected wounds or wounds with large amounts of exudate. Recurrent decubiti may require surgical closure. Myocutaneous flaps are the primary means of surgical management; however, they may not be the definitive answer. Innervated, vascularized flaps that allow for sensory input have been developed. Few data are available regarding their effectiveness.

Other Common Medical Problems

Eye Problems Astigmatism and refractive errors are common in children with meningomyelo-

cele. Strabismus occurs in 30%–40% of these children, and horizontal nystagmus and other ocular motility problems are common (Lennerstrand, Gallo, & Samuelsson, 1990). Visual loss and optic atrophy can occur as complications of hydrocephalus. Recent onset or change in strabismus may indicate shunt malfunction and should be evaluated promptly.

Seizures Seizures occur in about 15% of children with meningomyelocele. In one study (Talwar, Baldwin, & Horbatt, 1995), seizures were present in 17% of 81 children followed in a multidisciplinary clinic. All of the children had shunted hydrocephalus, and 12 of the 14 had other CNS pathology to explain their seizures. Recent onset of seizures or worsening of seizure control may be a sign of shunt dysfunction and should prompt further evaluation of hydrocephalus.

Obesity and Short Stature Obesity is a problem in almost all children and adults with high motor function levels and in some individuals with low motor function levels (McLaughlin & Shurtleff, 1979). Children and adults with meningomyelocele also have short stature. In one study (Ekvall, 1988), 80% of children with high lesions, 43% of those with midlesions, and none of the children with low lesions were in less than the third percentile for height. Ambulatory status is an important factor in linear growth and rate of weight gain. Obesity begins to be a significant problem after 5 years of age and is correlated with the presence of hydrocephalus in community ambulators (Mita, Akataki, Itoh, et al., 1993).

Monitor the growth of infants and children with meningomyelocele closely (both length or height and weight). Supplement the measurement of standing height with measurement of arm span (or upper-arm length). Standing or sitting height is a poor measure of linear growth in children with meningomyelocele because of the presence of scoliosis, flexion contractures, and undergrowth of the legs related to the paralysis. Also, supplement the measurement of weight with a measurement of arm circumference and triceps skinfold thickness.

The nutritionist is an important team member for the prevention and management of obesity and the treatment of constipation. Prevention is the treatment of choice for obesity. It involves regular review and counseling about diet and daily exercise. In one study (Ekvall, 1988), the mean caloric intake to maintain growth in children with meningomyelocele older than 8 years of age was 50% of that for children without meningomyelocele. Swimming, bicycling, and many wheelchair sports are appropriate exercises for cardiovascular fitness. Ideally, children and adults with meningomyelocele would exercise vigorously at least once daily. Walks with friends or family (preferably using braces and assistive devices as needed) should be encouraged but do not provide the same level of conditioning as swimming or bicycling.

Some children with spina bifida have an apparent growth hormone deficiency and show improved linear growth when treated with recombinant human growth hormone (RHGH) (Rotenstein & Breen, 1996). The possibility of a symptomatic tethered cord must be considered prior to initiation of treatment with RHGH (Rotenstein, Reigel, & Lucke, 1996).

Latex Allergy Type III, immunoglobulin E (IgE)–mediated, immediate hypersensitivity to latex is a frequent problem among children with meningomyelocele. Multidisciplinary clinics report rates of hypersensitivity to latex that vary from 20% to 47% (Leger & Meeropol, 1992; Pittman, Kiburz, Gabriel, et al., 1995; Shah, Cawley, Gleeson, et al., 1998). Symptoms include urticaria and life-threatening anaphylaxis, and at times exposure may appear to be trivial. Individuals who have a history of allergies to rubber products (e.g., balloons, rubber bands, ad-

hesive tape) or food allergies (e.g., bananas, avocados, water chestnuts, other fruits) or people who have had multiple surgeries are at increased risk of having a serious allergic reaction to latex (Kelly, Pearson, Kurup, et al., 1994). In addition, children with spina bifida who have a history of atopic disease (e.g., asthma, eczema) are at higher risk of developing a latex allergy (Nieto, Estornell, Maxon, et al., 1997). Children with latex allergies can be detected by a positive history and by the latex skin test or radioimmunoassay test (RAST). The skin test (prick test) has high sensitivity and specificity but can provoke an allergic reaction, and standardized latex extract is not commercially available. The RAST has acceptable sensitivity and specificity (89% sensitivity and 69% specificity in one study [Eghrari-Sabet & Slater, 1993]) and is safer than the skin test.

Most spina bifida clinics regularly ask questions about allergic reactions to rubber products and foods, test all preschool-age children, and repeat testing in older children. All children who have a positive RAST should be considered allergic, even if they do not have a history of a definite reaction. Children who are allergic to latex should carry an emergency kit with epinephrine and an oral antihistamine and should wear a bracelet that makes their allergy known (Eghrari-Sabet & Slater, 1993). The primary treatment of latex allergy is prevention. Families with children with spina bifida should be counseled to avoid use or exposure to latex products. Families with children who are allergic to latex should be extremely careful to avoid latex exposure, especially in medical and dental offices. Exposure to powder from latex gloves or any mucous membrane exposure to latex may result in a potentially serious immediate hypersensitivity reaction. All children with spina bifida should receive surgery in a latex-free environment. The benefits of medication prior to and during surgery to prevent anaphylactic reactions in children who are allergic remain controversial. One regimen, in which medications are started 24 hours before and continued for 24 hours after surgery, is as follows:

- Diphenhydramine 1 milligram per kilogram every 6 hours intravenously or by mouth
- Methylprednisolone 1 milligram per kilogram every 6 hours intravenously or by mouth
- Cimetidine 5 milligrams per kilogram every 6 hours intravenously or by mouth (Eghrari-Sabet & Slater, 1993)

A principal factor in the increasing incidence of latex allergy in children with spina bifida and health care workers is the use of latex gloves. All medical and dental offices should provide latex-safe environments, all mucosal examinations should be done with nonlatex gloves, and low-allergenic latex gloves should be used when the use of latex gloves is necessary. Information for physicians, dentists, families, and school staff is available at a number of World Wide Web sites, including http://www.latexallergyhelp.com. School staff also should be counseled about the importance of a latex-free environment for children who are allergic to latex.

Autonomic Dysreflexia Autonomic dysreflexia is a potentially life-threatening problem that occurs in individuals with spinal cord injury above thoracic vertebra (T) 4–6. Children and adults with meningomyelocele with paralysis above the midthoracic level also are at risk. A variety of stimuli can initiate this reaction, including overdistention of the bladder (usual cause), bladder spasms or stones, instrumentation, distention of the rectum and rectal examination, skin pressure or breakdown, and tight clothing or shoes. The syndrome is characterized by a pounding headache, sweating above the level of injury, flushed or dry and pale skin, chills without fever, goose bumps (cutis anserina), nausea, anxiety, and severely elevated blood pressure. Immediate treatment as described in the following list of steps includes identification and removal of the noxious stimulus and treatment of the hypertension as needed:

- Place the child in the upright position (e.g., elevate the head of the bed), and monitor the blood pressure every few minutes.
- Loosen the child's tight clothing, and remove the child's shoes.
- Catheterize and drain the child's bladder; if a catheter is in place, check for obstruction, irrigate, or replace the catheter as needed; or stop the procedure that initiated the response.
- If the child's blood pressure remains elevated, do a digital examination of rectum to check for impaction using 2% Xylocaine jelly or Nupercainal ointment.
- Consider use of sublingual nifedipine, Procardia (10 milligrams for a school-age child, 5 milligrams for a preschool-age child) before examination of the rectum and removal of the impaction.
- Check for a decubitus or an ingrown toenail.

If necessary, subsequent treatment may involve irrigation of the bladder with pontocaine solution, insertion of nupercainal ointment into the rectum, and intravenous medications to treat the malignant hypertension (Children's Orthopedic Hospital and Medical Center [COHMC], 1992). The long-term management of autonomic dysreflexia includes 1) regular bladder and bowel programs to ensure regular and complete emptying of the bladder and rectum and 2) the prevention of stool impaction. A number of medications have been reported to be effective in treating recurrent episodes of autonomic dysreflexia when the noxious stimulus cannot be identified. These medications include alpha-adrenergic blocking agents (phenoxybenzamine, terazosin, and prozasin) and the beta blocker metoprolol (Pasquina, Houston, & Belandres, 1998). In one study (Chancellor, Erhard, Hirsch, & Stass, 1994), terazosin was effective in reducing episodes of autonomic dysreflexia during a 3-month trial in 21 individuals with spinal cord injury (see also the Appendix at the end of Chapter 16).

Developmental and Learning Problems

Developmental Delay and Mental Retardation

As many as 50% of children with high lumbar and thoracic motor levels manifest developmental delay or mental retardation. Only approximately 15% of children with low lumbar and sacral levels have developmental delay or mental retardation (Shurtleff, 1986). Children with meningomyelocele who have not been shunted have higher IQ scores than children who have been shunted. The primary factors affecting IQ scores in this population are complications due to the treatment of hydrocephalus, especially ventriculitis, and the presence of additional CNS anomalies.

Refer infants with meningomyelocele for EI services based on their risk for global developmental delay and the extent of their motor delays. In addition, monitor the development of all infants and preschool-age children with meningomyelocele regularly. Please review the discussion of developmental screening and surveillance in Chapter 2 and the discussion of EI/early childhood special education (EI/ECSE) services in Chapter 5.

Nonverbal Learning Disabilities Many children with meningomyelocele and hydrocephalus manifest a pattern of learning problems referred to as *nonverbal learning disabilities* (NVLD). Children with above average, average, or below average IQ scores can have NVLD. NVLD is a syndrome characterized by impairments in visual-perceptual and fine motor skills, language comprehension and problem solving, mathematics, executive functions (initiation, planning, organization, and attention), and social skills. Children with meningomyelocele may have relatively well-developed single-word and rote language skills (reading and spelling) but may have difficulty with complex and novel material (Rourke, 1988). These problems may be misdiagnosed as the child's being unmotivated, sloppy or disobedient, or not paying attention.

Children with NVLD do benefit from education programs tailored to meet their individual needs; therefore, prompt identification of NVLD is important. The executive function impairments of children with NVLD may not be apparent at younger ages, but they become increasingly problematic for older children as learning and behavioral expectations become increasingly complex. Children with spina bifida are evaluated for NVLD prior to school entry and again at the third to fourth grade and seventh to eighth grade levels as needed. The evaluation for NVLD includes a traditional measure of intellectual potential (e.g., the Wechsler Intelligence Scale for Children [WISC-III]; Wechsler, 1991), tests of fine motor and visual-perceptual skills, and neuropsychological testing. Children with NVLD often manifest a significant verbal versus performance discrepancy on intellectual test-ing. Many of these evaluations can be completed by school staff (occupational therapist, psychologist, and special educator), depending on school resources and the experience of school personnel. Implementation of treatment recommendations is a collaborative effort of spina bifida clinic and school staff, parents, and the child.

Social Competence, Sexuality and Infertility, and Transition to Adult Services

Critical issues for adolescents with spina bifida and their families are promotion of social competence, sexuality and infertility, and transition to adult services and independent living. Recommendations for anticipatory guidance on other clinical issues are presented in the Guidelines for Care located in the Appendix at the end of this chapter. A variety of brief educational materials on clinical issues are available to families and health professionals through the Spina Bifida Association of America (SBAA) and many regional spina bifida programs. Many adolescents and young adults with spina bifida also report being depressed. The prevention of depression in individuals with spina bifida is based in large part on the promotion of social competence and self-esteem through activities such as those described in the subsections that follow.

Promotion of Social Competence, Self-Care, and Individual Responsibility Adolescents with meningomyelocele report low self-esteem and less competence in academic, athletic, and social skills than their peers without disabilities (Appleton, Minchom, Ellis, et al., 1994). Even individuals with mild physical impairments may have markedly low

self-esteem. Teenagers with meningomyelocele value having friends but have few out-of-school contacts with peers, participate in few organized social events, and generally choose sedentary activities (Blum, Resnick, Nelson, & St. Germaine, 1991). Teens with meningomyelocele have a high level of dependence on their parents for personal care and a low level of responsibility at home.

Parents of children with meningomyelocele report that they receive much greater support from professionals for medical and physical issues than for psychosocial matters (Rinck et al., 1989). They desire more assistance with their children's psychosocial issues, including sexuality (45%), vocational needs (68%), and teen issues (57%). Comprehensive care of the child with meningomyelocele and his or her family must include attention to psychosocial development and related family support issues beginning in infancy. The following are general recommendations with regard to caring for this population:

- Encourage the child's independence and self-care at all ages, and discourage overprotection of the child by parents or teachers.
- Encourage the child's participation in organized social and sports events (e.g., parks and recreation programs, clubs, Scouts, summer camp, Special Olympics).
- Provide child and family educational materials regularly, and discuss the child's medical problems and treatment directly with older children and adolescents.
- Emphasize the child's individual responsibility (e.g., jobs at home, management of continence programs).
- Involve the child with adult role models (e.g., an adult with a disability) in the clinic, in the school, or in community programs.
- Link the child and family to advocacy groups (e.g., local and national chapters of the SBAA).
- Provide the teenager with spina bifida with information on Internet resources (e.g., the e-mail discussion group SB-TEENS at http://www.members.tripod.com/~sbteens).
- Refer the child, parent(s), and siblings to counseling services as needed; involve community agencies with the child's care at appropriate ages (e.g., refer the child for EI services, refer the adolescent to the Vocational Rehabilitation division and developmental disabilities services).

Sexuality and Infertility The SBAA (Sloan, Leibold, & Henry-Atkinson, 1995) published an excellent manual entitled, *Sexuality and the Person with Spina Bifida.* In general, all females with spina bifida are fertile; however, pregnancy may be complicated or contraindicated because of their urologic problems. Vaginal lubrication usually is limited. Both males and females with spina bifida need to lubricate before and during sexual activity with a water-soluble lubricating jelly (Sloan et al., 1995). Most males with spina bifida are infertile. Many males with low lumbar or sacral motor level are able to have erections and can ejaculate; however, males with thoracic or high lumbar motor levels are unable to have erections or ejaculate or have retrograde ejaculations (Shurtleff & Dunne, 1986). Erection aids are available, and electroejaculation (i.e., ejaculation by electrical stimulation) has been used with limited success with men with spinal cord injuries (Sloan et al., 1995).

Sexual development is also complicated by perineal sensory loss, bowel and bladder incontinence, the child's dependence for basic care on parents, a lack of close friends, and impairments in social skills. The child also may lack an understanding of privacy and modesty that is due in part to frequent medical examinations and daily continence programs (Sloan, Leibold, & Henry-Atkinson, 1995). In addition, precocious puberty is more common in girls with meningomyelocele than among girls without disabilities. In one study (Elias & Sadeghi-Nejad, 1994), precocious puberty had occurred in 5 of the 30 girls who were older than 10 years of age at the time of the study. Treatment, if indicated, is with leuprolide (Depo-Lupron). Precocious puberty is strongly associated with hydrocephalus.

Transition to Adult Services and Independent Living Transition from high school to higher education or to work in the community and transition from living at home to living in the community can be highly stressful for the individual with meningomyelocele and his or her family. Transition planning begins early in high school and may involve staff from the Vocational Rehabilitation division, Developmental Disability Services, and independent living programs in addition to the school, the child development team of specialists, the primary care physician, and the family.

Employment Young adults with spina bifida have low levels of employment, are often socially isolated, and remain dependent on their parents. In one survey (Shurtleff & Dunne, 1986) of young adults with spina bifida, only 25% were fully employed, 24% lived alone, 33% lived with partners or friends, 36% lived with their parents, and 8% lived in institutions. Intelligence and level of impairment correlated highly with employment status and inde-

pendent living. The rates of employment reported in other studies have varied from 20% to 70% (Shurtleff & Friedrich, 1986). These studies, however, do not include individuals born and cared for in the 1980s and 1990s. Lack of mobility, frequent health problems (e.g., UTIs), fine motor problems, NVLD, depression, poor self-image, and poor motivation, as well as the resistance of some employers to modify the workplace to accommodate employees with disabilities, are all factors that contribute to these individuals' high levels of unemployment.

Medical Care Most young adults make the transition from care in the multidisciplinary clinic to health care services in the community. Studies (Kaufman et al., 1994; Shurtleff & Dunne, 1986) have documented a large number of unmet health needs in this population, including recurrent decubiti, obesity, recurrent UTIs, incontinence, scoliosis, arthritis, and mental health problems. Kaufman and co-workers (1994) reported the results of a survey of 87 individuals with meningomyelocele 3 years after a multidisciplinary clinic was disbanded. Of the total number of individuals studied, 45%–52% had not received regular medical and specialty care. Older individuals received less care and had an increase in the rate of serious morbidity. Neither the individual, nor the family, nor the primary care physician was able to provide the coordination of care needed by this population (Kaufman et al., 1994). Many multidisciplinary clinics have extended care to young adults. The challenge for the future is to continue to provide the highest quality of care to children and adults with meningomyelocele within the financial constraints of managed care.

Important Care Coordination Issues

Educational staff are responsible for supervision and at times for conducting the child's continence programs when the child is at school. In addition, the teacher or the school therapist may be the first to notice changes in school performance or gait related to neurosurgical complications. The school staff need information about clinical issues, and they may require training in specific procedures such as intermittent catheterization. Collaboration among the primary care office, the schools, and the spina bifida team is essential for optimal management of children with meningomyelocele. In addition to the recommendations for care coordination provided earlier in this chapter, the primary care office should identify the school district contact people who supervise health procedures in education settings and facilitate the exchange of information.

REFERENCES

Acs, G., & Cozzi, E. (1992). Antibiotic prophylaxis for patients with hydrocephalus shunts: A survey of pediatric dentistry and neurosurgery program directors. *Pediatric Dentistry, 14,* 246–250.

Adzick, N.S., Sutton, L.N., Crombleholme, T.M., & Flake, A.W. (1998). Successful fetal surgery for spina bifida. *Lancet, 352,* 1675–1676.

Appleton, P.L., Minchom, P.E., Ellis, N.C., et al. (1994). The self-concept of young people with spina bifida: A population-based study. *Developmental Medicine and Child Neurology, 36,* 198–215.

Ashcraft, K.W., Garred, J.L., Holder, T.M., et al. (1990). Rectal prolapse: 17-year experience with the posterior repair and suspension. *Journal of Pediatric Surgery, 25*(9), 992–994.

Babcook, C.J. (1995). Ultrasound evaluation of prenatal and neonatal spina bifida. *Neurosurgery Clinics of North America, 6*(2), 203–218.

Babcook, C.J., Goldstein, R.B., & Filly, R.A. (1995). Prenatally detected fetal myelomeningocele: Is karyotype analysis warranted? *Radiology, 194*(2), 491–494.

Bailey, R.B. (1991). Urologic management of spina bifida. In H.L. Rekate (Ed.), *Comprehensive management of spina bifida* (pp. 185–213). Boca Raton, FL: CRC Press.

Balcom, A.H., Wiatrak, M., Biefeld, T., et al. (1997). Initial experience with home therapeutic electrical stimulation for continence in the myelomeningocele population. *Journal of Urology, 158,* 1272–1276.

Banta, J.V. (1990). Combined anterior and posterior fusion for spinal deformity in myelomeningocele. *Spine, 15*(9), 946–952.

Banta, J.V., Romness, M.J., Thomson, J.D., et al. (1999, September). *Treatment of neuromuscular scoliosis: Instructional course.* Paper presented at the annual meeting of the American Academy for Cerebral Palsy and Developmental Medicine, Washington, DC.

Barnet, A.B., Weiss, I.P., & Shaer, C. (1993). Evoked potentials in infant brainstem syndrome associated with Arnold-Chiari malformation. *Developmental Medicine and Child Neurology, 35*(1), 42–48.

Bauer, S.B., & Joseph, D.B. (1990). Management of the obstructed urinary tract associated with neurogenic bladder dysfunction. *Urologic Clinics of North America, 17*(2), 395–406.

Biggar, W.D., Morrison, S.A., Chait, P., et al. (1999, September). *Cecostomy for bowel management in children with myelomeningocele.* Paper presented at the annual meeting of the American Academy for Cerebral Palsy and Developmental Medicine, Washington, DC.

Blum, R.W., Resnick, M.D., Nelson, R., & St. Germaine, A. (1991). Family and peer issues among adolescents with spina bifida and cerebral palsy. *Pediatrics, 88*(2), 280–285.

Boemers, T.M., Soorani-Lunsing, I.J., de Jong, T.P., & Pruijs, H.E. (1996). Urological problems after surgical treatment of scoliosis in children with myelomeningocele. *Journal of Urology, 155*(3), 1066–1069.

Boemers, T.M., van Gool, J.D., & de Jong, T.P. (1995). Tethered spinal cord: The effect of neurosurgery on the lower urinary tract and male sexual function. *British Journal of Urology, 76*(6), 747–751.

Bomalaski, M.D., Bloom, D.A., McGuire, E.J., & Panzl, A. (1996). Glutaraldehyde cross-linked collagen in the treatment of urinary incontinence in children. *Journal of Urology, 155*(2), 699–702.

Boone, T.B., Roehrborn, C.G., & Hurt, G. (1992). Transurethral intravesical electrotherapy for neurogenic bladder dysfunction in children with myelodysplasia: A prospective, randomized clinical trial. *Journal of Urology, 148*(2 pt. 2), 550–554.

Boor, R., Schwarz, M., Reitter, B., & Voth, D. (1993). Tethered cord after spina bifida aperta: A longitudinal study of somatosensory evoked potentials. *Child's Nervous System, 9*(6), 328–330.

Bouchard, J., & D'Astous, J. (1991). Postoperative heterotopic ossification in children: A comparison of children with spina bifida and with cerebral palsy. *Canadian Journal of Surgery, 34*(5), 545–546.

Bruner, J.P., Tulipan, N.E., & Richards, W.O. (1996). Endoscopic coverage of fetal open myelomeningocele in utero [Letter, comment]. *American Journal of Obstetrics and Gynecology, 174,* 1255–1264.

Byrd, S.E., & Radkowski, M.A. (1991). The radiological evaluation of the child with a meningomyelocele. *Journal of the National Medical Association, 83*(7), 608–614.

Carroll, N.C. (1987). Assessment and management of the lower extremity in myelodysplasia. *Orthopedic Clinics of North America, 18*(4), 709–724.

Centers for Disease Control and Prevention (CDC). (1992). Recommendations for the use of folic acid to reduce the number of cases of spina bifida and other neural tube defects. *Morbidity and Mortality Weekly Report, 41*(RR-14), 1–7.

Chancellor, M.D., Erhard, M.J., Hirsch, I.H., & Stass, W.E., Jr. (1994). Prospective evaluation of terazosin for the treatment of autonomic dysreflexia. *Journal of Urology, 151*(1), 111–113.

Charney, E.B., Melchionni, J.B., & Smith, D.R. (1991). Community ambulation by children with myelomeningocele and high-level paralysis. *Journal of Pediatric Orthopedics, 11*(5), 579–582.

Charney, E.B., Weller, S.C., Sutton, L.N., et al. (1985). Management of the newborn with myelomeningocele: Time for a decision-making process. *Pediatrics, 75*(1), 58–64.

Chatkupt, S., Hol, F.A., Shugart, Y.Y., et al. (1995). Absence of linkage between familial neural tube defects and *PAX-3* gene. *Journal of Medical Genetics, 32,* 200–204.

Chatkupt, S., Skurnick, J.H., Jaggi, M., et al. (1994). Study of genetics, epidemiology, and vitamin usage in familial spina bifida in the United States in the 1990s. *Neurology, 44*(1), 65–70.

Cheskin, L.J., Kamal, N., Crowell, M.D., et al. (1995). Mechanisms of constipation in older persons and effects of fiber compared with placebo. *Journal of the American Geriatrics Society, 43*(6), 666–669.

Children's Orthopedic Hospital and Medical Center (COHMC). (1992). *Autonomic hyperreflexia (dysreflexia)* (pp. 1–5). Seattle, WA: Author.

Cochrane, D., Aronyk, K., Sawatzky, B., et al. (1991). The effects of labor and delivery on spinal cord function and ambulation in patients with meningomyelocele. *Child's Nervous System, 7*(6), 312–315.

Crandall, B.F., Corson, V.L., Evans, M.I., et al. (1998). American College of Medical Genetics Statement on Folic Acid: Fortification and supplementation [Letter to the editor]. *American Journal of Medical Genetics, 78*, 381.

Crandall, R.C., Birkebak, R.C., & Winter, R.B. (1989). The role of hip location and dislocation in the functional status of the myelodysplastic patient: A review of 100 patients. *Orthopedics, 12*(5), 675–684.

Czeizel, A.E., & Dudas, I. (1992). Prevention of the first occurrence of neural-tube defects by preconceptional vitamin supplementation. *New England Journal of Medicine, 327*(26), 1832–1833.

Decter, R.M., Snyder, P., & Laudermilch, C. (1994). Transurethral electrical bladder stimulation: A follow-up report. *Journal of Urology, 152*(2 pt. 2), 812–814.

DePeppo, F., Iacobelli, B.D., DeGennaro, M., et al. (1999). Percutaneous endoscopic cecostomy for antegrade colonic irrigation in fecally incontinent children. *Endoscopy, 31*(6), 501–503.

Desch, L.W. (in press). Longitudinal reliability of visual evoked potentials in children with hydrocephalus. *Developmental Medicine and Child Neurology.*

Dias, M.S., & McLone, D.G. (1993). Hydrocephalus in the child with dysraphism. *Neurosurgery Clinics of North America, 4*(4), 715–726.

Dodson, W.E. (1989). Deleterious effects of drugs on the developing nervous system. *Neonatal Neurology, 16*(2), 339–353.

Duckett, J.W., & Lotfi, A.H. (1993). Appendicovesicostomy (and variations) in bladder reconstruction. *Journal of Urology, 149*(3), 567–569.

Eghrari-Sabet, J.S., & Slater, J.E. (1993). Who is at risk, how to evaluate, and what to do? Latex allergy: A potentially serious respiratory disorder. *Journal of Respiratory Diseases, 14*(3), 473–482.

Ekvall, S.M. (1988). Myelomeningocele: Nutrition implications. *Topics in Clinical Nutrition, 3*(3), 41–54.

Elias, E.R., & Sadeghi-Nejad, A. (1994). Precocious puberty in girls with myelodysplasia. *Pediatrics, 93*(3), 521–522.

Fernandes, E.T., Reinberg, Y., Vernier, R., & Gonzalez, R. (1994). Neurogenic bladder dysfunction in children: Review of pathophysiology and current management. *Journal of Pediatrics, 124*(1), 1–7.

Folio, M.R., & Fewell, R. (1983). *Peabody Developmental Motor Scales and Activity Cards (PDMS).* Itasca, IL: Riverside Publishing Co.

Fraser, R.K., Bourke, H.M., Broughton, N.S., & Menelaus, M.B. (1995). Unilateral dislocation of the hip in spina bifida: A long-term follow-up. *Journal of Bone and Joint Surgery, British, 77*(4), 615–619.

Gaston, H. (1991). Ophthalmic complications of spina bifida and hydrocephalus. *Eye, 5*(pt. 3), 279–290.

Goh, D., & Minns, R.A. (1995). Intracranial pressure and cerebral arterial flow velocity indices in childhood hydrocephalus: Current review. *Child's Nervous System, 11*(7), 392–396.

Gonzalez, R., Merino, F.G., & Vaughn, M. (1995). Long-term results of the artificial urinary sphincter in male patients with neurogenic bladder. *Journal of Urology, 154*(2 Pt 2), 769–770.

Graf, J.L., Strear, C., Bratton, B., et al. (1998). The antegrade continence enema procedure: A review of the literature. *Journal of Pediatric Surgery, 33*(8), 1294–1296.

Greenland, S., & Ackerman, D.L. (1995). Clomiphene citrate and neural tube defects: A pooled analysis of controlled epidemiologic studies and recommendations for further studies. *Fertility and Sterility, 64*(5), 936–941.

Haley, S.M., Coster, W.J., Ludlow, L.H., et al. (1992). *Pediatric Evaluation of Disability Inventory (PEDI), version 1.1: Developmental, standardization and administration manual.* Boston: New England Medical Center Hospitals.

Hanlo, P.W., Gooskens, R.H., Nijhuis, I.J., et al. (1995). Value of transcranial Doppler indices in predicting raised ICP in infantile hydrocephalus: A study with review of literature. *Child's Nervous System, 11*(10), 595–603.

Hartford, J.M., Banta, J.V., & Smith, B.G. (1995). Tethered cord release: Effects on scoliosis. *European Journal of Pediatric Surgery, 5*(Suppl. 1), 49.

Helpin, M.L., Rosenberg, H.M., Sayany, Z., & Sanford, R.A. (1998). Antibiotic prophylaxis in dental patients with ventriculoperitoneal shunts: A pilot study. *ASDC Journal of Dentistry in Children, 65*(4), 244–247.

Herman, J.M., McLone, D.G., Storrs, B.B., & Dauser, R.C. (1993). Analysis of 153 patients with myelomeningocele or spinal lipoma reoperated upon for a tethered cord: Presentation, management, and outcome. *Pediatric Neurosurgery, 19*(5), 243–249.

Hernandez, R.D., Hurwitz, R.S., Foote, J.E., et al. (1994). Nonsurgical management of threatened upper urinary tracts and incontinence in children with myelomeningocele. *Journal of Urology, 152*(5 pt. 1), 1582–1585.

Herschorn, S., Rangaswamy, S., & Radomski, S.B. (1994). Urinary undiversion in adults with myelodysplasia: Long-term followup. *Journal of Urology, 152*(2 pt. 1), 329–333.

Hill, A.E., & Beattie, F. (1994). Does caesarean section delivery improve neurological outcome in open spina bifida? *European Journal of Pediatric Surgery, 4*(Suppl. 1), 32–34.

Hoberman, A., & Wald, E.R. (1997). UTI in young children: New light on old questions, *Contemporary Pediatrics, 14*(11), 140–156.

Jones, K.L. (1997). *Smith's recognizable patterns of human malformation* (5th ed.). Philadelphia: W.B. Saunders Co.

Jones, R.F., Kowk, B.C., Stening, W.A., & Vonau, M. (1996). Third ventriculostomy for hydrocephalus associated with spinal dysraphism: Indications and contraindications. *European Journal of Pediatric Surgery, 6*(Suppl. 1), 5–6.

Kanev, P.M., & Park, T.S. (1993). The treatment of hydrocephalus. *Neurosurgery Clinics of North America, 4*(4), 611–619.

Kaplan, W.E., Richards, T.W., & Richards, I. (1989). Intravesical transurethral bladder stimulation to increase bladder capacity. *Journal of Urology, 142*(2 pt. 2), 600–602.

Karol, L.A. (1995). Orthopedic management in myelomeningocele. *Neurosurgery Clinics of North America, 6*(2), 259–268.

Kasabian, N.G., Bauer, S.B., Dyro, F.M., et al. (1992). The prophylactic value of clean intermittent catheterization and anticholinergic medication in newborns and infants with myelodysplasia at risk of developing urinary tract deterioration. *American Journal of Diseases of Children, 146*(7), 840–843.

Kaufman, B.A., Terbrock, A., Winters, N., et al. (1994). Disbanding a multidisciplinary clinic: Effects on the health care of myelomeningocele patients. *Pediatric Neurosurgery, 21*(1), 36–44.

Keggi, J.M., Banta, J.V., & Walton, C. (1992). The myelodysplastic hip and scoliosis. *Developmental Medicine and Child Neurology, 34*(3), 240–246.

Kelly, K.J., Pearson, M.L., Kurup, V.P., et al. (1994). A cluster of anaphylactic reactions in children with spina bifida during general anesthesia: Epidemiologic features, risk factors, and latex hypersensitivity. *Journal of Allergy and Clinical Immunology, 94*(1), 53–61.

Keynes, R., & Krumlauf, R. (1994). HOX genes and regionalization of the nervous system. *Annual Review of Neuroscience, 17*, 109–132.

Kimura, D.K., Mayo, M., & Shurtleff, D.B. (1986). Urinary tract management. In D.B. Shurtleff (Ed.), *Myelodysplasias and exstrophies: Significance, prevention, and treatment* (pp. 243–266). Orlando, FL: Harcourt, Brace & Co.

Knutson, L.M., & Clark, D.E. (1991). Orthotic devices for ambulation in children with cerebral palsy and myelomeningocele. *Physical Therapy, 71*(12), 947–960.

Koch, M.O., McDougal, W.S., Hall, M.C., et al. (1992). Long-term metabolic effects of urinary diversion. *Journal of Urology, 147*(5), 1343–1347.

Krahn, C.G., & Johnson, H.W. (1993). Cutaneous vesicostomy in the young child: Indications and results. *Urology, 41*(6), 558–563.

Krieger, D., & Sclabassi, R.J. (1995). Neurophysiologic assessment in the management of spinal dysraphism. *Neurosurgery Clinics of North America, 6*(2), 219–230.

Kropp, K.A., & Angwao, F.F. (1986). Urethral lengthening and reimplantation for neurogenic incontinence in children. *Journal of Urology, 135*, 533–536.

Lary, J.M., & Edmonds, L.D. (1996). Prevalence of spina bifida at birth: United States, 1983–1990: A comparison of two surveillance systems. *Morbidity and Mortality Weekly Report, 45*(SS-2), 15–27.

Leger, R.R., & Meeropol, E. (1992). Children at risk: Latex allergy and spina bifida. *Journal of Pediatric Nursing, 7*(6), 371–376.

Lennerstrand, G., Gallo, J.E., & Samuelsson, L. (1990). Neuro-ophthalmological findings in relation to CNS lesions in patients with myelomeningocele. *Developmental Medicine and Child Neurology, 32*, 423–431.

Lindseth, R.E., Dias, L.S., & Drennan, J.C. (1991). Myelomeningocele. *Instructional Course Lectures, 40*, 271–291.

Liptak, G.S. (1995). Tethered spinal cord: Update of an analysis of published articles. *European Journal of Pediatric Surgery, 5*(Suppl. 1), 21–23.

Liptak, G.S., Campbell, J., Stewart, R., & Hulbert, W.C., Jr. (1993). Screening for urinary tract infection in children with neurogenic bladders. *American Journal of Physical Medicine and Rehabilitation, 72*(3), 122–126.

Liptak, G.S., & Revell, G.M. (1992). Management of bowel dysfunction in children with spinal cord disease or injury by means of the enema continence catheter. *Journal of Pediatrics, 120*(2 pt. 1), 190–194.

Liptak, G.S., Gellerstedt, M.D., & Klionsky, N. (1992). Isosorbide in the medical management of hydrocephalus in children with myelodysplasia. *Developmental Medicine and Child Neurology, 34*(2), 150–154.

Lopez, B.C., David, K.M., & Crockard, H.A. (1997). Inadequate PAX-1 gene expression as a cause of agenesis of the thoracolumbar spine with failure of segmentation. *Journal of Neurosurgery, 86*, 1018–1021.

Luthy, D.A., Wardinsky, T., Shurtleff, D.B., et al. (1991). Cesarean section before the onset of labor and subsequent motor function in infants with meningomyelocele diagnosed antenatally. *New England Journal of Medicine, 324*(10), 690–691.

Malone, P.S., Curry, J.I., & Osborne, A. (1998). The antegrade continence enema procedure: Why, when, and how? *World Journal of Urology, 16*(4), 274–278.

Marlett, J.A., Li, B.U., Patrow, C.J., & Bass, P. (1987). Comparative laxation of psyllium with and without senna in an ambulatory constipated population. *American Journal of Gastroenterology, 82*(4), 333–337.

Mayfield, J.K. (1991). Comprehensive orthopedic management in myelomeningocele. In H.L. Rekate (Ed.), *Comprehensive management of spina bifida* (pp. 113–163). Boca Raton, FL: CRC Press.

McGuire, E.J., Woodside, J.R., Bordeu, T.A., & Weiss, R.M. (1981). Prognostic value of urodynamic testing in myelodysplastic patients. *Journal of Urology, 126*, 205–209.

McLaughlin, J.F., & Shurtleff, D.B. (1979). Management of the newborn with myelodysplasia. *Clinical Pediatrics, 18*(8), 463–476.

McLone, D.G., & Partington, M.D. (1993). Arrest and compensation of hydrocephalus. *Neurosurgery Clinics of North America, 4*(4), 621–624.

McMichael, A.J., Dreosti, I.F., Ryan, P., & Robertson, E.F. (1994). Neural tube defects and maternal serum zinc and copper concentrations in mid-pregnancy: A case-control study. *Medical Journal of Australia, 161*(8), 478–482.

Medical Research Council (MRC) Vitamin Study Research Group. (1991). Prevention of neural tube defects: Results of the Medical Research Council Vitamin Study. *Lancet, 338*(8760), 131–137.

Meuli, M., Meuli-Simmen, C., Yingling, C.D., et al. (1996). In utero repair of experimental myelomeningocele saves neurological function at birth. *Journal of Pediatric Surgery, 31*, 397–402.

Meuli-Simmen, C., Meuli, M., Hutchins, G.M., et al. (1995). Fetal reconstructive surgery: Experimental use of the latissimus dorsi flap to correct myelomeningocele in utero. *Plastic Reconstruction Surgery, 96*(5), 1007–1011.

Milhorat, T.H., Miller, J.I., Johnson, W.D., et al. (1993). Anatomical basis of syringomyelia occurring with hindbrain lesions. *Neurosurgery, 32*(5), 748–754.

Miller, P.D., Pollack, I.F., Pang, D., & Albright, A.L. (1996). Comparison of simultaneous versus delayed ventriculoperitoneal shunt insertion in children undergoing myelomeningocele repair. *Journal of Child Neurology, 11*(5), 370–372.

Milunsky, A., Ulcickas, M., Rothman, K.J., et al. (1992). Maternal heat exposure and neural tube defects. *JAMA: Journal of the American Medical Association, 268*(7), 882–885.

Mita, K., Akataki, K., Itoh, K., et al. (1993). Assessment of obesity of children with spina bifida. *Developmental Medicine and Child Neurology, 35*(4), 305–311.

Muller, E.B., & Nordwall, A. (1994). Brace treatment of scoliosis in children with myelomeningocele. *Spine, 19*(2), 151–155.

Nickel, R.E., & Magenis, R.E. (1996). Neural tube defects and deletions of chromosome 22q11. *American Journal of Medical Genetics, 66*(1), 25–27.

Nickel, R.E., Pillers, D.A., Merkens, M., et al. (1994). Velo-cardiofacial syndrome and DiGeorge sequence with meningomyelocele and deletions of the 22q11 region. *American Journal of Medical Genetics, 52*(4), 445–449.

Nieto, A., Estornell, F., Maxon, A., et al. (1997). Allergy to latex in spina bifida: A multivariate study of associated factors in 100 consecutive patients. *Journal of Allergy and Clinical Immunology, 98,* 501–507.

Noetzel, M.J. (1989). Myelomeningocele: Current concepts of management. *Neonatal Neurology, 16*(2), 311–329.

Nohria, V., & Oakes, W.J. (1994). Chiari malformations, hydrosyringomyelia and the tethered cord syndrome. In S.L. Weinstein (Ed.), *The pediatric spine: Principles and practice* (pp. 685–705). Philadelphia: Lippincott-Raven.

Omtzigt, J.G., Los, F.J., Hagenaars, A.M., et al. (1992). Prenatal diagnosis of spina bifida aperta after first-trimester valproate exposure. *Prenatal Diagnosis, 12*(11), 893–897.

Pacific Northwest Regional Genetics Group (PacNoRGG). (1999, August). *Family genetics update: Preventing neural tube defects for couples at increased risk: Fact sheet.* Eugene, OR: Author.

Pandya, A., Xia, X.J., Landa, B.L., et al. (1996). Phenotypic variation in Waardenburg syndrome: Mutational heterogeneity, modifier, genes or polygenic background? *Human Molecular Genetics, 5*(4), 497–502.

Pang, D. (1995). Surgical complications of open spinal dysraphism. *Neurosurgery Clinics of North America, 6*(2), 243–257.

Parent, A.D., & McMillan, T. (1995). Contemporaneous shunting with repair of myelomeningocele. *Pediatric Neurosurgery, 22*(3), 132–135.

Pasquina, P.F., Houston, R.M., & Belandres, P.V. (1998). Beta blockade in the treatment of autonomic dysreflexia: A case report and review. *Archives of Physical Medicine and Rehabilitation, 79,* 582–584.

Passmore, A.P., Davies, K.W., Flanagan, P.G., et al. (1993). A comparison of Agiolax and lactulose in elderly patients with chronic constipation. *Pharmacology, 47*(Suppl. 1), 249–252.

Pittman, T., Kiburz, J., Gabriel, K., et al. (1995). Latex allergy in children with spina bifida. *Pediatric Neurosurgery, 22*(2), 96–100.

Platt, L.D., Feuchtbaum, L., Filly, R., et al. (1992). The California Maternal Serum Alpha-Fetoprotein Screening Program: The role of ultrasonography in the detection of spina bifida. *American Journal of Obstetrics and Gynecology, 166*(5), 1328–1329.

Quigley, S.M., & Curley, M.A.Q. (1996). Skin integrity in the pediatric population: Preventing and managing pressure ulcers. *Journal of the Society of Pediatric Nurses, 1*(1), 7–18.

Ramasastry, S.S., & Cohen, M. (1995). Soft tissue closure and plastic surgical aspects of large open myelomeningoceles. *Neurosurgery Clinics of North America, 6*(2), 279–291.

Rauzzino, M., & Oakes, W.J. (1995). Chiari II malformation and syringomyelia. *Neurosurgery Clinics of North America, 6*(2), 293–309.

Reigel, D.H., Tchernoukha, K., Bazmi, B., et al. (1994). Change in spinal curvature following release of tethered spinal cord associated with spina bifida. *Pediatric Neurosurgery, 20*(1), 30–42.

Rekate, H.L. (1991a). Neurosurgical management of the child with spina bifida. In H.L. Rekate (Ed.), *Comprehensive management of spina bifida* (pp. 93–111). Boca Raton, FL: CRC Press.

Rekate, H.L. (1991b). Neurosurgical management of the newborn with spina bifida. In H.L. Rekate (Ed.), *Comprehensive management of spina bifida* (pp. 2–29). Boca Raton, FL: CRC Press.

Rekate, H.L. (1991c). Shunt revision: Complications and their prevention. *Pediatric Neurology, 17,* 155–162.

Rinck, C., Berg, J., & Hafeman, C. (1989). The adolescent with myelomeningocele: A review of parent experiences and expectations. *Adolescence, 24*(95), 699–710.

Roach, M.B., Switters, D.M., & Stone, A.R. (1993). The changing urodynamic pattern in infants with myelomeningocele. *Journal of Urology, 150*(3), 944–947.

Rose, N.C., & Mennuti, M.T. (1993). Maternal serum screening for neural tube defects and fetal chromosome abnormalities. *Fetal Medicine, 159,* 312–317.

Rotenstein, D., & Breen, T.J. (1996). Growth hormone treatment of children with myelomeningocele. *Journal of Pediatrics, 128,* S28–S31.

Rotenstein, D., Reigel, D.H., & Lucke, J.F. (1996). Growth of growth hormone-treated and nontreated children before and after tethered spinal cord release. *Pediatric Neurosurgery, 24*(5), 238–241.

Rothman, K.J., Moore, L.L., Singer, M.R., et al. (1995). Teratogenicity of high vitamin A intake. *New England Journal of Medicine, 333*(21), 1369–1373.

Rourke, B.P. (1988). The syndrome of nonverbal learning disabilities: Developmental manifestations in neurological disease, disorder, and dysfunction. *Clinical Neuropsychologist, 2*(4), 93–330.

Rudy, D.C., & Woodside, J.R. (1991). The incontinent myelodysplastic patient. *Urologic Clinics of North America, 18*(2), 295–308.

Ryan, K.D., Ploski, C., & Emans, J.B. (1991). Myelodysplasia: The musculoskeletal problem: Habilation from infancy to adulthood. *Physical Therapy, 71*(12), 935–946.

Schafer, M.F., & Dias, L.S. (1983a). Ankle. In M.F. Schafer & L.S. Dias, *Myelomeningocele: Orthopaedic treatment* (pp. 160–178). Philadelphia: Lippincott Williams & Wilkins.

Schafer, M.F., & Dias, L.S. (1983b). Foot. In M.F. Schafer & L.S. Dias, *Myelomeningocele: Orthopaedic treatment* (pp. 179–213). Philadelphia: Lippincott Williams & Wilkins.

Schafer, M.F., & Dias, L.S. (1983c). Knee. In M.F. Schafer & L.S. Dias, *Myelomeningocele: Orthopaedic treatment* (pp. 147–159). Philadelphia: Lippincott Williams & Wilkins.

Schell, S.R., Toogood, G.J., & Dudley, N.E. (1997). Control of fecal incontinence: Continued success with the Malone procedure. *Surgery, 122*(3), 626–631.

Shaffer, J., & Friedrich, W. (1986). Young adult psychosocial adjustment. In D.B. Shurtleff (Ed.), *Myelodysplasias and exstrophies: Significance, prevention, and treatment* (pp. 421–432). Orlando, FL: Grune & Stratton.

Shah, S., Cawley, M., Gleeson, R., et al. (1998). Latex allergy and latex sensitization in children and adolescents with meningomyelocele. *Journal of Allergy and Clinical Immunology, 101,* 741–746.

Sherk, H.H., Melchionne, J., & Smith, R. (1987). The natural history of hip dislocations in ambulatory myelomeningoceles. *Zeitschrift fur Kinderchirurgie, 42*(Suppl. 1), 48–49.

Shinnar, S., Gammon, K., Bergman, E.W., Jr., et al. (1985). Management of hydrocephalus in infancy: Use of acetazolamide and furosemide to avoid cerebrospinal fluid shunts. *Journal of Pediatrics, 107*(1), 31–37.

Shurtleff, D.B., Lemire, R., & Warkany, J. (1986). Embryology, etiology, and epidemiology. In D.B. Shurtleff (Ed.), *Myelodysplasias and exstrophies: Significance, prevention, and treatment* (pp. 39–64). Orlando, FL: Grune & Stratton.

Shurtleff, D.B., Luthy, D.A., Nyberg, D.A., et al. (1994). Meningomyelocele: Management in utero and post natum. *Ciba Foundation Symposium, 181*, 270–280.

Shurtleff, D.B., & Stuntz, T. (1986). Back closure. In D.B. Shurtleff (Ed.), *Myelodysplasias and exstrophies: Significance, prevention, and treatment* (pp. 117–138). Orlando, FL: Harcourt, Brace & Co.

Shurtleff, D.B. (1986). Selection process for the care of congenitally malformed infants. In D.B. Shurtleff (Ed.), *Myelodysplasias and exstrophies: Significance, prevention, and treatment* (pp. 89–116). Orlando, FL: Harcourt, Brace & Co.

Shurtleff, D.B., & Dunne, K. (1986). Adults and adolescents with meningomyelocele. In D.B. Shurtleff (Ed.), *Myelodysplasias and exstrophies: Significance, prevention, and treatment* (pp. 433–448). Orlando, FL: Grune & Stratton.

Shurtleff, D.B., & Lemire, R.J. (1995). Epidemiology, etiologic factors, and prenatal diagnosis of open spinal dysraphism. *Neurosurgery Clinics of North America, 6*(2), 183–192.

Shurtleff, D.B., Stuntz, T., & Hayden, P. (1986). Hydrocephalus. In D.B. Shurtleff (Ed.), *Myelodysplasias and exstrophies: Significance, prevention, and treatment* (pp. 139–180). Orlando, FL: Harcourt, Brace & Co.

Sloan, S.L., Leibold, S.R., & Henry-Atkinson, J. (1995). *Sexuality and the person with spina bifida* [Booklet]. Washington, DC: Spina Bifida Association of America.

Spina Bifida Association of America (SBAA). (1995). *Guidelines for spina bifida health care services throughout life.* Washington, DC: Author.

Stafstrom, C.E., Gilmore, H.E., & Kurtin, P.S. (1992). Nephrocalcinosis complicating medical treatment of posthemorrhagic hydrocephalus. *Pediatric Neurology, 8*(3), 79–82.

Stone, A.R. (1995). Neurourologic evaluation and urologic management of spinal dysraphism. *Neurosurgery Clinics of North America, 6*(2), 269–277.

Swartz, M.L. (1989). Citrucel (methylcellulose/bulk-forming laxative). *Gastroenterology Nursing, 12*(1), 50–52.

Tachdjian, M.O. (1990). *Pediatric orthopedics* (2nd ed.). Philadelphia: W.B. Saunders & Co.

Talwar, D., Baldwin, M.A., & Horbatt, C.L. (1995). Epilepsy in children with meningomyelocele. *Pediatric Neurology, 13*(1), 29–32.

Tassabehji, M., Read, A.P., Newton, V.E., et al. (1992). Waardenburg's syndrome patients have mutations in the human homologue of the *Pax-3* paired box gene. *Nature, 355*(6361), 635–636.

Teo, C., & Jones, R. (1996). Management of hydrocephalus by endoscopic third ventriculostomy in patients with myelomeningocele. *Pediatric Neurosurgery, 25*(2), 57–63.

Wechsler, D. (1991). *Wechsler Intelligence Scale for Children* (3rd ed.). San Antonio, TX: The Psychological Corporation.

Werler, M.M., Louik, C., Shapiro, S., & Mitchell, A.A. (1996). Prepregnant weight in relation of risk of neural tube defects. *JAMA: Journal of the American Medical Association, 275*(14), 1089–1092.

Whitehead, W.E., Parker, L., Bosmajian, L., et al. (1986). Treatment of fecal incontinence in children with spina bifida: Comparison of biofeedback and behavior modification. *Archives of Physical Medicine and Rehabilitation, 67*(4), 218–224.

Wicks, K., & Shurtleff, D.B. (1986). Stool management. In D.B. Shurtleff (Ed.), *Myelodysplasias and exstrophies: Significance, prevention, and treatment* (pp. 221–242). Orlando, FL: Harcourt, Brace & Co.

Worley, G., Erwin, C.W., Schuster, J.M., et al. (1994). BAEPs in infants with myelomeningocele and later development of Chiari II malformation-related brainstem dysfunction. *Developmental Medicine and Child Neurology, 36*(8), 707–715.

Yarkony, G.M. (1994). Pressure ulcers: A review. *Archives of Physical Medicine and Rehabilitation, 75*, 908–917.

13

Appendix

Guidelines for the Care of
Children and Adolescents with Meningomyelocele

Basic Team

The special care needs of children with meningomyelocele are best met by an experienced, co-ordinated team of pediatric specialists working collaboratively with parents, the primary care physician, and other service providers. Not all members of the basic team may be needed at each visit, and other professionals may be required. These include but are not limited to an or-thotist, a child neurologist, an ophthalmologist, a speech-language pathologist, and a special educator. Parents of children with spina bifida and adults with spina bifida should be encour-aged to participate actively as part of the team. Please note that though a coordinated team is needed to manage the specialty services, all children require a medical home. The primary care physician is responsible for preventive and acute illness care and for assisting parents in coor-dinating the special services their children require.

Regular team members include a developmental pediatrician, a medical social worker, a neuro-surgeon, a nurse, a nutritionist, an orthopedist, a pediatric physiatrist, physical or occupational therapists, a psychologist, and a urologist.

Initial Evaluation

The initial evaluation should be performed as soon as possible after birth. The responsibilities of the primary care physician are to 1) initiate treatment of the exposed neural tube defect; 2) obtain family, pregnancy, and perinatal histories; 3) perform a physical examination to iden-tify additional congenital defects and musculoskeletal deformities and to determine the appar-ent motor and sensory levels; 4) request radiologic and laboratory tests that include cranial and renal or bladder ultrasounds, urinalysis and culture, serum creatinine (Cr), and blood urea ni-trogen (BUN); and 5) arrange for consultation by the team of specialists.

Frequency of Visits

Children with spina bifida require regular follow-up by the team of specialists. They are at risk for a number of neurosurgical problems as well as deterioration in urologic status. As the child grows and develops, additional needs (e.g., incontinence, learning disabilities) become evident that require other disciplines and treatments.

Clear and regular communication among service providers is critical. The child should be re-evaluated by the team of professionals several times per year in the first 2–3 years, twice annu-ally to 5 years of age, and then at least annually thereafter. The spina bifida team works collab-oratively with many health care professionals. In general, the primary care office should review the child's progress and update the office management plan at least yearly and more often for young children.

Please also review "Guidelines for Spina Bifida Health Care Services Throughout Life," Spina Bifida Association of America, 1995.

Guidelines for the Care of Children and Adolescents with Meningomyelocele

The following elements are recommended by age group, and the listing is cumulative. Review all items indicated up through the actual age group of a child entering your practice for the first time as part of the initial evaluation.

AGE	KEY CLINICAL ISSUES/CONCERNS	EVALUATIONS/KEY PROCEDURES	SPECIALISTS
Newborn	Feeding/Nutrition	Growth parameters, evaluation by feeding specialist as needed	Developmental pediatrician (DPed), nutritionist
	Cause of the Neural Tube Defect (NTD)	Blood chromosome or fluorescent in situ hybridization (FISH) testing as needed; discuss use of folate to prevent NTDs	DPed, medical geneticist as needed
	Evaluation and Treatment of Hydrocephalus Surgical Closure of NTD	Cranial ultrasound (US) or computed tomography (CT) scan	Neurosurgeon, plastic surgeon
	Monitor for Symptomatic Chiari Type II Malformations	Cranial magnetic resonance imaging (MRI) scan, pneumocardiogram; direct laryngoscopy as needed	Neurosurgeon, DPed as needed
	Identification of High-Risk Bladder, Hydronephrosis, Increased Outlet Resistance, Vesicoureteral Reflux (VUR)	Urinalysis/culture, serum creatinine and blood urea nitrogen, renal/bladder US, postvoid residual, voiding cystourethrogram, urodynamics if available at age 8 weeks. Initiate clean intermittent catheterization (CIC), anticholinergics as needed	DPed, urologist
	Determine Motor and Sensory Levels	Complete neuromotor examination, including passive range-of-motion (ROM) testing	Physical therapist, DPed, orthopedist
	Treatment of Clubfeet, Flexion Contractures, Hip Subluxation or Dislocation	X rays, serial casts (or strapping then brace) for clubfeet, passive ROM exercises	Orthopedist, physical therapist
	Parent Education and Anticipatory Guidance	Initiate care notebook; provide educational materials on shunt dysfunction, Chiari type II malformation tethered cord, urinary tract infections (UTIs), folic acid	DPed, nurse, medical social worker, referral to community health nurse, early intervention (EI) specialist as needed
	Care Coordination and Family Support	Link to other family with child with meningomyelocele as appropriate	

The Physician's Guide to Caring for Children with Disabilities and Chronic Conditions, edited by Robert E. Nickel and Larry W. Desch, copyright © 2000 Paul H. Brookes Publishing Co.

Guidelines for the Care of Children and Adolescents with Meningomyelocele *(continued)*

The following elements are recommended by age group, and the listing is cumulative. Review all items indicated up through the actual age group of a child entering your practice for the first time as part of the initial evaluation.

AGE	KEY CLINICAL ISSUES/CONCERNS	EVALUATIONS/KEY PROCEDURES	SPECIALISTS
First year to age 5 years (pre-school age)	*Growth/Nutrition* Oral motor dysfunction Prevention of obesity	Growth parameters, diet record, evaluation by feeding specialist or nutritionist as needed	DPed, nurse specialist, nutritionist
	Dental Care	Review oral hygiene	Dentist
	Respiratory Problems Stridor, apnea Sleep disordered breathing	Cranial MRI (if not already done), sleep study, direct laryngoscopy, surgery for symptomatic Chiari type II malformation as needed, respiratory support as needed	DPed, neurosurgeon, pediatric pulmonary specialist as needed
	Neurosurgical Problems Hydrocephalus or shunt dysfunction Symptomatic Chiari II malformation Symptomatic hydromyelia and/or syringomyelia Symptomatic tethered cord	Repeat cranial US or CT; follow head circumference, revision of shunt as needed Cranial MRI, pneumocard ogram, direct laryngoscopy as needed, posterior fossa decompression as needed Cranial and spinal MRI as needed Repeat passive ROM and muscle-strength testing, urodynamics, electromyogram (EMG) or somatosensory evoked potentials (SSEPs) as needed, surgical untethering as needed	Neurosurgeon, DPed, physical therapist, occupational therapist, urologist
	Urologic Problems High-risk bladder Recurrent UTIs, renal damage Hydronephrosis VUR High or low outlet resistance Continence program	Urodynamics at 6–12 months of age, repeat as needed, anticholinergics, and CIC as needed; vesicostomy if CIC is unsuccessful Screen with nitrite and leukocyte esterase test strips each clinic visit, urinalysis and culture as needed, antibiotic prophylaxis as needed Repeat renal and bladder US at 1–3 months and every 6–12 months, antibiotic prophylaxis as needed VCUG at age 6–12 months if not done as newborn and repeat as needed; renal scan as needed; antibiotic prophylaxis CIC and anticholinergics as needed Initiate continence program at age 3–4 years (*Note:* If change in continence occurs, evaluate for UTI or neurosurgical complication)	Urologist, DPed, nurse specialist

The Physician's Guide to Caring for Children with Disabilities and Chronic Conditions, edited by Robert E. Nickel and Larry W. Desch, copyright © 2000 Paul H. Brookes Publishing Co.

Guidelines for the Care of Children and Adolescents with Meningomyelocele *(continued)*

The following elements are recommended by age group, and the listing is cumulative. Review all items indicated up through the actual age group of a child entering your practice for the first time as part of the initial evaluation.

AGE	KEY CLINICAL ISSUES/CONCERNS	EVALUATIONS/KEY PROCEDURES	SPECIALISTS
First year to age 5 years (pre-school age) *(continued)*	*Musculoskeletal Problems*	Repeat passive ROM and muscle-strength testing (at least yearly)	Orthopedist, physical therapist
	Hip subluxation or dislocation	X rays: Anterior/posterior and lateral of the pelvis; if surgery pursued, after 2 years of age	
	Clubfeet	Surgery at 8–12 months of age	
	Joint contractures/equinus	Consider surgery if hip flexion contracture (FC) > 30°, knee FC > 20°, fixed equinus > 10°	
	Rotational deformities of leg	Gait analysis as needed, surgery as needed (usually by school-age)	
	Foot–ankle deformities	X ray: Standing anterior/posterior and lateral of the foot–ankle, surgery after 4–5 years as needed	
	Congenital kyphosis or scoliosis	X ray: Supine anterior/posterior and lateral of the spine, thoracolumbar-sacral orthosis (TLSO) as needed	
	Osteopenia and fractures	X rays as needed, treat fracture with soft case or usual brace (fracture of the epiphysis); take vitamin D and adequate calcium, encourage standing activities	
	Bowel Problems		
	Constipation	Diet plus bulk agent, adequate fluid intake/activity	DPed, nurse
	Impaction	X ray: Flat plate of abdomen as needed, oil or saline enemas, then oral cathartic as needed	
	Rectal prolapse	Rule out intussception, treat constipation	
	Continence program	Initiate timed continence program at 2–3 years of age with or without digital stimulation	
	Associated Medical Problems		
	Seizures	Electroencephalogram (EEG)	DPed, nurse, child neurologist, and ophthalmologist as needed
	Strabismus or visual problems	Ophthalmologic referral by 3–4 years of age and as needed	
	Latex allergy	Repeat history of rubber/food allergies each appointment, obtain a radioimmunoassay test (RAST) at 3–5 years or as needed, discuss primary and secondary prevention	
	Obesity	Growth parameters, education on diet, regular exercise, consult by nutritionist as needed	

The Physician's Guide to Caring for Children with Disabilities and Chronic Conditions, edited by Robert E. Nickel and Larry W. Desch, copyright © 2000 Paul H. Brookes Publishing Co.

Guidelines for the Care of Children and Adolescents with Meningomyelocele *(continued)*

The following elements are recommended by age group, and the listing is cumulative. Review all items indicated up through the actual age group of a child entering your practice for the first time as part of the initial evaluation.

AGE	KEY CLINICAL ISSUES/CONCERNS	EVALUATIONS/KEY PROCEDURES	SPECIALISTS
First year to age 5 years (pre-school age) *(continued)*	Skin care	Education on daily skin checks, pressure relief, good hygiene; review seating/positioning	
	Autonomic dysreflexia (midthoracic level or above)	Educational materials, effective continence programs, treat constipation, review treatment protocol	
	Ambulation and Mobility	Repeat passive ROM and muscle-strength testing at least yearly, gait analysis as needed	Physical therapist, DPed, orthotist, orthopedist, physiatrist
	Need for therapy services	Referral for regular PT services as needed	
	Bracing/adaptive equipment	Initial brace for T, L1, L2, or L3 motor level, parapodium or standing frame	
		Initial brace for L4, 5, KAFO or AFO	
	Seating and Positioning	Prescribe wheelchair if it enhances mobility (as early as age 18 months)	Physical therapist, physiatrist
	Wheelchair use		
	Upper-Extremity Function/Visual Motor Skills	Regularly monitor grip strength, passive ROM	Occupational therapist, neurosurgeon
	Need for occupational therapy (OT) services	Referral for OT services as needed	
	Upper-extremity weakness or spasticity	If increasing weakness or spasticity occurs, evaluate for symptomatic hydromyelia and syringomyelia	
	Developmental Progress	Audiologic testing	DPed, nurse, psychologist, occupational therapist, collaboration with EI/ECSE and school staff
	Developmental delay	Monitor developmental progress	
		Refer for early intervention/early childhood special education (EI/ECSE) services (L3 motor level and above) or as needed (low lumbar and sacral)	
	Nonverbal learning disability (NVLD)	Evaluation by occupational therapist and psychologist at age 3 years and prior to school entry	
	Social Skills	School-based program, and encourage participation in community services	DPed, nurse, school staff
	Involvement in peer group activities at school and in community (determine which supports are needed)		

The Physician's Guide to Caring for Children with Disabilities and Chronic Conditions, edited by Robert E. Nickel and Larry W. Desch, copyright © 2000 Paul H. Brookes Publishing Co.

Guidelines for the Care of Children and Adolescents with Meningomyelocele *(continued)*

The following elements are recommended by age group, and the listing is cumulative. Review all items indicated up through the actual age group of a child entering your practice for the first time as part of the initial evaluation.

AGE	KEY CLINICAL ISSUES/CONCERNS	EVALUATIONS/KEY PROCEDURES	SPECIALISTS
First year to age 5 years (pre-school age) *(continued)*	*Family Support Services* Respite care Parent group Community health nurse Advocacy Financial services (Supplemental Security Income [SSI]) Other enabling services	Family interview; use parent questionnaire (e.g., Family Needs Survey); provide resource information Referral to local or national Spina Bifida Association of America organization	DPed, nurse, social worker, psychologist as needed; referral to community health nurse as needed
	Anticipatory Guidance Importance of fostering independence and self-care Information on clinical issues	Educational materials on NVLD, latex allergy, obesity, skin care, continence programs	Primary care office in collaboration with spina bifida team
	Collaboration with Community Services School Community health nurse Developmental Disability Services	Comprehensive care coordination, with regular exchange of written information (at least yearly) with other providers; care conference as needed	Primary care office in collaboration with spina bifida team
School-age children and adolescents	*Neurosurgical Problems*	Yearly, detailed neuromotor and musculoskeletal examinations School reports at least yearly Repeat CT, spinal MRI scans as needed Repeat psychological testing as needed Repeat urodynamics, EMG, SSEPs as needed	Neurosurgeon, physical therapist, collaboration with school staff
	Musculoskeletal Problems Scoliosis, developmental Kyphosis, congenital Recurrent flexion contractures Recurrent foot–ankle deformities	Yearly, detailed neuromotor and musculoskeletal examinations Repeat X rays: Sitting and/or supine anterior/posterior and lateral of the spine as needed; TLSO if spinal curve is greater than 20°, consider surgery if spinal curve is greater than 40° Surgery if severe or progressive deformity, recurrent decubiti are present Other X rays as needed, gait analysis as needed	Orthopedist, physical therapist

The Physician's Guide to Caring for Children with Disabilities and Chronic Conditions, edited by Robert E. Nickel and Larry W. Desch, copyright © 2000 Paul H. Brookes Publishing Co.

Guidelines for the Care of Children and Adolescents with Meningomyelocele *(continued)*

The following elements are recommended by age group, and the listing is cumulative. Review all items indicated up through the actual age group of a child entering your practice for the first time as part of the initial evaluation.

AGE	KEY CLINICAL ISSUES/CONCERNS	EVALUATIONS/KEY PROCEDURES	SPECIALISTS
School-age children and adolescents *(continued)*	*Bowel Problems* Constipation and impaction Continence program	Treat constipation and impaction, regular emptying program (e.g., use of suppositories, enemas), encourage self-care, consider alternative programs as needed (e.g., antegrade continence enema)	DPed, nurse
	Ambulation and Mobility Reevaluate need for PT/OT services	Evaluation includes functional assessment (e.g., Pediatric Evaluation of Disability Inventory [PEDI]), review of adaptive equipment needs	Physical therapist, occupational therapist, orthotist
	Associated Developmental and Learning Problems NVLD Mental retardation	Reevaluation as needed, particularly at third or fourth grade and seventh or eighth grade	Occupational therapist, psychologist, collaboration with school staff
	Associated Behavior and Mental Health Problems Inattention, poor motivation Social isolation Anxiety Obsessive-compulsive behaviors Depression	Behavioral checklist, school information Referral to mental health professional as needed Encourage participation in organized clubs, sports, parks and recreation programs, camps Involve in mentoring program	DPed, nurse, social worker, psychologist, collaboration with school staff
	Self-Care and Independent Living Determine which supports are needed	Outpatient PT and OT services as needed; consider inpatient rehabilitation evaluation Independent living skills program, social skills training as needed	Social worker, physical and occupational therapists, psychologist, and/or vocational specialist
	Parent and Child Education and Anticipatory Guidance Discuss diagnosis and treatment with child Review genetics and prevention (use of folic acid) Transition to middle school, high school, or higher education Transition to adult medical services Vocational or career planning Encourage healthy behaviors (e.g., exercise, diet) Recreation and leisure activities Sexuality and high-risk behavior (e.g., substance abuse)	Child, family, and teacher interview; school conference as needed Referral to Department of Vocational Rehabilitation, career counseling, life skills program as needed Referral to community services as needed Begin gynecologic care for sexually active females Educational materials on folic acid, sexuality, family planning	Primary care office in collaboration with spina bifida team

The Physician's Guide to Caring for Children with Disabilities and Chronic Conditions, edited by Robert E. Nickel and Larry W. Desch, copyright © 2000 Paul H. Brookes Publishing Co.

Family and Physician Management Plan Summary for Children and Adolescents with Meningomyelocele

This form will help you and your physician review current services and service needs. Please answer the questions about your current services on this page. Your physician will review your responses and complete the rest of the form.

Child's name _____ Today's date _____

Person completing the form _____

CURRENT SERVICES

1. Please list your/your child's current medications and any side effects.

2. What braces and special equipment do you/does your child use now?

3. What is your/your child's current school program?

   School name _____ Grade _____

   Teacher _____ Telephone _____

4. Do you/does your child receive any support services or other special programs at school (e.g., physical therapy, resource room)? Please list.

5. Who are your/your child's other medical and dental service providers?

   Dentist _____

   Neurosurgeon _____

   Orthopedist _____

   Urologist _____

   Other _____

The Physician's Guide to Caring for Children with Disabilities and Chronic Conditions, edited by Robert E. Nickel and Larry W. Desch,
copyright © 2000 Paul H. Brookes Publishing Co.

Family and Physician Management Plan Summary for Children and Adolescents with Meningomyelocele *(continued)*

6. Who are your/your child's other community service providers?

    Physical therapist _____

    Community health nurse _____

    Other _____

7. Do you/does your child also receive services from a spina bifida team of specialists?

    Contact person _____

    Location _____

8. Have you/has your child had any blood tests, radiologic (X-ray) examinations, or other procedures since your last visit? If yes, please describe.

9. Have you/has your child been hospitalized or received surgery since your last visit? If yes, describe.

10. Please note accomplishments since your last visit. Consider activities at home, in your neighborhood, or at school, as well as success with treatments.

11. What goals (i.e., skills) would you/your child like to accomplish in the next year? Consider activities at home, in your neighborhood, or at school, as well as success with a treatment.

12. What questions or concerns would you like addressed today?

Family and Physician Management Plan Summary for Children and Adolescents with Meningomyelocele

The Management Plan Summary should be completed at each annual review and more often as needed. It is intended to be used with the Guidelines for Care, which provide a more complete listing of clinical issues at different ages as well as recommended evaluations and treatments.

Child's name _____ Person completing form _____ Today's date _____

Clinical issues	Currently a problem?	Evaluations needed	Treatment recommendations	Referrals made	Date for status check
Family's Questions					
Cause of the Neural Tube Defect (NTD) Counsel about folic acid use					
Growth/Nutrition Feeding problems, obesity					
Dental Care					
Respiratory Problems Stridor, apnea Sleep disordered breathing					
Skin Care and Decubiti Performing regular skin checks					
Latex Allergy Discuss primary and secondary prevention					

The Physician's Guide to Caring for Children with Disabilities and Chronic Conditions, edited by Robert E. Nickel and Larry W. Desch, copyright © 2000 Paul H. Brookes Publishing Co.

Family and Physician Management Plan Summary for Children and Adolescents with Meningomyelocele *(continued)*

Child's name _____ Person completing form _____ Today's date _____

Clinical issues	Currently a problem?	Evaluations needed	Treatment recommendations	Referrals made	Date for status check
Neurosurgical Problems Rapid head growth Recent change in neurologic examination or upper-extremity weakness					
Urologic Problems Current continence program Recent change in continence Today's urinalysis results					
Bowel Problems Describe current continence program Constipation or impaction					
Musculoskeletal Problems Recent change in contractures, gait, or scoliosis					
Ambulation and Mobility Describe current ambulatory status Questions about physical therapy (PT) services, braces, or adaptive equipment					
Seating and Positioning					

The Physician's Guide to Caring for Children with Disabilities and Chronic Conditions, edited by Robert E. Nickel and Larry W. Desch, copyright © 2000 Paul H. Brookes Publishing Co.

Family and Physician Management Plan Summary for Children and Adolescents with Meningomyelocele *(continued)*

Child's name _____ Person completing form _____ Today's date _____

Clinical issues	Currently a problem?	Evaluations needed	Treatment recommendations	Referrals made	Date for status check
Upper-Extremity Function/ Visual Motor Skills Increase in upper-extremity weakness or spasticity Questions about services					
Associated Medical Problems Seizures Strabismus/visual concerns Autonomic dysreflexia Precocious puberty **Note any side effects of medications.**					
Associated Developmental and Learning Problems Review early intervention or school services (individual-ized family service plan [IFSP], individualized educa-tion program [IEP]) Describe current school achievement Nonverbal learning disabilities (NVLD) Developmental delay or mental retardation					

The Physician's Guide to Caring for Children with Disabilities and Chronic Conditions, edited by Robert E. Nickel and Larry W. Desch, copyright © 2000 Paul H. Brookes Publishing Co.

Family and Physician Management Plan Summary for Children and Adolescents with Meningomyelocele *(continued)*

Child's name _____ Person completing form _____ Today's date _____

Clinical issues	Currently a problem?	Evaluations needed	Treatment recommendations	Referrals made	Date for status check
Associated Behavior and Mental Health Problems					
Social Skills Involvement in peer-group activities in school and in the community					
Self-Care and Independence					
Family Support Services					
Anticipatory Guidance List issues discussed and materials provided					

The Physician's Guide to Caring for Children with Disabilities and Chronic Conditions, edited by Robert E. Nickel and Larry W. Desch, copyright © 2000 Paul H. Brookes Publishing Co.

Family and Physician Management Plan Summary for Children and Adolescents with Meningomyelocele *(continued)*

Child's name _____ Person completing form _____ Today's date _____

Clinical issues	Currently a problem?	Evaluations needed	Treatment recommendations	Referrals made	Date for status check
Collaboration with Community Agencies School Developmental Disability Services Vocational Rehabilitation					
Comments					

Next update of the Management Plan Summary _____

Signature _____ Date _____
(Child and parent)

Signature _____ Date _____
(Health professional)

The Physician's Guide to Caring for Children with Disabilities and Chronic Conditions, edited by Robert E. Nickel and Larry W. Desch, copyright © 2000 Paul H. Brookes Publishing Co.

RESOURCES ON MENINGOMYELOCELE AND RELATED NEURAL TUBE DEFECTS

Readings

Bunnett, R. (1992). *Friends in the park*. New York: Checkerboard Press.

Chapman, W., Hill, M., & Shurtleff, D.B. (1993). *Management of the neurogenic bowel and bladder*. Oak Brook, IL: Eterna Press. (Post Office Box 1344, Oak Brook, IL 60522-1344)

Dwight, L. (1992). *We can do it*. New York: Checkerboard Press.

Engelman, B.E., Loomis, J.W., & Klieback, L. (1994). *Confronting the challenges of spina bifida: A group curriculum addressing self-care, self-esteem, and social skills in 8 to 13 year old children*. Newington, CT: Newington Children's Hospital. (860-545-9000)

Field, J. (1992). *Toobie: Self-cath coloring book for boys and girls*. Santa Barbara, CA: Mentor Urology.

Lutenhoff, M., & Oppenheimer, S.G. (Eds.). (1997). *Spinabilities: A young person's guide to spina bifida*. Bethesda, MD: Woodbine House. (1-800-843-7323)

McLone, D. (n.d.). *An introduction to spina bifida*. Chicago: Children's Memorial Hospital. (312-880-4373; available in English and Spanish versions)

Rose, J. (1988). *Spike speaks on self-catheterization for boys*. Austin, TX: Children's Hospital of Austin at Brackenridge, The Specialty Care Center, and the Spina Bifida Association of Texas.

Rowley-Kelly, F.L., & Reigel, D.H. (1993). *Teaching the student with spina bifida*. Baltimore: Paul H. Brookes Publishing Co. (1-800-638-3775)

Sandler, A. (1997). *Living with spina bifida: A guide for families and professionals*. Chapel Hill: University of North Carolina Press. (1-800-848-6224)

Sloan, S.L., Leibold, S.R., & Henry-Atkinson, J.H. (1995), *Sexuality and the person with spina bifida*. Washington, DC: Spina Bifida Association of America (SBAA). (1-800-621-3141)

Spina Bifida and Hydrocephalus Association of Ontario. (1995). *A guide to hydrocephalus*. Toronto: Spina Bifida and Hydrocephalus Association of Ontario.

Spina Bifida Association of Kentucky. (n.d.). *Becoming the me I want to be*. Louisville: Transition to Independence Project, Spina Bifida Association of Kentucky. (982 Eastern Parkway, Louisville, KY 40217-1566)

Spina Bifida Association of Kentucky. (n.d.). *Building skills: A guide for parents and professionals working with people who have spina bifida*. Louisville: Transition to Independence Project, Spina Bifida Association of Kentucky. (982 Eastern Parkway, Louisville, KY 40217-1566)

Spina Bifida Association of Kentucky. (n.d.). *Making choices*. Louisville: Transition to Independence Project, Spina Bifida Association of Kentucky. (982 Eastern Parkway, Louisville, KY 40217-1566) (a journal/workbook for teens and young adults with spina bifida that provides opportunities for making choices about their lives)

University of Colorado Health Sciences Center, School of Nursing. (1986). *User's manual: Clean intermittent catheterization*. Denver: University of Colorado, School of Nursing, Health Sciences Center. (Distributed by Learner Managed Designs, Inc., Post Office Box 747, Lawrence, KS 66044; 913-842-9088, 1-800-467-1644)

Wolraich, M.L., & Lozes, M.H. (1985). *What you should know about your child with spina bifida*. Iowa City, IA: University Hospital School. (319-353-6390)

Latex Allergy Information

LatexAllergyHelp.com
World Wide Web site: http://www.latexallergyhelp.com/

This site provides detailed information for families, physicians, and dentists.

National Organizations

Hydrocephalus Association
870 Market Street, Suite 955
San Francisco, California 94102
Telephone: (415) 732-7040
Fax: (415) 732-7044
E-mail: hydroassoc@aol.com
World Wide Web site: http://www.HydroAssoc.org/

This association provides information and referrals and publishes a resource guide, a directory of pediatric neurosurgeons, and a quarterly newsletter.

Hydrocephalus, Syringomyelia, Spina Bifida, and Allied Disorders Resources
World Wide Web site: http://neurosurgery.mgh.harvard.edu/hyd-rsrc.htm

This site offers links to a variety of resources and other World Wide Web sites on these chronic conditions.

Spina Bifida Association of America (SBAA)
4590 MacArthur Boulevard NW, Suite 250
Washington, D.C. 20007-4226
Telephone: (800) 621-3141, (202) 944-3285
Fax: (202) 944-3295
E-mail: sbaa@sbaa.org
World Wide Web site: http://www.sbaa.org/

A national organization with more than 100 local chapters that provides information and referrals and publishes a variety of materials, including a newsletter, as well as supports research and conducts conferences for parents and professionals.

Other Internet Resources

Children with Spina Bifida: A Resource Page for Parents
World Wide Web site: http://www.waisman.wisc.edu/
~rowley/sb-kids/

This site provides information and support to new parents of infants with spina bifida, including links to personal home pages of other parents of children with spina bifida.

SB-TEENS
E-mail: c_tdsnetz@yahoo.com
World Wide Web site: http://www.members.tripod.com/
~sbteens

Teens with spina bifida can "meet" on-line. This site provides information and links to other World Wide Web sites for teens. The co-sponsor of SB-TEEN list is Carrie Bloss, a teenager with spina bifida.

14

Craniofacial Disorders

Lisa Letcher-Glembo

KEY COMPETENCIES

- Discuss the classification of craniofacial anomalies, and describe clefts of the primary palate, clefts of the secondary palate, and submucous clefts
- Discuss the common causes of cleft lip and/or palate (CLP), including syndromes associated with clefting
- Perform a dysmorphology screen and an evaluation for minor physical anomalies to assist in referral of infants with CLP who may have a syndromic birth defect
- Discuss the feeding problems of infants with CLP and appropriate management techniques
- Describe the management of middle-ear problems of children with CLP
- Monitor the developmental progress of infants and toddlers with CLP using parent report measures, developmental screening tools, and a targeted screen for psychosocial functioning as needed
- Construct an overall management plan for a child with CLP, including the specialists involved and the usual timing of surgeries

DESCRIPTION

Definition and Terminology

The term *craniofacial* refers to bones of the cranium and face. Facial structure can be divided into upper face, midface, and lower face. A person with an abnormality that involves any or all parts of the cranium, upper face, or midface is said to have a *craniofacial anomaly* or a *craniofacial disorder*. Craniofacial anomalies range from simple (e.g., cleft lip) to complex (e.g., Treacher Collins syndrome) and may be isolated or associated with other congenital defects.

The lips, gum line, and roof of the mouth are formed during the seventh through thirteenth weeks of fetal life. Interruption of this formation results in a group of disorders known as *orofacial clefts* (Blackman, 1997). Clefts differ in type and in severity. Variations are attributed to the timing of the interference during the fetal period. Because orofacial clefts are the most common craniofacial anomalies, the emphasis in this chapter is on the evaluation and management of infants and children with cleft conditions.

Etiology and Incidence

Congenital craniofacial anomalies may occur as an isolated defect, as part of a birth defect syndrome (e.g., fetal alcohol syndrome [FAS]), or as part of a developmental sequence (e.g., Pierre Robin sequence).

A *birth defect syndrome* refers to a pattern of malformations that are related pathogenically (Brodsky, Holt, & Ritter-Schmidt, 1992). A *developmental sequence* refers to conditions that occur together as a result of an initial precipitating cause (McWilliams, Morris, & Shelton, 1990). For example, the midline U-shaped cleft in Pierre Robin sequence results from micrognathia and posterior displacement of the tongue during fetal development. Craniofacial disorders can result from teratogens (e.g., FAS); chromosomal disorders (e.g., deletion of 4p); microdeletion syndromes (e.g., velocardiofacial [VCF] syndrome, the microdeletion of chromosome 22q11); and autosomal dominant disorders (e.g., Stickler syndrome). They also can be due to autosomal recessive disorders (e.g., Roberts-SC phocomelia); polygenic, multifactorial disorders (e.g., isolated cleft lip and palate); or sporadic disorders (e.g., amniotic rupture sequence).

More complex congenital craniofacial anomalies include Crouzon syndrome, Treacher Collins syndrome, and hemifacial microsomia. The predominant features of several major syndromes and sequences that professionals are likely to encounter in their practices are outlined in Table 14.1 (Blackman, 1997; Jones, 1997; McWilliams et al., 1990).

Traumatic injuries to the face and oral musculature from motor vehicle accidents, surgical removal of tumors, or gunshot wounds can result in complex craniofacial defects. In addition, some craniofacial disorders may result from causes other than genetics or trauma. For example, in the mid-1990s, an increase in plagiocephaly without actual craniosynostosis was observed (Kane, Mitchell, Craven, & Marsh, 1996). It has been questioned whether there is a relationship between this craniofacial nontraumatic, noncongenital condition and the increased prevalence of recommendations to position infants in a supine position during sleep to avoid sudden infant death syndrome (SIDS).

Cleft lip and/or palate (CLP) is the most common of the congenital craniofacial anomalies and affects approximately 1 in 600 Caucasian newborns; its incidence is somewhat lower in the African American population and higher among people of Chinese and Japanese descent (Moller & Starr, 1993). The following statements review the etiology, incidence, and recurrence risks for nonsyndromic, isolated clefts:

- Multifactorial inheritance (i.e., a combination of genetic and environmental factors) is the cause for the majority of isolated clefts.
- The combination of cleft lip and palate is more common than cleft lip only or cleft palate only; cleft lip *and* palate composes about 50% of all

Table 14.1. Selected craniofacial syndrome conditions and their associated characteristics

Apert syndrome: Craniosynostosis, hypertelorism, exorbitism, midface hypoplasia, high-arched and narrow maxillary arch, and syndactyly of hands and feet (1:169,000)

Crouzon syndrome: Craniosynostosis, hypertelorism, exorbitism, midface hypoplasia, high-arched and narrow maxillary arch

Hemifacial microsomia: Hypoplasia of malar, maxillary, and mandibular regions; cleftlike extension of the corner of the mouth; hypoplasia of facial musculature; microtia; preauricular tags, pits, or both; middle-ear anomalies; malfunction of the tongue and the soft palate; clefts of lip and/or palate (CLP); associated heart malformations (1:3,000 with 3:2 male predominance)

Pierre Robin sequence: Micrognathia that leads to glossoptosis; midline, typically wide, U-shaped palatal clefts; feeding and respiratory difficulties as well as occasionally occurring congenital heart, eye, and ear defects

Stickler syndrome: Flat facies, epicanthal folds, midfacial or mandibular hypoplasia, palatal clefts, micrognathia, sensory and conductive deafness, dental anomalies, severe myopia and/or cataracts present typically prior to age 10 years

Treacher Collins syndrome: Malar hypoplasia with down-slanting palpebral (eyelid) fissures, colobomas of lower eyelid, malformation of auricles, defect of external auditory canal, cleft palate, projection of scalp hair onto cheek, and occasional skin tags (1:3,000 to 1:5,000 births; male-to-female ratio is 3:2)

Velocardiofacial (VCF) syndrome: Congenital velopharyngeal incompetence, cardiac anomalies, prominent nose, narrow palpebral fissures, malar deficiency, vertical maxillary excess with long face, microcephaly, slender hands and digits, associated learning and language impairments

Sources: Blackman (1997); Jones (1997); McWilliams, Morris, and Shelton (1990).

Note: When available, the incidence rate of the disorder listed is given in parentheses.

cases of clefting; cleft lip, about 25%; and cleft palate, about 25%.

- Isolated cleft palate appears to be distinct from cleft lip with or without cleft palate. Specifically, individuals with isolated cleft palate demonstrate a higher incidence of learning disabilities than people with CLP; CLP is more common in males than in females; the female-to-male ratio is 2:1 for clefts involving both hard and soft palate without lip involvement; female-to-male ratio is equal for clefts that involve the soft palate only (Gorlin, 1993).
- The incidence of cleft varies by race; Native Americans demonstrate the highest incidence of

CLP, Japanese and Chinese populations demonstrate the second- and third-highest incidences of CLP, and African Americans display the lowest incidence of CLP.

- Severity of a facial cleft affects the recurrence risks. Specifically, if a parent has isolated unilateral cleft lip, recurrence risk is about 2.5%; if a parent has isolated unilateral cleft lip *and* palate, recurrence risk is about 4%; if a parent has isolated bilateral cleft lip and palate (BCLP), recurrence risk is higher than 5.5% (Gorlin, 1993; Vanderas, 1987).

Review of Anatomy, Physiology, and Clinical Problems

Nose and Upper Lip Nasal and oral features can be affected greatly by the cleft condition. It is helpful to be knowledgeable of normal facial, oral, and pharyngeal anatomy and physiology to best understand the problems associated with orofacial clefts and their management. Figure 14.1 demonstrates the nasal tip, nasal ala, columella, and philtrum, as well as the Cupid's bow. The *nasal ala* is the rounded cartilage that helps to define the nasal airway on each side of the nose. The *columella* is the strip of tissue between the tip of the nose and the base of the nose. The *philtrum* is the vertical groove connecting the upper lip to the nose.

Common nasal sequelae of clefting include partial collapse or flattening of the nose, flaring of the alar base on the side of the cleft, and nasal septum deviations (McWilliams et al., 1990; Moller & Starr, 1993). These sequelae can occur on one side, as in the case of unilateral cleft, or on both sides, as in the case of bilateral cleft. Another frequent occurrence is the shortening or the absence of the columella. These deviations alone or in combination can produce nasal airway difficulties and can affect the quality of an individual's speech.

The *Cupid's bow* refers to the symmetric, V-shaped border of the midline of the upper lip. The reddened tissue of the lip is known as the *vermilion*. The lips, consisting of cutaneous, muscular, glandular, and mucosal tissue, are defined by their vermilion border (Zemlin, 1998). Lip activity is achieved most predominantly by an oval ring of muscle known as the *orbicularis oris*. Lip closure assists in saliva control as well as in the speech production of the bilabial consonants "b," "p," "m," and "w." Proper lip function assists in the acts of blowing, sucking, and kissing.

The upper lip appears particularly vulnerable to clefting. The initial lip repair surgery, typically completed when the child is approximately 10 weeks of

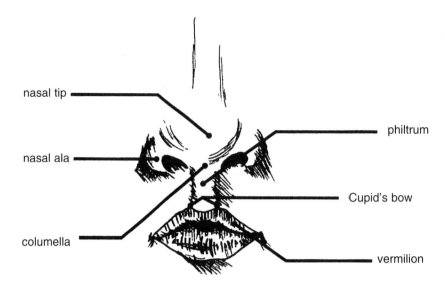

Figure 14.1.   Frontal view of the face.

age, can be made easier, at times, by narrowing the cleft preoperatively. This narrowing can be achieved by a simple preliminary operation known as a *lip adhesion* (Edwards & Watson, 1993). A lip adhesion involves exposing and suturing the muscles of the upper lip. The lip adhesion does not restore proper labial muscular function; however, it does serve to draw the two halves of the maxilla together. This makes the later full lip repair not only easier but also better (Millard, 1976–1980). An alternative method of narrowing the cleft preoperatively is by the use of presurgical orthopedics. Extraoral and/or intraoral orthopedic techniques are increasingly being recommended during the early postnatal state to assist in decreasing maxillary protrusion in the case of children with bilateral cleft lip (Figueroa, Reisberg, Polley, & Cohen, 1996).

Postsurgical defects of the lip that are associated with both unilateral and bilateral repaired clefts include muscle discontinuity of the orbicularis oris; philtral deformities; and irregularity of the vermilion border, particularly at the midline of the upper lip (i.e., in the area of the Cupid's bow). These deviations are generally improved but not fully corrected by the initial surgical lip repair.

Alveolar Process and Dentition   Figure 14.2 illustrates the nose, lip, oral, and pharyngeal structures. The *alveolar process* serves as the bony housing structure for the primary, and ultimately the permanent, maxillary teeth. A number of consonants are produced by lower lip or tongue tip contact against the upper teeth of the alveolar process. An individual can experience a cleft that can affect the bony gum line of the alveolar process of the maxilla. This type of cleft is referred to as an *alveolar cleft* or *alveolar defect*. When a cleft involves the alveolar process, missing and/or malpositioned teeth in and around the cleft site are expected. Narrowing or collapse of the upper dental arch may occur and can cause *dental crossbite*, which is overlapping of the maxillary teeth by the mandibular teeth (Zemlin, 1998).

Malocclusion   The dental and orthognathic differences of individuals with craniofacial anomalies can impair their eating and speech and can negatively affect their appearance and psychosocial function. Symmetric or nonsymmetric undergrowth (*hypoplasia*) or overgrowth (*hyperplasia*) of either the maxilla and/or the mandible can result.

According to Zemlin (1998), *Class I occlusion* provides a normal facial profile. In *Class I malocclusion,* the dental arches line up properly in relationship to each other; however, the dentition within the arches may be rotated or crowded. *Class II malocclusion* occurs when the cusps of the first mandibular molars are behind and inside the opposing molars. Individuals with Treacher Collins syndrome and those with Pierre Robin sequence are at particular risk for Class II malocclusion. *Class III malocclusion* occurs when the cusps of the first mandibular molars are ahead of the maxillary incisors. This condition results in the appearance of a prognathic or protruding lower jaw or a retrusive midface. Following initial surgical repair of the lip and palate, children born with congenital clefts have been found to be at increased risk for Class III malocclusion.

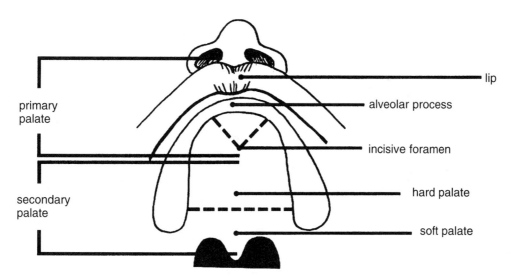

Figure 14.2. Schematic drawing of facial, intraoral, and pharyngeal structures.

Roba and Bochacki (1992) pointed out that when caring for individuals with craniofacial differences, the clinician should recognize as early as possible whether dentoskeletal anomalies are treatable with orthodontic treatment alone or whether they require orthognathic surgery in addition to orthodontics. Typically, the correction of significant skeletal discrepancies requires orthognathic surgical intervention. Orthognathic surgery can involve surgical manipulation of the upper jaw, the lower jaw, or both jaws. For optimal results, such surgery traditionally is deferred until facial growth and development are at or near completion.

Hard and Soft Palate   Posterior to the alveolar process is the hard palate. The hard palate consists of the palatine bones and a portion of the maxilla covered by mucosa. The hard palate, when intact, contributes to the separation of the oral and nasal cavities. Infants with yet-to-be-repaired palatal clefts are at particular risk for malnutrition, dehydration, and weight loss as a result of their inability to build up adequate suction for feeding activities. Any opening in the hard palate, such as an unrepaired cleft or *fistula(e),* can lead to the transfer of food or fluids into the nasal cavity and can reduce intraoral pressure necessary for speech, sucking, and blowing.

The soft palate, also referred to as the *velum,* is made up of muscle covered by mucosa. It consists primarily of levator palatine and palatopharyngeus muscles, which, when functioning properly, contribute greatly to successful speech and swallow functions. Like the levator palatine and palatopharyngeus muscles, the *uvula* is a portion of the soft palate made up of muscular tissue. A *bifid uvula* can indicate a greater underlying problem such as *submucous cleft palate* (McWilliams et al., 1990).

The terms *primary palate* and *secondary palate* serve as the most common basis for the classification of clefts (Fritzell, 1993). The primary and secondary palates are derived from the fusion of palatal shelves during embryologic development. The primary palate consists of the lip, alveolar process, and anterior triangular portion of the bony hard palate up to the level of the incisive foramen. It is this portion of the upper jaw that should later house the right and left maxillary central and lateral incisors. The secondary palate consists of the remainder of the hard palate and all of the soft palate (i.e., from the level of the incisive foramen of the hard palate through the uvula of the soft palate).

Middle Ear Function   Children with craniofacial anomalies are at increased risk for permanent or fluctuating hearing loss and demonstrate a higher incidence of middle-ear disease (Volk, Arnold, & Brodsky, 1992). Commonly, eustachian tube function in children with orofacial clefts is faulty and accounts for their increased risk of middle-ear disease and fluctuating hearing acuity. Hearing loss can negatively affect these individuals' linguistic, educational, psychosocial, and long-term vocational function. Bilateral myringotomies with tube placement are usually done prophylactically at the time of the initial lip repair of infants with CLP.

Abnormalities of the auditory structures are common in individuals with craniofacial anomalies (American Cleft Palate–Craniofacial Association [ACPA], 1993). Individuals with craniofacial anom-

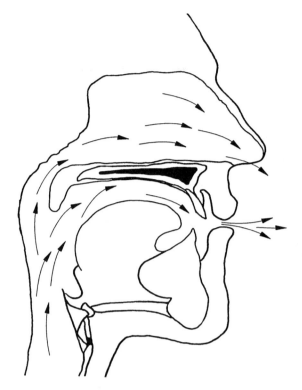

Figure 14.3.   Lateral view of oral, palatal, and pharyngeal structures while soft palate is at rest.

alies may demonstrate differences of the pinna, including microtia of the outer ear, ear pits, and extraneous skin tags. Atresia of the ear canal may occur, and children with more involved craniofacial anomalies are at increased risk for cochlear malformations.

Velopharyngeal Closure   A relationship exists between speech and the function of the soft palate and pharyngeal walls. At rest, the soft palate hangs down and airflow can be directed out the oral cavity, the nasal cavity, or both (see Figure 14.3). During certain activities, such as swallowing, blowing, sucking, and whistling, the nasal cavity must be separated from the oral cavity. The separation of oral and nasal cavities is achieved by a process known as *velopharyngeal closure*. Velopharyngeal closure occurs when there is adequate elevation of the soft palate sufficient in length to make contact with the posterior pharyngeal wall. Soft palate elevation during velopharyngeal closure is typically coupled with medial movement of the lateral pharyngeal walls. Anterior movement of the posterior pharyngeal wall is observed with less frequency than lateral pharyngeal wall movement in individuals with competent velopharyngeal closure mechanisms. The hard and soft palates must be intact for velopharyngeal closure to be accomplished successfully.

Velopharyngeal closure is responsible for the direction of the airstream for sound production and is involved in the resonance phenomenon known as *nasality*. The nasal sounds of "m," "n," and "ng" are the only sounds of the English language that do not require velopharyngeal closure. Velopharyngeal closure, coupled with tongue and lip movements for articulation, is required for correct production of all oral sounds of the English language: "p," "b," "t," "d," "k," "g," "f," "v," "s," and "z," as well as "th," "sh," "ch," and "j." During production of these sounds, the airstream should solely be directed out of the mouth if the hard and soft palates are intact and palatal and pharyngeal musculature is of proper configuration, strength, and coordination (see Figure 14.4).

Velopharyngeal Incompetence   An individual who is unable to build up sufficient intraoral pressure by the decoupling of the nasal and oral cavities is said to have *velopharyngeal incompetence* (VPI). VPI is the umbrella term for any neurologic, muscular, or structural defect that causes an impairment in velopharyngeal valving. VPI can lead to impaired speech intelligibility, hypernasality, and audible or inaudible nasal air emission.

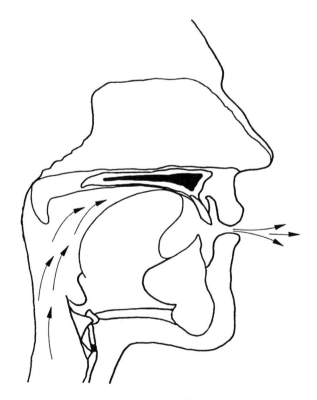

Figure 14.4.   Lateral view of intraoral and pharyngeal structures during process of velopharyngeal closure.

Individuals with clefting are at particular risk for a certain type of VPI known as *velopharyngeal insufficiency*, which is a type of VPI in which the soft palate is too short in relation to the posterior and lateral pharyngeal walls (see Figure 14.5). *Velopharyngeal inadequacy* is the term applied to those cases that involve an impairment in palatal and/or pharyngeal wall movement. Children who have intact hard and soft palates but have a history of facial asymmetry and/or neuromuscular disorders also are at increased risk for velopharyngeal inadequacy and corresponding nasality problems secondary to reduced strength, range of motion, and coordination of the velopharyngeal closure mechanism.

A person may be able to obtain adequate velopharyngeal closure for swallowing to prohibit nasal reflux but may be unable to achieve and maintain appropriate velopharyngeal closure during speech. VPI also may become more apparent with advancing age because of continued facial growth and development, adenoidal tissue atrophy, and lengthier verbal productions.

Instrumental evaluation techniques such as frontal and lateral videofluoroscopy and the more invasive procedure of nasoendoscopy are useful supplements to the intraoral examination in the assessment of the velopharyngeal closure mechanism.

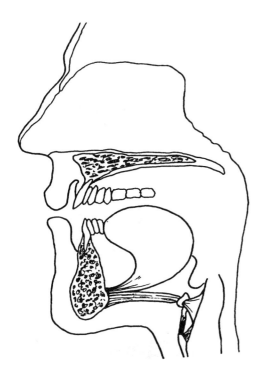

Figure 14.5. Schematic view of velopharyngeal insufficiency. The soft palate is too short in relation to the posterior pharyngeal wall.

Velopharyngeal closure occurs at a higher-level plane than can be viewed intraorally. These procedures should be coupled with in-depth evaluation of articulation and resonance characteristics in cases in which VPI is suspected.

Classification of Orofacial Clefts

Clefts have been described by the principal oral structures involved, that is, cleft lip (CL), cleft palate (CP), or cleft lip and palate (CLP) (Edmondson & Reinhartsen, 1998). In publications and professional reports, the abbreviation CL+P is used with great frequency to indicate *cleft lip with or without coexisting cleft palate*. This system, though adequate in some situations, lacks the detail necessary in others. Clefts that involve the lip up to the level of the incisive foramen and clefts that involve the lip through at least a portion of the soft palate are known to be different etiologically from clefts that involve solely the palate posterior to the level of the incisive foramen (Fogh-Andersen, 1993). Kernahan and Stark (1958) developed a classification system based on embryologic and etiologic differences that continues to be used widely. Their classification system addresses unilateral versus bilateral clefts, complete versus incomplete clefts, clefts of the primary palate, clefts of the secondary palate, clefts of both the primary and the secondary palates, and submucous clefts.

Unilateral versus Bilateral and Complete versus Incomplete Clefts Clefts are described as *unilateral* or *bilateral* depending, respectively, on whether one or both sides are affected. Clefts are also described as being complete or incomplete. A *complete cleft* affects every component of either the primary palate or the secondary palate. An *incomplete cleft* or partial cleft affects only some structures or parts of structures of the primary palate or secondary palate. Figure 14.6 demonstrates unilateral (A, B, C) and bilateral clefts (D) as well as incomplete (A, B, and portion of D) and complete (C and portion of D) clefts.

Clefts of the Primary Palate A *cleft of the primary palate* can be unilateral or bilateral and can be complete or incomplete. A cleft of the primary palate may involve lack of fusion of the lip, alveolar ridge, and/or a portion of the hard palate up to the level of the incisive foramen. Figure 14.7 schematically demonstrates a unilateral complete cleft of the primary palate.

Clefts of the Secondary Palate A *cleft of the secondary palate* may involve portions of both the hard and soft palates. This term is used to describe the lack of fusion of any or all portions of the hard palate posterior to the incisive foramen as well as the lack of fusion of any or all portions of the soft

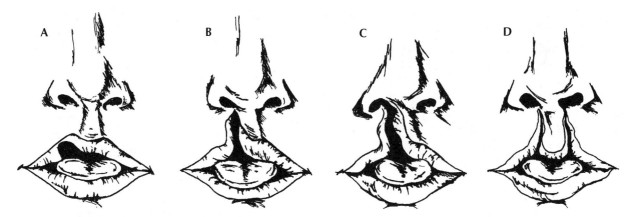

Figure 14.6.   Examples of incomplete and complete clefts of the primary palate. (A, unilateral incomplete cleft; B, unilateral complete [portion] and incomplete [portion] cleft; C, unilateral cleft; D, bilateral incomplete [portion] and complete [portion] cleft.)

palate. Figure 14.8 demonstrates a complete cleft of the secondary palate.

Clefts of the Primary and Secondary Palates   A *cleft of both the primary and secondary palates* is more severe than a cleft of either palate alone. At minimum, it entails both bony and muscular involvement in that at least portions, if not all, of the hard and soft palates are involved. Figure 14.9 demonstrates a unilateral complete cleft of the primary and secondary palates that extends from the lip through the velum in its entirety.

Submucous Clefts   A less common condition known as *submucous cleft palate* (SMCP) or *submu-*

cosal cleft occurs when there is a lack of joining of the underlying musculature of the soft palate (see Figure 14.10). The overlying skin or mucosa, however, is intact. In the most severe form of a submucous cleft, the levator and other palatal muscles fail to connect fully at midline and instead travel anteriorly to insert into the hard palate. Possible outward signs of a submucous cleft palate include bifid uvula, palatal muscle diastasis, and bony notch on the most posterior aspect of the hard palate (Edwards & Watson, 1993). A submucous cleft may interfere with velopharyngeal closure, which can result in nasal reflux during oral intake as well as

Figure 14.7.   Schematic drawing of unilateral complete cleft of the primary palate.

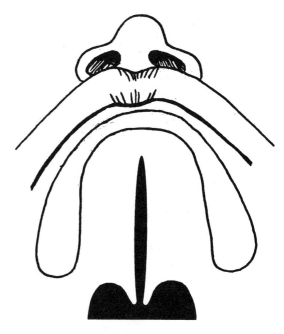

Figure 14.8.   Schematic drawing of complete cleft of the secondary palate.

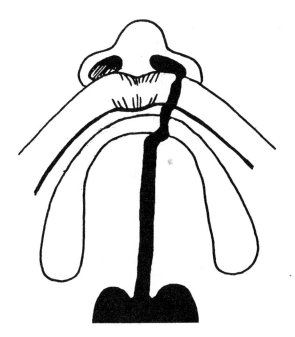

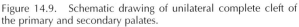

Figure 14.9. Schematic drawing of unilateral complete cleft of the primary and secondary palates.

Figure 14.10. Schematic drawing of a submucous cleft palate.

hypernasality in speech. Paradise (1983, as cited by McWilliams et al., 1990) recommended that *all* children for whom adenoidectomy is being considered be examined carefully for the traditional triad of symptoms associated with submucous cleft palate (McWilliams et al., 1990). If any signs of submucous cleft are present, proceeding with adenoidectomy without further evaluation is contraindicated. Such children should be referred to a cleft palate team or, at minimum, to a speech-language pathologist who has in-depth experience in the evaluation of the velopharyngeal closure mechanism. This evaluation is likely to prevent some of the unexpected and unwanted results of adenoidectomy, such as hypernasality.

DIAGNOSIS AND EVALUATION

Children with craniofacial anomalies should be evaluated fully within the first few days after birth or at the latest within the first few weeks of life (ACPA, 1993). Subsequent, ongoing evaluations are required because of the complex and longitudinal nature of difficulties associated with craniofacial anomalies. The frequency, type, and timing of evaluations are dependent on the needs of the child and his or her family. The primary health care provider can promote optimal care by prompt identification and referral of the infant and family to a craniofacial disorders team. The following are the responsibilities of the primary health care provider in the initial evaluation of infants with craniofacial anomalies:

- Perform an evaluation for minor physical anomalies (see Chapter 5) to determine the need for further evaluation (e.g., blood chromosomal analysis) and referral to a medical geneticist to assist with the diagnosis of a birth defect syndrome and for counseling regarding the risk of recurrence.

- Evaluate the infant for other associated defects such as a cervical spine anomaly or a congenital heart defect.

- Identify newborns and children with feeding and/or swallowing difficulties who are at risk for weight loss, malnutrition, and/or dehydration, and make a referral as needed to professional(s) with expertise in feeding children with orofacial clefts.

- Refer the child and family to a plastic surgeon and craniofacial team of specialists for initial evaluation.

- Provide advocacy, information, and ongoing support to the family in conjunction with the craniofacial team.

Optimal care of infants and children with CLP or other craniofacial anomalies is provided best by a team of professionals. The professionals who represent the various disciplines on the craniofacial disorders team should evaluate and treat large enough numbers of individuals each year to maintain their clinical expertise. These professionals include but are not limited to the plastic or reconstructive surgeon, the otolaryngologist (ENT), the pediatric dentist, the oral surgeon, the orthodontist, the speech-language pathologist, the audiologist, the nurse, the psychologist, the developmental pediatrician, and the medical social worker.

Evaluation

Delineation and diagnosis of isolated and syndromic conditions involve evaluation of the infant for minor anomalies; craniofacial dysmorphology screening; and, for some infants, chromosome testing, anthropometric measurement, and cranial imaging techniques. A craniofacial dysmorphology screening tool is included in the Appendix at the end of this chapter, and an evaluation for minor anomalies is provided in the Appendix at the end of Chapter 5. (The reader also is referred to "Basic Anthropometric Measurements and Proportions in Various Regions of the Craniofacial Complex," an excellent chapter in *Craniofacial Anomalies: An Interdisciplinary Approach* [Brodsky et al., 1992], a reference guide on how to obtain basic linear, angular, and surface measurements and proportion indices in the seven regions of the craniofacial complex: head, face, orbits, nose, lips, mouth, and ears.)

Identification of Associated Malformations

With advances in prenatal diagnosis, the presence of associated defects and the etiology of the congenital defects may be established prior to birth. It continues to be the norm, however, that craniofacial deformities such as CLP are detected at or shortly following birth. Other congenital anomalies are more often associated with cleft palate only (20%–50%) than with either cleft lip only (7%–13%) or CLP (2%–11%) (Gorlin, 1993). Twenty-eight percent of clefts of all types are accompanied by one or more malformations. More malformations have been found in infants with bilateral cleft lip with or without cleft palate than in those with unilateral cleft lip, and associated anomalies are noted more frequently in individuals without a family history of clefting than in people with relatives who have clefts (Gorlin, 1993). Congenital velopharyngeal incompetence has been found to be associated frequently with cervical spine anomalies (Gorlin, 1993).

Infants with Feeding Difficulties

Neonates with craniofacial anomalies often demonstrate feeding difficulties. The primary health care provider should monitor nutritional intake and weight gain weekly during the first month of life. Although gavage feedings are at times unavoidable because of nutritional risk, long-term gavage feedings should be avoided because they fail to promote normal suck-and-swallow reflexes and can result in oral hypersensitivity. Clefting can result in nasal reflux and difficulty with breast and bottle feeding because of inadequate buildup of pressure for sucking activities. These children often require longer feeding times, which can cause them to experience fatigue and irritability. Their air intake during eating attempts is increased, and as a result they may experience increased stomach discomfort, vomiting, and spitting. They are at increased risk for inadequate weight gain because of their inability to take in sufficient amounts of breast milk or formula.

Consultation with a trained professional to provide assistance with feeding is critical. Typically, professionals involved are a nurse or a speech-language pathologist with specialized training in cleft palate and other craniofacial deformities (Letcher-Glembo & Scott, 2000). Techniques for both breast feeding and/or bottle feeding as preferred by the parent can be explored (Bennett, 1986). Verbal and printed instruction should be provided. The goal is for infants to take in enough liquids to promote oral motor control without becoming overly fatigued, demonstrate proper growth and development, and show readiness for upcoming surgical procedures. Use of a *supplemental nursing system,* which is a device that consists of a bag containing expressed breast milk with tubing that is placed in the infant's mouth while at the mother's breast, can help maintain adequate intake and the benefits of breast milk. Soft, pliable bottles and cross-cut nipples coupled with upright positioning can improve the success of oral feeding. Another technique that has been found to be of benefit to many children with impaired sucking abilities is the *Haberman Feeder* (Haberman, 1988). The Haberman Feeder is a small, nonflexible bottle with a larger-than-average nipple. The nipple contains a one-way valve that traps fluids within the nipple. This decreases the pressure buildup required for expression of the fluid from the bottle. The following is a summary of factors to consider in selection of nipples and bottles:

1. Nipples should
   a. Compress easily
   b. Have soft, thin walls to reduce fatigue
   c. Allow for a normal swallow
   d. Aid in strengthening orofacial muscles without requiring excessive effort
2. Liquid should flow
   a. Easily
   b. Slowly enough to prevent choking (Arvedson, 1992)

Counseling the Family
About Recurrence Risks and Prognosis

A key component in the management of children with congenital craniofacial anomalies includes not only adequate diagnosis but also recurrence risk counseling and counseling regarding prognosis (ACPA, 1993). The specific diagnosis of a complex syndrome may not be apparent in the first year of life; therefore, genetic follow-up evaluations may be necessary for some children. The indications for referral for a complete genetic evaluation include but are not limited to

- Positive family history
- Prenatal growth deficiency
- Unexplained postnatal growth deficiency
- Developmental delay or mental retardation
- Associated major malformations and/or disorders
- Associated minor malformations (three or more)
- Family request
- Recognized genetic diagnosis

Families living in remote areas should be referred to an accessible source where genetic services can be provided. Families should be encouraged to follow through on genetic evaluation referral. In addition, genetic counseling should be offered to the maturing adolescent.

The recurrence risks and prognoses for syndromic conditions vary depending on the specific disorder. For example, FAS is characterized by dysmorphic facial features such as indistinct philtrum and micrognathia, occasionally cleft palate, microcephaly, pre- and postnatal growth deficiency, and learning and behavior problems (Jones, 1997). The etiology of FAS can be traced to the effects of prenatal alcohol exposure. The recurrence risk for a mother's future children being affected by FAS would be zero if the mother ceased her alcohol consumption during subsequent pregnancies.

The results of large epidemiologic studies suggest that the recurrence risk of isolated craniofacial malformations for first-degree relatives is in the range of 3%–5%; however, this figure varies with the number and gender of affected family members (Brodsky et al., 1992). Genetic counseling by an experienced professional can be instrumental in clarifying these issues and alleviating questions and feelings of guilt held by the parents of children with these conditions. Prognosis is highly dependent on the impact of the craniofacial anomaly and associated malformations on the child's overall health status as well as cognitive and intellectual function, educational progress, and psychosocial development.

MANAGEMENT

The impact of a craniofacial anomaly on an individual's life and on his or her family is typically complex and multifaceted. Individuals with congenital craniofacial anomalies are served best by an interdisciplinary team of specialists with expertise in the diagnosis and treatment of craniofacial disorders (ACPA, 1993). Evaluation and treatment planning for these children are essential, as is long-term follow-up. Inadequate care can lead to diagnostic errors; inappropriate, poorly performed, or poorly timed procedures; and failure to recognize and treat the full spectrum of health problems associated with the craniofacial anomalies (ACPA, 1993). By referral to a team and continued long-term care, the primary health care provider helps to ensure that the needs of these individuals are fully identified and appropriately treated.

The role the primary health care provider plays in this process is vital. Ongoing communication among patient and family, primary health care provider, and cleft palate and craniofacial disorders team should be maintained so that all parties are knowledgeable about an individual's stage of treatment planning and goals. The following are specific activities that the primary health care provider performs for infants and children with craniofacial disorders:

- Monitor nutritional intake, weight gain, and height and weight parameters to ensure the child's proper growth and to help determine his or her readiness for surgery (e.g., readiness for closure of the palate), and assist with the child's postsurgical recovery, including feeding, hydration, restraints, and surgical site protection.
- Monitor the child's otologic health and hearing status.
- Monitor the individual's speech-language development.
- Be instrumental in the care of children with compromised airways and in techniques of airway maintenance.
- Provide preliminary evaluation of the child's primary dentition, offer counseling regarding the importance of oral care and prevention of dental caries, and make referrals to specialists as needed.
- Monitor the child's self-concept, developmental and educational progress, and social development.
- Review parent–child adaptation and acceptance of the child's disability, parenting skills, behav-

ior management, and nurturance, and provide advocacy and support for the child and family.

- Be knowledgeable about the treatment recommendations of the craniofacial team and the desired short- and long-term outcomes.

Surgical Management

Primary care physicians assist in the preparation of children and families for surgical procedures. They also provide support for postsurgical recovery, including feeding, hydration, restraints, airway management, surgical site protection, and adjustment needs. For the most part, the attending surgeon and nursing staff prepare children and families for what to expect before and after surgery. The primary care physician can provide additional support and assurance regarding surgical procedures. Table 14.2 lists the common surgical procedures that may be necessary for children with CLP and the typical timing of the surgery. It is helpful for health care providers to assist with authorization and ordering of items such as arm restraints and adaptive feeding equipment that are needed during the recovery process.

Clefts of the Alveolar Process   Typically, clefts of the alveolar process are not repaired at the time of initial lip repair or at the time of initial palate repair. Differences of opinion exist regarding the ideal timing of surgical repair of alveolar clefts. Timing of alveolar bone grafting ranges from 3 years of age to completion during the early teen years. Research (El Deeb, Waite, & Curran, 1993) has suggested that early correction of the alveolar defect may contribute to limited facial growth and development in some individuals. For this reason, alveolar bone grafting is deferred most commonly until between 9 and 12 years of age when the canine root is one fourth to one third formed. El Deeb and colleagues (1993) noted that when an alveolar defect remains,

Table 14.2.   Typical cleft lip/palate surgical procedures and the age for completion

Surgical procedure	Age for completion
Lip adhesion	1–2 days
Initial lip repair	3–10 weeks
Palate repair	6–18 months
Pharyngeal flap and/or pharyngoplasty, if needed	2–7 years
Lip and/or nasal revision	4–6 years
Alveolar bone grafting	8–12 years
Cleft nasoseptal reconstruction	15–16 years
Orthognathic surgery	15 years or older

the alveolar process fails to support the base of the nose adequately, and bony support for dental root formation is lacking until the defect is repaired. Improper delay of alveolar bone grafting can result in premature tooth loss. Panoramic X rays, coupled with direct examination, can shed light on the presence and severity of alveolar cleft defects.

Velopharyngeal Incompetence   Many children demonstrate adequate velopharyngeal closure for speech after cleft palate repair. For those who do not, the primary methods of surgical improvement include pharyngoplasty and *pharyngeal flap surgery,* a procedure in which the surgeon creates a flap or a bridge of tissue that connects the soft palate to the back wall of the throat to improve velopharyngeal closure. Prosthetic options involve a *palatal lift–type prosthesis* for use when the soft palate is of sufficient length but lacks sufficient mobility. The posterior acrylic portion of the palatal lift prosthesis elevates the soft palate to decrease the space between the soft palate and the posterior and lateral pharyngeal walls. A *speech bulb prosthesis* can be constructed when the soft palate is too short in relation to the posterior and lateral pharyngeal walls. In such a case, the posterior portion of the device is bulked up and configured to form a bulb of acrylic that the lateral pharyngeal walls meet during velopharyngeal closure attempts for oral direction of the airstream. An additional type of prosthetic speech appliance, an *obturator,* serves to occlude a residual palatal fistula.

Medical Management

Routine Primary Care   Primary care physicians should provide continuity of routine pediatric care, including assessment and monitoring of nutritional intake, weight gain, and height and weight parameters to ensure proper growth and development and to help determine an individual's surgical readiness. It is essential that families receive instruction and educational materials about feeding, breast pumps, special bottles, equipment, and feeding devices. Children with clefts from birth to age 20 months have been found to experience a drop in weight percentile by 35% for males and 29% for females (McWilliams et al., 1990). At least 71% of all children had *lower* relative weights at 20 and 24 months than at birth. Furthermore, McWilliams and colleagues reported in a related study that the height percentiles of children with clefts followed during an 11-year period decreased. These findings support the critical nature of continued inspection of growth and developmental parameters. Standard and alternative methods of measurement of nutrition and growth disorders are discussed in Chapter 4. These methods can be used to document and share information among the child's various health care providers. Health and growth status should be evaluated prior to any surgical procedure to help ascertain the child's surgical readiness.

Otolaryngologic and Audiologic Follow-Up
Up to 90% of children with craniofacial anomalies have an associated hearing loss that is due to outer-, middle-, and/or inner-ear defects. Of these children (i.e., the 90% who have an associated hearing loss), 50% have congenital hearing loss and 40% have acquired hearing loss (Volk et al. 1992).

Following the common cold, otitis media is the second most common illness of children. Although it is a common occurrence for many children, its prevalence is even greater in children with craniofacial disorders. Bilateral myringotomies with tube placement are usually done prophylactically in children with orofacial clefts at the time of the initial lip repair.

The following protocol is recommended for primary health care providers to follow in their care of children with craniofacial anomalies:

- Hearing should be tested in the neonatal period for early identification of potential hearing loss.
- Otologic inspection of the ear, nose, velopharyngeal closure mechanism, and, if indicated, laryngeal mechanism should be carried out within the first few months of life or sooner if respiratory obstruction so dictates.
- Each child with craniofacial anomalies should have an appropriate assessment of hearing sensitivity before age 1 year.
- Tympanometry results should be obtained as a part of each audiologic evaluation to monitor the child's middle-ear status.
- Amplification should be considered when a persisting hearing loss is present.
- Audiologic and otologic follow-up examinations should continue through adolescence; the timing of recall appointments is determined on the basis of each child's particular history of ear disease.

Speech-Language Development In addition to defects of external or inner auditory structures and increased risk of middle-ear disease, children with craniofacial disorders demonstrate increased incidence of speech-language deviations. For example, children with orofacial clefts are at particular risk for the resonance disorder of hypernasality. In cases of children with incompetent velopharyngeal mechanisms, referral for surgical and/or prosthetic in-

tervention may be necessary. Primary health care providers should ensure that families receive information about typical speech-language development, speech-language impairments for which the child may be at risk, and ways to facilitate the child's speech-language development. Specifically, the following protocol is recommended:

- The physician should facilitate referral for speech-language evaluations with appropriate documentation for children with craniofacial disorders every 6–12 months until the age of 4 years. The speech-language pathologist completing such services should have specialized training in craniofacial anomalies.
- Continued periodic speech-language evaluation is needed after age 4 years because individuals with certain craniofacial disorders are at risk for increased hypernasality with atrophy of adenoidal tissue and continued facial growth and development.
- Evaluations should address speech, language, and cognitive status, including perceptual and, if needed, instrumental evaluation of velopharyngeal and laryngeal function. Instrumental ratings of speech include videofluoroscopic and nasoendoscopic examination of the velopharyngeal closure mechanism.
- Referral for enrollment in speech-language services is required for some children.

Airway Maintenance Primary health care providers should be instrumental in the care of children with compromised airways and in techniques of airway maintenance. Table 14.3 summarizes common causes and management techniques for chronic upper-airway obstruction (Volk et al., 1992). A flexible fiberoptic endoscopic examination may be necessary to determine the precise etiology of the airway problem. An airway obstruction may be due to the posterior displacement of a tongue of typical size. This condition, known as *glossoptosis*, causes reduced airflow because of tongue base-to-posterior pharyngeal wall contact (Volk et al., 1992). The etiology and severity of obstruction determine the management course. Short-term treatments include positioning and the use of a nasopharyngeal airway while waiting for growth and, ideally, neurologic maturation. Detailed instructions for making a positioning frame that allows nursing in the prone position while also decreasing airway obstruction are available (Edwards & Watson, 1993). The caregiver may need to be trained in the use of apnea-bradycardia monitors and tracheostomy care.

Table 14.3. Causes of chronic upper-airway obstruction and potential surgical management techniques

Anatomical variant	Surgical management
Nasal hypoplasia	Nasal reconstruction
Nasal septal deviation	Septoplasty
Maxillary hypoplasia	Maxillary advancement and/or tracheostomy
Adenotonsillary hyperplasia	Tonsillectomy and possibly lateral adenoidectomy
Narrowed nasopharynx (secondary to constricted skull base)	Maxillary advancement and/or tracheostomy
Obstructing pharyngeal flap	Revision of pharyngeal flap
Pharyngeal hypotonia	Uvulopalatopharyngoplasty and/or tracheostomy
Macroglossia	Tongue reduction and/or tracheostomy

Evaluation of Dentition and Counseling Regarding Oral Care and Caries Prevention Individuals with clefts and other craniofacial anomalies are at increased risk for missing and impacted teeth, supernumerary or extra malformed teeth, and enamel defects. As El Deeb and colleagues (1993) pointed out, dental decay and periodontal disease may ravage the adolescent dentition and complicate late orthodontic, surgical, or fixed prosthodontic procedures. The necessity for good, ongoing dental care and a high standard of oral hygiene must be emphasized as an essential precursor to the initiation of orthodontic and surgical treatments. The primary health care provider should keep the following points in mind with regard to dental care for children with craniofacial disorders:

• Refer the child for initial dental consult at approximately 2–2.5 years of age.
• Refer the child for initial orthodontic consult at approximately 6–6.5 years of age.

Identification of Developmental, Educational, and Psychosocial Difficulties Primary health care providers should monitor the development of preschool-age children and regularly review the school progress and psychosocial adjustment of older children. Children and families may require referral to early intervention/early childhood special education (EI/ECSE) services or to counseling and other child and family support services. Developmental screening and surveillance are discussed in Chapter 2. A psychosocial screening form is included in the Appendix at the end of this chapter. The presence of craniofacial anomalies affects not only the child with the diagnosis but most likely the entire family constellation as well. Research (see Brodsky et al., 1992; Clifford & Crocker, 1971; Richman & Harper, 1978) has demonstrated that these individuals are at in-creased risk for experiencing differences in social adjustment and self-concept, as well as disproportionate degrees of stress. Attention should be paid to the child's psychological status, the appropriateness of surgery, and available support systems for the child (Nash & Zevon, 1992).

Parent–Child Adaptation

From the time of first contact with the child and family, every effort must be made to assist the family in adjusting to the birth of a child with a craniofacial anomaly and to the consequent demands and stress placed upon the family. Parents and caregivers must be given information about recommended treatment procedures, options, risk factors, benefits, and costs to assist them in (a) making informed decisions on the child's behalf, and (b) preparing the child and themselves for all recommended procedures. (ACPA, 1993, pp. 4–5)

Primary health care providers should review the parents' and the child's understanding of the child's condition as well as the treatment plan, and they should identify for the parents and the child the support services necessary to ensure consistent follow-through. To help the primary care physician provide the child and family with educational information and guidance, Guidelines for the Care of Children and Adolescents with Cleft Lip and Palate are included in the Appendix at the end of this chapter. In addition, the physician should assess the adequacy of the family's financial and social support; the family's adjustment to the disability; and cultural, linguistic, and environmental influences that affect the family. The family should be provided with information about local support groups and other agencies that can provide assistance. The Cleft Palate Foundation (CPF), a national organization, provides information about potential community sources of specialized expertise in craniofacial disorders, a variety of publications, and a listing of professionals who are registered members of the national American Cleft Palate–Craniofacial Association (ACPA). The CPF supports CLEFTLINE (1-800-24-CLEFT), a telephone resource line for parents of newborns with craniofacial anomalies. Information regarding CPF and ACPA is included in the "Resources" section of the Appendix at the end of this chapter.

Important Care Coordination Issues

The complex nature of craniofacial anomalies often necessitates the need for the child with this diagnosis to have numerous health care providers. It is the responsibility of both the primary health care provider and the craniofacial team serving the child to make appropriate referrals and to communicate clearly and directly with all service providers. The primary health care provider is often the vital link between the client, the family, and the craniofacial disorders team. Following are key strategies that primary health care providers should implement:

- Identify an experienced craniofacial disorders team in the local area.
- Identify an individual with expertise in feeding infants with CLP and a resource for in-home nursing support.
- Maintain an updated file of local and national resources for children with craniofacial disorders and their families.
- Follow the general recommendations for care coordination reviewed in Chapter 1.

REFERENCES

American Cleft Palate–Craniofacial Association (ACPA). (1993). Parameters for the evaluation and treatment of patients with cleft lip/palate or other craniofacial anomalies. *Cleft Palate–Craniofacial Journal, 30*(Suppl. 1), 1–32.

American Speech-Language-Hearing Association (ASHA). (1993). *Delineation and diagnosis of craniofacial syndromes: Effect on case management* [Teleconference and booklet]. Rockville, MD: Author.

Arvedson, J. (1992). Infant oral-motor function and feeding. In L. Brodsky, L. Holt, & D.H. Ritter-Schmidt (Eds.), *Craniofacial anomalies: An interdisciplinary approach* (pp. 188–195). St. Louis: Mosby–Year Book.

Bennett, V. (1986). *Feeding young children with cleft lip and palate*. St. Paul, MN: American Dietetic Association.

Blackman, J.A. (Ed.). (1997). *Medical aspects of developmental disabilities in children birth to three* (3rd ed.). Gaithersburg, MD: Aspen Publishers.

Brodsky, L., Holt, L., & Ritter-Schmidt, D.H. (1992). *Craniofacial anomalies: An interdisciplinary approach*. St. Louis: Mosby–Year Book.

Clifford, E., & Crocker, E.C. (1971). Maternal responses: The birth of a normal child as compared to the birth of a child with a cleft. *Cleft Palate Journal, 8,* 298–306.

Edmondson, R., & Reinhartsen, D. (1998). The young child with cleft lip and palate: Intervention needs in the first three years. *Infants and Young Children, 11*(2), 12–20.

Edwards, M., & Watson, A.C.H. (Eds.). (1993). *Advances in the management of cleft palate*. London: Colin Whurr Publishers.

El Deeb, M., Waite, D.E., & Curran, J. (1993). Oral and maxillofacial surgery and the management of cleft lip and palate. In K.T. Moller & C.D. Starr (Eds.), *Cleft palate: Interdisciplinary issues and treatment* (pp. 79–120). Austin, TX: PRO-ED.

Figueroa, A., Reisberg, D., Polley, J., & Cohen, M. (1996). Intraoral-appliance modification to retract the premaxilla in patients with bilateral cleft lip. *Cleft Palate–Craniofacial Journal, 33,* 497–500.

Fogh-Andersen, P. (1993). Incidence and aetiology. In M. Edwards & A.C.H. Watson (Eds.), *Advances in the management of cleft palate* (pp. 43–48). London: Colin Whurr Publishers.

Fritzell, B. (1993). Anatomical and physiological considerations. In M. Edwards & A.C.H. Watson (Eds.), *Advances in the management of cleft palate* (pp. 49–63). London: Colin Whurr Publishers.

Gorlin, R.J. (1993). Development and genetic aspects of cleft lip and palate. In K.T. Moller & C.D. Starr (Eds.), *Cleft palate: Interdisciplinary issues and treatment* (pp. 25–48). Austin, TX: PRO-ED.

Haberman, M. (1988). A mother of invention. *Nursing Times, 84*(2), 52–53.

Jones, K.L. (1997). *Smith's recognizable patterns of human malformation* (5th ed.). Philadelphia: W.B. Saunders Co.

Kane, A.A., Mitchell, L.E., Craven, K.P., & Marsh, J. (1996). Observations on a recent increase in plagiocephaly without synostosis. *American Journal of Pediatrics, 97,* 877–885.

Kernahan, D.A., & Stark, R.B. (1958). A new classification for cleft lip and palate. *Plastic and Reconstructive Surgery, 22,* 435.

Letcher-Glembo, L., & Scott, M. (2000, April). *A survey of health care professionals' attitudes and practices regarding maternal breastfeeding of infants with cleft lip ± palate: Pacific Northwest findings*. Paper presented at the 57th annual meeting of the American Cleft Palate-Craniofacial Association, Atlanta, GA.

McWilliams, B.J., Morris, H.L., & Shelton, R.L. (1990). *Cleft palate speech* (2nd ed.). Philadelphia: B.C. Decker.

Millard, D.R., Jr. (1976–1980). *Cleft craft: The evolution of its surgery* (3 vols.). Boston: Little, Brown.

Moller, K.T., & Starr, C.D. (Eds.). (1993). *Cleft palate: Interdisciplinary issues and treatment*. Austin, TX: PRO-ED.

Nash, L., & Zevon, M. (1992). Psychosocial aspects: Family, patient, and treatment issues. In L. Brodsky, L. Holt, & D.H. Ritter–Schmidt (Eds.), *Craniofacial anomalies: An interdisciplinary approach* (pp. 27–40). St. Louis: Mosby–Year Book.

Richman, L.C., & Harper, D. (1978). School adjustment of children with observable difficulties. *Journal of Abnormal Child Psychology, 6,* 11.

Roba, C., & Bochacki, V. (1992). Orthodontic considerations. In L. Brodsky, L. Holt, & D.H. Ritter-Schmidt (Eds.), *Craniofacial anomalies: An interdisciplinary approach* (pp. 127–136). St. Louis: Mosby–Year Book.

Vanderas, A.P. (1987). Incidence of cleft lip, cleft palate, and cleft lip and palate among races: A review. *Cleft Palate Journal, 24,* 216–223.

Volk, M.S., Arnold, S., & Brodsky, L. (1992). Otolaryngology and audiology. In L. Brodsky, L. Holt, & D.H. Ritter-Schmidt (Eds.), *Craniofacial anomalies: An interdisciplinary approach* (pp. 168–187). St. Louis: Mosby–Year Book.

Zemlin, W. (1998). *Speech and hearing sciences: Anatomy and physiology* (4th ed.). Needham Heights, MA: Allyn & Bacon.

14

Appendix

Guidelines for the Care of Children and Adolescents with Cleft Lip and Palate

Basic Team

The special care needs of the child with cleft lip and/or palate (CLP) are met best by an interdisciplinary team of specialists who work in collaboration with the child, the child's parents, and the primary care health professional. The craniofacial team coordinator, if desired, can assist in the coordination of special services that these children require.

A CLP team typically consists of a plastic or reconstructive surgeon, an otolaryngologist, a nurse, an orthodontist, a dentist, an oral surgeon, a speech-language pathologist, a medical social worker, and an audiologist. Furthermore, consultation with or ready availability of the following disciplines is desirable: a genetic counselor, a medical geneticist, a developmental pediatrician, a radiologist, a prosthodontist, a dental hygienist, a psychologist, a physical therapist, and an occupational therapist.

Initial Evaluation

The optimal time for the first evaluation is at or shortly after birth; however, referral for team evaluation and management can be considered for individuals of any age. When the diagnosis has been made prior to delivery, prenatal counseling should be made available. The critical issues for the young infant with CLP are feeding and nutrition, initial surgical correction of the cleft, and pre- and postoperative support of the child and the family. The responsibilites of the primary care physician are to refer to the craniofacial disorders team (the team members initially involved are the plastic or reconstructive surgeon, the feeding specialist, the nurse, and the speech-language pathologist); identify associated defects; closely monitor growth and nutrition; and determine the need for other referrals (e.g., to the medical geneticist).

Frequency of Visits

The frequency and timing of visits to the specialty team are dependent on the child's needs and overall status. In general, the team evaluates the infant or toddler and the family at least twice yearly, and then yearly or as needed after the toddler years. The timing of the usual surgeries for children with CLP is as follows:

Surgical procedure	Age for completion
Lip adhesion	1–2 days
Initial lip repair	3–10 weeks
Palate repair	6–18 months
Pharyngeal flap and/or pharyngoplasty, if needed	2–7 years
Lip and/or nasal revision	4–6 years
Alveolar bone grafting	8–12 years
Cleft nasoseptal reconstruction	15–16 years
Orthognathic surgery	15 years or older

The primary care office monitors growth and nutrition, developmental and school progress, and middle-ear function; identifies associated medical problems; assists the family with care coordination; and provides ongoing child and family support and education in conjunction with the CLP team. The child's progress is reviewed at least annually (more frequently for younger children), and an office management plan is updated at that time.

The Physician's Guide to Caring for Children with Disabilities and Chronic Conditions, edited by Robert E. Nickel and Larry W. Desch, copyright © 2000 Paul H. Brookes Publishing Co.

Guidelines for the Care of Children and Adolescents with Cleft Lip and Palate

The following elements are recommended by age group, and the listing is cumulative. Review all items indicated up through the actual age group of a child entering your practice for the first time as part of the initial evaluation.

AGE	KEY CLINICAL ISSUES/CONCERNS	EVALUATIONS/KEY PROCEDURES	SPECIALISTS
Birth– 1 month	Feeding/Nutrition/Risk for Dehydration	Growth parameters, evaluation by feeding specialist as needed	Feeding specialist, nutritionist
	Cause of the Cleft Lip and/or Palate (CLP)	Evaluation for minor anomalies, craniofacial dysmorphology screen	Developmental pediatrician (DPed), medical geneticist as needed
	Evaluation for Associated Congenital Defects	Blood chromosomes, other tests as needed Cranial ultrasonography (US) or computed tomography (CT) scan, echocardiogram, other tests as needed	DPed and/or medical geneticist
	Closure of the Lip	Pre- and postoperative care	Plastic or reconstructive surgeon, CLP team
	Hearing Status/Risk for Middle-Ear Effusion and Infection	Schedule neonatal hearing examination with auditory brainstem screening (ALGO) or otoacoustic emissions (OAEs), prophylactic bilateral myringotomies and ventilation tube placement	Audiologist, otolaryngologist (ENT)
	Risk for Airway Obstruction (e.g., Pierre Robin sequence) or Aspiration (e.g., laryngeal cleft)	Detailed otolaryngologic examination, positioning, other interventions	ENT, plastic or reconstructive surgeon, DPed, nurse
	Need for Intraoral Prosthetic Appliance	Evaluation for bilateral and/or severe clefting	Plastic or reconstructive surgeon, dental specialist
	Parent Education/Anticipatory Guidance Care Coordination/Family Support	Initiate care notebook, provide educational materials and resource list; complete family interview using parent questionnaire (e.g., Family Needs Survey) or CLP psychosocial screening form as needed	Speech-language pathologist (SLP), ENT CLP team coordinator, medical social worker, DPed, referral to community health nurse as needed
1 month– 5 years	Growth/Nutrition Oral motor dysfunction Gastroesophageal reflux (GER)	Growth parameters, diet record, evaluation by feeding specialist, workup for GER as needed	Nutritionist, feeding specialist, DPed as needed
	Initial Palate Repair (6–18 months of age) Pre- or postoperative support	Confirm that family is established with plastic or reconstructive surgeon	Plastic or reconstructive surgeon, nurse, SLP, other team members as needed
	Monitor Hearing Status/Middle-Ear Function	Audiologic testing at least annually or as needed	Audiologist, ENT as needed

The Physician's Guide to Caring for Children with Disabilities and Chronic Conditions, edited by Robert E. Nickel and Larry W. Desch, copyright © 2000 Paul H. Brookes Publishing Co.

Guidelines for the Care of Children and Adolescents with Cleft Lip and Palate *(continued)*

The following elements are recommended by age group, and the listing is cumulative. Review all items indicated up through the actual age group of a child entering your practice for the first time as part of the initial evaluation.

AGE	KEY CLINICAL ISSUES/CONCERNS	EVALUATIONS/KEY PROCEDURES	SPECIALISTS
1 month–5 years *(continued)*	*Dental Care* Prevention of dental caries	Review dental hygiene and potential dental issues (e.g., missing and supernumerary teeth)	Dentist
	Associated Medical Problems Visual problems or strabismus Seizures Craniosynostosis	Vision testing Electroencephalogram (EEG) Skull X rays, cranial computed tomography (CT) scan as needed	Pediatric ophthalmologist Neurologist Neurosurgeon
	Associated congenital defects (e.g., heart or renal defects, hand or foot anomalies)	Additional tests dependent on type and severity of associated problems	Cardiologist, orthopedist
	Speech-Language Progress Language delay Speech disorder (due to dental and anatomic differences)	Monitor language progress	SLP SLP, orthodontist, oral surgeon
	Voice quality and need for pharyngeal flap for velopharyngeal incompetence (2–7 years of age)	Assessment of velopharyngeal incompetence and voice quality	SLP, ENT, plastic or reconstructive surgeon as needed
	Developmental Progress/Need for Early Intervention (EI) or Early Childhood Special Education (ECSE) Services Speech-language delay Developmental delay	Developmental surveillance and screening Refer for eligibilty testing for EI services as needed	Referral to child development team as needed
	Family Support Services Respite care Parent group Community health nurse Advocacy Financial services (e.g., Supplemental Security Income [SSI])	Family interview, parent questionnaires (e.g., Family Needs Survey) Provide resource information (e.g., Cleft Palate Foundation) Care coordination	Medical social worker, referral to community health nurse, other community services as needed

The Physician's Guide to Caring for Children with Disabilities and Chronic Conditions, edited by Robert E. Nickel and Larry W. Desch, copyright © 2000 Paul H. Brookes Publishing Co.

Guidelines for the Care of Children and Adolescents with Cleft Lip and Palate *(continued)*

The following elements are recommended by age group, and the listing is cumulative. Review all items indicated up through the actual age group of a child entering your practice for the first time as part of the initial evaluation.

AGE	KEY CLINICAL ISSUES/CONCERNS	EVALUATIONS/KEY PROCEDURES	SPECIALISTS
1 month–5 years *(continued)*	*Anticipatory Guidance* Review individualized family service plan (IFSP) with family as needed Transition from preschool to kindergarten Risk for dental, orthognathic, or facial differences and their treatment Risk for behavior problems, low self-esteem Promote self-care and independence	Family interview, educational materials, resource information Teacher interview, school conference as needed	Primary care office in collaboration with CLP team
	Collaboration with Community Services Community health nurse Educational services	Comprehensive care coordination with regular exchange of written information (at least yearly) with other service providers	Primary care office in collaboration with CLP team
6–12 years (school-age)	*Dental Care* (e.g., missing or impacted teeth)	Full set of dental X rays	Dentist, oral surgeon
	Facial Differences Lip or nasal revision (ages 4–6 years)	Evaluation of facial aesthetics and function	Plastic or reconstructive surgeon
	Orthognathic Differences Alveolar bone grafting (ages 8–12 years)	Establish orthodontic care and, if indicated, oral surgical care	Orthodontist, oral surgeon
	Speech-Language Progress Increased risk for hypernasality as adenoidal tissue atrophies	Evaluation of speech-language skills, voice quality, and assessment of velopharyngeal incompetence as needed	SLP, ENT as needed
	School Progress Learning disabilities Mental retardation (if birth defect syndrome is present)	Regular exchange of information with school behavioral questionnaires; child, parent, and teacher interviews; school progress report; intellectual and achievement testing as needed	Referral to child development team or individual psychology appointment as needed Collaborate with school staff
	Social Skills Involvement in peer-group activities at school and in the community	Encourage participation in community services, social skills program at school as needed	Psychologist, behavioral specialist, school counselor as needed

The Physician's Guide to Caring for Children with Disabilities and Chronic Conditions, edited by Robert E. Nickel and Larry W. Desch, copyright © 2000 Paul H. Brookes Publishing Co.

Guidelines for the Care of Children and Adolescents with Cleft Lip and Palate *(continued)*

The following elements are recommended by age group, and the listing is cumulative. Review all items indicated up through the actual age group of a child entering your practice for the first time as part of the initial evaluation.

AGE	KEY CLINICAL ISSUES/CONCERNS	EVALUATIONS/KEY PROCEDURES	SPECIALISTS
6–12 years (school-age) *(continued)*	*Anticipatory Guidance* Discuss diagnosis and management with the child Need for cleft nasoseptal reconstruction, orthognathic surgery Transition to middle school Recreation and leisure activities	Child and family interviews, provide educational materials and resource information Encourage participation in community recreation and leisure activities	Primary care office in collaboration with CLP team and school staff
13–21 years (adolescents and young adults)	*Cleft Nasoseptal Reconstruction* (ages 15–16 years)	Evaluation of airway and appearance of nose	Plastic or reconstructive surgeon and/or ENT
	Orthognathic Surgery for Class III Malocclusion (ages 15 years and older) Retrusive midface Prognathism	Evaluation of dentoskeletal facial balance and function	Oral surgeon, orthodontist
	Persisting Speech Differences Risk for velopharyngeal incompetence Continuing articulation difficulties Continuing vocal quality deviations	Monitor voice quality, assess velopharyngeal competence as needed	SLP, ENT as needed
	Anticipatory Guidance Review genetics and recurrence risk with adolescent and family Promote healthy behaviors (e.g., diet, exercise) Sexuality and high-risk behaviors (e.g., substance abuse) Transition to high school Career planning/higher education Transition to adult medical services	Adolescent and family interviews Teacher interview, school conference, review individualized education program (IEP) with family as needed Referral to gynecologist, mental health specialist as needed	Primary care office in collaboration with CLP team

The Physician's Guide to Caring for Children with Disabilities and Chronic Conditions, edited by Robert E. Nickel and Larry W. Desch, copyright © 2000 Paul H. Brookes Publishing Co.

Family and Physician Management Plan Summary for Children and Adolescents with Cleft Lip and Palate

This form will help you and your physician review current services and service needs. Please answer the questions about your current services on this page. Your physician will review your responses and complete the rest of the form.

Child's name _____ Today's date _____

Person completing the form _____

CURRENT SERVICES

1. Please list your/your child's current medications and any side effects.

2. What is your/your child's current school program?

   School name _____ Grade _____

   Teacher _____ Telephone _____

3. Do you/does your child receive any support services or other special programs at school (e.g., speech pathologist)? Please list.

4. Who is your/your child's surgeon? _____

   Date last seen _____

5. Who are your/your child's other medical and dental service providers?

   Dentist _____

   Orthodontist _____

   Plastic surgeon _____

   Otolaryngologist _____

   Speech-language pathologist _____

   Audiologist _____ Date hearing was last tested _____

   Any hearing concerns?

Family and Physician Management Plan Summary
for Children and Adolescents with Cleft Lip and Palate *(continued)*

6. Who are your/your child's other community service providers?

   Community health nurse _____

   Other _____

7. Do you also receive services from a cleft lip and palate team of specialists?

   Contact person _____

   Location _____

8. Have you/has your child had any blood tests, radiologic (X-ray) examinations, or other proce-dures since your last visit? If yes, please describe.

9. Have you/has your child been hospitalized or received surgery since your last visit? If yes, describe.

10. Please note your/your child's accomplishments since your last visit. Consider activities at home, in your neighborhood, or at school, as well as success with treatments.

11. What goals (i.e., skills) would you/your child like to accomplish in the next year? Consider activities at home, in your neighborhood, or at school, as well as success with a treatment.

12. What questions or concerns would you like addressed today?

The Physician's Guide to Caring for Children with Disabilities and Chronic Conditions, edited by Robert E. Nickel and Larry W. Desch, copyright © 2000 Paul H. Brookes Publishing Co.

Family and Physician Management Plan Summary for Children and Adolescents with Cleft Lip and Palate

The Family and Physician Management Plan Summary should be completed at each annual review and more often as needed. It is intended to be used with the Guidelines for Care, which provide a more complete listing of clinical issues at different ages as well as recommended evaluations and treatments.

Child's name _____ Person completing form _____ Today's date _____

Clinical issues	Currently a problem?	Evaluations needed	Treatment recommendations	Referrals made	Date for status check
Family's Questions					
Cause of the Cleft Lip and/or Palate (CLP)					
Growth/Nutrition Feeding problems					

Surgical Checklist
  Initial lip repair
  Initial palate repair
  Lip or nasal revisions
  Myringotomy/tube placement
  Alveolar bone grafting
  Cleft septorhinoplasty
  Surgical improvement of velo-
    pharyngeal closure if indicated
  Orthognathic surgery
  Other					

Dental and Orthodontic Care					

The Physician's Guide to Caring for Children with Disabilities and Chronic Conditions, edited by Robert E. Nickel and Larry W. Desch, copyright © 2000 Paul H. Brookes Publishing Co.

Family and Physician Management Plan Summary
for Children and Adolescents with Cleft Lip and Palate *(continued)*

Child's name _____   Person completing form _____   Today's date _____

Clinical issues	Currently a problem?	Evaluations needed	Treatment recommendations	Referrals made	Date for status check
Hearing Status/Middle-Ear Function					
Risk for Airway Obstruction					
Associated Medical Problems Visual problems or strabismus Seizures Craniosynostosis Other congenital defects					
Speech-Language Progress Need for speech-language therapy Poor speech intelligibility Voice quality (nasality)					
Developmental/School Progress Current school achievement Review individualized family services plan (IFSP) or individ-ualized education program (IEP) with family					

The Physician's Guide to Caring for Children with Disabilities and Chronic Conditions, edited by Robert E. Nickel and Larry W. Desch, copyright © 2000 Paul H. Brookes Publishing Co.

Family and Physician Management Plan Summary
for Children and Adolescents with Cleft Lip and Palate *(continued)*

Child's name _____   Person completing form _____   Today's date _____

Clinical issues	Currently a problem?	Evaluations needed	Treatment recommendations	Referrals made	Date for status check
Social Skills Involvement in peer-group activities at school and in the community					
Self-Care/Independence					
Family Support Services					
Anticipatory Guidance List issues discussed and materials provided					
Collaboration with Community Agencies School Community health nurse					

The Physician's Guide to Caring for Children with Disabilities and Chronic Conditions, edited by Robert E. Nickel and Larry W. Desch, copyright © 2000 Paul H. Brookes Publishing Co.

Family and Physician Management Plan Summary
for Children and Adolescents with Cleft Lip and Palate (continued)

Child's name _____ Person completing form _____ Today's date _____

Clinical issues	Currently a problem?	Evaluations needed	Treatment recommendations	Referrals made	Date for status check
Comments					

Next update of the Management Plan Summary _____

Signature _____ Date _____
           (Child and parent)

Signature _____ Date _____
           (Health professional)

CRANIOFACIAL DISORDERS PSYCHOSOCIAL SCREENING FORM

Child's name _____ Age _____ Date of birth _____

Diagnosis _____ Today's date _____ Examiner _____

Surgical variables

Motivation for treatment _____

_____

_____

Understanding of risk-to-benefit ratio _____

_____

_____

Expectations of surgery _____

_____

_____

Number of prior surgeries _____

_____

_____

Psychosocial variables

Body image _____

_____

_____

Self-concept _____

_____

_____

CRANIOFACIAL DISORDERS PSYCHOSOCIAL SCREENING FORM *(continued)*

Emotional status _____

_____

_____

Social skills _____

_____

_____

Behavior problems _____

_____

_____

Family and social support

Parents' motivation for treatment _____

_____

_____

Parental relationship _____

_____

_____

Family climate _____

_____

_____

Family cohesion _____

_____

_____

The Physician's Guide to Caring for Children with Disabilities and Chronic Conditions, edited by Robert E. Nickel and Larry W. Desch, copyright © 2000 Paul H. Brookes Publishing Co.

CRANIOFACIAL DISORDERS PSYCHOSOCIAL SCREENING FORM *(continued)*

Available social support _____

_____

_____

Educational variables

Child's age _____ Grade _____ School placement _____ Special services? Yes _____ No _____

CRANIOFACIAL DISORDERS DYSMORPHOLOGY SCREENING FORM

Child's name _____ Age_____ Date of birth _____

Diagnosis _____ Today's date _____ Examiner _____

Cranial deviations

Cranial size _____

_____

_____

Cranial shape _____

_____

_____

Hair growth pattern _____

_____

_____

Other _____

_____

_____

Craniomaxillofacial deviations

Craniofacial deviations _____

_____

_____

Ear structure, size, and position _____

_____

_____

CRANIOFACIAL DISORDERS DYSMORPHOLOGY SCREENING FORM (*continued*)

Presence or absence of skin tags and pits _____

_____

_____

Size, shape, and function of nose, including nasal ala and columella _____

_____

_____

Philtrum _____

_____

_____

Lip intactness, shape, thickness, and function, including potential lip pits _____

_____

_____

Contour and intactness of alveolar process _____

_____

_____

Dentition _____

_____

_____

Dental occlusion _____

_____

_____

The Physician's Guide to Caring for Children with Disabilities and Chronic Conditions, edited by Robert E. Nickel and Larry W. Desch, copyright © 2000 Paul H. Brookes Publishing Co.

CRANIOFACIAL DISORDERS DYSMORPHOLOGY SCREENING FORM (*continued*)

Contour and intactness of hard palate _____

_____

_____

Contour and intactness of soft palate _____

_____

_____

Appearance of face (e.g., malar eminences, midface) _____

_____

_____

Length, mobility, and symmetry of soft palate _____

_____

_____

Depth of oropharynx in relationship to soft palate _____

_____

_____

Other _____

_____

_____

Cranioorbital deviations
Eye structure, position, orientation, and function _____

_____

_____

CRANIOFACIAL DISORDERS DYSMORPHOLOGY SCREENING FORM (*continued*)

Other _____

_____

_____

Craniomandibular deviations

Tongue size, structure, and function _____

_____

_____

Size and symmetry of mandible _____

_____

_____

Other _____

_____

_____

Source: American Speech-Language-Hearing Association (1993).

RESOURCES ON CRANIOFACIAL DISORDERS

Readings

American Cleft Palate–Craniofacial Association (ACPA). (1993). Parameters for the evaluation and treatment of patients with cleft lip and palate or other craniofacial anomalies. *American Cleft Palate-Craniofacial Journal, 30*(Suppl. 11) [Entire issue]. (919-933-9044)

Brodsky, L., Holt, L., & Ritter-Schmidt, D.H. (1992). *Craniofacial anomalies: An interdisciplinary approach.* St. Louis, MO: Mosby–Year Book. (1-800-325-4177)

Cleft Palate Foundation. (n.d.). *Feeding an infant with a cleft* [Booklet]. Pittsburgh, PA: Cleft Palate Foundation (1218 Grandview Avenue, Pittsburgh, PA 15211).

Coulter-Danner, S. (n.d.). *Nursing your baby with a cleft palate or cleft lip* [Pamphlet]. Rochester, NY: Childbirth Graphics, Ltd. (1210 Culver Road, Rochester, NY 14609-5454).

Fishbaugh, M., & Erwin, C. (n.d.). *Someone like me: A booklet for children born with cleft lip and palate* [Booklet] (Address requests for copies to A. Michael Sadove, M.D., Department of Surgery, James Whitcomb Riley Hospital for Children, 702 Barnhill Drive, Room 2514, Indianapolis, IN 46202-5200).

MacDonald, S.K. (n.d.). *Hearing and behavior in children born with cleft palate.* Quincy, MA: Prescription Parents (Prescription Parents, Inc., P.O. Box 855, Quincy, MA 02169).

McWilliams, B., Morris, H., & Shelton, R. (1990). *Cleft palate speech* (2nd ed.). Philadelphia: B.C. Decker.

Mead Johnson Nutritionals. (n.d.). *Guidelines for feeding and care of the cleft lip/palate infant* [Pamphlet]. Evansville, IN: Author (Mead Johnson Nutritionals, 2404 Pennsylvania Avenue, Evansville, IN 47721-0001).

Moller, K.T., Starr, C.D., & Johnson S.A. (1990). *A parent's guide to cleft lip and palate.* Minneapolis: University of Minnesota Press. (612-627-1970)

Salyer, K.E., & Rogers-Salyer, M. (Eds.). (1985). *Craniofacial deformity: A booklet for parents* (2nd ed.). Dallas: Foundation for Craniofacial Deformities.

Organizations

AboutFace International
123 Edward Street, Suite 1003
Toronto, Ontario M5G 1E2
Canada
Telephone: (800) 225-FACE [3223]
Fax: (416) 597-8494
E-mail: info@aboutfaceinternational.org
World Wide Web site: http://www.
  aboutfaceinternational.org/

This international organization provides information, support, and education programs to individuals with facial differences and their families.

AboutFace USA
Rickey Anderson, Executive Director
Post Office Box 458
Crystal Lake, Illinois 60014
Telephone: (888) 486-1209
E-mail: AboutFace2000@aol.com
World Wide Web site: http://www.aboutface2000.org/

This is the U.S. affiliate of the international organization that provides information, support, and education programs to individuals with facial differences and their families.

American Cleft Palate-Craniofacial Association (ACPA)/ Cleft Palate Foundation (CPF)
104 South Estes Drive, Suite 204
Chapel Hill, North Carolina 27514
Telephone: (919) 933-9044
Fax: (919) 933-9604
Telephone: "CLEFTLINE" (800) 24-CLEFT (toll-free service that provides information and referral to parent support groups and cleft palate/craniofacial teams)
E-mail: cleftline@aol.com
World Wide Web site: http://www.cleft.com/

Professional organization dedicated to research and improvement of clinical services to people with cleft palate and associated deformities; CPF is an affiliate of ACPA that provides information and support, educates the public about cleft lip and palate and other craniofacial anomalies, and operates CLEFTLINE.

15

Traumatic Brain Injury

Janice L. Cockrell
Robert E. Nickel

514 Cockrell and Nickel

KEY COMPETENCIES

- Assess a child with a traumatic brain injury (TBI)
- Define *mild, moderate,* and *severe TBI*
- Discuss likely motor outcomes for children and adolescents with mild, moderate, and severe TBI
- Discuss likely language and cognitive outcomes for children and adolescents with mild, moderate, and severe TBI
- Identify medical and psychological conditions associated with childhood TBI
- Discuss assessment tools for motor, language, and cognitive function in children with TBI
- Construct an appropriate diagnostic plan for a child with TBI
- Construct an appropriate treatment plan for a child with TBI

DESCRIPTION

Definition

Traumatic brain injury (TBI) is an injury to the brain resulting from rapidly accelerating and decelerating external forces. Direct trauma may result from a penetrating injury, such as a bullet or a depressed skull fracture, or from the brain's striking the inside of the cranium. Indirect injury may result from the rotational forces generated by acceleration or deceleration; by shearing forces; or by secondary injury from edema, hypoxia, hypoperfusion, and/or free radical injury. TBI may cause impairment of cognitive and motor abilities and disturbances of behavioral or emotional functioning that are either temporary or permanent.

Classification

Traumatic brain injuries may be open or closed. The severity of the injury is defined by the affected person's responsiveness at the time of injury as measured by the Glasgow Coma Scale (GCS) (Teasdale & Jennett, 1974) and/or by the duration of posttraumatic amnesia (PTA) using the Children's Orientation and Amnesia Test (COAT) (Ewing-Cobbs, Levin, Fletcher, et al., 1990) or the Galveston Orientation and Amnesia Test (GOAT) (Levin, O'Donnell, & Grossman, 1979). Modifications of the GCS for children and infants are available (Hahn, Chyung, Barthel, et al., 1988; Raimondi & Hirschauer, 1984). TBIs are classified as follows:

- Mild—GCS score of 13–15
- Moderate—GCS score of 9–12
- Severe—GCS score of 8 or less

The level of severity as determined by the duration of PTA is usually classified as follows:

- Mild—PTA less than 30 minutes
- Moderate—PTA from 30 minutes to 24 hours
- Severe—PTA longer than 24 hours

Children who are younger than 4 years of age cannot be assessed reliably for PTA, so this definition is rarely used in pediatrics. The Abbreviated Injury Scale (AIS) assesses individual organ systems, and the Injury Severity Score (ISS) is the sum of the squares of the three highest AIS scores (MacKenzie, Shapiro, & Eastham, 1985). The ISS and the AIS weigh each organ system equally and thus are not able to predict a child's central nervous system (CNS) outcome accurately.

Incidence, Mortality, and Morbidity

The NIH consensus conference (NIH Consensus Development Panel on Rehabilitation of Persons with Traumatic Brain Injury, 1999) on traumatic brain injury estimated that the incidence of TBI is 100 per 100,000 individuals, with 52,000 deaths occurring annually. The highest incidence is among individuals 15–24 years of age and among individuals ages 75 years and older, with a smaller peak in children 15 years of age and younger. Kraus, Fife, and Conroy (1987) estimated that 7,000 deaths from TBI occurred among people ages birth–19 years in 1975 in the United States, or 29% of all deaths from injury in this age group. They also estimated that the prevalence of disability from TBI is about 29,000 children and youth per year and that 10% of mild injuries, 90% of moderate injuries, and 100% of severe injuries result in disabilities each year (Kraus et al., 1987; Kraus, Rock, & Humyari, 1990). In addition, a National Pediatric Trauma Registry survey (Di Scala, Osber, Gans, et al., 1991) found that 16.2 % of 4,870 children admitted to the hospital with TBI had from one to three impairments at discharge and that 5.9% had four or more impairments.

Pathophysiology

The *primary injury* to the brain is caused by the transmission of extreme acceleration then deceleration forces to the brain, initially beneath the site of impact and then on the contralateral side (i.e., coup-contrecoup). These forces cause stretching and breaking of the bridging vessels as well as of the axons; this stretching and breaking activity is exacerbated by rotational forces generated by the acceleration then deceleration on the soft tissues of the brain rotating around the relatively fixed brain stem. The rotatory forces also cause direct trauma to the brain at the sites of bony outcroppings in the cranium, specifically on the floor of the frontal and temporal lobe areas.

Breakage of blood vessels can result in subdural hematomas, epidural hematomas, intraparenchmal contusions, and/or subarachnoid hemorrhages. Punctate hemorrhages throughout the cerebrum and/or brain stem may be seen by microscopic examination. *Diffuse axonal injury* refers to the tearing of axons and subsequent dying back of the neurons that can be seen microscopically but may escape detection by computed tomography (CT) or magnetic resonance imaging (MRI) scan. Widespread diffuse axonal injury is often associated with a slower recovery and a worse overall prognosis, as are deep cerebral contusions and hemorrhages. The injuries just described are known as *primary injuries* to the brain resulting directly from the impact forces.

Secondary injury is caused when reduced cerebral perfusion fails to deliver adequate oxygen and clear waste or when hypoxic injury accompanies or follows the direct trauma. Meticulous management by a pediatric intensivist and neurosurgeon as well as a well-organized and rapidly responding emergency medical system can reduce secondary injuries greatly. Children younger than age 6 years may have an unusual autonomic response to brain injury with a delayed and occasionally fatal increase in intracranial pressure following a relatively mild injury. This phenomenon is well known to physicians with expertise in pediatric traumatic brain injury but may be missed by those who work primarily with adults. For this reason, any child with a significant brain injury should be observed for 24 hours following the injury.

Release of excitotoxic amino acids, calcium, nitric oxide, and free radicals contributes to the secondary neuronal injury. Research has focused on treatments that block the N-methyl-D-aspartate (NMDA) receptor and other strategies to minimize the production of the free radicals, including the use of hypothermia (Biagas & Gaeta, 1998; Globus, Alonso, Dietrich, et al., 1995; Lynch & Dawson, 1994).

Long-Term Outcomes

Mild and Moderate Traumatic Brain Injury
Several studies (Fay, Jaffe, Pollisar, et al., 1993; Fay, Jaffe, Polisar, et al., 1994; Klonoff, Clark, & Klonoff, 1993) have looked at complex neuropsychologic tasks of children and adolescents with mild TBIs within the first year following injury, and all demonstrated a small but significant decrement in function compared to controls. In one study (Fay et al., 1994), children followed to 3 years postinjury continued to show impairments, although the impairments were not functionally significant. A retrospective study (Klonoff et al., 1993) of children with

primarily mild TBI reported a 31% incidence of subjective sequelae such as learning and memory difficulties, depressed mood, and anxiety disorders and a 15.1% rate of recurrent TBI. The rates of sequelae and subsequent TBI were significantly higher than those found in the general population. Social problem solving also has been found to be impaired in children following TBI (Warschausky, Cohen, Parker, et al., 1997).

Severe Traumatic Brain Injury
Kriel, Krach, and Jones-Saete (1993) evaluated 37 children with TBI who had been in a coma of 3 months' duration or longer. Seventy-five percent of the children eventually regained consciousness; however, all of the children studied had significant disabilities. They also found that 50% of the children who remained in a persistent vegetative state (PVS) had died within 5 years after sustaining their injuries. PVS, which is defined as complete and prolonged unresponsiveness to external stimulation, is relatively unusual in children with TBI.

The best outcomes are achieved if the child's TBI occurs between the ages of 2 and 18 years, in part because of differences in physiology and in part because of the etiology of the injury. In a retrospective review of children treated for severe or mild TBI matched with children with orthopedic injuries, significant impairment of adaptive function was found in the children with severe and mild TBI but not in the children with orthopedic injuries (Max, Koele, Lindgren, et al., 1998). Family function, psychiatric disorders, and verbal and nonverbal IQ score deficits were significant predictors of outcome, and the severity of the child's TBI was less important than the investigators had hypothesized. In a review (Cattelani, Lombardi, Brianti, & Mazzuchi, 1998) of adults with a history of pediatric head trauma who had been referred to a psychiatric program, not IQ score and functional status but social maladjustment and poor quality of life were the prevailing problems. Prospective long-term studies are necessary to assess the impact of childhood TBI over the course of years and decades.

Motor, Sensory, Language, Cognitive, and Behavior Problems

Motor Impairments
Motor impairments following TBI may include weakness, spasticity, rigidity, ataxia, dystonia, or motor apraxia, depending on the site of cerebral injury. The distribution of impairment is exceedingly variable and can include the trunk, any or all of the limbs, and the oculomotor and/or bulbar muscles. Weakness and spasticity often resolve quickly, and most children are able

to walk with or without assistive devices within 6 months of the injury (Brink, Garrett, Hale, et al., 1970). The ataxic or dystonic components tend to be more persistent and can be detected even in relatively mild cases for several years following the injury. Rigidity is a sign of severe subcortical injury and generally does not resolve. Motor apraxia may resolve or persist; however, it is important that severe subcortical injury be identified as a source of dysfunction and be treated appropriately. Children with a significant TBI may develop progressive contractures rapidly in the weeks postinjury. Treatment with botulinum toxin can help prevent the development of permanent contractures (e.g., plantarflexion contracture at the ankle) (see discussion of the use of botulinum toxin in Chapter 6).

Oculomotor impairments are variable. It is important to determine that the abnormality is not due to muscle entrapment. When an oculomotor impairment is accompanied by orbital fractures, an ophthalmology consult must be obtained immediately. Children younger than 5 years of age who have a TBI with disconjugate gaze should be evaluated by a pediatric ophthalmologist as soon as possible following the injury. They are at high risk for amblyopia and need a treatment such as a patching program.

Bulbar weakness or incoordination can result in *dysphagia*. Dysphagia may be due to oral apraxia and incoordination of the posterior pharyngeal structures with intact gag and cough reflexes. Inadequate retropulsion of the bolus (food) and/or ineffective swallow may prevent safe oral feeding. If the gag and cough reflexes are absent, oral feeding is contraindicated. A speech-language pathologist (SLP) or an occupational therapist with expertise in dysphagia can often identify the risk; but, on occasion, a videofluoroscopic swallowing assessment (modified barium swallow) is necessary to ascertain whether silent aspiration is present, as well as to determine the safety of oral feeding and recommendations for an oral feeding program (see Chapter 6).

Sensory Impairments and Cranial Nerve Dysfunction   The child's ability to describe or to recognize sensory impairment is inversely proportional to the child's age. Younger children require careful monitoring to determine whether sensory impairments are present. Visual impairments are common (Duhaime, Alario, Lewander, et al., 1992; Griffith & Dodge, 1968). If oculomotor dysfunction is present, diplopia can be assumed to be present. Some children, however, have cognitive impairments that prevent them from recognizing the diplopia. Most of the muscle imbalances resolve within the first year fol-

lowing the injury. In young children, however, the risk of amblyopia exists, and a pediatric ophthalmologist must be consulted as soon as possible. Visual field cuts are often present and most often accompany a profound hemiplegic motor impairment. Accommodation defects causing blurry vision are usually temporary but are typically quite bothersome to the child. Most resolve within a few months.

Anosmia is common and can be one of the major causes of the child's refusal to eat and failure to thrive (FTT). Hearing loss can be found in up to 20% of children immediately following TBI and may be conductive or sensorineural (Cockrell & Gregory, 1992; Sakai & Mateer, 1984). Conductive hearing loss may be caused by dissociation of the ossicles. If hearing loss due to dissociation of the ossicles is suspected, immediate surgery is indicated. Otherwise, the hearing loss can be followed longitudinally. If isolated sensory or motor cranial nerve dysfunction is apparent, a workup in the acute phase is warranted. This workup would include an MRI scan and nerve conduction studies and an electromyogram (EMG) to determine whether decompression or a nerve graft is indicated. Sensory impairments in the limbs usually resolve as motor function returns. Any persistent sensory impairments in the extremities likewise warrant a search for peripheral nerve entrapment and should be evaluated with nerve conduction studies.

Vertigo or lightheadedness is common after TBI and may persist for months. In the absence of cerebellar findings and orthostatic hypotension, inner-ear concussion and/or fistula must be ruled out. An otolaryngologist (ENT) can assist in the evaluation. Paralysis of the face can be central or peripheral. If entrapment of the facial nerve is suspected, an ENT should be consulted immediately because early detection and treatment can yield excellent results.

Speech-Language Impairments   Because language and cognition are so closely related, most speech-language impairments are addressed in this chapter under the "Motor, Sensory, Language, Cognitive, and Behavior Problems" heading. Dysarthria, apraxia, and aphasia are conditions found in the acute phase following injury (see Table 15.1). During the early stages, when the child's consciousness is impaired, these conditions may be difficult to identify. In particular, apraxia and aphasia may be difficult to differentiate until standardized testing or skilled observation by a therapist or knowledgeable physician can be carried out.

Subtle difficulties in word finding often persist throughout the lifetime of the individual with TBI

Table 15.1. Posttrauma language impairments

Aphasia	Inability to produce (expressive) or understand (receptive) spoken language
Apraxia	Dysfluency that is due to difficulty with motor planning
Aprosodia	Lack of inflection of speech, usually caused by acquired brain injury
Dysarthria	Difficulty with pronouncing words because of incoordination of the lips, the tongue, or the palate
Spastic dysphonia	Difficulty with controlling tone or inflection of speech because of spasticity of the vocal cords or palate

(Vargha-Khadem, O'Gorman, & Watters, 1985; Ylvisaker, 1986). Most types of dysarthria resolve with therapy, but spastic dysphonia may persist and can be addressed with temporary paralysis using botulinum toxin (Botox; see Chapter 6) or surgically. Vocal cord paralysis resulting from prolonged intubation or cranial nerve dysfunction must be assessed. If vocal cord paralysis persists longer than 1 year, latex injection of one or both cords can be performed.

Central auditory processing (CAP) difficulties can be found in 10%–20% of individuals following mild, moderate, or severe TBI (Cockrell & Gregory, 1992). These can present as difficulties with attention or as language dysfunction. In most cases, CAP difficulties persist for years, making it difficult for individuals with TBI to follow group conversations, attend to the spoken word in the presence of background noise, or follow complex one-to-one conversations. Conductive or sensorineural hearing loss may mimic CAP disorders, so evaluation by an audiologist who is experienced with CAP disorders is important.

Cognitive Impairments Because the temporal and frontal lobes are almost invariably affected by TBI, memory, integrative language function, attention span, attention to detail, and other executive functions are usually impaired as well. Impairments of memory may include difficulty with encoding (i.e., acquiring information) or decoding (i.e., retrieving information), problems with auditory memory, or problems with visual memory. Integrative language skills include verbal reasoning and problem solving, concept formation, and concept flexibility. As mentioned previously, attention span may be impaired, as may attention to visual or auditory detail. Executive functions include mental flexibility, abstract thinking, organizational skills, judgment, and ability to do several tasks at once. These functions emerge in young children and continue to

evolve throughout their lifetimes. The development of executive functions is associated with myelination of the deep cortical tracts, which is effectively completed by an individual's mid-20s (Thatcher, Walker, & Giudice, 1987). It is these deep tracts that are most affected by the shearing and twisting of the brain upon its stalk (i.e., the brain stem) during and immediately following impact. When assessing children with TBI, one must keep in mind that although executive function impairments may exist, their impact may not be noted fully until adolescence.

Although all cognitive impairments secondary to TBI improve markedly during the first year following injury, almost all persist to some degree throughout the individual's lifetime. Warschausky and colleagues (1997) assessed the social problem-solving skills of children with TBI at a median time of 9 months after the injury. They found that children with TBI generated fewer total solutions in social problem-solving situations than individuals without TBI and that children with TBI had fewer positive assertive and more indirect responses as well as a higher number of anomalous strategies than children without TBI (e.g., a child with TBI may sit near someone to make friends but not say anything). These cognitive impairments have obvious implications for a child's behavioral functioning (see the discussion of behavior problems in this chapter under the "Motor, Sensory, Language, Cognitive, and Behavior Problems" heading). With appropriate academic support, however, most children with TBI can complete high school successfully, and many, even some with severe injuries, can complete a course of higher education. These individuals' career success may be limited by executive function impairment, however.

As many as 20% of children with TBI have preexisting attention-deficit/hyperactivity disorder (ADHD), and there is some evidence that the outcome of children with premorbid ADHD and TBI is worse than that of children with TBI without ADHD (e.g., increase in affective lability and aggression) (Max, Robin, Lindgren, et al., 1997). In a study (Williams, Ris, Ayyangar, et al., 1998) of 10 children with posttraumatic ADHD, the children performed no differently when taking methylphenidate or placebo on measures of behavior, attention, memory, and processing speed. Some individuals did appear to respond to methylphenidate, and clinical experience suggests that those who do respond to methylphenidate are children who had premorbid ADHD. In general, posttraumatic ADHD is unresponsive to methylphenidate. Furthermore, in a study (Max, Arndt, Castillo, et al., 1998) of posttraumatic ADHD, when family psychiatric history and socioeconomic status were controlled, family function emerged as the variable most closely related to the severity of the child's ADHD symptoms.

Behavior Problems All of the impairments discussed in the previous subsections can contribute to reactive emotional problems such as anger, depression, or acting-out behavior. Any behavioral difficulties that the child exhibited prior to sustaining the TBI are usually exacerbated, not only during the weeks following injury but often for years afterward.

Frontal lobe behaviors such as lack of initiation or disinhibition are common, particularly in the acute phase. In most cases, poor initiation and disinhibition resolve spontaneously or respond to a behavior management program. These behaviors may persist, however, and become particularly problematic as the child moves into adolescence or adulthood. In such cases, conducting a careful functional analysis of the child's behavior is important (see Chapters 5 and 8). Irritability, severe mood swings, and persistent depression or mania may also persist. A higher percentage of children and adults with mild, moderate, or severe TBI than among the general population without TBI develop full-blown psychiatric illness, including schizophrenia, paranoia, and bipolar disorders (Klonoff et al., 1993). In a study (Max, Koele, Smith, et al., 1998) of 24 children with severe TBI matched to children with mild TBI and children with orthopedic injuries, severe TBI was a significant predictor of the development of a psychiatric disorder, most commonly organic personality disorder. Sixty-three percent of those with severe TBI, as compared with 21% of those with mild TBI and 4% of children with orthopedic injuries, manifested clinically significant new psychiatric symptoms 2 years postinjury. Preinjury psychiatric disorders were similar across the groups. The novel psychiatric findings were unrelated to age, sex, race, social class, family, or personal psychiatric history and family stress.

Sleep–wake cycle disturbances are present in nearly all children with TBI in the acute phase, and these disturbances persist in a high percentage of individuals for months or even for years afterward. Postconcussion syndrome (PCS) manifests differently in adults and children. Younger children may present with irritability, sleep disturbance, and hyperkinesis. Older children and adolescents usually complain of headaches, irritability, and sleep disturbance. Treatment of the sleep disturbance usually relieves the PCS. Some authors (e.g., Sbordone, 1999) consider PCS a manifestation of posttraumatic stress syndrome; the sleep disturbance is related to emotional reactivity to the event that caused the individual's TBI (Sbordone, 1999). Eating disorders are often seen following TBI in both the acute and postacute phases and may include anorexia nervosa, bulimia, or hyperphagia. Hyperphagia is most often related to disinhibition following TBI. When assessing eating disorders, an endocrine abnormality must be excluded.

Other Associated Problems In the *acute* injury phase, bladder and bowel incontinence, occult fractures or intraabdominal injury, nutritional and endocrine disorders, pain, and seizure activity may complicate the child's recovery and rehabilitation. Early seizures (i.e., those that occur within 24 hours postinjury) are quite common in children. No evidence exists, however, that they lead to late seizures. Furthermore, no evidence has been found that prophylaxis with anticonvulsant drugs (ACDs) prevents late seizures, and clear evidence exists that ACDs impair cognition. For this reason, ACD prophylaxis (e.g., diphenylhydantoin or Dilantin) in the absence of a penetrating brain injury or late seizures is not recommended (Dikmen, Temkin, Miller, et al., 1991; Temkin, Dikmen, Wilensky, et al., 1990). The presence or absence of each of the above problems must be determined and appropriately addressed.

In the *postacute* phase of TBI, nutritional, endocrine, and seizure disorders are common. Late seizures are often partial complex seizures resulting from trauma to the temporal lobes. Carbamazepine (Tegretol) is the drug of choice in treating temporal lobe seizures, although some pediatric neurologists may continue diphenylhydantoin if started in the acute injury phase for prophylaxis. If disinhibited behavior or poor attention span are also present, carbamazepine is a better initial choice because some evidence of improved attention and self-control in individuals treated with carbamazepine exists (Mitchell, Zhou, Chavez, & Guzman, 1993).

EVALUATION

Initial Evaluation After Acute Injury

The initial evaluation is likely to be done by emergency personnel. The child should be assessed acutely for level of consciousness and any accompanying bony or soft tissue trauma. The airway should be determined to be patent, cardiac perfusion should be assessed, and then the spine should be stabilized. Gently position the child's head and neck in a neutral position using a backboard and sandbags or tape to prevent further injury should vertebral fractures or subluxation be present. Airway and spinal stabilization precautions should be considered in cases involving infants and toddlers as well as in larger children. Any obvious fractures should also be stabilized, and any sources of bleeding should be stopped. If possible, a GCS score should be assigned to the child in the field, and intravenous (IV) access should be established. Emergency personnel should then transport the child to the most appropriate trauma center. A small child or infant with severe TBI should never be picked up and transported in a car. In the trauma center, the child can be triaged and discharged home, admitted to the general ward for observation, taken to surgery, or admitted to the intensive care unit (ICU).

Management of the child with acute TBI is beyond the scope of this discussion. The primary care physician participates in and coordinates the care of the child following the acute TBI. If the child is discharged to home from the emergency department or the physician's office, the child's parents should be instructed to awaken the child every hour for the next 24 hours to assess the child's level of alertness.

Assessment of the child who has been in the ICU and has been transferred to the hospital floor can be difficult. Often the parents of the child with TBI are so relieved that he or she has survived the accident that they may fail to notice their child's memory problems or unsafe behavior in the hospital. It is up to the pediatrician to determine whether the child is safe to return home or needs further medical supervision or consultation regarding rehabilitation services. The COAT can be useful in assessing older children and adolescents with TBI in determining whether PTA has resolved. If the child is still confused or lethargic, the Rancho Los Amigos Scale of Cognitive Functioning (RLA) (Hagen, 1982) is used to assign a stage of emergence from coma and to determine whether the child is able to benefit from intensive rehabilitative services. The RLA consists of eight levels, with Level 1 representing unresponsiveness to the environment and Level 8 representing normal and appropriate cognitive responses. In general, an individual with an RLA score of Level 4 or less usually is not yet ready for inpatient rehabilitation and may need to be placed in a subacute facility until he or she is more aware of the environment. An individual in RLA Level 5 may or may not be ready for inpatient rehabilitation, depending on how quickly he or she appears to be recovering. At RLA Level 6 or 7, inpatient rehabilitation services are usually needed, depending on the availability of supervision in the home and outpatient therapy services.

In order for a child to benefit from inpatient rehabilitation services, other factors must be taken into consideration:

- The child must be medically stable.
- The child should be able to tolerate about 3 hours of therapy daily.
- Significant impairments in at least two functional skill areas must be present.
- Realistic goals for rehabilitation must be set.
- The child's caregivers must be willing to participate in the rehabilitation process.

In exceptional instances, one or two of the previous criteria may be waived; but experience has shown that these criteria lead to the most successful long-term outcomes. In addition to the previous criteria, funding for inpatient rehabilitation must be identified. If inpatient or outpatient rehabilitation services are considered, the hospital social worker and the admissions coordinator of the rehabilitation program can be of assistance with the process of preauthorization and resource identification.

Assessment After Hospital Discharge
Each child with TBI is different, and a standard frequency of assessment cannot be recommended for all children, particularly in the first 2 years following the injury. In the case of mild TBI, follow-up by the physician at 3, 6, and 12 months postinjury is probably adequate. For children with moderate to severe TBI, follow-up is determined by the rate of improvement, the need for ancillary services, and function in school and in the family. Some individuals may require weekly follow-up by the physician for 1–2 months, and others may need to be seen only twice per year.

Families or school personnel may refer a child to a pediatrician for review of cognitive or behavior problems and not identify a TBI as one of the precipitating factors of the problem. The primary care physician also may have been reassured by a child's return to apparently normal motor and language function and not realize that higher-level cognitive and/or language skills may have been damaged. Later difficulties in academic performance or interpersonal skills may be due to a serious TBI that the child incurred as a toddler.

The following activities assist the primary care health professional to determine the need for further evaluation of or services for a child with TBI:

- Obtain complete medical, developmental, and family histories.
- Interview the parents and the child.
- Obtain behavioral questionnaires (parent, teacher, and older child).
- Do a mental status examination (with older children).
- Perform a complete neurologic examination.

- Screen for vision, visual-motor and visual-perceptual problems (as needed).
- Obtain school information, and interview the child's teacher (as needed).

The medical, developmental, and family histories should clarify the child's pre- and postinjury behavior and developmental and school status. A mental status examination is appropriate for older children. The components of the mental status examination may include the following:

- *Attention:* Forward digit span and the A test
- *Memory:* Orientation and three-word recall, historical data, and visual memory
- *Language:* Spontaneous speech quality and content; ability to follow one-, two-, and three-step commands; naming and reading; and repetition skills
- *Visuospatial skills:* Ability to draw a flower, a house, and/or a clock face
- *Executive function:* Word-list generation and ability to abstract (Cummings, 1993)

The use of behavioral questionnaires and the child, parent, and teacher interviews is discussed in Chapter 7. Further evaluation may include the following:

- Neuropsychologic evaluation
- Physical therapy (PT) assessment of higher-level gross motor skills
- Occupational therapy (OT) assessment of fine motor skills and visual-perceptual or visual-motor deficit
- Speech-language pathology evaluation of higher-level language skills
- Audiologic evaluation (to include CAP assessment)
- Evaluation of oral motor function and feeding skills
- Neuroimaging and other radiographic studies (e.g., modified barium swallow)

When results of premorbid standardized testing are available, the issues are frequently easier to identify and define. The psychology, speech-language, OT, PT, and feeding evaluations are best obtained from an experienced team of rehabilitation professionals or from a child development team (in cases involving younger children).

Assessment Tools This section is designed to familiarize physicians briefly with the most commonly available tools for evaluation of children with TBI.

Assessment of Motor Function In very young children, the Bayley Scales of Infant Development (Bayley, 1993) and the Peabody Developmental Motor Scales and Activity Cards (PDMS) (Folio & Fewell, 1983) can be used to evaluate a child's fine and gross motor function objectively. In older children, the Bruininks-Oseretsky Scale (Bruininks, 1978) is a useful assessment of a child's gross and fine motor function. It is standardized to age 14.5 years but can be used with older children to quantify their motor impairments. The Gross Motor Function Measure (GMFM) (Russell, Rosenbaum, Cadman, et al., 1989) is a well-validated scale of motor function that is useful for following the motor progress of children with TBI. If indicated, the Index Finger Tapping Test of the Halstead-Reitan Neuropsychological Test Battery (Reitan & Wolfson, 1993) and the Purdue Pegboard Test (Tiffin, 1983) can evaluate a child's fine motor speed, and a child's balance can be assessed further by using a tilt platform.

As mentioned previously, a child with TBI may need to be evaluated for dysphagia with a modified barium swallow. This test, however, should be done by the radiologist with the assistance of an SLP or an occupational therapist with expertise in dysphagia. Thin and thick liquids as well as purées and solids can be used to evaluate how the child handles various textures to assist in making recommendations for the child's feeding program.

Assessment of Language and Cognition A full neuropsychologic battery takes up to 6 hours. Most children and adults with TBI cannot concentrate for such a prolonged period, and the testing will need to be divided into several sessions for accurate data. The Wechsler intelligence scales are used commonly in the assessment of cognition. They are standardized for use with individuals ages 4 years through adulthood and include the Wechsler Preschool and Primary Scale of Intelligence–Revised (WPPSI–R) (Wechsler, 1989), the Wechsler Intelligence Scale for Children–Third Edition (WISC-III) (Wechsler, 1991), and the Wechsler Adult Intelligence Scale–Third Edition (WAIS-III) (Wechsler, 1997). These assessments evaluate verbal and nonverbal cognitive skills and include a series of subtests that allow the psychologist to examine multiple areas of the individual's language and cognition. Another broad cognitive assessment tool is the Kaufman Assessment Battery for Children (Kaufman & Kaufman, 1983). Please also review the discussion of evaluation tools in Chapter 5.

Receptive language can be assessed by the Peabody Picture Vocabulary Test–Revised (PPVT–R) (Dunn & Dunn, 1981), the Token Test for Children (DiSimoni, 1978), and the Token Test (DiRenzi & Vignolo, 1962) for older children and adults. Free and cued recall can also be evaluated in a standardized fashion. Expressive language can be evaluated by using the Boston Diagnostic Aphasia Test (Goodglass & Kaplan, 1983) as well as other tests. The Detroit Test of Learning Aptitude (Hammill, 1991) and the Woodcock-Johnson Psycho-Educational Battery–Revised (Woodcock & Johnson, 1990) may be used for evaluation of integrative language.

Because of the high incidence of significant behavioral and cognitive impairments following TBI, it is important to identify a local psychologist and, if possible, a local psychiatrist with expertise in both pediatrics and TBI. Adaptations that may be necessary in testing individuals with TBI may include nonverbal responses, shortening of directions, using the most functional modality for the individual (e.g., auditory versus written cues or vice versa), enlarging print, and obtaining timed and untimed scores (Ylvisaker & Feeney, 1996). Any adaptations to the testing method must be described in the final report. A word of caution is in order regarding the use of achievement testing to assess the cognitive skills of children with TBI. Achievement tests evaluate only old learning and do not assess new learning. For this reason, the child with TBI may appear to function at a premorbid level if achievement tests are the only tests administered for the purpose of school programming. If the child is placed in a classroom without appropriate academic support or without modifications to his or her homework or testing, the resulting unrealistic expectations most likely will lead to academic failure.

Assessment of Behavior and Mood A number of standard psychological scales can be used to assess children for depression and mood and other mental health disorders following TBI. Similar adaptations to those used in cognitive testing may be required with regard to the testing environment. The Child Behavior Checklist (CBCL) (Achenbach, 1991a) remains a valid tool for the evaluation for possible internalizing and externalizing behavior disorders, both at home and in the classroom. Parent, youth, and teacher CBCL forms are available (Achenbach, 1991a, 1991b, 1991c). CBCL can be used by the primary care professional or by the rehabilitation specialist.

Assessment of Visual-Perceptual and Visual-Motor Skills Visual-perceptual and visual-motor skills usually are assessed by the occupational therapist. Test instruments include The Beery-Buktenica Visuomotor Integration (VMI) test (Beery, 1997) and the Purdue Pegboard Test (Tiffin, 1983). Subtests

from a neuropsychologic battery may also be useful (e.g., the Trail Making Test of the Halstead-Reitan Neuropsychological Test Battery; Reitan, 1979).

Assessment of Functional Skills Three methods that are used to quantitate functional skills in daily life are the Vineland Adaptive Behavior Scales (VABS) (Sparrow, Balla, & Cicchetti, 1984), the Functional Independence Measure (FIMSM) (Corrigan, Smith-Knapp, & Granger, 1997; State University of New York at Buffalo, 1993a), the Functional Independence Measure for Children (WeeFIMSM) (Hamilton & Granger, 1991; State University of New York at Buffalo, 1993b), and the Pediatric Evaluation of Disability Inventory (PEDI) (Feldman, Haley, & Coryell, 1990; Haley, Coster, Ludlow, et al., 1992). The VABS is completed by interview and measures communication, daily living, socialization, and motor skills. It has a long history of use by psychologists in conjunction with intellectual assessments. The FIM (used with adolescents and adults) and WeeFIM (used with children), as well as the PEDI, are broad functional scales that include self-care, mobility, and communication. One advantage of the PEDI is the score is expressed as a percentage of the child's chronological age. Thus, improvement in function can be monitored relative to the child's expected development. The WeeFIM and FIM scores are unrelated to age, so any improvement in these scores does not reflect anticipated developmental improvement. Please also review Chapter 6.

Impact on the Family

The occurrence of TBI in a family member can be a major stressor on families. The TBI may exacerbate existing dysfunctional family patterns. The primary health care professional can assist the family and rehabilitation professionals in identifying the family's support needs and community resources. A formal evaluation of the level of stress and coping skills of individual family members and an initial counseling session are indicated at an early stage of a child's inpatient rehabilitation stay. Please also review Chapter 3.

MANAGEMENT

Treatment Plan in the Postemergency Period

The first part of this section focuses on the postemergency period (after treatment of acute medical problems)—for example, after transfer of the child with moderate or severe TBI from the ICU to the general hospital ward. In the case of the child with mild TBI, postemergency treatment planning begins in the emergency room. The child may be admitted for observation or discharged home for observation. The areas to be addressed in the formulation of a treatment plan are as follows:

- Mentation
- Gross motor skills
- Fine motor skills
- Presence or absence of sensory impairments
- Nutrition and other medical issues
- Cognition and language
- Bowel and bladder management
- Behavioral issues, including safety
- Academic reentry (see Ylvisaker, Hartwick, & Stevens, 1991)
- Impact of the child's TBI on the family

The availability and funding of services are also major considerations that affect the overall treatment plan. Table 15.2 outlines management considerations for individuals with TBI in the postemergency period. A table of commonly used medications and their indications is provided in the Appendix at the end of this chapter. Discharge planning must begin early during inpatient rehabilitation.

Outpatient Management Plan

Outpatient management of the child with TBI and the child's family encompasses regular review of the issues described previously, along with recommendations for reevaluation and referral to specialists as needed. Please review the key components of care forms located in the Appendix at the end of this chapter. These forms are intended to assist primary health care professionals and families in an ongoing review of service needs. Management decisions are also assisted by the regular use of behavioral questionnaires and close collaboration with school staff and other community service providers. Management plans must include family support needs (e.g., respite care, training in behavioral management). As mentioned previously, the primary care physician is the primary care coordinator of the child's services and thus needs to follow the child regularly to monitor the success of the treatment plan.

A number of the principles of the management of TBI in children are highlighted in the discussion of two specific situations: a 13-year-old with irritability, restlessness, and inattention following a mild TBI and a 10-year-old who sustained a severe TBI.

> A 13-year-old boy has been a good student and has no known behavior problems. His mother reports that he had a concussion 3 months ago while visiting relatives in another state. Since that time, he has been irritable, inattentive, and restless. He is having difficulty with sleeping at night and has some balance problems during athletic activities but

denies true vertigo. He has exhibited a drop in academic performance.

The differential diagnosis at this point would be one of the following:

1. Postconcussive syndrome with secondary sleep cycle disturbance and fatigue
2. New psychosocial issues in the family (e.g., marital strife, illness of family member)
3. New-onset behavioral or emotional issue unrelated to concussion (e.g., drug use, depression)
4. Inner-ear concussion, inner-ear fistula due to concussion or trauma (absence of true vertigo would make this highly unlikely), or posttraumatic arteriovenous malformation (AVM; also unlikely in the absence of severe head trauma)

If diagnoses 2 and 3 can be ruled out, the first step is to address the sleep cycle disturbance. If the child describes a pattern of difficulty with falling asleep with frequent waking at night, a trial of 25–75 milligrams of trazodone at bedtime is appropriate. Often the symptoms of irritability, inattentiveness, restlessness, and mild balance difficulties clear up with management of the sleep cycle disturbance, particularly following mild to moderate injuries. Medical treatment may need to continue for up to 6 months before the sleep cycle normalizes. Psychological assessment or educational services may need to be pursued if the sleep problem resolves and the inattentiveness persists. Individuals with TBI often need to be retrained to attend to conversation, prioritize their activities, and use good social and study skills.

It is also important to review the contribution of psychosocial factors to a child's behavior change. A 13-year-old is at an age when experimentation with drugs and alcohol may produce acute behavior and academic problems among previously "good" kids, and thus the TBI may be a secondary rather than a primary issue. Obtaining a careful history and examination would permit the physician to evaluate the child's dizziness. An assessment by a physical therapist and an audiologic examination or referral to an ENT may be necessary to make the final diagnosis.

> A 10-year-old boy who sustained a severe TBI required intensive care in the ICU for 3 weeks followed by 4 weeks of intensive inpatient rehabilitation services. At the time of discharge, he had a left spastic hemiparesis, dysarthria, significant memory impairment, and hyperactivity. Cognitive evaluation showed strengths in mathematics, problem-solving skills, and overall information but severe weakness in expressive and receptive language skills, visual and auditory memory, and attention to detail. His

Table 15.2.   Treatment considerations for children with acute traumatic brain injury

Functional issue	Mild injury	Moderate injury	Severe injury
Mentation	RLA score of 8: Observe RLA score of less than 8: speech-language/cognitive screen (e.g., Children's Orientation and Amnesia Test [COAT]); if impairment is found, refer for speech-language consultation	RLA 8: Observe RLA less than 8: Refer for speech-language and occupational therapy (OT) consultation Consider inpatient or outpatient rehab services Never appropriate for skilled nursing facility (SNF) placement	RLA 7: Refer for speech-language and OT consultation RLA 5–7: Consider inpatient rehabilitation or home health if services are available RLA less than 6 with slow recovery: Consider SNF or home health if adequate support exists at home
Gross motor skills	Observe for decreased motor speed and balance difficulty; if impairment is found, refer for consultation with physical therapist May need outpatient physical therapy (PT) services	Observe for decreased motor speed and balance difficulty; if impairment is found, refer for consultation with a physical therapist May need outpatient PT services	PT consult; if mobility not safe or independent, consider inpatient rehab if another functional area is impaired; if multiple fractures *and* non-weight bearing, SNF or home health services are needed
Fine motor skills	Look for difficulty with writing and drawing May need outpatient OT services	Look for difficulties with activities of daily living, writing, and drawing; upper-extremity ataxia; if impaired, OT consult May need outpatient OT services	Assess ability to engage in activities of daily living (ADLs) Assess degree of upper-extremity ataxia Consult with occupational therapist
Sensory impairments	Observe for increase in visual or auditory distractibility; may need audiology referral Look for visual-perceptual impairments; may need outpatient OT services Presence of vertigo or dizziness; may need audiology/otolaryngology referral	Assess visual fields, extra-ocular movements, hearing (may screen using tuning fork); ask if "blurry vision" is present; may need outpatient audiology or ophthalmology referral Screen for visual-perceptual impairments; if impaired, OT consult May need outpatient OT services	Assess visual fields, extra-ocular movements, hearing (screen using tuning fork); ask if "blurry vision" is present, if patient able to respond OT consultation
Nutrition, metabolism, and so forth	Look for weight loss or gain since accident	Monitor weight every other day until eating well; may need nutrition consult Do multichemistry panel hematocrit and prealbumin level, if indicated Assess for anosmia if appetite decreased May need speech consult for dysphagia	Monitor weight every other day until eating well; nutrition consult Do multichemistry panel, hematocrit, and prealbumin level Consider tube feedings or hyperalimentation; monitor fluid intake/output, calorie intake Speech referral to begin dysphagia treatment
Cognition and language	Look for memory impairments, word-finding, or calculation problems May need outpatient speech services	Look for memory deficits, word-finding or calculation problems, or do Mini-Mental Status Examination; if positive, refer to speech-language pathologist (SLP) for formal assessment	SLP referral to begin coma stimulation or language assessment and treatment

(continued)

Table 15.2.   (continued)

Functional issue	Mild injury	Moderate injury	Severe injury
Bowel and bladder	Look for new-onset enuresis; assess and treat accordingly	Assess continence, screen for urinary tract infection; begin timed voids and bowel program (stool softener and daily suppository); use commode instead of bedpan	Assess continence, screen for urinary tract infection (UTI), begin timed voids and bowel program as soon as patient shows awareness of wetness (if previously potty trained); use commode if possible
Behavior, sleep, safety, and family issues	Look for new onset sleep disorder, nightmares, hyperactivity, irritability, poor safety awareness, family reaction to accident; observe for 1–2 months	Observe sleep pattern, initiation, attention, safety, impulsivity May need to treat with trazodone at bedtime; may need clonidine or Ritalin, esp if premorbid ADHD	If severely agitated (RLA 4–5) use Inderal or clonidine (may use patch if cannot give by mouth); for evening agitation ("sundowning") use imipramine at bedtime if younger than 5 years of age or trazodone if age 5 years or older
Funding	May have liability or medical insurance available; may qualify for Medicaid	May have liability or medical insurance available; may qualify for Medicaid or Title V funds	Liability insurance probably exhausted; check for medical insurance; patient may qualify for Medicaid or Title V funds; have family apply for Supplemental Security Income (SSI) immediately
Type of rehabilitative services to consider	Follow-up by primary care physican and by the school; referral to physiatrist or developmental pediatrician if symptoms persist for more than 6 months	May need brief inpatient rehabilitation stay if unsafe or if mobility issues (e.g., lower-extremity fractures) are present Outpatient physical therapy, occupational therapy, or speech therapy two to three times per week; follow-up with physiatrist MAKE CERTAIN FUNDING IS IN PLACE BEFORE DISCHARGE	Inpatient rehabilitation unless cannot tolerate intensive therapy or too obtunded to benefit SNF or home health if not suitable for inpatient rehabilitation MAKE CERTAIN FUNDING IS IN PLACE BEFORE DISCHARGE
Academic reentry	Have parents notify the school of the accident Observe academic progress during the year	Notify school and make plans for return to school as soon as patient is safe and mobile Refer for early intervention/early childhood special education (EI/ECSE) if preschooler	Inpatient rehab team will arrange school reentry If in SNF or home health program, request home tutor from school Refer to EI/ECSE if preschooler

RLA, Rancho Los Amigos Scale of Cognitive Functioning.

discharge plan included regular outpatient speech-language, OT, and PT services; but because of the family's rural residence, he was treated by therapists with little experience in pediatric TBI cases.

He made poor progress, and funding for outpatient services was terminated by the payor with the recommendation that the services be delivered in the educational setting. Prior to sustaining the TBI,

he had been an active child; however, his classroom behavior had been good, and he had had many friends. Following the TBI, however, the boy was unable to complete modified classroom work, and his former friends avoided him. The parents advocated for additional educational services but were unsuccessful. The local school district did not implement several of the recommendations that the rehabilitation team school liaison made. The family requested the physician's assistance 1 year later.

This boy's situation illustrates the difficulties in providing services to children with TBI and their families who live in rural areas, as well as the need for close collaboration among the rehabilitation team, the school system, and the primary care physician. Children with severe TBI make the most progress during the first 2–3 years following their injuries. This is the time during which strengths must be identified, compensatory strategies must be developed, and behavior problems and interpersonal skills must be addressed. The physician must be aware of local and regional resources that can be useful to the child and his or her family.

This 10-year-old needs reassessment by a neuropsychologist, a physical therapist, an occupational therapist, and an SLP. This information will assist the physician, the school, and the family to agree and implement a plan for services. It is also important to encourage the child's integration into typical community activities such as summer camp or Scouts. Family functioning should be assessed, and appropriate services for parents and/or siblings should be recommended. The parents may benefit from individual or couples counseling to facilitate their adaptation to their child's disability.

The two children represent two situations along a continuum. Using the postemergency format and addressing the various areas of function, the primary care physician can work with families, schools, and specialists to implement effective treatment plans. Consultation with experienced specialists can be essential. The 10-year-old boy did have 2 weeks of daily therapy services by the rehabilitation team approved by the insurance company because of the lack of local services. The child's gross motor function increased from a 5-year functional level to 10 years within that period, with similar improvement in his speech-language skills. His visual-perceptual performance and upper-extremity coordination improved from 5 years to 7 years. Self-monitoring noticeably improved, and impulsivity decreased with a structured behavioral program.

REFERENCES

Achenbach, T.M. (1991a). *Manual for the Child Behavior Checklist and Revised Child Behavior Profile*. Burlington: University of Vermont.

Achenbach, T.M. (1991b). *Manual for the Child Behavior Checklist–Youth Self-Report*. Burlington: University of Vermont.

Achenbach, T.M. (1991c). *Manual for the Teacher Report Form and the Child Behavior Profile*. Burlington: University of Vermont.

Bayley, N. (1993). *Bayley Scales of Infant Development* (2nd ed.). San Antonio, TX: The Psychological Corporation.

Beery, K.E. (1997). *The Beery-Buktenica VMI: Developmental test of visual-motor integration with supplemental developmental tests of visual perception and motor coordination: Administration, scoring, and teaching manual* (4th ed. rev.). Parsippany, NJ: Modern Curriculum Press.

Biagas, K.V., & Gaeta, M.L. (1998). Treatment of traumatic brain injury with hypothermia. *Current Opinions in Pediatrics, 10*(3), 271–277.

Blosser, J.L., & DePompei, R. (1995, April). *Successful school transition for students with TBI*. Paper presented at Current Concepts in Pediatric Neurodevelopment and Rehabilitation, Columbia, MO.

Brink, J.L., Garrett, A.L., Hale, W.R., et al. (1970). Recovery of motor and intellectual function in children sustaining severe head injuries. *Developmental Medicine and Child Neurology, 12*, 565–571.

Bruininks, R.H. (1978). *Bruininks-Oseretsky Test of Motor Proficiency: Examiner's manual*. Circle Pines, MN: American Guidance Service.

Cattelani, R., Lombardi, F., Brianti, R., & Mazzuchi, A. (1998). Traumatic brain injury in childhood: Intellectual, behavioural and social outcome into adulthood. *Brain Injury, 12*, 283–296.

Cockrell, J.L., & Gregory, S.A. (1992). Audiological deficits in brain-injured children and adolescents. *Brain Injury, 6*, 261–266.

Corrigan, J.D., Smith-Knapp, K., & Granger C.V. (1997). Validity of the Functional Independence Measure for persons with traumatic brain injury. *Archives of Physical Medicine and Rehabilitation, 78*, 828–834.

Cummings, J.L. (1993). The mental status examination. *Hospital Practice (Off Ed), 28*(5A), 56–58, 60, 65–68.

Di Scala, C., Osber, J.S., Gans, B.M., et al. (1991). Children with traumatic head injury: Morbidity and postacute treatment. *Archives of Physical Medicine and Rehabilitation, 72*(9), 662–666.

Dikmen, S.S., Temkin, N.R., Miller, B., et al. (1991). Neurobehavioral effects of phenytoin prophylaxis of posttraumatic seizures. *JAMA: Journal of the American Medical Association, 265*, 1271–1277.

DiRenzi, E., & Vignolo, L.A. (1962). Token Test. *Brain, 85*, 665–678.

DiSimoni, F. (1978). *Token Test for Children*. Austin, TX: PRO-ED.

Duhaime, A.C., Alario, A.J., Lewander, W.J., et al. (1992). Head injury in very young children: Mechanisms, injury types, and ophthalmologic findings in 100 hospitalized patients younger than 2 years of age. *Pediatrics, 90*, 179–185.

Dunn, L.M., & Dunn, L.M. (1981). *Peabody Picture Vocabulary Test–Revised* (PPVT–R). Circle Pines, MN: American Guidance Service.

Ewing-Cobbs, L., Levin, H.S., Fletcher, J.M., et al. (1990). The Children's Orientation and Amnesia Test: Relationship to severity of acute head injury and to recovery of memory. *Neurosurgery, 27*, 683–691.

Fay, G.C., Jaffe, K.M., Polissar, N.L., et al. (1993). Mild pediatric traumatic brain injury: A cohort study. *Archives of Physical Medicine and Rehabilitation, 74,* 895–901.

Fay, G.C., Jaffe, K.M., Polissar, N.L., et al. (1994). Outcome of pediatric traumatic brain injury at three years: A cohort study. *Archives of Physical Medicine and Rehabilitation, 75,* 733–741.

Feldman, A.B., Haley, S.M., & Coryell, J. (1990). Concurrent and construct validity of the Pediatric Evaluation of Disability Inventory. *Physical Therapy, 70,* 602–610.

Folio, M.R., & Fewell, R.R. (1983). *Peabody Developmental Motor Scales and Activity Cards* (PDMS). Itasca, IL: Riverside Publishing Co.

Globus, M.Y., Alonso, O., Dietrich, W.D., et al. (1995). Glutamate release and free radical production following brain injury: Effects of posttraumatic hypothermia. *Journal of Neurochemistry, 65*(4), 1704–1711.

Goodglass, H., & Kaplan, E. (1983). *Boston Diagnostic Aphasia Test.* Philadelphia: Lea & Febiger.

Griffith, J.F., & Dodge, P.R. (1968). Transient blindness following head injury in children. *New England Journal of Medicine, 278,* 648–651.

Hagen, C. (1982). Language cognitive disorganization following closed head injury: A conceptualization. In L.E. Trexler (Ed.), *Cognitive rehabilitation: Conceptualization and intervention* (pp. 131–151). New York: Plenum Publishing Corp.

Hahn, Y.S., Chyung, C., Barthel, M.J., et al. (1988). Head injuries in children under 36 months of age: Demography and outcome. *Child's Nervous System, 4,* 34–40.

Haley, S.M., Coster, W.J., Ludlow, L.H., et al. (1992). *Pediatric Evaluation of Disability Inventory (PEDI): Version 1.0, Developmental, Standardization, and Administration Manual.* Boston: New England Medical Center Hospitals.

Hamilton, B.B., & Granger, C.V. (1991). *Functional Independence Measure for Children (WeeFIM^{SM}).* Buffalo: State University of New York.

Hammill, D.D. (1991). *Detroit Tests of Learning Aptitude–III.* Austin, TX: PRO-ED.

Kaufman, A.S., & Kaufman, N.L. (1983). *Kaufman Assessment Battery for Children.* Circle Pines, MN: American Guidance Service.

Klonoff, H., Clark, C., & Klonoff, P.S. (1993). Long-term outcome of head injuries: A 23-year follow-up study of children with head injuries. *Journal of Neurology, Neurosurgery, and Psychiatry, 56,* 410–415.

Kraus, J.F., Fife, D., & Conroy, C. (1987). Pediatric brain injuries: The nature, clinical course, and early outcomes in a defined United States population. *Pediatrics, 79,* 501–507.

Kraus, J.F., Rock, A., & Humyari, P. (1990). Brain injuries among infants, children, adolescents and young adults. *American Journal of Diseases of Children, 144,* 684–691.

Kriel, R.L., Krach, L.E., & Jones-Saete, C. (1993). Outcomes of children with prolonged unconsciousness and vegetative states. *Pediatric Neurology, 9*(5), 362–368.

Levin, H.S., O'Donnell, V.M., & Grossman, R.G. (1979). The Galveston Orientation and Amnesia Test: A practical scale to assess cognition after head injury. *Journal of Nervous and Mental Disease, 167*(11), 675–684.

Lynch, D.R., & Dawson, T.M. (1994). Secondary mechanisms in neuronal trauma. *Current Opinions in Neurology, 7*(6), 510–516.

MacKenzie, E.J., Shapiro, S., & Eastham, J.N. (1985). The Abbreviated Injury Scale and Injury Severity Score: Levels of inter-and intrarater reliability. *Medical Care, 23*(6), 823–835.

Max, J., Robin, D., Lindgren, S., et al. (1997). *Predicting outcome following childhood traumatic brain injury.* Symposium at the annual meeting of the American Academy of Child and Adolescent Psychiatry, Toronto.

Max, J.E., Arndt, S., Castillo, C.S., et al. (1998). Attention-deficit hyperactivity symptomatology after traumatic brain injury: A prospective study. *Journal of the American Academy of Child and Adolescent Psychiatry, 37,* 841–847.

Max, J.E., Koele, S.L., Lindgren, S.D., et al. (1998). Adaptive functioning following traumatic brain injury and orthopedic injury: A controlled study. *Archives of Physical Medicine and Rehabilitation, 79,* 893–899.

Max, J.E., Koele, S.L., Smith, W.L., et al. (1998). Psychiatric disorders in children and adolescents after severe traumatic brain injury: A controlled study. *Journal of the American Academy of Child and Adolescent Psychiatry, 37,* 832–840.

Mitchell, W.G., Zhou, Y., Chavez, J.M., & Guzman, B.L. (1993). Effects of antiepileptic drugs on reaction time, attention, and impulsivity in children. *Pediatrics, 91*(1), 101–105.

NIH Consensus Development Panel on Rehabilitation of Persons with Traumatic Brain Injury. (1999). Consensus conference: Rehabilitation of persons with traumatic brain injury. *JAMA: Journal of the American Medical Association, 282*(10), 974–983.

Raimondi, A., & Hirschauer, J. (1984). Head injury in the infant and toddler: Coma severity and outcome scale. *Child's Brain, 11,* 12–35.

Reilly, P.L., Simpson, D.A., Sprod, R., & Thomas, L. (1988). Assessing the conscious level in infants and young children: A paediatric version of the Glasgow Coma Scale. *Child's Nervous System, 4*(1), 30–33.

Reitan, R.M. (1979). *Manual for administration of neuropsychological test batteries for adults and children.* Tucson, AZ: Reitan Neuropsychological Laboratory.

Reitan, R.M., & Wolfson, D. (1993). *The Halstead-Reitan Neuropsychological Test Battery: Theory and clinical interpretation.* Tucson, AZ: Neuropsychology Press.

Russell, D., Rosenbaum, P., Cadman, D., et al. (1989). The gross motor function measure: A means to evaluate the effects of physical therapy. *Developmental Medicine and Child Neurology, 31,* 341–352.

Russell, E.W., & Starkey, R.I. (1993). *Halstead Russell Neuropsychological Examination System (HRNES).* Los Angeles: Western Psychological Services.

Sakai, C.S., & Mateer, C. (1984). Otological and audiological sequelae of closed head injury. *Seminars in Hearing, 5,* 157–173.

Sbordone, R. (1999). Posttraumatic stress disorder: An overview and its relationship to closed head injuries. *Neurorehabilitation, 13,* 69–78.

Sparrow, S.S., Balla, D.A., & Cicchetti, D.V. (1984). *The Vineland Adaptive Behavior Scales (VABS).* Circle Pines, MN: American Guidance Services.

State University of New York at Buffalo. (1993a). *Guide for the Uniform Data Set for Medical Rehabilitation (Adult FIM^{SM}), version 4.0.* Buffalo, NY: Author.

State University of New York at Buffalo. (1993b). *Guide for the Uniform Data Set for Medical Rehabilitation for Children (WeeFIM^SM), version 4.0–inpatient.* Buffalo, NY: Author.

Teasdale, G., & Jennett, B. (1974). Assessment of coma and impaired consciousness: A practical scale. *Lancet, 2*(7872), 81–84.

Temkin, N.R., Dikmen, S.S., Wilensky, A.J., et al. (1990). A randomized, double blind study of phenytoin for the prevention of post-traumatic seizures. *New England Journal of Medicine, 323*(8), 497–502.

Thatcher, R.W., Walker, R.A., & Giudice, S. (1987). Human cerebral hemispheres develop at different rates and ages. *Science, 236*(4805), 1110–1113.

Tiffin, J. (1983). *The Purdue Pegboard Test.* Lafayette, IN: Lafayette Instrument Co.

Vargha-Khadem, F., O'Gorman, A.M., & Watters, G.V. (1985). Aphasia and handedness in relation to hemispheric side, age at injury, and severity of cerebral lesion during childhood. *Brain, 108,* 677–696.

Warschausky, S., Cohen, E.H., Parker, J.G., et al. (1997). Social problem-solving skills of children with traumatic brain injury. *Pediatric Rehabilitation, 1,* 77–81.

Wechsler, D. (1989). *Wechsler Preschool and Primary Scale of Intelligence–Revised* (WPPSI–R). San Antonio, TX: The Psychological Corporation.

Wechsler, D. (1991). *Wechsler Intelligence Scale for Children–Third Edition* (WISC–III). San Antonio, TX: The Psychological Corporation.

Wechsler, D. (1997). *Wechsler Adult Intelligence Scale–Third Edition* (WAIS–III). San Antonio, TX: The Psychological Corporation.

Williams, S.E., Ris, M.D., Ayyangar, R., et al. (1998). Recovery in pediatric brain injury: Is psychostimulant medication beneficial? *Journal of Head Trauma Rehabilitation, 13*(3), 73–81.

Woodcock, R.E., & Johnson, M.B. (1990). *Woodcock-Johnson Psycho-Educational Battery–Revised.* Itasca, IL: Riverside Publishing Co.

Ylvisaker, M. (1986). Language and communication disorders following pediatric head injury. *Journal of Head Trauma Rehabilitation, 1*(4), 48–56.

Ylvisaker, M., & Feeney, T.J. (1996). Executive functions after traumatic brain injury: Supported cognition and self-advocacy. *Seminars in Speech and Language, 17*(3), 217–232.

Ylvisaker, M., Hartwick, P., & Stevens, M. (1991). School reentry following head injury: Managing the transition from hospital to school. *Journal of Head Trauma Rehabilitation, 61,* 10–22.

15

Appendix

Guidelines for the Care of Children and Adolescents with Traumatic Brain Injury

Basic Team

The special care needs of children and adolescents with traumatic brain injury (TBI) are best met by an experienced, coordinated team of specialists working collaboratively with parents, the primary care physician, and other service providers. Younger children with TBI may be followed by a team headed by a developmental pediatrician. Not all members of the basic team may be needed at each visit, and other professionals may be required. These professionals include but are not limited to an orthotist, an orthopedist, a child neurologist, an ophthalmologist, a nutritionist, and a feeding specialist. Parents of children with TBI and the individuals with TBI themselves should be encouraged to participate actively as part of the team. Please note that though a coordinated team may be needed to manage the range of specialty services required, all children require a medical home.

Regular members of the child development team include a developmental pediatrician or a pediatric physiatrist, a medical social worker, a neurosurgeon, a nurse, an occupational therapist, a physical therapist, a psychologist, and a speech-language pathologist.

Initial Evaluation

The initial evaluation of rehabilitation needs should be performed as soon as the child is stable following the injury. Some children are discharged for outpatient follow-up, others are discharged and then readmitted for inpatient rehabilitation, and others are transferred for inpatient rehabilitation.

The responsibilities of the primary care physician are to 1) coordinate acute medical care; 2) follow the child's progress with the physiatrist during inpatient rehabilitation; 3) coordinate follow-up after hospital discharge; 4) obtain family, medical, and developmental histories; and 5) request school information. An initial management plan for community services should be developed prior to hospital (acute care or rehabilitation) discharge, inclusive of all needed services.

Frequency of Visits

As the child with TBI grows and develops, additional needs may become evident that require other treatments and consultations with professionals from other disciplines. The child may require evaluation by the team of professionals two to four times during the first year following the TBI, two times during the second and third years, and annually as needed thereafter, depending on the severity of the child's TBI and co-morbid disabilities.

The rehabilitation team works collaboratively with the primary health care professionals. In general, the primary care office should review the child's progress and update the office management plan at least yearly, more often for younger children and in the first year or two after the injury occurs.

The Physician's Guide to Caring for Children with Disabilities and Chronic Conditions, edited by Robert E. Nickel and Larry W. Desch, copyright © 2000 Paul H. Brookes Publishing Co.

Guidelines for the Care of Children and Adolescents with Traumatic Brain Injury

The following elements are recommended by age group, and the listing is cumulative. Review all items indicated up through the actual age group of a child entering the program for the first time as part of the initial evaluation.

AGE	KEY CLINICAL ISSUES/CONCERNS	EVALUATIONS/KEY PROCEDURES	SPECIALISTS
Birth–5 years (pre–school age)	*Growth/Nutrition* Oral motor dysfunction, dysphagia Failure to thrive (FTT)	Growth parameters, diet record, nutrition and feeding assessment, evaluation of gastroesophageal reflux (GER), video fluoroscopy of swallowing as needed	Physiatrist or developmental pediatrician (DPed), nurse, feeding specialist as needed
	Dental Care	Review oral hygiene, refer to dentist	Primary care physician, nurse, and dentist
	Associated Medical Problems Strabismus or visual problems Hearing loss Dizziness (vertigo) Seizures	Hearing testing and referral to ophthalmologist as needed Referral to otolaryngologist (ENT) as needed Electroencephalogram, referral to child neurologist as needed	Physiatrist, DPed, nurse, audiologist, ophthalmologist, child neurologist, urologist, speech-language pathologist (SLP) needed
	Chronic respiratory problems/aspiration GER Constipation Enuresis, urinary incontinence Sleep disorder	Chest X ray, workup for GER, swallowing dysfunction, gastrointestinal consult as needed Diet, medication (e.g., bulk agent, stool softener) Referral to urologist as needed Behavior management, occasional short-term medications	
	Drooling	Oral-motor therapy (ages birth–3 years), other behavioral therapies, medication, and (rarely) surgery (as older child)	
	Note any side effects of medications.		
	Musculoskeletal Issues Joint contractures Hip subluxation or dislocation Scoliosis Other foot–ankle deformities	Detailed musculoskeletal examination Use of stretching, braces, botulinum toxin injections to prevent contractures as needed	Physiatrist or DPed, physical and occupational therapists, orthopedist as needed
	Ambulation and Mobility Need for physical therapy services Bracing and adaptive equipment Treatment of hypertonicity	Detailed neuromotor examination, gait analysis as needed	Physiatrist or DPed, physical and occupational therapists
	Seating and Positioning Need for specialized seating device	Detailed neuromotor and musculoskeletal examination	Physiatrist or DPed, physical and occupational therapists

The Physician's Guide to Caring for Children with Disabilities and Chronic Conditions, edited by Robert E. Nickel and Larry W. Desch, copyright © 2000 Paul H. Brookes Publishing Co.

Guidelines for the Care of Children and Adolescents with Traumatic Brain Injury (continued)

The following elements are recommended by age group, and the listing is cumulative. Review all items indicated up through the actual age group of a child entering your practice for the first time as part of the initial evaluation.

AGE	KEY CLINICAL ISSUES/CONCERNS	EVALUATIONS/KEY PROCEDURES	SPECIALISTS
Birth–5 years (pre–school age) *(continued)*	*Upper-Extremity Function/Visual Motor Skills* Need for occupational therapy (OT) services	Neuromotor examination, screen of visual perceptual skills, assess fine motor skills	Occupational therapist, ophthalmologist
	Associated Behavior/ Mental Health Problems Inattention, hyperactivity, impulsivity Aggression, agitation Oppositional behaviors Anxiety	Interviews, behavioral rating scales (parents and teachers) as needed and regularly if on medication, referral to mental health professional as needed Parent training in behavior management	Physiatrist or DPed, nurse, psychologist, collaboration with EI/ECSE staff (or community preschool)
	Communication and Developmental Progress Need for early intervention (EI) or early childhood special education (ECSE) services Language delay/speech-language disorder Developmental delay	Developmental screening and surveillance Referral to speech-language pathologist (SLP) or child development team as needed Referral for eligibility testing for EI/ECSE services as needed	DPed or physiatrist, nurse, SLP, psychologist, or child development team as needed
	Need for Special Technology Power-drive wheelchair, augmentative and alternative communication devices such as computer keyboard for written evaluation	AAC clinic, power-drive wheelchair assessment, assessment of visual acuity as needed	Physical therapist, occupational therapist, SLP, ophthalmologist as needed
	Family Support Services Respite care Parent group Community health services Financial services (e.g., SSI)	Interview, use parent questionnaires as needed, parent resource materials (e.g., Family Needs Survey) Referral to community services as needed	DPed, nurse, social worker

The Physician's Guide to Caring for Children with Disabilities and Chronic Conditions, edited by Robert E. Nickel and Larry W. Desch, copyright © 2000 Paul H. Brookes Publishing Co.

Guidelines for the Care of Children and Adolescents with Traumatic Brain Injury *(continued)*

The following elements are recommended by age group, and the listing is cumulative. Review all items indicated up through the actual age group of a child entering your practice for the first time as part of the initial evaluation.

AGE	KEY CLINICAL ISSUES/CONCERNS	EVALUATIONS/KEY PROCEDURES	SPECIALISTS
Birth–5 years (pre-school age) *(continued)*	*Review of Diagnosis and Anticipatory Guidance* School reentry Need for parent training in behavior management Review individualized family service plan (IFSP) with family Accident prevention Transition from EI to ECSE and from ECSE to elementary school (or community preschool) Encourage self-care and independence	Interview, educational materials, school conference as needed, initiate care notebook	Primary care office in collaboration with specialists and education staff
6–12 years (school-age)	*Associated Learning Problems* Learning disabilities Attention-deficit/hyperactivity disorder (ADHD) Executive function problems Difficulties with memory, information processing Central auditory processing impairment Mental retardation	Behavior checklists, intellectual and achievement testing, referral to child development team as needed; may require neuropsychological assessment	DPed or physiatrist, nurse, psychologist, SLP, occupational therapist as needed, collaboration with school staff
	Reassess Need for Physical or Occupational Therapy Services	Complete neuromotor examination, assessment of fine and gross motor skills and functional skills	DPed or physiatrist, physical therapist, occupational therapist
	Social Skills Promote social competence Involvement in peer group activities at school and in community (determine which supports are needed)	Care coordination, referral to community resources, mentor program	DPed, nurse, physical therapist and occupational therapist, school staff
	Anticipatory Guidance Reentry to school after traumatic brain injury (TBI) Recreation skills/adaptive sports Transition to middle school Educate child about diagnosis Encourage healthy behaviors (e.g., diet, exercise, muscle stretching)	Teacher interview, school conference Referral to community recreation programs, sports Education materials for child with TBI	Primary care office in collaboration with specialists and school staff

The Physician's Guide to Caring for Children with Disabilities and Chronic Conditions, edited by Robert E. Nickel and Larry W. Desch, copyright © 2000 Paul H. Brookes Publishing Co.

Guidelines for the Care of Children and Adolescents with Traumatic Brain Injury *(continued)*

The following elements are recommended by age group, and the listing is cumulative. Review all items indicated up through the actual age group of a child entering your practice for the first time as part of the initial evaluation.

AGE	KEY CLINICAL ISSUES/CONCERNS	EVALUATIONS/KEY PROCEDURES	SPECIALISTS
13–21 years (adolescent and young adult)	*Community Mobility/Driver Training*	Driver training assessment	Physiatrist, occupational therapist, medical social worker
	Associated Behavior/ Mental Health Problems Aggression ADHD Anxiety disorders Depression Other mental health disorders Follow-up of medication treatment	Behavioral rating scales (parent, child, and teacher) as needed, regularly if on medication Referral to child psychiatrist as needed Review medication management; check growth, blood pressure, heart rate, tics, side effects at least twice yearly if stable and doing well; electrocardiogram (EKG); lab work as needed for specific medications	Physiatrist or DPed, mental health professional as needed Collaboration with school staff
	Self-Care and Independent living Determine which supports are needed	Outpatient PT and OT services as needed, consider inpatient rehabilitation evaluation Independent living skills program, social skills training as needed Care coordination	Social worker, physical and occupational therapists, psychologist, and/or vocational specialist
	Anticipatory Guidance Promote healthy behaviors (exercise program, weight control, muscle-stretching program) Sexuality and birth control High-risk behavior Career planning and/or higher education Transition to adult medical services Social isolation	Patient educational materials, gynecologic examination for sexually active women Referral to counseling, mental health professional as needed Teacher interview, school conference; referral to Department of Vocational Rehabilitation, career counseling, or life skills program as needed Encourage involvement in after-school and community activities, mentor programs	Primary care office in collaboration with specialists and school staff

The Physician's Guide to Caring for Children with Disabilities and Chronic Conditions, edited by Robert E. Nickel and Larry W. Desch, copyright © 2000 Paul H. Brookes Publishing Co.

Family and Physician Management Plan Summary for Children and Adolescents with Traumatic Brain Injury

This form will help you and your physician review current services and service needs. Please answer the questions about your current services on this page. Your physician will review your responses and complete the rest of the form.

Child's name _____ Today's date _____

Person completing the form _____

CURRENT SERVICES

1. Please list your/your child's current medications and any side effects.

2. What braces and special equipment do you/does your child use now?

3. What is your/your child's current school program?

    School name _____ Grade _____

    Teacher _____ Telephone _____

4. Do you/does your child receive any support services and other special programs at school (e.g., physical therapy, resource room)? Please list.

5. Who are your/your child's other medical and dental service providers?

    Dentist _____

    Neurologist _____

    Orthopedist _____

    Other _____

6. Who are your/your child's other community service providers?

    Physical therapist _____

    Community health nurse _____

    Other _____

The Physician's Guide to Caring for Children with Disabilities and Chronic Conditions, edited by Robert E. Nickel and Larry W. Desch, copyright © 2000 Paul H. Brookes Publishing Co.

Family and Physician Management Plan Summary
for Children and Adolescents with Traumatic Brain Injury *(continued)*

7. Do you/does your child also receive services from a neurodevelopmental team of specialists?

    Contact person _____

    Location _____

8. Have you/has your child had any blood tests, radiologic (X-ray) examinations, or other procedures since your last visit? If yes, please describe.

9. Have you/has your child been hospitalized or undergone surgery since your last visit? If yes, describe.

10. Please note your/your child's accomplishments since the last visit. Consider activities at home, in your neighborhood, or at school, as well as success with treatments.

11. What goals (i.e., skills) would you/your child like to accomplish in the next year? Consider activities at home, in your neighborhood, or at school, as well as success with a treatment.

12. What questions or concerns would you like addressed today?

Family and Physician Management Plan Summary for Children and Adolescents with Traumatic Brain Injury

The Management Plan Summary should be completed at each annual review and more often as needed. It is intended to be used with the Guidelines for Care, which provide a more complete listing of clinical issues at different ages as well as recommended evaluations and treatments.

Child's name _____ Person completing form _____ Today's date _____

Clinical issues	Currently a problem?	Evaluations needed	Treatment recommendations	Referrals made	Date for status check
Family's Questions					
Growth/Nutrition Concerns Feeding problems, dysphagia Slow weight gain, linear growth Questions about specialized feeding, gastrostomy care					
Dental Care					
Musculoskeletal Issues Change in range of motion, gait, scoliosis					
Ambulation and Mobility Describe ambulatory status Questions about physical therapy (PT), braces, adaptive equipment Assess need for power-drive wheelchair					

The Physician's Guide to Caring for Children with Disabilities and Chronic Conditions, edited by Robert E. Nickel and Larry W. Desch, copyright © 2000 Paul H. Brookes Publishing Co.

Family and Physician Management Plan Summary
for Children and Adolescents with Traumatic Brain Injury *(continued)*

Child's name _____ Person completing form _____ Today's date _____

Clinical issues	Currently a problem?	Evaluations needed	Treatment recommendations	Referrals made	Date for status check
Seating and Positioning					
Upper-Extremity Function/ Visual-Motor Skills					
Treatment of Hypertonicity					
Other Medical Issues Recurrent respiratory problems or aspiration problems Gastroesophageal reflux (GER) Seizures Dizziness (vertigo) Toilet training (determine need for adaptive seating) Constipation, enuresis, urinary incontinence Drooling Muscle cramps Hearing loss Strabismus/visual problems Sleep disorder **Note any side effects of medications.**					

The Physician's Guide to Caring for Children with Disabilities and Chronic Conditions, edited by Robert E. Nickel and Larry W. Desch, copyright © 2000 Paul H. Brookes Publishing Co.

Family and Physician Management Plan Summary
for Children and Adolescents with Traumatic Brain Injury *(continued)*

Child's name _____ Person completing form _____ Today's date _____

Clinical issues	Currently a problem?	Evaluations needed	Treatment recommendations	Referrals made	Date for status check
Communication and Speech Progress Questions about speech services Need for augmentative and alternative communication (AAC) devices or a computer for written communication					
Associated Developmental/ Learning Issues Describe current school progress Review early intervention or other school services (individualized family service plan [IFSP] or individualized education program [IEP]) School reentry Memory problems Executive function problems Difficulty with information processing Central auditory processing impairment					

The Physician's Guide to Caring for Children with Disabilities and Chronic Conditions, edited by Robert E. Nickel and Larry W. Desch, copyright © 2000 Paul H. Brookes Publishing Co.

Family and Physician Management Plan Summary
for Children and Adolescents with Traumatic Brain Injury *(continued)*

Child's name _____ Person completing form _____ Today's date _____

Clinical issues	Currently a problem?	Evaluations needed	Treatment recommendations	Referrals made	Date for status check
Associated Behavior/ Mental Health Issues					
Social Skills Involvement in peer-group activities in school or in the community (determine which supports needed)					
Self-Care and Independence					
Family Support Services					
Anticipatory Guidance List issues discussed and materials provided					
Collaboration with Community Agencies School Developmental Disability Services Vocational Rehabilitation					

The Physician's Guide to Caring for Children with Disabilities and Chronic Conditions, edited by Robert E. Nickel and Larry W. Desch, copyright © 2000 Paul H. Brookes Publishing Co.

Family and Physician Management Plan Summary
for Children and Adolescents with Traumatic Brain Injury *(continued)*

Child's name _____ Person completing form _____ Today's date _____

Clinical issues	Currently a problem?	Evaluations needed	Treatment recommendations	Referrals made	Date for status check
Comments					

Next update of the Management Plan Summary _____

Signature _____ Date _____
(Child and parent)

Signature _____ Date _____
(Health professional)

The Physician's Guide to Caring for Children with Disabilities and Chronic Conditions, edited by Robert E. Nickel and Larry W. Desch, copyright © 2000 Paul H. Brookes Publishing Co.

Children with Traumatic Brain Injury and Other Types of Disabilities: Differentiating Characteristics

Students with traumatic brain injury are different from other students with disabilities as their learning disabilities are acquired. Following are some of the characteristics of children with TBI that make them different from individuals with other disabilities. Educators must be aware of these differences and their effect on learning in order to plan appropriately for classroom placement and participation. The student with TBI has

- A previous successful experience in academic and social environments
- A premorbid self-concept of being a child without a disability
- Discrepancies in ability levels with regard to different skills and behaviors
- Inconsistent patterns of performance
- Variability and fluctuation in the recovery process, resulting in unpredictable and unexpected spurts of progress
- More extreme problems than other children with or without disabilities with generalizing, integrating, or structuring information
- Poor judgment and loss of emotional control, which make the student with TBI appear to have emotional difficulties at times
- Cognitive impairments that are present as in other children with disabilities but are uneven in terms of their extent and the child's rate of recovery from TBI
- Combinations of conditions resulting from the closed head injury that are unique and are not generally experienced by children with other disabilities
- Inappropriate behaviors that may be exaggerated:

    Impulsivity

    Distractibility

    Emotional lability

    Difficulties with memory, information processing, organization, and flexibility

- A learning style that requires the use of a variety of compensatory and adaptive strategies
- Some high-level skills that may be intact, making it difficult for teachers and others to understand why the child has problems in performing lower-level tasks
- A previously learned base of information that assists in his or her relearning skills rapidly

From Blosser, J.L., & DePompei, R. (1995, April). *Successful school transition for students with TBI.* Paper presented at Current Concepts in Pediatric Neurodevelopment and Rehabilitation, Columbus, OH; adapted by permission.

Commonly Used Medications and Doses

Name of medication	Dosage	Side effects
Acetaminophen	10–15 milligrams/kilogram/dose every 4 hours Maximum five doses/24 hours	Hepatotoxity from overdose
Baclofen (Lioresal)	1–4 years of age: 2.5–5 milligrams two or three times a day 5–12 years of age: 2.5–10 milligrams three times a day	Drowsiness, constipation, nausea, muscle weakness, hallucination with abrupt withdrawal
Carbamazepine (Tegretol)	Initial 10 milligrams/kilogram/24 hours, increase in increments to 20 milligrams/kilogram/24 hours Maximum 100-milligram dose twice a day	Drowsiness, dizziness, diplopia, urinary retention, rare Stevens-Johnson syndrome, hepatotoxicity
Chlorazepate dipotassium (Tranxene)	1–3 years of age: 1/2 of a 3.75-milligram tablet two or three times a day 4–9 years of age: 3.75 milligrams two or three times a day 9–12 years of age: 7.5 milligrams two or three times a day	Excessive sedation, confusion
Clonidine (Catapres)	5–12 years of age: 0.05 milligrams two times a day increasing in increments of 0.05 milligrams/day to a maximum of 0.2 milligrams/day	Sedation; rare hypotension; hypertension, risk for cardiac arrhythmia, hypertension with abrupt withdrawal
Codeine	0.5–1.0 milligrams/kilogram/dose every 4–6 hours intramuscularly or orally Maximum 30–60 milligrams/dose	Constipation, cramping, dowsiness
Dantrolene (Dantrium)	0.5 milligrams/kilogram/dose twice a day; gradually increase to maximum dose of 3 milligrams/kilogram four times a day Maximum 100 milligrams four times a day	Drowsiness, weakness, lethargy, diarrhea
Diazepam (Valium) *As sedative:*	0.12–0.8 milligrams/kilogram/24 hours every 6–8 hours by mouth; maximum 0.6 milligrams/kilogram within an 8-hour period	Excessive sedation, hypotension, respiratory depression, confusion
Docusate (Colace)	< 3 years of age: 10–40 milligrams/24 hours orally 3–6 years of age: 20–60 milligrams/24 hours 6–12 years of age: 40–120 milligrams/24 hours >12 years of age: 50–240 milligrams/24 hours	Diarrhea
Imipramine (Tofranil)	0.5 milligrams/kilogram/every night orally; increase by 0.5 milligrams/kilogram Maximum oral dose 1.5 milligrams/kilogram	Drowsiness, dry mouth, constipation, dizziness
Lithium	15–60 milligrams/kilogram/day two or three times a day by mouth	Sedation, goiter, pancreatitis, nephrogenic diabetes insipidus; seizures or death at levels >2.5 milliequivalents
Lorazepam (Ativan)	Status epilepticus: 0.05 milligrams/kilogram dose intravenously by rectum up to maximum of 4 milligrams/dose. May repeat in 15–20 minutes × 1	Sedation, dizziness, respiratory depression, ataxia
Methylphenidate (Ritalin)	0.3–0.6 milligrams/kilogram dose orally at breakfast and lunch; may add late afternoon dose	Insomnia, weight loss, decreased appetite, may increase tics
Phenytoin (Dilantin)	4–7 milligrams/kilogram/24 hours twice a day intravenously orally Maximum 300 milligrams/24 hours	Ataxia, hepatotoxicity, nystagmus, gingival overgrowth, rare Stevens-Johnson syndrome
Ranitidine (Zantac)	2–4 milligrams/kilogram/24 hours twice a day orally	Headache, malaise, insomnia, sedation, arthralgia, hepatotoxicity
Trazodone (Desyrel)	25–150 milligrams every night orally; not approved for children < 13 years	Nausea/vomiting

Adapted from Horn and Zasler (1996).

The Physician's Guide to Caring for Children with Disabilities and Chronic Conditions, edited by Robert E. Nickel and Larry W. Desch, copyright © 2000 Paul H. Brookes Publishing Co.

Comparison of Glasgow Coma Scale, Children's Coma Scales, and Pediatric Coma Scale

Glasgow Coma Scale	Children's Coma Scale[1]	Children's Coma Scale[2]	Pediatric Coma Scale
Eye Opening	**Eyes**	**Eye Opening**	**Eyes Open**
4 Spontaneous	4 Pursuit	4 Spontaneous	4 Spontaneous
3 Reaction to speech	3 Extraocular muscle intact, pupils reactive	3 Reaction to speech	3 To speech
2 Reaction to pain	2 Fixed pupils or extra-ocular movement impaired	2 Reaction to pain	2 To pain
1 No response	1 Fixed pupils or extra-ocular movement paralyzed	1 No response	1 None
Verbal	**Verbal**	**Verbal**	**Best Verbal Response**
5 Oriented	3 Cries	5 Smiles, oriented to sound, follows objects, interacts	5 Oriented
4 Confused/disordered	2 Spontaneous respiration		4 Words
3 Inappropriate words	1 Apneic	*Crying* *Interacts*	3 Vocal sounds
2 Incomprehensible sounds		4 Consolable Inappropriate	2 Cries
1 No response		3 Inconsistently consolable Moaning	1 None
		2 Inconsolable Irritable, restless	
		1 No response	
Motor	**Motor**	**Motor**	**Best/Most Correct Response**
6 Spontaneous (obeys verbal commands)	4 Flexes and extends	6 Spontaneous (obeys verbal command)	5 Obeys commands
5 Localizes pain	3 Withdrawal from painful stimuli	5 Localizes pain	4 Localizes to pain
4 Withdraws in response to pain	2 Hypertonic	4 Withdraws to pain	3 Flexion to pain
3 Abnormal flexion to pain (decorticate posture)	1 Flaccid	3 Decorticate response to pain	2 Extension to pain
2 Abnormal extension response to pain (decerebrate posture)		2 Decerebrate response to pain	1 None
1 No response		1 No response	

Glasgow Coma Scale (Teasdale & Jennett, 1974), Children's Coma Scale[1] (Raimondi & Hirschauer, 1984), Children's Coma Scale[2] (Hahn, Chyung, Barthel, et al., 1988), and Pediatric Coma Scale (Reilly, Simpson, Sprod, & Thomas, 1988).

RESOURCES ON TRAUMATIC BRAIN INJURY

Readings

Begail, V. (1997). *Head injury in children and adolescents: A resource and review for school and allied professionals.* Brandon, VT: Clinical Psychology Publishing Co. (1-800-433-0234)

Cockrell, J. (1995). Pediatric brain injury rehabilitation. In L.J. Horn & N.D. Zasler (Eds.), *Medical rehabilitation of traumatic brain injury.* Philadelphia: Hanley & Belfus. (1-800-962-1892)

DeBoskey, D.S. (1995). *An educational challenge: Meeting the needs of students with brain injury.* Houston, TX: HDI Publishing. (1-800-321-7037)

DeBoskey, D.S., Hecht, J.S., & Calub, C.J. (1991). *Educating families: A guide to medical, cognitive & social issues.* Gaithersburg, MD: Aspen Publishers. (1-800-638-8437)

Glang, A., Singer, G.H.S., & Todis, B. (Eds.). (1997). *Students with acquired brain injury: The school's response.* Baltimore: Paul H. Brookes Publishing Co. (1-800-638-3775)

Lehr, E. (1990). *Psychological management of traumatic brain injuries in children and adolescents.* Gaithersburg, MD: Aspen Publishers. (1-800-638-8437)

León-Carrión, J. (1994). *Daño cerebral: Guìa para familares y cuidadores.* Houston, TX: HDI Publishers. (1-800-321-7037)

Nowicki, S., Duke, M.P., & Martin, E. (1992). *Helping the child who doesn't fit in.* Atlanta, GA: Peachtree Publishers. (1-800-241-0113)

Raines, S.R., & Waaland, P.K., (n.d.). *For kids only: A guide to brain injury.* Richmond: Medical College of Virginia, Department of Physical Medicine and Rehabilitation. (804-828-9000)

Savage, R.C., & Wolcott, G.F. (Eds.). (1994). *Educational dimensions of acquired brain injury.* Austin, TX: PRO-ED. (1-800-897-3202)

Sellars, C.W., Vegter, C., & Ellerbusch, S. (1997). *Pediatric brain injury: The case of the very young child.* Houston, TX: HDI Publishers. (1-800-321-7037)

Singer, G.H.S., Glang, A., & Williams, J.M. (Eds.). (1996). *Children with acquired brain injury: Educating and supporting families.* Baltimore: Paul H. Brookes Publishing Co. (1-800-638-3775)

Specht, K.Q. (1996). *Physical management of students who have sustained a TBI.* Houston, TX: HDI Publishers. (1-800-321-7037)

Williams, J.M., & Kay, T. (Eds). (1991). *Head injury—A family matter.* Baltimore: Paul H. Brookes Publishing Co. (1-800-638-3775)

Wolcott, G., Lash, M., & Pearson, S. (1995). *Signs and strategies for educating students with brain injuries: A practical guide for teachers and schools.* Houston, TX: HDI Publishers. (1-800-321-7037)

Ylvisaker, M. (Ed.). (1995). *Head injury rehabilitation: Children and adolescents.* Pittsburgh, PA: Rehabilitation Institute of Pittsburgh. (412-420-2345)

Government Agency

National Institute on Disability and Rehabilitation Research (NIDRR)
Office of Special Education and Rehabilitative Services
U.S. Department of Education
400 Maryland Avenue SW
Washington, D.C. 20202
Telephone: (800) USA-LEARN (872-53276)
World Wide Web site: http://www.ed.gov/offices/OSERS/NIDRR/

General Information

The Brain Injury Information Network
E-mail: jlyon@tbinet.org
World Wide Web site: http://tbinet.org/

This web site provides information, support, and referrals to other related Internet traumatic and acquired brain injury World Wide Web sites and information.

National Rehabilitation Information Center (NARIC)
1010 Wayne Avenue, Suite 800
Silver Spring, Maryland 20910
Telephone: (800) 346-2742, (301) 562-2400; TTY: (301) 495-5626
Fax: (301) 562-2401
World Wide Web site: http://www.naric.com/naric/

NARIC provides information, referrals, and access to literature searches and publishes several directories and resource guides.

The Perspective Network
Post Office Box 1859
Cumming, Georgia 30028-1859
Telephone: (800) 685-6302, (770) 844-6898
Fax: (770) 844-6898
E-mail: TPN@tbi.org
World Wide Web site: http://www.tbi.org/

This network provides information, support, and referrals, including materials, books, "chat rooms," and lists of service agencies and organizations.

National Organization

Brain Injury Association, Inc.
105 North Alfred Street
Alexandria, Virginia 22314
Telephone: (703) 236-6000
Fax: (703) 236-6001
World Wide Web site: http://www.biausa.org/

This organization provides information to families and professionals and educates the public about brain injury, including its effects, causes, and prevention.

16

Spinal Cord Injury

Janice L. Cockrell

KEY COMPETENCIES

- Discuss the American Spinal Injury Association (ASIA) classification of spinal cord injury (SCI)
- Assess a child who has had an SCI
- Discuss functional expectations for level of SCI
- Discuss the long-term medical complications of SCI
- Identify and treat autonomic dysreflexia
- Discuss home ventilation issues
- Establish a treatment plan for a child with SCI following the acute injury
- Establish a treatment plan for a child with SCI in the postacute phase

DESCRIPTION

Definition

Spinal cord injury (SCI) is defined by the level and type of the neurologic injury and the distribution of the impairment.

Neurologic Injury The level of the neurologic injury is defined as the lowest neurologic segment with normal motor and normal sensory function (American Spinal Injury Association [ASIA], 1992). If the child has C6 quadriplegia, he or she has full motor and sensory function at the C6 level and above and probably partial motor and/or sensory function at the C7 level. If a child has asymmetrical levels of function (e.g., C5 on the left and C7 on the right), he or she would have C5 quadriplegia. Such an individual may be described clinically, however, as a C5/C7 quadriplegic, indicating the asymmetry.

SCI can be complete or incomplete. In a complete SCI, the motor and sensory axons are severed or crushed completely, whereas axonal sparing occurs in incomplete SCI. In a complete injury, no motor and/or sensory function exists below the zone of injury. Since high-dose steroid protocols have been introduced for the treatment of acute SCI in trauma centers, more children have shown spotty preservation of motor and/or sensory function below the level of injury. In most cases, this finding is nonfunctional to the individual; however, it makes ascertaining whether the lesion is complete or incomplete difficult. In an incomplete injury, there is preservation of some motor and/or sensory function below the zone of injury. During the acute phase of injury, the presence of sensation or of movement anywhere below the level of injury suggests an incomplete lesion. Most typically, sensation may be present in the perianal area and is known as *sacral sparing*.

Distribution of the Impairment SCI is also defined by the distribution of impairment. Children and adolescents with quadriplegia have involvement of the upper and lower extremities and the trunk. Impairment results from loss of motor and/or sensory function in the cervical neurologic segments secondary to damage to neural elements in the spinal cord. Children with paraplegia have involvement of the trunk and the lower extremities. Impairment results from loss of motor and/or sensory function in the thoracic, lumbar, or sacral neurologic segments secondary to damage of neural elements in the spinal cord. In the case of a T1 injury, the individual may be functionally quadriplegic, although strictly by definition he or she has a paraplegia.

Classification

The ASIA (1992) classification of SCI follows:

A Complete injury, no motor or sensory function is present below the level of injury
B Incomplete, preserved sensation only, excluding phantom sensations, below the level of injury
C Incomplete, preserved motor (nonfunctional) (i.e., preservation of voluntary motor function below the level of injury, which is nonfunctional); sensation may or may not be preserved
D Incomplete, preserved motor (functional) (i.e., preservation of voluntary and functional motor capability below the level of injury)
E Complete return of all motor and sensory functions but still with possibility of abnormal reflexes

Incomplete injuries are classified as different clinical syndromes based on the location of injury within the spinal cord. These include anterior cord syndrome, central cord syndrome, Brown-Sequard syndrome, posterior cord syndrome, and mixed syndrome (see Table 16.1).

Causes

Complete SCI is most often associated with a gunshot wound or a complete fracture or dislocation of vertebral bodies with resulting compromise of the spinal canal. Spinal cord strokes, contusions, and knife wounds are more often associated with incomplete injuries. Pediatric "lap belt" injuries can present with complete or incomplete lesions. Other causes of SCI include falls, motor vehicle accidents, equestrian injuries, and bicycle injuries. Child abuse is an infrequent cause of quadriplegia.

In children, an incomplete spinal cord lesion that is not associated with an anatomic disruption of the cord may be followed by nearly complete re-

Table 16.1. Anatomic classification of spinal cord injury

Anterior cord syndrome	Motor paralysis with hypesthesia and hypalgesia with preservation of posterior column sensory function
Brown-Sequard syndrome	Homolateral paralysis and contralateral sensory loss
Central cord syndrome	Dissociation in degree of motor weakness with lower limbs stronger than upper limbs and with sacral sensory sparing
Posterior cord syndrome	Motor paralysis with loss of posterior column sensory function (rare)
Mixed syndrome	Unclassifiable combination of the previous syndromes (very common)

covery. If nerve roots are involved, as in the case of some cauda equina or conus injuries, complete recovery is less likely. Because of the relatively large size of a young child's head, rapid acceleration or deceleration injuries in the absence of neck support increase the risk for quadriplegia. Young children and youth, however, also have a relatively large cervical spinal canal, which can be protective. In those youth for whom an apparently minor trauma has resulted in an SCI, congenital vertebral fusion along with relative spinal stenosis may be identified by imaging.

ASSESSMENT AND MANAGEMENT IMMEDIATELY FOLLOWING INJURY

Stabilization of the Spine in the Child with Acute Injury

At the scene of an accident, the child may be conscious or unconscious. If the child is conscious and crying, lack of movement of any of the extremities should be assumed to be due to SCI until proved otherwise. If the child is unconscious at the accident scene, SCI must likewise be assumed until the child awakens and moves all four extremities. The child's spine must be immobilized with a backboard before being moved. Although immobilization is done in the case of adolescents and adults, it is not uncommon for infants and children to be picked up and carried to another spot prior to spinal immobilization. In the presence of intervertebral instability without neural injury, such a maneuver may well lead to actual subluxation and secondary neural injury. It is thus of vital importance that physicians instruct parents and participants in cardiopulmonary resuscitation (CPR) classes to observe the same spinal precautions with infants and children as with adolescents and adults with spinal injuries.

Radiographic Evaluation

In the emergency room, the child's spinal stability can be assessed with plain radiographs. Normal alignment of the vertebrae on cross-table lateral films only suggests stability, and therefore flexion and extension films may be necessary. Because the films may place the spinal cord at risk, they should be done only in the presence of the neurosurgeon or the orthopedist. In young children, vertebral bodies are not well ossified, and ligaments are more lax. In these cases, false positive vertebral instability may be noted. For this reason, the treating physicians should have expertise in reading pediatric spine films.

SCI without radiographic abnormalities (SCIWORA) is a well-described entity (Pang & Wilberger, 1982) that is more common in children than in adults. If SCI is suspected but vertebral alignment appears normal on plain radiographs, a magnetic resonance imaging (MRI) or computed tomography (CT) scan of the spine is indicated. In the case of acute contusion or spinal cord infarction secondary to trauma, only subtle edema may be present on the initial films, in which case the films need to be repeated in 24–48 hours.

Acute Management

The results of the second (Bracken, Shepard, Collins, et al., 1992) and third (Bracken, Shepard, Holford, et al., 1997) National Acute Spinal Cord Injury studies demonstrated that methylprednisolone treatment improves neurologic outcomes if given within 8 hours after the acute injury. If methylprednisolone treatment is initiated by 3 hours after the injury, it should be continued for 24 hours (Bracken et al., 1997). If treatment is initiated 3–8 hours after the acute SCI, methylprednisolone treatment should be continued for 48 hours. The use of methylprednisolone after 8 hours appears to offer no benefit. In addition to these recommendations, rapid reduction and/or stabilization of injuries causing spinal cord compression are critical to optimize neurologic outcomes (Delamarter & Coyle, 1999).

Physical Examination

The physical examination is limited by the need for spinal stabilization. If the child is still unconscious, then vital signs, assessment of mentation and cranial nerves, response to pain above and below the suspected level of injury, and evaluation of abdominal, cremasteric, anal wink, bulbocavernosus, and deep tendon reflexes (DTRs) should be attempted. If the child is conscious, further assessment of sensation to pain, touch, position, vibration, and cold should be done if the child is old enough to cooper-

Table 16.2.   Presence or absence of anal wink, bulbocavernosus, and cremasteric reflexes in conus and cauda equina injuries

Reflex	Conus	Cauda equina
Anal wink	May be present or absent	Absent
Bulbocavernosus	May be present or absent	Absent
Cremasteric	May be present or absent	May be asymmetrical

ate. In cases involving thoracic SCI, which is rare, abdominal reflexes can help to localize the level of injury. Assessment of anal wink, cremasteric, and bulbocavernosus reflexes (the latter being done by inserting a gloved finger in the rectum, then pressing the penis or the clitoris) can help differentiate between a conus medullaris or cauda equina injury (see Table 16.2). In evaluating the level of injury, dermatome charts (see the Appendix at the end of this chapter) may be used to evaluate sensory levels. Table 16.3 presents the segmental innervation of different muscles as a guide to determining the level of the child's motor impairment.

After the child's admission to the acute care setting, daily evaluation of motor and sensory levels is indicated because function levels may rise or fall during the first few days following injury. Immediately following the injury, DTRs below the level of injury are absent, except where motor sparing has occurred. The emergence of previously absent DTRs indicates the end of spinal shock. In the case of injuries above T4 (or above T8, according to some authorities), once the child has emerged from spinal shock, autonomic dysreflexia precautions should be instituted (see subsequent discussion under the "Autonomic Dysreflexia" heading in this chapter).

Table 16.3.   Segmented innervation and function of specific muscles

Function	Muscles	Level
Inspiration	Diaphragm	C3, C4, C5
Elbow flexion	Biceps brachii Brachioradialis	C5, C6
Wrist extension	Extensor carpi radialis	C6, C7
Elbow extension	Triceps	C7, C8
Fine finger control	Interossei Thenar muscles	C8, T1
Hip flexion	Iliopsoas	L2, L3
Knee extension	Quadriceps	L3, L4
Ankle dorsiflexion	Tibialis anterior	L4, L5
Great toe extension	Extensor hallucis longus	L5, S1
Ankle plantarflexion	Gastrocsoleus	S1, S2

Skin   The child's skin must be examined daily, particularly pressure points such as the heels, sacrum, elbows, scapulae, and occiput. Skin breakdown under a halovest or Minerva jacket for spinal stabilization is not uncommon and should be looked for meticulously. Infants and toddlers are especially prone to occipital breakdown. Implementing precautionary measures such as "moon boots," air beds, and careful attention to position change helps prevent breakdown. Even when such measures are instituted, however, poor nutrition, impaired sensation, and impaired blood flow to the skin may still lead to breakdown.

Pulmonary Status   Ongoing evaluation of pulmonary status and aggressive management of pulmonary dysfunction must be performed, even in individuals with low paraplegia. Chest physical therapy and postural drainage, incentive spirometry, resistance spirometry, frequent position changes, and even activities such as blowing bubbles or singing loudly in the case of younger children are techniques that can be employed to improve the child's pulmonary function and address or prevent microatelectasis.

Bladder Function   During the acute phase of injury, the bladder is usually atonic. Once the Foley catheter is discontinued, staff may misinterpret intermittent overflow voiding as spontaneous bladder functioning. For this reason, upon discontinuance of an indwelling catheter, clean intermittent catheterization (CIC) must be instituted. If spontaneous voiding seems to be occurring, postvoid residuals should be done at least three times. If the residuals are less than 100 cubic centimeters (or in the case of children under age 13 years, less than 30 cubic centimeters plus the child's age in years multiplied by 5 cubic centimeters), the detrusor may be assumed to be working and CIC may be discontinued. Detrusor dyssynergia is not ruled out, however, and further urologic workup may be indicated (see subsequent discussion under "Evaluation and Management of Medical Issues" heading in this chapter).

Bowel Function   Immediately following SCI, gastrointestinal motility is inhibited and rectal tone is usually flaccid. Thus, as soon as enteral feeding is begun, an aggressive bowel program must be instituted, usually consisting of a stool softener such as docusate sodium, fiber, adequate fluids, and a glycerin or bisacodyl suppository administered daily at the same time of day, usually right after breakfast or right after dinner. It may be necessary to address gastrointestinal motility using metoclopramide or cisapride, but often an aggressive, scheduled bowel program in combination with enteral feeding stimulates peristalsis (see the Medications Frequently Used in Spinal Cord Injury form in the Appendix at the end of this chapter).

Other Medical Complications Other medical complications of SCI that must be sought and addressed include the common ones such as hypertension or hypotension; pneumothorax; ileus; aspiration pneumonia; gastrointestinal hemorrhage; urinary tract infections (UTIs); fractures of extremities; contusions of the kidney(s), liver, spleen, gut, or lung(s); thrombophlebitis (particularly with regard to children older than 14 years of age); and acute malnutrition. Less common complications are myocardial contusion, inappropriate antidiuretic hormone (ADH) secretion, adrenocortical insufficiency, renal tubular acidosis, renal and bladder calculi, fat emboli, and superior mesenteric artery (SMA) insufficiency. SMA is also known as *cast syndrome* and represents the combined result of the supine positioning of a thin, malnourished individual and the external compression of the individual's abdominal contents, usually by a body cast or a body jacket. SMA insufficiency is difficult to treat, particularly in the presence of an unstable spine requiring an orthosis; but measures such as jejunal feeding, upright positioning as often as possible, avoidance of the supine position, and (sometimes) hyperalimentation can be employed. Spinal stabilization of an unstable cervical spine injury is addressed by the neurosurgeon or the orthopedist and may consist of initial traction, then placement of a halovest; a thoracolumbosacral orthosis (TLSO); or, in the case of a thoracic or lumbar fracture or dislocation, anterior or posterior fusion and instrumentation followed by fitting of a halovest or a TLSO. Children with quadriplegia have difficulty with regulating their body temperature. This poikilothermia may lead to wide temperature swings; but in the case of persistent high or low body temperature, infection must be ruled out. In young children with quadriplegia, elevated temperatures have been associated with autonomic dysreflexia; but inappropriate ambient temperature or infection should always be the initial presumption.

INPATIENT REHABILITATION PROGRAM

The inpatient rehabilitation team consists of the following professionals:

- *Physiatrist:* Medical director of the team; if the physiatrist is also a pediatrician, he or she can manage medical complications that are unique to pediatric cases
- *Pediatrician:* Addresses medical complications during the child's inpatient stay at the hospital
- *Physical therapist:* Counsels with regard to mobility and transfer skills; assists with the prescription of braces, wheelchairs, and other positioning equipment
- *Occupational therapist:* Advises with regard to hygiene, grooming, dressing, bathing, and other fine motor skills; in cases of quadriplegia, may work on switch accessibility and academic skills such as writing or computer skills
- *Speech-language pathologist (SLP):* Involved if there is also a traumatic brain injury (TBI) or if the child has quadriplegia; in the latter case, works on the child's vocalization, breath support, and respiratory control and dysphagia issues
- *Respiratory therapist:* In the case of quadriplegia, carries out treatment and instructs caregivers on respiratory hygiene, including chest physical therapy, postural draining, and nebulizers; works closely with the SLP on voicing issues
- *Medical social worker:* Identifies resources and provides family counseling; updates the insurance case manager
- *Psychologist:* Assists the child and the child's family with adjustment issues; addresses behavioral issues on the inpatient unit
- *Educator:* Assists the child and the child's family with regard to the child's school reentry and provides tutoring to children who are hospitalized during the academic year
- *Rehabilitation nurse:* Performs and instructs the child and the child's family with regard to continuing care issues such as bowel and bladder management and nutrition; carries out the rehabilitation team plan on a 24-hour basis, including transfers, mobility, self-care, behavior, and adjustment issues

Functional Expectations for Level of Injury

Once the child has stabilized medically, inpatient rehabilitation is usually indicated. In order to meet the criteria for intensive inpatient rehabilitation, the child must

- Be medically stable
- Be able to tolerate at least 3 hours of therapy per day

- Have an appropriate discharge location in place (e.g., a biological or foster family that is willing and able to care for the child)
- Have realistic goals for rehabilitation based on the severity of the injury

The primary care physician can play an important role in assessing the likelihood of a successful discharge to the family's home, identifying important psychosocial issues that may affect the success of the rehabilitation program, assisting with the setting of realistic goals, and advocating for the most appropriate location and level of rehabilitation services for the child. The level of injury can assist the physician in setting realistic long-term goals (see Table 16.4). A halovest or a TLSO inhibits mobility enough that mobility goals often are not achievable until the orthosis is discontinued, which may be as long as 3 months postinjury.

Until the advent of managed care, inpatient rehabilitation stays for SCIs lasted 3–6 months. By discharge, the individual was out of spinal shock, no longer needed to use an orthosis, and was able to achieve appropriate functional goals. In the 1990s, the length of hospital stays for SCI decreased significantly (Eastwood, Hagglund, Ragnarsson, et al., 1999). Unfortunately, this situation has resulted in increased adverse events at 1 year following SCI (Eastwood et al., 1999). Most individuals with paraplegia do not remain in the acute rehabilitation setting for more than 4 weeks, and most individuals with quadriplegia stay for 6–8 weeks. Since the orthoses usually must be worn for 2–3 months, individuals with SCI must try to complete many of their rehabilitation goals as outpatients. Depending on the availability of services where the individual lives, these goals may or may not be accomplished. On occasion, an individual must be readmitted to inpatient rehabilitation to achieve the maximum level of function. Table 16.4 reviews reasonable functional goals for different levels of neurologic injury.

Evaluation and Management of Medical Complications

A brief review of medical problems associated with SCI is located in the Appendix at the end of this chapter. It provides information for health professionals and families on recognition of SCI and the appropriate rehabilitative actions to take. The most common complications during the postacute injury phase of SCI include recurrent UTIs, bowel and bladder incontinence, skin breakdown, spasticity, heterotopic ossification, joint contractures, scoliosis, and osteopenia and fractures. As mentioned previously, in people with an SCI above T4, autonomic dysreflexia is a

dangerous and important complication. Other initial management issues are the diagnosis and treatment of syringomyelia and the home ventilation program.

Urologic Issues

Recurrent Urinary Tract Infections   During the month following SCI, a renal and bladder ultrasonography (US) should be obtained in order to identify anatomical abnormalities as well as the presence of renal or bladder stones. Subsequently, renal and bladder US should be obtained every 6 months in order to monitor the urinary tract. Periodic urine cultures and sensitivities should be obtained so that when a febrile UTI occurs, the likely organisms are identified already. Antibiotic treatment and prophylaxis should be used with caution because development of resistance to a wide range of antibiotics is common. Colonization of the urinary tract is to be expected with CIC. Asymptomatic bacteriuria should not be treated with antibiotics.

If renal or bladder stones are present, the individual should be seen by a pediatric urologist or a renal specialist if possible. Bladder stones need to be removed cystoscopically and analyzed, and the child's diet must be adjusted appropriately to prevent further formation of bladder stones. Large renal stones that cause obstruction may also need to be removed. The stones serve as a nidus of infection and must thus be identified as soon as possible and treated aggressively.

Upper Motor Neuron Bladder   The choice of bladder management depends on whether the bladder is spastic (upper motor neuron) or flaccid (lower motor neuron). On occasion, when bladder spasticity is mild, a balanced bladder can be achieved with low-dose anticholinergics such as oxybutynin and suprapubic stimulation to initiate voiding, either by tapping with the forefinger for about 1 minute or by applying a cold, damp washcloth. In most cases, however, the upper motor neuron bladder is characterized by strong spastic detrusor contractions that may or may not be in synergy with the sphincter. Typically, a feedback loop ensures that contraction of the detrusor is accompanied by relaxation of the sphincter and that appropriate bladder volumes and pressures are maintained. In the case of dyssynergia, the sphincter does not necessarily relax when detrusor contractions occur. High bladder pressures cause reflux into the upper tract as well as thickening of the bladder wall, which results in a small, noncompliant bladder.

Urodynamic studies can quantify bladder pressures, bladder volume, and contractions of the detrusor and sphincter muscles. This information can

Table 16.4. Functional outcomes for different levels of neurologic injury

Injury level	Functional expectations
C1–C3	Relies on ventilator, but family understands ventilator and tracheostomy care, can perform bag and mask respiration and suction, and is trained in cardiopulmonary resuscitation (CPR)
	Patient can use Passey-Muir valve for verbal communication
	Patient may drive wheelchair using sip-and-puff mechanism or head switch
	Patient can use computer and environmental control unit (ECU) with modified scanning or voice activation
	Family trained in dependent transfers
C4	Patient can drive wheelchair using sip-and-puff mechanism or head or tongue switch
	Patient is skillful using mouthstick to write, or paint, or to use ECU
	Patient is skillful using mouthstick, switches, or voice activation to access computer or ECU
	Family understands pulmonary toilet and is trained in CPR
	Family trained in dependent transfers with or without a lift
C5	Dresses upper trunk
	Turns self in bed with side rails
	Propels manual wheelchair with hand rim projections over level surfaces
	Propels power wheelchair with joystick for uneven surfaces or rough terrain, long distances, or improved efficiency
	Feeds self by using hand splints
	Sliding board transfers with moderate assistance to and from bed
C6	All of C5 goals
	Transfers from wheelchair to auto with moderate assistance
	Skilled in use of tenodesis splint and/or universal cuff
	Assists with transfer to and from commode by using sliding board
C7	Independent transfers to bed, car, toilet, and/or commode chair
	Self-feeds with universal cuff or built-up utensils
	Dresses upper and lower extremities with assistive devices and modified fasteners
	Propels manual wheelchair with friction-coated rims; may need power chair for uneven terrain or greater efficiency
C8, T1–T4	Self-feeds without assistive devices
	Dresses without assistive devices; may need modified fasteners
	Transfers from wheelchair to floor and returns independently
	Propels manual chair up and down curbs
	Transfers in and out of tub
T5–T11	Total manual wheelchair independence with advanced skills
	Can be considered for ambulation using knee-ankle-foot orthoses (KAFOs) or ground-reaction AFOs (GRAFOs) and crutches or walker (for exercise)
T12–L1	Functional ambulation with KAFOs or GRAFOs and crutches or walker
L2–L4	Ambulation with AFOs and forearm crutches
L5	Ambulation with or without AFOs having plantarflexion assist and with crutches or cane
S1	May achieve partial or complete bowel and/or bladder control

be used to develop an appropriate bladder management program. Urodynamic studies are invalid while the child is still in spinal shock and, because of neurologic changes during the first few months following injury, may need to be repeated 1 year after the initial study. When urodynamic studies are not available, the force and frequency of voids as well as the volumes and information from the renal and bladder US can give the treating physi-

cian a fair idea of bladder function and compliance. The voiding cystourethrogram (VCUG) is an essential study for the diagnosis and management of vesicoureteral reflux (VUR). The child or adolescent with VUR is at increased risk of febrile UTIs and resultant renal damage. Antibiotic prophylaxis is indicated for children with VUR.

If a spastic bladder is present when the child is no longer in spinal shock, he or she will be incontinent between catheterizations. The bladder can then be paralyzed partially with oxybutynin (see Medications Frequently Used in Spinal Cord Injury form in the Appendix at the end of this chapter) beginning at the lowest appropriate dose and titrating upward until continence between clean intermittent catheterizations (CICs) is achieved. Sometimes sphincter tone needs to be augmented by using ephedrine or pseudoephedrine; imipramine can also act with any of the previous medications in a synergistic manner to promote continence in a CIC program. The Mitrofanoff procedure (Mitrofanoff, 1980) may allow some individuals with low quadriplegia to perform CIC independently. It involves use of the child's appendix to make a continent catheterizable conduit to the bladder. Please also see the discussion in Chapter 13.

Lower Motor Neuron Bladder   If a flaccid bladder with sphincter insufficiency is present, incontinence between catheterizations may still occur. In such a case, close attention to the bowel program is extremely important because a mass of stool pressing on the bladder can cause incontinence. Ephedrine, pseudoephedrine, and/or imipramine can also be used. Sometimes full continence is not achievable with a lower motor neuron bladder, however, and peripads or large diapers may be necessary.

Other Bladder Management Options   Other bladder management options for adults with quadriplegia, such as indwelling urethral catheters or suprapubic catheters, are not recommended for children because long-term use of these methods results in a small, noncompliant bladder. Once the individual is older than age 18 years and wishes to live independently, a suprapubic catheter may be an acceptable option. Indwelling urethral catheters are associated with irreparable damage to the urethra and are not recommended for ongoing use. They can be useful during travel when rest rooms may not be easily available or accessible. Condom catheters are sometimes helpful to young males who have sphincter insufficiency; however, most individuals complain of leakage, and skin breakdown beneath the condom is common. Epididymitis is a complication seen in chronic users of condom catheters or indwelling urethral catheters. The use of implantable anterior sacral root stimulators (Egon, Barat, Colombel, et al., 1998), as well as the use of functional electrical stimulation (Fall, 1998) to improve bladder continence, continues to be primarily of research interest.

Decubiti   Skin breakdown is more often seen in adolescents and adults than in children, but it is

Table 16.5.   Classification of decubiti

Grade I	Erythema without involvement of subcutaneous tissue
Grade II	Partial penetration through the epidermis
Grade III	Penetration through the dermis with exposure of muscle or fascia
Grade IV	Penetration through the subcutaneous tissues with exposure of bone

a danger in all age groups. The breakdown is a result of shearing that is due to improper weight transfer or weight shifts (including reclining wheelchairs, which actually promote shear), moisture (from excessive sweating, urinary incontinence, or plastic seat materials), unrelieved pressure on bony prominences, or a combination of all three. Decubitus ulcers are classified as shown in Table 16.5. The most effective management of skin breakdown, of course, is prevention (see Table 16.6). Children and their families must understand the importance of daily (preferably twice daily) skin inspection. Children who are old enough should be provided with long-handled mirrors. Good nutrition, safe transfers, effective pressure relief every 20 minutes, and appropriate seating and positioning must be emphasized. Many times, in spite of vigorous preventive and educational efforts regarding skin care, breakdown does occur. When skin breakdown develops, the most important step is to determine the cause of the breakdown. Did the child or the child's family forget to adjust the gel in the cushion on a daily basis? Is the child's seating system inappropriate? Are the child's weight transfers traumatic to the skin? If a Grade I lesion is present, correction of the offending practice is usually adequate. The treatment of skin breakdown is reviewed in Table 16.7. The wound can be covered with a semipermeable dressing until the redness is gone. If a Grade II or Grade III skin breakdown is noted, the child must be kept off the decubitus until healing is nearly complete. Devitalized tissue can be debrided chemically by using a product such as Santyl. Wet-to-dry dressings are no longer recommended, be-

Table 16.6.   Prevention of decubiti

Twice-daily skin inspection of buttocks, heels, and other pressure points
Good nutrition
Safe transfers
Effective pressure relief every 15–20 minutes
Appropriate cushion
Appropriate positioning

Table 16.7.   Treatment of skin breakdown

Grade I	Identify and correct the cause of the breakdown Semipermeable dressing Strict adherence to pressure reliefs
Grade II	Strictly limit weight-bearing on affected area (i.e., no more than ½ hour two to three times per day) Cleanse gently with water or soap and water twice daily Apply calcium alginate powder or gel and cover with an occlusive dressing, if no devitalization is present Alternatively, leave dressing on for 2–3 days and then cleanse and apply occlusive dressing
Grade III	No weight-bearing on affected area Consider a specialized mattress (such as a One-Step, which can be provided in the home, or admission to a skilled nursing facility for a Clinitron or a Kinn-Air bed) If devitalized tissue is present, chemically debride with daily cleansing and application of Santyl If no devitalized tissue is present, dress as per Grade II If tunneling is present, *lightly* pack with Nugauze
Grade IV	Consult plastic surgeon

cause they appear to prolong the healing process by traumatizing the newly formed tissue. If devitalized tissue is not present, a calcium alginate powder or gel can be placed in the wound and occlusive dressings can be applied. In the case of a Grade IV skin breakdown, involvement of the periosteum must be ruled out and a plastic surgeon should be consulted to determine whether primary removal and closure or rotation of a musculocutaneous flap is required. On occasion, tunneling or deep breakdown at the interface between the bone and tissue may be present, even though it is not obvious on visual inspection of a Grade II or Grade III skin breakdown. Exploration of the wound with a cotton swab rules out significant tunneling. Deep breakdown cannot be ruled out; but the treating physician or nurse must always be suspicious, particularly if the wound is over a bony prominence and is caused primarily by pressure.

Spasticity   The management of spasticity in SCI is slightly different from that caused by cerebral dysfunction. Spasticity is more often associated with widespread extensor and/or flexor spasms in response to stimulation than with the cogwheeling tone noted in cerebral palsy. These spasms may cause discomfort or, in quadriplegia, respiratory

distress. They are generally tolerated well, unless they cause severe discomfort or interfere with transfers or seating. Children with incomplete SCI may experience spasticity that is more severe than that of those with a complete injury, and individuals with quadriplegia appear to have more difficulty than people with paraplegia, probably because of their relative immobility. Frequent joint ranging and position changes help to reduce spasticity, but many individuals require medication.

Oral baclofen is quite effective in the majority of SCI cases, and supplementation with low-dose diazepam may be needed. Other medications have been found to be useful in some individuals who did not respond to that regimen (Gracies, Nance, Elovic, et al., 1997; Katz, 1988). When spasticity is severe, however, it is important to look for an irritant below the level of injury. Renal or bladder calculi, a UTI, an untreated spastic bladder, fecal impaction, skin breakdown, or an ingrown toenail may cause increased spasticity. If any of these conditions is found, it must be treated before any change in treatment regimen is considered. Although splinting to prevent excessive spasm is useful in combination with passive range of motion, the use of tone-reducing ankle–foot orthoses (AFOs) has not been found to be as effective in SCI cases as in cerebral spasticity cases.

Continuous intrathecal baclofen infusion (CIBI) with a subcutaneous programmable pump offers another treatment alternative if other treatments have been unsuccessful. For a discussion of the complications and disadvantages of CIBI treatments, please see Chapter 6. The use of botulinum toxin intramuscularly has not been studied in the control of spasms but probably is not of practical use because of the widespread involvement of large muscle groups below the level of injury. In cases of severe spasms of adults that are unresponsive to any of these measures, laser rhizotomy or myelotomy is sometimes used. It is rarely recommended, however, because the resulting flaccidity causes an increased incidence of skin breakdown and may be associated with increased bladder and bowel incontinence.

Deep Vein Thrombosis   Children are at significant risk for deep vein thrombosis (DVT) during the first 8–12 weeks following SCI. Their risk is only slightly lower than that of adults. Therefore, children should be treated with prophylactic subcutaneous low-molecular-weight heparin (e.g., Lovenox) and techniques to prevent venous stasis in the legs, such as the use of support stockings (Radecki & Gaebler-Spira, 1994).

Heterotopic Ossification Heterotopic ossification (HO) is the deposition of calcium in periarticular regions and must be differentiated from myositis ossificans, which is the deposition of calcium in muscle, usually following trauma. HO is seen most often following central nervous system (CNS) injury, is seen more frequently in adults than in children, is observed more often following SCI than following TBI, and is seen most frequently within the first 6 months postinjury. In SCI, HO occurs below the level of injury and may present as a low-grade, persistent elevation of temperature. Asymmetrical limitation of joint movement or asymmetric swelling or warmth of a joint should also raise the suspicion that HO may be present. If the child is at least 1 month postinjury, plain radiographs of the joint may show the presence of HO. If the radiographs are negative and the index of suspicion is high, or if the child is less than 1 month postinjury, a triplephase bone scan is the most sensitive method for diagnosing the condition.

If HO is present, the treatment of choice is frequent passive ranging of the joint. Splinting or casting the joint is strongly contraindicated. Physical management (i.e., passive range of motion) is often adequate to control the progress of HO in children and adolescents. Medical management with sodium etidronate is used in adults but is contraindicated in children and adolescents because the development of rickets has been reported in association with its long-term use (Chiodo & Nelson, 1987; Silverman, Hurvitz, Nelson, & Chiodo, 1994). Indomethacin has also been found to be effective; however, it should be used cautiously. If HO remains untreated, the joint may ankylose. Surgery is not effective until the HO has matured, a process that usually takes 1–3 years. It is not unusual for HO to recur following surgery of the joint. Fortunately, joint ankylosis due to HO is less common in children with SCI than in older teenagers and adults with SCI.

Other Orthopedic Complications Children must be monitored for joint contractures, scoliosis, and osteopenia and fractures. All are difficult to prevent.

Joint Contractures and Hip Dislocation Although splinting and position changes help prevent contractures, most children with SCI develop hip and knee flexion contractures after years of wheelchair use. Even those individuals who are ambulatory and use knee-ankle-foot orthoses (KAFOs) and crutches or walkers also develop flexion contractures of the lower extremities. Although meticulous use of a standing frame for several hours per day has been

used, its efficacy is unproved. It also may be difficult for a family or a classroom to be able to fit such a regimen into their schedule. Use of the standing frame is important because lower-extremity flexion contractures may ultimately result in improper pressures in both sitting and lying and contribute to skin breakdown.

It is important to monitor joint range of motion every 6–12 months. Goniometry by an experienced physical therapist or physician is the most accurate monitoring method. In most cases, if the contracture of the hip or knee is less than 20°, an interval physical therapy program (e.g., three times per week for 3–4 weeks) with the use of prone positioning with or without weights may be effective. In the case of knees, dynamic splinting or serial casting also can improve the child's joint range of motion. Unless the child and his or her family are dedicated to maintaining the joint range of motion, the gains may be lost within several months. If the contractures are interfering with a standing or walking program and are greater than 30°, then surgical intervention may be warranted.

In one study (Betz, 1997), 87% of children who sustained an SCI before age 5 years developed dislocated hips. Ranging and weight bearing should not be discouraged, however, unless the hip dislocation produces pain or dysreflexia. The status of the hips should also be monitored regularly by examinations and plain radiographs.

Scoliosis Virtually all children who sustain an SCI before 10 years of age develop scoliosis (Betz, 1997). Scoliosis is a particularly difficult management problem in infants and children with quadriplegia. TLSOs have questionable efficacy and may impair pulmonary function. Premature surgical intervention retards growth, ultimately leading to pulmonary function impairment; however, delayed surgical intervention can result in an uncorrectable curvature and ventilation impairment. Improper seating hastens the appearance of scoliosis, although no firm evidence that proper seating slows the onset of paralytic scoliosis exists.

It is important to monitor the spine with plain radiographs at least every year and every 6 months during rapid growth. It is likely, although unproved, that proper use of a standing frame may delay the onset of paralytic scoliosis. If the child's spinal curve is progressing at the rate of 5° every 6 months or if the curve is 20°–40°, most clinicians prescribe a brace. Once the child's spinal curve reaches 40°, it is usually best to stabilize the spine surgically. Bracing has been shown to slow the progression of the spinal curve in 50% of individuals with SCI (Betz, 1997), but it also decreases the child's abilities to transfer and toilet and increases dependence on caregivers. Thus, the decision to brace should be weighed against the decrease in the child's independence.

Osteopenia and Fractures Osteopenia is inevitable in individuals who spend the majority of their time in a wheelchair. Children with SCI have been shown to have a bone density that is 60% that of children without disabilities of the same age and gender (Betz, 1997). Regular weight bearing by use of a standing frame has been prescribed to prevent osteopenia. Unfortunately, controlled experiments (Kunkel, Scremin, Eisenberg, et al., 1993) have not supported this treatment but do suggest that active loading and unloading of muscles and bones during exercise reduce osteoporosis. Prevention or correction of osteopenia by using a functional electrical stimulation (FES) program appears to be most effective. In FES, muscle contraction is stimulated via electrodes that are in contact with the skin; the electrodes are usually embedded in spandex clothing and are connected to a computer program that times the firing of muscles to allow for stationary bicycling or ambulation. Research studies (BeDell, Scremin, Perell, & Kunkel, 1996; Bloomfield, Mysiw, & Jackson, 1996) have shown that FES preserves muscle bulk below the level of the lesion and decreases osteopenia and the attendant fractures. FES, however, is still primarily of research interest. Such a program is time consuming and expensive, and few spinal cord centers use it regularly. Furthermore, its cost is not reimbursed by most insurance companies, and the equipment would be difficult to use at home. The treatment recommended most often for children with SCI is adequate dietary intake of calcium and vitamin D. High doses of calcium and vitamin D have not been found to be more effective than the Food and Drug Administration's (FDA's) recommended daily allowance.

Upper-Extremity Function Selected muscle and tendon transfers (James, 1996) and the use of FES can improve upper-extremity function and an individual's independence. If the neurologic injury is complete, upper-extremity surgery should be delayed until at least 1 year after the injury. If the injury is incomplete, wait until motor recovery has plateaued. A representative surgery is transfer of the deltoid to the triceps to improve elbow extension and to enable the individual to reach overhead and assist with pressure relief in the wheelchair. An eight-channel FES system, the Freehand System, may be implanted to restore lateral pinch and palmar grasp to improve the individual's self-care,

writing, and socialization (Davis, Mulcahey, Smith, & Betz, 1998; Mulcahey, Betz, Smith, et al., 1997). Data on the use of the Freehand System are limited. Contraindications to the use of FES are lower motor neuron damage (flaccid paralysis) and upper-extremity contractures. Problems with the use of the Freehand System include difficulty with transfers and the need for assistance in donning the system.

Syringomyelia As many as 50% of children with SCI develop syringomyelia (Betz, 1997). The presence of syringomyelia does not correlate with pain, dysreflexia, hyperesthesia, or hyperhidrosis but does correlate with spasticity. It is imperative to track sensation, muscle strength and tone, and bowel and/or bladder function. Posttraumatic syringomyelia can occur at any time following the injury and may present with decreased sensation and muscle strength, increased spasticity and muscle spasms, severe pain, or a decrease in bowel and/or bladder function. If changes are noted in any of the preceding symptoms without an obvious cause, posttraumatic syringomyelia should be considered. In addition, if the child has unexplained pain or dysreflexia, consider syringomyelia in the differential diagnosis.

Syringomyelia is best diagnosed by an MRI scan, but if the child has been instrumented, a CT scan gives a satisfactory diagnosis. The presence of a syrinx on neuroimaging that is not accompanied by symptoms is not an indication for intervention. Syringomyelia is a clinical diagnosis that is supported by the neuroimaging studies. If the child is symptomatic and a syrinx is present, the child should be referred to a neurosurgeon who is experienced in the care of individuals with SCI.

Autonomic Dysreflexia Acute autonomic dysreflexia (AAD) is a life-threatening discharge of the sympathetic nervous system that can occur when sympathetic outflow is blocked, as in injury above the T4 level. It is precipitated by a noxious stimulus below the level of injury. It manifests itself with acute and sometimes severe hypertension, bradycardia, flushing above the injury level, and headache. Because the autonomic nervous system in young children is immature, AAD may present with tachycardia in lieu of bradycardia, no flushing, and elevation of temperature. Hypertension is present, however. AAD is a medical emergency, and all caregivers must be aware of it. The first line of treatment is to identify and remove the offending stimulus. Make sure that the child and his or her family are given a laminated AAD protocol to present to medical personnel who may not have experience with AAD (see the Appendix at the end of this chapter). If AAD occurs, the following steps must be taken:

- The child should be placed in or should remain in an upright sitting position.
- If the child has a catheter, it should be checked to be certain it is draining properly. If the catheter is not draining properly, it must be changed immediately.
- If the child has no catheter, he or she should be catheterized immediately to empty the bladder.
- If catheterization does not relieve the child's AAD symptoms, tight clothing or shoes should be removed and hypertension should be treated as per the protocol.

Once the child's hypertension is controlled, the examiner should do a rectal examination using lidocaine jelly and remove any impacted stool. He or she should also look for skin breakdown, fracture, ingrown toenail, or any other potentially noxious stimulus below the level of injury, such as acute thrombophlebitis. If the child is an adolescent female, menstrual cramping or miscarriage can precipitate AAD.

Chronic autonomic dysreflexia with low-grade hypertension and chronic headache is not uncommon. Although it is not an emergency, a process similar to that used to treat AAD must be followed. An occult fracture, UTI, detrusor dyssynergia, or low-grade skin breakdown or infection below the level of injury must be sought. No satisfactory pharmaceutical treatment of chronic dysreflexia has been found, although a variety of medications have been tried, including phenoxybenzamine, clonidine, and other antihypertensive agents. Regular bladder and bowel continence programs are important preventative measures.

Home Ventilation In most cases, families wish to take home a child who uses a ventilator to breathe. Home ventilation is associated with a lower incidence of complications such as pneumonia, skin breakdown, and joint contractures than ventilation in a hospital or an institutional setting, and home therefore is the most appropriate setting for a child who is dependent on a ventilator (Nelson, Carroll, Hurvitz, & Dean, 1996). Relatively few long-term care facilities exist that are able to take care of children who use ventilators. In the rare instance in which the family is unable or unwilling to care for such a child at home, medical foster care has been a successful alternative.

The discharge-planning process for a child requiring ventilation takes about 3 weeks, particularly if the child is being discharged to a rural environment. In most cases, the home care agency that provides the services needs to hire and train the home nursing team. This process may be extremely challenging in a rural environment, which may have a limited number of medical professionals with pediatric and/or respiratory expertise. Typically, the home health agency requires a minimum of 2 weeks to hire and train the home nursing team, which consists of six to eight nurses who provide 12–16 hours of nursing daily. It is best if the agency can be notified at least 3 weeks prior to the child's discharge from the hospital or acute care facility. Therefore, on the day the child or youth is admitted to the rehabilitation service for home ventilation training, the home health agency must be notified.

By the time of discharge, the family must be trained in CPR; must know how to suction and bag the child and change the tracheostomy; must have a working knowledge of the portable ventilator and be able to do some basic troubleshooting; and must understand the use of mist, a portable nose, and a Passey-Muir valve. They must possess these skills in addition to the many other caregiving skills that any parent of a child or adolescent with SCI needs.

The list of equipment and supplies required for home ventilation is formidable (see the Appendix at the end of this chapter) and includes a backup ventilator, a home generator in remote rural locations, a chair with a ventilator tray, portable and stationary suction machines, portable oxygen, mist, additional tracheostomy tubes, a hospital bed, bagging equipment, and suction catheters. Most of this equipment must be special-ordered and should be delivered to the family's home prior to the first weekend pass or before discharge.

An excellent resource for medical professionals who are handling home ventilation cases is *Ventilator-Assisted Patient Care: Planning for Hospital Discharge and Home Care* (Johnson, Giovannoni, & Driscoll, 1986), which contains teaching and monitoring flow sheets, equipment lists and emergency protocols, and a great deal of basic physiologic information.

Other Complications Another long-term issue in pediatric SCI cases is latex allergy, which develops in as many as 6%–18% of children with SCI (Vogel, 1997). For this reason, children's exposure to latex-containing compounds should be minimized. Please see the discussion in Chapter 13. In addition, individuals with SCI are more prone to severe respiratory infection than the population at large. For that reason, pneumococcal and yearly influenza vaccines are indicated. DVT can occur late in the course of SCI, but its incidence is rare.

Two studies of adults with SCI have reported that from 51% (Anderson, 1997) to 67% (Kannisto & Sintonen, 1997) are gainfully employed. One of the studies (Kannisto & Sintonen, 1997) evaluated quality-of-life indicators in 28 adults with SCI. The individuals studied rated continence, mobility, social participation, and working relatively low and communication, hearing, seeing, breathing, mental functioning, depression, and distress relatively high in importance with regard to quality of life. In another study (Vogel, Klaas, Lubicky, et al., 1998), psychosocial factors such as education, employment, and social opportunities were rated more important to long-term life satisfaction of adults who had sustained SCIs as children than were level of injury, age at injury, or duration of injury.

The physiatrist and/or the pediatrician also need to discuss the issues of sexuality and fertility with older children and adolescents and their parents. In males with complete SCI, conception may require electroejaculation techniques. Females with SCI are able to conceive; however, the pregnancy may be complicated by urologic deterioration and an increased risk for AAD. The risk for AAD is especially increased during labor and delivery.

OUTPATIENT REHABILITATION

After discharge from inpatient rehabilitation, a limited outpatient program is usually indicated so that the child can develop self-care and mobility skills further. Therapy services serve primarily to monitor the child's function and progress and to update the home program. If the child is discharged with a TLSO, he or she is not likely to be able to perform advanced wheelchair skills, which include going up curbs, getting from the chair to the floor safely, and vice versa. The outpatient therapists may need to see the child two to three times per week to complete the motor goals of the rehabilitation plan. In addition, the child needs ongoing support to become independent with the bowel and bladder programs and with bathroom transfers.

Home health nursing is probably the most appropriate service for completion of the bladder and bowel independence program. The home health component should be prescribed first (e.g., occupational therapy [OT] for bathroom safety and transfers and nursing for bowel and bladder independence) because home health and outpatient services may not be authorized simultaneously under insurance restrictions. After the home health component is prescribed, the outpatient physical therapy (PT) component for advanced mobility skills can be set up.

In most cases, the outpatient goals can be accomplished in a short time (e.g., four to eight visits to the outpatient department). Then monitoring can take place on a monthly to a semiannual basis, depending on the child's age and the time elapsed since injury. Medical therapy services must be coordinated with educational and school-based therapy services. Table 16.8 reviews specific issues in the care of the child with SCI that should be monitored every 6–12 months. The regular monitoring is best performed by an experienced rehabilitation team of therapists and other specialists working in conjunction with the primary care physician.

ROLE OF THE PRIMARY CARE PHYSICIAN

The primary care physician (PCP) can play an active role during all phases of the child's care. Immediately following injury, particularly in rural areas, it may be the PCP who sees the child in the local emergency room and transfers the child to a trauma center. In urban areas, the PCP often follows the child's progress in the intensive care unit and then takes over as the attending physician when the child is transferred to the acute pediatric ward.

During inpatient rehabilitation, the PCP can follow the patient jointly with the physiatrist and function as the pediatric consultant when necessary. He or she also plays an important support role for the family as the one who knows the family well. The PCP can also advocate for appropriate inpatient rehabilitation services for the child in con-

Table 16.8. Clinical issues in the care of a child with spinal cord injury

Clinical issues	Methods used to monitor
Mobility	History, observation
Self-care	History, observation
Academic performance	History, school report
Adjustment	History
Pain	History, observation, examination
Equipment	History, observation (e.g., inspect wheelchair brakes, tires, cushion)
Skin integrity	Physical examination
Bladder and bowel function	History, urinalysis/culture, rectal examination, renal and bladder ultrasound
Nutrition	Weight, skinfold thickness, lab
Joint range of motion	Goniometry
Muscle strength	Manual muscle testing
Sensation	Physical examination

junction with the rehabilitation team. Following inpatient rehabilitation, the PCP takes over once again as the primary medical manager of the child and is responsible for making the necessary referrals, providing care coordination, advocating for appropriate school-based medical and therapy services, and assisting the family and the child with regard to adjustment issues.

REFERENCES

American Spinal Injury Association (ASIA). (1992). *International standards for neurological and functional classification of spinal cord injury.* Chicago: Author.

Anderson, C.J. (1997). Unique management needs of pediatric spinal cord injury patients: Social issues. *Journal of Spinal Cord Medicine, 20*(1), 21–24.

BeDell, K.K., Scremin, A.M.E., Perell, K.L., & Kunkel, C.F. (1996). Effects of functional electrical stimulation-induced lower extremity cycling on bone density of spinal cord-injured patients. *American Journal of Physical Medicine and Rehabilitation, 75*(1), 29–34.

Betz, R.R. (1997). Unique management needs of pediatric spinal cord injury patients: Orthopedic problems in the child with spinal cord injury. *Journal of Spinal Cord Medicine, 20*(1), 14–16.

Bloomfield, S.A., Mysiw, W.J., & Jackson, R.D. (1996). Bone mass and endocrine adaptations to training in spinal cord injured individuals. *Bone, 19*(1), 61–68.

Bracken, M.B., Shepard, M.J., Collins, W.F., Jr., et al. (1992). Methylprednisolone or naloxone treatment after acute spinal cord injury: 1-year follow-up data. Results of the Second National Acute Spinal Cord Injury Study. *Journal of Neurosurgery, 76*(1), 23–31.

Bracken, M.B., Shepard, M.J., Holford, T.R., et al. (1997). Administration of methylprednisolone for 24 or 48 hours in the treatment of acute spinal cord injury: Results of the Third National Acute Spinal Cord Injury Randomized Controlled Trial: National Acute Spinal Cord Injury Study. *JAMA: Journal of the American Medical Association, 277*(20), 1597–1604.

Camay, A., & Tschantz, P. (1972). Mechanical influences in bone remodeling: Experimental research on Wolff's law. *Journal of Biomechanics, 5,* 173–180.

Chiodo, A.E., & Nelson, V.S. (1987). Rickets associated with etidronate use in a pediatric head injured patient. *Archives of Physical Medicine and Rehabilitation, 68,* 539–542.

Davis, S.E., Mulcahey, M.J., Smith, B.T., & Betz, R.R. (1998). Self-reported use of an implanted FES hand system by adolescents with tetraplegia. *Journal of Spinal Cord Medicine, 21*(3), 220–226.

Delamarter, R.B., & Coyle, J. (1999). Acute management of spinal cord injury. *Journal of the American Academy of Orthopaedic Surgeons, 7*(3), 166–175.

Eastwood, E.A., Hagglund, K.J., Ragnarsson, K.T., et al. (1999). Medical rehabilitation length of stay and outcomes for persons with traumatic spinal cord injury: 1990–1997. *Archives of Physical Medicine and Rehabilitation, 80,* 1457–1631.

Egon, G., Barat, M., Colombel, P., et al. (1998). Implantation of anterior sacral root stimulators combined with posterior sacral rhizotomy in spinal injury patients. *World Journal of Urology, 16*(5), 342–349.

Fall, M. (1998). Advantages and pitfalls of functional electrical stimulation. *Acta Obstetrica Gynecologica Scandinavia, 77*(Suppl. 168), 16–21.

Gracies, J.M., Nance, P., Elovic, E., et al. (1997). Traditional pharmacologic treatments for spasticity: Part II. General and regional treatments. *Muscle and Nerve Supplement, 6,* S92–S120.

James, M.A. (1996). Surgical treatment of the upper extremity: Indications, patient assessment, and procedures. In R.R. Betz & M.J. Mulcahey (Eds.), *The child with a spinal cord injury* (pp. 394–404). Rosemont, IL: American Academy of Orthopedic Surgeons.

Johnson, D.L., Giovannoni, R.M., & Driscoll, S.A. (Eds.). (1986). *Ventilator-assisted patient care: Planning for hospital discharge and home care.* Gaithersburg, MD: Aspen Publishers.

Kannisto, M., & Sintonen, H. (1997). Later health-related quality of life in adults who have sustained spinal cord injury in childhood. *Spinal Cord, 35*(11), 747–751.

Katz, R.T. (1988). Management of spasticity. *American Journal of Physical Medicine and Rehabilitation, 67*(3), 108–116.

Kunkel, C.F., Scremin, A.M., Eisenberg, B., et al. (1993). Effect of "standing" on spasticity, contracture, and osteoporosis in paralyzed males. *Archives of Physical Medicine and Rehabilitation, 74*(1), 73–78.

McBride, W.J., Gadowski, G.R., Keller, M.S., & Vane, D.W. (1994). Pulmonary embolism in pediatric trauma patients. *Journal of Trauma, 37*(6), 913–915.

Mitrofanoff, P. (1980). Trans-appendicular continent cystotomy in the management of the neurogenic bladder. *Chirugie Pediatrie, 21,* 297–305.

Mulcahey, M.J., Betz, R.R., Smith, B.T., et al. (1997). Implanted functional electrical stimulation hand system in adolescents with spinal injuries: An evaluation. *Archives of Physical Medicine and Rehabilitation, 78*(6), 597–607.

Nelson, V.S., Carroll, J.C., Hurvitz, E.A., & Dean, J.M. (1996). Home mechanical ventilation of children. *Developmental Medicine and Child Neurology, 38,* 704–715.

Pang, D., & Wilberger, J.E. (1982). Spinal cord injury without radiologic abnormalities in children. *Journal of Neurosurgery, 57,* 114–129.

Radecki, R.T., & Gaebler-Spira, D. (1994). Deep vein thrombosis in the disabled pediatric population. *Archives of Physical Medicine and Rehabilitation, 75,* 248–250.

Silverman, S.L., Hurvitz, E.A., Nelson, V.S., & Chiodo, A.E. (1994). Rachitic syndrome after disodium etidronate therapy in an adolescent. *Archives of Physical Medicine and Rehabilitation, 75*(1), 118–120.

Vogel, L.C. (1997). Unique management needs of pediatric spinal cord injury patients: Medical issues. *Spinal Cord Medicine, 20*(1), 17–20.

Vogel, L.C., Klaas, S.J., Lubicky, J.P., et al. (1998). Long-term outcomes and life satisfaction of adults who had spinal cord injuries. *Archives of Physical Medicine and Rehabilitation, 79,* 1496–1503.

Appendix

Guidelines for the Care of Children and Adolescents with Spinal Cord Injury

Basic Team

The special care needs of children with spinal cord injury (SCI) are best met by an experienced, coordinated team of specialists working collaboratively with parents, the primary care physician, and other service providers. Some young children with SCI may be followed by a team headed by a developmental pediatrician. Not all members of the basic team may be needed at each visit, and other professionals may be required. These professionals include but are not limited to an orthotist and a neurologist. Parents of children with SCI and/or children with SCI themselves should be encouraged to participate actively as part of the team. Please note that though a coordinated team is needed to manage the specialty services, all children require a medical home. The primary care physician is responsible for preventive and acute illness care and for assisting parents in coordinating the special services.

Regular members of the child development team include a pediatric physiatrist, a medical social worker, a neurosurgeon, a nurse, a nutritionist, an occupational therapist, an orthopedist, a physical therapist, a psychologist, and a urologist.

Initial Evaluation

The initial evaluation for rehabilitation needs should be performed as soon as possible after the child is medically stable following the injury. Some children are discharged for outpatient follow-up, others are discharged and then readmitted for inpatient rehabilitation, and others are transferred for inpatient rehabilitation.

The responsibilities of the primary care physician are to 1) coordinate acute medical care; 2) follow the child with the physiatrist during inpatient rehabilitation; 3) coordinate follow-up after hospital discharge; 4) obtain family, medical, and developmental histories; and 5) request school information. An initial management plan for community services should be developed prior to hospital discharge, inclusive of all needed services.

Frequency of Visits

Children and adolescents with SCI require regular follow-up by the team of specialists. As the child or adolescent recovers from the injury, additional needs (e.g., mental health problems) may become evident that require other treatments and the involvement of professionals from other disciplines.

Clear, regular communication among service providers is essential. The child or adolescent should be evaluated by the team of professionals two to four times in the year following the SCI, and once or twice annually thereafter. The rehabilitation team works collaboratively with the primary health care professionals. In general, the primary care office should review the child's progress and update the office management plan at least yearly, more often for younger children and in the first year or two after the injury.

The Physician's Guide to Caring for Children with Disabilities and Chronic Conditions, edited by Robert E. Nickel and Larry W. Desch, copyright © 2000 Paul H. Brookes Publishing Co.

Guidelines for the Care of Children and Adolescents with Spinal Cord Injury

The following elements are recommended by age group, and the listing is cumulative. Review all items indicated up through the actual age group of a child entering your practice for the first time as part of the initial evaluation.

AGE	KEY CLINICAL ISSUES/CONCERNS	EVALUATIONS/KEY PROCEDURES	SPECIALISTS
Hospital-ization	*Growth/Nutrition*	Growth parameters, evaluation by nutritionist as needed	Primary care pediatrician, nurse, physiatrist
	Respiratory Care	Pulmonary function studies, tracheostomy, assisted ventilation as needed	Primary care pediatrician, nurse, physiatrist, consult with pulmonologist as needed
	Stabilization of Spine	Surgical stabilization as needed, use thoracolumbo-sacral orthosis (TLSO) as needed	Orthopedist, neurosurgeon
	Treatment of Associated Injuries	Radiologic and laboratory studies as needed	Primary care pediatrician, others as needed
	Determine Motor and Sensory Levels	Detailed musculoskeletal and neurologic examinations	Physiatrist, physical therapist
	Evaluation for Neurogenic Bladder, Incontinence; Monitor for Urinary Tract Infections (UTIs)	Urinalysis/culture, serum creatinine and blood urea nitrogen (BUN), postvoid residual, voiding cys-tourethrogram (VCUG) and urodynamics as needed	Physiatrist, urologist
	Prevent/Treat Joint Contractures, Other Orthopedic Problems; Treat Spasticity	Examination with passive range of motion (ROM) and muscle-strength testing, X rays, passive ROM exercises, braces, medications	Physiatrist, orthopedist, and physical therapist
	Initiate Urine and Stool Continence Programs; Prevent/Treat Constipation	Clean intermittent catheterization (CIC) and anticho-linergics; timed bowel program with or without dig-ital stimulation, use bulk agent, other as needed	Physiatrist, urologist, nurse
	Parent and Child Education and Anticipatory Guidance	Initiate care notebook, provide educational materials on spinal cord injury (SCI), autonomic dysreflexia, continence programs	Physiatrist, nurse
	Care Coordination/Family Support Services	Referral to community services as needed	Primary care pediatrician, nurse, medical social worker, psychologist as needed
Birth–12 years (pre-school and school age)	*Urologic Issues* Continence program Recurrent renal damage, UTIs High-risk bladder Hydronephrosis Vesicoureteral reflux (VUR) Renal/bladder stones	CIC plus anticholinergic, or other as needed Screen for UTIs with nitrite/leukocyte esterase test strips, urinalysis/culture as needed Urodynamics as needed; repeat renal/bladder ultra-sonography (US) scans regularly (e.g., every 6–12 months); VCUG and renal scan as needed, anti-biotic prophylaxis of VUR	Urologist, physiatrist or developmental pediatri-cian (DPed), nurse

The Physician's Guide to Caring for Children with Disabilities and Chronic Conditions, edited by Robert E. Nickel and Larry W. Desch, copyright © 2000 Paul H. Brookes Publishing Co.

Guidelines for the Care of Children and Adolescents with Spinal Cord Injury (continued)

The following elements are recommended by age group, and the listing is cumulative. Review all items indicated up through the actual age group of a child entering your practice for the first time as part of the initial evaluation.

AGE	KEY CLINICAL ISSUES/CONCERNS	EVALUATIONS/KEY PROCEDURES	SPECIALISTS
Birth–12 years (pre-school and school age) (continued)	*Bowel Problems* Constipation	Diet plus bulk agent, adequate fluid intake/activity, other as needed	Physiatrist or DPed, nurse
	Impaction	X-ray: Flat plate of abdomen as needed, saline or oil enemas, after impaction removed, oral cathartic as needed	
	Continence program	Timed bowel program with or without digital stimulation, other as needed	
	Musculoskeletal Problems Joint contractures Foot–ankle deformities	Regular passive ROM and muscle-strength testing Regular passive ROM exercises, use of standing frame; consider surgery if hip flexion/contracture (FC) > 30%, knee FC > 20%, fixed equinus > 10% if ambulation potential	Orthopedist, physical therapist, occupational therapist, physiatrist, or DPed
	Scoliosis, kyphosis, lordosis	X ray: Sitting or standing anterior/posterior and lateral (AP/lat) of spine (repeat at least every 6 months or yearly if child has quadriplegia), spinal orthosis as needed (may compromise respiratory function)	
	Heterotropic ossification Osteopenia and fractures	Regular passive ROM exercises Encourage weight-bearing (use of standing frame), regular activity, supplemental calcium/vitamin D, X rays as needed to diagnose fracture	
	Other Medical Problems Pneumovax and influenza vaccine Seizures (especially if associated brain injury)	Electroencephalogram (EEG), referral to neurologist as needed	Physiatrist or DPed, child neurologist, nurse as needed
	Obesity	Growth parameters, education on diet, regular exercise, consult by nutritionist as needed	
	Skin care (decubiti)	Education on daily skin checks, pressure relief, good hygiene; review seating and positioning	
	Respiratory problems/recurrent infection/tracheostomy care/ventilator management	Pulmonary function studies, training in tracheostomy care, home ventilation program as needed, referral to pulmonologist as needed	

The Physician's Guide to Caring for Children with Disabilities and Chronic Conditions, edited by Robert E. Nickel and Larry W. Desch, copyright © 2000 Paul H. Brookes Publishing Co.

Guidelines for the Care of Children and Adolescents with Spinal Cord Injury *(continued)*

The following elements are recommended by age group, and the listing is cumulative. Review all items indicated up through the actual age group of a child entering your practice for the first time as part of the initial evaluation.

AGE	KEY CLINICAL ISSUES/CONCERNS	EVALUATIONS/KEY PROCEDURES	SPECIALISTS
Birth–12 years (pre-school and school age) *(continued)*	*Ambulation and Mobility* Need for therapy services Bracing/adaptive equipment Seating/positioning Treatment of spasticity Environmental control	Regular passive ROM and muscle-strength testing Referral for physical therapy and occupational therapy services, including gait training with brace or adaptive equipment Evaluation for power-drive wheelchair Medications, botulinum toxin injections as needed; consider intrathecal baclofen Evaluation for environmental control unit as needed	Physical therapist, occupational therapist, physiatrist or DPed
	Developmental/School Progress Associated traumatic brain injury School reentry Written communication Oral communication (need for Passey-Muir valve, augmentative and alternative communication [AAC] devices)	Monitor child's developmental and school progress Evaluation for computer use; AAC evaluation as needed	Physiatrist or DPed; evaluations by psychologist, occupational therapist, child development team as needed Collaboration with school staff
	Social Skills Involvement in peer-group activities at school and in the community (determine which supports are needed)	Coordinate with school-based program and encourage participation in community services	Psychologist, occupational therapist, physical therapist, nurse as needed Collaborate with school staff
	Family Support Services Respite care Parent group Community health nurse Advocacy Financial services (Supplemental Security Income [SSI])	Interview, family assessment, behavioral rating scales, referral to counseling as needed Referral to SCI support group, other family with child with SCI, or Easter Seals Society	Nurse, medical social worker, psychologist as needed
	Parent and Child Education and Anticipatory Guidance Information on clinical issues Encourage self-care/independence	Educational materials on SCI, obesity, skin care, continence, autonomic dysreflexia	Primary care office in collaboration with specialists and school staff

The Physician's Guide to Caring for Children with Disabilities and Chronic Conditions, edited by Robert E. Nickel and Larry W. Desch, copyright © 2000 Paul H. Brookes Publishing Co.

Guidelines for the Care of Children and Adolescents with Spinal Cord Injury (continued)

The following elements are recommended by age group, and the listing is cumulative. Review all items indicated up through the actual age group of a child entering your practice for the first time as part of the initial evaluation.

AGE	KEY CLINICAL ISSUES/CONCERNS	EVALUATIONS/KEY PROCEDURES	SPECIALISTS
13–21 years (adolescent and young adult)	*Neurosurgical Problems* Treatment of spasticity Syringomyelia	Yearly passive ROM/muscle-strength testing, monitor grip strength Consider intrathecal baclofen as appropriate after trial of oral medications Spinal magnetic resonance imaging scan as needed Repeat urodynamics, electromyogram (EMG), as needed	Physiatrist or DPed, neurosurgeon, physical therapist, occupational therapist as needed
	Urologic Problems	Screen for UTI with nitrite/leukocyte esterase test strips at each visit Repeat renal/bladder US scan every other year or as needed Repeat VCUG, urodynamics as needed Serum creatinine, BUN, renal scan as needed	Physiatrist or DPed, urologist, nurse
	Bowel Problems Continence program Prevention of constipation/impaction	Encourage independence/self-care, prevention of constipation	Physiatrist or DPed, nurse as needed
	Musculoskeletal Problems Scoliosis, kyphosis, lordosis Recurrent joint contractures Recurrent fractures	Perform year early passive ROM/muscle-strength testing Repeat X rays: Sitting or standing AP/lat of spine (at least every 6 months or yearly if child has quadriplegia) Consider brace (e.g., TLSO) for progressive curve or surgery if curve > 40% Other X rays as needed, gait analysis as needed Supplemental calcium and vitamin D, weight bearing, use of functional electrical stimulation	Orthopedist, physiatrist or DPed, physical therapist, occupational therapist
	Upper-Extremity Function Indications for muscle/tendon transfers Provide info about use of functional electrical stimulation (FES)	Detailed evaluation of upper-extremity function, strength, range of motion	Occupational therapist, physiatrist, orthopedist as needed

The Physician's Guide to Caring for Children with Disabilities and Chronic Conditions, edited by Robert E. Nickel and Larry W. Desch, copyright © 2000 Paul H. Brookes Publishing Co.

Guidelines for the Care of Children and Adolescents with Spinal Cord Injury *(continued)*

The following elements are recommended by age group, and the listing is cumulative. Review all items indicated up through the actual age group of a child entering your practice for the first time as part of the initial evaluation.

AGE	KEY CLINICAL ISSUES/CONCERNS	EVALUATIONS/KEY PROCEDURES	SPECIALISTS
13–21 years (adolescent and young adult) *(continued)*	*School Performance*	Reevaluation as needed; request school information yearly Behavioral rating scales (parent, child, teacher) as needed	Individual appointments with occupational therapist, psychologist, or child development team evaluation Collaboration with school staff
	Associated Behavior/ Mental Health Problems Inattention, poor motivation Social isolation Anxiety Depression High-risk behaviors (substance abuse, promiscuity)	Encourage participation in organized clubs, sports, parks and recreation programs, camps Involve in mentoring program Referral to mental health professional as needed	Physiatrist or DPed, social worker, psychologist, collaboration with school staff
	Self-Care and Independent Living Determine which supports are needed Need for personal attendant, canine companion, environmental control unit	Inpatient rehabilitation program for self-care/ independent living skills as needed	Social worker, physical and occupational therapists, psychologist and/or vocational specialist
	Parent and Child Education and Anticipatory Guidance Transition to middle school or high school or higher education Transition to adult medical services Vocational/career planning Sexuality/family planning Promote healthy behaviors (e.g., diet, exercise)	Teacher/school interview/conference Referral to Department of Vocational Rehabilitation, career counseling as needed Referral to community services as needed Educational materials on sexuality/family planning Begin gynecologic care for sexually active females Consultation by nutritionist as needed	Primary care office in collaboration with school staff
	Collaboration with Community Services (e.g., school, community health nurse, Department of Vocational Rehabilitation)	Regular exchange of information (at least yearly), conference as needed	Physiatrist, nurse, or social worker

The Physician's Guide to Caring for Children with Disabilities and Chronic Conditions, edited by Robert E. Nickel and Larry W. Desch, copyright © 2000 Paul H. Brookes Publishing Co.

Family and Physician Management Plan Summary for Children and Adolescents with Spinal Cord Injury

This form will help you and your physician review current services and service needs. Please answer the questions about your current services on this page. Your physician will review your responses and complete the rest of the form.

Child's name _____ Today's date _____

Person completing the form _____

CURRENT SERVICES

1. Please list your/your child's current medications and any side effects.

2. What braces and special equipment do you/does your child use now?

3. What is your/your child's current school program?

   School name _____ Grade _____

   Teacher _____ Telephone _____

4. Do you/does your child receive any support services and other special programs at school (e.g., physical therapy, resource room)? Please list.

5. Who are your/your child's other medical and dental service providers?

   Dentist _____

   Neurosurgeon _____

   Orthopedist _____

   Urologist _____

   Other _____

6. Who are your/your child's other community service providers?

   Physical therapist _____

   Community health nurse _____

   Other _____

Family and Physician Management Plan Summary
for Children and Adolescents with Spinal Cord Injury *(continued)*

7. Do you also receive services from a spinal cord injury (SCI) team of specialists?

    Contact person _____

    Location _____

8. Have you/has your child had any blood tests, radiologic (X-ray) examinations, or other procedures since your last visit? If yes, please describe.

9. Have you/has your child been hospitalized or received surgery since your last visit? If yes, describe.

10. Please note accomplishments since your last visit. Consider activities at home, in your neighborhood, or at school, as well as success with treatments.

11. What goals (i.e., skills) would you/your child like to accomplish in the next year? Consider activities at home, in your neighborhood, or at school, as well as success with a treatment.

12. What questions or concerns would you like addressed today?

Family and Physician Management Plan Summary for Children and Adolescents with Spinal Cord Injury

The Management Plan Summary should be completed at each annual review and more often as needed. It is intended to be used with the Guidelines for Care, which provide a more complete listing of clinical issues at different ages as well as recommended evaluations and treatments.

Child's name _____ Person completing form _____ Today's date _____

Clinical issues	Currently a problem?	Evaluations needed	Treatment recommendations	Referrals made	Date for status check
Family's Questions					
Growth/Nutrition Slow weight gain, obesity					
Dental Care					
Respiratory Problems Recurrent infections Tracheostomy care/home ventilation program					
Skin Care (Decubiti) Performing regular skin checks?					
Urologic Problems Describe current continence program Recent change in continence? Today's urinalysis result					

The Physician's Guide to Caring for Children with Disabilities and Chronic Conditions, edited by Robert E. Nickel and Larry W. Desch, copyright © 2000 Paul H. Brookes Publishing Co.

Family and Physician Management Plan Summary for Children and Adolescents with Spinal Cord Injury *(continued)*

Child's name _____ Person completing form _____ Today's date _____

Clinical issues	Currently a problem?	Evaluations needed	Treatment recommendations	Referrals made	Date for status check
Bowel Problems Describe current continence program Constipation/impaction					
Autonomic Dysreflexia					
Neurosurgical Problems Syringomyelia Change in neurologic examination, upper-extremity weakness?					
Treatment of Hypertonicity, Muscle Spasms					
Musculoskeletal Problems Change in contractures, gait, scoliosis? Osteopenia, taking calcium, vitamin D?					
Ambulation and Mobility Describe ambulatory status Need for physical therapy services Questions about braces, adaptive equipment?					

Family and Physician Management Plan Summary for Children and Adolescents with Spinal Cord Injury *(continued)*

Child's name _____ Person completing form _____ Today's date _____

Clinical issues	Currently a problem?	Evaluations needed	Treatment recommendations	Referrals made	Date for status check
Upper-Extremity Function Need for occupational therapy services Indications for orthopedic surgery Provide information about other treatments (e.g., functional electrical stimulation [FES])					
Seating and Positioning Need for power-drive wheelchair					
Other Medical Problems Seizures (if traumatic brain injury [TBI] is also present) Hearing loss/strabismus/visual problems (if TBI is also present) **Note any side effects of medications.**					
Associated Developmental/ Learning Problems School reentry Current school achievement Review school services (individualized family service plan [IFSP] or individualized education program [IEP])					

The Physician's Guide to Caring for Children with Disabilities and Chronic Conditions, edited by Robert E. Nickel and Larry W. Desch, copyright © 2000 Paul H. Brookes Publishing Co.

Family and Physician Management Plan Summary for Children and Adolescents with Spinal Cord Injury *(continued)*

Child's name _____   Person completing form _____   Today's date _____

Clinical issues	Currently a problem?	Evaluations needed	Treatment recommendations	Referrals made	Date for status check
Associated Behavior/ Mental Health Problems Inattention, impulsivity Anxiety, depression Social isolation High-risk behaviors (e.g., drug or alcohol abuse)					
Social Skills Involvement in peer-group activities at school and in the community (determine which supports are needed)					
Self-Care/Independence					
Family Support Services					
Anticipatory Guidance List issues discussed and materials provided					

The Physician's Guide to Caring for Children with Disabilities and Chronic Conditions, edited by Robert E. Nickel and Larry W. Desch, copyright © 2000 Paul H. Brookes Publishing Co.

Family and Physician Management Plan Summary for Children and Adolescents with Spinal Cord Injury *(continued)*

Child's name _____ Person completing form _____ Today's date _____

Clinical issues	Currently a problem?	Evaluations needed	Treatment recommendations	Referrals made	Date for status check
Collaboration with Community Agencies School Vocational Rehabilitation					
Comments					

Next update of the Management Plan Summary _____

Signature _____ Date _____
(Child and parent)

Signature _____ Date _____
(Health professional)

The Physician's Guide to Caring for Children with Disabilities and Chronic Conditions, edited by Robert E. Nickel and Larry W. Desch, copyright © 2000 Paul H. Brookes Publishing Co.

MEDICAL PROBLEMS TO RECOGNIZE AFTER SPINAL CORD INJURY

BLADDER	Recognition of Problem	Action
Infection	Chills and/or fever	• Take temperature
	Cloudy or bloody urine	• Call doctor to request urine test and/or medication
	Foul-smelling urine Increased continence Decreased ability to urinate Painful urination Increased spasticity Increased dysreflexia	• Increase fluids within the limits of your bladder program
Stones	Large particles or stonelike material in urine	• Report to doctor; strain out stones if possible
	Blood in the urine Flank pain Autonomic dysreflexia	• Increase fluids within the limits of your bladder program • Begin treatment program for autonomic dysreflexia

BOWEL		
Constipation	Hard stools	• Increase bulk and fluids in diet
	Infrequent stools	• Resume daily bowel program if less frequent
	Bloating or abdominal discomfort	• Mild laxative such as Senokot tablets daily until regular
	Hard mass of stool in rectum with possible oozing of liquid stool (impaction)	• If using glycerine suppository, try Dulcolax suppositories temporarily • Manually remove mass in rectum, then proceed with regular bowel program
	Autonomic dysreflexia	• Begin treatment program for autonomic dysreflexia
Diarrhea	Large, loose, or frequent watery stools	• Take temperature • Discontinue stool softeners and laxatives until problem subsides • Eliminate possible foods in diet that may be causes, such as spicy foods or alcohol • Meticulous skin care around anus • Call doctor if problem persists
Hemorroids	Rectal bleeding Painful bowel program Red bulging tissue in or around rectum	• Prevent constipation and straining • Notify doctor if it worsens or bleeds heavily • For temporary relief, try wyanoid suppositiories

RESPIRATORY		
Common cold	Runny nose Slight cough Slight sore throat	• Drink plenty of fluids • Take temperature—call doctor if over 101° • Take deep breaths and cough (with assistance if necessary) every hour while awake • If symptoms continue longer than 3 days, call doctor

The Physician's Guide to Caring for Children with Disabilities and Chronic Conditions, edited by Robert E. Nickel and Larry W. Desch, copyright © 2000 Paul H. Brookes Publishing Co.

MEDICAL PROBLEMS TO RECOGNIZE AFTER SPINAL CORD INJURY *(continued)*

RESPIRATORY	Recognition of Problem	Action
Pneumonia or chest congestion	Fever Chest tightness or pain Cough—may be productive	• Call doctor • Take temperature—call doctor if over 101° • Take deep breath and cough (with assistance if necessary) every hour while awake • Drink plenty of fluids within limits of bladder program • Use cool mist humidifier • Rest, but do not stay in bed at all times
SKIN		
Rash	Pimples Red spots	• Keep area clean and dry—leave open to air 30 minutes twice daily • If no improvement in 2–3 days, contact doctor
Burn	Red or blistered skin	• Apply cold water immediately • Watch for signs of infection, such as pus or slow healing • Protect area to allow healing • Do not open or pop blisters
Pressure ulcer	Mild—reddened skin	• Keep pressure off until redness gone • Limit pressure or increase pressure releases to prevent recurrence
	Moderate—skin broken, but without a deep ulcer	• Keep pressure off until healed • Cleanse with soap and water twice daily • Leave open to air twice daily • Gradually build up pressure time after healing and increase pressure releases • Notify doctor if area does not heal or shows signs of infection
	Severe—deep sore with drainage or blackened area	• Eliminate all pressure • Consult with doctor for care of ulcer • High-protein diet • Adequate fluids
OTHER PROBLEMS		
Inflammation of leg	Calf or thigh swollen and red area is warm to touch Area may be painful	• Notify doctor • Rest in bed • Do not bend leg • Do not rub leg • Check temperature • Elevate leg at all times
Ingrown toenails	Red, inflamed area around great toenail (usually) May have some draining	• Cut toenail straight across • Soak foot in warm water twice daily • Put some cotton wisp under edge of toenail to elevate it
Temperature regulation	Become hot or cold in reaction to air temperature or environment Dizziness Headache Faintness Nausea	• If hot, sponge body with tepid water to get temperature below 100° • Call doctor if it does not drop • Drink cool liquids • If cool, warm body with a blanket and clothing • Drink warm liquids • Do not use hot water bottles or heating pads, as they may cause burns

The Physician's Guide to Caring for Children with Disabilities and Chronic Conditions, edited by Robert E. Nickel and Larry W. Desch,
copyright © 2000 Paul H. Brookes Publishing Co.

MEDICATIONS FREQUENTLY USED IN SPINAL CORD INJURY

Medication	Dosage	Side Effects
Baclofen (Lioresal)	2–7 years: 30–40 milligrams a day, given 3 times a day ≥ 8 years: 60 milligrams a day, given 3 times a day	Drowsiness, weakness, insomnia, nausea **Do not** discontinue abruptly—may cause hallucinations
Bisacodyl (Dulcolax)	By mouth: 0.3 milligrams/kilogram/24 hours every 6 hours until desired effect By rectum: < 2 years: 5 milligrams > 2 years: 10 milligrams	Abdominal cramps
Cisapride (Propulsid)	0.2–0.3 milligrams/kilogram dose 3–4 times a day up to 40 milligrams	Cardiac arrhythmias (contraindicated if structural heart disease), abdominal cramps, nausea, anorexia, headaches
Docusate (Colace)	By mouth: < 3 years: 10–40 milligrams/24 hours 3–6 years: 20–60 milligrams/24 hours 6–12 years: 40–120 milligrams/24 hours > 12 years: 40–250 milligrams/24 hours	Oral solution very bitter
Imipramine (Tofranil)	Not recommended for children < 6 years 10–25 milligrams at bedtime by mouth	Dry mouth, drowsiness, constipation, dizziness Monitor electrocardiogram (EKG), blood pressure, complete blood count (CBC)
Indomethacin (Indocin)	1–3 milligrams/kilogram a day given 3 times a day	Gastrointestinal (GI) distress, ulcer, headache, blood dyscrasias Monitor CBC
Metoclopramide hydrochloride (Reglan)	0.1 milligrams/kilogram/dose 4 times a day up to 10 milligrams	Extrapyramidal symptoms
Nifedipine (Procardia)	0.25–0.5 milligrams/kilogram/dose by mouth or sublingual up to 30 milligrams every 6–8 hours	Hypotension, flushing, headache, tachycardia, dizziness, nausea, syncope
Oxybutynin chloride (Ditropan)	< 5 years: 0.5 milligrams/kilogram a day given three times a day > 5 years: 5 milligrams 2–3 times a day	Dry mouth, drowsiness, constipation Contraindicated in GI obstruction, megacolon, colitis
Pseudoephedrine hydrochloride (Sudafed)	4 milligrams per kilogram a day given 4 times a day by mouth up to 30 milligrams per dose	Nervousness, insomnia

The Physician's Guide to Caring for Children with Disabilities and Chronic Conditions, edited by Robert E. Nickel and Larry W. Desch, copyright © 2000 Paul H. Brookes Publishing Co.

TREATMENT OF ACUTE EPISODES OF AUTONOMIC DYSREFLEXIA

CHILDREN YOUNGER THAN 13 YEARS OF AGE

MILD TO MODERATE EPISODE—DIASTOLIC PRESSURE BELOW 100

- Sit up patient
- Check blood pressure every 3–5 minutes as indicated
- Insert straight catheter or check Foley and tubing for obstruction; maintain free drainage
- Check rectum using a small amount of lidocaine jelly and gently remove fecal material
- Check for pressure sores, abscess, epididymitis, penoscrotal fistula, swelling of lower extremities
- Notify physician of assessment, treatment, and patient response
- If antihypertensive medication is used, monitor for s/s orthostatic hypertension

SEVERE EPISODE—DIASTOLIC PRESSURE ABOVE 100 (systolic pressure may be 150–250)—OR IF ABOVE ARE UNSUCCESSFUL OR PERSISTENT ≥ 10 MINUTES

- Implement all of the above
- Call physician for intravenous (IV) and oxygen therapy orders—monitor vital signs and urine output
- Transport patient to emergency department
  - Give hydralazine (Apresoline) (20 mg/1 cc) .1–.5 milligrams/kilogram/dose up to 5–10 milligrams intramuscular (IM) or IV, under the direction of a physician and repeat every 4 hours as necessary
  - If condition is not stabilized, obtain blood urea nitrogen, creatinine, complete blood count (CBC), electrolytes, urinalysis with culture, electrocardiogram (EKG), X rays: chest and flat plate of abdomen

PATIENTS AGES 13 YEARS AND OLDER

MILD TO MODERATE EPISODE—DIASTOLIC PRESSURE BELOW 120

- Sit up patient
- Check blood pressure every 3–5 minutes as indicated
- Insert straight catheter or check Foley and tubing for obstruction; maintain free drainage
- If pressure does not decrease below 180/90 in 5–10 minutes, give
  - Clonidine (Catapres) .1 milligram every 20–30 minutes to maximum of .4 milligrams **OR**
  - Nifedipine (Adalat, Procardia) 10-milligram sublingual (SD) every 2–4 hours to maximum of 40 milligrams
- Check rectum using 2% lidocaine jelly and gently remove fecal material
- Check for pressure sores, abscess, epididymitis, penoscrotal fistula, swelling of lower extremities
- Notify physician of assessment, treatment, and patient response

SEVERE EPISODE—DIASTOLIC PRESSURE ABOVE 120 (systolic pressure may be 200–400)—OR IF ABOVE ARE UNSUCCESSFUL

- Implement all of the above
- Call physician for IV and oxygen therapy orders—monitor vital signs and urine output
- Transport patient to emergency department, where the following may be used under the direction of physician:
  - Nifedipine 10 milligrams SL every 30–60 minutes **OR**
  - Sodium nitroprusside intravenous titrated to effect to a maximum of 8 micrograms/kilogram/minute **OR**
  - Hydralazine 5–10 milligrams IM or IV; repeat as necessary

RESOURCES ON SPINAL CORD INJURY

Readings

Ducharme, S.H., & Gill, K.M. (1997). *Sexuality after spinal cord injury: Answers to your questions.* Baltimore: Paul H. Brookes Publishing Co. (1-800-638-3775)

Krotoski, D.N., Nosek, M.A., & Turk, M.A. (Eds.). (1996). *Women with physical disabilities: Achieving and maintaining health and well-being.* Baltimore: Paul H. Brookes Publishing Co. (1-800-638-3775)

Lash, M. (1991). *When your child is seriously injured: The emotional impact on families.* Hackensack, NJ: Exceptional Parent. (1-800-372-7368)

Lash, M. (1992). *When your child goes to school after an injury.* Hackensack, NJ: Exceptional Parent. (1-800-372-7368)

Maddox, S. (1993). *Spinal network* (2nd ed.). New York: Demos Medical Publishing. (1-800-532-8663)

Marsh, J.D.B., & Boggis, C. (Eds.). (1995). *From the heart: On being the mother of a child with special needs.* Bethesda, MD: Woodbine House. (1-800-843-7323)

Mulcahey, M.J., & Betz, R.R. (Eds.). (1996). *The child with a spinal injury.* Rosemont, IL: American Academy of Orthopedic Surgeons. (1-800-626-6726)

Russell, L.M., et al. (1995). *Planning for the future: Providing a meaningful life for a child with a disability after your death* (3rd ed.). Evanston, IL: American Publishing Co.

Yarkony, G.M. (Ed.). (1994). *Spinal cord injury: Medical management and rehabilitation.* Gaithersburg, MD: Aspen Publishers.(1-800-638-8437)

Books for Children

Muldoon, K.M. (1989). *Princess Pooh.* Niles, IL: A. Whitman. (1-800-255-7675)

Osofsky, A. (1992). *My buddy.* New York: Henry Holt & Co. (1-888-330-8477)

National Organization

National Spinal Cord Injury Association (NSCIA)
Zalco Building
8701 Georgia Avenue, Suite 500
Silver Spring, Maryland 20910
Telephone: (301) 588-6959; Helpline: (800) 962-9629;
   Hotline: (800) 526-3456 (information and referral)
Fax: (301) 588-9414
E-mail: nscia2@aol.com
World Wide Web site: http://www.spinalcord.org/

A national organization with local chapters that provides information, support, and referral services and a number of publications. NSCIA also is compiling a children's peer support registry called In Touch with Kids (ITWK).

17

Seizure Disorders

Ronda M. Roberts

KEY COMPETENCIES

- Become familiar with the classification system of seizures and epileptic syndromes
- Recognize paroxysmal nonepileptic events that mimic seizures
- Recognize developmental disabilities commonly associated with seizures
- Plan the diagnostic workup for a child with a suspected seizure disorder
- Discuss the indications for initiating antiepilepsy drug therapy
- Become familiar with antiepilepsy drugs, associated side effects, and appropriate monitoring
- Discuss the guidelines for withdrawal of antiepilepsy drugs
- Review the indications for surgical management of seizure disorders
- Become familiar with the psychosocial aspects of managing a child with a seizure disorder

DESCRIPTION

Definitions of Seizure, Epilepsy, Epileptic Syndrome, and Status Epilepticus

A *seizure* is defined as a behavioral, motor, sensory, or cognitive event that is due to abnormal neuronal activity characterized by excessive hypersynchronous neuronal discharges. The manifestations can be quite varied. Lip smacking without any associated loss of consciousness and generalized tonic-clonic activity with complete loss of consciousness can both be manifestations of seizure activity. *Epilepsy* is defined as recurrent seizures secondary to central nervous system (CNS) dysfunction. An *epileptic syndrome* is an identifiable constellation of seizure types, developmental and family history, neurological examination, electroencephalogram (EEG) features, and natural history. *Status epilepticus* is defined as 30 minutes of continuous

Table 17.1. Cumulative incidence of convulsive disorders by age 20 years

Neonatal	0.1% of the population (33% will develop epilepsy)
Febrile seizure	2%–4% of the population (3%–5% will develop epilepsy)
Acute symptomatic nonfebrile seizure	0.5% of the population (15%–20% will develop epilepsy)
Epilepsy	1% of the population

Adapted from Hauser (1994).

seizure activity or recurrent seizures without the return of consciousness in between (Pellock, 1994). It is considered a true neurologic emergency. The mortality rate of children who suffer from an episode of status epilepticus is 3%–6% (Phillips & Shanahan, 1989).

Incidence of Seizures, Epilepsy, Epileptic Syndromes, and Status Epilepticus

Between 4% and 10% of all children experience a seizure at some time in their lives; however, by age 20, only 1% of the population will have epilepsy (Hauser, 1994). Febrile seizures occur in 2%–4% of the population. The highest incidence of all seizure types combined occurs in the second year of life, and the highest incidence of specific epileptic syndromes occurs in the first year of life (see Tables 17.1 and Table 17.2). Status epilepticus occurs in 25,000–50,000 children per year in the United States (Hauser, 1990). The majority of individuals with status epilepticus are children with acute neurologic conditions such as meningitis, encephalitis, or trauma; children with degenerative or progressive neurologic conditions; children with an intercurrent illness or who have not complied with medication prescriptions; and children with atypical febrile seizures (Mitchell, 1996).

Table 17.2. Incidence of childhood epileptic syndromes

Epileptic syndrome	Percentage of all childhood epileptic syndromes
West syndrome	2% (25% of epileptic syndromes that occur in the first year of life)
Lennox-Gastaut syndrome	1%–2% (10% of epileptic syndromes that occur in the first year of life)
Childhood absence epilepsy	10%–15%
Juvenile myoclonic epilepsy	10%–30%
Benign childhood epilepsy with centrotemporal spikes	10% (25% of epileptic syndromes that occur between ages 5 and 15 years)
Epilepsy with generalized tonic-clonic seizures upon awakening	22%–37%

Adapted from Delgado-Escueta, Medina, Serratosa, et al. (1999) and Hauser (1994).

Factors that Predispose a Child to Develop a Seizure Disorder

Any interference with the brain's integrity can contribute to the development of seizures, including inherent (i.e., genetic) and external influences. The immature brain of a child may have a propensity for seizures by virtue of its neuroanatomic and neurophysiologic uniqueness (Johnston, 1996). Age-dependent seizure types, age-specific EEG changes, and sensitivity to medications at different ages underscore the importance of the developing CNS. In neonates and infants, severe hypoxia, metabolic defects, developmental brain defects (e.g., migration defects), and perinatal injuries are the most common insults that predispose a child to the development of a seizure disorder. During *early childhood*, fever (caused by an infection at a site outside the brain) and brain infections (e.g., meningitis, encephalitis, brain abscess) and, less commonly, tumors, toxins, trauma, vascular disease, and degenerative disease become important etiologic factors. In *older children and adolescents*, trauma is a common predisposing factor (Epilepsy Foundation of America [EFA], 1992). Children with developmental disabilities often have one of these insults and therefore are at a high risk for subsequent development of a seizure disorder. It is important to recognize that seizures do not occur because of the developmental disability but rather because of the underlying brain abnormality that causes the disability.

Pathophysiology of a Seizure

The basic pathophysiologic mechanism of a seizure requires excessive neuronal hyperexcitability and abnormal neuronal synchronization. The neuronal hyperexcitability is characterized by cellular depolarization secondary to a massive influx of sodium and calcium. A number of insults (e.g., severe hypoxia) cause metabolic derangements in the microenvironment of the neuron, which can precipitate this depolarization. In addition, neurotransmitters can modulate neuronal function. Experimental models show that the neurotransmitter gamma-aminobutyric acid (GABA) has an inhibitory effect on hyperexcitability and that the amino acid glutamate produces excitability (Meldrum, 1989). Corticotropin-releasing hormone (CRH) may play a role in generating developmentally regulated, triggered seizures (Baram & Hatalski, 1998).

Classification of Seizures and Epileptic Syndromes

Fundamental to the management of epilepsy is classifying the seizure type properly and determining whether the individual's seizure disorder is part of

an epileptic syndrome. Most experts use the classification system established by the International League Against Epilepsy. The International Classification of Epileptic Seizures (ICES) (Commission on Classification and Terminology, 1981) defines the seizure type based on its origin and divides seizures into the categories *generalized seizures* (involvement of both hemispheres) and *partial seizures* (originating from a specific locus). Partial seizures are then divided into those that are *simple* (no loss of consciousness) or *complex* (consciousness is impaired), or those that evolve into *secondarily generalized seizures*. See Table 17.3 for a comparison of the terminology used previously with that of the ICES.

Although the ICES system is useful, it provides little prognostic information to the child and the child's family. The International Classification of Epilepsies and Epileptic Syndromes (ICE) (Commission on Classification and Terminology, 1985) was designed subsequently to help the clinician to

- Decide on appropriate diagnostic studies
- Decide on appropriate management, including the selection of antiepilepsy drugs (AEDs); avoid contraindicated medications; and time the cessation of medication
- Give information about the prognosis of a particular disorder
- Prepare the child and the family to decide on appropriate activities, career decisions, and family planning for the child
- Consider surgical management and controversial therapies (Penry, 1986)

The newer classification (Table 17.4) is based on whether the predominant seizure type in the epilepsy or epileptic syndrome is localized (i.e., a localization-related syndrome) or generalized (i.e., a generalized syndrome). It further divides these

Table 17.3. Comparison of terminology

International classification	Previous terminology
Generalized seizures	
Absence	Petit mal
Myoclonic	Minor motor
Tonic-clonic	Grand mal, major motor
Atonic	Akinetic, drop attacks, astatic
Partial seizures	Focal, local
Simple partial with motor symptoms	Jacksonian
Complex partial	Psychomotor
	Temporal lobe

Source: Pedley and De Vivo (1987).

Table 17.4.   International Classification of Epilepsies and Epileptic Syndromes

I.   Localization-related (partial) epilepsies and syndromes
   A.   Idiopathic (with age-related onset):
      •   Benign childhood epilepsy with centrotemporal spike (BECTS)
      •   Childhood epilepsy with occipital paroxysms
   B.   Symptomatic: This category comprises syndromes of great variability and includes epilepsies based on anatomical location (e.g., temporal lobe epilepsy)
II.   Generalized epilepsies and syndromes
   A.   Idiopathic (with age-related onset, in order of appearance)
      •   Benign neonatal familial convulsions
      •   Benign neonatal convulsions
      •   Benign myoclonic epilepsy in infancy
      •   Childhood absence epilepsy (pyknolepsy, petit mal)
      •   Juvenile absence epilepsy
      •   Juvenile myoclonic epilepsy (impulsive petit mal)
      •   Epilepsy with generalized tonic-clonic seizures on awakening
   B.   Idiopathic and/or symptomatic (in order of age of appearance)
      •   West syndrome (infantile spasms)
      •   Lennox-Gastaut syndrome
      •   Epilepsy with myoclonic-astatic seizures
      •   Epilepsy with myoclonic absences
   C.   Symptomatic
III.   Epilepsies and syndromes undetermined as to whether they are localized or generalized
   A.   With both generalized and focal seizures
      •   Neonatal seizures
      •   Severe myoclonic epilepsy in infancy
      •   Epilepsy with continuous spikes and waves during slow-wave sleep
      •   Acquired epileptic aphasia (Landau-Kleffner)
   B.   Without unequivocal generalized or focal features
IV.   Special syndromes
   A.   Situation-related seizures (e.g., febrile convulsions or seizures related to other identifiable situations, such as stress, hormones, drugs, alcohol)
   B.   Isolated, apparently unprovoked epileptic events
   C.   Chronic progressive partialis continua of childhood

From the Commission on Classification and Terminology of the International League Against Epilepsy. (1985). Proposal for revised classification of epilepsies and epileptic syndromes. *Epilepsia, 26,* 268–278; adapted by permission from Lippincott Williams & Wilkins.

two main categories into *idiopathic*, which usually refers to epilepsies with a strong hereditary component and a normal neurologic status; and *symptomatic*, which implies that a neuropathologic process has been identified. In addition to the previous two main groups, a third group includes epilepsies and syndromes whose etiologies are undetermined with regard to whether they are localized or generalized (e.g., neonatals), as well as a fourth group that includes special syndromes such as those provoked by an identifiable cause (e.g., febrile seizures).

The importance of recognizing whether a particular seizure type belongs to an epileptic syndrome is demonstrated in the following example. Assume that a 6-month-old begins having myoclonic seizures. Because of the characteristic motor behavior, age of onset, developmental history, and EEG changes, a diagnosis of West syndrome is suspected, and a variety of anatomic, infectious, ge-

netic, and metabolic etiologies are investigated. Although a variety of medications to treat myoclonic seizures are available, adrenocorticotropic hormone (ACTH) is considered the treatment of choice for West syndrome.

Characteristics of Seizures that Occur During the Neonatal Period, Infancy, Childhood, and Adolescence

It is helpful for practitioners caring for children with seizure disorders to consider the age of presentation as a guide while making the diagnosis. The discussion of the characteristics of seizures in this chapter is presented in this manner. Table 17.5 (Duchowny & Harvey, 1996) lists several epilepsies and epileptic syndromes according to typical age of onset.

Seizures During the Neonatal Period   Most neonatal seizures appear to be epiphenomena of insults occurring before, during, or after birth or of

Table 17.5. Classification of epileptic syndromes according to usual age of onset

Neonatal period
 Miscellaneous neonatal seizures
 Benign neonatal convulsions
 Benign neonatal familial convulsions

Infancy
 Febrile seizures
 Early infantile epileptic encephalopathy
 Early myoclonic encephalopathy
 Infantile spasms (West syndrome)
 Severe myoclonic epilepsy of infancy
 Benign myoclonic epilepsy of infancy
 Benign partial epilepsy of infancy
 Benign infantile familial convulsions
 Symptomatic or cryptogenic partial epilepsies

Early childhood (toddler and preschool)
 Epilepsy with myoclonic absences
 Lennox-Gastaut syndrome
 Acquired epileptic aphasia (Landau-Kleffner syndrome)
 Epilepsy with continuous spike waves during slow sleep
 Symptomatic or cryptogenic partial epilepsies

Childhood (school-age), adolescence, and young adulthood
 Childhood absence epilepsy
 Benign partial epilepsy with centrotemporal spikes
 Benign occipital epilepsy
 Reflex epilepsies (e.g., photosensitive epilepsy, reading epilepsy)
 Juvenile absence epilepsy
 Epilepsy with tonic-clonic seizures on awakening
 Juvenile myoclonic epilepsy
 Autosomal dominant nocturnal frontal lobe epilepsy
 Symptomatic or cryptogenic partial epilepsies

Adapted from Duchowny and Harvey (1996).

transient metabolic or systemic abnormalities (Lombroso, 1990). When grouped statistically, neonatal seizures occur in approximately 0.1% of the population, and approximately 33% of infants who experience neonatal seizures develop epilepsy later in life (Hauser, 1994). Their etiology can be diverse, often prompting an extensive medical workup (see Table 17.6). Two neonatal epilepsies, benign neonatal familial convulsions and benign neonatal convulsions, are classified as idiopathic generalized epilepsies. To make their diagnosis, a workup to exclude metabolic, infectious, developmental, or traumatic etiologies must be performed.

Fenichel (1997) categorized neonatal seizures as *subtle* (e.g., eye blinking, sucking, bicycling, apnea), *clonic* (rhythmic flexion or extension), *tonic* (sustained posture), or *myoclonic* (sudden flexion or extension without rhythmicity). Some neonatal behaviors may not be epileptic in origin but may rep-

resent brainstem reflexes released from cortical inhibition (Murphy & Dehkharghani, 1994). These behaviors are often difficult to distinguish from seizure activity. Gathering information regarding what the infant was doing at the time of the event (e.g., eating, sleeping) as well as determining the presence or absence of autonomic activity may help with the diagnosis (e.g., apnea associated with seizures is usually accompanied by an increase in blood pressure and heart rate, whereas apnea from other causes usually is accompanied by bradycardia). Controversy exists regarding the relationship between EEG findings and clinical manifestations.

Legido, Clancy, and Berman (1991) reported unfavorable developmental outcomes in 79% of pediatric cases with an EEG confirmed neonatal seizure, and global abnormalities on neuroimaging studies clearly are associated with unfavorable outcomes (Ortibus, Sum, & Hahn, 1997; Bye, Cunningham, Chee, et al., 1997). Uncertainty exists with regard to whether neonatal seizures are simply markers of a neurologic insult or whether they can cause brain injury and subsequent developmental sequelae. Treatment is directed toward correcting the abnormality whenever possible. Benzodiazepines, phenobarbital, and phenytoin are commonly used for neonatal seizure control (see the discussion under the subsequent "Medication Management" heading in this chapter).

Benign Neonatal Familial Convulsions Benign neonatal familial convulsions usually occur on the second or third day of life and manifest as apnea or clonic motor activity. Most families show an autosomal dominant pattern of inheritance, and linkage has been identified on the long arms of chromosomes 20 and 8 (Leppert, Anderson, & Quattlebaum, 1989). The seizures typically disappear within 1–6 months, and normal neurologic development ensues; however, approximately 14% of these newborns develop epilepsy later in life.

Benign Neonatal Convulsions Benign neonatal convulsions typically begin on the fifth day of life. They present as apnea or clonic motor activity; however, there is no family history of seizure disorders, and the EEG shows a characteristic pattern (Plouin, 1985). They usually disappear within 1–2 days without any neurologic sequelae.

Seizures During Infancy Seizures during infancy can be due to developmental brain anomalies, metabolic defects, brain infection, fever, tumors, toxins, vascular disease, degenerative disease, and trauma. These should be investigated based on the child's clinical presentation. The seizures may be

Table 17.6.   Differential diagnosis of neonatal seizures by peak time of onset

24 hours	*72 hours to 1 week*
Hypoxic-ischemic encephalopathy	Benign familial neonatal convulsions
Bacterial meningitis and sepsis	Benign neonatal convulsions
Subarachnoid hemorrhage	Cerebral dysgenesis
Intrauterine infection	Cerebral infarction
Trauma	Intracerebral hemorrhage
	Kernicterus
24–72 hours	Nutritional hypocalcemia
Intraventricular hemorrhage in premature	Metabolic or genetic (e.g., tuberous sclerosis)
infants	
Cerebral contusion	*1 week to 4 weeks*
Subarachnoid hemorrhage	Cerebral dysgenesis
Bacterial meningitis and sepsis	Herpes simplex encephalitis
Cerebral dysgenesis	Metabolic or genetic
Cerebral infarction	(e.g., amino acidopathies, peroxisomal disorders,
Drug withdrawal	neonatal adrenoleukodystrophy)
Metabolic or genetic (e.g., pyridoxine	
dependency, hypocalcemia)	

Adapted from Fenichel (1997).

generalized or localized, and it is important to determine if they are part of an epileptic syndrome.

Febrile Seizures   Febrile seizures fit under the classification of situation-related seizures and are the most common seizures of early life, occurring in approximately 2%–4% of the population (Hauser, 1994). Febrile seizures usually occur between 6 months and 5 years of age. Certain factors can increase the risk to 6%–10%, including 1) a complicated neonatal course, 2) developmental delay, 3) family history of febrile seizures, and 4) attendance at child care programs (Bethune, Gordon, Dooley, et al., 1993). Approximately one third of children who experience one febrile seizure have a second episode, and 9% have three or more. Children who have the first febrile seizure before 1 year of age or have a family history of febrile seizures show the highest recurrence rates.

Simple febrile seizures are defined as lasting less than 15 minutes, are associated with temperature greater than 38.5° C, and are nonfocal. The risk of developing subsequent epilepsy among children who have simple febrile seizures is only slightly higher than that found in the general population (2% compared to 1%). Complex febrile seizures are those that last longer than 15 minutes, have focality, or occur repeatedly in a 24-hour period. They do not increase the risk of recurrent febrile seizures to greater than that of simple febrile seizures (Murphy & Dehkharghani, 1994). The occurrence of many febrile seizures carries an increased risk of subsequent epilepsy (MacDonald, Johnson, Sander, & Shorvon, 1999).

Acute management consists of determining the underlying cause of the fever. Lumbar puncture does not need to be done routinely but must be performed in any individual showing signs of meningitis or in an ill-appearing infant too young to show the classic meningeal signs. Electrolytes, glucose, blood urea nitrogen (BUN), calcium, phosphorous, and magnesium testing should be performed when a clinical suspicion arises that an abnormality may exist. In addition, if a structural lesion is suspected (e.g., febrile seizure with focality), cranial computed tomography (CT) or magnetic resonance imaging (MRI) scans should be performed.

Counseling is also an important part of care. Parents should be counseled to be calm and reassuring during the episode. They should place the child on his or her side on a protected surface and to observe the child carefully. If the seizure lasts longer than 10 minutes, the child should be brought in for medical attention. Physicians usually provide information on the use of the proper dosage of antipyretics during a febrile illness; however, use of antipyretics has not been shown to decrease the likelihood of recurrence of a febrile seizure.

Controversy exists regarding the use of prophylactic phenobarbital. Concerns regarding its effects on the child's cognitive functioning and behavior as well as a lack of evidence that AEDs prevent the development of subsequent epilepsy have been raised. This information, as well as studies that have shown no adverse developmental outcomes among children who have had simple febrile seizures, has changed care recommendations for these children (Knudsen, Paerregaard, Andersen, & Andresen, 1996). Multiple or prolonged attacks are commonly treated with rectal or oral benzodiazepines, which can be given preventively during a high fever. Indications for the use of prophylactic AEDs for febrile seizures include

- Prior neurodevelopmental abnormality associated with increased risk for seizures
- A child with many recurrences, especially at a young age
- A child whose parents are extremely anxious despite maximal reassurance from the physician
- A child who cannot be transported to medical care within a reasonable amount of time

Myoclonic Epilepsies *Infantile spasms* are classified as idiopathic and/or symptomatic generalized epilepsies and occur in approximately 0.29–0.41 per 1,000 live births (Rantala & Putkonen, 1999; Trevathan, Murphy, & Yeargin-Allsopp, 1999). The spasms consist of sudden extension or flexion of the trunk and/or extremities and tend to occur in clusters, with the highest frequencies occurring during the transition between sleep and wake. These spasms can occur up to 100 times per day. Peak age of onset is between 4 and 6 months of age, but spasms have been noted to begin as early as 1 week of age (Bobele & Bodensteiner, 1990). West syndrome consists of the triad of infantile spasms, psychomotor retardation, and hypsarrhythmic changes on the EEG (Hrachovy & Frost, 1989). The etiology of infantile spasms is diverse (Bobele & Bodensteiner, 1990) (see Table 17.7).

Evaluation of a child with infantile spasms should be directed toward identification of the underlying etiology (see subsequent discussion under the "Diagnosis and Evaluation" heading). The mainstay of treatment is ACTH, which alters the CNS concentrations of various biogenic amines and increases GABA receptor affinity. Another mechanism that may be important in seizure control is in-

Table 17.7. Etiology of infantile spasms

Prenatal factors	Perinatal factors
Intrauterine infections (e.g., cytomegalovirus)	Hypoxic-ischemic encephalopathy
Cerebral malformations (including focal cortical dysplasias)	Periventricular hemorrhage
	Other intracranial hemorrhage
Genetic conditions (e.g., tuberous sclerosis, Aicardi syndrome)	Neonatal herpes
	Postnatal factors
Metabolic disorders (e.g., lactic acidosis, phenylketonuria, pyridoxine dependency, leukodystrophies)	Neonatal sepsis or meningitis
	Kernicterus
	Traumatic brain injury
	Central nervous system infections

Adapted from Bobele and Bodensteiner (1990) and Hrachovy and Frost (1989).

hibiting the release of corticotropin-releasing factor (CRF), which is an excitatory neuropeptide. Of all individuals treated with ACTH, 50%–75% experience complete seizure control within 4 weeks of beginning treatment (Haines & Casto, 1994). Treatment is subsequently tapered based on clinical response. A variety of treatment protocols are used; however, early initiation and high-dose regimen protocols have resulted in the best response rates (Zupanc, 1996). Other drugs used include valproic acid, benzodiazepines, pyridoxine, and vigabatrin. With children who do not respond well to medication or who have clinical evidence of lateralized findings, the primary care physician should refer for a single photon emission computed tomography (SPECT) or positron emission tomography (PET) scan to search for a focal metabolic abnormality that may be amenable to surgical resection. The ketogenic diet has also been used with some success in these patients.

In general, the developmental prognosis of infants with infantile spasms is poor, with more than 90% having major cognitive impairments. Up to 50% of these individuals continue to have seizures and are at high risk for developing Lennox-Gastaut syndrome. Even if seizure control treatment is obtained, it does not translate into an improved prognosis for cognitive development. Less than 5% of these individuals are classified as idiopathic and seem to have a better prognosis than those with a defined underlying etiology. About 30%–70% of these individuals will have typical intellectual functioning (Haines & Casto, 1994). Typical development before the onset of spasms, short duration of seizures before seizure control treatment is implemented, and absence of abnormal physical findings are favorable prognostic indicators (Riikonen, 1982).

Two additional myoclonic epilepsies that may be early variants of infantile spasms have also been described. *Early infantile epileptic encephalopathy* (Ohtahara syndrome) is typically associated with severe structural CNS abnormalities and leads to severe developmental delay and persistent seizures. Tonic spasms can occur singly or in clusters early in infancy. The EEG shows a burst suppression pattern that may evolve into hypsarrhythmia. AEDs and corticosteroids are rarely effective (Duchowny & Harvey, 1996). *Early myoclonic encephalopathy* is differentiated from early infantile epileptic encephalopathy by the presence of erratic myoclonias. It typically begins before 3 months of age and shows a burst suppression pattern on EEG. It also is associated with severe neurologic impairment. A metabolic etiology must be investigated for both of these diagnoses, and the prognosis for individuals with either one is generally dismal (Lombroso, 1990).

Benign infantile myoclonic epilepsy is an epileptic syndrome characterized by seizures that usually begin in the first 2 years of life. A history of febrile seizures is frequently present, and apparently typical neurologic development is present prior to the onset of the myoclonic seizures. One third of patients have a family history of epilepsy. The seizures consist of brief myoclonic attacks that can range in severity from a brief head nod to contractions that throw the infant to the floor. The EEG shows a generalized 3-hertz spike-wave pattern or poly-spike-wave discharges. High-dose valproic acid is very effective for treating myoclonic seizures; however, other seizure types may ensue (Lin, Itomi, Takada, et al., 1998). For example, rare major motor seizures can occur during adolescence. The prognosis for favorable neurodevelopmental outcome is good if treatment is started early (Dravet, Bureau, & Genton, 1992).

Severe myoclonic epilepsy of infancy is also characterized by multiple febrile seizures and typical development until the first seizure; however, children subsequently develop uncontrollable myoclonic, generalized tonic-clonic seizures and often other seizure types (e.g., atonic) (Hurst, 1990). In a longitudinal study (Lin, Itomi, Takada, et al., 1998), tonic-clonic convulsions were seen throughout the entire course of the study. Myoclonic, complex partial, and atypical absence seizures disappeared and reappeared repeatedly. EEG patterns show generalized and multifocal poly-spike-wave, spike-wave, and slow-wave discharges. The prognosis for infants with severe myoclonic epilepsy is poor. The infant's psychomotor development slows, and ataxia and corticospinal tract signs become evident. An extensive metabolic workup must be performed; however, the cause of severe myoclonic epilepsy remains unknown and seizures are usually refractory to AED therapy. Lamotrogine (lamictal) has been reported to aggravate seizures in 17 of 20 children with severe myoclonic epilepsy (Guerrini, Dravet, Genton, et al., 1998), and the authors recommend against its use in this disorder.

Localization-Related Epilepsies Epilepsies that are related to symptomatic or cryptogenic localization can be caused by a variety of CNS lesions, and manifestations vary depending on the intracranial location (temporal, frontal, parietal, or occipital). (Please see the following discussion of localization during early childhood.)

Seizures During Early Childhood Seizures that occur during the toddler and preschool-age period can be due to a variety of causes, as mentioned previously under the "Factors that Predispose a Child to the Development of a Seizure Disorder" heading in this chapter. They can be either generalized or localized, and it is important to become familiar with the common epilepsies and epileptic syndromes that can occur during early childhood. Febrile seizures can occur during early childhood (see previous discussion).

Lennox-Gastaut Syndrome Lennox-Gastaut syndrome is defined by three necessary components:

1. Generalized seizures (usually a combination of tonic, atypical absence, atonic, and tonic-clonic)
2. An EEG pattern of interictal diffuse, slow spike-wave discharges over a slow background
3. Severe cognitive impairments

The etiologies (see Table 17.7) must be investigated. A premorbid history of West syndrome is present in approximately 25% of children with Lennox-Gastaut syndrome. The age of onset is typically between 1 and 8 years, with a peak occurrence at age 5 years. The seizures are often difficult to treat, and the long-term prognosis for children with this diagnosis is poor (Talwar & Swaiman, 1994). In a study with greater than 10-year follow-up, Oguni, Hayashi, and Osawa (1996) found that two thirds of the children studied continued to have seizures on a weekly or a daily basis despite medical therapy. In addition, a significant decline in intellectual ability occurred in 82% of those with idiopathic Lennox-Gastaut syndrome and 78% with symptomatic Lennox-Gastaut syndrome. Gait ability declined (i.e., children became more clumsy), and the frequency of drop attacks increased over time. The multiple types of seizures characteristic of Lennox-Gastaut syndrome often evolve into a predominant seizure type. Standard AEDs generally are not successful, but corticosteroids and ketogenic diet have achieved moderate success. Lamotrigine has shown promising effects; however, precautions against its use have been issued (Arky, 1999). Surgical corpus callostomy may be beneficial in reducing the number of seizures that the child experiences. Even if seizure control is obtained, the child's neurodevelopmental outcome remains poor. Videotelemetry can sometimes be helpful in differentiating between atypical absence seizures and stereotypic movements common in this disorder (Bare, Glauser, & Strawsburg, 1998).

Acquired Epileptic Aphasia (Landau-Kleffner Syndrome) Landau-Kleffner syndrome is characterized by a deterioration in receptive and expressive language skills, inattentiveness to sound (auditory agnosia), behavioral disturbances, and EEG changes that usually occur in the toddler or preschooler age range. Seventy percent of children with Landau-Kleffner syndrome have clinically overt seizures (Hirsch, Marescaux, & Maquet, 1990) that can be atypical absence seizures, generalized tonic-clonic seizures, or partial seizures. These can occur before, concurrently with, or after the loss of language. The EEG changes can be focal or multifocal and are always increased during sleep; therefore, a prolonged EEG record during sleep is helpful with the diagnosis. The syndrome may be confused with infantile autism; however, with Landau-Kleffner syndrome, language loss usually occurs after the development of phrases. A related epilepsy syndrome, *continuous spike-wave discharges during slow-wave sleep (CSWS)*, also is associated with language loss and behavioral symptoms (Soprano, Garcia, Caraballo, & Fejerman, 1994).

Treatment with the usual AEDs may control seizures in Landau-Kleffner syndrome; however, aphasia is generally not affected. Corticosteroids and immunoglobulins have been tried (Prasad, Stafstrom, & Holmes, 1996). Lerman, Lerman-Sagie, and Kivity (1991) described four individuals who were treated with various corticosteroids (prednisone, dexamethasone, and ACTH), and all showed dramatic improvement with regard to seizure control and aphasia. Multiple subpial surgical transection of the perisylvian cortex has been tried in a select group of individuals with Landau-Kleffner syndrome, with 11 of 14 showing some improvement in speech (Morrell, Whistler, Smith, et al., 1995).

Localization-Related Epilepsies Epilepsies that are related to symptomatic or cryptogenic localization include those that are characterized by simple partial, complex partial, and secondarily generalized seizures. Their symptoms are highly dependent on anatomic location. Some characteristics follow:

- *Temporal:* Begins as simple partial with olfactory or auditory phenomena, followed by alteration in consciousness, motor arrest, and automatisms; in younger children, motor phenomena and simple automatisms (such as blinking) typically occur, followed by dystonic posturing
- *Frontal:* Motor manifestations are prominent; secondarily, generalized seizures typically occur; and status epilepticus is a frequent complication
- *Parietal:* Often associated with sensory phenomena and may produce speech-language difficulties
- *Occipital:* Visual perturbations, headaches, and hallucinations

Carbamazepine, phenytoin, and phenobarbital are used frequently for the treatment of these seizures. In addition, many children with localization-related epilepsies are found to have focal cortical dysplasias and may be amenable to surgical therapy (Wyllie, Rothner, & Luders, 1989).

Seizures During Childhood, Adolescence, and Young Adulthood Trauma is a leading cause of seizures during childhood, adolescence, and young adulthood. In addition, infection, tumors, toxins, vascular disease, degenerative disease, metabolic defects, and developmental anomalies can still play a role in seizure development. The most common epilepsies during this period are described in the subsections that follow.

Benign Childhood Epilepsy with Centrotemporal Spikes Benign childhood epilepsy with centrotemporal spikes (BECTS) is also known as *benign rolandic epilepsy.* This disorder accounts for 10% of all epileptic seizures, and it occurs in children 5–14 years of age. It is inherited as an autosomal dominant trait with variable penetrance. The seizures involve sensorimotor phenomena and typically consist of paraesthesias on one side of the mouth followed by ipsilateral twitching of the face, mouth, and pharynx, resulting in speech arrest and drooling (Holmes, 1993). Seventy to seventy-five percent of children experience these seizures nocturnally. The EEG shows unilateral or bilateral drowsiness or sleep-activated spike discharges in the central or centrotemporal regions. Treatment is not necessary if the seizures are infrequent. If treatment is necessary, carbamazepine or valproic acid have been shown to be effective. Almost all children who experience BECTS outgrow their seizures by midadolescence.

Another form of epilepsy believed to be caused by the same genetic trait as the one that causes BECTS is *benign occipital epilepsy.* This form of epilepsy has a strong hereditary component, with almost 50% of children with benign occipital epilepsy having a family history of seizures (Panayiotopoulos, 1989). Benign occipital epilepsy is believed to be inherited in an autosomal dominant fashion with variable penetrance. The age of onset is between 2 and 9 years, usually peaking at 5–7 years of age. The seizures are characterized by visual symptoms, including visual hemianopia and visual hallucinations, often in the form of flashing lights or spots. The visual symptoms are usually followed by hemiclonic seizures, automatisms, generalized tonic-clonic seizures, or dysarthria, and 33% of children experience severe throbbing migraine headaches postictally. The greatest frequency of seizures is seen during the transition from wake to sleep. The EEG shows high amplitude spike-wave discharges at 2–3 hertz in the occipital and posterotemporal regions. Seizures are usually treatable with carbamazepine, phenytoin, or valproic acid. Seizures typically remit in adolescence.

Childhood Absence Epilepsy (Petit Mal, Pyknolepsy) Childhood absence epilepsy accounts for 10%–15% of all cases of epilepsy. It occurs in children ages 1–14 years and peaks between the ages of 4 and 8 years (Wirrell, Camfield, Camfield, et al., 1997). It has a strong hereditary component, with 15%–44% of first-degree relatives having an abnormal EEG. Seizures consist of brief staring spells usually lasting between 5 and 10 seconds. The staring occurs in conjunction with unresponsiveness and sometimes with eyelid fluttering, automatisms, and mild clonic movements of the upper extremities. This type of seizure can be hyperventilation-induced and can be differentiated from a complex partial seizure in that no postictal confusion is present. Wirrell and colleagues (1997) showed 65% of children presenting with childhood absence seizures had remission of their epilepsy. Children with cognitive delays, history of absence status, development of generalization tonic-clonic or myoclonic seizures, abnormal background on EEG, older age at time of onset, and family history of generalized seizures in first-degree relatives were less likely to become seizure-free. The EEG shows bilaterally synchronous and symmetric 3-hertz spike-wave discharges, with the amplitude being highest in the frontocentral region (Porter, 1993). Treatment consists of ethosuximide, or valproic acid if tonic-clonic seizures also are present.

Juvenile absence epilepsy may be related to childhood absence seizures (Porter, 1993). With this form of epilepsy, seizures typically begin near puberty (between the ages of 10 and 17 years). Only 20% have absence seizures as the only seizure type and approximately 80% have associated generalized tonic-clonic seizures (Obeid, 1994). The generalized tonic-clonic seizures are easily controlled with valproic acid; however, absence seizures become less frequent during treatment but often don't completely stop (Obeid, 1994).

Juvenile Myoclonic Epilepsy (Impulsive Petit Mal, Janz Syndrome) Age of onset for juvenile myoclonic epilepsy is between 12 and 18 years of age. It occurs in approximately 10%–30% of people with epilepsy. There is a question whether juvenile myoclonic epilepsy, juvenile absence epilepsy, and epilepsy with generalized tonic-clonic seizures upon awakening are clinically distinct, even though they

have different predominant seizure types (Reutens & Berkovic, 1995). For example, Wirrell and colleagues (1997) reported that 44% of children without remission of childhood absence seizures went on to develop juvenile myoclonic epilepsy. Evidence exists, however, that the gene locus for classic juvenile myoclonic epilepsy is on chromosome 6, while that of childhood absence epilepsy, which evolves into juvenile myoclonic epilepsy, is on chromosome 1.

Generalized tonic-clonic seizures occur in approximately 90% of adolescents with juvenile myoclonic epilepsy, and approximately 33% of children with juvenile myoclonic epilepsy have associated absence seizures (Panayiotopoulos, Obeid, & Tanan, 1994). The myoclonic seizures that occur in all patients typically occur in the early morning with mild, sudden jerks of the shoulders and arms and no loss of consciousness or often go unrecognized. Factors that may provoke seizures include sleep deprivation, alcohol abuse, and photic stimulation (Ercegovac, Vojvodic, Sokic, et al., 1998; Ishida, Yamashita, Matsuishi, et al., 1998). The EEG characteristically shows multiple spike-wave complexes and spike-wave discharges at 3–4 hertz (Panayiotopoulos et al., 1994). Valproic acid is the treatment of choice; and if therapy is started early, remission occurs in most patients. If therapy begins after many severe generalized tonic-clonic seizures, the response to medication is incomplete (Ercegovac et al., 1998).

Paroxysmal Events that Mimic Seizures
A complete history is crucial to determine whether a paroxysmal event is a result of seizure activity. Williams, Grant, Jackson, and colleagues (1996) reported behavioral descriptors which help to differentiate between seizure and nonseizure events (Table 17.8). In addition, home videotape monitoring, with its widespread availability, is becoming an important adjunct to the history. Sheth and Bodensteiner (1994) outlined guidelines for parents to use while videotaping an event to ensure that the quality of the recording is sufficient for interpretation (Table 17.9). Table 17.10 describes specific childhood events and their differentiation from seizures.

Developmental Disorders that Are Frequently Associated with Seizure Disorders
Children with developmental disabilities are at a significantly increased risk for developing a seizure disorder and often have complex seizure patterns that are difficult to control (Steffenburg, Hagberg, & Kyllerman, 1996). These factors may lead to poly-

Table 17.8. Behavioral descriptors frequently reported to occur during seizure activity

Does not remember what happened
Moves mouth in an atypical way
Eyes turn or head turns to one side
Drools
Jerks or twitches
Becomes stiff
Stares off into space
Bites or chews tongue
Eyes look glassy
Does not respond
Mumbles or slurs words
Changes in breathing

Adapted from Williams, Grant, Jackson, et al. (1996).

pharmacy and multiple medication changes. Monitoring for possible side effects, drug interactions, and drug levels can often overwhelm a family. Parents of children with developmental disabilities rank seizures as a major disruptive factor (Devinsky & Vazquez, 1993). They often are concerned more about the seizure disorder than the developmental disability. Parents may feel helplessness, worry about further brain damage, and feel stress with every seizure. In addition, children with seizures and developmental disabilities frequently require prolonged, if not lifelong, therapy. Table 17.11 lists some developmental and neurodegenerative disorders that have epilepsy as a prominent feature.

Table 17.9   Checklist for parents to use when recording a possible seizure

Prerecording	Have the camera ready in an accessible position.
Technique	The background should be a dark color.
	Turn the lights on, or use a camera that can record well at low levels of light.
	Remove obstructions such as furniture, bed coverings, or clothing.
Recording	Frame the child's entire body without excessive surrounding space. If jerking of a limb or automatisms are present, then zooming in is desirable as long as part of the recording shows the entire body.
	Ideally, recording begins before the event, encompasses the spell, and finishes with the postictal period.
Postrecording	Mark the tape counter and preview the recording.

Adapted from Sheth and Bodensteiner (1994).

Table 17.10.   Differentiation of physiologic paroxysmal events from epileptic seizures in young children

Physiologic spell	Differentiation from epileptic seizures
Syncope	Rarely occurs lying down
Breath holding	Provoked or preceded by frustration, injury, or anger
Paroxysmal vertigo	Nausea and the fear of walking
Gastroesophageal reflux	Tonic neck deviation shortly after feeding
Tremors	Abolished by change in posture
Myoclonus	Provoked by sudden startle
Opisthotonus	Spasticity accentuated by crying
Rhythmic sleep myoclonus	Exclusively in sleep; normal electroencephalogram
Staring spells	Frequent when bored
Tics	Head and neck movements become worse with stress
Masturbation	Pelvic thrusting with preserved consciousness
Pseudo seizure	Thrashing movements rather than tonic-clonic movements
Shuddering attacks	Brief shivering spells; may be a family history of essential tremor
Night terrors	Brief nocturnal episodes of terror without typical convulsive movements
Rages	Provoked and goal directed

Adapted from Sheth and Bodensteiner (1994) and Murphy and Dehkharghani (1994).

DIAGNOSIS AND EVALUATION

Comprehensive Evaluation of a Child with a Suspected Seizure Disorder

The objectives of the diagnostic evaluation of a child with a suspected seizure disorder are to

• Confirm the presence of an epileptic seizure (versus a paroxysmal nonepileptic event)
• Identify the seizure type (partial versus generalized)
• Determine whether the seizure disorder belongs to a specific epilepsy or an epileptic syndrome
• Identify associated developmental, mental health, or learning disabilities
• Determine the presence of associated medical problems
• Determine the need for family support services

The responsibilities of the primary care physician and the nurse are listed in Table 17.12. Often, referral to a pediatric neurologist or to another specialist (e.g., a developmental pediatrician) is necessary during the initial stages of evaluation and management.

Table 17.11.   Seizures in developmental disorders

Developmental disorder	Prevalence of seizure disorder
Neurofibromatosis 1	6%
Tuberous sclerosis	93%
Down syndrome	6%
Cerebral palsy	25%
Mental retardation (idiopathic)	8%–15%
Neural tube defects	25%
Autism	10%
Cerebral dysgenesis	Highly associated
Schizencephaly	Highly associated
Rett syndrome	>50%
Angelman syndrome	79%

Adapted from Granata, Battaglia, D'Incerti, et al. (1996), Hunt (1993), Korf, Carrazana, and Holmes (1993), Leitner and Smith (1996), Sansom, Krishanan, Corbett, et al. (1993), and Wallace (1990).

Parent, Child, and Teacher Interviews   A critical part of the diagnostic evaluation of a seizure disorder is obtaining a detailed history. This history should include

- A detailed description of the ictal event as well as information about the period immediately preceding and immediately after the episode (Table 17.13)
- A videotape recording, if possible (see discussion in the previous section)
- A family history that includes questions about family members with a seizure disorder, birth defects, neonatal deaths, motor impairments, developmental problems, learning difficulties including mental retardation, childhood-onset hearing loss, birthmarks, or behavior problems
- A detailed developmental history, including questions about motor and language milestones as well as any loss of skills that may suggest a neurodegenerative process
- A past medical history that includes the prenatal and perinatal history; a general medical and diet history; and questions about possible ingestions, previous seizure or seizure-like behaviors, CNS infections or head trauma, and current medications
- Information about previous studies that have been performed, including, for example, laboratory work, an EEG, a cranial ultrasonography (US) scan, a head CT scan, or an MRI scan

Developmental Screening   A seizure may be the first clue that a developmental deviation is present. It is important for all children with a suspected

Table 17.12.   Components of the comprehensive evaluation of children with a suspected seizure disorder

History (child and family)
Videotape recordings of seizure events and seizure record as needed
Medical examination (with emphasis on neurologic examination)
- May include Infant Motor Screen (Nickel, Renken, & Gallenstein, 1989)
- May include screening for minor congenital anomalies (see the Appendix at the end of Chapter 5).
Laboratory studies (electroencephalogram, neuroimaging, blood work)
Developmental screening
- Ages & Stages Questionnaires (Bricker & Squires, 1999)
- Revised Developmental Screening Inventory (Knobloch, Stevens, Malone, et al., 1980)
Behavioral assessment
May include Child Behavior Checklist (CBCL) (Achenbach & Edelbrock, 1983)
Conners' Parent and Teachers Rating Scales–Revised (Conners, 1997)
School information
Cognitive, achievement, and neuropsychologic testing as needed
Assessment of family stress and coping
May include Parenting Stress Index (Abidin, 1995)

seizure to be screened for any delays. This screening can be done with a parent-completed questionnaire such as the *Ages & Stages Questionnaires, Second Edition* (Bricker & Squires, 1999), or a general office screen such as the *Revised Developmental Screening Inventory* (Knobloch, Stevens, Malone, et al., 1980). Please refer to Chapter 2 for further discussion of screening and surveillance.

Medical Examination   The medical examination of a child with a suspected seizure disorder should include

- A general physical examination, including blood pressure and pulse rate
- Growth parameters, including head circumference
- A thorough examination of the skin for café au lait spots, depigmented macules, adenoma sebaceum, Shagreen's patch, subungual fibromas, angiomas, and neurofibromas
- A fundoscopic examination
- A thorough neurologic examination, including a neuromotor examination (e.g., Infant Motor Screen; Nickel, Renken, & Gallenstein, 1989)
- An examination for minor congenital anomalies (see form located in the Appendix at the end of Chapter 5)

Table 17.13. Pertinent clinical history questions

For the observers	For the older child who is able to respond
What was the child doing immediately before the seizure?	What is the last event the child recalled?
Where did the seizure occur?	Could the child understand people talking during the event?
At what time of day did the seizure occur?	What happened after the seizure?
What was the first abnormality?	Were there any precipitating events? Extrasensory stimulation?
What happened during the seizure (including direction of gaze)?	Has the child experienced aura?
Could the child be aroused?	
Was incontinence of urine or stool present?	
What happened after the seizure?	

Adapted from Epilepsy Foundation of America (1992).

- Hyperventilation for 1–2 minutes if absence seizures are suspected or symptoms are thought to be due directly to hyperventilation

Electroencephalogram EEGs are almost always performed in children with a suspected seizure disorder, with some exceptions including straightforward simple febrile seizures or seizures that are due to a transient metabolic abnormality (e.g., those that can occur with dehydration). An EEG is a critical component of classifying particular seizure types. A major limitation of EEG study is that ictal abnormalities may not be present during the standard 30-minute recording. In addition, the skill of the interpreter must be considered because of the normal maturational changes. Ajmone-Marsan and Zivin (1970) found that the sensitivity of a single EEG for identifying specific epileptiform events is about 50%, increasing to about 90% by the third recording. Recording during wake and sleep states is desired, and hyperventilation and photic stimulation can be used in older children to increase the yield of capturing an ictal event. Prolonged monitoring with videotelemetry or ambulatory monitoring can also be helpful in the following circumstances:

- If routine EEGs are normal
- In children with suspected pseudo seizures
- When an exact seizure count is needed
- In candidates for epilepsy surgery

Videotelemetry or ambulatory monitoring is helpful in detecting seizure activity only if seizures occur during the recording.

Neuroimaging Neuroimaging is an important tool in the diagnosis and management of children with seizure disorders (Duncan, 1997). Holmes (1989) showed that 30%–40% of children with a seizure disorder had an abnormal CT scan. Since the advent of MRI technology, the percentage of children with an identified brain abnormality is probably much higher because MRI is excellent at detecting areas of focal dysgenesis and tumors that were not previously delineated well with CT. In addition, further advancements (e.g., interactive segmentation techniques) have identified abnormalities not previously detected on routine MRI scans. Using this technique, 40% of individuals with juvenile myclonic epilepsy were found to have significant abnormalities (Woermann, Free, Koepp, et al., 1999). Duncan (1997) found that 85% of individuals with refractory partial seizures who were candidates for surgical treatment had a relevant MRI abnormality. In addition, MRI has an advantage over CT by not exposing the child to radiation and enabling better visualization of the temporal lobes and posterior fossa.

CT continues to be important in the detection of calcifications and is often the only neuroimaging study available. Skull X ray has a limited role in the evaluation of a child with a seizure disorder. US is the imaging modality of choice for infants born prematurely and is excellent for detecting intraventricular, periventricular, and intracerebral hemorrhage. It also can detect hydrocephalus readily and is useful in the diagnosis of hypoxic-ischemic encephalopathy (Carson, Hertzberg, Bowie, & Burger, 1990). Although a US scan can detect certain developmental anomalies, a MRI is usually needed to study these malformations.

PET, which is not readily available, and SPECT, which is more readily available but less sensitive, are instrumental in detecting focal metabolic abnormalities. They are often used when evaluating children for surgery. Children with Sturge-Weber syndrome, Lennox-Gastaut syndrome, Landau-Kleffner syndrome, and children with intractable seizures, are often candidates for this form of evaluation. Magnetic resonance relaxometry, magnetic resonance spectroscopy, functional MRI, and receptor PET studies are newer imaging techniques (Kuzniecky, 1996).

A neuroimaging study is indicated in children with seizures and any of the following:

- Evidence of developmental delay or regression
- A history or a physical examination suggestive of a CNS abnormality (e.g., those with a focal abnormality on neurological examination, neurocutaneous stigmata, macrocephaly, microcephaly)
- A predisposition to have a structural abnormality (e.g., those who present with a seizure in the first few years of life or those with partial seizures)
- Seizures that are refractory to treatment

When ordering a neuroimaging study, it is important to include the child's age as well as the suspected clinical diagnosis in order for the proper study to be performed. Chloral hydrate is the medication of choice for sedation (Greenberg, Faerber, Aspinall, & Adams, 1993).

Laboratory Assessment   The following are laboratory studies that are recommended for evaluation of a child with seizures:

- *Neonate:* EEG, electrolytes, BUN, calcium, magnesium, glucose, blood gas, urine metabolic screen, lumbar puncture (LP), lactate, ammonia, cranial US, complete blood count (CBC)
- *Well infant:* EEG; consider calcium, magnesium, BUN, and CT or MRI
- *Ill infant:* EEG, glucose, calcium, magnesium, CBC, BUN, electrolytes; consider blood culture, LP, urine metabolic screen, lactate, ammonia, urine toxicology screen, CT or MRI, ophthalmologic examination, and glucose
- *Well older child:* EEG; consider CT or MRI
- *Ill older child:* EEG, CBC, electrolytes, BUN; consider blood culture, LP, urine toxicology screen, CT or MRI, ophthalmologic exam, glucose, calcium, magnesium
- *Infant or child with developmental delays or a child who has atypical absence seizures, myoclonic seizures, or infantile spasms or Lennox-Gastaut syndrome:* EEG, MRI, electrolytes, CBC, BUN, ophthalmologic evaluation, urine organic acids and plasma amino acids, chromosomes; consider lysosomal enzymes; LP for protein, enzymes, and immunoglobulin G (IgG); long-chain fatty acids; skin biopsy; PET or SPECT scan

Behavioral Assessment   Children with epilepsy are at an increased risk for developing behavior problems (Kim, 1991). Hoare and Russell (1995)

reported psychiatric dysfunction in 48% of children with epilepsy. Arbelle, Caplan, Guthrie, and colleagues (1997) reported that 54% of children with primary generalized epilepsy with absences and 63% of children with complex partial epilepsy have one or more psychiatric diagnoses. Children with a seizure disorder and developmental disability have significantly more behavior problems than children with other chronic conditions not involving the CNS (Dunn & Austin, 1999). Poor seizure control, biological factors, family stress and resources, gender, and cognitive function are predictors of behavior problems in children with seizure disorders (Austin, Risinger, & Beckett, 1992; Strang, 1990). Behavior problems may be due to the side effects of AEDs, but large-scale studies do not show conclusive evidence. Phenobarbital may cause both behavioral and cognitive difficulties. ADHD, depression, and autistic behaviors were cited as the most frequent behavioral disorders in a population of children with mental retardation and epilepsy (Steffenburg et al., 1996). Children with temporal lobe epilepsy may be prone to exhibiting acting-out behaviors, whereas those with generalized epilepsy may be more anxious and inhibited (Corbett, 1983). Devinsky and Vazquez (1993) reported that as many as 80% of adults with epilepsy say they are depressed.

Information regarding a child's behavior is obtained by conducting child and parent interviews, making observations in the office, and obtaining school information. A behavioral rating scale such as the Child Behavioral Checklist (parent and teacher forms) (Achenbach & Edelbrock, 1983), or the Conners' Parent and Teacher Rating Scales–Revised (1997) can help identify children who are experiencing significant behavior problems and may need further psychological or psychiatric evaluation.

Assessment of Cognitive Skills and School Achievement   Children with seizure disorders have lower scores on cognitive testing compared to their peers without seizure disorders (Farwell, Dodrill, & Batzel, 1985) and have poorer academic performance. Austin, Huberty, Huster, et al. (1998) reported that impaired adaptive functioning at school, negative attitude toward illness, and more severe illness correlated with academic underachievement. Any child who has school difficulties, behavior problems, or developmental delay should undergo cognitive and achievement testing. The school psychologist, a clinical psychologist, or a child development team can complete this testing. Neuropsychological testing also can be useful when assessing a child who is having school diffi-culties. In addition, the possible impact of poor sei-zure control and possible side effects of medication on cognitive and behavioral functioning need to be investigated.

Clinical research has led to a better understand-ing regarding the correlation between specific epi-lepsies and the learning disabilities with which they frequently are associated (e.g., left temporal lobe epilepsy is associated with difficulties with lan-guage and verbal skills as well as verbal learning) (Svoboda, 1979). Epilepsy per se, except in the case of absence seizures, does not cause learning disabil-ities, but rather the underlying neurologic abnormal-ity and associated behavior problems contribute to the child's learning difficulties.

MANAGEMENT

Medication Management

Indications for Initiating Antiepilepsy Drug Ther-apy Once the diagnosis of a seizure is made, a deci-sion must be made regarding the necessity of anti-epilepsy medication. It is important that the child, the parent, and the physician make this decision to-gether. Debate continues with regard to whether the seizure itself is harmful (Jones, 1998). Studies (e.g., Zacharowicz & Moshe, 1995) have shown that most seizures are self-limiting and do not produce harm except in cases of prolonged seizures or status epilepticus. Initiating therapy is a highly individual-ized decision that is based on considering the risks versus the benefits of treatment. This decision is in-fluenced by

- Risk factors associated with high likelihood of recurrence
- Natural history of epileptic syndromes
- Level of parental anxiety
- Accessibility to medical care
- Safety factors during a recurrence (e.g., adoles-cent driver)

Earlier retrospective studies (Camfield, Cam-field, Dooley, et al., 1985; Elwes, Chesterman, & Reynolds, 1985) reported recurrence rates after a first unprovoked seizure in the range of 27%–71%; however, more recent prospective studies (see, e.g., So, 1993) reported recurrence rates after a first un-provoked seizure between 14% and 37% at 1 year and between 34% and 52% at 4–5 years. Based on this information, a child having a first unprovoked seizure is not started on AED therapy automati-cally. Assessing for associated risk factors can be helpful when considering AED therapy. Risk fac-tors associated with higher likelihood of recurrence include the following:

- The presence of an underlying neurologic ab-normality or developmental disorder
- An abnormal EEG
- A partial seizure versus a generalized unpro-voked seizure

The probability of recurrence is even higher when two or more of these risk factors are present.

Many clinicians choose to observe without treat-ment if no risk factors are present. If one or more risk factors are present, AED therapy is usually consid-ered. It is important to note that absence epilepsies, infantile spasms, neonatal seizures, Lennox-Gastaut syndrome, and myoclonic epilepsies usually present as multiple seizures, and prompt initiation of ther-apy is indicated (Zacharowicz & Moshe, 1995). In ad-dition, if a first seizure is followed rapidly by a sec-ond seizure, treatment is usually initiated (Leppik, 1996). A pediatric neurologist is often consulted re-garding the initial evaluation and management of a child with a seizure disorder; however, the primary care physician has a central role in the child's long-term medical management.

General Principles of Antiepilepsy Drug Therapy The general principles of AED therapy include

- Investigating and classifying the seizure disor-der properly
- The use of monotherapy before polytherapy is initiated
- Monitoring for adequate seizure control by using a seizure record form (see the Appendix at the end of this chapter)
- Keeping an accurate record of antiepilepsy medications (see the Appendix at the end of this chapter)
- Monitoring for medication side effects, includ-ing behavioral and cognitive functioning
- Monitoring serum drug levels when indicated and following appropriate laboratory results
- Providing psychosocial support and education to the child, parents, family members, and educators
- Reevaluating the child with regard to treatment on a regular basis to consider the child's candi-dacy for drug withdrawal
- Discontinuing AEDs gradually
- Working closely with the consulting neurologist on management decisions (Penry, 1986)

It is also important to recognize that individuals vary with respect to their metabolism of AEDs. Seizure control may be achieved at AED dosage levels that are lower than the recommended therapeutic range, or some individuals may require higher dosage levels than the recommended range. This consideration also applies to toxic effects, which can be highly individualized. Precipitants of seizures in children who are being treated with AEDs include

- Noncompliance (can be determined by checking AED blood level)
- Illness, especially with high fever
- Excessive fatigue
- Use of illicit drugs and alcohol
- Emotional stress

In certain circumstances, AEDs may aggravate pre-existing seizures or trigger new seizure types (Guerrini, Belmonte, Genton, et al., 1998). Overdosage of phenytoin may result in an increase in seizure frequency. An inappropriate choice of an AED may cause seizure exacerbation, for example, the use of carbamazepine and vigabatrin to treat absence and myoclonic seizures (Guerrini et al., 1998).

Parents and families should be counseled on these factors. The treatments commonly used for a variety of seizures and epileptic syndromes are listed in Table 17.14.

Important Issues in Educating the Child and Parents About Medications Before initiating AED

Table 17.14. Use of antiepileptic drugs in the treatment of epilepsy

Types of seizures/ epilepsies/syndromes	Common treatments
Neonatal seizures	Phenobarbital Diazepam
Infantile spasms	Adrenocorticotropic hormone Corticosteroids Ketogenic diet Surgery
Simple partial or focal seizures	Carbamazepine Phenytoin Phenobarbital
Complex partial (psychomotor, temporal lobe)	Carbamazepine Phenytoin Phenobarbital
Benign epilepsy of childhood with centrotemporal spikes	Carbamazepine Phenytoin
Juvenile myoclonic epilepsy	Valproic acid
Absence	Valproic acid Ethosuximide
Generalized tonic-clonic	Phenobarbital Carbamazepine Valproic acid

Adapted from Morton and Pellock (1996).

therapy, it is important to address the parents' and the child's concerns in a supportive and relaxed manner. The following medication issues should be discussed:

- The goals of the medication therapy
- Side effects of medications
- Advantages of brand name versus generic drugs
- The importance of not using another person's AEDs
- The need to store medications out of children's reach
- Relative drug interactions
- The importance of compliance with the recommended, prescribed dosing regimen
- Warning against discontinuing AEDs suddenly

Common Antiepilepsy Drugs, Associated Side Effects, and Appropriate Monitoring AEDs used in children include carbamazepine (Tegretol and Carbatrol), phenytoin (Dilantin), valproic acid (Depakene), ethosuximide (Zarontin), phenobarbital, vigabatrin (Sabrilex), lamotrigine (Lamictal), gabapentin (Neurontin), felbamate (Felbatol), tiagabine (Gabatril), and topiramate (Topomax). Each of these drugs, their associated side effects, and appropriate monitoring of children once these drugs have been prescribed are outlined in the list that follows.

Carbamazepine (CBZ) (Tegretol, Carbatrol)
- Used for partial and generalized tonic-clonic seizures; its use is contraindicated in treating typical absence seizures (Parker, Agathonikou, Robinson, & Panayiotopoulos, 1998)
- Dosage
  Ages 6–11 years:
  a. Usual starting dose is 100 milligrams twice per day (doses of 5–8 milligrams per kilogram per day are generally sufficient during the first week of treatment)
  b. Add up to 100 milligrams per day at weekly intervals, three or four times per day
  c. Usual maintenance dose is 10–20 milligrams per kilogram per day divided three or four times per day
  d. Maximum dose is 1 gram per day
  Ages 12–15 years:
  a. Usual starting dose is 200 milligrams, twice per day
  b. Add up to 200 milligrams per day at weekly intervals
  c. Usual maintenance dose is 10–20 milligrams per kilogram per day, divided three to four times per day.
  d. Maximum dose is 1 gram per day

- CBZ induces its own metabolism in the liver; therefore, the gradual increase in dosage is recommended
- Check blood level approximately 3 weeks after initiating treatment (therapeutic range = 4–12 micrograms per milliliter)
- Peaks in 1.5 hours with suspension and 4–5 hours with tablet
- New steady state is reached approximately 3–4 days after each dosage change once therapy has been established
- Prior to initiating therapy, draw blood for CBC and liver function tests (LFTs); repeat in 6 weeks, and monitor closely during the first 6 months of treatment
- Side effects
  a. *Dose-related:* Sedation, dizziness, visual disturbances, ataxia
  b. *Non-dose-related:* Gastrointestinal upset, diarrhea, fluid retention
  c. *Idiosyncratic:* Allergic dermatitis, granulocyte depression (can expect mild decrease in absolute neutrophil count; if neutrophil count is less than 1,000, discontinue medication), Stevens-Johnson syndrome, aplastic anemia, hepatic failure, kidney failure, developmental regression
- Phenobarbital, phenytoin, and valproic acid increase CBZ levels
- Macrolide antibiotics (e.g., erythromycin) increase CBZ levels; if unable to avoid their use, CBZ dose should be decreased by approximately 30%, and side effects and drug levels should be monitored closely
- Low potential for long-term negative cognitive and behavioral effects
- Chemically related to tricyclics and may have calming effect on ADHD-related behaviors

Phenytoin (Dilantin)

- Use for generalized tonic-clonic seizures and partial seizures
- Available in different dosage forms that have clinical significance for the rate of absorption and the delivered dose of phenytoin acid
- In general, use the prompt-release phenytoin sodium capsules or the oral suspension
- Loading dose
  a. 15–20 milligrams per kilogram if no doses have been administered in the previous 24 hours or estimate for every 1 milligram per kilogram administered; serum level increases by 1 microgram per milliliter; pheny-

toin follows nonlinear regression between dosage and serum concentration, so wide fluctuations in blood levels may occur at higher therapeutic levels; administer the oral loading dose in three to four doses every 2–4 hours in a clinic or hospital
- Maintenance dose
  Children younger than 3 years of age:
  a. 5–8 milligrams per kilogram per day in divided doses every 8–12 hours
  Children older than 3 years of age:
  b. 5–8 milligrams per kilogram per day in divided doses every 12–24 hours
- If started at the maintenance dose (without the loading dose), it takes 7–10 days to reach steady state
- Therapeutic range is 10–20 micrograms per milliliter
- Peak blood level when using oral suspension is 1.5–3 hours after administration
- Obtain blood for CBC and LFTs before starting therapy and during the initiation of treatment
- Side effects
  a. *Dose-related:* Nystagmus, ataxia, incoordination
  b. *Non-dose-related:* Gingival hyperplasia, coarsening of facial features, hirsutism, osteopenia, neuropathy
  c. *Idiosyncratic:* Allergic dermatitis, lupus-like syndrome, hepatic failure, fetal drug effects, aplastic anemia, hyperglycemia
- Metabolized in liver
- Can see elevation of LFTs
- Good dental hygiene reduces gum hyperplasia
- Consider supplemental vitamin D

Valproic acid (Depakene)

- Depakene (valproic acid) is rapidly absorbed and therefore blood levels fluctuate; also has a tendency to cause gastritis
- Depakote (Divalproex) is enteric-coated and produces more consistent blood levels and less gastritis; also comes in a palatable sprinkle form
- Use for mixed (absence and generalized tonic-clonic seizures), generalized tonic-clonic seizures, and partial seizures with secondary generalization
- Dosage
  a. *Initial dose:* 15 milligrams per kilogram per day, increasing at 1 week intervals by 5–10 milligrams per kilogram per day until seizures are controlled or side effects preclude further increases

b. *Maintenance dose:* Usually 30–60 milligrams per kilograms per day, unless the child is receiving more than one anticonvulsant; then a maintenance dose of 100 milligrams per kilogram per day may be required

c. If total daily dose is less than 250 milligrams, divide dose into a two or three times per day regimen

- Therapeutic range is 50–100 micrograms per milliliter
- Side effects
  a. *Dose-related:* Liver enzyme elevations, tremor, hyperammonemia, initial somnolence, behavioral changes, gastrointestinal upset, thrombocytopenia
  b. *Non-dose-related:* Weight gain, nausea, hair loss, polycystic ovaries (Vainionpaa, Rattya, Knip, et al., 1999)
  c. *Idiosyncratic:* Hepatotoxicity usually occurs during the first 3 months of therapy; initial signs of hepatotoxicity are lethargy, vomiting, and anorexia; hepatic failure occurs in 1 in 10,000 individuals; fatal hepatotoxicity has occurred primarily in children younger than age 2 years who have neurologic abnormalities and are being treated with multiple AEDs; risk in this group is 1 in 500
- Supplemental carnitine is recommended for children younger than 2 years of age (30–100 milligrams per kilogram per day)
- Obtain blood for CBC with platelets and LFTs prior to initiating therapy, and monitor the child monthly for the first 3 months of therapy
- Drug interaction with phenobarbital and other high-protein binding medications

Ethosuximide (Zarontin)

- Use for absence seizures
- Dosage
  Ages younger than 6 years:
  a. Initial dose of 15 milligrams per kilogram per day in two divided doses
  b. Maintenance dose usually 15–40 milligrams per kilogram per day in two divided doses
  Ages 6 years and older:
  a. 250 milligrams twice daily to start; increase as needed to 1.5 grams per day in two divided doses; usual maintenance dose is 20–40 milligrams per kilogram in two divided doses
- Side effects
  a. *Dose-related:* Fatigue, dizziness, intractable hiccups

b. *Non-dose-related:* Nausea, gastric discomfort

c. *Idiosyncratic:* Hepatotoxicity, lupus-like syndrome, bone marrow depression

Phenobarbital

- Use for generalized tonic-clonic seizures, partial seizures, and neonatal seizures
- Dosage
  a. *Loading dose:* 15–20 milligrams per kilogram produces a blood level of approximately 20 micrograms per milliliter
  b. *Maintenance dose:* For children younger than 2 years of age, 5–10 milligrams per kilogram per day in one dose or two divided doses; for children older than 2 years of age, 3–6 milligrams per kilogram per day in one dose or two divided doses
- Therapeutic range is 15–40 micrograms per milliliter
- Peak effect occurs 8–12 hours after dose
- Can take almost 3 weeks to achieve steady-state level after dose is changed
- Side effects
  a. *Dose-related:* Sedation, cognitive impairment, ataxia, hyperactivity, sleep problems
  b. *Non-dose-related:* Hyperactivity, osteopenia, decreased attention, sleep problems
  c. *Idiosyncratic:* Allergic dermatitis, Stevens-Johnson syndrome, hepatic failure, granulocyte suppression
- Hyperactivity, attention problems, concentration problems, aggressive behaviors, and sleep problems can occur in up to 50% of children ages 2–10 years; sedation is more common after the age of 10 years

Approximately 70% of seizures respond to traditional AED monotherapy (Appleton, 1996). The remaining 30% often present a clinical challenge, and the advent of new AEDs has offered some therapeutic options. It remains important to use the older recommended drugs appropriately in view of the lack of long-term efficacy and safety studies with the newer AEDs. Economic (i.e., high cost) factors may also be an issue with many of the newer AEDs.

Vigabatrin (Sabrilex) (not approved by the U.S. Food and Drug Administration [FDA])

- Use with partial seizures with or without secondary generalization as add-on therapy; its use for typical absence seizures is contraindicated (Parker et al., 1998)
- Emerging as an effective drug for infantile spasms, particularly those associated with tuberous sclerosis

- Side effects include transient sedation, dizziness, agitation, blood dyscrasias, and rash
- No correlation with plasma concentration and clinical efficacy; therefore, blood levels usually are not monitored

Lamotrigine (Lamictal)

- Use for partial seizures, atypical absence seizures, generalized tonic-clonic seizures, atonic seizures, myoclonic seizures, and Lennox-Gastaut syndrome
- Reports (Arky, 1999) have shown a 1 in 50 to a 1 in 100 risk of developing a life-threatening rashes in the pediatric population; therefore, lamotrigine is not recommended for use with children younger than age 16 years; this reaction has also been reported in the adult population, but it occurs in approximately 1 in 1,000 adults
- May have positive effects on attention and mood
- Side effects include drowsiness, rash, vomiting, Stevens-Johnson syndrome, and toxic epidermal necrolysis (Arky, 1999)
- Often used as an add-on drug with sodium valproic acid, and dosage recommendations depend on whether this or another AED is being administered (this may increase risk of side effects)

Gabapentin (Neurontin)

- Use as add-on treatment for partial seizures
- Also being used as monotherapy for BECTS
- Side effects include dizziness, ataxia, and drowsiness
- Reports of adverse behavioral side effects (e.g., aggressiveness and hyperactivity, especially in those with underlying encephalopathy)
- Dosage
  Older than age 12 years:
  a. 25–35 milligrams per kilogram per day, with total daily dose usually being 900–1,800 milligrams per day in three doses

Felbamate (Felbatol)

- Use has been associated with aplastic anemia and hepatic toxicity; therefore, it is contraindicated for treatment of most epilepsies except Lennox-Gastaut syndrome or seizures that are so refractory that no other reasonable alternative exists
- Therapy should not begin without the child's and family's knowing the considerable risk of serious side effects

Tiagabine (Gabatril)

- Use as adjunctive therapy in partial complex seizures in children younger than age 16 years

- Side effects
  a. Stomachache (give tiagabine with meals)
  b. Headaches, irritability

Topiramate (Topomax)

- Use as adjunctive therapy in partial complex seizures (as many as 50% of children experience a significant reduction in seizures)
- Use in intractable epilepsy, including Lennox-Gastaut syndrome, generalized seizures, and myoclonic seizures and infantile spasms
- Side effects
  a. Irritability
  b. Slurred speech
  c. Dulled mental status
  d. Kidney stones
- Should not be used in conjunction with diuretics, acetazolamide, or the ketogenic diet

Indications for Discontinuing Antiepilepsy Drug Therapy Shinnar, Berg, Moshe, and colleagues (1994) advocate considering AED therapy withdrawal in children who have been seizure-free for 2 years on AED therapy. Etiology of seizures, age of onset, family history, seizure type, the presence of an abnormal EEG, and a specific epileptic syndrome are all predictors of outcome. Children with neurologic impairment have higher recurrence rates; however, AED therapy can be discontinued successfully in more than half of these children (Shinnar et al., 1994).

Gordon, MacSween, Dooley, and associates (1996) reported wide variability in the risk of recurrence that different families are willing to accept before discontinuing AEDs. They also found that physicians are not always able to assess the degree of risk that is acceptable to a particular family. A thorough discussion between the physician and the child and family is imperative, and the importance of using an individualized approach cannot be overstressed. The decision process must take into account the statistical risk of seizure recurrence, the potential consequences of such a recurrence, and the potential adverse effects of continuing AED therapy (Shinnar et al., 1994).

Management of Status Epilepticus Because of the acute nature of status epilepticus, the primary focus is on stopping the seizure activity and concomitantly determining the etiology. Most treatment protocols include the following steps:

- Follow the ABCs of cardiopulmonary resuscitation
- With regard to the child's airway, position the child to prevent aspiration or physical injury; intubation may be necessary

- With regard to breathing, administer oxygen
- With regard to circulation, take the child's pulse and blood pressure readings and monitor vital signs
- Obtain intravenous access; measure blood sugar, electrolytes, calcium, magnesium, CBC, BUN, and drug levels
- Obtain blood gas levels
- Administer 2 milliliters per kilogram of 25% glucose if indicated
- Administer medication (most protocols use a benzodiazepine followed by phenytoin)
  a. Diazepam .1–.3 milligrams per kilogram over 1–5 minutes or lorazepam .05–.1 milligrams per kilogram (longer-acting than diazepam); respiratory depression may be a side effect of both medications
  b. If seizures continue, repeat diazepam or lorazepam (may repeat in 5–20 minutes); if seizures have stopped, give phenytoin
  c. Phenytoin 10–20 milligrams per kilogram over 5–20 minutes; monitor blood pressure and electrocardiogram (EKG); administer slowly, no faster than 1 milligram per kilogram per minute; not compatible with glucose-containing solutions
  d. Phenobarbital 5–20 milligrams per kilogram; especially useful in neonatal seizures; may produce respiratory depression, especially if used with a benzodiazepine
- Correct metabolic abnormalities
- Consider underlying causes
- Obtain CT scan if structural disorders are suspected
- Perform lumbar puncture, blood culture, and antibiotics as indicated
- Consider toxicology screen, theophylline level as indicated

Indications for Surgical Management

Advances in neuroimaging are helping to select children who may be candidates for surgery. Features of surgical candidacy include

- Intractable, disabling epilepsy
- Temporal epilepsy with hippocampal sclerosis or abnormal tissue
- Extratemporal epilepsy with abnormal tissue in a resectable site
- Epilepsy with infantile or childhood hemiplegia
- Rasmussen's encephalitis
- Drop attacks
- Landau-Kleffner syndrome
- Localized epileptogenic zone

- Low risk of new impairments postoperatively (Kennedy, 1996; Wyllie, 1998)

Alternative Epilepsy Therapies

Despite the development of new AEDs, a population of children remains that does not respond to AED therapy or who experience side effects that limit its use. Many of these children also are not candidates for surgical resection and therefore other therapies, including the ketogenic diet, immunoglobulins, and steroids, may be considered. Prasad and associates (1996) emphasized the need for critical evaluation of alternative therapies.

The *ketogenic diet* refers to dietary manipulation that results in ketone bodies instead of glucose becoming the brain's main energy source. It is a diet that is high in fat and low in protein and carbohydrates. The precise mechanism of action is not known. This therapy is used for the treatment of children with difficult-to-control seizures, such as children with infantile spasms or Lennox-Gastaut, who have not responded to AEDs. One third to two thirds of children will respond positively to the diet with a cessation of seizures or a marked decrease in seizure frequency (Freeman, Vining, Pillas, et al., 1998; Freeman & Vining, 1999; Hassan, Keene, Whiting, et al., 1999). In one study (Freeman et al., 1998), 27% of children treated continued to experience a greater than 90% reduction in seizures after 1 year of treatment. The ketogenic diet seems to work best in younger children with refractory seizures who have motivated parents working closely with an experienced dietitian. It is a difficult diet to follow, and gastrointestinal side effects may limit its use as a treatment modality (Vining, Freeman, Ballaban-Gil, et al., 1998).

Immunoglobulins have been used intravenously to treat infantile spasms, Landau-Kleffner syndrome, and Rasmussen's encephalitis. Most of the reports have been anecdotal, and therefore the appropriate dosage, frequency of administration, and duration of therapy are not well known. Steroids have been shown to be quite effective with certain seizure types, for example, infantile spasms (Hancock & Osborne, 1998; Prasad et al., 1996); however, their use in Landau-Kleffner syndrome is more controversial. Marescaux, Hirsch, Finck, and coworkers (1990) reported improved speech, suppression of seizures, and normalization of the EEG in all three children treated with corticosteroids; other researchers have found ACTH, prednisone, and dexamethasone to have some benefit (Lerman et al., 1991).

Behavior management can be a useful adjunct to medical therapy. Kuhn, Allen, and Shriver (1995) outlined behavioral intervention guidelines that can be used in a primary care physician's office. This intervention consists of getting a baseline assessment of seizure activity to evaluate for environmental factors playing a role in seizure evocation as well as for record keeping. A behavioral intervention using the following guidelines can then be used:

- Affirm the child's disability and normalize the role of the environment.
- Teach the child anticonvulsant coping behaviors such as relaxation techniques.
- Teach immediate caregivers these guidelines to encourage the child's and family's independent functioning.
- Recommend that teachers and other supervising adults respond in a similar fashion (see the Appendix at the end of this chapter for specific recommendations).

Counseling the Child and the Family

Counsel children and families about seizure recognition, first aid, and other education issues, as well as communication with schools. Please also review the discussion of family support services in Chapters 1 and 3.

Recognition of Seizures Most families can recognize a generalized tonic-clonic seizure easily; however, other subtle behavioral changes may not be recognized as seizure activity. These behavioral changes include

- Short attention blackouts that look like daydreaming
- Sudden falls for no reason
- Lack of response for brief periods
- Dazed behavior
- Unusual sleepiness and irritability when awakened from sleep
- Head nodding
- Rapid blinking
- Frequent complaints from the child that objects look, sound, taste, smell, or feel funny
- Clusters of jackknife movements in babies
- Clusters of grabbing with both arms in babies
- Sudden stomach pain followed by confusion and sleepiness
- Repeated movements that look out of place or unnatural (EFA, 1994)

First Aid for Seizures Family members and other caregivers should be instructed on first aid during a seizure. For generalized tonic-clonic sei-

zures, family members should observe the following precautions:

- Move sharp objects out of the way.
- Remember that even though the child looks as if in pain, the child actually feels nothing during the seizure.
- If the child stops breathing for a few moments or shows some temporary blueness or paleness, be aware that this is a naturally occurring part of the seizure.
- Loosen tight clothing around the neck, and wipe away saliva around the mouth.
- Turn the child on his or her side in case he or she vomits during the seizure.
- Do not try to bring the child out of the seizure by using cold water or slapping or shaking the child.
- Do not try to hold the child down or restrain the child in any way.
- Do not try to give the child medication by mouth during the seizure.
- Do not put anything hard in the child's mouth to keep the child from biting his or her lips or tongue.
- Do try to observe what happens during the seizure; check a wristwatch and note when the child regains consciousness.
- If a seizure lasts longer than 5 minutes or if two seizures occur in a row, the child should be brought to the physician for medical attention (EFA, 1994).

Sports and Recreation Activities Most professionals recognize that the psychological benefits of sports participation can outweigh the physical risks it entails. Common sense should prevail when deciding on appropriate sporting events for children with epilepsy. Sports such as scuba diving or rock climbing should be avoided; but most other sports, including swimming, should be allowed. As with all pediatric patients, it is important that the child with epilepsy never swim alone.

Parenting Parents of a child with a seizure disorder have a natural tendency to give special attention to that child. This special attention can influence the emotional development of the child as well as the relationship between the parents and the other children in the family as well as the marital relationship. The following suggestions for parents have been helpful:

- Try to give the child with epilepsy responsibilities, duties, and privileges just like other family members.

- Take time to talk with the child about his or her understanding of epilepsy, and encourage the child's siblings to express their concerns.
- Do not encourage that the siblings of the child with seizures become the child's permanent caregivers.
- Do not "give in" to a child with epilepsy because of a threatened tantrum out of the fear that a tantrum might trigger a seizure; it is important to provide the child with consistent discipline.
- A child who is exhibiting significant behavior problems may need a referral for individual and possibly family counseling.

Communication with the Schools Direct communication with the school regarding a child's seizure disorder is an important way to create a more accepting school environment for the child. The Epilepsy Foundation of America provides pamphlets and educational videotapes to help with this process. In addition, it is helpful for the child's par-

ents to meet with teachers to provide specific information about their child's seizure disorder, medications, and possible medication side effects. A reassuring letter from a physician to the child's teachers and/or school administrators can also be helpful.

Important Care Coordination Issues
General recommendations for changes in office procedures to facilitate the care of children with disabilities and chronic conditions are discussed in Chapter 1. In addition, specific responsibilities of the primary health care professional for the management of a child with a seizure disorder are to

- Maintain an updated list of neurologists who specialize in pediatric seizure disorders
- Identify clearly who is responsible for medication management (the primary care physician, the neurologist, or the developmental pediatrician)
- Exchange reports with schools and other service providers regularly, and update school staff on changes in seizure management

REFERENCES

Achenbach, T.M., & Edelbrock, C. (1983). *Manual for the Child Behavior Checklist and Revised Child Behavior Profile.* Burlington: University of Vermont, Department of Psychiatry.

Ajmone-Marsan, C., & Zivin, L.S. (1970). Factors related to the occurrence of typical paroxysmal abnormalities in the EEG recordings of epileptic patients. *Epilepsia, 11,* 361–381.

Appleton, R.E. (1996). The new antiepileptic drugs. *Archives of Diseases in Childhood, 75,* 256–262.

Arbelle, C.R., Caplan, R., Guthrie, D., et al. (1997). Formal thought disorder and psychopathology in pediatric primary generalized and complex partial epilepsy. *Journal of the American Academy of Child and Adolescent Psychiatry, 36*(9), 1286–1294.

Arky, R. (1999). *Physician's desk reference* (53rd ed.). Montvale, NJ: Medical Economics Co.

Austin, J.K., Huberty, T.J., Huster, G.A., & Dunn, D.W. (1998). Academic achievement in children with epilepsy or asthma. *Developmental Medicine and Child Neurology, 40*(4), 248–255.

Austin, J.K., Risinger, M.W., & Beckett, L.A. (1992). Correlates of behavior problems in children with epilepsy. *Epilepsia, 33*(6), 1115–1122.

Baram, T.Z., & Hatalski, C.G. (1998). Neuropeptide-mediated excitability: A key triggering mechanism for seizure generation in the developing brain. *Trends in Neuroscience, 21*(11), 471–476.

Bare, M.A., Glauser, T.A., & Strawsburg, R.H. (1998). Need for electroencephalogram video confirmation of atypical absence seizures in children with Lennox-Gastaut syndrome. *Journal of Child Neurology, 13*(10), 498–500.

Bethune, P., Gordon, K.G., Dooley, J.M., et al. (1993). Which child will have a febrile seizure? *American Journal of Diseases of Children, 147,* 35–39.

Bobele, G.B., & Bodensteiner, J.B. (1990). Infantile spasms. *Neurologic Clinics, 8*(3), 633–645.

Bricker, D., & Squires, J. (1999). *Ages and Stages Questionnaires (ASQ): A parent-completed, child-monitoring system* (2nd ed.). Baltimore: Paul H. Brookes Publishing Co.

Bye, A.M., Cunningham, C.A., Chee, K.Y., et al. (1997). Outcome of neonates with electrographically identified seizures, or at risk of seizures. *Pediatric Neurology, 16*(3), 225–231.

Camfield, P.R., Camfield, C.S., Dooley, J.M., et al. (1985). Epilepsy after a first unprovoked seizure in childhood. *Neurology, 35*(11), 1657–1660.

Carson, S., Hertzberg, B., Bowie, J., & Burger, P. (1990). Value of sonography in the diagnosis of intracranial haemorrhage and periventricular leukomalacia: A postmortem study of 35 cases. *American Journal of Neuroradiology, 11,* 677–684.

Commission on Classification and Terminology of the International League Against Epilepsy. (1981). Proposal for revised clinical and electroencephalographic classification of epileptic seizures. *Epilepsia, 22*(4), 489–501.

Commission on Classification and Terminology of the International League Against Epilepsy. (1985). Proposal for the classification of epilepsies and epileptic syndromes. *Epilepsia, 26,* 268–278.

Conners, C.K. (1997). *Conners' Parent and Teacher Rating Scales–Revised.* North Tonawanda, NY: Multi-Health Systems.

Corbett, J.A. (1983). In M. Rutter (Ed.), *Developmental neuropsychiatry.* New York: Guilford Press.

Delgado-Escueta, A.V., & Enrile-Bascal, F.E. (1984). Juvenile myoclonic epilepsy of Janz. *Neurology, 34,* 285–294.

Delgado-Escueta, A.V., Medina, M.T., Serratosa, J.M., et al. (1999). Mapping and positional cloning of common idiopathic generalized epilepsies: Juvenile myoclonus epilepsy and childhood absence epilepsy. *Advances in Neurology, 79,* 351–374.

Devinsky, O., & Vazquez, B. (1993). Behavioral changes associated with epilepsy. *Neurology Clinics, 11*(1), 127–149.

Dravet, C., Bureau, M., & Genton, P. (1992). Benign myoclonic epilepsy of infancy: Electroclinical symptomatology and differential diagnosis from the other types of generalized epilepsy of infancy. *Epilepsy Research Supplement, 6,* 131–135.

Duchowny, M., & Harvey, A.S. (1996). Pediatric epilepsy syndromes: An update and critical review. *Epilepsia, 37*(Suppl. 1), S26–S40.

Duncan, J.S. (1997). Imaging and epilepsy. *Brain, 120,* 339–377.

Dunn, D.W., & Austin, J.K. (1999). Behavioral issues in pediatric epilepsy. *Neurology, 53*(5 Suppl. 2), S96–S100.

Elwes, R.D., Chesterman, P., & Reynolds, E.H. (1985). Prognosis after a first untreated tonic-clonic seizure. *Lancet, 2*(8458), 752–753.

Epilepsy Foundation of America (EFA). (1992). *Seizure recognition and observation* [Monograph]. Landover, MD: Author.

Epilepsy Foundation of America (EFA). (1994). *How to recognize and classify seizures and epilepsy* [Monograph]. Landover, MD: Author.

Ercegovac, M.D., Vojvodic, N., Sokic, D.V., et al. (1998). Juvenile myoclonic epilepsy [Serbo-Croatian (Cyrillic)]. *Srpski Arhiv Za Celokupno Lekarstvo, 126*(9–10), 335–344.

Farwell, J.R., Dodrill, C.B., & Batzel, L.W. (1985). Neuropsychological abilities of children with epilepsy. *Epilepsia, 26*(5), 395–400.

Fenichel, G.M. (1997). Paroxysmal disorders. In G.M. Fenichel, *Clinical pediatric neurology: A signs and symptoms approach* (3rd ed., pp. 1–47). Philadelphia: W.B. Saunders Co.

Freeman, J.M., & Vining, E.P. (1999). Seizures decrease rapidly after fasting: Preliminary studies of the ketogenic diet. *Archives of Paediatrics and Adolescent Medicine, 153*(9), 946–949.

Freeman, J.M., Vining, E.P.G., Pillas, D.J., et al. (1998). The efficacy of the ketogenic diet—1998: A prospective evaluation of intervention in 150 children. *Pediatrics, 102,* 1358–1363.

Gordon, K., MacSween, J., Dooley, J., et al. (1996). Families are content to discontinue antiepileptic drugs at different risks than their physicians. *Epilepsia, 37*(6), 557–562.

Granata, T., Battaglia, G., D'Incerti, L., et al. (1996). Schizencepaly: Neuroradiologic and epileptologic findings. *Epilepsia, 37*(12), 1185–1193.

Greenberg, S.B., Faerber, E.N., Aspinall, C.L., & Adams, R.C. (1993). High-dose chloral hydrate sedation for children undergoing MR imaging: Safety and efficacy in relation to age. *American Journal of Roentgenology, 161*(3), 639–641.

Guerrini, R., Belmonte, A., & Genton, P. (1998). Antiepileptic drug-induced worsening of seizures in children. *Epilepsia, 39*(Suppl. 3), S2–S10.

Guerrini, R., Dravet, C., Genton, P., et al. (1998). Lamotrigine and seizure aggravation in severe myoclonic epilepsy. *Epilepsia, 39*(5), 508–512.

Haines, S.T., & Casto, D.T. (1994). Treatment of infantile spasms. *Annals of Pharmacotherapy, 38*(6), 779–791.

Hancock, E., & Osborne, J. (1998). Treatment of infantile spasms with high-dose oral prednisolone. *Developmental Medicine and Child Neurology, 40*(7), 500.

Hassan, A.M., Keene, D.L., Whiting, S.E., et al. (1999). Ketogenic diet in the treatment of refractory epilepsy in childhood. *Pediatric Neurology, 21*(2), 548–552.

Hauser, W.A. (1990). Risk factors for epilepsy. *Epilepsy Research, 4,* 45–52.

Hauser, W.A. (1994). The prevalence and incidence of convulsive disorders in children. *Epilepsia, 35*(Suppl. 2), S1–S5.

Hirsch, E., Marescaux, C., & Maquet, P. (1990). Landau-Kleffner syndrome: A clinical and EEG study of five cases. *Epilepsia, 31,* 756–767.

Hoare, P., & Russell, M. (1995). The quality of life of children with chronic epilepsy and their families: Preliminary findings with a new assessment measure. *Developmental Medicine and Child Neurology, 37*(8), 689–696.

Holmes, G.L. (1989). Electroencephalographic and neuroradiologic evaluation of children with epilepsy. *Pediatric Clinics of North America, 36*(2), 395–420.

Holmes, G.L. (1993). Benign focal epilepsies of childhood. *Epilepsia, 34*(Suppl. 3), S49–S61.

Hrachovy, R., & Frost, J. (1989). Infantile spasms. *Pediatric Clinics of North America, 36*(2), 311–330.

Hunt, A. (1993). Development, behaviour, and seizures in 300 cases of tuberous sclerosis. *Journal of Intellectual Disability Research, 37*(pt. 1), 41–51.

Hurst, D.L. (1990). Epidemiology of severe myoclonic epilepsy of infancy. *Epilepsia, 31*(4), 397–400.

Ishida, S., Yamashita, Y., Matsuishi, T., et al. (1998). Photosensitive seizures provoked while viewing "pocket monsters," a made-for-telelvision animation program in Japan. *Epilepsia, 39*(12), 1340–1344.

Johnston, M.V. (1996). Developmental aspects of epileptogenesis. *Epilepsia, 37*(Suppl. 1), S2–S9.

Jones, M.W. (1998). Consequences of epilepsy: Why do we treat seizures? *Canadian Journal of Neurological Sciences, 25*(4), S24–S26.

Kennedy, C.R. (1996). Advances in neurology. *Archives of Diseases in Childhood, 75,* 251–255.

Kim, W.J. (1991). Psychiatric aspects of epileptic children and adolescents. *Journal of the American Academy of Child and Adolescent Psychiatry, 30*(6), 874–886.

Knobloch, H., Stevens, F., Malone, A., et al. (1980). Manual of Developmental Diagnosis. The Administration and Interpretation of the Revised Gesell and Amatruda Developmental Neurological Examination. New York: Harper & Row.

Knudsen, F.U., Paerregaard, A., Andersen, R., & Andresen, J. (1996). Long term outcome of prophylaxis for febrile convulsions. *Archives of Diseases in Childhood, 74,* 13–18.

Korf, B.R., Carrazana, E., & Holmes, G.L. (1993). Patterns of seizures observed in association with neurofibromatosis 1. *Epilepsia, 34*(4), 616–620.

Kuhn, B., Allen, K., & Shriver, M. (1995). Behavioral management of children's seizure activity. *Clinical Pediatrics, 11,* 570–575.

Kuzniecky, R.I. (1996). Neuroimaging in pediatric epilepsy. *Epilepsia, 37*(Suppl. 1), S10–S21.

Legido, A., Clancy, R., & Berman, P.H. (1991). Neurologic outcome after electro-encephalographically proven neonatal seizures. *Pediatrics, 88*(3), 583–596.

Leitner, R.P., & Smith, A. (1996). An Angelman syndrome clinic: Report on 24 patients. *Journal of Paediatrics and Child Health, 32*(2), 94–98.

Leppert, M., Anderson, V.E., & Quattlebaum, T.G. (1989). Benign familial neonatal convulsions linked to genetic markers on chromosome 20. *Nature, 337*, 647–648.

Leppik, I.E. (1996). Rational monotherapy for epilepsy. *Baillieres Clinical Neurology, 5*(4), 749–755.

Lerman, P., Lerman-Sagie, T., & Kivity, S. (1991). Effect of early corticosteroid therapy for Landau-Kleffner syndrome. *Developmental Medicine and Child Neurology, 33*, 257–260.

Lin, Y., Itomi, K., Takada, H., et al. (1998). Benign myoclonic epilepsy in infants: Video-EEG features and long-term follow-up. *Neuropediatrics, 29*(5), 268–271.

Lombroso, C.T. (1990). Early myoclonic encephalopathy, early infantile epileptic encephalopathy, and benign and severe infantile myoclonic epilepsies: A critical review and personal contributions. *Journal of Clinical Neurophysiology, 7*, 380.

MacDonald, B.K., Johnson, A.L., Sander, J.W., & Shorvon, S.D. (1999). Febrile convulsions in 220 children: Neurological sequelae at 12 years follow-up. *European Neurology, 41*(4), 179–186.

Marescaux, C., Hirsch, E., Finck, S., et al. (1990). Landau-Kleffner syndrome: A pharmacologic study of five cases. *Epilepsia, 31*(6), 768–777.

Meldrum, B.S. (1989). GABAergic mechanisms in the pathogenesis and treatment of epilepsy. *British Journal of Clinical Pharmacology, 27*, 35–115.

Mitchell, W.G. (1996). Status epilepticus and acute repetitive seizures in children, adolescents, and young adults: Etiology, outcome, and treatment. *Epilepsia, 37*(Suppl. 1), S74–S80.

Morrell, F., Whistler, W.W., & Smith, M.C. (1995). Landau-Kleffner syndrome: Treatment with subpial intracortical transection. *Brain, 118*, 1529–1546.

Morton, L.D., & Pellock, J.M. (1996). Diagnosis and treatment of epilepsy in children and adolescents. *Drugs, 51*(3), 399–414.

Murphy, J.V., & Dehkharghani, F. (1994). Diagnosis of childhood seizure disorders. *Epilepsia, 35*(Suppl. 2), 7–17.

Nickel, R.E., Renken, C.A., & Gallenstein, J.S. (1989). The Infant Motor Screen. *Developmental Medicine and Child Neurology, 31*, 35–42.

Obeid, T. (1994). Clinical and genetic aspects of juvenile absence epilepsy. *Journal of Neurology, 241*, 487–491.

Oguni, H., Hayashi, K., & Osawa, M. (1996). Long-term prognosis of Lennox-Gastaut syndrome. *Epilepsia, 37*(Supp. 3), 44–47.

Ortibus, E.L., Sum, J.M., & Hahn, J.S. (1997). Predictive value of EEG for outcome and epilepsy following neonatal seizures. *Electroencephalogy Clinics of Neurophysiology, 98*(3), 175–185.

Panayiotopoulos, C.P. (1989). Benign childhood epilepsy with occipital paroxysms: A 15-year prospective study. *Annals of Neurology, 26*, 51–56.

Panayiotopoulos, C.P., Obeid, T., & Tanan, A.R. (1994). Juvenile myoclonic epilepsy: A 5-year prospective study. *Epilepsia, 35*(5), 285–296.

Parker, A.P.J., Agathonikou, A., Robinson, R.O., & Panayiotopoulos, C.P. (1998). Inappropriate use of car-bamazepine and vigabatrin in typical absence seizures. *Developmental Medicine and Child Neurology, 40*, 517–519.

Pedley, T.A., & De Vivo, D.C. (1987). Seizure disorders in infants and children. In A.M. Rudolph (Ed.), *Pediatrics* (18th ed.). Stamford, CT: Appleton & Lange.

Pellock, J.M. (1994). Status epilepticus in children: Update and review. *Journal of Child Neurology, 9*(Suppl. 2), 27–35.

Penry, J.K. (Ed.). (1986). *Epilepsy: Diagnosis, management, quality of life.* Philadelphia: Lippincott-Raven.

Phillips, S.A., & Shanahan, R.J. (1989). Etiology and mortality of status epilepticus in children: A recent update. *Archives of Neurology, 46*(1), 74–76.

Plouin, P. (1985). Benign neonatal convulsions. In J. Roger, C. Dravet, M. Bureau, F.E. Dreifuss, & P. Wolf (Eds.), *Epileptic syndromes in infancy, childhood and adolescence* (pp. 2–11). London: John Libbey Eurotext.

Porter, R.J. (1993). The absence epilepsies. *Epilepsia, 34*(Supp. 3), 42–48.

Prasad, A.N., Stafstrom, C.F., & Holmes, G.L. (1996). Alternative epilepsy therapies: The ketogenic diet, immunoglobulins, and steroids. *Epilepsia, 37*(Suppl. 1), S81–S95.

Rantala, H., & Putkonen, T. (1999). Occurrence, outcome, and prognostic factors of infantile spasms and Lennox-Gastaut syndrome. *Epilepsia, 40*(3), 286–289.

Reutens, D.C., & Berkovic, S.F. (1995). Idiopathic generalized epilepsy of adolescence: Are the syndromes clinically distinct? *Neurology, 45*(8), 1469–1476.

Riikonen, R. (1982). A long-term follow-up study of 214 children with the syndrome of infantile spasms. *Neuropediatrics, 13*, 14–23.

Sansom, D., Krishanan, V.H., Corbett, J., et al. (1993). Emotional and behavioural aspects of Rett syndrome. *Developmental Medicine and Child Neurology, 35*(4), 340–345.

Sheth, R.D., & Bodensteiner, J.B. (1994). Effective utilization of home-video recordings for the evaluation of paroxysmal events in pediatrics. *Clinical Pediatrics, 33*(10), 578–582.

Shinnar, S., Berg, A., Moshe, S.L., et al. (1994). Discontinuing antiepileptic drugs in children with epilepsy: A prospective study. *Annals of Neurology, 35*, 534–545.

So, N.K. (1993). Recurrence, remission, and relapse of seizures. *Cleveland Clinic Journal of Medicine, 60*, 439–444.

Soprano, A.M., Garcia, E.F., Caraballo, R., & Fejerman, N. (1994). Acquired epileptic aphasia: Neuropsychologic follow-up of 12 patients. *Pediatric Neurology, 11*(3), 230–235.

Steffenburg, U., Hagberg, G., & Kyllerman, M. (1996). Characteristics of seizures in a population-based series of mentally retarded children with active epilepsy. *Epilepsia, 37*(9), 850–856.

Strang, J.D. (1990). Cognitive deficits in children. *Epilepsia, 31*(Supp. 4), 54–58.

Svoboda, W.B. (1979). *Learning about epilepsy.* Baltimore: University Park Press.

Swaiman, K.F., & Ashwal, S. (Eds.). (1999). *Pediatric neurology: Principles and practice* (3rd ed.). St. Louis: Mosby.

Talwar, D., & Swaiman, D. (1994). Myoclonic seizures. In K.F. Swaiman (Ed.), *Pediatric neurology: Principles and practice* (2nd ed., pp. 543–544). St. Louis: Mosby.

Trevathan, E., Murphy, C.C., & Yeargin-Allsopp, M. (1999). The descriptive epidemiology of infantile spasms among Atlanta children. *Epilepsia, 40*(6), 748–751.

Vainionpaa, L.K., Rattya, J., Knip, M., et al. (1999). Valproate-induced hyperandrogenism during pubertal maturation in girls with epilepsy. *Annals of Neurology, 45*(4), 444–450.

Vining, E.P., Freeman, J.M., Ballaban-Gil, K., et al. (1998). A multicenter study of the efficacy of the ketogenic diet. *Archives of Neurology, 55*(11), 1433–1437.

Wallace, S.J. (1990). Risk of seizures. *Developmental Medicine and Child Neurology, 32*(7), 645–649.

Williams, J., Grant, M., Jackson, M., et al. (1996). Behavioral descriptors that differentiate between seizure and nonseizure events in a pediatric population. *Clinical Pediatrics, 5*, 243–249.

Wirrell, E.C., Camfield, C.S., Camfield, P.R., et al. (1997). Long-term psychosocial outcome in typical absence epilepsy: Sometimes a wolf in sheep's clothing. *Archives of Pediatrics and Adolescent Medicine, 151*(2), 152–158.

Woermann, F.G., Free, S.L., Koepp, M.J., et al. (1999). Abnormal cerebral structure in juvenile myoclonic epilepsy demonstrated with voxel-based analysis of MRI. *Brain, 12*(pt. 11), 2101–2108.

Wolf, P. (1985). Juvenile absence epilepsy. In J. Roger, C. Dravet, M. Bureau, F.E. Dreifuss, & P. Wolf (Eds.), *Epileptic syndromes in infancy, childhood and adolescence.* London: John Libbey Eurotext.

Wyllie, E. (1998). Surgical treatment of epilepsy in children. *Pediatric Neurology, 19*(3), 179–188.

Wyllie, E., Rothner, D., & Luders, H. (1989). Partial seizures in children. *Pediatric Clinics of North America, 36*(2), 343–364.

Zacharowicz, L., & Moshe, S.L. (1995). Anti-epileptic drug therapy in younger patients: When to start, when to stop. *Cleveland Clinic Journal of Medicine, 62*, 176–183.

Zupanc, M.L. (1996). Update on epilepsy in pediatric patients. *Mayo Clinic Proceedings, 71*, 899–916.

Appendix

Guidelines for the Care of Children and Adolescents with a Seizure Disorder

Basic Team

The special care needs of children with a seizure disorder can be met by an experienced primary care physician working collaboratively with parents, a pediatric neurologist, and school staff. Some children and families require referral to an experienced neurodevelopmental or child development team headed by a developmental pediatrician, and other children may need referral to a mental health professional. Please note that the primary care physician continues to be responsible for coordinating the special services that these children require.

Initial Evaluation

The objectives of the initial evaluation are to document the seizure type or the presence of an epilepsy syndrome, identify associated medical and developmental problems, and clarify the cause of the seizures if possible. The responsibilities of the primary care physician and nurse are to complete parent and child interviews, perform a complete medical and laboratory evaluation, initiate treatment, determine the need for referrals, and counsel the parents and child about the diagnosis and recommended treatment.

Frequency of Visits

The child and family should be followed at least monthly by the primary care office following the initiation of the antiepilepsy drug treatment until the child's seizures are being controlled well, the medical evaluation is complete, and the child is receiving recommended services. The child and the family are reevaluated best in the office twice yearly if the child is stable and doing well with the treatment program, and more frequently for younger children and in the first year of treatment. In addition, the physician and office staff may need to have frequent telephone interviews with parents and/or teachers and obtain behavior rating scales as needed. Many children need ongoing management by the pediatric neurologist. The office management plan should be updated as needed at each reevaluation and not less than yearly.

Guidelines for the Care of Children and Adolescents with a Seizure Disorder

The following elements are recommended by age group, and the listing is cumulative. Review all items indicated up through the actual age group of a child entering your practice for the first time as part of the initial evaluation.

AGE	KEY CLINICAL ISSUES/CONCERNS	EVALUATIONS/KEY PROCEDURES	SPECIALISTS
Birth–5 years (pre–school age)	*Growth/Nutrition* (if associated developmental disability) Oral motor dysfunction Failure to thrive (FTT) Intrauterine growth retardation (IUGR) Microcephaly or macrocephaly	Growth parameters, diet history Cranial magnetic resonance imaging (MRI) or computed tomography (CT) scan	Nutritionist or feeding specialist as needed
	Dental Care	Review oral hygiene	Dentist
	Associated Medical Problems Hearing and vision problems Neuromotor concerns (e.g., cerebral palsy, ataxia) Constipation Enuresis Sleep disorder **Note any side effects of medications.**	Hearing and vision testing as needed Detailed musculoskeletal and neuromotor examinations Diet, medication (e.g., bulk agent), gastrointestinal referral as needed Urinalysis culture as needed, behavioral or other management, urology referral as needed Behavioral management and occasionally medication	Audiologist, ophthalmologist as needed Developmental pediatrician (DPed), physical therapist or neurodevelopmental team as needed
	Cause of Seizures Epilepsy syndrome present? Possible degenerative disorder?	Evaluation for minor anomalies, careful skin/physical examination Electroencephalogram (EEG), MRI or CT scan, blood chromosomes, other laboratory studies	Pediatric neurologist, DPed, medical geneticist, metabolic specialist as needed
	Management of Seizures Follow-up of antiepilepsy drugs (AEDs) Ketogenic diet Other (e.g., adrenocorticotropic hormone [ACTH])	Behavioral rating scales and teacher report as needed Check growth, blood pressure, and heart rate; side effects as needed and at least twice yearly if stable and doing well EEG, blood AED level, other lab work as needed for specific seizure types or medications	Pediatric neurologist, dietitian as needed Collaborate with school staff

The Physician's Guide to Caring for Children with Disabilities and Chronic Conditions, edited by Robert E. Nickel and Larry W. Desch, copyright © 2000 Paul H. Brookes Publishing Co.

Guidelines for the Care of Children and Adolescents with a Seizure Disorder (continued)

The following elements are recommended by age group, and the listing is cumulative. Review all items indicated up through the actual age group of a child entering your practice for the first time as part of the initial evaluation.

AGE	KEY CLINICAL ISSUES/CONCERNS	EVALUATIONS/KEY PROCEDURES	SPECIALISTS
Birth–5 years (pre-school age) *(continued)*	*Associated Behavior/ Mental Health Problems* Inattention or hyperactivity Aggression Oppositional behaviors Anxiety Lethargy	Family interview, behavior rating scales, school information as needed Parent training in behavior management as needed Referral to mental health professional as needed	DPed, behavioral specialist, mental health professional as needed
	Developmental Progress, Need for Early Intervention/Early Childhood Special Education (EI/ECSE) Services Language delay/speech disorder Developmental delay	Developmental screening and surveillance Referral for eligibility testing for EI/ECSE services as needed	Psychologist, speech-language pathologist, child development team as needed
	Family Support Services Respite care Parent group Community health nurse Advocacy Financial support (e.g., Supplemental Security Income [SSI])	Family interview, use parent questionnaire (e.g., Family Needs Survey), provide resource materials, referral to community services as needed	Medical social worker, referral to community health nurse as needed
	Review of Diagnosis and Anticipatory Guidance Review of seizure recognition Review first aid for seizure Warn against sudden discontinuation of AEDs Communication with school (e.g., type of seizures, medications, possible side effects) Advice regarding accident prevention and protection (e.g., need for helmet) Review individualized family service plan (IFSP) with family Transition to ECSE grade school	Family interview, educational materials, initiate care notebook Review IFSP with family; hold teacher interview, school conference as needed	Primary care office in collaboration with specialists
	Collaboration with Community Services Community health nurse Educational services	Comprehensive care coordination with regular exchange of written information (at least yearly) with other service providers	Primary care office in collaboration with specialists

The Physician's Guide to Caring for Children with Disabilities and Chronic Conditions, edited by Robert E. Nickel and Larry W. Desch, copyright © 2000 Paul H. Brookes Publishing Co.

Guidelines for the Care of Children and Adolescents with a Seizure Disorder *(continued)*

The following elements are recommended by age group, and the listing is cumulative. Review all items indicated up through the actual age group of a child entering your practice for the first time as part of the initial evaluation.

AGE	KEY CLINICAL ISSUES/CONCERNS	EVALUATIONS/KEY PROCEDURES	SPECIALISTS
6–12 years (school age)	*Management of Seizures* Review indications for discontinuation of AEDs (if child is currently seizure-free) Review indications for epilepsy surgery (if child has had uncontrolled seizures)	Continue to monitor for side effects of AEDs, blood AED levels and laboratory tests as indicated Repeat EEG as needed, referral to epilepsy center	Pediatric neurologist, epilepsy center as needed Collaborate with school staff
	School Progress Learning disabilities Mental retardation	Intellectual and achievement testing as needed	Psychologist or referral to child development team as needed
	Associated Behavior/Mental Health Problems Attention-deficit/hyperactivity disorder (ADHD) Oppositional behaviors Aggression Anxiety, depression Schizophrenia, psychotic disorder	Child and parent interviews, behavioral rating scales, school report, teacher interview as neeeded Review medication management	DPed, child psychiatrist, mental health professional as needed; collaborate with school staff
	Social Skills Promote social competence Involvement in peer group activities at school and in the community (determine which supports are needed)	School-based program; encourage participation in community programs	Psychologist, adaptive physical education specialist as needed Collaborate with school staff
13–21 years (adolescent–young adult)	*Anticipatory Guidance* Transition to high school Encourage healthy behaviors (e.g., diet, exercise) High-risk behaviors (e.g., substance use or abuse, promiscuity) Career planning Transition to adult services and independent living	Adolescent, family interviews Teacher interview, school conference as needed Referral to mental health professional as needed Referral to Department of Vocational Rehabilitation, career counseling, or life skills program as needed	Primary care office in collaboration with specialists and school staff

The Physician's Guide to Caring for Children with Disabilities and Chronic Conditions, edited by Robert E. Nickel and Larry W. Desch, copyright © 2000 Paul H. Brookes Publishing Co.

Family and Physician Management Plan Summary for Children and Adolescents with a Seizure Disorder

This form will help you and your physician review current services and service needs. Please answer the questions about your current services on this page. Your physician will review your responses and complete the rest of the form.

Child's name _____ Today's date _____

Person completing the form _____

CURRENT SERVICES

1. Please list your/your child's current medications and any side effects.

2. When was your/your child's last seizure?

   How many seizures do you/does your child have per week or per month?

3. What is your/your child's current school program?

   School name _____ Grade _____

   Teacher _____ Telephone _____

4. Do you/does your child receive any support services and other special programs at school (e.g., physical therapy, access to resource room)? Please list.

5. Who are your/your child's other medical and dental service providers?

   Dentist _____

   Neurologist _____

   Other _____

6. Who are your/your child's other community service providers?

   Community health nurse _____

   Other _____

The Physician's Guide to Caring for Children with Disabilities and Chronic Conditions, edited by Robert E. Nickel and Larry W. Desch, copyright © 2000 Paul H. Brookes Publishing Co.

Family and Physician Management Plan Summary
for Children and Adolescents with a Seizure Disorder *(continued)*

7.   Have you/has your child had any electroencephalogram (EEG), any blood tests, radiologic (X-ray) examinations, or other procedures since your last visit? If yes, please describe.

8.   Have you/has your child been hospitalized or received surgery since your last visit? If yes, describe.

9.   Please note your/your child's accomplishments since your last visit. Consider activities at home, in your neighborhood, or at school, as well as success with treatments.

10.   What goals (i.e., skills) would you/your child like to accomplish in the next year? Consider activities at home, in your neighborhood, or at school, as well as success with a treatment.

11.   What questions or concerns would you like addressed today?

Family and Physician Management Plan Summary for Children and Adolescents with a Seizure Disorder

The Management Plan Summary should be completed at each annual review and more often as needed. It is intended to be used with the Guidelines for Care, which provide a more complete listing of clinical issues at different ages as well as recommended evaluations and treatments.

Child's name _____   Person completing form _____   Today's date _____

Clinical issues	Currently a problem?	Evaluations needed	Treatment recommendations	Referrals made	Date for status check
Family's Questions					
Growth and Nutrition					
Dental Care					
Other Medical Problems Hearing loss or vision concerns Neuromotor problems Constipation, enuresis Sleep disorder **Note any side effects of medications.**					

The Physician's Guide to Caring for Children with Disabilities and Chronic Conditions, edited by Robert E. Nickel and Larry W. Desch, copyright © 2000 Paul H. Brookes Publishing Co.

Family and Physician Management Plan Summary for Children and Adolescents with a Seizure Disorder *(continued)*

Child's name _____   Person completing form _____   Today's date _____

Clinical issues	Currently a problem?	Evaluations needed	Treatment recommendations	Referrals made	Date for status check
Associated Developmental/ Learning Issues Describe current school achievement Review early intervention (EI) or other school services (individualized family service plan [IFSP] or individualized education program [IEP]) Learning disability Speech-language disorder Developmental delay or mental retardation					
Associated Behavior/ Mental Health Problems Inattention or hyperactivity Aggression Oppositional behavior Anxiety, depression Schizophrenia (psychotic disorder) High-risk behaviors					
Social Skills Involvement in peer-group activities at school and in the community (determine which supports are needed)					

The Physician's Guide to Caring for Children with Disabilities and Chronic Conditions, edited by Robert E. Nickel and Larry W. Desch, copyright © 2000 Paul H. Brookes Publishing Co.

Family and Physician Management Plan Summary for Children and Adolescents with a Seizure Disorder *(continued)*

Child's name _____ Person completing form _____ Today's date _____

Clinical issues	Currently a problem?	Evaluations needed	Treatment recommendations	Referrals made	Date for status check
Self-Care and Independence					
Family Support Services					
Anticipatory Guidance List issues discussed and materials provided					
Collaboration with Community Agencies Communication with school					
Comments					

Next update of the Management Plan Summary _____

Signature _____ Date _____
      (Child and parent)

Signature _____ Date _____
      (Health professional)

The Physician's Guide to Caring for Children with Disabilities and Chronic Conditions, edited by Robert E. Nickel and Larry W. Desch, copyright © 2000 Paul H. Brookes Publishing Co.

SEIZURE RECORD

Child's name _____ Date of birth _____ Person completing form _____

Date	Time	Length of seizure	Events before seizure	Description of seizure and events after seizure

The Physician's Guide to Caring for Children with Disabilities and Chronic Conditions, edited by Robert E. Nickel and Larry W. Desch,
copyright © 2000 Paul H. Brookes Publishing Co.

MEDICATION RECORD

Child's name _____ Date of birth _____ Person completing form _____

Date prescribed	Medication	Dose	Date changed	Comments (including drug levels)

RESOURCES ON SEIZURE DISORDERS

Readings

Dotty the Dalmation Has Epilepsy (Wellbook Collection). (1993). New York: Tim Peters & Co.

Epilepsy Foundation of America. (n.d.). *Epilepsy USA [Newsletter]*. Landover, MD: Author (Epilepsy Foundation of America, 4351 Garden City Drive, Landover, MD 20785-2267; 1-301-459-3700, 1-800-EFA-1000).

Epilepsy Foundation of America Staff. (1993). *Issues and answers: A guide for parents of children with seizures, ages six to twelve*. Landover, MD: Author (Epilepsy Foundation of America, 1-301-459-3700, 1-800-EFA-1000).

Freeman, J.M., Vining, E.P.G., & Pillas, D.J. (1997). *Seizures and epilepsy in childhood: A guide for parents* (2nd ed.). Baltimore: The Johns Hopkins University Press (1-800-537-5487).

Garcìa-Mèndez, L. (1994). *Seizures and convulsions in infants, children, and adolescents: Practical informative guide for parents, teachers, and paramedical personnel*. Columbia, MO: Lemar Publishers.

Gumnit, R.J. (1995). *Your child and epilepsy: A guide to living well*. New York: Demos Vermande. (1-800-532-8663)

Jan, J.E., Ziegler, R.G., & Erba, G. (1991). *Does your child have epilepsy?* (2nd ed.). Austin, TX: PRO-ED (1-800-897-3202).

Kaplan, P.W. (1995). *Epilepsy A to Z: A glossary of epilepsy terminology*. New York: Demos Medical Publishing. (1-800-532-8663)

Moss, D. (1989). *Lee, the Rabbit with Epilepsy*. Bethesda, MD: Woodbine House (1-800-843-7323).

Reisner, H. (Ed.). (1988). *Children with epilepsy: A parent's guide*. Bethesda, MD: Woodbine House (1-800-843-7323).

Schacter, S.C. (Ed.). (1993). *Brainstorms: Epilepsy in our own words: Personal accounts of living with seizures*. Philadelphia: Lippincott-Raven. (1-800-638-3030)

Schachter, S.C., Montouris, G.D., & Pellock, J.M. (1996). *The brainstorms family: Epilepsy on our terms: Stories by children with seizures and their parents*. Philadelphia: Lippincott-Raven. (1-800-638-3030)

Schachter, S.C., & Rowan, A.J. (Eds.). (1998). *The brainstorms healer: Epilepsy in our experience: Stories of health care professionals as care providers and patients*. Philadelphia: Lippincott-Raven.(1-800-638-3030)

Wilner, A.N. (1996). *Epilepsy: 199 answers: A doctor responds to his patients' questions*. New York: Demos Vermande. (1-800-532-8663)

National Organization

Epilepsy Foundation of America
4351 Garden City Drive
Landover, Maryland 20785-2267
Telephone: 800-332-1000, 800-332-2070 (TDD),
  (301) 459-3700
Fax: (301) 577-4941
E-mail: webmaster@efa.org
World Wide Web site: http://www.efa.org/

National organization with local affiliates that provides information, referral, public and professional education, employment assistance, advocacy, and self-help; publishes pamphlets, brochures, and newsletter.

18

Chronic Respiratory Disorders

Jay D. Eisenberg

KEY COMPETENCIES

- Discuss the etiology and risk factors of asthma, cystic fibrosis, and bronchopulmonary dysplasia (BPD)
- Describe the diagnostic techniques useful in evaluating children with respiratory diseases
- Delineate the diagnostic criteria for asthma and describe the diagnostic classifications for asthma
- Describe the diagnostic criteria for cystic fibrosis and know the indications for sweat testing
- Describe the most common congenital anomalies of the respiratory tract and their presentation and evaluation
- Describe the stepwise pharmacologic approach to asthma therapy
- Delineate and understand the modalities of therapy for cystic fibrosis pulmonary disease
- Delineate the modalities of therapy used to treat BPD
- Be familiar with guidelines for home mechanical ventilation for children

DESCRIPTION

Definition and Classification

Acute and chronic respiratory diseases in children occur with problems in the upper-respiratory tract, lower-respiratory tract, the pleura, and the pleural space, as well as with neurologic and neuromuscular abnormalities. An exhaustive listing of childhood respiratory diseases can be found in any general pediatric or pediatric pulmonary textbook (Behrman, Kliegman, & Jenson, 2000; Loughlin & Eigen, 1994). Only those childhood respiratory diseases that are chronic in nature are discussed in this chapter. A classification of acute and chronic respiratory diseases is presented in Table 18.1.

Prevalence

The epidemiology of chronic childhood respiratory disorders is best defined in terms of specific diseases. Asthma is the most common chronic illness in chil-

dren. It occurs in approximately 5%–10% of children (Centers for Disease Control and Prevention [CDC], 1996). Cystic fibrosis occurs in approximately 1 in 2,500 births among European Americans; 1 in 17,000 among African Americans; and 1 in 90,000 Asian Americans (Davis, Drumm, & Konstan, 1996). About 15%–20% of infants with cystic fibrosis are born with neonatal intestinal obstruction that is usually related to meconium ileus (Cystic Fibrosis Foundation [CFF], 1996).

Bronchopulmonary dysplasia (BPD) is reported in about 20% of newborns who require ventilators, with an estimated prevalence of 3,000–7,000 infants in the United States. Wide variability with regard to BPD exists between cystic fibrosis centers. The risk of BPD increases with decreasing birth weight and gestational age (Abman & Groothius 1994). Alpha-1 antitrypsin deficiency PiZZ (proteinase inhibitor zz) genotype is present in approximately 1 in 2,500 individuals. Lung disease in children that is due to alpha-1 antitrypsin deficiency is extremely rare (Wall, Moe, Eisenberg, et al., 1990).

Etiology

Chronic pulmonary disease is a major cause of morbidity and mortality throughout life. Childhood respiratory disease probably predisposes people to chronic lung disease in later life (Burrows, Knudson, & Lebowitz, 1977; Colley, Douglas, & Reid, 1973). Whether respiratory symptoms during childhood identify those individuals with a predisposition to chronic lung disease or respiratory illnesses to further illness is not known.

Some chronic pulmonary diseases have a clear-cut genetic basis, such as cystic fibrosis, alpha-1 antitrypsin deficiency, ciliary dyskinesia, and some of the immunodeficiency syndromes such as Bruton agammaglobulinemia and ataxia-telangiectasia. Other chronic respiratory diseases have important genetic components such as asthma and some immunodeficiency syndromes such as immunoglobulin G (IgG) subclass deficiency and immunoglobu-

Table 18.1.   Classification of childhood respiratory diseases

Airway/pulmonary	Neuromuscular and chest wall	Control of breathing
Asthma	Muscular dystrophies	Congenital central hypoventilation syndrome
Cystic fibrosis	Spinal muscular atrophy	Arnold-Chiari malformation
Bronchopulmonary dysplasia (BPD)	Scoliosis	Neurodegenerative syndromes
Alpha-1 antitrypsin deficiency	Asphyxiating thoracic dystrophy	
Ciliary dyskinesia	Other conditions associated with muscle weakness or congenital chest wall deformities	
Immunodeficiency syndromes		

lin A (IgA) deficiency, although the genetic component is defined less clearly and environmental factors are important contributors (Landau, 1994). Nonpulmonary diseases with a significant respiratory component include neuromuscular diseases, chest wall abnormalities, and problems with control of breathing.

Gender contributes to some chronic pulmonary conditions. Males are more prone to develop lower respiratory tract illness during the first 2 years of life and to have more severe asthma during childhood. Lung function tests suggest that boys have smaller airways relative to lung size than girls, which may predispose boys to increased lower respiratory tract disease (Taussig, Cota, & Kaltenborn, 1981).

In utero influences likely contribute to subsequent lung disease. Smoking during pregnancy increases bronchial responsiveness after birth (Young, Le Souef, Geelhoed, et al., 1991). Cord blood immunoglobulin E (IgE) levels are higher in babies with a family history of asthma (Kjellman, 1981). Premature birth and development of respiratory distress syndrome increase an infant's risk of chronic lung disease such as BPD (Abman & Groothius, 1994). Oxygen toxicity and barotrauma that are secondary to treatment of infants who are born prematurely contribute to development of BPD.

DIAGNOSIS AND EVALUATION

In general, the diagnosis of a chronic respiratory disease in a child can be made after a medical evaluation. This evaluation should include a complete history, physical examination, and appropriate laboratory and diagnostic tests. Diagnostic techniques that are useful in evaluating children with respiratory diseases are presented in Table 18.2. Specific diagnostic modalities are discussed in the following sections as they pertain to specific diseases.

Asthma

Clinical judgment is required in making the correct diagnosis of asthma. Signs and symptoms vary widely from child to child as well as within each individual over time. A careful medical history, physical examination, pulmonary function tests, and additional tests provide the information needed to ensure the correct diagnosis of asthma. To establish the diagnosis of asthma, the clinician must determine that episodic symptoms of airflow obstruction are present, that airflow obstruction is at least partially reversible, and that alternative diagnoses are excluded. *Asthma* can be defined as an obstructive airways disease with the following characteristics:

- Reversible airway obstruction
- Airway inflammation in all individuals with asthma
- Airway hyperreactivity

Medical History A detailed medical history of the new patient known or thought to have asthma should address symptoms, the pattern of symptoms, precipitating factors, development of the disease and treatments, family and social history, profile of a typical exacerbation, impact of asthma on the patient and

Table 18.2.   Diagnostic techniques

History and physical examination	Inspection, auscultation, percussion, palpation
	Upper-airway examination
	Extremities
Lung function testing	Spirometry
	Bronchoprovocation testing
	Exercise testing
	Lung volumes
	Carbon monoxide diffusing capacity
	Inspiratory muscle strength
Imaging	Chest radiograph
	Computed tomography (CT) scan
	Magnetic resonance imaging (MRI) scan
	Ultrasonography (US) scan
	Radionuclide scintigraphy
	Angiography
	Bronchography
Bronchoscopy	Flexible bronchoscopy (rigid bronchoscopy)
	Bronchoalveolar lavage (BAL)
	Nasopharyngoscopy
Laboratory evaluation	Sweat chloride
	Microbiological evaluation
	BAL
	Cell count and differential
	Cytology
	Blood gases
	Immunologic evaluation
	Allergy testing
	Quantitative immunoglobulins
	Immunoglobulin G subclasses
	Ciliary ultrastructure
Assessment of respiratory control	Ventilatory responses
	Response to hypercapnia
	Response to hypoxia
	Diaphragm electromyogram (EMG)
	Mouth occlusion pressure
	Arousal responses

the patient's family, and assessment of the patient's and family's perceptions of the disease. Symptoms of asthma include coughing, wheezing, shortness of breath, chest tightness, and sputum production.

Physical Examination   The physical examination should focus on the child's respiratory tract, chest, and skin. Physical findings that increase the probability of asthma include hyperexpansion of the thorax, use of accessory muscles, wheezing and/or a prolonged expiratory phase, increased nasal secretions and mucosal swelling, and manifestations of allergic skin disease.

Spirometry   Spirometry (forced expired volume in 1 second [FEV1], forced vital capacity [FVC], and FEV1/FVC) before and after the patient inhales a short-acting bronchodilator should be undertaken for individuals for whom the diagnosis of asthma is being considered (Bye, Kerstein, & Barsh, 1992). Spirometry is useful in children older than age 4 years, but some children cannot perform spirometry adequately until they reach age 7 years. Airflow obstruction is indicated by reduced FEV1 and FEV1/FVC values relative to reference values or predicted values. In severe cases, the FVC may also be reduced. Significant reversibility is indicated by an increase of greater than or equal to 12% and 200 milliliters in FEV1 after inhaling a bronchodilator (American Thoracic Society, 1991). A trial of oral corticosteroid therapy may be required to demonstrate reversibility. Although asthma is usually associated with these pulmonary function abnormalities, other diseases are also associated with the same pattern of abnormalities. The patient's pattern of symptoms and the exclusion of other possible diagnoses are also data that are needed to make an accurate diagnosis. Office-based spirometry is useful both for diagnosis and monitoring of patients with asthma. Equipment and techniques should meet published standards (American Thoracic Society, 1995). When office spirometry shows severe abnormalities, further assessment should be performed in a specialized pulmonary function laboratory.

Additional Studies   The following additional studies may be useful to define characteristics of the patient's asthma better or when considering alternative diagnoses:

- Lung volumes and inspiratory and expiratory flow volume loops to evaluate other obstructive pulmonary diseases, restrictive impairments, or central-airway obstruction
- Assessment of diurnal variation in peak expiratory flow rates for patients with normal spirometry who have asthma symptoms

- Bronchoprovocation with methacholine, histamine, or exercise when asthma is suspected but spirometry is normal
- Chest radiograph to rule out other diagnoses
- Allergy testing
- Evaluation for gastroesophageal reflux (GER)

Recurrent episodes of cough and wheezing in children are almost always due to asthma. Children who wheeze when they have respiratory tract infections are often labeled as having bronchitis, bronchiolitis, or pneumonia. Some infants with asthma wheeze when they have an acute upper respiratory tract infection (URTI). As these infants grow, their airways become larger and wheezing becomes less prominent. Other infants with asthma wheeze when they have a URTI but also in between these infections, and they continue to wheeze as they become older. This group of infants may have eczema, allergic rhinitis, or other allergic manifestations. NIH guidelines for asthma management recommend assessing asthma severity based on the frequency and the severity of asthma symptoms (see Table 18.3) (National Heart, Lung, and Blood Institute [NHLBI], 1997). Some children with asthma should be referred to a specialist in asthma care (usually a trained pediatric pulmonologist or an allergist) consultation or care (NHLBI, 1997). Reasons for referral are discussed in more detail under the "Management" heading in this chapter.

Cystic Fibrosis

Cystic fibrosis is the most common lethal genetic disease affecting European Americans. It is inherited in an autosomal recessive manner. About 4% of European Americans are carriers (i.e., of heterozygotes) who have no recognizable clinical manifestations. Progressive chronic obstructive pulmonary disease, pancreatic exocrine insufficiency, and elevated sweat electrolyte concentrations are present in most cases of cystic fibrosis.

The cystic fibrosis gene codes for a protein called the *cystic fibrosis transmembrane conductance regulator (CFTR)*. The most common mutation in the cystic fibrosis gene is a three base pair deletion that leads to a deletion of phenylalanine at position 508 of CFTR (ΔF508). ΔF508 is present on about 70% of cystic fibrosis chromosomes. The remaining cases are accounted for by more than 800 different mutations that are present on another 15% of cystic fibrosis chromosomes. The remainder of cystic fibrosis chromosomes have mutations that are not identified easily.

Cystic fibrosis is diagnosed if the patient has an elevated sweat chloride concentration (see subsequent discussion in this chapter) and pulmonary

Table 18.3. Asthma severity based on symptoms

Severity	Symptoms	Nighttime symptons
Mild intermittent	Symptoms less than or equal to twice per week	Equal to or less than twice per month
	Asymptomatic, normal peak expiratory flow (PEF) between exacerbations	
	Brief exacerbations (less than 2 or 3 days), intensity may vary	
Mild persistent	Symptoms more than twice per week	More than twice per month
	Exacerbations may affect activity	
Moderate persistent	Daily symptoms	More than once per week
	Daily use of inhaled beta-agonist	
	Exacerbations affect activity	
	Exacerbations equal to or more than twice per week; may last days	
Severe persistent	Continual symptoms	Frequent
	Limited physical activity	
	Frequent exacerbations	

From National Heart, Lung, and Blood Institute (NHLBI). (1997). *National Asthma Education and Prevention Program expert panel report 2: Guidelines for the diagnosis and management of asthma* (p. 20). Rockville, MD: National Institutes of Health.

disease consistent with cystic fibrosis and/or pancreatic exocrine insufficiency and/or a family history of cystic fibrosis. The clinician should consider the diagnosis of cystic fibrosis in a wide range of clinical situations. Two thirds of the cases are diagnosed by age 1 year, but 10% escape diagnosis until adolescence or adulthood. About 15%–20% of patients are born with neonatal intestinal obstruction that usually is related to meconium ileus (Cystic Fibrosis Foundation [CFF], 1996).

Sweat Test The standard *sweat test* method is the quantitative pilocarpine iontophoresis sweat test (Gibson & Cooke, 1959). Localized sweating is stimulated by the iontophoresis of pilocarpine into the skin. At least 100 milligrams of sweat are collected, and the chloride concentrations are measured by accepted techniques (LeGrys, 1996). Interpretation of the sweat test result is made with regard to the patient's clinical presentation. Reference values for sweat chloride are as follows:

- *Negative:* Less than 40 millimoles per liter
- *Borderline:* 40–60 millimoles per liter
- *Consistent with cystic fibrosis:* Greater than 60 millimoles per liter

Approximately 98% of patients with cystic fibrosis have sweat chloride concentrations greater than 60 millimoles per liter, and 1%–2% have sweat chloride concentrations less than 60 millimoles per liter.

Patients with sweat chloride concentrations of less than 60 millimoles per liter can be diagnosed on the basis of genotype, nasal potential differences, or clinical presentation.

Qualitative sweat tests are screening tests and should not be used to make a definitive diagnosis of cystic fibrosis. Any patient with a positive or borderline qualitative sweat test result should be given a *quantitative sweat test*. All accredited cystic fibrosis care centers perform the quantitative sweat test. Indications for sweat testing are detailed in Table 18.4.

No correlation exists between the magnitude of the sweat chloride and the severity of cystic fibrosis. Some patients with borderline or sweat chloride values in the low end of the abnormal range have pancreatic exocrine sufficiency. Normal sweat chloride values may occur in patients with cystic fibrosis in the presence of edema and hypoproteinemia, but values become abnormal with resolution of the edema (MacLean & Tripp, 1973). Elevated concentrations of sweat electrolytes have been reported in conditions other than cystic fibrosis (see Table 18.5).

Genotyping Genotyping may help with the diagnosis of cystic fibrosis in some cases. All patients with cystic fibrosis have mutations in both copies of the cystic fibrosis gene on chromosome 7, but not everyone with two mutant alleles at the cystic fibrosis gene manifests the full cystic fibrosis syndrome. For example, some patients with mild

Table 18.4. Indications for sweat testing

Pulmonary/upper respiratory	Gastrointestinal	Metabolic or other
Atelectasis	Steatorrhea	Positive family history
Bronchiectasis	Chronic diarrhea	Failure to thrive (FTT)
Chronic cough	Meconium ileus	Hypoproteinemia and edema
Chronic wheezing	Meconium plug syndrome	Hypoprothrombinemia
Recurrent or chronic pneumonia	Intestinal atresia	Hypochloremic metabolic alkalosis
Digital clubbing	Rectal prolapse	Azoospermia
Pseudomonas colonization	Fat-soluble vitamin deficiency	Absence of the vas deferens
Nasal polyposis	Biliary cirrhosis	
Pansinusitis	Portal hypertension	
Hemoptysis	Prolonged neonatal jaundice	
	Recurrent intussusception	
	Recurrent pancreatitis	
	Mucoid-impacted appendix	

Adapted from Rosenstein (1994).

mutations on both chromosomes may exhibit only congenital bilateral absence of the vas deferens as their cystic fibrosis phenotype, without apparent pulmonary or pancreatic involvement. In cases in which the sweat chloride is borderline and/or the patient does not exhibit the full clinical syndrome of cystic fibrosis, genotyping may be useful in making the diagnosis of cystic fibrosis. The most common mutation present in the cystic fibrosis gene, ΔF508, is present on about 70% of cystic fibrosis chromosomes. The remaining cases are accounted for by more than 800 different mutations. DNA analysis for cystic fibrosis mutations analyzes for about 70 mutations. Other than ΔF508, the additional 70 mutations account for another 15%–20% of cystic fibrosis alleles. The remaining 10%–15% of cystic fibrosis chromosomes have mutations that are not identified easily. Use of deoxyribonucleic acid (DNA) analysis to diagnose cystic fibrosis is not as sensitive as the sweat test but might aid in the diagnosis of unusual cases (Davis et al., 1996).

Bronchopulmonary Dysplasia

BPD is the chronic cardiopulmonary disease of infancy that follows ventilator and oxygen therapy for neonatal respiratory disease in infants who are born prematurely. Northway, Rosan, and Porter first described BPD in 1967. Since then, therapeutic advances such as surfactant therapy, permissive ventilation strategies, and nutritional intervention have modified the course of treatment for infants with BPD. Infants with BPD may exhibit growth, nutritional, developmental, and cardiovascular problems in addition to their chronic pulmonary disease. Table 18.6 delineates useful diagnostic modalities for children with BPD.

Chronic Pulmonary Disease   BPD is characterized clinically by chronic respiratory distress, radiographic abnormalities, and a persistent oxygen requirement to correct hypoxemia in room air. This nonspecific description does not account for differences in gestational age, physiologic abnormalities, histologic and biochemical changes, or radiographic differences (Abman & Groothius, 1994). The diagnosis of BPD is likely to be made before the infant leaves the neonatal intensive care unit (NICU). Serial clinical evaluations, pulse oximetry, and chest radiographs should provide information for evaluation of infants with BPD on an outpatient basis. Pathophysiologic features of the respiratory tract in patients with BPD include

Table 18.5. Causes of false-positive sweat test

Adrenal insufficiency
Ectodermal dysplasia
Nephrogenic diabetes insipidus
Type I glycogen storage disease
Anorexia nervosa
Hypoparathyroidism
Mauriac syndrome
Familial cholestatic syndromes
Malnutrition
Hypothyroidism
Mucopolysaccharidoses
Fucosidosis

Table 18.6. Evaluation of infants with bronchopulmonary dysplasia

System and symptoms	Diagnostic modalities
Respiratory system	Pulse oximetry (awake, asleep, feedings)
Oxygenation and gas exchange	Transcutaneous partial pressure (tension) of carbon dioxide (pCO$_2$)
	Blood gasses
Airway obstruction or structural abnormalities	Bronchoscopy, computed tomography (CT) scan, magnetic resonance imaging (MRI) scan
Cardiovascular system	
Anatomic heart disease	Echocardiogram, cardiac catheterization
Pulmonary hypertension	Echocardiogram, cardiac catheterization
Systemic hypertension	Renal evaluation, serial blood pressures
Gastrointestinal system	
Failure to thrive (FTT)	Dietary evaluation
Chronic aspiration, gastroesophageal reflux	Radiographic evaluation, esophageal pH study
Neurodevelopment	Developmental evaluation

- Increased airways resistance and abnormal lung mechanics
- Pulmonary edema
- Pulmonary hypertension

Increased airways resistance is present within the first 2 weeks after birth and may itself contribute to the pathogenesis of BPD. Bronchial hyperreactivity is present and may persist in older children and adolescents (Tepper, Morgan, Cota, & Taussig, 1986). Structural obstructive lesions, including tracheal, subglottic, and bronchial stenosis; polyps; granulomas; tracheomalacia; and bronchomalacia may be present. These lesions usually are acquired and should be ruled out in infants with severe BPD. Pulmonary function testing in children with BPD who are older than 5 years of age should be obtained as described under the "Asthma" heading in this chapter.

Pulmonary edema is present in BPD because of both hydrostatic and permeability causes (Jefferies, Coates, & O'Brodovich, 1984). BPD contributes to pulmonary edema by disruption of the alveolar-capillary unit, increased pulmonary blood flow that is due to a patent ductus arteriosis, fluid overload, salt and water retention, *pulmonary hypertension*, decreased pulmonary vascular surface area, decreased lymphatic clearance, and heart failure. Serial chest radiographs with persistent pulmonary infiltrates and physical findings such as persistent crackles are evidence of chronic pulmonary edema. Pulse oximetry provides a simple, reliable, noninvasive method to evaluate arterial oxygen saturation for infants with BPD. Therapeutic goals for long-term oxygen therapy in BPD are discussed under the "Management" heading in this chapter.

Cardiovascular Disease Pulmonary and systemic hypertension are significant problems in infants with BPD (Abman, Warady, Lum, & Koops, 1984; Goodman, Perkin, Anas, et al., 1988). Pulmonary hypertension is caused by pulmonary vascular abnormalities such as vascular remodeling and decreased arterial number. Babies with BPD and cardiovascular disease may have cor pulmonale and are at risk of morbidity and mortality due to viral infections. The onset of systemic hypertension in infants with BPD usually occurs between 2 and 4 months of age. The cause(s) of systemic hypertension is not known. Serial blood pressure measurements, an electrocardiogram (EKG), and echocardiography should be considered for infants with BPD.

Growth and Nutritional Status Poor growth and nutritional status may affect the outcome of infants with BPD (Meisels, Plunkett, Roloff, et al., 1986). Malnutrition may affect the infant's lung growth and development. Poor growth in babies with BPD is due to increased oxygen consumption, inadequate caloric intake, the effects of hypoxia, and increased catecholamine effects. Poor growth can occur despite high caloric intake. A dietitian who is familiar with BPD should be included in evaluating an infant with severe BPD and poor growth. Chronic aspiration and gastroesophageal reflux (GER) can exacerbate lung injury in children with BPD. Modalities to evaluate GER include barium studies, technetium-99 nuclear medicine studies, and esophageal pH evaluation (see Chapter 4).

Neurodevelopmental Status   Infants with BPD are at risk for various neurodevelopmental problems, including seizures, cerebral palsy, hearing and vision impairments, speech delay, and learning disabilities (Luchi, Bennett, & Jackson, 1991). Regular assessment of the developmental status of these infants should be provided.

Other Childhood Respiratory Diseases

Children Who Are Dependent on Ventilators for Respiration   With advancements in medical care, some children who are critically ill survive the acute phase of their illnesses but are not capable of maintaining adequate respiratory function without supportive technology. Areas requiring diagnosis and evaluation are discussed briefly in this section, and the details of management are discussed under the "Management" heading in this chapter. Guidelines for the management of home mechanical ventilation in pediatric patients have been published (see Eigen & Zander, 1990) and should be followed. Chronic respiratory failure as a result of pulmonary parenchymal disease, abnormalities of respiratory control, mechanical impairment, or neuromuscular disease are the primary indications for home mechanical ventilation.

Congenital Anomalies of the Respiratory Tract   Congenital anomalies of the lungs and airways can cause chronic respiratory signs and symptoms in infants and children. Some of these malformations present early in life, but others may not be apparent until adolescence or adulthood.

Laryngeal Anomalies   Laryngeal anomalies are relatively common, occurring in about 1 in every 2,000 live births. *Laryngomalacia* is the most common congenital abnormality of the larynx. It is not truly a malformation but a delayed maturation of the supporting structures. Infants with laryngomalacia present with stridor before 6 weeks of age. Stridor may be worse when the infant is crying, feeding, and in the supine position. Laryngomalacia is usually a benign, self-limited condition that resolves by 1–2 years of age. The diagnosis usually is based on the history and physical findings. Further evaluation is warranted if the stridor is high-pitched, progressive, associated with marked retractions at rest, or persists beyond 1 year of age. The supraglottic and subglottic areas and the lower airways should be evaluated with bronchoscopy.

Other congenital anomalies of the larynx are not very common. Most children with laryngeal anomalies present with stridor, an abnormal cry, feeding problems, and occasionally respiratory distress at birth. A definitive diagnosis requires visualization of the upper and lower airways with a bronchoscope. Even if an upper-airway anomaly is encoun-

Table 18.7.   Congenital anomalies of the larynx

Malformation	Signs and symptoms
Laryngomalacia	Stridor, normal cry
Laryngotracheal esophageal cleft	Stridor, apnea, feeding problems
Laryngeal webs	Distress at birth, stridor, abnormal cry
Laryngeal cysts	Distress at birth, stridor, hoarseness, aphonia
Vocal cord dysfunction	Stridor, abnormal cry, aspiration
Vocal cord paralysis: Unilateral	Stridor, hoarse or weak cry, aspiration
Vocal cord paralysis: Bilateral	Distress at birth, stridor, abnormal cry, aspiration
Subglottic stenosis: Congenital	Distress at birth, stridor
Subglottic hemangioma	Stridor, hoarse cry

tered, the lower airways should be evaluated to rule out associated lesions (Wood, 1984). Congenital anomalies of the larynx are listed with associated common signs and symptoms in Table 18.7.

Tracheal Anomalies   Tracheal malformations include lesions that are primary tracheal anomalies or malformations of other thoracic organs that involve the trachea. *Tracheomalacia* is caused by inadequate or malformed cartilaginous support of the trachea. It may occur as a primary malformation or secondary to other anomalies such as *tracheoesophageal fistula* (TEF) or vascular ring. If the intrathoracic portion of the trachea is involved, collapse of the affected area occurs during expiration and the patient may exhibit wheezing. If the extrathoracic portion of the trachea is involved, collapse of the affected area occurs during inspiration and the patient may have stridor.

The diagnosis of tracheomalacia should be suspected in a child with low-pitched or coarse wheezing or stridor that does not respond to bronchodilators or inhaled topical vasoconstrictors such as epinephrine. A plain chest radiograph and barium swallow to rule out a vascular ring should be performed. If the child is old enough, pulmonary function testing with flow-volume curves that may reveal a flattened inspiratory limb can be performed. The final diagnosis should be made with flexible bronchoscopy, with the child breathing spontaneously in order to evaluate airway dynamics. The common causes of *vascular rings* are double aortic arch, right aortic arch, aberrant right subclavian artery, aberrant innominate artery, and vascular sling. An MRI scan can be performed to define anatomy. Arteriography usually is not needed.

TEF is associated with esophageal atresia in about 85% of cases. This is usually diagnosed soon after birth because of feeding problems and respiratory distress. The remaining 15% of TEF cases have an intact esophagus and present in infancy with feeding problems, recurrent aspiration, and pneumonia. Older children with TEF present with recurrent, severe pneumonias. The diagnosis of TEF with intact esophagus such as the H-type fistula can be difficult to make. Multiple examinations including barium swallow and combined bronchoscopy and esophagoscopy with injection of methylene blue into the esophagus may be needed. Congenital anomalies of the trachea are listed with associated common signs and symptoms in Table 18.8.

Lung Malformations Congenital malformations of the lung are associated with variable acute and chronic respiratory symptoms. Some congenital lung malformations present in the newborn period because of respiratory distress. In older children, establishing the diagnosis of lung malformation requires a degree of suspicion. Infants with *pulmonary hypoplasia* who survive the newborn period may be left with severe chronic lung disease similar to BPD. *Congenital lobar emphysema* (CLE) and *cystic adenomatoid malformation* (CAM) usually present in the newborn period with respiratory distress. CAM can present with recurrent pneumonias after the age of 1 year. Obtaining a chest CT scan is the modality used to make the diagnosis.

Bronchogenic cysts arise from abnormal lung budding and can present with respiratory signs and symptoms secondary to extrinsic airway compression. Diagnosis is suspected when a mass is seen on a chest radiograph. A chest CT scan usually delineates the cyst and surrounding structures. *Pulmonary sequestration* is nonfunctioning pulmonary tissue separated from the tracheobronchial tree and pulmonary circulation. Pulmonary sequestration usually presents with multiple episodes of pneumonia. The diagnosis is made with chest radiographs and chest CT or MRI scans to delineate the vascular supply.

Abnormalities of the Diaphragm Congenital malformations of the diaphragm that present with clinical problems include eventration, agenesis of a phrenic nerve, and diaphragmatic hernia. Eventration of the diaphragm results when the muscular component of the diaphragm fails to develop. Evaluation should include a chest radiograph and ultrasonography (US) or fluoroscopy, which confirm paradoxical motion of the diaphragm on the affected side (Oh, Newman, Bender, & Bowen, 1988). Congenital diaphragmatic hernias (CDH) occur when the pleuroperitoneal membrane fails to form completely prior to return of the abdominal viscera to the peritoneal cavity. CDH is associated with bilateral pulmonary hypoplasia mostly on the ipsilateral side. Most newborns with CDH are diagnosed prenatally or soon after birth.

Ciliary Dyskinesia Syndrome Ultrastructural abnormalities of the cilia are associated with ciliary dyskinesia syndrome. Signs and symptoms of ciliary dyskinesia syndrome include chronic otitis media and sinusitis, recurrent pneumonia, inspiratory crackles and wheezing, digital clubbing, and nasal polyps. Bronchiectasis is the primary pulmonary lesion and can be diagnosed radiographically with a high-resolution chest CT scan. Pulmonary function testing demonstrates an obstructive pattern. Ciliary evaluation includes brushing or biopsy of ciliated respiratory epithelium, usually from the nasal mucosa, and ultrastructural evaluation with electron microscopy (Schidlow, 1994).

Disorders of the Chest Wall and Muscles

Chest wall abnormalities can be congenital or acquired. Primary abnormalities of the ribs and spine can lead to asymmetry of the thorax and lung function impairment. Neuromuscular disease can lead to secondary chest wall abnormalities such as scoliosis and cause lung function impairment.

Pectus Excavatum Pectus excavatum is characterized by a depression of the midsternum between the manubrium and the xiphoid. In most cases, the etiology is not known, although it is associated with some conditions such as Marfan syndrome. Diagnosis is made by conducting a visual inspection of the thorax. Generally, pectus excavatum does not cause significant respiratory dysfunction.

Scoliosis Scoliosis may be primary or secondary to vertebral body abnormalities and neuromuscular disease. Pulmonary function usually is affected by severe scoliosis, especially when associated with neuromuscular disease. Pulmonary function tests reveal a restrictive impairment. When assessing lung function in patients with progressive scoliosis, the use of arm span instead of standing

Table 18.8. Congenital anomalies of the trachea

Malformation	Signs and symptoms
Tracheomalacia	Stridor, wheezing, exertional dyspnea
Tracheal stenosis	Stridor, apnea, feeding problems
Vascular ring	Stridor, wheezing, feeding problems
Tracheoesophageal fistula	Wheezing, feeding problems, recurrent pneumonia

height predicts normal values more accurately. Serial measurement of the thoracic deformity and lung function should be used to evaluate a patient with scoliosis. Respiratory dysfunction is a sequelae of muscle weakness associated with neuromuscular disease. Pulmonary evaluation of children with neuromuscular disease includes assessment of respiratory muscle strength, respiratory muscle endurance, and respiratory muscle fatigue. Muscle strength is measured by obtaining inspiratory and expiratory static pressures at the mouth. Muscle endurance can be measured with the maximum voluntary ventilation (MVV) assessment. Spirometry and measurement of lung volumes by body plethysmography should be performed for serial assessment of lung function.

Unilateral Diaphragmatic Paralysis Unilateral diaphragmatic paralysis usually occurs as a result of birth injury or following cardiothoracic surgery. Evaluation should include a chest radiograph to evaluate elevation of the affected hemidiaphragm and either fluoroscopy or US to evaluate paradoxical diaphragmatic motion.

Problems with Control of Breathing Obstructive apnea occurs when there is cessation of airflow at the nose and mouth despite respiratory efforts. Central apnea occurs with cessation of airflow that is not accompanied by respiratory effort. *Obstructive sleep apnea syndrome* (OSAS) refers to the spectrum of sleep apnea associated with a mixture of obstructive and central apnea. In children, adenotonsillar hypertrophy is the most common condition leading to OSAS. Conditions associated with craniofacial anomalies and neuromuscular disease are associated with OSAS (see Table 18.9).

Children with OSAS have a history of 1) difficulty with breathing during sleep and 2) restlessness. Daytime somnolence, developmental delay, and behavioral disturbances can result from OSAS. Cardiovascular complications include pulmonary hypertension, cor pulmonale, and systemic hypertension. The method of establishing the diagnosis of OSAS is overnight polysomnography. Ideally, this can be performed at a sleep laboratory that has extensive experience with studying children. Cardiovascular evaluation of children with OSAS should include a chest radiograph, an EKG, and echocardiography.

Central alveolar hypoventilation is defined as persistently elevated arterial carbon dioxide tension (more than 45 millimeters of mercury) that is due to a decrease in central nervous system (CNS) ventilatory drive. Patients with central alveolar hypoventilation have normal lungs, chest walls, and upper airways. Central alveolar hypoventilation may be congenital or acquired and may be primary or secondary. Causes of central alveolar hypoventilation are listed in Table 18.10.

Most patients with congenital central hypoventilation syndrome (CCHS) present at or soon after birth with respiratory depression, apnea, and cyanosis. Occasionally, patients present later with cor pulmonale, lethargy, seizures, or respiratory failure precipitated by a respiratory tract infection. The physical examination of these patients may be normal when the child is awake. Because a spectrum of severity with CCHS exists, presentation is variable and an index of suspicion is needed to make the diagnosis. Patients with CCHS have decreased or absent ventilatory chemosensitivity in response to progressive hypoxia and hypercarbia.

MANAGEMENT

Management of children with chronic respiratory disease depends on the age and diagnosis of the patient. For children with asthma, treatment guidelines are based on age. Most patients with BPD are infants or toddlers. Treatment modalities available for children with chronic respiratory disease are shown in Table 18.11. A detailed list and a description are presented in the sections on specific respiratory diseases.

Table 18.9. Medical conditions associated with obstructive sleep apnea syndrome

Achondroplasia
Apert syndrome
Beckwith-Wiedemann syndrome
Cerebral palsy
Choanal atresia
Crouzon syndrome
Cystic hygroma
Down syndrome
Hallermann-Strieff syndrome
Hypothyroidism
Klippel-Feil syndrome
Mucopolysaccharidosis
Obesity
Osteopetrosis
Oropharyngeal papillomatosis
Pierre Robin sequence
Pfeiffer syndrome
Prader-Willi syndrome
Sickle cell disease
Treacher Collins syndrome

Adapted from Marcus and Carroll (1994).

Table 18.10. Causes of central hypoventilation

Primary
Congenital central hypoventilation
Central hypoventilation syndromes associated
  with endocrine dysfunction

Secondary

Obesity hypoventilation syndrome

Increased intracranial pressure
  Arnold-Chiari malformation type I
  Arnold-Chiari malformation type II
  Ventriculoperitoneal shunt malfunction
  Achondroplasia

Brainstem lesions
  Hypoxic-ischemic encephalopathy
  Trauma
  Hemorrhage
  Tumor
  Congenital anomalies

Neurologic syndromes
  Familial dysautonomia
  Leigh disease
  Mitochondrial defects
  Neurodegenerative syndromes

Asthma

Asthma is a chronic inflammatory disease. Treatment regimens for patients with asthma should be developed by taking both the chronic and inflammatory components of the disease into consideration. Asthma therapy regimens for children should include pharmacotherapy, patient and family education, environmental controls, and objective measures of lung function in children who are old enough to perform these tests.

The aim of asthma therapy is to maintain control of the asthma with the least amount of medication and minimal risk for adverse effects. *Control of asthma* is defined as

- Preventing chronic and troublesome symptoms
- Preventing recurrent exacerbations and minimizing the need for emergency visits or hospitalizations
- Maintaining normal activity levels and lifestyle
- Maintaining nearly normal pulmonary function
- Providing optimal pharmacotherapy with minimal or no adverse side effects
- Meeting patients' and families' expectations of and satisfaction with asthma care

Referral to a specialist for diagnosis and evaluation is recommended in the following circumstances:

- The patient has had a life-threatening asthma exacerbation.
- Signs and symptoms are atypical.
- Other conditions complicate the patient's asthma or its diagnosis (e.g., sinusitis, nasal polyps, aspergillosis, severe rhinitis, vocal cord dysfunction, GER).
- Additional diagnostic testing is indicated (e.g., skin testing, complete pulmonary function testing, bronchial provocation testing, nasopharyngoscopy or bronchoscopy).

Pharmacotherapy In asthma management guidelines (National Heart, Lung, and Blood Institute [NHLBI], 1997), National Institutes of Health (NIH) recommended a stepwise approach to pharmacologic therapy for asthma (see Figure 18.1). After determining asthma severity as outlined in the previous section, the clinician should take a stepwise approach to pharmacologic therapy to gain and maintain control of a patient's asthma. Therapy should be initiated at a higher level than the patient's step of severity at onset to establish control. Regular follow-up visits at 1- to 6-month intervals are essential to ensure that asthma control is maintained and appropriate step-down in therapy is considered. Table 18.12 provides recommendations for initial pharmacologic therapy based on asthma severity. There are two approaches to gaining control of asthma:

1. Start treatment at the step that is appropriate to the severity of the patient's asthma at the time of evaluation, and gradually step up the treatment if control is not achieved.
2. Start treatment at a level higher than the patient's level of severity to gain rapid control of the patient's asthma. Once control is gained, step down the level of therapy.

Table 18.13 provides a list of pharmacologic agents used to treat asthma.

Diagnosing and managing asthma in infants is often difficult, yet underdiagnosis and undertreat-

Table 18.11. Therapeutic modalities

Pharmacotherapy	Airway management
Bronchodilators	Airway clearance techniques
Anti-inflammatory agents	Tracheostomy
Antibiotics	Mechanical airway support
Diuretics	Continuous positive
Oxygen	airway pressure (CPAP)
Mucolytics	Bilevel positive airway
	pressure (BiPAP)
	Mechanical ventilation

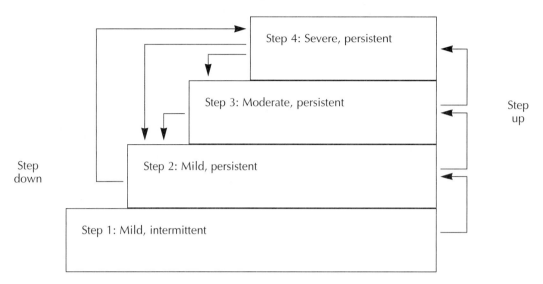

Figure 18.1.   The stepwise approach to asthma management. (From National Heart, Lung, and Blood Institute [NHLBI]. [1997]. *National Asthma Education and Prevention Program expert panel report 2: Guidelines for the diagnosis and management of asthma* [p. 82]. Rockville, MD: National Institutes of Health.)

ment are key problems in this age group. A diagnostic trial of inhaled bronchodilators and anti-inflammatory medications may be helpful. Infants and young children who require symptomatic treatment more than two times per week consistently should be prescribed daily anti-inflammatory therapy. When initiating daily anti-inflammatory therapy in infants, a trial of cromolyn or nedocromil is often given first because of the safety profile of these medications. Response to therapy should be monitored carefully. If control of asthma symptoms is established and sustained, a careful step-down in therapy should be attempted. If no clear benefit is observed, alternative therapies, including inhaled corticosteroids, should be considered.

Several delivery devices for inhaled medications are available: a metered-dose inhaler (MDI), a breath-activated MDI, a dry powder inhaler (DPI), a spacer or holding chamber, and a nebulizer. Spacers or holding chambers are useful for all patients who use metered-dose inhalers. The dose received may vary considerably among devices and age groups.

Table 18.12.   Treatment approach based on asthma severity

STEP 1:	Mild, intermittent asthma	Short-acting inhaled beta-agonist administered as needed
STEP 2:	Mild, persistent asthma	Long-term daily anti-inflammatory medication (low-dose corticosteroids or cromolyn/nedocromil)
		Leukotriene modifier as an alternative long-term control medication
		Short-acting inhaled beta-agonist administered as needed
STEP 3:	Moderate, persistent asthma	Increase inhaled corticosteroids to medium dose AND/OR
		Add long-acting bronchodilator AND/OR
		Add cromolyn/nedocromil OR
		Increase inhaled corticosteroids to high dose
		Short-acting inhaled beta-agonist administered as needed
STEP 4:	Severe, persistent asthma	As in step 3 and oral systemic corticosteroids on a long-term basis

From National Heart, Lung, and Blood Institute (NHLBI). (1997). *National Asthma Education and Prevention Program expert panel report 2: Guidelines for the diagnosis and management of asthma* (pp. 84, 85). Rockville, MD: National Institutes of Health.

Table 18.13. Pharmacologic agents for asthma

Classified by therapeutic action	
Bronchodilators	Beta-sympathomimetics
	Anticholinergics
	Methylxanthines
Anti-inflammatory agents	Corticosteroids
	Cromolyn/nedocromil
	Zafirlukast (Accolate)
	Montelukast (Singulair)
Classified by length of administration	
Long-term control medications	Inhaled corticosteroids
	Oral corticosteroids (severe persistent asthma)
	Cromolyn/nedocromil
	Long-acting beta-agonists
	Methylxanthines
	Leukotriene modifiers
Short-term control medications	Short-acting inhaled beta-agonists
	Anticholinergics
	Systemic corticosteroids (short courses or bursts)

The child's caregivers must be instructed in the proper use of appropriate-size face masks, spacers or holding chambers with face masks, and spacers or holding chambers for medication delivery to be effective and efficient. For children younger than 2 years of age, nebulizer therapy may be preferred for administering cromolyn and for high doses of beta-agonists during exacerbations. Children between 3 and 5 years of age may begin therapy with an MDI and a spacer or holding chamber alone; but if the desired therapeutic effects are not achieved, they may require a nebulizer or an MDI plus spacer or holding chamber and face mask. Doses and dosing forms of medications used to treat asthma and the estimated comparative daily dosages for inhaled corticosteroids are provided in the Appendix at the end of this chapter.

Objective Measures of Lung Function Regular monitoring of pulmonary function at home should be a component of asthma management. Peak expiratory flow (PEF) monitoring provides a simple, quantitative, and reproducible measure of the presence and severity of airflow obstruction. Patients need instructions on techniques with frequent reviews to maintain skills. PEF monitoring can be used for short-term monitoring, managing exacerbations, and daily long-term monitoring. The patient's personal best is the most appropriate reference value. Patients with moderate to severe persistent asthma and those who experience severe exacerba-

tions should learn how to monitor PEF. Patients should be given a written management plan with instructions. Patients should measure their PEF once daily after waking in the morning before using a bronchodilator. If the PEF is below 80% of the patient's personal best, PEF should be measured more than once daily and additional medication may be indicated. PEF below 50% indicates a severe exacerbation. The cut points of 80% and 50% are suggested but may be tailored to meet individual patients' needs. The traffic light system shown in Table 18.14 is useful for monitoring PEF.

Environmental Controls Exposure of asthma patients to irritants and allergens can increase asthma symptoms and precipitate exacerbations. For successful long-term asthma management, it is essential to identify and reduce exposures to relevant allergens and irritants and to control other factors that have been shown to increase asthma symptoms and/or precipitate asthma exacerbations. These factors fall into four categories: inhalant allergens, occupational exposures, irritants, and other factors. Examples for each category are shown in Table 18.15.

In patients with persistent asthma, an attempt should be made to identify allergen sensitivity with skin testing or in vitro testing. The significance of positive immunologic testing should be assessed in the context of each patient. Patients with asthma should avoid allergens to which they are sensitive, environmental tobacco smoke, and exertion when levels of air pollution are high. In addition, they should avoid beta blockers, foods to which they are sensitive, and aspirin and nonsteroidal anti-inflammatory drugs if they have a known sensitivity. Patients with persistent asthma, as with all

Table 18.14. Asthma action plan

Green zone	80%–100% of personal best: GO!!
	No asthma symptoms
	Continue with usual medications
Yellow zone	50%–80% of personal best: CAUTION!!
	Asthma symptoms present
	Actions: Should be listed in plan, including medications and telephone numbers
Red zone	Less than 50% of personal best: DANGER!!
	Actions: Should be listed in plan, including medications and telephone numbers

From National Heart, Lung, and Blood Institute (NHLBI). (1997). *National Asthma Education and Prevention Program expert panel report 2: Guidelines for the diagnosis and management of asthma* (p. 138). Rockville, MD: National Institutes of Health.

Table 18.15.   Environmental factors important in asthma

Inhalant allergens	Animal allergens
	House dust mites
	Cockroach allergens
	Indoor fungi (molds)
	Outdoor allergens
Occupational exposures	
Irritants	Tobacco smoke
	Indoor and outdoor air pollution
Other factors	Viral respiratory infections
	Rhinitis and sinusitis
	Gastroesophageal reflux (GER)
	Aspirin, nonsteroidal anti-inflammatory sensitivity
	Beta-blockers

From National Heart, Lung, and Blood Institute (NHLBI). (1997). *National Asthma Education and Prevention Program expert panel report 2: Guidelines for the diagnosis and management of asthma* (p. 42). Rockville, MD: National Institutes of Health.

chronic respiratory disorders, should be given an annual influenza vaccine.

Patient and Family Education   Patient and family education should begin at the time of diagnosis and should be integrated into *every* step of clinical asthma care. It is essential that education be provided by *all* members of the health care team. The principal clinician should introduce the key educational messages and negotiate agreements with patients; these messages should be reinforced and expanded by all members of the health care team. Teach asthma self-management, tailoring the approach to the needs of each patient. To encourage an active partnership with the patient and the family, provide all patients and families with a written daily self-management plan and an action plan for exacerbations. Action plans are especially important for patients with moderate to persistent asthma and patients with a history of severe exacerbations. Provide appropriate patients with a daily asthma diary. Encourage adherence by promoting open communication; individualizing, reviewing, and adjusting plans as needed; emphasizing goals and outcomes; and encouraging family involvement.

Cystic Fibrosis

Much of the information in this section is based on *Clinical Practice Guidelines for Cystic Fibrosis* (Cystic Fibrosis Foundation [CFF], 1997). The care of children with cystic fibrosis is complex and multifaceted. Medical management of a child with cystic fibrosis is best carried out through a close collaboration between the patient's primary care physician and the specialized staff of a cystic fibrosis center. Cystic fibrosis center accreditation is performed by the CFF. The physician who provides primary care for a cystic fibrosis patient should be responsible for health maintenance visits, management of intercurrent, non–cystic fibrosis–related medical problems, management of mild cystic fibrosis–related infections, and patient and family counseling, support, and advocacy.

The standard of care for monitoring patients at a cystic fibrosis center is every 3 months ("Cystic Fibrosis Foundation's Guidelines," 1990). The cystic fibrosis care center should be responsible for quarterly visits, respiratory tract culture and sensitivity, special imaging procedures, and bronchoscopy and gastrointestinal endoscopy. Cystic fibrosis–related evaluations and interventions, which are best carried out by the specialized multidisciplinary team of a cystic fibrosis center, include

- Annual psychosocial evaluation by the cystic fibrosis center social worker
- Annual nutritional evaluation by the cystic fibrosis center dietitian
- Annual respiratory therapy evaluation and teaching by the cystic fibrosis center respiratory therapist
- Genetic counseling
- Management of cystic fibrosis–related complications (e.g., pneumothorax, hemoptysis, respiratory failure, distal intestinal obstruction syndrome, diabetes mellitus, gastrointestinal bleeding, pancreatitis)
- Management of recurrent or persistent moderate to severe respiratory tract infections or exacerbations
- Evaluation and management of the newly diagnosed patient with cystic fibrosis
- Patient and family education, teaching, advocacy, and care coordination
- Cystic fibrosis–related surgical interventions for cystic fibrosis patients who require anesthesia for cystic fibrosis–related and non–cystic fibrosis–related surgical problems should be cared for by anesthesia staff with experience in managing airway complications in patients with cystic fibrosis

The major morbidity and mortality in cystic fibrosis patients is associated with chronic pulmonary disease and gastrointestinal or nutritional abnormalities. In this chapter, the management of these disease manifestations is discussed in separate sections. As previously discussed, management of patients with cystic fibrosis requires a multidisciplinary, specialized team approach.

Chronic Pulmonary Disease The goals of therapy in cystic fibrosis lung disease are to maintain pulmonary function and prevent progression of pulmonary disease. Excessive, poorly cleared airway secretions should be mobilized, infections should be treated, and inflammation should be suppressed. Therapy for cystic fibrosis pulmonary disease includes airway mucous clearance (mechanical and pharmacologic), antibiotics, bronchodilators, anti-inflammatory therapy, and supplemental oxygen. Ramsey (1996) wrote an excellent review of management of pulmonary disease in patients with cystic fibrosis.

Mechanical Airway Clearance Mechanical airway clearance techniques include chest percussion and postural drainage (CPT), Flutter, positive expiratory pressure (PEP), active cycle of breathing technique (ACBT), autogenic drainage, and mechanical vest therapy. CPT is labor intensive and time consuming, and it usually requires skilled personnel to be performed correctly. The other techniques just listed have been found, in general, to be as effective as CPT for improvement in sputum production and pulmonary function (Arens, Gozal, Omlin, et al., 1994; Giles, Wagener, Accurso, & Butler-Simon, 1995; Homnick, White, & de Castro, 1995; Kluft, Beker, Castagnino, et al., 1996). The Flutter is a hand-held device that vibrates the airway walls during exhalation. Use of the Flutter can increase sputum production up to threefold compared to CPT (Konstan, Stern, & Doershuk, 1994). Some form of airway clearance should be performed on all patients on a daily basis with augmentation of the usual regimen during a pulmonary exacerbation when sputum production is increased.

Recombinant Human Deoxyribonuclease Recombinant human deoxyribonuclease (rhDNase [Pulmozyme]; manufactured by Genentech in South San Francisco, California) cleaves extracellular DNA in sputum. When administered by aerosol to patients with cystic fibrosis, Pulmozyme reduces the risk of their developing a pulmonary exacerbation and improves pulmonary function and quality of life (Fuchs, Borowitz, Christiansen, et al., 1994). Pulmozyme is administered once daily with specific nebulizer and compressor combinations as detailed in the package insert. Patients who use Pulmozyme must be able to keep a nebulizer mouthpiece in their mouths for the 15 minutes of daily administration. Pulmozyme is prescribed for cystic fibrosis patients who are older than ages 4–5 years who exhibit chronic sputum production, physical findings consistent with lung disease, radiographic abnormalities, or pulmonary function abnormalities (Ramsey & Dorkin, 1994).

Antibiotics Patients with cystic fibrosis develop a chronic endobronchial infection, probably as a result of the ion transport abnormality associated with cystic fibrosis. Administration of antibiotics is one of the cornerstones of therapy for pulmonary disease in patients with cystic fibrosis. *Pseudomonas aeruginosa, Staphylococcus aureus,* and *Hemophilus influenza* are the most common bacterial pathogens that are present in the sputum of people with cystic fibrosis (Burns, Ramsey, & Smith, 1993; FitzSimmons, 1994; Koch & Hoiby, 1993). Eradication of the infection once it is established is rare. The proper choice of antibiotics for the treatment of pulmonary disease in cystic fibrosis is based on the epidemiology of the bacterial pathogens present in the airway, microbiologic information obtained from the clinical laboratory, and a knowledge of the clinical response to antimicrobial agents administered previously (Eisenberg, 1996). Table 18.16 lists antibiotics commonly used to treat patients with cystic fibrosis.

Indications for antibiotic therapy in patients with cystic fibrosis include both acute and chronic administration. Acute administration of antibiotics to a patient with cystic fibrosis is indicated for a pulmonary exacerbation. A pulmonary exacerbation results when a patient's clinical, laboratory, and pulmonary function parameters decline from their usual baseline levels (see Table 18.17).

In general, mild pulmonary exacerbations can be treated on an outpatient basis with oral or inhaled antibiotics. Severe exacerbations are treated with intravenous (IV) antibiotics in the hospital or at home. The length of therapy is determined by improvement in clinical, pulmonary function, radiographic, and laboratory parameters. Improvement in pulmonary function usually occurs within 5 days of initiation of inpatient therapy and continues thereafter. Some patients return to baseline within 10 days, and others require up to 21 days of therapy (Redding, Restuccia, Cotton, & Brooks, 1982; Rosenberg & Schramm, 1993).

Combination therapy with at least two antibiotics is recommended to treat pulmonary exacerbations in patients infected with *P. aeruginosa.* The most common combinations include an aminoglycoside with a beta-lactam or a fluoroquinolone with a beta-lactam. Prescription of antibiotic therapy for patients who are not infected with *P. aeruginosa* depends on the bacterial pathogens present. Antibiotic susceptibility data provided by the clinical microbiological laboratory may guide antibiotic therapy, but the clinician's knowledge of a patient's response to a particular therapy is important. The accuracy of commercial antibiotic susceptibility systems is not

Table 18.16.   Antibiotics for treating children with cystic fibrosis

Classification	Antibiotic	Method of administration
Aminoglycosides	Amikacin	IV
	Gentamicin	IV, inhaled
	Tobramycin	IV, inhaled
Beta-lactams	Amoxicillin-clavulanate	Oral
	Cepharadine (first-generation cephalosporin)	Oral
	Cefuroxime (third-generation cephalosporin)	Oral, IV
	Dicloxacillin	Oral
	Aztreonam	IV
	Cefazolin	IV
	Cefoperazone	IV
	Ceftazidime	IV
	Imipenem-cilastatin	IV
	Piperacillin-tazobactam	IV
	Ticarcillin-clavulanate	IV
Fluoroquinolones	Ciprofloxacin	Oral, IV
	Ofloxacin	Oral
Sulfonamides	Trimethoprim-sulfamethoxazole	Oral
Other	Vancomycin	IV
	Colistin	Inhaled

IV, intravenous.

well documented for the types of *P. aeruginosa* found in the sputum of patients with cystic fibrosis (Gilligan, 1994).

Chronic administration of antibiotics to maintain lung function includes oral, inhaled, and IV regimens. Chronic antibiotic administration by aerosol provides a safe and efficacious method of delivering high concentrations of aminoglycosides to the lower respiratory tract of cystic fibrosis patients with minimal systemic toxicity (Smith & Ramsey, 1995; Touw, Brimicombe, Hodson, et al., 1995). Aerosol formulations of tobramycin are listed in Table 18.18.

Bronchodilators   Inhaled bronchodilator therapy should be considered in cystic fibrosis patients who exhibit pulmonary function or subjective improvement after an inhaled bronchodilator and in those who carry a diagnosis of asthma. Infants and young children with recurrent episodes of wheezing may benefit as well. Some evidence exists that chronic bronchodilator therapy in cystic fibrosis patients may slow the decline in their pulmonary function (Hordvik, Konig, Morris, et al., 1985; Konig, Gayer, Barbero, & Shaffer, 1995). Doses and product selection are detailed in the Appendix at the end of this chapter.

Anti-inflammatory Therapy   High levels of chronic inflammation contribute to the progression of cystic fibrosis pulmonary disease (Khan, Wag-

Table 18.17.   Elements of a pulmonary exacerbation

Subjective parameters	Objective parameters
Increased cough	Decreased lung function parameters
Increased dyspnea	Changes in chest sounds from baseline
Increased sputum production	Decreased oxygen saturation from baseline
Report of fever	Elevated blood leukocyte count
Malaise, fatigue, or lethargy	Hemoptysis
Anorexia	Weight loss
Sinus pain	

Table 18.18.   Aerosol formulation of tobramycin

Formulation	Delivery device and dose
80 milligrams in a 2-milliliter vial[a]	Jet nebulizer, one or two vials two to three times daily
600 milligrams per 30 milliliters	Ultrasonic nebulizer, two to three times daily
300 milligrams per 5 milliliters	Jet nebulizer, twice daily

[a]Parenteral formulation.

ener, Bost, et al., 1995; Konstan, Hilliard, Norvell, & Berger, 1994). Chronic anti-inflammatory therapy is used with many children and adolescents with cystic fibrosis. Chronic ibuprofen therapy has been shown to slow decline of pulmonary function in patients with cystic fibrosis. The greatest effect was found among children 5–13 years of age, especially those younger than 13 years who had relatively well-preserved lung function (Konstan, Byard, Hoppel, & Davis, 1995). Ibuprofen is administered at a high dose after the correct dose is determined by using pharmacokinetic data from ibuprofen blood levels (peak serum concentration of 50–100 micrograms per milliliter) provided by a special laboratory. These levels are not available routinely from clinical laboratories. Liver and renal function should be followed serially. Chronic prednisone therapy has been shown to be effective at slowing decline in pulmonary function in children 6–14 years old, but not without corticosteroid side effects (Eigen, Rosenstein, FitzSimmons, & Schidlow, 1995; Price & Greally, 1993). Doses of 1 milligram per kilogram cause fewer side effects than 2 milligrams per kilogram every other day. In general, chronic prednisone therapy has been reserved for patients whose cystic fibrosis is more severe, in whom some corticosteroid side effects may be less of a concern.

Supplemental Oxygen Supplemental oxygen is administered to patients who exhibit hypoxemia. As the pulmonary disease progresses, most patients require nocturnal supplemental oxygen initially and then supplemental oxygen around the clock. Patients with unrecognized nocturnal hypoxemia may complain of morning headaches and fatigue. Hypoxemia can be evaluated using pulse oximetry. Usually, a pulse oxygen saturation of 90%–92% is adequate to minimize symptoms and prevent pulmonary hypertension.

Gastrointestinal Disease The overall therapy for patients with cystic fibrosis includes treatment for gastrointestinal disease. Pancreatic exocrine insufficiency is treated with supplemental pancreatic enzymes administered with every meal. Vitamin supplementation should include vitamin preparations with high doses of vitamins A, D, E, and K. Patients with laboratory confirmation of a vitamin deficiency should be treated with appropriate doses of the vitamin with close follow-up of vitamin levels. Nutritional status should be followed closely, and supplementation should be provided in cases of failure to thrive (FTT). A dietitian familiar with cystic fibrosis should be involved with decisions about nutritional supplementation for these patients.

Approximately 15%–20% of people with cystic fibrosis are born with meconium ileus. Treatment of infants with this condition should be undertaken by a multidisciplinary team familiar with cystic fibrosis care. Recurrent episodes of distal small bowel obstruction (distal intestinal obstruction syndrome [DIOS] or meconium ileus equivalent) in patients older than newborns may require acute therapy to relieve the obstruction as well as chronic therapy to prevent recurrent episodes. A pediatric gastroenterologist who is familiar with cystic fibrosis should be involved in caring for these patients.

Biliary cirrhosis with hepatomegaly, elevated liver enzymes, or portal hypertension with splenomegaly can develop in patients with cystic fibrosis. These conditions tend to develop in preadolescent or adolescent patients. Treatment usually includes ursodiol (Actigall). Close monitoring of biochemical, physical, and radiographic parameters is essential.

Bronchopulmonary Dysplasia

Treatment modalities used for treating patients with BPD include supplemental oxygen, bronchodilators, diuretics, anti-inflammatory medications, and mechanical ventilation. In addition, infants with BPD may require nutritional, cardiovascular, and neurodevelopmental therapies.

Oxygen Therapy The goals of oxygen therapy in BPD are to treat hypoxemia, optimize growth and development, and prevent pulmonary hypertension. Oxygen can be delivered by nasal cannula at levels to maintain oxygen saturations between 92% and 96% (Goodman et al., 1988; Hudak, Allen, Hudak, & Loughlin, 1989). As the patient improves, oxygen therapy can be weaned carefully. Criteria for weaning oxygen in infants and children with BPD are shown in Table 18.19.

Bronchodilators Infants with BPD exhibit acute improvement in pulmonary function in response to inhaled beta-agonists, anticholinergic agents, and theophylline (Davis, Sinkin, & Aranda, 1990; Logvinoff, Lemen, Taussig, & Lamont, 1985). Inhaled bronchodilator therapy in children with BPD is much the same as it is in children with asthma. Doses and product selections are provided in the Appendix at the end of this chapter. The frequency of inhaled bronchodilator administration to these patients varies widely, with some patients requiring as-needed dosing and others requiring medication as often as every 4 hours. Increased frequency of administration is likely to be necessary during intercurrent respiratory tract infections.

Theophylline is an effective bronchodilator in patients with BPD, but it also causes adverse effects

Table 18.19. Criteria for weaning oxygen therapy in bronchopulmonary dysplasia

Awake oxygen	Adequate growth rate
	Oxygen saturation greater than 92% on room air for 15 minutes
	Echocardiogram without evidence of pulmonary hypertension
Nocturnal oxygen	Stable off awake oxygen for 4–6 weeks
	Adequate growth rate
	Oxygen saturation greater than 92% asleep on room air
	Electrocardiogram or echocardiogram without evidence of pulmonary hypertension
Follow-up	Adequate growth and development
	Follow-up echocardiogram in 4–6 months
	Assess oxygen needs during acute illnesses

that may limit its use. Dosing and serum levels must be monitored closely. Adverse effects that are common with theophylline include vomiting, GER, irritability, seizures, tachycardia, hypertension, and arrhythmias.

Diuretics   Diuretics are used to treat the persistent pulmonary edema in BPD. Diuretics, including furosemide, thiazides, and spironolactone, improve lung function in infants with BPD (Kao, Warburton, Cheng, et al., 1984). The probable mechanism for this improvement is likely to involve diuresis and local pulmonary effects. Long-term diuretic therapy can cause hypokalemia, hypochloremia, hyponatremia, metabolic alkalosis, hypercalciuria, and nephrocalcinosis. The addition of thiazide diuretics to furosemide therapy may help reduce hypercalciuria, along with its associated problems. Diuretic therapy is continued until the patient demonstrates a period of stability with improving pulmonary status and decreasing clinical and radiographic evidence of pulmonary edema.

Anti-inflammatory Medications   The rationale for steroid use in BPD cases is in part based on the role of inflammation in the pathogenesis of BPD. Steroids should be beneficial in reducing bronchial hyperreactivity. Despite widespread use of corticosteroids, no studies as of 2000 have documented the long-term benefit of corticosteroid treatment for infants with BPD. Chronic steroid use in these infants is associated with significant adverse effects,

including electrolyte imbalance, fluid retention, hypertension, glucose intolerance, growth alterations, immunosuppression, prolonged suppression of the hypothalamic-pituitary-adrenal axis, and hypertrophic cardiomyopathy.

Inhaled steroids have been administered to infants with BPD. Although neither the safety nor the efficacy of inhaled steroids have been documented in long-term trials with these infants, the inhaled route of administration offers an alternative to long-term systemic administration with potentially fewer adverse effects. Alternate-day oral systemic steroids should be considered for infants with BPD who require long-term steroid therapy. Cromolyn may be beneficial for infants with BPD, but it has not been evaluated adequately. Long-term mechanical ventilation for infants with BPD is discussed under the "Children Who Are Dependent on Ventilators for Respiration" heading in this chapter.

Other Childhood Respiratory Diseases
Children Who Are Dependent on Ventilators for Respiration   Please review Table 18.20 prior to reading this subsection. Prior to discharge, an infant or child who is being considered for home mechanical ventilation should meet certain criteria, including the following:

• Stable disease process
• Stable ventilator settings, oxygen requirements, and blood gasses
• Stable growth while following an established nutritional regimen
• Established medication schedule

The family's resources and home physical environment should be evaluated. Issues surrounding family stresses that should be explored prior to discharge include finances, extended family emotional support, and comprehensive discharge planning.

Home care equipment vendors and respiratory therapists should have adequate experience in caring for children. Most children receiving home mechanical ventilation have a tracheostomy. Proper understanding of home tracheostomy care in children is essential. The *Tracheostomy Care Manual for Parents* (Kingston et al., 1995) is a useful tool for parent education and support.

Outpatient visits to the multidisciplinary management team are logistically difficult and should be scheduled at intervals that allow adequate time for the child to have a change in clinical status. The home care management team should be in frequent contact with the medical team that is managing the

Table 18.20. Guidelines for home mechanical ventilation for children

Health care team	Pediatric pulmonologist
	Other specialists when indicated (e.g., otolaryngologist [ENT])
	Primary care physician
	Pediatric pulmonary nurse specialist
	Home medical equipment vendor
	Home health care agency
	Medical social worker
	Respiratory therapist
	Occupational therapist, physical therapist, speech-language therapist, registered dietitian, psychologist
Patient selection	Cardiopulmonary stability
	Established growth pattern
	Freedom from frequent respiratory tract infections
	Child and family are suitable candidates based on psychosocial parameters
	Home care environment
	Local hospital and emergency services
	Available space in home
	Adequate utilities (e.g., electricity, heat, plumbing, telephone)
	Family support available (e.g., other family members, friends, nurses)
	Funding
Family preparation	Cardiopulmonary resuscitation (CPR) training
	Equipment instruction (e.g., use, maintenance, troubleshooting)
	Comprehensive home care plan
	Discussion of family responsibilities

Adapted from Eigen and Zander (1990).

patient, and management decisions frequently can be carried out by telephone.

Weaning criteria for each patient depend on the underlying illness. Improvement in blood gas parameters, decreased work of breathing, regular weight gain, and increasing stability during acute illnesses are signals that the child requires less mechanical ventilation. The ventilator rate is decreased by a specified number of breaths per minute at regular intervals (e.g., two breaths per minute every 10 days) while pulse oximetry and clinical parameters are monitored. The decrease of the ventilator rate is performed during waking

hours at first, then during sleeping hours. An alternative method is to remove the patient from the ventilator for short periods of time (e.g., 15 minutes every 2–4 hours, which is known as *sprinting*) and increase the periods of time off the ventilator if the patient tolerates less support. The final step is to wean the child from supplemental oxygen in much the same way as discussed previously under the "Management Plan for a Child with Bronchopulmonary Dysplasia" heading (DeWitt, Jansen, Ward, & Keens, 1993; Eigen & Zander, 1990; Fields, Rosenblatt, Pollack, & Kaufman, 1991; Schreiner, Donar, & Kettrick, 1987).

Congenital Anomalies of the Respiratory Tract

Laryngeal Anomalies Laryngomalacia is usually a benign, self-limited condition. Severe laryngomalacia that causes chronic airway obstruction and feeding problems may require surgical intervention or even a tracheostomy. More severe laryngeal anomalies such as clefts, webs, cysts, vocal cord paralysis, subglottic stenosis, and hemangioma usually require surgical intervention. A tracheostomy may be placed to bypass the area of obstruction and provide an airway until the infant grows larger, at which time definitive surgery can be performed.

Tracheal Anomalies Localized, primary tracheomalacia is usually a benign, self-limited condition. Severe primary tracheomalacia that causes episodes of airway obstruction may require a tracheostomy with or without positive pressure support with continuous positive airway pressure (CPAP) (Wiseman, Duncan, & Cameron, 1985). Tracheal stenosis is difficult to manage. Patients with tracheal stenosis require endotracheal intubation or tracheostomy, and even with surgical intervention such as resection with end-to-end anastomosis, long-term airway obstruction is common. Children diagnosed with vascular rings require surgical treatment and may have residual tracheomalacia, which usually improves with growth. TEF with or without esophageal atresia requires surgical intervention. After surgical intervention, children with TEF commonly have recurrent respiratory infections, asthma, and esophageal dysmotility.

Congenital Lung Malformations Infants and children with lung malformations such as congenital lobar emphysema, cystic adenomatoid malformation, bronchogenic cyst, and pulmonary sequestration require surgical intervention. Patients with pulmonary hypoplasia require supportive care and frequently require long-term mechanical ventilation in severe cases.

Abnormalities of the Diaphragm Children with congenital diaphragmatic eventration and paralysis who can maintain adequate gas exchange and good growth require observation. Newborns may require support with mechanical ventilation for approximately 2 weeks. If diaphragm function does not improve, plication should be performed. Congenital diaphragmatic hernia (CDH) usually requires emergent surgical intervention. CDH is associated with high mortality and morbidity. Long-term abnormalities in lung function persist in individuals who survive CDH (Falconer, Brown, Helms, et al., 1990).

Ciliary Dyskinesia Syndrome Treatment for ciliary dyskinesia syndrome includes inhaled beta-agonist bronchodilators, airway clearance with some form of mechanical airway clearance, and liberal use of antibiotics. Most patients have recurrent upper and lower respiratory tract infections with *Hemophilus influenza, Streptococcus pneumonia, Staphylococcus aureus,* and occasionally *Pseudomonas aeruginosa.* Management of the bronchiectasis depends on its severity and localization. Severe, localized bronchiectasis may be amenable to surgical resection with the realization that in the future, other parts of the lung will develop bronchiectasis.

Disorders of the Chest Wall and Chest Muscles Mild to moderate pectus excavatum can be observed. In severe cases, surgical correction has not been shown to definitively improve either lung function or exercise tolerance on a consistent basis. The most appropriate time for surgery has not been well established. The management of scoliosis includes serial lung function testing, including lung volumes when the spinal curve exceeds 50°–60°. Patients with gas exchange abnormalities may require supplemental oxygen or ventilatory support. Orthopedic management includes stabilization with bracing or surgical spinal stabilization.

Management of respiratory dysfunction associated with neuromuscular disease includes airway clearance techniques to help mobilize secretions. These techniques are discussed under the "Cystic Fibrosis" heading in this chapter. Intermittent positive pressure breathing (IPPB) may be useful for some children with muscle weakness who do not have much intrinsic lung disease. Respiratory muscle training appears to be most beneficial only in patients with static neuromuscular disease. Mechanical ventilation with either negative or positive pressure ventilators can be used in patients with severe respiratory compromise. Positive pressure ventilation is administered via a tracheostomy or mouthpiece. Positive pressure ventilation can be delivered with a mechanical ventilator or bilevel positive airway pressure (BiPAP). The physician and multidisciplinary team should discuss the use of life-sustaining treatment with the patient and the family.

Control of Breathing Problems The treatment of children with obstructive sleep apnea syndrome (OSAS) depends on the severity of the OSAS (Marcus & Carroll, 1994). Patients with documented OSAS should be considered for adenotonsillectomy. Underlying risk factors such as obesity should be treated if possible. Patients with hypoxemia should receive supplemental oxygen during sleep. If the polysomnogram continues to be abnormal despite initial treatment, then treatment with CPAP, uvulopharyngopalatoplasty, or even tracheostomy should be considered.

Treatment of central hypoventilation syndromes (CCHS) should include treatment of the primary cause of the hypoventilation if possible. For example, patients with hydrocephalus and Arnold-Chiari malformation may improve following the decrease of intracranial pressure with a shunt or surgical decompression of the posterior fossa (see Chapter 13). Pharmacotherapy for CCHS has not been found to be effective. The primary mode of therapy for patients with CCHS is ventilatory support. In young children, mechanical ventilation is administered with a tracheostomy. As children who require mechanical ventilation become older, their ventilatory support can be administered via a face mask if they can tolerate wearing the face mask during sleep. Diaphragmatic pacing has been used with some children, but these children still require a tracheostomy to prevent the occurrence of obstructive apnea. As the child grows, gas exchange and ventilatory support should be reevaluated every 6–12 months or when a change in clinical status occurs.

Family Support Needs

Families of children with chronic respiratory disorders often are expected to provide a variety of medical and nonmedical treatments, manage supplies and equipment, attend office appointments with their primary care physician as well as specialists, and continue to attend to the needs of other individual family members. Please review the discussion on "enabling" or support services in Chapter 1, and please review Chapter 3 also. Families of children with chronic respiratory disorders may need basic support services such as assistance with constructing a daily schedule and prioritizing care.

REFERENCES

Abman, S.H., & Groothius, J.R. (1994). Pathophysiology and treatment of bronchopulmonary dysplasia: Current issues. *Pediatric Clinics of North America, 41*(2), 277–315.

Abman, S.H., Warady, B.A., Lum, G.M., & Koops, B.L. (1984). Systemic hypertension in infants with bronchopulmonary dysplasia. *Journal of Pediatrics, 104*(6), 928–931.

American Thoracic Society. (1991). Lung function testing: Selection of reference values and interpretive strategies. *American Review of Respiratory Diseases, 144*(5), 1202–1218.

American Thoracic Society. (1995). Standardization of spirometry: 1994 update. *American Journal of Respiratory and Critical Care Medicine, 152*(3), 1107–1136.

Arens, R., Gozal, D., Omlin, K.J., et al. (1994). Comparison of high frequency chest compression and conventional chest physiotherapy in hospitalized patients with cystic fibrosis. *American Journal of Respiratory and Critical Care Medicine, 150*(4), 1154–1157.

Behrman, R.E., Kliegman, R.M., & Jenson, H.B. (Eds.). (2000). *Nelson textbook of pediatrics* (16th ed.). Philadelphia: W.B. Saunders Co.

Burns, J.L., Ramsey, B.W., & Smith, A.L. (1993). Clinical manifestations and treatment of pulmonary infections in cystic fibrosis. *Advances in Pediatric Infectious Diseases, 8*, 53–66.

Burrows, B., Knudson, R.J., & Lebowitz, M.D. (1977). The relationship of childhood respiratory illness to adult obstructive airway disease. *American Review of Respiratory Diseases, 115*(5), 751–760.

Bye, M.R., Kerstein, D., & Barsh, E. (1992). The importance of spirometry in the assessment of childhood asthma. *American Journal of Diseases of Childhood, 146*(8), 977–978.

Centers for Disease Control and Prevention (CDC). (1996). Asthma mortality and hospitalization among children and young adults: United States, 1980–1993. *JAMA: Journal of the American Medical Association, 275*(20), 1535–1537.

Colley, J.R.T., Douglas, J.W., & Reid, D.D. (1973). Respiratory disease in young adults: Influence of early childhood lower respiratory tract illness, social class, air pollution, and smoking. *British Medical Journal, 3*(873), 195–198.

Cystic Fibrosis Foundation (CFF). (1996). *Patient registry 1995 annual data report.* Bethesda, MD: Author.

Cystic Fibrosis Foundation (CFF). (1997). *Clinical Practice Guidelines for Cystic Fibrosis.* Bethesda, MD: Author.

Cystic Fibrosis Foundation's guidelines for patient services, evaluation, and monitoring in cystic fibrosis centers. (1990, December). *American Journal of Diseases of Childhood, 144*(12), 1311–1312.

Davis, J.M., Sinkin, R.A., & Aranda, J.V. (1990). Drug therapy for bronchopulmonary dysplasia. *Pediatric Pulmonology, 8*(2), 117–125.

Davis, P.B., Drumm, M., & Konstan, M.W. (1996). Cystic fibrosis: State of the art. *American Journal of Respiratory and Critical Care Medicine, 154*, 1229–1256.

DeWitt, P.K., Jansen, M.T., Ward, S.L., & Keens, T.G. (1993). Obstacles to discharge of ventilator-assisted children from the hospital to home. *Chest, 103*(5), 1560–1565.

Eigen, H., & Zander, J. (1990). Home mechanical ventilation of pediatric patients: American Thoracic Society. *American Review of Respiratory Diseases, 141*(1),258–259.

Eigen, H., Rosenstein, B.J., FitzSimmons, S., & Schidlow, D.V. (1995). A multicenter study of alternate-day prednisone therapy in patients with cystic fibrosis: Cystic Fibrosis Foundation Prednisone Trial Group. *Archives of the Disease of Childhood, 126*(4), 515–523.

Eisenberg, J.D. (1996). Antibiotic use in cystic fibrosis. *Current Opinion in Pulmonary Medicine, 2*, 439–446.

Falconer, A.R., Brown, R.A., Helms, P., et al. (1990). Pulmonary sequelae in survivors of congenital diaphragmatic hernia. *Thorax, 45*(2), 126–129.

Fields, A.I., Rosenblatt, A., Pollack, M.M., & Kaufman, J. (1991). Home care cost-effectiveness for respiratory technology-dependent children. *American Journal of Diseases of Children, 145*(7), 729–733.

FitzSimmons, S.C. (1994). The changing epidemiology of cystic fibrosis. *Current Problems in Pediatrics, 24*, 171– 179.

Fuchs, H.J., Borowitz, D.S., Christiansen, D.H., et al. (1994). Effect of aerosolized recombinant human DNase on exacerbations of respiratory symptoms and on pulmonary function in patients with cystic fibrosis: The Pulmozyme Study Group. *New England Journal of Medicine, 331*(10), 637–642.

Gibson, L.E., & Cooke, R.E. (1959). A test for the concentration of electrolytes in sweat in cystic fibrosis of the pancreas utilizing pilocarpine by iontophoresis. *Pediatrics, 24*, 545–549.

Giles, D.R., Wagener, J.S., Accurso, F.J., & Butler-Simon, N. (1995). Short-term effects of postural drainage with clapping vs. autogenic drainage on oxygen saturation and sputum recovery in patients with cystic fibrosis. *Chest, 108*(4), 952–954.

Gilligan, P.H. (1994). The role of the clinical microbiology laboratory in management of chronic lung infections in patients with cystic fibrosis. *Pediatric Pulmonology,* (Suppl. 10), 79–80.

Goodman, G., Perkin, R.M., Anas, N.G., et al. (1988). Pulmonary hypertension in infants with bronchopulmonary dysplasia. *Journal of Pediatrics, 112*(1), 67–72.

Homnick, D.N., White, F., & de Castro, C. (1995). Comparison of effects of an intrapulmonary percussive ventilator to standard aerosol and chest physiotherapy in treatment of cystic fibrosis. *Pediatric Pulmonology, 20*(1), 50–55.

Hordvik, N.L., Konig, P., Morris, D., et al. (1985). A longitudinal study of bronchodilator responsiveness in cystic fibrosis. *American Review of Respiratory Disease, 131*(6), 889–893.

Hudak, B.B., Allen, M.C., Hudak, M.L., & Loughlin, G.M. (1989). Home oxygen therapy for chronic lung disease in extremely low-birth-weight infants. *American Journal of Diseases of Children, 143*, 357–360.

Jefferies, A.L., Coates, G., & O'Brodovich, H. (1984). Pulmonary epithelial permeability in hyaline-membrane disease. *New England Journal of Medicine, 311*, 1075–1080.

Kao, L.C., Warburton, D., Cheng, M.H., et al. (1984). Effect of oral diuretics on pulmonary mechanics in infants with chronic bronchopulmonary dysplasia: Results of a double-blind crossover sequential trial. *Pediatrics, 74*, 37–44.

Khan, T.Z., Wagener, J.S., Bost, T., et al. (1995). Early pulmonary inflammation in infants with cystic fibrosis. *American Journal of Respiratory and Critical Care Medicine, 151*, 1075–1082.

Kingston, L., et al. (1995). *Tracheotomy care manual for parents.* Buffalo, NY: Children's Hospital of Buffalo, Department of Pediatric Otolaryngology, Pediatric ENT Associates.

Kjellman, N.I. (1981). Effect of parental smoking on IgE levels in children. *Lancet, 1*(8227), 993–994.

Kluft, J., Beker, L., Castagnino, M., et al. (1996). A comparison of bronchial drainage treatments in cystic fibrosis. *Pediatric Pulmonology, 22*(4), 271–274.

Koch, C., & Hoiby, N. (1993). Pathogenesis of cystic fibrosis. *Lancet, 341*, 1065–1069.

Konig, P., Gayer, D., Barbero, G.J., & Shaffer, J. (1995). Short-term and long-term effects of albuterol aerosol therapy in cystic fibrosis: A preliminary report. *Pediatric Pulmonology, 20*, 205–214.

Konstan, M.W., Byard, P.J., Hoppel, C.L., & Davis, P.B. (1995). Effect of high-dose ibuprofen in patients with cystic fibrosis. *New England Journal of Medicine, 332*(13), 848–854.

Konstan, M.W., Hilliard, K.A., Norvell, T.M., & Berger, M. (1994). Bronchoalveolar lavage findings in cystic fibrosis patients with stable, clinically mild lung disease suggest ongoing infection and inflammation. *American Journal of Respiratory and Critical Care Medicine, 150*, 448–454 (see erratum *151*(1), 260).

Konstan, M.W., Stern, R.C., & Doershuk, C.F. (1994). Efficacy of the Flutter device for airway mucus clearance in patients with cystic fibrosis. *Journal of Pediatrics, 124*(5 pt. 1), 689–693.

Landau, L.I. (1994). Origins of chronic lung disease. In G.M. Loughlin & H. Eigen (Eds.), *Respiratory disease in children: Diagnosis and management* (pp. 47–52). Philadelphia: Lippincott Williams & Wilkins.

LeGrys, V.A. (1996). Sweat testing for the diagnosis of cystic fibrosis: Practical considerations. *Journal of Pediatrics, 129*, 892–897.

Logvinoff, M.M., Lemen, R.J., Taussig, L.M., & Lamont, B.A. (1985). Bronchodilators and diuretics in children with bronchopulmonary dysplasia. *Pediatric Pulmonology, 1*, 98–203.

Loughlin, G.M., & Eigen, H. (1994). *Respiratory disease in children: Diagnosis and management.* Philadelphia: Lippincott Williams & Wilkins.

Luchi, J.M., Bennett, F.C., & Jackson, J.C. (1991). Predictors of neurodevelopmental outcome following bronchopulmonary dysplasia. *American Journal of Diseases of Childhood, 145*, 813–817.

MacLean, W.C., Jr., & Tripp, R.W. (1973). Cystic fibrosis with edema and falsely negative sweat test. *Journal of Pediatrics, 83*, 86–88.

Mahesh, V.K., McDougal, J.A., & Haluszka, L. (1996). Efficacy of the Flutter device for airway mucus clearance in patients with cystic fibrosis. *Journal of Pediatrics, 128*(1), 165–166.

Marcus, C.L., & Carroll, J.L. (1994). Obstructive sleep apnea syndrome. In G.M. Loughlin & H. Eigen (Eds.), *Respiratory disease in children: Diagnosis and management*

(pp. 475–499). Philadelphia: Lippincott Williams & Wilkins.

Meisels, S.J., Plunkett, J.W., Roloff, D.W., et al. (1986). Growth and development of preterm infants with respiratory distress syndrome and bronchopulmonary dysplasia. *Pediatrics, 77*, 345–352.

National Heart, Lung, and Blood Institute (NHLBI). (1997). National Asthma Education and Prevention Program expert panel report 2: Guidelines for the diagnosis and management of asthma. (Electronic document available at http://www.nhlbi.nih.gov/guidelines/asthma/asthgdln.htm).

Northway, W.H., Jr., Rosan, R.C., & Porter, D.Y. (1967). Pulmonary disease following respiratory therapy of hyaline membrane disease: Bronchopulmonary dysplasia. *New England Journal of Medicine, 276*(7), 357–368.

Oh, K.S., Newman, B., Bender, T.M., & Bowen, A. (1988). Radiologic evaluation of the diaphragm. *Radiologic Clinics of North America, 26*(2), 355–364.

Price, J.F., & Greally, P. (1993). Corticosteroid treatment in cystic fibrosis. *Archives of the Diseases of Childhood, 68*(6), 719–721.

Ramsey, B.W. (1996). Management of pulmonary disease in patients with cystic fibrosis. *New England Journal of Medicine, 335*(3), 179–188.

Ramsey, B.W., & Dorkin, H.L. (1994). Consensus conference: Practical applications of Pulmozyme. *Pediatric Pulmonology, 17*, 404–408.

Redding, G.J., Restuccia, R., Cotton, E.K., & Brooks, J.G. (1982). Serial changes in pulmonary function in children hospitalized with cystic fibrosis. *American Review of Respiratory Disease, 126*, 31–36.

Rosenberg, S.M., & Schramm, C.M. (1993). Predictive value of pulmonary function testing during pulmonary exacerbations in cystic fibrosis. *Pediatric Pulmonology, 16*, 227–235.

Rosenstein, B.J. (1994). Cystic fibrosis. In G.M. Loughlin & H. Eigen (Eds.), *Respiratory disease in children: Diagnosis and management* (pp. 263–289). Philadelphia: Lippincott Williams & Wilkins.

Schidlow, D.V. (1994). Primary ciliary dyskinesia (the immotile cilia syndrome). *Annals of Allergy, 73*(6), 457–470.

Schreiner, M.S., Donar, M.E., & Kettrick, R.G. (1987). Pediatric home mechanical ventilation. *Pediatric Clinics of North America, 34*, 47–60.

Smith, A.L., & Ramsey, B. (1995). Aerosol administration of antibiotics. *Respiration, 62*(Suppl. 1), 19–24.

Taussig, L.M., Cota, K., & Kaltenborn, W. (1981). Different mechanical properties of the lung in boys and girls. *American Review of Respiratory Disease, 123*, 640–643.

Tepper, R.S., Morgan, W.J., Cota, K., & Taussig, L.M. (1986). Expiratory flow limitation in infants with bronchopulmonary dysplasia. *Journal of Pediatrics, 109*, 1040–1046.

Touw, D.J., Brimicombe, R.W., Hodson, M.E., et al. (1995). Inhalation of antibiotics in cystic fibrosis. *European Respiratory Journal, 8*, 1594–1604.

Wall, M., Moe, E., Eisenberg, J., et al. (1990). Long-term follow-up of a cohort of children with alpha-1-antitrypsin deficiency. *Journal of Pediatrics, 116*, 248–251.

Wiseman, N.E., Duncan, P.G., & Cameron, C.B. (1985). Management of tracheobronchomalacia with continuous positive airway pressure. *Journal of Pediatric Surgery, 20,* 489–493.

Wood, R.E. (1984). Spelunking in the pediatric air-ways: Explorations with the flexible fiberoptic bronchoscope. *Pediatric Clinics of North America, 31,* 785–799.

Young, S., Le Souef, P.N., Geelhoed, G.C., et al. (1991). The influence of a family history of asthma and parental smoking on airway responsiveness in early infancy. *New England Journal of Medicine, 324*(17), 1168–1173 (erratum: 325[10], 747).

18

Appendix

Guidelines for the Care of Children and Adolescents with Cystic Fibrosis

Basic Team

The special care needs of children with cystic fibrosis are complex and multifaceted. The management of a patient with cystic fibrosis is best carried out through a close collaboration between the patient's primary care physician and the specialized staff of a cystic fibrosis care center. Continuity of care provided by both the primary care physician and the center staff is crucial to the cystic fibrosis patient's well-being. Cystic fibrosis care centers are accredited by the Cystic Fibrosis Foundation and must meet specific criteria pertinent to personnel, facilities and services, teaching resources, and research to maintain accreditation.

Regular members of the cystic fibrosis care center team include but are not limited to a pediatric pulmonologist, a pediatric gastroenterologist, a center nurse, a respiratory or physical therapist, a dietitian or nutritionist, and a medical social worker. Not all members of the team may be needed at each visit. Consultation with personnel who have pediatric expertise and experience in managing complications of children and adolescents with cystic fibrosis may be needed. The primary care physician continues to be responsible for preventative and acute illness care and coordinating the special services that these children require.

Initial Evaluation

The initial evaluation should be performed as soon as the diagnosis of cystic fibrosis is made or is suspected. The initial evaluation may require more than one visit. The components of the initial evaluation include medical, family, and social histories; physical examination; nutritional assessment; psychosocial assessment; and other tests as indicated. Other tests may include pulmonary function testing; sweat chloride evaluation; chest and other radiographs; sputum culture; and laboratory tests to evaluate renal, hepatic, and nutritional function. The evaluation should include patient and family education, including materials provided by the Cystic Fibrosis Foundation and the cystic fibrosis care center. An initial management plan should be formulated and provided to the family and the primary care physician.

Frequency of Visits

The optimal visit interval for monitoring patients at the cystic fibrosis care center is 3 months. This interval is the standard of care and is based on the primary outcome measures for nutritional status in the growing child and pulmonary function assessment in all patients. These measures provide more reliable and useful data if they are monitored on a quarterly basis. This visit frequency is also necessary for patient education and motivation to adhere to the ongoing medical regimen. In the presence of other associated conditions, more frequent monitoring may be necessary. An overall management plan should be formulated by specialists at the cystic fibrosis care center and modified as necessary, and they should be provided to the family and the primary care physician. The primary care physician should evaluate the child and the family in the office at least twice yearly if the child is stable and doing well to review the child's progress and provide ongoing support to the child and the family.

Guidelines for the Care of Children and Adolescents with Cystic Fibrosis

The following elements are recommended by age group, and the listing is cumulative. Review all items indicated up through the actual age group of a child entering your practice for the first time as part of the initial evaluation.

AGE	KEY CLINICAL ISSUES/CONCERNS	EVALUATIONS/KEY PROCEDURES	SPECIALISTS

Birth–5 years (pre–school age)	*Growth/Nutrition/Gastrointestinal Issues*
	Slow weight gain/failure to thrive (FTT)
	Dietary intake
	Bowel habits
	Medication usage
	Abdominal symptoms
	Gastroesophageal reflux (GER)
		Growth parameters, diet record, dietary assessment
		Gastrostomy as needed
		Medications
		  Pancreatic enzymes
		  Vitamin K for infants younger than 1 year old or presence of liver disease or prolonged pro-thrombin time
		  Multivitamin with 5,000 international units (IU) vitamin A and 200–800 IU vitamin E
		  Antacids, hydrogen-blockers, prokinetic agents
		  Laxatives, stool softeners
		Annual labs: Complete blood count (CBC), liver function tests
		Labs as indicated: Vitamin A, D, or E levels, pro-thrombin time, albumin, 72-hour fecal fat
			Pediatric gastroenterologist, dietitian, feeding specialist, or team nurse

	Pulmonary/Respiratory Issues
	Cough
	Sputum production
	Pain
	Upper-respiratory symptoms
	Exercise tolerance
	Shortness of breath
	Medication usage
	Respiratory treatments
	Complications
		Vital signs, oximetry, respiratory tract examination
		Annual respiratory tract culture
		Chest radiograph every 2–4 years if stable
		Chest radiograph annually with frequent infections
		Airway clearance techniques (review technique)
		Medication usage
		  Bronchodilators
		  Anti-inflammatory agents
		  Mucolytic agents
		  Antibiotics
			Pediatric pulmonologist, respiratory therapist, nurse

	Other Medical Problems
	Diabetes-related symptoms
		Oral glucose tolerance test, if indicated
		If child has diabetes:
		  Hemoglobin A_{1c} every 3 months
		  Home glucose monitoring
		  Urinalysis (UA) annually
			Dietitian, pediatric endocrinologist as needed

	Developmental Progress Need for early intervention (EI) services	Developmental surveillance Referral for eligibility testing for EI services as needed	
	Family Support Services Respite care Parents' group Community health nurse Advocacy Financial services	Family interview, questionnaires; provide resource information Care coordination, referral to community services as needed	Medical social worker, referral to community health nurse as needed

The Physician's Guide to Caring for Children with Disabilities and Chronic Conditions, edited by Robert E. Nickel and Larry W. Desch, copyright © 2000 Paul H. Brookes Publishing Co.

Guidelines for the Care of Children and Adolescents with Cystic Fibrosis *(continued)*

The following elements are recommended by age group, and the listing is cumulative. Review all items indicated up through the actual age group of a child entering your practice for the first time as part of the initial evaluation.

AGE	KEY CLINICAL ISSUES/CONCERNS	EVALUATIONS/KEY PROCEDURES	SPECIALISTS
Birth–5 years (pre-school age) *(continued)*	*Review of Diagnosis and Anticipatory Guidance with Family* Information on diagnosis and management	Family interview, provide educational materials, initiate care notebook	Primary care office in collaboration with cystic fibrosis team
	Collaboration with Community Services Community health nurse Other community providers	Comprehensive care coordination with regular exchange of written information (at least yearly) with other service providers, care conference as needed	Primary care office in collaboration with cystic fibrosis team
6–12 years	*School Progress* Need for support services	Exchange of information with the school as needed	Collaborate with school staff
	Anticipatory Guidance Discuss the diagnosis with the child Promote self-care and independence	Family interview, provide educational materials	Cystic fibrosis team in collaboration with primary care office
13–21 years (adolescent and young adult)	*Pulmonary/Respiratory*	In addition to evaluations from birth through age 5 years, conduct spirometry every 3–6 months	Pediatric pulmonologist, respiratory therapist, nurse
	Other Medical Problems Diabetes-related symptoms Liver disease	Consider oral glucose tolerance test annually or every other year, other lab tests as needed	Pediatrician, dietitian, pediatric endocrinologist
	Anticipatory Guidance Review genetics Promote healthy behaviors (e.g., nutrition, compliance with treatment plan) Sexuality, fertility Career planning/higher education Depression, social isolation, high-risk behaviors Transition to adult medical services	Adolescent, family, and teacher interviews as needed Educational materials Referral for genetic counseling and mutation analysis Education or counseling regarding male infertility, impact of pregnancy on health of women with cystic fibrosis, birth control	Cystic fibrosis team in collaboration with primary care office and school staff Referral to mental health professional as needed
	Collaboration with Community Services School Other community service providers	Comprehensive care coordination with regular exchange of information (at least yearly) with other providers	Primary care office in collaboration with Cystic Fibrosis Foundation

[a]Appropriate respiratory tract culture techniques are outlined in Appendix VIII of *Clinical Practice Guidelines for Cystic Fibrosis* (Cystic Fibrosis Foundation, 1997).

The Physician's Guide to Caring for Children with Disabilities and Chronic Conditions, edited by Robert E. Nickel and Larry W. Desch, copyright © 2000 Paul H. Brookes Publishing Co.

Family and Physician Management Plan Summary for Children and Adolescents with Cystic Fibrosis

This form will help you and your physician review current services and service needs. Please answer the questions about your current services on this page. Your physician will review your responses and complete the rest of the form.

Child's name _____ Today's date _____

Person completing the form _____

CURRENT SERVICES

1. Please list your/your child's current medications and any side effects.

2. What is your/your child's current school program?

    School name _____ Grade _____

    Teacher _____ Telephone _____

3. Do you/does your child receive any support services and other special programs at school (e.g., audiology, speech-language therapy, resource room)? Please list.

4. Who are your/your child's other medical and dental service providers?

    Pediatric pulmonologist _____

    Gastroenterologist _____

    Dentist _____

    Other _____

5. Who are your/your child's other community service providers?

    Respiratory therapist _____

    Dietitian _____

    Other _____

Family and Physician Management Plan Summary
for Children and Adolescents with Cystic Fibrosis *(continued)*

6. Do you also receive services from a cystic fibrosis center?

    Contact person _____

    Location _____

7. Have you/has your child had any laboratory tests or radiologic (X-ray) examinations, or other procedures since your last visit? If yes, please describe.

8. Have you/has your child been hospitalized or received surgery since your last visit? If yes, describe.

9. Please note accomplishments since your last visit. Consider activities at home, in your neighborhood, or at school, as well as success with treatments.

10. What goals (i.e., skills) would you/your child like to accomplish in the next year? Consider activities at home, in your neighborhood, or at school, as well as success with a treatment.

11. What questions or concerns would you like addressed today?

Family and Physician Management Plan Summary for Children and Adolescents with Cystic Fibrosis

The Management Plan Summary should be completed at each annual review and more often as needed. It is intended to be used with the Guidelines for Care, which provide a more complete listing of clinical issues at different ages as well as recommended evaluations and treatments.

Child's name _____ Person completing form _____ Today's date _____

Clinical issues	Currently a problem?	Evaluations needed	Treatment recommendations	Referrals made	Date for status check
Family's Questions					
Review of Genetics of Cystic Fibrosis					
Dental Care					
Growth/Nutrition/ Gastrointestinal Issues Slow weight gain/linear growth Monitor dietary intake, bowel habits, abdominal symptoms					
Pulmonary/Respiratory Issues Monitor presence/severity of: Cough Sputum production Pain Upper-respiratory symptoms Exercise tolerance Shortness of breath Respiratory treatments Complications					

The Physician's Guide to Caring for Children with Disabilities and Chronic Conditions, edited by Robert E. Nickel and Larry W. Desch, copyright © 2000 Paul H. Brookes Publishing Co.

Family and Physician Management Plan Summary for Children and Adolescents with Cystic Fibrosis *(continued)*

Child's name _____ Person completing form _____ Today's date _____

Clinical issues	Currently a problem?	Evaluations needed	Treatment recommendations	Referrals made	Date for status check
Medications/Treatments Update medications, dosages, frequency					
Other Medical Problems Diabetes-related symptoms Liver disease					
Developmental/School Progress Describe child's educational achievement Review of early intervention (EI) or school services (individualized family service plan [IFSP] or individualized education program [IEP]) as needed					
Social Skills Involvement in group activities at school and in the community (determine which supports are needed)					
Self-Care and Independence Compliance with treatment program					

The Physician's Guide to Caring for Children with Disabilities and Chronic Conditions, edited by Robert E. Nickel and Larry W. Desch, copyright © 2000 Paul H. Brookes Publishing Co.

Family and Physician Management Plan Summary for Children and Adolescents with Cystic Fibrosis *(continued)*

Child's name _____ Person completing form _____ Today's date _____

Clinical issues	Currently a problem?	Evaluations needed	Treatment recommendations	Referrals made	Date for status check
Family Support Services					
Collaboration with Community Services School Other community service providers					
Comments					

Next update of the Management Plan Summary _____

Signature _____ Date _____
          (Child and parent)

Signature _____ Date _____
          (Health professional)

The Physician's Guide to Caring for Children with Disabilities and Chronic Conditions, edited by Robert E. Nickel and Larry W. Desch, copyright © 2000 Paul H. Brookes Publishing Co.

USAGE DOSAGES OF ASTHMA MEDICATIONS

Medications	Dosage form	Pediatric dose	Adult dose
Inhaled corticosteroids Beclomethasone Budesonide Flunisolide Fluticasone Triamcinolone	See "Estimated Comparative Daily Doses for Inhaled Corticosteroids" in this Appendix		
Systemic corticosteroids Methylprednisolone Prednisolone Prednisone	2-, 4-, 8-, 16-, 32-milligram tablets 5-milligram tablets, 5 milligrams per milliliter 15 milligrams per milliliter 1-, 2.5-, 5-, 10-, 20-, 25-milligram tablets; 5 milligrams per milliliter	.25–2 milligrams per kilogram daily in a single dose up to 4 times daily *Short course:* 1–2 milligrams per kilogram per day up to 60 milligrams per day for 3–10 days	7.5–60 milligrams daily in a single dose Up to four times daily *Short course:* 40–60 milligrams per day as a once- or twice-daily dose for 3–10 days
Cromolyn and nedocromil Cromolyn	Metered-dose-inhaler (MDI) 1 milligram per puff Nebulizer solution 20-milligram ampule	1–2 puffs three or four times per day 1 ampule three or four times per day	2–4 puffs three or four times per day 1 ampule three or four times per day
Nedocromil	MDI 1.75 milligrams per puff	1–2 puffs two to four times per day	2–4 puffs two to four times per day
Long-acting beta-agonists Salmeterol	*Inhaled* MDI 21-micrograms per puff, 60 or 120 puffs Dry powder inhaler (DPI) 50 micrograms per puff *Tablet* 4-milligram tablet	1–2 puffs every 12 hours 1 puff every 12 hours .3–.6 milligrams per kilogram, up to 8 milligrams per day	2 puffs every 12 hours 1 puff every 12 hours 4 milligrams every 12 hours
Sustained-release albuterol			
Methylxanthines	Liquids, sustained-release tablets, and capsules	*Starting dose:* 10 milligrams per kilogram per day *Usual maximum dose:* Children younger than age 1 year: .2 × (age in weeks) + 5 = milligrams per kilogram per day Children age 1 year and older: 16 mg/kg/day	*Starting dose:* 10 milligrams per kilogram per day, up to 300 milligrams *Usual maximum dose:* 800 milligrams per day
Leukotriene modifiers Zafirlukast	20-milligram tablet		4 milligrams daily (one tablet twice daily)
Zieluton	300-, 600-milligram tablet		2,400 milligrams daily (two 300-milligram tablets or one 600-milligram tablet, four times daily)

(continued)

USAGE DOSAGES OF ASTHMA MEDICATIONS *(continued)*			
Medications	Dosage form	Pediatric dose	Adult dose
Montelukast	5-milligram chewable tablet, 10-milligram tablet	Children ages 5–14 years: 5 milligrams at bedtime Children ages 14 years and older and adults: 10 milligrams at bedtime	
Short-acting beta-agonists			
	MDIs		
Albuterol Albuterol HFA Bitolterol Pirbuterol Terbutaline	90 micrograms per puff, 200 puffs 90 micrograms per puff, 200 puffs 370 micrograms per puff, 300 puffs 200 micrograms per puff, 400 puffs 200 micrograms per puff, 300 puffs	1–2 puffs 5 minutes prior to exercise 2 puffs three or four times per day as needed	2 puffs 5 minutes prior to exercise 2 puffs three or four times per day as needed
	DPI		
Albuterol rotahaler	200-microgram puff	1 puff every 4–6 hours as needed prior to exercise	1–2 puffs every 4–6 hours as needed prior to exercise
	Nebulizer solution		
Albuterol	5 milligrams per milliliter (.5%)	.05 milligrams per kilogram (minimum, 1.25 milligrams, maximum, 2.5 milligrams) in 2–3 cubic centimeters of saline solution every 4–6 hours	1.25–5 milligrams (.25–1 mL) in 2–3 cubic centimeters of saline solution every 4–8 hours
Bitolterol	2 milligrams per milliliter (.2%)	Not established	.5–3.5 milligrams (.25–1 milliliter) in 2–3 cubic centimeters of saline solution every 4–8 hours
Anticholinergics			
	MDI		
Ipratropium	18 micrograms per puff, 200 puffs	1–2 puffs every 6 hours	2–3 puffs every 6 hours
	Nebulizer solution .25 milligrams per milliliter (.025%)	.25 milligrams every 6 hours	.25–.5 milligrams every 6 hours
Systemic corticosteroids			
Methylprednisolone Prednisolone Prednisone	2-, 4-, 8-, 16-, 32-milligram tablets 5-milligram tablets, 5 milligrams per cubic centimeter, 15 milligrams per cubic centimeter 1-, 2.5-, 5-, 10-, 20-, 25-milligram tablets 5 milligrams per cubic centimeter	*Short course:* 1–2 milligrams per kilogram per day up to 60 milligrams per day for 3–10 days	*Short course:* 40–60 milligrams per day as single or two divided doses for 3–10 days

ESTIMATED COMPARATIVE DAILY DOSES FOR INHALED CORTICOSTEROIDS

Children

Drug	Low dose	Medium dose	High dose
Beclomethasone 42 micrograms per puff 84 micrograms per puff	84–336 micrograms (2–8 puffs)	336–672 micrograms (8–16 puffs)	More than 672 micrograms (more than 16 puffs)
Budesonide Turbuhaler 200 micrograms per puff	100–200 micrograms	200–400 micrograms (1–2 inhalations)	More than 400 micrograms (more than 2 inhalations)
Flunisolide 250 micrograms per puff	500–750 micrograms (2–3 puffs)	1,000–1,250 micrograms (4–5 puffs)	More than 1,250 micrograms (more than 5 puffs)
Fluticasone Metered-dose inhaler (MDI); 44, 110, 220 micrograms per puff	88–176 micrograms (2–4 puffs, 44 micrograms)	176–440 micrograms (4–10 puffs, 44 micrograms) or (2–4 puffs, 110 micrograms)	More than 440 micrograms (more than 4 puffs, 110 micrograms)
Dry powder inhaler (DPI); 50-, 100-, 200-microgram dose	(2–4 inhalations, 50 micrograms)	(2–4 inhalations, 100 micrograms)	(more than 4 inhalations, 100 micrograms)
Triamcinolone 100 micrograms per puff	40–800 micrograms (4–8 puffs)	800–1,200 micrograms (8–12 puffs)	More than 1,200 micrograms (more than 12 puffs)

Adults

Drug	Low dose	Medium dose	High dose
Beclomethasone 42 micrograms per puff 84 micrograms per puff	168–504 micrograms (4–12 puffs, 42 micrograms) (2–6 puffs, 84 micrograms)	504–840 micrograms (12–20 puffs, 42 micrograms) (6–10 puffs, 84 micrograms)	More than 840 micrograms (more than 20 puffs, 42 micrograms) (more than 10 puffs, 84 micrograms)
Budesonide Turbuhaler 200 micrograms per puff	200–400 micrograms (1–2 inhalations)	400–600 micrograms (2–3 inhalations)	More than 600 micrograms (more than 3 inhalations)
Flunisolide 250 micrograms per puff	500–1,000 micrograms (2–4 puffs)	1,000–2,000 micrograms (4–8 puffs)	More than 2,000 micrograms (more than 8 puffs)
Fluticasone Metered-dose inhaler (MDI); 44, 110, 220 micrograms per puff	88–264 micrograms (2–4 puffs, 44 micrograms) or (2 puffs, 110 micrograms)	264–660 micrograms (2–6 puffs, 110 micrograms)	More than 660 micrograms (more than 6 puffs, 100 micrograms) or (more than 3 puffs, 220 micrograms)
Dry powder inhaler (DPI); 50-, 100-, 200-microgram dose	(2–6 inhalations, 50 micrograms)	(3–6 inhalations, 100 micrograms)	(more than 6 inhalations, 100 micrograms)
Triamcinolone 100 micrograms per puff	400–1,000 micrograms (4–10 puffs)	1,000–2,000 micrograms (10–20 puffs)	More than 2,000 micrograms (more than 20 puffs)

From National Heart, Lung, and Blood Institute (NHLBI). (1997). *National Asthma Education and Prevention Program expert panel report 2: Guidelines for the diagnosis and management of asthma* (p. 88). Rockville, MD: National Institutes of Health.

RESOURCES ON CHRONIC RESPIRATORY DISORDERS

Readings

Bierman, C.W., Pearlman, D.S., & Shapiro, G.G. (Eds.). (1996). *Allergy, asthma, and immunology from infancy to adulthood* (3rd ed.). Philadelphia: W.B. Saunders Co. (1-800-545-2522)

Bluebond-Langner, M. (1996). *In the shadow of illness: Parents and siblings of the chronically ill child.* Princeton, NJ: Princeton University Press. (1-800-777-4726)

DeFord, F. (1997). *Alex: The life of a child.* Nashville, TN: Rutledge Hill Press. (1-800-234-4234)

Edelman, N.H., & The American Lung Association Asthma Advisory Group. (1997). *The American Lung Association family guide to asthma and allergies.* Boston: Little, Brown. (1-800-759-0190)

Harris, A., & Super, M. (1995). *Cystic fibrosis: The facts* (3rd ed.). New York: Oxford University Press. (1-800-445-9714)

Orenstein, D.M. (1997). *Cystic fibrosis: A guide for patient and family.* Philadelphia: Lippincott-Raven. (1-800-638-3030)

Ostrow, W., Ostrow, W., & Ostrow, V. (1989). *All about asthma.* Niles, IL: A. Whitman. (1-800-255-7675)

Sander, N. (1994). *A parent's guide to asthma: How you can help your child control asthma at home, school, and play.* New York: Plume. (212-366-2000)

Sheperd, R.W., & Cleghorn, G.J. (1989). *Cystic fibrosis: Nutritional and intestinal disorders.* Boca Raton, FL: CRC Press. (1-800-272-7737, 561-994-0555)

Weiss, J.H. (1994). *Breathe easy: Young people's guide to asthma.* Washington, DC: Magination Press of the American Psychological Association. (1-800-374-2721)

National Organizations

Cystic Fibrosis Foundation
6931 Arlington Road
Bethesda, Maryland 20814
Telephone: (301) 951-4422, (800) FIGHT-CF (344-4823)
Fax: (301) 951-6378
E-mail: info@cff.org
World Wide Web site: http://www.cff.org/

This organization provides public and professional education, referrals to services, and a directory of local chapters in addition to supporting research and professional training.

Allergy, Asthma and Immunology Online
American College of Allergy, Asthma, and Immunology
85 West Algonquin Road, Suite 550
Arlington Heights, Illinois 60005
E-mail: mail@acaai.org
World Wide Web site: http://www.allergy.mcg.edu/

This organization maintains a World Wide Web site and provides information to individuals, their families, and professionals.

Allergy and Asthma Network: Mothers of Asthmatics, Inc.
2751 Properity Ave, Suite 150
Fairfax, Virginia 22031
Telephone: (800) 878-4403, (703) 641-9595
Fax: (703) 573-7794
E-mail: aanma@aol.com
World Wide Web site: http://www.aanma.org/

This parent organization provides information, support, and referrals and publishes a monthly newsletter, *The Ma Report.*

Index

Page numbers followed by "f" or "t" indicate figures or tables, respectively.

653